PREMIER LEAGUE
LEAGUE
RECORD FILE

BRUCE SMITH

First published in Great Britain in 2000 by
Virgin Books
an imprint of Virgin Publishing Ltd
Thames Wharf Studios
Rainville Road
London W6 9HA

A catalogue record for this book is available from the British Library.

ISBN 0 7535 0468 5

Designed by Roger Kohn
Typeset by Bruce Smith
Printed and bound by Mackays of Chatham plc, Chatham, Kent

CONTENTS

CONTENTS

PREMIER LEAGUE RECORD FILE

The first eight years of the Premier League are chronicled in this Record File. Every table, every result, every scorer, every player – and there have been a lot of each.

The Record File is divided into three distinctive sections and these are detailed more fully below. It is taken from an extensive database of results and line-ups I have compiled on my computer since day one of the 1992-93 season. For those inclined to know, the data is maintained in Excel and Access formats and Visual Basic macros are used to massage the raw data into the various forms in which it has been regurgitated herein.

I would like to say a particular thanks to John Russell. John has acted as my chief statistician for the past few years and his diligent checking, re-checking and chasing of detail have taken a huge weight off my own shoulders, for which I am gratefully indebted.

WHOSE GOAL IS IT ANYWAY?

A word about goals. I often get letters saying such-and-such scored a certain goal and not the person you have stated. Sometimes the confusion arises because the scorer of the goal has been re-assigned. The Premier League run a Dubious Goals committee which adjudicates on whether person a or person b scores a particular goal. More often that not it has to determine whether a goal should be re-assigned as an own goal. A couple of examples. The most famous instances came a few years back when Egil Ostenstad thought he had notched a hat-trick in Southampton's 6-3 demolition of grey-suited Manchester United. The player duly gathered the ball, had it signed and took it home. The Dubious Goals committee ruled, however, that his third goal should be credited to Manchester's Gary Neville as an OG, and so the record books were amended. During the 1999-00 season, Lee Dixon was credited with a goal at Leicester which was later re-assigned as an own goal. At the time of writing the club still had this goal allocated to Lee but the pages of this book have toed the official line, so to speak.

KEY MATTERS

Numerous abbreviations are used throughout and many of these are repeated at different places in the book. The most common ones in use are detailed below while others that appear occasionally are listed at the end of the appropriate section.

P	Played	games played
W	Won	games won
D	Drawn	games drawn
L	Lost	games lost
F	For	goals scored by (For) the team/player
A	Against	goals scored against the team/player
Pts	Points	points won by the team
Tot	Total	normally related to appearances
St	Start	normally relates to number of starting appearances made by player, ie, the times player was in the starting line-up.
Sb	Sub	normally relates to number of appearances as a substitute made by player, ie, the times player was brought on from the bench during a game.
Ps	Player Subbed	number of times player in question has been substituted, ie, replaced.
Snu	Sub Not Used	number of times a player has not been used, ie, started as a substitute and was not called upon during the game.

THE TABLES AND STATS

This first section starts off by documenting the eight seasons, 1992-93 through to 1999-00. It lists final tables, stats from the season and then has results and attendance acrostic grids. This is followed by over two pages of general stats relating to the Premier League. It covers everything from record wins and draws through to players that have made the most appearances, scored the most goals and even those who have been used as a sub the most! It also covers goalkeepers, managers and referees.

THE CLUBS

This section details the 33 clubs who have played in the Premier League from 1992-93 to 1999-00. Clubs are listed alphabetically (page 8 provides a convenient alphabetical list of the clubs). Included here are details of club honours, a summary of their Premier League highs and lows, and playing records on a season-by-season basis. It is completed with a list of results against each of the other teams. This list is arranged by opposition club and includes details of date, score, scorers, attendance and referee. Browsing through this can throw up some interesting items. Look at Arsenal's record against Liverpool for instance. The Gunners have only managed five goals against the Merseyside club in 16 Premiership encounters. Three of those were scored by Ian Wright, and none have come in the last six games! (Painful for an Arsenal Season Ticket holder!)

THE PLAYERS

This section provides a complete A-Z of players who have appeared in the Premier League during the period 1992-93 to 1999-00. The only requirement is that the player must have appeared – even if it was once as a sub in the dying seconds of a game. Again this section throws up some interesting detail. Check out some of the goalkeepers who may have made only a handful of appearances down the years but have spent many years sitting on the bench as a SNU. This section does not include players who may have appeared on the bench but have not made it onto the field of play.

ACKNOWLEDGEMENTS

As already mentioned, a big thank-you to John Russell for his help in producing the stats for this Record File. Thanks also to Sports.com for always being on-hand to sort out various queries that have arisen and Mark Webb for accepting the task of completing these pages while business commitments meant that I could not.

YEAR BY YEAR

AND

ALL-TIME

STATISTICS

ALL-TIME PLAYING RECORDS BY CLUB

	Club	P	W	D	L	F	A	Pts	S	B	W
1	Arsenal	316	149	91	76	456	272	538	8	1	12
2	Aston Villa	316	129	86	101	399	344	473	8	2	18
3	Barnsley	38	10	5	23	37	82	35	1	19	19
4	Blackburn Rovers	278	122	74	82	409	315	440	7	1	19
5	Bolton Wanderers	76	17	18	41	80	132	69	2	18	20
6	Bradford City	38	9	9	20	38	68	36	1	17	17
7	Charlton Athletic	38	8	12	18	41	56	36	1	18	18
8	Chelsea	316	126	95	95	435	368	473	8	3	14
9	Coventry City	316	91	102	123	351	427	375	8	11	17
10	Crystal Palace	122	30	37	55	119	181	127	3	19	20
11	Derby County	152	49	44	59	181	209	191	4	8	16
12	Everton	316	97	92	127	389	422	383	8	6	17
13	Ipswich Town	126	28	38	60	121	206	122	3	16	22
14	Leeds United	316	129	91	96	426	357	478	8	3	17
15	Leicester City	194	59	56	79	237	276	233	5	8	21
16	Liverpool	316	145	83	88	505	339	518	8	3	8
17	Manchester City	164	45	54	65	180	222	189	4	9	18
18	Manchester United	316	196	80	40	623	284	668	8	1	2
19	Middlesbrough	194	58	58	78	234	291	229	5	9	21
20	Newcastle United	274	122	71	81	434	317	437	7	2	13
21	Norwich City	126	43	39	44	163	180	168	3	3	20
22	Nottingham Forest	198	60	59	79	229	287	239	5	3	22
23	Oldham Athletic	84	22	23	39	105	142	89	2	19	21
24	QPR	164	59	39	66	224	232	216	4	5	19
25	Sheffield United	84	22	28	34	96	113	94	2	14	20
26	Sheffield Wednesday	316	101	89	126	409	453	392	8	7	19
27	Southampton	316	93	80	143	380	479	359	8	10	18
28	Sunderland	76	26	20	30	92	109	98	2	7	18
29	Swindon Town	42	5	15	22	47	100	30	1	22	22
30	Tottenham Hotspur	316	109	90	117	422	427	417	8	7	15
31	Watford	38	6	6	26	35	77	24	1	20	20
32	West Ham United	274	97	72	105	327	369	363	7	5	14
33	Wimbledon	316	99	94	123	384	472	391	8	6	18

ALL-TIME PLAYING RECORDS BY POINTS

		P	W	D	L	F	A	Pts	S	B	W
1	Manchester United	316	196	80	40	623	284	668	8	1	2
2	Arsenal	316	149	91	76	456	272	538	8	1	12
3	Liverpool	316	145	83	88	505	339	518	8	3	8
4	Leeds United	316	129	91	96	426	357	478	8	3	17
5	Aston Villa	316	129	86	101	399	344	473	8	2	18
6	Chelsea	316	126	95	95	435	368	473	8	3	14
7	Blackburn Rovers	278	122	74	82	409	315	440	7	1	19
8	Newcastle United	274	122	71	81	434	317	437	7	2	13
9	Tottenham Hotspur	316	109	90	117	422	427	417	8	7	15
10	Sheffield Wednesday	316	101	89	126	409	453	392	8	7	19
11	Wimbledon	316	99	94	123	384	472	391	8	6	18
12	Everton	316	97	92	127	389	422	383	8	6	17
13	Coventry City	316	91	102	123	351	427	375	8	11	17
14	West Ham United	274	97	72	105	327	369	363	7	5	14
15	Southampton	316	93	80	143	380	479	359	8	10	18
16	Nottingham Forest	198	60	59	79	229	287	239	5	3	22
17	Leicester City	194	59	56	79	237	276	233	5	8	21
18	Middlesbrough	194	58	58	78	234	291	229	5	9	21
19	QPR	164	59	39	66	224	232	216	4	5	19
20	Derby County	152	49	44	59	181	209	191	4	8	16
21	Manchester City	164	45	54	65	180	222	189	4	9	18
22	Norwich City	126	43	39	44	163	180	168	3	3	20
23	Crystal Palace	122	30	37	55	119	181	127	3	19	20
24	Ipswich Town	126	28	38	60	121	206	122	3	16	22
25	Sunderland	76	26	20	30	92	109	98	2	7	18
26	Sheffield United	84	22	28	34	96	113	94	2	14	20
27	Oldham Athletic	84	22	23	39	105	142	89	2	19	21
28	Bolton Wanderers	76	17	18	41	80	132	69	2	18	20
29	Bradford City	38	9	9	20	38	68	36	1	17	17
30	Charlton Athletic	38	8	12	18	41	56	36	1	18	18
31	Barnsley	38	10	5	23	37	82	35	1	19	19
32	Swindon Town	42	5	15	22	47	100	30	1	22	22
33	Watford	38	6	6	26	35	77	24	1	20	20

Key:
S=Seasons – number of seasons competed in Premier League.
B=Best position obtained.
W=Worst position obtained.

COMPOSITE FINAL TABLE

Pos	Team	P	W	D	L	F	A	Pts	
1	Manchester United	42	24	12	6	67	31	84	Champions' Cup
2	Aston Villa	42	21	11	10	57	40	74	UEFA Cup
3	Norwich City	42	21	9	12	61	65	72	UEFA Cup
4	Blackburn Rovers	42	20	11	11	68	46	71	
5	QPR	42	17	12	13	63	55	63	
6	Liverpool	42	16	11	15	62	55	59	
7	Sheffield Wednesday	42	15	14	13	55	51	59	
8	Tottenham Hotspur	42	16	11	15	60	66	59	
9	Manchester City	42	15	12	15	56	51	57	
10	Arsenal	42	15	11	16	40	38	56	Cup Winners' Cup
11	Chelsea	42	14	14	14	51	54	56	
12	Wimbledon	42	14	12	16	56	55	54	
13	Everton	42	15	8	19	53	55	53	
14	Sheffield United	42	14	10	18	54	53	52	
15	Coventry City	42	13	13	16	52	57	52	
16	Ipswich Town	42	12	16	14	50	55	52	
17	Leeds United	42	12	15	15	57	62	51	
18	Southampton	42	13	11	18	54	61	50	
19	Oldham Athletic	42	13	10	19	63	74	49	
20	Crystal Palace	42	11	16	15	48	61	49	Relegated
21	Middlesbrough	42	11	11	20	54	75	44	Relegated
22	Nottingham Forest	42	10	10	22	41	62	40	Relegated

HOME & AWAY FINAL TABLE

Pos	Team	P	Home					Away					Pts
			W	D	L	F	A	W	D	L	F	A	
1	Manchester United	42	14	5	2	39	14	10	7	4	28	17	84
2	Aston Villa	42	13	5	3	36	16	8	6	7	21	24	74
3	Norwich City	42	13	6	2	31	19	8	3	10	30	46	72
4	Blackburn Rovers	42	13	4	4	38	18	7	7	7	30	28	71
5	QPR	42	11	5	5	41	32	6	7	8	22	23	63
6	Liverpool	42	13	4	4	41	18	3	7	11	21	37	59
7	Sheffield Wednesday	42	9	8	4	34	26	6	6	9	21	25	59
8	Tottenham Hotspur	42	11	5	5	40	25	5	6	10	20	41	59
9	Manchester City	42	7	8	6	30	25	8	4	9	26	26	57
10	Arsenal	42	8	6	7	25	20	7	5	9	15	18	56
11	Chelsea	42	9	7	5	29	22	5	7	9	22	32	56
12	Wimbledon	42	9	4	8	32	23	5	8	8	24	32	54
13	Everton	42	7	6	8	26	27	8	2	11	27	28	53
14	Sheffield United	42	10	6	5	33	19	4	4	13	21	34	52
15	Coventry City	42	7	4	10	29	28	6	9	6	23	29	52
16	Ipswich Town	42	8	9	4	29	22	4	7	10	21	33	52
17	Leeds United	42	12	8	1	40	17	0	7	14	17	45	51
18	Southampton	42	10	6	5	30	21	3	5	13	24	40	50
19	Oldham Athletic	42	10	6	5	43	30	3	4	14	20	44	49
20	Crystal Palace	42	6	9	6	27	25	5	7	9	21	36	49
21	Middlesbrough	42	8	5	8	33	27	3	6	12	21	48	44
22	Nottingham Forest	42	6	4	11	17	25	4	6	11	24	37	40

1992-93 – SEASON FACTS

TOP SCORERS

Player	Club	Gls
Sheringham, Teddy†	Tottenham H.	22
Ferdinand, Les	QPR	20
Holdsworth, Dean	Wimbledon	19
Quinn, Mick	Coventry C.	17
Shearer, Shearer	Blackburn R.	16
White, David	Manchester C.	16

†Including 1 for Nottingham Forest.

EVER-PRESENT PLAYERS

Player	Club	Tot	St	Sb	Ps	Gls
Barrett, Earl	Aston Villa	42	42	0	0	1
Bowen, Mark	Norwich C.	42	42	0	0	1
Flowers, Tim	Southampton	42	42	0	0	0
Gunn, Bryan	Norwich C.	42	42	0	0	0
Martyn, Nigel	Crystal P.	42	42	0	0	0
Mimms, Bobby	Blackburn R.	42	42	0	0	0
Pallister, Gary	Manchester U.	42	42	0	0	1
Schmeichel, Peter	Manchester U.	42	42	0	0	0
Bruce, Steve	Manchester U.	42	42	0	1	5
Clough, Nigel	Nottingham F.	42	42	0	1	10
Earle, Robbie	Wimbledon	42	42	0	1	7
McGoldrick, Eddie	Crystal P.	42	42	0	1	8
McGrath, Ray	Aston Villa	42	42	0	1	4
Milligan, Mike	Oldham A.	42	42	0	1	3
Richardson, Kevin	Aston Villa	42	42	0	1	2
Staunton, Steve	Aston Villa	42	42	0	1	2
Linighan, David	Ipswich T.	42	42	0	2	1
Phillips, David	Norwich C.	42	42	0	2	9
White, David	Manchester C.	42	42	0	3	16
McClair, Brian	Manchester U.	42	41	1	2	9

ATTENDANCES BY CLUB

Club	Total	Average
Arsenal	512,466	24,403
Aston Villa	622,472	29,642
Blackburn R.	341,207	16,248
Chelsea	393,865	18,755
Coventry C.	314,897	14,995
Crystal P.	330,698	15,748
Everton	429,588	20,457
Ipswich T.	381,881	18,185
Leeds U.	613,798	29,228
Liverpool	777,213	37,010
Manchester C.	518,628	24,697
Manchester U.	737,768	35,132
Middlesbrough	351,162	16,722
Norwich C.	342,338	16,302
Nottingham F.	459,194	21,866
Oldham A.	270,032	12,859
QPR	315,342	15,016
Sheffield U.	394,826	18,801
Sheffield W.	572,534	27,264
Southampton	323,018	15,382
Tottenham H.	585,241	27,869
Wimbledon	176,505	8,405
Total	9,764,673	21,136

TOP SCORERS BY CLUB

Club	Scorers
Arsenal	Wright 15, Merson 6, Campbell 4
Aston Villa	Saunders 13, Atkinson 11, Parker 9
Blackburn R.	Shearer 16, Newell 13, Ripley 7
Chelsea	Harford 9, Stuart 9, Spencer 7
Coventry C.	Quinn 17, J Williams 8, Ndlovu 7
Crystal Palace	Armstrong 15, McGoldrick 8, Young 6
Everton	Cottee 12, Beardsley 10, Barlow 5
Ipswich T.	Kiwomya 10, Dozzell 7, Wark 6
Leeds U.	Chapman 15, Speed 7, Wallace 7
Liverpool	Rush 14, Walters 11, Hutchison 7
Manchester C.	White 16, Sheron 11, Quinn 9
Manchester U.	Hughes 15, Cantona 9, Giggs 9, McClair 9
Middlesbrough	Wilkinson 15, Hendrie 9, Falconer 5, Wright 5
Norwich C.	Robins 15, Phillips 9, Sutton 8
Nottingham Forest	Clough 10, Bannister 8, Keane 6
Oldham A.	Olney 12, Adams 9, Sharp 7
QPR	Ferdinand 20, Allen 10, Sinton 7
Sheffield U.	Deane 15, Littlejohn 8, Whitehouse 5
Sheffield W.	Bright 11, Hirst 11, Bart-Williams 6, Warhurst 6
Southampton	Le Tissier 15, Dowie 11, Banger 6
Tottenham H.	Sheringham 21, Anderton 6, Barmby 6
Wimbledon	Holdsworth 19, Fashanu 6, Clark 5

11

1992-93 – RESULTS GRID

	Arsenal	A.Villa	Blackb'n	Chelsea	Coventry	Crystal P.	Everton	Ipswich	Leeds	Liverpool	Man.C.
Arsenal	–	0-1	0-1	2-1	3-0	3-0	2-0	0-0	0-0	0-1	1-0
Aston Villa	1-0	–	0-0	1-3	0-0	3-0	2-1	2-0	1-1	4-2	3-1
Blackburn R.	1-0	3-0	–	2-0	2-5	1-2	2-3	2-1	3-1	4-1	1-0
Chelsea	1-0	0-1	0-0	–	2-1	3-1	2-1	2-1	1-0	0-0	2-4
Coventry C.	0-2	3-0	0-2	1-2	–	2-2	0-1	2-2	3-3	5-1	2-3
Crystal P.	1-2	1-0	3-3	1-1	0-0	–	0-2	3-1	1-0	1-1	0-0
Everton	0-0	1-0	2-1	1-0	1-1	0-2	–	3-0	2-0	2-1	1-3
Ipswich T.	1-2	1-1	2-1	1-1	0-0	2-2	1-0	–	4-2	2-2	3-1
Leeds U.	3-0	1-1	5-2	1-1	2-2	0-0	2-0	1-0	–	2-2	1-0
Liverpool	0-2	1-2	2-1	2-1	4-0	5-0	1-0	0-0	2-0	–	1-1
Manchester C.	0-1	1-1	3-2	0-1	1-0	0-0	2-5	3-1	4-0	1-1	–
Manchester U.	0-0	1-1	3-1	3-0	5-0	1-0	0-3	1-1	2-0	2-2	2-1
Middlesbrough	1-0	2-3	3-2	0-0	0-2	0-1	1-2	2-2	4-1	1-2	2-0
Norwich C.	1-1	1-0	0-0	2-1	1-1	4-2	1-1	0-2	4-2	1-0	2-1
Nottingham F.	0-1	0-1	1-3	3-0	1-1	1-1	0-1	0-1	1-1	1-0	0-2
Oldham A.	0-1	1-1	0-1	3-1	0-1	1-1	1-0	4-2	2-2	3-2	0-1
QPR	0-0	2-1	0-3	1-1	2-0	1-3	4-2	0-0	2-1	0-1	1-1
Sheffield U.	1-1	0-2	1-3	4-2	1-1	0-1	1-0	3-0	2-1	1-0	1-1
Sheffield W.	1-0	1-2	0-0	3-3	1-2	2-1	3-1	1-1	1-1	1-1	0-3
Southampton	2-0	2-0	1-1	1-0	2-2	1-0	0-0	4-3	1-1	2-1	0-1
Tottenham H.	1-0	0-0	1-2	1-2	0-2	2-2	2-1	0-2	4-0	2-0	3-1
Wimbledon	3-2	2-3	1-1	0-0	1-2	4-0	1-3	0-1	1-0	2-0	0-1

	Man.U.	Middlesb'	Norwich	N.Forest	Oldham	QPR	Sheff.U.	Sheff.W.	South'ton	Tottenham	Wim'don
Arsenal	0-1	1-1	2-4	1-1	2-0	0-0	1-1	2-1	4-3	1-3	0-1
Aston Villa	1-0	5-1	2-3	2-1	0-1	2-0	3-1	2-0	1-1	0-0	1-0
Blackburn R.	0-0	1-1	7-1	4-1	2-0	1-0	1-0	1-0	0-0	0-2	0-0
Chelsea	1-1	4-0	2-3	0-0	1-1	1-0	1-2	0-2	1-1	1-1	4-2
Coventry C.	0-1	2-1	1-1	0-1	3-0	0-1	1-3	1-0	2-0	1-0	0-2
Crystal P.	0-2	4-1	1-2	1-1	2-2	1-1	2-0	1-1	1-2	1-3	2-0
Everton	0-2	2-2	0-1	3-0	2-2	3-5	0-2	1-1	2-1	1-2	0-0
Ipswich T.	2-1	0-1	3-1	2-1	1-2	1-1	0-0	0-1	0-0	1-1	2-1
Leeds U.	0-0	3-0	0-0	1-4	2-0	1-1	3-1	3-1	2-1	5-0	2-1
Liverpool	1-2	4-1	4-1	0-0	1-0	2-1	1-0	1-1	1-1	6-2	2-3
Manchester C.	1-1	0-1	3-1	2-2	3-3	1-1	2-0	1-2	1-0	0-1	1-1
Manchester U.	–	3-0	1-0	2-0	3-0	0-0	2-1	2-1	2-1	4-1	0-1
Middlesbrough	1-1	–	3-3	1-2	2-3	0-1	2-0	1-1	2-1	3-0	2-0
Norwich C.	1-3	1-1	–	3-1	1-0	2-1	2-1	1-0	1-0	0-0	2-1
Nottingham F.	0-2	1-0	0-3	–	2-0	1-0	0-2	1-2	1-2	2-1	1-1
Oldham A.	1-0	4-1	2-3	5-3	–	2-2	1-1	1-1	4-3	2-1	6-2
QPR	1-3	3-3	3-1	4-3	3-2	–	3-2	3-1	3-1	4-1	1-2
Sheffield U.	2-1	2-0	0-1	0-0	2-0	1-2	–	1-1	2-0	6-0	2-2
Sheffield W.	3-3	2-3	1-0	2-0	2-1	1-0	1-1	–	5-2	2-0	1-1
Southampton	0-1	2-1	3-0	1-2	1-0	1-2	3-2	1-2	–	0-0	2-2
Tottenham H.	1-1	2-2	5-1	2-1	4-1	3-2	2-0	0-2	4-2	–	1-1
Wimbledon	1-2	2-0	3-0	1-0	5-2	0-2	2-0	1-1	1-2	1-1	–

	Arsenal	A.Villa	Blackb'n	Chelsea	Coventry	Crystal P.	Everton	Ipswich	Leeds	Liverpool	Man.C.
Arsenal	–	27,125	28,643	27,780	27,693	25,225	28,052	26,198	21,061	27,580	21,504
Aston Villa	35,170	–	30,398	19,125	38,543	17,120	33,913	25,395	29,151	37,863	33,108
Blackburn R.	16,454	15,127	–	14,780	15,215	14,163	19,563	14,071	19,910	15,032	19,433
Chelsea	17,725	20,081	19,575	–	14,186	17,141	12,739	16,702	24,345	20,981	15,939
Coventry C.	15,437	24,245	14,541	15,626	–	11,808	11,285	11,294	19,591	19,779	14,590
Crystal P.	20,734	12,270	17,086	12,610	12,248	–	13,227	18,881	14,462	18,688	14,005
Everton	19,044	22,372	18,086	17,418	17,587	18,080	–	15,638	21,031	35,826	20,242
Ipswich T.	20,358	16,818	21,431	17,444	16,698	17,861	18,032	–	21,200	20,109	16,833
Leeds U.	30,516	27,815	31,791	28,135	28,018	27,545	27,915	28,848	–	29,597	30,840
Liverpool	34,961	40,826	43,688	34,199	33,328	36,380	44,619	36,680	34,992	–	43,037
Manchester C.	25,047	23,525	29,122	22,420	20,092	21,167	25,180	20,680	27,255	28,098	–
Manchester U.	37,301	36,163	40,447	40,139	36,025	29,736	31,901	31,704	31,296	33,243	35,408
Middlesbrough	12,726	20,905	20,096	15,559	14,008	21,123	16,627	14,255	18,649	22,463	15,369
Norwich C.	14,820	19,528	15,821	15,164	13,613	13,543	14,150	20,032	18,613	20,610	16,386
Nottingham F.	24,862	26,742	20,467	23,249	17,553	20,603	20,941	21,411	25,148	20,038	25,956
Oldham A.	12,311	13,457	13,742	11,762	11,254	11,063	13,013	11,150	13,848	15,381	14,903
QPR	20,868	18,904	10,677	15,806	12,453	14,571	14,802	12,806	19,326	21,056	13,003
Sheffield U.	19,105	18,773	18,186	24,850	15,625	18,857	16,266	16,758	20,562	20,632	18,231
Sheffield W.	23,645	29,964	31,044	26,338	22,874	26,459	24,979	24,270	26,855	33,964	27,169
Southampton	17,286	19,087	16,626	15,135	12,306	13,397	16,911	15,428	16,229	17,216	16,730
Tottenham H.	33,709	32,852	23,097	31,540	24,388	25,237	26,303	23,738	32,040	32,917	27,247
Wimbledon	12,906	6,849	6,117	14,687	3,759	12,275	3,039	4,954	6,704	11,294	4,714

	Man.U.	Middlesb'	Norwich	N.Forest	Oldham	QPR	Sheff.U.	Sheff.W.	South'ton	Tottenham	Wim'don
Arsenal	29,739	23,197	24,030	19,024	20,796	18,817	23,818	23,389	24,149	26,393	18,253
Aston Villa	39,063	19,977	28,837	29,015	37,247	20,140	20,266	38,024	17,894	37,727	34,496
Blackburn R.	20,305	14,041	16,312	16,180	18,383	15,850	16,057	14,956	13,566	17,305	14,504
Chelsea	34,496	13,043	16,880	19,760	20,699	22,910	13,763	16,261	18,344	25,157	13,138
Coventry C.	24,429	12,681	16,436	15,264	10,544	13,563	12,993	13,206	10,463	15,348	11,774
Crystal P.	30,115	15,123	12,033	15,330	11,224	14,705	12,361	14,005	13,829	20,937	16,825
Everton	30,002	24,391	20,301	21,271	18,025	19,057	15,197	27,687	14,051	16,164	18,118
Ipswich T.	22,068	15,430	21,081	22,093	15,025	17,354	16,353	16,538	15,722	20,100	13,333
Leeds U.	34,166	30,344	30,282	29,364	27,654	31,408	29,706	29,770	26,071	28,218	25,795
Liverpool	44,374	34,974	36,318	40,463	36,129	30,370	33,107	35,785	30,024	43,385	29,574
Manchester C.	37,136	25,244	23,182	22,571	27,255	24,471	27,455	23,619	20,089	25,496	19,524
Manchester U.	–	36,251	34,500	36,085	33,497	33,287	36,156	40,102	36,257	35,648	32,622
Middlesbrough	24,172	–	15,155	15,639	12,290	15,616	15,179	18,414	13,921	14,472	14,524
Norwich C.	20,582	14,499	–	14,104	19,597	16,009	14,874	14,367	12,452	19,413	14,161
Nottingham F.	19,694	16,897	20,799	–	21,240	22,436	26,752	19,420	19,942	25,682	19,362
Oldham A.	17,106	12,401	11,018	11,632	–	10,946	14,795	12,312	14,597	11,735	11,606
QPR	21,142	12,272	13,892	15,815	11,800	–	10,932	12,177	10,925	19,845	12,270
Sheffield U.	28,070	15,184	15,583	19,152	14,628	16,366	–	30,039	15,842	16,654	15,463
Sheffield W.	37,708	25,949	23,360	29,623	24,485	23,164	38,688	–	26,183	24,895	20,918
Southampton	15,623	13,003	12,969	18,005	10,827	14,125	13,814	17,426	–	19,654	11,221
Tottenham H.	33,296	24,735	31,425	32,118	26,663	32,341	21,322	25,702	20,098	–	24,473
Wimbledon	30,115	5,821	10,875	9,358	3,386	6,771	3,979	5,740	4,534	8,628	–

1993-94 FINAL TABLES

COMPOSITE FINAL TABLE

Pos	Team	P	W	D	L	F	A	Pts	
1	Manchester United	42	27	11	4	80	38	92	Champions' Cup
2	Blackburn Rovers	42	25	9	8	63	36	84	UEFA Cup
3	Newcastle United	42	23	8	11	82	41	77	UEFA Cup
4	Arsenal	42	18	17	7	53	28	71	Cup-Winners' Cup
5	Leeds United	42	18	16	8	65	39	70	
6	Wimbledon	42	18	11	13	56	53	65	
7	Sheffield Wednesday	42	16	16	10	76	54	64	
8	Liverpool	42	17	9	16	59	55	60	
9	QPR	42	16	12	14	62	61	60	
10	Aston Villa	42	15	12	15	46	50	57	UEFA Cup (League Cup winners)
11	Coventry City	42	14	14	14	43	45	56	
12	Norwich City	42	12	17	13	65	61	53	
13	West Ham United	42	13	13	16	47	58	52	
14	Chelsea	42	13	12	17	49	53	51	Cup-Winners' Cup
15	Tottenham Hotspur	42	11	12	19	54	59	45	
16	Manchester City	42	9	18	15	38	49	45	
17	Everton	42	12	8	22	42	63	44	
18	Southampton	42	12	7	23	49	66	43	
19	Ipswich Town	42	9	16	17	35	58	43	
20	Sheffield United	42	8	18	16	42	60	42	Relegated
21	Oldham Athletic	42	9	13	20	42	68	40	Relegated
22	Swindon Town	42	5	15	22	47	100	30	Relegated

HOME & AWAY FINAL TABLE

Pos	Team	P	Home					Away					Pts
			W	D	L	F	A	W	D	L	F	A	
1	Manchester United	42	14	6	1	39	13	13	5	3	41	25	92
2	Blackburn Rovers	42	14	5	2	31	11	11	4	6	32	25	84
3	Newcastle United	42	14	4	3	51	14	9	4	8	31	27	77
4	Arsenal	42	10	8	3	25	15	8	9	4	28	13	71
5	Leeds United	42	13	6	2	37	18	5	10	6	28	21	70
6	Wimbledon	42	12	5	4	35	21	6	6	9	21	32	65
7	Sheffield Wednesday	42	10	7	4	48	24	6	9	6	28	30	64
8	Liverpool	42	12	4	5	33	23	5	5	11	26	32	60
9	QPR	42	8	7	6	32	29	8	5	8	30	32	60
10	Aston Villa	42	8	5	8	23	18	7	7	7	23	32	57
11	Coventry City	42	9	7	5	23	17	5	7	9	20	28	56
12	Norwich City	42	4	9	8	26	29	8	8	5	39	32	53
13	West Ham United	42	6	7	8	26	31	7	6	8	21	27	52
14	Chelsea	42	11	5	5	31	20	2	7	12	18	33	51
15	Tottenham Hotspur	42	4	8	9	29	33	7	4	10	25	26	45
16	Manchester City	42	6	10	5	24	22	3	8	10	14	27	45
17	Everton	42	8	4	9	26	30	4	4	13	16	33	44
18	Southampton	42	9	2	10	30	31	3	5	13	19	35	43
19	Ipswich Town	42	5	8	8	21	32	4	8	9	14	26	43
20	Sheffield United	42	6	10	5	24	23	2	8	11	18	37	42
21	Oldham Athletic	42	5	8	8	24	33	4	5	12	18	35	40
22	Swindon Town	42	4	7	10	25	45	1	8	12	22	55	30

TOP SCORERS

Player	Club	Gls
COLE, Andy	Newcastle U.	34
SHEARER, Alan	Blackburn R.	31
SUTTON, Chris	Norwich C.	25
Le TISSIER, Matt	Southampton	25
WRIGHT, Ian	Arsenal	23
BEARDSLEY, Peter	Newcastle U.	21
BRIGHT, Mark	Sheffield W.	19
CANTONA, Eric	Manchester U.	18
FERNINAND, Les	QPR	17
HOLDSWORTH, Dean	Wimbledon	17
WALLACE, Rod	Leeds U.	17
COTTEE, Tony	Everton	16
CAMPBELL, Kevin	Arsenal	14
RUSH, Ian	Liverpool	14
SHERINGHAM, Teddy	Tottenham H.	14

EVER-PRESENT PLAYERS

Player	Club	Tot	St	Sb	Ps	Gl
Culverhouse, Ian	Norwich C.	42	42	0	0	1
Earle, Robbie	Wimbledon	42	42	0	0	0
Kelly, Gary	Leeds U.	42	42	0	0	0
McAllister, Gary	Leeds U.	42	42	0	0	8
Miklosko, Ludek	West Ham U.	42	42	0	0	0
Southall, Neville	Everton	42	42	0	0	0
Stockwell, Mick	Ipswich T.	42	42	0	0	1
Taylor, Shaun	Swindon T.	42	42	0	0	4
Wilson, Clive	QPR	42	42	0	0	3
Irwin, Denis	Manchester U.	42	42	0	1	2
Sedgely, Steve	Tottenham H.	42	42	0	2	6
Walker, Des	Sheffield W.	42	42	0	2	0
Houldsworth, Dean	Wimbledon	42	42	0	3	0
Rush, Ian	Liverpool	42	41	1	2	14
Morley, Trevor	West Ham U.	42	39	3	5	13

ATTENDANCES BY CLUB

Club	Total	Average
Arsenal	641,833	30,563
Aston Villa	609,314	29,015
Blackburn R.	372,145	17,721
Chelsea	406,732	19,368
Coventry C.	280,389	13,352
Everton	480,391	22,876
Ipswich T.	343,825	16,373
Leeds U.	724,363	34,493
Liverpool	808,361	38,493
Manchester C.	565,899	26,948
Manchester U.	929,133	44,244
Newcastle U.	707,269	33,679
Norwich C.	381,436	18,164
Oldham A.	263,815	12,563
QPR	298,782	14,228
Sheffield U.	410,805	19,562
Sheffield W.	571,002	27,191
Southampton	309,765	14,751
Swindon T.	320,761	15,274
Tottenham H.	570,359	27,160
West Ham U.	432,008	20,572
Wimbledon	219,961	10,474

TOP SCORERS BY CLUB

Club	Scorers
Arsenal	Wright 23, Campbell 14, Merson 8
Aston Villa	Saunders 10, Atkinson 8, Richardson 5
Blackburn R.	Shearer 31, Gallagher 7, Newell 6, Wilcox 6
Chelsea	Stein 13, Peacock 8, Shipperley 4
Coventry C.	Ndlovu 11, Quinn 8, Wegerle 6
Everton	Cottee 16, Rideout 6, Ebbrell 4
Ipswich T.	Marshall 10, Kiwomya 5
Leeds U.	Rod Wallace 17, Deane 11, McAllister 9
Liverpool	Rush 14, Fowler 12, Clough 7
Manchester C.	Sheron 6, Quinn 5
Manchester U.	Cantona 18, Giggs 13, Hughes 12
Newcastle U.	Cole 34, Beardlsey 21, Lee 7
Norwich C.	Sutton 25, Ekoku 12
QPR	Ferdinand 17, White 8, Penrice 8
Sheffield W.	Bright 19, Watson 12
Southampton	Le Tissier 25, Dowie 5
Tottenham H.	Sheringham 14, Dozzell 8, Anderton 6
West Ham U.	Morley 13, Allen M 7, Chapman 7
Wimbledon	Holdsworth 17, Fashanu 11, Earle 9

1993-94 RESULTS GRIDS

	Arsenal	Aston Villa	Blackburn R.	Chelsea	Coventry C.	Everton	Ipswich T.	Leeds U.	Liverpool	Manchester C.	Manchester U.
Arsenal	–	1-2	1-0	1-0	0-3	2-0	4-0	2-1	1-0	0-0	2-2
Aston Villa	1-2	–	0-1	1-0	0-0	0-0	0-1	1-0	2-1	0-0	1-2
Blackburn R.	1-1	1-0	–	2-0	2-1	2-0	0-0	2-1	2-0	2-0	2-0
Chelsea	0-2	1-1	1-2	–	1-2	4-2	1-1	1-1	1-0	0-0	1-0
Coventry C.	1-0	0-1	2-1	1-1	–	2-1	1-0	0-2	1-0	4-0	0-1
Everton	1-1	0-1	0-3	4-2	0-0	–	0-0	1-1	2-0	1-0	0-1
Ipswich T.	1-5	1-2	1-0	1-0	0-2	0-2	–	0-0	1-2	2-2	1-2
Leeds U.	2-1	2-0	3-3	4-1	1-0	3-0	0-0	–	2-0	3-2	0-2
Liverpool	0-0	2-1	0-1	2-1	1-0	2-1	1-0	2-0	–	2-1	3-3
Manchester C.	0-0	3-0	0-2	2-2	1-1	1-0	2-1	1-1	1-1	–	2-3
Manchester U.	1-0	3-1	1-1	0-1	0-0	1-0	0-0	0-0	1-0	2-0	–
Newcastle U.	2-0	5-1	1-1	0-0	4-0	1-0	2-0	1-1	3-0	2-0	1-1
Norwich C.	1-1	1-2	2-2	1-1	1-0	3-0	1-0	2-1	2-2	1-1	0-2
Oldham A.	0-0	1-1	1-2	2-1	3-3	0-1	0-3	1-1	0-3	0-0	2-5
QPR	1-1	2-2	1-0	1-1	5-1	2-1	3-0	0-4	1-3	1-1	2-3
Sheffield U.	1-1	1-2	1-2	1-0	0-0	0-0	1-1	2-2	0-0	0-1	0-3
Sheffield W.	0-1	0-0	1-2	3-1	0-0	5-1	5-0	3-3	3-1	1-1	2-3
Southampton	0-4	4-1	3-1	3-1	1-0	0-2	0-1	0-2	4-2	0-1	1-3
Swindon T.	0-4	1-2	1-3	1-3	3-1	1-1	2-2	0-5	0-5	1-3	2-2
Tottenham H.	0-1	1-1	0-2	1-1	1-2	3-2	1-1	1-1	3-3	1-0	0-1
West Ham U.	0-0	0-0	1-2	1-0	3-2	0-1	2-1	0-1	1-2	3-1	2-2
Wimbledon	0-3	2-2	4-1	1-1	1-2	1-1	0-2	1-0	1-1	1-0	1-0

	Newcastle U.	Norwich C.	Oldham A.	QPR	Sheffield U.	Sheffield W.	Southampton	Swindon T.	Tottenham H.	West Ham U.	Wimbledon
Arsenal	2-1	0-0	1-1	0-0	3-0	1-0	1-0	1-1	1-1	0-2	1-1
Aston Villa	0-2	0-0	1-2	4-1	1-0	2-2	0-2	5-0	1-0	3-1	0-1
Blackburn R.	1-0	2-3	1-0	1-1	0-0	1-1	2-0	3-1	1-0	0-2	3-0
Chelsea	1-0	1-2	0-1	2-0	3-2	1-1	2-0	2-0	4-3	2-0	2-0
Coventry C.	2-1	2-1	1-1	0-1	0-0	1-1	1-1	1-1	1-0	1-1	1-2
Everton	0-2	1-5	2-1	0-3	4-2	0-2	1-0	6-2	0-1	0-1	3-2
Ipswich T.	1-1	2-1	0-0	1-3	3-2	1-4	1-0	1-1	2-2	1-1	0-0
Leeds U.	1-1	0-4	1-0	1-1	2-1	2-2	0-0	3-0	2-0	1-0	4-0
Liverpool	0-2	0-1	2-1	3-2	1-2	2-0	4-2	2-2	1-2	2-0	1-1
Manchester C.	2-1	1-1	1-1	3-0	0-0	1-3	1-1	2-1	0-2	0-0	0-1
Manchester U.	1-1	2-2	3-2	2-1	3-0	5-0	2-0	4-2	2-1	3-0	3-1
Newcastle U.	–	3-0	3-2	1-2	4-0	4-2	1-2	7-1	0-1	2-0	4-0
Norwich C.	1-2	–	1-1	3-4	0-1	1-1	4-5	0-0	1-2	0-0	0-1
Oldham A.	1-3	2-1	–	4-1	1-1	0-0	2-1	2-1	0-2	1-2	1-1
QPR	1-2	2-2	2-0	–	2-1	1-2	2-1	1-3	1-1	0-0	1-0
Sheffield U.	2-0	1-2	2-1	1-1	–	1-1	0-0	3-1	2-2	3-2	2-1
Sheffield W.	0-1	3-3	3-0	3-1	3-1	–	2-0	3-3	1-0	5-0	2-2
Southampton	2-1	0-1	1-3	0-1	3-3	1-1	–	5-1	1-0	0-2	1-0
Swindon T.	2-2	3-3	0-1	1-0	0-0	0-1	2-1	–	2-1	1-1	2-4
Tottenham H.	1-2	1-3	5-0	1-2	2-2	1-3	3-0	1-1	–	1-4	1-1
West Ham U.	2-4	3-3	2-0	0-4	0-0	2-0	3-3	0-0	1-3	–	0-2
Wimbledon	4-2	3-1	3-0	1-1	2-0	2-1	1-0	3-0	2-1	1-2	–

1993-94 ATTENDANCE GRIDS

	Arsenal	Aston Villa	Blackburn R.	Chelsea	Coventry C.	Everton	Ipswich T.	Leeds U.	Liverpool	Manchester C.	Manchester U.
Arsenal	–	31,773	35,030	34,314	26,397	29,063	28,563	29,042	35,556	29,567	36,203
Aston Villa	31,580	–	40,903	29,706	31,181	36,044	23,732	26,919	45,347	19,254	39,624
Blackburn R.	14,410	19,287	–	16,756	16,376	22,061	20,633	17,475	20,831	19,479	20,866
Chelsea	26,839	18,348	29,189	–	8,923	18,338	13,208	18,544	31,271	10,128	37,064
Coventry C.	12,632	14,323	16,646	13,586	–	11,550	11,244	13,933	16,735	11,739	17,009
Everton	19,760	24,067	27,463	18,201	23,352	–	19,641	17,102	38,157	26,025	35,455
Ipswich T.	18,803	16,658	14,436	17,355	12,782	15,094	–	17,532	22,270	12,871	22,478
Leeds U.	37,289	33,126	37,827	35,050	30,023	35,487	31,317	–	40,029	33,820	41,127
Liverpool	42,750	38,484	37,355	38,629	38,547	44,281	30,485	44,068	–	41,872	42,795
Manchester C.	25,642	26,075	25,185	33,594	21,537	25,513	28,188	32,366	30,403	–	35,155
Manchester U.	44,009	44,499	44,511	44,745	44,717	44,750	43,300	44,724	44,751	44,333	–
Newcastle U.	32,216	32,217	33,987	32,218	32,210	34,490	32,234	36,342	36,246	35,585	36,332
Norwich C.	17,667	20,650	15,124	19,472	16,239	16,432	18,976	16,586	19,746	16,626	19,705
Oldham A.	12,105	12,836	13,887	12,002	10,817	13,666	12,074	11,136	14,573	16,462	16,708
QPR	11,442	14,915	17,636	15,735	12,979	13,330	12,292	15,365	19,625	13,474	21,267
Sheffield U.	20,019	18,402	19,124	16,119	15,394	15,135	17,932	19,425	22,932	20,067	26,744
Sheffield W.	26,023	28,450	24,655	20,433	23,379	24,080	23,854	31,892	32,177	33,589	34,548
Southampton	16,790	18,803	19,105	14,221	12,397	14,051	9,028	13,511	18,306	16,377	16,189
Swindon T.	17,214	16,322	15,847	16,261	14,635	14,437	13,860	17,228	17,364	16,067	18,102
Tottenham H.	28,355	17,452	30,236	27,567	26,015	27,487	26,653	31,275	31,394	24,535	31,343
West Ham U.	20,279	20,416	22,186	18,917	17,243	20,243	18,307	20,468	26,106	16,605	28,382
Wimbledon	16,584	7,564	10,537	11,263	4,739	6,934	7,756	9,035	13,819	8,533	28,553

	Newcastle U.	Norwich C.	Oldham A.	QPR	Sheffield U.	Sheffield W.	Southampton	Swindon T.	Tottenham H.	West Ham U.	Wimbledon
Arsenal	36,091	30,516	26,524	34,935	27,035	22,026	26,902	31,635	35,669	33,700	21,292
Aston Villa	37,336	25,416	21,214	32,944	24,686	20,304	16,180	27,637	32,498	28,869	17,940
Blackburn R.	20,798	14,260	14,397	19,193	14,276	14,495	17,343	20,046	17,462	14,437	17,264
Chelsea	22,133	16,923	15,372	20,191	21,782	16,652	19,801	11,180	19,398	19,545	11,903
Coventry C.	15,760	13,515	11,792	12,065	10,439	13,052	9,837	15,869	14,487	12,864	11,312
Everton	25,362	20,631	18,881	17,326	24,177	16,471	13,265	20,760	23,460	19,602	31,233
Ipswich T.	19,126	19,751	11,789	14,653	11,468	14,767	14,958	14,760	19,437	20,988	11,849
Leeds U.	40,005	32,008	28,717	39,124	33,879	33,575	30,829	32,630	33,658	34,588	30,255
Liverpool	44,601	44,339	32,661	24,561	36,642	43,792	32,818	32,739	42,456	42,254	32,232
Manchester C.	33,774	28,020	21,401	24,445	25,448	23,416	24,712	26,360	21,566	29,118	23,981
Manchester U.	41,829	44,694	44,686	44,663	41,949	43,669	44,705	44,583	44,655	44,613	44,748
Newcastle U.	–	32,228	32,214	33,801	35,029	33,519	32,067	32,219	34,565	34,179	33,371
Norwich C.	19,564	–	20,394	16,499	18,474	18,311	17,150	17,614	21,181	20,175	14,851
Oldham A.	13,821	10,198	–	10,440	14,779	12,973	9,982	9,771	14,283	11,669	9,633
QPR	15,774	13,359	13,218	–	11,113	16,858	10,613	9,875	17,694	10,850	11,368
Sheffield U.	29,013	18,254	17,066	14,183	–	30,044	19,522	20,904	21,325	13,646	15,555
Sheffield W.	33,153	25,175	18,509	22,437	34,959	–	22,503	30,570	32,514	26,350	21,752
Southampton	13,804	16,556	14,101	11,946	11,619	16,391	–	12,505	16,017	13,258	14,790
Swindon T.	15,393	15,341	11,940	14,674	12,882	13,927	13,565	–	16,464	15,929	13,309
Tottenham H.	30,780	31,130	24,614	26,105	25,741	23,078	25,959	31,394	–	31,502	17,744
West Ham U.	23,132	20,738	17,211	18,084	20,365	19,441	26,952	15,777	20,787	–	20,369
Wimbledon	13,358	7,206	6,766	9,478	6,728	5,536	6,036	7,758	20,875	10,903	–

1994-95 FINAL TABLES

COMPOSITE FINAL TABLE

Pos	Team	P	W	D	L	F	A	Pts	
1	Blackburn Rovers	42	27	8	7	80	39	89	Champions' Cup
2	Manchester United	42	26	10	6	77	28	88	UEFA Cup
3	Nottingham Forest...	42	22	11	9	72	43	77	UEFA Cup
4	Liverpool	42	21	11	10	65	37	74	UEFA Cup (League Cup winners)
5	Leeds United	42	20	13	9	59	38	73	UEFA Cup
6	Newcastle United	42	20	12	10	67	47	72	
7	Tottenham Hotspur	42	16	14	12	66	58	62	
8	QPR	42	17	9	16	61	59	60	
9	Wimbledon	42	15	11	16	48	65	56	
10	Southampton	42	12	18	12	61	63	54	
11	Chelsea	42	13	15	14	50	55	54	
12	Arsenal	42	13	12	17	52	49	51	
13	Sheffield Wednesday	42	13	12	17	49	57	51	
14	West Ham United	42	13	11	18	44	48	50	
15	Everton	42	11	17	14	44	51	50	Cup-Winners' Cup
16	Coventry City	42	12	14	16	44	62	50	
17	Manchester City	42	12	13	17	53	64	49	
18	Aston Villa	42	11	15	16	51	56	48	
19	Crystal Palace	42	11	12	19	34	49	45	Relegated
20	Norwich City	42	10	13	19	37	54	43	Relegated
21	Leicester City	42	6	11	25	45	80	29	Relegated
22	Ipswich Town	42	7	6	29	36	93	27	Relegated

HOME & AWAY FINAL TABLE

Pos	Team	P	Home					Away					Pts
			W	D	L	F	A	W	D	L	F	A	
1	Blackburn Rovers	42	17	2	2	54	21	10	6	5	26	18	89
2	Manchester United	42	16	4	1	42	4	10	6	5	35	24	88
3	Nottingham Forest... ...	42	12	6	3	36	18	10	5	6	36	25	77
4	Liverpool	42	13	5	3	38	13	8	6	7	27	24	74
5	Leeds United	42	13	5	3	35	15	7	8	6	24	23	73
6	Newcastle United	42	14	6	1	46	20	6	6	9	21	27	72
7	Tottenham Hotspur	42	10	5	6	32	25	6	9	6	34	33	62
8	QPR	42	11	3	7	36	26	6	6	9	25	33	60
9	Wimbledon	42	9	5	7	26	26	6	6	9	22	39	56
10	Southampton	42	8	9	4	33	27	4	9	8	28	36	54
11	Chelsea	42	7	7	7	25	22	6	8	7	25	33	54
12	Arsenal	42	6	9	6	27	21	7	3	11	25	28	51
13	Sheffield Wednesday	42	7	7	7	26	26	6	5	10	23	31	51
14	West Ham United	42	9	6	6	28	19	4	5	12	16	29	50
15	Everton	42	8	9	4	31	23	3	8	10	13	28	50
16	Coventry City	42	7	7	7	23	25	5	7	9	21	37	50
17	Manchester City	42	8	7	6	37	28	4	6	11	16	36	49
18	Aston Villa	42	6	9	6	27	24	5	6	10	24	32	48
19	Crystal Palace	42	6	6	9	16	23	5	6	10	18	26	45
20	Norwich City	42	8	8	5	27	21	2	5	14	10	33	43
21	Leicester City	42	5	6	10	28	37	1	5	15	17	43	29
22	Ipswich Town	42	5	3	13	24	34	2	3	16	12	59	27

TOP SCORERS

Player	Club	Gls
SHEARER, ALan	Blackburn R.	34
FOWLER, Robbie	Liverpool	25
COLLYMORE, Stan	Nottingham F.	23
FERDINAND. Les	QPR	23
KLINSMANN, Jurgen	Tottenham H.r	22
COLE, Andy	Newcastle U. &	
	Manchester U.	21
LE TISSIER, Matt	Southampton	20
WRIGHT, Ian	Arsenal	18
SHERRINGHAM, Teddy	Tottenham H.	17
ROSLER, Uwe	Manchester C.	15
SAUNDERS, Dean	Aston Villa	15
SUTTON, Chris	Blackburn R.	15
KANCHELSKIS, Andrei	Manchester U.	14
BEARDSLEY, Peter	Newcastle U.	13
COTTEE, Tony	West Ham U.	13
DUBLIN, Dion	Coventry C.	13
ROY, Bryan	Nottingham F.	13
Paul RIDEOUT, Paul	Everton	13

EVER-PRESENT PLAYERS

Player	Club	Tot	St	Sb	Ps	Gl
CROSSLEY, Mark	Nottingham F.	42	42	0	0	0
FOWLER, Robbie	Liverpool	42	42	0	3	25
JAMES, David	Liverpool	42	42	0	0	0
KELLY, Gary	Leeds U.	42	42	0	3	0
LUKIC, John	Leeds U.	42	42	0	0	0
MAGILTON, Jim	Southampton	42	42	0	2	6
MIKLOSKO, Ludek	West Ham U.	42	42	0	0	0
NOLAN, Ian	Sheffield W.	42	42	0	1	3
PALLISTER, Gary	Manchester U.	42	42	0	0	2
POTTS, Steve	West Ham U.	42	42	0	2	0
SHEARER, Alan	Blackburn R.	42	42	0	2	34
SHERINGHAM, Teddy	Tottenham H.	42	41	1	0	17
SOUTHGATE, Gareth	Crystal P.	42	42	0	0	3

ATTENDANCES BY CLUB

Club	Total	Average
Arsenal	741,650	35,317
Aston Villa	624,881	29,756
Blackburn R.	530,705	25,272
Chelsea	442,346	21,064
Coventry C.	336,854	16,041
Crystal P.	312,703	14,891
Everton	658,727	31,368
Ipswich T.	355,044	16,907
Leeds U.	692,257	32,965
Leicester C.	410,172	19,532
Liverpool	717,792	34,181
Manchester C.	477,620	22,744
Manchester U.	917,318	43,682
Newcastle U.	728,537	34,692
Norwich C.	391,034	18,621
Nottingham F.	495,188	23,580
QPR	306,569	14,599
Sheffield W.	558,527	26,597
Southampton	308,465	14,689
Tottenham H.	572,436	27,259
West Ham U.	423,568	20,170
Wimbledon	214,834	10,230

TOP SCORERS BY CLUB

Club	Scorers
Arsenal	Wright 18, Hartson 7, Campbell 4
Aston Villa	Saunders 15, Staunton 5, Johnson 4
Blackburn R.	Shearer 34, Sutton 15, Atkins 6, Sherwood 6
Chelsea	Spencer 11, Furlong 10, Stein 8
Coventry C.	Dublin 13, Ndlovu 11, Flynn 4
Crystal Palace	Armstrong 8, Salako 4, Preece 4, Dowie 4
Everton	Rideout 13, Ferguson 5, Amokachi 4
Ipswich T.	Thomsen 5, Wark 4, Sedgley 4
Leeds U.	Yeboah 11, Whelan 7, Dean 7
Leicester C.	Roberts 9, Lowe 8, Robins 5
Liverpool	Fowler 25, Rush 12, McManaman 7, Barnes 7
Manchester C.	Rosler 15, Walsh 12, Quinn 8
Manchester U.	Kanchelskis 14, Cantona 12, Cole 12, Hughes 7
Newcastle U.	Beardsley 13, Fox 10, Cole 9, Lee 9
Norwich C.	Ward 8, Robins 4, Cureton 4
Nottingham F.	Collymore 23, Roy 13, Pearce 8
QPR	Ferdinand 23, Gallen 10, Sinclair 4, Barker 4
Sheffield W.	Bright 11, Whittingham 9, Hyde 5
Southampton	Le Tissier 20, Magilton 6, Dowie 5, Ekelund 5
Tottenham H.	Klinsmann 22, Sheringham 17, Barmby 9
West Ham U.	Cottee 13, Hutchinson 8, Boere 6
Wimbledon	Ekoku 9, Holdsworth 7, Harford 6

1994-95 RESULT GRIDS

	Arsenal	Aston Villa	Blackburn R.	Chelsea	Coventry C.	Crystal P.	Everton	Ipswich T.	Leeds U.	Leicester C.	Liverpool
Arsenal	–	0-0	0-0	3-1	2-1	1-2	1-1	4-1	1-3	1-1	0-1
Aston Villa	0-4	–	0-1	3-0	0-0	1-1	0-0	2-0	0-0	4-4	2-0
Blackburn R.	3-1	3-1	–	2-1	4-0	2-1	3-0	4-1	1-1	3-0	3-2
Chelsea	2-1	1-0	1-2	–	2-2	0-0	0-1	2-0	0-3	4-0	0-0
Coventry C.	0-1	0-1	1-1	2-2	–	1-4	0-0	2-0	2-1	4-2	1-1
Crystal P.	0-3	0-0	0-1	0-1	0-2	–	1-0	3-0	1-2	2-0	1-6
Everton	1-1	2-2	1-2	3-3	0-2	3-1	–	4-1	3-0	1-1	2-0
Ipswich T.	0-2	0-1	1-3	2-2	2-0	0-2	0-1	–	2-0	4-1	1-3
Leeds U.	1-0	1-0	1-1	2-3	3-0	3-1	1-0	4-0	–	2-1	0-2
Leicester C.	2-1	1-1	0-0	1-1	2-2	0-1	2-2	2-0	1-3	–	1-2
Liverpool	3-0	3-2	2-1	3-1	2-3	0-0	0-0	0-1	0-1	2-0	–
Manchester C.	1-2	2-2	1-3	1-2	0-0	1-1	4-0	2-0	0-0	0-1	2-1
Manchester U.	3-0	1-0	1-0	0-0	2-0	3-0	2-0	9-0	0-0	1-1	2-0
Newcastle U.	1-0	3-1	1-1	4-2	4-0	3-2	2-0	1-1	1-2	3-1	1-1
Norwich C.	0-0	1-1	2-1	3-0	2-2	0-0	0-0	3-0	2-1	2-1	1-2
Nottingham F.	2-2	1-2	0-2	0-1	2-0	1-0	2-1	4-1	3-0	1-0	1-1
QPR	3-1	2-0	0-1	1-0	2-2	0-1	2-3	1-2	3-2	2-0	2-1
Sheffield W.	3-1	1-2	0-1	1-1	5-1	1-0	0-0	4-1	1-1	1-0	1-2
Southampton	1-0	2-1	1-1	0-1	0-0	3-1	2-0	3-1	1-3	2-2	0-2
Tottenham H.	1-0	3-4	3-1	0-0	1-3	0-0	2-1	3-0	1-1	1-0	0-0
West Ham U.	0-2	1-0	2-0	1-2	0-1	1-0	2-2	1-1	0-0	1-0	3-0
Wimbledon	1-3	4-3	0-3	1-1	2-0	2-0	2-1	1-1	0-0	2-1	0-0

	Arsenal	Aston Villa	Blackburn R.	Chelsea	Coventry C.	Crystal P.	Everton	Ipswich T.	Leeds U.	Leicester C.	Liverpool
Arsenal	3-0	0-0	2-3	5-1	1-0	1-3	0-0	1-1	1-1	0-1	0-0
Aston Villa	1-1	1-2	0-2	1-1	0-2	2-1	1-1	1-1	1-0	0-2	7-1
Blackburn R.	2-3	2-4	1-0	0-0	3-0	4-0	3-1	3-2	2-0	4-2	2-1
Chelsea	3-0	2-3	1-1	2-0	0-2	1-0	1-1	0-2	1-1	1-2	1-1
Coventry C.	1-0	2-3	0-0	1-0	0-0	0-1	2-0	1-3	0-4	2-0	1-1
Crystal P.	2-1	1-1	0-1	0-1	1-2	0-0	2-1	0-0	1-1	1-0	0-0
Everton	1-1	1-0	2-0	2-1	1-2	2-2	1-4	0-0	0-0	1-0	0-0
Ipswich T.	1-2	3-2	0-2	1-2	0-1	0-1	1-2	2-1	1-3	1-1	2-2
Leeds U.	2-0	2-1	0-0	2-1	1-0	4-0	0-1	0-0	1-1	2-2	3-1
Leicester C.	0-1	0-4	1-3	1-0	2-4	1-1	0-1	4-3	3-1	1-2	3-4
Liverpool	2-0	2-0	2-0	4-0	1-0	1-1	4-1	3-1	1-1	0-0	3-0
Manchester C.	–	0-3	0-0	2-0	3-3	2-3	3-2	3-3	5-2	3-0	2-0
Manchester U.	5-0	–	2-0	1-0	1-2	2-0	1-0	2-1	0-0	1-0	3-0
Newcastle U.	0-0	1-1	–	3-0	2-1	2-1	2-1	5-1	3-3	2-0	2-1
Norwich C.	1-1	0-2	2-1	–	0-1	4-2	0-0	2-2	0-2	1-0	1-2
Nottingham F.	1-0	1-1	0-0	1-0	–	3-2	4-1	3-0	2-2	1-1	3-1
QPR	1-2	2-3	3-0	2-0	1-1	–	3-2	2-2	2-1	2-1	0-1
Sheffield W.	1-1	1-0	0-0	0-0	1-7	0-2	–	1-1	3-4	1-0	0-1
Southampton	2-2	2-2	3-1	1-1	1-1	2-1	0-0	–	4-3	1-1	2-3
Tottenham H.	2-1	0-1	4-2	1-0	1-4	1-1	3-1	1-2	–	3-1	1-2
West Ham U.	3-0	1-1	1-3	2-2	3-1	0-0	0-2	2-0	1-2	–	3-0
Wimbledon	2-0	0-1	3-2	1-0	2-2	1-3	0-1	0-2	1-2	1-0	–

1994-95 ATTENDANCE GRIDS

	Manchester C.	Manchester U.	Newcastle U.	Norwich C.	Nottingham F.	QPR	Sheffield W.	Southampton	Tottenham H.	West Ham U.	Wimbledon
Arsenal	–	34,452	37,629	38,234	31,725	34,136	34,473	36,818	38,098	31,373	38,036
Aston Villa	32,005	–	40,114	32,901	26,186	23,305	29,678	22,241	35,038	30,825	40,154
Blackburn R.	23,452	22,694	–	25,490	21,657	28,005	26,538	21,325	28,561	21,050	30,263
Chelsea	29,542	17,051	17,513	–	17,090	14,130	28,115	15,068	20,174	18,397	27,050
Coventry C.	14,468	12,218	18,547	13,429	–	10,732	21,814	9,526	15,389	20,663	21,029
Crystal P.	17,092	12,606	14,232	16,030	11,891	–	15,026	13,450	14,453	12,707	18,084
Everton	32,003	35,544	37,905	33,180	28,233	23,733	–	25,659	25,897	28,003	39,866
Ipswich T.	22,054	15,710	17,329	17,296	12,893	15,570	14,951	–	15,956	15,803	22,519
Leeds U.	34,218	32,955	39,426	32,212	29,179	30,942	30,793	28,600	–	28,547	38,563
Leicester C.	20,774	20,896	20,559	18,140	19,372	20,022	20,447	15,248	20,068	–	21,393
Liverpool	30,117	32,158	40,014	32,855	27,183	30,972	39,505	32,733	37,454	36,012	–
Manchester C.	20,500	22,513	23,387	21,880	20,632	19,971	19,867	21,430	22,892	21,007	27,055
Manchester U.	43,623	43,795	43,742	43,728	43,130	43,788	43,803	43,804	43,712	43,789	43,740
Newcastle U.	35,611	34,637	34,344	34,435	34,163	35,626	34,465	34,459	35,626	34,400	34,435
Norwich C.	17,768	19,374	18,146	18,246	14,024	19,015	18,377	17,510	17,390	20,567	21,843
Nottingham F.	21,662	24,598	22,131	22,092	26,253	21,326	24,526	21,340	26,299	21,601	25,418
QPR	16,341	16,037	16,508	15,103	11,398	14,227	14,488	12,456	17,416	10,189	18,295
Sheffield W.	23,468	24,063	24,207	25,450	26,056	21,930	27,880	30,213	23,227	22,551	31,932
Southampton	15,201	13,874	14,209	14,404	14,505	15,151	15,163	13,246	15,202	15,101	15,190
Tottenham H.	28,747	26,899	28,124	27,037	24,134	27,730	24,553	24,930	33,040	30,851	31,988
West Ham U.	18,498	18,326	24,202	21,500	17,251	16,959	21,081	20,542	18,610	18,780	22,446
Wimbledon	10,842	6,221	12,341	7,022	7,349	8,835	9,506	6,341	10,211	7,683	12,041

	Manchester C.	Manchester U.	Newcastle U.	Norwich C.	Nottingham F.	QPR	Sheffield W.	Southampton	Tottenham H.	West Ham U.	Wimbledon
Arsenal	38,368	38,301	36,819	36,942	35,441	32,393	33,705	27,213	38,377	36,295	32,822
Aston Villa	30,133	32,136	29,960	22,468	29,217	26,578	25,082	24,179	40,017	28,682	23,982
Blackburn R.	27,857	30,260	30,545	25,579	27,510	21,302	22,223	23,372	26,933	25,503	20,586
Chelsea	21,740	31,161	22,987	23,098	17,890	21,704	17,285	16,738	30,812	18,696	16,105
Coventry C.	15,804	21,885	17,233	11,885	19,224	15,740	17,015	11,784	19,951	17,556	10,962
Crystal P.	13,312	18,224	17,739	12,252	15,886	16,372	10,422	14,186	18,149	18,224	12,366
Everton	28,485	40,011	34,811	23,293	26,689	27,285	37,080	36,840	32,809	28,338	33,063
Ipswich T.	13,504	22,559	18,639	17,447	18,882	11,767	13,073	16,067	22,559	19,099	11,367
Leeds U.	30,938	39,396	39,337	31,982	38,191	28,780	33,750	28,953	39,224	28,987	27,284
Leicester C.	19,006	21,281	20,048	15,992	20,423	18,695	20,624	20,020	21,300	20,375	15,489
Liverpool	38,122	38,906	39,300	34,709	33,329	35,996	31,493	29,881	35,007	30,907	31,139
Manchester C.	–	26,368	27,389	21,031	23,150	27,850	23,355	21,589	25,473	19,150	21,131
Manchester U.	43,738	–	43,795	43,789	43,744	43,214	43,868	43,479	43,802	43,795	43,440
Newcastle U.	34,437	34,471	–	35,518	34,471	34,278	34,408	34,181	35,603	34,595	34,374
Norwich C.	16,266	21,824	21,172	–	19,005	19,431	13,530	18,361	21,814	19,110	18,261
Nottingham F.	28,882	22,072	22,102	20,010	–	21,449	22,022	24,146	28,711	28,361	20,187
QPR	13,631	18,948	16,576	10,519	13,363	–	12,788	16,078	18,367	12,780	11,061
Sheffield W.	26,776	33,441	31,215	25,072	30,060	22,766	–	28,424	34,051	25,350	20,395
Southampton	14,902	15,204	14,676	12,976	14,505	15,201	15,189	–	15,105	15,178	14,603
Tottenham H.	27,410	24,502	28,002	32,304	24,558	25,799	25,912	22,387	–	26,271	27,258
West Ham U.	17,286	24,783	18,580	21,464	20,544	22,932	14,554	18,853	24,573	–	21,804
Wimbledon	5,268	18,224	14,203	8,242	15,341	9,176	7,453	10,521	16,802	11,212	–

COMPOSITE FINAL TABLE

Pos	Team	P	W	D	L	F	A	Pts	
1	Manchester United	38	25	7	6	73	35	82	Champions' Cup
2	Newcastle United	38	24	6	8	66	37	78	UEFA Cup
3	Liverpool	38	20	11	7	70	34	71	Cup-Winners' Cup
4	Aston Villa	38	18	9	11	52	35	63	UEFA Cup (League Cup winners)
5	Arsenal	38	17	12	9	49	32	63	UEFA Cup
6	Everton	38	17	10	11	64	44	61	
7	Blackburn Rovers	38	18	7	13	61	47	61	
8	Tottenham Hotspur	38	16	13	9	50	38	61	
9	Nottingham Forest	38	15	13	10	50	54	58	
10	West Ham United	38	14	9	15	43	52	51	
11	Chelsea	38	12	14	12	46	44	50	
12	Middlesbrough	38	11	10	17	35	50	43	
13	Leeds United	38	12	7	19	40	57	43	
14	Wimbledon	38	10	11	17	55	70	41	
15	Sheffield Wednesday	38	10	10	18	48	61	40	
16	Coventry City	38	8	14	16	42	60	38	
17	Southampton	38	9	11	18	34	52	38	
18	Manchester City	38	9	11	18	33	58	38	Relegated
19	QPR	38	9	6	23	38	57	33	Relegated
20	Bolton Wanderers	38	8	5	25	39	71	29	Relegated

HOME & AWAY FINAL TABLE

Pos	Team	P	Home					Away					Pts
			W	D	L	F	A	W	D	L	F	A	
1	Manchester United	38	15	4	0	36	9	10	3	6	37	26	82
2	Newcastle United	38	17	1	1	38	9	7	5	7	28	28	78
3	Liverpool	38	14	4	1	46	13	6	7	6	24	21	71
4	Aston Villa	38	11	5	3	32	15	7	4	8	20	20	63
5	Arsenal	38	10	7	2	30	16	7	5	7	19	16	63
6	Everton	38	10	5	4	35	19	7	5	7	29	25	61
7	Blackburn Rovers	38	14	2	3	44	19	4	5	10	17	28	61
8	Tottenham Hotspur	38	9	5	5	26	19	7	8	4	24	19	61
9	Nottingham Forest	38	11	6	2	29	17	4	7	8	21	37	58
10	West Ham United	38	9	5	5	25	21	5	4	10	18	31	51
11	Chelsea	38	7	7	5	30	22	5	7	7	16	22	50
12	Middlesbrough	38	8	3	8	27	27	3	7	9	8	23	43
13	Leeds United	38	8	3	8	21	21	4	4	11	19	36	43
14	Wimbledon	38	5	6	8	27	33	5	5	9	28	37	41
15	Sheffield Wednesday	38	7	5	7	30	31	3	5	11	18	30	40
16	Coventry City	38	6	7	6	21	23	2	7	10	21	37	38
17	Southampton	38	7	7	5	21	18	2	4	13	13	34	38
18	Manchester City	38	7	7	5	21	19	2	4	13	12	39	38
19	QPR	38	6	5	8	25	26	3	1	15	13	31	33
20	Bolton Wanderers	38	5	4	10	16	31	3	1	15	23	40	29

TOP SCORERS

Player	Club	Gls Tot	St	Sb	Ps
SHEARER, Alan	Blackburn Rovers	31			
FOWLER, Robbie	Liverpool	28			
FERDINAND, Les	Newcastle United	25			
YORKE, Dwight	Aston Villa	17			
SHERINGHAM, Teddy	Tottenham Hotspur	16			
KANCHELSKIS, Andrei	Everton	16			
WRIGHT, Ian	Arsenal	15			
ARMSTRONG, Chris	Tottenham Hotspur	15			
COLLYMORE, Stan	Liverpool	14			
CANTONA, Eric	Manchester United	14			
DUBLIN, Dion	Coventry City	14			
HIRST, David	Sheffield Wednesday	13			
SPENCER, John	Chelsea	13			

EVER-PRESENT PLAYERS

Player	Club	Tot	St	Sb	Ps	Gl
BERG, Henning	Blackburn R.	38	38	0	0	0
BOSNICH, Mark	Aston Villa	38	38	0	1	0
CROSSLEY, Mark	Nottingham F.	38	38	0	0	0
DIXON, Lee	Arsenal	38	38	0	1	2
FOWLER, Robbie	Liverpool	38	36	2	2	28
IMMEL, Eike	Manchester C.	38	38	0	0	0
JAMES, David	Liverpool	38	38	0	0	0
McMANAMAN, Steve	Liverpool	38	38	0	1	6
MERSON, Paul	Arsenal	38	38	0	2	5
SEAMAN, David	Arsenal	38	38	0	0	0
SHERINGHAM, Teddy	Tottenham H.	38	38	0	1	16
SOUTHALL, Neville	Everton	38	38	0	0	0
SYMONS, Kit	Manchester C.	38	38	0	0	2
WALKER, Ian	Tottenham H.	38	38	0	0	0
WRIGHT, Alan	Aston Villa	38	38	0	0	2

ATTENDANCES BY CLUB

Club	Total	Average
Arsenal	713,797	37,568
Aston Villa	619,650	32,613
Blackburn R.	526,564	27,714
Bolton W.	357,625	18,822
Chelsea	486,361	25,598
Coventry C.	351,646	18,508
Everton	673,407	35,442
Leeds U.	619,946	32,629
Liverpool	751,501	39,553
Manchester C.	528,885	27,836
Manchester U.	791,940	41,681
Middlesbrough	549,486	28,920
Newcastle U.	693,580	36,504
Nottingham F.	492,395	25,916
QPR	297,775	15,672
Sheffield W.	472,665	24,877
Southampton	281,615	14,822
Tottenham H.	579,834	30,518
West Ham U.	424,015	22,317
Wimbledon	250,422	13,180

TOP SCORERS BY CLUB

Club	Scorers
Arsenal	Wright 15, Bergkamp 11, Platt 6
Aston Villa	Yorke 17, Milosevic 12, Johnson 5
Blackburn Rovers	Shearer 31, Fenton 6, Bohinen 4, Sherwood 4
Bolton Wanderers	McGinlay 6, De Freitas 5
Chelsea	Spencer 13, Hughes 8, Wise 7
Coventry City	Dublin 14, Whelan 8, Ndlovu 5
Everton	Kanchelskis 16, Stuart 9, Amokachi 6, Rideout 6
Leeds United	Yeboah 12, Deane 7, McAllister 5
Liverpool	Fowler 28, Collymore 14, McManaman 6
Manchester City	Rosler 9, Quinn 8, Kinkladze 4
Manchester United	Cantona 14, Andy Cole 11, Ryan Giggs 11
Middlesbrough	Barmby 7, Fjortoft 6, Hignett 5
Newcastle United	Ferdinand 25, Beardsley 8, Lee 8
Nottingham Forest	Woan 8, Lee 8, Roy 8
QPR	Dichio 10, Gallen 8, Barker 5
Sheffield Wednesday	Hirst 13, Degryse 8, Bright 7
Southampton	Shipperley 8, Le Tissier 7, Watson 3
Tottenham Hotspur	Sheringham 16, Armstrong 15, Fox 6
West Ham United	Cottee 10, Dicks 10, Dowie 8
Wimbledon	Earle 11, Holdsworth 10, Ekoku 7

	Arsenal	Aston Villa	Blackburn R.	Bolton W.	Chelsea	Coventry C.	Everton	Leeds U.	Liverpool	Manchester C.
Arsenal	–	2-0	0-0	2-1	1-1	1-1	1-2	2-1	0-0	3-1
Aston Villa	1-1	–	2-0	1-0	0-1	4-1	1-0	3-0	0-2	0-1
Blackburn R.	1-1	1-1	–	3-1	3-0	5-1	0-3	1-0	2-3	2-0
Bolton W.	1-0	0-2	2-1	–	2-1	1-2	1-1	0-2	0-1	1-1
Chelsea	1-0	1-2	2-3	3-2	–	2-2	0-0	4-1	2-2	1-1
Coventry C.	0-0	0-3	5-0	0-2	1-0	–	2-1	0-0	1-0	2-1
Everton	0-2	1-0	1-0	3-0	1-1	2-2	–	2-0	1-1	2-0
Leeds U.	0-3	2-0	0-0	0-1	1-0	3-1	2-2	–	1-0	0-1
Liverpool	3-1	3-0	3-0	5-2	2-0	0-0	1-2	5-0	–	6-0
Manchester C.	0-1	1-0	1-1	1-0	0-1	1-1	0-2	0-0	2-2	–
Manchester U.	1-0	0-0	1-0	3-0	1-1	1-0	2-0	1-0	2-2	1-0
Middlesbrough	2-3	0-2	2-0	1-4	2-0	2-1	0-2	1-1	2-1	4-1
Newcastle U.	2-0	1-0	1-0	2-1	2-0	3-0	1-0	2-1	2-1	3-1
Nottingham F.	0-1	1-1	1-5	3-2	0-0	0-0	3-2	2-1	1-0	3-0
QPR	1-1	1-0	0-1	2-1	1-2	1-1	3-1	1-2	1-2	1-0
Sheffield W.	1-0	2-0	2-1	4-2	0-0	4-3	2-5	6-2	1-1	1-1
Southampton	0-0	0-1	1-0	1-0	2-3	1-0	2-2	1-1	1-3	1-1
Tottenham H.	2-1	0-1	2-3	2-2	1-1	3-1	0-0	2-1	1-3	1-0
West Ham U.	0-1	1-4	1-1	1-0	1-3	3-2	2-1	1-2	0-0	4-2
Wimbledon	0-3	3-3	1-1	3-2	1-1	0-2	2-3	2-4	1-0	3-0

	Manchester U.	Middlesbrough	Newcastle U.	Nottingham F.	QPR	Sheffield W.	Southampton	Tottenham H.	West Ham U.	Wimbledon
Arsenal	1-0	1-1	2-0	1-1	3-0	4-2	4-2	0-0	1-0	1-3
Aston Villa	3-1	0-0	1-1	1-1	4-2	3-2	3-0	2-1	1-1	2-0
Blackburn R.	1-2	1-0	2-1	7-0	1-0	3-0	2-1	2-1	4-2	3-2
Bolton W.	0-6	1-1	1-3	1-1	0-1	2-1	0-1	2-3	0-3	1-0
Chelsea	1-4	5-0	1-0	1-0	1-1	0-0	3-0	0-0	1-2	1-2
Coventry C.	0-4	0-0	0-1	1-1	1-0	0-1	1-1	2-3	2-2	3-3
Everton	2-3	4-0	1-3	3-0	2-0	2-2	2-0	1-1	3-0	2-4
Leeds U.	3-1	0-1	0-1	1-3	1-3	2-0	1-0	1-3	2-0	1-1
Liverpool	2-0	1-0	4-3	4-2	1-0	1-0	1-1	0-0	2-0	2-2
Manchester C.	2-3	0-1	3-3	1-1	2-0	1-0	2-1	1-1	2-1	1-0
Manchester U.	–	2-0	2-0	5-0	2-1	2-2	4-1	1-0	2-1	3-1
Middlesbrough	0-3	–	1-2	1-1	1-0	3-1	0-0	0-1	4-2	1-2
Newcastle U.	0-1	1-0	–	3-1	2-1	2-0	1-0	1-1	3-0	6-1
Nottingham F.	1-1	1-1	1-1	–	3-0	1-0	1-0	2-1	1-1	4-1
QPR	1-1	1-1	2-3	1-1	–	0-3	3-0	2-3	3-0	0-3
Sheffield W.	0-0	0-1	0-2	1-3	1-3	–	2-2	1-3	0-1	2-1
Southampton	3-1	2-1	1-0	3-4	2-0	0-1	–	0-0	0-0	0-0
Tottenham H.	4-1	1-1	1-1	0-1	1-0	1-0	1-0	–	0-1	3-1
West Ham U.	0-1	2-0	2-0	1-0	1-0	1-1	2-1	1-1	–	1-1
Wimbledon	2-4	0-0	3-3	1-0	2-1	2-2	1-2	0-1	0-1	–

1995-96 ATTENDANCE GRIDS

	Arsenal	Aston Villa	Blackburn R.	Bolton W.	Chelsea	Coventry C.	Everton	Leeds U.	Liverpool	Manchester C.
Arsenal	–	38,271	37,695	38,104	38,295	35,623	38,275	37,619	38,323	34,519
Aston Villa	37,770	–	28,008	31,770	34,922	28,476	32,792	35,982	39,332	39,336
Blackburn R.	29,834	27,084	–	30,419	27,733	24,382	29,468	23,358	30,895	28,915
Bolton W.	18,682	18,099	20,253	–	18,021	16,678	20,427	18,414	21,042	21,050
Chelsea	31,048	23,530	28,436	17,495	–	24,398	30,189	22,131	31,137	17,078
Coventry C.	20,081	21,004	13,409	17,168	20,629	–	16,638	22,769	23,037	16,568
Everton	36,047	40,127	30,097	37,974	34,968	34,517	–	40,009	40,120	37,354
Leeds U.	38,552	35,086	31,285	30,106	36,209	30,161	29,425	–	35,852	33,249
Liverpool	39,806	39,508	39,502	40,104	40,820	39,079	40,818	40,254	–	39,267
Manchester C.	23,994	28,027	29,078	28,397	28,668	25,710	28,432	26,390	31,436	–
Manchester U.	50,028	42,667	42,681	32,812	42,019	50,332	42,459	48,382	34,934	35,707
Middlesbrough	29,359	28,535	29,462	29,354	28,286	27,882	29,407	29,467	29,390	29,469
Newcastle U.	36,530	36,510	36,463	36,534	36,225	36,485	36,557	36,572	36,547	36,501
Nottingham F.	27,222	25,790	25,273	25,426	27,007	24,629	24,786	24,465	29,058	25,620
QPR	17,970	14,778	13,957	11,456	14,904	11,189	18,349	13,991	18,405	14,212
Sheffield W.	24,349	22,964	25,544	24,872	25,094	16,229	32,724	24,573	32,747	24,422
Southampton	15,238	13,582	14,793	14,404	15,226	14,461	15,136	15,212	15,245	15,172
Tottenham H.	32,894	26,726	31,803	30,702	32,918	26,808	32,894	30,034	31,254	31,438
West Ham U.	24,217	23,637	21,776	23,086	19,228	18,884	21,085	22,901	24,324	24,017
Wimbledon	18,335	12,193	7,105	9,317	17,048	15,540	11,121	13,307	19,530	11,844

	Manchester U.	Middlesbrough	Newcastle U.	Nottingham F.	QPR	Sheffield W.	Southampton	Tottenham H.	West Ham U.	Wimbledon
Arsenal	38,317	37,308	38,271	38,248	38,259	34,556	38,136	38,273	38,065	37,640
Aston Villa	34,655	23,933	39,167	33,972	28,221	27,893	34,059	35,666	26,768	26,928
Blackburn R.	29,843	27,996	30,717	27,660	25,932	24,732	26,780	30,004	26,638	24,174
Bolton W.	21,381	18,376	20,243	17,342	17,362	18,368	18,795	17,829	19,047	16,216
Chelsea	31,019	21,060	31,098	24,482	25,590	23,216	26,237	31,059	25,252	21,906
Coventry C.	23,344	17,979	20,553	17,238	22,916	14,002	16,822	17,545	17,448	12,496
Everton	39,496	40,091	33,080	33,163	30,009	35,898	33,668	33,629	31,778	31,382
Leeds U.	39,801	31,778	38,862	39,220	31,504	34,076	26,077	30,061	30,658	27,984
Liverpool	40,546	40,782	40,702	39,206	37,548	40,535	38,007	40,628	40,326	34,063
Manchester C.	29,688	25,865	31,115	25,660	27,509	30,898	29,550	30,827	24,024	23,617
Manchester U.	–	36,580	42,024	53,926	41,890	41,849	39,301	50,157	31,966	32,226
Middlesbrough	29,921	–	30,011	23,392	29,293	29,751	29,188	29,487	28,640	29,192
Newcastle U.	36,584	36,483	–	36,531	36,583	36,567	36,554	36,589	36,331	36,434
Nottingham F.	29,263	27,027	28,280	–	22,910	27,810	23,321	27,053	26,645	20,810
QPR	18,817	17,546	18,254	17,549	–	12,459	17,615	15,659	18,828	11,837
Sheffield W.	34,101	21,177	24,815	21,930	22,442	–	25,115	26,565	23,917	19,085
Southampton	15,262	15,151	15,237	15,165	15,137	13,216	–	15,238	13,568	15,172
Tottenham H.	32,852	32,036	32,279	32,876	28,851	32,047	26,320	–	29,781	25,321
West Ham U.	24,197	23,850	23,843	21,257	21,504	23,790	18,501	23,516	–	20,402
Wimbledon	24,432	13,780	18,002	9,807	9,123	6,352	7,982	16,193	9,411	–

COMPOSITE FINAL TABLE

Pos	Team	P	W	D	L	F	A	Pts	
1	Manchester United ... .38	38	21	12	5	76	44	75	Champions' League Group
2	Newcastle United ... .38	38	19	11	8	73	40	68	Champions' League Qualifying
3	Arsenal 38	38	19	11	8	62	32	68	UEFA Cup
4	Liverpool 38	38	19	11	8	62	37	68	UEFA Cup
5	Aston Villa 38	38	17	10	11	47	34	61	UEFA Cup
6	Chelsea... 38	38	16	11	11	58	55	59	Cup-Winners' Cup
7	Sheffield Wednesday 38	38	14	15	9	50	51	57	
8	Wimbledon 38	38	15	11	12	49	46	56	
9	Leicester City 38	38	12	11	15	46	54	47	UEFA Cup (League Cup winners)
10	Tottenham Hotspur 38	38	13	7	18	44	51	46	
11	Leeds United 38	38	11	13	14	28	38	46	
12	Derby County 38	38	11	13	14	45	58	46	
13	Blackburn Rovers 38	38	9	15	14	42	43	42	
14	West Ham United ... .38	38	10	12	16	39	48	42	
15	Everton 38	38	10	12	16	44	57	42	
16	Southampton 38	38	10	11	17	50	56	41	
17	Coventry City 38	38	9	14	15	38	54	41	
18	Sunderland... 38	38	10	10	18	35	53	40	Relegated
19	Middlesbrough ... .38	38	10	12	16	51	60	39	Relegated – three points deducted
20	Nottingham Forest... 38	38	6	16	16	31	59	34	Relegated

HOME & AWAY FINAL TABLE

Pos	Team	P	Home					Away					Pts
			W	D	L	F	A	W	D	L	F	A	
1	Manchester United 38	38	12	5	2	38	17	9	7	3	38	27	75
2	Newcastle United ... .38	38	13	3	3	54	20	6	8	5	19	20	68
3	Arsenal 38	38	10	5	4	36	18	9	6	4	26	14	68
4	Liverpool 38	38	10	6	3	38	19	9	5	5	24	18	68
5	Aston Villa 38	38	11	5	3	27	13	6	5	8	20	21	61
6	Chelsea... 38	38	9	8	2	33	22	7	3	9	25	33	59
7	Sheffield Wednesday 38	38	8	10	1	25	16	6	5	8	25	35	57
8	Wimbledon 38	38	9	6	4	28	21	6	5	8	21	25	56
9	Leicester City 38	38	7	5	7	22	26	5	6	8	24	28	47
10	Tottenham Hotspur 38	38	8	4	7	19	17	5	3	11	25	34	46
11	Leeds United 38	38	7	7	5	15	13	4	6	9	13	25	46
12	Derby County 38	38	8	6	5	25	22	3	7	9	20	36	46
13	Blackburn Rovers 38	38	8	4	7	28	23	1	11	7	14	20	42
14	West Ham United ... .38	38	7	6	6	27	25	3	6	10	12	23	42
15	Everton 38	38	7	4	8	24	22	3	8	8	20	35	42
16	Southampton 38	38	6	7	6	32	24	4	4	11	18	32	41
17	Coventry City 38	38	4	8	7	19	23	5	6	8	19	31	41
18	Sunderland... 38	38	7	6	6	20	18	3	4	12	15	35	40
19	Middlesbrough ... .38	38	8	5	6	34	25	2	7	10	17	35	39
20	Nottingham Forest... 38	38	3	9	7	15	27	3	7	9	16	32	34

Middlesbrough deducted three points. The club called off their match at Everton when their squad was struck down by flu. The Premier League ruled that they should not have done so and punished them with the points penalty. Middlesbrough lost the re-arranged game.

TOP SCORERS

Player	Club	Gls
SHEARER, ALan	Newcastle United	25
WRIGHT, Ian	Arsenal	23
FOWLER, Robbie	Liverpool	18
SOLSKJAER, OG	Manchester United	18
YORKE, Dwight	Aston Villa	17
FERDINAND, Les	Newcastle United	16
RAVANELLI, Fabrizio	Middlesbrough	16
DUBLIN, Dion	Coventry City	14
LE TISSIER, Matt	Southampton	13
BERGKAMP, Dennis	Arsenal	12
COLLYMORE, Stan	Liverpool	12
CLARIDGE, Steve	Leicester City	12
JUNINHO	Middlesbrough	12

EVER-PRESENT PLAYERS

Player	Club	Tot	St	Sb	Ps	Gl
BJORNEBYE, Stig Inge	Liverpool	38	38	0	3	2
BRACEWELL, Paul	Sunderland	38	38	0	6	0
CAMPBELL, Sol	Tottenham H.	38	38	0	2	0
EHIOGU, Ugo	Aston Villa	38	38	0	0	3
JAMES, David	Liverpool	38	38	0	0	0
McALLISTER, Gary	Coventry C.	38	38	0	0	6
NOLAN, Ian	Sheffield W.	38	38	0	1	1
OGRIZOVIC, Steve	Coventry C.	38	38	0	1	0
PRESSMAN, Kevin	Sheffield W.	38	38	0	1	0
WINTERBURN, Nigel	Arsenal	38	38	0	3	0
WRIGHT, Alan	Aston Villa	38	38	0	0	0

ATTENDANCES BY CLUB

Club	Total	Average
Arsenal	718,603	37,821
Aston Villa	684,383	36,020
Blackburn R.	473,999	24,947
Chelsea	524,677	27,615
Coventry C.	372,560	19,608
Derby Co.	339,885	17,889
Everton	687,672	36,193
Leeds U.	610,235	32,118
Leicester C.	383,490	20,184
Liverpool	755,757	39,777
Manchester U.	1,046,527	55,080
Middlesbrough	567,541	29,871
Newcastle U.	692,866	36,467
Nottingham F.	467,151	24,587
Sheffield W.	488,475	25,709
Southampton	286,986	15,105
Sunderland	398,497	20,974
Tottenham H.	590,278	31,067
West Ham U.	441,131	23,217
Wimbledon	287,637	15,139

TOP SCORERS BY CLUB

Club	Scorers
Arsenal	Wright 23, Bergkamp 12, Merson 6
Aston Villa	Yorke 17, Milosevic 10, Johnson 4
Blackburn Rovers	Sutton 11, Gallagher 10, Sherwood 3
Chelsea	Vialli 9, M. Hughes 8, Zola 8
Coventry City	Dublin 14, Whelan 6, McAllister 6
Derby County	Sturridge 11, Ward 10, Asanovic 6
Everton	Ferguson 10, Speed 9, Stuart 5, Unsworth 5
Leeds United	Deane 5, Sharpe 5, Bowyer 4
Leicester City	Claridge 12, Heskey 10, Marshall 9
Liverpool	Fowler 18, Collymore 12, McManaman 7
Manchester United	Solskjaer 18, Cantona 11, Beckham 8
Middlesbrough	Ravanelli 16, Juninho 12, Beck 5
Newcastle United	Shearer 25, Ferdinand 16, R. Elliot 7
Nottingham Forest	Campbell 6, Haaland 6, Pearce 5
Sheffield Wednesday	Booth 10, Hirst 6, Pembridge 6
Southampton	Le Tissier 13, Ostenstad 10, Berkovic 4
Sunderland	Russell 4, Stewart 3, Quinn 3, Rae 3, Gray 3, Ball 3
Tottenham Hotspur	Sheringham 7, Iversen 6, Sinton 6
West Ham United	Kitson 8, Dicks 6, Hartson 5
Wimbledon	Ekoku 11, Gayle 8, Earle 7

27

	Arsenal	Aston Villa	Blackburn R.	Chelsea	Coventry C.	Derby Co.	Everton	Leeds U.	Leicester C.	Liverpool
Arsenal	–	2-2	1-1	3-3	0-0	2-2	3-1	3-0	2-0	1-2
Aston Villa	2-2	–	1-0	0-2	2-1	2-0	3-1	2-0	1-3	1-0
Blackburn R.	0-2	0-2	–	1-1	4-0	1-2	1-1	0-1	2-4	3-0
Chelsea	0-3	1-1	1-1	–	2-0	3-1	2-2	0-0	2-1	1-0
Coventry C.	1-1	1-2	0-0	3-1	–	1-2	0-0	2-1	0-0	0-1
Derby Co.	1-3	2-1	0-0	3-2	2-1	–	0-1	3-3	2-0	0-1
Everton	0-2	0-1	0-2	1-2	1-1	1-0	–	0-0	1-1	1-1
Leeds U.	0-0	0-0	0-0	2-0	1-3	0-0	1-0	–	3-0	0-2
Leicester C.	0-2	1-0	1-1	1-3	0-2	4-2	1-2	1-0	–	0-3
Liverpool	2-0	3-0	0-0	5-1	1-2	2-1	1-1	4-0	1-1	–
Manchester U.	1-0	0-0	2-2	1-3	3-1	2-3	2-2	1-0	3-1	1-0
Middlesbrough	0-2	3-2	2-1	1-0	4-0	6-1	4-2	0-0	0-2	3-3
Newcastle U.	1-2	4-3	2-1	3-1	4-0	3-1	4-1	3-0	4-3	1-1
Nottingham F.	2-1	0-0	2-2	2-0	0-1	1-1	0-1	1-1	0-0	1-1
Sheffield W.	0-0	2-1	1-1	0-2	0-0	0-0	2-1	2-2	2-1	1-1
Southampton	0-2	0-1	2-0	0-0	2-2	3-1	2-2	0-2	2-2	0-1
Sunderland	1-0	1-0	0-0	3-0	1-0	2-0	2-0	0-1	0-0	1-2
Tottenham H.	0-0	1-0	2-1	1-2	1-2	1-1	0-0	1-0	1-2	0-2
West Ham U.	1-2	0-2	2-1	3-2	1-1	1-1	2-2	0-2	1-0	1-2
Wimbledon	2-2	0-2	1-0	0-1	2-2	1-1	4-0	2-0	1-3	2-1

	Manchester U.	Middlesbrough	Newcastle U.	Nottingham F.	Sheffield W.	Southampton	Sunderland	Tottenham H.	West Ham U.	Wimbledon
Arsenal	1-2	2-0	0-1	2-0	4-1	3-1	2-0	3-1	2-0	0-1
Aston Villa	0-0	1-0	2-2	2-0	0-1	1-0	1-0	1-1	0-0	5-0
Blackburn R.	2-3	0-0	1-0	1-1	4-1	2-1	1-0	0-2	2-1	3-1
Chelsea	1-1	1-0	1-1	1-1	2-2	1-0	6-2	3-1	3-1	2-4
Coventry C.	0-2	3-0	2-1	0-3	0-0	1-1	2-2	1-2	1-3	1-1
Derby Co.	1-1	2-1	0-1	0-0	2-2	1-1	1-0	4-2	1-0	0-2
Everton	0-2	1-2	2-0	2-0	2-0	7-1	1-3	1-0	2-1	1-3
Leeds U.	0-4	1-1	0-1	2-0	0-2	0-0	3-0	0-0	1-0	1-0
Leicester C.	2-2	1-3	2-0	2-2	1-0	2-1	1-1	1-1	0-1	1-0
Liverpool	1-3	5-1	4-3	4-2	0-1	2-1	0-0	2-1	0-0	1-1
Manchester U.	–	3-3	0-0	4-1	2-0	2-1	5-0	2-0	2-0	2-1
Middlesbrough	2-2	–	0-1	1-1	4-2	0-1	0-1	0-3	4-1	0-0
Newcastle U.	5-0	3-1	–	5-0	1-2	0-1	1-1	7-1	1-1	2-0
Nottingham F.	0-4	1-1	0-0	–	0-3	1-3	1-4	2-1	0-2	1-1
Sheffield W.	1-1	3-1	1-1	2-0	–	1-1	2-1	2-1	0-0	3-1
Southampton	6-3	4-0	2-2	2-2	2-3	–	3-0	0-1	2-0	0-0
Sunderland	2-1	2-2	1-2	1-1	1-1	0-1	–	0-4	0-0	1-3
Tottenham H.	1-2	1-0	1-2	0-1	1-1	3-1	2-0	–	1-0	1-0
West Ham U.	2-2	0-0	0-0	0-1	5-1	2-1	2-0	4-3	–	0-2
Wimbledon	0-3	1-1	1-1	1-0	4-2	3-1	1-0	1-0	1-1	–

1996-97 ATTENDANCE GRIDS

	Arsenal	Aston Villa	Blackburn R.	Chelsea	Coventry C.	Derby Co.	Everton	Leeds U.	Leicester C.	Liverpool
Arsenal	–	38,130	38,086	38,132	38,140	38,018	38,095	38,076	38,044	38,068
Aston Villa	37,944	–	32,257	39,339	30,409	34,646	39,339	39,051	36,193	39,399
Blackburn R.	24,303	24,274	–	27,229	24,055	19,214	27,091	23,226	25,881	29,598
Chelsea	28,182	27,729	25,784	–	25,024	28,293	28,418	28,277	27,723	28,239
Coventry C.	19,998	21,340	17,032	19,917	–	22,839	19,497	17,297	19,220	23,021
Derby Co.	18,287	18,071	17,847	18,039	18,042	–	17,252	17,927	18,010	18,102
Everton	36,980	39,115	30,427	38,321	31,477	32,240	–	36,954	30,368	40,177
Leeds U.	35,502	26,897	27,264	32,671	36,465	27,549	32,055	–	29,486	39,981
Leicester C.	20,429	20,626	19,306	20,766	20,038	20,323	20,975	20,359	–	20,987
Liverpool	38,103	40,489	40,747	40,739	40,079	39,515	40,751	38,957	40,786	–
Manchester U.	55,210	55,113	54,178	55,198	55,230	55,243	54,943	55,256	55,196	55,128
Middlesbrough	29,629	30,074	29,891	29,811	29,811	29,739	29,673	30,018	29,709	30,039
Newcastle U.	36,565	36,400	36,424	36,320	36,571	36,553	36,143	36,489	36,396	36,570
Nottingham F.	27,384	25,239	17,525	28,358	22,619	27,771	19,892	25,565	24,105	29,181
Sheffield W.	23,245	26,861	22,191	30,983	21,793	23,934	24,175	30,373	17,657	38,943
Southampton	15,144	15,232	15,247	15,186	15,251	14,901	15,134	15,241	15,044	15,222
Sunderland	21,154	21,059	20,850	19,683	19,459	22,512	22,108	21,890	19,262	21,938
Tottenham H.	33,039	32,847	22,943	33,027	33,029	28,219	29,696	33,040	24,159	32,899
West Ham U.	24,382	19,105	23,947	24,502	21,580	24,576	24,525	19,441	22,285	25,064
Wimbledon	25,521	9,015	13,246	14,601	10,307	11,467	13,684	7,979	11,487	20,016

	Manchester U.	Middlesbrough	Newcastle U.	Nottingham F.	Sheffield W.	Southampton	Sunderland	Tottenham H.	West Ham U.	Wimbledon
Arsenal	38,172	37,573	38,179	38,206	33,461	38,033	38,016	38,264	38,056	37,854
Aston Villa	39,339	39,053	39,339	35,310	26,726	39,339	32,491	39,339	35,995	28,875
Blackburn R.	30,476	27,411	30,398	20,485	20,845	23,018	24,208	26,960	21,994	23,333
Chelsea	28,336	28,272	28,401	27,673	27,467	28,079	24,072	28,373	28,315	28,020
Coventry C.	23,085	20,617	21,538	19,468	17,267	15,485	17,700	19,675	22,291	15,273
Derby Co.	18,026	17,350	18,092	18,087	18,060	17,839	17,692	18,083	18,057	17,022
Everton	40,079	39,250	40,117	32,567	34,160	35,669	40,087	36,380	36,571	36,733
Leeds U.	39,694	38,567	36,070	29,225	31,011	25,913	31,667	33,783	30,575	25,860
Leicester C.	21,068	20,561	21,134	20,833	20,793	17,562	17,883	20,593	20,327	18,927
Liverpool	40,892	39,491	40,751	36,126	39,507	39,189	40,503	40,003	40,102	39,027
Manchester U.	–	54,489	55,236	54,984	55,267	55,269	55,081	54,943	55,249	55,314
Middlesbrough	30,063	–	30,063	29,888	29,485	29,509	30,106	30,215	30,060	29,758
Newcastle U.	36,579	36,577	–	36,554	36,452	36,446	36,582	36,308	36,552	36,385
Nottingham F.	29,032	24,705	25,762	–	21,485	25,134	22,874	27,303	23,352	19,865
Sheffield W.	37,671	28,206	33,798	16,390	–	20,106	20,294	22,667	22,231	26,957
Southampton	15,253	15,230	15,251	14,450	15,062	–	15,225	15,251	15,244	14,418
Sunderland	22,225	20,936	22,037	22,120	20,644	21,521	–	20,785	18,642	19,672
Tottenham H.	33,028	29,947	32,535	32,805	30,996	30,549	31,867	–	32,999	32,654
West Ham U.	25,045	23,988	24,617	22,358	24,490	21,227	24,077	23,998	–	21,924
Wimbledon	25,786	15,046	23,175	12,608	10,512	8,572	21,338	17,506	15,771	–

COMPOSITE FINAL TABLE

Pos	Team	P	W	D	L	F	A	Pts	
1	Arsenal	38	23	9	6	68	33	78	Champions' League Group
2	Manchester United	38	23	8	7	73	26	77	Champions' League qualifying
3	Liverpool	38	18	11	9	68	42	65	UEFA Cup
4	Chelsea	38	20	3	15	71	43	63	Cup-Winners' Cup
5	Leeds United	38	17	8	13	57	46	59	UEFA Cup
6	Blackburn Rovers	38	16	10	12	57	52	58	UEFA Cup
7	Aston Villa	38	17	6	15	49	48	57	Aston Villa (League Cup winners)
8	West Ham United	38	16	8	14	56	57	56	
9	Derby County	38	16	7	15	52	49	55	
10	Leicester City	38	13	14	11	51	41	53	
11	Coventry City	38	12	16	10	46	44	52	
12	Southampton	38	14	6	18	50	55	48	
13	Newcastle United	38	11	11	16	35	44	44	
14	Tottenham Hotspur	38	11	11	16	44	56	44	
15	Wimbledon	38	10	14	14	34	46	44	
16	Sheffield Wednesday	38	12	8	18	52	67	44	
17	Everton	38	9	13	16	41	56	40	
18	Bolton Wanderers	38	9	13	16	41	61	40	Relegated
19	Barnsley	38	10	5	23	37	82	35	Relegated
20	Crystal Palace	38	8	9	21	37	71	33	Relegated

HOME & AWAY FINAL TABLE

Pos	Team	P	Home					Away					Pts
			W	D	L	F	A	W	D	L	F	A	
1	Arsenal	38	15	2	2	43	10	8	7	4	25	23	78
2	Manchester United	38	13	4	2	42	9	10	4	5	31	17	77
3	Liverpool	38	13	2	4	42	16	5	9	5	26	26	65
4	Chelsea	38	13	2	4	37	14	7	1	11	34	29	63
5	Leeds United	38	9	5	5	31	21	8	3	8	26	25	59
6	Blackburn Rovers	38	11	4	4	40	26	5	6	8	17	26	58
7	Aston Villa	38	9	3	7	26	24	8	3	8	23	24	57
8	West Ham United	38	13	4	2	40	18	3	4	12	16	39	56
9	Derby County	38	12	3	4	33	18	4	4	11	19	31	55
10	Leicester City	38	6	10	3	21	15	7	4	8	30	26	53
11	Coventry City	38	8	9	2	26	17	4	7	8	20	27	52
12	Southampton	38	10	1	8	28	23	4	5	10	22	32	48
13	Newcastle United	38	8	5	6	22	20	3	6	10	13	24	44
14	Tottenham Hotspur	38	7	8	4	23	22	4	3	12	21	34	44
15	Wimbledon	38	5	6	8	18	25	5	8	6	16	21	44
16	Sheffield Wednesday	38	9	5	5	30	26	3	3	13	22	41	44
17	Everton	38	7	5	7	25	27	2	8	9	16	29	40
18	Bolton Wanderers	38	7	8	4	25	22	2	5	12	16	39	40
19	Barnsley	38	7	4	8	25	35	3	1	15	12	47	35
20	Crystal Palace	38	2	5	12	15	39	6	4	9	22	32	33

TOP SCORERS

Player	Club	Gls
Dion DUBLIN	Coventry City	18
Michael OWEN	Liverpool	18
Chris SUTTON	Blackburn Rovers	18
Dennis BERGKAMP	Arsenal	16
Kevin GALLACHER	Blackburn Rovers	16
Jimmy HASSELBAINK	Leeds United	16
Andy COLE	Manchester United	15
John HARTSON	West Ham United	15
Darren HUCKERBY	Coventry City	14
Paulo WANCHOPE	Derby County	13

EVER-PRESENT PLAYERS

Player	Club	Tot	St	Sb	Ps	Gl
CARR, Stephen	Tottenham H.	38	37	1	3	0
FRANDSEN, Per	Bolton W.	38	38	0	5	2
JONES, Paul	Southampton	38	38	0	0	0
MILLER, Kevin	Crystal P.	38	38	0	0	0
SULLIVAN, Neil	Wimbledon	38	38	0	0	0
WALKER, Des	Sheffield W.	38	38	0	1	0

ATTENDANCES BY CLUB

Club	Total	Average
Arsenal	722,907	38,048
Aston Villa	686,592	36,136
Barnsley	350,412	18,443
Blackburn R.	483,804	25,463
Bolton W.	472,703	24,879
Chelsea	636,357	33,492
Coventry C.	374,722	19,722
Crystal P.	417,673	21,983
Derby Co.	553,417	29,127
Everton	673,133	35,428
Leeds U.	658,292	34,647
Leicester C.	391,409	20,600
Liverpool	771,926	40,628
Manchester U.	1,031,314	54,280
Newcastle U.	697,208	36,695
Sheffield W.	545,463	28,709
Southampton	288,189	15,168
Tottenham H.	553,731	29,144
West Ham U.	474,372	24,967
Wimbledon	316,969	16,683

TOP SCORERS BY CLUB

Club	Scorers
Arsenal	Bergkamp 16, Overmars 12, Wright 10
Aston Villa	Yorke 12, Joachim 8, Milosevic 7
Barnsley	Redfearn 10, Ward 8, Fjortoft 6
Blackburn Rovers	Sutton 18, Gallacher 16, Sherwood 5
Bolton Wanderers	Blake 12, Thompson 9
Chelsea	Flo, Vialli 11, M. Hughes 9, Zola 8
Coventry City	Dublin 18, Huckerby 14, Whelan 6
Crystal Palace	Shipperley 7, Bent, Lombardo 5
Derby County	Wanchope 13, Baiano, 12 Sturridge 9
Everton	Ferguson 11, Speed 7, Madar 6
Leeds United	Hasselbaink 16, Radebe 10
Leicester City	Heskey 10, Elliott 7
Liverpool	Owen 18, McManaman 11, Fowler 9
Manchester United	Cole 16, Sheringham 9, Giggs, Scholes 8
Newcastle United	Barnes 6, Lee, Gillespie 4
Sheffield Wednesday	Di Canio 12, Carbone 9
Southampton	Le Tissier, Ostenstad 11, Davies, Hirst 9
Tottenham Hotspur	Klinsmann 9, Ferdinand, Armstrong 5
West Ham United	Hartson 15, Berkovic, Sinclair 7
Wimbledon	Cort, Ekoku, Euell, M. Hughes, Leaburn 4

	Arsenal	Aston Villa	Barnsley	Blackburn R.	Bolton W.	Chelsea	Coventry C.	Crystal P.	Derby Co.	Everton
Arsenal	–	0-0	5-0	1-3	4-1	2-0	2-0	1-0	1-0	4-0
Aston Villa	1-0	–	0-1	0-4	1-3	0-2	3-0	3-1	2-1	2-1
Barnsley	0-2	0-3	–	1-1	2-1	0-6	2-0	1-0	1-0	2-2
Blackburn R.	1-4	5-0	2-1	–	3-1	1-0	0-0	2-2	1-0	3-2
Bolton W.	0-1	0-1	1-1	2-1	–	1-0	1-5	5-2	3-3	0-0
Chelsea	2-3	0-1	2-0	0-1	2-0	–	3-1	6-2	4-0	2-0
Coventry C.	2-2	1-2	1-0	2-0	2-2	3-2	–	1-1	1-0	0-0
Crystal P.	0-0	1-1	0-1	1-2	2-2	0-3	0-3	–	3-1	1-3
Derby Co.	3-0	0-1	1-0	3-1	4-0	0-1	3-1	0-0	–	3-1
Everton	2-2	1-4	4-2	1-0	3-2	3-1	1-1	1-2	1-2	–
Leeds U.	1-1	1-1	2-1	4-0	2-0	3-1	3-3	0-2	4-3	0-0
Leicester C.	3-3	1-0	1-0	1-1	0-0	2-0	1-1	1-1	1-2	0-1
Liverpool	4-0	3-0	0-1	0-0	2-1	4-2	1-0	2-1	4-0	1-1
Manchester U.	0-1	1-0	7-0	4-0	1-1	2-2	3-0	2-0	2-0	2-0
Newcastle U.	0-1	1-0	2-1	1-1	2-1	3-1	0-0	1-2	0-0	1-0
Sheffield W.	2-0	1-3	2-1	0-0	5-0	1-4	0-0	1-3	2-5	3-1
Southampton	1-3	1-2	4-1	3-0	0-1	1-0	1-2	1-0	0-2	2-1
Tottenham H.	1-1	3-2	3-0	0-0	1-0	1-6	1-1	0-1	1-0	1-1
West Ham U.	0-0	2-1	6-0	2-1	3-0	2-1	1-0	4-1	0-0	2-2
Wimbledon	0-1	2-1	4-1	0-1	0-0	0-2	1-2	0-1	0-0	0-0

	Leeds U.	Leicester C.	Liverpool	Manchester U.	Newcastle U.	Sheffield W.	Southampton	Tottenham H.	West Ham U.	Wimbledon
Arsenal	2-1	2-1	0-1	3-2	3-1	1-0	3-0	0-0	4-0	5-0
Aston Villa	1-0	1-1	2-1	0-2	0-1	2-2	1-1	4-1	2-0	1-2
Barnsley	2-3	0-2	2-3	0-2	2-2	2-1	4-3	1-1	1-2	2-1
Blackburn R.	3-4	5-3	1-1	1-3	1-0	7-2	1-0	0-3	3-0	0-0
Bolton W.	2-3	2-0	1-1	0-0	1-0	3-2	0-0	1-1	1-1	1-0
Chelsea	0-0	1-0	4-1	0-1	1-0	1-0	4-2	2-0	2-1	1-1
Coventry C.	0-0	0-2	1-1	3-2	2-2	1-0	1-0	4-0	1-1	0-0
Crystal P.	0-2	0-3	0-3	0-3	1-2	1-0	1-1	1-3	3-3	0-3
Derby Co.	0-5	0-4	1-0	2-2	1-0	3-0	4-0	2-1	2-0	1-1
Everton	2-0	1-1	2-0	0-2	0-0	1-3	0-2	0-2	2-1	0-0
Leeds U.	–	0-1	0-2	1-0	4-1	1-2	0-1	1-0	3-1	1-1
Leicester C.	1-0	–	0-0	0-0	0-0	1-1	3-3	3-0	2-1	0-1
Liverpool	3-1	1-2	–	1-3	1-0	2-1	2-3	4-0	5-0	2-0
Manchester U.	3-0	0-1	1-1	–	1-1	6-1	1-0	2-0	2-1	2-0
Newcastle U.	1-1	3-3	1-2	0-1	–	2-1	2-1	1-0	0-1	1-3
Sheffield W.	1-3	1-0	3-3	2-0	2-1	–	1-0	1-0	1-1	1-1
Southampton	0-2	2-1	1-1	1-0	2-1	2-3	–	3-2	3-0	0-1
Tottenham H.	0-1	1-1	3-3	0-2	2-0	3-2	1-1	–	1-0	0-0
West Ham U.	3-0	4-3	2-1	1-1	0-1	1-0	2-4	2-1	–	3-1
Wimbledon	1-0	2-1	1-1	2-5	0-0	1-1	1-0	2-6	1-2	–

	Arsenal	Aston Villa	Barnsley	Blackburn R.	Bolton W.	Chelsea	Coventry C.	Crystal P.	Derby Co.	Everton
Arsenal	–	38,081	38,049	38,147	38,138	38,083	37,324	38,094	38,121	38,269
Aston Villa	39,372	–	29,519	37,112	38,392	39,372	33,250	33,781	35,444	36,389
Barnsley	18,691	18,649	–	18,665	18,661	18,170	17,463	17,819	18,686	18,672
Blackburn R.	28,212	24,834	24,179	–	29,503	27,683	19,086	23,872	23,557	25,397
Bolton W.	25,000	24,196	35,000	25,000	–	24,080	25,000	24,449	23,037	23,131
Chelsea	33,012	33,018	34,442	33,311	34,845	–	34,647	31,917	36,544	34,148
Coventry C.	22,864	22,792	20,265	18,794	16,633	22,686	–	15,900	18,705	18,760
Crystal P.	26,180	21,097	21,547	20,849	17,134	26,186	21,810	–	18,101	23,311
Derby Co.	30,004	30,251	27,232	27,823	29,126	30,062	29,351	26,950	–	27,828
Everton	35,457	36,471	32,659	33,423	37,149	32,355	40,109	35,716	34,876	–
Leeds U.	37,993	36,287	37,749	32,933	31,163	37,276	36,522	29,076	33,572	34,986
Leicester C.	21,089	20,304	21,293	19,921	20,564	21,335	21,137	19,191	19,385	20,628
Liverpool	44,417	34,843	41,001	43,890	44,532	36,647	39,707	43,007	38,017	44,501
Manchester U.	55,174	55,151	55,142	38,094	55,156	55,163	55,074	55,143	55,170	55,167
Newcastle U.	36,571	36,783	36,534	36,716	36,767	36,710	36,767	36,565	36,289	36,705
Sheffield W.	34,373	34,177	29,086	33,502	25,067	28,334	21,087	22,072	22,391	24,486
Southampton	15,246	15,238	15,018	15,162	15,206	15,231	15,091	15,032	15,202	15,102
Tottenham H.	29,610	26,317	28,232	26,573	29,032	28,476	33,463	25,634	25,886	35,624
West Ham U.	25,717	24,976	23,714	24,733	24,867	25,829	22,477	23,335	25,155	25,905
Wimbledon	22,291	13,131	7,976	15,600	11,356	22,237	11,210	16,747	13,031	15,131

	Leeds U.	Leicester C.	Liverpool	Manchester U.	Newcastle U.	Sheffield W.	Southampton	Tottenham H.	West Ham U.	Wimbledon
Arsenal	38,018	38,023	38,094	38,083	38,102	38,087	38,056	38,102	38,012	38,024
Aston Villa	39,027	36,429	39,377	39,372	38,266	32,044	29,343	38,644	39,372	32,087
Barnsley	18,690	18,660	18,684	18,694	18,687	18,692	18,368	18,692	18,667	17,102
Blackburn R.	21,956	24,854	30,187	30,547	29,300	19,618	24,130	30,388	21,653	24,848
Bolton W.	25,000	25,000	25,000	25,000	24,494	24,847	23,333	23,433	25,000	22,703
Chelsea	34,690	33,356	34,639	34,511	31,563	29,075	30,008	34,149	34,382	34,100
Coventry C.	17,770	18,309	22,721	23,054	22,679	18,375	18,659	19,499	18,289	17,968
Crystal P.	25,248	18,771	25,790	26,180	26,085	16,876	22,853	26,116	19,129	14,410
Derby Co.	30,217	29,855	30,492	30,014	30,302	30,203	25,625	30,187	29,300	28,595
Everton	37,099	33,642	41,112	40,079	37,972	35,497	29,958	36,670	34,356	28,533
Leeds U.	–	29,620	39,775	39,952	39,834	33,166	28,791	31,394	30,031	38,172
Leicester C.	21,244	–	21,633	21,221	21,699	20,800	20,708	20,683	20,217	18,553
Liverpool	43,854	35,007	–	41,027	42,791	34,705	43,550	38,005	44,414	38,011
Manchester U.	55,167	55,156	55,171	–	55,194	55,529	55,008	55,281	55,068	55,306
Newcastle U.	36,511	36,574	36,718	36,767	–	36,771	37,759	36,709	36,736	36,256
Sheffield W.	31,520	24,851	35,405	39,427	29,446	–	29,677	29,871	28,036	22,655
Southampton	15,102	15,121	15,252	15,241	15,242	15,442	–	15,225	15,212	14,815
Tottenham H.	26,441	28,355	30,245	26,359	35,847	25,097	35,995	–	30,284	26,261
West Ham U.	24,107	25,781	25,908	25,892	25,884	24,344	25,878	25,354	–	24,516
Wimbledon	15,718	13,229	26,106	26,309	15,478	11,503	12,009	25,820	22,087	–

COMPOSITE FINAL TABLE

Pos	Team	P	W	D	L	F	A	Pts	
1	Manchester United	38	22	13	3	53	37	79	Champions' League Group
2	Arsenal	38	22	12	4	30	17	78	Champions' League Group
3	Chelsea	38	18	15	3	41	30	75	Champions' League Qualifying
4	Leeds United	38	17	13	7	39	34	67	UEFA Cup
5	West Ham United	38	16	9	13	40	53	57	InterToto Cup
6	Aston Villa	38	15	10	13	46	46	55	
7	Liverpool	38	15	9	14	48	49	54	
8	Derby County	38	13	13	12	37	45	52	
9	Middlesbrough	38	12	15	11	41	54	51	
10	Leicester City	38	11	13	13	40	46	49	
11	Tottenham Hotspur	38	13	14	13	45	50	47	UEFA Cup (League Cup winners)
12	Sheffield Wednesday	38	11	7	18	36	42	46	
13	Newcastle United	38	12	13	14	47	54	46	UEFA Cup (FA Cup finalists)
14	Everton	38	9	10	17	32	47	43	
15	Coventry City	38	11	9	18	34	51	42	
16	Wimbledon	38	9	12	16	39	63	42	
17	Southampton	38	13	8	19	34	64	41	
18	Charlton Athletic	38	5	12	18	41	56	36	Relegated
19	Blackburn Rovers	38	10	14	17	41	52	35	Relegated
20	Nottingham Forest	38	3	9	22	48	69	30	Relegated

HOME & AWAY FINAL TABLE

Pos	Team	P	Home					Away					Pts
			W	D	L	F	A	W	D	L	F	A	
1	Manchester United	38	14	4	1	45	18	8	9	2	35	19	79
2	Arsenal	38	14	5	0	34	5	8	7	4	25	12	78
3	Chelsea	38	12	6	1	29	13	8	9	2	28	17	75
4	Leeds United	38	12	5	2	32	9	6	8	5	30	25	67
5	West Ham United	38	11	3	5	32	26	5	6	8	14	27	57
6	Aston Villa	38	10	3	6	33	28	5	7	7	18	18	55
7	Liverpool	38	10	5	4	44	24	5	4	10	24	25	54
8	Derby County	38	8	7	4	22	19	5	6	8	18	26	52
9	Middlesbrough	38	7	9	3	25	18	5	6	8	23	36	51
10	Leicester City	38	7	6	6	25	25	5	7	7	15	21	49
11	Tottenham Hotspur	38	7	7	5	28	26	4	7	8	19	24	47
12	Sheffield Wednesday	38	7	5	7	20	15	6	2	11	21	27	46
13	Newcastle United	38	7	6	6	26	25	4	7	8	22	29	46
14	Everton	38	6	8	5	22	12	5	2	12	20	35	43
15	Coventry City	38	8	6	5	26	21	3	3	13	13	30	42
16	Wimbledon	38	7	7	5	22	21	3	5	11	18	42	42
17	Southampton	38	9	4	6	29	26	2	4	13	8	38	41
18	Charlton Athletic	38	4	7	8	20	20	4	5	10	21	36	36
19	Blackburn Rovers	38	6	5	8	21	24	1	9	9	17	28	35
20	Nottingham Forest	38	3	7	9	18	31	4	2	13	17	38	30

TOP SCORERS

Player	Club	Gls
HASSELBAINK, JF	Leeds United	18
OWEN, Michael	Liverpool	18
YORKE, Dwight	Manchester United	18
ANELKA, Nicolas	Arsenal	17
COLE, Andy	Manchester United	17
RICARD, Hamilton	Middlesbrough	15
DUBLIN, Dion	Coventry C./Aston Villa	14
FOWLER, Robbie	Liverpool	14
JOACHIM, Julian	Aston Villa	14
SHEARER, ALan	Newcastle United	14
ZOLA, Gianfranco	Chelsea	13
BERGKAMP, Dennis	Arsenal	12
SOLSKJAER, OG	Manchester United	12
POYET, Gus	Chelsea	11

EVER-PRESENT PLAYERS

Player	Club	Tot	St	Sb	Ps	Gls
ATHERTON, Peter	Sheffield W.	38	38	0	0	2
GORDON, Dean	Middlesbrough	38	38	0	0	3
GUPPY, Steve	Leicester C.	38	38	0	0	4
JONK, Wim	Sheffield W.	38	38	0	6	2
KEWELL, Harry	Leeds U.	38	36	2	9	6
KINSELLA, Mark	Charlton A.	38	38	0	8	3
LAMPARD, Frank	West Ham U.	38	38	0	0	5
MYRHE, Thomas	Everton	38	38	0	0	0
POWELL, Chris	Charlton A.	38	38	0	2	0
SOUTHGATE, Gareth	Aston Villa	38	38	0	0	1
SPEED, Gary	Newcastle U.	38	34	4	3	4
SULLIVAN, Neil	Wimbledon	38	38	0	0	0
THOME, Emerson	Sheffield W.	38	38	0	1	1
WRIGHT, Alan	Aston Villa	38	38	0	1	0

ATTENDANCES BY CLUB

Club	Total	Average
Arsenal	722,450	38,024
Aston Villa	701,795	36,937
Blackburn R.	493,341	25,965
Charlton A.	376,637	19,823
Chelsea	660,273	34,751
Coventry C.	394,791	20,778
Derby Co.	554,998	29,210
Everton	687,856	36,203
Leeds U.	681,074	35,846
Leicester C.	388,910	20,469
Liverpool	823,105	43,321
Manchester U.	1,048,580	55,188
Middlesbrough	653,393	34,389
Newcastle U.	696,631	36,665
Nottingham F.	465,894	24,521
Sheffield W.	508,521	26,764
Southampton	287,653	15,140
Tottenham H.	650,298	34,226
West Ham U.	487,996	25,684
Wimbledon	346,468	18,235

TOP SCORERS BY CLUB

Club	Scorers
Arsenal	Anelka 17, Bergkamp 12
Aston Villa	Joachim 14, Dublin 11, Merson 5
Blackburn Rovers	Gallacher 5, Ward 5
Charlton Athletic	Mendonca 8, Hunt 6
Chelsea	Zola 13, Poyet 11, Flo 10
Coventry City	Whelan 10, Huckerby 9, Aloisi 5
Derby County	Burton 9, Wanchope 9
Everton	Campbell 9, Jeffers 6
Leeds United	Hasselbaink 18, Bowyer 9, Smith 7
Leicester City	Cottee 10, Heskey 6, Izzet 5
Liverpool	Owen 18, Fowler 14, Redknapp 8
Manchester United	Yorke 18, Cole 17, Solskjaer 12
Middlesbrough	Ricard 15, Deane 6, Beck 5
Newcastle United	Shearer 14, Solano 6, Ketsbaia 5
Nottingham Forest	Freedman 9, Van Hooijdonk 6, Rogers 4
Sheffield Wednesday	Carbone 8, Booth 6, Rudi 6
Southampton	Le Tissier 7, Ostenstad 7
Tottenham Hotspur	Iversen 9, Armstrong 7, Campbell 6
West Ham United	Wright 9, Sinclair 7, Lampard 5, Keller 5
Wimbledon	Euell 10, Gayle 10, Ekoku 6

	Arsenal	Aston Villa	Blackburn R.	Charlton A.	Chelsea	Coventry C.	Derby Co.	Everton	Leeds U.	Leicester C.
Arsenal	–	1-0	1-0	0-0	1-0	2-0	1-0	1-0	3-1	5-0
Aston Villa	3-2	–	1-3	3-4	0-3	1-4	1-0	3-0	1-2	1-1
Blackburn R.	1-2	2-1	–	1-0	3-4	1-2	0-0	1-2	1-0	1-0
Charlton A.	0-1	0-1	0-0	–	0-1	1-1	1-2	1-2	1-1	0-0
Chelsea	0-0	2-1	1-1	2-1	–	2-1	2-1	3-1	1-0	2-2
Coventry C.	0-1	1-2	1-1	2-1	2-1	–	1-1	3-0	2-2	1-1
Derby Co.	0-0	2-1	1-0	0-2	2-2	0-0	–	2-1	2-2	2-0
Everton	0-2	0-0	0-0	4-1	0-0	2-0	0-0	–	0-0	0-0
Leeds U.	1-0	0-0	1-0	4-1	0-0	2-0	4-1	1-0	–	0-1
Leicester C.	1-1	2-2	1-1	1-1	2-4	1-0	1-2	2-0	1-2	–
Liverpool	0-0	0-1	2-0	3-3	1-1	2-0	1-2	3-2	1-3	0-1
Manchester U.	1-1	2-1	3-2	4-1	1-1	2-0	1-0	3-1	3-2	2-2
Middlesbrough	1-6	0-0	2-1	2-0	0-0	2-0	1-1	2-2	0-0	0-0
Newcastle U.	1-1	2-1	1-1	0-0	0-1	4-1	2-1	1-3	0-3	1-0
Nottingham F.	0-1	2-2	2-2	0-1	1-3	1-0	2-2	0-2	1-1	1-0
Sheffield W.	1-0	0-1	3-0	3-0	0-0	1-2	0-1	0-0	0-2	0-1
Southampton	0-0	1-4	3-3	3-1	0-2	2-1	0-1	2-0	3-0	2-1
Tottenham H.	1-3	1-0	2-1	2-2	2-2	0-0	1-1	4-1	3-3	0-2
West Ham U.	0-4	0-0	2-0	0-1	1-1	2-0	5-1	2-1	1-5	3-2
Wimbledon	1-0	0-0	1-1	2-1	1-2	2-1	2-1	1-2	1-1	0-1

	Liverpool	Manchester U.	Middlesbrough	Newcastle U.	Nottingham F.	Sheffield W.	Southampton	Tottenham H.	West Ham U.	Wimbledon
Arsenal	0-0	3-0	1-1	3-0	2-1	3-0	1-1	0-0	1-0	5-1
Aston Villa	2-4	1-1	3-1	1-0	2-0	2-1	3-0	3-2	0-0	2-0
Blackburn R.	1-3	0-0	0-0	0-0	1-2	1-4	0-2	1-1	3-0	3-1
Charlton A.	1-0	0-1	1-1	2-2	0-0	0-1	5-0	1-4	4-2	2-0
Chelsea	2-1	0-0	2-0	1-1	2-1	1-1	1-0	2-0	0-1	3-0
Coventry C.	2-1	0-1	1-2	1-5	4-0	1-0	1-0	1-1	0-0	2-1
Derby Co.	3-2	1-1	2-1	3-4	1-0	1-0	0-0	0-1	0-2	0-0
Everton	0-0	1-4	5-0	1-0	0-1	1-2	1-0	0-1	6-0	1-1
Leeds U.	0-0	1-1	2-0	0-1	3-1	2-1	3-0	2-0	4-0	2-2
Leicester C.	1-0	2-6	0-1	2-0	3-1	0-2	2-0	2-1	0-0	1-1
Liverpool	–	2-2	3-1	4-2	5-1	2-0	7-1	3-2	2-2	3-0
Manchester U.	2-0	–	2-3	0-0	3-0	3-0	2-1	2-1	4-1	5-1
Middlesbrough	1-3	0-1	–	2-2	1-1	4-0	3-0	0-0	1-0	3-1
Newcastle U.	1-4	1-2	1-1	–	2-0	1-1	4-0	1-1	0-3	3-1
Nottingham F.	2-2	1-8	1-2	1-2	–	2-0	1-1	0-1	0-0	0-1
Sheffield W.	1-0	3-1	3-1	1-1	3-2	–	0-0	0-0	0-1	1-2
Southampton	1-2	0-3	3-3	2-1	1-2	1-0	–	1-1	1-0	3-1
Tottenham H.	2-1	2-2	0-3	2-0	0-3	0-3	3-0	–	1-2	0-0
West Ham U.	2-1	0-0	4-0	2-0	2-1	0-4	1-0	2-1	–	3-4
Wimbledon	1-0	1-1	2-2	1-1	1-3	2-1	0-2	3-1	0-0	–

	Arsenal	Aston Villa	Blackburn R.	Charlton A.	Chelsea	Coventry C.	Derby Co.	Everton	Leeds U.	Leicester C.
Arsenal	–	38,308	37,762	38,014	38,121	38,073	37,323	38,088	38,025	38,069
Aston Villa	39,217	–	37,404	37,705	39,217	38,799	38,007	32,488	37,510	39,241
Blackburn R.	30,867	27,536	–	22,568	23,113	23,779	24,007	27,219	27,620	22,544
Charlton A.	20,043	20,043	20,041	–	20,046	20,043	19,516	20,043	20,043	20,021
Chelsea	34,644	34,765	34,382	34,639	–	34,869	35,016	34,909	34,762	34,535
Coventry C.	23,040	22,654	19,701	20,259	23,042	–	16,627	19,290	23,049	19,894
Derby Co.	29,018	26,836	27,386	27,853	29,056	32,450	–	27,603	27,034	26,738
Everton	38,049	40,112	36,404	40,089	36,430	32,341	39,206	–	36,687	32,792
Leeds U.	40,142	33,446	30,652	32,487	36,292	31,802	38,971	36,344	–	32,606
Leicester C.	21,628	20,652	21,083	20,220	21,401	20,224	20,535	21,037	18,101	–
Liverpool	44,429	44,306	41,753	44,526	44,404	41,771	44,020	44,852	44,305	36,019
Manchester U.	55,171	55,189	55,198	55,147	55,159	55,193	55,174	55,182	55,172	55,052
Middlesbrough	34,630	34,643	34,413	34,529	34,406	34,293	34,121	34,563	34,162	34,631
Newcastle U.	36,708	36,766	36,623	36,719	36,711	36,352	36,750	36,775	36,783	36,718
Nottingham F.	26,021	25,753	22,013	22,661	26,351	22,546	24,014	25,610	23,911	25,353
Sheffield W.	27,949	25,989	20,846	26,010	21,652	28,136	24,440	26,952	28,142	33,513
Southampton	15,255	15,242	15,209	15,222	15,253	15,152	14,762	15,254	15,236	15,228
Tottenham H.	36,019	35,963	28,338	32,202	36,878	34,376	35,392	36,053	35,535	35,415
West Ham U.	26,042	26,002	25,529	26,041	26,023	25,662	25,485	25,998	25,997	25,642
Wimbledon	26,003	15,582	12,526	19,106	21,577	11,717	12,732	16,054	16,437	11,801

	Liverpool	Manchester U.	Middlesbrough	Newcastle U.	Nottingham F.	Sheffield W.	Southampton	Tottenham H.	West Ham U.	Wimbledon
Arsenal	38,107	38,142	38,075	38,102	38,064	37,792	38,027	38,278	38,098	37,982
Aston Villa	39,241	39,241	29,559	39,241	34,492	39,217	32,203	39,241	36,813	32,959
Blackburn R.	29,944	30,463	27,482	27,569	24,565	24,643	22,812	29,643	25,213	21,754
Charlton A.	20,043	20,043	20,043	20,043	20,007	20,043	16,488	20,043	20,043	20,002
Chelsea	34,822	34,741	34,811	34,795	34,809	34,451	34,920	34,881	34,765	34,757
Coventry C.	23,056	22,596	19,231	22,656	17,172	16,006	21,402	23,098	20,818	21,200
Derby Co.	32,913	30,867	32,726	32,039	32,217	26,209	26,557	30,083	31,666	25,747
Everton	40,185	40,079	31,606	30,357	34,175	35,270	32,073	39,378	40,049	32,574
Leeds U.	39,451	40,255	37,473	40,202	39,645	30,012	30,637	34,521	36,320	39,816
Leicester C.	21,837	22,091	20,635	21,125	20,891	20,113	18,423	20,787	20,402	17,725
Liverpool	–	44,702	44,384	44,605	44,595	40,003	44,011	44,007	44,511	41,902
Manchester U.	55,181	–	55,152	55,174	55,216	55,270	55,316	55,189	55,180	55,265
Middlesbrough	34,626	34,665	–	34,629	34,223	34,163	33,387	34,687	34,623	33,999
Newcastle U.	36,740	36,500	36,552	–	36,760	36,698	36,454	36,655	36,744	36,623
Nottingham F.	28,374	30,025	21,468	22,852	–	20,480	23,456	25,181	28,463	21,362
Sheffield W.	27,383	39,475	24,534	21,545	19,321	–	30,078	28,204	30,236	24,116
Southampton	15,202	15,251	15,202	15,244	14,942	15,201	–	15,204	15,240	14,354
Tottenham H.	36,521	36,070	30,437	36,047	35,832	32,129	28,580	–	36,089	32,422
West Ham U.	26,029	26,039	25,902	25,997	25,458	25,642	23,153	26,044	–	25,311
Wimbledon	26,080	26,121	14,114	21,172	12,149	13,163	24,068	23,031	23,035	–

COMPOSITE FINAL TABLE

Pos	Team	P	W	D	L	F	A	Pts	
1	Manchester United	38	28	7	3	97	45	91	Champions' League Group
2	Arsenal	38	22	7	9	73	43	73	Champions' League Group
3	Leeds United	38	21	6	11	58	43	69	Champions' League Qualifying
4	Liverpool	38	19	10	9	51	30	67	UEFA Cup
5	Chelsea	38	18	11	9	53	34	65	UEFA Cup (FA Cup winners)
6	Aston Villa	38	15	13	10	46	35	58	InterToto Cup
7	Sunderland	38	16	10	12	57	56	58	
8	Leicester City	38	16	7	15	55	55	55	UEFA Cup (League Cup winners)
9	West Ham United	38	15	10	13	52	53	55	
10	Tottenham Hotspur	38	15	8	15	57	49	53	
11	Newcastle United	38	14	10	14	63	54	52	
12	Middlesbrough	38	14	10	14	46	52	52	
13	Everton	38	12	14	12	59	49	50	
14	Coventry City	38	12	8	18	47	54	44	
15	Southampton	38	12	8	18	45	62	44	
16	Derby County	38	9	11	18	44	57	38	
17	Bradford City	38	9	9	20	38	68	36	InterToto Cup
18	Wimbledon	38	7	12	19	46	74	33	Relegated
19	Sheffield Wednesday	38	8	7	23	38	70	31	Relegated
20	Watford	38	6	6	26	35	77	24	Relegated

HOME & AWAY FINAL TABLE

Pos	Team	P	Home					Away					Pts
			W	D	L	F	A	W	D	L	F	A	
1	Manchester United	38	15	4	0	59	16	13	3	3	38	29	91
2	Arsenal	38	14	3	2	42	17	8	4	7	31	26	73
3	Leeds United	38	12	2	5	29	18	9	4	6	29	25	69
4	Liverpool	38	11	4	4	28	13	8	6	5	23	17	67
5	Chelsea	38	12	5	2	35	12	6	6	7	18	22	65
6	Aston Villa	38	8	8	3	23	12	7	5	7	23	23	58
7	Sunderland	38	10	6	3	28	17	6	4	9	29	39	58
8	Leicester City	38	10	3	6	31	24	6	4	9	24	31	55
9	West Ham United	38	11	5	3	32	23	4	5	10	20	30	55
10	Tottenham Hotspur	38	10	3	6	40	26	5	5	9	17	23	53
11	Newcastle United	38	10	5	4	42	20	4	5	10	21	34	52
12	Middlesbrough	38	8	5	6	23	26	6	5	8	23	26	52
13	Everton	38	7	9	3	36	21	5	5	9	23	28	50
14	Coventry City	38	12	1	6	38	22	0	7	12	9	32	44
15	Southampton	38	8	4	7	26	22	4	4	11	19	40	44
16	Derby County	38	6	3	10	22	25	3	8	8	22	32	38
17	Bradford City	38	6	8	5	26	29	3	1	15	12	39	36
18	Wimbledon	38	6	7	6	30	28	1	5	13	16	46	33
19	Sheffield Wednesday	38	6	3	10	21	23	2	4	13	17	47	31
20	Watford	38	5	4	10	24	31	1	2	16	11	46	24

- Manchester United – undefeated at home, 91 points and 97 goals – both records
- Coventry City – no away wins all season
- Bradford City – least number of points not to be relegated

TOP SCORERS

Players	Club	Goals
PHILLIPS, Kevin	Sunderland	30
SHEARER, Alan	Newcastle Utd	23
YORKE, Dwight	Manchester Utd	20
BRIDGES, Michael	Leeds Utd	19
COLE, Andy	Manchester Utd	19
HENRY, Thierry	Arsenal	17
DI CANIO, Paolo	West Ham Utd	16
QUINN, Niall	Sunderland	14
ARMSTRONG, Chris	Tottenham Hotspur	14
IVERSON, Steffen	Tottenham Hotspur	14
COTTEE, Tony	Leicester City	13
PAHARS, Marian	Southampton	13
CAMPBELL, Kevin	Everton	12
DUBLIN, Dion	Aston Villa	12
KANU, Nwankwo	Arsenal	12
KEANE, Robbie	Coventry City	12
RICARD, Hamilton	Middlesbrough	12
SOLSKJAER, Ole Gunnar	Manchester Utd	12
WANCHOPE, Paolo	West Ham Utd	12
McALLISTER, Gary	Coventry City	11
OWEN, Michael	Liverpool	11
DE BILDE, Gilles	Sheffield Wednesday	10
FLO, Tore Andre	Chelsea	10
POYET, Gustavo	Chelsea	10
KEWELL, Harry	Leeds Utd	10
WINDASS, Dean	Bradford City	10

EVER-PRESENT PLAYERS

Player	Club	Tot	St	Sb	Ps	Gls
DE BILDE, Gilles	Sheffield W.	38	37	1	17	10
HALLE, Gunnar	Bradford C.	38	37	1	6	0
HYYPIA, Sami	Liverpool	38	38	0	1	2
MARTYN, Nigel	Leeds U.	38	38	0	0	0
McALLISTER, Gary	Coventry C.	38	38	0	3	11
PALMER, Steve	Watford	38	38	0	1	0
WALKER, Ian	Tottenham H.	38	38	0	0	0
WETHERALL, David	Bradford C.	38	38	0	0	2
WINDASS, Dean	Bradford C.	38	36	2	7	10

ATTENDANCES BY CLUB

Club	Total	Average
Arsenal	722,630	38,033
Aston Villa	602,237	31,697
Bradford C.	324,294	17,068
Chelsea	656,102	34,532
Coventry C.	395,369	20,809
Derby Co.	557,678	29,351
Everton	661,720	34,827
Leeds U.	743,942	39,155
Leicester C.	376,720	19,827
Liverpool	837,402	44,074
Manchester U.	1,102,324	58,017
Middlesbrough	644,474	33,920
Newcastle U.	690,153	36,324
Sheffield W.	472,253	24,855
Southampton	287,516	15,132
Sunderland	786,131	41,375
Tottenham H.	663,324	34,912
Watford	351,708	18,511
West Ham U.	453,813	23,885
Wimbledon	325,185	17,115

TOP SCORERS BY CLUB

Club	Scorers
Arsenal	Henry 17, Kanu 12, Suker 8
Aston Villa	Dublin 12, Thompson 11
Bradford City	Windass 10, Beagrie 7, Mills 5
Chelsea	Flo, Poyet 10, Petrescu, Wise, Zola 4, Morris, Weah 3
Coventry City	Keane 12, McAllister 11, Hadji, Roussel 6
Derby County	Delap 8, Christie, Sturridge 6 Burley, Strupar 5
Everton	Campbell 12, Barmby 9 Hutchison, Jeffers, Moore, Unsworth 6
Leeds United	Bridges 19, Kewell 10, Harte 6
Leicester City	Cottee 13, Izzet 8, Heskey 7
Liverpool	Owen 11, Berger, Camara 9
Manchester United	Yorke 20, Cole 19, Solskjaer 12
Middlesbrough	Ricard 12, Deane 9, Ziege 6
Newcastle United	Shearer 23, Speed 9
Sheffield Wednesday	De Bilde 10, Alexandersson, Sibon 5
Southampton	Pahars 13, Davies 6
Sunderland	Phillips 30, Quinn 14
Tottenham Hotspur	Armstrong, Iversen 14, Sherwood 8
Watford	Helguson, Ngonge, Smart 5
West Ham United	Di Canio 16, Wanchope 12, Lampard, Sinclair 7
Wimbledon	Cort, Hartson 9, Gayle 7, Euell 4

1999-00 RESULT GRIDS

	Arsenal	Aston Villa	Bradford C.	Chelsea	Coventry C.	Derby Co.	Everton	Leeds U.	Leicester C.	Liverpool
Arsenal	–	3-1	2-0	2-1	3-0	2-1	4-1	2-0	2-1	0-1
Aston Villa	1-1	–	1-0	0-0	1-0	2-0	3-0	1-0	2-2	0-0
Bradford C.	2-1	1-1	–	1-1	1-1	4-4	0-0	1-2	3-1	1-0
Chelsea	2-3	1-0	1-0	–	2-1	4-0	1-1	0-2	1-1	2-0
Coventry C.	3-2	2-1	4-0	2-2	–	2-0	1-0	3-4	0-1	0-3
Derby Co.	1-2	0-2	0-1	3-1	0-0	–	1-0	0-1	3-0	0-2
Everton	0-1	0-0	4-0	1-1	1-1	2-1	–	4-4	2-2	0-0
Leeds U.	0-4	1-2	2-1	0-1	3-0	0-0	1-1	–	2-1	1-2
Leicester C.	0-3	3-1	3-0	2-2	1-0	0-1	1-1	2-1	–	2-2
Liverpool	2-0	0-0	3-1	1-0	2-0	2-0	0-1	3-1	0-2	–
Manchester U.	1-1	3-0	4-0	3-2	3-2	3-1	5-1	2-0	2-0	1-1
Middlesbrough	2-1	0-4	0-1	0-1	2-0	1-4	2-1	0-0	0-3	1-0
Newcastle U.	4-2	0-1	2-0	0-1	2-0	2-0	1-1	2-2	0-2	2-2
Sheffield W.	1-1	0-1	2-0	1-0	0-0	0-2	0-2	0-3	4-0	1-2
Southampton	0-1	2-0	1-0	1-2	0-0	3-3	2-0	0-3	1-2	1-1
Sunderland	0-0	2-1	0-1	4-1	1-1	1-1	2-1	1-2	2-0	0-2
Tottenham H.	2-1	2-4	1-1	0-1	3-2	1-1	3-2	1-2	2-3	1-0
Watford	2-3	0-1	1-0	1-0	1-0	0-0	1-3	1-2	1-1	2-3
West Ham U.	2-1	1-1	5-4	0-0	5-0	1-1	0-4	0-0	2-1	1-0
Wimbledon	1-3	2-2	3-2	0-1	1-1	2-2	0-3	2-0	2-1	1-2

	Manchester U.	Middlesbrough	Newcastle U.	Sheffield W.	Southampton	Sunderland	Tottenham H.	Watford	West Ham U.	Wimbledon
Arsenal	1-2	5-1	0-0	3-3	3-1	4-1	2-1	1-0	2-1	1-1
Aston Villa	0-1	1-0	0-1	2-1	0-1	1-1	1-1	4-0	2-2	1-1
Bradford C.	0-4	1-1	2-0	1-1	1-2	0-4	1-1	3-2	0-3	3-0
Chelsea	5-0	1-1	1-0	3-0	1-1	4-0	1-0	2-1	0-0	3-1
Coventry C.	1-2	2-1	4-1	4-1	0-1	3-2	0-1	4-0	1-0	2-0
Derby Co.	1-2	1-3	0-0	3-3	2-0	0-5	0-1	2-0	1-2	4-0
Everton	1-1	0-2	0-2	1-1	4-1	5-0	2-2	4-2	1-0	4-0
Leeds U.	0-1	2-0	3-2	2-0	1-0	2-1	1-0	3-1	1-0	4-1
Leicester C.	0-2	2-1	1-2	3-0	2-1	5-2	0-1	1-0	1-3	2-1
Liverpool	2-3	0-0	2-1	4-1	0-0	1-1	2-0	0-1	1-0	3-1
Manchester U.	–	1-0	5-1	4-0	3-3	4-0	3-1	4-1	7-1	1-1
Middlesbrough	3-4	–	2-2	1-0	3-2	1-1	2-1	1-1	2-0	0-0
Newcastle U.	3-0	2-1	–	8-0	5-0	1-2	2-1	1-0	2-2	3-3
Sheffield W.	0-1	1-0	0-2	–	0-1	0-2	1-2	2-2	3-1	5-1
Southampton	1-3	1-1	4-2	1-1	–	1-2	0-1	2-0	2-1	2-0
Sunderland	2-2	1-1	2-2	1-0	2-0	–	2-1	2-0	1-0	2-1
Tottenham H.	3-1	2-3	3-1	0-1	7-2	3-1	–	4-0	0-0	2-0
Watford	2-3	1-3	1-1	1-0	3-2	2-3	1-1	–	1-2	2-3
West Ham U.	2-4	0-1	2-1	-	2-0	1-1	1-0	1-0	–	2-1
Wimbledon	2-2	2-3	2-0	0-2	1-1	1-0	1-1	5-0	2-2	–

	Arsenal	Aston Villa	Bradford C.	Chelsea	Coventry C.	Derby Co.	Everton	Leeds U.	Leicester C.	Liverpool
Arsenal	–	38,093	38,073	38,119	38,027	37,964	38,042	38,096	38,026	38,098
Aston Villa	36,930	–	28,083	33,704	33,177	28,613	30,337	33,889	31,229	39,217
Bradford C.	18,276	18,276	–		17,587	18,276	18,276	18,276	17,655	18,276
Chelsea	34,958	35,071	31,591	–	32,316	35,084	35,113	35,106	35,063	34,957
Coventry C.	22,757	20,184	19,201	20,164	–	17,685	18,518	21,532	22,021	23,098
Derby Co.	25,901	33,222	31,035	28,614	28,381	–	26,550	29,455	25,763	33,378
Everton	35,919	34,750	30,646	38,225	34,839	33,260	–	37,355	30,490	40,052
Leeds U.	39,307	40,027	39,937	40,162	38,710	40,118	37,713	–	40,105	39,703
Leicester C.	20,495	19,917	21,103	21,068	19,196	18,581	18,705	21,095	–	21,623
Liverpool	44,886	43,615	40,483	44,826	44,024	44,467	44,802	44,793	43,456	–
Manchester U.	58,293	55,211	55,188	61,593	61,380	61,619	55,193	55,187	55,191	61,592
Middlesbrough	34,244	31,571	33,762	34,183	32,798	32,745	33,916	34,800	33,126	34,783
Newcastle U.	36,450	36,517	36,572	36,448	36,408	35,614	36,164	36,460	36,426	36,445
Sheffield W.	26,155	18,136	24,682	21,743	23,296	20,943	23,539	23,416	21,656	34,853
Southampton	15,242	15,218	15,027	15,232	15,168	14,208	15,232	15,206	15,178	15,241
Sunderland	41,680	41,045	40,628	41,377	39,427	41,940	41,934	41,947	40,105	42,015
Tottenham H.	36,085	35,304	35,472	36,041	35,224	33,044	34,539	36,012	35,591	36,044
Watford	19,670	19,161	15,564	21,244	18,977	16,579	17,346	19,677	16,184	21,367
West Ham U.	26,009	24,237	25,417	26,041	24,719	24,998	26,025	26,044	23,631	26,043
Wimbledon	25,858	19,188	10,029	22,167	10,635	12,282	13,172	18,747	14,316	26,102

	Manchester U.	Middlesbrough	Newcastle U.	Sheffield W.	Southampton	Sunderland	Tottenham H.	Watford	West Ham U.	Wimbledon
Arsenal	38,147	38,082	38,106	37,271	38,044	38,039	38,131	38,127	38,093	38,052
Aston Villa	39,217	28,728	34,531	23,885	26,474	33,949	39,217	27,647	26,250	27,160
Bradford C.	18,276	17,708	18,276	18,276	17,439	18,204	18,141	16,864	17,936	18,276
Chelsea	34,909	34,467	35,092	32,938	34,956	34,831	34,969	34,920	34,935	34,826
Coventry C.	22,024	19,435	23,031	19,921	19,915	22,101	23,077	21,700	19,993	19,012
Derby Co.	33,370	24,045	32,724	30,100	29,403	28,264	29,815	28,072	31,202	28,384
Everton	39,141	34,663	32,512	32,020	31,755	40,017	36,144	31,960	35,154	32,818
Leeds U.	40,160	34,122	40,192	39,437	39,288	39,064	40,127	36,324	40,190	39,256
Leicester C.	22,170	17,550	21,225	19,046	19,556	20,432	19,764	17,920	19,019	18,255
Liverpool	44,929	44,324	44,743	42,517	44,015	44,693	44,536	44,174	44,012	44,107
Manchester U.	–	61,267	55,190	54,941	55,249	61,613	61,629	55,188	61,611	55,189
Middlesbrough	34,775	–	34,744	32,748	32,165	44,793	33,129	32,930	31,862	31,400
Newcastle U.	36,470	36,421	–	36,619	35,623	36,500	36,460	36,433	36,314	35,809
Sheffield W.	39,640	28,531	29,212	–	23,470	28,072	24,027	21,658	21,147	18,077
Southampton	15,245	15,223	15,030	14,815	–	15,245	15,248	15,252	15,257	15,249
Sunderland	42,026	42,013	42,192	41,132	40,860	–	41,904	40,630	41,684	41,592
Tottenham H.	36,072	31,796	28,701	35,897	36,024	36,070	–	36,089	36,233	33,086
Watford	20,250	16,081	19,539	15,840	18,459	21,590	20,050	–	18,619	15,511
West Ham U.	26,037	25,472	25,817	-	23,484	26,081	26,010	25,310	–	22,438
Wimbledon	26,129	11,036	22,118	8,248	15,754	17,621	17,368	14,021	20,394	–

PREMIERSHIP TITLES BY NUMBER

6	Manchester United	1992-93, 1993-94, 1995-96, 1996-97, 1998-99, 1999-00
1	Arsenal	1997-98
1	Blackburn Rovers	1994-95

PREMIERSHIP RUNNERS-UP BY NUMBER

2	Arsenal	1998-99, 1999-00
2	Manchester United	1994-95, 1997-98
2	Newcastle United	1995-96, 1996-97
1	Aston Villa	1992-93
1	Blackburn Rovers	1993-94

CHAMPIONSHIP RECORDS

Season	Champions	P	W	D	L	F	A	Pts
1992-93	Manchester U.	42	24	12	6	67	31	84
1993-94	Manchester U.	42	27	11	4	80	38	92
1994-95	Blackburn R.	42	27	8	7	80	39	89
1995-96	Manchester U.	38	25	7	6	73	35	82
1996-97	Manchester U.	38	21	12	5	76	44	75
1997-98	Arsenal	38	23	9	6	68	33	78
1998-99	Manchester U.	38	22	13	3	80	37	79
1999-00	Manchester U.	38	28	7	3	97	45	91

ALL-TIME BIGGEST HOME WINS

9-0	Manchester United v Ipswich Town	04/03/95
8-0	Newcastle United v Sheffield Wednesday	19/09/99
7-0	Blackburn Rovers v Nottingham Forest	18/11/95
7-0	Manchester United v Barnsley	25/10/97
7-1	Aston Villa v Wimbledon	11/02/93
7-1	Blackburn Rovers v Norwich City	02/10/92
7-1	Newcastle United v Swindon Town	12/03/94
7-1	Everton v Southampton	28/12/96
7-1	Newcastle United v Tottenham Hotspur	05/03/97
7-1	Liverpool v Southampton	16/01/99
7-1	Manchester United v West Ham United	01/04/00
7-2	Blackburn Rovers v Sheffield Wednesday	28/08/97
7-2	Tottenham Hotspur v Southampton	11/03/00

ALL-TIME BIGGEST AWAY WINS

1-8	Nottingham Forest v Manchester United	06/02/99
1-7	Sheffield Wednesday v Nottingham Forest	01/04/95
0-6	Bolton Wanderers v Manchester United	25/02/96
1-6	Crystal Palace v Liverpool	20/08/94
1-6	Tottenham Hotspur v Chelsea	02/05/98
1-6	Middlesbrough v Arsenal	24/04/99
2-6	Wimbledon v Tottenham Hotspur	06/12/97
2-6	Leicester City v Manchester United	16/01/99

ALL-TIME HIGHEST SCORE DRAW

4-4	Aston Villa v Leicester City	22/02/95
	Everton v Leeds United	24/10/99
	Bracdford City v Derby County	21/04/00

ALL-TIME HIGHEST AGGREGATE SCORES

9 Goals

4-5	Norwich City v Southampton	09/04/94
9-0	Manchester United v Ipswich Town	04/03/95
1-8	Nottingham Forest v Manchester United	06/02/99
7-2	Blackburn Rovers v Sheffield United	11/03/98
6-3	Southampton v Manchester United	26/10/96
5-4	West Ham United v Bradford City	12/02/00
7-2	Tottenham Hotspur v Southampton	11/03/00

ALL-TIME SEASON GENERAL RECORDS

Record/Team	No	Season	P
Most Goals Scored			
Manchester United	97	1999-00	38
Newcastle United	84	1993-94	42
Fewest Goals Scored			
Crystal Palace	34	1994-95	42
Manchester City	31	1996-97	38
Most Goals Conceded			
Swindon Town	100	1993-94	42
Barnsley	82	1997-98	38
Fewest Goals Conceded			
Arsenal	28	1993-94	42
Manchester United	28	1994-95	42
Arsenal	17	1998-99	38
Most Points			
Manchester United	92	1993-94	42
Manchester United	91	1999-00	38
Fewest Points			
Watford	24	1999-00	38
Ipswich Town	27	1994-95	42
Most Wins			
Manchester United	28	1999-00	38
Manchester United	27	1993-94	42
Fewest Wins			
Swindon Town	5	1993-94	42
Watford	6	1999-00	38
Fewest Defeats			
Manchester United	3	1998-99	38

Chelsea	3	1998-99	38
Manchester United	3	1999-00	38
Manchester United	4	1993-94	42

Most Defeats

Ipswich Town	29	1994-95	42
Watford	26	1999-00	38

Most Draws

Manchester City	18	1993-94	42
Sheffield United	18	1993-94	42
Southampton	18	1994-95	42
Nottingham Forest	16	1996-97	38
Coventry City	16	1997-98	38

NB: 38 or 42 refers to the number of games played in that season.

LAST DAY CHAMPIONSHIPS

The FA Premier League Championship has been decided on the last day of the season three times.

1994-95

	P	W	D	L	F	A	Pts	GD
Blackburn Rovers	41	27	8	6	79	37	89	+42
Manchester United	41	26	9	6	76	27	87	+48

On the last day of the season Blackburn travelled to Liverpool needing a win to secure the title. Manchester United went to Upton Park needing three points from West Ham and hoping that Rovers would fail to win. A last minute goal gave Liverpool a 2-1 win over Blackburn, but despite a succession of missed chances Manchester United could only draw and the title went to Blackburn Rovers.

1995-96

	P	W	D	L	F	A	Pts	GD
Manchester United	37	24	7	6	70	35	79	+35
Newcastle United	37	24	5	8	65	36	77	+29

At one point Newcastle led the table by 12 points but a string of last-minute reversals and a relentless attack by the Red Devils allowed them to peg the Magpies back. On the final day of the season the former won 3-0 at Middlesbrough while the latter could only draw 1-1 at home with Spurs.

1998-99

	P	W	D	L	F	A	Pts	GD
Manchester United	37	21	13	3	78	36	76	+42
Arsenal	37	21	12	4	58	17	75	+41

It was so close that the two protagonists went into the final day of the season with only a goal difference of one separating them. Manchester United knew a win over Tottenham would ensure the title. Arsenal knew a win over Aston Villa wouldn't be sufficient and that they needed arch-rivals Tottenham Hotspur to get some sort of result at Old Trafford. Tottenham – involved in the final day drama for the second time – took the lead at Old Trafford and raised the Highbury hopes. But goals either side of the interval from Beckham and Cole meant that Kanu's second-half winner for Arsenal didn't re-direct the championship outcome.

PROMOTIONS TO PREMIERSHIP

1999-00
Promoted: Charlton Athletic (1st), Manchester City (2nd), Ipswich Town (3rd)

1998-99
Promoted: Sunderland (1st), Bradford City (2nd), Watford (5th)

1997-98
Promoted: Nottingham Forest (1st), Middlesbrough (2nd), Charlton Atheltic (4th)

1996-97
Promoted: Bolton Wanderers (1st), Barnsley (2nd), Crystal Palace (6th)

1995-96
Promoted: Sunderland (1st), Derby Co. (2nd), Leicester City (5th)

1994-95*
Promoted: Middlesbrough (1st), Bolton Wanderers (3rd)

1993-94
Promoted: Crystal Palace (1st), N. Forest (2nd), Leicester City (4th)

1992-93
Promoted: Newcastle United (1st), West Ham United (2nd), Swindon Town (5th)

1991-92†
Promoted: Ipswich Town (1st), Middlesbrough (2nd), Blackburn Rovers (6th)

* FA Premier League reduced to 20 clubs.
† Promoted from Division 2 to newly formed FA Premier League.

PLAYERS WITH MOST PREMIERSHIP APPEARANCES

Fullname	Tot	St	Sb	Snu	Ps
ATHERTON,Peter	292	291	1	2	6
SPEED,Gary	287	282	5	0	7
SHERWOOD,Tim	276	267	9	2	14
McALLISTER,Gary	270	270	0	0	18
WINTERBURN,Nigel	270	260	10	7	17
HUGHES,Mark	267	257	10	10	39
WALKER,Des	264	264	0	0	11
DIXON,Lee	263	259	4	6	17
IRWIN,Denis	263	256	7	8	22
FLOWERS,Tim	260	258	2	21	3
LE TISSIER,Matthew	258	232	26	8	49
SEAMAN,David	256	256	0	0	2
PALLISTER,Gary	253	253	0	1	14
SHEARER,Alan	253	243	10	1	10
SCHMEICHEL,Peter	252	252	0	0	5
GIGGS,Ryan	250	234	16	7	48
PALMER,Carlton	246	242	4	1	3
BARMBY,Nicky	245	228	17	7	58
EARLE,Robbie	244	240	4	6	23
SHERINGHAM,Teddy	244	216	28	12	15
JAMES,David	243	242	1	50	2
YORKE,Dwight	243	221	22	14	35
McMANAMAN,Steve	240	232	8	3	18
KEOWN,Martin	239	221	18	7	16
WETHERALL,David	239	226	13	31	11
SUTTON,Chris	237	219	18	6	29
KENNA,Jeff	236	232	4	9	8
WALKER,Ian	236	235	1	58	3
BENALI,Francis	235	216	19	20	22
SOUTHGATE,Gareth	235	235	0	2	6
CAMPBELL,Sol	234	225	9	6	26
DEANE,Brian	234	225	9	0	19
FERDINAND,Les	232	222	10	2	38
WRIGHT,Alan	232	223	9	14	16
BARTON,Warren	231	210	21	27	19
PEACOCK,Darren	231	223	8	15	5
RIPLEY,Stuart	231	205	26	9	67
LEE,Robert	229	220	9	0	33
PARLOUR,Ray	229	197	32	5	48
SHAW,Richard	229	225	4	7	8
EHIOGU,Ugo	227	218	9	14	5
REDKNAPP,Jamie	226	200	26	10	18
KEANE,Roy	225	217	8	0	21
MARTYN,Nigel	225	225	0	1	2
WISE,Dennis	225	217	8	1	17
BERG,Henning	224	203	21	24	2
WATSON,Dave	224	221	3	18	10
COLE,Andy	223	197	26	8	35
FOX,Ruel	223	208	15	27	40
SINCLAIR,Frank	222	215	7	8	14

PLAYERS WHO HAVE STARTED THE MOST GAMES

Fullname	St	Tot	Sb	Snu	Ps
ATHERTON,Peter	291	292	1	2	6
SPEED,Gary	282	287	5	0	7
McALLISTER,Gary	270	270	0	0	18
SHERWOOD,Tim	267	276	9	2	14
WALKER,Des	264	264	0	0	11
WINTERBURN,Nigel	260	270	10	7	17
DIXON,Lee	259	263	4	6	17
FLOWERS,Tim	258	260	2	21	3
HUGHES,Mark	257	267	10	10	39
IRWIN,Denis	256	263	7	8	22
SEAMAN,David	256	256	0	0	2
PALLISTER,Gary	253	253	0	1	14
SCHMEICHEL,Peter	252	252	0	0	5
SHEARER,Alan	243	253	10	1	10
JAMES,David	242	243	1	50	2
PALMER,Carlton	242	246	4	1	3
EARLE,Robbie	240	244	4	6	23
SOUTHGATE,Gareth	235	235	0	2	6
WALKER,Ian	235	236	1	58	3
GIGGS,Ryan	234	250	16	7	48
KENNA,Jeff	232	236	4	9	8
LE TISSIER,Matthew	232	258	26	8	49
McMANAMAN,Steve	232	240	8	3	18
BARMBY,Nicky	228	245	17	7	58
WETHERALL,David	226	239	13	31	11
CAMPBELL,Sol	225	234	9	6	26
DEANE,Brian	225	234	9	0	19
MARTYN,Nigel	225	225	0	1	2
SHAW,Richard	225	229	4	7	8
PEACOCK,Darren	223	231	8	15	5
WRIGHT,Alan	223	232	9	14	16
FERDINAND,Les	222	232	10	2	38
KEOWN,Martin	221	239	18	7	16
WATSON,Dave	221	224	3	18	10
YORKE,Dwight	221	243	22	14	35
LEE,Robert	220	229	9	0	33

Fullname	St	Tot	Sb	Snu	Ps
SUTTON,Chris	219	237	18	6	29
EHIOGU,Ugo	218	227	9	14	5
KEANE,Roy	217	225	8	0	21
WISE,Dennis	217	225	8	1	17
ADAMS,Tony	216	219	3	0	11
BENALI,Francis	216	235	19	20	22
SHERINGHAM,Teddy	216	244	28	12	15
SINCLAIR,Frank	215	222	7	8	14
KELLY,Gary	214	219	5	2	6
INCE,Paul	213	213	0	1	13
HENDRY,Colin	212	213	1	0	10
BARTON,Warren	210	231	21	27	19
HINCHCLIFFE,Andy	210	219	9	5	14
TOWNSEND,Andy	210	213	3	1	23

PLAYERS WHO HAVE MADE MOST APPEARANCES AS A SUBSTITUTE

Fullname	Sb	Tot	St	Snu	Ps
CLARKE,Andy	70	124	54	35	26
McCLAIR,Brian	56	162	106	49	18
FENTON,Graham	55	93	38	52	19
WATSON,Gordon	48	109	61	13	21
ROSENTHAL,Ronny	47	118	71	12	18
JOACHIM,Julian	46	136	90	31	27
CADAMARTERI,Danny	45	74	29	16	14
FLO,Tore Andre	44	98	54	7	19
SCHOLES,Paul	43	160	117	25	47
BARLOW,Stuart	41	62	21	20	7
HYDE,Graham	40	157	117	15	27
MARSHALL,Ian	40	157	117	15	26
BUTT,Nicky	38	178	140	11	32
SOLSKJAER,Ole Gunnar	38	102	64	22	28
KETSBAIA,Temuri	37	78	41	12	19
HUCKERBY,Darren	34	128	94	3	30
HUMPHREYS,Richie	33	60	27	26	18
CLARK,Lee	32	101	69	25	9
EKOKU,Efan	32	160	128	7	56
GOODMAN,Jon	32	60	28	9	16
HUGHES,David Robert	32	53	21	15	5
LEE,Jason	32	63	31	17	3
PARLOUR,Ray	32	229	197	5	48
SPENCER,John	32	112	80	16	22
DOMINGUEZ,Jose	31	43	12	16	8
WARHURST,Paul	31	112	81	23	23
WHITTINGHAM,Guy	31	138	107	22	30

Fullname	Sb	Tot	St	Snu	Ps
BART-WILLIAMS,Chris	30	181	151	9	35
BOHINEN,Lars	30	154	124	15	32
GAYLE,Marcus	30	204	174	6	63

PLAYERS WHO HAVE SAT ON THE BENCH MOST WITHOUT BEING USED (SUB NOT USED)

Fullname	Snu	Tot	St	Sb	Ps
HITCHCOCK,Kevin	178	61	57	4	1
SEALEY,Les	161	4	2	2	0
BEENEY,Mark	144	35	35	0	0
KEARTON,Jason	135	6	3	3	0
HEALD,Paul	127	23	22	1	1
BAARDSEN,Espen	124	23	22	1	0
GOULD,Jonathan	110	25	25	0	0
VAN DER GOUW,Raimond	108	26	21	5	1
OAKES,Michael	107	51	49	2	0
CLARKE,Matt	101	25	23	2	1
GERRARD,Paul	93	84	82	2	1
MIMMS,Bobby	92	61	59	2	0
WARNER,Tony	89	0	0	0	0
SULLIVAN,Neil	88	179	178	1	1
FORREST,Craig	86	103	99	4	0
LUKIC,John	86	144	144	0	1
MOSS,Neil	86	19	17	2	0
PRESSMAN,Kevin	86	207	205	2	3
SPINK,Nigel	86	55	51	4	0
FILAN,John	85	49	48	1	2
ARPHEXAD,Pegguy	84	20	16	4	0
HOOPER,Mike	81	34	31	3	0
ANDREWS,Ian	79	5	5	0	0
DAY,Chris	78	11	11	0	0
MILLER,Alan	75	24	22	2	0
OGRIZOVIC,Steve	75	191	191	0	1
MARGETSON,Martyn	74	1	1	0	1
MARRIOTT,Andy	74	6	6	0	0
SRNICEK,Pavel	72	141	140	1	1
BEASANT,Dave	71	131	129	2	0
ROBINSON,Paul	71	5	4	1	0
MANNINGER,Alex	70	28	27	1	0
FETTIS,Alan	67	14	13	1	0
GIVEN,Shay	66	71	71	0	1
HOULT,Russell	63	67	66	1	1
BERESFORD,Marlon	61	5	5	0	0
GROBBELAAR,Bruce	61	66	66	0	2
WARD,Gavin	61	17	15	2	0

APPEARANCE STATISTICS

Fullname	Snu	Tot	St	Sb	Ps
SIMONSEN,Steve	60	30	27	3	4
WALKER,Ian	58	236	235	1	3
BAKER,Clive	56	48	47	1	0
BARTRAM,Vince	54	11	11	0	0
ROBERTS,Tony	53	80	80	0	1
FENTON,Graham	52	93	38	55	19
DIBBLE,Andy	51	29	27	2	0
JAMES,David	50	243	242	1	2
MADDISON,Neil	50	184	157	27	29
McCLAIR,Brian	49	162	106	56	18
FRIEDEL,Brad	48	25	25	0	0
THORSTVEDT,Erik	48	60	58	2	2
WALSH,Gary	48	73	72	1	0

PLAYERS WHO HAVE BEEN SUBSTITUTED THE MOST

Fullname	Ps	St	Sb	Snu
RIPLEY,Stuart	67	205	26	9
GAYLE,Marcus	63	174	30	6
BARMBY,Nicky	58	228	17	7
EKOKU,Efan	56	128	32	7
COTTEE,Tony	51	193	25	10
LE TISSIER,Matthew	49	232	26	8
GALLACHER,Kevin	48	163	16	4
GIGGS,Ryan	48	234	16	7
GINOLA,David	48	154	4	10
PARLOUR,Ray	48	197	32	5
PETRESCU,Dan	48	162	25	3
SCHOLES,Paul	47	117	43	25
OVERMARS,Marc	45	91	9	0
HIRST,David	44	121	14	0
MERSON,Paul	44	198	23	9
WALLACE,Rod	43	153	25	15
ZOLA,Gianfranco	42	105	15	8
SINTON,Andy	41	156	23	10
FOX,Ruel	40	208	15	27
HOLDSWORTH,Dean	40	165	24	4
HUGHES,Mark	39	257	10	10
FERDINAND,Les	38	222	10	2
OAKLEY,Matthew	36	107	18	2
WILCOX,Jason	36	192	20	7
WRIGHT,Ian	36	202	11	0
BART-WILLIAMS,Chris	35	151	30	9
BERKOVIC,Eyal	35	88	5	7
COLE,Andy	35	197	26	8
YORKE,Dwight	35	221	22	14

Fullname	Ps	St	Sb	Snu
BAIANO,Francesco	34	52	12	3
HOWELLS,David	34	140	12	7
ARDLEY,Neal	33	141	29	12
CARBONE,Benito	33	108	12	1
GILLESPIE,Keith	33	110	28	14
LEE,Robert	33	220	9	0
SAUNDERS,Dean	33	178	8	2
ANDERTON,Darren	32	184	17	3
BERGKAMP,Dennis	32	140	7	2
BOHINEN,Lars	32	124	30	15
BUTT,Nicky	32	140	38	11
PEMBRIDGE,Mark	32	117	7	2
ROY,Bryan	32	70	15	12
STAUNTON,Steve	32	206	8	22
LEONHARDSEN,Oyvind	31	128	7	5
HUCKERBY,Darren	30	94	34	3
IMPEY,Andy	30	208	8	13
JENSEN,John	30	93	5	8
WHITTINGHAM,Guy	30	107	31	22
GEMMILL,Scot	29	128	21	26
MADDISON,Neil	29	157	27	50
ROCASTLE,David	29	65	10	6
SOLANO,Norberto	29	53	6	7
SUTTON,Chris	29	219	18	6
WHELAN,Noel	29	155	27	11

TOP PREMIERSHIP GOAL SCORERS (ALL CLUBS)

Fullname	Gls	Tot	St	Sb
SHEARER,Alan	176	253	243	10
COLE,Andy	124	223	197	26
FERDINAND,Les	113	232	222	10
WRIGHT,Ian	113	213	202	11
FOWLER,Robbie	109	199	187	12
LE TISSIER,Matthew	101	258	232	26
YORKE,Dwight	98	243	221	22
SHERINGHAM,Teddy	91	244	216	28
DUBLIN,Dion	87	215	197	18
SUTTON,Chris	81	237	219	18
COTTEE,Tony	78	218	193	25
CANTONA,Eric	70	156	154	2
ARMSTRONG,Chris	69	207	189	18
DEANE,Brian	62	234	225	9
HUGHES,Mark	62	267	257	10
HOLDSWORTH,Dean	61	189	165	24
COLLYMORE,Stan	60	150	131	19
BEARDSLEY,Peter	59	185	179	6
BERGKAMP,Dennis	57	147	140	7
GALLACHER,Kevin	54	179	163	16
GIGGS,Ryan	54	250	234	16
CAMPBELL,Kevin	52	169	150	19
EKOKU,Efan	52	160	128	32
SPEED,Gary	52	287	282	5
BRIGHT,Mark	50	143	118	25
HARTSON,John	49	143	129	14
OWEN,Michael	48	95	87	8
RUSH,Ian	48	176	158	18
SOLSKJAER,Ole Gunnar	48	102	64	38
QUINN,Niall	47	169	143	26
BARMBY,Nicky	46	245	228	17
EARLE,Robbie	45	244	240	4
FERGUSON,Duncan	45	146	134	12
McALLISTER,Gary	44	270	270	0
SAUNDERS,Dean	44	186	178	8
HIRST,David	43	135	121	14
KANCHELSKIS,Andrei	43	140	119	21
WALLACE,Rod	42	178	153	25
McMANAMAN,Steve	41	240	232	8
SCHOLES,Paul	41	160	117	43
MERSON,Paul	38	221	198	23
WHELAN,Noel	38	182	155	27
BECKHAM,David	36	175	158	17
FOX,Ruel	36	223	208	15

Fullname	Gls	Tot	St	Sb
HESKEY,Emile	36	136	135	1
INCE,Paul	36	213	213	0
SHERWOOD,Tim	36	276	267	9
SPENCER,John	36	112	80	32
DI CANIO,Paolo	35	84	80	4
JOACHIM,Julian	35	136	90	46
NDLOVU,Peter	35	154	132	22
WANCHOPE,Paulo	35	107	98	9

TOP STRIKE RATES FOR GOALSCORERS
(GOAL EVERY SR GAME)

	SR	Gls	Tot	St	Sb
SHEARER,Alan	1.438	176	253	243	10
COLE,Andy	1.798	124	223	197	26
KLINSMANN,Jurgen	1.806	31	56	56	0
FOWLER,Robbie	1.826	109	199	187	12
WRIGHT,Ian	1.885	113	213	202	11
OWEN,Michael	1.979	48	95	87	8
HASSELBAINK,Jimmy	2.029	34	69	66	3
FERDINAND,Les	2.053	113	232	222	10
SOLSKJAER,Ole Gunnar	2.125	48	102	64	38
CANTONA,Eric	2.229	70	156	154	2
DI CANIO,Paolo	2.400	35	84	80	4
DUBLIN,Dion	2.471	87	215	197	18
YORKE,Dwight	2.480	98	243	221	22
COLLYMORE,Stan	2.500	60	150	131	19
LE TISSIER,Matthew	2.554	101	258	232	26
QUINN,Mick	2.560	25	64	57	7
BERGKAMP,Dennis	2.579	57	147	140	7
RICARD,Hamilton	2.593	27	70	60	10
BRIDGES,Michael	2.636	22	58	42	16
SHERINGHAM,Teddy	2.681	91	244	216	28
ROSLER,Uwe	2.724	29	79	75	4
VIALLI,Gianluca	2.762	21	58	46	12
COTTEE,Tony	2.795	78	218	193	25
ANELKA,Nicolas	2.826	23	65	50	15
BRIGHT,Mak	2.860	50	143	118	25
HARTSON,John	2.918	49	143	129	14
SUTTON,Chris	2.926	81	237	219	18
ALLEN,Bradley	2.950	20	59	42	17
ARMSTRONG,Chris	3.000	69	207	189	18
POYET,Gustavo	3.000	25	75	57	18
WANCHOPE,Paulo	3.057	35	107	98	9
EKOKU,Efan	3.077	52	160	128	32
HOLDSWORTH,Dean	3.098	61	189	165	24

	SR	Gls	Tot	St	Sb	Player	Team	Gls	Tot
MILOSEVIC,Savo	3.103	29	90	84	6	CANTONA, Eric	Manchester U.	64	143
SPENCER,John	3.111	36	112	80	32	SHEARER, Alan	Newcastle U.	64	115
BEARDSLEY,Peter	3.136	59	185	179	6	DUBLIN, Dion	Coventry C.	62	153
HIRST,David	3.140	43	135	121	14	FERDINAND, Les	QPR	60	110
FLO,Tore Andre	3.161	31	98	54	44	YORKE, Dwight	Aston Villa	60	179
IVERSEN,Steffen	3.172	29	92	82	10	HOLDSWORTH, Dean	Wimbledon	58	169
FERGUSON,Duncan	3.244	45	146	134	12	BERGKAMP, Dennis	Arsenal	57	147
CAMPBELL,Kevin	3.250	52	169	150	19	GIGGS, Ryan	Manchester U.	54	250
KANCHELSKIS,Andrei	3.256	43	140	119	21	BRIGHT, Mark	Sheffield W.	48	133
OSTENSTAD,Egil	3.310	29	96	80	16	OWEN, Michael	Liverpool	48	95
GALLACHER,Kevin	3.315	54	179	163	16	SOLSKJAER, Ole Gunnar	Manchester U.	48	102
ATKINSON,Dalian	3.318	22	73	68	5	BEARDSLEY, Peter	Newcastle U.	47	129
WARD,Ashley	3.355	31	104	97	7	SUTTON, Chris	Blackburn R.	47	130
FJORTOFT,Jan-Aage	3.360	25	84	67	17	ARMSTRONG, Chris	Tottenham H.	46	132
SHARP,Graeme	3.438	16	55	51	4	GALLAGHER, Kevin	Blackburn R.	46	139
WALSH,Paul	3.438	16	55	55	0	EARLE, Robbie	Wimbledon	45	244
ROBINS,Mark	3.538	26	92	78	14	RUSH, Ian	Liverpool	45	130
ROY,Bryan	3.542	24	85	70	15	COLE, Andy	Newcastle U.	43	58
QUINN,Niall	3.596	47	169	143	26	WALLACE, Rod	Leeds U.	42	178
KITSON,Paul	3.600	25	90	69	21	FERDINAND, Les	Newcastle U.	41	68
BLAKE,Nathan	3.619	21	76	65	11	McMANAMAN, Steve	Liverpool	41	240
ZOLA,Gianfranco	3.636	33	120	105	15	SCHOLES, Paul	Manchester U.	41	160
GALLEN,Kevin	3.667	18	66	57	9	YORKE, Dwight	Manchester U.	38	64
RUSH,Ian	3.667	48	176	158	18	EKOKU, Efan	Wimbledon	37	123
STURRIDGE,Dean	3.677	31	114	90	24	FERGUSON, Duncan	Everton	37	116
PENRICE,Gary	3.706	17	63	42	21	SAUNDERS, Dean	Aston Villa	37	112
DEANE,Brian	3.774	62	234	225	9	BECKHAM, David	Manchester U.	36	175
HESKEY,Emile	3.778	36	136	135	1	SPENCER, John	Chelsea	36	103
RIDEOUT,Paul	3.828	29	111	86	25	NDLOVU, Peter	Coventry C.	35	154
WHITE,David	3.846	26	100	86	14	GAYLE, Marcus	Wimbledon	34	204
JOACHIM,Julian	3.886	35	136	90	46	HASSELBAINK, Jimmy	Leeds U.	34	69
FASHANU,John	3.900	20	78	73	5	HIRST, David	Sheffield W.	34	105
SCHOLES,Paul	3.902	41	160	117	43	HUGHES, Mark	Manchester U.	34	111
BAIANO,Francesco	4.000	16	64	52	12	HESKEY, Emile	Leicester C.	33	124
OVERMARS,Marc	4.000	25	100	91	9	SUTTON, Chris	Norwich C.	33	79
SAUNDERS,Dean	4.227	44	186	178	8	DEANE, Brian	Leeds U.	32	138
						JOACHIM, Julian	Aston Villa	32	121
						LEE, Robert	Newcastle U.	32	229
						FLO, Tore Andre	Chelsea	31	98
						KLINSMANN, Jurgen	Tottenham H.	31	56
						STURRIDGE, Dean	Derby Co.	31	114
						WHELAN, Noel	Coventry C.	31	134
						WISE, Dennis	Chelsea	31	225
						PHILLIPS, Kevin	Sunderland	30	36
						QUINN, Niall	Manchester C.	30	120

TOP GOAL SCORERS FOR SINGLE CLUB

Player	Team	Gls	Tot
SHEARER, Alan	Blackburn R.	112	138
FOWLER, Robbie	Liverpool	109	199
WRIGHT, Ian	Arsenal	104	191
LE TISSIER, Matthew	Southampton	101	258
COLE, Andy	Manchester U.	81	165
SHERINGHAM, Teddy	Tottenham H.	74	166

MOST GOALS IN ONE GAME BY A PLAYER

Gls	Player	Match/Date	Res
5	COLE Andy	Manchester U. v Ipswich T. 04/03/95	9-0
	SHEARER, Alan	Newcastle U. v Sheffield W. 18/09/99	8-0
4	EKOKU Efan	Everton v Norwich C. 25/09/93	1-5
	FOWLER Robbie	Liverpool v Middlesbrough 14/12/96	5-1
	VIALLI Gianluca	Barnsley v Chelsea 24/08/97	6-0
	KLINSMANN Jurgen	Wimbledon v Tottenham H. 02/05/98	6-2
	OWEN Michael	Liverpool v N.Forest 14/10/98	5-1
	SOLSKJAER Ole G.	N.Forest v Manchester U. 06/02/99	1-8
	COLE, Andy	Manchester U. v Newcastle U. 30/08/99	5-1
	SOLSKJAER, Ole G.	Manchester U. v Everton 04/12/99	5-1

PLAYERS: CONSECUTIVE GAMES WITH GOAL

7   Mark Stein, Chelsea – 1993-94

Dec 27	Southampton	Away	1-3	1 goal
Dec 28	Newcastle U.	Home	1-0	1 goal
Jan 1	Swindon T.	Away	3-0	1 goal
Jan 3	Everton	Home	4-2	2 (1 pen)
Jan 15	Norwich C.	Away	1-1	1 goal
Jan 22	Aston Villa	Home	1-1	1 goal
Feb 5	Everton	Away	2-4	2 (1pen)

(Stein actually scored 9 goals – inc. two penalties – in this sequence. These goals were scored in consecutive Chelsea matches as well.)

7   Alan Shearer, Newcastle United – 1996-97

Sep 14	Blackburn R.	Home	2-1	1 pen
Sep 21	Leeds U.	Away	1-0	1 goal
Sep 30	Aston Villa	Home	4-3	1 goal
Oct 12	Derby Co.	Away	1-0	1 goal
Oct 20	Manchester U.	Home	5-0	1 goal
Nov 23	Chelsea	Away	1-1	1 goal
Nov 30	Arsenal	Home	1-2	1 goal

(Newcastle played Leicester City, Middlesbrough and West Ham after playing Man. United and before Chelsea but Shearer was injured for these matches.)

7   Thierry Henry, Arsenal – 1999-00

Mar 19	Tottenham H.	Home	2-1	1pen
Mar 26	Coventry C.	Home	3-0	1 goal
Apr 1	Wimbledon	Away	3-1	1 pen
Apr 16	Leeds U.	Away	4-0	1 goal
Apr 23	Watford	Away	3-2	2 goals
May 6	Chelsea	Home	2-1	2 goal
May 9	Sheffield W.	Home	3-3	1 gaol

Henry scored nine goals including two penalties in this sequence. Henry missed two Arsenal games (v Everton and West Ham before the final game in the seuqnece).

FASTEST GOALS IN A GAME

April fools? Two of the fastest goals to have been scored in the Premier League have both come on the 1st April!

13 seconds
SUTTON, Chris   Blackburn R. v Everton   01/04/94

17 seconds
SPENCER, John   Chelsea v Leicester C.   08/10/94

25 seconds
HASSELBAINK, JF   West Ham U. v Leeds U.   01/04/99

FASTEST HAT-TRICK IN A GAME

4 mins 33 secs
FOWLER Robbie   Liverpool v Arsenal   28/08/94

BEST HAT-TRICK

BERGKAMP, Dennis   Leicester v Arsenal
The Dutchman's three strikes won first, second and third place in the monthly Match of the Day, Goal of the Month competition!

PLAYER: MOST HAT-TRICKS IN A SEASON

5   Alan Shearer, Blackburn Rovers – 1995-96
v Coventry City, Nottingham Forest, West Ham United, Bolton Wanderers and Tottenham Hotspur

Season	Date	Player	Gls	Pens	Match	Score
1992-93	25-Aug-92	Cantona, Eric	3		LEEDS U. v Tottenham H.	(5-0)
1992-93	9-Nov-92	Robins, Mark	3		Oldham A. v NORWICH C.	(2-3)
1992-93	5-Dec-92	Hendrie, John	3		MIDDLESBROUGH v Blackburn R.	(3-2)
1992-93	28-Dec-92	Sinton, Andy	3		QPR v Everton	(4-2)
1992-93	16-Jan-93	Deane, Brian	3		SHEFFIELD U. v Ipswich T.	(3-0)
1992-93	20-Feb-93	Sheringham, Teddy	3		TOTTENHAM H. v Leeds U.	(4-0)
1992-93	10-Apr-93	Strachan, Gordon	3		LEEDS U. v Blackburn R.	(5-0)
1992-93	10-Apr-93	Ferdinand, Les	3		QPR v Nottingham F.	(4-3)
1992-93	12-Apr-93	Ferdinand, Les	3		Everton v QPR	(3-5)
1992-93	12-Apr-93	Bart-Williams, Chris	3		SHEFFIELD W. v Southampton	(5-2)
1992-93	14-Apr-93	Sutton, Chris	3		NORWICH C. v Leeds U.	(4-2)
1992-93	17-Apr-93	Walters, Mark	3	1	LIVERPOOL v Coventry C/	(4-0)
1992-93	8-May-93	Le Tissier, Matt	3		Oldham A. v SOUTHAMPTON	(4-3)
1992-93	5-May-93	Wallace, Rod	3		Coventry C. v LEEDS U.	(3-3)
1993-94	14-Aug-93	Quinn, Mick	3		Arsenal v COVENTRY C.	(0-3)
1993-94	18-Aug-93	Cottee, Tony	3		EVERTON v Sheffield U.	(4-2)
1993-94	11-Sep-93	Campbell, Kevin	3		ARSENAL v Ipswich T.	(4-0)
1993-94	25-Sep-93	Ekoku, Efan	4		Everton v NORWICH C.	(1-5)
1993-94	23-Oct-93	Shearer, Alan	3		Leeds U. v BLACKBURN R.	(3-3)
1993-94	30-Oct-93	Fowler, Robbie	3		LIVERPOOL v Southampton	(4-2)
1993-94	30-Oct-93	Beardsley, Peter	3		NEWCASTLE U. v Wimbledon	(4-0)
1993-94	20-Nov-93	Allen, Bradley	3		Everton v QPR	(0-3)
1993-94	21-Nov-93	Cole, Andy	3		NEWCASTLE U. v Liverpool	(3-0)
1993-94	27-Dec-93	Campbell, Kevin	3		Swindon T. v ARSENAL	(0-4)
1993-94	15-Jan-94	Cottee, Tony	3		EVERTON v Swindon T.	(6-2)
1993-94	5-Feb-94	Fjortoft, Jan Aage	3		SWINDON T. v Coventry	(3-1)
1993-94	12-Feb-94	Saunders, Dean	3		ASTON VILLA v Swindon T.	(5-0)
1993-94	14-Feb-94	Le Tissier, Matt	3		SOUTHAMPTON v Liverpool	(4-2)
1993-94	23-Feb-94	Cole, Andy	3		NEWCASTLE U. v Coventry	(4-0)
1993-94	5-Feb-94	Wright, Ian	3		Ipswich T. v ARSENAL	(1-5)
1993-94	19-Mar-94	Wright, Ian	3		Southampton v ARSENAL	(0-4)
1993-94	9-Apr-94	Le Tissier, Matt	3		Norwich C. v SOUTHAMPTON	(4-5)
1993-94	26-Apr-94	Holdsworth, Dean	3		WIMBLEDON v Oldham A.	(3-0)
1994-95	27-Aug-94	Sutton, Chris	3		BLACKBURN v Coventry C.	(4-0)
1994-95	28-Aug-94	Fowler, Robbie	3		LIVERPOOL v Arsenal	(3-0)
1994-95	10-Nov-94	Kanchelskis, Andre	3		MANCHESTER U. v Manchester C.	(5-0)
1994-95	26-Nov-94	Shearer, Alan	3		BLACKBURN R. v QPR	(4-0)
1994-95	3-Dec-94	Sheringham, Teddy	3		TOTTENHAM H. v Newcastle U.	(4-2)
1994-95	17-Dec-94	Cottee, Tony	3		WEST HAM U. v Manchester C.	(3-0)
1994-95	2-Jan-95	Shearer, Alan	3		BLACKBURN R. v West Ham U.	(4-2)
1994-95	28-Jan-95	Shearer, Alan	3		BLACKBURN R. v Ipswich T.	(4-1)
1994-95	11-Feb-95	Johnson, Tommy	3		ASTON VILLA v Winbledon	(7-1)
1994-95	4-Mar-95	Cole, Andy	5		MANCHESTER U. v Ipswich T.	(9-0)
1994-95	4-Mar-95	Ndlovu, Peter	3		Liverpool v COVENTRY C.	(2-3)
1994-95	5-Apr-95	Yeboah, Anthony	3		LEEDS U. v Ipswich T.	(4-0)
1994-95	15-Apr-95	Wright, Ian	3		ARSENAL v Ipswich T.	(4-1)
1995-96	19-Aug-95	Le Tissier, Matt	3	2	SOUTHAMPTON v Nottingham F.	(3-4)
1995-96	23-Sep-95	Shearer, Alan	3		BLACKBURN R. v Coventry C.	(5-1)
1995-96	23-Sep-95	Yeboah, Tony	3		Wimbledon v LEEDS U.	(4-2)
1995-96	23-Sep-95	Fowler, Robbie	4		LIVERPOOL v Bolton W.	(5-2)

Season	Date	Player	Gls	Pens	Match	Score
1995-96	21-Oct-95	Ferdinand, Les	3		NEWCASTLE U. v Wimbledon	(6-1)
1995-96	28-Oct-95	McAllister, Gary	3	1	LEEDS U. v Coventry C.	(3-1)
1995-96	18-Nov-95	Shearer, Alan	3		BLACKBURN R. v Nottingahm F.	(7-0)
1995-96	2-Dec-95	Shearer, Alan	3	1	BLACKBURN R. v West Ham U.	(4-2)
1995-96	3-Dec-95	Dublin, Dion	3		Sheffield W. v COVENTRY C.	(4-3)
1995-96	16-Dec-95	Milosevic, Savo	3		ASTON VILLA v Coventry C.	(4-1)
1995-96	23-Dec-95	Fowler, Robbie	3		LIVERPOOL v Arsenal	(3-1)
1995-96	3-Feb-96	Shearer, Alan	3		BLACKBURN R. v Bolton W.	(3-1)
1995-96	4-Feb-96	Peacock, Gavin	3		CHELSEA v Middlesbrough	(5-0)
1995-96	16-Mar-96	Shearer, Alan	3	1	Tottenham H. v BLACKBURN R.	(3-2)
1995-96	13-Apr-96	Hughes, Mark	3	1	CHELSEA v Leeds U.	(4-1)
1995-96	27-Apr-96	Kanchelskis, Andre	3		Sheffield W. v EVERTON	(5-2)
1996-97	17-Aug-96	Campbell, Kevin	3		Coventry C. v NOTTINGHAM F.	(0-3)
1996-97	17-Aug-96	Ravanelli, Fabrizio	3	1	MIDDLESBROUGH v Liverpool	(3-3)
1996-97	16-Sep-96	Wright, Ian	3	1	ARSENAL v Sheffield W.	(4-1)
1996-97	30-Sep-96	Yorke, Dwight	3		Newcastle U. v ASTON VILLA	(4-3)
1996-97	16-Nov-96	Speed, Gary	3		EVERTON v Southampton	(7-1)
1996-97	14-Dec-96	Fowler, Robbie	4		LIVERPOOL v Middlesbrough	(5-1)
1996-97	2-Feb-97	Shearer, Alan	3		NEWCASTLE U. v Leicester C.	(4-3)
1996-97	22-Feb-97	Marshall, Ian	3		LEICESTER C. v Derby Co.	(4-2)
1996-97	4-Mar-97	Iversen, Steffen	3		Sunderland v TOTTENHAM H.	(0-4)
1996-97	5-Mar-97	Ravanelli, Fabrizio	3		MIDDLESBROUGH v Derby Co.	(6-1)
1996-97	15-Mar-97	Gallacher, Kevin	3		BLACKBURN R. v Wimbledon	(3-1)
1996-97	3-May-97	Kitson, Paul	3		WEST HAM U. v Sheffield W.	(5-1)
1997-98	9-Aug-97	Dublin, Dion	3		COVENTRY C. v Chelsea	(3-2)
1997-98	13-Aug-97	Sutton, Chris	3		Aston Villa v BLACKBURN R.	(0-4)
1997-98	24-Aug-97	Vialli, Gianluca	4		Barnsley v CHELSEA	(0-6)
1997-98	27-Aug-97	Bergkamp, Dennis	3		Leicester C. v ARSENAL	(3-3)
1997-98	13-Sep-97	Wright, Ian	3		ARSENAL v Bolton W.	(4-1)
1997-98	6-Oct-98	Berger, Patrik	3		LIVERPOOL v Chelsea	(4-2)
1997-98	25-Oct-97	Cole, Andy	3		MANCHESTER U. v Barnsley	(7-0)
1997-98	8-Nov-97	Booth, Andy	3		SHEFFIELD W. v Bolton W.	(5-0)
1997-98	29-Nov-97	Zola, Gianfranco	3		CHELSEA v Derby Co.	(4-0)
1997-98	6-Dec-97	Flo, Tore Andre	3		Tottenham H. v CHELSEA	(1-6)
1997-98	28-Dec-97	Ferguson, Duncan	3		EVERTON v Bolton W.	(3-2)
1997-98	17-Jan-98	Gallacher, Kevin	3		BLACKBURN R. v Aston Villa	(5-0)
1997-98	14-Feb-98	Owen, Michael	3		Sheffield W. v LIVERPOOL	(3-3)
1997-98	28-Feb-98	Sutton, Chris	3		BLACKBURN R. v Leicester C.	(5-3)
1997-98	25-Apr-98	Huckerby, Darren	3		Leeds U. v COVENTRY C.	(3-3)
1997-98	2-May-98	Klinsmann, Jurgen	4		Wimbledon v TOTTENHAM H.	(2-6)
1998-99	22-Aug-98	Mendonca, Clive	3	1	CHARLTON A. v Southampton	(5-0)
1998-99	30-Aug-98	Owen, Micheal	3		Newcastle U. v LIVERPOOL	(1-4)
1998-99	24-Oct-98	Owen, Michael	4		LIVERPOOL v Nottingham F.	(5-1)
1998-99	14-Nov-98	Dublin, Dion	3		Southampton v ASTON VILLA	(1-4)
1998-99	21-Nov-98	Fowler, Robbie	3		Aston Villa v LIVERPOOL	(2-4)
1998-99	28-Dec-98	Armstrong, Chris	3		TOTTENHAM H. v Everton	(4-1)
1998-99	9-Jan-99	Huckerby, Darren	3		COVENTRY C. v Nottingham F.	(4-0)
1998-99	16-Jan-99	Yorke, Dwight	3		Leicester C. v MANCHESTER U.	(2-6)
1998-99	16-Jan-99	Fowler, Robbie	3		LIVERPOOL v Southampton	(7-1)
1998-99	6-Feb-99	Solskjaer, Ole Gunnar	4		Nottingham F. v MANCHESTER U.	(1-8)

HAT-TRICKS AS THEY HAPPENED

Season	Date	Player	Gls	Pens	Match	Score
1998-99	20-Feb-99	Anelka, Nicolas	3		ARSENAL v Leicester C.	(5-0)
1998-99	8-May-99	Campbell, Kevin	3		EVERTON v West Ham U.	(6-0)
1999-00	11-Aug-99	Bridges, Michael	3		Southampton v LEEDS U.	(0-3)
1999-00	30-Aug-99	Cole, Andy	4		MANCHESTER U. v Newcastle U.	(5-1)
1999-00	18-Sep-99	Phillips , Kevin	3		Derby Co. v SUNDERLAND	(0-5)
1999-00	18-Sep-99	Shearer, Alan	5		NEWCASTLE U. v Sheffield W.	(8-0)
1999-00	23-Oct-99	Kanu,	3		Chelsea v ARSENAL	(2-3)
1999-00	20-Nov-99	Overmars, Marc	3		ARSENAL v Middlesbrough	(5-1)
1999-00	4-Dec-99	Solskjaer, Ole Gunnar	4		MANCHESTER U. v Everton	(5-1)
1999-00	26-Feb-00	Barmby, Nick	3		West Ham U. v EVERTON	(0-4)
1999-00	5-Mar-00	Collymore, Stan	3		LEICESTER C. v Sunderland	(5-2)
1999-00	11-Mar-00	Yorke, Dwight	3		MANCHESTER U. v Derby Co.	(3-1)
1999-00	11-Mar-00	Iversen, Steffen	3		TOTTENHAM H. v Southampton	(7-2)
1999-00	1-Apr-00	Scholes, Paul	3	1	MANCHESTER U. v West Ham U.	(7-1)
1999-00	21-Apr-00	Windass, Dean	3		BRADFORD C. v Derby Co.	(4-4)

PLAYERS – MOST HAT-TRICKS

No	Player	Club(s)
11	Shearer, Alan	Blackburn R. (9) and Newcastle U. (2)
7	Fowler, Robbie	Liverpool
5	Cole, Andy	Newcastle U. (2) and Manchester U. (3)
5	Wright, Ian	Arsenal
4	Campbell, Kevin	Arsenal (2) and Nottingham F. (2)
4	Le Tissier, Matt	Southampton
4	Sutton, Chris	Norwich C. (1) and Blackburn R. (3)
3	Cottee, Tony	Everton (2) and West Ham U. (1)
3	Dublin, Dion	Coventry C. (2) and Aston Villa (1)
3	Ferdinand, Les	QPR (2) and Newcastle U. (1)
3	Owen, Michael	Liverpool
3	Yorke, Dwight	Aston Villa (1) and Manchester U. (2)
2	Gallacher, Kevin	Blackburn R.
2	Huckerby, Darren	Coventry C.
2	Iversen, Steffen	Tottenham H.
2	Kanchelskis, Andre	Manchester U. and Everton
2	Ravanelli, Fabrizio	Middlesbrough
2	Sheringham, Teddy	Totttenham H.
2	Solskjaer, Ole Gunnar	Manchester U.
2	Yeboah, Tony	Leeds U.
1	Allen, Bradley	QPR
1	Anelka, Nicolas	Arsenal
1	Armstrong, Chris	Tottenham H.
1	Barmby, Nick	Everton
1	Bart-Williams, Chris	Sheffield W.
1	Beardsley, Peter	Newcastle U.
1	Berger, Patrik	Liverpool
1	Bergkamp, Dennis	Arsenal
1	Booth, Andy	Sheffield W.
1	Bridges, Michael	Leeds U.
1	Cantona, Eric	Leeds U.
1	Collymore, Stan	Leicester C.
1	Deane, Brian	Sheffield U.
1	Ekoku, Efan	Norwich C.
1	Ferguson, Duncan	Everton
1	Fjortoft, Jan Aage	Swindon T.
1	Flo, Tore Andre	Chelsea
1	Hendrie, John	Middlesbrough
1	Holdsworth, Dean	Wimbledon
1	Hughes, Mark	Chelsea
1	Johnson, Tommy	Aston Villa
1	Kanu	Arsenal
1	Kitson, Paul	West Ham U.
1	Klinsmann, Jurgen	Tottenham
1	Marshall, Ian	Leicester C.
1	McAllister, Gary	Leeds U.
1	Mendonca, Clive	Charlton A.
1	Milosevic, Savo	Aston Villa
1	Ndlovu, Peter	Coventry C.
1	Overmars, Marc	Arsenal
1	Peacock, Gavin	Chelsea
1	Phillips , Kevin	Sunderland
1	Quinn, Mick	Coventry C.
1	Robins, Mark	Norwich C.

1	Saunders, Dean	Aston Villa
1	Scholes, Paul	Manchester U.
1	Sinton, Andy	QPR
1	Speed, Gary	Everton
1	Strachan, Gordon	Leeds U.
1	Vialli, Gianluca	Chelsea
1	Wallace, Rod	Leeds U.
1	Walters, Mark	Liverpool
1	Windass, Dean	Bradford C.
1	Zola, Gianfranco	Chelsea

PLAYERS WITH MOST YELLOW CARDS

Fullname	Y	R	Tot	St	Sb
HUGHES,Mark	70	2	267	257	10
PALMER,Carlton	53	4	246	242	4
WRIGHT,Ian	53	2	213	202	11
KEANE,Roy	52	4	225	217	8
WISE,Dennis	51	3	225	217	8
LE TISSIER,Matthew	50	1	258	232	26
BATTY,David	48	4	202	198	4
MONCUR,John	47	2	174	159	15
SUTTON,Chris	47	2	237	219	18
SHERWOOD,Tim	46	4	276	267	9
MONKOU,Ken	44	1	198	190	8
BURROWS,David	43	1	194	187	7
SINCLAIR,Frank	41	5	222	215	7
TOWNSEND,Andy	41	3	213	210	3
INCE,Paul	40	0	213	213	0
JONES,Vinny	40	6	184	178	6
RUDDOCK,Neil	40	2	196	188	8
EDINBURGH,Justin	39	2	174	154	20
WINTERBURN,Nigel	39	1	270	260	10
KEOWN,Martin	38	5	239	221	18
SPEED,Gary	38	0	287	282	5
ATHERTON,Peter	37	1	292	291	1
BENALI,Francis	37	5	235	216	19
BOULD,Steve	37	2	195	183	12
UNSWORTH,David	37	3	213	204	9
VIEIRA,Patrick	36	3	128	124	4
WETHERALL,David	36	0	239	226	13
EHIOGU,Ugo	34	1	227	218	9
DEANE,Brian	33	0	234	225	9
WILLIAMS,Paul D	33	3	134	122	12
HARTSON,John	32	5	143	129	14
HUTCHISON,Don	32	4	152	131	21
LE SAUX,Graeme	32	1	209	200	9
TELFER,Paul	32	0	160	151	9

Fullname	Y	R	Tot	St	Sb
WHELAN,Noel	32	0	182	155	27
COOPER,Colin	31	0	166	165	1
DOWIE,Iain	31	0	175	163	12
FERDINAND,Les	31	2	232	222	10
FLITCROFT,Garry	31	1	187	175	12
HENDRY,Colin	31	0	213	212	1
LEBOEUF,Franck	31	4	119	119	0
PEACOCK,Darren	31	0	231	223	8
STIMAC,Igor	31	1	81	81	0
TAYLOR,Ian	31	0	189	170	19
ADAMS,Tony	30	4	219	216	3
BARTON,Warren	30	1	231	210	21
BOWYER,Lee	30	0	125	119	6
PARLOUR,Ray	30	0	229	197	32
PERRY,Chris	30	0	202	193	9

PLAYERS WHO HAVE RECEIVED THE MOST RED
CARDS IN THE PREMIERSHIP

Fullname	R	Y	Tot	St	Sb
JONES,Vinny	6	40	184	178	6
BENALI,Francis	5	37	235	216	19
HARTSON,John	5	32	143	129	14
KEOWN,Martin	5	38	239	221	18
SINCLAIR,Frank	5	41	222	215	7
WILCOX,Jason	5	21	212	192	20
ADAMS,Tony	4	30	219	216	3
BATTY,David	4	48	202	198	4
BUTT,Nicky	4	29	178	140	38
FERGUSON,Duncan	4	21	146	134	12
HUTCHISON,Don	4	32	152	131	21
KEANE,Roy	4	52	225	217	8
LEBOEUF,Franck	4	31	119	119	0
LOMAS,Steve	4	28	171	162	9
PALMER,Carlton	4	53	246	242	4
SHERWOOD,Tim	4	46	276	267	9
SRNICEK,Pavel	4	2	141	140	1
BILIC,Slaven	3	16	76	74	2
CALDERWOOD,Colin	3	26	189	175	14
CANTONA,Eric	3	18	156	154	2
CHETTLE,Steve	3	18	174	171	3
DABIZAS,Nikos	3	15	70	64	6
DUNNE,Richard	3	13	56	50	6
FLOWERS,Tim	3	9	260	258	2
PETIT,Manu	3	15	85	82	3
TOWNSEND,Andy	3	41	213	210	3

Fullname	R	Y	Tot	St	Sb
UNSWORTH,David	3	37	213	204	9
VIEIRA,Patrick	3	36	128	124	4
WILLIAMS,Paul D	3	33	134	122	12
WISE,Dennis	3	51	225	217	8

REFEREES GAMES

Referee	Games	HW	D	AW	HF	HA
A.Buksh	12	4	4	4	15	17
A.D'Urso	20	14	3	3	37	13
A.Gunn	36	10	11	15	41	46
A.Wiley	21	9	6	6	32	24
A.Wilkie	145	69	42	34	225	165
A.Wilkie	147	70	43	34	227	167
B.Hill	42	21	12	9	76	49
B.Knight	12	8	1	3	21	12
C.Dunn	1	0	1	0	1	1
D.Allison	34	17	6	11	51	35
D.Crick	1	0	1	0	1	1
D.Elleray	142	65	35	42	219	177
D.Frampton	10	3	2	5	12	15
D.Gallagher	136	60	32	44	190	166
G.Ashby	111	55	23	33	194	128
G.Barber	88	34	31	23	114	107
G.Hegley	1	0	0	1	0	1
G.Poll	142	62	43	37	217	165
G.Powler	1	0	0	1	1	2
G.Willard	99	50	29	20	152	92
H.King	13	6	5	2	20	13
I.Mitchell	1	1	0	0	2	0
J.Borrett	24	8	9	7	33	30
J.Key	5	4	1	0	11	5
J.Lloyd	13	5	3	5	23	19
J.Martin	11	5	4	2	17	9
J.Winter	102	48	30	24	171	96
J.Worrall	60	36	14	10	113	41
K.Barratt	30	10	8	12	42	45
K.Burge	122	64	23	35	185	130
K.Cooper	71	33	23	15	121	71
K.Hackett	37	14	12	11	42	36
K.Morton	61	25	22	14	106	76
K.Redfern	13	6	2	5	22	20
L.Dilkes	2	0	1	1	0	1
M.Bodenham	119	39	37	43	134	144
M.Halsey	13	4	5	4	19	18
M.Peck	12	7	1	4	19	13

Referee	Games	HW	D	AW	HF	HA
M.Peck	1	1	0	0	2	1
M.Reed	165	82	43	40	268	169
M.Riley	76	37	24	15	132	81
N.Barry	60	35	17	8	121	62
P.Alcock	96	52	24	20	159	102
P.Crabtree	1	0	0	1	0	3
P.Danson	57	19	25	13	67	54
P.Don	59	27	17	15	87	76
P.Durkin	155	74	42	39	253	172
P.Foakes	21	7	9	5	30	29
P.Jones	118	56	31	31	175	126
P.Sampson	1	1	0	0	2	1
P.Wright	4	1	1	2	5	6
R.Bigger	4	1	2	1	4	5
R.Dilkes	73	32	25	16	107	70
R.Gifford	43	14	16	13	46	45
R.Groves	11	7	4	0	24	11
R.Hamer	2	0	2	0	3	3
R.Harris	39	21	6	12	60	54
R.Hart	78	36	20	22	117	85
R.Lewis	16	6	4	6	21	15
R.Milford	34	15	11	8	48	33
R.Nixon	4	2	2	0	9	5
S.Bennett	12	6	2	4	14	13
S.Dunn	98	43	25	30	149	105
S.Lodge	157	71	49	37	222	151
T.Holbrook	33	16	9	8	46	25
T.Ward	8	4	1	3	12	9
U.Rennie	60	23	19	18	82	67
V.Callow	34	14	11	9	52	42

HW+Home Wins, D=Draws, AW=Away Wins, HF=Home For, HA=Home Against.

Injuries: When referees are injured and replaced during a game the stats for the game are allocated to the starting, ie, injured, referee.
A.Wilkie was injured in two games and was replaced in one by M.Smims and another by M.Tomlin. H.King was injured in one game and replaced by P.Rejer. I.Mitchell and M.Peck were injured in their only Premiership games and were replaced by G.Pearson. and J.Hilditch respectively. P.Durkin has been injured twice and replaced by D.Elleray and J.Petit.

THE GOALKEEPERS

GOALKEEPER RECORDS BY SURNAME

Goalkeeper	St	Sb	GKGA	TCS	AGR
ANDREWS, Ian	5	0	6	2	1.20
BAARDSEN, Espen	22	1	28	8	1.22
BAKER, Clive	47	1	71	13	1.48
BARTRAM, Vince	11	0	18	2	1.64
BEASANT, Dave	129	2	202	25	1.54
BEENEY, Mark	35	0	40	13	1.14
BERESFORD, Marlon	5	0	11	0	2.20
BOOTH *, Andy	1	0	1	0	1.00
BOSNICH, Mark	201	0	200	73	1.00
BRANAGAN, Keith	65	0	109	14	1.68
BROWN, Steve	0	1	0	1	0.00
BURRIDGE, John	3	1	5	0	1.25
BYWATER, Steve	3	1	7	1	1.75
CHAMBERLAIN, Alec	27	0	61	3	2.26
CLARKE, Matt	23	2	43	6	1.72
COLGAN, Nick	1	0	3	0	3.00
COLLETT, Andy	2	0	5	0	2.50
COTON, Tony	103	1	118	27	1.13
CROSSLEY, Mark	162	0	219	39	1.35
CUDICINI, Carle	1	0	0	1	0.00
CULKIN, Nick	0	1	0	0	0.00
CUTLER, Neil	0	1	0	0	0.00
DAVISON, Aiden	7	1	17	0	2.13
DAY, Chris	13	0	22	3	1.69
DE GOEY, Ed	104	0	93	42	0.89
DEARDEN, Kevin	0	1	0	1	0.00
DIBBLE, Andy	26	2	38	10	1.36
DIGBY, Frank	28	0	64	3	2.29
DYKSTRA, Sieb	11	0	19	3	1.73
ENCKELMAN, Peter	9	1	9	4	0.90
FETTIS, Alan	12	1	26	3	2.00
FEUER, Ian	3	0	2	1	0.67
FILAN, John	46	1	65	12	1.38
FINN, Neil	1	0	2	0	2.00
FLOWERS, Tim	258	2	298	74	1.15
FORREST, Craig	99	4	161	25	1.56
FRIEDEL, Brad	25	0	31	6	1.24
GERRARD, Paul	82	2	127	17	1.51
GIVEN, Shay	71	0	92	21	1.30
GOULD, Jon	25	0	36	8	1.44
GROBBELAAR, Bruce	66	0	98	18	1.48
GRODAS, Frode	20	1	30	4	1.43
GUNN, Bryan	104	0	158	23	1.52
HALLWORTH, Jon	35	0	61	2	1.74
HAMMOND, Micky	11	2	23	1	1.77
HARPER, Steve	26	1	31	8	1.15
HEALD, Paul	22	1	36	3	1.57
HEDMAN, Magnus	85	0	107	22	1.26
HISLOP, Shaka	112	0	127	32	1.13
HITCHCOCK, Kevin	57	4	72	11	1.18
HOOPER, Mike	31	3	36	9	1.06
HORNE, Brian	3	1	4	2	1.00
HOULT, Russell	66	1	96	14	1.43
HOWELLS, David	0	1	3	0	3.00
HOWIE, Scott	1	1	3	1	1.50
ILIC, Sasa	24	0	37	6	1.54
IMMEL, Eike	38	0	58	3	1.53
IRONSIDE, Ian	11	1	19	2	1.58
JAMES, David	242	1	243	85	1.00
JONES, Paul	100	0	157	23	1.57
KARELSE, John	3	0	7	1	2.33
KEARTON, Jason	3	3	10	1	1.67
KEELEY, John	1	0	1	0	1.00
KELLER, Kasey	67	0	84	23	1.25
KELLY, Alan	61	2	83	19	1.32
KEY, Lance	2	0	3	1	1.50
KHARINE, Dmitri	114	0	147	38	1.29
LAMA, Bernard	12	0	21	3	1.75
LEESE, Lars	9	1	24	1	2.40
LUKIC, John	144	0	169	49	1.17
MANNINGER, Alex	27	1	22	15	0.79
MARGETSON, Martyn	1	1	3	0	1.50
MARRIOTT, Andy	6	0	8	0	1.33
MARSHALL, Andy	20	1	17	7	0.81
MARTYN, Nigel	225	0	255	82	1.13
MAUNTONE, Steve	1	0	0	1	0.00
MIKLOSKO, Ludek	170	0	222	47	1.31
MILLER,A., Alan	22	2	34	5	1.42
MILLER,K., Kevin	38	0	71	6	1.87
MIMMS, Bobby	59	2	66	24	1.08
MORGAN, Phillip	1	0	2	0	2.00
MOSS, Neil	17	2	24	6	1.26
MYHRE, Thomas	64	0	78	23	1.22
NICOL *,	0	1	2	0	2.00
OAKES, Michael	49	2	65	15	1.27
OGRIZOVIC, Steve	191	0	257	46	1.35
PEARS, Stephen	26	0	47	4	1.81
PEREZ, Lionel	28	1	45	7	1.55
PETTERSON, Andy	8	3	19	2	1.73

Goalkeeper	St	Sb	GKGA	TCS	AGR
PEYTON, Gerry	1	0	1	0	1.00
PILKINGTON, Kevin	4	1	8	1	1.60
POOLE, Kevin	43	0	80	4	1.86
POOM, Mart	83	2	110	30	1.29
PRESSMAN, Kevin	205	2	308	50	1.49
RACHEL, Adam	0	1	1	0	1.00
ROBERTS,B., Ben	9	1	12	0	1.20
ROBERTS,T., Tony	80	0	111	15	1.39
ROYCE, Simon	8	0	5	5	0.63
SCHMEICHAEL, Peter	254	0	222	115	0.87
SCHWARZER, Mark	78	0	102	24	1.31
SEALEY, Les	2	2	5	0	1.25
SEAMAN, David	256	0	209	109	0.82
SEGERS, Hans	117	2	155	31	1.30
SHEFFIELD, Jon	2	0	7	0	3.50
SIMONSEN, Steve	0	1	2	0	2.00
SOMMER, Jurgen	33	0	49	4	1.48
SORENSEN, Thomas	37	0	55	9	1.49
SOUTHALL, Neville	208	0	275	63	1.32
SPINK, Nigel	51	4	64	15	1.16
SRNICEK, Pavel	140	1	153	44	1.09
STEJSKAL, Jan	40	1	53	11	1.29
SULLIVAN, Neil	178	1	275	46	1.54
TAIBI, Massimo	4	0	11	0	2.75
TAYLOR,M., Maik	18	0	19	7	1.06
TAYLOR,MJ., Martin	3	0	3	1	1.00
THORSTVEDT, Erik	58	2	76	17	1.27
TRACEY, Simon	28	2	45	8	1.50
VAN DER GOUW, Raimond	19	5	17	7	0.71
WALKER, Ian	235	1	322	60	1.36
WALSH, Gary	73	1	102	19	1.38
WARD, Gavin	15	2	32	0	1.88
WATSON, David	30	0	58	4	1.93
WESTERVELD, Sander	36	0	29	14	0.81
WILMOTT, Chris	5	1	8	1	1.33
WOODS, Chris	69	1	89	17	1.27
WRIGHT,R., Richard	3	0	5	1	1.67
WRIGHT,T., Tommy	6	1	14	1	2.00

Key:
St=Starting appearances; Sb=Substitute appearances
GKGA=Goalkeeper Goals Against
TCS=Total number of Clean Sheets
ACG=Average Goals Conceded per Game
*=Outfield player in goal

KEEPERS BY BEST AGR (MIN. 30 GAMES)

Goalkeeper	St	Sb	GKGA	TCS	AGR
WESTERVELD, Sander	36	0	29	14	0.81
SEAMAN, David	256	0	209	109	0.82
SCHMICHAEL, Peter	254	0	222	115	0.87
DE GOEY, Ed	104	0	93	42	0.89
BOSNICH, Mark	201	0	200	73	1.00
JAMES, David	242	1	243	85	1.00
HOOPER, Mike	31	3	36	9	1.06
MIMMS, Bobby	59	2	66	24	1.08
SRNICEK, Pavel	140	1	153	44	1.09
MARTYN, Nigel	225	0	255	82	1.13
HISLOP, Shaka	112	0	127	32	1.13
COTON, Tony	103	1	118	27	1.13
BEENEY, Mark	35	0	40	13	1.14
FLOWERS, Tim	258	2	298	74	1.15
SPINK, Nigel	51	4	64	15	1.16
LUKIC, John	144	0	169	49	1.17
HITCHCOCK, Kevin	57	4	72	11	1.18
MYHRE, Thomas	64	0	78	23	1.22
KELLER, Kasey	67	0	84	23	1.25
HEDMAN, Magnus	85	0	107	22	1.26
THORSTVEDT, Erik	58	2	76	17	1.27
WOODS, Chris	69	1	89	17	1.27
OAKES, Michael	49	2	65	15	1.27
KHARINE, Dmitri	114	0	147	38	1.29
STEJSKAL, Jan	40	1	53	11	1.29
POOM, Mart	83	2	110	30	1.29
GIVEN, Shay	71	0	92	21	1.30
SEGERS, Hans	117	2	155	31	1.30
MIKLOSKO, Ludek	170	0	222	47	1.31
SCHWARZER, Mark	78	0	102	24	1.31
KELLY, Alan	61	2	83	19	1.32
SOUTHALL, Neville	208	0	275	63	1.32
OGRIZOVIC, Steve	191	0	257	46	1.35
CROSSLEY, Mark	162	0	219	39	1.35
WALKER, Ian	235	1	322	60	1.36
WALSH, Gary	73	1	102	19	1.38
FILAN, John	46	1	65	12	1.38
ROBERTS,T., Tony	80	0	111	15	1.39
HOULT, Russell	66	1	96	14	1.43
BAKER, Clive	47	1	71	13	1.48
GROBBELAAR, Bruce	66	0	98	18	1.48
SOMMER, Jurgen	33	0	49	4	1.48
SORENSEN, Thomas	37	0	55	9	1.49
PRESSMAN, Kevin	205	2	308	50	1.49

THE GOALKEEPERS

Goalkeeper	St	Sb	GKGA	TCS	AGR
GERRARD, Paul	82	2	127	17	1.51
GUNN, Bryan	104	0	158	23	1.52
IMMEL, Eike	38	0	58	8	1.53
SULLIVAN, Neil	178	1	275	46	1.54
BEASANT, Dave	129	2	202	25	1.54
FORREST, Craig	99	4	161	25	1.56
JONES, Paul	100	0	157	23	1.57
BRANAGAN, Keith	65	0	109	14	1.68
HALLWORTH, Jon	35	0	61	2	1.74
POOLE, Kevin	43	0	80	4	1.86
MILLER,K., Kevin	38	0	71	6	1.87
WATSON, David	30	0	58	4	1.93

Goalkeeper	St	Sb	GKGA	TCS	AGR
HEDMAN, Magnus	85	0	107	22	1.26
GIVEN, Shay	71	0	92	21	1.30
KELLY, Alan	61	2	83	19	1.32
WALSH, Gary	73	1	102	19	1.38
GROBBELAAR, Bruce	66	0	98	18	1.48
THORSTVEDT, Erik	58	2	76	17	1.27
WOODS, Chris	69	1	89	17	1.27
GERRARD, Paul	82	2	127	17	1.51
MANNINGER, Alex	27	1	22	15	0.79
SPINK, Nigel	51	4	64	15	1.16
OAKES, Michael	49	2	65	15	1.27
ROBERTS,T., Tony	80	0	111	15	1.39
WESTERVELD, Sander	36	0	29	14	0.81
HOULT, Russell	66	1	96	14	1.43
BRANAGAN, Keith	65	0	109	14	1.68
BEENEY, Mark	35	0	40	13	1.14
BAKER, Clive	47	1	71	13	1.48
FILAN, John	46	1	65	12	1.38
HITCHCOCK, Kevin	57	4	72	11	1.18
STEJSKAL, Jan	40	1	53	11	1.29
DIBBLE, Andy	26	2	38	10	1.36

KEEPERS BY MOST CLEAN SHEETS

Goalkeeper	St	Sb	GKGA	TCS	AGR
SCHMEICHEL, Peter	254	0	222	115	0.87
SEAMAN, David	256	0	209	109	0.82
JAMES, David	242	1	243	85	1.00
MARTYN, Nigel	225	0	255	82	1.13
FLOWERS, Tim	258	2	298	74	1.15
BOSNICH, Mark	201	0	200	73	1.00
SOUTHALL, Neville	208	0	275	63	1.32
WALKER, Ian	235	1	322	60	1.36
PRESSMAN, Kevin	205	2	308	50	1.49
LUKIC, John	144	0	169	49	1.17
MIKLOSKO, Ludek	170	0	222	47	1.31
OGRIZOVIC, Steve	191	0	257	46	1.35
SULLIVAN, Neil	178	1	275	46	1.54
SRNICEK, Pavel	140	1	153	44	1.09
DE GOEY, Ed	104	0	93	42	0.89
CROSSLEY, Mark	162	0	219	39	1.35
KHARINE, Dmitri	114	0	147	38	1.29
HISLOP, Shaka	112	0	127	32	1.13
SEGERS, Hans	117	2	155	31	1.30
POOM, Mart	83	2	110	30	1.29
COTON, Tony	103	1	118	27	1.13
BEASANT, Dave	129	2	202	25	1.54
FORREST, Craig	99	4	161	25	1.56
MIMMS, Bobby	59	2	66	24	1.08
SCHWARZER, Mark	78	0	102	24	1.31
MYHRE, Thomas	64	0	78	23	1.22
KELLER, Kasey	67	0	84	23	1.25
GUNN, Bryan	104	0	158	23	1.52
JONES, Paul	100	0	157	23	1.57

MANAGERS RECORDS BY THEIR CLUBS

ARSENAL

Manager	T	Start	End	P	W	D	L	F	A	Pts	PPG
GRAHAM, George	F	14-May-86	21-Feb-95	112	0	0	0	0	0	161	1.44
HOUSTON, Stuart	C	21-Feb-95	8-Jun-95	14	0	0	0	0	0	17	1.21
RIOCH, Bruce	F	8-Jun-95	12-Aug-96	38	0	0	0	0	0	63	1.66
HOUSTON, Stuart	C	12-Aug-96	13-Sep-96	5	2	2	1	9	7	8	1.60
RICE, Pat	C	13-Sep-96	30-Sep-96	3	3	0	0	8	1	9	3.00
WENGER, Arsene	F	1-Oct-96		144	81	37	26	245	117	280	1.94

ASTON VILLA

Manager	T	Start	End	P	W	D	L	F	A	Pts	PPG
ATKINSON, Ron	F	1-Jun-91	10-Nov-94	98	0	0	0	0	0	141	1.44
BARRON, Jim	C	10-Nov-94	25-Nov-94	1	0	0	0	0	0	3	3.00
LITTLE, Brian	F	25-Nov-94	25-Feb-98	130	51	36	43	159	136	189	1.45
GREGORY, John	F	25-Feb-98		87	39	23	25	108	91	140	1.61

BARNSLEY

Manager	T	Start	End	P	W	D	L	F	A	Pts	PPG
WILSON, Danny	F			38	10	5	23	37	82	35	0.92

BLACKBURN ROVERS

Manager	T	Start	End	P	W	D	L	F	A	Pts	PPG
DALGLISH, Kenny	F	1-Oct-91	1-May-95	126	0	0	0	0	0	244	1.94
HARFORD, Ray	F	1-May-95	25-Oct-96	58	0	19	21	79	89	69	1.19
PARKES, Tony	C	26-Oct-96	11-May-97	28	9	11	8	36	29	38	1.36
HODGSON, Ray	F	1-Jun-97	21-Nov-98	52	18	13	21	70	64	67	1.29
PARKES, Tony	C	29-Nov-98		2	1	0	1	1	2	3	1.50
KIDD, Brian	F	12-Dec-98		22	4	11	7	24	28	23	1.05

BOLTON WANDERERS

Manager	T	Start	End	P	W	D	L	F	A	Pts	PPG
McFARLAND, Roy	F	1-Jun-95	1-Jan-96	22	0	0	0	0	0	10	0.45
TODD, Colin	F	2-Jan-96		54	15	14	25	59	88	59	1.09

BRADFORD CITY

Manager	T	Start	End	P	W	D	L	F	A	Pts	PPG
JEWELL, Paul	F	6-Jan-98		38	9	9	20	38	68	36	0.95

CHARLTON ATHLETIC

Manager	T	Start	End	P	W	D	L	F	A	Pts	PPG
CURBISHLEY, Alan				38	8	12	18	41	56	36	0.95

CHELSEA

Manager	T	Start	End	P	W	D	L	F	A	Pts	PPG
PORTERFIELD, Ian	F	11-Jun-91	15-Feb-93	29	0	0	0	0	0	37	1.28
WEBB, David	F	15-Feb-93	11-May-93	13	0	0	0	0	0	19	1.46
HODDLE, Glenn	F	4-Jun-93	31-May-96	122	0	0	0	0	0	155	1.27
GULLITT, Ruud	PM	1-Jun-96	12-Feb-98	64	30	14	19	110	82	104	1.63
VIALLI, Gianluca	PM/F	12-Feb-98		89	44	26	19	129	80	158	1.78

COVENTRY CITY

Manager	T	Start	End	P	W	D	L	F	A	Pts	PPG
GOULD, Bobby	F	24-Jun-92	23-Oct-93	54	0	0	0	0	0	67	1.24
NEAL, Phil	F	23-Oct-93	14-Feb-95	58	0	0	0	0	0	72	1.24
ATKINSON, Ron	F	15-Feb-95	21-Oct-96	62	17	17	28	56	81	68	1.10
STRACHAN, Gordon	F	22-Oct-96		142	43	44	55	166	189	173	1.22

CRYSTAL PALACE

Manager	T	Start	End	P	W	D	L	F	A	Pts	PPG
COPPELL, Steve	F	7-Jun-90	20-May-93	42	0	0	0	0	0	49	1.17
SMITH, Alan	F	3-Jun-93	15-May-95	42	0	0	0	0	0	45	1.07
COPPLE, Steve	F		13-Mar-98	27	5	8	14	21	41	24	0.89
LOMBARDO, Atillio	PM	14-Mar-98	23-Apr-98	7	2	0	5	10	19	6	0.86
LEWINGTON, Ray	C	23-Apr-98		4	1	1	2	6	11	4	1.00

DERBY COUNTY

Manager	T	Start	End	P	W	D	L	F	A	Pts	PPG
SMITH, Jim	F	15-Jun-95		152	49	44	59	181	209	191	1.26

EVERTON

Manager	T	Start	End	P	W	D	L	F	A	Pts	PPG
KENDALL, Howard	F	1-Nov-90	4-Dec-93	60	0	0	0	0	0	77	1.28
HARVEY, Colin	C	4-Dec-93	6-Jan-94	7	0	0	0	0	0	1	0.14
WALKER, Mike	F	7-Jan-94	8-Nov-94	31	0	0	0	0	0	27	0.87
ROYLE, Joe	F	10-Nov-94	23-Mar-97	97	36	31	30	136	116	139	1.43
WATSON, Dave	C	5-Apr-97	31-May-97	7	1	3	3	7	12	6	0.86
KENDALL, Howard	F	27-Jun-97	1-Jul-98	38	9	13	16	41	56	40	1.05
SMITH, Walter	F	1-Jul-98		76	23	24	29	101	96	93	1.22

IPSWICH TOWN

Manager	T	Start	End	P	W	D	L	F	A	Pts	PPG
LYALL, John	F	11-May-90	5-Dec-94	101	0	0	0	0	0	106	1.05
GODDARD, Paul	C	5-Dec-94	28-Dec-94	3	0	0	0	0	0	2	0.67
BURLEY, George	F	28-Dec-94		22	0	0	0	0	0	14	0.64

LEEDS UNITED

Manager	T	Start	End	P	W	D	L	F	A	Pts	PPG
WILKINSON, Howard	F	10-Oct-88	8-Sep-96	174	66	53	55	231	214	250	1.44

THE MANAGERS

	T	Start	End	P	W	D	L	F	A	Pts	PPG
GRAHAM, George	F	10-Sep-96	28-Sep-98	78	28	25	25	88	79	109	1.40
OLEARY, David	F	28-Sep-98		69	37	14	18	112	73	125	1.81

LEICESTER CITY

Manager	T	Start	End	P	W	D	L	F	A	Pts	PPG
LITTLE, Brian	F	1-May-91	22-Nov-94	14	0	0	0	0	0	9	0.64
EVANS, Allan	C	22-Nov-94	13-Dec-94	4	0	0	0	0	0	4	1.00
McGHEE, Mark	F	14-Dec-94	1-Dec-95	24	0	0	0	0	0	16	0.67
O'NEILL, Martin	F	21-Dec-95		152	53	45	54	192	206	204	1.34

LIVERPOOL

Manager	T	Start	End	P	W	D	L	F	A	Pts	PPG
SOUNESS, Graeme	F	14-Jun-90	28-Jan-94	68	0	0	0	0	0	102	1.50
EVANS, Roy	F	28-Jan-94	12-Nov-98	172	83	46	43	280	173	295	1.72
EVANS/HOULLIER	JM	1-Jul-98	12-Nov-98	12	4	4	4	19	14	16	1.33
HOULLIER, Gerard	F	12-Nov-98		64	30	15	19	100	65	105	1.64

MANCHESTER CITY

Manager	T	Start	End	P	W	D	L	F	A	Pts	PPG
REID, Peter	F	13-Jun-90	26-Aug-93	46	0	0	0	0	0	58	1.26
HORTON, Brian	F	27-Aug-93	16-May-95	80	0	0	0	0	0	93	1.16
BALL, Alan	F	1-Jul-95		38	0	0	0	0	0	38	1.00

MANCHESTER UNITED

Manager	T	Start	End	P	W	D	L	F	A	Pts	PPG
FERGUSON, Alex	F	6-Nov-86		316	196	80	40	623	284	668	2.11

MIDDLESBROUGH

Manager	T	Start	End	P	W	D	L	F	A	Pts	PPG
LAWRENCE, Lennie	F	10-Jul-91	2-May-94	42	0	0	0	0	0	44	1.05
ROBSON, Bryan	F	1-May-94		152	47	47	58	180	216	185	1.22

NEWCASTLE UNITED

Manager	T	Start	End	P	W	D	L	F	A	Pts	PPG
KEEGAN, Kevin	F	5-Feb-92	8-Jan-97	143	78	30	35	253	147	264	1.85
McDERMOTT, Terry	C	11-Jan-97	13-Jan-97	1	0	1	0	2	2	1	1.00
DALGLISH, Kenny	F	14-Jan-97	23-Aug-98	56	19	19	18	69	61	76	1.36
GUILLIT, Rudd	F	24-Mar-98	28-Aug-99	41	11	12	18	54	66	45	1.10
CLARKE, Steve	C	28-Aug-99	2-Sep-99	1	0	0	1	1	5	0	
ROBSON, Bobby	F	2-Sep-99		32	14	9	9	55	36	51	1.59

NORWICH CITY

Manager	T	Start	End	P	W	D	L	F	A	Pts	PPG
WALKER, Mike	F	1-Jun-92	7-Jan-94	65	31	0	0	0	0	109	1.68
DEEHAN, John	F	7-Jan-94	18-Jun-09	61	0	0	0	0	0	59	0.97

NOTTINGHAM FOREST

Manager	T	Start	End	P	W	D	L	F	A	Pts	PPG
CLOUGH, Brian	F	6-Jan-75	1-May-93	42	0	0	0	0	0	40	0.95
CLARK, Frank	F	12-May-93	19-Dec-96	97	38	31	28	136	126	145	1.49
PEARCE, Stuart	PM	20-Dec-96		21	5	9	7	17	30	24	1.14
BASSETT, Dave	F	1-May-98	5-Jan-99	20	2	7	11	18	36	13	0.65
ADAMS, Micky	C	5-Jan-99	12-Jan-99	1	0	0	1	0	4	0	0.00
ATKINSON, Ron	F	12-Jan-99	1-Jun-99	17	5	2	10	17	29	17	1.00

OLDHAM ATHLETIC

Manager	T	Start	End	P	W	D	L	F	A	Pts	PPG
ROYLE, Joe	F	14-Jul-82	10-Nov-94	84	0	0	0	0	0	89	1.06

QPR

Manager	T	Start	End	P	W	D	L	F	A	Pts	PPG
FRANCIS, Gerry	F	1-Jun-91	11-Nov-94	56	0	0	0	0	0	86	1.54
WILKINS, Ray	F	15-Nov-94		108	0	0	0	0	0	130	1.20

SHEFFIELD UNITED

Manager	T	Start	End	P	W	D	L	F	A	Pts	PPG
BASSETT, Dave	F	21-Jan-88	12-Dec-95	84	0	0	0	0	0	94	1.12

SHEFFIELD WEDNESDAY

Manager	T	Start	End	P	W	D	L	F	A	Pts	PPG
FRANCIS, Trevor	F	17-Jun-91	20-May-95	126	0	0	0	0	0	174	1.38
PLEAT, David	F	17-Jun-95	3-Nov-97	89	26	28	35	116	147	106	1.19
SHREEVES, Peter	C	3-Nov-97	14-Nov-97	1	1	0	0	5	0	3	3.00
ATKINSON, Ron	F	14-Nov-97	17-May-98	24	9	5	10	29	32	32	1.33
WILSON, Danny	F	6-Jul-98	21-Mar-00	29	5	6	18	27	56	21	0.72
SHREEVES, Peter	C	21-Mar-00		9	3	1	5	11	14	10	1.11

SOUTHAMPTON

Manager	T	Start	End	P	W	D	L	F	A	Pts	PPG
BRANFOOT, Ian	F	1-Jun-91	11-Jan-94	66	0	0	0	0	0	68	1.03
MORTIMORE, John	C	11-Jan-94	20-Jan-94	1	0	0	0	0	0	3	3.00
BALL, Alan	F	20-Jan-94	13-Jul-95	60	0	0	0	0	0	79	1.32
MERRINGTON, Dave	F	14-Jul-95	14-Jun-96	38	0	0	0	0	0	38	1.00
SOUNESS, Graeme	F	3-Jul-96	1-Jun-97	38	10	11	17	50	56	41	1.08
JONES, Dave	F	23-Jun-97	21-Jan-00	98	31	19	48	113	156	112	1.14
HODDLE, Glenn	C	28-Jan-00		16	6	3	7	19	25	21	1.31

SUNDERLAND

Manager	T	Start	End	P	W	D	L	F	A	Pts	PPG
REID, Peter	F	29-Mar-95		76	26	20	30	92	109	98	1.29

SWINDON TOWN

Manager	T	Start	End	P	W	D	L	F	A	Pts	PPG
GORMAN, John	F	4-Jun-93	21-Nov-94	42	0	0	0	0	0	30	0.71

TOTTENHAM HOTSPUR

Manager	T	Start	End	P	W	D	L	F	A	Pts	PPG
LIVERMORE/CLEMENCE, Doug/Ray											
	F	27-May-92	1-Jun-93	42	0	0	0	0	0	59	1.40
ARDILES, Ossie	F	19-Jun-93	30-Oct-94	54	0	0	0	0	0	62	1.15
PERRYMAN, Steve	C	1-Nov-94	14-Nov-94	1	0	0	0	0	0	0	0.00
FRANCIS, Gerry	F	15-Nov-94	19-Nov-97	119	43	36	40	156	151	165	1.39
HOUGHTON, Chris	C	20-Nov-97	24-Nov-97	1	0	0	1	0	1	0	0.00
GROSS, Christian	F	25-Nov-98	1-Sep-98	26	9	7	10	29	31	34	1.31
PLEAT, David	C	2-Sep-98	29-Sep-98	4	1	2	1	6	8	5	1.25
GRAHAM, George	F	30-Sep-98		69	24	20	25	96	85	92	1.33

WATFORD

Manager	T	Start	End	P	W	D	L	F	A	Pts	PPG
TAYLOR, Graham	F	21-Feb-96		38	6	6	26	35	77	24	0.63

WEST HAM UNITED

Manager	T	Start	End	P	W	D	L	F	A	Pts	PPG
BONDS, Billy	F	23-Apr-90	10-Aug-94	42	0	0	0	0	0	52	1.24
REDKNAPP, Harry	F	10-Aug-94		232	84	59	89	280	311	311	1.34

WIMBLEDON

Manager	T	Start	End	P	W	D	L	F	A	Pts	PPG
KINNEAR, Joe	F	19-Jan-92	9-Jun-99	278	92	82	104	338	398	358	1.29
OLSEN, Egil	F	9-Jun-99	28-Apr-00	36	7	11	18	44	70	32	0.89
BURTON, Terry	C	28-Apr-00		2	0	1	1	2	4	1	0.50

Key:

T=Type of Manager – F=Fulltime, PM=Player/Manager, C=Caretaker.

PPG=Points Per Game – number of points scored, on average, for each Premiership game.

THE CLUBS

INTRODUCTION

Formed as Dial Square, a workshop in Woolwich Arsenal with a sundial over the entrance, in October 1886, becoming Royal Arsenal, the 'Royal' possibly from a local public house, later the same year. Turned professional and became Woolwich Arsenal in 1891. Selected for an expanded Football League Division Two in 1893, the first southern team to join. Moved from the Manor Ground, Plumstead, south-east London, to Highbury, north London, in 1913, changing name again at the same time. Elected from fifth in Division Two to the expanded First Division for the 1919-20 season and never relegated. Premier League founder members 1992. In 1997-98 performed the Double for the second time.

Ground: Arsenal Stadium, Avenell Road, Highbury,
            London N5 1BU
Nickname: Gunners
Internet: www.arsenal.co.uk

HONOURS

FA Premier League: Champions 1997-98
                        Runners-up 1998-99, 1999-00
Football League: Div 1: Champions 1930-31, 1932-33,
                        1933-34, 1934-35, 1937-38,
                        1947-48, 1952-53, 1970-71,
                        1988-89, 1990-91; Runners-up
                        1925-26, 1931-32, 1972-73
Football League: Div 2: Runners-up 1903-04
FA Cup: Winners 1929-30, 1935-36,
                        1949-50, 1970-71, 1978-79,
                        1992-93, 1997-98
                        Runners-up 1926-27, 1931-32,
                        1951-52, 1971-72, 1977-78,
                        1979-80
Football League Cup: Winners 1986-87, 1992-93
                        Runners-up 1967-68, 1968-69,
                        1987-88
Cup-Winners' Cup   Winners 1993-94; Runners-up
                        1979-80, 1994-95
Fairs Cup: Winners 1969-70
UEFA Cup: Runners-up 1999-2000
European Super Cup: Runners-up 1994-95

EUROPEAN RECORD

Champions' League (4): 71-72 (QF), 91-92 (2), 98-99 (L),
                        99-00 (L1)
Cup-Winners' Cup (3):   79-80 (F), 93-94 (W), 94-95 (F)
UEFA Cup (9)   63-64 (2), 69-70 (W), 71-70 (Q),
                        78-79 (3), 81-82 (2), 82-83 (1),
                        96-97 (1), 97-98 (1), 99-00 (F)

FAPL RECORD SUMMARY

Most Total:	WINTERBURN, Nigel	270
Most Starts:	WINTERBURN, Nigel	260
Most Subs:	PARLOUR, Ray	32
Most SNU:	MILLER, Alan	71
Most PS:	PARLOUR, Ray	48
Most Goals:	WRIGHT, Ian	104
Most Yel:	WRIGHT, Ian	44
Most Red:	KEOWN, Martin	5

PLAYING RECORD – SEASON TOTALS

Season	Pn	P	W	D	L	F	A	Pts
1992-93	10	42	15	11	16	40	38	56
1993-94	4	42	18	17	7	53	28	71
1994-95	12	42	13	12	17	52	49	51
1995-96	5	38	17	12	9	49	32	63
1996-97	3	38	19	11	8	62	32	68
1997-98	1	38	23	9	6	68	33	78
1998-99	2	38	22	12	4	59	17	78
1999-00	2	38	22	7	9	73	43	73
Totals		316	149	91	76	456	272	538

PLAYING RECORD – HOME TOTALS

Season	Pn	P	W	D	L	F	A	Pts
1992-93	10	21	8	6	7	25	20	30
1993-94	4	21	10	8	3	25	15	38
1994-95	12	21	6	9	6	27	21	27
1995-96	5	19	10	7	2	30	16	37
1996-97	3	19	10	5	4	36	18	35
1997-98	1	19	15	2	2	43	10	47
1998-99	2	19	14	5	0	34	5	47
1999-00	2	19	14	3	2	42	17	45
Totals		158	87	45	26	262	122	306

PLAYING RECORD – AWAY TOTALS

Season	Pn	P	W	D	L	F	A	Pts
1992-93	10	21	7	5	9	15	18	26
1993-94	4	21	8	9	4	28	13	33
1994-95	12	21	7	3	11	25	28	24
1995-96	5	19	7	5	7	19	16	26
1996-97	3	19	9	6	4	26	14	33
1997-98	1	19	8	7	4	25	23	31
1998-99	2	19	8	7	4	25	12	31
1999-00	2	19	8	4	7	31	26	28
Totals		158	62	46	50	194	150	232

HIGHEST HOME ATTENDANCES

	Attendance	Opponents	Date	Season
1	38,377	Tottenham H.	29-Apr-95	1994-95
2	38,368	Manchester C.	20-Aug-94	1994-95
3	38,323	Liverpool	1-May-96	1995-96
4	38,317	Manchester U.	4-Nov-95	1995-96
5	38,308	Aston Villa	16-May-99	1998-99

LOWEST HOME ATTENDANCES

	Attendance	Opponents	Date	Season
1	18,253	Wimbledon	10-Feb-93	1992-93
2	18,817	QPR	4-May-93	1992-93
3	19,024	Nottingham F.	21-Apr-93	1992-93
4	20,796	Oldham A.	26-Aug-92	1992-93
5	21,061	Leeds U.	24-Feb-93	1992-93

TOP SCORER – SEASON BY SEASON

Season	Player	Goals
1992-93	Wright	15
1993-94	Wright	23
1994-95	Wright	18
1995-96	Wright	15
1996-97	Wright	23
1997-98	Bergkamp	16

1998-99	Anelka	17
1999-00	Henry	17

PLAYERS WITH MOST PREMIERSHIP APPEARANCES

Tot	Player	St	Sb	Gls
270	WINTERBURN, Nigel	260	10	4
263	DIXON, Lee	259	4	8
256	SEAMAN, David	256	0	0
229	PARLOUR, Ray	197	32	17
226	KEOWN, Martin	208	18	4
219	ADAMS, Tony	216	3	11
191	WRIGHT, Ian	182	9	104
175	BOULD, Steve	164	11	2
160	MERSON, Paul	150	10	28
147	BERGKAMP, Dennis	140	7	57
128	VIEIRA, Patrick	124	4	9
100	OVERMARS, Marc	91	9	25
98	JENSEN, John	93	5	1
97	CAMPBELL, Kevin	79	18	22
91	LINIGHAN, Andy	79	12	5

CLUB-BY-CLUB RESULTS

ASTON VILLA

Season	Venue	Date	Res	Scorers	Attendance	Referee
1992-93	Away	28-Dec-92	0-1		35,170	M.Bodenham
1992-93	Home	12-Apr-93	0-1		27,125	G.Ashby
1993-94	Home	6-Nov-93	1-2	Wright (58)	31,773	M.Bodenham
1993-94	Away	23-Apr-94	2-1	Wright (30 pen, 90)	31,580	K.Cooper
1994-95	Home	26-Dec-94	0-0		34,452	K.Morton
1994-95	Away	17-Apr-95	4-0	Hartson (31,87); Wright (32,72 pen)	32,005	K.Morton
1995-96	Home	21-Oct-95	2-0	Merson (47); Wright (78)	38,271	R.Hart
1995-96	Away	2-Dec-95	1-1	Platt (60)	37,770	J.Winter
1996-97	Away	7-Sep-96	2-2	Merson (70); Linighan (89)	37,944	M.Riley
1996-97	Home	28-Dec-96	2-2	Wright (12); Merson (73)	38,130	J.Winter
1997-98	Home	26-Oct-97	0-0		38,081	P.Durkin
1997-98	Away	10-May-98	0-1		39,372	G.Poll
1998-99	Away	13-Dec-98	2-3	Bergkamp (14, 45)	39,217	S.Lodge
1998-99	Home	16-May-99	1-0	Kanu (66)	38,308	D.Gallagher
1999-00	Home	11-Sep-99	3-1	Suker (45,49); Kanu (82)	38,093	D.Elleray
1999-00	Away	5-Mar-00	1-1	Dixon (84)	36,930	G.Poll

BARNSLEY

Season	Venue	Date	Res	Scorers	Attendance	Referee
1997-98	Home	4-Oct-97	5-0	Bergkamp (25, 31);Wright (26); Parlour (44); Platt (63)	38,049	P.Jones
1997-98	Away	25-Apr-98	2-0	Bergkamp (23); Overmars (76)	18,691	M.Riley

BLACKBURN ROVERS

Season	Venue	Date	Res	Scorers	Attendance	Referee
1992-93	Away	18-Aug-92	0-1		16,454	J.Worrall
1992-93	Home	12-Sep-92	0-1		28,643	M.Reed
1993-94	Away	1-Sep-93	1-1	Campbell (75)	14,410	D.Allison
1993-94	Home	25-Feb-94	1-0	Merson (73)	35,030	J.Worrall
1994-95	Home	31-Aug-94	0-0		37,629	K.Morton
1994-95	Away	8-Mar-95	1-3	Morrow (49)	23,452	A.Wilkie
1995-96	Home	26-Nov-95	0-0		37,695	G.Poll
1995-96	Away	27-Apr-96	1-1	Wright (75 pen)	29,834	K.Cooper
1996-97	Away	12-Oct-96	2-0	Wright (3, 51)	24,303	S.Dunn
1996-97	Home	19-Apr-97	1-1	Platt (19)	38,086	M.Riley
1997-98	Home	13-Dec-97	1-3	Overmars (18)	38,147	G.Willard
1997-98	Away	13-Apr-98	4-1	Bergkamp (2); Parlour (7, 14); Anelka (42)	28,212	M.Bodenham
1998-99	Away	25-Oct-98	2-1	Anelka (25); Petit (39)	30,867	D.Gallagher
1998-99	Home	6-Apr-99	1-0	Bergkamp (42)	37,762	G.Poll

BOLTON WANDERERS

Season	Venue	Date	Res	Scorers	Attendance	Referee
1995-96	Away	30-Oct-95	0-1		18,682	K.Cooper
1995-96	Home	5-May-96	2-1	Platt (82); Bergkamp (84)	38,104	G.Willard
1997-98	Home	13-Sep-97	4-1	Wright (20, 25, 81); Parlour (44)	38,138	N.Barry
1997-98	Away	31-Mar-98	1-0	Wreh (47)	25,000	K.Burge

BRADFORD CITY

Season	Venue	Date	Res	Scorers	Attendance	Referee
1999-00	Home	25-Aug-99	2-0	Vieira (8); Kanu (17 pen)	38,073	A.Wiley
1999-00	Away	5-Feb-00	1-2	Henry (13)	18,276	A.D'Urso

CHARLTON ATHELTIC

Season	Venue	Date	Res	Scorers	Attendance	Referee
1998-99	Home	29-Aug-98	0-0		38,014	G.Poll
1998-99	Away	28-Dec-98	1-0	Overmars (53 pen)	20,043	U.Rennie

CHELSEA

Season	Venue	Date	Res	Scorers	Attendance	Referee
1992-93	Home	3-Oct-92	2-1	Merson (10); Wright (85)	27,780	K.Morton
1992-93	Away	1-Mar-93	0-1		17,725	T.Ward
1993-94	Away	20-Nov-93	2-0	Smith (27); Wright (45pen)	26,839	P.Don
1993-94	Home	16-Apr-94	1-0	Wright (72)	34,314	A.Wilkie
1994-95	Home	15-Oct-94	3-1	Wright (40,63); Campbell (54)	38,234	D.Gallagher
1994-95	Away	14-May-95	1-2	Hartson (23)	29,542	J.Worrall
1995-96	Away	30-Sep-95	0-1		31,048	M.Bodenham
1995-96	Home	16-Dec-95	1-1	Dixon (88)	38,295	G.Ashby
1996-97	Home	3-Sep-96	3-3	Merson (44); Keown (66); Wright (77)	38,132	K.Burge

1996-97	Away	5-Apr-97	3-0	Wright (22); Platt (53); Bergkamp (81)	28,182	R.Dilkes
1997-98	Away	21-Sep-97	3-2	Bergkamp (45, 59); Winterburn (89)	33,012	D.Gallagher
1997-98	Home	8-Feb-98	2-0	Hughes (4, 42)	38,083	D.Gallagher
1998-99	Away	9-Sep-98	0-0		34,644	S.Lodge
1998-99	Home	31-Jan-99	1-0	Bergkamp (32)	38,121	G.Poll
1999-00	Away	23-Oct-99	3-2	Kanu (75, 83, 90)	34,958	A.Wilkie
1999-00	Home	6-May-00	2-1	Henry (21, 48)	38,119	M.Reed

COVENTRY CITY

Season	Venue	Date	Res	Scorers	Attendance	Referee
1992-93	Home	7-Nov-92	3-0	Smith (8); Wright (30); Campbell (45)	27,693	J.Worrall
1992-93	Away	13-Mar-93	2-0	Campbell (28); Wright (29)	15,437	D.Allison
1993-94	Home	14-Aug-93	0-3		26,397	A.Wilkie
1993-94	Away	4-Dec-93	0-1		12,632	R.Hart
1994-95	Home	23-Oct-94	2-1	Wright (13,32)	31,725	A.Wilkie
1994-95	Away	21-Jan-95	1-0	Hartson (78)	14,468	J.Worrall
1995-96	Away	26-Aug-95	0-0		20,081	S.Dunn
1995-96	Home	3-Feb-96	1-1	Bergkamp (24)	35,623	S.Dunn
1996-97	Home	19-Oct-96	0-0		38,140	P.Jones
1996-97	Away	21-Apr-97	1-1	Wright (19 pen)	19,998	K.Burge
1997-98	Home	11-Aug-97	2-0	Wright (29, 47)	37,324	K.Burge
1997-98	Away	17-Jan-98	2-2	Bergkamp (50); Anelka (57)	22,864	S.Lodge
1998-99	Away	31-Oct-98	1-0	Anelka (63)	23,040	U.Rennie
1998-99	Home	21-Mar-99	2-0	Parlour (16); Overmars (80)	38,073	P.Alcock
1999-00	Away	26-Dec-99	2-3	Ljungberg (67); Suker (86)	22,757	R.Harris
1999-00	Home	26-Mar-00	3-0	Henry (50); Grimandi (79); Kanu (80)	38,027	B.Knight

CRYSTAL PALACE

Season	Venue	Date	Res	Scorers	Attendance	Referee
1992-93	Away	2-Nov-92	2-1	Merson (5); Wright (73)	20,734	V.Callow
1992-93	Home	8-May-93	3-0	Wright (9); Dickov (82); Campbell (89)	25,225	K.Burge
1994-95	Home	1-Oct-94	1-2	Wright (72)	34,136	M.Bodenham
1994-95	Away	25-Feb-95	3-0	Merson (24); Kiwomya (39,78)	17,092	K.Morton
1997-98	Away	18-Oct-97	0-0		26,180	S.Dunn
1997-98	Home	21-Feb-98	1-0	Grimandi (49)	38,094	J.Winter

DERBY COUNTY

Season	Venue	Date	Res	Scorers	Attendance	Referee
1996-97	Home	7-Dec-96	2-2	Adams (45); Vieira (90)	38,018	M.Bodenham
1996-97	Away	11-May-97	3-1	Wright (55, 90); Bergkamp (82)	18,287	P.Durkin
1997-98	Away	1-Nov-97	0-3		30,004	P.Alcock
1997-98	Home	28-Apr-98	1-0	Petit (34)	38,121	N.Barry
1998-99	Away	5-Dec-98	0-0		29,018	M.Reed
1998-99	Home	2-May-99	1-0	Anelka (14)	37,323	N.Barry
1999-00	Away	10-Aug-99	2-1	Petit (40); Bergkamp (47)	25,901	S.Lodge
1999-00	Home	28-Nov-99	2-1	Henry (11, 51)	37,964	A.D'Urso

EVERTON

Season	Venue	Date	Res	Scorers	Attendance	Referee
1992-93	Home	24-Oct-92	2-0	Wright (5); Limpar (58)	28,052	K.Hackett
1992-93	Away	1-May-93	0-0		19,044	A.Gunn

1993-94	Home	28-Aug-93	2-0	Wright (48, 78)	29,063	K.Burge
1993-94	Away	19-Feb-94	1-1	Merson (56)	19,760	D.Allison
1994-95	Away	29-Oct-94	1-1	Schwarz (24)	32,003	K.Burge
1994-95	Home	14-Jan-95	1-1	Wright (4)	34,473	R.Hart
1995-96	Away	23-Aug-95	2-0	Platt (69); Wright (86)	36,047	K.Burge
1995-96	Home	20-Jan-96	1-2	Wright (38)	38,275	M.Bodenham
1996-97	Home	19-Jan-97	3-1	Bergkamp (54); Vieira (56); Merson (68)	38,095	K.Burge
1996-97	Away	1-Mar-97	2-0	Bergkamp (21); Wright (27)	36,980	P.Danson
1997-98	Away	27-Sep-97	2-2	Wright (32); Overmars (41)	35,457	A.Wilkie
1997-98	Home	3-May-98	4-0	OG (6, Bilic); Overmars (28, 57); Adams (89)	38,269	G.Ashby
1998-99	Home	8-Nov-98	1-0	Anelka (6)	38,088	G.Willard
1998-99	Away	13-Mar-99	2-0	Parlour (16); Bergkamp (69 pen)	38,049	U.Rennie
1999-00	Home	16-Oct-99	4-1	Dixon (40); Suker (54, 61); Kanu (90)	38,042	S.Dunn
1999-00	Away	29-Apr-00	1-0	Overmars (34)	35,919	D.Gallagher

IPSWICH TOWN

Season	Venue	Date	Res	Scorers	Attendance	Referee
1992-93	Home	26-Dec-92	0-0		26,198	R.Milford
1992-93	Away	10-Apr-93	2-1	Smith (2); Merson (87)	20,358	R.Lewis
1993-94	Home	11-Sep-93	4-0	Wright (30); Campbell (38, 55, 64)	28,563	J.Worrall
1993-94	Away	5-Mar-94	5-1	Wright (18, 40 pen, 86); OG (24, Youds); Parlour (52)	18,803	K.Barratt
1994-95	Away	28-Dec-94	2-0	Wright (16); Campbell (79)	22,054	P.Danson
1994-95	Home	15-Apr-95	4-1	Merson (33); Wright (47,50,56)	36,818	T.Holbrook

LEEDS UNITED

Season	Venue	Date	Res	Scorers	Attendance	Referee
1992-93	Away	21-Nov-92	0-3		30,516	R.Hart
1992-93	Home	24-Feb-93	0-0		21,061	K.Redfern
1993-94	Home	24-Aug-93	2-1	OG (1, Newsome); Merson (57)	29,042	K.Hackett
1993-94	Away	18-Dec-93	1-2	Campbell (27)	37,289	K.Burge
1994-95	Away	23-Aug-94	0-1		34,218	R.Dilkes
1994-95	Home	17-Dec-94	1-3	Linighan (86)	38,098	G.Poll
1995-96	Away	14-Oct-95	3-0	Merson (43); Bergkamp (56); Wright (86)	38,552	P.Crabtree
1995-96	Home	6-Apr-96	2-1	Wright (44, 90)	37,619	J.Winter
1996-97	Home	26-Oct-96	3-0	Dixon (1); Bergkamp (5); Wright (65)	38,076	A.Wilkie
1996-97	Away	1-Feb-97	0-0		35,502	D.Elleray
1997-98	Away	9-Aug-97	1-1	Wright (35)	37,993	D.Gallagher
1997-98	Home	10-Jan-98	2-1	Overmars (60, 72)	38,018	G.Ashby
1998-99	Home	20-Dec-98	3-1	Bergkamp (28); Vieira (53); Petit (82)	38,025	P.Durkin
1998-99	Away	11-May-99	0-1		40,142	G.Willard
1999-00	Home	28-Dec-99	2-0	Ljungberg (32); Henry (58)	38,096	G.Poll
1999-00	Away	16-Apr-00	4-0	Henry (21); Keown (70); Kanu (83); Overmars (90)	39,307	S.Dunn

LEICESTER CITY

Season	Venue	Date	Res	Scorers	Attendance	Referee
1994-95	Away	23-Nov-94	1-2	Wright (19 pen)	20,774	D.Elleray
1994-95	Home	11-Feb-95	1-1	Merson (52)	31,373	G.Poll
1996-97	Away	24-Aug-96	2-0	Bergkamp (26 pen); Wright (90)	20,429	G.Barber
1996-97	Home	12-Apr-97	2-0	Adams (34); Platt (64)	38,044	S.Lodge
1997-98	Away	27-Aug-97	3-3	Bergkamp (9, 22, 90)	21,089	G.Barber

1997-98	Home	26-Dec-97	2-1	Platt (36); OG (56, Walsh)	38,023	D.Elleray
1998-99	Away	12-Sep-98	1-1	Hughes,S. (90)	21,628	P.Durkin
1998-99	Home	20-Feb-99	5-0	Anelka (23, 27, 44); Parlour (42, 48)	38,069	P.Durkin
1999-00	Home	7-Aug-99	2-1	Bergkamp (65); OG (90, Sinclair)	38,026	A.Wilkie
1999-00	Away	4-Dec-99	3-0	Grimandi (23); OG (53); Overmars (75)	20,495	D.Gallagher

LIVERPOOL

Season	Venue	Date	Res	Scorers	Attendance	Referee
1992-93	Away	23-Aug-92	2-0	Limpar (53); Wright (80)	34,961	K.Redfern
1992-93	Home	31-Jan-93	0-1		27,580	K.Cooper
1993-94	Away	2-Oct-93	0-0		42,750	G.Ashby
1993-94	Home	26-Mar-94	1-0	Merson (47)	35,556	R.Hart
1994-95	Away	28-Aug-94	0-3		30,117	A.Wilkie
1994-95	Home	12-Apr-95	0-1		38,036	M.Bodenham
1995-96	Away	23-Dec-95	1-3	Wright (8 pen)	39,806	K.Cooper
1995-96	Home	1-May-96	0-0		38,323	G.Ashby
1996-97	Away	19-Aug-96	0-2		38,103	G.Willard
1996-97	Home	24-Mar-97	1-2	Wright (78)	38,068	G.Ashby
1997-98	Home	30-Nov-97	0-1		38,094	G.Poll
1997-98	Away	6-May-98	0-4		44,417	A.Wilkie
1998-99	Away	22-Aug-98	0-0		44,429	D.Elleray
1998-99	Home	9-Jan-99	0-0		38,107	G.Barber
1999-00	Away	28-Aug-99	0-2		44,886	D.Gallagher
1999-00	Home	13-Feb-00	0-1		38,098	S.Dunn

MANCHESTER CITY

Season	Venue	Date	Res	Scorers	Attendance	Referee
1992-93	Home	28-Sep-92	1-0	Wright (19)	21,504	J.Martin
1992-93	Away	16-Jan-93	1-0	Merson (79)	25,047	K.Burge
1993-94	Home	16-Oct-93	0-0		29,567	R.Milford
1993-94	Away	15-Jan-94	0-0		25,642	D.Allison
1994-95	Home	20-Aug-94	3-0	Campbell (2); Smith (36); Wright (76)	38,368	P.Durkin
1994-95	Away	12-Dec-94	2-1	Smith (31); Schwarz (34)	20,500	G.Ashby
1995-96	Away	10-Sep-95	1-0	Wright (90)	23,994	D.Gallagher
1995-96	Home	5-Mar-96	3-1	Hartson (29, 55); Dixon (41)	34,519	P.Jones

MANCHESTER UNITED

Season	Venue	Date	Res	Scorers	Attendance	Referee
1992-93	Home	28-Nov-92	0-1		29,739	H.King
1992-93	Away	24-Mar-93	0-0		37,301	V.Callow
1993-94	Away	19-Sep-93	0-1		44,009	V.Callow
1993-94	Home	22-Mar-94	2-2	OG (36, Pallister); Merson (78)	36,203	V.Callow
1994-95	Home	26-Nov-94	0-0		38,301	K.Morton
1994-95	Away	22-Mar-95	0-3		43,623	K.Cooper
1995-96	Home	4-Nov-95	1-0	Bergkamp (14)	38,317	P.Durkin
1995-96	Away	20-Mar-96	0-1		50,028	G.Willard
1996-97	Away	16-Nov-96	0-1		55,210	G.Poll
1996-97	Home	19-Feb-97	1-2	Bergkamp (69)	38,172	M.Bodenham
1997-98	Home	9-Nov-97	3-2	Anelka (9); Viera (26); Platt (83)	38,083	M.Bodenham
1997-98	Away	14-Mar-98	1-0	Overmars (79)	55,174	A.Wilkie
1998-99	Home	20-Sep-98	3-0	Adams (13); Anelka (44); Ljungberg (84)	38,142	G.Barber

1998-99	Away	17-Feb-99	1-1	Anelka (48)	55,171	G.Willard
1999-00	Home	22-Aug-99	1-2	Ljungberg (41)	38,147	G.Poll
1999-00	Away	24-Jan-00	1-1	Ljungberg (11)	58,293	P.Durkin

MIDDLESBROUGH

Season	Venue	Date	Res	Scorers	Attendance	Referee
1992-93	Home	19-Dec-92	1-1	Wright (81)	23,197	S.Lodge
1992-93	Away	6-Apr-93	0-1		12,726	K.Hackett
1995-96	Home	20-Aug-95	1-1	Wright (36)	37,308	G.Ashby
1995-96	Away	13-Jan-96	3-2	Merson (6); Platt (59); Helder(62)	29,359	G.Poll
1996-97	Away	21-Sep-96	2-0	Hartson (3); Wright (27)	29,629	M.Bodenham
1996-97	Home	1-Jan-97	2-0	Bergkamp (14); Wright (44)	37,573	M.Reed
1998-99	Home	29-Nov-98	1-1	Anelka (89)	38,075	G.Barber
1998-99	Away	24-Apr-99	6-1	Overmars (4 pen); Anelka (38, 78); Vieria (58); Kanu (45,60)	34,630	M.Riley
1999-00	Home	20-Nov-99	5-1	Overmars (26, 61, 78); Bergkamp (40, 49)	38,082	N.Barry
1999-00	Away	12-Mar-00	1-2	Bergkamp (70)	34,244	R.Harris

NEWCASTLE UNITED

Season	Venue	Date	Res	Scorers	Attendance	Referee
1993-94	Home	27-Nov-93	2-1	Wright (15); Smith (60)	36,091	A.Gunn
1993-94	Away	7-May-94	0-2		32,216	R.Dilkes
1994-95	Home	18-Sep-94	2-3	Adams (9); Wright (88)	36,819	T.Holbrook
1994-95	Away	19-Mar-95	0-1		35,611	G.Willard
1995-96	Away	2-Jan-96	0-2		36,530	D.Gallagher
1995-96	Home	23-Mar-96	2-0	Marshall (3); Wright (17)	38,271	P.Durkin
1996-97	Away	30-Nov-96	2-1	Dixon (10); Wright (59)	36,565	G.Barber
1996-97	Home	3-May-97	0-1		38,179	M.Bodenham
1997-98	Away	6-Dec-97	1-0	Wright (36)	36,571	S.Dunn
1997-98	Home	11-Apr-98	3-1	Anelka (41, 64); Vieira (72)	38,102	G.Willard
1998-99	Home	4-Oct-98	3-0	Bergkamp (22, 66 pen); Anelka (29)	38,102	M.Reed
1998-99	Away	28-Feb-99	1-1	Anelka (36)	36,708	M.Reed
1999-00	Home	30-Oct-99	0-0		38,106	P.Jones
1999-00	Away	14-May-00	2-4	Kanu (7); Malz (53)	36,450	G.Poll

NORWICH CITY

Season	Venue	Date	Res	Scorers	Attendance	Referee
1992-93	Home	15-Aug-92	2-4	Bould (28); Campbell (39)	24,030	A.Gunn
1992-93	Away	3-Mar-93	1-1	Wright (81)	14,820	J.Martin
1993-94	Home	30-Oct-93	0-0		30,516	R.Dilkes
1993-94	Away	13-Feb-94	1-1	Campbell (33)	17,667	R.Dilkes
1994-95	Away	10-Sep-94	0-0		17,768	R.Hart
1994-95	Home	1-Apr-95	5-1	Hartsen (4,13); Dixon (6); Merson (75); OG (90, Newman)	36,942	P.Jones

NOTTINGHAM FOREST

Season	Venue	Date	Res	Scorers	Attendance	Referee
1992-93	Away	17-Oct-92	1-0	Smith (38)	24,862	J.Worrall
1992-93	Home	21-Apr-93	1-1	Wright (67)	19,024	M.Bodenham
1994-95	Away	3-Dec-94	2-2	Keown (59); Davis (76)	21,662	B.Hill
1994-95	Home	21-Feb-95	1-0	Kiwomya (81)	35,441	P.Durkin

1995-96	Home	29-Aug-95	1-1	Platt (41)	38,248	R.Dilkes
1995-96	Away	10-Feb-96	1-0	Bergkamp (59)	27,222	R.Hart
1996-97	Away	21-Dec-96	1-2	Wright (63)	27,384	S.Lodge
1996-97	Home	8-Mar-97	2-0	Bergkamp (49, 78)	38,206	M.Reed
1998-99	Home	17-Aug-98	2-1	Petit (58); Overmars (80)	38,064	M.Riley
1998-99	Away	16-Jan-99	1-0	Keown (34)	26,021	P.Durkin

OLDHAM ATHLETIC

Season	Venue	Date	Res	Scorers	Attendance	Referee
1992-93	Home	26-Aug-92	2-0	Winterburn (25); Wright (31)	20,796	R.Milford
1992-93	Away	20-Feb-93	1-0	Linighan (50)	12,311	K.Hackett
1993-94	Away	23-Oct-93	0-0		12,105	M.Reed
1993-94	Home	22-Jan-94	1-1	Wright (45pen)	26,524	P.Foakes

QPR

Season	Venue	Date	Res	Scorers	Attendance	Referee
1992-93	Away	2-Sep-92	0-0		20,868	R.Groves
1992-93	Home	4-May-93	0-0		18,817	R.Gifford
1993-94	Home	3-Jan-94	0-0		34,935	J.Borrett
1993-94	Away	27-Apr-94	1-1	Merson (46)	11,442	J.Borrett
1994-95	Home	31-Dec-94	1-3	Jensen (64)	32,393	G.Willard
1994-95	Away	8-Apr-95	1-3	Adams (90)	16,341	P.Don
1995-96	Home	26-Dec-95	3-0	Wright (44); Merson (81, 83)	38,259	M.Reed
1995-96	Away	2-Mar-96	1-1	Bergkamp (50)	17,970	P.Alcock

SHEFFIELD UNITED

Season	Venue	Date	Res	Scorers	Attendance	Referee
1992-93	Away	19-Sep-92	1-1	Wright (85)	19,105	R.Dilkes
1992-93	Home	9-Jan-93	1-1	Hillier (43)	23,818	G.Ashby
1993-94	Home	29-Dec-93	3-0	Campbell (11, 55); Wright (40)	27,035	R.Milford
1993-94	Away	4-Apr-94	1-1	Campbell (69)	20,019	D.Frampton

SHEFFIELD WEDNESDAY

Season	Venue	Date	Res	Scorers	Attendance	Referee
1992-93	Home	29-Aug-92	2-1	Parlour (8); Merson (27)	23,389	P.Durkin
1992-93	Away	6-May-93	0-1		23,645	R.Hart
1993-94	Away	21-Aug-93	1-0	Wright (8)	26,023	R.Hart
1993-94	Home	12-Dec-93	1-0	Wright (90)	22,026	D.Gallagher
1994-95	Home	6-Nov-94	0-0		33,705	R.Gifford
1994-95	Away	4-Feb-95	1-3	Linighan (3)	23,468	K.Burge
1995-96	Home	21-Nov-95	4-2	Bergkamp (3); Winterburn (53); Dickov (64); Hartson (86)	34,556	R.Dilkes
1995-96	Away	8-Apr-96	0-1		24,349	S.Dunn
1996-97	Home	16-Sep-96	4-1	Platt (58); Wright (62 pen, 78, 89)	33,461	M.Reed
1996-97	Away	26-Dec-96	0-0		23,245	R.Dilkes
1997-98	Away	22-Nov-97	0-2		34,373	K.Burge
1997-98	Home	28-Mar-98	1-0	Bergkamp (35)	38,087	S.Dunn
1998-99	Away	27-Sep-98	0-1		27,949	P.Alcock
1998-99	Home	9-Mar-99	3-0	Bergkamp (83, 88): Kanu (86)	37,792	D.Elleray
1999-00	Away	3-Jan-00	1-1	Petit (40)	26,155	M.Reed
1999-00	Home	9-May-00	3-3	Dixon (34); Silvinho (77); Henry (80)	37,271	J.Winter

SOUTHAMPTON

Season	Venue	Date	Res	Scorers	Attendance	Referee
1992-93	Away	5-Dec-92	0-2		17,286	J.Key
1992-93	Home	20-Mar-93	4-3	Linighan (15); Merson (16); Carter (20, 79)	24,149	K.Barratt
1993-94	Home	25-Sep-93	1-0	Merson (45)	26,902	K.Morton
1993-94	Away	19-Mar-94	4-0	Wright (18, 30, 68 pen); Campbell (84)	16,790	D.Frampton
1994-95	Away	19-Nov-94	0-1		15,201	R.Dilkes
1994-95	Home	24-Jan-95	1-1	Hartson (21)	27,213	D.Gallagher
1995-96	Home	23-Sep-95	4-2	Bergkamp (17, 68); Adams (23); Wright (73)	38,136	R.Hart
1995-96	Away	9-Dec-95	0-0		15,238	P.Danson
1996-97	Home	4-Dec-96	3-1	Merson (43); Wright (57 pen); Shaw (89)	38,033	P.Jones
1996-97	Away	15-Mar-97	2-0	Hughes (41); Shaw (72)	15,144	J.Winter
1997-98	Away	23-Aug-97	3-1	Overmars (19); Bergkamp (57, 78)	15,246	D.Elleray
1997-98	Home	31-Jan-98	3-0	Bergkamp (62); Adams (67); Anelka (68)	38,056	P.Jones
1998-99	Home	17-Oct-98	1-0	Anelka (34)	38,027	J.Winter
1998-99	Away	3-Apr-99	0-0		15,255	P.Jones
1999-00	Away	18-Sep-99	1-0	Henry (79)	15,242	G.Barber
1999-00	Home	26-Feb-00	3-1	Ljungberg (22, 68); Bergkamp (36)	38,044	J.Winter

SUNDERLAND

Season	Venue	Date	Res	Scorers	Attendance	Referee
1996-97	Home	28-Sep-96	2-0	Hartson (76); Parlour (88)	38,016	P.Danson
1996-97	Away	11-Jan-97	0-1		21,154	M.Riley
1999-00	Away	14-Aug-99	0-0		41,680	U.Rennie
1999-00	Home	15-Jan-00	4-1	Henry (3, 81); Suker (27, 32)	38,039	P.Alcock

SWINDON TOWN

Season	Venue	Date	Res	Scorers	Attendance	Referee
1993-94	Away	27-Dec-93	4-0	Campbell (19, 26, 68); Wright (90)	17,214	S.Lodge
1993-94	Home	2-Apr-94	1-1	Smith (4)	31,635	B.Hill

TOTTENHAM HOTSPUR

Season	Venue	Date	Res	Scorers	Attendance	Referee
1992-93	Away	12-Dec-92	0-1		33,709	A.Buksh
1992-93	Home	11-May-93	1-3	Dickov (52)	26,393	K.Cooper
1993-94	Away	16-Aug-93	1-0	Wright (87)	28,355	D.Elleray
1993-94	Home	6-Dec-93	1-1	Wright (65)	35,669	P.Don
1994-95	Away	2-Jan-95	0-1		28,747	M.Reed
1994-95	Home	29-Apr-95	1-1	Wright (61 pen)	38,377	R.Hart
1995-96	Away	18-Nov-95	1-2	Bergkamp (14)	32,894	A.Wilkie
1995-96	Home	15-Apr-96	0-0		38,273	M.Reed
1996-97	Home	24-Nov-96	3-1	Wright (27 pen); Adams (87); Bergkamp (89)	38,264	D.Elleray
1996-97	Away	15-Feb-97	0-0		33,039	G.Poll
1997-98	Home	30-Aug-97	0-0		38,102	G.Willard
1997-98	Away	28-Dec-97	1-1	Parlour (62)	29,610	M.Riley
1998-99	Home	14-Nov-98	0-0		38,278	A.Wilkie
1998-99	Away	5-May-99	3-1	Petit (17); Anelka (33); Kanu (85)	36,019	S.Dunn
1999-00	Away	7-Nov-99	1-2	Vieira (39)	36,085	D.Elleray
1999-00	Home	19-Mar-00	2-1	OG (19, Armstrong); Henry (45 pen)	38,131	P.Durkin

WATFORD

Season	Venue	Date	Res	Scorers	Attendance	Referee
1999-00	Home	25-Sep-99	1-0	Kanu (86)	38,127	P.Durkin
1999-00	Away	23-Apr-00	3-2	Henry (18, 45); Parlour (43)	19,670	R.Harris

WEST HAM UNITED

Season	Venue	Date	Res	Scorers	Attendance	Referee
1993-94	Away	24-Nov-93	0-0		20,279	P.Durkin
1993-94	Home	30-Apr-94	0-2		33,700	R.Milford
1994-95	Away	25-Sep-94	2-0	Adams (17); Wright (53)	18,498	K.Cooper
1994-95	Home	5-Mar-95	0-1		36,295	B.Hill
1995-96	Home	16-Sep-95	1-0	Wright (75 pen)	38,065	A.Wilkie
1995-96	Away	24-Feb-96	1-0	Hartson (1)	24,217	D.Elleray
1996-97	Home	17-Aug-96	2-0	Hartson (22); Bergkamp (39 pen)	38,056	P.Durkin
1996-97	Away	29-Jan-97	2-1	Parlour (7); Wright (66)	24,382	M.Bodenham
1997-98	Home	24-Sep-97	4-0	Bergkamp (12); Overmars (39, 45); Wright (12 pen)	38,012	P.Alcock
1997-98	Away	2-Mar-98	0-0		25,717	P.Durkin
1998-99	Home	26-Dec-98	1-0	Overmars (7)	38,098	P.Jones
1998-99	Away	6-Feb-99	4-0	Bergkamp (35); Overmars (45); Anelka (83); Parlour (87)	26,042	J.Winter
1999-00	Away	3-Oct-99	1-2	Suker (77)	26,009	M.Reed
1999-00	Home	2-May-00	2-1	Overmars (69); Petit (90)	38,093	P.Durkin

WIMBLEDON

Season	Venue	Date	Res	Scorers	Attendance	Referee
1992-93	Away	5-Sep-92	2-3	Wright 2 (34, 82)	12,906	K.Burge
1992-93	Home	10-Feb-93	0-1		18,253	P.Don
1993-94	Away	1-Jan-94	3-0	Campbell (18); Parlour (23); Wright (55)	16,584	G.Ashby
1993-94	Home	19-Apr-94	1-1	Bould (51)	21,292	R.Gifford
1994-95	Away	8-Oct-94	3-1	Wright (11); Smith (57); Campbell (65)	10,842	G.Ashby
1994-95	Home	4-May-95	0-0		32,822	R.Gifford
1995-96	Home	30-Dec-95	1-3	Wright (27)	37,640	S.Lodge
1995-96	Away	16-Mar-96	3-0	Winterburn (61); Platt (65); Bergkamp (83)	18,335	D.Gallagher
1996-97	Away	2-Nov-96	2-2	Wright (6); Merson (65)	25,521	P.Alcock
1996-97	Home	23-Feb-97	0-1		37,854	P.Jones
1997-98	Away	11-Mar-98	1-0	Wreh (21)	22,291	D.Gallagher
1997-98	Home	18-Apr-98	5-0	Adams (11); Overmars (17); Bergkamp (19); Petit (54); Wreh (88)	38,024	P.Jones
1998-99	Away	21-Nov-98	0-1		26,003	M.Riley
1998-99	Home	19-Apr-99	5-1	Parlour (34); Vieira (49); OG (56, Thatcher); Bergkamp (57); Kanu (59)	37,982	S.Lodge
1999-00	Home	18-Dec-99	1-1	Henry (61)	38,052	G.Barber
1999-00	Away	1-Apr-00	3-1	Kanu (33, 41); Henry (89 pen)	25,858	U.Rennie

INTRODUCTION

Founded in 1874 by cricketers from the Aston Wesleyan Chapel, Lozells, who played on Aston Park, moving to a field in Wellington Road, Perry Barr in 1876. Prominent nationally, the club was a founder member of the Football League in 1888. The landlord at Perry Barr made such demands that the club sought its own ground and eventually moved back to Aston occupying the Aston Lower Grounds, which had already been used for some big games. Not known as Villa Park until some time later, the ground first saw league football in 1897. Premier League founder members 1992.

Ground: Villa Park, Trinity Rd,
            Birmingham, B6 6HE
Nickname: The Villains
Internet: www.astonvilla-fc.co.uk

HONOURS

FA Premier League:	Runners-up 1992-93
Football League: Div 1 :	Champions 1893-94, 1895-96, 1896-97, 1898-99, 1899-1900, 1909-10, 1980-81; Runners-up 1888-89, 1902-03, 1907-08, 1910-11, 1912-13, 1913-14, 1930-31, 1932-33, 1989-90;
Football League: Div 2 :	1937-38, 1959-60; Runners-up 1974-75, 1987-88;
Football League: Div 3:	Champions 1971-72.
FA Cup:	Winners 1887, 1895, 1897, 1905, 1913, 1920, 1957; Runners-up 1892, 1924.
Football League Cup:	Winners 1961, 1975, 1977, 1994, 1996; Runners-up 1963, 1971.
Champions' Cup:	Winners 1981-82.
European Super Cup:	Winners 1982-83.
World Club Cup:	Runners-up 1982-83.

EUROPEAN RECORD

Champions' League (2):	81-82 (W), 82-83 (QF);
Cup–Winners' Cup (0);	
UEFA Cup (9):	75-76 (1), 77-78 (Q), 83-84 (2), 90-91 (2), 93-94 (2), 94-95 (2), 96-97 (1), 97-98 (QF), 98-99 (2)

FAPL RECORD SUMMARY

Most Total:	EHIOGU, Ugo	227
Most Starts:	EHIOGU, Ugo	218
Most Subs:	JOACHIM, Julian	42
Most SNU:	OAKES, Michael	107
Most PS:	JOACHIM, Julian	25
Most Goals:	YORKE, Dwight	60
Most Yel:	EHIOGU, Ugo	34
Most Red:	TOWNSEND, Andy	3

PLAYING RECORD – SEASON TOTALS

Season	Pn	P	W	D	L	F	A	Pts
1992-93	2	42	21	11	10	57	40	74
1993-94	10	42	15	12	15	46	50	57
1994-95	18	42	11	15	16	51	56	48
1995-96	4	38	18	9	11	52	35	63
1996-97	5	38	17	10	11	47	34	61
1997-98	7	38	17	6	15	49	48	57
1998-99	6	38	15	10	13	51	46	55
1999-00	6	38	15	13	10	46	35	58
Totals		316	129	86	101	399	344	473

PLAYING RECORD – HOME TOTALS

Season	Pn	P	W	D	L	F	A	Pts
1992-93	2	21	13	5	3	36	16	44
1993-94	10	21	8	5	8	23	18	29
1994-95	18	21	6	9	6	27	24	27
1995-96	4	19	11	5	3	32	15	38
1996-97	5	19	11	5	3	27	13	38
1997-98	7	19	9	3	7	26	24	30
1998-99	6	19	10	3	6	33	28	33
1999-00	6	19	8	8	3	23	12	32
Totals		158	76	43	39	227	150	271

PLAYING RECORD – AWAY TOTALS

Season	Pn	P	W	D	L	F	A	Pts
1992-93	2	21	8	6	7	21	24	30
1993-94	10	21	7	7	7	23	32	28
1994-95	18	21	5	6	10	24	32	21
1995-96	4	19	7	4	8	20	20	25
1996-97	5	19	6	5	8	20	21	23
1997-98	7	19	8	3	8	23	24	27
1998-99	6	19	5	7	7	18	18	22
1999-00	6	19	7	5	7	23	23	26
Totals		158	53	43	62	172	194	202

HIGHEST HOME ATTENDANCES

	Attendance	Opponents	Date	Season
1	45,347	Liverpool	7-May-94	1993-94
2	40,903	Blackburn R.	1-Jan-94	1993-94
3	40,154	Liverpool	6-May-95	1994-95
4	40,114	Blackburn R.	4-Mar-95	1994-95
5	40,017	Tottenham H.	25-Jan-95	1994-95

LOWEST HOME ATTENDANCES

	Attendance	Opponents	Date	Season
1	16,180	Southampton	24-Nov-93	1993-94
2	17,120	Crystal P.	5-Sep-92	1992-93
3	17,894	Southampton	22-Aug-92	1992-93
4	17,940	Wimbledon	11-Dec-93	1993-94
5	19,125	Chelsea	2-Sep-92	1992-93

TOP SCORER – SEASON BY SEASON

Season	Player	Goals
1992-93	Saunders	13
1993-94	Saunders	10
1994-95	Saunders	15
1995-96	Yorke	17
1996-97	Yorke	17
1997-98	Yorke	12

1998-99	Joachim	14
1999-00	Dublin	12

PLAYERS WITH MOST PREMIERSHIP APPEARANCES

Tot	Player	St	Sb	Gls
227	EHIOGU, Ugo	218	9	12
191	WRIGHT, Alan	188	3	4
179	YORKE, Dwight	160	19	60
178	BOSNICH, Mark	178	0	0
175	TAYLOR, Ian	161	14	21
171	STAUNTON, Steve	168	3	13
160	SOUTHGATE, Gareth	160	0	5
142	McGRATH, Paul	137	5	6
132	TOWNSEND, Andy	131	1	8
121	JOACHIM, Julian	79	42	32
120	DRAPER, Mark	108	12	7
112	SAUNDERS, Dean	111	1	37
106	BARRETT, Earl	105	1	1
105	TEALE, Shaun	104	1	2
101	RICHARDSON, Kevin	100	1	7
95	HOUGHTON, Ray	83	12	6
90	MILOSEVIC, Savo	84	6	29

CLUB-BY-CLUB RESULTS

ARSENAL

Season	Venue	Date	Res	Scorers	Attendance	Referee
1992-93	Home	28-Dec-92	1-0	Saunders (45 pen)	35,170	M.Bodenham
1992-93	Away	12-Apr-93	1-0	Daley (68)	27,125	G.Ashby
1993-94	Away	6-Nov-93	2-1	Whittingham (74); Townsend (90)	31,773	M.Bodenham
1993-94	Home	23-Apr-94	1-2	Houghton (57)	31,580	K.Cooper
1994-95	Away	26-Dec-94	0-0		34,452	K.Morton
1994-95	Home	17-Apr-95	0-4		32,005	K.Morton
1995-96	Away	21-Oct-95	0-2		38,271	R.Hart
1995-96	Home	2-Dec-95	1-1	Yorke (65)	37,770	J.Winter
1996-97	Home	7-Sep-96	2-2	Milosevic (39, 63)	37,944	M.Riley
1996-97	Away	28-Dec-96	2-2	Milosevic (67); Yorke (74)	38,130	J.Winter
1997-98	Away	26-Oct-97	0-0		38,081	P.Durkin
1997-98	Home	10-May-98	1-0	Yorke (37 pen)	39,372	G.Poll
1998-99	Home	13-Dec-98	3-2	Joachim (62); Dublin (65, 83)	39,217	S.Lodge
1998-99	Away	16-May-99	0-1		38,308	D.Gallagher
1999-00	Away	11-Sep-99	1-3	Joachim (44)	38,093	D.Elleray
1999-00	Home	5-Mar-00	1-1	Walker (62)	36,930	G.Poll

BARNSLEY

Season	Venue	Date	Res	Scorers	Attendance	Referee
1997-98	Away	13-Sep-97	3-0	Ehiogu (25); Draper (50); Taylor (72)	18,649	G.Barber
1997-98	Home	11-Mar-98	0-1		29,519	P.Jones

BLACKBURN ROVERS

Season	Venue	Date	Res	Scorers	Attendance	Referee
1992-93	Home	19-Oct-92	0-0		30,398	H.King
1992-93	Away	21-Apr-93	0-3		15,127	J.Worrall
1993-94	Home	1-Jan-94	0-1		40,903	R.Dilkes
1993-94	Away	11-Apr-94	0-1		19,287	D.Allison
1994-95	Away	24-Sep-94	1-3	Ehiogu (90)	22,694	M.Bodenham
1994-95	Home	4-Mar-95	0-1		40,114	R.Gifford
1995-96	Away	9-Sep-95	1-1	Milosevic (33)	27,084	R.Dilkes
1995-96	Home	28-Feb-96	2-0	Joachim (55); Southgate (71)	28,008	S.Lodge
1996-97	Home	20-Aug-96	1-0	Southgate (64)	32,257	A.Wilkie
1996-97	Away	22-Mar-97	2-0	Johnson (64); Yorke (79)	24,274	A.Wilkie
1997-98	Home	13-Aug-97	0-4		37,112	P.Alcock
1997-98	Away	17-Jan-98	0-5		24,834	K.Burge
1998-99	Away	26-Dec-98	1-2	Scimeca (81)	27,536	D.Gallagher
1998-99	Home	6-Feb-99	1-3	Joachim (69)	37,404	K.Burge

BOLTON WANDERERS

Season	Venue	Date	Res	Scorers	Attendance	Referee
1995-96	Home	30-Aug-95	1-0	Yorke (75)	31,770	P.Jones
1995-96	Away	10-Feb-96	2-0	Yorke (40, 53)	18,099	G.Ashby
1997-98	Away	4-Oct-97	1-0	Milosevic (12)	24,196	G.Poll
1997-98	Home	25-Apr-98	1-3	Taylor (57)	38,392	D.Elleray

BRADFORD CITY

Season	Venue	Date	Res	Scorers	Attendance	Referee
1999-00	Home	18-Sep-99	1-0	Dublin (71)	28,083	S.Lodge
1999-00	Away	26-Feb-00	1-1	Merson (38)	18,276	M.Halsey

CHARLTON ATHLETIC

Season	Venue	Date	Res	Scorers	Attendance	Referee
1998-99	Away	21-Dec-98	1-0	OG (3, Rufus)	20,043	G.Willard
1998-99	Home	8-May-99	3-4	Barry (7); Joachim (66, 79)	37,705	M.Riley

CHELSEA

Season	Venue	Date	Res	Scorers	Attendance	Referee
1992-93	Home	2-Sep-92	1-3	Richardson (30)	19,125	P.Foakes
1992-93	Away	13-Feb-93	1-0	Houghton (22)	20,081	M.Peck
1993-94	Home	23-Oct-93	1-0	Atkinson (6)	29,706	D.Allison
1993-94	Away	22-Jan-94	1-1	Saunders (39)	18,348	G.Poll
1994-95	Home	28-Dec-94	3-0	OG (9, Sinclair); Yorke (32); Taylor (82)	32,901	K.Burge
1994-95	Away	15-Apr-95	0-1		17,051	K.Burge
1995-96	Home	14-Oct-95	0-1		34,922	S.Dunn
1995-96	Away	6-Apr-96	2-1	Milosevic (40); Yorke (59)	23,530	G.Poll
1996-97	Away	15-Sep-96	1-1	Townsend (18)	27,729	J.Winter
1996-97	Home	26-Dec-96	0-2		39,339	P.Danson
1997-98	Home	1-Nov-97	0-2		39,372	S.Dunn
1997-98	Away	8-Mar-98	1-0	Joachim (50)	33,018	S.Lodge
1998-99	Away	9-Dec-98	1-2	Hendrie (31)	34,765	A.Wilkie
1998-99	Home	22-Mar-99	0-3		39,217	G.Barber
1999-00	Away	21-Aug-99	0-1		35,071	N.Barry
1999-00	Home	22-Jan-00	0-0		33,704	A.Wilkie

COVENTRY CITY

Season	Venue	Date	Res	Scorers	Attendance	Referee
1992-93	Away	26-Dec-92	0-3		24,245	R.Dilkes
1992-93	Home	10-Apr-93	0-0		38,543	A.Gunn
1993-94	Home	11-Sep-93	0-0		31,181	M.Bodenham
1993-94	Away	6-Mar-94	1-0	Daley (20)	14,323	K.Hackett
1994-95	Away	29-Aug-94	1-0	Yorke (3)	12,218	P.Durkin
1994-95	Home	6-Mar-95	0-0		26,186	G.Poll
1995-96	Away	30-Sep-95	3-0	Yorke (1); Milosevic (84, 87)	21,004	A.Wilkie
1995-96	Home	16-Dec-95	4-1	Johnson (12); Milosevic (48, 64, 80)	28,476	P.Alcock
1996-97	Away	23-Nov-96	2-1	Joachim (29); Staunton (85)	21,340	P.Durkin
1996-97	Home	19-Feb-97	2-1	Yorke (43, 75)	30,409	K.Burge
1997-98	Home	6-Dec-97	3-0	Collymore (21); Hendrie (71); Joachim (84)	33,250	G.Barber
1997-98	Away	11-Apr-98	2-1	Yorke (5, 48)	22,792	D.Gallagher
1998-99	Away	3-Oct-98	2-1	Taylor (29, 39)	22,654	S.Lodge
1998-99	Home	27-Feb-99	1-4	Dublin (55 pen)	38,799	U.Rennie
1999-00	Away	22-Nov-99	1-2	Dublin (41)	20,184	G.Barber
1999-00	Home	11-Mar-00	1-0	Ehiogu (45)	33,177	U.Rennie

CRYSTAL PALACE

Season	Venue	Date	Res	Scorers	Attendance	Referee
1992-93	Home	5-Sep-92	3-0	Yorke (18); Staunton (42); Froggatt (72)	17,120	K.Redfern
1992-93	Away	10-Feb-93	0-1		12,270	K.Redfern
1994-95	Home	27-Aug-94	1-1	Staunton (46)	23,305	J.Worrall
1994-95	Away	4-Apr-95	0-0		12,606	K.Cooper
1997-98	Away	8-Nov-97	1-1	Joachim (86)	21,097	J.Winter
1997-98	Home	14-Mar-98	3-1	Taylor (1); Milosevic (14 pen, 36)	33,781	G.Barber

DERBY COUNTY

Season	Venue	Date	Res	Scorers	Attendance	Referee
1996-97	Home	24-Aug-96	2-0	Joachim (18); Johnson (46 pen)	34,646	P.Alcock
1996-97	Away	12-Apr-97	1-2	Joachim (84)	18,071	P.Danson
1997-98	Home	20-Sep-97	2-1	Yorke (73); Joachim (75)	35,444	J.Winter
1997-98	Away	7-Feb-98	1-0	Yorke (90)	30,251	P.Alcock
1998-99	Home	27-Sep-98	1-0	Merson (15)	38,007	S.Dunn
1998-99	Away	10-Mar-99	1-2	Thompson (44)	26,836	G.Willard
1999-00	Away	26-Dec-99	2-0	Boateng (68); Taylor (78)	33,222	A.Wilkie
1999-00	Home	25-Mar-00	2-0	Carbone (40); Boateng (57)	28,613	P.Alcock

EVERTON

Season	Venue	Date	Res	Scorers	Attendance	Referee
1992-93	Away	25-Aug-92	0-1		22,372	M.Bodenham
1992-93	Home	20-Feb-93	2-1	Cox (12); Barrett (18)	33,913	T.Ward
1993-94	Away	31-Aug-93	1-0	Whittingham (32)	24,067	R.Gifford
1993-94	Home	30-Mar-94	0-0		36,044	R.Gifford
1994-95	Away	20-Aug-94	2-2	Fashanu (68); Saunders (74)	35,544	K.Morton
1994-95	Home	10-Dec-94	0-0		29,678	R.Gifford
1995-96	Home	28-Oct-95	1-0	Yorke (76)	32,792	K.Burge
1995-96	Away	5-May-96	0-1		40,127	R.Hart
1996-97	Away	3-Sep-96	1-0	Ehiogu (62)	39,115	M.Bodenham
1996-97	Home	5-Apr-97	3-1	Milosevic (41); Staunton (50); Yorke (54)	39,339	J.Winter

1997-98	Home	22-Nov-97	2-1	Milosevic (38); Ehiogu (56)	36,389	U.Rennie
1997-98	Away	28-Mar-98	4-1	Joachim (11): Charles (62); Yorke (72 pen, 81)	36,471	N.Barry
1998-99	Away	15-Aug-98	0-0		40,112	A.Wilkie
1998-99	Home	18-Jan-99	3-0	Joachim (40, 51); Merson (78)	32,488	N.Barry
1999-00	Home	11-Aug-99	3-0	Joachim (9); Dublin (57); Taylor (85)	30,337	G.Barber
1999-00	Away	27-Nov-99	0-0		34,750	P.Jones

IPSWICH TOWN

Season	Venue	Date	Res	Scorers	Attendance	Referee
1992-93	Away	15-Aug-92	1-1	Atkinson (84)	16,818	A.Buksh
1992-93	Home	6-Feb-93	2-0	Yorke (32); Saunders (42)	25,395	P.Durkin
1993-94	Away	18-Sep-93	2-1	Saunders (19); Townsend (55)	16,658	R.Dilkes
1993-94	Home	12-Mar-94	0-1		23,732	A.Wilkie
1994-95	Home	10-Sep-94	2-0	Staunton (15); Saunders (85)	22,241	G.Willard
1994-95	Away	1-Apr-95	1-0	OG (90, Swales)	15,710	J.Worrall

LEEDS UNITED

Season	Venue	Date	Res	Scorers	Attendance	Referee
1992-93	Home	19-Aug-92	1-1	Atkinson (77)	29,151	K.Hackett
1992-93	Away	13-Sep-92	1-1	Parker (19)	27,815	J.Worrall
1993-94	Home	6-Feb-94	1-0	Townsend (70)	26,919	J.Borrett
1993-94	Away	16-Mar-94	0-2		33,126	D.Allison
1994-95	Home	2-Jan-95	0-0		35,038	P.Danson
1994-95	Away	29-Apr-95	0-1		32,955	D.Elleray
1995-96	Away	26-Aug-95	0-2		35,086	D.Gallagher
1995-96	Home	3-Feb-96	3-0	Yorke (11, 23); Wright (61)	35,982	R.Hart
1996-97	Home	19-Oct-96	2-0	Yorke (58); Johnson (65)	39,051	G.Poll
1996-97	Away	22-Apr-97	0-0		26,897	G.Barber
1997-98	Home	30-Aug-97	1-0	Yorke (67)	39,027	P.Jones
1997-98	Away	28-Dec-97	1-1	Milosevic (85)	36,287	D.Gallagher
1998-99	Away	19-Sep-98	0-0		33,446	J.Winter
1998-99	Home	17-Feb-99	1-2	Scimeca (76)	37,510	D.Gallagher
1999-00	Away	3-Jan-00	2-1	Southgate (19, 62)	40,027	U.Rennie
1999-00	Home	9-Apr-00	1-0	Joachim (39)	33,889	B.Knight

LEICESTER CITY

Season	Venue	Date	Res	Scorers	Attendance	Referee
1994-95	Away	3-Dec-94	1-1	Whittingham (61)	20,896	M.Bodenham
1994-95	Home	22-Feb-95	4-4	Saunders (8); Staunton (37); Yorke (60); Johnson (65)	30,825	K.Morton
1996-97	Home	16-Nov-96	1-3	Yorke (16)	36,193	D.Elleray
1996-97	Away	5-Mar-97	0-1		20,626	G.Poll
1997-98	Away	9-Aug-97	0-1		20,304	S.Lodge
1997-98	Home	10-Jan-98	1-1	Joachim (87)	36,429	M.Riley
1998-99	Home	24-Oct-98	1-1	Ehiogu (68)	39,241	K.Burge
1998-99	Away	6-Apr-99	2-2	Hendrie (2); Joachim (49)	20,652	S.Lodge
1999-00	Away	25-Sep-99	1-3	Dublin (73)	19,917	J.Winter
1999-00	Home	22-Apr-00	2-2	Thompson (31); Merson (48)	31,229	G.Barber

LIVERPOOL

Season	Venue	Date	Res	Scorers	Attendance	Referee
1992-93	Home	19-Sep-92	4-2	Saunders (44, 66); Atkinson (54); Parker (78)	37,863	P.Don
1992-93	Away	9-Jan-93	2-1	Parker (54); Saunders (64)	40,826	K.Hackett
1993-94	Away	28-Nov-93	1-2	Atkinson (53)	38,484	A.Wilkie
1993-94	Home	7-May-94	2-1	Yorke 2 (65,81)	45,347	K.Burge
1994-95	Away	8-Oct-94	2-3	Whittingham (37); Staunton (90)	32,158	K.Burge
1994-95	Home	6-May-95	2-0	Yorke (25,36)	40,154	R.Hart
1995-96	Home	31-Jan-96	0-2		39,332	R.Dilkes
1995-96	Away	3-Mar-96	0-3		39,508	K.Cooper
1996-97	Away	18-Jan-97	0-3		40,489	R.Dilkes
1996-97	Home	2-Mar-97	1-0	Taylor (83)	39,399	S.Dunn
1997-98	Away	22-Sep-97	0-3		34,843	M.Bodenham
1997-98	Home	28-Feb-98	2-1	Collymore (10, 64)	39,377	G.Poll
1998-99	Home	21-Nov-98	2-4	Dublin (47, 63)	39,241	P.Jones
1998-99	Away	17-Apr-99	1-0	Taylor (33)	44,306	J.Winter
1999-00	Home	2-Oct-99	0-0		39,217	R.Harris
1999-00	Away	15-Mar-00	0-0		43,615	S.Bennett

MANCHESTER CITY

Season	Venue	Date	Res	Scorers	Attendance	Referee
1992-93	Away	19-Dec-92	1-1	Parker (34)	23,525	R.Bigger
1992-93	Home	18-Apr-93	3-1	Saunders (47); Parker (67pen); Houghton (89)	33,108	P.Don
1993-94	Home	22-Feb-94	0-0		19,254	M.Bodenham
1993-94	Away	2-Apr-94	0-3		26,075	P.Durkin
1994-95	Away	31-Dec-94	2-2	OG (54, Brightwell,I); Saunders (59)	22,513	J.Worrall
1994-95	Home	3-May-95	1-1	Eghiogu (9)	30,133	S.Lodge
1995-96	Away	25-Nov-95	0-1		28,027	G.Ashby
1995-96	Home	27-Apr-96	0-1		39,336	D.Elleray

MANCHESTER UNITED

Season	Venue	Date	Res	Scorers	Attendance	Referee
1992-93	Home	7-Nov-92	1-0	Atkinson (12)	39,063	D.Elleray
1992-93	Away	14-Mar-93	1-1	Staunton (53)	36,163	A.Gunn
1993-94	Home	23-Aug-93	1-2	Atkinson (45)	39,624	D.Elleray
1993-94	Away	19-Dec-93	1-3	Cox (90)	44,499	J.Worrall
1994-95	Home	6-Nov-94	1-2	Atkinson (29)	32,136	P.Don
1994-95	Away	4-Feb-95	0-1		43,795	D.Elleray
1995-96	Home	19-Aug-95	3-1	Taylor (14); Draper (27); Yorke (36 pen)	34,655	R.Hart
1995-96	Away	13-Jan-96	0-0		42,667	G.Willard
1996-97	Home	21-Sep-96	0-0		39,339	S.Lodge
1996-97	Away	1-Jan-97	0-0		55,113	D.Elleray
1997-98	Away	15-Dec-97	0-1		55,151	P.Durkin
1997-98	Home	18-Feb-98	0-2		39,372	M.Bodenham
1998-99	Home	5-Dec-98	1-1	Joachim (55)	39,241	M.Riley
1998-99	Away	1-May-99	1-2	Joachim (33)	55,189	K.Burge
1999-00	Away	30-Oct-99	0-3		55,211	A.Wilkie
1999-00	Home	14-May-00	0-1		39,217	P.Durkin

MIDDLESBROUGH

Season	Venue	Date	Res	Scorers	Attendance	Referee
1992-93	Away	26-Sep-92	3-2	Saunders 2 (22, 74); Atkinson (71)	20,905	D.Elleray
1992-93	Home	17-Jan-93	5-1	Parker (26); McGrath (32); Yorke (44); Saunders (58); Teale (68)	19,977	K.Cooper
1995-96	Away	1-Jan-96	2-0	Wright (21); Johnson (40)	28,535	M.Bodenham
1995-96	Home	19-Mar-96	0-0		23,933	P.Alcock
1996-97	Home	30-Nov-96	1-0	Yorke (39 pen)	39,053	G.Willard
1996-97	Away	3-May-97	2-3	Ehiogu (58); Milosevic (76)	30,074	P.Alcock
1998-99	Home	23-Aug-98	3-1	Joachim (6); Charles (52); Thompson (78)	29,559	P.Alcock
1998-99	Away	9-Jan-99	0-0		34,643	U.Rennie
1999-00	Home	28-Aug-99	1-0	Dublin (5)	28,728	M.Halsey
1999-00	Away	14-Feb-00	4-0	Carbone (11); OG (65, Summerbell); Joachim (70, 75)	31,571	A.Wilkie

NEWCASTLE UNITED

Season	Venue	Date	Res	Scorers	Attendance	Referee
1993-94	Home	2-Oct-93	0-2		37,336	P.Durkin
1993-94	Away	27-Apr-94	1-5	Beinlich (10)	32,217	J.Lloyd
1994-95	Home	1-Oct-94	0-2		29,960	D.Gallagher
1994-95	Away	25-Feb-95	1-3	Townsend (40)	34,637	P.Don
1995-96	Home	18-Nov-95	1-1	Johnson (22)	39,167	S.Lodge
1995-96	Away	14-Apr-96	0-1		36,510	M.Bodenham
1996-97	Away	30-Sep-96	3-4	Yorke (5, 59, 69)	36,400	D.Elleray
1996-97	Home	11-Jan-97	2-2	Yorke (39); Milosevic (52)	39,339	G.Poll
1997-98	Away	23-Aug-97	0-1		36,783	G.Willard
1997-98	Home	1-Feb-98	0-1		38,266	S.Lodge
1998-99	Home	9-Sep-98	1-0	Hendrie (63 pen)	39,241	G.Poll
1998-99	Away	30-Jan-99	1-2	Merson (61)	36,766	R.Harris
1999-00	Away	7-Aug-99	1-0	Joachim (75)	36,517	U.Rennie
1999-00	Home	4-Dec-99	0-1		34,531	M.Riley

NORWICH CITY

Season	Venue	Date	Res	Scorers	Attendance	Referee
1992-93	Home	28-Nov-92	2-3	Houghton (45); Parker (46)	28,837	A.Buksh
1992-93	Away	24-Mar-93	0-1		19,528	R.Hart
1993-94	Away	29-Dec-93	2-1	Houghton (55); Saunders (58)	20,650	D.Elleray
1993-94	Home	4-Apr-94	0-0		25,416	M.Bodenham
1994-95	Home	15-Oct-94	1-1	Saunders (62)	22,468	A.Wilkie
1994-95	Away	14-May-95	1-1	Staunton (7)	19,374	K.Cooper

NOTTINGHAM FOREST

Season	Venue	Date	Res	Scorers	Attendance	Referee
1992-93	Home	12-Dec-92	2-1	Regis (33); McGrath (47)	29,015	J.Worrall
1992-93	Away	4-Apr-93	1-0	McGrath (63)	26,742	K.Burge
1994-95	Home	22-Oct-94	0-2		29,217	K.Cooper
1994-95	Away	21-Jan-95	2-1	Fashanu (32); Saunders (68)	24,598	K.Cooper
1995-96	Home	23-Sep-95	1-1	Townsend (67)	33,972	P.Danson
1995-96	Away	10-Dec-95	1-1	Yorke (47)	25,790	P.Durkin
1996-97	Home	2-Nov-96	2-0	Tiler (20); Yorke (65)	35,310	R.Dilkes
1996-97	Away	22-Feb-97	0-0		25,239	G.Barber

1998-99	Away	28-Nov-98	2-2	Joachim (58, 63)	25,753	G.Willard
1998-99	Home	24-Apr-99	2-0	Draper (45); Barry (57)	34,492	P.Durkin (J.Pettitt

after 27 mins - Durkin injured)

OLDHAM ATHLETIC

Season	Venue	Date	Res	Scorers	Attendance	Referee
1992-93	Away	24-Oct-92	1-1	Atkinson (81)	13,457	R.Gifford
1992-93	Home	2-May-93	0-1		37,247	D.Allison
1993-94	Away	25-Sep-93	1-1	Saunders (51)	12,836	H.King (P.Rejer, 46)
1993-94	Home	19-Mar-94	1-2	OG (58, Redmond)	21,214	J.Worrall

QPR

Season	Venue	Date	Res	Scorers	Attendance	Referee
1992-93	Home	1-Nov-92	2-0	Saunders (43); Atkinson (79)	20,140	M.Peck
1992-93	Away	9-May-93	1-2	Daley (38)	18,904	P.Durkin
1993-94	Home	14-Aug-93	4-1	Atkinson (38, 89); Saunders (62); Staunton (90)	32,944	K.Morton
1993-94	Away	4-Dec-93	2-2	Richardson (26); Parker (47)	14,915	K.Hackett
1994-95	Away	29-Oct-94	0-2		16,037	R.Hart
1994-95	Home	14-Jan-95	2-1	Fashanu (7); Ehiogu (76)	26,578	A.Wilkie
1995-96	Away	23-Dec-95	0-1		14,778	A.Wilkie
1995-96	Home	9-Mar-96	4-2	Milosevic (18); Yorke (65, 80); OG (82, Yates)	28,221	A.Wilkie

SHEFFIELD UNITED

Season	Venue	Date	Res	Scorers	Attendance	Referee
1992-93	Away	29-Aug-92	2-0	Parker 2 (2, 86)	18,773	R.Milford
1992-93	Home	27-Jan-93	3-1	McGrath (54); Saunders (58); Richardson (89)	20,266	K.Burge
1993-94	Home	20-Nov-93	1-0	Whittingham (76)	24,686	D.Frampton
1993-94	Away	16-Apr-94	2-1	Richardson (23); Fenton (25)	18,402	G.Poll

SHEFFIELD WEDNESDAY

Season	Venue	Date	Res	Scorers	Attendance	Referee
1992-93	Away	5-Dec-92	2-1	Atkinson (19, 67)	29,964	R.Hart
1992-93	Home	20-Mar-93	2-0	Yorke 2 (2, 56)	38,024	R.Milford
1993-94	Away	18-Aug-93	0-0		28,450	P.Foakes
1993-94	Home	8-Dec-93	2-2	Cox (29); Saunders (53pen)	20,304	P.Foakes
1994-95	Home	27-Nov-94	1-1	Atkinson (15)	25,082	G.Poll
1994-95	Away	18-Feb-95	2-1	Saunders (26,44)	24,063	D.Gallagher
1995-96	Home	6-Mar-96	3-2	Milosevic (61, 62); Townsend (75)	27,893	D.Elleray
1995-96	Away	16-Mar-96	0-2		22,964	P.Jones
1996-97	Away	17-Aug-96	1-2	Johnson (88)	26,861	R.Dilkes
1996-97	Home	29-Jan-97	0-1		26,726	P.Alcock
1997-98	Home	27-Sep-97	2-2	Stanton (32);Taylor (49)	32,044	N.Barry
1997-98	Away	2-May-98	3-1	Yorke (21); Hendrie (25); Joachim (50)	34,177	M.Bodenham
1998-99	Away	29-Aug-98	1-0	Joachim (37)	25,989	K.Burge
1998-99	Home	28-Dec-98	2-1	Southgate (7); Ehiogu (85)	39,217	G.Barber
1999-00	Home	18-Dec-99	2-1	Merson (69); Taylor (82)	23,885	S.Bennett
1999-00	Away	5-Apr-00	1-0	Thompson (90)	18,136	G.Poll

SOUTHAMPTON

Season	Venue	Date	Res	Scorers	Attendance	Referee
1992-93	Home	22-Aug-92	1-1	Atkinson (64)	17,894	K.Morton
1992-93	Away	30-Jan-93	0-2		19,087	P.Wright
1993-94	Home	24-Nov-93	0-2		16,180	K.Morton
1993-94	Away	30-Apr-94	1-4	OG (58, Charlton)	18,803	S.Lodge
1994-95	Home	24-Aug-94	1-1	Saunders (32)	24,179	P.Don
1994-95	Away	19-Dec-94	1-2	Houghton (80)	13,874	S.Lodge
1995-96	Away	20-Nov-95	1-0	Johnson (3)	13,582	D.Elleray
1995-96	Home	8-Apr-96	3-0	Taylor (64)	34,059	P.Danson
1996-97	Away	7-Dec-96	1-0	Townsend (34)	15,232	S.Lodge
1996-97	Home	11-May-97	1-0	OG (12, Dryden)	39,339	G.Willard
1997-98	Home	20-Dec-97	1-1	Taylor (64)	29,343	D.Elleray
1997-98	Away	18-Apr-98	2-1	Hendrie (6); Yorke (60)	15,238	A.Wilkie
1998-99	Away	14-Nov-98	4-1	Dublin (3, 56, 85); Merson	15,242	N.Barry
1998-99	Home	10-Apr-99	3-0	Draper (13); Joachim (66); Dublin (89)	32,203	N.Barry
1999-00	Home	6-Nov-99	0-1		26,474	A.D'Urso
1999-00	Away	18-Mar-00	0-2		15,218	M.Riley

SUNDERLAND

Season	Venue	Date	Res	Scorers	Attendance	Referee
1996-97	Away	26-Oct-96	0-1		21,059	P.Alcock
1996-97	Home	1-Feb-97	1-0	Milosevic (37)	32,491	S.Lodge
1999-00	Away	18-Oct-99	1-2	Dublin (46)	41,045	D.Elleray
1999-00	Home	29-Apr-00	1-1	Barry (60)	33,949	A.D'Urso

SWINDON TOWN

Season	Venue	Date	Res	Scorers	Attendance	Referee
1993-94	Away	30-Oct-93	2-1	Teale (43); Atkinson (68)	16,322	K.Burge
1993-94	Home	12-Feb-94	5-0	Saunders (31, 66pen, 84pen); Froggatt (55); Richardson (73)	27,637	R.Hart

TOTTENHAM HOTSPUR

Season	Venue	Date	Res	Scorers	Attendance	Referee
1992-93	Away	21-Nov-92	0-0		32,852	J.Borrett
1992-93	Home	10-Mar-93	0-0		37,727	K.Hackett
1993-94	Home	28-Aug-93	1-0	Staunton (71pen)	32,498	K.Cooper
1993-94	Away	2-Mar-94	1-1	Parker (9)	17,452	K.Morton
1994-95	Away	19-Nov-94	4-3	Atkinson (8); Fenton (20,26); Saunders (90)	26,899	P.Durkin
1994-95	Home	25-Jan-95	1-0	Saunders (18)	40,017	R.Hart
1995-96	Away	23-Aug-95	1-0	Ehiogu (69)	26,726	S.Dunn
1995-96	Home	21-Jan-96	2-1	McGrath (23); Yorke (79)	35,666	G.Poll
1996-97	Away	12-Oct-96	0-1		32,847	P.Jones
1996-97	Home	19-Apr-97	1-1	Yorke (81)	39,339	M.Bodenham
1997-98	Away	27-Aug-97	2-3	Yorke (27); Collymore (87)	26,317	M.Riley
1997-98	Home	26-Dec-97	4-1	Draper (38, 68); Collymore (81, 88)	38,644	A.Wilkie
1998-99	Home	7-Nov-98	3-2	Dublin (31, 35); Collymore (48)	39,241	R.Harris
1998-99	Away	13-Mar-99	0-1		35,963	P.Jones
1999-00	Home	29-Dec-99	1-1	Taylor (75)	39,217	G.Barber
1999-00	Away	15-Apr-00	4-2	Dublin (62 pen, 69); Carbone (70); Wright (74)	35,304	R.Harris

WATFORD

Season	Venue	Date	Res	Scorers	Attendance	Referee
1999-00	Away	24-Aug-99	1-0	Delaney (68)	19,161	S.Bennett
1999-00	Home	5-Feb-00	4-0	Stone (47); Merson (57, 59); Walker (81)	27,647	P.Jones

WEST HAM UNITED

Season	Venue	Date	Res	Scorers	Attendance	Referee
1993-94	Away	16-Oct-93	0-0		20,416	S.Lodge
1993-94	Home	15-Jan-94	3-1	Richardson (15); Atkinson (43, 68)	28,869	S.Lodge
1994-95	Away	17-Sep-94	0-1		18,326	S.Lodge
1994-95	Home	18-Mar-95	0-2		28,682	M.Bodenham
1995-96	Away	4-Nov-95	4-1	Milosevic (33, 89); Johnson (49); Yorke (54)	23,637	P.Jones
1995-96	Home	17-Apr-96	1-1	McGrath (27)	26,768	S.Dunn
1996-97	Away	4-Dec-96	2-0	Ehiogu (37); Yorke (73)	19,105	M.Riley
1996-97	Home	15-Mar-97	0-0		35,995	D.Elleray
1997-98	Away	29-Nov-97	1-2	Yorke (46)	24,976	P.Alcock
1997-98	Home	4-Apr-98	2-0	Joachim (75); Milosevic (83)	39,372	S.Dunn
1998-99	Away	17-Oct-98	0-0		26,002	P.Alcock
1998-99	Home	2-Apr-99	0-0		36,813	G.Willard
1999-00	Home	16-Aug-99	2-2	Dublin (5,52)	26,250	M.Riley
1999-00	Away	15-Jan-00	1-1	Taylor (24)	24,237	G.Poll

WIMBLEDON

Season	Venue	Date	Res	Scorers	Attendance	Referee
1992-93	Away	3-Oct-92	3-2	Saunders (5, 29); Atkinson (77)	6,849	S.Lodge
1992-93	Home	27-Feb-93	1-0	Yorke (79)	34,496	S.Lodge
1993-94	Away	21-Aug-93	2-2	Richardson (18); Staunton (82)	7,564	J.Borrett
1993-94	Home	11-Dec-93	0-1		17,940	A.Gunn
1994-95	Away	9-Nov-94	3-4	Parker (19); Saunders (38,50)	6,221	D.Elleray
1994-95	Home	11-Feb-95	7-1	OG (12, Reeves); Johnson (22,26,38); Saunders (48, 66 pen); Yorke (83)	23,982	B.Hill
1995-96	Home	16-Sep-95	2-0	Draper (7); Taylor (47)	26,928	D.Elleray
1995-96	Away	24-Feb-96	3-3	OG (33, Reeves); Yorke (49 pen); OG (58, Cunningham)	12,193	J.Winter
1996-97	Home	22-Dec-96	5-0	Yorke (38, 86); Milosevic (41, 75); Taylor (61)	28,875	S.Dunn
1996-97	Away	9-Apr-97	2-0	Milosevic (26); Wright (78)	9,015	R.Dilkes
1997-98	Home	18-Oct-97	1-2	Taylor (44)	32,087	K.Burge
1997-98	Away	21-Feb-98	1-2	Milosevic (41)	13,131	G.Ashby
1998-99	Home	12-Sep-98	2-0	Merson (45); Taylor (57)	32,959	D.Elleray
1998-99	Away	21-Feb-99	0-0		15,582	P.Alcock
1999-00	Home	23-Oct-99	1-1	Dublin (35)	27,160	U.Rennie
1999-00	Away	6-May-00	2-2	Hendrie (54); Dublin (74)	19,188	M.Halsey

BARNSLEY

INTRODUCTION

Formed in 1887 by the Rev. Preedy as Barnsley St Peter, a
reflection of the church connection. St Peter was dropped
ten years later, a year before Barnsley were elected to the
Second Division of the Football League. The early years
were unremarkable save the fact that the FA Cup was won in
1912, two years after they had been beaten finalists.
The club remained in the lower reaches of the League,
dropping down to the old Fourth Division for three seasons
from 1965-68. Division One status was achieved in 1992
and the club completed a remarkable rise into the
Premiership at the end of 1997. Relegation followed
immediately, however.

Ground: Oakwell Ground, Barnsley,
            South Yorkshire, S71 1ET
Nickname: The Tykes or Reds
Internet: www.barnsleyfc.co.uk

HONOURS

Football League Div 1:   Runners-up 1996-97
Football League Div 3N: Champions 1933-34, 1938-39,
                         1954-55 ;Runners-up 1953-54;
Football League Div 3:   Runners-up 1980-81;
Football League Div 4:   Runners-up 1967-68
                         Promoted 1978-79.
FA Cup: Winners 1911-12; Runners-up
                         1909-10.

EUROPEAN RECORD
Never qualified.

FAPL RECORD SUMMARY

Most Total:	REDFEARN, Neil	37
Most Starts:	REDFEARN, Neil	37
Most Subs:	HENDRIE, John	13
Most SNU:	LEESE, Lars	23
Most PS:	LIDDELL, Andy	11
Most Goals:	REDFEARN, Neil	10
Most Yel:	BOSANCIC, Jovo	8
Most Red:	BARNARD, Darren	1

PLAYING RECORD – SEASON TOTALS

Season	Pn	P	W	D	L	F	A	Pts
1997-98	19	38	10	5	23	37	82	35
Totals		38	10	5	23	37	82	35

PLAYING RECORD – HOME TOTALS

Season	Pn	P	W	D	L	F	A	Pts
1997-98	19	19	7	4	8	25	35	25
Totals		19	7	4	8	25	35	25

PLAYING RECORD – AWAY TOTALS

Season	Pn	P	W	D	L	F	A	Pts
1997-98	19	19	3	1	15	12	47	10
Barnsley		19	3	1	15	12	47	10

HIGHEST HOME ATTENDANCES

	Attendance	Opponents	Date	Season
1	18,694	Manchester U.	10-May-98	1997-98
2	18,692	Sheffield W.	11-Apr-98	1997-98
3	18,692	Tottenham H.	18-Apr-98	1997-98
4	18,691	Arsenal	25-Apr-98	1997-98
5	18,690	Leeds U.	29-Nov-97	1997-98

LOWEST HOME ATTENDANCES

	Attendance	Opponents	Date	Season
1	17,102	Wimbledon	28-Feb-98	1997-98
2	17,463	Coventry C.	20-Oct-97	1997-98
3	17,819	Crystal P.	17-Jan-98	1997-98
4	18,170	Chelsea	24-Aug-97	1997-98
5	18,368	Southampton	14-Mar-98	1997-98

TOP SCORER – SEASON BY SEASON

Season	Player	Goals
1997-98	Redfearn	10

PLAYERS WITH MOST PREMIERSHIP APPEARANCES

Tot	Player	St	Sb	Gls
37	REDFEARN, Neil	37	0	10
35	BARNARD, Darren	33	2	2
35	EADEN, Nicky	32	3	0
35	MOSES, Adrian	32	3	0
33	BULLOCK, Martin	23	10	0
30	WATSON, David	30	0	0
29	WARD, Ashley	28	1	8
26	DE ZEEUW, Arjan	26	0	0
26	LIDDELL, Andy	13	13	1
26	SHERIDAN, Darren	20	6	0
25	TINKLER, Eric	21	4	2
23	HRISTOV, Georgi	11	12	4
20	HENDRIE, John	7	13	1
20	MARCELLE, Clint	9	11	0

CLUB-BY-CLUB RESULTS

ARSENAL

Season	Venue	Date	Res	Scorers	Attendance	Referee
1997-98	Away	4-Oct-97	0-5		38,049	P.Jones
1997-98	Home	25-Apr-98	0-2		18,691	M.Riley

ASTON VILLA

Season	Venue	Date	Res	Scorers	Attendance	Referee
1997-98	Home	13-Sep-97	0-3		18,649	G.Barber
1997-98	Away	11-Mar-98	1-0	Ward (17)	29,519	P.Jones

BLACKBURN ROVERS

Season	Venue	Date	Res	Scorers	Attendance	Referee
1997-98	Home	1-Nov-97	1-1	Bosanacic (79)	18,665	G.Poll
1997-98	Away	31-Mar-98	1-2	Hristov (68)	24,179	M.Reed

BOLTON WANDERERS

Season	Venue	Date	Res	Scorers	Attendance	Referee
1997-98	Home	27-Aug-97	2-1	Tinkler (12); Hristov (47)	18,661	D.Gallagher
1997-98	Away	26-Dec-97	1-1	Hristov (20)	35,000	S.Dunn

CHELSEA

Season	Venue	Date	Res	Scorers	Attendance	Referee
1997-98	Home	24-Aug-97	0-6		18,170	G.Poll
1997-98	Away	31-Jan-98	0-2		34,442	J.Winter

COVENTRY CITY

Season	Venue	Date	Res	Scorers	Attendance	Referee
1997-98	Home	20-Oct-97	2-0	Ward (11); Redfearn (66 pen)	17,463	P.Alcock
1997-98	Away	21-Feb-98	0-1		20,265	A.Wilkie

CRYSTAL PALACE

Season	Venue	Date	Res	Scorers	Attendance	Referee
1997-98	Away	12-Aug-97	1-0	Redfearn (56)	21,547	N.Barry
1997-98	Home	17-Jan-98	1-0	Ward (26)	17,819	M.Reed

DERBY COUNTY

Season	Venue	Date	Res	Scorers	Attendance	Referee
1997-98	Away	30-Aug-97	0-1		27,232	P.Durkin
1997-98	Home	28-Dec-97	1-0	Ward (67)	18,686	G.Barber

EVERTON

Season	Venue	Date	Res	Scorers	Attendance	Referee
1997-98	Away	20-Sep-97	2-4	Redfearn (32); Barnard (78)	32,659	G.Ashby
1997-98	Home	7-Feb-98	2-2	Fjortoft (24); Barnard (63)	18,672	M.Bodenham

LEEDS UNITED

Season	Venue	Date	Res	Scorers	Attendance	Referee
1997-98	Home	29-Nov-97	2-3	Liddell (8); Ward (28)	18,690	M.Reed
1997-98	Away	4-Apr-98	1-2	Hristov (44)	37,749	K.Burge

LEICESTER CITY

Season	Venue	Date	Res	Scorers	Attendance	Referee
1997-98	Home	27-Sep-97	0-2		18,660	G.Poll
1997-98	Away	2-May-98	0-1		21,293	D.Gallagher

LIVERPOOL

Season	Venue	Date	Res	Scorers	Attendance	Referee
1997-98	Away	22-Nov-97	1-0	Ward (35)	41,001	J.Winter
1997-98	Home	28-Mar-98	2-3	Redfearn (37, 85 pen)	18,684	G.Willard

MANCHESTER UNITED

Season	Venue	Date	Res	Scorers	Attendance	Referee
1997-98	Away	25-Oct-97	0-7		55,142	M.Riley
1997-98	Home	10-May-98	0-2		18,694	P.Durkin

NEWCASTLE UNITED

Season	Venue	Date	Res	Scorers	Attendance	Referee
1997-98	Home	13-Dec-97	2-2	Redfearn (9); Hendrie (75)	18,687	P.Alcock
1997-98	Away	13-Apr-98	1-2	Fjortoft (50)	36,534	S.Dunn

SHEFFIELD WEDNESDAY

Season	Venue	Date	Res	Scorers	Attendance	Referee
1997-98	Away	8-Dec-97	1-2	Redfearn (29)	29,086	G.Willard
1997-98	Home	11-Apr-98	2-1	Ward (65); Fjortoft (71)	18,692	P.Alcock

SOUTHAMPTON

Season	Venue	Date	Res	Scorers	Attendance	Referee
1997-98	Away	8-Nov-97	1-4	Bosanacic (37 pen)	15,018	G.Ashby
1997-98	Home	14-Mar-98	4-3	Ward (17); S.Jones (32); Fjortoft (42); Redfearn (57 pen)	18,368	G.Ashby

TOTTENHAM HOTSPUR

Season	Venue	Date	Res	Scorers	Attendance	Referee
1997-98	Away	20-Dec-97	0-3		28,232	M.Reed
1997-98	Home	18-Apr-98	1-1	Redfearn (19)	18,692	M.Bodenham

WEST HAM UNITED

Season	Venue	Date	Res	Scorers	Attendance	Referee
1997-98	Home	9-Aug-97	1-2	Redfearn (9)	18,667	A.Wilkie
1997-98	Away	10-Jan-98	0-6		23,714	N.Barry

WIMBLEDON

Season	Venue	Date	Res	Scorers	Attendance	Referee
1997-98	Away	23-Sep-97	1-4	Tinkler (41)	7,976	J.Winter
1997-98	Home	28-Feb-98	2-1	Fjortoft (25, 63)	17,102	G.Barber

BLACKBURN ROVERS

INTRODUCTION
Founded in 1875 by local school-leavers. Used several pitches, including Alexander Meadows, the East Lancashire Cricket Club ground, and became known nationally for their FA Cup exploits, eclipsing the record of Blackburn Olympic, the first club to take the trophy away from London. Three consecutive wins in the 1880s, when in the finals Queen's Park (twice) and West Bromwich Albion were beaten, brought recognition by way of a special shield awarded by the FA to commemorate the achievement. Founder members of the Football League in 1888, the club settled at Ewood Park in 1890, purchasing the ground outright in 1893-94. Premier League founder members 1992 and champions in 1994-95. Relegated to Football League at end of 1998-99.

Ground: Ewood Park, Blackburn, BB2 4JF
Nickname: Blue and Whites
Internet: www.rovers.co.uk

HONOURS
FA Premier League:	Champions 1994-95; Runners-up 1993-94
Football League Div 1:	Champions 1911-12, 1913-14;
Football League Div 2:	Champions 1938-39; Runners-up 1957-58;
Football League Div 3:	Champions 1974-75; Runners-up 1979-1980
FA Cup:	Winners 1884, 1885, 1886, 1890, 1891, 1928; Runners-up 1882, 1960
Full Members' Cup:	Win ners 1986-87.

EUROPEAN RECORD
Champions' League (1):	95-96
Cup-Winners' Cup (0):	–
UEFA Cup (2)	94-95 (1), 98-99 (1)

FAPL RECORD SUMMARY
Most Total:	SHERWOOD, Tim	235
Most Starts:	SHERWOOD, Tim	232
Most Subs:	WARHURST, Paul	27
Most SNU:	MIMMS, Bobby	92
Most PS:	RIPLEY, Stuart	51
Most Goals:	SHEARER, Alan	112
Most Yel:	SHERWOOD, Tim	36
Most Red:	WILCOX, Jason	5

PLAYING RECORD – SEASON TOTALS
Season	Pn	P	W	D	L	F	A	Pts
1992-93	4	42	20	11	11	68	46	71
1993-94	2	42	25	9	8	63	36	84
1994-95	1	42	27	8	7	80	39	89
1995-96	7	38	18	7	13	61	47	61
1996-97	13	38	9	15	14	42	43	42
1997-98	6	38	16	10	12	57	52	58
1998-99	19	38	7	14	17	38	52	35
Totals		278	122	74	82	409	315	440

PLAYING RECORD – HOME TOTALS
Season	Pn	P	W	D	L	F	A	Pts
1992-93	4	21	13	4	4	38	18	43
1993-94	2	21	14	5	2	31	11	47
1994-95	1	21	17	2	2	54	21	53
1995-96	7	19	14	2	3	44	19	44
1996-97	13	19	8	4	7	28	23	28
1997-98	6	19	11	4	4	40	26	37
1998-99	19	19	6	5	8	21	24	23
Totals		139	83	26	30	256	142	275

PLAYING RECORD – AWAY TOTALS
Season	Pn	P	W	D	L	F	A	Pts
1992-93	4	21	7	7	7	30	28	28
1993-94	2	21	11	4	6	32	25	37
1994-95	1	21	10	6	5	26	18	36
1995-96	7	19	4	5	10	17	28	17
1996-97	13	19	1	11	7	14	20	14
1997-98	6	19	5	6	8	17	26	21
1998-99	19	19	1	9	9	17	28	12
Totals		139	39	48	52	153	173	165

HIGHEST HOME ATTENDANCES
	Attendance	Opponents	Date	Season
1	30,895	Liverpool	24-Feb-96	1995-96
2	30,867	Arsenal	25-Oct-98	1998-99
3	30,717	Newcastle U.	8-Apr-96	1995-96
4	30,547	Manchester U.	6-Apr-98	1997-98
5	30,545	Newcastle U.	8-May-95	1994-95

LOWEST HOME ATTENDANCES
	Attendance	Opponents	Date	Season
1	13,566	Southampton	9-Mar-93	1992-93
2	14,041	Middlesbrough	20-Mar-93	1992-93
3	14,071	Ipswich T.	12-Apr-93	1992-93
4	14,163	Crystal P.	2-Feb-93	1992-93
5	14,260	Norwich C.	18-Aug-93	1993-94

BLACKBURN ROVERS

TOP SCORER – SEASON BY SEASON

Season	Player	Goals
1992-93	Shearer	16
1993-94	Shearer	31
1994-95	Shearer	34
1995-96	Shearer	31
1996-97	Sutton	11
1997-98	Sutton	18
1998-99	Gallacher	5

PLAYERS WITH MOST PREMIERSHIP APPEARANCES

Tot	Player	St	Sb	Gls
235	SHERWOOD, Tim	232	3	26
204	HENDRY, Colin	203	1	8
192	WILCOX, Jason	177	15	26
186	RIPLEY, Stuart	171	15	13
177	FLOWERS, Tim	175	2	0

159	BERG, Henning	154	5	4
139	GALLAGHER, Kevin	129	10	46
138	KENNA, Jeff	137	1	1
138	SHEARER, Alan	132	6	112
130	LE SAUX, Graeme	128	2	7
130	SUTTON, Chris	125	5	47
110	NEWELL, Mike	95	15	22
90	McKINLAY, Billy	76	14	3
84	ATKINS, Mark	62	22	12
74	MAY, David	74	0	2
72	FLITCROFT, Garry	66	6	5
70	HENCHOZ, Stephane	70	0	0

CLUB-BY-CLUB RESULTS

ARSENAL

Season	Venue	Date	Res	Scorers	Attendance	Referee
1992-93	Home	18-Aug-92	1-0	Shearer (84)	16,454	J.Worrall
1992-93	Away	12-Sep-92	1-0	Newell (71)	28,643	M.Reed
1993-94	Home	1-Sep-93	1-1	Gallacher (37)	14,410	D.Allison
1993-94	Away	25-Feb-94	0-1		35,030	J.Worrall
1994-95	Away	31-Aug-94	0-0		37,629	K.Morton
1994-95	Home	8-Mar-95	3-1	Shearer (4,48 pen); Le Saux (18)	23,452	A.Wilkie
1995-96	Away	26-Nov-95	0-0		37,695	G.Poll
1995-96	Home	27-Apr-96	1-1	Gallacher (12)	29,834	K.Cooper
1996-97	Home	12-Oct-96	0-2		24,303	S.Dunn
1996-97	Away	19-Apr-97	1-1	Flitcroft (89)	38,086	M.Riley
1997-98	Away	13-Dec-97	3-1	Wilcox (57); Gallacher (65): Sherwood (89)	38,147	G.Willard
1997-98	Home	13-Apr-98	1-4	Gallagher (51)	28,212	M.Bodenham
1998-99	Home	25-Oct-98	1-2	Johnson (64)	30,867	D.Gallagher
1998-99	Away	6-Apr-99	0-1		37,762	G.Poll

ASTON VILLA

Season	Venue	Date	Res	Scorers	Attendance	Referee
1992-93	Away	19-Oct-92	0-0		30,398	H.King
1992-93	Home	21-Apr-93	3-0	Newell (9, 40); Gallacher (15)	15,127	J.Worrall
1993-94	Away	1-Jan-94	1-0	Shearer (38)	40,903	R.Dilkes
1993-94	Home	11-Apr-94	1-0	Shearer (11)	19,287	D.Allison
1994-95	Home	24-Sep-94	3-1	Shearer (17 pen,72); Sutton (56)	22,694	M.Bodenham
1994-95	Away	4-Mar-95	1-0	Hendry (12)	40,114	R.Gifford
1995-96	Home	9-Sep-95	1-1	Shearer (82)	27,084	R.Dilkes
1995-96	Away	28-Feb-96	0-2		28,008	S.Lodge
1996-97	Away	20-Aug-96	0-1		32,257	A.Wilkie
1996-97	Home	22-Mar-97	0-2	Johnson (64)	24,274	A.Wilkie

1997-98	Away	13-Aug-97	4-0	Sutton (21, 25, 41); Gallacher (71)	37,112	P.Alcock
1997-98	Home	17-Jan-98	5-0	Sherwood (22);Gallacher (30, 54, 69); Ripley (81)	24,834	K.Burge
1998-99	Home	26-Dec-98	2-1	Gallacher (44); Sherwood (88)	27,536	D.Gallagher
1998-99	Away	6-Feb-99	3-1	OG (32, Southgate); Ward (62); Dunn (64)	37,404	K.Burge

BARNSLEY

Season	Venue	Date	Res	Scorers	Attendance	Referee
1997-98	Away	1-Nov-97	1-1	Sherwood (30)	18,665	G.Poll
1997-98	Home	31-Mar-98	2-1	Dahlin (9); Gallacher (87)	24,179	M.Reed

BOLTON WANDERERS

Season	Venue	Date	Res	Scorers	Attendance	Referee
1995-96	Away	26-Aug-95	1-2	Holmes (61)	20,253	K.Burge
1995-96	Home	3-Feb-96	3-1	Shearer (12, 83, 90)	30,419	P.Alcock
1997-98	Home	6-Dec-97	3-1	Gallagher (3); Sutton (20); Wilcox (90)	29,503	M.Riley
1997-98	Away	11-Apr-98	1-2	Duff (51)	25,000	M.Riley

CHARLTON ATHLETIC

Season	Venue	Date	Res	Scorers	Attendance	Referee
1998-99	Home	5-Dec-98	1-0	Davies (75)	22,568	G.Poll
1998-99	Away	1-May-99	0-0		20,041	G.Willard

CHELSEA

Season	Venue	Date	Res	Scorers	Attendance	Referee
1992-93	Away	26-Aug-92	0-0		19,575	R.Bigger
1992-93	Home	21-Feb-93	2-0	Newell (8, 63)	14,780	D.Allison
1993-94	Away	14-Aug-93	2-1	Ripley (63); Newell (78)	29,189	A.Gunn
1993-94	Home	5-Dec-93	2-0	La Saux (15); Shearer (90)	16,756	G.Ashby
1994-95	Away	18-Sep-94	2-1	OG (27, Johnsen); Sutton (66)	17,513	P.Durkin
1994-95	Home	18-Mar-95	2-1	Shearer (16); Sherwood (37)	25,490	P.Danson
1995-96	Home	28-Oct-95	3-0	Sherwood (39); Shearer (49); Newell (57)	27,733	P.Durkin
1995-96	Away	5-May-96	3-2	Sherwood (37); McKinlay (48); Fenton (59)	28,436	M.Bodenham
1996-97	Home	16-Nov-96	1-1	Gallacher (56)	27,229	G.Barber
1996-97	Away	5-Mar-97	1-1	Pedersen (62)	25,784	G.Barber
1997-98	Home	22-Nov-97	1-0	Croft (11)	27,683	S.Lodge
1997-98	Away	29-Apr-98	1-0	Gallacher (48)	33,311	P.Alcock
1998-99	Home	21-Sep-98	3-4	Sutton (22, 79 pen); Perez (57)	23,113	P.Jones
1998-99	Away	17-Feb-99	1-1	Ward (83)	34,382	U.Rennie

COVENTRY CITY

Season	Venue	Date	Res	Scorers	Attendance	Referee
1992-93	Away	29-Aug-92	2-0	Shearer (69 pen); Atkins (79)	14,541	R.Lewis
1992-93	Home	26-Jan-93	2-5	Newell (13); Hendry (71)	15,215	K.Redfern
1993-94	Home	23-Nov-93	2-1	Shearer (32, 63)	16,376	K.Burge
1993-94	Away	2-May-94	1-2	Le Saux (29)	16,646	P.Don
1994-95	Home	27-Aug-94	4-0	Sutton (67,74,88); Wilcox (77)	21,657	G.Poll
1994-95	Away	11-Mar-95	1-1	Shearer (79)	18,547	T.Holbrook
1995-96	Home	23-Sep-95	5-1	Shearer (8, 60, 67); Hendry (23); Pearce (75)	24,382	K.Cooper
1995-96	Away	9-Dec-95	0-5		13,409	S.Dunn
1996-97	Away	28-Sep-96	0-0		17,032	J.Winter

1996-97	Home	11-Jan-97	4-0	Sutton (16, 34); Gallacher (30); Donis (76)	24,055	P.Durkin
1997-98	Home	28-Sep-97	0-0		19,086	P.Jones
1997-98	Away	2-May-98	0-2		18,794	S.Lodge
1998-99	Home	7-Nov-98	1-2	Sherwood (73)	23,779	P.Durkin
1998-99	Away	13-Mar-99	1-1	Wilcox (67)	19,701	C.Dunn

CRYSTAL PALACE

Season	Venue	Date	Res	Scorers	Attendance	Referee
1992-93	Away	15-Aug-92	3-3	Ripley (42); Shearer 2 (66, 81)	17,086	R.Milford
1992-93	Home	2-Feb-93	1-2	Wegerle (16)	14,163	P.Wright
1994-95	Away	31-Dec-94	1-0	Sherwood (66)	14,232	D.Elleray
1994-95	Home	20-Apr-95	2-1	Kenna (47); Gallacher (51)	28,005	B.Hill
1997-98	Away	30-Aug-97	2-1	Sutton (23); Gallacher (32)	20,849	K.Burge
1997-98	Home	28-Dec-97	2-2	Gallagher (26);Sutton (77)	23,872	P.Jones

DERBY COUNTY

Season	Venue	Date	Res	Scorers	Attendance	Referee
1996-97	Home	9-Sep-96	1-2	Sutton (11)	19,214	S.Lodge
1996-97	Away	28-Dec-96	0-0		17,847	D.Elleray
1997-98	Home	9-Aug-97	1-0	Gallacher (21)	23,557	D.Elleray
1997-98	Away	11-Jan-98	1-3	Sutton (87)	27,823	G.Poll
1998-99	Home	15-Aug-98	0-0		24,007	S.Lodge
1998-99	Away	16-Jan-99	0-1		27,386	D.Gallagher

EVERTON

Season	Venue	Date	Res	Scorers	Attendance	Referee
1992-93	Home	15-Sep-92	2-3	Shearer (12 pen, 74)	19,563	D.Allison
1992-93	Away	3-Mar-93	1-2	May (42)	18,086	P.Foakes
1993-94	Home	29-Dec-93	2-0	Shearer (24, 42)	22,061	T.Holbrook
1993-94	Away	4-Apr-94	3-0	Newell (27, 81); Wilcox (60)	27,463	K.Morton
1994-95	Home	10-Sep-94	3-0	Shearer (17,60 pen); Wilcox (43)	26,538	R.Dilkes
1994-95	Away	1-Apr-95	2-1	Sutton (13 secs); Shearer (6)	37,905	D.Gallagher
1995-96	Away	5-Nov-95	0-1		30,097	A.Wilkie
1995-96	Home	30-Mar-96	0-3		29,468	J.Winter
1996-97	Home	21-Sep-96	1-1	Donis (31)	27,091	D.Elleray
1996-97	Away	1-Jan-97	2-0	Sherwood (18); Sutton (32)	30,427	G.Barber
1997-98	Home	8-Nov-97	3-2	Gallacher (37); Duff (81); Sherwood (85)	25,397	P.Alcock
1997-98	Away	14-Mar-98	0-1		33,423	G.Willard
1998-99	Away	27-Sep-98	0-0		36,404	M.Riley
1998-99	Home	10-Mar-99	1-2	Ward (2)	27,219	P.Alcock

IPSWICH TOWN

Season	Venue	Date	Res	Scorers	Attendance	Referee
1992-93	Away	28-Dec-92	1-2	Wegerle (72)	21,431	A.Gunn
1992-93	Home	12-Apr-93	2-1	Ripley (6); OG (43, Whelan)	14,071	K.Hackett
1993-94	Away	27-Nov-93	0-1		14,436	P.Durkin
1993-94	Home	7-May-94	0-0		20,633	J.Lloyd
1994-95	Away	19-Nov-94	3-1	Sutton (8); Sherwood (41); Shearer (70)	17,329	K.Burge
1994-95	Home	28-Jan-95	4-1	Shearer (3,29,90 pen); Sherwood (49)	21,325	G.Poll

LEEDS UNITED

Season	Venue	Date	Res	Scorers	Attendance	Referee
1992-93	Home	26-Dec-92	3-1	Wilcox (8); Shearer (45, 58)	19,910	S.Lodge
1992-93	Away	10-Apr-93	2-5	Gallacher (72); Atkins (85)	31,791	D.Elleray
1993-94	Away	23-Oct-93	3-3	Shearer (25, 46, 75)	37,827	K.Morton
1993-94	Home	23-Jan-94	2-1	Shearer (11, 90)	17,475	V.Callow
1994-95	Home	1-Feb-95	1-1	Shearer (6 pen)	28,561	R.Gifford
1994-95	Away	15-Apr-95	1-1	Hendry (44)	39,426	G.Poll
1995-96	Away	1-Jan-96	0-0		31,285	R.Dilkes
1995-96	Home	13-Mar-96	1-0	Fenton (47)	23,358	S.Dunn
1996-97	Home	3-Sep-96	0-1		23,226	L.Dilkes
1996-97	Away	7-Apr-97	0-0		27,264	M.Reed
1997-98	Home	14-Sep-97	3-4	Gallacher (8); Sutton (16 pen); Dahlin (33)	21,956	S.Dunn
1997-98	Away	11-Mar-98	0-4		32,933	D.Elleray
1998-99	Away	24-Aug-98	0-1		30,652	D.Gallagher
1998-99	Home	9-Jan-99	1-0	Gillespie (22)	27,620	R.Harris

LEICESTER CITY

Season	Venue	Date	Res	Scorers	Attendance	Referee
1994-95	Home	23-Aug-94	3-0	Sutton (18); Berg (59); Shearer (73)	21,050	K.Burge
1994-95	Away	17-Dec-94	0-0		20,559	P.Don
1996-97	Away	7-Dec-96	1-1	Sutton (33)	19,306	M.Riley
1996-97	Home	11-May-97	2-4	Flitcroft (25); Fenton (66)	25,881	S.Dunn
1997-98	Away	24-Sep-97	1-1	Sutton (36)	19,921	N.Barry
1997-98	Home	28-Feb-98	5-3	Dahlin (11): Sutton (25, 45, 47); Hendry (63)	24,854	N.Barry
1998-99	Home	29-Aug-98	1-0	Gallacher (12)	22,544	U.Rennie
1998-99	Away	28-Dec-98	1-1	Gallacher (38)	21,083	A.Wilkie

LIVERPOOL

Season	Venue	Date	Res	Scorers	Attendance	Referee
1992-93	Away	13-Dec-92	1-2	Shearer (80)	43,688	P.Don
1992-93	Home	3-Apr-93	4-1	Newell (13); Moran (25); Gallacher (41); Wilcox (65)	15,032	K.Redfern
1993-94	Away	12-Sep-93	1-0	Newell (54)	37,355	M.Reed
1993-94	Home	5-Mar-94	2-0	Wilcox (17); Sherwood (65)	20,831	G.Ashby
1994-95	Home	15-Oct-94	3-2	Atkins (52); Sutton (57,72)	30,263	B.Hill
1994-95	Away	14-May-95	1-2	Shearer (20)	40,014	D.Elleray
1995-96	Away	16-Sep-95	0-3		39,502	G.Willard
1995-96	Home	24-Feb-96	2-3	Wilcox (25); Sherwood (84)	30,895	A.Wilkie
1996-97	Home	3-Nov-96	3-0	Sutton (3 pen, 55); Wilcox (24)	29,598	S.Lodge
1996-97	Away	22-Feb-97	0-0		40,747	M.Bodenham
1997-98	Home	23-Aug-97	1-1	Dahllin (84)	30,187	S.Lodge
1997-98	Away	31-Jan-98	0-0		43,890	P.Durkin
1998-99	Away	29-Nov-98	0-2		41,753	J.Winter
1998-99	Home	24-Apr-99	1-3	Duff (63)	29,944	R.Harris

MANCHESTER CITY

Season	Venue	Date	Res	Scorers	Attendance	Referee
1992-93	Home	22-Aug-92	1-0	Newell (69)	19,433	R.Hart
1992-93	Away	30-Jan-93	2-3	Newell (4); OG (14, Phelan)	29,122	M.Peck
1993-94	Away	24-Aug-93	2-0	Newell (10); Gallacher (50)	25,185	J.Lloyd

1993-94	Home	18-Dec-93	2-0	Gallacher; (13); Shearer (76)	19,479	S.Lodge
1994-95	Away	26-Dec-94	3-1	Shearer (9); Atkins (16); Le Saux (67)	23,387	P.Danson
1994-95	Home	17-Apr-95	2-3	Shearer (7); Hendry (39)	27,857	K.Cooper
1995-96	Home	26-Dec-95	2-0	Shearer (11); Batty (50)	28,915	K.Cooper
1995-96	Away	2-Mar-96	1-1	Shearer (57)	29,078	P.Danson

MANCHESTER UNITED

Season	Venue	Date	Res	Scorers	Attendance	Referee
1992-93	Home	24-Oct-92	0-0		20,305	M.Reed
1992-93	Away	3-May-93	1-3	Gallacher (8)	40,447	J.Borrett
1993-94	Away	26-Dec-93	1-1	Gallacher (15)	44,511	D.Gallagher
1993-94	Home	2-Apr-94	2-0	Shearer (46, 76)	20,866	R.Milford
1994-95	Home	23-Oct-94	2-4	Warhurst (13); Hendry (31)	30,260	G.Ashby
1994-95	Away	22-Jan-95	0-1		43,742	P.Durkin
1995-96	Home	28-Aug-95	1-2	Shearer (59)	29,843	D.Elleray
1995-96	Away	10-Feb-96	0-1		42,681	K.Burge
1996-97	Away	25-Aug-96	2-2	Warhurst (33); Bohinen (50)	54,178	S.Dunn
1996-97	Home	12-Apr-97	2-3	McKinlay (35); Warhurst (88)	30,476	M.Bodenham
1997-98	Away	30-Nov-97	0-4		38,094	A.Wilkie
1997-98	Home	6-Apr-98	1-3	Sutton (32 pen)	30,547	G.Ashby
1998-99	Away	14-Nov-98	2-3	Marcolin (65); Blake (74)	55,198	M.Reed
1998-99	Home	12-May-99	0-0		30,463	M.Reed

MIDDLESBROUGH

Season	Venue	Date	Res	Scorers	Attendance	Referee
1992-93	Away	5-Dec-92	2-3	Wilcox (44); OG (74, Phillips)	20,096	B.Hill
1992-93	Home	20-Mar-93	1-1	Atkins (23)	14,041	G.Ashby
1995-96	Away	30-Sep-95	0-2		29,462	P.Alcock
1995-96	Home	16-Dec-95	1-0	Shearer (42)	27,996	P.Danson
1996-97	Away	19-Mar-97	1-2	Sutton (68)	29,891	D.Gallagher
1996-97	Home	8-May-97	0-0		27,411	G.Poll
1998-99	Away	17-Oct-98	1-2	Sherwood (56)	34,413	U.Rennie
1998-99	Home	3-Apr-99	0-0		27,482	A.Wilkie

NEWCASTLE UNITED

Season	Venue	Date	Res	Scorers	Attendance	Referee
1993-94	Away	29-Aug-93	1-1	Shearer (75)	33,987	S.Lodge
1993-94	Home	19-Feb-94	1-0	May (76)	20,798	K.Burge
1994-95	Away	9-Oct-94	1-1	Shearer (58 pen)	34,344	S.Lodge
1994-95	Home	8-May-95	1-0	Shearer (29)	30,545	P.Don
1995-96	Away	8-Nov-95	0-1		36,463	D.Gallagher
1995-96	Home	8-Apr-96	2-1	Fenton (86, 90)	30,717	G.Willard
1996-97	Away	14-Sep-96	1-2	Sutton (85)	36,424	K.Burge
1996-97	Home	26-Dec-96	1-0	Gallacher (75)	30,398	M.Reed
1997-98	Away	25-Oct-97	1-1	Sutton (57)	36,716	J.Winter
1997-98	Home	10-May-98	1-0	Sutton (88)	29,300	D.Elleray
1998-99	Home	12-Dec-98	0-0		27,569	R.Harris
1998-99	Away	16-May-99	1-1	Wilcox (37)	36,623	J.Winter

NORWICH CITY

Season	Venue	Date	Res	Scorers	Attendance	Referee
1992-93	Home	3-Oct-92	7-1	Wegerle (8, 32); Sherwood (27); Shearer (43, 76); Cowans (63); Ripley (70)	16,312	R.Dilkes
1992-93	Away	28-Feb-93	0-0		15,821	P.Don
1993-94	Home	18-Aug-93	2-3	Atkins (7); Wilcox (55)	14,260	R.Hart
1993-94	Away	22-Feb-94	2-2	Gallacher (32, 58)	15,124	K.Barratt
1994-95	Away	1-Oct-94	1-2	Sutton (4)	18,146	P.Jones
1994-95	Home	25-Feb-95	0-0		25,579	M.Reed

NOTTINGHAM FOREST

Season	Venue	Date	Res	Scorers	Attendance	Referee
1992-93	Home	5-Sep-92	4-1	Shearer (3, 59 pen); Aitkins (52); OG (62,Crossley)	16,180	R.Nixon
1992-93	Away	7-Apr-93	3-1	Wilcox (7); Ripley (67); Newell (76)	20,467	T.Ward
1994-95	Away	29-Oct-94	2-0	Sutton (6,68)	22,131	P.Danson
1994-95	Home	14-Jan-95	3-0	Warhurst (54); Wilcox (78); OG (88, Chettle)	27,510	J.Worrall
1995-96	Home	18-Nov-95	7-0	Shearer (20, 58, 68); Bohinen (28, 76); Newell (82); Le Saux (90)	27,660	J.Winter
1995-96	Away	13-Apr-96	5-1	Shearer (27); McKinlay (30); Wilcox (45, 69); Fenton (86)	25,273	P.Jones
1996-97	Away	25-Nov-96	2-2	Gallacher (53); Wilcox (57)	17,525	P.Alcock
1996-97	Home	11-Mar-97	1-1	Gallacher (64)	20,485	M.Riley
1998-99	Away	19-Dec-98	2-2	Blake (49, 90)	22,013	S.Lodge
1998-99	Home	8-May-99	1-2	Gallacher (25)	24,565	G.Poll

OLDHAM ATHLETIC

Season	Venue	Date	Res	Scorers	Attendance	Referee
1992-93	Home	26-Sep-92	2-0	Shearer (30); Ripley (61)	18,383	V.Callow
1992-93	Away	16-Jan-93	1-0	Ripley (80)	13,742	A.Buksh
1993-94	Home	21-Aug-93	1-0	Moran (9)	14,397	J.Worrall
1993-94	Away	11-Dec-93	2-1	Shearer (27, 49)	13,887	J.Worrall

QPR

Season	Venue	Date	Res	Scorers	Attendance	Referee
1992-93	Home	28-Nov-92	1-0	Shearer (17)	15,850	K.Hackett
1992-93	Away	24-Mar-93	3-0	Ripley (23); Moran (55); Atkins (65)	10,677	A.Gunn
1993-94	Away	6-Nov-93	0-1		17,636	A.Gunn
1993-94	Home	24-Apr-94	1-1	Shearer (45)	19,193	R.Gifford
1994-95	Home	26-Nov-94	4-0	Sutton (9); Shearer (56,66 pen,85)	21,302	J.Worrall
1994-95	Away	4-Apr-95	1-0	Sutton (67)	16,508	R.Hart
1995-96	Home	19-Aug-95	1-0	Shearer (6 pen)	25,932	A.Wilkie
1995-96	Away	13-Jan-96	1-0	Shearer (77)	13,957	G.Ashby

SHEFFIELD UNITED

Season	Venue	Date	Res	Scorers	Attendance	Referee
1992-93	Home	19-Dec-92	1-0	Moran (27)	16,057	D.Gallagher
1992-93	Away	17-Apr-93	3-1	Gallacher (39); Newell (54); Sherwood (68)	18,186	D.Allison
1993-94	Home	18-Oct-93	0-0		14,276	T.Holbrook
1993-94	Away	15-Jan-94	2-1	Shearer (38, 64)	19,124	P.Foakes

BLACKBURN ROVERS

SHEFFIELD WEDNESDAY

Season	Venue	Date	Res	Scorers	Attendance	Referee
1992-93	Away	31-Oct-92	0-0		31,044	R.Lewis
1992-93	Home	8-May-93	1-0	Sherwood (65)	14,956	P.Don
1993-94	Home	25-Sep-93	1-1	Shearer (81)	14,495	V.Callow
1993-94	Away	20-Mar-94	2-1	Wilcox (18); Newell (89)	24,655	R.Dilkes
1994-95	Away	2-Nov-94	1-0	Shearer (53)	24,207	R.Hart
1994-95	Home	12-Feb-95	3-1	Sherwood (26); Atkins (35); Shearer (66)	22,223	P.Jones
1995-96	Away	23-Aug-95	1-2	Shearer (60)	25,544	P.Danson
1995-96	Home	20-Jan-96	3-0	Shearer (28); Bohinen (31); Gallacher (84)	24,732	G.Willard
1996-97	Away	19-Oct-96	1-1	Bohinen (74)	22,191	P.Danson
1996-97	Home	22-Apr-97	4-1	Berg (6); Sherwood (24); Le Saux (40); Flitcroft (59)	20,845	G.Willard
1997-98	Home	25-Aug-97	7-2	Gallacher (2, 6); OG (10, Hyde); Wilcox (19); Sutton (23, 74); Bohinen (53)	19,618	J.Winter
1997-98	Away	26-Dec-97	0-0		33,502	J.Winter
1998-99	Away	12-Sep-98	0-3		20,846	A.Wilkie
1998-99	Home	20-Feb-99	1-4	McAteer (68)	24,643	A.Wilkie

SOUTHAMPTON

Season	Venue	Date	Res	Scorers	Attendance	Referee
1992-93	Away	22-Nov-92	1-1	Moran (38)	16,626	M.Bodenham
1992-93	Home	9-Mar-93	0-0		13,566	S.Lodge
1993-94	Home	20-Nov-93	2-0	Shearer (24 pen, 77)	17,343	K.Cooper
1993-94	Away	16-Apr-94	1-3	Ripley (48)	19,105	J.Worrall
1994-95	Away	20-Aug-94	1-1	Shearer (60)	14,209	K.Cooper
1994-95	Home	10-Dec-94	3-2	Atkins (6); Shearer (13,74)	23,372	A.Wilkie
1995-96	Home	14-Oct-95	2-1	Bohinen (16); Shearer (77)	26,780	M.Reed
1995-96	Away	6-Apr-96	0-1		14,793	D.Elleray
1996-97	Home	30-Nov-96	2-1	Sherwood (27); Sutton (87)	23,018	R.Dilkes
1996-97	Away	3-May-97	0-2		15,247	G.Ashby
1997-98	Home	18-Oct-97	1-0	Sherwood (26)	24,130	G.Willard
1997-98	Away	21-Feb-98	0-3		15,162	U.Rennie
1998-99	Home	21-Nov-98	0-2		22,812	S.Dunn
1998-99	Away	17-Apr-99	3-3	Ward (14); Peacock (25); Wilcox (47)	15,209	G.Barber

SUNDERLAND

Season	Venue	Date	Res	Scorers	Attendance	Referee
1996-97	Away	18-Jan-97	0-0		20,850	P.Alcock
1996-97	Home	1-Mar-97	1-0	Gallacher (84)	24,208	R.Dilkes

SWINDON TOWN

Season	Venue	Date	Res	Scorers	Attendance	Referee
1993-94	Away	2-Oct-93	3-1	Shearer (15, 90); Ripley (51)	15,847	D.Frampton
1993-94	Home	26-Mar-94	3-1	Shearer (6, 82 pen); Sherwood (27)	20,046	K.Morton

TOTTENHAM HOTSPUR

Season	Venue	Date	Res	Scorers	Attendance	Referee
1992-93	Home	7-Nov-92	0-2		17,305	K.Barratt
1992-93	Away	5-May-93	2-1	Newell (22, 54)	23,097	K.Morton
1993-94	Home	30-Oct-93	1-0	Shearer (15)	17,462	A.Wilkie

95

1993-94	Away	12-Feb-94	2-0	Shearer (60); Gallacher (72)	30,236	J.Borrett
1994-95	Home	5-Nov-94	2-0	Wilcox (8); Shearer (49 pen)	26,933	T.Holbrook
1994-95	Away	5-Feb-95	1-3	Sherwood (46)	28,124	M.Bodenham
1995-96	Home	30-Dec-95	2-1	Marker (31); Shearer (41)	30,004	P.Jones
1995-96	Away	16-Mar-96	3-2	Shearer (7 pen, 34, 90)	31,803	P.Durkin
1996-97	Home	17-Aug-96	0-2		26,960	P.Jones
1996-97	Away	29-Jan-97	1-2	Hendry (57)	22,943	P.Danson
1997-98	Away	20-Sep-97	0-0		26,573	G.Barber
1997-98	Home	7-Feb-98	0-3		30,388	G.Barber
1998-99	Away	9-Sep-98	1-2	Gallacher (11)	28,338	P.Alcock
1998-99	Home	30-Jan-99	1-1	Jansen (43)	29,643	N.Barry

WEST HAM UNITED

Season	Venue	Date	Res	Scorers	Attendance	Referee
1993-94	Home	18-Sep-93	0-2		14,437	K.Hackett
1993-94	Away	27-Apr-94	2-1	Berg (11); Pearce (75)	22,186	T.Holbrook
1994-95	Home	2-Jan-95	4-2	Shearer (14 pen,75,79 pen); Le Saux (61)	25,503	K.Morton
1994-95	Away	30-Apr-95	0-2		24,202	K.Morton
1995-96	Away	21-Oct-95	1-1	Shearer (89)	21,776	S.Lodge
1995-96	Home	2-Dec-95	4-2	Shearer (3, 17, 65 pen); Newell (32)	26,638	K.Burge
1996-97	Away	26-Oct-96	1-2	Berg (8)	23,947	M.Reed
1996-97	Home	1-Feb-97	2-1	Gallacher (36); Sutton (39)	21,994	A.Wilkie
1997-98	Home	20-Dec-97	3-0	Ripley (22);Duff (50, 72)	21,653	G.Ashby
1997-98	Away	18-Apr-98	1-2	Wilcox (44)	24,733	P.Durkin
1998-99	Home	3-Oct-98	3-0	Flitcroft (10, 87); Davidson (68)	25,213	K.Burge
1998-99	Away	27-Feb-99	0-2		25,529	S.Dunn

WIMBLEDON

Season	Venue	Date	Res	Scorers	Attendance	Referee
1992-93	Away	19-Sep-92	1-1	Shearer (32)	6,117	M.Bodenham
1992-93	Home	9-Jan-93	0-0		14,504	R.Hart
1993-94	Home	5-Feb-94	3-0	Shearer (7 pen); Wilcox (30); Ripley (39)	17,264	A.Wilkie
1993-94	Away	29-Mar-94	1-4	Wilcox (15)	10,537	J.Lloyd
1994-95	Away	3-Dec-94	3-0	Atkins (51); Wilcox (72); Shearer (74)	12,341	P.Jones
1994-95	Home	22-Feb-95	2-1	Shearer (3); Atkins (25)	20,586	S.Lodge
1995-96	Away	23-Dec-95	1-1	Sherwood (27)	7,105	M.Bodenham
1995-96	Home	17-Apr-96	3-2	Shearer (13, 46); Fenton (58)	24,174	R.Hart
1996-97	Away	14-Dec-96	0-1		13,246	A.Wilkie
1996-97	Home	15-Mar-97	3-1	Gallacher (6, 26, 57)	23,333	G.Poll
1997-98	Away	4-Oct-97	1-0	Sutton (6)	15,600	D.Gallagher
1997-98	Home	25-Apr-98	0-0		24,848	G.Poll
1998-99	Away	31-Oct-98	1-1	Sutton (47 pen)	12,526	G.Willard
1998-99	Home	21-Mar-99	3-1	Ward (7); Jansen (18, 26)	21,754	G.Willard

INTRODUCTION

Formed in 1874 as a Sunday School side, Christ Church. This connection ended in 1877 when they adopted their present name. Turned professional in 1895 and were Football League founder members. Moved from Pikes Lane to present ground in 1895. Members of the reorganised Division One on formation of the Premier League, they were promoted to the Premier League for the 1995-96 season and, after being relegated straight back, bounced back into the top flight at the first attempt as Division One Champions.

Ground: The Reebok Stadium, Mansell Way, Horwich, Bolton
Nickname: The Trotters
Internet: www.boltonwfc.co.uk

HONOURS

Football League Div 1:   Champions 1996-97.
Football League Div 2:   Champions 1908-09, 1977-78;
Football League Div 3:   Champions 1972-73
FA Cup: Winners 1922-23, 1925-26, 1928-29, 1957-58; Runners-up 1883-84, 1903-04, 1952-53.
League Cup: Runners-up 1994-95
FA Charity Shield: Winners 1958
Sherpa Van Trophy: Winners 1988-89
Freight Rover Trophy: Runners-up 1985-86.

EUROPEAN RECORD

Never qualified.

FAPL RECORD SUMMARY

Most Total:	BERGSSON, Gundi	69
Most Starts:	BERGSSON, Gundi	68
Most Subs:	GUNNLAUGSSON, Arnar	13
Most SNU:	WARD, Gavin	28
Most PS:	McGINLAY, John	11
Most Goals:	BLAKE, Nathan	13
Most Yel:	BERGSSON, Gundi	17
Most Red:	BERGSSON, Gundi	2

PLAYING RECORD – SEASON TOTALS

Season	Pn	P	W	D	L	F	A	Pts
1995-96	20	38	8	5	25	39	71	29
1997-98	18	38	9	13	16	41	61	40
Totals		76	17	18	41	80	132	69

PLAYING RECORD – HOME TOTALS

Season	Pn	P	W	D	L	F	A	Pts
1995-96	20	19	5	4	10	16	31	19
1997-98	18	19	7	8	4	25	22	29
Totals		38	12	12	14	41	53	48

PLAYING RECORD – AWAY TOTALS

Season	Pn	P	W	D	L	F	A	Pts
1995-96	20	19	3	1	15	23	40	10
1997-98	18	19	2	5	12	16	39	11
Totals		38	5	6	27	39	79	21

HIGHEST HOME ATTENDANCES

	Attendance	Opponents	Date	Season
1	25,000	Manchester U.	20-Sep-97	1997-98
2	25,000	Liverpool	1-Nov-97	1997-98
3	24,494	Newcastle U.	1-Dec-97	1997-98
4	24,196	Aston Villa	4-Oct-97	1997-98
5	24,080	Chelsea	26-Oct-97	1997-98

LOWEST HOME ATTENDANCES

	Attendance	Opponents	Date	Season
1	16,216	Wimbledon	13-Jan-96	1995-96
2	16,678	Coventry C.	30-Dec-95	1995-96
3	17,342	Nottingham F.	2-Dec-95	1995-96
4	17,362	QPR	30-Sep-95	1995-96
5	17,829	Tottenham H.	20-Mar-96	1995-96

TOP SCORER – SEASON BY SEASON

Season	Player	Goals
1995-96	McGINLAY	6
1997-98	Blake	12

PLAYERS WITH MOST PREMIERSHIP APPEARANCES

Tot	Player	St	Sb	Gls
69	BERGSSON, Gundi	68	1	6
65	BRANAGAN, Keith	65	0	0
59	PHILLIPS, Jimmy	58	1	1
59	THOMPSON, Alan	56	3	10
53	BLAKE, Nathan	49	4	13
44	FAIRCLOUGH, Chris	43	1	0
44	SELLARS, Scott	44	0	5
40	McGINLAY, John	34	6	6
38	FRANDSEN, Per	38	0	2

CLUB-BY-CLUB RESULTS

ARSENAL

Season	Venue	Date	Res	Scorers	Attendance	Referee
1995-96	Home	30-Oct-95	1-0	McGinlay (35)	18,682	K.Cooper
1995-96	Away	5-May-96	1-2	Todd (76)	38,104	G.Willard
1997-98	Away	13-Sep-97	1-4	Thompson (13)	38,138	N.Barry
1997-98	Home	31-Mar-98	0-1		25,000	K.Burge

ASTON VILLA

Season	Venue	Date	Res	Scorers	Attendance	Referee
1995-96	Away	30-Aug-95	0-1		31,770	P.Jones
1995-96	Home	10-Feb-96	0-2		18,099	G.Ashby
1997-98	Home	4-Oct-97	0-1		24,196	G.Poll
1997-98	Away	25-Apr-98	3-1	Cox (18); Taylor (41); Blake (83)	38,392	D.Elleray

BARNSLEY

Season	Venue	Date	Res	Scorers	Attendance	Referee
1997-98	Away	27-Aug-97	1-2	Beardsley (31)	18,661	D.Gallagher
1997-98	Home	26-Dec-97	1-1	Bergsson (38)	35,000	S.Dunn

BLACKBURN ROVERS

Season	Venue	Date	Res	Scorers	Attendance	Referee
1995-96	Home	26-Aug-95	2-1	De Freitas (21); Stubbs (80)	20,253	K.Burge
1995-96	Away	3-Feb-96	1-3	Green (29)	30,419	P.Alcock
1997-98	Away	6-Dec-97	1-3	Frandsen (83)	29,503	M.Riley
1997-98	Home	11-Apr-98	2-1	Holdsworth (20); Taylor (67)	25,000	M.Riley

CHELSEA

Season	Venue	Date	Res	Scorers	Attendance	Referee
1995-96	Away	22-Nov-95	2-3	Curcic (10); Green (67)	17,495	G.Poll
1995-96	Home	8-Apr-96	2-1	McGinlay (40); Curcic (44)	18,021	S.Lodge
1997-98	Home	26-Oct-97	1-0	Holdsworth (72)	24,080	P.Jones
1997-98	Away	10-May-98	0-2		34,845	A.Wilkie

COVENTRY CITY

Season	Venue	Date	Res	Scorers	Attendance	Referee
1995-96	Home	30-Dec-95	1-2	McGinlay (16)	16,678	A.Wilkie
1995-96	Away	16-Mar-96	2-0	Stubbs (68, 70)	17,168	K.Burge
1997-98	Away	23-Aug-97	2-2	Blake (69, 76)	16,633	M.Riley
1997-98	Home	31-Jan-98	1-5	Sellars (22)	25,000	D.Gallagher

CRYSTAL PALACE

Season	Venue	Date	Res	Scorers	Attendance	Referee
1997-98	Away	27-Sep-97	2-2	Beardsley (36); Johanson (66)	17,134	D.Elleray
1997-98	Home	2-May-98	5-2	Blake (6); Fish (20); Phillips (30); Thompson (74); Holdsworth (79)	24,449	N.Barry

DERBY COUNTY

Season	Venue	Date	Res	Scorers	Attendance	Referee
1997-98	Home	14-Dec-97	3-3	Thompson (50); Blake (72); Pollock (77)	23,037	U.Rennie
1997-98	Away	13-Apr-98	0-4		29,126	D.Gallagher

EVERTON

Season	Venue	Date	Res	Scorers	Attendance	Referee
1995-96	Home	14-Oct-95	1-1	Paatelainen (1)	20,427	P.Alcock
1995-96	Away	6-Apr-96	0-3		37,974	M.Bodenham
1997-98	Home	1-Sep-97	0-0		23,131	S.Lodge
1997-98	Away	28-Dec-97	2-3	Bergsson (42): Sellars (43)	37,149	K.Burge

LEEDS UNITED

Season	Venue	Date	Res	Scorers	Attendance	Referee
1995-96	Home	27-Dec-95	0-2		18,414	D.Elleray
1995-96	Away	2-Mar-96	1-0	Bergsson (16)	30,106	G.Willard
1997-98	Away	20-Dec-97	0-2		31,163	A.Wilkie
1997-98	Home	18-Apr-98	2-3	Thompson (57); Fish (90)	25,000	J.Winter

LEICESTER CITY

Season	Venue	Date	Res	Scorers	Attendance	Referee
1997-98	Away	22-Nov-97	0-0		20,564	G.Barber
1997-98	Home	28-Mar-98	2-0	Thompson (62,90)	25,000	U.Rennie

LIVERPOOL

Season	Venue	Date	Res	Scorers	Attendance	Referee
1995-96	Away	23-Sep-95	2-5	Todd (78); Patterson (81)	40,104	M.Bodenham
1995-96	Home	9-Dec-95	0-1		21,042	M.Bodenham
1997-98	Home	1-Nov-97	1-1	Blake (84)	25,000	D.Gallagher
1997-98	Away	5-Mar-98	1-2	Thompson (7)	44,532	K.Burge

MANCHESTER CITY

Season	Venue	Date	Res	Scorers	Attendance	Referee
1995-96	Away	4-Nov-95	0-1		28,397	R.Hart
1995-96	Home	30-Mar-96	1-1	McGinlay (74)	21,050	R.Dilkes

MANCHESTER UNITED

Season	Venue	Date	Res	Scorers	Attendance	Referee
1995-96	Away	16-Sep-95	0-3		32,812	S.Dunn
1995-96	Home	25-Feb-96	0-6		21,381	D.Gallagher
1997-98	Home	20-Sep-97	0-0		25,000	P.Durkin
1997-98	Away	7-Feb-98	1-1	Taylor (60)	55,156	S.Lodge

MIDDLESBROUGH

Season	Venue	Date	Res	Scorers	Attendance	Referee
1995-96	Home	9-Sep-95	1-1	McGinlay (24)	18,376	P.Danson
1995-96	Away	17-Feb-96	4-1	Blake (12); Coleman (45); De Freitas (62); Lee (73)	29,354	P.Danson

BOLTON WANDERERS

NEWCASTLE UNITED

Season	Venue	Date	Res	Scorers	Attendance	Referee
1995-96	Home	22-Aug-95	1-3	Bergsson (51)	20,243	S.Lodge
1995-96	Away	20-Jan-96	1-2	Bergsson (19)	36,534	K.Cooper
1997-98	Home	1-Dec-97	1-0	Blake (22)	24,494	N.Barry
1997-98	Away	17-Jan-98	1-2	Blake (72)	36,767	G.Poll

NOTTINGHAM FOREST

Season	Venue	Date	Res	Scorers	Attendance	Referee
1995-96	Away	21-Oct-95	2-3	Sneekes (24); De Freitas (78)	25,426	D.Elleray
1995-96	Home	2-Dec-95	1-1	De Freitas (67)	17,342	R.Dilkes

QPR

Season	Venue	Date	Res	Scorers	Attendance	Referee
1995-96	Home	30-Sep-95	0-1		17,362	J.Winter
1995-96	Away	16-Dec-95	1-2	Sellars (43)	11,456	S.Lodge

SHEFFIELD WEDNESDAY

Season	Venue	Date	Res	Scorers	Attendance	Referee
1995-96	Away	1-Jan-96	2-4	Curcic (51); Taggart (77)	24,872	P.Durkin
1995-96	Home	23-Mar-96	2-1	Sellars (44); Curcic (52)	18,368	J.Winter
1997-98	Away	8-Nov-97	0-5		25,067	M.Reed
1997-98	Home	14-Mar-98	3-2	Fradsen (31); Blake (53); Thompson (68 pen)	24,847	G.Poll

SOUTHAMPTON

Season	Venue	Date	Res	Scorers	Attendance	Referee
1995-96	Away	25-Nov-95	0-1		14,404	P.Jones
1995-96	Home	27-Apr-96	0-1		18,795	G.Ashby
1997-98	Away	9-Aug-97	1-0	Blake (42)	15,206	M.Bodenham
1997-98	Home	10-Jan-98	0-0		23,333	G.Willard

TOTTENHAM HOTSPUR

Season	Venue	Date	Res	Scorers	Attendance	Referee
1995-96	Away	23-Dec-95	2-2	Green (76); Bergsson (78)	30,702	P.Danson
1995-96	Home	20-Mar-96	2-3	Stubbs (74); Sellars (84)	17,829	S.Dunn
1997-98	Home	23-Sep-97	1-1	Thompson (20 pen)	23,433	U.Rennie
1997-98	Away	1-Mar-98	0-1		29,032	P.Jones

WEST HAM UNITED

Season	Venue	Date	Res	Scorers	Attendance	Referee
1995-96	Home	18-Nov-95	0-3		19,047	P.Durkin
1995-96	Away	13-Apr-96	0-1		23,086	A.Wilkie
1997-98	Away	18-Oct-97	0-3		24,867	G.Ashby
1997-98	Home	21-Feb-98	1-1	Blake (86)	25,000	P.Alcock

WIMBLEDON

Season	Venue	Date	Res	Scorers	Attendance	Referee
1995-96	Away	19-Aug-95	2-3	Thompson (26 pen); De Freitas (40)	9,317	K.Cooper
1995-96	Home	13-Jan-96	1-0	McGinlay (44 pen)	16,216	M.Reed
1997-98	Home	29-Nov-97	1-0	Blake (90)	22,703	J.Winter
1997-98	Away	4-Apr-98	0-0		11,356	M.Bodenham

BRADFORD CITY

INTRODUCTION

Founded as a football club in 1903 after the club had started life as a rugby side – Manningham RC – which had got into financial difficulties. It worked as the club were immediately voted into the Football League not least because the organising body wished to get a foothold in that part of the country. The club immediately turned professional and within five years were in Division 1 and three years later lifted the FA Cup. Following relegation in 1922 the club bounced around the lower divisions and as recently as 1992 were playing in Division 3. In 1985, 56 people died when the old Main Stand was consumed by flames, after a discarded cigarette butt turned litter into tinder. In 1996 the club won promotion to Division 1 and on the last day of the 1999 season confirmed promotion to the Premier League for the first time since the rugby club played its first game at Valley Parade all those years ago. Confounding all the odds they maintained their place in the top flight at the end of their debut season.

Ground: Valley Parade, Bradford, BD8 7DY
Nickname: The Bantams
Internet: www.bradfordcityfc.co.uk

HONOURS

Football League Div 1: Runners-up 1998-99
Football League Div 2: Champions 1907-08
Football League Div 3: Champions 1984-85
Football League Div 3N: Champions 1928-29
Football League Div 4: Runners-up 1981-82
FA Cup Winners 1910-11

EUROPEAN RECORD

Never qualified.

FAPL RECORD SUMMARY

Most Total:	HALLE, Gunnar	38
Most Starts:	WETHERALL, David	38
Most Subs:	BLAKE, Robbie	12
Most SNU:	DAVISON, Aidan	16
Most PS:	SAUNDERS, Dean	10
Most Goals:	WINDASS, Dean	10
Most Yel:	HALLE, Gunnar	8
Most Red:	MYERS, Andy	1

PLAYING RECORD – SEASON TOTALS

Season	Pn	P	W	D	L	F	A	Pts
1999-00	17	38	9	9	20	38	68	36
Totals		38	9	9	20	38	68	36

PLAYING RECORD – HOME TOTALS

Season	Pn	P	W	D	L	F	A	Pts
1999-00	17	19	6	8	5	26	29	26
Totals		19	6	8	5	26	29	26

PLAYING RECORD – AWAY TOTALS

Season	Pn	P	W	D	L	F	A	Pts
1999-00	17	19	3	1	15	12	39	10
Totals		19	3	1	15	12	39	10

HIGHEST HOME ATTENDANCES

	Attendance	Opponents	Date	Season
1	18,276	Sheffield W.	14-Aug-99	1999-00
2	18,276	Newcastle U.	18-Dec-99	1999-00
3	18,276	Everton	28-Dec-99	1999-00
4	18,276	Chelsea	8-Jan-00	1999-00
5	18,276	Arsenal	5-Feb-00	1999-00

LOWEST HOME ATTENDANCES

	Attendance	Opponents	Date	Season
1	16,864	Watford	22-Jan-00	1999-00
2	17,439	Southampton	8-Apr-00	1999-00
3	17,587	Coventry C.	6-Nov-99	1999-00
4	17,655	Leicester C.	23-Oct-99	1999-00
5	17,708	Middlesbrough	4-Dec-99	1999-00

TOP SCORER – SEASON BY SEASON

Season	Player	Goals
1999-00	Windass	10

PLAYERS WITH MOST PREMIERSHIP APPEARANCES

Tot	Player	St	Sb	Gls
38	HALLE, Gunnar	37	1	0
38	WETHERALL, David	38	0	2
38	WINDASS, Dean	36	2	10
36	O'BRIEN, Andy	36	0	1
35	BEAGRIE, Peter	30	5	7
34	McCALL, Stuart	33	1	1
34	SAUNDERS, Dean	28	6	3
27	BLAKE, Robbie	15	12	2
24	JACOBS, Wayne	22	2	0
23	LAWRENCE, Jamie	19	4	3
21	CLARKE, Matt	21	0	0
21	MILLS, Lee	19	2	5

CLUB-BY-CLUB RESULTS

ARSENAL

Season	Venue	Date	Res	Scorers	Attendance	Referee
1999-00	Away	25-Aug-99	0-2		38,073	A.Wiley
1999-00	Home	5-Feb-00	2-1	Windass (10); Saunders (57)	18,276	A.D'Urso

ASTON VILLA

Season	Venue	Date	Res	Scorers	Attendance	Referee
1999-00	Away	18-Sep-99	0-1		28,083	S.Lodge
1999-00	Home	26-Feb-00	1-1	Windass (76)	18,276	M.Halsey

CHELSEA

Season	Venue	Date	Res	Scorers	Attendance	Referee
1999-00	Away	28-Nov-99	0-1		31,591	A.Wiley
1999-00	Home	8-Jan-00	1-1	Mills (2)		

COVENTRY CITY

Season	Venue	Date	Res	Scorers	Attendance	Referee
1999-00	Home	6-Nov-99	1-1	Mills (43)	17,587	B.Knight
1999-00	Away	18-Mar-00	0-4		19,201	S.Lodge

DERBY COUNTY

Season	Venue	Date	Res	Scorers	Attendance	Referee
1999-00	Away	25-Sep-99	1-0	OG (66, Carbonari)	31,035	M.Halsey
1999-00	Home	21-Apr-00	4-4	Windass (11,18,44); Beagrie (27 pen)	18,276	A.Wilkie

EVERTON

Season	Venue	Date	Res	Scorers	Attendance	Referee
1999-00	Home	28-Dec-99	0-0		18,276	U.Rennie
1999-00	Away	15-Apr-00	0-4		30,646	P.Alcock

LEEDS UNITED

Season	Venue	Date	Res	Scorers	Attendance	Referee
1999-00	Away	20-Nov-99	1-2	Windass (90)	39,937	P.Durkin
1999-00	Home	12-Mar-00	1-2	Beagrie (75)	18,276	P.Durkin

LEICESTER CITY

Season	Venue	Date	Res	Scorers	Attendance	Referee
1999-00	Home	23-Oct-99	3-1	Blake (12); Mills (40); Redfearn (66)	17,655	M.Reed
1999-00	Away	6-May-00	0-3		21,103	S.Dunn

LIVERPOOL

Season	Venue	Date	Res	Scorers	Attendance	Referee
1999-00	Away	1-Nov-99	1-3	Windass (12)	40,483	J.Winter
1999-00	Home	14-May-00	1-0	Wetherall (12)	18,276	D.Gallagher

BRADFORD CITY

MANCHESTER UNITED

Season	Venue	Date	Res	Scorers	Attendance	Referee
1999-00	Away	26-Dec-99	0-4		55,188	P.Jones
1999-00	Home	25-Mar-00	0-4		18,276	G.Poll

MIDDLESBROUGH

Season	Venue	Date	Res	Scorers	Attendance	Referee
1999-00	Away	7-Aug-99	1-0	Saunders (89)	33,762	N.Barry
1999-00	Home	4-Dec-99	1-1	Mills (60)	17,708	R.Harris

NEWCASTLE UNITED

Season	Venue	Date	Res	Scorers	Attendance	Referee
1999-00	Home	18-Dec-99	2-0	Saunders (56); Wetherall (71)	18,276	N.Barry
1999-00	Away	1-Apr-00	0-2		36,572	A.D'Urso

SHEFFIELD WEDNESDAY

Season	Venue	Date	Res	Scorers	Attendance	Referee
1999-00	Home	14-Aug-99	1-1	Beagrie (89 pen)	18,276	D.Gallagher
1999-00	Away	15-Jan-00	0-2		24,682	J.Winter

SOUTHAMPTON

Season	Venue	Date	Res	Scorers	Attendance	Referee
1999-00	Away	3-Jan-00	0-1		15,027	D.Elleray
1999-00	Home	8-Apr-00	1-2	Blake (77)	17,439	D.Elleray

SUNDERLAND

Season	Venue	Date	Res	Scorers	Attendance	Referee
1999-00	Home	2-Oct-99	0-4		18,204	S.Bennett
1999-00	Away	24-Apr-00	1-0	Dreyer (60)	40,628	S.Lodge

TOTTENHAM HOTSPUR

Season	Venue	Date	Res	Scorers	Attendance	Referee
1999-00	Home	12-Sep-99	1-1	McCall (90)	18,141	A.Wilkie
1999-00	Away	4-Mar-00	1-1	Lawrence (42)	35,472	P.Jones

WATFORD

Season	Venue	Date	Res	Scorers	Attendance	Referee
1999-00	Away	21-Aug-99	0-1		15,564	R.Harris
1999-00	Home	22-Jan-00	3-2	Beagrie (25 pen); Whalley (37); O'Brien (49)	16,864	P.Alcock

WEST HAM UNITED

Season	Venue	Date	Res	Scorers	Attendance	Referee
1999-00	Home	28-Aug-99	0-3		17,936	P.Jones
1999-00	Away	12-Feb-00	4-5	Windass (30); Beagrie (45 pen); Lawrence (47, 51)	25,417	N.Barry

WIMBLEDON

Season	Venue	Date	Res	Scorers	Attendance	Referee
1999-00	Away	16-Oct-99	2-3	Mills (45); Windass (90)	10,029	P.Alcock
1999-00	Home	30-Apr-00	3-0	Beagrie (43 pen, 50); Windass (83)	18,276	J.Winter

INTRODUCTION
Reformed in 1984 after a traumatic period in their history that saw them move away from The Valley and play for a while at West Ham. Revitalised and regenerated the club achieved Premiership status for the first time in 1998 having won through the play-offs. Originally formed in 1905 by a number of youths, they joined the Football League in 1921 as members of Division 3 South. Played largely in Division 2 and 3 throughout their years. The Addicks flirted briefly with the old Division 1 at the end of the 1980s, having been runners-up in their first season in the top flight (1936-37). Promoted to Premier League in 1998 but relegated back in 1999.

Ground: The Valley, Floyd Road, Charlton, London SE7 8BL
Nickname: Addicks
Internet: www.charlton-athletic.co.uk

HONOURS
Football League Div 1:	Runners-up 1936-37; Play-Off winners 1997-98
Football League Div 2:	Runners-up 1935-36, 1985-86
Football League Div 3S:	Champions 1928-29, 1934-35
FA Cup:	Winners 1946-47
Full Members' Cup:	Runners-up 1986-87

EUROPEAN RECORD
Never qualified.

FAPL RECORD SUMMARY
Most Total:	KINSELLA, Mark	38
Most Starts:	KINSELLA, Mark	38
Most Subs:	JONES, Steve	19
Most SNU:	BROWN, Steve	15
Most PS:	HUNT, Andy	14
Most Goals:	MENDONCA, Clive	8
Most Yel:	MILLS, Danny	9
Most Red:	RUFUS, Richard	2

PLAYING RECORD – SEASON TOTALS
Season	Pn	P	W	D	L	F	A	Pts
1998-99	18	38	8	12	18	41	56	36
Totals		38	8	12	18	41	56	36

PLAYING RECORD – HOME TOTALS
Season	Pn	P	W	D	L	F	A	Pts
1998-99	18	19	4	7	8	20	20	19
Totals		19	4	7	8	20	20	1

PLAYING RECORD – AWAY TOTALS
Season	Pn	P	W	D	L	F	A	Pts
1998-99	18	19	4	5	10	21	36	17
Totals		19	4	5	10	21	36	17

HIGHEST HOME ATTENDANCES
	Attendance	Opponents	Date	Season
1	20,046	Chelsea	3-Apr-99	1998-99
2	20,043	Coventry C.	27-Sep-98	1998-99
3	20,043	West Ham U.	24-Oct-98	1998-99
4	20,043	Middlesbrough	14-Nov-98	1998-99
5	20,043	Everton	28-Nov-98	1998-99

LOWEST HOME ATTENDANCES
	Attendance	Opponents	Date	Season
1	16,488	Southampton	22-Aug-98	1998-99
2	19,516	Derby Co.	12-Sep-98	1998-99
3	20,002	Wimbledon	8-Feb-99	1998-99
4	20,007	Nottingham F.	27-Feb-99	1998-99
5	20,021	Leicester C.	7-Nov-98	1998-99

TOP SCORER – SEASON BY SEASON
Season	Player	Goals
1998-99	Mendonca	8

PLAYERS WITH MOST PREMIERSHIP APPEARANCES
Tot	Player	St	Sb	Gls
38	KINSELLA, Mark	38	0	3
38	POWELL, Chris	38	0	0
36	MILLS, Danny	36	0	2
34	HUNT, Andy	32	2	6
30	REDFEARN, Neil	29	1	3
30	ROBINSON, John	27	3	3
27	RUFUS, Richard	27	0	1
27	TILER, Carl	27	0	1
26	JONES, Steve	7	19	1
25	MENDONCA, Clive	19	6	8
23	ILIC, Sasa	23	0	0
22	YOUDS, Eddie	21	1	2
22	JONES, Keith	13	9	1
18	PRINGLE, Martin	15	3	3
18	BROWN, Steve	13	5	0
17	MORTIMER, Paul	10	7	1
16	NEWTON, Shaun	13	3	0
12	BARNES, John	2	10	0
10	PETTERSON, Andy	7	3	0

CHARLTON ATHLETIC

ARSENAL

Season	Venue	Date	Res	Scorers	Attendance	Referee
1998-99	Away	29-Aug-98	0-0		38,014	G.Poll
1998-99	Home	28-Dec-98	0-1		20,043	U.Rennie

ASTON VILLA

Season	Venue	Date	Res	Scorers	Attendance	Referee
1998-99	Home	21-Dec-98	0-1		20,043	G.Willard
1998-99	Away	8-May-99	4-3	OG (3, Barry); Mendonca (56); Robinson (68); Mills (89)	37,705	M.Riley

BLACKBURN ROVERS

Season	Venue	Date	Res	Scorers	Attendance	Referee
1998-99	Away	5-Dec-98	0-1		22,568	G.Poll
1998-99	Home	1-May-99	0-0		20,041	G.Willard

CHELSEA

Season	Venue	Date	Res	Scorers	Attendance	Referee
1998-99	Away	17-Oct-98	1-2	Youds (58)	34,639	S.Dunn
1998-99	Home	3-Apr-99	0-1		20,046	R.Harris

COVENTRY CITY

Season	Venue	Date	Res	Scorers	Attendance	Referee
1998-99	Home	27-Sep-98	1-1	Hunt (74)	20,043	J.Winter
1998-99	Away	6-Mar-99	1-2	Robinson (55)	20,259	J.Winter

DERBY COUNTY

Season	Venue	Date	Res	Scorers	Attendance	Referee
1998-99	Home	12-Sep-98	1-2	Mendonca (89 pen)	19,516	M.Reed
1998-99	Away	20-Feb-99	2-0	Hunt (64); Pringle (86)	27,853	U.Rennie

EVERTON

Season	Venue	Date	Res	Scorers	Attendance	Referee
1998-99	Home	28-Nov-98	1-2	Kinsella (72)	20,043	K.Burge
1998-99	Away	24-Apr-99	1-4	Stuart (81 pen)	40,089	P.Alcock

LEEDS UNITED

Season	Venue	Date	Res	Scorers	Attendance	Referee
1998-99	Away	21-Nov-98	1-4	Mortimer (65)	32,487	R.Harris
1998-99	Home	17-Apr-99	1-1	Stuart (20)	20,043	A.Wilkie

LEICESTER CITY

Season	Venue	Date	Res	Scorers	Attendance	Referee
1998-99	Home	7-Nov-98	0-0		20,021	D.Elleray
1998-99	Away	13-Mar-99	1-1	Mendonca (90)	20,220	A.Wilkie

LIVERPOOL

Season	Venue	Date	Res	Scorers	Attendance	Referee
1998-99	Away	19-Sep-98	3-3	Rufus (24); Mendonca (61); Jones,S. (83)	44,526	P.Alcock
1998-99	Home	13-Feb-99	1-0	Jones,K. (70)	20,043	M.Reed

MANCHESTER UNITED

Season	Venue	Date	Res	Scorers	Attendance	Referee
1998-99	Away	9-Sep-98	1-4	Kinsella	55,147	P.Durkin
1998-99	Home	31-Jan-99	0-1		20,043	G.Willard

MIDDLESBROUGH

Season	Venue	Date	Res	Scorers	Attendance	Referee
1998-99	Home	14-Nov-98	1-1	Mendonca (37 pen)	20,043	M.Riley
1998-99	Away	10-Apr-99	0-2		34,529	U.Rennie

NEWCASTLE UNITED

Season	Venue	Date	Res	Scorers	Attendance	Referee
1998-99	Away	15-Aug-98	0-0		36,719	D.Gallagher
1998-99	Home	17-Jan-99	2-2	Bright (64); Pringle (90)	20,043	P.Jones

NOTTINGHAM FOREST

Season	Venue	Date	Res	Scorers	Attendance	Referee
1998-99	Away	3-Oct-98	1-0	Youds (5)	22,661	P.Jones
1998-99	Home	27-Feb-99	0-0		20,007	S.Lodge

SHEFFIELD WEDNESDAY

Season	Venue	Date	Res	Scorers	Attendance	Referee
1998-99	Away	12-Dec-98	0-3		26,010	D.Gallagher
1998-99	Home	16-May-99	0-1		20,043	M.Reed

SOUTHAMPTON

Season	Venue	Date	Res	Scorers	Attendance	Referee
1998-99	Home	22-Aug-98	5-0	Robinson (3); Redfearn (46); Mendonca (63 pen, 80, 90)	16,488	R.Harris
1998-99	Away	9-Jan-99	1-3	Hunt (13)	15,222	G.Poll

TOTTENHAM HOTSPUR

Season	Venue	Date	Res	Scorers	Attendance	Referee
1998-99	Away	2-Nov-98	2-2	Hunt (32, 75)	32,202	M.Reed
1998-99	Home	20-Apr-99	1-4	Kinsella (5)	20,043	D.Gallagher

WEST HAM UNITED

Season	Venue	Date	Res	Scorers	Attendance	Referee
1998-99	Home	24-Oct-98	4-2	Tiler (29); Mills (73); Hunt (87); Redfearn (90 pen)	20,043	N.Barry
1998-99	Away	5-Apr-99	1-0	Stuart (76)	26,041	S.Dunn

WIMBLEDON

Season	Venue	Date	Res	Scorers	Attendance	Referee
1998-99	Away	26-Dec-98	1-2	Redfearn (29)	19,106	G.Barber
1998-99	Home	8-Feb-99	2-0	Pringle (36); OG (69, Blackwell)	20,002	D.Elleray

INTRODUCTION

Founded in 1905. The Mears brothers developed Stamford Bridge Athletic Ground, which they owned, into a football stadium for prestigious matches and, prospectively, nearby Fulham FC. But Fulham did not take up the chance so the Mears brothers established their own club, rejecting possible names such as 'London' and 'Kensington' in favour, eventually, of Chelsea. Judging that the club would not be accepted into the Southern League, it sought membership of the Football League. This was gained at the first attempt and it started the 1906-07 season in Division Two. Premier League founder members 1992. Completed League Cup and Cup-Winners' Cup double in 1997-98.

Ground: Stamford Bridge, London SW6 1HS
Nickname: The Blues
Internet: www.chelseafc.co.uk

HONOURS

Football League Div 1:	Champions 1954-55
Football League Div 2:	Champions 1983-84, 1988-89
	Runners-up 1906-07, 1911-12,
	1929-30,1962-63, 1976-77
FA Cup:	Winners 1969-70, 1996-97
	Runners-up 1914-15, 1966-67,
	1993-94
Football League Cup:	Winners 1964-65, 1997-98
	Runners-up 1971-72
Cup-Winners' Cup:	Winners 1970-71, 1997-98
Full Members' Cup:	Winners 1985-86
Zenith Data Systems Cup:	Winners 1989-90.

EUROPEAN RECORD

Champions' League (1):	99-00 (SF)
Cup-Winners' Cup (5):	70-71 (W), 71-72 (2), 94-95
	(SF), 97-98 (W), 99-98 (F)
UEFA Cup (3):	58-60(QF), 65-66 (SF), 68-69
	(2).

FAPL RECORD SUMMARY

Most Total:	WISE, Dennis	225
Most Starts:	WISE, Dennis	217
Most Subs:	FLO, Tore Andre	44
Most SNU:	HITCHCOCK, Kevin	178
Most PS:	PETRESCU, Dan	39
Most Goals:	SPENCER, John	36
Most Yel:	WISE, Dennis	51
Most Red:	LEBOEUF, Franck	4

PLAYING RECORD – SEASON TOTALS

Season	Pn	P	W	D	L	F	A	Pts
1992-93	11	42	14	14	14	51	54	56
1993-94	14	42	13	12	17	49	53	51
1994-95	11	42	13	15	14	50	55	54
1995-96	11	38	12	14	12	46	44	50
1996-97	6	38	16	11	11	58	55	59
1997-98	4	38	20	3	15	71	43	63
1998-99	3	38	20	15	3	57	30	75
1999-00	5	38	18	11	9	53	34	65
Totals		316	126	95	95	435	368	473

PLAYING RECORD – HOME TOTALS

Season	Pn	P	W	D	L	F	A	Pts
1992-93	11	21	9	7	5	29	22	34
1993-94	14	21	11	5	5	31	20	38
1994-95	11	21	7	7	7	25	22	28
1995-96	11	19	7	7	5	30	22	28
1996-97	6	19	9	8	2	33	22	35
1997-98	4	19	13	2	4	37	14	41
1998-99	3	19	12	6	1	29	13	42
1999-00	5	19	12	5	2	35	12	41
Totals		158	80	47	31	249	147	287

PLAYING RECORD – AWAY TOTALS

Season	Pn	P	W	D	L	F	A	Pts
1992-93	11	21	5	7	9	22	32	22
1993-94	14	21	2	7	12	18	33	13
1994-95	11	21	6	8	7	25	33	26
1995-96	11	19	5	7	7	16	22	22
1996-97	6	19	7	3	9	25	33	24
1997-98	4	19	7	1	11	34	29	22
1998-99	3	19	8	9	2	28	17	33
1999-00	5	19	6	6	7	18	22	24
Totals		158	46	48	64	186	221	186

HIGHEST HOME ATTENDANCES

	Attendance	Opponents	Date	Season
1	37,064	Manchester U.	11-Sep-93	1993-94
2	36,544	Derby Co.	29-Nov-97	1997-98
3	35,113	Everton	11-Mar-00	1999-00
4	35,106	Leeds U.	19-Dec-99	1999-00
5	35,092	Newcastle U.	11-Sep-99	1999-00

LOWEST HOME ATTENDANCES

	Attendance	Opponents	Date	Season
1	8,923	Coventry C.	4-May-94	1993-94
2	10,128	Manchester C.	22-Nov-93	1993-94
3	11,180	Swindon T.	27-Apr-94	1993-94
4	11,903	Wimbledon	16-Mar-94	1993-94
5	12,739	Everton	10-Mar-93	1992-93

TOP SCORER – SEASON BY SEASON

Season	Player	Goals
1992-93	Harford	9
1993-94	Stein	13
1994-95	Spencer	11
1995-96	Spencer	13
1996-97	Vialli	9
1997-98	Flo, Vialli	11
1998-99	Zola	13
1999-00	Flo, Poyet	10

PLAYERS WITH MOST PREMIERSHIP APPEARANCES

Tot	Player	St	Sb	Gls
225	WISE, Dennis	217	8	31
167	CLARKE, Steve	160	7	1
164	NEWTON, Eddie	139	25	7
157	SINCLAIR, Frank	151	6	6
150	PETRESCU, Dan	134	16	18
119	LEBOEUF, Franck	119	0	17
118	KHARINE, Dmitri	118	0	0
114	JOHNSEN, Erland	105	9	1
112	DI MATTEO, Roberto	101	11	14
104	BURLEY, Craig	79	25	7
103	PEACOCK, Gavin	92	11	17
103	SPENCER, John	75	28	36
100	DE GOEY, Ed	100	0	0
98	FLO, Tore Andre	54	44	31
95	HUGHES, Mark	88	7	25
86	DUBERRY, Michael	77	9	1

CLUB-BY-CLUB RESULTS

ARSENAL

Season	Venue	Date	Res	Scorers	Attendance	Referee
1992-93	Away	3-Oct-92	1-2	Wise (79)	27,780	K.Morton
1992-93	Home	1-Mar-93	1-0	Stuart (81)	17,725	T.Ward
1993-94	Home	20-Nov-93	0-2		26,839	P.Don
1993-94	Away	16-Apr-94	0-1		34,314	A.Wilkie
1994-95	Away	15-Oct-94	1-3	Wise (34)	38,234	D.Gallagher
1994-95	Home	14-May-95	2-1	Furlong (21); Stein (53)	29,542	J.Worrall
1995-96	Home	30-Sep-95	1-0	Hughes (51)	31,048	M.Bodenham
1995-96	Away	16-Dec-95	1-1	Spencer (25)	38,295	G.Ashby
1996-97	Away	3-Sep-96	3-3	Leboeuf (6 pen); Vialli (30); Wise (90)	38,132	K.Burge
1996-97	Home	5-Apr-97	0-3		28,182	R.Dilkes
1997-98	Home	21-Sep-97	2-3	Poyet (40); Zola (60)	33,012	D.Gallagher
1997-98	Away	8-Feb-98	0-2		38,083	D.Gallagher
1998-99	Home	9-Sep-98	0-0		34,644	S.Lodge
1998-99	Away	31-Jan-99	0-1		38,121	G.Poll
1999-00	Home	23-Oct-99	2-3	Flo (32); Petrescu (52)	34,958	A.Wilkie
1999-00	Away	6-May-00	1-2	Poyet (79)	38,119	M.Reed

ASTON VILLA

Season	Venue	Date	Res	Scorers	Attendance	Referee
1992-93	Away	2-Sep-92	3-1	Fleck (40); Newton (42); Wise (57)	19,125	P.Foakes
1992-93	Home	13-Feb-93	0-1		20,081	M.Peck
1993-94	Away	23-Oct-93	0-1		29,706	D.Allison
1993-94	Home	22-Jan-94	1-0	Stein (67)	18,348	G.Poll
1994-95	Away	28-Dec-94	0-3		32,901	K.Burge
1994-95	Home	15-Apr-95	1-0	Stein (30)	17,051	K.Burge
1995-96	Away	14-Oct-95	1-0	Wise (72)	34,922	S.Dunn
1995-96	Home	6-Apr-96	1-2	Spencer (8)	23,530	G.Poll
1996-97	Home	15-Sep-96	1-1	Leboeuf (45)	27,729	J.Winter

1996-97	Away	26-Dec-96	2-0	Zola (66, 70)	39,339	P.Danson
1997-98	Away	1-Nov-97	2-0	Hughes,M. (38); Flo (82)	39,372	S.Dunn
1997-98	Home	8-Mar-98	0-1		33,018	S.Lodge
1998-99	Home	9-Dec-98	2-1	Zola (29); Flo (90)	34,765	A.Wilkie
1998-99	Away	22-Mar-99	3-0	Flo (59, 90); Goldbaek (86)	39,217	G.Barber
1999-00	Home	21-Aug-99	1-0	OG (52, Ehiogu)	35,071	N.Barry
1999-00	Away	22-Jan-00	0-0		33,704	A.Wilkie

BARNSLEY

Season	Venue	Date	Res	Scorers	Attendance	Referee
1997-98	Away	24-Aug-97	6-0	Petrescu (25); Poyet (37); Vialli (43, 57, 64, 81)	18,170	G.Poll
1997-98	Home	31-Jan-98	2-0	Vialli (22); Hughes,M. (47)	34,442	J.Winter

BLACKBURN ROVERS

Season	Venue	Date	Res	Scorers	Attendance	Referee
1992-93	Home	26-Aug-92	0-0		19,575	R.Bigger
1992-93	Away	21-Feb-93	0-2		14,780	D.Allison
1993-94	Home	14-Aug-93	1-2	Peacock (46)	29,189	A.Gunn
1993-94	Away	5-Dec-93	0-2		16,756	G.Ashby
1994-95	Home	18-Sep-94	1-2	Spencer (55)	17,513	P.Durkin
1994-95	Away	18-Mar-95	1-2	Stein (3)	25,490	P.Danson
1995-96	Away	28-Oct-95	0-3		27,733	P.Durkin
1995-96	Home	5-May-96	2-3	Wise (35); Spencer (88)	28,436	M.Bodenham
1996-97	Away	16-Nov-96	1-1	Petrescu (82)	27,229	G.Barber
1996-97	Home	5-Mar-97	1-1	Minto (63)	25,784	G.Barber
1997-98	Away	22-Nov-97	0-1		27,683	S.Lodge
1997-98	Home	29-Apr-98	0-1		33,311	P.Alcock
1998-99	Away	21-Sep-98	4-3	Zola (15); Leboeuf (51 pen); Flo (82, 86)	23,113	P.Jones
1998-99	Home	17-Feb-99	1-1	Morris (43)	34,382	U.Rennie

BOLTON WANDERERS

Season	Venue	Date	Res	Scorers	Attendance	Referee
1995-96	Home	22-Nov-95	3-2	Lee (17); Hall (59); Newton (85)	17,495	G.Poll
1995-96	Away	8-Apr-96	1-2	Spencer (13)	18,021	S.Lodge
1997-98	Away	26-Oct-97	0-1		24,080	P.Jones
1997-98	Home	10-May-98	2-0	Vialli (73); Morris (90)	34,845	A.Wilkie

BRADFORD CITY

Season	Venue	Date	Res	Scorers	Attendance	Referee
1999-00	Home	28-Nov-99	1-0	Flo (16)	31,591	A.Wiley
1999-00	Away	8-Jan-00	1-1	Petrescu (58)		

CHARLTON ATHLETIC

Season	Venue	Date	Res	Scorers	Attendance	Referee
1998-99	Home	17-Oct-98	2-1	Leboeuf (18 pen); Poyet (88)	34,639	S.Dunn
1998-99	Away	3-Apr-99	1-0	Di Matteo (11)	20,046	R.Harris

COVENTRY CITY

Season	Venue	Date	Res	Scorers	Attendance	Referee
1992-93	Away	24-Oct-92	2-1	Harford (32); Stuart (70)	15,626	M.Peck
1992-93	Home	1-May-93	2-1	Spencer (13); Cascarino (71)	14,186	R.Groves

1993-94	Away	18-Sep-93	1-1	Peacock (36)	13,586	P.Durkin
1993-94	Home	4-May-94	1-2	Cascarino (43)	8,923	J.Borrett
1994-95	Home	6-Nov-94	2-2	Spencer (46); Kjeldbjerg (69)	17,090	S.Lodge
1994-95	Away	4-Feb-95	2-2	Stein (14); Spencer (33 pen)	13,429	R.Hart
1995-96	Home	30-Aug-95	2-2	Wise (6 pen); Hughes (10)	24,398	G.Willard
1995-96	Away	10-Feb-96	0-1		20,629	R.Dilkes
1996-97	Home	24-Aug-96	2-0	Leboeuf (28); Vialli (74)	25,024	P.Danson
1996-97	Away	9-Apr-97	1-3	Hughes P. (43)	19,917	D.Gallagher
1997-98	Away	9-Aug-97	2-3	Sinclair (39); Flo (71)	22,686	P.Durkin
1997-98	Home	10-Jan-98	3-1	Nicholls (65, 70); Di Matteo (77)	34,647	M.Reed
1998-99	Away	15-Aug-98	1-2	Poyet (37)	23,042	G.Barber
1998-99	Home	16-Jan-99	2-1	Leboeuf (45); DiMatteo (90)	34,869	J.Winter
1999-00	Away	4-Jan-00	2-2	Flo (55, 82)	20,164	P.Durkin
1999-00	Home	12-Apr-00	2-1	OG (Hendry 53); Zola (58)	33,316	G.Poll

CRYSTAL PALACE

Season	Venue	Date	Res	Scorers	Attendance	Referee
1992-93	Home	7-Nov-92	3-1	OG (4,Shaw); Stuart (40); Hartford (58)	17,141	R.Groves
1992-93	Away	15-Mar-93	1-1	Stuart (4)	12,610	K.Cooper
1994-95	Away	24-Sep-94	1-0	Furlong (50)	16,030	R.Dilkes
1994-95	Home	5-Mar-95	0-0		14,130	M.Reed
1997-98	Away	13-Sep-97	3-0	Hughes,M. (20); Lebeof (26 pen); Le Saux (89)	26,186	G.Ashby
1997-98	Home	11-Mar-98	6-2	Vialli (14, 43); Zola (16); Wise (85); Flo (88, 90)	31,917	M.Riley

DERBY COUNTY

Season	Venue	Date	Res	Scorers	Attendance	Referee
1996-97	Home	18-Jan-97	3-1	Wise (38); Leboeuf (45 pen); Hughes, P. (85)	28,293	G.Poll
1996-97	Away	1-Mar-97	2-3	Minto (16); Leboeuf (53)	18,039	A.Wilkie
1997-98	Home	29-Nov-97	4-0	Zola (11, 62, 76); Hughes,M. (34)	36,544	U.Rennie
1997-98	Away	5-Apr-98	1-0	Hughes,M. (37)	30,062	J.Winter
1998-99	Away	12-Dec-98	2-2	Flo (55); Poyet (59)	29,056	P.Jones
1998-99	Home	16-May-99	2-1	Babayaro (40); Vialli (68)	35,016	M.Riley
1999-00	Away	30-Oct-99	1-3	Leboeuf (10)	28,614	R.Harris
1999-00	Home	14-May-00	4-0	Zola (47); Poyet (55); Di Matteo (69); Flo (90)	35,084	J.Winter

EVERTON

Season	Venue	Date	Res	Scorers	Attendance	Referee
1992-93	Away	21-Nov-92	0-1	Fleck (45)	17,418	M.Reed
1992-93	Home	10-Mar-93	2-1	Stuart (39); Spencer (79)	12,739	M.Bodenham
1993-94	Home	3-Jan-94	4-2	Burley (22); Stein (40 pen, 88); Shipperley (62)	18,338	K.Barratt
1993-94	Away	5-Feb-94	2-4	Stein (24, 86pen)	18,201	B.Hill
1994-95	Home	26-Nov-94	0-1		28,115	R.Hart
1994-95	Away	3-May-95	3-3	Furlong (29, 77); Hopkin (52)	33,180	B.Hill
1995-96	Home	19-Aug-95	0-0		30,189	M.Reed
1995-96	Away	13-Jan-96	1-1	Spencer (20)	34,968	R.Hart
1996-97	Home	7-Dec-96	2-2	Zola (12); Vialli (55)	28,418	P.Durkin
1996-97	Away	11-May-97	2-1	Wise (14); Di Matteo (36)	38,321	P.Jones
1997-98	Home	26-Nov-97	2-0	Wise (80 pen); Zola (90 pen)	34,148	N.Barry
1997-98	Away	18-Jan-98	1-3	Flo (37)	32,355	A.Wilkie
1998-99	Away	5-Dec-98	0-0		36,430	G.Willard
1998-99	Home	1-May-99	3-1	Zola (25, 81); Petrescu (50)	34,909	D.Gallagher

| 1999-00 | Away | 20-Nov-99 | 1-1 | Flo (90) | 38,225 | M.Halsey |
| 1999-00 | Home | 11-Mar-00 | 1-1 | Wise (29) | 35,113 | D.Elleray |

IPSWICH TOWN

Season	Venue	Date	Res	Scorers	Attendance	Referee
1992-93	Home	17-Oct-92	2-1	Hall (28); Harford (78)	16,702	B.Hill
1992-93	Away	6-Apr-93	1-1	Spencer (58)	17,444	J.Lloyd
1993-94	Away	21-Aug-93	0-1		17,355	D.Elleray
1993-94	Home	11-Dec-93	1-1	Peacock (23)	13,208	A.Wilkie
1994-95	Home	23-Oct-94	2-0	Wise (74); Shipperley (83)	15,068	B.Hill
1994-95	Away	21-Jan-95	2-2	Stein (67); Burley (88)	17,296	P.Don

LEEDS UNITED

Season	Venue	Date	Res	Scorers	Attendance	Referee
1992-93	Home	29-Nov-92	1-0	Townsend (87)	24,345	M.Bodenham
1992-93	Away	24-Mar-93	1-1	Donaghy (53)	28,135	A.Wilkie
1993-94	Away	6-Nov-93	1-4	Shipperley (84)	35,050	D.Gallagher
1993-94	Home	23-Apr-94	1-1	Spencer (63)	18,544	P.Foakes
1994-95	Away	27-Aug-94	3-2	Wise (37 pen); Spencer (61,88)	32,212	G.Ashby
1994-95	Home	11-Mar-95	0-3		20,174	P.Jones
1995-96	Away	18-Nov-95	0-1		36,209	M.Reed
1995-96	Home	13-Apr-96	4-1	Hughes (18, 35, 48 pen); Spencer (19)	22,131	D.Gallagher
1996-97	Away	1-Dec-96	0-2		32,671	S.Dunn
1996-97	Home	3-May-97	0-0		28,277	J.Winter
1997-98	Home	13-Dec-97	0-0		34,690	G.Poll
1997-98	Away	8-Apr-98	1-3	Charvet (11)	37,276	D.Elleray
1998-99	Away	24-Oct-98	0-0		36,292	M.Reed
1998-99	Home	5-May-99	1-0	Poyet (68)	34,762	J.Winter
1999-00	Home	19-Dec-99	0-2		35,106	J.Winter
1999-00	Away	1-Apr-00	1-0	Harley (62)	40,162	J.Winter

LEICESTER CITY

Season	Venue	Date	Res	Scorers	Attendance	Referee
1994-95	Home	8-Oct-94	4-0	Spencer (1,49); Peacock (4); Shipperley (77)	18,397	J.Worrall
1994-95	Away	6-May-95	1-1	Furlong (15)	18,140	G.Willard
1996-97	Away	12-Oct-96	3-1	Vialli (48); Di Matteo (64); Hughes, M (80)	20,766	M.Reed
1996-97	Home	19-Apr-97	2-1	Minto (13); Hughes M. (72)	27,723	A.Wilkie
1997-98	Home	18-Oct-97	1-0	Lebeof (86)	33,356	U.Rennie
1997-98	Away	21-Feb-98	0-2		21,335	P.Durkin
1998-99	Away	21-Nov-98	4-2	Zola (28, 90); Poyet (39); Flo (56)	21,401	P.Durkin
1998-99	Home	18-Apr-99	2-2	Zola (30); Petrescu (69)	34,535	M.Reed
1999-00	Away	14-Aug-99	2-2	Wise (48); OG (90, Sinclair)	21,068	S.Lodge
1999-00	Home	15-Jan-00	1-1	Wise (85)	35,063	G.Barber

LIVERPOOL

Season	Venue	Date	Res	Scorers	Attendance	Referee
1992-93	Away	5-Sep-92	1-2	Harford (72)	34,199	J.Key
1992-93	Home	10-Feb-93	0-0		20,981	J.Martin
1993-94	Home	25-Sep-93	1-0	Shipperley (48)	31,271	K.Hackett
1993-94	Away	19-Mar-94	1-2	Burley (50)	38,629	R.Gifford
1994-95	Away	9-Nov-94	1-3	Spencer (3)	32,855	G.Poll

1994-95	Home	18-Dec-94	0-0		27,050	D.Gallagher
1995-96	Home	30-Dec-95	2-2	Spencer (9, 44)	31,137	K.Burge
1995-96	Away	16-Mar-96	0-2		40,820	S.Dunn
1996-97	Away	21-Sep-96	1-5	Leboeuf (89 pen)	40,739	S.Dunn
1996-97	Home	1-Jan-97	1-0	Di Matteo (44)	28,239	S.Lodge
1997-98	Away	5-Oct-97	2-4	Zola (22); Poyet (85 pen)	36,647	D.Elleray
1997-98	Home	25-Apr-98	4-1	Hughes,M. (10, 75); Clarke (69); Flo (70)	34,639	G.Ashby
1998-99	Away	4-Oct-98	1-1	Casiraghi (10)	44,404	G.Poll
1998-99	Home	27-Feb-99	2-1	Leboeuf (7 pen); Goldbaek (38)	34,822	P.Durkin
1999-00	Away	16-Oct-99	0-1		44,826	M.Reed
1999-00	Home	29-Apr-00	2-0	Weah (2); Di Matteo (14)	34,957	G.Barber

MANCHESTER CITY

Season	Venue	Date	Res	Scorers	Attendance	Referee
1992-93	Away	20-Sep-92	1-0	Harford (40)	22,420	K.Hackett
1992-93	Home	9-Jan-93	2-4	Stuart (77); Spencer (83)	15,939	V.Callow
1993-94	Home	22-Nov-93	0-0		10,128	M.Reed
1993-94	Away	30-Apr-94	2-2	Fleck (15); Cascarino (19)	33,594	G.Poll
1994-95	Home	31-Aug-94	3-0	Peacock (4); Wise (73); Vonk (OG 83)	21,740	M.Reed
1994-95	Away	8-Mar-95	2-1	Stein (5, 81)	21,880	D.Elleray
1995-96	Away	23-Dec-95	1-0	Peacock (76)	28,668	G.Willard
1995-96	Home	12-Mar-96	1-1	Gullit (25)	17,078	P.Durkin

MANCHESTER UNITED

Season	Venue	Date	Res	Scorers	Attendance	Referee
1992-93	Home	19-Dec-92	1-1	Lee (67)	34,496	R.Lewis
1992-93	Away	17-Apr-93	0-3		40,139	H.King
1993-94	Home	11-Sep-93	1-0	Peacock (17)	37,064	P.Foakes
1993-94	Away	5-Mar-94	1-0	Peacock (65)	44,745	D.Gallagher
1994-95	Home	26-Dec-94	2-3	Spencer (58 pen); Newton (77)	31,161	M.Reed
1994-95	Away	17-Apr-95	0-0		43,728	S.Lodge
1995-96	Home	21-Oct-95	1-4	Hughes (76)	31,019	A.Wilkie
1995-96	Away	2-Dec-95	1-1	Wise (53)	42,019	M.Bodenham
1996-97	Away	2-Nov-96	3-1	Duberry (30); Vialli (59)	55,198	K.Burge
1996-97	Home	22-Feb-97	1-1	Zola (3)	28,336	G.Ashby
1997-98	Away	24-Sep-97	2-2	OG (25, Berg); Hughes,M. (68)	55,163	G.Willard
1997-98	Home	28-Feb-98	0-1		34,511	S.Dunn
1998-99	Away	16-Dec-98	1-1	Zola (83)	55,159	G.Barber
1998-99	Home	29-Dec-98	0-0		34,741	M.Riley
1999-00	Home	3-Oct-99	5-0	Poyet (1, 54); Sutton (16); OG (59, Berg); Morris (81)	34,909	D.Gallagher
1999-00	Away	24-Apr-00	2-3	Petrescu (22); Zola (36)	61,593	S.Dunn

MIDDLESBROUGH

Season	Venue	Date	Res	Scorers	Attendance	Referee
1992-93	Away	11-Dec-92	0-0		15,559	K.Barratt
1992-93	Home	3-Apr-93	4-0	Donaghy (52); Spencer (61); Stuart (73); Barnard (89)	13,043	J.Worrall
1995-96	Away	26-Aug-95	0-2		28,286	S.Lodge
1995-96	Home	4-Feb-96	5-0	Peacock (28, 38, 55); Spencer (31); Furlong (52)	21,060	K.Cooper
1996-97	Home	21-Aug-96	1-0	Di Matteo (85)	28,272	G.Willard
1996-97	Away	22-Mar-97	0-1		29,811	M.Riley
1998-99	Home	27-Sep-98	2-0	OG (26, Pallister); Zola (81)	34,811	M.Reed

Season	Venue	Date	Res	Scorers	Attendance	Referee
1998-99	Away	14-Apr-99	0-0		34,406	N.Barry
1999-00	Away	25-Sep-99	1-0	Lambourde (54)	34,183	P.Alcock
1999-00	Home	22-Apr-00	1-1	Poyet (10)	34,467	U.Rennie

NEWCASTLE UNITED

Season	Venue	Date	Res	Scorers	Attendance	Referee
1993-94	Home	28-Dec-93	1-0	Stein (11)	22,133	J.Worrall
1993-94	Away	4-Apr-94	0-0		32,218	S.Lodge
1994-95	Away	10-Sep-94	2-4	Peacock (15); Furlong (27)	34,435	P.Jones
1994-95	Home	1-Apr-95	1-1	Peacock (38)	22,987	M.Bodenham
1995-96	Away	24-Sep-95	0-2		36,225	P.Jones
1995-96	Home	9-Dec-95	1-0	Petrescu (43)	31,098	R.Dilkes
1996-97	Home	23-Nov-96	1-1	Vialli (25)	28,401	M.Reed
1996-97	Away	16-Apr-97	1-3	Burley (62)	36,320	R.Dilkes
1997-98	Home	27-Sep-97	1-0	Poyet (75)	31,563	M.Riley
1997-98	Away	2-May-98	1-3	Di Matteo (78)	36,710	K.Burge
1998-99	Home	22-Aug-98	1-1	Babayaro (23)	34,795	U.Rennie
1998-99	Away	9-Jan-99	1-0	Petrescu (39)	36,711	D.Gallagher
1999-00	Home	11-Sep-99	1-0	Leboeuf (37 pen)	35,092	G.Poll
1999-00	Away	4-Mar-00	1-0	Poyet (22)	36,448	M.Riley

NORWICH CITY

Season	Venue	Date	Res	Scorers	Attendance	Referee
1992-93	Away	19-Aug-92	1-2	Stuart (15)	15,164	G.Ashby
1992-93	Home	12-Sep-92	2-3	Harford (2); Townsend (29)	16,880	K.Barratt
1993-94	Home	16-Oct-93	1-2	Peacock (83)	16,923	V.Callow
1993-94	Away	15-Jan-94	1-1	Stein (42)	19,472	K.Cooper
1994-95	Home	20-Aug-94	2-0	Sinclair (44); Furlong (75)	23,098	T.Holbrook
1994-95	Away	10-Dec-94	0-3		18,246	J.Worrall

NOTTINGHAM FOREST

Season	Venue	Date	Res	Scorers	Attendance	Referee
1992-93	Home	26-Sep-92	0-0		19,760	J.Worrall
1992-93	Away	16-Jan-93	0-3		23,249	P.Durkin
1994-95	Away	19-Nov-94	1-0	Spencer (28)	22,092	T.Holbrook
1994-95	Home	25-Jan-95	0-2		17,890	M.Bodenham
1995-96	Away	23-Aug-95	0-0		27,007	J.Winter
1995-96	Home	20-Jan-96	1-0	Spencer (55)	24,482	J.Winter
1996-97	Home	28-Sep-96	1-1	Vialli (51)	27,673	G.Poll
1996-97	Away	11-Jan-97	0-2		28,358	K.Burge
1998-99	Home	12-Sep-98	2-1	Zola (1); Poyet (35)	34,809	P.Alcock
1998-99	Away	20-Feb-99	3-1	Forssell (6); Goldbaek (25, 83)	26,351	J.Winter

OLDHAM ATHLETIC

Season	Venue	Date	Res	Scorers	Attendance	Referee
1992-93	Home	15-Aug-92	1-1	Harford (9)	20,699	J.Borrett
1992-93	Away	6-Feb-93	1-3	Harford (89)	11,762	R.Milford
1993-94	Home	30-Oct-93	0-1		15,372	D.Frampton
1993-94	Away	12-Feb-94	1-2	Spencer (52)	12,002	A.Gunn

QPR

Season	Venue	Date	Res	Scorers	Attendance	Referee
1992-93	Home	29-Aug-92	1-0	Harford (59)	22,910	A.Buksh
1992-93	Away	27-Jan-93	1-1	Spencer (47)	15,806	T.Ward
1993-94	Home	25-Aug-93	2-0	Peacock (17); Cascarino (51)	20,191	K.Burge
1993-94	Away	13-Apr-94	1-1	Wise (79)	15,735	R.Milford
1994-95	Away	22-Mar-95	0-1		15,103	B.Hill
1994-95	Home	29-Apr-95	1-0	Sinclair (64)	21,704	G.Ashby
1995-96	Away	2-Jan-96	2-1	OG (78, Brazier); Furlong (90)	14,904	D.Elleray
1995-96	Home	23-Mar-96	1-1	Spencer (9)	25,590	M.Reed

SHEFFIELD UNITED

Season	Venue	Date	Res	Scorers	Attendance	Referee
1992-93	Home	31-Oct-92	1-2	Townsend (41)	13,763	D.Allison
1992-93	Away	8-May-93	2-4	Lee (86); Townsend (87)	24,850	A.Gunn
1993-94	Away	27-Nov-93	0-1		16,119	R.Milford
1993-94	Home	7-May-94	3-2	Kjeldjerg (58); Stein (76, 90)	21,782	K.Cooper

SHEFFIELD WEDNESDAY

Season	Venue	Date	Res	Scorers	Attendance	Referee
1992-93	Away	22-Aug-92	3-3	Jones (49); Stuart (57); Newton (64)	26,338	R.Dilkes
1992-93	Home	30-Jan-93	0-2		16,261	P.Foakes
1993-94	Home	28-Aug-93	1-1	Lee (34)	16,652	K.Morton
1993-94	Away	30-Mar-94	1-3	Spencer (65)	20,433	D.Allison
1994-95	Away	29-Oct-94	1-1	Wise (40)	25,450	M.Reed
1994-95	Home	14-Jan-95	1-1	Spencer (34)	17,285	G.Willard
1995-96	Home	4-Nov-95	0-0		23,216	P.Danson
1995-96	Away	17-Apr-96	0-0		25,094	G.Willard
1996-97	Away	7-Sep-96	2-0	Burley (28); Myers (83)	30,983	P.Jones
1996-97	Home	28-Dec-96	2-2	Zola (10); Hughes, M. (22)	27,467	P.Durkin
1997-98	Away	20-Dec-97	4-1	Petrescu (30); Vialli (56); Leboeuf (65 pen); Flo (84)	28,334	G.Barber
1997-98	Home	19-Apr-98	1-0	Lebeof (22 pen)	29,075	G.Willard
1998-99	Home	28-Nov-98	1-1	Zola (27)	34,451	N.Barry
1998-99	Away	25-Apr-99	0-0		21,652	S.Dunn
1999-00	Home	29-Dec-99	3-0	Wise (31); Flo (34); Morris (83)	32,938	A.D'Urso
1999-00	Away	15-Apr-00	0-1		21,743	P.Durkin

SOUTHAMPTON

Season	Venue	Date	Res	Scorers	Attendance	Referee
1992-93	Home	26-Dec-92	1-1	Newton (89)	18,344	A.Gunn
1992-93	Away	10-Apr-93	0-1		15,135	K.Burge
1993-94	Away	27-Dec-93	1-3	Stein (42)	14,221	P.Durkin
1993-94	Home	2-Apr-94	2-0	Spencer (44); Johnsen (80)	19,801	M.Reed
1994-95	Away	3-Dec-94	1-0	Furlong (89)	14,404	R.Gifford
1994-95	Home	12-Apr-95	0-2		16,738	A.Wilkie
1995-96	Home	16-Sep-95	3-0	Sinclair (74); Gullit (86); Hughes (90)	26,237	P.Alcock
1995-96	Away	24-Feb-96	3-2	Wise (20, 26 pen); Gullit (53)	15,226	G.Ashby
1996-97	Away	18-Aug-96	0-0		15,186	M.Bodenham
1996-97	Home	19-Mar-97	1-0	Zola (21)	28,079	S.Lodge
1997-98	Home	30-Aug-97	4-2	Petrescu (7); Lebeof (30); M.Hughes (31); Wise (34)	30,008	A.Wilkie

1997-98	Away	29-Dec-97	0-1		15,231	M.Bodenham
1998-99	Away	26-Dec-98	2-0	Flo (20); Poyet (48)	15,253	D.Elleray
1998-99	Home	6-Feb-99	1-0	Zola (11)	34,920	R.Harris
1999-00	Away	26-Dec-99	2-1	Flo (18, 43)	15,232	P.Alcock
1999-00	Home	25-Mar-00	1-1	OG (75, Richards)	34,956	D.Gallagher

SUNDERLAND

Season	Venue	Date	Res	Scorers	Attendance	Referee
1996-97	Away	14-Dec-96	0-3		19,683	M.Bodenham
1996-97	Home	16-Mar-97	6-2	Zola (38); Sinclair (42); Petrescu (50); Hughes, M. (76, 89); Di Matteo (90)	24,072	G.Willard
1999-00	Home	7-Aug-99	4-0	Poyet (20, 78); Zola (32); Flo (77)	34,831	M.Riley
1999-00	Away	4-Dec-99	1-4	Poyet (81)	41,377	S.Dunn

SWINDON TOWN

Season	Venue	Date	Res	Scorers	Attendance	Referee
1993-94	Away	1-Jan-94	3-1	Shipperley (19); Stein (44); Wise (89)	16,261	K.Hackett
1993-94	Home	27-Apr-94	2-0	Wise (25pen); Peacock (39)	11,180	B.Hill

TOTTENHAM HOTSPUR

Season	Venue	Date	Res	Scorers	Attendance	Referee
1992-93	Away	5-Dec-92	2-1	Newton (76, 85)	31,540	R.Dilkes
1992-93	Home	20-Mar-93	1-1	Cascarino (52)	25,157	R.Dilkes
1993-94	Away	1-Sep-93	1-1	Cascarino (23)	27,567	V.Callow
1993-94	Home	27-Feb-94	4-3	Donaghy (29); Stein (33, 90 pen); Spencer (41)	19,398	J.Lloyd
1994-95	Away	23-Nov-94	0-0		27,037	G.Willard
1994-95	Home	11-Feb-95	1-1	Wise (79)	30,812	P.Durkin
1995-96	Home	25-Nov-95	0-0		31,059	S.Lodge
1995-96	Away	27-Apr-96	1-1	Hughes (35)	40,782	A.Wilkie
1996-97	Home	26-Oct-96	3-1	Gullit (27); Lee (55 pen); Di Matteo (81)	28,373	R.Dilkes
1996-97	Away	1-Feb-97	2-1	OG (1, Campbell); Di Matteo (52)	33,027	P.Alcock
1997-98	Away	6-Dec-97	6-1	Flo (39, 62, 89); Di Matteo (47); Petrescu (59); Nicholls (77)	28,476	D.Gallagher
1997-98	Home	11-Apr-98	2-0	Flo (75); Vialli (88)	34,149	P.Durkin
1998-99	Home	19-Dec-98	2-0	Poyet (80); Flo (90)	34,881	G.Poll
1998-99	Away	10-May-99	2-2	Poyet (4); Goldbaek (72)	36,878	D.Elleray
1999-00	Home	12-Jan-00	1-0	Weah (87)	34,969	N.Barry
1999-00	Away	5-Feb-00	1-0	Lambourde (52)	36,041	G.Poll

WATFORD

Season	Venue	Date	Res	Scorers	Attendance	Referee
1999-00	Away	18-Sep-99	0-1		21,244	M.Reed
1999-00	Home	26-Feb-00	2-1	Desailly (2); Harley (65)	34,920	S.Dunn

WEST HAM UNITED

Season	Venue	Date	Res	Scorers	Attendance	Referee
1993-94	Away	2-Oct-93	0-1		18,917	R.Hart
1993-94	Home	26-Mar-94	2-0	Barnard (39); Hoddle (75)	19,545	M.Bodenham
1994-95	Home	2-Oct-94	1-2	Furlong (62)	18,696	P.Don
1994-95	Away	25-Feb-95	2-1	Burley (67); Stein (75)	21,500	G.Ashby

1995-96	Away	11-Sep-95	3-1	Wise (31); Spencer (33, 89)	19,228	R.Hart
1995-96	Home	17-Feb-96	1-2	Peacock (13)	25,252	G.Willard
1996-97	Home	21-Dec-96	3-1	Hughes, M. (5, 36); Zola (10)	28,315	A.Wilkie
1996-97	Away	12-Mar-97	2-3	Vialli (26); Hughes, M. (87)	24,502	K.Burge
1997-98	Home	9-Nov-97	2-1	OG (56, Ferdinand); Zola (81)	34,382	G.Barber
1997-98	Away	14-Mar-98	1-2	Charvet (52)	25,829	M.Bodenham
1998-99	Away	8-Nov-98	1-1	Babayaro (76)	26,023	G.Barber
1998-99	Home	13-Mar-99	0-1		34,765	S.Lodge
1999-00	Home	7-Nov-99	0-0		34,935	M.Riley
1999-00	Away	18-Mar-00	0-0		26,041	S.Dunn

WIMBLEDON

Season	Venue	Date	Res	Scorers	Attendance	Referee
1992-93	Away	28-Dec-92	0-0		14,687	D.Elleray
1992-93	Home	12-Apr-93	4-2	Wise (45 pen); Hall (50); Spencer (81); Shipperley (85)	13,138	D.Elleray
1993-94	Away	17-Aug-93	1-1	Wise (78)	11,263	M.Reed
1993-94	Home	16-Mar-94	2-0	OG (21, Fashanu); Burley (73)	11,903	K.Morton
1994-95	Home	31-Dec-94	1-1	Furlong (65)	16,105	K.Morton
1994-95	Away	10-Apr-95	1-1	Sinclair (35)	7,022	K.Morton
1995-96	Home	26-Dec-95	1-2	Petrescu (12)	21,906	D.Gallagher
1995-96	Away	2-Mar-96	1-1	Furlong (35)	17,048	P.Jones
1996-97	Home	19-Oct-96	2-4	Minto (11); Vialli (84 pen)	28,020	D.Elleray
1996-97	Away	22-Apr-97	1-0	Petrescu (14)	14,601	P.Danson
1997-98	Away	26-Aug-97	2-0	Di Matteo (60); Petrescu (62)	22,237	M.Bodenham
1997-98	Home	26-Dec-97	1-1	Vialli (8)	34,100	G.Willard
1998-99	Home	14-Nov-98	3-0	Zola (32); Poyet (55); Petrescu (70)	34,757	J.Winter
1998-99	Away	11-Apr-99	2-1	Flo (24); Poyet (53)	21,577	G.Willard
1999-00	Away	28-Aug-99	1-0	Petrescu (78)	22,167	S.Dunn
1999-00	Home	12-Feb-00	3-1	Poyet (79); Weah (80); Morris (90)	34,826	P.Jones

INTRODUCTION

Founded as Singer's FC, cycle manufacturers, in 1883. Joined the Birmingham and District League in 1894; in 1898 changed name to Coventry City; and in 1905 moved to the Athletic Ground, Highfield Road. Elected to Division One of the Southern League in 1908, but relegated to the Second in 1914.

Joined the Wartime Midland Section of the Football League in 1918 and elected to an expanded Second Division of the Football League for 1919-20. Founder members of the Fourth Division in 1958. Promoted to Division One for the first time in 1967 and never relegated. Premier League founder members 1992.

Ground: Highfield Road Stadium, King Richard St, Coventry, CV2 4FW
Nickname: Sky Blues
Internet: www.ccfc.co.uk

HONOURS

Football League Div 2:	Champions 1966-67
Football League Div 3:	Champions 1963-64
Football League Div 3S:	Champions 1935-36
	Runners-up 1933-34
Football League Div 4:	Runners-up 1958-59
FA Cup:	Winners 1986-87

EUROPEAN RECORD

Champions League (0)	–
Cup-Winners' Cup (0)	–
UEFA Cup (1):	70-71 (2)

FAPL RECORD SUMMARY

Most Total:	OGRIZOVIC, Steve	191
Most Starts:	OGRIZOVIC, Steve	191
Most Subs:	NDLOVU, Peter	22
Most SNU:	GOULD, Jonathan	110
Most PS:	HUCKERBY, Darren	27
Most Goals:	DUBLIN, Dion	62
Most Yel:	WILLIAMS, Paul	33
Most Red:	WILLIAMS, Paul	3

PLAYING RECORD – SEASON TOTALS

Season	Pn	P	W	D	L	F	A	Pts
1992-93	15	42	13	13	16	52	57	52
1993-94	11	42	14	14	14	43	45	56
1994-95	16	42	12	14	16	44	62	50
1995-96	16	38	8	14	16	42	60	38
1996-97	17	38	9	14	15	38	54	41
1997-98	11	38	12	16	10	46	44	52
1998-99	15	38	11	9	18	39	51	42
1999-00	14	38	12	8	18	47	54	44
Totals		316	91	102	123	351	427	375

PLAYING RECORD – HOME TOTALS

Season	Pn	P	W	D	L	F	A	Pts
1992-93	15	21	7	4	10	29	28	25
1993-94	11	21	9	7	5	23	17	34
1994-95	16	21	7	7	7	23	25	28
1995-96	16	19	6	7	6	21	23	25
1996-97	17	19	4	8	7	19	23	20
1997-98	11	19	8	9	2	26	17	33
1998-99	15	19	8	6	5	26	21	30
1999-00	14	19	12	1	6	38	22	37
Totals		158	61	49	48	205	176	232

PLAYING RECORD – AWAY TOTALS

Season	Pn	P	W	D	L	F	A	Pts
1992-93	15	21	6	9	6	23	29	27
1993-94	11	21	5	7	9	20	28	22
1994-95	16	21	5	7	9	21	37	22
1995-96	16	19	2	7	10	21	37	13
1996-97	17	19	5	6	8	19	31	21
1997-98	11	19	4	7	8	20	27	19
1998-99	15	19	3	3	13	13	30	12
1999-00	14	19	0	7	12	9	32	7
Totals		158	30	53	75	146	251	143

HIGHEST HOME ATTENDANCES

	Attendance	Opponents	Date	Season
1	24,429	Manchester U.	12-Apr-93	1992-93
2	24,245	Aston Villa	26-Dec-92	1992-93
3	23,344	Manchester U.	22-Nov-95	1995-96
4	23,098	Tottenham H.	26-Dec-98	1998-99
5	23,098	Liverpool	1-Apr-00	1999-00

LOWEST HOME ATTENDANCES

	Attendance	Opponents	Date	Season
1	9,526	Ipswich T.	10-Oct-94	1994-95
2	9,837	Southampton	16-Oct-93	1993-94
3	10,439	Sheffield U.	31-Oct-93	1993-94
4	10,463	Southampton	3-Apr-93	1992-93
5	10,544	Oldham A.	23-Jan-93	1992-93

TOP SCORER – SEASON BY SEASON

Season	Player	Goals
1992-93	Quinn	17
1993-94	Ndlovu	11
1994-95	Dublin	13
1995-96	Dublin	14
1996-97	Dublin	14
1997-98	Dublin	18
1998-99	Whelan	10
1999-00	Keane	12

PLAYERS WITH MOST PREMIERSHIP APPEARANCES

Tot	Player	St	Sb	Gls
191	OGRIZOVIC, Steve	191	0	0
160	TELFER, Paul	151	9	6
155	SHAW, Richard	152	3	0
154	NDLOVU, Peter	132	22	35
153	DUBLIN, Dion	146	7	62
145	BORROWS, Brian	134	11	2
134	WHELAN, Noel	127	7	31
134	WILLIAMS, Paul	122	12	5
119	McALLISTER, Gary	119	0	20
101	BURROWS, David	96	5	0
94	HUCKERBY, Darren	85	9	28
85	HEDMAN, Magnus	85	0	0
85	BREEN, Gary	79	6	1
82	RENNIE, David	80	2	3
82	HALL, Marcus	65	17	1
80	WILLIAMS, John	66	14	11
79	ATHERTON, Peter	78	1	0
78	RICHARDSON, Kevin	75	3	0
77	BABB, Phil	70	7	3
75	FLYNN, Sean	69	6	7

CLUB-BY-CLUB RESULTS

ARSENAL

Season	Venue	Date	Res	Scorers	Attendance	Referee
1992-93	Away	7-Nov-92	0-3		27,693	J.Worrall
1992-93	Home	13-Mar-93	0-2		15,437	D.Allison
1993-94	Away	14-Aug-93	3-0	Quinn (34 pen, 62, 65)	26,397	A.Wilkie
1993-94	Home	4-Dec-93	1-0	Quinn (78)	12,632	R.Hart
1994-95	Away	23-Oct-94	1-2	Wegerle (81 pen)	31,725	A.Wilkie
1994-95	Home	21-Jan-95	0-1		14,468	J.Worrall
1995-96	Home	26-Aug-95	0-0		20,081	S.Dunn
1995-96	Away	3-Feb-96	1-1	Whelan (23)	35,623	S.Dunn
1996-97	Away	19-Oct-96	0-0		38,140	P.Jones
1996-97	Home	21-Apr-97	1-1	Dublin (1)	19,998	K.Burge
1997-98	Away	11-Aug-97	0-2		37,324	K.Burge
1997-98	Home	17-Jan-98	2-2	Whelan (21); Dublin (66 pen)	22,864	S.Lodge
1998-99	Home	31-Oct-98	0-1		23,040	U.Rennie
1998-99	Away	21-Mar-99	0-2		38,073	P.Alcock
1999-00	Home	26-Dec-99	3-2	McAllister (6); Hadji (40); Keane (71)	22,757	R.Harris
1999-00	Away	26-Mar-00	0-3		38,027	B.Knight

ASTON VILLA

Season	Venue	Date	Res	Scorers	Attendance	Referee
1992-93	Home	26-Dec-92	3-0	Quinn (52, 55); Rosario (59)	24,245	R.Dilkes
1992-93	Away	10-Apr-93	0-0		38,543	A.Gunn
1993-94	Away	11-Sep-93	0-0		31,181	M.Bodenham
1993-94	Home	6-Mar-94	0-1		14,323	K.Hackett
1994-95	Home	29-Aug-94	0-1		12,218	P.Durkin
1994-95	Away	6-Mar-95	0-0		26,186	G.Poll
1995-96	Home	30-Sep-95	0-3		21,004	A.Wilkie
1995-96	Away	16-Dec-95	1-4	Dublin (59)	28,476	P.Alcock
1996-97	Home	23-Nov-96	1-2	Dublin (75)	21,340	P.Durkin

1996-97	Away	19-Feb-97	1-2	OG (78, Staunton)	30,409	K.Burge
1997-98	Away	6-Dec-97	0-3		33,250	G.Barber
1997-98	Home	11-Apr-98	1-2	Whelan (59)	22,792	D.Gallagher
1998-99	Home	3-Oct-98	1-2	Soltvedt (71)	22,654	S.Lodge
1998-99	Away	27-Feb-99	4-1	Aloisi (25, 73); Boateng (51, 84)	38,799	U.Rennie
1999-00	Home	22-Nov-99	2-1	Roussel (8); Keane (65)	20,184	G.Barber
1999-00	Away	11-Mar-00	0-1		33,177	U.Rennie

BARNSLEY

Season	Venue	Date	Res	Scorers	Attendance	Referee
1997-98	Away	20-Oct-97	0-2		17,463	P.Alcock
1997-98	Home	21-Feb-98	1-0	Dublin (89 pen)	20,265	A.Wilkie

BLACKBURN ROVERS

Season	Venue	Date	Res	Scorers	Attendance	Referee
1992-93	Home	29-Aug-92	0-2		14,541	R.Lewis
1992-93	Away	26-Jan-93	5-2	OG (19, May); Hurst (44); Williams,J. (48); Quinn (85, 89)	15,215	K.Redfern
1993-94	Away	23-Nov-93	1-2	Ndlovu (62)	16,376	K.Burge
1993-94	Home	2-May-94	2-1	Darby (11, 55)	16,646	P.Don
1994-95	Away	27-Aug-94	0-4		21,657	G.Poll
1994-95	Home	11-Mar-95	1-1	Dublin (30)	18,547	T.Holbrook
1995-96	Away	23-Sep-95	1-5	Ndlovu (34)	24,382	K.Cooper
1995-96	Home	9-Dec-95	5-0	Busst (40); Dublin (60); Rennie (64); Ndlovu (74); Salako (88)	13,409	S.Dunn
1996-97	Home	28-Sep-96	0-0		17,032	J.Winter
1996-97	Away	11-Jan-97	0-4		24,055	P.Durkin
1997-98	Away	28-Sep-97	0-0		19,086	P.Jones
1997-98	Home	2-May-98	2-0	Dublin (19 pen); Boateng (34)	18,794	S.Lodge
1998-99	Away	7-Nov-98	2-1	Huckerby (54); Whelan (74)	23,779	P.Durkin
1998-99	Home	13-Mar-99	1-1	Aloisi (22)	19,701	C.Dunn

BOLTON WANDERERS

Season	Venue	Date	Res	Scorers	Attendance	Referee
1995-96	Away	30-Dec-95	2-1	Whelan (44); Salako (90 pen)	16,678	A.Wilkie
1995-96	Home	16-Mar-96	0-2		17,168	K.Burge
1997-98	Home	23-Aug-97	2-2	Telfer (8); Huckerby (20)	16,633	M.Riley
1997-98	Away	31-Jan-98	5-1	Whelan (25); Huckerby (57, 65); Dublin (73, 79)	25,000	D.Gallagher

BRADFORD CITY

Season	Venue	Date	Res	Scorers	Attendance	Referee
1999-00	Away	6-Nov-99	1-1	McAllister (1)	17,587	B.Knight
1999-00	Home	18-Mar-00	4-0	Roussel (7); Whelan (21); Eustace (85 pen); Zuniga (86)	19,201	S.Lodge

CHARLTON ATHLETIC

Season	Venue	Date	Res	Scorers	Attendance	Referee
1998-99	Away	27-Sep-98	1-1	Whelan (69)	20,043	J.Winter
1998-99	Home	6-Mar-99	2-1	Whelan (67); Soltvedt (85)	20,259	J.Winter

CHELSEA

Season	Venue	Date	Res	Scorers	Attendance	Referee
1992-93	Home	24-Oct-92	1-2	Rosario (58)	15,626	M.Peck
1992-93	Away	1-May-93	1-2	Quinn (15)	14,186	R.Groves
1993-94	Home	18-Sep-93	1-1	Morgan (49)	13,586	P.Durkin
1993-94	Away	4-May-94	2-1	Ndlovu (32); Morgan (34)	8,923	J.Borrett
1994-95	Away	6-Nov-94	2-2	Dublin (45); Ndlovu (77)	17,090	S.Lodge
1994-95	Home	4-Feb-95	2-2	Flyn (26); OG (36, Burley)	13,429	R.Hart
1995-96	Away	30-Aug-95	2-2	Isaias (40); Ndlovu (54)	24,398	G.Willard
1995-96	Home	10-Feb-96	1-0	Whelan (43)	20,629	R.Dilkes
1996-97	Away	24-Aug-96	0-2		25,024	P.Danson
1996-97	Home	9-Apr-97	3-1	Dublin (49); Williams (51); Whelan (58)	19,917	D.Gallagher
1997-98	Home	9-Aug-97	3-2	Dublin (41, 82, 88)	22,686	P.Durkin
1997-98	Away	10-Jan-98	1-3	Telfer (30)	34,647	M.Reed
1998-99	Home	15-Aug-98	2-1	Huckerby (10); Dublin (16)	23,042	G.Barber
1998-99	Away	16-Jan-99	1-2	Huckerby (9)	34,869	J.Winter
1999-00	Home	4-Jan-00	2-2	Roussel (54); Keane (81)	20,164	P.Durkin
1999-00	Away	12-Apr-00	1-2	McAllister (18)	33,316	G.Poll

CRYSTAL PALACE

Season	Venue	Date	Res	Scorers	Attendance	Referee
1992-93	Home	3-Oct-92	2-2	Pearce (7); Gallacher (18)	11,808	G.Ashby
1992-93	Away	27-Feb-93	0-0		12,248	P.Foakes
1994-95	Home	2-Nov-94	1-4	Dublin (23)	10,732	P.Jones
1994-95	Away	11-Feb-95	2-0	Jones (74); Dublin (86)	11,891	M.Bodenham
1997-98	Home	24-Sep-97	1-1	Dublin (8)	15,900	G.Barber
1997-98	Away	28-Feb-98	3-0	Telfer (1); Moldovan (40); Dublin (77)	21,810	D.Elleray

DERBY COUNTY

Season	Venue	Date	Res	Scorers	Attendance	Referee
1996-97	Away	30-Nov-96	1-2	Dublin (42)	18,042	M.Riley
1996-97	Home	3-May-97	1-2	McAllister (59)	22,839	R.Dilkes
1997-98	Away	22-Nov-97	1-3	Huckerby (71)	29,351	D.Elleray
1997-98	Home	28-Mar-98	1-0	Huckerby (44)	18,705	K.Burge
1998-99	Home	19-Dec-98	1-1	Whelan (16)	16,627	U.Rennie
1998-99	Away	8-May-99	0-0		32,450	P.Alcock
1999-00	Home	21-Aug-99	2-0	Keane (43,67)	17,685	J.Winter
1999-00	Away	22-Jan-00	0-0		28,381	G.Barber

EVERTON

Season	Venue	Date	Res	Scorers	Attendance	Referee
1992-93	Away	17-Oct-92	1-1	Ndlovu (44)	17,587	R.Hamer
1992-93	Home	7-Mar-93	0-1		11,285	D.Elleray
1993-94	Home	6-Nov-93	2-1	Quinn (27, 49)	11,550	A.Wilkie
1993-94	Away	23-Apr-94	0-0		23,352	R.Dilkes
1994-95	Away	15-Oct-94	2-0	Dublin (6); Wegerle (17)	28,233	D.Elleray
1994-95	Home	14-May-95	0-0		21,814	P.Jones
1995-96	Home	23-Dec-95	2-1	Busst (48); Whelan (84)	16,638	S.Lodge
1995-96	Away	9-Mar-96	2-2	Daish (38); Williams,P. (85)	34,517	P.Danson
1996-97	Away	4-Nov-96	1-1	McAllister (68)	31,477	G.Poll
1996-97	Home	22-Feb-97	0-0		19,497	J.Winter

1997-98	Home	25-Oct-97	0-0		18,760	S.Lodge
1997-98	Away	10-May-98	1-1	Dublin (89)	40,109	P.Alcock
1998-99	Home	15-Nov-98	3-0	Froggatt (15); Huckerby (48); Whelan (89)	19,290	G.Poll
1998-99	Away	11-Apr-99	0-2		32,341	R.Harris
1999-00	Away	2-Oct-99	1-1	McAllister (11)	34,839	N.Barry
1999-00	Home	15-Mar-00	1-0	McAllister (86)	18,518	M.Halsey

IPSWICH TOWN

Season	Venue	Date	Res	Scorers	Attendance	Referee
1992-93	Home	5-Dec-92	2-2	Gallacher (16); Quinn (54)	11,294	K.Hackett
1992-93	Away	20-Mar-93	0-0		16,698	J.Worrall
1993-94	Home	2-Feb-94	1-0	Flynn (5)	11,244	D.Allison
1993-94	Away	4-Apr-94	2-0	Flynn (55); Ndlovu (66)	12,782	R.Gifford
1994-95	Home	10-Oct-94	2-0	OG (45, Wark); Cook (76 pen)	9,526	R.Hart
1994-95	Away	6-May-95	0-2		12,893	M.Reed

LEEDS UNITED

Season	Venue	Date	Res	Scorers	Attendance	Referee
1992-93	Away	31-Oct-92	2-2	OG (12, McAllister); Ndlovu (77)	28,018	B.Hill
1992-93	Home	8-May-93	3-3	Williams (5); Quinn (40); Ndlovu (73)	19,591	K.Morton
1993-94	Home	25-Sep-93	0-2		13,933	K.Cooper
1993-94	Away	19-Mar-94	0-1		30,023	A.Wilkie
1994-95	Home	17-Sep-94	2-1	Dublin (50); Cook (83)	15,389	B.Hill
1994-95	Away	18-Mar-95	0-3		29,179	R.Hart
1995-96	Away	28-Oct-95	1-3	Dublin (12)	30,161	G.Ashby
1995-96	Home	5-May-96	0-0		22,769	D.Elleray
1996-97	Home	14-Sep-96	2-1	Salako (57); Whelan (65)	17,297	G.Willard
1996-97	Away	26-Dec-96	3-1	Huckerby (30); Dublin (38); McAllister (40)	36,465	M.Bodenham
1997-98	Home	4-Oct-97	0-0		17,770	A.Wilkie
1997-98	Away	25-Apr-98	3-3	Huckerby (20, 34, 62)	36,522	M.Reed
1998-99	Away	14-Dec-98	0-2		31,802	G.Poll
1998-99	Home	16-May-99	2-2	Aloisi (63); Telfer (72)	23,049	S.Lodge
1999-00	Home	11-Sep-99	3-4	McAllister (2 pen); Aloisi (17); Chippo (54)	21,532	S.Dunn
1999-00	Away	5-Mar-00	0-3		38,710	J.Winter

LEICESTER CITY

Season	Venue	Date	Res	Scorers	Attendance	Referee
1994-95	Away	3-Oct-94	2-2	Wegerle (11); Dublin (73)	19,372	K.Cooper
1994-95	Home	25-Feb-95	4-2	Flynn (18,76); Marsh (27); Ndlovu (87)	20,663	R.Gifford
1996-97	Away	21-Dec-96	2-0	Dublin (10, 71)	20,038	G.Barber
1996-97	Home	8-Mar-97	0-0		19,220	P.Alcock
1997-98	Home	29-Nov-97	0-2		18,309	M.Bodenham
1997-98	Away	4-Apr-98	1-1	Whelan (80)	21,137	G.Barber
1998-99	Home	28-Nov-98	1-1	Huckerby (78)	19,894	M.Riley
1998-99	Away	24-Apr-99	0-0		20,224	G.Barber
1999-00	Away	11-Aug-99	0-1		19,196	N.Barry
1999-00	Home	27-Nov-99	0-1		22,021	S.Lodge

COVENTRY CITY

LIVERPOOL

Season	Venue	Date	Res	Scorers	Attendance	Referee
1992-93	Home	19-Dec-92	5-1	Borrows (37 pen, 54); Gallacher (61); Quinn (71, 74)	19,779	K.Morton
1992-93	Away	17-Apr-93	0-4		33,328	T.Ward
1993-94	Home	1-Sep-93	1-0	Babb (21)	16,735	K.Burge
1993-94	Away	25-Feb-94	0-1		38,547	D.Elleray
1994-95	Home	3-Dec-94	1-1	Flynn (57)	21,029	K.Burge
1994-95	Away	14-Mar-95	3-2	Ndlovu (21,36 pen,87)	27,183	M.Reed
1995-96	Away	14-Oct-95	0-0		39,079	P.Danson
1995-96	Home	6-Apr-96	1-0	Whelan (18)	23,037	P.Jones
1996-97	Home	4-Sep-96	0-1		23,021	G.Poll
1996-97	Away	6-Apr-97	2-1	Whelan (65); Dublin (90)	40,079	P.Danson
1997-98	Away	20-Dec-97	0-1		39,707	P.Alcock
1997-98	Home	19-Apr-98	1-1	Dublin (47 pen)	22,721	G.Willard
1998-99	Away	9-Sep-98	0-2		41,771	D.Gallagher
1998-99	Home	30-Jan-99	2-1	Boateng (60); Whelan (71)	23,056	M.Riley
1999-00	Away	18-Dec-99	0-2		44,024	A.D'Urso
1999-00	Home	1-Apr-00	0-3		23,098	M.Reed

MANCHESTER CITY

Season	Venue	Date	Res	Scorers	Attendance	Referee
1992-93	Home	21-Nov-92	2-3	Quinn (13, 49)	14,590	P.Durkin
1992-93	Away	10-Mar-93	0-1		20,092	P.Durkin
1993-94	Away	27-Aug-93	1-1	Wegerle (85)	21,537	P.Don
1993-94	Home	19-Feb-94	4-0	Rennie (54); Quinn (75); Wiliams,J. (87); Ndlovu (90)	11,739	G.Ashby
1994-95	Home	29-Oct-94	1-0	Dublin (85)	15,804	M.Bodenham
1994-95	Away	14-Jan-95	0-0		20,632	D.Gallagher
1995-96	Home	23-Aug-95	2-1	Telfer (12); Dublin (86)	16,568	P.Alcock
1995-96	Away	20-Jan-96	1-1	Dublin (66)	25,710	R.Hart

MANCHESTER UNITED

Season	Venue	Date	Res	Scorers	Attendance	Referee
1992-93	Away	28-Dec-92	0-5		36,025	R.Groves
1992-93	Home	12-Apr-93	0-1		24,429	R.Gifford
1993-94	Home	27-Nov-93	0-1		17,009	S.Lodge
1993-94	Away	8-May-94	0-0		44,717	S.Lodge
1994-95	Away	3-Jan-95	0-2		43,130	G.Willard
1994-95	Home	1-May-95	2-3	Ndlovu (39); Pressley (72)	21,885	P.Don
1995-96	Home	22-Nov-95	0-4		23,344	K.Burge
1995-96	Away	8-Apr-96	0-1		50,332	D.Gallagher
1996-97	Home	18-Jan-97	0-2		23,085	S.Dunn
1996-97	Away	1-Mar-97	1-3	Huckerby (85)	55,230	G.Barber
1997-98	Away	30-Aug-97	0-3		55,074	G.Ashby
1997-98	Home	28-Dec-97	3-2	Whelan (12); Dublin (86 pen); Huckerby (87)	23,054	N.Barry
1998-99	Away	12-Sep-98	0-2		55,193	U.Rennie
1998-99	Home	20-Feb-99	0-1		22,596	D.Gallagher
1999-00	Home	25-Aug-99	1-2	Aloisi (80)	22,024	A.Wilkie
1999-00	Away	5-Feb-00	2-3	Roussel (65, 90)	61,380	A.Wilkie

MIDDLESBROUGH

Season	Venue	Date	Res	Scorers	Attendance	Referee
1992-93	Home	15-Aug-92	2-1	Williams,J. (9); Smith (51)	12,681	H.King
1992-93	Away	6-Feb-93	2-0	Ndlovu (67); Quinn (79)	14,008	J.Borrett
1995-96	Away	16-Sep-95	1-2	Isaias (47)	27,882	G.Poll
1995-96	Home	24-Feb-96	0-0		17,979	P.Durkin
1996-97	Away	7-Sep-96	0-4		29,811	G.Barber
1996-97	Home	28-Dec-96	3-0	Huckerby (29); McAllister (64 pen); OG (85, Liddle)	20,617	S.Lodge
1998-99	Away	21-Nov-98	0-2		34,293	G.Willard
1998-99	Home	17-Apr-99	1-2	McAllister (72)	19,231	P.Jones
1999-00	Away	19-Feb-00	0-2		32,798	G.Barber
1999-00	Home	15-Apr-00	2-1	OG (32, Ince); Keane (61)	19,435	N.Barry

NEWCASTLE UNITED

Season	Venue	Date	Res	Scorers	Attendance	Referee
1993-94	Home	18-Aug-93	2-1	Ndlovu (58); Harford (85)	15,760	J.Borrett
1993-94	Away	23-Feb-94	0-4		32,210	R.Hart
1994-95	Away	24-Aug-94	0-4		34,163	P.Danson
1994-95	Home	17-Dec-94	0-0		17,233	P.Danson
1995-96	Away	19-Aug-95	0-3		36,485	R.Dilkes
1995-96	Home	14-Jan-96	0-1		20,553	P.Jones
1996-97	Home	17-Dec-96	2-1	Huckerby (6); McAllister (31)	21,538	P.Jones
1996-97	Away	15-Mar-97	0-4		36,571	G.Ashby
1997-98	Home	8-Nov-97	2-2	Dublin (4, 82)	22,679	P.Durkin
1997-98	Away	14-Mar-98	0-0		36,767	P.Jones
1998-99	Home	19-Sep-98	1-5	Whelan (4)	22,656	R.Harris
1998-99	Away	17-Feb-99	1-4	Whelan (17)	36,352	S.Dunn
1999-00	Home	16-Oct-99	4-1	Palmer (13); Williams (21); Keane (39); Hadji (90)	23,031	A.Wiley
1999-00	Away	29-Apr-00	0-2		36,408	P.Jones

NORWICH CITY

Season	Venue	Date	Res	Scorers	Attendance	Referee
1992-93	Home	26-Sep-92	1-1	Ndlovu (37)	16,436	A.Buksh
1992-93	Away	16-Jan-93	1-1	Quinn (57)	13,613	A.Gunn
1993-94	Away	2-Oct-93	0-1		16,239	D.Gallagher
1993-94	Home	26-Mar-94	2-1	Flynn (28); Quinn (70)	13,515	D.Frampton
1994-95	Home	19-Nov-94	1-0	Jones (62)	11,885	G.Willard
1994-95	Away	25-Jan-95	2-2	Dublin (22); Jenkinson (76)	14,024	P.Don

NOTTINGHAM FOREST

Season	Venue	Date	Res	Scorers	Attendance	Referee
1992-93	Away	21-Sep-92	1-1	Rosario (45)	17,553	K.Morton
1992-93	Home	9-Jan-93	0-1		15,264	M.Bodenham
1994-95	Home	26-Dec-94	0-0		19,224	A.Wilkie
1994-95	Away	17-Apr-95	0-2		26,253	P.Durkin
1995-96	Home	9-Sep-95	1-1	Dublin (12)	17,238	P.Jones
1995-96	Away	17-Apr-96	0-0		24,629	M.Reed
1996-97	Home	17-Aug-96	0-3		19,468	A.Wilkie
1996-97	Away	29-Jan-97	1-0	Huckerby (50)	22,619	A.Wiley
1998-99	Away	22-Aug-98	0-1		22,546	K.Burge
1998-99	Home	9-Jan-99	4-0	Huckerby (45, 46, 75); Telfer (54)	17,172	P.Jones

OLDHAM ATHLETIC

Season	Venue	Date	Res	Scorers	Attendance	Referee
1992-93	Away	5-Sep-92	1-0	Gallacher (55)	11,254	D.Allison
1992-93	Home	23-Jan-93	3-0	Gallacher (6, 18); Ndlovu (12)	10,544	R.Lewis
1993-94	Away	24-Aug-93	3-3	Williams,J. (9); Ndlovu (74); Wegerle (84 pen)	10,817	P.Foakes
1993-94	Home	18-Dec-93	1-1	Wegerle (28)	11,792	D.Gallagher

QPR

Season	Venue	Date	Res	Scorers	Attendance	Referee
1992-93	Home	26-Aug-92	0-1		13,563	S.Lodge
1992-93	Away	20-Feb-93	0-2		12,453	P.Durkin
1993-94	Away	23-Oct-93	1-5	Ndlovu (75)	12,979	G.Ashby
1993-94	Home	22-Jan-94	0-1		12,065	A.Wilkie
1994-95	Away	10-Sep-94	2-2	Cook (22); Dublin (86)	11,398	J.Worrall
1994-95	Home	1-Apr-95	0-1		15,740	P.Danson
1995-96	Away	19-Dec-95	1-1	Dublin (75)	11,189	M.Bodenham
1995-96	Home	13-Apr-96	1-0	Jess (70)	22,916	K.Cooper

SHEFFIELD UNITED

Season	Venue	Date	Res	Scorers	Attendance	Referee
1992-93	Away	28-Nov-92	1-1	Quinn (7)	15,625	P.Don
1992-93	Home	24-Mar-93	1-3	Williams,J. (17)	12,993	P.Wright
1993-94	Home	31-Oct-93	0-0		10,439	A.Gunn
1993-94	Away	12-Feb-94	0-0		15,394	J.Worrall

SHEFFIELD WEDNESDAY

Season	Venue	Date	Res	Scorers	Attendance	Referee
1992-93	Away	2-Sep-92	2-1	Ndlovu (42); Hurst (49)	22,874	R.Gifford
1992-93	Home	3-Mar-93	1-0	Gynn (43)	13,206	K.Cooper
1993-94	Away	20-Nov-93	0-0		23,379	G.Poll
1993-94	Home	16-Apr-94	1-1	Ndlovu (25 pen)	13,052	R.Hart
1994-95	Away	28-Dec-94	1-5	Ndlovu (17 pen)	26,056	K.Morton
1994-95	Home	15-Apr-95	2-0	Dublin (3); Ndlovu (88)	17,015	G.Willard
1995-96	Home	21-Oct-95	0-1		14,002	J.Winter
1995-96	Away	3-Dec-95	3-4	Dublin (18, 37, 55)	16,229	M.Reed
1996-97	Home	26-Oct-96	0-0		17,267	K.Burge
1996-97	Away	1-Feb-97	0-0		21,793	M.Bodenham
1997-98	Away	20-Sep-97	0-0		21,087	G.Willard
1997-98	Home	7-Feb-98	1-0	Dubin (74 pen)	18,375	G.Ashby
1998-99	Home	18-Oct-98	1-0	Dublin (74)	16,006	D.Elleray
1998-99	Away	3-Apr-99	2-1	McAllister (19 pen); Whelan (84)	28,136	K.Burge
1999-00	Away	23-Oct-99	0-0		23,296	M.Riley
1999-00	Home	6-May-00	4-1	McAllister (38, 70); Zuniga (67); Hadji (80)	19,921	S.Bennett

SOUTHAMPTON

Season	Venue	Date	Res	Scorers	Attendance	Referee
1992-93	Away	12-Dec-92	2-2	Quinn (6, 25)	12,306	R.Nixon
1992-93	Home	3-Apr-93	2-0	Quinn (7 pen); Williams,J. (80)	10,463	K.Cooper
1993-94	Home	16-Oct-93	1-1	Babb (87)	9,837	J.Worrall
1993-94	Away	15-Jan-94	0-1		12,397	P.Don
1994-95	Home	24-Sep-94	1-3	Dublin (2)	11,784	K.Morton

1994-95	Away	4-Mar-95	0-0		14,505	K.Morton
1995-96	Home	1-Jan-96	1-1	Whelan (83)	16,822	K.Cooper
1995-96	Away	25-Mar-96	0-1		14,461	S.Lodge
1996-97	Home	13-Oct-96	1-1	Dublin (90)	15,485	P.Durkin
1996-97	Away	19-Apr-97	2-2	Ndlovu (62); Whelan (74)	15,251	P.Jones
1997-98	Home	13-Sep-97	1-0	Soltvedt (65)	18,659	U.Rennie
1997-98	Away	18-Feb-98	2-1	Whelan (14); Huckerby (29)	15,091	P.Alcock
1998-99	Home	24-Oct-98	1-2	Dublin (60)	15,152	R.Harris
1998-99	Home	5-Apr-99	1-0	Boateng (64)	21,402	U.Rennie
1999-00	Home	7-Aug-99	0-1		19,915	P.Jones
1999-00	Away	4-Dec-99	0-0		15,168	J.Winter

SUNDERLAND

Season	Venue	Date	Res	Scorers	Attendance	Referee
1996-97	Away	21-Sep-96	0-1		19,459	M.Riley
1996-97	Home	1-Jan-97	2-2	Dublin (10); Daish (28)	17,700	G.Poll
1999-00	Away	29-Aug-99	1-1	Keane (33)	39,427	S.Lodge
1999-00	Home	12-Feb-00	3-2	Keane (2); Hadji (13); Roussel (18)	22,101	P.Alcock

SWINDON TOWN

Season	Venue	Date	Res	Scorers	Attendance	Referee
1993-94	Home	3-Jan-94	1-1	Wegerle (73)	15,869	B.Hill
1993-94	Away	5-Feb-94	1-3	Darby (53)	14,635	K.Burge

TOTTENHAM HOTSPUR

Season	Venue	Date	Res	Scorers	Attendance	Referee
1992-93	Away	19-Aug-92	2-0	Williams,J. (4, 29)	24,388	D.Gallagher
1992-93	Home	14-Sep-92	1-0	Williams,J. (61)	15,348	M.Bodenham
1993-94	Away	1-Jan-94	2-1	Babb (25); Wegerle (77)	26,015	T.Holbrook
1993-94	Home	9-Apr-94	1-0	Ndlovu (62 pen)	14,487	M.Reed
1994-95	Home	31-Dec-94	0-4		19,951	G.Ashby
1994-95	Away	9-May-95	3-1	Ndlovu (33, 64 pen); Dublin (68)	24,134	A.Wilkie
1995-96	Home	4-Nov-95	2-3	Dublin (9); Williams P. (48)	17,545	J.Winter
1995-96	Away	30-Mar-96	1-3	Dublin (20)	26,808	R.Hart
1996-97	Home	7-Dec-96	1-2	Whelan (61)	19,675	G.Willard
1996-97	Away	11-May-97	2-1	Dublin (13); Williams (39)	33,029	M.Bodenham
1997-98	Home	13-Dec-97	4-0	Huckerby (42, 84); Breen (63); Hall (87)	19,499	S.Dunn
1997-98	Away	13-Apr-98	1-1	Dublin (86)	33,463	M.Riley
1998-99	Home	26-Dec-98	1-1	Aloisi (81)	23,098	K.Burge
1998-99	Away	6-Feb-99	0-0		34,376	S.Lodge
1999-00	Away	19-Sep-99	2-3	Keane (54); Chippo (75)	35,224	A.D'Urso
1999-00	Home	26-Feb-00	0-1		23,077	P.Durkin

WATFORD

Season	Venue	Date	Res	Scorers	Attendance	Referee
1999-00	Home	31-Oct-99	4-0	Keane (17); Froggatt (33); Hadji (49); McAllister (62 pen)	21,700	P.Durkin
1999-00	Away	14-May-00	0-1		18,977	U.Rennie

WEST HAM UNITED

Season	Venue	Date	Res	Scorers	Attendance	Referee
1993-94	Home	21-Aug-93	1-1	Wegerle (57)	12,864	S.Lodge
1993-94	Away	11-Dec-93	2-3	Darby (41, 76)	17,243	K.Cooper
1994-95	Away	26-Nov-94	1-0	Buust (58)	17,251	M.Reed
1994-95	Home	18-Feb-95	2-0	Marsh (25); Ndlovu (67)	17,556	R.Dilkes
1995-96	Away	31-Jan-96	2-3	Dublin (62); Whelan (82)	18,884	G.Poll
1995-96	Home	2-Mar-96	2-2	Salako (7); Whelan (15)	17,448	M.Bodenham
1996-97	Away	21-Aug-96	1-1	McAllister (11)	21,580	S.Dunn
1996-97	Home	22-Mar-97	1-3	Dublin (9)	22,291	M.Reed
1997-98	Home	27-Aug-97	1-1	Huckerby (38)	18,289	N.Barry
1997-98	Away	26-Dec-97	0-1		22,477	G.Poll
1998-99	Home	29-Aug-98	0-0		20,818	N.Barry
1998-99	Away	28-Dec-98	0-2		25,662	P.Durkin
1999-00	Home	25-Sep-99	1-0	Hadji (36)	19,993	D.Elleray
1999-00	Away	22-Apr-00	0-5		24,719	A.D'Urso

WIMBLEDON

Season	Venue	Date	Res	Scorers	Attendance	Referee
1992-93	Away	22-Aug-92	2-1	Gynn (13); Rosario (46)	3,759	J.Borrett
1992-93	Home	30-Jan-93	0-2		11,774	R.Gifford
1993-94	Away	26-Dec-93	2-1	Ndlovu (16); J.Williams (71)	4,739	M.Bodenham
1993-94	Home	2-Apr-94	1-2	Ndlovu (64)	11,312	M.Bodenham
1994-95	Home	20-Aug-94	1-1	Busst (70)	10,962	R.Gifford
1994-95	Away	10-Dec-94	0-2		7,349	R.Dilkes
1995-96	Home	25-Nov-95	3-3	OG (14, Heald); Dublin (67); Rennie (83)	12,496	R.Hart
1995-96	Away	27-Apr-96	2-0	Ndlovu (52, 89)	15,540	S.Dunn
1996-97	Away	16-Nov-96	2-2	Whelan (54); Dublin (68)	10,307	M.Bodenham
1996-97	Home	3-Mar-97	1-1	Dublin (37)	15,273	D.Elleray
1997-98	Away	1-Nov-97	2-1	Huckerby (16); Dublin (22)	11,210	U.Rennie
1997-98	Home	29-Apr-98	0-0		17,968	J.Winter
1998-99	Away	5-Dec-98	1-2	McAllister (54 pen)	11,717	S.Dunn
1998-99	Home	1-May-99	2-1	Huckerby (16); Whelan (29)	21,200	G.Poll
1999-00	Away	14-Aug-99	1-1	McAllister (90 pen)	10,635	M.Halsey
1999-00	Home	15-Jan-00	2-0	McAllister (56 pen); Keane (74)	19,012	S.Bennett

CRYSTAL PALACE

INTRODUCTION

Founded in 1905 to play at the Crystal Palace Ground where, earlier, a Crystal Palace staff team had successfully played. Joined the Southern League for 1905-06 when they were Champions of Division Two. Soon moved to Herne Hill, then to The Nest, Selhurst. Founder members and first champions of the Football League Third Division 1920-21. Moved to Selhurst Park in 1924.

Founder members of the old Fourth Division in 1958, they reached the First Division for the first time as Second Division runners-up in 1969. Premier League founder members 1992. Relegated after one season, but promoted back at the first attempt, only to be relegated in 1994-95, winning their place back through the play-offs at the end of the 1996-97 season only to face immediate relegation.

Ground: Selhurst Park, South Norwood,
            London SE25 6PU
Nickname: The Eagles
Internet: www.c-palace.org

HONOURS

Football League Div 1:	Champions 1993-94
Football League Div 2:	Champions 1978-79
	Runners-up 1968-69
	Play-off Winners 1996-97
Football League Div 3:	Runners-up 1963-64
Football League Div 3S:	Champions 1920-21
	Runners-up 1928-29, 1930-31,
	1938-39
Football League Div 4:	Runners-up 1960-61
FA Cup:	Runners-up 1989-90
Zenith Data System Cup:	Winners 1991

EUROPEAN RECORD

Never qualified.

FAPL RECORD SUMMARY

Most Total:	MARTYN, Nigel	79
Most Starts:	MARTYN, Nigel	79
Most Subs:	NDAH, George	17
Most SNU:	WILMOT, Rhys	36
Most PS:	DYER, Bruce	15
Most Goals:	ARMSTRONG, Chris	23
Most Yel:	FULLARTON, Jamie	11
Most Red:	ARMSTRONG, Chris	1

PLAYING RECORD – SEASON TOTALS

Season	Pn	P	W	D	L	F	A	Pts
1992-93	20	42	11	16	15	48	61	49
1994-95	19	42	11	12	19	34	49	45
1997-98	20	38	8	9	21	37	71	33
Totals		122	30	37	55	119	181	127

PLAYING RECORD – HOME TOTALS

Season	Pn	P	W	D	L	F	A	Pts
1992-93	20	21	6	9	6	27	25	27
1994-95	19	21	6	6	9	16	23	24
1997-98	20	19	2	5	12	15	39	11
Totals		61	14	20	27	58	87	62

PLAYING RECORD – AWAY TOTALS

Season	Pn	P	W	D	L	F	A	Pts
1992-93	20	21	5	7	9	21	36	22
1994-95	19	21	5	6	10	18	26	21
1997-98	20	19	6	4	9	22	32	22
Totals		61	16	17	28	61	94	65

HIGHEST HOME ATTENDANCES

	Attendance	Opponents	Date	Season
1	30,115	Manchester U.	21-Apr-93	1992-93
2	26,186	Chelsea	13-Sep-97	1997-98
3	26,180	Arsenal	18-Oct-97	1997-98
4	26,180	Manchester U.	27-Apr-98	1997-98
5	26,116	Tottenham H.	28-Mar-98	1997-98

LOWEST HOME ATTENDANCES

	Attendance	Opponents	Date	Season
1	10,422	Sheffield W.	14-Mar-95	1994-95
2	11,224	Oldham A.	12-Sep-92	1992-93
3	11,891	Coventry C.	11-Feb-95	1994-95
4	12,033	Norwich C.	29-Aug-92	1992-93
5	12,248	Coventry C.	27-Feb-93	1992-93

TOP SCORER – SEASON BY SEASON

Season	Player	Goals
1992-93	Armstrong	15
1994-95	Armstrong	8
1997-98	Shipperley	7

PLAYERS WITH MOST PREMIERSHIP APPEARANCES

Tot	Player	St	Sb	Gls
79	MARTYN, Nigel	79	0	0
75	ARMSTRONG, Chris	75	0	23
75	SOUTHGATE, Gareth	75	0	6
74	SHAW, Richard	73	1	0
73	COLEMAN, Chris	66	7	6

CRYSTAL PALACE

56	RODGER, Simon	53	3	4
53	HUMPHREY, John	47	6	0
52	SALAKO, John	51	1	4
51	YOUNG, Eric	51	0	6
51	GORDON, Dean	44	7	2
42	McGOLDRICK, Eddie	42	0	8
40	DYER, Bruce	28	12	5
38	MILLER, Kevin	38	0	0
37	GORDON, Dean	36	1	2
37	NEWMAN, Ricky	33	4	3
34	THORN, Andy	34	0	1
34	EDWORTHY, Marc	33	1	0
31	OSBORN, Simon	27	4	2
30	HREIDARSSON, Hermann	26	4	2

CLUB-BY-CLUB RESULTS

ARSENAL

Season	Venue	Date	Res	Scorers	Attendance	Referee
1992-93	Home	2-Nov-92	1-2	McGoldrick (69)	20,734	V.Callow
1992-93	Away	8-May-93	0-3		25,225	K.Burge
1994-95	Away	1-Oct-94	2-1	Salako (19,41)	34,136	M.Bodenham
1994-95	Home	25-Feb-95	0-3		17,092	K.Morton
1997-98	Home	18-Oct-97	0-0		26,180	S.Dunn
1997-98	Away	21-Feb-98	0-1		38,094	J.Winter

ASTON VILLA

Season	Venue	Date	Res	Scorers	Attendance	Referee
1992-93	Away	5-Sep-92	0-3		17,120	K.Redfern
1992-93	Home	10-Feb-93	1-0	Bowry (9)	12,270	K.Redfern
1994-95	Away	27-Aug-94	1-1	Southgate (86)	23,305	J.Worrall
1994-95	Home	4-Apr-95	0-0		12,606	K.Cooper
1997-98	Home	8-Nov-97	1-1	Shipperly (42)	21,097	J.Winter
1997-98	Away	14-Mar-98	1-3	Jansen (62)	33,781	G.Barber

BARNSLEY

Season	Venue	Date	Res	Scorers	Attendance	Referee
1997-98	Home	12-Aug-97	0-1		21,547	N.Barry
1997-98	Away	17-Jan-98	0-1		17,819	M.Reed

BLACKBURN ROVERS

Season	Venue	Date	Res	Scorers	Attendance	Referee
1992-93	Home	15-Aug-92	3-3	Bright (37); Southgate (63); Osborn (90)	17,086	R.Milford
1992-93	Away	2-Feb-93	2-1	Armstrong (9); Rodger (59)	14,163	P.Wright
1994-95	Home	31-Dec-94	0-1		14,232	D.Elleray
1994-95	Away	20-Apr-95	1-2	Houghton (71)	28,005	B.Hill
1997-98	Home	30-Aug-97	1-2	Dyer (51)	20,849	K.Burge
1997-98	Away	28-Dec-97	2-2	Dyer (11); Warhurst (48)	23,872	P.Jones

BOLTON WANDERERS

Season	Venue	Date	Res	Scorers	Attendance	Referee
1997-98	Home	27-Sep-97	2-2	Warhurst (9); Gordan (19)	17,134	D.Elleray
1997-98	Away	2-May-98	2-5	Gordon (8); Bent (16)	24,449	N.Barry

CHELSEA

Season	Venue	Date	Res	Scorers	Attendance	Referee
1992-93	Away	7-Nov-92	1-3	Young (70)	17,141	R.Groves
1992-93	Home	15-Mar-93	1-1	Armstrong (41)	12,610	K.Cooper
1994-95	Home	24-Sep-94	0-1		16,030	R.Dilkes
1994-95	Away	5-Mar-95	0-0		14,130	M.Reed
1997-98	Home	13-Sep-97	0-3		26,186	G.Ashby
1997-98	Away	11-Mar-98	2-6	Hreidarsson (7); Bent (87)	31,917	M.Riley

COVENTRY CITY

Season	Venue	Date	Res	Scorers	Attendance	Referee
1992-93	Away	3-Oct-92	2-2	Coleman (8); McGoldrick (38)	11,808	G.Ashby
1992-93	Home	27-Feb-93	0-0		12,248	P.Foakes
1994-95	Away	2-Nov-94	4-1	Preece (18,49); Salako (20); Newman (80)	10,732	P.Jones
1994-95	Home	11-Feb-95	0-2		11,891	M.Bodenham
1997-98	Away	24-Sep-97	1-1	Fullerton (9)	15,900	G.Barber
1997-98	Home	28-Feb-98	0-3		21,810	D.Elleray

DERBY COUNTY

Season	Venue	Date	Res	Scorers	Attendance	Referee
1997-98	Away	20-Dec-97	0-0		26,950	M.Bodenham
1997-98	Home	18-Apr-98	3-1	Jansen (73); Curcic (80); Bent (90)	18,101	P.Alcock

EVERTON

Season	Venue	Date	Res	Scorers	Attendance	Referee
1992-93	Away	19-Sep-92	2-0	Armstrong (8, 17)	18,080	D.Gallagher
1992-93	Home	9-Jan-93	0-2		13,227	R.Milford
1994-95	Home	22-Oct-94	1-0	Preece (53)	15,026	S.Lodge
1994-95	Away	21-Jan-95	1-3	Coleman (79)	23,733	P.Jones
1997-98	Away	9-Aug-97	2-1	Lombardo (34); Dyer (62 pen)	35,716	S.Dunn
1997-98	Home	10-Jan-98	1-3	Dyer (16 pen)	23,311	G.Barber

IPSWICH TOWN

Season	Venue	Date	Res	Scorers	Attendance	Referee
1992-93	Away	24-Oct-92	2-2	Armstrong (60); Coleman (75)	17,861	G.Ashby
1992-93	Home	1-May-93	3-1	Young (8); Armstrong (17); McGoldrick (60)	18,881	P.Don
1994-95	Home	5-Nov-94	3-0	Newman (19); Armstrong (83); Salako (87)	13,450	A.Wilkie
1994-95	Away	4-Feb-95	2-0	Dowie (55); Gordon (86 pen)	15,570	S.Lodge

LEEDS UNITED

Season	Venue	Date	Res	Scorers	Attendance	Referee
1992-93	Home	20-Dec-92	1-0	Thorn (30)	14,462	A.Gunn
1992-93	Away	17-Apr-93	0-0		27,545	R.Hart
1994-95	Home	30-Aug-94	1-2	Gordon (55)	14,453	D.Gallagher
1994-95	Away	9-May-95	1-3	Armstrong (67)	30,942	J.Worrall

1997-98	Away	23-Aug-97	2-0	Warhurst (22); Lombardo (51)	29,076	U.Rennie
1997-98	Home	31-Jan-98	0-2		25,248	U.Rennie

LEICESTER CITY

Season	Venue	Date	Res	Scorers	Attendance	Referee
1994-95	Away	29-Oct-94	1-0	Preece (36)	20,022	P.Don
1994-95	Home	14-Jan-95	2-0	Newman (23); Ndah (44)	12,707	P.Durkin
1997-98	Away	6-Dec-97	1-1	Padovano (43)	19,191	U.Rennie
1997-98	Home	11-Apr-98	0-3		18,771	A.Wilkie

LIVERPOOL

Season	Venue	Date	Res	Scorers	Attendance	Referee
1992-93	Away	28-Nov-92	0-5		36,380	S.Lodge
1992-93	Home	23-Mar-93	1-1	Armstrong (78)	18,688	R.Dilkes
1994-95	Home	20-Aug-94	1-6	Armstrong (49)	18,084	R.Hart
1994-95	Away	11-Dec-94	0-0		30,972	K.Morton
1997-98	Home	13-Dec-97	0-3		25,790	N.Barry
1997-98	Away	13-Apr-98	1-2	Bent (72)	43,007	G.Barber

MANCHESTER CITY

Season	Venue	Date	Res	Scorers	Attendance	Referee
1992-93	Home	17-Oct-92	0-0		14,005	M.Bodenham
1992-93	Away	5-May-93	0-0		21,167	S.Lodge
1994-95	Away	10-Sep-94	1-1	Dyer (31)	19,971	K.Burge
1994-95	Home	1-Apr-95	2-1	Armstrong (34); Patterson (65)	13,312	T.Holbrook

MANCHESTER UNITED

Season	Venue	Date	Res	Scorers	Attendance	Referee
1992-93	Away	2-Sep-92	0-1		29,736	V.Callow
1992-93	Home	21-Apr-93	0-2		30,115	K.Barratt
1994-95	Away	19-Nov-94	0-3		43,788	B.Hill
1994-95	Home	25-Jan-95	1-1	Southgate (80)	18,224	A.Wilkie
1997-98	Away	4-Oct-97	0-2		55,143	S.Lodge
1997-98	Home	27-Apr-98	0-3		26,180	P.Jones

MIDDLESBROUGH

Season	Venue	Date	Res	Scorers	Attendance	Referee
1992-93	Away	28-Dec-92	1-0	Osborn (63)	21,123	K.Hackett
1992-93	Home	12-Apr-93	4-1	Rodger (54); Young (61); Armstrong (81); Coleman (85)	15,123	M.Bodenham

NEWCASTLE UNITED

Season	Venue	Date	Res	Scorers	Attendance	Referee
1994-95	Home	15-Oct-94	0-1		17,739	K.Morton
1994-95	Away	14-May-95	2-3	Armstrong (51); Houghton (81)	35,626	G.Ashby
1997-98	Home	29-Nov-97	1-2	Shipperly (66)	26,085	M.Riley
1997-98	Away	18-Mar-98	2-1	Lombardo (14); Jansen (23)	36,565	S.Lodge

NORWICH CITY

Season	Venue	Date	Res	Scorers	Attendance	Referee
1992-93	Home	29-Aug-92	1-2	McGoldrick (20)	12,033	D.Allison
1992-93	Away	27-Jan-93	2-4	Armstrong (2); Thomas (45)	13,543	V.Callow
1994-95	Away	24-Aug-94	0-0		19,015	B.Hill
1994-95	Home	17-Dec-94	0-1		12,252	R.Hart

NOTTINGHAM FOREST

Season	Venue	Date	Res	Scorers	Attendance	Referee
1992-93	Home	21-Nov-92	1-1	Armstrong (23)	15,330	K.Hackett
1992-93	Away	3-Mar-93	1-1	Southgate (23)	20,603	J.Borrett
1994-95	Away	2-Jan-95	0-1		21,326	G.Ashby
1994-95	Home	29-Apr-95	1-2	Dowie (79)	15,886	K.Burge

OLDHAM ATHLETIC

Season	Venue	Date	Res	Scorers	Attendance	Referee
1992-93	Away	19-Aug-92	1-1	McGoldrick (50)	11,063	M.Peck
1992-93	Home	12-Sep-92	2-2	Armstrong (64, 66)	11,224	B.Hill

QPR

Season	Venue	Date	Res	Scorers	Attendance	Referee
1992-93	Away	12-Dec-92	3-1	McGoldrick (46, 89); Armstrong (71)	14,571	R.Hart
1992-93	Home	3-Apr-93	1-1	OG (62, Bardsley)	14,705	A.Wilkie
1994-95	Home	26-Dec-94	0-0		16,372	B.Hill
1994-95	Away	17-Apr-95	1-0	Dowie (56)	14,227	A.Wilkie

SHEFFIELD UNITED

Season	Venue	Date	Res	Scorers	Attendance	Referee
1992-93	Home	5-Dec-92	2-0	Armstrong (43); Southgate (76)	12,361	H.King
1992-93	Away	20-Mar-93	1-0	Coleman (44)	18,857	J.Martin

SHEFFIELD WEDNESDAY

Season	Venue	Date	Res	Scorers	Attendance	Referee
1992-93	Home	25-Aug-92	1-1	Young (41)	14,005	J.Martin
1992-93	Away	20-Feb-93	1-2	Armstrong (62)	26,459	M.Reed
1994-95	Away	3-Dec-94	0-1		21,930	K.Cooper
1994-95	Home	14-Mar-95	2-1	Armstrong (55); Dowie (65)	10,422	P.Don
1997-98	Away	25-Oct-97	3-1	Hreidarsson (27); Rodger (52); Shipperly (60)	22,072	D.Gallagher
1997-98	Home	10-May-98	1-0	Morrison (90)	16,876	M.Reed

SOUTHAMPTON

Season	Venue	Date	Res	Scorers	Attendance	Referee
1992-93	Home	26-Sep-92	1-2	Young (54)	13,829	J.Borrett
1992-93	Away	16-Jan-93	0-1		13,397	P.Don
1994-95	Home	26-Nov-94	0-0		14,186	P.Danson
1994-95	Away	3-May-95	1-3	Southgate (26)	15,151	G.Poll
1997-98	Away	27-Aug-97	0-1		15,032	J.Winter
1997-98	Home	26-Dec-97	1-1	Shipperley (61)	22,853	P.Alcock

TOTTENHAM HOTSPUR

Season	Venue	Date	Res	Scorers	Attendance	Referee
1992-93	Away	22-Aug-92	2-2	McGoldrick (21); Young (80)	25,237	P.Don
1992-93	Home	30-Jan-93	1-3	OG (54, Ruddock)	20,937	D.Elleray
1994-95	Away	27-Dec-94	0-0		27,730	G.Willard
1994-95	Home	14-Apr-95	1-1	Armstrong (41)	18,149	P.Don
1997-98	Away	24-Nov-97	1-0	Shipperly (57)	25,634	P.Durkin
1997-98	Home	28-Mar-98	1-3	Shipperley (82)	26,116	M.Reed

WEST HAM UNITED

Season	Venue	Date	Res	Scorers	Attendance	Referee
1994-95	Away	8-Oct-94	0-1		16,959	G.Poll
1994-95	Home	6-May-95	1-0	Armstrong (51)	18,224	S.Lodge
1997-98	Away	3-Dec-97	1-4	Shipperly (41)	23,335	D.Elleray
1997-98	Home	5-May-98	3-3	Bent (44); Rodger (48); Lombardo (63)	19,129	G.Poll

WIMBLEDON

Season	Venue	Date	Res	Scorers	Attendance	Referee
1992-93	Home	26-Dec-92	2-0	Coleman (3); Thomas (37)	16,825	R.Lewis
1992-93	Away	9-Apr-93	0-4		12,275	V.Callow
1994-95	Home	17-Sep-94	0-0		12,366	K.Cooper
1994-95	Away	18-Mar-95	0-2		8,835	D.Gallagher
1997-98	Away	20-Sep-97	1-0	Lombardo (79)	16,747	P.Alcock
1997-98	Home	9-Feb-98	0-3		14,410	K.Burge

INTRODUCTION

In 1884 members of the Derbyshire County Cricket team formed the football club as a way of boosting finances in the cricket close season. They played their first season at the Racecourse Ground and entered the FA Cup. A year later the club moved to the Baseball Ground where they remained until a move to Pride Park Stadium for the 1997-98 season. In 1888 they became founder members of the Football League. Since their formation they have fluctuated through the top divisions, but enjoyed a sparkling spell during the 1970s.

Ground: Pride Park Stadium, Derby, DE24 8XL
Nickname: The Rams
Internet: www.dcfc.co.uk

HONOURS

Football League Div 1:	Champions 1971-72, 1974-75
	Runners-up 1895-96, 1929-30,
	1935-36, 1995-96
Football League Div 2:	Champions 1911-12, 1914-15,
	1968-69, 1986-87
	Runners-up 1925-26
Football League Div 3N:	Champions 1956-57
	Runners-up 1955-56
FA Cup:	Winners 1945-46
	Runners-up 1897-98, 1888-89,
	1902-03
Anglo Italian Cup:	Runners-up 1992-93

EUROPEAN RECORD

Champions' Cup (2):	1972-73 (SF), 1975-76 (2)
Cup Winners' Cup (0):	–
UEFA Cup(2):	1974-75 (3), 1976-77 (2)

FAPL RECORD SUMMARY

Most Total:	LAURSEN, Jacob	137
Most Starts:	LAURSEN, Jacob	135
Most Subs:	BURTON, Deon	28
Most SNU:	HOULT, Russell	61
Most PS:	BAIANO, Francesco	34
Most Goals:	STURRIDGE, Dean	31
Most Yel:	POWELL, Darryl	26
Most Red:	ERANIO, Stefano	2

PLAYING RECORD – SEASON TOTALS

Season	Pn	P	W	D	L	F	A	Pts
1996-97	12	38	11	13	14	45	58	46
1997-98	9	38	16	7	15	52	49	55
1998-99	8	38	13	13	12	40	45	52
1999-00	16	38	9	11	18	44	57	38
Totals		152	49	44	59	181	209	191

PLAYING RECORD – HOME TOTALS

Season	Pn	P	W	D	L	F	A	Pts
1996-97	12	19	8	6	5	25	22	30
1997-98	9	19	12	3	4	33	18	39
1998-99	8	19	8	7	4	22	19	31
1999-00	16	19	6	3	10	22	25	21
Totals		76	34	19	23	102	84	121

PLAYING RECORD – AWAY TOTALS

Season	Pn	P	W	D	L	F	A	Pts
1996-97	12	19	3	7	9	20	36	16
1997-98	9	19	4	4	11	19	31	16
1998-99	8	19	5	6	8	18	26	21
1999-00	16	19	3	8	8	22	32	17
Totals		76	15	25	36	79	125	70

HIGHEST HOME ATTENDANCES

	Attendance	Opponents	Date	Season
1	33,378	Liverpool	18-Mar-00	1999-00
2	33,370	Manchester U.	20-Nov-99	1999-00
3	33,222	Aston Villa	26-Dec-99	1999-00
4	32,913	Liverpool	13-Mar-99	1998-99
5	32,726	Middlesbrough	28-Dec-98	1998-99

LOWEST HOME ATTENDANCES

	Attendance	Opponents	Date	Season
1	17,022	Wimbledon	28-Sep-96	1996-97
2	17,252	Everton	16-Dec-96	1996-97
3	17,350	Middlesbrough	17-Nov-96	1996-97
4	17,692	Sunderland	14-Sep-96	1996-97
5	17,839	Southampton	9-Apr-97	1996-97

TOP SCORER – SEASON BY SEASON

Season	Player	Goals
1996-97	Sturridge	11
1997-98	Wanchope	13
1998-99	Burton	9
1999-00	Delap	8

DERBY COUNTY

PLAYERS WITH MOST PREMIERSHIP APPEARANCES

Tot	Player	St	Sb	Gls
137	LAURSEN, Jacob	135	2	3
121	POWELL, Darryl	101	20	3
114	STURRIDGE, Dean	90	24	31
85	POOM, Mart	83	2	0
80	CARSLEY, Lee	69	11	2
72	WANCHOPE, Paulo	65	7	23
71	POWELL, Chris	69	2	1
70	ROWETT, Gary	67	3	3
70	DELAP, Rory	65	5	8
69	BURTON, Deon	41	28	16
67	HOULT, Russell	66	1	0
67	DAILLY, Christian	62	5	4
67	ERANIO, Stefano	58	9	5
64	BAIANO, Francesco	52	12	16
58	CARBONARI, Horacio	57	1	7
57	STIMAC, Igor	57	0	2
54	PRIOR, Spencer	48	6	1
54	BOHINEN, Lars	46	8	1
52	SCHNOOR, Stefan	42	10	2
41	DORIGO, Tony	37	4	1

CLUB-BY-CLUB RESULTS

ARSENAL

Season	Venue	Date	Res	Scorers	Attendance	Referee
1996-97	Away	7-Dec-96	2-2	Sturridge (62); Powell D. (71)	38,018	M.Bodenham
1996-97	Home	11-May-97	1-3	Ward (9)	18,287	P.Durkin
1997-98	Home	1-Nov-97	3-0	Wanchope (46, 65); Sturridge (82)	30,004	P.Alcock
1997-98	Away	28-Apr-98	0-1		38,121	N.Barry
1998-99	Home	5-Dec-98	0-0		29,018	M.Reed
1998-99	Away	2-May-99	0-1		37,323	N.Barry
1999-00	Home	10-Aug-99	1-2	Delap (45)	25,901	S.Lodge
1999-00	Away	28-Nov-99	1-2	Sturridge (2)	37,964	A.D'Urso

ASTON VILLA

Season	Venue	Date	Res	Scorers	Attendance	Referee
1996-97	Away	24-Aug-96	0-2		34,646	P.Alcock
1996-97	Home	12-Apr-97	2-1	Rowett (21); van der Laan (35)	18,071	P.Danson
1997-98	Away	20-Sep-97	1-2	Biano (15)	35,444	J.Winter
1997-98	Home	7-Feb-98	0-1		30,251	P.Alcock
1998-99	Away	27-Sep-98	0-1		38,007	S.Dunn
1998-99	Home	10-Mar-99	2-1	Baiano (17); Burton (21)	26,836	G.Willard
1999-00	Home	26-Dec-99	0-2		33,222	A.Wilkie
1999-00	Away	25-Mar-00	0-2		28,613	P.Alcock

BARNSLEY

Season	Venue	Date	Res	Scorers	Attendance	Referee
1997-98	Home	30-Aug-97	1-0	Eranio (43 pen)	27,232	P.Durkin
1997-98	Away	28-Dec-97	0-1		18,686	G.Barber

BLACKBURN ROVERS

Season	Venue	Date	Res	Scorers	Attendance	Referee
1996-97	Away	9-Sep-96	2-1	Willems (1); Flynn (85)	19,214	S.Lodge
1996-97	Home	28-Dec-96	0-0		17,847	D.Elleray
1997-98	Away	9-Aug-97	0-1		23,557	D.Elleray
1997-98	Home	11-Jan-98	3-1	Sturridge (15, 41); Wanchope (88)	27,823	G.Poll
1998-99	Away	15-Aug-98	0-0		24,007	S.Lodge
1998-99	Home	16-Jan-99	1-0	Burton (84)	27,386	D.Gallagher

BOLTON WANDERERS

Season	Venue	Date	Res	Scorers	Attendance	Referee
1997-98	Away	14-Dec-97	3-3	Eranio (54); Bainano (64, 68)	23,037	U.Rennie
1997-98	Home	13-Apr-98	4-0	Wanchope (27); Burton (37, 40); Baiano (45)	29,126	D.Gallagher

BRADFORD CITY

Season	Venue	Date	Res	Scorers	Attendance	Referee
1999-00	Home	25-Sep-99	0-1		31,035	M.Halsey
1999-00	Away	21-Apr-00	4-4	Delap (1); Strupar (6); Burley (36 pen, 52 pen)	18,276	A.Wilkie

CHARLTON ATHLETIC

Season	Venue	Date	Res	Scorers	Attendance	Referee
1998-99	Away	12-Sep-98	2-1	Wanchope (5); Baiano (60)	19,516	M.Reed
1998-99	Home	20-Feb-99	0-2		27,853	U.Rennie

CHELSEA

Season	Venue	Date	Res	Scorers	Attendance	Referee
1996-97	Away	18-Jan-97	1-3	Asanovic (25)	28,293	G.Poll
1996-97	Home	1-Mar-97	3-2	Ward (50, 90); Asanovic (61 pen)	18,039	A.Wilkie
1997-98	Away	29-Nov-97	0-4		36,544	U.Rennie
1997-98	Home	5-Apr-98	0-1		30,062	J.Winter
1998-99	Home	12-Dec-98	2-2	Carbonari (26); Sturridge (90)	29,056	P.Jones
1998-99	Away	16-May-99	1-2	Carbonari (87)	35,016	M.Riley
1999-00	Home	30-Oct-99	3-1	Burton (7); Delap (80, 88)	28,614	R.Harris
1999-00	Away	14-May-00	0-4		35,084	J.Winter

COVENTRY CITY

Season	Venue	Date	Res	Scorers	Attendance	Referee
1996-97	Home	30-Nov-96	2-1	Asanovic (12 pen); Ward (79)	18,042	M.Riley
1996-97	Away	3-May-97	2-1	Rowett (50); Sturridge (62)	22,839	R.Dilkes
1997-98	Home	22-Nov-97	3-1	Biano (3); Eranio (30 pen); Wanchope (39)	29,351	D.Elleray
1997-98	Away	28-Mar-98	0-1		18,705	K.Burge
1998-99	Away	19-Dec-98	1-1	Carsley (50)	16,627	U.Rennie
1998-99	Home	8-May-99	0-0		32,450	P.Alcock
1999-00	Away	21-Aug-99	0-2		17,685	J.Winter
1999-00	Home	22-Jan-00	0-0		28,381	G.Barber

CRYSTAL PALACE

Season	Venue	Date	Res	Scorers	Attendance	Referee
1997-98	Home	20-Dec-97	0-0		26,950	M.Bodenham
1997-98	Away	18-Apr-98	1-3	Bohinen (85)	18,101	P.Alcock

EVERTON

Season	Venue	Date	Res	Scorers	Attendance	Referee
1996-97	Home	16-Dec-96	0-1		17,252	M.Reed
1996-97	Away	15-Mar-97	0-1		32,240	G.Barber
1997-98	Home	13-Sep-97	3-1	Hunt(23); Powell,C. (33); Sturridge (66)	27,828	M.Riley
1997-98	Away	14-Feb-98	2-1	Stimac (21): Wanchope (50)	34,876	S.Dunn
1998-99	Away	26-Dec-98	0-0		39,206	S.Lodge
1998-99	Home	7-Feb-99	2-1	Burton (51, 85)	27,603	G.Poll

Season	Venue	Date	Res	Scorers	Attendance	Referee
1999-00	Home	28-Aug-99	1-0	Fuertes (47)	26,550	A.D'Urso
1999-00	Away	12-Feb-00	1-2	Nimni (59)	33,260	U.Rennie

LEEDS UNITED

Season	Venue	Date	Res	Scorers	Attendance	Referee
1996-97	Home	17-Aug-96	3-3	Sturridge (77, 78); Simpson (88)	17,927	P.Danson
1996-97	Away	29-Jan-97	0-0		27,549	K.Burge
1997-98	Away	8-Nov-97	3-4	Sturridge (4, 11); Asanovic(33 pen)	33,572	N.Barry
1997-98	Home	15-Mar-98	0-5		30,217	S.Lodge
1998-99	Home	31-Oct-98	2-2	Schnoor (3 pen); Sturridge (56)	27,034	N.Barry
1998-99	Away	21-Mar-99	1-4	Baiano (4 pen)	38,971	M.Reed
1999-00	Away	7-Aug-99	0-0		40,118	G.Barber
1999-00	Home	5-Dec-99	0-1		29,455	P.Alcock

LEICESTER CITY

Season	Venue	Date	Res	Scorers	Attendance	Referee
1996-97	Home	2-Nov-96	2-0	Ward (55); OG (88, Whitlow)	18,010	G.Barber
1996-97	Away	22-Feb-97	2-4	Sturridge (2, 47)	20,323	P.Durkin
1997-98	Away	6-Oct-97	2-1	Biano (21, 62)	19,385	G.Ashby
1997-98	Home	26-Apr-98	0-4		29,855	G.Willard
1998-99	Home	19-Sep-98	2-0	Schnoor (34); Wanchope (51)	26,738	G.Poll
1998-99	Away	5-May-99	2-1	Sturridge (17); Beck (60)	20,535	N.Barry
1999-00	Away	18-Dec-99	1-0	Powell (69)	18,581	D.Elleray
1999-00	Home	2-Apr-00	3-0	Burley (15); Delap (45); Sturridge (45)	25,763	G.Poll

LIVERPOOL

Season	Venue	Date	Res	Scorers	Attendance	Referee
1996-97	Away	27-Oct-96	1-2	Ward (88)	39,515	G.Willard
1996-97	Home	1-Feb-97	0-1		18,102	P.Jones
1997-98	Away	25-Oct-97	0-4		38,017	G.Willard
1997-98	Home	10-May-98	1-0	Wanchope (63)	30,492	S.Lodge
1998-99	Away	7-Nov-98	2-1	Harper (6); Wanchope (27)	44,020	U.Rennie
1998-99	Home	13-Mar-99	3-2	Burton (12); Wanchope (44, 49)	32,913	G.Barber
1999-00	Away	6-Nov-99	0-2		44,467	U.Rennie
1999-00	Home	18-Mar-00	0-2		33,378	B.Knight

MANCHESTER UNITED

Season	Venue	Date	Res	Scorers	Attendance	Referee
1996-97	Home	3-Sep-96	1-1	Laursen (25)	18,026	M.Reed
1996-97	Away	5-Apr-97	3-2	Ward (29); Wanchope (35); Sturridge (75)	55,243	D.Elleray
1997-98	Home	18-Oct-97	2-2	Biano (23); Wanchope (38)	30,014	G.Poll
1997-98	Away	21-Feb-98	0-2		55,170	M.Reed
1998-99	Home	24-Oct-98	1-1	Burton (74)	30,867	P.Durkin
1998-99	Away	3-Feb-99	0-1		55,174	S.Lodge
1999-00	Home	20-Nov-99	1-2	Delap (90)	33,370	M.Reed
1999-00	Away	11-Mar-00	1-3	Strupar (66)	61,619	J.Winter

MIDDLESBROUGH

Season	Venue	Date	Res	Scorers	Attendance	Referee
1996-97	Home	17-Nov-96	2-1	Asanovic (15); Ward (47)	17,350	P.Durkin
1996-97	Away	5-Mar-97	1-6	Simpson (90)	29,739	M.Reed

1998-99	Away	29-Aug-98	1-1	Wanchope (31)	34,121	M.Riley
1998-99	Home	28-Dec-98	2-1	Sturridge (29); Hunt (85)	32,726	R.Harris
1999-00	Home	14-Aug-99	1-3	Burton (41)	24,045	S.Bennett
1999-00	Away	15-Jan-00	4-1	Christie (8, 59); Burton (47); Burley (90)	32,745	M.Halsey

NEWCASTLE UNITED

Season	Venue	Date	Res	Scorers	Attendance	Referee
1996-97	Home	12-Oct-96	0-1		18,092	M.Bodenham
1996-97	Away	19-Apr-97	1-3	Sturridge (1)	36,553	D.Gallagher
1997-98	Away	17-Dec-97	0-0		36,289	K.Burge
1997-98	Home	26-Dec-97	1-0	Eranio (4 pen)	30,302	M.Reed
1998-99	Away	17-Oct-98	1-2	Burton (73)	36,750	K.Burge
1998-99	Home	3-Apr-99	3-4	Burton (8); Baiano (22 pen); Wanchope (90)	32,039	D.Gallagher
1999-00	Away	25-Oct-99	0-2		35,614	S.Dunn
1999-00	Home	6-May-00	0-0		32,724	A.Wiley

NOTTINGHAM FOREST

Season	Venue	Date	Res	Scorers	Attendance	Referee
1996-97	Away	19-Oct-96	1-1	Dailly (57)	27,771	J.Winter
1996-97	Home	23-Apr-97	0-0		18,087	G.Poll
1998-99	Away	16-Nov-98	2-2	Dorigo (56 pen); Carbonari (72)	24,014	G.Barber
1998-99	Home	10-Apr-99	1-0	Carbonari (85)	32,217	G.Barber

SHEFFIELD WEDNESDAY

Season	Venue	Date	Res	Scorers	Attendance	Referee
1996-97	Away	21-Sep-96	0-0		23,934	G.Barber
1996-97	Home	19-Feb-97	2-2	Sturridge (34); Stimac (71)	18,060	P.Alcock
1997-98	Away	24-Sep-97	5-2	Biano (8, 48);Burton (74); Wanchope (33); Lausen (79)	22,391	M.Reed
1997-98	Home	28-Feb-98	3-0	Wanchope (3, 49); Rowett (67)	30,203	A.Wilkie
1998-99	Home	9-Sep-98	1-0	Sturridge (23)	26,209	P.Jones
1998-99	Away	30-Jan-99	1-0	Prior (54)	24,440	D.Elleray
1999-00	Away	25-Aug-99	2-0	Delap (54); Sturridge (79)	20,943	M.Reed
1999-00	Home	5-Feb-00	3-3	Strupar (71); Burley (90); Christie (90)	30,100	D.Elleray

SOUTHAMPTON

Season	Venue	Date	Res	Scorers	Attendance	Referee
1996-97	Away	21-Dec-96	1-3	Dailly (8)	14,901	P.Danson
1996-97	Home	9-Apr-97	1-1	Ward (66)	17,839	G.Willard
1997-98	Home	27-Sep-97	4-0	Biano (82, 83); Wanchope (79); Eranio (75 pen)	25,625	K.Burge
1997-98	Away	2-May-98	2-0	Dailly (50); Sturridge (88)	15,202	M.Riley
1998-99	Away	28-Nov-98	1-0	Carbonari (33)	14,762	S.Lodge
1998-99	Home	24-Apr-99	0-0		26,557	A.Wilkie
1999-00	Away	4-Oct-99	3-3	Delap (21); Laursen (75); Beck (90)	14,208	G.Poll
1999-00	Home	24-Apr-00	2-0	Powell (5); Christie (42)	29,403	P.Jones

SUNDERLAND

Season	Venue	Date	Res	Scorers	Attendance	Referee
1996-97	Home	14-Sep-96	1-0	Asanovic (84 pen)	17,692	D.Elleray
1996-97	Away	26-Dec-96	0-2		22,512	J.Winter

DERBY COUNTY

Season	Venue	Date	Res	Scorers	Attendance	Referee
1999-00	Home	18-Sep-99	0-5		28,264	P.Jones
1999-00	Away	26-Feb-00	1-1	Christie (60)	41,940	A.Wiley

TOTTENHAM HOTSPUR

Season	Venue	Date	Res	Scorers	Attendance	Referee
1996-97	Away	21-Aug-96	1-1	Dailly (90)	28,219	K.Burge
1996-97	Home	22-Mar-97	4-2	Van de Laan (10); Trollope (22); Sturridge (68); Ward (69)	18,083	S.Dunn
1997-98	Away	23-Aug-97	0-1		25,886	M.Bodenham
1997-98	Home	31-Jan-98	2-1	Sturridge (25); Wanchope (76)	30,187	G.Willard
1998-99	Home	3-Oct-98	0-1		30,083	D.Gallagher
1998-99	Away	27-Feb-99	1-1	Burton (46)	35,392	J.Winter
1999-00	Home	16-Oct-99	0-1		29,815	P.Durkin
1999-00	Away	29-Apr-00	1-1	Carbonari (63)	33,044	N.Barry

WATFORD

Season	Venue	Date	Res	Scorers	Attendance	Referee
1999-00	Home	3-Jan-00	2-0	Strupar (2, 72)	28,072	B.Knight
1999-00	Away	8-Apr-00	0-0		16,579	S.Bennett

WEST HAM UNITED

Season	Venue	Date	Res	Scorers	Attendance	Referee
1996-97	Away	23-Nov-96	1-1	Sturridge (42)	24,576	S.Lodge
1996-97	Home	15-Feb-97	1-0	Asanovic (53 pen)	18,057	G.Ashby
1997-98	Home	6-Dec-97	2-0	OG (10, Miklosko); Sturridge (49)	29,300	A.Wilkie
1997-98	Away	11-Apr-98	0-0		25,155	G.Barber
1998-99	Home	22-Nov-98	0-2		31,666	A.Wilkie
1998-99	Away	17-Apr-99	1-5	Wanchope (89)	25,485	K.Burge
1999-00	Away	28-Dec-99	1-1	Sturridge (4)	24,998	A.Wiley
1999-00	Home	15-Apr-00	1-2	Sturridge (84)	31,202	M.Halsey

WIMBLEDON

Season	Venue	Date	Res	Scorers	Attendance	Referee
1996-97	Home	28-Sep-96	0-2		17,022	A.Wilkie
1996-97	Away	11-Jan-97	1-1	Willems (84)	11,467	R.Dilkes
1997-98	Home	22-Oct-97	1-1	Baiano (53)	28,595	U.Rennie
1997-98	Away	17-Jan-98	0-0		13,031	P.Jones
1998-99	Home	22-Aug-98	0-0		25,747	J.Winter
1998-99	Away	9-Jan-99	1-2	Wanchope (76)	12,732	A.Wilkie
1999-00	Away	11-Sep-99	2-2	Cabonari (14); Johnson (81)	12,282	A.Wiley
1999-00	Home	4-Mar-00	4-0	Kinkladze (65); Christie (71); Burton (90); Sturridge (90)	28,384	A.D'Urso

INTRODUCTION

The cricket team of St Domingo's Church turned to football around 1878. Playing in Stanley Park, in late 1879 changed name to Everton FC, the name of the district to the west of the park. Moved to a field at Priory Road in 1882 and then, in 1884, moved to a site in Anfield Road. As one of the country's leading teams, became founder members of the Football League in 1888. Moved to Goodison Park, a field on the north side of Stanley Park, in 1892 following a dispute with the ground's landlord. Premier League founder members 1992.

Ground: Goodison Park, Liverpool, L4 4EL
Nickname: The Toffees
Internet: www.evertonfc.com

HONOURS

Football League Div 1:	Champions 1890-91, 1914-15, 1927-28, 1931-32, 1938-39, 1962-63, 1969-70, 1984-85, 1986-87. Runners-up 1889-90, 1894-95, 1901-02, 1904-05, 1908-09, 1911-12, 1985-86
Football League Div 2:	Champions 1930-31 Runners-up 1953-54
FA Cup:	Winners 1906, 1933, 1966, 1984, 1995. Runners-up 1893, 1897, 1907, 1968, 1985, 1986, 1989
Football League Cup:	Runners-up 1976-77, 1983-84
League Super Cup:	Runners-up 1986
Cup-Winners' Cup:	Winners 1984-85
Simod Cup:	Runners-up 1989
Zenith Data Systems Cup:	Runners-up 1991

EUROPEAN RECORD

Champions' League (2):	63-64 (1), 70-71 (QF)
CupWinners' Cup (3):	66-67 (2), 84-85 (W), 95-96 (2)
UEFA Cup (6):	62-63 (1), 64-65 (3), 65-66 (2), 75-76 (1), 78-79 (2), 79-80 (1).

FAPL RECORD SUMMARY

Most Total:	WATSON, Dave	224
Most Starts:	WATSON, Dave	221
Most Subs:	CADAMARTERI, Danny	45
Most SNU:	KEARTON, Jason	135
Most PS:	BARMBY, Nicky	33
Most Goals:	FERGUSON, Duncan	37
Most Yel:	WATSON, Dave	25
Most Red:	FERGUSON, Duncan	4

PLAYING RECORD – SEASON TOTALS

Season	Pn	P	W	D	L	F	A	Pts
1992-93	13	42	15	8	19	53	55	53
1993-94	17	42	12	8	22	42	63	44
1994-95	15	42	11	17	14	44	51	50
1995-96	6	38	17	10	11	64	44	61
1996-97	15	38	10	12	16	44	57	42
1997-98	17	38	9	13	16	41	56	40
1998-99	14	38	11	10	17	42	47	43
1999-00	13	38	12	14	12	59	49	50
Totals		316	97	92	127	389	422	383

PLAYING RECORD – HOME TOTALS

Season	Pn	P	W	D	L	F	A	Pts
1992-93	13	21	7	6	8	26	27	27
1993-94	17	21	8	4	9	26	30	28
1994-95	15	21	8	9	4	31	23	33
1995-96	6	19	10	5	4	35	19	35
1996-97	15	19	7	4	8	24	22	25
1997-98	17	19	7	5	7	25	27	26
1998-99	14	19	6	8	5	22	12	26
1999-00	13	19	7	9	3	36	21	30
Everton		158	60	50	48	225	181	230

PLAYING RECORD – AWAY TOTALS

Season	Pn	P	W	D	L	F	A	Pts
1992-93	13	21	8	2	11	27	28	26
1993-94	17	21	4	4	13	16	33	16
1994-95	15	21	3	8	10	13	28	17
1995-96	6	19	7	5	7	29	25	26
1996-97	15	19	3	8	8	20	35	17
1997-98	17	19	2	8	9	16	29	14
1998-99	14	19	5	2	12	20	35	17
1999-00	13	19	5	5	9	23	28	20
Totals		158	37	42	79	164	241	153

HIGHEST HOME ATTENDANCES

	Attendance	Opponents	Date	Season
1	41,112	Liverpool	18-Oct-97	1997-98
2	40,185	Liverpool	17-Oct-98	1998-99
3	40,177	Liverpool	16-Apr-97	1996-97
4	40,127	Aston Villa	5-May-96	1995-96
5	40,120	Liverpool	16-Apr-96	1995-96

LOWEST HOME ATTENDANCES

	Attendance	Opponents	Date	Season
1	13,265	Southampton	4-Dec-93	1993-94
2	14,051	Southampton	19-Dec-92	1992-93
3	15,197	Sheffield U.	4-May-93	1992-93

| 4 | 15,638 | Ipswich T. | 24-Mar-93 | 1992-93 |
| 5 | 16,164 | Tottenham H. | 10-Feb-93 | 1992-93 |

TOP SCORER – SEASON BY SEASON

Season	Player	Goals
1992-93	Cottee	12
1993-94	Cottee	16
1994-95	Rideout	13
1995-96	Kanchelskis	* 16
1996-97	Ferguson	10
1997-98	Ferguson	11
1998-99	Campbell	9
1999-00	Campbell	12

PLAYERS WITH MOST PREMIERSHIP APPEARANCES

Tot	Player	St	Sb	Gls
224	WATSON, Dave	221	3	6
207	SOUTHALL, Neville	207	0	0
143	HINCHCLIFFE, Andy	134	9	6

136	STUART, Graham	116	20	22
123	HORNE, Barry	118	5	3
121	EBBRELL, John	120	1	9
116	FERGUSON, Duncan	110	6	37
116	BARMBY, Nicky	105	11	18
114	UNSWORTH, David	107	7	10
111	ABLETT, Gary	111	0	5
111	RIDEOUT, Paul	86	25	29
108	JACKSON, Matt	102	6	3
99	SHORT, Craig	90	9	4
92	BALL, Michael	73	19	5
90	PARKINSON, Joe	88	2	3
75	HUTCHISON, Don	68	7	10
74	BARRETT, Earl	73	1	0
74	CADAMARTERI, Danny	29	45	9

CLUB-BY-CLUB RESULTS

ARSENAL

Season	Venue	Date	Res	Scorers	Attendance	Referee
1992-93	Away	24-Oct-92	0-2		28,052	K.Hackett
1992-93	Home	1-May-93	0-0		19,044	A.Gunn
1993-94	Away	28-Aug-93	0-2		29,063	K.Burge
1993-94	Home	19-Feb-94	1-1	Cottee (80)	19,760	D.Allison
1994-95	Home	29-Oct-94	1-1	Unsworth (14)	32,003	K.Burge
1994-95	Away	14-Jan-95	1-1	Watson (13)	34,473	R.Hart
1995-96	Home	23-Aug-95	0-2		36,047	K.Burge
1995-96	Away	20-Jan-96	2-1	Stuart (50); Kanchelskis (84)	38,275	M.Bodenham
1996-97	Away	19-Jan-97	1-3	Ferguson (89)	38,095	K.Burge
1996-97	Home	1-Mar-97	0-2		36,980	P.Danson
1997-98	Home	27-Sep-97	2-2	Ball (49); Cadamarteri (56)	35,457	A.Wilkie
1997-98	Away	3-May-98	0-4		38,269	G.Ashby
1998-99	Away	8-Nov-98	0-1		38,088	G.Willard
1998-99	Home	13-Mar-99	0-2		38,049	U.Rennie
1999-00	Away	16-Oct-99	1-4	Collins (16)	38,042	S.Dunn
1999-00	Home	29-Apr-00	0-1		35,919	D.Gallagher

ASTON VILLA

Season	Venue	Date	Res	Scorers	Attendance	Referee
1992-93	Home	25-Aug-92	1-0	Johnston (88)	22,372	M.Bodenham
1992-93	Away	20-Feb-93	1-2	Beardsley (24 pen)	33,913	T.Ward
1993-94	Home	31-Aug-93	0-1		24,067	R.Gifford
1993-94	Away	30-Mar-94	0-0		36,044	R.Gifford
1994-95	Home	20-Aug-94	2-2	Stuart (22); Rideout (70)	35,544	K.Morton
1994-95	Away	10-Dec-94	0-0		29,678	R.Gifford
1995-96	Away	28-Oct-95	0-1		32,792	K.Burge

1995-96	Home	5-May-96	1-0	Parkinson (78)	40,127	R.Hart
1996-97	Home	3-Sep-96	0-1		39,115	M.Bodenham
1996-97	Away	5-Apr-97	1-3	Unsworth (15)	39,339	J.Winter
1997-98	Away	22-Nov-97	1-2	Speed (11 pen)	36,389	U.Rennie
1997-98	Home	28-Mar-98	1-4	Madar (38)	36,471	N.Barry
1998-99	Home	15-Aug-98	0-0		40,112	A.Wilkie
1998-99	Away	18-Jan-99	0-3		32,488	N.Barry
1999-00	Away	11-Aug-99	0-3		30,337	G.Barber
1999-00	Home	27-Nov-99	0-0		34,750	P.Jones

BARNSLEY

Season	Venue	Date	Res	Scorers	Attendance	Referee
1997-98	Home	20-Sep-97	4-2	Speed (12, 72 pen); Oster (84); Cadarmarteri (42)	32,659	G.Ashby
1997-98	Away	7-Feb-98	2-2	Ferguson (40); Grant (50)	18,672	M.Bodenham

BLACKBURN ROVERS

Season	Venue	Date	Res	Scorers	Attendance	Referee
1992-93	Away	15-Sep-92	3-2	Cottee (22, 81); Ebbrell (39)	19,563	D.Allison
1992-93	Home	3-Mar-93	2-1	OG (56, Hendry); Cottee (71)	18,086	P.Foakes
1993-94	Away	29-Dec-93	0-2		22,061	T.Holbrook
1993-94	Home	4-Apr-94	0-3		27,463	K.Morton
1994-95	Away	10-Sep-94	0-3		26,538	R.Dilkes
1994-95	Home	1-Apr-95	1-2	Stuart (23)	37,905	D.Gallagher
1995-96	Home	5-Nov-95	1-0	Stuart (23)	30,097	A.Wilkie
1995-96	Away	30-Mar-96	3-0	Amokachi (71); Kanchelskis (77, 90)	29,468	J.Winter
1996-97	Away	21-Sep-96	1-1	Unsworth (38)	27,091	D.Elleray
1996-97	Home	1-Jan-97	0-2		30,427	G.Barber
1997-98	Away	8-Nov-97	2-3	Speed (7); Ferguson (55)	25,397	P.Alcock
1997-98	Home	14-Mar-98	1-0	Madar (62)	33,423	G.Willard
1998-99	Home	27-Sep-98	0-0		36,404	M.Riley
1998-99	Away	10-Mar-99	2-1	Bakayoko (15, 65)	27,219	P.Alcock

BOLTON WANDERERS

Season	Venue	Date	Res	Scorers	Attendance	Referee
1995-96	Away	14-Oct-95	1-1	Rideout (85)	20,427	P.Alcock
1995-96	Home	6-Apr-96	3-0	Hottiger (21); Kanchelskis (86); Amokachi (90)	37,974	M.Bodenham
1997-98	Away	1-Sep-97	0-0		23,131	S.Lodge
1997-98	Home	28-Dec-97	3-2	Ferguson (17, 41, 67)	37,149	K.Burge

BRADFORD CITY

Season	Venue	Date	Res	Scorers	Attendance	Referee
1999-00	Away	28-Dec-99	0-0		18,276	U.Rennie
1999-00	Home	15-Apr-00	4-0	Pembridge (2); Unsworth (15 pen); Barmby (54); Collins (83)	30,646	P.Alcock

CHARLTON ATHLETIC

Season	Venue	Date	Res	Scorers	Attendance	Referee
1998-99	Away	28-Nov-98	2-1	Cadamarteri (45,73)	20,043	K.Burge
1998-99	Home	24-Apr-99	4-1	Hutchison (24); Campbell (31, 60); Jeffers (75)	40,089	P.Alcock

CHELSEA

Season	Venue	Date	Res	Scorers	Attendance	Referee
1992-93	Home	21-Nov-92	1-0		17,418	M.Reed
1992-93	Away	10-Mar-93	1-2	Kenny (45)	12,739	M.Bodenham
1993-94	Away	3-Jan-94	2-4	Cottee (46); Barlow (55)	18,338	K.Barratt
1993-94	Home	5-Feb-94	4-2	Ebbrell (5); Rideout (26, 39); Angell (85)	18,201	B.Hill
1994-95	Away	26-Nov-94	1-0	Rideout (39)	28,115	R.Hart
1994-95	Home	3-May-95	3-3	Hinchcliffe (39); Ablett (50); Amokachi (70)	33,180	B.Hill
1995-96	Away	19-Aug-95	0-0		30,189	M.Reed
1995-96	Home	13-Jan-96	1-1	Unsworth (35 pen)	34,968	R.Hart
1996-97	Away	7-Dec-96	2-2	Branch (17); Kanchelskis (28)	28,418	P.Durkin
1996-97	Home	11-May-97	1-2	Barmby (77)	38,321	P.Jones
1997-98	Away	26-Nov-97	0-2		34,148	N.Barry
1997-98	Home	18-Jan-98	3-1	Speed (39); Ferguson (62); OG (82, Duberry)	32,355	A.Wilkie
1998-99	Home	5-Dec-98	0-0		36,430	G.Willard
1998-99	Away	1-May-99	1-3	Jeffers (69)	34,909	D.Gallagher
1999-00	Home	20-Nov-99	1-1	Campbell (15)	38,225	M.Halsey
1999-00	Away	11-Mar-00	1-1	Cadamarteri (69)	35,113	D.Elleray

COVENTRY CITY

Season	Venue	Date	Res	Scorers	Attendance	Referee
1992-93	Home	17-Oct-92	1-1	Beagrie (28)	17,587	R.Hamer
1992-93	Away	7-Mar-93	1-0	Ward,Mark (8)	11,285	D.Elleray
1993-94	Away	6-Nov-93	1-2	Rideout (69)	11,550	A.Wilkie
1993-94	Home	23-Apr-94	0-0		23,352	R.Dilkes
1994-95	Home	15-Oct-94	0-2		28,233	D.Elleray
1994-95	Away	14-May-95	0-0		21,814	P.Jones
1995-96	Away	23-Dec-95	1-2	Rideout (67)	16,638	S.Lodge
1995-96	Home	9-Mar-96	2-2	Ferguson (17, 25)	34,517	P.Danson
1996-97	Home	4-Nov-96	1-1	Stuart (45 pen)	31,477	G.Poll
1996-97	Away	22-Feb-97	0-0		19,497	J.Winter
1997-98	Away	25-Oct-97	0-0		18,760	S.Lodge
1997-98	Home	10-May-98	1-1	Farrelly (7)	40,109	P.Alcock
1998-99	Away	15-Nov-98	0-3		19,290	G.Poll
1998-99	Home	11-Apr-99	2-0	Campbell (29, 88)	32,341	R.Harris
1999-00	Home	2-Oct-99	1-1	Jeffers (2)	34,839	N.Barry
1999-00	Away	15-Mar-00	0-1		18,518	M.Halsey

CRYSTAL PALACE

Season	Venue	Date	Res	Scorers	Attendance	Referee
1992-93	Home	19-Sep-92	0-2		18,080	D.Gallagher
1992-93	Away	9-Jan-93	2-0	Jackson (50); Beardsley (85)	13,227	R.Milford
1994-95	Away	22-Oct-94	0-1		15,026	S.Lodge
1994-95	Home	21-Jan-95	3-1	Ferguson (2,87); Rideout (53)	23,733	P.Jones
1997-98	Home	9-Aug-97	1-2	Ferguson (85)	35,716	S.Dunn
1997-98	Away	10-Jan-98	3-1	Barmby (3); Ferguson (12); Madar (34)	23,311	G.Barber

DERBY COUNTY

Season	Venue	Date	Res	Scorers	Attendance	Referee
1996-97	Away	16-Dec-96	1-0	Barmby (86)	17,252	M.Reed
1996-97	Home	15-Mar-97	1-0	Watson (79)	32,240	G.Barber

Season	Venue	Date	Res	Scorers	Attendance	Referee
1997-98	Away	13-Sep-97	1-3	Stuart (28)	27,828	M.Riley
1997-98	Home	14-Feb-98	1-2	Thomsen (85)	34,876	S.Dunn
1998-99	Home	26-Dec-98	0-0		39,206	S.Lodge
1998-99	Away	7-Feb-99	1-2	Barmby (37)	27,603	G.Poll
1999-00	Away	28-Aug-99	0-1		26,550	A.D'Urso
1999-00	Home	12-Feb-00	2-1	Moore (24); Ball (45 pen)	33,260	U.Rennie

IPSWICH TOWN

Season	Venue	Date	Res	Scorers	Attendance	Referee
1992-93	Away	28-Nov-92	0-1		18,032	B.Hill
1992-93	Home	24-Mar-93	3-0	Barlow (18); Jackson (49); Cottee (66)	15,638	B.Hill
1993-94	Away	30-Oct-93	2-0	Barlow (13); OG (61, Whelan)	15,094	P.Don
1993-94	Home	12-Feb-94	0-0		19,641	R.Milford
1994-95	Home	31-Dec-94	4-1	Ferguson (27); Rideout (70,73); Watson (89)	25,659	R.Dilkes
1994-95	Away	9-May-95	1-0	Rideout (49)	14,951	R.Hart

LEEDS UNITED

Season	Venue	Date	Res	Scorers	Attendance	Referee
1992-93	Away	26-Sep-92	0-2		27,915	K.Redfern
1992-93	Home	16-Jan-93	2-0	Cottee (30, 49)	21,031	D.Elleray
1993-94	Home	23-Nov-93	1-1	Cottee (66)	17,102	K.Cooper
1993-94	Away	30-Apr-94	0-3		35,487	V.Callow
1994-95	Home	5-Dec-94	3-0	Rideout (7); Ferguson (58); Unsworth (66 pen)	25,897	P.Durkin
1994-95	Away	22-Feb-95	0-1		30,793	D.Gallagher
1995-96	Home	30-Dec-95	2-0	OG (5, Wetherall); Kanchelskis (51)	40,009	J.Winter
1995-96	Away	17-Mar-96	2-2	Stuart (28); Kanchelskis (50)	29,425	G.Ashby
1996-97	Home	21-Dec-96	0-0		36,954	G.Ashby
1996-97	Away	8-Mar-97	0-1		32,055	M.Bodenham
1997-98	Away	6-Dec-97	0-0		34,986	P.Durkin
1997-98	Home	11-Apr-98	2-0	Hutchison (10); Ferguson (38)	37,099	U.Rennie
1998-99	Home	12-Sep-98	0-0		36,687	N.Barry
1998-99	Away	20-Feb-99	0-1		36,344	D.Elleray
1999-00	Home	24-Oct-99	4-4	Campbell (4, 28); Hutchison (37); Weir (90)	37,355	D.Gallagher
1999-00	Away	8-May-00	1-1	Barmby (60)	37,713	A.D'Urso

LEICESTER CITY

Season	Venue	Date	Res	Scorers	Attendance	Referee
1994-95	Home	24-Sep-94	1-1	Ablett (50)	28,003	T.Holbrook
1994-95	Away	4-Mar-95	2-2	Limpar (5); Samways (45)	20,447	P.Durkin
1996-97	Away	23-Nov-96	2-1	Hinchcliffe (12); Unsworth (52)	20,975	J.Winter
1996-97	Home	9-Apr-97	1-1	Branch (17)	30,368	S.Dunn
1997-98	Away	20-Dec-97	1-0	Speed (89 pen)	20,628	J.Winter
1997-98	Home	18-Apr-98	1-1	Madar (2)	33,642	S.Lodge
1998-99	Away	22-Aug-98	0-2		21,037	S.Lodge
1998-99	Home	9-Jan-99	0-0		32,792	P.Durkin
1999-00	Home	3-Jan-00	2-2	Hutchison (15); Unsworth (56 pen)	30,490	J.Winter
1999-00	Away	8-Apr-00	1-1	Hutchison (27)	18,705	A.Wiley

LIVERPOOL

Season	Venue	Date	Res	Scorers	Attendance	Referee
1992-93	Home	7-Dec-92	2-1	Johnston (63); Beardsley (84)	35,826	M.Bodenham
1992-93	Away	20-Mar-93	0-1		44,619	P.Don
1993-94	Home	18-Sep-93	2-0	Ward,Mark (27); Cottee (85)	38,157	D.Elleray
1993-94	Away	13-Mar-94	1-2	Watson (21)	44,281	K.Cooper
1994-95	Home	21-Nov-94	2-0	Ferguson (56); Rideout (89)	39,866	D.Gallagher
1994-95	Away	24-Jan-95	0-0		39,505	B.Hill
1995-96	Away	18-Nov-95	2-1	Kancheslskis (53, 68)	40,818	G.Ashby
1995-96	Home	16-Apr-96	1-1	Kanchelskis (19)	40,120	D.Elleray
1996-97	Away	20-Nov-96	1-1	Speed (81)	40,751	S.Lodge
1996-97	Home	16-Apr-97	1-1	Ferguson (65)	40,177	S.Lodge
1997-98	Home	18-Oct-97	2-0	OG (45, Ruddock); Cadamarteri (75)	41,112	M.Reed
1997-98	Away	23-Feb-98	1-1	Ferguson (58)	44,501	P.Jones
1998-99	Home	17-Oct-98	0-0		40,185	P.Durkin
1998-99	Away	3-Apr-99	2-3	Dacourt (1); Jeffers (84)	44,852	D.Elleray
1999-00	Away	27-Sep-99	1-0	Campbell (4)	44,802	M.Riley
1999-00	Home	21-Apr-00	0-0		40,052	G.Poll

MANCHESTER CITY

Season	Venue	Date	Res	Scorers	Attendance	Referee
1992-93	Home	31-Oct-92	1-3	OG (68, Brightwell)	20,242	J.Worrall
1992-93	Away	8-May-93	5-2	Jackson (6); Beagrie (19, 84); Beardsley (32); Radosavljievic 'Preki' (51)	25,180	K.Redfern
1993-94	Home	17-Aug-93	1-0	Rideout (18)	26,025	V.Callow
1993-94	Away	8-Dec-93	0-1		25,513	P.Durkin
1994-95	Away	27-Aug-94	0-4		19,867	P.Don
1994-95	Home	15-Mar-95	1-1	Unsworth (80 pen)	28,485	G.Willard
1995-96	Away	30-Aug-95	2-0	Parkinson (58); Amokachi (75)	28,432	S.Lodge
1995-96	Home	10-Feb-96	2-0	Parkinson (37); Hinchcliffe (47 pen)	37,354	P.Alcock

MANCHESTER UNITED

Season	Venue	Date	Res	Scorers	Attendance	Referee
1992-93	Away	19-Aug-92	3-0	Beardsley (45); Warzycha (80); Johnston (90)	31,901	K.Barratt
1992-93	Home	12-Sep-92	0-2		30,002	M.Peck
1993-94	Home	23-Oct-93	0-1		35,455	K.Hackett
1993-94	Away	22-Jan-94	0-1		44,750	R.Gifford
1994-95	Away	1-Oct-94	0-2		43,803	G.Poll
1994-95	Home	25-Feb-95	1-0	Ferguson (58)	40,011	J.Worrall
1995-96	Home	9-Sep-95	2-3	Limpar (27); Rideout (55)	39,496	G.Poll
1995-96	Away	21-Feb-96	0-2		42,459	M.Bodenham
1996-97	Away	21-Aug-96	2-2	Ferguson (34, 40)	54,943	G.Poll
1996-97	Home	22-Mar-97	0-2		40,079	D.Gallagher
1997-98	Home	27-Aug-97	0-2		40,079	K.Burge
1997-98	Away	26-Dec-97	0-2		55,167	U.Rennie
1998-99	Home	31-Oct-98	1-4	Ferguson (30)	40,079	P.Jones
1998-99	Away	22-Mar-99	1-3	Hutchison (80)	55,182	M.Riley
1999-00	Home	8-Aug-99	1-1	OG (86, Stam)	39,141	D.Gallagher
1999-00	Away	4-Dec-99	1-5	Jeffers (7)	55,193	G.Poll

MIDDLESBROUGH

Season	Venue	Date	Res	Scorers	Attendance	Referee
1992-93	Home	26-Dec-92	2-2	Rideout (47); Beardsley (66pen)	24,391	R.Groves
1992-93	Away	10-Apr-93	2-1	Watson (26); Radosavljevic 'Preki' (80)	16,627	J.Lloyd
1995-96	Home	26-Dec-95	4-0	Short (10); Stuart (45, 59); Kanchelskis (67)	40,091	P.Jones
1995-96	Away	2-Mar-96	2-0	Grant (28); Hinchcliffe (44 pen)	29,407	D.Gallagher
1996-97	Home	14-Sep-96	1-2	Short (8)	39,250	P.Danson
1996-97	Away	26-Dec-96	2-4	Unsworth (31); Ferguson (45)	29,673	S.Dunn
1998-99	Away	19-Sep-98	2-2	Ball (47 pen); Collins (48)	34,563	D.Gallagher
1998-99	Home	17-Feb-99	5-0	Barmby (1, 16); Dacourt (61); Materazzi (67); Unsworth (73)	31,606	K.Burge
1999-00	Away	30-Oct-99	1-2	Campbell (3)	33,916	A.D'Urso
1999-00	Home	14-May-00	0-2		34,663	R.Harris

NEWCASTLE UNITED

Season	Venue	Date	Res	Scorers	Attendance	Referee
1993-94	Away	25-Aug-93	0-1		34,490	G.Ashby
1993-94	Home	18-Dec-93	0-2		25,362	M.Bodenham
1994-95	Away	1-Feb-95	0-2		34,465	D.Elleray
1994-95	Home	14-Apr-95	2-0	Amokachi (23,49)	34,811	R.Gifford
1995-96	Home	1-Oct-95	1-3	Limpar (81)	33,080	K.Cooper
1995-96	Away	16-Dec-95	0-1		36,557	P.Durkin
1996-97	Home	17-Aug-96	2-0	Unsworth (28 pen); Speed (40)	40,117	M.Reed
1996-97	Away	29-Jan-97	1-4	Speed (2)	36,143	M.Riley
1997-98	Away	24-Sep-97	0-1		36,705	G.Poll
1997-98	Home	28-Feb-98	0-0		37,972	M.Riley
1998-99	Home	23-Nov-98	1-0	Ball (18)	30,357	N.Barry
1998-99	Away	17-Apr-99	3-1	Campbell (1,44); Gemmill (88)	36,775	G.Poll
1999-00	Away	7-Nov-99	1-1	Campbell (62)	36,164	M.Reed
1999-00	Home	19-Mar-00	0-2		32,512	G.Barber

NORWICH CITY

Season	Venue	Date	Res	Scorers	Attendance	Referee
1992-93	Away	22-Aug-92	1-1	Beardsley (55)	14,150	J.Key
1992-93	Home	30-Jan-93	0-1		20,301	R.Lewis
1993-94	Home	25-Sep-93	1-5	Rideout (13)	20,631	P.Durkin
1993-94	Away	21-Mar-94	0-3		16,432	K.Burge
1994-95	Away	5-Nov-94	0-0		18,377	P.Danson
1994-95	Home	4-Feb-95	2-1	Stuart (42); Rideout (65)	23,293	A.Wilkie

NOTTINGHAM FOREST

Season	Venue	Date	Res	Scorers	Attendance	Referee
1992-93	Away	7-Nov-92	1-0	Rideout (52)	20,941	S.Lodge
1992-93	Home	13-Mar-93	3-0	Cottee (15, 26); Hinchcliffe (38)	21,271	V.Callow
1994-95	Home	30-Aug-94	1-2	Rideout (68)	26,689	G.Ashby
1994-95	Away	8-Mar-95	1-2	Barlow (45)	24,526	R.Dilkes
1995-96	Away	17-Sep-95	2-3	Rideout (62, 81)	24,786	M.Bodenham
1995-96	Home	24-Feb-96	3-0	Kanchelskis (52); Watson (56); Ferguson (60)	33,163	K.Cooper
1996-97	Away	28-Oct-96	1-0	Short (4)	19,892	P.Durkin
1996-97	Home	1-Feb-97	2-0	Ferguson (47); Barmby (67)	32,567	S.Dunn

| 1998-99 | Away | 8-Sep-98 | 2-0 | Ferguson (72, 84) | 25,610 | R.Harris |
| 1998-99 | Home | 30-Jan-99 | 0-1 | | 34,175 | G.Barber |

OLDHAM ATHLETIC

Season	Venue	Date	Res	Scorers	Attendance	Referee
1992-93	Away	4-Oct-92	0-1		13,013	P.Don
1992-93	Home	27-Feb-93	2-2	Beardsley (20 pen); Barlow (61)	18,025	K.Cooper
1993-94	Away	11-Sep-93	1-0	Cottee (32)	13,666	S.Lodge
1993-94	Home	5-Mar-94	2-1	Redosavlljevic 'Preki' (40); Stuart (61)	18,881	D.Elleray

QPR

Season	Venue	Date	Res	Scorers	Attendance	Referee
1992-93	Away	28-Dec-92	2-4	Barlow (65, 72)	14,802	G.Ashby
1992-93	Home	12-Apr-93	3-5	Cottee (31); Barlow (87); Radosavljevic 'Preki' (89)	19,057	S.Lodge
1993-94	Home	20-Nov-93	0-3		17,326	R.Hart
1993-94	Away	16-Apr-94	1-2	Cottee (64)	13,330	M.Bodenham
1994-95	Home	17-Sep-94	2-2	Amokachi (10); Rideout (24)	27,285	R.Gifford
1994-95	Away	18-Mar-95	3-2	Barlow (58); OG (69, McDonald); Hinchcliffe (90)	14,488	K.Morton
1995-96	Home	22-Nov-95	2-0	Stuart (18); Rideout (36)	30,009	P.Danson
1995-96	Away	8-Apr-96	1-3	Ebbrell (80)	18,349	P.Durkin

SHEFFIELD UNITED

Season	Venue	Date	Res	Scorers	Attendance	Referee
1992-93	Away	12-Dec-92	0-1		16,266	K.Morton
1992-93	Home	4-May-93	0-2		15,197	V.Callow
1993-94	Home	21-Aug-93	4-2	Cottee (35, 83, 90); Ebbrell (45)	24,177	D.Gallagher
1993-94	Away	11-Dec-93	0-0		15,135	V.Callow

SHEFFIELD WEDNESDAY

Season	Venue	Date	Res	Scorers	Attendance	Referee
1992-93	Home	15-Aug-92	1-1	Horne (44)	27,687	K.Morton
1992-93	Away	6-Feb-93	1-3	Cottee (83)	24,979	K.Morton
1993-94	Home	27-Dec-93	0-2		16,471	R.Dilkes
1993-94	Away	2-Apr-94	1-5	Cottee (76)	24,080	G.Ashby
1994-95	Home	26-Dec-94	1-4	Ferguson (36)	37,080	T.Holbrook
1994-95	Away	17-Apr-95	0-0		27,880	M.Reed
1995-96	Home	25-Nov-95	2-2	Kanchelskis (45); Amokachi (53)	35,898	M.Bodenham
1995-96	Away	27-Apr-96	5-2	Amokachi (4); Ebbrell (10); Kanchelskis (21, 54, 65)	32,724	M.Reed
1996-97	Home	28-Sep-96	2-0	Kanchelskis (17); Stuart (60)	34,160	P.Alcock
1996-97	Away	11-Jan-97	1-2	Ferguson (63)	24,175	A.Wilkie
1997-98	Away	4-Oct-97	1-3	Cadamarteri (84)	24,486	P.Durkin
1997-98	Home	25-Apr-98	1-3	Ferguson (72)	35,497	G.Barber
1998-99	Away	24-Oct-98	0-0		26,952	J.Winter
1998-99	Home	5-Apr-99	1-2	Jeffers (12)	35,270	M.Reed
1999-00	Away	11-Sep-99	2-0	Barmby (14); Gemmill (18)	23,539	M.Halsey
1999-00	Home	4-Mar-00	1-1	Weir (33)	32,020	G.Barber

SOUTHAMPTON

Season	Venue	Date	Res	Scorers	Attendance	Referee
1992-93	Home	19-Dec-92	2-1	Beardsley (11pen); Rideout (36)	14,051	M.Peck
1992-93	Away	17-Apr-93	0-0		16,911	M.Bodenham
1993-94	Away	14-Aug-93	2-0	Beagrie (10); Ebbrell (44)	14,051	K.Cooper
1993-94	Home	4-Dec-93	1-0	Cottee (35)	13,265	K.Burge
1994-95	Away	8-Oct-94	0-2		15,163	B.Hill
1994-95	Home	6-May-95	0-0		36,840	T.Holbrook
1995-96	Home	26-Aug-95	2-0	Limpar (34); Amokachi (42)	33,668	J.Winter
1995-96	Away	3-Feb-96	2-2	Stuart (53); Horne (57)	15,136	D.Elleray
1996-97	Home	16-Nov-96	7-1	Stuart (13); Kanchelskis (22, 35); Speed (30, 32, 72); Barmby (58)	35,669	M.Riley
1996-97	Away	5-Mar-97	2-2	Ferguson (10); Speed (27)	15,134	P.Durkin
1997-98	Home	2-Nov-97	0-2		29,958	A.Wilkie
1997-98	Away	7-Mar-98	1-2	Tiler (89)	15,102	D.Elleray
1998-99	Home	12-Dec-98	1-0	Bakayoko (31)	32,073	A.Wilkie
1998-99	Away	16-May-99	0-2		15,254	G.Barber
1999-00	Home	21-Aug-99	4-1	Gough (36); OG (47, Ludekvam); Jeffers (48); Campbell (54)	31,755	B.Knight
1999-00	Away	22-Jan-00	0-2		15,232	A.D'Urso

SUNDERLAND

Season	Venue	Date	Res	Scorers	Attendance	Referee
1996-97	Home	30-Nov-96	1-3	Ferguson (64)	40,087	P.Jones
1996-97	Away	3-May-97	0-2		22,108	K.Burge
1999-00	Home	26-Dec-99	5-0	Hutchison (16, 26); Jeffers (41); Pembridge (61); Campbell (72)	40,017	S.Lodge
1999-00	Away	25-Mar-00	1-2	Barmby (38)	41,934	S.Bennett

SWINDON TOWN

Season	Venue	Date	Res	Scorers	Attendance	Referee
1993-94	Away	16-Oct-93	1-1	Beagrie (27)	14,437	K.Morton
1993-94	Home	15-Jan-94	6-2	Ebbrell (4); Cottee (42, 84, 89 pen); Ablett (71); Beagrie (90)	20,760	G.Ashby

TOTTENHAM HOTSPUR

Season	Venue	Date	Res	Scorers	Attendance	Referee
1992-93	Away	5-Sep-92	1-2	Beardsley (42)	26,303	R.Hart
1992-93	Home	10-Feb-93	1-2	Sansom (29)	16,164	K.Barratt
1993-94	Away	3-Oct-93	2-3	Rideout (16); Cottee (67 pen)	27,487	R.Milford
1993-94	Home	26-Mar-94	0-1		23,460	K.Barratt
1994-95	Away	24-Aug-94	1-2	Rideout (46)	24,553	G.Willard
1994-95	Home	17-Dec-94	0-0		32,809	K.Cooper
1995-96	Home	22-Oct-95	1-1	Stuart (12)	33,629	R.Dilkes
1995-96	Away	2-Dec-95	0-0		32,894	S.Dunn
1996-97	Away	24-Aug-96	0-0		29,696	L.Dilkes
1996-97	Home	12-Apr-97	1-0	Speed (11)	36,380	G.Willard
1997-98	Home	29-Nov-97	0-2		36,670	P.Jones
1997-98	Away	4-Apr-98	1-1	Madar (24)	35,624	A.Wilkie
1998-99	Home	29-Aug-98	0-1		39,378	P.Jones
1998-99	Away	28-Dec-98	1-4	Bakayoko (31)	36,053	G.Poll

| 1999-00 | Away | 14-Aug-99 | 2-3 | Unsworth (24 pen, 77 pen) | 34,539 | P.Alcock |
| 1999-00 | Home | 15-Jan-00 | 2-2 | Campbell (22); Moore (90) | 36,144 | A.Wiley |

WATFORD

Season	Venue	Date	Res	Scorers	Attendance	Referee
1999-00	Away	18-Dec-99	3-1	Barmby (4); Hutchison (37); Unsworth (86 pen)	17,346	A.Wilkie
1999-00	Home	1-Apr-00	4-2	Hughes,M. (18); Moore (30, 36); Hughes,S. (86)	31,960	S.Dunn

WEST HAM UNITED

Season	Venue	Date	Res	Scorers	Attendance	Referee
1993-94	Home	1-Jan-94	0-1		19,602	J.Lloyd
1993-94	Away	9-Apr-94	1-0	Cottee (72)	20,243	P.Foakes
1994-95	Home	1-Nov-94	1-0	Ablett (54)	28,338	M.Bodenham
1994-95	Away	13-Feb-95	2-2	Rideout (44); Limpar (79)	21,081	M.Reed
1995-96	Away	23-Sep-95	1-2	Samways (40)	21,085	P.Durkin
1995-96	Home	11-Dec-95	3-0	Stuart (33); Unsworth (43 pen); Ebbrell (68)	31,778	M.Reed
1996-97	Home	12-Oct-96	2-1	Stuart (14); Speed (78)	36,571	G.Barber
1996-97	Away	19-Apr-97	2-2	Branch (78); Ferguson (89)	24,525	P.Alcock
1997-98	Home	23-Aug-97	2-1	Speed (67); Stuart (83)	34,356	P.Jones
1997-98	Away	31-Jan-98	2-2	Barmby (25); Madar (58)	25,905	M.Reed
1998-99	Away	19-Dec-98	1-2	Cadamarteri (71)	25,998	R.Harris
1998-99	Home	8-May-99	6-0	Campbell (14,52,77); Ball (25pen); Hutchison (38); Jeffers (87)	40,049	A.Wilkie
1999-00	Home	19-Sep-99	1-0	Jeffers (64)	35,154	S.Bennett
1999-00	Away	26-Feb-00	4-0	Barmby (8, 64, 67); Moore (71)	26,025	P.Alcock

WIMBLEDON

Season	Venue	Date	Res	Scorers	Attendance	Referee
1992-93	Home	29-Aug-92	0-0		18,118	H.King
1992-93	Away	26-Jan-93	3-1	Cottee (61, 71); Snoddin (73)	3,039	K.Hackett
1993-94	Away	27-Nov-93	1-1	Barlow (33)	6,934	M.Reed
1993-94	Home	7-May-94	3-2	Stuart (24pen, 81); Horne (67)	31,233	R.Hart
1994-95	Away	2-Jan-95	1-2	Rideout (16)	9,506	K.Burge
1994-95	Home	29-Apr-95	0-0		33,063	P.Danson
1995-96	Away	1-Jan-96	3-2	Ebbrell (1); Ferguson (23,25)	11,121	A.Wilkie
1995-96	Home	23-Mar-96	2-4	Short (21); Kanchelskis (61)	31,382	R.Dilkes
1996-97	Away	7-Sep-96	0-4		13,684	K.Burge
1996-97	Home	28-Dec-96	1-3	Stuart (23)	36,733	M.Bodenham
1997-98	Home	13-Dec-97	0-0		28,533	G.Ashby
1997-98	Away	13-Apr-98	0-0		15,131	K.Burge
1998-99	Away	3-Oct-98	2-1	Cadamarteri (32); Ferguson (59)	16,054	P.Alcock
1998-99	Home	27-Feb-99	1-1	Jeffers (57)	32,574	N.Barry
1999-00	Home	25-Aug-99	4-0	Unsworth (16); Barmby (46); Jeffers (50); Campbell (68)	32,818	J.Winter
1999-00	Away	6-Feb-00	3-0	Campbell (53, 61); Moore (63)	13,172	G.Barber

INTRODUCTION

Originally founded in the 1880s, a strictly amateur set up and founder member of the AFA's Southern Amateur League in 1907. Four times League champions and seven times County Cup winners. In 1936 under the leadership of the Cobbold family a professional Ipswich Town was formed. The new club used Portman Road, only recently occupied by the amateur side and the site of several sporting activities. After two Southern League campaigns and one championship, elected to Football League Division Three (South) in 1938. Football League Champions in 1963, the club's debut season in the top section. Premier League founder member 1992.

Ground: Portman Road, Ipswich, Suffolk, IP1 2DA
Nickname: Blues or Town
Internet: www.itfc.co.uk

HONOURS

Football League Div 1:	Champions:1961-62
	Runners-up: 1980-81, 1981-82
Football League Div 2:	Champions: 1960-61, 1967-68,
	1991-92
Football League Div 3N:	Champions: 1953-54, 1956-57
FA Cup Winners:	1977-78
UEFA Cup Winners:	1980-81

EUROPEAN RECORD

Champions' League (1):	62-63(2)
Cup-Winners' Cup (1):	78-79(QF)
UEFA Cup (8):	73-74(QF), 74-75(1), 75-76(2), 77-78(3), 79-80(2), 80-81(W), 81-82(1), 82-83(1)

FAPL RECORD SUMMARY

Most Total:	LINIGHAN, David	112
Most Starts:	LINIGHAN, David	111
Most Subs:	GUENTCHEV, Bontcho	22
Most SNU:	BAKER, Clive	56
Most PS:	WHELAN, Phil	12
Most Goals:	KIWOMYA, Chris	18
Most Yel:	WHELAN, Phil	15
Most Red:	FORREST, Craig	1

PLAYING RECORD – SEASON TOTALS

Season	Pn	P	W	D	L	F	A	Pts
1992-93	16	42	12	16	14	50	55	52
1993-94	19	42	9	16	17	35	58	43
1994-95	22	42	7	6	29	36	93	27
Totals		126	28	38	60	121	206	122

PLAYING RECORD – HOME TOTALS

Season	Pn	P	W	D	L	F	A	Pts
1992-93	16	21	8	9	4	29	22	33
1993-94	19	21	5	8	8	21	32	23
1994-95	22	21	5	3	13	24	34	18
Totals		63	18	20	25	74	88	74

PLAYING RECORD – AWAY TOTALS

Season	Pn	P	W	D	L	F	A	Pts
1992-93	16	21	4	7	10	21	33	19
1993-94	19	21	4	8	9	14	26	20
1994-95	22	21	2	3	16	12	59	9
Totals		63	10	18	35	47	118	48

HIGHEST HOME ATTENDANCES

	Attendance	Opponents	Date	Season
1	22,559	Tottenham H.	30-Aug-94	1994-95
2	22,559	Manchester U.	24-Sep-94	1994-95
3	22,519	Liverpool	29-Oct-94	1994-95
4	22,478	Manchester U.	1-May-94	1993-94
5	22,270	Liverpool	1-Jan-94	1993-94

LOWEST HOME ATTENDANCES

	Attendance	Opponents	Date	Season
1	11,367	Wimbledon	16-Dec-94	1994-95
2	11,468	Sheffield U.	22-Feb-94	1993-94
3	11,767	QPR	11-Apr-95	1994-95
4	11,789	Oldham A.	4-Dec-93	1993-94
5	11,849	Wimbledon	22-Jan-94	1993-94

TOP SCORER – SEASON BY SEASON

Season	Player	Goals
1992-93	Kiwomya	10
1993-94	Marshall	10
1994-95	Thomsen	5
1992-93	Chapman	15

IPSWICH TOWN

PLAYERS WITH MOST PREMIERSHIP APPEARANCES

Tot	Player	St	Sb	Gls
112	LINIGHAN, David	111	1	4
109	WILLIAMS, Geraint	109	0	1
101	WARK, John	100	1	13
96	STOCKWELL, Mike	94	2	5
90	KIWOMYA, Chris	85	5	18
74	FORREST, Craig	74	0	0
74	WHELAN, Phil	68	6	0
73	THOMPSON, Neil	72	1	3
73	JOHNSON, Gavin	69	4	6
61	GUENTCHEV, Bontcho	39	22	6
55	SLATER, Stuart	50	5	2
55	PALMER, Steve	45	10	1

54	YALLOP, Frank	48	6	3
52	MILTON, Simon	37	15	5
49	YOUDS, Eddie	37	12	1
48	BAKER, Clive	47	1	0
47	MARSHALL, Ian	42	5	13
43	MASON, Paul	37	6	6
41	DOZZELL, Jason	41	0	7

CLUB-BY-CLUB RESULTS

ARSENAL

Season	Venue	Date	Res	Scorers	Attendance	Referee
1992-93	Away	26-Dec-92	0-0		26,198	R.Milford
1992-93	Home	10-Apr-93	1-2	Wark (27 pen)	20,358	R.Lewis
1993-94	Away	11-Sep-93	0-4		28,563	J.Worrall
1993-94	Home	5-Mar-94	1-5	OG (70, Dixon)	18,803	K.Barratt
1994-95	Home	28-Dec-94	0-2		22,054	P.Danson
1994-95	Away	15-Apr-95	1-4	Marshall (71)	36,818	T.Holbrook

ASTON VILLA

Season	Venue	Date	Res	Scorers	Attendance	Referee
1992-93	Home	15-Aug-92	1-1	Johnson,G. (31)	16,818	A.Buksh
1992-93	Away	6-Feb-93	0-2		25,395	P.Durkin
1993-94	Home	18-Sep-93	1-2	Marshall (9)	16,658	R.Dilkes
1993-94	Away	12-Mar-94	1-0	Johnson (8)	23,732	A.Wilkie
1994-95	Away	10-Sep-94	0-2		22,241	G.Willard
1994-95	Home	1-Apr-95	0-1		15,710	J.Worrall

BLACKBURN ROVERS

Season	Venue	Date	Res	Scorers	Attendance	Referee
1992-93	Home	28-Dec-92	2-1	Guentchev (79); Kiwomya (81)	21,431	A.Gunn
1992-93	Away	12-Apr-93	1-2	Milton (68)	14,071	K.Hackett
1993-94	Home	27-Nov-93	1-0	Youds (40)	14,436	P.Durkin
1993-94	Away	7-May-94	0-0		20,633	J.Lloyd
1994-95	Home	19-Nov-94	1-3	Thomsen (28)	17,329	K.Burge
1994-95	Away	28-Jan-95	1-4	Wark (76 pen)	21,325	G.Poll

CHELSEA

Season	Venue	Date	Res	Scorers	Attendance	Referee
1992-93	Away	17-Oct-92	1-2	Whitton (79)	16,702	B.Hill
1992-93	Home	6-Apr-93	1-1	Guentchev (38)	17,444	J.Lloyd
1993-94	Home	21-Aug-93	1-0	Marshall (34)	17,355	D.Elleray
1993-94	Away	11-Dec-93	1-1	Kiwomya (60)	13,208	A.Wilkie

1994-95	Away	23-Oct-94	0-2		15,068	B.Hill
1994-95	Home	21-Jan-95	2-2	Slater (74); Wark (80 pen)	17,296	P.Don

COVENTRY CITY

Season	Venue	Date	Res	Scorers	Attendance	Referee
1992-93	Away	5-Dec-92	2-2	Kiwomya (13); Whitton (70 pen)	11,294	K.Hackett
1992-93	Home	20-Mar-93	0-0		16,698	J.Worrall
1993-94	Away	2-Feb-94	0-1		11,244	D.Allison
1993-94	Home	4-Apr-94	0-2		12,782	R.Gifford
1994-95	Away	10-Oct-94	0-2		9,526	R.Hart
1994-95	Home	6-May-95	2-0	Marshall (52); OG (62, Pressley)	12,893	M.Reed

CRYSTAL PALACE

Season	Venue	Date	Res	Scorers	Attendance	Referee
1992-93	Home	24-Oct-92	2-2	Dozzell (72, 83)	17,861	G.Ashby
1992-93	Away	1-May-93	1-3	Gregory (37)	18,881	P.Don
1994-95	Away	5-Nov-94	0-3		13,450	A.Wilkie
1994-95	Home	4-Feb-95	0-2		15,570	S.Lodge

EVERTON

Season	Venue	Date	Res	Scorers	Attendance	Referee
1992-93	Home	28-Nov-92	1-0	Johnson (72)	18,032	B.Hill
1992-93	Away	24-Mar-93	0-3		15,638	B.Hill
1993-94	Home	30-Oct-93	0-2		15,094	P.Don
1993-94	Away	12-Feb-94	0-0		19,641	R.Milford
1994-95	Away	31-Dec-94	1-4	Sedgley (14)	25,659	R.Dilkes
1994-95	Home	9-May-95	0-1		14,951	R.Hart

LEEDS UNITED

Season	Venue	Date	Res	Scorers	Attendance	Referee
1992-93	Home	3-Oct-92	4-2	Kiwomya (25); Wark (36, 44pen); Dozzell (70)	21,200	D.Elleray
1992-93	Away	27-Feb-93	0-1		28,848	M.Reed
1993-94	Home	17-Oct-93	0-0		17,532	M.Bodenham
1993-94	Away	15-Jan-94	0-0		31,317	K.Hackett
1994-95	Home	1-Nov-94	2-0	Sedgley (7); Williams (64)	15,956	D.Gallagher
1994-95	Away	5-Apr-95	0-4		28,600	G.Willard

LEICESTER CITY

Season	Venue	Date	Res	Scorers	Attendance	Referee
1994-95	Home	2-Jan-95	4-1	Kiwomya (34,62); Tanner (54); Yallop (73)	15,803	T.Holbrook
1994-95	Away	29-Apr-95	0-2		15,248	A.Wilkie

LIVERPOOL

Season	Venue	Date	Res	Scorers	Attendance	Referee
1992-93	Home	25-Aug-92	2-2	Dozzell (56); Kiwomya (90)	20,109	R.Hamer
1992-93	Away	20-Feb-93	0-0		36,680	A.Gunn
1993-94	Home	1-Jan-94	1-2	Marshall (75)	22,270	A.Gunn
1993-94	Away	9-Apr-94	0-1		30,485	D.Gallagher
1994-95	Home	29-Oct-94	1-3	Paz (64)	22,519	P.Durkin
1994-95	Away	14-Jan-95	1-0	Tanner (30)	32,733	R.Gifford

MANCHESTER CITY

Season	Venue	Date	Res	Scorers	Attendance	Referee
1992-93	Home	12-Dec-92	3-1	Stockwell (57); Johnson (61); Goddard (88)	16,833	R.Lewis
1992-93	Away	3-Apr-93	1-3	Johnson (2)	20,680	R.Gifford
1993-94	Away	5-Feb-94	1-2	Marshall (16)	28,188	R.Hart
1993-94	Home	29-Mar-94	2-2	Linighan (23); Guentchev (67 pen)	12,871	P.Don
1994-95	Home	3-Dec-94	1-2	Mason (73)	13,504	S.Lodge
1994-95	Away	22-Feb-95	0-2		21,430	K.Cooper

MANCHESTER UNITED

Season	Venue	Date	Res	Scorers	Attendance	Referee
1992-93	Away	22-Aug-92	1-1	Kiwomya (56)	31,704	G.Ashby
1992-93	Home	30-Jan-93	2-1	Kiwomya (20); Yallop (47)	22,068	J.Key
1993-94	Away	24-Nov-93	0-0		43,300	T.Holbrook
1993-94	Home	1-May-94	1-2	Kiwomya (20)	22,478	A.Gunn
1994-95	Home	24-Sep-94	3-2	Mason (15,43); Sedgley (80)	22,559	P.Jones
1994-95	Away	4-Mar-95	0-9		43,804	G.Poll

MIDDLESBROUGH

Season	Venue	Date	Res	Scorers	Attendance	Referee
1992-93	Away	1-Sep-92	2-2	Wark (26); Goddard (59)	14,255	R.Nixon
1992-93	Home	2-Mar-93	0-1		15,430	K.Barratt

NEWCASTLE UNITED

Season	Venue	Date	Res	Scorers	Attendance	Referee
1993-94	Home	31-Aug-93	1-1	Kiwomya (77)	19,126	D.Gallagher
1993-94	Away	23-Mar-94	0-2		32,234	K.Cooper
1994-95	Away	26-Nov-94	1-1	Thomsen (89)	34,459	K.Cooper
1994-95	Home	28-Feb-95	0-2		18,639	G.Ashby

NORWICH CITY

Season	Venue	Date	Res	Scorers	Attendance	Referee
1992-93	Away	21-Dec-92	2-0	Kiwomya (51); Thompson (87)	20,032	D.Elleray
1992-93	Home	19-Apr-93	3-1	Dozzell (21, 57); Stockwell (52)	21,081	V.Callow
1993-94	Away	25-Aug-93	0-1		18,976	A.Gunn
1993-94	Home	18-Dec-93	2-1	Wark (8pen); OG (90, Megson)	19,751	M.Reed
1994-95	Home	19-Sep-94	1-2	Wark (45 pen)	17,447	R.Dilkes
1994-95	Away	20-Mar-95	0-3		17,510	P.Durkin

NOTTINGHAM FOREST

Season	Venue	Date	Res	Scorers	Attendance	Referee
1992-93	Away	31-Oct-92	1-0	Dozzell (6)	21,411	M.Bodenham
1992-93	Home	8-May-93	2-1	Milton (40); Whitton (52pen)	22,093	M.Reed
1994-95	Home	20-Aug-94	0-1		18,882	S.Lodge
1994-95	Away	10-Dec-94	1-4	Thomsen (45)	21,340	M.Reed

OLDHAM ATHLETIC

Season	Venue	Date	Res	Scorers	Attendance	Referee
1992-93	Away	19-Sep-92	2-4	Wark (75); Thompson (88)	11,150	J.Key
1992-93	Home	9-Jan-93	1-2	Kiwomya (60)	15,025	K.Redfern

1993-94	Away	14-Aug-93	3-0	Marshall (41); Palmer (45); Mason (69)	12,074	K.Barratt
1993-94	Home	4-Dec-93	0-0		11,789	S.Lodge

QPR

Season	Venue	Date	Res	Scorers	Attendance	Referee
1992-93	Away	5-Sep-92	0-0		12,806	D.Gallagher
1992-93	Home	9-Feb-93	1-1	Thompson (40)	17,354	R.Milford
1993-94	Away	2-Oct-93	0-3		12,292	K.Cooper
1993-94	Home	26-Mar-94	1-3	Guentchev (90)	14,653	B.Hill
1994-95	Away	27-Aug-94	2-1	OG (19, Yates); Guentchev (50)	12,456	P.Danson
1994-95	Home	11-Apr-95	0-1		11,767	R.Gifford

SHEFFIELD UNITED

Season	Venue	Date	Res	Scorers	Attendance	Referee
1992-93	Home	26-Sep-92	0-0		16,353	R.Groves
1992-93	Away	16-Jan-93	0-3		16,758	D.Allison
1993-94	Away	28-Aug-93	1-1	Whitton (89)	17,932	P.Foakes
1993-94	Home	22-Feb-94	3-2	Linighan (2); Marshall (8); Slater (36)	11,468	K.Burge

SHEFFIELD WEDNESDAY

Season	Venue	Date	Res	Scorers	Attendance	Referee
1992-93	Away	21-Nov-92	1-1	Kiwomya (74)	24,270	K.Barratt
1992-93	Home	10-Mar-93	0-1		16,538	T.Ward
1993-94	Home	6-Nov-93	1-4	Marshall (81)	14,767	V.Callow
1993-94	Away	23-Apr-94	0-5		23,854	J.Worrall
1994-95	Home	16-Oct-94	1-2	Wark (50)	13,073	M.Reed
1994-95	Away	14-May-95	1-4	Mathie (50)	30,213	G.Poll

SOUTHAMPTON

Season	Venue	Date	Res	Scorers	Attendance	Referee
1992-93	Home	7-Nov-92	0-0		15,722	R.Dilkes
1992-93	Away	13-Mar-93	3-4	Linighan (13); Goddard (35); Kiwomya (87)	15,428	D.Elleray
1993-94	Home	17-Aug-93	1-0	Marshall (58)	14,958	A.Wilkie
1993-94	Away	8-Dec-93	1-0	Kiwomya (54)	9,028	G.Ashby
1994-95	Away	1-Oct-94	1-3	Marshall (77)	13,246	G.Ashby
1994-95	Home	25-Feb-95	2-1	Mathie (70); Chapman (77)	16,067	P.Jones

SWINDON TOWN

Season	Venue	Date	Res	Scorers	Attendance	Referee
1993-94	Away	20-Nov-93	2-2	Wark (17, 63 pen)	13,860	R.Dilkes
1993-94	Home	16-Apr-94	1-1	Marshall (60)	14,760	V.Callow

TOTTENHAM HOTSPUR

Season	Venue	Date	Res	Scorers	Attendance	Referee
1992-93	Home	30-Aug-92	1-1	Wark (45)	20,100	K.Hackett
1992-93	Away	27-Jan-93	2-0	Yallop (47); Guentchev (79)	23,738	S.Lodge
1993-94	Home	26-Sep-93	2-2	Milton (58); Marshall (80)	19,437	G.Ashby
1993-94	Away	19-Mar-94	1-1	Kiwomya (12)	26,653	G.Ashby
1994-95	Home	30-Aug-94	1-3	Kiwomya (86)	22,559	R.Gifford
1994-95	Away	8-Mar-95	0-3		24,930	B.Hill

WEST HAM UNITED

Season	Venue	Date	Res	Scorers	Attendance	Referee
1993-94	Home	27-Dec-93	1-1	Linighan (36)	20,988	G.Poll
1993-94	Away	2-Apr-94	1-2	Mason (87)	18,307	D.Elleray
1994-95	Away	26-Dec-94	1-1	Thomsen (70)	20,542	P.Durkin
1994-95	Home	17-Apr-95	1-1	Thomsen (11)	19,099	M.Bodenham

WIMBLEDON

Season	Venue	Date	Res	Scorers	Attendance	Referee
1992-93	Away	18-Aug-92	1-0	Johnson,G. (37)	4,954	R.Hart
1992-93	Home	12-Sep-92	2-1	Stockwell (14, 48)	13,333	S.Lodge
1993-94	Away	25-Oct-93	2-0	Mason (72); Stockwell (81)	7,756	A.Gunn
1993-94	Home	22-Jan-94	0-0		11,849	B.Hill
1994-95	Away	23-Aug-94	1-1	Milton (61)	6,341	J.Worrall
1994-95	Home	16-Dec-94	2-2	Milton (7); Sedgley (83)	11,367	D.Elleray

INTRODUCTION

Leeds City, founded in 1904, took over the Elland Road ground of the defunct Holbeck Club and in 1905 gained a Football League Division Two place. The club was, however, expelled in 1919 for disciplinary reasons associated with payments to players during the War. The club closed down. Leeds United FC, a new professional club, emerged the same year and competed in the Midland League. The club was elected to Football League Division Two for season 1920-21. The club has subsequently never been out of the top two divisions. Premier League founder members 1992.

Ground: Elland Road, Leeds, LS11 0ES
Nickname: United
Internet: www.lufc.co.uk

HONOURS

Football League Div 1:	Champions 1968-69, 1973-74, 1991-92. Runners-up 1964-65, 1965-66, 1969-70, 1970-71, 1971-72
Football League Div 2:	Champions 1923-24, 1963-64, 1989-90. Runners-up 1927-28, 1931-32, 1955-56
FA Cup:	Winners 1971-72 Runners-up 1964-65, 1969-70, 1972-73
Football League Cup:	Winners 1967-68 Runners-up 1995-96
Champions' Cup:	Runners-up 1974-75
Cup-Winners' Cup:	Runners-up 1972-73
UEFA Cup:	Winners 1967-68, 1970-71 Runners-up 1966-67

EUROPEAN RECORD

Champions' League (3):	69-70 (SF), 74-75 (F), 92-93 (2);
Cup-Winners' Cup (1):	72-73 (F)
UEFA Cup (11):	65-66 (SF), 66-67 (F), 67-68 (W), 68-69 (QF), 70-71 (W), 71-72 (1), 73-74 (3), 79-80 (2), 95-96 (2), 98-99 (2); 99-00 (SF).

FAPL RECORD SUMMARY

Most Total:	KELLY, Gary	219
Most Starts:	KELLY, Gary	214
Most Subs:	WALLACE, Rod	25
Most SNU:	BEENEY, Mark	144
Most PS:	WALLACE, Rod	43
Most Goals:	WALLACE, Rod	42
Most Yel:	BOWYER, Lee	30
Most Red:	KELLY, Gary	2

PLAYING RECORD – SEASON TOTALS

Season	Pn	P	W	D	L	F	A	Pts
1992-93	17	42	12	15	15	57	62	51
1993-94	5	42	18	16	8	65	39	70
1994-95	5	42	20	13	9	59	38	73
1995-96	13	38	12	7	19	40	57	43
1996-97	11	38	11	13	14	28	38	46
1997-98	5	38	17	8	13	57	46	59
1998-99	4	38	18	13	7	62	34	67
1999-00	3	38	21	6	11	58	43	69
Totals		316	129	91	96	426	357	478

PLAYING RECORD – HOME TOTALS

Season	Pn	P	W	D	L	F	A	Pts
1992-93	17	21	12	8	1	40	17	44
1993-94	5	21	13	6	2	37	18	45
1994-95	5	21	13	5	3	35	15	44
1995-96	13	19	8	3	8	21	21	27
1996-97	11	19	7	7	5	15	13	28
1997-98	5	19	9	5	5	31	21	32
1998-99	4	19	12	5	2	32	9	41
1999-00	3	19	12	2	5	29	18	38
Totals		158	86	41	31	240	132	299

PLAYING RECORD – AWAY TOTALS

Season	Pn	P	W	D	L	F	A	Pts
1992-93	17	21	0	7	14	17	45	7
1993-94	5	21	5	10	6	28	21	25
1994-95	5	21	7	8	6	24	23	29
1995-96	13	19	4	4	11	19	36	16
1996-97	11	19	4	6	9	13	25	18
1997-98	5	19	8	3	8	26	25	27
1998-99	4	19	6	8	5	30	25	26
1999-00	3	19	9	4	6	29	25	31
Totals		158	43	50	65	186	225	179

HIGHEST HOME ATTENDANCES

	Attendance	Opponents	Date	Season
1	41,127	Manchester U.	27-Apr-94	1993-94
2	40,255	Manchester U.	25-Apr-99	1998-99
3	40,202	Newcastle U.	6-Feb-99	1998-99
4	40,192	Newcastle U.	25-Sep-99	1999-00
5	40,190	West Ham U.	30-Oct-99	1999-00

LOWEST HOME ATTENDANCES

	Attendance	Opponents	Date	Season
1	25,795	Wimbledon	15-Aug-92	1992-93
2	25,860	Wimbledon	26-Aug-96	1996-97
3	25,913	Southampton	12-Mar-97	1996-97

| 4 | 26,071 | Southampton | 9-Jan-93 | 1992-93 |
| 5 | 26,077 | Southampton | 3-Apr-96 | 1995-96 |

TOP SCORER – SEASON BY SEASON

Season	Player	Goals
1993-94	Rod Wallace	17
1994-95	Yeboah	11
1995-96	Yeboah	12
1996-97	Deane	5
1997-98	Hasselbaink	16
1998-99	Hasselbaink	18
1999-00	Bridges	19

PLAYERS WITH MOST PREMIERSHIP APPEARANCES

Tot	Player	St	Sb	Gls
219	KELLY, Gary	214	5	2
201	WETHERALL, David	188	13	12
178	WALLACE, Rod	153	25	42

151	McALLISTER, Gary	151	0	24
146	MARTYN, Nigel	146	0	0
144	RADEBE, Lucas	133	11	0
143	SPEED, Gary	142	1	22
138	DEANE, Brian	131	7	32
133	DORIGO, Tony	130	3	2
129	LUKIC, John	129	0	0
125	BOWYER, Lee	119	6	21
106	KEWELL, Harry	100	6	21
102	PALMER, Carlton	100	2	5
98	HARTE, Ian	91	7	12
75	FAIRCLOUGH, Chris	70	5	7

CLUB-BY-CLUB RESULTS

ARSENAL

Season	Venue	Date	Res	Scorers	Attendance	Referee
1992-93	Home	21-Nov-92	3-0	Fairclough (51); Chapman (56); McAllister (87)	30,516	R.Hart
1992-93	Away	24-Feb-93	0-0		21,061	K.Redfern
1993-94	Away	24-Aug-93	1-2	Strachan (70)	29,042	K.Hackett
1993-94	Home	18-Dec-93	2-1	McAllister (21); OG (60, Adams)	37,289	K.Burge
1994-95	Home	23-Aug-94	1-0	Whelan (89)	34,218	R.Dilkes
1994-95	Away	17-Dec-94	3-1	Masinga (24,85); Deane (88)	38,098	G.Poll
1995-96	Home	14-Oct-95	0-3		38,552	P.Crabtree
1995-96	Away	6-Apr-96	1-2		37,619	J.Winter
1996-97	Away	26-Oct-96	0-3		38,076	A.Wilkie
1996-97	Home	1-Feb-97	0-0		35,502	D.Elleray
1997-98	Home	9-Aug-97	1-1	Hasselbaink (42)	37,993	D.Gallagher
1997-98	Away	10-Jan-98	1-2	Hasselbaink (69)	38,018	G.Ashby
1998-99	Away	20-Dec-98	1-3	Hasselbaink (66)	38,025	P.Durkin
1998-99	Home	11-May-99	1-0	Hasselbaink (86)	40,142	G.Willard
1999-00	Away	28-Dec-99	0-2		38,096	G.Poll
1999-00	Home	16-Apr-00	0-4		39,307	S.Dunn

ASTON VILLA

Season	Venue	Date	Res	Scorers	Attendance	Referee
1992-93	Away	19-Aug-92	1-1	Speed (84)	29,151	K.Hackett
1992-93	Home	13-Sep-92	1-1	Hodge (85)	27,815	J.Worrall
1993-94	Away	6-Feb-94	0-1		26,919	J.Borrett
1993-94	Home	16-Mar-94	2-0	Rod Wallace (27); Deane (52)	33,126	D.Allison
1994-95	Away	2-Jan-95	0-0		35,038	P.Danson
1994-95	Home	29-Apr-95	1-0	Palmer (89)	32,955	D.Elleray
1995-96	Home	26-Aug-95	2-0	Speed (4); White (87)	35,086	D.Gallagher
1995-96	Away	3-Feb-96	0-3		35,982	R.Hart
1996-97	Away	19-Oct-96	0-2		39,051	G.Poll

1996-97	Home	22-Apr-97	0-0		26,897	G.Barber
1997-98	Away	30-Aug-97	0-1		39,027	P.Jones
1997-98	Home	28-Dec-97	1-1	Hasselbaink (79)	36,287	D.Gallagher
1998-99	Home	19-Sep-98	0-0		33,446	J.Winter
1998-99	Away	17-Feb-99	2-1	Hasselbaink (7,31)	37,510	D.Gallagher
1999-00	Home	3-Jan-00	1-2	Kewell (46)	40,027	U.Rennie
1999-00	Away	9-Apr-00	0-1		33,889	B.Knight

BARNSLEY

Season	Venue	Date	Res	Scorers	Attendance	Referee
1997-98	Away	29-Nov-97	3-2	Haaland (35); Wallace (72); Lilley (82)	18,690	M.Reed
1997-98	Home	4-Apr-98	2-1	Hasselbaink (20); OG (80, Moses)	37,749	K.Burge

BLACKBURN ROVERS

Season	Venue	Date	Res	Scorers	Attendance	Referee
1992-93	Away	26-Dec-92	1-3	McAllister (37)	19,910	S.Lodge
1992-93	Home	10-Apr-93	5-2	Strachan (8 pen, 26 pen, 50); Wallace,Rod (67); Chapman (89)	31,791	D.Elleray
1993-94	Home	23-Oct-93	3-3	McAllister (56 pen); Newsome (82); OG (85, Sherwood)	37,827	K.Morton
1993-94	Away	23-Jan-94	1-2	Speed (78)	17,475	V.Callow
1994-95	Away	1-Feb-95	1-1	McAllister (85 pen)	28,561	R.Gifford
1994-95	Home	15-Apr-95	1-1	Deane (90)	39,426	G.Poll
1995-96	Home	1-Jan-96	0-0		31,285	R.Dilkes
1995-96	Away	13-Mar-96	0-1		23,358	S.Dunn
1996-97	Away	3-Sep-96	1-1	Harte (40)	23,226	L.Dilkes
1996-97	Home	7-Apr-97	0-0		27,264	M.Reed
1997-98	Away	14-Sep-97	4-3	Wallace (3,17); Molenaar (6); Hopkin (23)	21,956	S.Dunn
1997-98	Home	11-Mar-98	4-0	Bowyer (48); Hasselbaink (53); Haaland (56, 89)	32,933	D.Elleray
1998-99	Home	24-Aug-98	1-0	Hasselbaink (18)	30,652	D.Gallagher
1998-99	Away	9-Jan-99	0-1		27,620	R.Harris

BOLTON WANDERERS

Season	Venue	Date	Res	Scorers	Attendance	Referee
1995-96	Away	27-Dec-95	2-0	Brolin (39); Wetherall (63)	18,414	D.Elleray
1995-96	Home	2-Mar-96	0-1		30,106	G.Willard
1997-98	Home	20-Dec-97	2-0	Ribeiro (68); Hasselbaink (81)	31,163	A.Wilkie
1997-98	Away	18-Apr-98	3-2	Haaland (17); Halle (34); Hasselbaink (86)	25,000	J.Winter

BRADFORD CITY

Season	Venue	Date	Res	Scorers	Attendance	Referee
1999-00	Home	20-Nov-99	2-1	Smith (54); Harte (80 pen)	39,937	P.Durkin
1999-00	Away	12-Mar-00	2-1	Bridges (12, 63)	18,276	P.Durkin

CHARLTON ATHLETIC

Season	Venue	Date	Res	Scorers	Attendance	Referee
1998-99	Home	21-Nov-98	4-1	Hasselbaink (34); Bowyer (51); Smith (67); Kewell(87)	32,487	R.Harris
1998-99	Away	17-Apr-99	1-1	Woodgate (24)	20,043	A.Wilkie

CHELSEA

Season	Venue	Date	Res	Scorers	Attendance	Referee
1992-93	Away	29-Nov-92	0-1		24,345	M.Bodenham
1992-93	Home	24-Mar-93	1-1	Wetherall (43)	28,135	A.Wilkie
1993-94	Home	6-Nov-93	4-1	Deane (46); Wallace,Rod (51, 56); Rocastle (70)	35,050	D.Gallagher
1993-94	Away	23-Apr-94	1-1	Speed (36)	18,544	P.Foakes
1994-95	Home	27-Aug-94	2-3	Masinga (3); Whelan (18)	32,212	G.Ashby
1994-95	Away	11-Mar-95	3-0	Yeboah (23,61); McAllister (25)	20,174	P.Jones
1995-96	Home	18-Nov-95	1-0	Yeboah (80)	36,209	M.Reed
1995-96	Away	13-Apr-96	1-4	McAllister (65)	22,131	D.Gallagher
1996-97	Home	1-Dec-96	2-0	Deane (8); Rush (10)	32,671	S.Dunn
1996-97	Away	3-May-97	0-0		28,277	J.Winter
1997-98	Away	13-Dec-97	0-0		34,690	G.Poll
1997-98	Home	8-Apr-98	3-1	Hasselbaink (7, 47); Wetherall (22)	37,276	D.Elleray
1998-99	Home	24-Oct-98	0-0		36,292	M.Reed
1998-99	Away	5-May-99	0-1		34,762	J.Winter
1999-00	Away	19-Dec-99	2-0	McPhail (66, 87)	35,106	J.Winter
1999-00	Home	1-Apr-00	0-1		40,162	J.Winter

COVENTRY CITY

Season	Venue	Date	Res	Scorers	Attendance	Referee
1992-93	Home	31-Oct-92	2-2	Chapman (70); Fairclough (90)	28,018	B.Hill
1992-93	Away	8-May-93	3-3	Wallace,Rod (6, 89, 90)	19,591	K.Morton
1993-94	Away	25-Sep-93	2-0	Wallace,Rod (20, 48)	13,933	K.Cooper
1993-94	Home	19-Mar-94	1-0	Rod Wallace (54)	30,023	A.Wilkie
1994-95	Away	17-Sep-94	1-2	Speed (85)	15,389	B.Hill
1994-95	Home	18-Mar-95	3-0	Yeboah (39); OG (50, Gould); Wallace (60)	29,179	R.Hart
1995-96	Home	28-Oct-95	3-1	McAllister (40, 44, 89 pen)	30,161	G.Ashby
1995-96	Away	5-May-96	0-0		22,769	D.Elleray
1996-97	Away	14-Sep-96	1-2	Couzens (1)	17,297	G.Willard
1996-97	Home	26-Dec-96	1-3	Deane (9)	36,465	M.Bodenham
1997-98	Away	4-Oct-97	0-0		17,770	A.Wilkie
1997-98	Home	25-Apr-98	3-3	Hasselbaink (16, 28); Kewell (75)	36,522	M.Reed
1998-99	Home	14-Dec-98	2-0	Hopkin (40); Bowyer (90)	31,802	G.Poll
1998-99	Away	16-May-99	2-2	Wijnhard (43); Hopkin (90)	23,049	S.Lodge
1999-00	Away	11-Sep-99	4-3	Bowyer (7); Huckerby (25); Harte (33 pen); Bridges (60)	21,532	S.Dunn
1999-00	Home	5-Mar-00	3-0	Kewell (5); Bridges (42); Wilcox (85)	38,710	J.Winter

CRYSTAL PALACE

Season	Venue	Date	Res	Scorers	Attendance	Referee
1992-93	Away	20-Dec-92	0-1		14,462	A.Gunn
1992-93	Home	17-Apr-93	0-0		27,545	R.Hart
1994-95	Away	30-Aug-94	2-1	White (17); Whelan (63)	14,453	D.Gallagher
1994-95	Home	9-May-95	3-1	Yeboah (6,59); Wetherall (41)	30,942	J.Worrall
1997-98	Home	23-Aug-97	0-2		29,076	U.Rennie
1997-98	Away	31-Jan-98	2-0	Wallace (7); Hasselbaink (13)	25,248	U.Rennie

DERBY COUNTY

Season	Venue	Date	Res	Scorers	Attendance	Referee
1996-97	Away	17-Aug-96	3-3	OG (19, Laursen); Harte (72); Bowyer (85)	17,927	P.Danson
1996-97	Home	29-Jan-97	0-0		27,549	K.Burge
1997-98	Home	8-Nov-97	4-3	Wallace (37); Kewell (40); Hasselbank (82 pen); Bowyer (90)	33,572	N.Barry
1997-98	Away	15-Mar-98	5-0	OG (8, Laurensen); Halle (32); Bowyer (42); Kewell (60); Hasselbaink (72)	30,217	S.Lodge
1998-99	Away	31-Oct-98	2-2	Molenaar (16); Kewell (43)	27,034	N.Barry
1998-99	Home	21-Mar-99	4-1	Bowyer (18); Hasselbaink (32); Korsten (45); Harte (85)	38,971	M.Reed
1999-00	Home	7-Aug-99	0-0		40,118	G.Barber
1999-00	Away	5-Dec-99	1-0	Harte (90 pen)	29,455	P.Alcock

EVERTON

Season	Venue	Date	Res	Scorers	Attendance	Referee
1992-93	Home	26-Sep-92	2-0	McAllister (61pen); Chapman (63)	27,915	K.Redfern
1992-93	Away	16-Jan-93	0-2		21,031	D.Elleray
1993-94	Away	23-Nov-93	1-1	Rod Wallace (53)	17,102	K.Cooper
1993-94	Home	30-Apr-94	3-0	McAllister (72); OG (82, Watson); White (90)	35,487	V.Callow
1994-95	Away	5-Dec-94	0-3		25,897	P.Durkin
1994-95	Home	22-Feb-95	1-0	Yeboah (81)	30,793	D.Gallagher
1995-96	Away	30-Dec-95	0-2		40,009	J.Winter
1995-96	Home	17-Mar-96	2-2	Deane (6, 45)	29,425	G.Ashby
1996-97	Away	21-Dec-96	0-0		36,954	G.Ashby
1996-97	Home	8-Mar-97	1-0	Molenaar (28)	32,055	M.Bodenham
1997-98	Home	6-Dec-97	0-0		34,986	P.Durkin
1997-98	Away	11-Apr-98	0-2		37,099	U.Rennie
1998-99	Away	12-Sep-98	0-0		36,687	N.Barry
1998-99	Home	20-Feb-99	1-0	Korsten (55)	36,344	D.Elleray
1999-00	Away	24-Oct-99	4-4	Bridges (15, 67); Kewell (35); Woodgate (72)	37,355	D.Gallagher
1999-00	Home	8-May-00	1-1	Bridges (30)	37,713	A.D'Urso

IPSWICH TOWN

Season	Venue	Date	Res	Scorers	Attendance	Referee
1992-93	Away	3-Oct-92	2-4	Chapman (55); Speed (64)	21,200	D.Elleray
1992-93	Home	27-Feb-93	1-0	Dorigo (71 pen)	28,848	M.Reed
1993-94	Away	17-Oct-93	0-0		17,532	M.Bodenham
1993-94	Home	15-Jan-94	0-0		31,317	K.Hackett
1994-95	Away	1-Nov-94	0-2		15,956	D.Gallagher
1994-95	Home	5-Apr-95	4-0	Yeboah (3,34,45); Speed (31)	28,600	G.Willard

LEICESTER CITY

Season	Venue	Date	Res	Scorers	Attendance	Referee
1994-95	Home	24-Oct-94	2-1	McAllister (35); Whelan (67)	28,547	K.Burge
1994-95	Away	15-Mar-95	3-1	Yeboah (32,59); Palmer (78)	20,068	D.Gallagher
1996-97	Away	28-Sep-96	0-1		20,359	S.Dunn
1996-97	Home	11-Jan-97	3-0	Bowyer (40); Rush (45, 69)	29,486	M.Reed
1997-98	Home	20-Sep-97	0-1		29,620	K.Burge
1997-98	Away	7-Feb-98	0-1		21,244	N.Barry
1998-99	Home	3-Oct-98	0-1		32,606	G.Barber
1998-99	Away	1-Mar-99	2-1	Kewell (24); Smith (60)	18,101	G.Barber

LEEDS UNITED

Season	Venue	Date	Res	Scorers	Attendance	Referee
1999-00	Home	26-Dec-99	2-1	Bridges (29); Bowyer (45)	40,105	M.Halsey
1999-00	Away	26-Mar-00	1-2	Kewell (38)	21,095	S.Lodge

LIVERPOOL

Season	Venue	Date	Res	Scorers	Attendance	Referee
1992-93	Home	29-Aug-92	2-2	McAllister (7); Chapman (87)	29,597	R.Dilkes
1992-93	Away	21-Apr-93	0-2		34,992	M.Reed
1993-94	Away	28-Aug-93	0-2		44,068	R.Hart
1993-94	Home	19-Feb-94	2-0	Wetherall (9); McAllister (86)	40,029	G.Poll
1994-95	Home	31-Dec-94	0-2		38,563	A.Wilkie
1994-95	Away	9-Apr-95	1-0	Deane (29)	37,454	D.Gallagher
1995-96	Home	21-Aug-95	1-0	Yeboah (51)	35,852	D.Elleray
1995-96	Away	20-Jan-96	0-5		40,254	P.Durkin
1996-97	Home	16-Nov-96	0-2		39,981	P.Jones
1996-97	Away	19-Feb-97	0-4		38,957	A.Wilkie
1997-98	Home	26-Aug-97	0-2		39,775	A.Wilkie
1997-98	Away	26-Dec-97	1-3	Haaland (85)	43,854	S.Lodge
1998-99	Away	14-Nov-98	3-1	Smith (79); Hasselbaink (81, 86)	44,305	D.Gallagher
1998-99	Home	12-Apr-99	0-0		39,451	P.Jones
1999-00	Home	23-Aug-99	1-2	OG (20, Song)	39,703	D.Elleray
1999-00	Away	5-Feb-00	1-3	Bowyer (62)	44,793	M.Reed

MANCHESTER CITY

Season	Venue	Date	Res	Scorers	Attendance	Referee
1992-93	Away	7-Nov-92	0-4		27,255	K.Morton
1992-93	Home	13-Mar-93	1-0	Rocastle (11)	30,840	K.Hackett
1993-94	Away	14-Aug-93	1-1	Deane (90)	32,366	D.Gallagher
1993-94	Home	4-Dec-93	3-2	Rod Wallace (11); Speed (22); Deane (85)	33,820	R.Gifford
1994-95	Home	1-Oct-94	2-0	Whelan (27,90)	30,938	T.Holbrook
1994-95	Away	25-Feb-95	0-0		22,892	T.Holbrook
1995-96	Away	21-Oct-95	0-0		26,390	M.Bodenham
1995-96	Home	2-Dec-95	0-1		33,249	P.Alcock

MANCHESTER UNITED

Season	Venue	Date	Res	Scorers	Attendance	Referee
1992-93	Away	6-Sep-92	0-2		31,296	P.Don
1992-93	Home	8-Feb-93	0-0		34,166	K.Morton
1993-94	Away	1-Jan-94	0-0		44,724	D.Elleray
1993-94	Home	27-Apr-94	0-2		41,127	P.Don
1994-95	Home	11-Sep-94	2-1	Wetherall (12); Deane (48)	39,396	D.Elleray
1994-95	Away	2-Apr-95	0-0		43,712	R.Gifford
1995-96	Home	24-Dec-95	3-1	McAllister (6 pen); Yeboah (35); Deane (72)	39,801	D.Gallagher
1995-96	Away	17-Apr-96	0-1		48,382	K.Cooper
1996-97	Home	7-Sep-96	0-4		39,694	M.Bodenham
1996-97	Away	28-Dec-96	0-1		55,256	P.Alcock
1997-98	Home	27-Sep-97	1-0	Wetherall (34)	39,952	M.Bodenham
1997-98	Away	4-May-98	0-3		55,167	G.Willard
1998-99	Away	29-Nov-98	2-3	Hasselbaink (29); Kewell (52)	55,172	G.Poll
1998-99	Home	25-Apr-99	1-1	Hasselbaink (32)	40,255	D.Gallagher
1999-00	Away	14-Aug-99	0-2		55,187	N.Barry
1999-00	Home	20-Feb-00	0-1		40,160	P.Jones

MIDDLESBROUGH

Season	Venue	Date	Res	Scorers	Attendance	Referee
1992-93	Away	22-Aug-92	1-4	Cantona (68)	18,649	D.Allison
1992-93	Home	30-Jan-93	3-0	Strandli (69); Batty (81); Fairclough (90)	30,344	J.Martin
1995-96	Away	4-Nov-95	1-1	Deane (44)	29,467	K.Burge
1995-96	Home	30-Mar-96	0-1	Deane (53)	31,778	D.Elleray
1996-97	Away	7-Dec-96	0-0		30,018	D.Elleray
1996-97	Home	11-May-97	1-1	Deane (77)	38,567	A.Wilkie
1998-99	Away	15-Aug-98	0-0		34,162	D.Elleray
1998-99	Home	16-Jan-99	2-0	Smith (21); Bowyer (27)	37,473	S.Lodge
1999-00	Home	19-Sep-99	2-0	Bridges (14); Kewell (64)	34,122	D.Gallagher
1999-00	Away	26-Feb-00	0-0		34,800	U.Rennie

NEWCASTLE UNITED

Season	Venue	Date	Res	Scorers	Attendance	Referee
1993-94	Away	22-Dec-93	1-1	Fairclough (66)	36,342	P.Don
1993-94	Home	1-Apr-94	1-1	Fairclough (89)	40,005	K.Cooper
1994-95	Home	26-Dec-94	0-0		39,337	J.Worrall
1994-95	Away	17-Apr-95	2-1	McAllister (25 pen); Yeboah (31)	35,626	P.Danson
1995-96	Away	25-Nov-95	1-2	Deane (30)	36,572	S.Dunn
1995-96	Home	29-Apr-96	0-1		38,862	K.Burge
1996-97	Home	21-Sep-96	0-1		36,070	P.Alcock
1996-97	Away	1-Jan-97	0-3		36,489	P.Danson
1997-98	Home	18-Oct-97	4-1	Ribeiro (30); Kewell (38) ; OG (43, Beresford); Wetherall (47)	39,834	D.Elleray
1997-98	Away	22-Feb-98	1-1	Wallace (83)	36,511	G.Willard
1998-99	Away	26-Dec-98	3-0	Kewell (38); Bowyer (62); Hasselbaink (90)	36,783	G.Willard
1998-99	Home	6-Feb-99	0-1		40,202	U.Rennie
1999-00	Home	25-Sep-99	3-2	Bowyer (11); Kewell (39); Bridges (77)	40,192	B.Knight
1999-00	Away	23-Apr-00	2-2	Bridges (12); Wilcox (17)	36,460	D.Elleray

NORWICH CITY

Season	Venue	Date	Res	Scorers	Attendance	Referee
1992-93	Home	28-Dec-92	0-0		30,282	P.Don
1992-93	Away	14-Apr-93	2-4	Chapman (2); Wallace,Rod (46)	18,613	K.Burge
1993-94	Home	21-Aug-93	0-4		32,008	M.Reed
1993-94	Away	13-Dec-93	1-2	Rod Wallace (67)	16,586	R.Milford
1994-95	Away	8-Oct-94	1-2	Wallace (89)	17,390	P.Don
1994-95	Home	6-May-95	2-1	McAllister (79 pen); Palmer (90)	31,982	A.Wilkie

NOTTINGHAM FOREST

Season	Venue	Date	Res	Scorers	Attendance	Referee
1992-93	Home	5-Dec-92	1-4	Speed (87)	29,364	A.Buksh
1992-93	Away	21-Mar-93	1-1	Wallace,Rod (13)	25,148	R.Lewis
1994-95	Home	26-Nov-94	1-0	Whelan (61)	38,191	P.Jones
1994-95	Away.	22-Mar-95	0-3		26,299	M.Reed
1995-96	Away	31-Jan-96	1-2	Palmer (54)	24,465	A.Wilkie
1995-96	Home	8-Apr-96	1-3	Wetherall (9)	29,220	R.Hart
1996-97	Home	12-Oct-96	2-0	Wallace (46, 90)	29,225	S.Lodge
1996-97	Away	19-Apr-97	1-1	Deane (66)	25,565	D.Elleray

1998-99	Away	17-Oct-98	1-1	Halle (53)	23,911	A.Wilkie
1998-99	Home	3-Apr-99	3-1	Hasselbaink (43); Harte (60); Smith (84)	39,645	P.Alcock

OLDHAM ATHLETIC

Season	Venue	Date	Res	Scorers	Attendance	Referee
1992-93	Away	1-Sep-92	2-2	Cantona (53, 76)	13,848	K.Barratt
1992-93	Home	13-Feb-93	2-0	McAllister (18 pen); Chapman (79)	27,654	R.Dilkes
1993-94	Home	30-Aug-93	1-0	Strachan (11)	28,717	G.Ashby
1993-94	Away	28-Feb-94	1-1	McAllister (2)	11,136	B.Hill

QPR

Season	Venue	Date	Res	Scorers	Attendance	Referee
1992-93	Away	24-Oct-92	1-2	Strachan (57)	19,326	H.King
1992-93	Home	1-May-93	1-1	Hodge (69)	31,408	V.Callow
1993-94	Home	29-Dec-93	1-1	Hodge (71)	39,124	M.Reed
1993-94	Away	4-Apr-94	4-0	Deane (9); Wallace,Rod (44); White (53, 84)	15,365	J.Worrall
1994-95	Away	19-Nov-94	2-3	OG (55, McDonald); Deane (72)	17,416	M.Bodenham
1994-95	Home	24-Jan-95	4-0	Masinga (30,64); White (33); Deane (83)	28,780	K.Morton
1995-96	Home	16-Sep-95	1-3	Wetherall (87)	31,504	S.Lodge
1995-96	Away	6-Mar-96	2-1	Yeboah (10, 25)	13,991	G.Powler

SHEFFIELD UNITED

Season	Venue	Date	Res	Scorers	Attendance	Referee
1992-93	Home	17-Oct-92	3-1	Chapman (36); Speed (74); Whyte (78)	29,706	R.Lewis
1992-93	Away	6-Apr-93	1-2	Strandli (34)	20,562	K.Barratt
1993-94	Home	18-Sep-93	2-1	McAllister (5); Strachan (29)	33,879	P.Don
1993-94	Away	13-Mar-94	2-2	Speed (28); Deane (58)	19,425	R.Dilkes

SHEFFIELD WEDNESDAY

Season	Venue	Date	Res	Scorers	Attendance	Referee
1992-93	Home	12-Dec-92	3-1	Speed (32); Chapman (46); Varadi (79)	29,770	J.Borrett
1992-93	Away	4-May-93	1-1	Chapman (35)	26,855	R.Milford
1993-94	Away	30-Oct-93	3-3	Fairclough (42); Rod Wallace (56); Speed (64)	31,892	P.Durkin
1993-94	Home	3-May-94	2-2	White (71); Rod Wallace (74)	33,575	A.Gunn
1994-95	Away	26-Sep-94	1-1	McAllister (13)	23,227	A.Wilkie
1994-95	Home	4-Mar-95	0-1		33,750	K.Cooper
1995-96	Home	30-Sep-95	2-0	Yeboah (33); Speed (59)	34,076	D.Allison
1995-96	Away	16-Dec-95	2-6	Brolin (28); Wallace (84)	24,573	R.Hart
1996-97	Home	20-Aug-96	0-2		31,011	J.Winter
1996-97	Away	22-Mar-97	2-2	Sharpe (17); Wallace (21)	30,373	P.Danson
1997-98	Away	13-Aug-97	3-1	Wallace (7, 62); Ribiero (36)	31,520	P.Durkin
1997-98	Home	17-Jan-98	1-2	OG (Pembridge 63)	33,166	M.Bodenham
1998-99	Home	8-Nov-98	2-1	Hasselbaink (40); Woodgate (61)	30,012	K.Burge
1998-99	Away	13-Mar-99	2-0	Hasselbaink (4); Hopkin (73)	28,142	G.Poll
1999-00	Home	16-Oct-99	2-0	Smith (72, 78)	39,437	G.Barber
1999-00	Away	30-Apr-00	3-0	Hopkin (1); Bridges (53); Kewell (68)	23,416	R.Harris

SOUTHAMPTON

Season	Venue	Date	Res	Scorers	Attendance	Referee
1992-93	Away	19-Sep-92	1-1	Speed (83)	16,229	A.Buksh
1992-93	Home	9-Jan-93	2-1	Chapman (50); Speed (72)	26,071	R.Groves
1993-94	Away	11-Sep-93	2-0	Deane (50); Speed (90)	13,511	K.Burge
1993-94	Home	5-Mar-94	0-0		30,829	R.Hart
1994-95	Away	29-Oct-94	3-1	OG (54, Maddison); Wallace (84,90)	15,202	R.Gifford
1994-95	Home	14-Jan-95	0-0		28,953	S.Dunn
1995-96	Away	30-Aug-95	1-1	Dorigo (70)	15,212	K.Cooper
1995-96	Home	3-Apr-96	1-0	Deane (73)	26,077	M.Bodenham
1996-97	Away	23-Nov-96	2-0	Kelly (82); Sharpe (89)	15,241	K.Burge
1996-97	Home	12-Mar-97	0-0		25,913	G.Ashby
1997-98	Away	24-Sep-97	2-0	Molenaar (36); Wallace (55)	15,102	S.Lodge
1997-98	Home	28-Feb-98	0-1		28,791	K.Burge
1998-99	Home	8-Sep-98	3-0	OG (38, Marshall); Harte (52); Wijnhard (86)	30,637	A.Wilkie
1998-99	Away	30-Jan-99	0-3		15,236	S.Dunn
1999-00	Away	11-Aug-99	3-0	Bridges (10, 51, 72)	15,206	A.Wiley
1999-00	Home	28-Nov-99	1-0	Bridges (90)	39,288	R.Harris

SUNDERLAND

Season	Venue	Date	Res	Scorers	Attendance	Referee
1996-97	Home	2-Nov-96	3-0	Ford (27); Sharpe (62); Deane (68)	31,667	S.Dunn
1996-97	Away	22-Feb-97	1-0	Bowyer (48)	21,890	G.Poll
1999-00	Home	21-Aug-99	2-1	Bowyer (52); Mills (71)	39,064	P.Alcock
1999-00	Away	23-Jan-00	2-1	Wilcox (24); Bridges (50)	41,947	P.Jones

SWINDON TOWN

Season	Venue	Date	Res	Scorers	Attendance	Referee
1993-94	Home	27-Nov-93	3-0	Deane (80); Rod Wallace (86); Speed (90)	32,630	V.Callow
1993-94	Away	7-May-94	5-0	Deane (18, 67); White (28); Rod Wallace (58); Fairclough (90)	17,228	M.Bodenham

TOTTENHAM HOTSPUR

Season	Venue	Date	Res	Scorers	Attendance	Referee
1992-93	Home	25-Aug-92	5-0	Wallace,Rod (19); Cantona (26, 31, 46); Chapman (66)	28,218	M.Reed
1992-93	Away	20-Feb-93	0-4		32,040	G.Ashby
1993-94	Away	20-Nov-93	1-1	Deane (53)	31,275	J.Worrall
1993-94	Home	17-Apr-94	2-0	Rod Wallace (61, 89)	33,658	R.Milford
1994-95	Home	15-Oct-94	1-1	Deane (62)	39,224	K.Cooper
1994-95	Away	14-May-95	1-1	Deane (67)	33,040	P.Durkin
1995-96	Away	9-Sep-95	1-2	Yeboah (51)	30,034	P.Durkin
1995-96	Home	2-May-96	1-3	Wetherall (13)	30,061	M.Bodenham
1996-97	Home	14-Dec-96	0-0		33,783	P.Durkin
1996-97	Away	15-Mar-97	0-1		33,040	D.Gallagher
1997-98	Away	1-Nov-97	1-0	Wallace (19)	26,441	K.Burge
1997-98	Home	4-Mar-98	1-0	Kewell (45)	31,394	P.Alcock
1998-99	Away	27-Sep-98	3-3	Halle (4); Hasselbaink (26); Wijnhard (61)	35,535	P.Durkin
1998-99	Home	10-Mar-99	2-0	Smith (42); Kewell (68)	34,521	N.Barry
1999-00	Away	28-Aug-99	2-1	Smith (53); Harte (83)	36,012	M.Reed
1999-00	Home	12-Feb-00	1-0	Kewell (23)	40,127	D.Gallagher

LEEDS UNITED

WATFORD

Season	Venue	Date	Res	Scorers	Attendance	Referee
1999-00	Away	3-Oct-99	2-1	Bridges (45); Kewell (70)	19,677	A.D'Urso
1999-00	Home	3-May-00	3-1	Bridges (20); Duberry (45); Huckerby (52)	36,324	P.Alcock

WEST HAM UNITED

Season	Venue	Date	Res	Scorers	Attendance	Referee
1993-94	Home	17-Aug-93	1-0	Speed (61)	34,588	R.Dilkes
1993-94	Away	8-Dec-93	1-0	Rod Wallace (84)	20,468	J.Borrett
1994-95	Away	20-Aug-94	0-0		18,610	K.Burge
1994-95	Home	10-Dec-94	2-2	Worthington (2); Deane (24)	28,987	R.Hart
1995-96	Away	19-Aug-95	2-1	Yeboah (48, 57)	22,901	K.Burge
1995-96	Home	13-Jan-96	2-0	Brolin (25, 62)	30,658	P.Danson
1996-97	Away	20-Jan-97	2-0	Kelly (52); Bowyer (69)	19,441	G.Poll
1996-97	Home	1-Mar-97	1-0	Sharpe (47)	30,575	P.Jones
1997-98	Home	23-Nov-97	3-1	Hasselbank (76, 90); Haaland (88)	30,031	G.Ashby
1997-98	Away	30-Mar-98	0-3		24,107	A.Wilkie
1998-99	Home	5-Dec-98	4-0	Bowyer (8,61); Molenaar (68); Hasselbaink (79)	36,320	J.Winter
1998-99	Away	1-May-99	5-1	Hasselbaink (1); Smith (45); Harte (62 pen); Bowyer (78); Haaland (79)	25,997	R.Harris
1999-00	Home	30-Oct-99	1-0	Harte (57)	40,190	G.Poll
1999-00	Away	14-May-00	0-0		26,044	G.Barber

WIMBLEDON

Season	Venue	Date	Res	Scorers	Attendance	Referee
1992-93	Home	15-Aug-92	2-1	Chapman (14, 86)	25,795	G.Ashby
1992-93	Away	6-Feb-93	0-1		6,704	V.Callow
1993-94	Home	2-Oct-93	4-0	Speed (2, 90); McAllister (18, 81)	30,255	J.Worrall
1993-94	Away	26-Mar-94	0-1		9,035	K.Burge
1994-95	Home	5-Nov-94	3-1	Wetherall (13); Speed (38); White (45)	27,284	B.Hill
1994-95	Away	4-Feb-95	0-0		10,211	G.Ashby
1995-96	Away	23-Sep-95	4-2	Palmer (32); Yeboah (42, 44, 74)	13,307	R.Dilkes
1995-96	Home	9-Dec-95	1-1	Jobson (75)	27,984	G.Poll
1996-97	Home	26-Aug-96	1-0	Sharpe (58)	25,860	M.Reed
1996-97	Away	16-Apr-97	0-2		7,979	P.Alcock
1997-98	Away	25-Oct-97	0-1		15,718	G.Barber
1997-98	Home	10-May-98	1-1	Haaland (81)	38,172	S.Dunn
1998-99	Away	29-Aug-98	1-1	Bowyer (61)	16,437	S.Dunn
1998-99	Home	29-Dec-98	2-2	Ribeiro (26); Hopkin (57)	39,816	P.Jones
1999-00	Away	7-Nov-99	0-2		18,747	P.Jones
1999-00	Home	19-Mar-00	4-1	Bakke (23, 39); Harte (28 pen); Kewell (83)	39,256	A.Wiley

INTRODUCTION

Founded in 1884 as Leicester Fosse by former pupils of the Wyggeston School from the western part of the city near the old Roman Fosse Way. Moved to their present ground in 1891 and from the Midland League joined Division Two of the Football League in 1894. Promoted for the first time in 1908, they have been relegated seven times from the top flight. FA Cup runners-up four times, they gained European Cup-Winners' Cup experience in 1961-62. Members of the new Division One in its first season, 1992-93, and promoted to the Premier League following play-off success in 1994. Relegated straight back but repromoted, again via the play-offs at the end of the 1995-96 season. Won the League Cup in 1997 and were losing finalists in 1999.

Ground:	City Stadium, Filbert Street, Leicester LE2 7FL
Nickname:	Filberts or Foxes
Internet:	www.lcfc.co.uk

HONOURS

Football League Div 1:	Runners-up 1928-29
Football League Div 2:	Champions 1924-25, 1936-37, 1953-54, 1956-57, 1970-71, 1979-80. Runners-up 1907-08
FA Cup:	Runners-up 1949, 1961, 1963, 1969
Football League Cup:	Winners 1964, 1997 Runners-up 1965, 1999

EUROPEAN RECORD

Champions' League (0)	–
Cup-Winners' Cup (1):	61-62 (1)
UEFA Cup(1)	97-98 (1).

FAPL RECORD SUMMARY

Most Total:	LENNON, Neil	140
Most Starts:	LENNON, Neil	140
Most Subs:	MARSHALL, Ian	34
Most SNU:	ARPHEXAD, Pegguy	84
Most PS:	COTTEE, Tony	30
Most Goals:	HESKEY, Emile	33
Most Yel:	LENNON, Neil	28
Most Red:	SINCLAIR, Frank	2

PLAYING RECORD – SEASON TOTALS

Season	Pn	P	W	D	L	F	A	Pts
1994-95	21	42	6	11	25	45	80	29
1996-97	9	38	12	11	15	46	54	47
1997-98	10	38	13	14	11	51	41	53
1998-99	10	38	12	13	13	40	46	49
1999-00	8	38	16	7	15	55	55	55
Totals		194	59	56	79	237	276	233

PLAYING RECORD – HOME TOTALS

Season	Pn	P	W	D	L	F	A	Pts
1994-95	21	21	5	6	10	28	37	21
1996-97	9	19	7	5	7	22	26	26
1997-98	10	19	6	10	3	21	15	28
1998-99	10	19	7	6	6	25	25	27
1999-00	8	19	10	3	6	31	24	33
Totals		97	35	30	32	127	127	135

PLAYING RECORD – AWAY TOTALS

Season	Pn	P	W	D	L	F	A	Pts
1994-95	21	21	1	5	15	17	43	8
1996-97	9	19	5	6	8	24	28	21
1997-98	10	19	7	4	8	30	26	25
1998-99	10	19	5	7	7	15	21	22
1999-00	8	19	6	4	9	24	31	22
Totals		97	24	26	47	110	149	98

HIGHEST HOME ATTENDANCES

	Attendance	Opponents	Date	Season
1	22,170	Manchester U.	18-Mar-00	1999-00
2	22,091	Manchester U.	16-Jan-99	1998-99
3	21,837	Liverpool	31-Oct-98	1998-99
4	21,699	Newcastle U.	29-Apr-98	1997-98
5	21,633	Liverpool	17-Jan-98	1997-98

LOWEST HOME ATTENDANCES

	Attendance	Opponents	Date	Season
1	15,248	Ipswich T.	29-Apr-95	1994-95
2	15,489	Wimbledon	1-Apr-95	1994-95
3	15,992	Norwich C.	5-Apr-95	1994-95
4	17,550	Middlesbrough	5-Feb-00	1999-00
5	17,562	Southampton	21-Aug-96	1996-97

TOP SCORER – SEASON BY SEASON

Season	Player	Goals
1994-95	Roberts	9
1996-97	Claridge	12
1997-98	Heskey	10
1998-99	Cottee	10
1999-00	Cottee	13

PLAYERS WITH MOST PREMIERSHIP APPEARANCES

Tot	Player	St	Sb	Ps	Gls
140	LENNON, Neil	140	0	5	
134	IZZET, Muzzy	133	1	20	
127	ELLIOTT, Matt	127	0	20	
124	HESKEY, Emile	123	1	33	
118	GUPPY, Steve	116	2	8	
104	SAVAGE, Robbie	92	12	4	
100	KELLER, Kasey	100	0	0	
86	WALSH, Steve	72	14	8	
83	COTTEE, Tony	66	17	27	
83	MARSHALL, Ian	49	34	18	
74	PARKER, Garry	53	21	7	
70	GRAYSON, Simon	70	0	0	
65	SINCLAIR, Frank	64	1	1	
64	PRIOR, Spencer	61	3	0	
64	KAAMARK, Pontus	59	5	0	
50	ZAGORAKIS, Theo	34	16	3	

CLUB-BY-CLUB RESULTS

ARSENAL

Season	Venue	Date	Res	Scorers	Attendance	Referee
1994-95	Home	23-Nov-94	2-1	Ormondroyd (16); Lowe (28)	20,774	D.Elleray
1994-95	Away	11-Feb-95	1-1	Draper (78)	31,373	G.Poll
1996-97	Home	24-Aug-96	0-2		20,429	G.Barber
1996-97	Away	12-Apr-97	0-2		38,044	S.Lodge
1997-98	Home	27-Aug-97	3-3	Heskey (84); Elliot (89); Walsh (90)	21,089	G.Barber
1997-98	Away	26-Dec-97	1-2	Lennon (77)	38,023	D.Elleray
1998-99	Home	12-Sep-98	1-1	Heskey (28)	21,628	P.Durkin
1998-99	Away	20-Feb-99	0-5		38,069	P.Durkin
1999-00	Away	7-Aug-99	1-2	Cottee (57)	38,026	A.Wilkie
1999-00	Home	4-Dec-99	0-3		20,495	D.Gallagher

ASTON VILLA

Season	Venue	Date	Res	Scorers	Attendance	Referee
1994-95	Home	3-Dec-94	1-1	Gee (5)	20,896	M.Bodenham
1994-95	Away	22-Feb-95	4-4	Robins (61); Roberts (67); Lowe (80,90)	30,825	K.Morton
1996-97	Away	16-Nov-96	3-1	Claridge (8); Parker (44 pen); Izzet (84)	36,193	D.Elleray
1996-97	Home	5-Mar-97	1-0	Claridge (66)	20,626	G.Poll
1997-98	Home	9-Aug-97	1-0	Marshall (37)	20,304	S.Lodge
1997-98	Away	10-Jan-98	1-1	Parker (53 pen)	36,429	M.Riley
1998-99	Away	24-Oct-98	1-1	Cottee (36)	39,241	K.Burge
1998-99	Home	6-Apr-99	2-2	Savage (63); Cottee (71)	20,652	S.Lodge
1999-00	Home	25-Sep-99	3-1	Izzet (40); OG (48, Southgate); Cottee (55)	19,917	J.Winter
1999-00	Away	22-Apr-00	2-2	Elliott (36); Lennon (67)	31,229	G.Barber

BARNSLEY

Season	Venue	Date	Res	Scorers	Attendance	Referee
1997-98	Away	27-Sep-97	2-0	Marshall (55); Fenton (63)	18,660	G.Poll
1997-98	Home	2-May-98	1-0	Zagorakis (57)	21,293	D.Gallagher

BLACKBURN ROVERS

Season	Venue	Date	Res	Scorers	Attendance	Referee
1994-95	Away	23-Aug-94	0-3		21,050	K.Burge
1994-95	Home	17-Dec-94	0-0		20,559	P.Don
1996-97	Home	7-Dec-96	1-1	Marshall (78)	19,306	M.Riley
1996-97	Away	11-May-97	4-2	Heskey (13, 56); Claridge (55); Wilson (81)	25,881	S.Dunn
1997-98	Home	24-Sep-97	1-1	Izzett (43)	19,921	N.Barry
1997-98	Away	28-Feb-98	3-5	Wilson (72); Izzet (79); Ullathorne (81)	24,854	N.Barry
1998-99	Away	29-Aug-98	0-1		22,544	U.Rennie
1998-99	Home	28-Dec-98	1-1	Walsh (44)	21,083	A.Wilkie

BOLTON WANDERERS

Season	Venue	Date	Res	Scorers	Attendance	Referee
1997-98	Home	22-Nov-97	0-0		20,564	G.Barber
1997-98	Away	28-Mar-98	0-2		25,000	U.Rennie

BRADFORD CITY

Season	Venue	Date	Res	Scorers	Attendance	Referee
1999-00	Away	23-Oct-99	1-3	Impey (21)	17,655	M.Reed
1999-00	Home	6-May-00	3-0	Elliot (59, 63);Cottee (68)	21,103	S.Dunn

CHARLTON ATHLETIC

Season	Venue	Date	Res	Scorers	Attendance	Referee
1998-99	Away	7-Nov-98	0-0		20,021	D.Elleray
1998-99	Home	13-Mar-99	1-1	Lennon (60)	20,220	A.Wilkie

CHELSEA

Season	Venue	Date	Res	Scorers	Attendance	Referee
1994-95	Away	8-Oct-94	0-4		18,397	J.Worrall
1994-95	Home	6-May-95	1-1	Willis (24)	18,140	G.Willard
1996-97	Home	12-Oct-96	1-3	Watts (44)	20,766	M.Reed
1996-97	Away	19-Apr-97	1-2	OG (47, Sinclair)	27,723	A.Wilkie
1997-98	Away	18-Oct-97	0-1		33,356	U.Rennie
1997-98	Home	21-Feb-98	2-0	Heskey (2, 89)	21,335	P.Durkin
1998-99	Home	21-Nov-98	2-4	Izzet (40); Guppy (60)	21,401	P.Durkin
1998-99	Away	18-Apr-99	2-2	OG (82, Duberry); Guppy (88)	34,535	M.Reed
1999-00	Home	14-Aug-99	2-2	Heskey (10); Izzet (90 pen)	21,068	S.Lodge
1999-00	Away	15-Jan-00	1-1	Taggart (41)	35,063	G.Barber

COVENTRY CITY

Season	Venue	Date	Res	Scorers	Attendance	Referee
1994-95	Home	3-Oct-94	2-2	Roberts (45,85)	19,372	K.Cooper
1994-95	Away	25-Feb-95	2-4	Lowe (64); Roberts (74)	20,663	R.Gifford
1996-97	Home	21-Dec-96	0-2		20,038	G.Barber
1996-97	Away	8-Mar-97	0-0		19,220	P.Alcock
1997-98	Away	29-Nov-97	2-0	Fenton (32); Elliot (74 pen)	18,309	M.Bodenham
1997-98	Home	4-Apr-98	1-1	Wilson (78)	21,137	G.Barber
1998-99	Away	28-Nov-98	1-1	Heskey (89)	19,894	M.Riley
1998-99	Home	24-Apr-99	1-0	Marshall (45)	20,224	G.Barber
1999-00	Home	11-Aug-99	1-0	Izzet (24 pen)	19,196	N.Barry
1999-00	Away	27-Nov-99	1-0	Heskey (60)	22,021	S.Lodge

CRYSTAL PALACE

Season	Venue	Date	Res	Scorers	Attendance	Referee
1994-95	Home	29-Oct-94	0-1		20,022	P.Don
1994-95	Away	14-Jan-95	0-2		12,707	P.Durkin
1997-98	Home	6-Dec-97	1-1	Izzet (90)	19,191	U.Rennie
1997-98	Away	11-Apr-98	3-0	Heskey (44, 60); Elliott (74)	18,771	A.Wilkie

DERBY COUNTY

Season	Venue	Date	Res	Scorers	Attendance	Referee
1996-97	Away	2-Nov-96	0-2		18,010	G.Barber
1996-97	Home	22-Feb-97	4-2	Marshall (6, 24, 27); Claridge (58)	20,323	P.Durkin
1997-98	Home	6-Oct-97	1-2	Elliot (67)	19,385	G.Ashby
1997-98	Away	26-Apr-98	4-0	Heskey (2, 9); Izzet (3); Marshall (15)	29,855	G.Willard
1998-99	Away	19-Sep-98	0-2		26,738	G.Poll
1998-99	Home	5-May-99	1-2	Sinclair (28)	20,535	N.Barry
1999-00	Home	18-Dec-99	0-1		18,581	D.Elleray
1999-00	Away	2-Apr-00	0-3		25,763	G.Poll

EVERTON

Season	Venue	Date	Res	Scorers	Attendance	Referee
1994-95	Away	24-Sep-94	1-1	Draper (81)	28,003	T.Holbrook
1994-95	Home	4-Mar-95	2-2	Draper (59); Roberts (83)	20,447	P.Durkin
1996-97	Home	23-Nov-96	1-2	Walsh (83)	20,975	J.Winter
1996-97	Away	9-Apr-97	1-1	Marshall (70)	30,368	S.Dunn
1997-98	Home	20-Dec-97	0-1		20,628	J.Winter
1997-98	Away	18-Apr-98	1-1	Marshall (38)	33,642	S.Lodge
1998-99	Home	22-Aug-98	2-0	Cottee (10); Izzet (38)	21,037	S.Lodge
1998-99	Away	9-Jan-99	0-0		32,792	P.Durkin
1999-00	Away	3-Jan-00	2-2	Elliott (26, 31)	30,490	J.Winter
1999-00	Home	8-Apr-00	1-1	Taggart (8)	18,705	A.Wiley

IPSWICH TOWN

Season	Venue	Date	Res	Scorers	Attendance	Referee
1994-95	Away	2-Jan-95	1-4	Roberts (53)	15,803	T.Holbrook
1994-95	Home	29-Apr-95	2-0	Whitlow (67); Lowe (90)	15,248	A.Wilkie

LEEDS UNITED

Season	Venue	Date	Res	Scorers	Attendance	Referee
1994-95	Away	24-Oct-94	1-2	Blake (53)	28,547	K.Burge
1994-95	Home	15-Mar-95	1-3	Roberts (21)	20,068	D.Gallagher
1996-97	Home	28-Sep-96	1-0	Heskey (60)	20,359	S.Dunn
1996-97	Away	11-Jan-97	0-3		29,486	M.Reed
1997-98	Away	20-Sep-97	1-0	Walsh (32)	29,620	K.Burge
1997-98	Home	7-Feb-98	1-0	Parker (44 pen)	21,244	N.Barry
1998-99	Away	3-Oct-98	1-0	Cottee (76)	32,606	G.Barber
1998-99	Home	1-Mar-99	1-2	Cottee (76)	18,101	G.Barber
1999-00	Away	26-Dec-99	1-2	Cottee (10)	40,105	M.Halsey
1999-00	Home	26-Mar-00	2-1	Collymore (14); Guppy (48)	21,095	S.Lodge

LIVERPOOL

Season	Venue	Date	Res	Scorers	Attendance	Referee
1994-95	Home	26-Dec-94	1-2	Roberts (87)	21,393	G.Ashby
1994-95	Away	17-Apr-95	0-2		36,012	G.Poll
1996-97	Home	15-Sep-96	0-3		20,987	P.Durkin
1996-97	Away	26-Dec-96	1-1	Claridge (76)	40,786	A.Wilkie
1997-98	Away	13-Aug-97	2-1	Elliot (2); Fenton (83)	35,007	J.Winter
1997-98	Home	17-Jan-98	0-0		21,633	S.Dunn
1998-99	Home	31-Oct-98	1-0	Cottee (59)	21,837	M.Reed
1998-99	Away	21-Apr-99	1-0	Marshall (90)	36,019	G.Poll
1999-00	Home	18-Sep-99	2-2	Cottee (2); Izzet (86)	21,623	U.Rennie
1999-00	Away	3-May-00	2-0	Cottee (2); Gilchrist (48)	43,456	G.Poll

MANCHESTER CITY

Season	Venue	Date	Res	Scorers	Attendance	Referee
1994-95	Home	20-Nov-94	0-1		19,006	K.Morton
1994-95	Away	25-Jan-95	1-0	Robins (69)	21,007	S.Lodge

MANCHESTER UNITED

Season	Venue	Date	Res	Scorers	Attendance	Referee
1994-95	Away	28-Dec-94	1-1	Whitlow (65)	43,789	D.Gallagher
1994-95	Home	15-Apr-95	0-4		21,281	M.Bodenham
1996-97	Away	30-Nov-96	1-3	Lennon (90)	55,196	M.Bodenham
1996-97	Home	3-May-97	2-2	Walsh (15); Marshall (20)	21,068	A.Wilkie
1997-98	Home	23-Aug-97	0-0		21,221	D.Gallagher
1997-98	Away	31-Jan-98	1-0	Cottee (28)	55,156	G.Ashby
1998-99	Away	15-Aug-98	2-2	Heskey (7); Cottee (76)	55,052	N.Barry
1998-99	Home	16-Jan-99	2-6	Zagorakis (35); Walsh (73)	22,091	S.Dunn
1999-00	Away	6-Nov-99	0-2		55,191	P.Durkin
1999-00	Home	18-Mar-00	0-2		22,170	R.Harris

MIDDLESBROUGH

Season	Venue	Date	Res	Scorers	Attendance	Referee
1996-97	Away	3-Dec-96	2-0	Claridge (45); Izzet (47)	29,709	P.Alcock
1996-97	Home	15-Mar-97	1-3	Marshall (47)	20,561	S.Lodge
1998-99	Home	9-Sep-98	0-1		20,635	K.Burge
1998-99	Away	30-Jan-99	0-0		34,631	D.Gallagher
1999-00	Away	24-Aug-99	3-0	Heskey (35, 83); Cottee (38)	33,126	R.Harris
1999-00	Home	5-Feb-00	2-1	OG (1, O'Neill); OG (41, Schwarzer)	17,550	S.Bennett

NEWCASTLE UNITED

Season	Venue	Date	Res	Scorers	Attendance	Referee
1994-95	Home	21-Aug-94	1-3	Joachim (90)	20,048	M.Reed
1994-95	Away	10-Dec-94	1-3	Oldfield (48)	34,400	G.Willard
1996-97	Home	26-Oct-96	2-0	Claridge (17); Heskey (79)	21,134	G.Poll
1996-97	Away	2-Feb-97	3-4	Elliott (55); Claridge (60); Heskey (68)	36,396	M.Reed
1997-98	Away	1-Nov-97	3-3	Marshall (12, 31); Elliot (54)	36,574	G.Willard
1997-98	Home	29-Apr-98	0-0		21,699	M.Bodenham
1998-99	Away	19-Dec-98	0-1		36,718	J.Winter
1998-99	Home	8-May-99	2-0	Izzet (20); Cottee (41)	21,125	U.Rennie

1999-00	Home	28-Dec-99	1-2	Zagorakis (83)	21,225	P.Durkin
1999-00	Away	15-Apr-00	2-0	Cottee (7); Savage (52)	36,426	U.Rennie

NORWICH CITY

Season	Venue	Date	Res	Scorers	Attendance	Referee
1994-95	Away	26-Nov-94	1-2	Draper (22)	20,567	R.Gifford
1994-95	Home	5-Apr-95	1-0	Parker (48)	15,992	T.Holbrook

NOTTINGHAM FOREST

Season	Venue	Date	Res	Scorers	Attendance	Referee
1994-95	Away	27-Aug-94	0-1		21,601	G.Willard
1994-95	Home	11-Mar-95	2-4	Lowe (16); Draper (71)	20,423	P.Don
1996-97	Away	7-Sep-96	0-0		24,105	P.Alcock
1996-97	Home	28-Dec-96	2-2	Heskey (10); Izzet (63)	20,833	K.Burge
1998-99	Home	12-Dec-98	3-1	Heskey (43); Elliott (55 pen); Guppy (75)	20,891	M.Riley
1998-99	Away	16-May-99	0-1		25,353	S.Dunn

QPR

Season	Venue	Date	Res	Scorers	Attendance	Referee
1994-95	Home	31-Aug-94	1-1	Gee (89)	18,695	S.Lodge
1994-95	Away	8-Mar-95	0-2		10,189	M.Reed

SHEFFIELD WEDNESDAY

Season	Venue	Date	Res	Scorers	Attendance	Referee
1994-95	Home	31-Dec-94	0-1		20,624	M.Reed
1994-95	Away	8-Apr-95	0-1		22,551	G.Ashby
1996-97	Away	2-Sep-96	1-2	Claridge (28)	17,657	G.Willard
1996-97	Home	7-May-97	1-0	Elliott (86)	20,793	G.Ashby
1997-98	Away	30-Aug-97	0-1		24,851	P.Alcock
1997-98	Home	28-Dec-97	1-1	Guppy (28)	20,800	G.Poll
1998-99	Away	26-Dec-98	1-0	Cottee (34)	33,513	M.Reed
1998-99	Home	6-Feb-99	0-2		20,113	G.Willard
1999-00	Home	30-Oct-99	3-0	Taggart (24, 36); Cottee (57)	19,046	P.Alcock
1999-00	Away	14-May-00	0-4		21,656	D.Elleray

SOUTHAMPTON

Season	Venue	Date	Res	Scorers	Attendance	Referee
1994-95	Home	15-Oct-94	4-3	Blake (3,54); Roberts (21); Carr (81)	20,020	R.Hart
1994-95	Away	14-May-95	2-2	Parker (58); Robins (87)	15,101	K.Burge
1996-97	Home	21-Aug-96	2-1	Heskey (5, 42)	17,562	M.Riley
1996-97	Away	22-Mar-97	2-2	Heskey (47); Claridge (71)	15,044	K.Burge
1997-98	Away	13-Dec-97	1-2	Savage (84)	15,121	S.Lodge
1997-98	Home	14-Apr-98	3-3	Lennon (18); Elliott (52); Parker (90 pen)	20,708	G.Poll
1998-99	Home	5-Dec-98	2-0	Heskey (61); Walsh (63)	18,423	D.Gallagher
1998-99	Away	1-May-99	1-2	Marshall (17)	15,228	P.Alcock
1999-00	Home	16-Oct-99	2-1	Guppy (8); Cottee (39)	19,556	B.Knight
1999-00	Away	29-Apr-00	2-1	Cottee (22); Izzet (60)	15,178	M.Reed

LEICESTER CITY

SUNDERLAND

Season	Venue	Date	Res	Scorers	Attendance	Referee
1996-97	Away	17-Aug-96	0-0		19,262	S.Lodge
1996-97	Home	29-Jan-97	1-1	Parker (32 pen)	17,883	G.Ashby
1999-00	Away	11-Sep-99	0-2		40,105	A.D'Urso
1999-00	Home	5-Mar-00	5-2	Collymore (17, 60, 87); Heskey (34); Oakes (90)	20,432	N.Barry

TOTTENHAM HOTSPUR

Season	Venue	Date	Res	Scorers	Attendance	Referee
1994-95	Home	17-Sep-94	3-1	Joachim (45,90); Lowe (87)	21,300	G.Ashby
1994-95	Away	18-Mar-95	0-1		30,851	S.Lodge
1996-97	Away	22-Sep-96	2-1	Claridge (22); Marshall (86)	24,159	A.Wilkie
1996-97	Home	19-Mar-97	1-1	Claridge (74)	20,593	R.Dilkes
1997-98	Home	13-Sep-97	3-0	Walsh (55); Guppy (68); Heskey (77)	20,683	A.Wilkie
1997-98	Away	14-Feb-98	1-1	Cottee (34)	28,355	S.Lodge
1998-99	Home	19-Oct-98	2-1	Heskey (37); Izzet (85)	20,787	M.Riley
1998-99	Away	3-Apr-99	2-0	Elliott (43); Cottee (67)	35,415	N.Barry
1999-00	Away	3-Oct-99	3-2	Izzett (25 pen, 69); Taggart (76)	35,591	G.Barber
1999-00	Home	19-Apr-00	0-1		19,764	J.Winter

WATFORD

Season	Venue	Date	Res	Scorers	Attendance	Referee
1999-00	Home	30-Aug-99	1-0	Izzet (44)	17,920	N.Barry
1999-00	Away	12-Feb-00	1-1	Elliott (39)	16,184	A.D'Urso

WEST HAM UNITED

Season	Venue	Date	Res	Scorers	Attendance	Referee
1994-95	Away	5-Nov-94	0-1		18,780	R.Dilkes
1994-95	Home	4-Feb-95	1-2	Robins (44)	20,375	J.Worrall
1996-97	Away	19-Oct-96	0-1		22,285	M.Riley
1996-97	Home	23-Apr-97	0-1		20,327	G.Hegley
1997-98	Home	27-Oct-97	2-1	Heskey (16); Marshall (82)	20,021	M.Reed
1997-98	Away	10-May-98	3-4	Cottee (59, 83); Heskey (66)	25,781	U.Rennie
1998-99	Away	14-Nov-98	2-3	Izzet (28); OG (87, Lampard)	25,642	S.Lodge
1998-99	Home	10-Apr-99	0-0		20,402	J.Winter
1999-00	Away	21-Aug-99	1-2	Heskey (2)	23,631	A.Wiley
1999-00	Home	22-Jan-00	1-3	Heskey (24)	19,019	D.Elleray

WIMBLEDON

Season	Venue	Date	Res	Scorers	Attendance	Referee
1994-95	Away	10-Sep-94	1-2	Lowe (23)	7,683	G.Poll
1994-95	Home	1-Apr-95	3-4	Robins (13); Willis (79); Lawrence (84)	15,489	D.Elleray
1996-97	Home	18-Jan-97	1-0	Heskey (72)	18,927	S.Lodge
1996-97	Away	1-Mar-97	3-1	Elliott (17, 27); Robins (23)	11,487	G.Ashby
1997-98	Home	10-Nov-97	0-1		18,553	M.Riley
1997-98	Away	14-Mar-98	1-2	Savage (57)	13,229	M.Riley
1998-99	Home	28-Sep-98	1-1	Elliott (86)	17,725	A.Wilkie
1998-99	Away	6-Mar-99	1-0	Guppy (6)	11,801	R.Harris
1999-00	Home	20-Nov-99	2-1	Cottee (22, 58)	18,255	A.Wiley
1999-00	Away	11-Mar-00	1-2	Taggart (55)	14,316	P.Alcock

INTRODUCTION

Following a dispute between Everton and its Anfield landlord a new club, Liverpool AFC, was formed in 1892 by the landlord, former Everton committee-man John Houlding, with its headquarters at Anfield. An application for Football League membership was rejected without being put to the vote. Instead the team joined the Lancashire League and immediately won the Championship. After that one campaign, when the Liverpool Cup was won but there was early FA Cup elimination, Liverpool was selected to fill one of two vacancies in an expanded Football League Second Division in 1893. Premier League founder members 1992.

Ground:	Anfield Road, Liverpool L4 0TH
Nickname:	Reds or Pool
Internet:	www.liverpoolfc.net

HONOURS

Football League Div 1:	Champions 1900-01, 1905-06, 1921-22, 1922-23, 1946-47, 1963-64, 1965-66, 1972-73, 1975-76, 1976-77, 1978-79, 1979-80, 1981-82, 1982-83, 1983-84, 1985-86, 1987-88, 1989-90
	Runners-up 1898-99, 1909-10, 1968-69, 1973-74, 1974-75, 1977-78, 1984-85, 1986-87, 1988-89, 1990-91
Football League Div 2:	Champions 1893-94, 1895-96, 1904-05, 1961-62
FA Cup:	Winners 1964-65, 1973-74, 1985-86, 1988-89, 1991-92
	Runners-up 1913-14, 1949-50, 1970-71, 1976-77, 1987-88, 1995-96
Football League Cup:	Winners 1980-81, 1981-82, 1982-83, 1983-84, 1994-95
	Runners-up 1977-78, 1986-87, 1995-96
League Super Cup:	Winners 1985-86
Champions' Cup:	Winners 1976-77, 1977-78, 1980-81; 1983-84
	Runners-up 1984-85
Cup-Winners' Cup:	Runners-up 1965-66
UEFA Cup:	Winners 1972-73, 1975-76
European Super Cup:	Winners 1977
	Runners-up 1984
World Club Championship:	Runners-up 1981, 1984.

EUROPEAN RECORD

Champions' League (12):	64-65 (SF), 66-67 (2), 73-74 (2), 76-77 (W), 77-78 (W), 78-79 (1), 79-80 (1), 80-81 (W), 81-82 (QF), 82-83 (QF), 83-84 (W), 84-85 (F)
Cup-Winners' Cup (5):	65-66 (F), 71-72 (2), 74-75 (2), 92-93 (2), 96-97 (SF)
UEFA Cup (10)	67-68 (3), 68-69 (1), 69-70 (2), 70-71 (SF), 72-73 (W), 75-76 (W), 91-92 (QF), 94-95 (2), 97-98 (2), 98-99 (3).

FAPL RECORD SUMMARY

Most Total:	McMANAMAN, Steve	240
Most Starts:	McMANAMAN, Steve	232
Most Subs:	BERGER, Patrik	28
Most SNU:	WARNER, Tony	89
Most PS:	OWEN, Michael	28
Most Goals:	FOWLER, Robbie	109
Most Yel:	REDKNAPP, Jamie	25
Most Red:	FOWLER, Robbie	2

PLAYING RECORD – SEASON TOTALS

Season	Pn	P	W	D	L	F	A	Pts
1992-93	6	42	16	11	15	62	55	59
1993-94	8	42	17	9	16	59	55	60
1994-95	4	42	21	11	10	65	37	74
1995-96	3	38	20	11	7	70	34	71
1996-97	4	38	19	11	8	62	37	68
1997-98	3	38	18	11	9	68	42	65
1998-99	7	38	15	9	14	68	49	54
1999-00	4	38	19	10	9	51	30	67
Totals		316	145	83	88	505	339	518

PLAYING RECORD – HOME TOTALS

Season	Pn	P	W	D	L	F	A	Pts
1992-93	6	21	13	4	4	41	18	43
1993-94	8	21	12	4	5	33	23	40
1994-95	4	21	13	5	3	38	13	44
1995-96	3	19	14	4	1	46	13	46
1996-97	4	19	10	6	3	38	19	36
1997-98	3	19	13	2	4	42	16	41
1998-99	7	19	10	5	4	44	24	35
1999-00	4	19	11	4	4	28	13	37
Totals		158	96	34	28	310	139	322

PLAYING RECORD – AWAY TOTALS

Season	Pn	P	W	D	L	F	A	Pts
1992-93	6	21	3	7	11	21	37	16
1993-94	8	21	5	5	11	26	32	20
1994-95	4	21	8	6	7	27	24	30
1995-96	3	19	6	7	6	24	21	25
1996-97	4	19	9	5	5	24	18	32
1997-98	3	19	5	9	5	26	26	24
1998-99	7	19	5	4	10	24	25	19
1999-00	4	19	8	6	5	23	17	30
Totals		158	49	49	60	195	200	196

HIGHEST HOME ATTENDANCES

	Attendance	Opponents	Date	Season
1	44,929	Manchester U.	11-Sep-99	1999-00
2	44,886	Arsenal	28-Aug-99	1999-00
3	44,852	Everton	3-Apr-99	1998-99
4	44,826	Chelsea	16-Oct-99	1999-00
5	44,802	Everton	27-Sep-99	1999-00

LOWEST HOME ATTENDANCES

	Attendance	Opponents	Date	Season
1	24,561	QPR	8-Dec-93	1993-94
2	27,183	Coventry C.	14-Mar-95	1994-95
3	29,574	Wimbledon	26-Sep-92	1992-93
4	29,881	Southampton	5-Apr-95	1994-95
5	30,024	Southampton	1-Sep-92	1992-93

TOP SCORER – SEASON BY SEASON

Season	Player	Goals
1992-93	Rush	14
1993-94	Rush	14
1994-95	Fowler	25
1995-96	Fowler	28
1996-97	Fowler	18
1997-98	Owen	18
1998-99	Owen	18
1999-00	Owen	11

PLAYERS WITH MOST PREMIERSHIP APPEARANCES

Tot	Player	St	Sb	Gls
240	McMANAMAN, Steve	232	8	41
226	REDKNAPP, Jamie	200	26	29
214	JAMES, David	213	1	0
199	FOWLER, Robbie	187	12	109
162	BARNES, John	158	4	15
155	JONES, Rob	154	1	0
139	BJORNEBYE, Stig Inge	132	7	2
137	WRIGHT, Mark	135	2	5
130	RUSH, Ian	118	12	45
128	BABB, Phil	124	4	1
126	MATTE, , Dominic	112	14	1
116	RUDDOCK, Neil	111	5	11
111	BERGER, Patrik	83	28	25
107	THOMAS,Michael	80	27	6

CLUB-BY-CLUB RESULTS

ARSENAL

Season	Venue	Date	Res	Scorers	Attendance	Referee
1992-93	Home	23-Aug-92	0-2		34,961	K.Redfern
1992-93	Away	31-Jan-93	1-0	Barnes (59 pen)	27,580	K.Cooper
1993-94	Home	2-Oct-93	0-0		42,750	G.Ashby
1993-94	Away	26-Mar-94	0-1		35,556	R.Hart
1994-95	Home	28-Aug-94	3-0	Fowler (26,29,31)	30,117	A.Wilkie
1994-95	Away	12-Apr-95	1-0	Fowler (90)	38,036	M.Bodenham
1995-96	Home	23-Dec-95	3-1	Fowler (40, 59, 78)	39,806	K.Cooper
1995-96	Away	1-May-96	0-0		38,323	G.Ashby
1996-97	Home	19-Aug-96	2-0	McManaman (68, 74)	38,103	G.Willard
1996-97	Away	24-Mar-97	2-1	Collymore (50); McAteer (65)	38,068	G.Ashby
1997-98	Away	30-Nov-97	1-0	McManaman (56)	38,094	G.Poll
1997-98	Home	6-May-98	4-0	Ince (28, 30); Owen (40); Leonhardsen (86)	44,417	A.Wilkie
1998-99	Home	22-Aug-98	0-0		44,429	D.Elleray
1998-99	Away	9-Jan-99	0-0		38,107	G.Barber
1999-00	Home	28-Aug-99	2-0	Fowler (8); Berger (76)	44,886	D.Gallagher
1999-00	Away	13-Feb-00	1-0	Camara (18)	38,098	S.Dunn

ASTON VILLA

Season	Venue	Date	Res	Scorers	Attendance	Referee
1992-93	Away	19-Sep-92	2-4	Walters (43); Rosenthal (84)	37,863	P.Don
1992-93	Home	9-Jan-93	1-2	Barnes (42)	40,826	K.Hackett
1993-94	Home	28-Nov-93	2-1	Fowler (45); Redknapp (63)	38,484	A.Wilkie
1993-94	Away	7-May-94	1-2	Fowler (17)	45,347	K.Burge
1994-95	Home	8-Oct-94	3-2	Ruddock (20); Fowler (26,57)	32,158	K.Burge
1994-95	Away	6-May-95	0-2		40,154	R.Hart
1995-96	Away	31-Jan-96	2-0	Collymore (62); Fowler (65)	39,332	R.Dilkes
1995-96	Home	3-Mar-96	3-0	McManaman (1); Fowler (5, 8)	39,508	K.Cooper
1996-97	Home	18-Jan-97	3-0	Carragher (50); Collymore (58); Fowler (63)	40,489	R.Dilkes
1996-97	Away	2-Mar-97	0-1		39,399	S.Dunn
1997-98	Home	22-Sep-97	3-0	Fowler (56 pen); McMananman (79); Riedle (90)	34,843	M.Bodenham
1997-98	Away	28-Feb-98	1-2	Owen (5 pen)	39,377	G.Poll
1998-99	Away	21-Nov-98	4-2	Ince (2); Fowler (7, 58, 66)	39,241	P.Jones
1998-99	Home	17-Apr-99	0-1		44,306	J.Winter
1999-00	Away	2-Oct-99	0-0		39,217	R.Harris
1999-00	Home	15-Mar-00	0-0		43,615	S.Bennett

BARNSLEY

Season	Venue	Date	Res	Scorers	Attendance	Referee
1997-98	Home	22-Nov-97	0-1		41,001	J.Winter
1997-98	Away	28-Mar-98	3-2	Riedle (44, 59); McManaman (90)	18,684	G.Willard

BLACKBURN ROVERS

Season	Venue	Date	Res	Scorers	Attendance	Referee
1992-93	Home	13-Dec-92	2-1	Walters (77,85)	43,688	P.Don
1992-93	Away	3-Apr-93	1-4	Rush (84)	15,032	K.Redfern
1993-94	Home	12-Sep-93	0-1		37,355	M.Reed
1993-94	Away	5-Mar-94	0-2		20,831	G.Ashby
1994-95	Away	15-Oct-94	2-3	Fowler (29); Barnes (59)	30,263	B.Hill
1994-95	Home	14-May-95	2-1	Barnes (63); Redknapp (90)	40,014	D.Elleray
1995-96	Home	16-Sep-95	3-0	Redknapp (12); Fowler (22); Collymore (29)	39,502	G.Willard
1995-96	Away	24-Feb-96	3-2	Collymore (11, 21); Thomas (70)	30,895	A.Wilkie
1996-97	Away	3-Nov-96	0-3		29,598	S.Lodge
1996-97	Home	22-Feb-97	0-0		40,747	M.Bodenham
1997-98	Away	23-Aug-97	1-1	Owen (53)	30,187	S.Lodge
1997-98	Home	31-Jan-98	0-0		43,890	P.Durkin
1998-99	Home	29-Nov-98	2-0	Ince (29); Owen (32)	41,753	J.Winter
1998-99	Away	24-Apr-99	3-1	McManaman (23); Redknapp (32); Leonhardsen (32)	29,944	R.Harris

BOLTON WANDERERS

Season	Venue	Date	Res	Scorers	Attendance	Referee
1995-96	Home	23-Sep-95	5-2	Fowler (12, 30, 47, 65); Harkness (84)	40,104	M.Bodenham
1995-96	Away	9-Dec-95	1-0	Collymore (61)	21,042	M.Bodenham
1997-98	Away	1-Nov-97	1-1	Fowler (1)	25,000	D.Gallagher
1997-98	Home	5-Mar-98	2-1	Ince (58); Owen (65)	44,532	K.Burge

BRADFORD CITY

Season	Venue	Date	Res	Scorers	Attendance	Referee
1999-00	Home	1-Nov-99	3-1	Camara (20); Redknapp (40 pen); Heggem (78)	40,483	J.Winter
1999-00	Away	14-May-00	0-1		18,276	D.Gallagher

CHARLTON ATHLETIC

Season	Venue	Date	Res	Scorers	Attendance	Referee
1998-99	Home	19-Sep-98	3-3	Fowler (33 pen, 82); Berger (67)	44,526	P.Alcock
1998-99	Away	13-Feb-99	0-1		20,043	M.Reed

CHELSEA

Season	Venue	Date	Res	Scorers	Attendance	Referee
1992-93	Home	5-Sep-92	2-1	Saunders (27); Redknapp (89)	34,199	J.Key
1992-93	Away	10-Feb-93	0-0		20,981	J.Martin
1993-94	Away	25-Sep-93	0-1		31,271	K.Hackett
1993-94	Home	19-Mar-94	2-1	Rush (8); OG (19, Burley)	38,629	R.Gifford
1994-95	Home	9-Nov-94	3-1	Fowler (8,9); Ruddock (24)	32,855	G.Poll
1994-95	Away	18-Dec-94	0-0		27,050	D.Gallagher
1995-96	Away	30-Dec-95	2-2	McManaman (34, 76)	31,137	K.Burge
1995-96	Home	16-Mar-96	2-0	Wright (2); Fowler (62)	40,820	S.Dunn
1996-97	Home	21-Sep-96	5-1	Fowler (14); Berger (42, 48); OG (45 Myers); Barnes (57)	40,739	S.Dunn
1996-97	Away	1-Jan-97	0-1		28,239	S.Lodge
1997-98	Home	5-Oct-97	4-2	Berger (20, 35, 57); Fowler (64)	36,647	D.Elleray
1997-98	Away	25-Apr-98	1-4	Riedle (45)	34,639	G.Ashby
1998-99	Home	4-Oct-98	1-1	Redknapp (83)	44,404	G.Poll
1998-99	Away	27-Feb-99	1-2	Owen (77)	34,822	P.Durkin
1999-00	Home	16-Oct-99	1-0	Thompson (47)	44,826	M.Reed
1999-00	Away	29-Apr-00	0-2		34,957	G.Barber

COVENTRY CITY

Season	Venue	Date	Res	Scorers	Attendance	Referee
1992-93	Away	19-Dec-92	1-5	Redknapp (64)	19,779	K.Morton
1992-93	Home	17-Apr-93	4-0	Walters (16, 33, 50 pen); Burrows (75)	33,328	T.Ward
1993-94	Away	1-Sep-93	0-1		16,735	K.Burge
1993-94	Home	25-Feb-94	1-0	Rush (2)	38,547	D.Elleray
1994-95	Away	3-Dec-94	1-1	Rush (2)	21,029	K.Burge
1994-95	Home	14-Mar-95	2-3	Molby (77 pen); OG (90, Burrows)	27,183	M.Reed
1995-96	Home	14-Oct-95	0-0		39,079	P.Danson
1995-96	Away	6-Apr-96	0-1		23,037	P.Jones
1996-97	Away	4-Sep-96	1-0	Babb (68)	23,021	G.Poll
1996-97	Home	6-Apr-97	1-2	Fowler (53)	40,079	P.Danson
1997-98	Home	20-Dec-97	1-0	Owen (14)	39,707	P.Alcock
1997-98	Away	19-Apr-98	1-1	Owen (33)	22,721	G.Willard
1998-99	Home	9-Sep-98	2-0	Berger (26); Redknapp (48)	41,771	D.Gallagher
1998-99	Away	30-Jan-99	1-2	McManaman (86)	23,056	M.Riley
1999-00	Home	18-Dec-99	2-0	Owen (45); Camara (74)	44,024	A.D'Urso
1999-00	Away	1-Apr-00	3-0	Owen (23, 38); Heskey (78)	23,098	M.Reed

CRYSTAL PALACE

Season	Venue	Date	Res	Scorers	Attendance	Referee
1992-93	Home	28-Nov-92	5-0	McManaman (7,18); Marsh; (9); Rosenthal (62); Hutchison (72)	36,380	S.Lodge
1992-93	Away	23-Mar-93	1-1	Rush (49)	18,688	R.Dilkes
1994-95	Away	20-Aug-94	6-1	Molby (11 pen); McManaman (14,69); Fowler (44); Rush (60,72)	18,084	R.Hart
1994-95	Home	11-Dec-94	0-0		30,972	K.Morton
1997-98	Away	13-Dec-97	3-0	McManaman (39); Owen (55); Leonardsen (61)	25,790	N.Barry
1997-98	Home	13-Apr-98	2-1	Leonhardsen (29); Thompson (85)	43,007	G.Barber

DERBY COUNTY

Season	Venue	Date	Res	Scorers	Attendance	Referee
1996-97	Home	27-Oct-96	2-1	Fowler (47, 51)	39,515	G.Willard
1996-97	Away	1-Feb-97	1-0	Collymore (75)	18,102	P.Jones
1997-98	Home	25-Oct-97	4-0	Fowler (27, 84); Leonardson (65); McManaman (88)	38,017	G.Willard
1997-98	Away	10-May-98	0-1		30,492	S.Lodge
1998-99	Home	7-Nov-98	1-2	Redknapp (84)	44,020	U.Rennie
1998-99	Away	13-Mar-99	2-3	Fowler (36 pen, 57)	32,913	G.Barber
1999-00	Home	6-Nov-99	2-0	Murphy (65); Redknapp (69)	44,467	U.Rennie
1999-00	Away	18-Mar-00	2-0	Owen (17); Camara (86)	33,378	B.Knight

EVERTON

Season	Venue	Date	Res	Scorers	Attendance	Referee
1992-93	Away	7-Dec-92	1-2	Wright (62)	35,826	M.Bodenham
1992-93	Home	20-Mar-93	1-0	Rosenthal (90)	44,619	P.Don
1993-94	Away	18-Sep-93	0-2		38,157	D.Elleray
1993-94	Home	13-Mar-94	2-1	Rush (22); Fowler (44)	44,281	K.Cooper
1994-95	Away	21-Nov-94	0-2		39,866	D.Gallagher
1994-95	Home	24-Jan-95	0-0		39,505	B.Hill
1995-96	Home	18-Nov-95	1-2	Fowler (88)	40,818	G.Ashby
1995-96	Away	16-Apr-96	1-1	Fowler (87)	40,120	D.Elleray
1996-97	Home	20-Nov-96	1-1	Fowler (30)	40,751	S.Lodge
1996-97	Away	16-Apr-97	1-1	Redknapp (27)	40,177	S.Lodge
1997-98	Away	18-Oct-97	0-2		41,112	M.Reed
1997-98	Home	23-Feb-98	1-1	Ince (66)	44,501	P.Jones
1998-99	Away	17-Oct-98	0-0		40,185	P.Durkin
1998-99	Home	3-Apr-99	3-2	Fowler (15 pen, 21); Berger (82)	44,852	D.Elleray
1999-00	Home	27-Sep-99	0-1		44,802	M.Riley
1999-00	Away	21-Apr-00	0-0		40,052	G.Poll

IPSWICH TOWN

Season	Venue	Date	Res	Scorers	Attendance	Referee
1992-93	Away	25-Aug-92	2-2	Walters (39); Molby (70 pen)	20,109	R.Hamer
1992-93	Home	20-Feb-93	0-0		36,680	A.Gunn
1993-94	Away	1-Jan-94	2-1	Ruddock (57); Rush (88)	22,270	A.Gunn
1993-94	Home	9-Apr-94	1-0	Dicks (75 pen)	30,485	D.Gallagher
1994-95	Away	29-Oct-94	3-1	Barnes (39); Fowler (56,60)	22,519	P.Durkin
1994-95	Home	14-Jan-95	0-1		32,733	R.Gifford

LEEDS UNITED

Season	Venue	Date	Res	Scorers	Attendance	Referee
1992-93	Away	29-Aug-92	2-2	Whelan (44); Molby (70 pen)	29,597	R.Dilkes
1992-93	Home	21-Apr-93	2-0	Barnes (54); Walters (73 pen)	34,992	M.Reed
1993-94	Home	28-Aug-93	2-0	Rush (24); Molby (40 pen)	44,068	R.Hart
1993-94	Away	19-Feb-94	0-2		40,029	G.Poll
1994-95	Away	31-Dec-94	2-0	Redknapp (17); Fowler (75)	38,563	A.Wilkie
1994-95	Home	9-Apr-95	0-1		37,454	D.Gallagher
1995-96	Away	21-Aug-95	0-1		35,852	D.Elleray
1995-96	Home	20-Jan-96	5-0	Ruddock (25, 90); Fowler (60 pen, 67); Collymore (88)	40,254	P.Durkin
1996-97	Away	16-Nov-96	2-0	Ruddock (13); McManaman (90)	39,981	P.Jones
1996-97	Home	19-Feb-97	4-0	Fowler (22); Collymore (36, 38); Redknapp (87)	38,957	A.Wilkie
1997-98	Away	26-Aug-97	2-0	McMannman (23); Riedlel (75)	39,775	A.Wilkie
1997-98	Home	26-Dec-97	3-1	Owen (46); Fowler (79, 83)	43,854	S.Lodge
1998-99	Home	14-Nov-98	1-3	Fowler (68 pen)	44,305	D.Gallagher
1998-99	Away	12-Apr-99	0-0		39,451	P.Jones
1999-00	Away	23-Aug-99	2-1	Camara (45); OG (55, Radebe)	39,703	D.Elleray
1999-00	Home	5-Feb-00	3-1	Hamann (19); Berger (69); Murphy (90)	44,793	M.Reed

LEICESTER CITY

Season	Venue	Date	Res	Scorers	Attendance	Referee
1994-95	Away	26-Dec-94	2-1	Fowler (67 pen); Rush (77)	21,393	G.Ashby
1994-95	Home	17-Apr-95	2-0	Fowler (74); Rush (80)	36,012	G.Poll
1996-97	Away	15-Sep-96	3-0	Berger (58, 77); Thomas (62)	20,987	P.Durkin
1996-97	Home	26-Dec-96	1-1	Collymore (80)	40,786	A.Wilkie
1997-98	Home	13-Aug-97	1-2	Ince (84)	35,007	J.Winter
1997-98	Away	17-Jan-98	0-0		21,633	S.Dunn
1998-99	Away	31-Oct-98	0-1		21,837	M.Reed
1998-99	Home	21-Apr-99	0-1		36,019	G.Poll
1999-00	Away	18-Sep-99	2-2	Owen (23 pen, 39)	21,623	U.Rennie
1999-00	Home	3-May-00	0-2		43,456	G.Poll

MANCHESTER CITY

Season	Venue	Date	Res	Scorers	Attendance	Referee
1992-93	Home	28-Dec-92	1-1	Rush (49)	43,037	D.Allison
1992-93	Away	12-Apr-93	1-1	Rush (61)	28,098	M.Reed
1993-94	Away	23-Oct-93	1-1	Rush (89)	30,403	M.Bodenham
1993-94	Home	22-Jan-94	2-1	Rush (22, 90)	41,872	R.Milford
1994-95	Home	28-Dec-94	2-0	OG (55, Phelan); Fowler (82)	38,122	R.Hart
1994-95	Away	14-Apr-95	1-2	McManaman (21)	27,055	J.Worrall
1995-96	Home	28-Oct-95	6-0	Rush (3, 64); Redknapp (6); Fowler (47, 60); Ruddock (53)	39,267	A.Wilkie
1995-96	Away	5-May-96	2-2	OG (6, Lomas); Rush (41)	31,436	S.Lodge

MANCHESTER UNITED

Season	Venue	Date	Res	Scorers	Attendance	Referee
1992-93	Away	18-Oct-92	2-2	Hutchison (23); Rush (44)	33,243	K.Hackett
1992-93	Home	6-Mar-93	1-2	Rush (50)	44,374	R.Milford
1993-94	Home	4-Jan-94	3-3	Clough (25, 38); Ruddock (79)	42,795	P.Don
1993-94	Away	30-Mar-94	0-1		44,751	K.Hackett
1994-95	Away	17-Sep-94	0-2		43,740	K.Morton

1994-95	Home	19-Mar-95	2-0	Redknapp (24); OG (86, Bruce)	38,906	G.Ashby
1995-96	Away	1-Oct-95	2-2	Fowler (32, 53)	34,934	D.Elleray
1995-96	Home	17-Dec-95	2-0	Fowler (44, 87)	40,546	G.Poll
1996-97	Away	12-Oct-96	0-1		55,128	D.Elleray
1996-97	Home	19-Apr-97	1-3	Barnes (19)	40,892	G.Poll
1997-98	Home	6-Dec-97	1-3	Fowler (60 pen)	41,027	D.Elleray
1997-98	Away	10-Apr-98	1-1	Owen (36)	55,171	G.Poll
1998-99	Away	24-Sep-98	0-2		55,181	S.Lodge
1998-99	Home	5-May-99	2-2	Redknapp (69 pen); Ince (89)	44,702	D.Elleray
1999-00	Home	11-Sep-99	2-3	Hyypia (23); Berger (68)	44,929	G.Barber
1999-00	Away	4-Mar-00	1-1	Berger (27)	61,592	D.Gallagher

MIDDLESBROUGH

Season	Venue	Date	Res	Scorers	Attendance	Referee
1992-93	Home	7-Nov-92	4-1	Rosenthal 2 (9,38); McManaman (45); Rush (89)	34,974	D.Gallagher
1992-93	Away	13-Mar-93	2-1	Hutchison (11); Rush (81)	22,463	M.Peck
1995-96	Away	25-Nov-95	1-2	Ruddock (63)	29,390	D.Gallagher
1995-96	Home	27-Apr-96	1-0	Collymore (70)	40,782	R.Dilkes
1996-97	Away	17-Aug-96	3-3	Bjornebye (4); Barnes (29); Fowler (65)	30,039	P.Alcock
1996-97	Home	14-Dec-96	5-1	Fowler (1, 28, 77, 85); Bjornebye (45)	39,491	K.Burge
1998-99	Away	26-Dec-98	3-1	Owen (17); Redknapp (35); Heggem (88)	34,626	G.Poll
1998-99	Home	6-Feb-99	3-1	Owen (9); Heggem (44); Ince (45)	44,384	P.Jones
1999-00	Away	21-Aug-99	0-1		34,783	S.Dunn
1999-00	Home	22-Jan-00	0-0		44,324	S.Dunn

NEWCASTLE UNITED

Season	Venue	Date	Res	Scorers	Attendance	Referee
1993-94	Away	21-Nov-93	0-3		36,246	G.Ashby
1993-94	Home	16-Apr-94	0-2		44,601	P.Don
1994-95	Away	24-Sep-94	1-1	Rush (70)	34,435	P.Don
1994-95	Home	4-Mar-95	2-0	Fowler (57); Rush 63)	39,300	P.Jones
1995-96	Away	4-Nov-95	1-2	Rush (11)	36,547	M.Reed
1995-96	Home	3-Apr-96	4-3	Fowler (2, 57); Collymore (63, 90)	40,702	M.Reed
1996-97	Away	23-Dec-96	1-1	Fowler (45)	36,570	P.Alcock
1996-97	Home	10-Mar-97	4-3	McManaman (29); Berger (30); Fowler (42, 90)	40,751	D.Elleray
1997-98	Away	28-Dec-97	2-1	McManaman (31, 43)	36,718	G.Ashby
1997-98	Home	20-Jan-98	1-0	Owen (17)	42,791	G.Barber
1998-99	Away	30-Aug-98	4-1	Owen (17, 18, 32); Berger (45)	36,740	G.Barber
1998-99	Home	28-Dec-98	4-2	Owen (67, 80); Riedle (71, 84)	44,605	S.Lodge
1999-00	Away	26-Dec-99	2-2	Owen (31, 52)	36,445	D.Elleray
1999-00	Home	25-Mar-00	2-1	Camara (51); Redknapp (88)	44,743	P.Durkin

NORWICH CITY

Season	Venue	Date	Res	Scorers	Attendance	Referee
1992-93	Home	25-Oct-92	4-1	Thomas (15); Hutchison (20); Burrows (52); Walters (89 pen)	36,318	R.Lewis
1992-93	Away	1-May-93	0-1		20,610	D.Elleray
1993-94	Away	5-Feb-94	2-2	OG (53, Culverhouse); Barnes (76)	19,746	D.Gallagher
1993-94	Home	30-Apr-94	0-1		44,339	B.Hill
1994-95	Home	2-Jan-95	4-0	Scales (14); Fowler (38,47); Rush (83)	34,709	K.Cooper
1994-95	Away	29-Apr-95	2-1	Harkness (7); Rush (84)	21,843	B.Hill

NOTTINGHAM FOREST

Season	Venue	Date	Res	Scorers	Attendance	Referee
1992-93	Away	16-Aug-92	0-1		20,038	M.Reed
1992-93	Home	6-Feb-93	0-0		40,463	K.Barratt
1994-95	Home	5-Nov-94	1-0	Fowler (14)	33,329	J.Worrall
1994-95	Away	4-Feb-95	1-1	Fowler (90)	25,418	G.Willard
1995-96	Home	1-Jan-96	4-2	Fowler (31,42); Collymore (62); OG (86, Cooper)	39,206	P.Alcock
1995-96	Away	23-Mar-96	0-1		29,058	P.Danson
1996-97	Home	17-Dec-96	4-2	Collymore (6, 63); Fowler (27); OG (51, Lyttle)	36,126	G.Barber
1996-97	Away	15-Mar-97	1-1	Fowler (3)	29,181	R.Dilkes
1998-99	Home	24-Oct-98	5-1	Owen (10, 38, 71 pen, 77); McManaman (23)	44,595	S.Dunn
1998-99	Away	5-Apr-99	2-2	Redknapp (15); Owen (72)	28,374	D.Gallagher

OLDHAM ATHLETIC

Season	Venue	Date	Res	Scorers	Attendance	Referee
1992-93	Home	10-Apr-93	1-0	Rush (60)	36,129	J.Worrall
1992-93	Away	5-May-93	2-3	Rush (30,59)	15,381	P.Durkin
1993-94	Home	16-Oct-93	2-1	Fowler (87); OG (90, Barlow)	32,661	A.Wilkie
1993-94	Away	15-Jan-94	3-0	Dicks (47); Fowler (53); Redknapp (80)	14,573	J.Lloyd

QPR

Season	Venue	Date	Res	Scorers	Attendance	Referee
1992-93	Away	23-Nov-92	1-0	Rosenthal (87)	21,056	R.Milford
1992-93	Home	10-Mar-93	1-0	Rush (72)	30,370	K.Burge
1993-94	Away	18-Aug-93	3-1	Rush (18); Nicol (38); Clough (41)	19,625	P.Durkin
1993-94	Home	8-Dec-93	3-2	Barnes (25); Rush (32); Molby (78pen)	24,561	V.Callow
1994-95	Away	31-Oct-94	1-2	Barnes (65)	18,295	T.Holbrook
1994-95	Home	11-Feb-95	1-1	Scales (71)	35,996	D.Gallagher
1995-96	Home	30-Aug-95	1-0	Ruddock (30)	37,548	S.Dunn
1995-96	Away	11-Feb-96	2-1	Wright (15); Fowler (30)	18,405	D.Gallagher

SHEFFIELD UNITED

Season	Venue	Date	Res	Scorers	Attendance	Referee
1992-93	Home	19-Aug-92	2-1	Walters (43); Stewart (65)	33,107	D.Elleray
1992-93	Away	12-Sep-92	0-1		20,632	J.Martin
1993-94	Away	26-Dec-93	0-0		22,932	A.Wilkie
1993-94	Home	2-Apr-94	1-2	Rush (3)	36,642	T.Holbrook

SHEFFIELD WEDNESDAY

Season	Venue	Date	Res	Scorers	Attendance	Referee
1992-93	Home	3-Oct-92	1-0	Hutchison (80)	35,785	M.Bodenham
1992-93	Away	27-Feb-93	1-1	Hutchison (20)	33,964	V.Callow
1993-94	Home	14-Aug-93	2-0	Clough 2 (39,47)	43,792	H.King
1993-94	Away	4-Dec-93	1-3	Fowler (37)	32,177	J.Borrett
1994-95	Home	1-Oct-94	4-1	Rush (51); McManaman (54,86); OG (66, Walker)	31,493	G.Willard
1994-95	Away	25-Feb-95	2-1	Barnes (42); McManaman (59)	31,932	D.Elleray
1995-96	Home	19-Aug-95	1-0	Collymore (60)	40,535	P.Durkin
1995-96	Away	13-Jan-96	1-1	Rush (87)	32,747	D.Elleray
1996-97	Home	7-Dec-96	0-1		39,507	M.Reed
1996-97	Away	11-May-97	1-1	Redknapp (83)	38,943	D.Elleray
1997-98	Home	13-Sep-97	2-1	Ince (55); Thomas (68)	34,705	G.Poll

1997-98	Away	14-Feb-98	3-3	Owen (27, 73, 78)	35,405	M.Reed
1998-99	Home	19-Dec-98	2-0	Berger (19); Owen (34)	40,003	A.Wilkie
1998-99	Away	8-May-99	0-1		27,383	P.Jones
1999-00	Away	7-Aug-99	2-1	Fowler (75); Camara (84)	34,853	G.Poll
1999-00	Home	5-Dec-99	4-1	Hyypia (21); Murphy (41); Gerrard (69); Thompson (79)	42,517	P.Durkin

SOUTHAMPTON

Season	Venue	Date	Res	Scorers	Attendance	Referee
1992-93	Home	1-Sep-92	1-1	Wright (60)	30,024	R.Hart
1992-93	Away	13-Feb-93	1-2	Hutchison (61)	17,216	A.Buksh
1993-94	Home	30-Oct-93	4-2	Fowler (14, 29, 85); Rush (63)	32,818	D.Gallagher
1993-94	Away	14-Feb-94	2-4	Dicks (69 pen); Rush (86)	18,306	P.Foakes
1994-95	Away	31-Aug-94	2-0	Fowler (21); Barnes (77)	15,190	M.Bodenham
1994-95	Home	5-Apr-95	3-1	Rush (28,50); Fowler (71 pen)	29,881	S.Lodge
1995-96	Away	22-Oct-95	3-1	McManaman (23, 55); Redknapp (73)	15,245	D.Gallagher
1995-96	Home	2-Dec-95	1-1	Collymore (67)	38,007	R.Hart
1996-97	Home	7-Sep-96	2-1	Collymore (40); McManaman (89)	39,189	A.Wilkie
1996-97	Away	29-Dec-96	1-0	Barnes (77)	15,222	S.Dunn
1997-98	Home	20-Sep-97	1-1	Riedle (27)	15,252	P.Jones
1997-98	Home	7-Feb-98	2-3	Owen (24, 90)	43,550	J.Winter
1998-99	Away	16-Aug-98	2-1	Riedle (39); Owen (72)	15,202	P.Alcock
1998-99	Home	16-Jan-99	7-1	Fowler (21, 36, 47); Matteo (35); Carragher (54); Owen (63); Thompson (73)	44,011	U.Rennie
1999-00	Away	23-Oct-99	1-1	Camara (81)	15,241	N.Barry
1999-00	Home	7-May-00	0-0		44,015	P.Alcock

SUNDERLAND

Season	Venue	Date	Res	Scorers	Attendance	Referee
1996-97	Home	24-Aug-96	0-0		40,503	M.Bodenham
1996-97	Away	13-Apr-97	2-1	Fowler (33); McManaman (47)	21,938	D.Gallagher
1999-00	Away	20-Nov-99	2-0	Owen (63); Berger (85)	42,015	D.Gallagher
1999-00	Home	11-Mar-00	1-1	Berger (2 pen)	44,693	G.Poll

SWINDON TOWN

Season	Venue	Date	Res	Scorers	Attendance	Referee
1993-94	Away	22-Aug-93	5-0	Ruddock (19); McManaman (36, 63); Whelan (70); Marsh (80)	17,364	P.Don
1993-94	Home	11-Dec-93	2-2	Barnes (71); Wright (86)	32,739	K.Morton

TOTTENHAM HOTSPUR

Season	Venue	Date	Res	Scorers	Attendance	Referee
1992-93	Away	31-Oct-92	0-2		32,917	G.Ashby
1992-93	Home	8-May-93	6-2	Rush (21,85); Barnes (44,88); Harkness (47); Walters (82 pen)	43,385	S.Lodge
1993-94	Home	25-Aug-93	1-2	Clough (18)	42,456	K.Barratt
1993-94	Away	18-Dec-93	3-3	Fowler (48, 54 pen); Redknapp (51)	31,394	R.Hart
1994-95	Home	26-Nov-94	1-1	Fowler (39 pen)	35,007	S.Lodge
1994-95	Away	22-Mar-95	0-0		31,988	P.Danson
1995-96	Away	26-Aug-95	3-1	Barnes (7, 42); Fowler (55)	31,254	K.Cooper
1995-96	Home	3-Feb-96	0-0		40,628	S.Lodge

1996-97	Away	2-Dec-96	2-0	Thomas (45); McManaman (49)	32,899	G.Poll
1996-97	Home	3-May-97	2-1	Collymore (15); Berger (43)	40,003	M.Reed
1997-98	Home	8-Nov-97	4-0	McManaman (48); Owen (80); Leonhardsen (50); Redknapp (65)	38,005	S.Lodge
1997-98	Away	14-Mar-98	3-3	McManaman (20, 88); Ince (63)	30,245	U.Rennie
1998-99	Away	5-Dec-98	1-2	Berger (55)	36,521	G.Barber
1998-99	Home	1-May-99	3-2	Redknapp (49 pen); Ince (77); McManaman (79)	44,007	S.Lodge
1999-00	Away	3-Jan-00	0-1		36,044	A.Wilkie
1999-00	Home	9-Apr-00	2-0	Berger (34); Owen (61)	44,536	S.Lodge

WATFORD

Season	Venue	Date	Res	Scorers	Attendance	Referee
1999-00	Home	14-Aug-99	0-1		44,174	A.Wilkie
1999-00	Away	15-Jan-00	3-2	Berger (10); Thompson (41); Smicer (71)	21,367	S.Lodge

WEST HAM UNITED

Season	Venue	Date	Res	Scorers	Attendance	Referee
1993-94	Home	6-Nov-93	2-0	Clough (57); OG (83, Martin)	42,254	K.Barratt
1993-94	Away	23-Apr-94	2-1	Fowler (14); Rush (87)	26,106	S.Lodge
1994-95	Home	10-Sep-94	0-0		30,907	P.Danson
1994-95	Away	10-May-95	0-3		22,446	P.Durkin
1995-96	Away	22-Nov-95	0-0		24,324	J.Winter
1995-96	Home	8-Apr-96	2-0	Collymore (22); Barnes (38)	40,326	P.Alcock
1996-97	Away	29-Sep-96	2-1	Collymore (2); Thomas (55)	25,064	K.Burge
1996-97	Home	11-Jan-97	0-0		40,102	J.Winter
1997-98	Away	27-Sep-97	1-2	Fowler (52)	25,908	D.Gallagher
1997-98	Home	2-May-98	5-0	Owen (4); McAteer (21, 25); Leonhardsen (45); Ince (61)	44,414	J.Winter
1998-99	Away	12-Sep-98	1-2	Riedle (88)	26,029	J.Winter
1998-99	Home	20-Feb-99	2-2	Fowler (22); Owen (45)	44,511	N.Barry
1999-00	Home	27-Oct-99	1-0	Camara (43)	44,012	S.Lodge
1999-00	Away	27-Nov-99	0-1		26,043	G.Barber

WIMBLEDON

Season	Venue	Date	Res	Scorers	Attendance	Referee
1992-93	Home	26-Sep-92	2-3	Molby (35 pen); McManaman (39)	29,574	R.Milford
1992-93	Away	16-Jan-93	0-2		11,294	R.Dilkes
1993-94	Home	28-Dec-93	1-1	OG (27, Scales)	32,232	K.Cooper
1993-94	Away	4-Apr-94	1-1	Redknapp (65)	13,819	J.Borrett
1994-95	Home	22-Oct-94	3-0	McManaman (20); Fowler (35); Barnes (63)	31,139	P.Jones
1994-95	Away	2-May-95	0-0		12,041	T.Holbrook
1995-96	Away	9-Sep-95	0-1		19,530	K.Burge
1995-96	Home	13-Mar-96	2-2	McManaman (35); Collymore (68)	34,063	G.Willard
1996-97	Home	23-Nov-96	1-1	Collymore (1)	39,027	P.Danson
1996-97	Away	6-May-97	1-2	Owen (74)	20,016	P.Durkin
1997-98	Away	9-Aug-97	1-1	Owen (72 pen)	26,106	G.Willard
1997-98	Home	10-Jan-98	2-0	Redknapp (72, 84)	38,011	M.Bodenham
1998-99	Away	13-Dec-98	0-1		26,080	G.Willard
1998-99	Home	16-May-99	3-0	Berger (12); Riedle (50); Ince (65)	41,902	N.Barry
1999-00	Home	28-Dec-99	3-1	Owen (58); Berger (68); Fowler (80)	44,107	N.Barry
1999-00	Away	16-Apr-00	2-1	Heskey (36, 64)	26,102	M.Riley

INTRODUCTION

Founded in 1880 as West Gorton AFC. Following ground difficulties, having lost the use of the Kirkmanshulme Cricket Ground, was relaunched as Gorton AFC in 1884. There were more ground problems before, in 1889, the club moved to Hyde Road, adopted the title of Ardwick, and employed its first professional.

Ardwick joined the Football Alliance in 1891, finishing seventh, and was founder member of Football League Division Two in 1892. Ardwick too encountered difficulties and the club was restarted as Manchester City in 1894, retaining the Football League place. In 1923 the club moved to Maine Road. Premier League founder member 1992.

Ground:	Maine Road, Moss Side, Manchester, M14 7WN
Nickname:	Blues or The Citizens
Internet:	www.mcfc.co.uk

HONOURS

Football League Div 1:	Champions: 1936-37, 1967-68 Runners-up: 1903-04, 1920-21, 1976-77
Football League Div 1:	Champions: 1898-99, 1902-03, 1909-10, 1927-28, 1946-47, 1965-66. Runners-up: 1895-96, 1950-51, 1987-88
FA Cup Winners:	1969-70. Runners-up: 1973-74, 1980-81
Cup-Winners' Cup:	Winners 1969-70

EUROPEAN RECORD

Champions' League (1):	68-69
Cup-Winners Cup (2):	69-70 (W), 70-71
UEFA Cup (4):	72-73, 76-77, 77-78, 78-79.

FAPL RECORD SUMMARY

Most Total:	CURLE, Keith	131
Most Starts:	CURLE, Keith	131
Most Subs:	QUINN, Niall	20
Most SNU:	MARGETSON, Martyn	74
Most PS:	ROSLER, Uwe	13
Most Goals:	QUINN, Niall	30
Most Yel:	FLITCROFT, Garry	20
Most Red:	EDGHILL, Richard	2

PLAYING RECORD – SEASON TOTALS

Season	Pn	P	W	D	L	F	A	Pts
1992-93	9	42	15	12	15	56	51	57
1993-94	16	42	9	18	15	38	49	45
1994-95	17	42	12	13	17	53	64	49
1995-96	18	38	9	11	18	33	58	38
Totals		164	45	54	65	180	222	189

PLAYING RECORD – HOME TOTALS

Season	Pn	P	W	D	L	F	A	Pts
1992-93	9	21	7	8	6	30	25	29
1993-94	16	21	6	10	5	24	22	28
1994-95	17	21	8	7	6	37	28	31
1995-96	18	19	7	7	5	21	19	28
Totals		82	28	32	22	112	94	116

PLAYING RECORD – AWAY TOTALS

Season	Pn	P	W	D	L	F	A	Pts
1992-93	9	21	8	4	9	26	26	28
1993-94	16	21	3	8	10	14	27	17
1994-95	17	21	4	6	11	16	36	18
1995-96	18	19	2	4	13	12	39	10
Totals		82	17	22	43	68	128	73

HIGHEST HOME ATTENDANCES

	Attendance	Opponents	Date	Season
1	37,136	Manchester U.	20-Mar-93	1992-93
2	35,155	Manchester U.	7-Nov-93	1993-94
3	33,774	Newcastle U.	9-Apr-94	1993-94
4	33,594	Chelsea	30-Apr-94	1993-94
5	32,366	Leeds U.	14-Aug-93	1993-94

LOWEST HOME ATTENDANCES

	Attendance	Opponents	Date	Season
1	19,150	West Ham U.	24-Aug-94	1994-95
2	19,524	Wimbledon	21-Apr-93	1992-93
3	19,867	Everton	27-Aug-94	1994-95
4	19,971	Crystal P.	10-Sep-94	1994-95
5	20,089	Southampton	24-Oct-92	1992-93

TOP SCORER – SEASON BY SEASON

Season	Player	Goals
1992-93	White	16
1993-94	Sheron	6
1994-95	Rosler	15
1995-96	Rosler	9

PLAYERS WITH MOST PREMIERSHIP APPEARANCES

Tot	Player	St	Sb	Gls
131	CURLE, Keith	131	0	6
120	QUINN, Niall	100	20	30
115	FLITCROFT, Garry	109	6	13
103	PHELAN, Terry	102	1	2
93	COTON, Tony	92	1	0
85	BRIGHTWELL, Ian	80	5	1
79	ROSLER, Uwe	75	4	29
78	SUMMERBEE, Nicky	72	6	2

76	LOMAS, Steve	67	9	5
71	SHERON, Mike	62	9	17
69	McMAHON, Steve	65	4	1
58	WHITE, David	58	0	17
56	VONK, Michael	53	3	1
55	WALSH, Paul	55	0	16
54	HILL, Andy	48	6	1
51	BEAGRIE, Peter	46	5	3
50	HOLDEN, Rick	49	1	3

CLUB-BY-CLUB RESULTS

ARSENAL

Season	Venue	Date	Res	Scorers	Attendance	Referee
1992-93	Away	28-Sep-92	0-1		21,504	J.Martin
1992-93	Home	16-Jan-93	0-1		25,047	K.Burge
1993-94	Away	16-Oct-93	0-0		29,567	R.Milford
1993-94	Home	15-Jan-94	0-0		25,642	D.Allison
1994-95	Away	20-Aug-94	0-3		38,368	P.Durkin
1994-95	Home	12-Dec-94	1-2	Simpson (80)	20,500	G.Ashby
1995-96	Home	10-Sep-95	0-1		23,994	D.Gallagher
1995-96	Away	5-Mar-96	1-3	Creaney (54)	34,519	P.Jones

ASTON VILLA

Season	Venue	Date	Res	Scorers	Attendance	Referee
1992-93	Home	19-Dec-92	1-1	Flitcroft (58)	23,525	R.Bigger
1992-93	Away	18-Apr-93	1-3	Quinn (34)	33,108	P.Don
1993-94	Away	22-Feb-94	0-0		19,254	M.Bodenham
1993-94	Home	2-Apr-94	3-0	Beagrie (39); Walsh (45); Rosler (53)	26,075	P.Durkin
1994-95	Home	31-Dec-94	2-2	Rosler (14,52)	22,513	J.Worrall
1994-95	Away	3-May-95	1-1	Rosler (63)	30,133	S.Lodge
1995-96	Home	25-Nov-95	1-0	Kinkladze (85)	28,027	G.Ashby
1995-96	Away	27-Apr-96	1-0	Lomas (70)	39,336	D.Elleray

BLACKBURN ROVERS

Season	Venue	Date	Res	Scorers	Attendance	Referee
1992-93	Away	22-Aug-92	0-1		19,433	R.Hart
1992-93	Home	30-Jan-93	3-2	Sheron (33); Curle (74pen); White (78)	29,122	M.Peck
1993-94	Home	24-Aug-93	0-2		25,185	J.Lloyd
1993-94	Away	18-Dec-93	0-2		19,479	S.Lodge
1994-95	Home	26-Dec-94	1-3	Quinn (21)	23,387	P.Danson
1994-95	Away	17-Apr-95	3-2	Curle (32 pen); Rosler (57); Walsh (71)	27,857	K.Cooper
1995-96	Away	26-Dec-95	0-2		28,915	K.Cooper
1995-96	Home	2-Mar-96	1-1	Lomas (84)	29,078	P.Danson

BOLTON WANDERERS

Season	Venue	Date	Res	Scorers	Attendance	Referee
1995-96	Home	4-Nov-95	1-0	Summerbee (11)	28,397	R.Hart
1995-96	Away	30-Mar-96	1-1	Quinn (2)	21,050	R.Dilkes

CHELSEA

Season	Venue	Date	Res	Scorers	Attendance	Referee
1992-93	Home	20-Sep-92	0-1		22,420	K.Hackett
1992-93	Away	9-Jan-93	4-2	White (26); Sheron (29,87); Phelan (54)	15,939	V.Callow
1993-94	Away	22-Nov-93	0-0		10,128	M.Reed
1993-94	Home	30-Apr-94	2-2	Rosler (22); Walsh (37)	33,594	G.Poll
1994-95	Away	31-Aug-94	0-3		21,740	M.Reed
1994-95	Home	8-Mar-95	1-2	Gaudino (4)	21,880	D.Elleray
1995-96	Home	23-Dec-95	0-1		28,668	G.Willard
1995-96	Away	12-Mar-96	1-1	Clough (43)	17,078	P.Durkin

COVENTRY CITY

Season	Venue	Date	Res	Scorers	Attendance	Referee
1992-93	Away	21-Nov-92	3-2	Sheron (56); Quinn (66); Curle (78 pen)	14,590	P.Durkin
1992-93	Home	10-Mar-93	1-0	Flitcroft (35)	20,092	P.Durkin
1993-94	Home	27-Aug-93	1-1	Sheron (34)	21,537	P.Don
1993-94	Away	19-Feb-94	0-4		11,739	G.Ashby
1994-95	Away	29-Oct-94	0-1		15,804	M.Bodenham
1994-95	Home	14-Jan-95	0-0		20,632	D.Gallagher
1995-96	Away	23-Aug-95	1-2	Rosler (82)	16,568	P.Alcock
1995-96	Home	20-Jan-96	1-1	Rosler (55)	25,710	R.Hart

CRYSTAL PALACE

Season	Venue	Date	Res	Scorers	Attendance	Referee
1992-93	Away	17-Oct-92	0-0		14,005	M.Bodenham
1992-93	Home	5-May-93	0-0		21,167	S.Lodge
1994-95	Home	10-Sep-94	1-1	Walsh (18)	19,971	K.Burge
1994-95	Away	1-Apr-95	1-2	Rosler (58)	13,312	T.Holbrook

EVERTON

Season	Venue	Date	Res	Scorers	Attendance	Referee
1992-93	Away	31-Oct-92	3-1	Sheron (12, 62); White (19)	20,242	J.Worrall
1992-93	Home	8-May-93	2-5	White (39); Curle (73 pen)	25,180	K.Redfern
1993-94	Away	17-Aug-93	0-1		26,025	V.Callow
1993-94	Home	8-Dec-93	1-0	Griffiths (10)	25,513	P.Durkin
1994-95	Home	27-Aug-94	4-0	Rosler (56,80); Walsh (61,63)	19,867	P.Don
1994-95	Away	15-Mar-95	1-1	Gaudino (25)	28,485	G.Willard
1995-96	Home	30-Aug-95	0-2		28,432	S.Lodge
1995-96	Away	10-Feb-96	0-2		37,354	P.Alcock

IPSWICH TOWN

Season	Venue	Date	Res	Scorers	Attendance	Referee
1992-93	Away	12-Dec-92	1-3	Flitcroft (37)	16,833	R.Lewis
1992-93	Home	3-Apr-93	3-1	Quinn (55); Holden (66); Vonk (70)	20,680	R.Gifford
1993-94	Home	5-Feb-94	2-1	Griffiths (32); Flitcroft (73)	28,188	R.Hart
1993-94	Away	29-Mar-94	2-2	Walsh (32); Rosler (62)	12,871	P.Don
1994-95	Away	3-Dec-94	2-1	Flitcroft (20); Rosler (42)	13,504	S.Lodge
1994-95	Home	22-Feb-95	2-0	Quinn (68); Rosler (71)	21,430	K.Cooper

LEEDS UNITED

Season	Venue	Date	Res	Scorers	Attendance	Referee
1992-93	Home	7-Nov-92	4-0	Sheron (13); White (37); Hill (75); Brightwell,I. (80)	27,255	K.Morton
1992-93	Away	13-Mar-93	0-1		30,840	K.Hackett
1993-94	Home	14-Aug-93	1-1	Flitcroft (86)	32,366	D.Gallagher
1993-94	Away	4-Dec-93	2-3	Sheron (54); Griffiths (60)	33,820	R.Gifford
1994-95	Away	1-Oct-94	0-2		30,938	T.Holbrook
1994-95	Home	25-Feb-95	0-0		22,892	T.Holbrook
1995-96	Home	21-Oct-95	0-0		26,390	M.Bodenham
1995-96	Away	2-Dec-95	1-0	Creaney (60)	33,249	P.Alcock

LEICESTER CITY

Season	Venue	Date	Res	Scorers	Attendance	Referee
1994-95	Away	20-Nov-94	1-0	Quinn (16)	19,006	K.Morton
1994-95	Home	25-Jan-95	0-1		21,007	S.Lodge

LIVERPOOL

Season	Venue	Date	Res	Scorers	Attendance	Referee
1992-93	Away	28-Dec-92	1-1	Quinn (39)	43,037	D.Allison
1992-93	Home	12-Apr-93	1-1	Flitcroft (12)	28,098	M.Reed
1993-94	Home	23-Oct-93	1-1	White (66)	30,403	M.Bodenham
1993-94	Away	22-Jan-94	1-2	Griffiths (3)	41,872	R.Milford
1994-95	Away	28-Dec-94	0-2		38,122	R.Hart
1994-95	Home	14-Apr-95	2-1	Summerbee (17); Gaudino (73)	27,055	J.Worrall
1995-96	Away	28-Oct-95	0-6		39,267	A.Wilkie
1995-96	Home	5-May-96	2-2	Rosler (71 pen); Symons (78)	31,436	S.Lodge

MANCHESTER UNITED

Season	Venue	Date	Res	Scorers	Attendance	Referee
1992-93	Away	6-Dec-92	1-2	Quinn (74)	35,408	G.Ashby
1992-93	Home	20-Mar-93	1-1	Quinn (57)	37,136	R.Hart
1993-94	Home	7-Nov-93	2-3	Quinn (21,32)	35,155	R.Hart
1993-94	Away	23-Apr-94	0-2		44,333	K.Morton
1994-95	Away	10-Nov-94	0-5		43,738	K.Cooper
1994-95	Home	11-Feb-95	0-3		26,368	P.Don
1995-96	Away	14-Oct-95	0-1		35,707	R.Dilkes
1995-96	Home	6-Apr-96	2-3	Kavelashvili (39); Rosler (71)	29,688	M.Reed

MIDDLESBROUGH

Season	Venue	Date	Res	Scorers	Attendance	Referee
1992-93	Away	19-Aug-92	0-2		15,369	S.Lodge
1992-93	Home	12-Sep-92	0-1		25,244	R.Lewis
1995-96	Home	23-Sep-95	0-1		25,865	G.Willard
1995-96	Away	9-Dec-95	1-4	Kinkladze (14)	29,469	S.Lodge

NEWCASTLE UNITED

Season	Venue	Date	Res	Scorers	Attendance	Referee
1993-94	Away	1-Jan-94	0-2		35,585	K.Morton
1993-94	Home	9-Apr-94	2-1	Walsh (33); D.Brightwell (48)	33,774	J.Borrett
1994-95	Away	2-Jan-95	0-0		34,437	A.Wilkie

1994-95	Home	29-Apr-95	0-0			27,389	G.Poll
1995-96	Away	16-Sep-95	1-3	Creaney (81)		36,501	J.Winter
1995-96	Home	24-Feb-96	3-3	Quinn (16, 62); Rosler (77)		31,115	M.Bodenham

NORWICH CITY

Season	Venue	Date	Res	Scorers	Attendance	Referee
1992-93	Home	26-Aug-92	3-1	White (45,80); McMahon (90)	23,182	D.Elleray
1992-93	Away	20-Feb-93	1-2	Sheron (46)	16,386	B.Hill
1993-94	Away	20-Nov-93	1-1	Quinn (59)	16,626	K.Hackett
1993-94	Home	16-Apr-94	1-1	Rosler (46)	28,020	D.Elleray
1994-95	Home	24-Sep-94	2-0	Quinn (53); Rosler (62)	21,031	G.Poll
1994-95	Away	4-Mar-95	1-1	Simpson (86)	16,266	D.Gallagher

NOTTINGHAM FOREST

Season	Venue	Date	Res	Scorers	Attendance	Referee
1992-93	Home	3-Oct-92	2-2	Holden (17); Simpson (64)	22,571	R.Milford
1992-93	Away	27-Feb-93	2-0	White (19); Flitcroft (89)	25,956	A.Buksh
1994-95	Home	8-Oct-94	3-3	Quinn (41,54); Lomas (59)	23,150	P.Durkin
1994-95	Away	6-May-95	0-1		28,882	P.Jones
1995-96	Away	30-Sep-95	0-3		25,620	M.Reed
1995-96	Home	18-Dec-95	1-1	Rosler (16)	25,660	K.Burge

OLDHAM ATHLETIC

Season	Venue	Date	Res	Scorers	Attendance	Referee
1992-93	Home	29-Aug-92	3-3	Quinn (4); Vonk (8); White (23)	27,255	D.Gallagher
1992-93	Away	26-Jan-93	1-0	Quinn (77)	14,903	J.Borrett
1993-94	Home	4-Oct-93	1-1	Sheron (87)	21,401	J.Borrett
1993-94	Away	26-Mar-94	0-0		16,462	K.Hackett

QPR

Season	Venue	Date	Res	Scorers	Attendance	Referee
1992-93	Home	17-Aug-92	1-1	White (37)	24,471	M.Bodenham
1992-93	Away	6-Feb-93	1-1	Sheron (77)	13,003	M.Reed
1993-94	Home	11-Sep-93	3-0	Quinn (17); Sheron (37); Flitcroft (70)	24,445	A.Wilkie
1993-94	Away	5-Mar-94	1-1	Rocastle (55)	13,474	S.Lodge
1994-95	Away	15-Oct-94	2-1	Flitcroft (56); Walsh (58)	13,631	G.Willard
1994-95	Home	14-May-95	2-3	Quinn (26); Curle (80 pen)	27,850	M.Reed
1995-96	Away	26-Aug-95	0-1		14,212	P.Danson
1995-96	Home	3-Feb-96	2-0	Clough (25); Symons (50)	27,509	G.Poll

SHEFFIELD UNITED

Season	Venue	Date	Res	Scorers	Attendance	Referee
1992-93	Home	26-Dec-92	2-0	White (20,55)	27,455	K.Barratt
1992-93	Away	9-Apr-93	1-1	OG (8, Pemberton)	18,231	K.Cooper
1993-94	Away	25-Sep-93	1-0	Sheron (56)	20,067	D.Elleray
1993-94	Home	19-Mar-94	0-0		25,448	A.Gunn

SHEFFIELD WEDNESDAY

Season	Venue	Date	Res	Scorers	Attendance	Referee
1992-93	Away	5-Sep-92	3-0	White (20,55); Vonk (75)	27,169	R.Bigger
1992-93	Home	23-Feb-93	1-2	Quinn (84)	23,619	M.Bodenham

1993-94	Home	27-Nov-93	1-3	Sheron (85)	23,416	H.King
1993-94	Away	7-May-94	1-1	Rosler (48)	33,589	T.Holbrook
1994-95	Away	17-Sep-94	1-1	Walsh (44)	26,776	D.Gallagher
1994-95	Home	18-Mar-95	3-2	Rosler (37,83); Walsh (52)	23,355	K.Burge
1995-96	Away	18-Nov-95	1-1	Lomas (55)	24,422	G.Poll
1995-96	Home	13-Apr-96	1-0	Rosler (65)	30,898	R.Hart

SOUTHAMPTON

Season	Venue	Date	Res	Scorers	Attendance	Referee
1992-93	Home	24-Oct-92	1-0	Sheron (74)	20,089	P.Don
1992-93	Away	1-May-93	1-0	White (42)	16,730	J.Lloyd
1993-94	Home	28-Dec-93	1-1	Phelan (29)	24,712	A.Wilkie
1993-94	Away	4-Apr-94	1-0	Karl (88)	16,377	B.Hill
1994-95	Home	5-Nov-94	3-3	Walsh (50,61); Beagrie (79)	21,589	M.Reed
1994-95	Away	4-Feb-95	2-2	Kernaghan (29); Flitcroft (88)	14,902	P.Durkin
1995-96	Away	31-Jan-96	1-1	Rosler (84)	15,172	S.Dunn
1995-96	Home	16-Mar-96	2-1	Kinkladze (32, 37)	29,550	J.Winter

SWINDON TOWN

Season	Venue	Date	Res	Scorers	Attendance	Referee
1993-94	Away	1-Sep-93	3-1	Vonk (74); Quinn (79); Mike (90)	16,067	K.Cooper
1993-94	Home	25-Feb-94	2-1	OG (25,Horlock); Rocastle (50)	26,360	P.Foakes

TOTTENHAM HOTSPUR

Season	Venue	Date	Res	Scorers	Attendance	Referee
1992-93	Home	28-Nov-92	0-1		25,496	D.Allison
1992-93	Away	24-Mar-93	1-3	Sheron (60)	27,247	J.Martin
1993-94	Away	21-Aug-93	0-1		24,535	K.Hackett
1993-94	Home	11-Dec-93	0-2		21,566	G.Poll
1994-95	Home	22-Oct-94	5-2	Walsh (15,45); Quinn (41); Lomas (52); Flitcroft (79)	25,473	D.Elleray
1994-95	Away	11-Apr-95	1-2	Rosler (49)	27,410	A.Wilkie
1995-96	Home	19-Aug-95	1-1	Rosler (52)	30,827	G.Poll
1995-96	Away	13-Jan-96	0-1		31,438	D.Gallagher

WEST HAM UNITED

Season	Venue	Date	Res	Scorers	Attendance	Referee
1993-94	Away	1-Nov-93	1-3	Curle (86 pen)	16,605	K.Morton
1993-94	Home	12-Feb-94	0-0		29,118	V.Callow
1994-95	Home	24-Aug-94	3-0	Walsh (14); Beagrie (42); Rosler (56)	19,150	R.Hart
1994-95	Away	17-Dec-94	0-3		17,286	T.Holbrook
1995-96	Home	1-Jan-96	2-1	Quinn (21, 78)	24,024	M.Reed
1995-96	Away	23-Mar-96	2-4	Quinn (76, 90)	24,017	K.Cooper

WIMBLEDON

Season	Venue	Date	Res	Scorers	Attendance	Referee
1992-93	Away	1-Sep-92	1-0	White (49)	4,714	M.Reed
1992-93	Home	21-Apr-93	1-1	Holden (84)	19,524	H.King
1993-94	Away	20-Sep-93	0-1		8,533	K.Barratt
1993-94	Home	12-Mar-94	0-1		23,981	D.Frampton
1994-95	Home	26-Nov-94	2-0	Flitcroft (7); Rosler (88)	21,131	A.Wilkie
1994-95	Away	21-Mar-95	0-2		5,268	R.Gifford
1995-96	Home	22-Nov-95	1-0	Quinn (90)	23,617	P.Durkin
1995-96	Away	8-Apr-96	0-3		11,844	G.Poll

INTRODUCTION

Came into being in 1902 upon the bankruptcy of Newton Heath. Predecessors appear to have been formed in 1878 as Newton Heath (LYR) when workers at the Carriage and Wagon Department at the Lancashire and Yorkshire Railway formed a club. This soon outgrew railway competition. Turned professional in 1885 and founder members of Football Alliance in 1889. In 1892 Alliance runners-up Newton Heath were elected to an enlarged Division One of the Football League. In 1902 the club became Manchester United and, in February 1910, moved from Bank Street, Clayton, to Old Trafford. Premier League founder members 1992. Five times Premiership champions and the only side to have completed the Treble to cap off their greatest season in 1998-99.

Ground:	Old Trafford, Manchester, M16 0RA
Nickname:	Red Devils
Internet:	www.manutd.com

HONOURS

FA Premier League:	Champions 1992-93, 1993-94, 1995-96, 1996-97, 1998-99
	Runners-up 1994-95, 1997-98
Football League Div 1:	Champions 1907-8, 1910-11, 1951-52, 1955-56, 1956-57, 1964-65, 1966-67
	Runners-up 1946-47, 1947-48, 1948-49, 1950-51, 1958-59, 1963-64, 1967-68, 1979-80, 1987-88, 1991-92
Football League Div 2:	Champions 1935-36, 1974-75
	Runners-up 1896-97, 1905-06, 1924-25, 1937-38
FA Cup:	Winners 1908-09, 1947-48, 1962-63, 1976-77, 1982-83, 1984-85, 1989-90, 1993-94, 1995-96, 1998-99
	Runners-up 1957, 1958, 1976, 1979, 1995
Football League Cup:	Winners 1991-92
	Runners-up 1982-83, 1990-91, 1993-94
Champions' League:	Winners 1967-68, 1998-99
Cup-Winners' Cup:	Winners 1990-91

EUROPEAN RECORD

Champions' League (11): 56-57 (SF), 57-58 (SF), 65-66 (SF), 67-68 (W), 68-69 (SF), 93-94 (SF), 94-95 (CL), 96-97 (SF), 97-98 (QF), 98-99 (W); 99-00 (QF).

Cup-Winners' Cup (5): 63-64 (QF), 77-78 (2), 83-84 (SF), 90-91 (W), 91-92 (2)

UEFA Cup (7): 64-65 (SF), 76-77 (2), 80-81 (1), 82-83 (1), 84-85 (QF), 92-93 (1), 95-96 (1).

FAPL RECORD SUMMARY

Most Total:	IRWIN, Denis	263
Most Starts:	IRWIN, Denis	256
Most Subs:	McCLAIR, Brian	56
Most SNU:	VAN DER GOUW, Raimond	108
Most PS:	GIGGS, Ryan	48
Most Goals:	COLE, Andy	81
Most Yel:	KEANE, Roy	45
Most Red:	BUTT, Nicky	4

PLAYING RECORD – SEASON TOTALS

Season	Pn	P	W	D	L	F	A	Pts
1992-93	1	42	24	12	6	67	31	84
1993-94	1	42	27	11	4	80	38	92
1994-95	2	42	26	10	6	77	28	88
1995-96	1	38	25	7	6	73	35	82
1996-97	1	38	21	12	5	76	44	75
1997-98	2	38	23	8	7	73	26	77
1998-99	1	38	22	13	3	80	37	79
1999-00	1	38	28	7	3	97	45	91
Totals		316	196	80	40	623	284	668

PLAYING RECORD – HOME TOTALS

Season	Pn	P	W	D	L	F	A	Pts
1992-93	1	21	14	5	2	39	14	47
1993-94	1	21	14	6	1	39	13	48
1994-95	2	21	16	4	1	42	4	52
1995-96	1	19	15	4	0	36	9	49
1996-97	1	19	12	5	2	38	17	41
1997-98	2	19	13	4	2	42	9	43
1998-99	1	19	14	4	1	45	18	46
1999-00	1	19	15	4	0	59	16	49
Totals		158	113	36	9	340	100	375

PLAYING RECORD – AWAY TOTALS

Season	Pn	P	W	D	L	F	A	Pts
1992-93	1	21	10	7	4	28	17	37
1993-94	1	21	13	5	3	41	25	44
1994-95	2	21	10	6	5	35	24	36
1995-96	1	19	10	3	6	37	26	33
1996-97	1	19	9	7	3	38	27	34
1997-98	2	19	10	4	5	31	17	34
1998-99	1	19	8	9	2	35	19	33
1999-00	1	19	13	3	3	38	29	42
Totals		158	83	44	31	283	184	293

MANCHESTER UNITED

HIGHEST HOME ATTENDANCES

	Attendance	Opponents	Date	Season
1	61,629	Tottenham H.	6-May-00	1999-00
2	61,619	Derby Co.	11-Mar-00	1999-00
3	61,612	Sunderland	15-Apr-00	1999-00
4	61,611	West Ham U.	1-Apr-00	1999-00
5	61,593	Chelsea	24-Apr-00	1999-00

LOWEST HOME ATTENDANCES

	Attendance	Opponents	Date	Season
1	29,736	Crystal P.	2-Sep-92	1992-93
2	31,296	Leeds U.	6-Sep-92	1992-93
3	31,704	Ipswich T.	22-Aug-92	1992-93
4	31,901	Everton	19-Aug-92	1992-93
5	31,966	West Ham U.	23-Aug-95	1995-96

TOP SCORER – SEASON BY SEASON

Season	Player	Goals
1992-93	Hughes	15
1993-94	Cantona	18
1994-95	Kanchelskis	14
1995-96	Cantona	14
1996-97	Solskjaer	18
1997-98	Cole	16
1998-99	Yorke	18
1999-00	Yorke	20

PLAYERS WITH MOST PREMIERSHIP APPEARANCES

Tot	Player	St	Sb	Gls
263	IRWIN, Denis	256	7	18
252	SCHMEICHEL, Peter	252	0	0
250	GIGGS, Ryan	234	16	54
206	PALLISTER, Gary	206	0	8
185	KEANE, Roy	177	8	24
178	BUTT, Nicky	140	38	15
175	BECKHAM, David	158	17	36
171	NEVILLE, Gary	167	4	2
165	COLE,, Andy	139	26	81

CLUB-BY-CLUB RESULTS

ARSENAL

Season	Venue	Date	Res	Scorers	Attendance	Referee
1992-93	Away	28-Nov-92	1-0	Hughes (27)	29,739	H.King
1992-93	Home	24-Mar-93	0-0		37,301	V.Callow
1993-94	Home	19-Sep-93	1-0	Cantona (37)	44,009	V.Callow
1993-94	Away	22-Mar-94	2-2	Sharpe (10, 53)	36,203	V.Callow
1994-95	Away	26-Nov-94	0-0		38,301	K.Morton
1994-95	Home	22-Mar-95	3-0	Hughes (27); Sharpe (32); Kanchelskis (79)	43,623	K.Cooper
1995-96	Away	4-Nov-95	0-1		38,317	P.Durkin
1995-96	Home	20-Mar-96	1-0	Cantona (66)	50,028	G.Willard
1996-97	Home	16-Nov-96	1-0	OG (61, Winterburn)	55,210	G.Poll
1996-97	Away	19-Feb-97	2-1	Cole (8)	38,172	M.Bodenham
1997-98	Away	9-Nov-97	2-3	Sheringham (32, 41)	38,083	M.Bodenham
1997-98	Home	14-Mar-98	0-1		55,174	A.Wilkie
1998-99	Away	20-Sep-98	0-3		38,142	G.Barber
1998-99	Home	17-Feb-99	1-1	Cole (60)	55,171	G.Willard
1999-00	Away	22-Aug-99	2-1	Keane (58, 88)	38,147	G.Poll
1999-00	Home	24-Jan-00	1-1	Sheringham (73)	58,293	P.Durkin

ASTON VILLA

Season	Venue	Date	Res	Scorers	Attendance	Referee
1992-93	Away	7-Nov-92	0-1		39,063	D.Elleray
1992-93	Home	14-Mar-93	1-1	Huges (57)	36,163	A.Gunn
1993-94	Away	23-Aug-93	2-1	Sharpe (17, 74)	39,624	D.Elleray
1993-94	Home	19-Dec-93	3-1	Cantona (21, 90); Ince (90)	44,499	J.Worrall
1994-95	Away	6-Nov-94	2-1	Ince (44); Kanchelskis (49)	32,136	P.Don

1994-95	Home	4-Feb-95	1-0	Cole (17)	43,795	D.Elleray
1995-96	Away	19-Aug-95	1-3	Beckham (82)	34,655	R.Hart
1995-96	Home	13-Jan-96	0-0		42,667	G.Willard
1996-97	Away	21-Sep-96	0-0		39,339	S.Lodge
1996-97	Home	1-Jan-97	0-0		55,113	D.Elleray
1997-98	Home	15-Dec-97	1-0	Giggs (51)	55,151	P.Durkin
1997-98	Away	18-Feb-98	2-0	Beckham (82); Giggs (89)	39,372	M.Bodenham
1998-99	Away	5-Dec-98	1-1	Scholes (47)	39,241	M.Riley
1998-99	Home	1-May-99	2-1	OG (20, Watson); Beckham (46)	55,189	K.Burge
1999-00	Home	30-Oct-99	3-0	Scholes (30); Cole (45); Keane (65)	55,211	A.Wilkie
1999-00	Away	14-May-00	1-0	Sheringham (65)	39,217	P.Durkin

BARNSLEY

Season	Venue	Date	Res	Scorers	Attendance	Referee
1997-98	Home	25-Oct-97	7-0	Cole (7, 18, 44); Giggs (42, 56); Scholes (58);Poborsky (79)	55,142	M.Riley
1997-98	Away	10-May-98	2-0	Cole (5); Sheringham (67)	18,694	P.Durkin

BLACKBURN ROVERS

Season	Venue	Date	Res	Scorers	Attendance	Referee
1992-93	Away	24-Oct-92	0-0		20,305	M.Reed
1992-93	Home	3-May-93	3-1	Giggs (21); Ince (59); Pallister (90)	40,447	J.Borrett
1993-94	Home	26-Dec-93	1-1	Ince (88)	44,511	D.Gallagher
1993-94	Away	2-Apr-94	0-2		20,866	R.Milford
1994-95	Away	23-Oct-94	4-2	Cantona (45 pen); Kanchelskis (52,82); Hughes (67)	30,260	G.Ashby
1994-95	Home	22-Jan-95	1-0	Cantona (80)	43,742	P.Durkin
1995-96	Away	28-Aug-95	2-1	Sharpe (46); Beckham (68)	29,843	D.Elleray
1995-96	Home	10-Feb-96	1-0	Sharpe (14)	42,681	K.Burge
1996-97	Home	25-Aug-96	2-2	Cruyff (38); Solskjaer (68)	54,178	S.Dunn
1996-97	Away	12-Apr-97	3-2	Cole (32); Scholes (42); Cantona (81)	30,476	M.Bodenham
1997-98	Home	30-Nov-97	4-0	Solskjaer (17, 53); OG (59, Henchoz); OG (85, Kenna)	38,094	A.Wilkie
1997-98	Away	6-Apr-98	3-1	Cole (56); Scholes (73); Beckham (90)	30,547	G.Ashby
1998-99	Home	14-Nov-98	3-2	Scholes (32, 58); Yorke (44)	55,198	M.Reed
1998-99	Away	12-May-99	0-0		30,463	M.Reed

BOLTON WANDERERS

Season	Venue	Date	Res	Scorers	Attendance	Referee
1995-96	Home	16-Sep-95	3-0	Scholes (17, 85); Giggs (33)	32,812	S.Dunn
1995-96	Away	25-Feb-96	6-0	Beckham (5); Bruce (15); Cole (70); Scholes (76, 79); Butt (90)	21,381	D.Gallagher
1997-98	Away	20-Sep-97	0-0		25,000	P.Durkin
1997-98	Home	7-Feb-98	1-1	Cole (85)	55,156	S.Lodge

BRADFORD CITY

Season	Venue	Date	Res	Scorers	Attendance	Referee
1999-00	Home	26-Dec-99	4-0	Fortune (75); Yorke (79); Cole (87); Keane (88)	55,188	P.Jones
1999-00	Away	25-Mar-00	4-0	Yorke (37, 40); Scholes (71); Beckham (79)	18,276	G.Poll

CHARLTON ATHLETIC

Season	Venue	Date	Res	Scorers	Attendance	Referee
1998-99	Home	9-Sep-98	4-1	Solskjaer (38, 63); Yorke (45, 48)	55,147	P.Durkin
1998-99	Away	31-Jan-99	1-0	Yorke (89)	20,043	G.Willard

CHELSEA

Season	Venue	Date	Res	Scorers	Attendance	Referee
1992-93	Away	19-Dec-92	1-1	Cantona (71)	34,496	R.Lewis
1992-93	Home	17-Apr-93	3-0	Hughes (23); OG (44, Clarke); Cantona (48)	40,139	H.King
1993-94	Away	11-Sep-93	0-1		37,064	P.Foakes
1993-94	Home	5-Mar-94	0-1		44,745	D.Gallagher
1994-95	Away	26-Dec-94	3-2	Hughes (21); Cantona (45 pen); McClair (78)	31,161	M.Reed
1994-95	Home	17-Apr-95	0-0		43,728	S.Lodge
1995-96	Away	21-Oct-95	4-1	Scholes (3, 10); Giggs (79); McClair (88)	31,019	A.Wilkie
1995-96	Home	2-Dec-95	1-1	Beckham (60)	42,019	M.Bodenham
1996-97	Home	2-Nov-96	1-3	Poborsky (80)	55,198	K.Burge
1996-97	Away	22-Feb-97	1-1	Beckham (68)	28,336	G.Ashby
1997-98	Home	24-Sep-97	2-2	Scholes (35); Solskjaer (86)	55,163	G.Willard
1997-98	Away	28-Feb-98	1-0	Neville,P. (31)	34,511	S.Dunn
1998-99	Home	16-Dec-98	1-1	Cole (45)	55,159	G.Barber
1998-99	Away	29-Dec-98	0-0		34,741	M.Riley
1999-00	Away	3-Oct-99	0-5		34,909	D.Gallagher
1999-00	Home	24-Apr-00	3-2	Yorke (10, 69); Solskjaer (39)	61,593	S.Dunn

COVENTRY CITY

Season	Venue	Date	Res	Scorers	Attendance	Referee
1992-93	Home	28-Dec-92	5-0	Giggs (6); Hughes (40); Cantona (64 pen); Sharpe (78); Irwin (83)	36,025	R.Groves
1992-93	Away	12-Apr-93	1-0	Irwin (40)	24,429	R.Gifford
1993-94	Away	27-Nov-93	1-0	Cantona (60)	17,009	S.Lodge
1993-94	Home	8-May-94	0-0		44,717	S.Lodge
1994-95	Home	3-Jan-95	2-0	Scholes (29); Cantona (50 pen)	43,130	G.Willard
1994-95	Away	1-May-95	3-2	Scholes (32); Cole (55,79)	21,885	P.Don
1995-96	Away	22-Nov-95	4-0	Irwin (28); McClair (47, 76); Beckham (57)	23,344	K.Burge
1995-96	Home	8-Apr-96	1-0	Cantona (47)	50,332	D.Gallagher
1996-97	Away	18-Jan-97	2-0	Giggs (60); Solskjaer (79)	23,085	S.Dunn
1996-97	Home	1-Mar-97	3-1	OG (4, Breen); Cole (5); Poborsky (47)	55,230	G.Barber
1997-98	Home	30-Aug-97	3-0	Cole (1); Keane (72); Poborsky (89)	55,074	G.Ashby
1997-98	Away	28-Dec-97	2-3	Solskjaer (30); Sheringham (47)	23,054	N.Barry
1998-99	Home	12-Sep-98	2-0	Yorke (21); Johnsen (48)	55,193	U.Rennie
1998-99	Away	20-Feb-99	1-0	Giggs (78)	22,596	D.Gallagher
1999-00	Away	25-Aug-99	2-1	Scholes (63); Yorke (75)	22,024	A.Wilkie
1999-00	Home	5-Feb-00	3-2	Cole (39, 54); Scholes (77)	61,380	A.Wilkie

CRYSTAL PALACE

Season	Venue	Date	Res	Scorers	Attendance	Referee
1992-93	Home	2-Sep-92	1-0	Hughes (88)	29,736	V.Callow
1992-93	Away	21-Apr-93	2-0	Hughes (64); Ince (89)	30,115	K.Barratt
1994-95	Home	19-Nov-94	3-0	Irwin (8); Cantona (33); Kanchelskis (50)	43,788	B.Hill
1994-95	Away	25-Jan-95	1-1	May (56)	18,224	A.Wilkie

1997-98	Home	4-Oct-97	2-0	Sheringham (77); OG (29, Hreidarsson)	55,143	S.Lodge
1997-98	Away	27-Apr-98	3-0	Scholes (6); Butt (21); Cole (84)	26,180	P.Jones

DERBY COUNTY

Season	Venue	Date	Res	Scorers	Attendance	Referee
1996-97	Away	3-Sep-96	1-1	Beckham (38)	18,026	M.Reed
1996-97	Home	5-Apr-97	2-3	Cantona (47); Solskjaer (76)	55,243	D.Elleray
1997-98	Away	18-Oct-97	2-2	Sheringham (51); Cole (83)	30,014	G.Poll
1997-98	Home	21-Feb-98	2-0	Giggs (19); Irwin (71 pen)	55,170	M.Reed
1998-99	Away	24-Oct-98	1-1	Cruyff (86)	30,867	P.Durkin
1998-99	Home	3-Feb-99	1-0	Yorke (65)	55,174	S.Lodge
1999-00	Away	20-Nov-99	2-1	Butt (53); Cole (83)	33,370	M.Reed
1999-00	Home	11-Mar-00	3-1	Yorke (12, 70, 72)	61,619	J.Winter

EVERTON

Season	Venue	Date	Res	Scorers	Attendance	Referee
1992-93	Home	19-Aug-92	0-3		31,901	K.Barratt
1992-93	Away	12-Sep-92	2-0	McClair (29); Bruce (76 pen)	30,002	M.Peck
1993-94	Away	23-Oct-93	1-0	Sharpe (53)	35,455	K.Hackett
1993-94	Home	22-Jan-94	1-0	Giggs (27)	44,750	R.Gifford
1994-95	Home	1-Oct-94	2-0	Kanchelskis (41); Sharpe (88)	43,803	G.Poll
1994-95	Away	25-Feb-95	0-1		40,011	J.Worrall
1995-96	Away	9-Sep-95	3-2	Sharpe (3, 49); Giggs (73)	39,496	G.Poll
1995-96	Home	21-Feb-96	2-0	Keane (30); Giggs (82)	42,459	M.Bodenham
1996-97	Home	21-Aug-96	2-2	Cruyff (70); OG (81, Unsworth)	54,943	G.Poll
1996-97	Away	22-Mar-97	2-0	Solskjaer (35); Cantona (79)	40,079	D.Gallagher
1997-98	Away	27-Aug-97	2-0	Beckham (29); Sheringham (51)	40,079	K.Burge
1997-98	Home	26-Dec-97	2-0	Berg (14); Cole (34)	55,167	U.Rennie
1998-99	Away	31-Oct-98	4-1	Yorke (14); OG (23, Short); Cole (59); Blomqvist (64)	40,079	P.Jones
1998-99	Home	22-Mar-99	3-1	Solskjaer (55); Neville,G. (63); Beckham (67)	55,182	M.Riley
1999-00	Away	8-Aug-99	1-1	Yorke (7)	39,141	D.Gallagher
1999-00	Home	4-Dec-99	5-1	Irwin (26 pen); Solskjaer (29, 43, 52, 58)	55,193	G.Poll

IPSWICH TOWN

Season	Venue	Date	Res	Scorers	Attendance	Referee
1992-93	Home	22-Aug-92	1-1	Irwin (57)	31,704	G.Ashby
1992-93	Away	30-Jan-93	1-2	McClair (85)	22,068	J.Key
1993-94	Home	24-Nov-93	0-0		43,300	T.Holbrook
1993-94	Away	1-May-94	2-1	Cantona (36); Giggs (47)	22,478	A.Gunn
1994-95	Away	24-Sep-94	2-3	Cantona (70); Scholes (73)	22,559	P.Jones
1994-95	Home	4-Mar-95	9-0	Keane (15); Cole (23,36,52,64,88); Hughes (54,58); Ince (72)	43,804	G.Poll

LEEDS UNITED

Season	Venue	Date	Res	Scorers	Attendance	Referee
1992-93	Home	6-Sep-92	2-0	Kanchelskis (28); Bruce (44)	31,296	P.Don
1992-93	Away	8-Feb-93	0-0		34,166	K.Morton
1993-94	Home	1-Jan-94	0-0		44,724	D.Elleray
1993-94	Away	27-Apr-94	2-0	Kanchelskis (47); Giggs (85)	41,127	P.Don
1994-95	Away	11-Sep-94	1-2	Cantona (73 pen)	39,396	D.Elleray

Season	Venue	Date	Res	Scorers	Attendance	Referee
1994-95	Home	2-Apr-95	0-0		43,712	R.Gifford
1995-96	Away	24-Dec-95	1-3	Cole (33)	39,801	D.Gallagher
1995-96	Home	17-Apr-96	1-0	Keane (72)	48,382	K.Cooper
1996-97	Away	7-Sep-96	4-0	OG (2, Martyn); Butt (46); Poborsky (76); Cantona (90)	39,694	M.Bodenham
1996-97	Home	28-Dec-96	1-0	Cantona (9 pen)	55,256	P.Alcock
1997-98	Away	27-Sep-97	0-1		39,952	M.Bodenham
1997-98	Home	4-May-98	3-0	Giggs (6); Irwin (31 pen); Beckham (59)	55,167	G.Willard
1998-99	Home	29-Nov-98	3-2	Solskjaer (45); Keane (46); Butt (77)	55,172	G.Poll
1998-99	Away	25-Apr-99	1-1	Cole (56)	40,255	D.Gallagher
1999-00	Home	14-Aug-99	2-0	Yorke (76, 80)	55,187	N.Barry
1999-00	Away	20-Feb-00	1-0	Cole (52)	40,160	P.Jones

LEICESTER CITY

Season	Venue	Date	Res	Scorers	Attendance	Referee
1994-95	Home	28-Dec-94	1-1	Kanchelskis (61)	43,789	D.Gallagher
1994-95	Away	15-Apr-95	4-0	Sharpe (33); Cole (45,52); Ince (90)	21,281	M.Bodenham
1996-97	Home	30-Nov-96	3-1	Butt (75, 86); Solskjaer (84)	55,196	M.Bodenham
1996-97	Away	3-May-97	2-2	Walsh (15); Marshall (20)	21,068	A.Wilkie
1997-98	Away	23-Aug-97	0-0		21,221	D.Gallagher
1997-98	Home	31-Jan-98	0-1		55,156	G.Ashby
1998-99	Home	15-Aug-98	2-2	Sheringham (79); Beckham (90)	55,052	N.Barry
1998-99	Away	16-Jan-99	6-2	Yorke (10, 63, 84); Cole (49, 61); Stam (89)	22,091	S.Dunn
1999-00	Home	6-Nov-99	2-0	Cole (30, 83)	55,191	P.Durkin
1999-00	Away	18-Mar-00	2-0	Beckham (33); Yorke (83)	22,170	R.Harris

LIVERPOOL

Season	Venue	Date	Res	Scorers	Attendance	Referee
1992-93	Home	18-Oct-92	2-2	Hughes (78, 90)	33,243	K.Hackett
1992-93	Away	6-Mar-93	2-1	Hughes (42); McClair (56)	44,374	R.Milford
1993-94	Away	4-Jan-94	3-3	Bruce (9); Giggs (20); Irwin (24)	42,795	P.Don
1993-94	Home	30-Mar-94	1-0	Ince (36)	44,751	K.Hackett
1994-95	Home	17-Sep-94	2-0	Kanchelskis (72); McClair (73)	43,740	K.Morton
1994-95	Away	19-Mar-95	0-2		38,906	G.Ashby
1995-96	Home	1-Oct-95	2-2	Butt (1); Cantona (70 pen)	34,934	D.Elleray
1995-96	Away	17-Dec-95	0-2		40,546	G.Poll
1996-97	Home	12-Oct-96	1-0	Beckham (23)	55,128	D.Elleray
1996-97	Away	19-Apr-97	3-1	Pallister (13, 42); Cole (63)	40,892	G.Poll
1997-98	Away	6-Dec-97	3-1	Cole (51,74); Beckham (70)	41,027	D.Elleray
1997-98	Home	10-Apr-98	1-1	Johnsen (12)	55,171	G.Poll
1998-99	Home	24-Sep-98	2-0	Irwin (18 pen); Scholes (79)	55,181	S.Lodge
1998-99	Away	5-May-99	2-2	Yorke (23); Irwin (56 pen)	44,702	D.Elleray
1999-00	Away	11-Sep-99	3-2	OGs (Carragher 3,44); Cole (18)	44,929	G.Barber
1999-00	Home	4-Mar-00	1-1	Solskjaer (45)	61,592	D.Gallagher

MANCHESTER CITY

Season	Venue	Date	Res	Scorers	Attendance	Referee
1992-93	Home	6-Dec-92	2-1	Ince (20); Hughes (73)	35,408	G.Ashby
1992-93	Away	20-Mar-93	1-1	Cantona (68)	37,136	R.Hart
1993-94	Away	7-Nov-93	3-2	Cantona (52, 77); Keane (86)	35,155	R.Hart
1993-94	Home	23-Apr-94	2-0	Cantona (40, 45)	44,333	K.Morton

1994-95	Home	10-Nov-94	5-0	Cantona (24); Kanchelskis (43,47,89); Hughes (70)	43,738	K.Cooper
1994-95	Away	11-Feb-95	3-0	Ince (58); Kanchelskis (74); Cole (77)	26,368	P.Don
1995-96	Home	14-Oct-95	1-0	Scholes (4)	35,707	R.Dilkes
1995-96	Away	6-Apr-96	3-2	Cantona (7 pen); Cole (41); Giggs (77)	29,688	M.Reed

MIDDLESBROUGH

Season	Venue	Date	Res	Scorers	Attendance	Referee
1992-93	Away	3-Oct-92	1-1	Bruce (43 pen)	24,172	M.Reed
1992-93	Home	27-Feb-93	3-0	Giggs (20); Irwin (79); Cantona (85)	36,251	K.Hackett
1995-96	Home	28-Oct-95	2-0	Pallister (43); Cole (87)	36,580	S.Lodge
1995-96	Away	5-May-96	3-0	May (15); Cole (54); Giggs (80)	29,921	P.Durkin
1996-97	Away	23-Nov-96	2-2	Keane (17); May (72)	30,063	A.Wilkie
1996-97	Home	5-May-97	3-3	Keane (34); Neville G. (42); Solskjaer (67)	54,489	D.Gallagher
1998-99	Home	19-Dec-98	2-3	Butt (62); Scholes (70)	55,152	G.Willard
1998-99	Away	9-May-99	1-0	Yorke (45)	34,665	G.Barber
1999-00	Home	30-Jan-00	1-0	Beckham (87)	61,267	A.D'Urso
1999-00	Away	10-Apr-00	4-3	Giggs (46); Cole (59); Scholes (74); Fortune (88)	34,775	P.Durkin

NEWCASTLE UNITED

Season	Venue	Date	Res	Scorers	Attendance	Referee
1993-94	Home	21-Aug-93	1-1	Giggs (40)	41,829	K.Morton
1993-94	Away	11-Dec-93	1-1	Ince (59)	36,332	K.Hackett
1994-95	Home	29-Oct-94	2-0	Pallister (12); Gillespie (76)	43,795	J.Worrall
1994-95	Away	15-Jan-95	1-1	Hughes (12)	34,471	S.Lodge
1995-96	Home	27-Dec-95	2-0	Cole (5); Keane (53)	42,024	P.Alcock
1995-96	Away	4-Mar-96	1-0	Cantona (51)	36,584	D.Elleray
1996-97	Away	20-Oct-96	0-5		36,579	S.Dunn
1996-97	Home	8-May-97	0-0		55,236	S.Dunn
1997-98	Away	21-Dec-97	1-0	Cole (67)	36,767	P.Jones
1997-98	Home	18-Apr-98	1-1	Beckham (37)	55,194	U.Rennie
1998-99	Home	8-Nov-98	0-0		55,174	S.Dunn
1998-99	Away	13-Mar-99	2-1	Cole (25, 51)	36,500	D.Elleray
1999-00	Home	30-Aug-99	5-1	Cole (14, 46, 65, 71); Giggs (80)	55,190	J.Winter
1999-00	Away	12-Feb-00	0-3		36,470	S.Lodge

NORWICH CITY

Season	Venue	Date	Res	Scorers	Attendance	Referee
1992-93	Home	12-Dec-92	1-0	Hughes (59)	34,500	R.Milford
1992-93	Away	5-Apr-93	3-1	Giggs (13); Kanchelskis (20); Cantona (21)	20,582	T.Ward
1993-94	Away	15-Aug-93	2-0	Giggs (26); Robson (58)	19,705	K.Hackett
1993-94	Home	4-Dec-93	2-2	Giggs (30); McClair (41)	44,694	M.Bodenham
1994-95	Home	3-Dec-94	1-0	Cantona (36)	43,789	T.Holbrook
1994-95	Away	22-Feb-95	2-0	Ince (2); Kanchelskis (16)	21,824	T.Holbrook

NOTTINGHAM FOREST

Season	Venue	Date	Res	Scorers	Attendance	Referee
1992-93	Away	29-Aug-92	2-0	Hughes (17); Giggs (50)	19,694	K.Redfern
1992-93	Home	27-Jan-93	2-0	Ince (47); Hughes (68)	36,085	J.Worrall
1994-95	Away	22-Aug-94	1-1	Kanchelskis (22)	22,072	A.Wilkie
1994-95	Home	17-Dec-94	1-2	Cantona (68)	43,744	K.Burge
1995-96	Away	27-Nov-95	1-1	Cantona (66 pen)	29,263	K.Cooper

1995-96	Home	28-Apr-96	5-0	Scholes (41); Beckham (44, 54); Giggs (69); Cantona (89)53,926		J.Winter
1996-97	Home	14-Sep-96	4-1	Solskjaer (21); Giggs (42); Cantona (82, 90 pen)	54,984	P.Jones
1996-97	Away	26-Dec-96	4-0	Beckham (25); Butt (44); Solskjaer (66); Cole (74)	29,032	G.Ashby
1998-99	Home	26-Dec-98	3-0	Johnsen (28, 59); Giggs (62)	55,216	J.Winter
1998-99	Away	6-Feb-99	8-1	Yorke (2,66); Cole (7, 49); Solskjaer (80, 87, 90, 90)30,025		P.Alcock

OLDHAM ATHLETIC

Season	Venue	Date	Res	Scorers	Attendance	Referee
1992-93	Home	21-Nov-92	3-0	McClair (10,28); Hughes (11)	33,497	A.Gunn
1992-93	Away	9-Mar-93	0-1		17,106	G.Ashby
1993-94	Away	29-Dec-93	5-2	Kanchelskis (4); Cantona (18 pen); Bruce (38); Giggs (54, 60)	16,708	V.Callow
1993-94	Home	4-Apr-94	3-2	Giggs (11); Dublin (66); Ince (67)	44,686	P.Durkin

QPR

Season	Venue	Date	Res	Scorers	Attendance	Referee
1992-93	Home	26-Sep-92	0-0		33,287	D.Allison
1992-93	Away	18-Jan-93	3-1	Ince (26); Giggs (30); Kanchelskis (48)	21,142	J.Martin
1993-94	Home	30-Oct-93	2-1	Cantona (52); Hughes (57)	44,663	S.Lodge
1993-94	Away	5-Feb-94	3-2	Kanchelskis (18); Cantona (45); Giggs (59)	21,267	G.Poll
1994-95	Home	20-Aug-94	2-0	Hughes (47); McClair (68)	43,214	D.Gallagher
1994-95	Away	10-Dec-94	3-2	Scholes (32,47); Keane (38)	18,948	G.Poll
1995-96	Home	30-Dec-95	2-1	Cole (44); Giggs (52)	41,890	R.Hart
1995-96	Away	16-Mar-96	1-1	Cantona (90)	18,817	R.Hart

SHEFFIELD UNITED

Season	Venue	Date	Res	Scorers	Attendance	Referee
1992-93	Away	15-Aug-92	1-2	Hughes (61)	28,070	B.Hill
1992-93	Home	6-Feb-93	2-1	McClair (64); Cantona (80)	36,156	M.Bodenham
1993-94	Home	18-Aug-93	3-0	Keane (16, 43); Hughes (85)	41,949	G.Ashby
1993-94	Away	7-Dec-93	3-0	Hughes (13); Sharpe (27); Cantona (60)	26,744	A.Gunn

SHEFFIELD WEDNESDAY

Season	Venue	Date	Res	Scorers	Attendance	Referee
1992-93	Away	26-Dec-92	3-3	McClair (67,80); Cantona (84)	37,708	A.Buksh
1992-93	Home	10-Apr-93	2-1	Bruce (86, 90)	40,102	M.Peck (J.Hilditch, 61)
1993-94	Away	2-Oct-93	3-2	Hughes (50, 66); Giggs (71)	34,548	D.Allison
1993-94	Home	16-Mar-94	5-0	Giggs (14); Hughes (15); Ince (21); Cantona (45, 55)	43,669	M.Bodenham
1994-95	Away	8-Oct-94	0-1		33,441	P.Danson
1994-95	Home	7-May-95	1-0	May (5)	43,868	B.Hill
1995-96	Away	23-Sep-95	0-0		34,101	K.Burge
1995-96	Home	9-Dec-95	2-2	Cantona (17, 84)	41,849	P.Jones
1996-97	Away	18-Dec-96	1-1	Scholes (62)	37,671	P.Danson
1996-97	Home	15-Mar-97	2-0	Cole (20); Poborsky (60)	55,267	P.Durkin
1997-98	Home	1-Nov-97	6-1	Cole (19, 38); Sheringham (13, 62); Solskjaer (40,74)	55,529	G.Ashby
1997-98	Away	7-Mar-98	0-2		39,427	P.Jones
1998-99	Away	21-Nov-98	1-3	Cole (29)	39,475	D.Elleray
1998-99	Home	17-Apr-99	3-0	Solskjaer (35); Sheringham (44); Scholes (62)	55,270	N.Barry

| 1999-00 | Home | 11-Aug-99 | 4-0 | Scholes (9); Yorke (35); Cole (54); Solskjaer (84) | 54,941 | M.Reed |
| 1999-00 | Away | 2-Feb-00 | 1-0 | Sheringham (73) | 39,640 | S.Dunn |

SOUTHAMPTON

Season	Venue	Date	Res	Scorers	Attendance	Referee
1992-93	Away	24-Aug-92	1-0	Dublin (89)	15,623	R.Lewis
1992-93	Home	20-Feb-93	2-1	Giggs (82,83)	36,257	R.Lewis
1993-94	Away	28-Aug-93	3-1	Sharpe (5); Cantona (15); Irwin (49)	16,189	A.Gunn
1993-94	Home	4-May-94	2-0	Kanchelskis (60); Hughes (90)	44,705	T.Holbrook
1994-95	Away	31-Dec-94	2-2	Butt (50); Pallister (79)	15,204	M.Bodenham
1994-95	Home	10-May-95	2-1	Cole (21); Irwin (82 pen)	43,479	P.Danson
1995-96	Home	18-Nov-95	4-1	Giggs (1, 4); Scholes (8); Cole (69)	39,301	P.Danson
1995-96	Away	13-Apr-96	1-3	Giggs (89)	15,262	G.Poll
1996-97	Away	26-Oct-96	3-6	Beckham (41); May (56); Scholes (88)	15,253	J.Winter
1996-97	Home	1-Feb-97	2-1	Pallister (18); Cantona (79)	55,269	M.Riley
1997-98	Home	13-Aug-97	1-0	Beckham (78)	55,008	G.Barber
1997-98	Away	19-Jan-98	0-1		15,241	M.Riley
1998-99	Away	3-Oct-98	3-0	Yorke (11); Cole (59); Cruyff (74)	15,251	D.Elleray
1998-99	Home	27-Feb-99	2-1	Keane (79); Yorke (83)	55,316	P.Jones
1999-00	Home	25-Sep-99	3-3	Sheringham (34); Yorke (37, 64)	55,249	S.Dunn
1999-00	Away	22-Apr-00	3-1	Beckham (7); OG (15, Benali); Solskjaer (29)	15,245	N.Barry

SUNDERLAND

Season	Venue	Date	Res	Scorers	Attendance	Referee
1996-97	Home	21-Dec-96	5-0	Solskjaer (35, 47); Cantona (43 pen, 79); Butt (58)	55,081	P.Durkin
1996-97	Away	8-Mar-97	1-2	OG (77, Melville)	22,225	P.Jones
1999-00	Away	28-Dec-99	2-2	Keane (27); Butt (86)	42,026	J.Winter
1999-00	Home	15-Apr-00	4-0	Solskjaer (2, 51); Butt (66); Berg (70)	61,612	P.Jones

SWINDON TOWN

Season	Venue	Date	Res	Scorers	Attendance	Referee
1993-94	Home	25-Sep-93	4-2	Kanchelskis (4); Cantona (40); Hughes (50, 90)	44,583	J.Worrall
1993-94	Away	19-Mar-94	2-2	Keane (13); Ince (62)	18,102	B.Hill

TOTTENHAM HOTSPUR

Season	Venue	Date	Res	Scorers	Attendance	Referee
1992-93	Away	19-Sep-92	1-1	Giggs (45)	33,296	R.Groves
1992-93	Home	9-Jan-93	4-1	Cantona (40); Irwin (52); McClair (53); Parker (58)	35,648	M.Peck
1993-94	Home	16-Oct-93	2-1	Keane (65); Sharpe (68)	44,655	K.Burge
1993-94	Away	15-Jan-94	1-0	OG (49, Calderwood)	31,343	R.Milford
1994-95	Away	27-Aug-94	1-0	Bruce (48)	24,502	K.Burge
1994-95	Home	15-Mar-95	0-0		43,802	K.Morton
1995-96	Away	1-Jan-96	1-4	Cole (36)	32,852	G.Ashby
1995-96	Home	24-Mar-96	1-0	Cantona (50)	50,157	G.Ashby
1996-97	Home	29-Sep-96	2-0	Solskjaer (38, 58)	54,943	G.Willard
1996-97	Away	12-Jan-97	2-1	Solskjaer (22); Beckham (75)	33,028	M.Bodenham
1997-98	Away	10-Aug-97	2-0	Butt (82);OG (83, Vega)	26,359	G.Poll
1997-98	Home	10-Jan-98	2-0	Giggs (44, 67)	55,281	P.Alcock
1998-99	Away	12-Dec-98	2-2	Solskjaer (11, 18)	36,070	U.Rennie
1998-99	Home	16-May-99	2-1	Beckham (42); Cole (47)	55,189	G.Poll

| 1999-00 | Away | 23-Oct-99 | 1-3 | Giggs (23) | 36,072 | J.Winter |
| 1999-00 | Home | 6-May-00 | 3-1 | Solskjaer (5); Beckham (34); Sheringham (36) | 61,629 | A.Wilkie |

WATFORD

Season	Venue	Date	Res	Scorers	Attendance	Referee
1999-00	Home	16-Oct-99	4-1	Yorke (39); Cole (42, 50); Irwin (44 pen)	55,188	P.Jones
1999-00	Away	29-Apr-00	3-2	Yorke (68); Giggs (75); Cruyff (86)	20,250	S.Lodge

WEST HAM UNITED

Season	Venue	Date	Res	Scorers	Attendance	Referee
1993-94	Home	1-Sep-93	3-0	Sharpe (6); Cantona (45pen); Bruce (88)	44,613	R.Milford
1993-94	Away	26-Feb-94	2-2	Hughes (6); Ince (87)	28,382	A.Wilkie
1994-95	Home	15-Oct-94	1-0	Cantona (45)	43,795	R.Gifford
1994-95	Away	14-May-95	1-1	McClair (52)	24,783	A.Wilkie
1995-96	Home	23-Aug-95	2-1	Scholes (50); Keane (68)	31,966	D.Gallagher
1995-96	Away	22-Jan-96	1-0	Cantona (8)	24,197	S.Lodge
1996-97	Away	8-Dec-96	2-2	Solskjaer (53); Beckham (74)	25,045	P.Jones
1996-97	Home	12-May-97	2-0	Solskjaer (11); Cruyff (84)	55,249	S.Lodge
1997-98	Home	13-Sep-97	2-1	Keane (21); Scholes (76)	55,068	D.Elleray
1997-98	Away	11-Mar-98	1-1	Scholes (65)	25,892	G.Willard
1998-99	Away	22-Aug-98	0-0		26,039	P.Jones
1998-99	Home	10-Jan-99	4-1	Yorke (10); Cole (39, 68); Solskjaer (80)	55,180	M.Reed
1999-00	Away	18-Dec-99	4-2	Yorke (9, 62); Giggs (13, 19)	26,037	U.Rennie
1999-00	Home	1-Apr-00	7-1	Scholes (24, 51, 62pen); Irwin (26); Cole (45); Beckham (66); Solskjaer (73)	61,611	M.Riley

WIMBLEDON

Season	Venue	Date	Res	Scorers	Attendance	Referee
1992-93	Home	31-Oct-92	0-1		32,622	K.Morton
1992-93	Away	9-May-93	2-1	Ince (63); Robson (70)	30,115	J.Worrall
1993-94	Home	20-Nov-93	3-1	Pallister (53); Hughes (64); Kanchelskis (80)	44,748	J.Lloyd
1993-94	Away	16-Apr-94	0-1		28,553	T.Holbrook
1994-95	Home	31-Aug-94	3-0	Cantona (40); McClair (81); Giggs (85)	43,440	T.Holbrook
1994-95	Away	7-Mar-95	1-0	Bruce (84)	18,224	R.Hart
1995-96	Home	26-Aug-95	3-1	Keane (27, 79); Cole (59)	32,226	P.Durkin
1995-96	Away	3-Feb-96	4-2	Cole (42); OG (45, Perry); Cantona (70, 80 pen)	24,432	P.Durkin
1996-97	Away	17-Aug-96	3-0	Cantona (25); Irwin (58); Beckham (87)	25,786	D.Elleray
1996-97	Home	29-Jan-97	2-1	Giggs (75); Cole (82)	55,314	M.Reed
1997-98	Away	22-Nov-97	5-2	Butt (47); Beckham (66, 74); Scholes (80); Cole (85)	26,309	P.Durkin
1997-98	Home	28-Mar-98	2-0	Johnsen (83); Scholes (90)	55,306	D.Gallagher
1998-99	Home	17-Oct-98	5-1	Cole (19, 88); Giggs (45); Beckham (48); Yorke (54)	55,265	G.Willard
1998-99	Away	3-Apr-99	1-1	Beckham (44)	26,121	G.Barber
1999-00	Home	18-Sep-99	1-1	Cruyff (73)	55,189	R.Harris
1999-00	Away	26-Feb-00	2-2	Cruyff (30); Cole (80)	26,129	D.Elleray

INTRODUCTION

Formed in 1876 and played first game in 1877. Turned professional in 1889, but reverted to amateur status shortly afterwards, being early winners of the FA Amateur Cup. League football was first played in Middlesbrough by the Ironpolis side for one season, 1893-94. Middlesbrough turned professional again, were elected to Division Two in 1899, and moved to Ayresome Park in 1903. They were founder members of the Premier League in 1993 but were relegated in their first season. Moved to purpose-built stadium in 1995 coinciding with return to Premiership. Reached and lost both Cup Finals in 1997 in addition to being relegated to Division 1.

Ground:	The Cellnet Riverside Stadium, Middlesbrough, TS3 6RS
Nickname:	The Boro
Internet::	www.mfc.co.uk

HONOURS

Football League Div 1:	Champions 1994-95 Runners-up 1997-98
Football League Div 2:	Champions 1926-27, 1928-29, 1973-74. Runners-up 1901-02, 1991-92
Football League Div 3:	Runners up 1966-67, 1986-87
FA Cup:	Runners-up 1996-97
League Cup:	Runners-up 1996-97, 1997-98
FA Amateur Cup:	Winners 1895, 1898
Anglo-Scottish Cup:	Winners 1975-76

EUROPEAN RECORD

Never qualified

FAPL RECORD SUMMARY

Most Total:	MUSTOE, Robbie	136
Most Starts:	MUSTOE, Robbie	123
Most Subs:	STAMP, Phil	23
Most SNU:	BERESFORD, Marlon	59
Most PS:	RICARD, Hamilton	27
Most Goals:	RICARD, Hamilton	27
Most Yel:	MUSTOE, Robbie	25
Most Red:	FALCONER, Willie	1

PLAYING RECORD – SEASON TOTALS

Season	Pn	P	W	D	L	F	A	Pts
1992-93	21	42	11	11	20	54	75	44
1995-96	12	38	11	10	17	35	50	43
1996-97	19	38	10	12	16	51	60	42
1998-99	9	38	12	15	11	48	54	51
1999-00	12	38	14	10	14	46	52	52
Totals	194	58	58	78	234	291	232	

PLAYING RECORD – HOME TOTALS

Season	Pn	P	W	D	L	F	A	Pts
1992-93	21	21	8	5	8	33	27	29
1995-96	12	19	8	3	8	27	27	27
1996-97	19	19	8	5	6	34	25	29
1998-99	9	19	7	9	3	25	18	30
1999-00	12	19	8	5	6	23	26	29
Totals	97	39	27	31	142	123	144	

PLAYING RECORD – AWAY TOTALS

Season	Pn	P	W	D	L	F	A	Pts
1992-93	21	21	3	6	12	21	48	15
1995-96	12	19	3	7	9	8	23	16
1996-97	19	19	2	7	10	17	35	13
1998-99	9	19	5	6	8	23	36	21
1999-00	12	19	6	5	8	23	26	23
Totals	97	19	31	47	92	168	88	

HIGHEST HOME ATTENDANCES

	Attendance	Opponents	Date	Season
1	44,793	Sunderland	6-Nov-99	1999-00
2	34,800	Leeds U.	26-Feb-00	1999-00
3	34,783	Liverpool	21-Aug-99	1999-00
4	34,775	Manchester U.	10-Apr-00	1999-00
5	34,744	Newcastle U.	2-May-00	1999-00

LOWEST HOME ATTENDANCES

	Attendance	Opponents	Date	Season
1	12,290	Oldham A.	22-Mar-93	1992-93
2	12,726	Arsenal	6-Apr-93	1992-93
3	13,921	Southampton	26-Jan-93	1992-93
4	14,008	Coventry C.	6-Feb-93	1992-93
5	14,255	Ipswich T.	1-Sep-92	1992-93

TOP SCORER – SEASON BY SEASON

Season	Player	Goals
1992-93	Wilkinson	15
1995-96	Barmby	7
1996-97	Ravanelli	16
1998-99	Ricard	15
1999-00	Ricard	12

MIDDLESBROUGH

PLAYERS WITH MOST PREMIERSHIP APPEARANCES

Tot	Player	St	Sb	Gls
136	MUSTOE, Robbie	123	13	8
124	VICKERS, Steve	118	6	2
109	FLEMING, Curtis	105	4	2
84	JUNINHO	78	6	18
81	WHYTE, Derek	78	3	0
78	SCHWARZER, Mark	78	0	0
70	RICARD, Hamilton	60	10	27
67	FESTA, Gianluca	65	2	5
66	COX, Neil	64	2	2
66	STAMP, Phil	43	23	5
65	HIGNETT, Craig	54	11	13
58	COOPER, Colin	57	1	1
55	DEANE, Brian	53	2	15
54	PEARSON, Nigel	53	1	0
53	POLLOCK, Jamie	48	5	2
52	MORRIS, Chris	47	5	3
52	BECK, Mikkel	35	17	10

CLUB-BY-CLUB RESULTS

ARSENAL

Season	Venue	Date	Res	Scorers	Attendance	Referee
1992-93	Away	19-Dec-92	1-1	Wilkinson (34)	23,197	S.Lodge
1992-93	Home	6-Apr-93	1-0	Hendrie (32)	12,726	K.Hackett
1995-96	Away	20-Aug-95	1-1	Barmby (31)	37,308	G.Ashby
1995-96	Home	13-Jan-96	2-3	Juninho (38); Stamp (55)	29,359	G.Poll
1996-97	Home	21-Sep-96	0-2		29,629	M.Bodenham
1996-97	Away	1-Jan-97	0-2		37,573	M.Reed
1998-99	Away	29-Nov-98	1-1	Deane (5)	38,075	G.Barber
1998-99	Home	24-Apr-99	1-6	Armstrong (87)	34,630	M.Riley
1999-00	Away	20-Nov-99	1-5	Ricard (68)	38,082	N.Barry
1999-00	Home	12-Mar-00	2-1	Ince (48); Ricard (63)	34,244	R.Harris

ASTON VILLA

Season	Venue	Date	Res	Scorers	Attendance	Referee
1992-93	Home	26-Sep-92	2-3	Slaven (62); OG (86, McGrath)	20,905	D.Elleray
1992-93	Away	17-Jan-93	1-5	Hignett (82)	19,977	K.Cooper
1995-96	Home	1-Jan-96	0-2		28,535	M.Bodenham
1995-96	Away	19-Mar-96	0-0		23,933	P.Alcock
1996-97	Away	30-Nov-96	0-1		39,053	G.Willard
1996-97	Home	3-May-97	3-2	Ravanelli (20, 90 pen); Beck 34)	30,074	P.Alcock
1998-99	Away	23-Aug-98	1-3	Beck (62)	29,559	P.Alcock
1998-99	Home	9-Jan-99	0-0		34,643	U.Rennie
1999-00	Away	28-Aug-99	0-1		28,728	M.Halsey
1999-00	Home	14-Feb-00	0-4		31,571	A.Wilkie

BLACKBURN ROVERS

Season	Venue	Date	Res	Scorers	Attendance	Referee
1992-93	Home	5-Dec-92	3-2	Hendrie (52, 55, 66)	20,096	B.Hill
1992-93	Away	20-Mar-93	1-1	Hendrie (32)	14,041	G.Ashby
1995-96	Home	30-Sep-95	2-0	Barmby (44); Hignett (72)	29,462	P.Alcock
1995-96	Away	16-Dec-95	0-1		27,996	P.Danson
1996-97	Home	19-Mar-97	2-1	Juninho (43); Ravanelli (60)	29,891	D.Gallagher
1996-97	Away	8-May-97	0-0		27,411	G.Poll
1998-99	Home	17-Oct-98	2-1	Ricard (83 pen); Fleming (90)	34,413	U.Rennie
1998-99	Away	3-Apr-99	0-0		27,482	A.Wilkie

BOLTON WANDERERS

Season	Venue	Date	Res	Scorers	Attendance	Referee
1995-96	Away	9-Sep-95	1-1	Hignett (77)	18,376	P.Danson
1995-96	Home	17-Feb-96	1-4	Pollock (36)	29,354	P.Danson

BRADFORD CITY

Season	Venue	Date	Res	Scorers	Attendance	Referee
1999-00	Home	7-Aug-99	0-1		33,762	N.Barry
1999-00	Away	4-Dec-99	1-1	Ricard (13)	17,708	R.Harris

CHARLTON ATHLETIC

Season	Venue	Date	Res	Scorers	Attendance	Referee
1998-99	Away	14-Nov-98	1-1	Stamp (74)	20,043	M.Riley
1998-99	Home	10-Apr-99	2-0	Ricard (35); Mustoe (60)	34,529	U.Rennie

CHELSEA

Season	Venue	Date	Res	Scorers	Attendance	Referee
1992-93	Home	11-Dec-92	0-0		15,559	K.Barratt
1992-93	Away	3-Apr-93	0-4		13,043	J.Worrall
1995-96	Home	26-Aug-95	2-0	Hignett (39); Fjortoft (76)	28,286	S.Lodge
1995-96	Away	4-Feb-96	0-5		21,060	K.Cooper
1996-97	Away	21-Aug-96	0-1		28,272	G.Willard
1996-97	Home	22-Mar-97	1-0	Juninho (53)	29,811	M.Riley
1998-99	Away	27-Sep-98	0-2		34,811	M.Reed
1998-99	Home	14-Apr-99	0-0		34,406	N.Barry
1999-00	Home	25-Sep-99	0-1		34,183	P.Alcock
1999-00	Away	22-Apr-00	1-1	Ricard (37)	34,467	U.Rennie

COVENTRY CITY

Season	Venue	Date	Res	Scorers	Attendance	Referee
1992-93	Away	15-Aug-92	1-2	Wilkinson (63)	12,681	H.King
1992-93	Home	6-Feb-93	0-2		14,008	J.Borrett
1995-96	Home	16-Sep-95	2-1	Vicars (57); Fjortoft (78)	27,882	G.Poll
1995-96	Away	24-Feb-96	0-0		17,979	P.Durkin
1996-97	Home	7-Sep-96	4-0	Ravenelli (3, 73); Juninho (28, 80)	29,811	G.Barber
1996-97	Away	28-Dec-96	0-3		20,617	S.Lodge
1998-99	Home	21-Nov-98	2-0	Gordon (66); Ricard (83)	34,293	G.Willard
1998-99	Away	17-Apr-99	2-1	Kinder (64); Gordon (82)	19,231	P.Jones
1999-00	Home	19-Feb-00	2-0	Festa (8); Ricard (20)	32,798	G.Barber
1999-00	Away	15-Apr-00	1-2	Ziege (64 pen)	19,435	N.Barry

CRYSTAL PALACE

Season	Venue	Date	Res	Scorers	Attendance	Referee
1992-93	Home	28-Dec-92	0-1		21,123	K.Hackett
1992-93	Away	12-Apr-93	1-4	Wilkinson (86)	15,123	M.Bodenham

DERBY COUNTY

Season	Venue	Date	Res	Scorers	Attendance	Referee
1996-97	Away	17-Nov-96	1-2	Ravenelli (73)	17,350	P.Durkin
1996-97	Home	5-Mar-97	6-1	Kinder (24); Ravanelli (54, 83, 85); Hignett (70); Beck (84)	29,739	M.Reed

1998-99	Home	29-Aug-98	1-1	Ricard (48)	34,121	M.Riley
1998-99	Away	28-Dec-98	1-2	Beck (77)	32,726	R.Harris
1999-00	Away	14-Aug-99	3-1	Deane (9); Ziege (20); Ricard (66 pen)	24,045	S.Bennett
1999-00	Home	15-Jan-00	1-4	Campbell (71)	32,745	M.Halsey

EVERTON

Season	Venue	Date	Res	Scorers	Attendance	Referee
1992-93	Away	26-Dec-92	2-2	Hignett (49, 82)	24,391	R.Groves
1992-93	Home	10-Apr-93	1-2	Wilkinson (64)	16,627	J.Lloyd
1995-96	Away	26-Dec-95	0-4		40,091	P.Jones
1995-96	Home	2-Mar-96	0-2		29,407	D.Gallagher
1996-97	Away	14-Sep-96	2-1	Barmby (61); Juninho (81)	39,250	P.Danson
1996-97	Home	26-Dec-96	4-2	Hignett (22); Blackmore (37); Juninho (58, 74)	29,673	S.Dunn
1998-99	Home	19-Sep-98	2-2	Ricard (27, 35)	34,563	D.Gallagher
1998-99	Away	17-Feb-99	0-5		31,606	K.Burge
1999-00	Home	30-Oct-99	2-1	Ziege (15); Deane (61)	33,916	A.D'Urso
1999-00	Away	14-May-00	2-0	Deane (8); Juninho (86)	34,663	R.Harris

IPSWICH TOWN

Season	Venue	Date	Res	Scorers	Attendance	Referee
1992-93	Home	1-Sep-92	2-2	Kernaghan (54); Wilkinson (82)	14,255	R.Nixon
1992-93	Away	2-Mar-93	1-0	Wilkinson (35)	15,430	K.Barratt

LEEDS UNITED

Season	Venue	Date	Res	Scorers	Attendance	Referee
1992-93	Home	22-Aug-92	4-1	Wilkinson (7, 8); Wright (47); Hendrie (59)	18,649	D.Allison
1992-93	Away	30-Jan-93	0-3		30,344	J.Martin
1995-96	Home	4-Nov-95	1-1	Fjortoft (9)	29,467	K.Burge
1995-96	Away	30-Mar-96	1-0	Kavanagh (4)	31,778	D.Elleray
1996-97	Home	7-Dec-96	0-0		30,018	D.Elleray
1996-97	Away	11-May-97	1-1	Juninho (79)	38,567	A.Wilkie
1998-99	Home	15-Aug-98	0-0		34,162	D.Elleray
1998-99	Away	16-Jan-99	0-2		37,473	S.Lodge
1999-00	Away	19-Sep-99	0-2		34,122	D.Gallagher
1999-00	Home	26-Feb-00	0-0		34,800	U.Rennie

LEICESTER CITY

Season	Venue	Date	Res	Scorers	Attendance	Referee
1996-97	Home	3-Dec-96	0-2		29,709	P.Alcock
1996-97	Away	15-Mar-97	3-1	Blackmore (8); Juninho (26); Beck (36)	20,561	S.Lodge
1998-99	Away	9-Sep-98	1-0	Gascoigne (45)	20,635	K.Burge
1998-99	Home	30-Jan-99	0-0		34,631	D.Gallagher
1999-00	Home	24-Aug-99	0-3		33,126	R.Harris
1999-00	Away	5-Feb-00	1-2	Campbell (52)	17,550	S.Bennett

LIVERPOOL

Season	Venue	Date	Res	Scorers	Attendance	Referee
1992-93	Away	7-Nov-92	1-4	Phillips (41)	34,974	D.Gallagher
1992-93	Home	13-Mar-93	1-2	OG (15, Nicol)	22,463	M.Peck
1995-96	Home	25-Nov-95	2-1	Cox (2); Barmby (64)	29,390	D.Gallagher
1995-96	Away	27-Apr-96	0-1		40,782	R.Dilkes

1996-97	Home	17-Aug-96	3-3	Ravanelli (26 pen, 35, 81)	30,039	P.Alcock
1996-97	Away	14-Dec-96	1-5	Fjortoft (75)	39,491	K.Burge
1998-99	Home	26-Dec-98	1-3	Deane (32)	34,626	G.Poll
1998-99	Away	6-Feb-99	1-3	Stamp (86)	44,384	P.Jones
1999-00	Home	21-Aug-99	1-0	Deane (49)	34,783	S.Dunn
1999-00	Away	22-Jan-00	0-0		44,324	S.Dunn

MANCHESTER CITY

Season	Venue	Date	Res	Scorers	Attendance	Referee
1992-93	Home	19-Aug-92	2-0	Slaven (15, 17)	15,369	S.Lodge
1992-93	Away	12-Sep-92	1-0	OG (42, Flitcroft)	25,244	R.Lewis
1995-96	Away	23-Sep-95	1-0	Barmby (16)	25,865	G.Willard
1995-96	Home	9-Dec-95	4-1	Barmby (33, 54); Stamp (53); Juninho (74)	29,469	S.Lodge

MANCHESTER UNITED

Season	Venue	Date	Res	Scorers	Attendance	Referee
1992-93	Home	3-Oct-92	1-1	Slaven (59)	24,172	M.Reed
1992-93	Away	27-Feb-93	0-3		36,251	K.Hackett
1995-96	Away	28-Oct-95	0-2		36,580	S.Lodge
1995-96	Home	5-May-96	0-3		29,921	P.Durkin
1996-97	Home	23-Nov-96	2-2	Ravanelli (27); Hignett (82 pen)	30,063	A.Wilkie
1996-97	Away	5-May-97	3-3	Juninho (15); Emerson (37); Hignett (40)	54,489	D.Gallagher
1998-99	Away	19-Dec-98	3-2	Ricard (23); Gordon (31); Deane (59)	55,152	G.Willard
1998-99	Home	9-May-99	0-1		34,665	G.Barber
1999-00	Away	30-Jan-00	0-1		61,267	A.D'Urso
1999-00	Home	10-Apr-00	3-4	Campbell (18); Ince (86); Juninho (90)	34,775	P.Durkin

NEWCASTLE UNITED

Season	Venue	Date	Res	Scorers	Attendance	Referee
1995-96	Away	30-Aug-95	0-1		36,483	R.Hart
1995-96	Home	10-Feb-96	1-2	OG (37, Beresford)	30,011	S.Dunn
1996-97	Away	3-Nov-96	1-3	Beck (88)	36,577	G.Willard
1996-97	Home	22-Feb-97	0-1		30,063	S.Dunn
1998-99	Home	6-Dec-98	2-2	Townsend (13); Cooper (59)	34,629	U.Rennie
1998-99	Away	1-May-99	1-1	Mustoe (60)	36,552	M.Reed
1999-00	Away	3-Oct-99	1-2	Deane (89)	36,421	S.Lodge
1999-00	Home	2-May-00	2-2	Juninho (5); Festa (78)	34,744	M.Riley

NORWICH CITY

Season	Venue	Date	Res	Scorers	Attendance	Referee
1992-93	Away	31-Oct-92	1-1	Wilkinson (64)	14,499	S.Lodge
1992-93	Home	8-May-93	3-3	Falconer (34); Wilkinson (65); Hendrie (74)	15,155	G.Ashby

NOTTINGHAM FOREST

Season	Venue	Date	Res	Scorers	Attendance	Referee
1992-93	Away	21-Oct-92	0-1		16,897	M.Peck
1992-93	Home	20-Feb-93	1-2	Phillips (59)	15,639	D.Elleray
1995-96	Away	30-Dec-95	0-1		27,027	G.Willard
1995-96	Home	16-Mar-96	1-1	Mustoe (57)	23,392	A.Wilkie
1996-97	Away	24-Aug-96	1-1	Juninho (48)	24,705	M.Riley
1996-97	Home	24-Mar-97	1-1	Beck (56)	29,888	P.Danson

1998-99	Home	1-Nov-98	1-1	Deane (22)	34,223	P.Durkin
1998-99	Away	21-Mar-99	2-1	Ricard (30); Deane (87)	21,468	S.Dunn

OLDHAM ATHLETIC

Season	Venue	Date	Res	Scorers	Attendance	Referee
1992-93	Away	28-Nov-92	1-4	Falconer (15)	12,401	K.Morton
1992-93	Home	22-Mar-93	2-3	Mohan (83); Hignett (88)	12,290	K.Morton

QPR

Season	Venue	Date	Res	Scorers	Attendance	Referee
1992-93	Away	19-Sep-92	3-3	Kernaghan (37); Wright (58); Falconer (86)	12,272	J.Borrett
1992-93	Home	9-Jan-93	0-1		15,616	R.Dilkes
1995-96	Home	21-Oct-95	1-0	Hignett (15 pen)	29,293	M.Reed
1995-96	Away	2-Dec-95	1-1	Morris (8)	17,546	P.Durkin

SHEFFIELD UNITED

Season	Venue	Date	Res	Scorers	Attendance	Referee
1992-93	Home	5-Sep-92	2-0	Falconer (35); Wright (83)	15,179	A.Buksh
1992-93	Away	9-Feb-93	0-2		15,184	T.Ward

SHEFFIELD WEDNESDAY

Season	Venue	Date	Res	Scorers	Attendance	Referee
1992-93	Home	24-Oct-92	1-1	Wilkinson (34)	18,414	P.Wright
1992-93	Away	1-May-93	3-2	Falconer (26); Pollock (38); Hendrie (51)	25,949	B.Hill
1995-96	Away	15-Oct-95	1-0	Hignett (68 pen)	21,177	G.Ashby
1995-96	Home	5-Apr-96	3-1	Fjortoft (53, 66); Freestone (71)	29,751	K.Cooper
1996-97	Home	18-Jan-97	4-2	Ravanelli (14 pen); Festa (23); Emerson (72 pen); Juninho (90)	29,485	P.Durkin
1996-97	Away	1-Mar-97	1-3	OG (71, Nicol)	28,206	G.Willard
1998-99	Home	3-Oct-98	4-0	Beck (27, 45); Ricard (49); Gascoigne (90)	34,163	R.Harris
1998-99	Away	27-Feb-99	1-3	Mustoe (78)	24,534	M.Riley
1999-00	Away	26-Dec-99	0-1		28,531	B.Knight
1999-00	Home	25-Mar-00	1-0	Campbell (11)	32,748	A.D'Urso

SOUTHAMPTON

Season	Venue	Date	Res	Scorers	Attendance	Referee
1992-93	Away	29-Aug-92	1-2	Wilkinson (75)	13,003	R.Gifford
1992-93	Home	26-Jan-93	2-1	Mohan (24); Wilkinson (71)	13,921	P.Foakes
1995-96	Home	12-Sep-95	0-0		29,188	P.Jones
1995-96	Away	20-Jan-96	1-2	Barmby (44)	15,151	K.Burge
1996-97	Away	28-Sep-96	0-4		15,230	R.Dilkes
1996-97	Home	11-Jan-97	0-1		29,509	G.Ashby
1998-99	Away	7-Nov-98	3-3	Gascoigne (47); OG (66, Lundekvam); Festa (90)	15,202	P.Alcock
1998-99	Home	14-Mar-99	3-0	Beck (44); Ricard (45); Vickers (62)	33,387	M.Reed
1999-00	Home	11-Sep-99	3-2	Pallister (17); Gascoigne (67 pen); Deane (78)	32,165	S.Lodge
1999-00	Away	4-Mar-00	1-1	Ricard (45 pen)	15,223	S.Dunn

SUNDERLAND

Season	Venue	Date	Res	Scorers	Attendance	Referee
1996-97	Away	14-Oct-96	2-2	Emerson (17); Ravanelli (52)	20,936	G.Poll
1996-97	Home	19-Apr-97	0-1		30,106	G.Ashby

1999-00	Home	6-Nov-99	1-1	Ricard (76)	44,793	G.Barber
1999-00	Away	18-Mar-00	1-1	Ziege (82)	42,013	D.Elleray

TOTTENHAM HOTSPUR

Season	Venue	Date	Res	Scorers	Attendance	Referee
1992-93	Away	17-Oct-92	2-2	Mustoe (1); Wilkinson (32)	24,735	P.Durkin
1992-93	Home	20-Apr-93	3-0	Wright (2, 26); Wilkinson (76)	14,472	D.Allison
1995-96	Home	21-Nov-95	0-1		29,487	M.Reed
1995-96	Away	8-Apr-96	1-1	Whelan (85)	32,036	P.Jones
1996-97	Home	19-Oct-96	0-3		30,215	S.Lodge
1996-97	Away	24-Apr-97	0-1		29,947	P.Durkin
1998-99	Away	13-Sep-98	3-0	Ricard (25, 32); Kinder (87)	30,437	S.Dunn
1998-99	Home	20-Feb-99	0-0		34,687	R.Harris
1999-00	Home	18-Dec-99	2-1	Ziege (34); Deane (67)	33,129	S.Dunn
1999-00	Away	3-Apr-00	3-2	OG (40, Carr); Ricard (64, 78)	31,796	A.Wiley

WATFORD

Season	Venue	Date	Res	Scorers	Attendance	Referee
1999-00	Away	24-Oct-99	3-1	OG (2, Williams); Juninho (18); Ince (83)	16,081	A.Wiley
1999-00	Home	6-May-00	1-1	Stockdale (27)	32,930	P.Jones

WEST HAM UNITED

Season	Venue	Date	Res	Scorers	Attendance	Referee
1995-96	Home	23-Dec-95	4-2	Fjortoft (20); Cox (21); Morris (28); Hendrie (82)	28,640	S.Dunn
1995-96	Away	9-Mar-96	0-2		23,850	M.Reed
1996-97	Home	3-Sep-96	4-1	Emerson (12); Mustoe (28); Ravanelli (53); Stamp (83)	30,060	P.Jones
1996-97	Away	9-Apr-97	0-0		23,988	P.Jones
1998-99	Home	12-Dec-98	1-0	Deane (40)	34,623	K.Burge
1998-99	Away	16-May-99	0-4		25,902	G.Willard
1999-00	Home	17-Oct-99	2-0	Deane (51); Armstrong (88)	31,862	U.Rennie
1999-00	Away	29-Apr-00	1-0	Deane (60 pen)	25,472	B.Knight

WIMBLEDON

Season	Venue	Date	Res	Scorers	Attendance	Referee
1992-93	Home	21-Nov-92	2-0	Hendrie (49); Morris (56)	14,524	J.Worrall
1992-93	Away	9-Mar-93	0-2		5,821	M.Reed
1995-96	Away	18-Nov-95	0-0		13,780	K.Cooper
1995-96	Home	13-Apr-96	1-2	Fleming (23)	29,192	G.Ashby
1996-97	Home	26-Oct-96	0-0		29,758	S.Dunn
1996-97	Away	1-Feb-97	1-1	Mustoe (75)	15,046	G.Barber
1998-99	Away	24-Oct-98	2-2	Mustoe (23); Ricard (37)	14,114	S.Lodge
1998-99	Home	5-Apr-99	3-1	Ricard (1, 29); Festa (8)	33,999	P.Durkin
1999-00	Away	10-Aug-99	3-2	Ziege (23); Ricard (28 pen, 64)	11,036	B.Knight
1999-00	Home	27-Nov-99	0-0		31,400	P.Durkin

INTRODUCTION

Formed 1882 as Newcastle East End on the amalgamation of Stanley and Rosewood. Founder members, as a professional club, of the Northern League in 1889. Moved from Chillington Road, Heaton, in 1892 to take over the home of the defunct Newcastle West End, with several of those associated with the West End side joining the newcomers.

Applied for Football League Division One membership in 1892, failed and decided against a place in the new Second Division, staying in the Northern League. Later in 1892 changed name to Newcastle United. Elected to an expanded Football League Division Two in 1893.

Ground: St James's Park,
               Newcastle-upon-Tyne, NE1 4ST
Nickname: Magpies
Internet: www.newcastle-utd.co.uk

HONOURS

FA Premier League:	Runners-up 1995-96, 1996-97
Football League Div 1:	Champions 1904-05, 1906-07, 1908-09, 1926-27, 1992-93
Football League Div 1:	Champions 1964-65 Runners-up 1897-98, 1947-48
FA Cup:	Winners 1909-10, 1923-24, 1931-32, 1950-51, 1951-52, 1954-55. Runners-up 1904-05, 1905-06, 1907-08, 1910-11, 1973-74, 1997-98
Football League Cup:	Runners-up 1975-76.
Texaco Cup:	Winners 1973-74, 1974-75
UEFA Cup:	Winners 1968-69

EUROPEAN RECORD

Champions' League (1)	97-98 (CL)
Cup-Winners' Cup (1):	98-99 (1)
UEFA Cup (7):	68-69 (W), 69-70 (QF), 70-71 (2), 77-78 (2), 94-95 (2), 96-97 (QF).

FAPL RECORD SUMMARY

Most Total:	LEE, Robert	229
Most Starts:	LEE, Robert	220
Most Subs:	KETSBAIA, Temuri	37
Most SNU:	SRNICEK, Pavel	57
Most PS:	LEE, Robert	33
Most Goals:	SHEARER, Alan	64
Most Yel:	LEE, Robert	29
Most Red:	BATTY, David	4

PLAYING RECORD – SEASON TOTALS

Season	Pn	P	W	D	L	F	A	Pts
1993-94	3	42	23	8	11	82	41	77
1994-95	6	42	20	12	10	67	47	72
1995-96	2	38	24	6	8	66	37	78
1996-97	2	38	19	11	8	73	40	68
1997-98	13	38	11	11	16	35	44	44
1998-99	13	38	11	13	14	48	54	46
1999-00	11	38	14	10	14	63	54	52
Totals		274	122	71	81	434	317	437

PLAYING RECORD – HOME TOTALS

Season	Pn	P	W	D	L	F	A	Pts
1993-94	3	21	14	4	3	51	14	46
1994-95	6	21	14	6	1	46	20	48
1995-96	2	19	17	1	1	38	9	52
1996-97	2	19	13	3	3	54	20	42
1997-98	13	19	8	5	6	22	20	29
1998-99	13	19	7	6	6	26	25	27
1999-00	11	19	10	5	4	42	20	35
Totals		137	83	30	24	279	128	279

PLAYING RECORD – AWAY TOTALS

Season	Pn	P	W	D	L	F	A	Pts
1993-94	3	21	9	4	8	31	27	31
1994-95	6	21	6	6	9	21	27	24
1995-96	2	19	7	5	7	28	28	26
1996-97	2	19	6	8	5	19	20	26
1997-98	13	19	3	6	10	13	24	15
1998-99	13	19	4	7	8	22	29	19
1999-00	11	19	4	5	10	21	34	17
Totals		137	39	41	57	155	189	158

HIGHEST HOME ATTENDANCES

	Attendance	Opponents	Date	Season
1	37,759	Southampton	22-Nov-97	1997-98
2	36,783	Aston Villa	23-Aug-97	1997-98
3	36,783	Leeds U.	26-Dec-98	1998-99
4	36,775	Everton	17-Apr-99	1998-99
5	36,771	Sheffield W.	9-Aug-97	1997-98

LOWEST HOME ATTENDANCES

	Attendance	Opponents	Date	Season
1	32,067	Southampton	22-Jan-94	1993-94
2	32,210	Coventry C.	23-Feb-94	1993-94
3	32,214	Oldham A.	23-Apr-94	1993-94
4	32,216	Arsenal	7-May-94	1993-94
5	32,217	Aston Villa	27-Apr-94	1993-94

NEWCASTLE UNITED

TOP SCORER – SEASON BY SEASON

Season	Player	Goals
1993-94	Cole	34
1994-95	Beardsley	13
1995-96	Ferdinand	25
1996-97	Shearer	25
1997-98	Barnes	6
1998-99	Shearer	14
1999-00	Shearer	23

PLAYERS WITH MOST PREMIERSHIP APPEARANCES

Tot	Player	St	Sb	Gls
229	LEE, Robert	220	9	32
154	WATSON, Steve	133	21	11
137	BERESFORD, John	134	3	2
133	PEACOCK, Darren	131	2	2
130	BARTON, Warren	111	19	4
129	BEARDSLEY, Peter	126	3	47
117	HOWEY, Steve	110	7	3
115	SHEARER, Alan	111	4	64
113	GILLESPIE, Keith	94	19	11
101	CLARK, Lee	69	32	7

CLUB-BY-CLUB RESULTS

ARSENAL

Season	Venue	Date	Res	Scorers	Attendance	Referee
1993-94	Away	27-Nov-93	1-2	Beardsley (61)	36,091	A.Gunn
1993-94	Home	7-May-94	2-0	Cole (46); Beardsley (66 pen)	32,216	R.Dilkes
1994-95	Away	18-Sep-94	3-2	Beardsley (6,45 pen); Fox (74)	36,819	T.Holbrook
1994-95	Home	19-Mar-95	1-0	Beardsley (89)	35,611	G.Willard
1995-96	Home	2-Jan-96	2-0	Ginola (1); Ferdinand (47)	36,530	D.Gallagher
1995-96	Away	23-Mar-96	0-2		38,271	P.Durkin
1996-97	Home	30-Nov-96	1-2	Shearer (20)	36,565	G.Barber
1996-97	Away	3-May-97	1-0	Elliot R. (44)	38,179	M.Bodenham
1997-98	Home	6-Dec-97	0-1		36,571	S.Dunn
1997-98	Away	11-Apr-98	1-3	Barton (79)	38,102	G.Willard
1998-99	Away	4-Oct-98	0-3		38,102	M.Reed
1998-99	Home	28-Feb-99	1-1	Hamann (77)	36,708	M.Reed
1999-00	Away	30-Oct-99	0-0		38,106	P.Jones
1999-00	Home	14-May-00	4-2	Speed (6, 59); Shearer (23); Griffin (63)	36,450	G.Poll

ASTON VILLA

Season	Venue	Date	Res	Scorers	Attendance	Referee
1993-94	Away	2-Oct-93	2-0	Allen (46 pen); Cole (80)	37,336	P.Durkin
1993-94	Home	27-Apr-94	5-1	Bracewell (15); Beardsley (23pen, 66); Cole (41); Sellars (79)	32,217	J.Lloyd
1994-95	Away	1-Oct-94	2-0	Lee (66); Cole (83)	29,960	D.Gallagher
1994-95	Home	25-Feb-95	3-1	Venison (31); Beardsley (55,66)	34,637	P.Don
1995-96	Away	18-Nov-95	1-1	Ferdinand (58)	39,167	S.Lodge
1995-96	Home	14-Apr-96	1-0	Ferdinand (64)	36,510	M.Bodenham
1996-97	Home	30-Sep-96	4-3	Ferdinand (5, 22); Shearer (38); Howey (67)	36,400	D.Elleray
1996-97	Away	11-Jan-97	2-2	Shearer (16); Clark (22)	39,339	G.Poll
1997-98	Home	23-Aug-97	1-0	Beresford (12)	36,783	G.Willard
1997-98	Away	1-Feb-98	1-0	Batty (58)	38,266	S.Lodge
1998-99	Away	9-Sep-98	0-1		39,241	G.Poll
1998-99	Home	30-Jan-99	2-1	Shearer (4); Ketsbaia (27)	36,766	R.Harris
1999-00	Home	7-Aug-99	0-1		36,517	U.Rennie
1999-00	Away	4-Dec-99	1-0	Ferguson (65)	34,531	M.Riley

BARNSLEY

Season	Venue	Date	Res	Scorers	Attendance	Referee
1997-98	Away	13-Dec-97	2-2	Gillespie (44, 49)	18,687	P.Alcock
1997-98	Home	13-Apr-98	2-1	Andersson (40); Shearer (86)	36,534	S.Dunn

BLACKBURN ROVERS

Season	Venue	Date	Res	Scorers	Attendance	Referee
1993-94	Home	29-Aug-93	1-1	Cole (60)	33,987	S.Lodge
1993-94	Away	19-Feb-94	0-1		20,798	K.Burge
1994-95	Home	9-Oct-94	1-1	OG (88, Flowers)	34,344	S.Lodge
1994-95	Away	8-May-95	0-1		30,545	P.Don
1995-96	Home	8-Nov-95	1-0	Lee (13)	36,463	D.Gallagher
1995-96	Away	8-Apr-96	1-2	Batty (76)	30,717	G.Willard
1996-97	Home	14-Sep-96	2-1	Shearer (44 pen); Ferdinand (60)	36,424	K.Burge
1996-97	Away	26-Dec-96	0-1		30,398	M.Reed
1997-98	Home	25-Oct-97	1-1	Gillespie (27)	36,716	J.Winter
1997-98	Away	10-May-98	0-1		29,300	D.Elleray
1998-99	Away	12-Dec-98	0-0		27,569	R.Harris
1998-99	Home	16-May-99	1-1	Hamann (51)	36,623	J.Winter

BOLTON WANDERERS

Season	Venue	Date	Res	Scorers	Attendance	Referee
1995-96	Away	22-Aug-95	3-1	Ferdinand (17, 84); Lee (77)	20,243	S.Lodge
1995-96	Home	20-Jan-96	2-1	Kitson (9); Beardsley (37)	36,534	K.Cooper
1997-98	Away	1-Dec-97	0-1		24,494	N.Barry
1997-98	Home	17-Jan-98	2-1	Barnes (6); Ketsbaia (90)	36,767	G.Poll

BRADFORD CITY

Season	Venue	Date	Res	Scorers	Attendance	Referee
1999-00	Away	18-Dec-99	0-2		18,276	N.Barry
1999-00	Home	1-Apr-00	2-0	Speed (6); Shearer (89)	36,572	A.D'Urso

CHARLTON ATHLETIC

Season	Venue	Date	Res	Scorers	Attendance	Referee
1998-99	Home	15-Aug-98	0-0		36,719	D.Gallagher
1998-99	Away	17-Jan-99	2-2	Ketsbaia (13); Solano (55)	20,043	P.Jones

CHELSEA

Season	Venue	Date	Res	Scorers	Attendance	Referee
1993-94	Away	28-Dec-93	0-1		22,133	J.Worrall
1993-94	Home	4-Apr-94	0-0		32,218	S.Lodge
1994-95	Home	10-Sep-94	4-2	Cole (7,66); Fox (21); Lee (55)	34,435	P.Jones
1994-95	Away	1-Apr-95	1-1	Hottiger (88)	22,987	M.Bodenham
1995-96	Home	24-Sep-95	2-0	Ferdinand (41, 57)	36,225	P.Jones
1995-96	Away	9-Dec-95	0-1		31,098	R.Dilkes
1996-97	Away	23-Nov-96	1-1	Shearer (42)	28,401	M.Reed
1996-97	Home	16-Apr-97	3-1	Shearer (11, 35); Asprilla (30)	36,320	R.Dilkes
1997-98	Away	27-Sep-97	0-1		31,563	M.Riley
1997-98	Home	2-May-98	3-1	Dabizas (38); Lee (42); Speed (58)	36,710	K.Burge
1998-99	Away	22-Aug-98	1-1	Andersson (42)	34,795	U.Rennie

1998-99	Home	9-Jan-99	0-1		36,711	D.Gallagher
1999-00	Away	11-Sep-99	0-1		35,092	G.Poll
1999-00	Home	4-Mar-00	0-1		36,448	M.Riley

COVENTRY CITY

Season	Venue	Date	Res	Scorers	Attendance	Referee
1993-94	Away	18-Aug-93	1-2	O'Brien (27)	15,760	J.Borrett
1993-94	Home	23-Feb-94	4-0	Cole (49, 70, 77); Mathie (86)	32,210	R.Hart
1994-95	Home	24-Aug-94	4-0	Lee (21,34); Watson (26); Cole (73)	34,163	P.Danson
1994-95	Away	17-Dec-94	0-0		17,233	P.Danson
1995-96	Home	19-Aug-95	3-0	Lee (7); Beardsley (82 pen); Ferdinand (83)	36,485	R.Dilkes
1995-96	Away	14-Jan-96	1-0	Watson (44)	20,553	P.Jones
1996-97	Away	17-Dec-96	1-2	Shearer (61)	21,538	P.Jones
1996-97	Home	15-Mar-97	4-0	Watson (11); Lee (44); Beardsley (75 pen); Elliott R. (86)	36,571	G.Ashby
1997-98	Away	8-Nov-97	2-2	Barnes (31); Lee (87)	22,679	P.Durkin
1997-98	Home	14-Mar-98	0-0		36,767	P.Jones
1998-99	Away	19-Sep-98	5-1	Dabizas (14); Shearer (42, 90); Speed (43); Glass (58)	22,656	R.Harris
1998-99	Home	17-Feb-99	4-1	Shearer (18, 75); Speed (55); Saha (58)	36,352	S.Dunn
1999-00	Away	16-Oct-99	1-4	Domi (81)	23,031	A.Wiley
1999-00	Home	29-Apr-00	2-0	Shearer (78 pen); Gavilan (84)	36,408	P.Jones

CRYSTAL PALACE

Season	Venue	Date	Res	Scorers	Attendance	Referee
1994-95	Away	15-Oct-94	1-0	Beardsley (89)	17,739	K.Morton
1994-95	Home	14-May-95	3-2	Fox (6); Lee (26); Gillespie (28)	35,626	G.Ashby
1997-98	Away	29-Nov-97	2-1	Ketsbia (45); Tomasson (64)	26,085	M.Riley
1997-98	Home	18-Mar-98	1-2	Shearer (77)	36,565	S.Lodge

DERBY COUNTY

Season	Venue	Date	Res	Scorers	Attendance	Referee
1996-97	Away	12-Oct-96	1-0	Shearer (76)	18,092	M.Bodenham
1996-97	Home	19-Apr-97	3-1	Elliot R. (11); Ferdinand (51); Shearer (74)	36,553	D.Gallagher
1997-98	Home	17-Dec-97	0-0		36,289	K.Burge
1997-98	Away	26-Dec-97	0-1		30,302	M.Reed
1998-99	Home	17-Oct-98	2-1	Dabizas (13); Glass (17)	36,750	K.Burge
1998-99	Away	3-Apr-99	4-3	Speed (11, 24); Ketsbaia (39); Solano (60)	32,039	D.Gallagher
1999-00	Home	25-Oct-99	2-0	OG (42, Eranio); Shearer (53)	35,614	S.Dunn
1999-00	Away	6-May-00	0-0		32,724	A.Wiley

EVERTON

Season	Venue	Date	Res	Scorers	Attendance	Referee
1993-94	Home	25-Aug-93	1-0	Allen (18)	34,490	G.Ashby
1993-94	Away	18-Dec-93	2-0	Cole (14); Beardsley (76)	25,362	M.Bodenham
1994-95	Home	1-Feb-95	2-0	Fox (74); Beardsley (80 pen)	34,465	D.Elleray
1994-95	Away	14-Apr-95	0-2		34,811	R.Gifford
1995-96	Away	1-Oct-95	3-1	Ferdinand (20); Lee (59); Kitson (65)	33,080	K.Cooper
1995-96	Home	16-Dec-95	1-0	Ferdinand (17)	36,557	P.Durkin
1996-97	Away	17-Aug-96	0-2		40,117	M.Reed
1996-97	Home	29-Jan-97	4-1	Ferdinand (74); Lee (79); Shearer (87 pen); Elliot R.(90)	36,143	M.Riley
1997-98	Home	24-Sep-97	1-0	Lee (87)	36,705	G.Poll

1997-98	Away	28-Feb-98	0-0		37,972	M.Riley
1998-99	Away	23-Nov-98	0-1		30,357	N.Barry
1998-99	Home	17-Apr-99	1-3	Shearer (82 pen)	36,775	G.Poll
1999-00	Home	7-Nov-99	1-1	Shearer (46 pen)	36,164	M.Reed
1999-00	Away	19-Mar-00	2-0	Hughes (81); Dyer (87)	32,512	G.Barber

IPSWICH TOWN

Season	Venue	Date	Res	Scorers	Attendance	Referee
1993-94	Away	31-Aug-93	1-1	Cole (47)	19,126	D.Gallagher
1993-94	Home	23-Mar-94	2-0	Sellars (37); Cole (73)	32,234	K.Cooper
1994-95	Home	26-Nov-94	1-1	Cole (86)	34,459	K.Cooper
1994-95	Away	28-Feb-95	2-0	Fox (12); Kitson (38)	18,639	G.Ashby

LEEDS UNITED

Season	Venue	Date	Res	Scorers	Attendance	Referee
1993-94	Home	22-Dec-93	1-1	Cole (85)	36,342	P.Don
1993-94	Away	1-Apr-94	1-1	Cole (3)	40,005	K.Cooper
1994-95	Away	26-Dec-94	0-0		39,337	J.Worrall
1994-95	Home	17-Apr-95	1-2	Elliott (30)	35,626	P.Danson
1995-96	Home	25-Nov-95	2-1	Lee (70); Beardsley (72)	36,572	S.Dunn
1995-96	Away	29-Apr-96	1-0	Gillespie (17)	38,862	K.Burge
1996-97	Away	21-Sep-96	1-0	Shearer (59)	36,070	P.Alcock
1996-97	Home	1-Jan-97	3-0	Shearer (4, 77); Ferdinand (87)	36,489	P.Danson
1997-98	Away	18-Oct-97	1-4	Gillespie (62)	39,834	D.Elleray
1997-98	Home	22-Feb-98	1-1	Ketsbaia (85)	36,511	G.Willard
1998-99	Home	26-Dec-98	0-3		36,783	G.Willard
1998-99	Away	6-Feb-99	1-0	Solano (63)	40,202	U.Rennie
1999-00	Away	25-Sep-99	2-3	Shearer (42, 54)	40,192	B.Knight
1999-00	Home	23-Apr-00	2-2	Shearer (24, 48)	36,460	D.Elleray

LEICESTER CITY

Season	Venue	Date	Res	Scorers	Attendance	Referee
1994-95	Away	21-Aug-94	3-1	Cole (51); Beardsley (58); Elliott (74)	20,048	M.Reed
1994-95	Home	10-Dec-94	3-1	Albert (32,70); Howey (50)	34,400	G.Willard
1996-97	Away	26-Oct-96	0-2		21,134	G.Poll
1996-97	Home	2-Feb-97	4-3	Elliott R. (3); Shearer (77, 83, 90)	36,396	M.Reed
1997-98	Home	1-Nov-97	3-3	Barnes (4 pen); Tomasson (45); Beresford (90)	36,574	G.Willard
1997-98	Away	29-Apr-98	0-0		21,699	M.Bodenham
1998-99	Home	19-Dec-98	1-0	Glass (66)	36,718	J.Winter
1998-99	Away	8-May-99	0-2		21,125	U.Rennie
1999-00	Away	28-Dec-99	2-1	Ferguson (21); Shearer (53)	21,225	P.Durkin
1999-00	Home	15-Apr-00	0-2		36,426	U.Rennie

LIVERPOOL

Season	Venue	Date	Res	Scorers	Attendance	Referee
1993-94	Home	21-Nov-93	3-0	Cole (4, 15, 30)	36,246	G.Ashby
1993-94	Away	16-Apr-94	2-0	Lee (4); Cole (56)	44,601	P.Don
1994-95	Home	24-Sep-94	1-1	Lee (50)	34,435	P.Don
1994-95	Away	4-Mar-95	0-2		39,300	P.Jones
1995-96	Home	4-Nov-95	2-1	Ferdinand (3); Watson (89)	36,547	M.Reed
1995-96	Away	3-Apr-96	3-4	Ferdinand (10); Ginola (14); Asprilla (60)	40,702	M.Reed

1996-97	Home	23-Dec-96	1-1	Shearer (29)	36,570	P.Alcock
1996-97	Away	10-Mar-97	3-4	Gillespie (71); Asprilla (87); Barton (88)	40,751	D.Elleray
1997-98	Home	28-Dec-97	1-2	Watson (16)	36,718	G.Ashby
1997-98	Away	20-Jan-98	0-1		42,791	G.Barber
1998-99	Home	30-Aug-98	1-4	Guivarc'h (28)	36,740	G.Barber
1998-99	Away	28-Dec-98	2-4	Solano (29); Andersson (56)	44,605	S.Lodge
1999-00	Home	26-Dec-99	2-2	Shearer (12); Ferguson (67)	36,445	D.Elleray
1999-00	Away	25-Mar-00	1-2	Shearer (67)	44,743	P.Durkin

MANCHESTER CITY

Season	Venue	Date	Res	Scorers	Attendance	Referee
1993-94	Home	1-Jan-94	2-0	Cole (28, 45)	35,585	K.Morton
1993-94	Away	9-Apr-94	1-2	Sellars (19)	33,774	J.Borrett
1994-95	Home	2-Jan-95	0-0		34,437	A.Wilkie
1994-95	Away	29-Apr-95	0-0		27,389	G.Poll
1995-96	Home	16-Sep-95	3-1	Beardsley (18 pen); Lee (38); Ferdinand (59)	36,501	J.Winter
1995-96	Away	24-Feb-96	3-3	Albert (44, 81); Asprilla (71)	31,115	M.Bodenham

MANCHESTER UNITED

Season	Venue	Date	Res	Scorers	Attendance	Referee
1993-94	Away	21-Aug-93	1-1	Cole (70)	41,829	K.Morton
1993-94	Home	11-Dec-93	1-1	Cole (71)	36,332	K.Hackett
1994-95	Away	29-Oct-94	0-2		43,795	J.Worrall
1994-95	Home	15-Jan-95	1-1	Kitson (67)	34,471	S.Lodge
1995-96	Away	27-Dec-95	0-2		42,024	P.Alcock
1995-96	Home	4-Mar-96	0-1		36,584	D.Elleray
1996-97	Home	20-Oct-96	5-0	Peacock (12); Ginola (30); Ferdinand (62); Shearer (74); Albert (83)	36,579	S.Dunn
1996-97	Away	8-May-97	0-0		55,236	S.Dunn
1997-98	Home	21-Dec-97	0-1		36,767	P.Jones
1997-98	Away	18-Apr-98	1-1	Andersson (11)	55,194	U.Rennie
1998-99	Away	8-Nov-98	0-0		55,174	S.Dunn
1998-99	Home	13-Mar-99	1-2	Solano (16)	36,500	D.Elleray
1999-00	Away	30-Aug-99	1-5	OG (31, Berg)	55,190	J.Winter
1999-00	Home	12-Feb-00	3-0	Ferguson (26); Shearer (76, 86)	36,470	S.Lodge

MIDDLESBROUGH

Season	Venue	Date	Res	Scorers	Attendance	Referee
1995-96	Home	30-Aug-95	1-0	Ferdinand (67)	36,483	R.Hart
1995-96	Away	10-Feb-96	2-1	Watson (73); Ferdinand (78)	30,011	S.Dunn
1996-97	Home	3-Nov-96	3-1	Beardsley (40 pen, 69); Lee (74)	36,577	G.Willard
1996-97	Away	22-Feb-97	1-0	Ferdinand (8)	30,063	S.Dunn
1998-99	Away	6-Dec-98	2-2	Charvet (38); Dabizas (83)	34,629	U.Rennie
1998-99	Home	1-May-99	1-1	Shearer (64 pen)	36,552	M.Reed
1999-00	Home	3-Oct-99	2-1	Shearer (17, 44)	36,421	S.Lodge
1999-00	Away	2-May-00	2-2	Speed (10); Pistone (18)	34,744	M.Riley

NORWICH CITY

Season	Venue	Date	Res	Scorers	Attendance	Referee
1993-94	Away	4-Jan-94	2-1	Beardsley (20); Cole (80)	19,564	T.Holbrook
1993-94	Home	29-Mar-94	3-0	Cole (50); Lee (50); Beardsley (70)	32,228	T.Holbrook

| 1994-95 | Away | 31-Dec-94 | 1-2 | Fox (39 pen) | 21,172 | B.Hill |
| 1994-95 | Home | 8-Apr-95 | 3-0 | Beardsley (8 pen, 42); Kitson (74) | 35,518 | M.Reed |

NOTTINGHAM FOREST

Season	Venue	Date	Res	Scorers	Attendance	Referee
1994-95	Away	7-Nov-94	0-0		22,102	K.Burge
1994-95	Home	11-Feb-95	2-1	Fox (47); Lee (73)	34,471	K.Morton
1995-96	Home	23-Dec-95	3-1	Lee (12, 74); Ginola (25)	36,531	D.Elleray
1995-96	Away	2-May-96	1-1	Beardsley (32)	28,280	R.Dilkes
1996-97	Away	9-Dec-96	0-0		25,762	D.Elleray
1996-97	Home	11-May-97	5-0	Asprilla (20); Ferdinand (23, 26); Shearer (36); Elliot (77)	36,554	M.Reed
1998-99	Home	26-Sep-98	2-0	Shearer (11, 89 pen)	36,760	D.Elleray
1998-99	Away	10-Mar-99	2-1	Shearer (45 pen); Hamann (73)	22,852	J.Winter

OLDHAM ATHLETIC

Season	Venue	Date	Res	Scorers	Attendance	Referee
1993-94	Away	8-Nov-93	3-1	Cole (53, 81); Beardsley (73)	13,821	R.Gifford
1993-94	Home	23-Apr-94	3-2	Fox (19); Beardsley (54); Lee (63)	32,214	D.Allison

QPR

Season	Venue	Date	Res	Scorers	Attendance	Referee
1993-94	Home	16-Oct-93	1-2	Allen (48)	33,801	K.Hackett
1993-94	Away	16-Jan-94	2-1	Clark (4); Beardsley (63)	15,774	D.Gallagher
1994-95	Home	5-Nov-94	2-1	Kitson (20); Beardsley (42)	34,278	G.Ashby
1994-95	Away	4-Feb-95	0-3		16,576	K.Cooper
1995-96	Away	14-Oct-95	3-2	Gillespie (48, 72); Ferdinand (57)	18,254	P.Durkin
1995-96	Home	6-Apr-96	2-1	Beardsley (77, 81)	36,583	P.Sampson

SHEFFIELD UNITED

Season	Venue	Date	Res	Scorers	Attendance	Referee
1993-94	Home	24-Nov-93	4-0	OG (9, Ward); Beardsley (12, 73); Cole (70)	35,029	J.Worrall
1993-94	Away	30-Apr-94	0-2		29,013	J.Worrall

SHEFFIELD WEDNESDAY

Season	Venue	Date	Res	Scorers	Attendance	Referee
1993-94	Home	13-Sep-93	4-2	Cole (21, 76); Mathie (81); Allen (88)	33,519	R.Dilkes
1993-94	Away	5-Mar-94	1-0	Cole (88)	33,153	P.Durkin
1994-95	Home	22-Oct-94	2-1	Watson (35); Cole (37)	34,408	G.Poll
1994-95	Away	21-Jan-95	0-0		31,215	R.Gifford
1995-96	Away	27-Aug-95	2-0	Ginola (53); Beardsley (75)	24,815	P.Alcock
1995-96	Home	3-Feb-96	2-0	Ferdinand (54); Clark (90)	36,567	P.Danson
1996-97	Home	24-Aug-96	1-2	Shearer (12 pen)	36,452	P.Jones
1996-97	Away	13-Apr-97	1-1	Elliot R. (38)	33,798	G.Barber
1997-98	Home	9-Aug-97	2-1	Asprilla (2, 71)	36,771	P.Jones
1997-98	Away	10-Jan-98	1-2	Tomasson (20)	29,446	D.Elleray
1998-99	Home	14-Nov-98	1-1	Dalglish (4)	36,698	P.Jones
1998-99	Away	21-Apr-99	1-1	Shearer (45 pen)	21,545	P.Alcock
1999-00	Home	19-Sep-99	8-0	Hughes (11); Shearer (30, 33pen, 42, 81, 84pen); Dyer (46); Speed (78)	36,619	N.Barry
1999-00	Away	26-Feb-00	2-0	Gallacher (11); Shearer (86)	29,212	M.Riley

SOUTHAMPTON

Season	Venue	Date	Res	Scorers	Attendance	Referee
1993-94	Away	24-Oct-93	1-2	Cole (72)	13,804	P.Don
1993-94	Home	22-Jan-94	1-2	Cole (38)	32,067	A.Gunn
1994-95	Home	27-Aug-94	5-1	Watson (30,37); Cole (40,73); Lee (85)	34,181	D.Elleray
1994-95	Away	22-Mar-95	1-3	Kitson (18)	14,676	J.Worrall
1995-96	Away	9-Sep-95	0-1		15,237	G.Ashby
1995-96	Home	17-Apr-96	1-0	Lee (10)	36,554	D.Gallagher
1996-97	Away	18-Jan-97	2-2	Ferdinand (13); Clark (82)	15,251	M.Reed
1996-97	Home	1-Mar-97	0-1		36,446	M.Bodenham
1997-98	Home	22-Nov-97	2-1	Barnes (54, 75)	37,759	D.Gallagher
1997-98	Away	28-Mar-98	1-2	Lee (46)	15,251	G.Barber
1998-99	Home	12-Sep-98	4-0	Shearer (8, 38 pen); Ketsbaia (90); OG (90, Marshall)	36,454	M.Riley
1998-99	Away	20-Feb-99	1-2	Hamann (86)	15,244	G.Poll
1999-00	Away	15-Aug-99	2-4	Shearer (23 pen); Speed (84)	15,030	D.Elleray
1999-00	Home	16-Jan-00	5-0	Ferguson (3, 4); Solano (17); OG (31, Dryden); OG (83, Monk)	35,623	N.Barry

SUNDERLAND

Season	Venue	Date	Res	Scorers	Attendance	Referee
1996-97	Away	3-Sep-96	2-1	Beardsley (52); Ferdinand (62)	22,037	J.Winter
1996-97	Home	5-Apr-97	1-1	Shearer (77)	36,582	P.Durkin
1999-00	Home	25-Aug-99	1-2	Dyer (28)	36,500	G.Poll
1999-00	Away	5-Feb-00	2-2	Domi (11); Helder (21)	42,192	D.Gallagher

SWINDON TOWN

Season	Venue	Date	Res	Scorers	Attendance	Referee
1993-94	Away	18-Sep-93	2-2	Clark (37); Allen (45 pen)	15,393	H.King
1993-94	Home	12-Mar-94	7-1	Beardsley (12pen, 70); Lee (17, 67); Watson (76, 79); Fox (84)	32,219	M.Reed

TOTTENHAM HOTSPUR

Season	Venue	Date	Res	Scorers	Attendance	Referee
1993-94	Home	14-Aug-93	0-1		34,565	D.Allison
1993-94	Away	4-Dec-93	2-1	Beardsley (54, 89)	30,780	M.Reed
1994-95	Away	3-Dec-94	2-4	Fox (29,41)	28,002	D.Gallagher
1994-95	Home	3-May-95	3-3	Gillespie (7); Peacock (10); Beardsley (70)	35,603	D.Gallagher
1995-96	Away	29-Oct-95	1-1	Ginola (47)	32,279	M.Bodenham
1995-96	Home	5-May-96	1-1	Ferdinand (71)	36,589	D.Gallagher
1996-97	Away	7-Sep-96	2-1	Ferdinand (36, 80)	32,535	P.Durkin
1996-97	Home	28-Dec-96	7-1	Shearer (19, 82); Ferdinand (22, 58); Lee (60, 87); Albert (78)	36,308	G.Ashby
1997-98	Home	4-Oct-97	1-0	Barton (89)	36,709	M.Bodenham
1997-98	Away	25-Apr-98	0-2		35,847	J.Winter
1998-99	Away	24-Oct-98	0-2		36,047	G.Barber
1998-99	Home	5-Apr-99	1-1	Ketsbaia (78)	36,655	M.Riley
1999-00	Away	9-Aug-99	1-3	Solano (16)	28,701	R.Harris
1999-00	Home	28-Nov-99	2-1	Glass (5); Dabizas (58)	36,460	P.Alcock

WATFORD

Season	Venue	Date	Res	Scorers	Attendance	Referee
1999-00	Away	20-Nov-99	1-1	Dabizas (59)	19,539	S.Dunn
1999-00	Home	11-Mar-00	1-0	Gallacher (59)	36,433	A.Wiley

WEST HAM UNITED

Season	Venue	Date	Res	Scorers	Attendance	Referee
1993-94	Home	25-Sep-93	2-0	Cole (51, 84)	34,179	M.Reed
1993-94	Away	19-Mar-94	4-2	OG (34, Potts); Lee (73); Cole (69); Mathie (90)	23,132	K.Morton
1994-95	Away	31-Aug-94	3-1	OG (31, Potts); Lee (35); Mathie (89)	18,580	B.Hill
1994-95	Home	8-Mar-95	2-0	Clark (17); Kitson (52)	34,595	T.Holbrook
1995-96	Away	21-Feb-96	0-2		23,843	P.Alcock
1995-96	Home	18-Mar-96	3-0	Albert (21); Asprilla (55); Ferdinand (65)	36,331	S.Lodge
1996-97	Home	16-Nov-96	1-1	Beardsley (82)	36,552	P.Danson
1996-97	Away	6-May-97	0-0		24,617	G.Poll
1997-98	Away	20-Sep-97	1-0	Barnes (43)	25,884	S.Dunn
1997-98	Home	7-Feb-98	0-1		36,736	U.Rennie
1998-99	Home	31-Oct-98	0-3		36,744	G.Poll
1998-99	Away	21-Mar-99	0-2		25,997	P.Durkin
1999-00	Home	3-Jan-00	2-2	Dabizas (18); Speed (65)	36,314	R.Harris
1999-00	Away	12-Apr-00	1-2	Speed (48)	25,817	P.Alcock

WIMBLEDON

Season	Venue	Date	Res	Scorers	Attendance	Referee
1993-94	Home	30-Oct-93	4-0	Beardsley (36 pen, 63, 71); Cole (60)	33,371	V.Callow
1993-94	Away	12-Feb-94	2-4	Beardsley (50pen, 89pen)	13,358	J.Lloyd
1994-95	Away	19-Nov-94	2-3	Beardsley (29); Kitson (32)	14,203	P.Don
1994-95	Home	25-Jan-95	2-1	Fox (34); Kitson (51)	34,374	M.Reed
1995-96	Home	21-Oct-95	6-1	Howey (31); Ferdinand (35, 41, 63); Clark (5); Albert (84)	36,434	G.Poll
1995-96	Away	3-Dec-95	3-3	Ferdinand (8, 29); Gillespie (35)	18,002	G.Ashby
1996-97	Home	21-Aug-96	2-0	Batty (4); Shearer (87)	36,385	S.Lodge
1996-97	Away	23-Mar-97	1-1	Asprilla (52)	23,175	S.Lodge
1997-98	Home	13-Sep-97	1-3	Barton (31)	36,256	M.Reed
1997-98	Away	31-Mar-98	0-0		15,478	N.Barry
1998-99	Home	28-Nov-98	3-1	Solano (38); Ferguson (59, 90)	36,623	U.Rennie
1998-99	Away	24-Apr-99	1-1	Shearer (18)	21,172	P.Jones
1999-00	Home	21-Aug-99	3-3	Speed (7); Domi (28); Solano (46 pen)	35,809	M.Reed
1999-00	Away	22-Jan-00	0-2		22,118	D.Gallagher

INTRODUCTION

Formed following a June 1902 public meeting organised by two local schoolteachers which agreed the desirability of a Norwich City Football Club. Started in the Norwich & Suffolk League. Turned professional and elected to the Southern League in 1905. Moved from Newmarket Road to The Nest, Rosary Road in 1908.

Founder members of Football League Divison Three with other Southern Leaguers in 1920, this becoming Division Three (South) in 1921. Moved to Carrow Road, the home of Boulton & Paul Sports Club in 1935. Founder members of Division Three on the end of regionalisation in 1958. Premier League founder members 1992.

Ground: Carrow Road, Norwich, NR1 1JE
Nickname: The Canaries
Internet: www.canaries.co.uk

HONOURS

Football League Div 2:	Champions: 1971-72,1985-86
Football League Div 3S:	Champions: 1933-34
Football League Div 3:	Runners-up: 1959-60.
Football League Cup:	Winners: 1962, 1985
	Runners-up: 1973, 1975

EUROPEAN RECORD

Champions' League (0):	–
Cup-Winners' Cup (0):	–
UEFA Cup (1):	93-94(2)

FAPL RECORD SUMMARY

Most Total:	BOWEN, Mark	119
Most Starts:	BOWEN, Mark	117
Most Subs:	SUTCH, Daryl	20
Most SNU:	HOWIE, Scott	45
Most PS:	ROBINS, Mark	19
Most Goals:	SUTTON, Chris	33
Most Yel:	GOSS, Jeremy	13
Most Red:	GUNN, Bryan	1

PLAYING RECORD – SEASON TOTALS

Season	Pn	P	W	D	L	F	A	Pts
1992-93	3	42	21	9	12	61	65	72
1993-94	12	42	12	17	13	65	61	53
1994-95	20	42	10	13	19	37	54	43
Totals		126	43	39	44	163	180	168

PLAYING RECORD – HOME TOTALS

Season	Pn	P	W	D	L	F	A	Pts
1992-93	3	21	13	6	2	31	19	45
1993-94	12	21	4	9	8	26	29	21
1994-95	20	21	8	8	5	27	21	32
Totals		63	25	23	15	84	69	98

PLAYING RECORD – AWAY TOTALS

Season	Pn	P	W	D	L	F	A	Pts
1992-93	3	21	8	3	10	30	46	27
1993-94	12	21	8	8	5	39	32	32
1994-95	20	21	2	5	14	10	33	11
Totals		63	18	16	29	79	111	70

HIGHEST HOME ATTENDANCES

	Attendance	Opponents	Date	Season
1	21,843	Liverpool	29-Apr-95	1994-95
2	21,824	Manchester U.	22-Feb-95	1994-95
3	21,814	Tottenham H.	26-Dec-94	1994-95
4	21,181	Tottenham H.	2-Apr-94	1993-94
5	21,172	Newcastle U.	31-Dec-94	1994-95

LOWEST HOME ATTENDANCES

	Attendance	Opponents	Date	Season
1	12,452	Southampton	5-Sep-92	1992-93
2	13,530	Sheffield W.	8-Mar-95	1994-95
3	13,543	Crystal P.	27-Jan-93	1992-93
4	13,613	Coventry C.	16-Jan-93	1992-93
5	14,024	Coventry C.	25-Jan-95	1994-95

TOP SCORER – SEASON BY SEASON

Season	Player	Goals
1992-93	Robins	15
1993-94	Sutton	25
1994-95	Ward	8

PLAYERS WITH MOST PREMIERSHIP APPEARANCES

Tot	Player	St	Sb	Gls
119	BOWEN, Mark	117	2	7
106	CROOK, Ian	103	3	3
104	GUNN, Bryan	104	0	0
96	POLSTON, John	96	0	1
84	GOSS, Jeremy	78	6	9
83	CULVERHOUSE, Ian	83	0	1
82	NEWMAN, Rob	71	11	5
79	SUTTON, Chris	73	6	33
67	ROBINS, Mark	57	10	20
59	FOX, Ruel	57	2	11
55	SUTCH, Daryl	35	20	3
51	BUTTERWORTH, Ian	49	2	1

CLUB-BY-CLUB RESULTS

ARSENAL

Season	Venue	Date	Res	Scorers	Attendance	Referee
1992-93	Away	15-Aug-92	4-2	Robins (69, 84); Phillips (72); Fox (82)	24,030	A.Gunn
1992-93	Home	3-Mar-93	1-1	Fox (35)	14,820	J.Martin
1993-94	Away	30-Oct-93	0-0		30,516	R.Dilkes
1993-94	Home	13-Feb-94	1-1	Ekoku (57)	17,667	R.Dilkes
1994-95	Home	10-Sep-94	0-0		17,768	R.Hart
1994-95	Away	1-Apr-95	1-5	Cureton (32)	36,942	P.Jones

ASTON VILLA

Season	Venue	Date	Res	Scorers	Attendance	Referee
1992-93	Away	28-Nov-92	3-2	Phillips (17); Beckford (30); Sutch (49)	28,837	A.Buksh
1992-93	Home	24-Mar-93	1-0	Polston (81)	19,528	R.Hart
1993-94	Home	29-Dec-93	1-2	Sutton (26)	20,650	D.Elleray
1993-94	Away	4-Apr-94	0-0		25,416	M.Bodenham
1994-95	Away	15-Oct-94	1-1	Milligan (49)	22,468	A.Wilkie
1994-95	Home	14-May-95	1-1	Goss (56)	19,374	K.Cooper

BLACKBURN ROVERS

Season	Venue	Date	Res	Scorers	Attendance	Referee
1992-93	Away	3-Oct-92	1-7	Newman (39)	16,312	R.Dilkes
1992-93	Home	28-Feb-93	0-0		15,821	P.Don
1993-94	Away	18-Aug-93	3-2	Sutton (44, 65); Newman (63)	14,260	R.Hart
1993-94	Home	22-Feb-94	2-2	Sutton (40 pen, 57)	15,124	K.Barratt
1994-95	Home	1-Oct-94	2-1	Bowen (30); Newsome (55)	18,146	P.Jones
1994-95	Away	25-Feb-95	0-0		25,579	M.Reed

CHELSEA

Season	Venue	Date	Res	Scorers	Attendance	Referee
1992-93	Home	19-Aug-92	2-1	Phillips (57); Robins (59)	15,164	G.Ashby
1992-93	Away	12-Sep-92	3-2	Robins (46,74); Phillips (79)	16,880	K.Barratt
1993-94	Away	16-Oct-93	2-1	Fox (23); Sutton (69)	16,923	V.Callow
1993-94	Home	15-Jan-94	1-1	Ekoku (59)	19,472	K.Cooper
1994-95	Away	20-Aug-94	0-2		23,098	T.Holbrook
1994-95	Home	10-Dec-94	3-0	Ward (23,45); Cureton (88)	18,246	J.Worrall

COVENTRY CITY

Season	Venue	Date	Res	Scorers	Attendance	Referee
1992-93	Away	26-Sep-92	1-1	Crook (13)	16,436	A.Buksh
1992-93	Home	16-Jan-93	1-1	Sutton (13)	13,613	A.Gunn
1993-94	Home	2-Oct-93	1-0	Fox (45)	16,239	D.Gallagher
1993-94	Away	26-Mar-94	1-2	Eadie (46)	13,515	D.Frampton
1994-95	Away	19-Nov-94	0-1		11,885	G.Willard
1994-95	Home	25-Jan-95	2-2	Adams (32 pen); Ward (58)	14,024	P.Don

CRYSTAL PALACE

Season	Venue	Date	Res	Scorers	Attendance	Referee
1992-93	Away	29-Aug-92	2-1	Power (16); Phillips (74)	12,033	D.Allison
1992-93	Home	27-Jan-93	4-2	Power (9,89); Sutton (26); Goss (50)	13,543	V.Callow
1994-95	Home	24-Aug-94	0-0		19,015	B.Hill
1994-95	Away	17-Dec-94	1-0	Ward (48)	12,252	R.Hart

EVERTON

Season	Venue	Date	Res	Scorers	Attendance	Referee
1992-93	Home	22-Aug-92	1-1	Fox (67)	14,150	J.Key
1992-93	Away	30-Jan-93	1-0	Sutton (16)	20,301	R.Lewis
1993-94	Away	25-Sep-93	5-1	Ekoku (44, 57, 63, 69); Sutton (77)	20,631	P.Durkin
1993-94	Home	21-Mar-94	3-0	Culverhouse (40); Sutton (49); Bowen (70)	16,432	K.Burge
1994-95	Home	5-Nov-94	0-0		18,377	P.Danson
1994-95	Away	4-Feb-95	1-2	Milligan (80)	23,293	A.Wilkie

IPSWICH TOWN

Season	Venue	Date	Res	Scorers	Attendance	Referee
1992-93	Home	21-Dec-92	0-2		20,032	D.Elleray
1992-93	Away	19-Apr-93	1-3	Sutton (41)	21,081	V.Callow
1993-94	Home	25-Aug-93	1-0	Goss (28)	18,976	A.Gunn
1993-94	Away	18-Dec-93	1-2	Bowen (40)	19,751	M.Reed
1994-95	Away	19-Sep-94	2-1	Newman (11); Bradshaw (52 pen)	17,447	R.Dilkes
1994-95	Home	20-Mar-95	3-0	Cureton (53); Ward (58); Eadie (77)	17,510	P.Durkin

LEEDS UNITED

Season	Venue	Date	Res	Scorers	Attendance	Referee
1992-93	Away	28-Dec-92	0-0		30,282	P.Don
1992-93	Home	14-Apr-93	4-2	Sutton (11, 14, 79); Phillips (15 pen)	18,613	K.Burge
1993-94	Away	21-Aug-93	4-0	Fox (3, 69); Sutton (41); Goss (61)	32,008	M.Reed
1993-94	Home	13-Dec-93	2-1	Sutton (44); Ekoku (80)	16,586	R.Milford
1994-95	Home	8-Oct-94	2-1	Robins (61); Adams (90)	17,390	P.Don
1994-95	Away	6-May-95	1-2	Ward (36)	31,982	A.Wilkie

LEICESTER CITY

Season	Venue	Date	Res	Scorers	Attendance	Referee
1994-95	Home	26-Nov-94	2-1	Newsome (56); Sutch (90)	20,567	R.Gifford
1994-95	Away	5-Apr-95	0-1		15,992	T.Holbrook

LIVERPOOL

Season	Venue	Date	Res	Scorers	Attendance	Referee
1992-93	Away	25-Oct-92	1-4	Butterworth (2)	36,318	R.Lewis
1992-93	Home	1-May-93	1-0	Phillips (62 pen)	20,610	D.Elleray
1993-94	Home	5-Feb-94	2-2	Sutton (12, 63)	19,746	D.Gallagher
1993-94	Away	30-Apr-94	1-0	Goss (35)	44,339	B.Hill
1994-95	Away	2-Jan-95	0-4		34,709	K.Cooper
1994-95	Home	29-Apr-95	1-2	Ullathorne (16)	21,843	B.Hill

MANCHESTER CITY

Season	Venue	Date	Res	Scorers	Attendance	Referee
1992-93	Away	26-Aug-92	1-3	Megson (58)	23,182	D.Elleray
1992-93	Home	20-Feb-93	2-1	Robins (28); Power (29)	16,386	B.Hill
1993-94	Home	20-Nov-93	1-1	Fox (58)	16,626	K.Hackett
1993-94	Away	16-Apr-94	1-1	Ullathorne (14)	28,020	D.Elleray
1994-95	Away	24-Sep-94	0-2		21,031	G.Poll
1994-95	Home	4-Mar-95	1-1	Cureton (82)	16,266	D.Gallagher

MANCHESTER UNITED

Season	Venue	Date	Res	Scorers	Attendance	Referee
1992-93	Away	12-Dec-92	0-1		34,500	R.Milford
1992-93	Home	5-Apr-93	1-3	Robins (61)	20,582	T.Ward
1993-94	Home	15-Aug-93	0-2		19,705	K.Hackett
1993-94	Away	4-Dec-93	2-2	Sutton (31); Fox (47 pen)	44,694	M.Bodenham
1994-95	Away	3-Dec-94	0-1		43,789	T.Holbrook
1994-95	Home	22-Feb-95	0-2		21,824	T.Holbrook

MIDDLESBROUGH

Season	Venue	Date	Res	Scorers	Attendance	Referee
1992-93	Home	31-Oct-92	1-1	Sutch (86)	14,499	S.Lodge
1992-93	Away	8-May-93	3-3	Ekoku (14, 66); Johnson (68)	15,155	G.Ashby

NEWCASTLE UNITED

Season	Venue	Date	Res	Scorers	Attendance	Referee
1993-94	Home	4-Jan-94	1-2	Bowen (4)	19,564	T.Holbrook
1993-94	Away	29-Mar-94	0-3		32,228	T.Holbrook
1994-95	Home	31-Dec-94	2-1	Adams (1); Ward (10)	21,172	B.Hill
1994-95	Away	8-Apr-95	0-3		35,518	M.Reed

NOTTINGHAM FOREST

Season	Venue	Date	Res	Scorers	Attendance	Referee
1992-93	Home	31-Aug-92	3-1	Crook (2); Power (76); Phillips (89)	14,104	B.Hill
1992-93	Away	17-Mar-93	3-0	Robins (45); Power (73); Crook (78)	20,799	S.Lodge
1994-95	Away	27-Dec-94	0-1		20,010	S.Lodge
1994-95	Home	12-Apr-95	0-1		19,005	K.Morton

OLDHAM ATHLETIC

Season	Venue	Date	Res	Scorers	Attendance	Referee
1992-93	Away	9-Nov-92	3-2	Robins (14, 27, 90)	11,018	R.Hart
1992-93	Home	13-Mar-93	1-0	OG (12, Henry)	19,597	R.Milford
1993-94	Away	27-Nov-93	1-2	Sutton (54)	10,198	P.Don
1993-94	Home	7-May-94	1-1	Ullathorne (72)	20,394	D.Frampton

QPR

Season	Venue	Date	Res	Scorers	Attendance	Referee
1992-93	Home	17-Oct-92	2-1	Bowen (53 pen); Sutton (64)	16,009	D.Gallagher
1992-93	Away	6-Mar-93	1-3	Robins (41)	13,892	R.Gifford
1993-94	Away	18-Sep-93	2-2	OG (23, McDonald); Eadie (37)	13,359	R.Milford
1993-94	Home	12-Mar-94	3-4	Ekoku (9, 55); Bowen (87)	16,499	D.Allison

1994-95	Home	22-Oct-94	4-2	Robins (46); Bowen (54); Sheron (57); OG (62, White)	19,431	M.Reed
1994-95	Away	15-Mar-95	0-2		10,519	G.Ashby

SHEFFIELD UNITED

Season	Venue	Date	Res	Scorers	Attendance	Referee
1992-93	Home	21-Nov-92	2-1	OG (60, Beesley); Robins (80)	14,874	M.Peck
1992-93	Away	10-Mar-93	1-0	Fox (55)	15,583	R.Lewis
1993-94	Away	6-Nov-93	2-1	Goss (26); Eadie (57)	18,254	K.Burge
1993-94	Home	23-Apr-94	0-1		18,474	R.Hart

SHEFFIELD WEDNESDAY

Season	Venue	Date	Res	Scorers	Attendance	Referee
1992-93	Home	19-Sep-92	1-0	Newman (44)	14,367	R.Nixon
1992-93	Away	10-Jan-93	0-1		23,360	D.Allison
1993-94	Away	1-Sep-93	3-3	Bowen (63); Ekoku (72); Sutton (76)	25,175	A.Wilkie
1993-94	Home	25-Feb-94	1-1	Sutton (90)	18,311	V.Callow
1994-95	Away	31-Aug-94	0-0		25,072	K.Cooper
1994-95	Home	8-Mar-95	0-0		13,530	P.Danson

SOUTHAMPTON

Season	Venue	Date	Res	Scorers	Attendance	Referee
1992-93	Home	5-Sep-92	1-0	Robins (87)	12,452	K.Hackett
1992-93	Away	10-Feb-93	0-3		12,969	J.Worrall
1993-94	Away	1-Jan-94	1-0	Sutton (44)	16,556	G.Poll
1993-94	Home	9-Apr-94	4-5	Robins (37); Goss (48); Sutton (55, 63)	17,150	K.Cooper
1994-95	Away	2-Nov-94	1-1	Robins (48)	12,976	P.Durkin
1994-95	Home	11-Feb-95	2-2	Newsome (37); Ward (90)	18,361	R.Hart

SWINDON TOWN

Season	Venue	Date	Res	Scorers	Attendance	Referee
1993-94	Home	28-Aug-93	0-0		17,614	D.Elleray
1993-94	Away	19-Feb-94	3-3	Sutton (15); Newman (41); Goss (83)	15,341	R.Gifford

TOTTENHAM HOTSPUR

Season	Venue	Date	Res	Scorers	Attendance	Referee
1992-93	Home	26-Dec-92	0-0		19,413	J.Martin
1992-93	Away	9-Apr-93	1-5	Ekoku (86)	31,425	K.Barratt
1993-94	Away	27-Dec-93	3-1	Sutton (27, 89); Ekoku (36)	31,130	A.Gunn
1993-94	Home	2-Apr-94	1-2	Sutton (71)	21,181	A.Wilkie
1994-95	Home	26-Dec-94	0-2		21,814	R.Dilkes
1994-95	Away	17-Apr-95	0-1		32,304	R.Gifford

WEST HAM UNITED

Season	Venue	Date	Res	Scorers	Attendance	Referee
1993-94	Home	23-Oct-93	0-0		20,175	J.Worrall
1993-94	Away	24-Jan-94	3-3	Sutton (5, 56); Fox (79)	20,738	J.Worrall
1994-95	Home	27-Aug-94	1-0	Robins (64)	19,110	P.Jones
1994-95	Away	11-Mar-95	2-2	Eadie (22); Ullathorne (55)	21,464	A.Wilkie (M.Sims 35)

WIMBLEDON

Season	Venue	Date	Res	Scorers	Attendance	Referee
1992-93	Home	5-Dec-92	2-1	Robins (77); Phillips (88)	14,161	R.Groves
1992-93	Away	20-Mar-93	0-3		10,875	K.Cooper
1993-94	Home	11-Sep-93	0-1		14,851	G.Ashby
1993-94	Away	5-Mar-94	1-3	Ekoku (6)	7,206	A.Gunn
1994-95	Away	30-Oct-94	0-1		8,242	D.Gallagher
1994-95	Home	14-Jan-95	1-2	Goss (22)	18,261	M.Bodenham

INTRODUCTION

Founded in 1865 by players of a hockey-like game, shinney, who played at the Forest Recreation Ground. They played their first game in 1866. Had several early homes, including a former Notts County ground, The Meadows, and Trent Bridge Cricket Ground.

Founder members of the Football Alliance in 1889 and champions in 1892 when elected to an extended Football League top division. In 1898 moved from the Town Ground to the City Ground at West Bridgford. Run by a committee until 1982, the last league club to become a limited company. Premier League founder members 1992. Relegated after one season, but promoted back at the first attempt, only to be relegated once again in 1997.

Ground:	City Ground, Nottingham NG2 5FJ
Nickname:	Reds
Internet:	www.nottinghamforest.co.uk

HONOURS

Football League Div 1:	Champions 1977-78
	Runners-up 1966-67, 1978-79
Football League Div 2:	Champions 1906-07, 1921-22
	Runners-up 1956-57
Football League Div 3S:	Champions 1950-51
FA Cup:	Winners 1898, 1959
	Runners-up 1991
Anglo-Scottish Cup:	Winners 1976-77
Football League Cup:	Winners 1977-78, 1978-79,
	1988-89, 1989-90
	Runners-up 1979-80, 1991-92
Simod Cup:	Winners 1989
Zenith Data Systems Cup:	Winners 1991-92
Champions' Cup:	Winners 1978-79, 1979-80
European Super Cup:	Winners 1979-80
	Runners-up 1980-81
World Club Championship:	Runners-up 1980-81.

EUROPEAN RECORD

Champions' League (3):	78-79 (W), 79-80 (W), 80-81 (1)
Cup-Winners' Cup (0):	–
UEFA Cup (5):	61-62 (1), 67-68 (2), 83-84 (3),
	84-85 (1), 95-96 (QF).

FAPL RECORD SUMMARY

Most Total:	CHETTLE, Steve	174
Most Starts:	CHETTLE, Steve	171
Most Subs:	LEE, Jason	32
Most SNU:	MARRIOTT, Andy	37
Most PS:	ROY, Bryan	32
Most Goals:	ROY, Bryan	24

Most Yel:	COOPER, Colin	20
Most Red:	CHETTLE, Steve	3

PLAYING RECORD – SEASON TOTALS

Season	Pn	P	W	D	L	F	A	Pts
1992-93	22	42	10	10	22	41	62	40
1994-95	3	42	22	11	9	72	43	77
1995-96	9	38	15	13	10	50	54	58
1996-97	20	38	6	16	16	31	59	34
1998-99	20	38	7	9	22	35	69	30
Totals		198	60	59	79	229	287	239

PLAYING RECORD – HOME TOTALS

Season	Pn	P	W	D	L	F	A	Pts
1992-93	22	21	6	4	11	17	25	22
1994-95	3	21	12	6	3	36	18	42
1995-96	9	19	11	6	2	29	17	39
1996-97	20	19	3	9	7	15	27	18
1998-99	20	19	3	7	9	18	31	16
Totals		99	35	32	32	115	118	137

PLAYING RECORD – AWAY TOTALS

Season	Pn	P	W	D	L	F	A	Pts
1992-93	22	21	4	6	11	24	37	18
1994-95	3	21	10	5	6	36	25	35
1995-96	9	19	4	7	8	21	37	19
1996-97	20	19	3	7	9	16	32	16
1998-99	20	19	4	2	13	17	38	14
Totals		99	25	27	47	114	169	102

HIGHEST HOME ATTENDANCES

	Attendance	Opponents	Date	Season
1	30,025	Manchester U.	6-Feb-99	1998-99
2	29,263	Manchester U.	27-Nov-95	1995-96
3	29,181	Liverpool	15-Mar-97	1996-97
4	29,058	Liverpool	23-Mar-96	1995-96
5	29,032	Manchester U.	26-Dec-96	1996-97

LOWEST HOME ATTENDANCES

	Attendance	Opponents	Date	Season
1	16,897	Middlesbrough	21-Oct-92	1992-93
2	17,525	Blackburn R.	25-Nov-96	1996-97
3	17,553	Coventry C.	21-Sep-92	1992-93
4	19,362	Wimbledon	20-Dec-92	1992-93
5	19,420	Sheffield W.	12-Sep-92	1992-93

NOTTINGHAM FOREST

TOP SCORER – SEASON BY SEASON

Season	Player	Goals
1994-95	Collymore	23
1992-93	Clough	10
1995-96	Woan	8
1996-97	Campbell	65
1998-99	Freedman	9

PLAYERS WITH MOST PREMIERSHIP APPEARANCES

Tot	Player	St	Sb	Gls
174	CHETTLE, Steve	171	3	2
162	CROSSLEY, Mark	162	0	0
132	WOAN, Ian	124	8	17
128	GEMMILL, Scot	115	13	3
123	PEARCE ,Stuart	123	0	18
118	STONE, Steve	117	1	16
113	LYTTLE, Des	105	8	2
108	COOPER, Colin	108	0	8
85	ROY, Bryan	70	15	24
83	PHILLIPS, David	76	7	1
72	BART-WILLIAMS, Chris	68	4	4
71	HAALAND, Alf Inge	63	8	7
63	LEE ,Jason	31	32	12

CLUB-BY-CLUB RESULTS

ARSENAL

Season	Venue	Date	Res	Scorers	Attendance	Referee
1992-93	Home	17-Oct-92	0-1		24,862	J.Worrall
1992-93	Away	21-Apr-93	1-1	Keane (90)	19,024	M.Bodenham
1994-95	Home	3-Dec-94	2-2	Pearce (36 pen); Roy (60)	21,662	B.Hill
1994-95	Away	21-Feb-95	0-1		35,441	P.Durkin
1995-96	Away	29-Aug-95	1-1	Campbell (61)	38,248	R.Dilkes
1995-96	Home	10-Feb-96	0-1		27,222	R.Hart
1996-97	Home	21-Dec-96	2-1	Haaland (64, 88)	27,384	S.Lodge
1996-97	Away	8-Mar-97	0-2		38,206	M.Reed
1998-99	Away	17-Aug-98	1-2	Thomas (77)	38,064	M.Riley
1998-99	Home	16-Jan-99	0-1		26,021	P.Durkin

ASTON VILLA

Season	Venue	Date	Res	Scorers	Attendance	Referee
1992-93	Away	12-Dec-92	1-2	Keane (9)	29,015	J.Worrall
1992-93	Home	4-Apr-93	0-1		26,742	K.Burge
1994-95	Away	22-Oct-94	2-0	Pearce (1 pen); Stone (70)	29,217	K.Cooper
1994-95	Home	21-Jan-95	1-2	Collymore (53 pen)	24,598	K.Cooper
1995-96	Away	23-Sep-95	1-1	Lyttle (87)	33,972	P.Danson
1995-96	Home	10-Dec-95	1-1	Stone (82)	25,790	P.Durkin
1996-97	Away	2-Nov-96	0-2		35,310	R.Dilkes
1996-97	Home	22-Feb-97	0-0		25,239	G.Barber
1998-99	Home	28-Nov-98	2-2	Bart-Williams (32); Freedman (44)	25,753	G.Willard
1998-99	Away	24-Apr-99	0-2		34,492	P.Durkin
						(J.Pettitt, 27)

BLACKBURN ROVERS

Season	Venue	Date	Res	Scorers	Attendance	Referee
1992-93	Away	5-Sep-92	1-4	Bannister (15)	16,180	R.Nixon
1992-93	Home	7-Apr-93	1-3	Clough (51 pen)	20,467	T.Ward
1994-95	Home	29-Oct-94	0-2		22,131	P.Danson
1994-95	Away	14-Jan-95	0-3		27,510	J.Worrall

227

1995-96	Away	18-Nov-95	0-7		27,660	J.Winter
1995-96	Home	13-Apr-96	1-5	Woan (40)	25,273	P.Jones
1996-97	Home	25-Nov-96	2-2	Pearce (44 pen); Cooper (90)	17,525	P.Alcock
1996-97	Away	11-Mar-97	1-1	Haaland (19)	20,485	M.Riley
1998-99	Home	19-Dec-98	2-2	Chettle (22 pen); Freedman (30)	22,013	S.Lodge
1998-99	Away	8-May-99	2-1	Freedman (12); Bart-Williams (56)	24,565	G.Poll

BOLTON WANDERERS

Season	Venue	Date	Res	Scorers	Attendance	Referee
1995-96	Home	21-Oct-95	3-2	Roy (27); Lee (68); Cooper (90)	25,426	D.Elleray
1995-96	Away	2-Dec-95	1-1	Cooper (90)	17,342	R.Dilkes

CHARLTON ATHLETIC

Season	Venue	Date	Res	Scorers	Attendance	Referee
1998-99	Home	3-Oct-98	0-1		22,661	P.Jones
1998-99	Away	27-Feb-99	0-0		20,007	S.Lodge

CHELSEA

Season	Venue	Date	Res	Scorers	Attendance	Referee
1992-93	Away	26-Sep-92	0-0		19,760	J.Worrall
1992-93	Home	16-Jan-93	3-0	Bannister (9, 58); Orlygsson (89)	23,249	P.Durkin
1994-95	Home	19-Nov-94	0-1		22,092	T.Holbrook
1994-95	Away	25-Jan-95	2-0	Collymore (33,54)	17,890	M.Bodenham
1995-96	Home	23-Aug-95	0-0		27,007	J.Winter
1995-96	Away	20-Jan-96	0-1		24,482	J.Winter
1996-97	Away	28-Sep-96	1-1	Lee (90)	27,673	G.Poll
1996-97	Home	11-Jan-97	2-0	Pearce (39); Bart-Williams (57)	28,358	K.Burge
1998-99	Away	12-Sep-98	1-2	Darcheville (89)	34,809	P.Alcock
1998-99	Home	20-Feb-99	1-3	Van Hooijdonk (39)	26,351	J.Winter

COVENTRY CITY

Season	Venue	Date	Res	Scorers	Attendance	Referee
1992-93	Home	21-Sep-92	1-1	Clough (69)	17,553	K.Morton
1992-93	Away	9-Jan-93	1-0	Woan (65)	15,264	M.Bodenham
1994-95	Away	26-Dec-94	0-0		19,224	A.Wilkie
1994-95	Home	17-Apr-95	2-0	Woan (9); Collymore (42)	26,253	P.Durkin
1995-96	Away	9-Sep-95	1-1	Roy (23)	17,238	P.Jones
1995-96	Home	17-Apr-96	0-0		24,629	M.Reed
1996-97	Away	17-Aug-96	3-0	Campbell (13, 36, 47)	19,468	A.Wilkie
1996-97	Home	29-Jan-97	0-1		22,619	A.Wiley
1998-99	Home	22-Aug-98	1-0	Stone (52)	22,546	K.Burge
1998-99	Away	9-Jan-99	0-4		17,172	P.Jones

CRYSTAL PALACE

Season	Venue	Date	Res	Scorers	Attendance	Referee
1992-93	Away	21-Nov-92	1-1	Bannister (84)	15,330	K.Hackett
1992-93	Home	3-Mar-93	1-1	Keane (24)	20,603	J.Borrett
1994-95	Home	2-Jan-95	1-0	Bull (76)	21,326	G.Ashby
1994-95	Away	29-Apr-95	2-1	Roy (14); Collymore (67)	15,886	K.Burge

DERBY COUNTY

Season	Venue	Date	Res	Scorers	Attendance	Referee
1996-97	Home	19-Oct-96	1-1	Saunders (1)	27,771	J.Winter
1996-97	Away	23-Apr-97	0-0		18,087	G.Poll
1998-99	Home	16-Nov-98	2-2	Freedman (57); Van Hooijdonk (62)	24,014	G.Barber
1998-99	Away	10-Apr-99	0-1		32,217	G.Barber

EVERTON

Season	Venue	Date	Res	Scorers	Attendance	Referee
1992-93	Home	7-Nov-92	0-1		20,941	S.Lodge
1992-93	Away	13-Mar-93	0-3		21,271	V.Callow
1994-95	Away	30-Aug-94	2-1	OG (24, Hinchcliffe); Cooper (60)	26,689	G.Ashby
1994-95	Home	8-Mar-95	2-1	Collymore (19); Pearce (54)	24,526	R.Dilkes
1995-96	Home	17-Sep-95	3-2	OG (17, Watson); Lee (20); Woan (64)	24,786	M.Bodenham
1995-96	Away	24-Feb-96	0-3		33,163	K.Cooper
1996-97	Home	28-Oct-96	0-1		19,892	P.Durkin
1996-97	Away	1-Feb-97	0-2		32,567	S.Dunn
1998-99	Home	8-Sep-98	0-2		25,610	R.Harris
1998-99	Away	30-Jan-99	1-0	Van Hooijdonk (51)	34,175	G.Barber

IPSWICH TOWN

Season	Venue	Date	Res	Scorers	Attendance	Referee
1992-93	Home	31-Oct-92	0-1		21,411	M.Bodenham
1992-93	Away	8-May-93	1-2	Clough (64 pen)	22,093	M.Reed
1994-95	Away	20-Aug-94	1-0	Roy (40)	18,882	S.Lodge
1994-95	Home	10-Dec-94	4-1	Collymore (4); Gemmill (11); Haarland (26); Pearce (42)	21,340	M.Reed

LEEDS UNITED

Season	Venue	Date	Res	Scorers	Attendance	Referee
1992-93	Away	5-Dec-92	4-1	Clough (27); Keane (53, 67); Black (54)	29,364	A.Buksh
1992-93	Home	21-Mar-93	1-1	Clough (25 pen)	25,148	R.Lewis
1994-95	Away	26-Nov-94	0-1		38,191	P.Jones
1994-95	Home	22-Mar-95	3-0	Roy (9,35); Collymore (44)	26,299	M.Reed
1995-96	Home	31-Jan-96	2-1	Campbell (39); Roy (57 pen)	24,465	A.Wilkie
1995-96	Away	8-Apr-96	3-1	Cooper (18); Lee (30); Woan (66)	29,220	R.Hart
1996-97	Away	12-Oct-96	0-2		29,225	S.Lodge
1996-97	Home	19-Apr-97	1-1	van Hooijdonk (6)	25,565	D.Elleray
1998-99	Home	17-Oct-98	1-1	Stone (85)	23,911	A.Wilkie
1998-99	Away	3-Apr-99	1-3	Rogers (53)	39,645	P.Alcock

LEICESTER CITY

Season	Venue	Date	Res	Scorers	Attendance	Referee
1994-95	Home	27-Aug-94	1-0	Collymore (38)	21,601	G.Willard
1994-95	Away	11-Mar-95	4-2	Pearce (8 pen); Collymore (64); Woan (68); Lee (90)	20,423	P.Don
1996-97	Home	7-Sep-96	0-0		24,105	P.Alcock
1996-97	Away	28-Dec-96	2-2	Clough (37); Cooper (87)	20,833	K.Burge
1998-99	Away	12-Dec-98	1-3	Van Hooijdonk (14)	20,891	M.Riley
1998-99	Home	16-May-99	1-0	Bart-Williams (76)	25,353	S.Dunn

LIVERPOOL

Season	Venue	Date	Res	Scorers	Attendance	Referee
1992-93	Home	16-Aug-92	1-0	Sheringham (29)	20,038	M.Reed
1992-93	Away	6-Feb-93	0-0		40,463	K.Barratt
1994-95	Away	5-Nov-94	0-1		33,329	J.Worrall
1994-95	Home	4-Feb-95	1-1	Collymore (10)	25,418	G.Willard
1995-96	Away	1-Jan-96	2-4	Stone (13); Woan (18)	39,206	P.Alcock
1995-96	Home	23-Mar-96	1-0	Stone (43)	29,058	P.Danson
1996-97	Away	17-Dec-96	2-4	Campbell (34); Pearce (60)	36,126	G.Barber
1996-97	Home	15-Mar-97	1-1	Woan (29)	29,181	R.Dilkes
1998-99	Away	24-Oct-98	1-5	Freedman (18)	44,595	S.Dunn
1998-99	Home	5-Apr-99	2-2	Freedman (60); Van Hooijdonk (90)	28,374	D.Gallagher

MANCHESTER CITY

Season	Venue	Date	Res	Scorers	Attendance	Referee
1992-93	Away	3-Oct-92	2-2	McKinnon (56); Pearce (83)	22,571	R.Milford
1992-93	Home	27-Feb-93	0-2		25,956	A.Buksh
1994-95	Away	8-Oct-94	3-3	Collymore (22,51); Woan (92)	23,150	P.Durkin
1994-95	Home	6-May-95	1-0	Collymore (18)	28,882	P.Jones
1995-96	Home	30-Sep-95	3-0	Lee (10, 46); Stone (82)	25,620	M.Reed
1995-96	Away	18-Dec-95	1-1	Campbell (69)	25,660	K.Burge

MANCHESTER UNITED

Season	Venue	Date	Res	Scorers	Attendance	Referee
1992-93	Home	29-Aug-92	0-2		19,694	K.Redfern
1992-93	Away	27-Jan-93	0-2		36,085	J.Worrall
1994-95	Home	22-Aug-94	1-1	Collymore (26)	22,072	A.Wilkie
1994-95	Away	17-Dec-94	2-1	Collymore (35); Pearce (62)	43,744	K.Burge
1995-96	Home	27-Nov-95	1-1	McGregor (19)	29,263	K.Cooper
1995-96	Away	28-Apr-96	0-5		53,926	J.Winter
1996-97	Away	14-Sep-96	1-4	Haaland (3)	54,984	P.Jones
1996-97	Home	26-Dec-96	0-4		29,032	G.Ashby
1998-99	Away	26-Dec-98	0-3		55,216	J.Winter
1998-99	Home	6-Feb-99	1-8	Rogers (6)	30,025	P.Alcock

MIDDLESBROUGH

Season	Venue	Date	Res	Scorers	Attendance	Referee
1992-93	Home	21-Oct-92	1-0	Black (66)	16,897	M.Peck
1992-93	Away	20-Feb-93	2-1	Clough (58); Stone (68)	15,639	D.Elleray
1995-96	Home	30-Dec-95	1-0	Pearce (8 pen)	27,027	G.Willard
1995-96	Away	16-Mar-96	1-1	Allen (56)	23,392	A.Wilkie
1996-97	Home	24-Aug-96	1-1	Pearce (67)	24,705	M.Riley
1996-97	Away	24-Mar-97	1-1	Haaland (4)	29,888	P.Danson
1998-99	Away	1-Nov-98	1-1	Harewood (88)	34,223	P.Durkin
1998-99	Home	21-Mar-99	1-2	Freedman (37)	21,468	S.Dunn

NEWCASTLE UNITED

Season	Venue	Date	Res	Scorers	Attendance	Referee
1994-95	Home	7-Nov-94	0-0		22,102	K.Burge
1994-95	Away	11-Feb-95	1-2	Lee (74)	34,471	K.Morton
1995-96	Away	23-Dec-95	1-3	Woan (14)	36,531	D.Elleray

1995-96	Home	2-May-96	1-1	Woan (75)	28,280	R.Dilkes
1996-97	Home	9-Dec-96	0-0		25,762	D.Elleray
1996-97	Away	11-May-97	0-5		36,554	M.Reed
1998-99	Away	26-Sep-98	0-2		36,760	D.Elleray
1998-99	Home	10-Mar-99	1-2	Freedman (45)	22,852	J.Winter

NORWICH CITY

Season	Venue	Date	Res	Scorers	Attendance	Referee
1992-93	Away	31-Aug-92	1-3	Clough (31)	14,104	B.Hill
1992-93	Home	17-Mar-93	0-3		20,799	S.Lodge
1994-95	Home	27-Dec-94	1-0	Bohinen (51)	20,010	S.Lodge
1994-95	Away	12-Apr-95	1-0	Stone (85)	19,005	K.Morton

OLDHAM ATHLETIC

Season	Venue	Date	Res	Scorers	Attendance	Referee
1992-93	Away	22-Aug-92	3-5	Pearce (66 pen); Bannister (86, 88)	11,632	R.Groves
1992-93	Home	30-Jan-93	2-0	Woan (14, 59)	21,240	P.Don

QPR

Season	Venue	Date	Res	Scorers	Attendance	Referee
1992-93	Home	24-Feb-93	1-0	Crosby (70)	22,436	R.Gifford
1992-93	Away	10-Apr-93	3-4	Bannister (8); Black (49, 54)	15,815	P.Foakes
1994-95	Home	2-Oct-94	3-2	Black (51); Roy (63); Collymore (88)	21,449	K.Morton
1994-95	Away	26-Feb-95	1-1	Stone (57)	13,363	P.Danson
1995-96	Away	28-Oct-95	1-1	Lee (47)	17,549	S.Dunn
1995-96	Home	5-May-96	3-0	Stone (44); Roy (63); Howe (77)	22,910	G.Ashby

SHEFFIELD UNITED

Season	Venue	Date	Res	Scorers	Attendance	Referee
1992-93	Away	24-Oct-92	0-0		19,152	R.Hart
1992-93	Home	1-May-93	0-2		26,752	P.Durkin

SHEFFIELD WEDNESDAY

Season	Venue	Date	Res	Scorers	Attendance	Referee
1992-93	Away	19-Aug-92	0-2		29,623	P.Don
1992-93	Home	12-Sep-92	1-2	Bannister (87)	19,420	G.Ashby
1994-95	Home	10-Sep-94	4-1	Black (34); Bohinen (52); Pearce (63 pen); Roy (82)	22,022	P.Don
1994-95	Away	1-Apr-95	7-1	Pearce (17); Woan (20); Roy (48,64); Collymore (78,80); Bohinen (85)	30,060	A.Wilkie
1995-96	Home	26-Dec-95	1-0	Lee (7)	27,810	G.Ashby
1995-96	Away	3-Mar-96	3-1	Howe (10); McGregor (46); Roy (80)	21,930	G.Poll
1996-97	Away	18-Nov-96	0-2		16,390	S.Dunn
1996-97	Home	5-Mar-97	0-3		21,485	P.Jones
1998-99	Away	7-Dec-98	2-3	Bonalair (55); Van Hooijdonk (70)	19,321	R.Harris
1998-99	Home	1-May-99	2-0	Porfirio (14); Rogers (16)	20,480	J.Winter

SOUTHAMPTON

Season	Venue	Date	Res	Scorers	Attendance	Referee
1992-93	Home	28-Nov-92	1-2	Clough (43)	19,942	D.Elleray
1992-93	Away	24-Mar-93	2-1	Clough (5); Keane (45)	18,005	M.Reed
1994-95	Away	17-Sep-94	1-1	Collymore (43)	14,185	M.Reed
1994-95	Home	18-Mar-95	3-0	Roy (38,81); Collymore (63)	24,146	K.Cooper
1995-96	Away	19-Aug-95	4-3	Cooper(8); Woan (36); Roy (41,79)	15,165	G.Willard
1995-96	Home	13-Jan-96	1-0	Cooper (44)	23,321	S.Lodge
1996-97	Away	4-Sep-96	2-2	Campbell (4); Saunders (23)	14,450	P.Danson
1996-97	Home	5-Apr-97	1-3	Pearce (88 pen)	25,134	A.Wilkie
1998-99	Away	29-Aug-98	2-1	Darcheville (52); Stone (68)	14,942	D.Gallagher
1998-99	Home	28-Dec-98	1-1	Chettle (54 pen)	23,456	M.Reed

SUNDERLAND

Season	Venue	Date	Res	Scorers	Attendance	Referee
1996-97	Home	21-Aug-96	1-4	Haaland (26)	22,874	G.Barber
1996-97	Away	22-Mar-97	1-1	Lyttle (86)	22,120	P.Alcock

TOTTENHAM HOTSPUR

Season	Venue	Date	Res	Scorers	Attendance	Referee
1992-93	Away	28-Dec-92	1-2	Gemmill (73)	32,118	M.Reed
1992-93	Home	12-Apr-93	2-1	Black (25); Rosario (35)	25,682	A.Wilkie
1994-95	Away	24-Sep-94	4-1	Stone (9); Roy (52,69);Bohinen (79)	24,558	R.Hart
1994-95	Home	4-Mar-95	2-2	Bohinen (84); Lee (85)	28,711	G.Ashby
1995-96	Away	14-Oct-95	1-0	Stone(63)	32,876	R.Hart
1995-96	Home	6-Apr-96	2-1	Stone (40); Woan (61)	27,053	P.Alcock
1996-97	Home	19-Jan-97	2-1	Roy (47, 61)	27,303	J.Winter
1996-97	Away	1-Mar-97	1-0	Saunders (17)	32,805	J.Winter
1998-99	Away	21-Nov-98	0-2		35,832	S.Lodge
1998-99	Home	17-Apr-99	0-1		25,181	G.Willard

WEST HAM UNITED

Season	Venue	Date	Res	Scorers	Attendance	Referee
1994-95	Away	31-Dec-94	1-3	McGregor (89)	20,544	D.Gallagher
1994-95	Home	8-Apr-95	1-1	Collymore (78)	28,361	G.Poll
1995-96	Home	26-Aug-95	1-1	Pearce (35pen)	26,645	G.Ashby
1995-96	Away	3-Feb-96	0-1		21,257	K.Burge
1996-97	Home	21-Sep-96	0-2		23,352	G.Willard
1996-97	Away	1-Jan-97	1-0	Campbell (37)	22,358	P.Durkin
1998-99	Home	19-Sep-98	0-0		28,463	M.Reed
1998-99	Away	13-Feb-99	1-2	Hjelde (84)	25,458	R.Harris

WIMBLEDON

Season	Venue	Date	Res	Scorers	Attendance	Referee
1992-93	Home	20-Dec-92	1-1	Clough (5)	19,362	R.Hart
1992-93	Away	17-Apr-93	0-1		9,358	K.Barratt
1994-95	Home	17-Oct-94	3-1	Bohinen (40); Collymore (66); Woan (75)	20,187	R.Hart
1994-95	Away	13-May-95	2-2	Phillips (13); Stone (75)	15,341	S.Lodge
1995-96	Home	6-Nov-95	4-1	Roy (8); Pearce (31); Lee (47); Gemmill (87)	20,810	P.Alcock
1995-96	Away	30-Mar-96	0-1		9,807	K.Burge
1996-97	Away	30-Nov-96	0-1		12,608	M.Reed

NOTTINGHAM FOREST

1996-97	Home	3-May-97	1-1	Roy (60)	19,865	G.Barber
1998-99	Home	7-Nov-98	0-1		21,362	G.Poll
1998-99	Away	13-Mar-99	3-1	Rogers (21); Freedman (59); Shipperley (84)	12,149	K.Burge

INTRODUCTION

Founded in 1897 as Pine Villa by the licensee of the Featherstall & Junction Hotel and played in the Oldham Junior League. In 1899 at a meeting at the Black Cow, Chadderton, the club became Oldham Athletic; it moved to the defunct Oldham County FC's ground; and joined the Manchester Alliance.

Changed to the Manchester League in 1900 and the Lancashire Combination in 1904. Moved to Boundary Park in 1906. Initially rejected by the Football League in 1907, an unexpected vacancy arose and Oldham started 1907-08 in Division Two. Founder member of Division Four 1958 and of the Premier League in 1992.

Ground:	Boundary Park, Oldham
Nickname:	The Latics
Internet:	www.oldhamathletic.co.uk

HONOURS

Football League Div 1:	Runners-up 1914-15
Football League Div 2:	Champions 1990-91
	Runners-up 1909-10;
Football League Div 3N:	Champions 1952-53
Football League Cup:	Runners-up 1990

EUROPEAN RECORD

Champions' League (0):	–
Cup-Winners' Cup (0):	–
UEFA Cup (1):	1964-65

FAPL RECORD SUMMARY

Most Total:	MILLIGAN, Mike	81
Most Starts:	MILLIGAN, Mike	81
Most Subs:	PALMER, Roger	18
Most SNU:	KEELEY, John	28
Most PS:	RITCHIE, Andy	10
Most Goals:	SHARP, Graeme	16
Most Yel:	JOBSON, Richard	12
Most Red:	MAKIN, Chris	2

PLAYING RECORD – SEASON TOTALS

Season	Pn	P	W	D	L	F	A	Pts
1992-93	19	42	13	10	19	63	74	49
1993-94	21	42	9	13	20	42	68	40
Totals		84	22	23	39	105	142	89

PLAYING RECORD – HOME TOTALS

Season	Pn	P	W	D	L	F	A	Pts
1992-93	19	21	10	6	5	43	30	36
1993-94	21	21	5	8	8	24	33	23
Totals		42	15	14	13	67	63	59

PLAYING RECORD – AWAY TOTALS

Season	Pn	P	W	D	L	F	A	Pts
1992-93	19	21	3	4	14	20	44	13
1993-94	21	21	4	5	12	18	35	17
Totals		42	7	9	26	38	79	30

HIGHEST HOME ATTENDANCES

	Attendance	Opponents	Date	Season
1	17,106	Manchester U.	9-Mar-93	1992-93
2	16,708	Manchester U.	29-Dec-93	1993-94
3	16,462	Manchester C.	26-Mar-94	1993-94
4	15,381	Liverpool	5-May-93	1992-93
5	14,903	Manchester C.	26-Jan-93	1992-93

LOWEST HOME ATTENDANCES

	Attendance	Opponents	Date	Season
1	9,633	Wimbledon	28-Aug-93	1993-94
2	9,771	Swindon T.	7-Dec-93	1993-94
3	9,982	Southampton	5-Feb-94	1993-94
4	10,198	Norwich C.	27-Nov-93	1993-94
5	10,440	QPR	2-Apr-94	1993-94

TOP SCORER – SEASON BY SEASON

Season	Player	Goals
1992-93	Olney	12

PLAYERS WITH MOST PREMIERSHIP APPEARANCES

Tot	Player	St	Sb	Gls
81	MILLIGAN, Mike	81	0	3
77	JOBSON, Richard	77	0	7
65	BERNARD, Paul	64	1	9
64	HALLE, Gunnar	63	1	6
64	REDMOND, Steve	59	5	1
61	FLEMING, Craig	60	1	0
57	POINTON, Neil	56	1	3
55	SHARP, Graeme	51	4	16
54	HENRY, Nick	54	0	6
45	ADAMS, Neil	33	12	9
44	OLNEY, Ian	42	2	13
41	GERRARD, Paul	40	1	0
35	HALLWORTH, Jon	35	0	0
34	RITCHIE, Andy	23	11	4

CLUB-BY-CLUB RESULTS

ARSENAL

Season	Venue	Date	Res	Scorers	Attendance	Referee
1992-93	Away	26-Aug-92	0-2		20,796	R.Milford
1992-93	Home	20-Feb-93	0-1		12,311	K.Hackett
1993-94	Home	23-Oct-93	0-0		12,105	M.Reed
1993-94	Away	22-Jan-94	1-1	Sharp (4)	26,524	P.Foakes

ASTON VILLA

Season	Venue	Date	Res	Scorers	Attendance	Referee
1992-93	Home	24-Oct-92	1-1	Olney (19)	13,457	R.Gifford
1992-93	Away	2-May-93	1-0	Henry (30)	37,247	D.Allison
1993-94	Home	25-Sep-93	1-1	Halle (14)	12,836	H.King (P.Rejer, 46)
1993-94	Away	19-Mar-94	2-1	Beckford (67); Holden (74)	21,214	J.Worrall

BLACKBURN ROVERS

Season	Venue	Date	Res	Scorers	Attendance	Referee
1992-93	Away	26-Sep-92	0-2		18,383	V.Callow
1992-93	Home	16-Jan-93	0-1		13,742	A.Buksh
1993-94	Away	21-Aug-93	0-1		14,397	J.Worrall
1993-94	Home	11-Dec-93	1-2	Holden (40)	13,887	J.Worrall

CHELSEA

Season	Venue	Date	Res	Scorers	Attendance	Referee
1992-93	Away	15-Aug-92	1-1	Henry (86)	20,699	J.Borrett
1992-93	Home	6-Feb-93	3-1	Henry (38); Adams (61); Brennan (71)	11,762	R.Milford
1993-94	Away	30-Oct-93	1-0	Beckford (20)	15,372	D.Frampton
1993-94	Home	12-Feb-94	2-1	Jobson (17); Sharp (81)	12,002	A.Gunn

COVENTRY CITY

Season	Venue	Date	Res	Scorers	Attendance	Referee
1992-93	Home	5-Sep-92	0-1		11,254	D.Allison
1992-93	Away	23-Jan-93	0-3		10,544	R.Lewis
1993-94	Home	24-Aug-93	3-3	Bernard (38); Ritchie (49 pen); Olney (63)	10,817	P.Foakes
1993-94	Away	18-Dec-93	1-1	Bernard (50)	11,792	D.Gallagher

CRYSTAL PALACE

Season	Venue	Date	Res	Scorers	Attendance	Referee
1992-93	Home	19-Aug-92	1-1	Sharp (16)	11,063	M.Peck
1992-93	Away	12-Sep-92	2-2	Olney (19); Sharp (78)	11,224	B.Hill

EVERTON

Season	Venue	Date	Res	Scorers	Attendance	Referee
1992-93	Home	4-Oct-92	1-0	Jobson (8)	13,013	P.Don
1992-93	Away	27-Feb-93	2-2	Adams (87 pen, 88)	18,025	K.Cooper
1993-94	Home	11-Sep-93	0-1		13,666	S.Lodge
1993-94	Away	5-Mar-94	1-2	Sharp (43)	18,881	D.Elleray

IPSWICH TOWN

Season	Venue	Date	Res	Scorers	Attendance	Referee
1992-93	Home	19-Sep-92	4-2	Marshall (32); Sharp (53); Halle (56); Henry (82)	11,150	J.Key
1992-93	Away	9-Jan-93	2-1	Brennan (16); Bernard (51)	15,025	K.Redfern
1993-94	Home	14-Aug-93	0-3		12,074	K.Barratt
1993-94	Away	4-Dec-93	0-0		11,789	S.Lodge

LEEDS UNITED

Season	Venue	Date	Res	Scorers	Attendance	Referee
1992-93	Home	1-Sep-92	2-2	Olney (85, 90)	13,848	K.Barratt
1992-93	Away	13-Feb-93	0-2		27,654	R.Dilkes
1993-94	Away	30-Aug-93	0-1		28,717	G.Ashby
1993-94	Home	28-Feb-94	1-1	Beckford (85)	11,136	B.Hill

LIVERPOOL

Season	Venue	Date	Res	Scorers	Attendance	Referee
1992-93	Away	10-Apr-93	0-1		36,129	J.Worrall
1992-93	Home	5-May-93	3-2	Beckford (20); Olney (35, 36)	15,381	P.Durkin
1993-94	Away	16-Oct-93	1-2	Beckford (73)	32,661	A.Wilkie
1993-94	Home	15-Jan-94	0-3		14,573	J.Lloyd

MANCHESTER CITY

Season	Venue	Date	Res	Scorers	Attendance	Referee
1992-93	Away	29-Aug-92	3-3	Jobson (11); Milligan (29); Halle (38)	27,255	D.Gallagher
1992-93	Home	26-Jan-93	0-1		14,903	J.Borrett
1993-94	Away	4-Oct-93	1-1	Sharp (57)	21,401	J.Borrett
1993-94	Home	26-Mar-94	0-0		16,462	K.Hackett

MANCHESTER UNITED

Season	Venue	Date	Res	Scorers	Attendance	Referee
1992-93	Away	21-Nov-92	0-3		33,497	A.Gunn
1992-93	Home	9-Mar-93	1-0	Adams (26)	17,106	G.Ashby
1993-94	Home	29-Dec-93	2-5	Sharp (15); Holden (26)	16,708	V.Callow
1993-94	Away	4-Apr-94	2-3	McCarthy (49); Sharp (70)	44,686	P.Durkin

MIDDLESBROUGH

Season	Venue	Date	Res	Scorers	Attendance	Referee
1992-93	Home	28-Nov-92	4-1	Halle (21); Pointon (24); Sharp (28); Adams (60)	12,401	K.Morton
1992-93	Away	22-Mar-93	3-2	Bernard (29); Olney (34); Ritchie (85)	12,290	K.Morton

NEWCASTLE UNITED

Season	Venue	Date	Res	Scorers	Attendance	Referee
1993-94	Home	8-Nov-93	1-3	Jobson (35)	13,821	R.Gifford
1993-94	Away	23-Apr-94	2-3	Jobson (43); Sharp (57)	32,214	D.Allison

NORWICH CITY

Season	Venue	Date	Res	Scorers	Attendance	Referee
1992-93	Home	9-Nov-92	2-3	Sharp (25); Marshall (43)	11,018	R.Hart
1992-93	Away	13-Mar-93	0-1		19,597	R.Milford
1993-94	Home	27-Nov-93	2-1	Sharp (47); Makin (62)	10,198	P.Don
1993-94	Away	7-May-94	1-1	McCarthy (14)	20,394	D.Frampton

NOTTINGHAM FOREST

Season	Venue	Date	Res	Scorers	Attendance	Referee
1992-93	Home	22-Aug-92	5-3	Adams (31); Sharp (38); Henry (43); Halle (46); Bernard (59)	11,632	R.Groves
1992-93	Away	30-Jan-93	0-2		21,240	P.Don

QPR

Season	Venue	Date	Res	Scorers	Attendance	Referee
1992-93	Away	5-Dec-92	2-3	Adams (41); Olney (46)	11,800	S.Lodge
1992-93	Home	20-Mar-93	2-2	Henry (1); Adams (88)	10,946	M.Bodenham
1993-94	Away	27-Dec-93	0-2		13,218	K.Morton
1993-94	Home	2-Apr-94	4-1	Jobson (44); Beckford (46); McCarthy (52); OG (89, McCarthy)	10,440	K.Burge

SHEFFIELD UNITED

Season	Venue	Date	Res	Scorers	Attendance	Referee
1992-93	Away	22-Feb-93	0-2		14,628	G.Ashby
1992-93	Home	13-Apr-93	1-1	Ritchie (10)	14,795	P.Foakes
1993-94	Away	1-Jan-94	1-2	Jobson (45)	17,066	R.Hart
1993-94	Home	3-May-94	1-1	Beckford (24)	14,779	A.Wilkie

SHEFFIELD WEDNESDAY

Season	Venue	Date	Res	Scorers	Attendance	Referee
1992-93	Away	17-Oct-92	1-2	Milligan (44)	24,485	R.Groves
1992-93	Home	7-Apr-93	1-1	Pointon (13)	12,312	A.Wilkie
1993-94	Away	24-Nov-93	0-3		18,509	K.Barratt
1993-94	Home	30-Apr-94	0-0		12,973	P.Foakes

SOUTHAMPTON

Season	Venue	Date	Res	Scorers	Attendance	Referee
1992-93	Away	31-Oct-92	0-1		10,827	P.Durkin
1992-93	Home	8-May-93	4-3	Pointon (29); Olney (44); Ritchie (55); Halle (64)	14,597	H.King
1993-94	Home	5-Feb-94	2-1	McCarthy (33); Bernard (39)	9,982	K.Morton
1993-94	Away	30-Mar-94	3-1	Sharp (14); OG (42, Benali); Holden (88)	14,101	V.Callow

SWINDON TOWN

Season	Venue	Date	Res	Scorers	Attendance	Referee
1993-94	Away	18-Aug-93	1-0	Bernard (90)	11,940	D.Gallagher
1993-94	Home	7-Dec-93	2-1	Holden (12); Redmond (84)	9,771	D.Allison

TOTTENHAM HOTSPUR

Season	Venue	Date	Res	Scorers	Attendance	Referee
1992-93	Home	19-Dec-92	2-1	Sharp (29); Olney (90)	11,735	R.Milford
1992-93	Away	17-Apr-93	1-4	Beckford (25)	26,663	K.Hackett
1993-94	Away	18-Sep-93	0-5		24,614	A.Gunn
1993-94	Home	5-May-94	0-2		14,283	R.Gifford

WEST HAM UNITED

Season	Venue	Date	Res	Scorers	Attendance	Referee
v1993-94	Away	20-Nov-93	0-2		17,211	D.Allison
1993-94	Home	16-Apr-94	1-2	Holden (43 pen)	11,669	K.Barratt

WIMBLEDON

Season	Venue	Date	Res	Scorers	Attendance	Referee
1992-93	Away	12-Dec-92	2-5	Brennan (46); Milligan (63)	3,386	K.Hackett
1992-93	Home	3-Apr-93	6-2	OG (5, Fashanu); Bernard (13); Olney (42, 69); Adams (73); Beckford (87)	11,606	J.Martin
1993-94	Home	28-Aug-93	1-1	Bernard (6)	9,633	P.Durkin
1993-94	Away	26-Apr-94	0-3		6,766	R.Milford

INTRODUCTION

Founded in 1885 as St. Jude's Institute. Changed name to Queens Park Rangers in 1887; joined the London League in 1896; and turned professional in 1898. Moved to the Southern League, 1899, and were twice champions.

Led a nomadic existence in West London but in 1917 took over the home of the amateurs Shepherds Bush, Loftus Road, where, apart from a couple of seasons at White City, it has stayed. Founder members of Football League Division Three in 1920 (this becoming Division Three (South) the following season); of Division Three at the end of regionalisation in 1958; and of the Premier League, 1992.

Ground: Loftus Road,
                South Africa Road, W12 7PA
Nickname: Rangers or Rs
Internet: www.qpr.co.uk

HONOURS

Football League Div 1:	Runners-up: 1975-76
Football League Div 2:	Champions: 1982-83
	Runners-up: 1967-68, 1972-73
Football League Div 3S:	Champions: 1947-48
	Runners-up: 1946-47
Football League Div 3:	Champions: 1966-67
FA Cup:	Runners-up: 1982
Football League Cup:	Winners: 1966-67
	Runners-up: 1985-86.

EUROPEAN RECORD

Champions' League (0):	–
Cup-Winners' Cup (0):	–
UEFA Cup (2):	76-77(QF), 84-85(2).

FAPL RECORD SUMMARY

Most Total:	IMPEY, Andy	142
Most Starts:	IMPEY, Andy	138
Most Subs:	PENRICE, Gary	21
Most SNU:	ROBERTS, Tony	53
Most PS:	GALLEN, Kevin	19
Most Goals:	FERDINAND, Les	60
Most Yel:	BARKER, Simon	26
Most Red:	FERDINAND, Les	2

PLAYING RECORD – SEASON TOTALS

Season	Pn	P	W	D	L	F	A	Pts
1992-93	5	42	17	12	13	63	55	63
1993-94	9	42	16	12	14	62	61	60
1994-95	8	42	17	9	16	61	59	60
1995-96	19	38	9	6	23	38	57	33
Totals		164	59	39	66	224	232	216

PLAYING RECORD – HOME TOTALS

Season	Pn	P	W	D	L	F	A	Pts
1992-93	5	21	11	5	5	41	32	38
1993-94	9	21	8	7	6	32	29	31
1994-95	8	21	11	3	7	36	26	36
1995-96	19	19	6	5	8	25	26	23
Totals		82	36	20	26	134	113	128

PLAYING RECORD – AWAY TOTALS

Season	Pn	P	W	D	L	F	A	Pts
1992-93	5	21	6	7	8	22	23	25
1993-94	9	21	8	5	8	30	32	29
1994-95	8	21	6	6	9	25	33	24
1995-96	19	19	3	1	15	13	31	10
Totals		82	23	19	40	90	119	88

HIGHEST HOME ATTENDANCES

	Attendance	Opponents	Date	Season
1	21,267	Manchester U.	5-Feb-94	1993-94
2	21,142	Manchester U.	18-Jan-93	1992-93
3	21,056	Liverpool	23-Nov-92	1992-93
4	20,868	Arsenal	2-Sep-92	1992-93
5	19,845	Tottenham H.	3-Oct-92	1992-93

LOWEST HOME ATTENDANCES

	Attendance	Opponents	Date	Season
1	9,875	Swindon T.	30-Apr-94	1993-94
2	10,189	Leicester C.	8-Mar-95	1994-95
3	10,519	Norwich C.	15-Mar-95	1994-95
4	10,613	Southampton	21-Aug-93	1993-94
5	10,677	Blackburn R.	24-Mar-93	1992-93

TOP SCORER – SEASON BY SEASON

Season	Player	Goals
1992-93	Ferdinand	20
1993-94	Ferdinand	17
1994-95	Ferdinand	23
1995-96	Dichio	10

PLAYERS WITH MOST PREMIERSHIP APPEARANCES

Tot	Player	St	Sb	Gls
142	IMPEY, Andy	138	4	11
131	BARDSLEY, David	130	1	3
131	BARKER, Simon	126	5	15
119	WILSON, Clive	119	0	8
116	McDONALD, Alan	115	1	3
110	FERDINAND, Les	109	1	60
107	HOLLOWAY, Ian	96	11	4
102	SINCLAIR, Trevor	99	3	10
82	YATES, Steve	79	3	1
80	ROBERTS, Tony	80	0	0

CLUB-BY-CLUB RESULTS

ARSENAL

Season	Venue	Date	Res	Scorers	Attendance	Referee
1992-93	Home	2-Sep-92	0-0		20,868	R.Groves
1992-93	Away	4-May-93	0-0		18,817	R.Gifford
1993-94	Away	3-Jan-94	0-0		34,935	J.Borrett
1993-94	Home	27-Apr-94	1-1	Penrice (3)	11,442	J.Borrett
1994-95	Away	31-Dec-94	3-1	Gallen (3); Allen (76); Impey (77)	32,393	G.Willard
1994-95	Home	8-Apr-95	3-1	Impey (27); Gallen (59): Ready (82)	16,341	P.Don
1995-96	Away	26-Dec-95	0-3		38,259	M.Reed
1995-96	Home	2-Mar-96	1-1	Gallen (20)	17,970	P.Alcock

ASTON VILLA

Season	Venue	Date	Res	Scorers	Attendance	Referee
1992-93	Away	1-Nov-92	0-2		20,140	M.Peck
1992-93	Home	9-May-93	2-1	Ferdinand (67); Allen (78)	18,904	P.Durkin
1993-94	Away	14-Aug-93	1-4	Ferdinand (44)	32,944	K.Morton
1993-94	Home	4-Dec-93	2-2	OG (6, McGrath); Penrice (40)	14,915	K.Hackett
1994-95	Home	29-Oct-94	2-0	Dichio (36); Penrice (90)	16,037	R.Hart
1994-95	Away	14-Jan-95	1-2	Yates (88)	26,578	A.Wilkie
1995-96	Home	23-Dec-95	1-0	Gallen (54)	14,778	A.Wilkie
1995-96	Away	9-Mar-96	2-4	Dichio (50); Gallen (59)	28,221	A.Wilkie

BLACKBURN ROVERS

Season	Venue	Date	Res	Scorers	Attendance	Referee
1992-93	Away	28-Nov-92	0-1		15,850	K.Hackett
1992-93	Home	24-Mar-93	0-3		10,677	A.Gunn
1993-94	Home	6-Nov-93	1-0	OG (82, Hendry)	17,636	A.Gunn
1993-94	Away	24-Apr-94	1-1	Ready (83)	19,193	R.Gifford
1994-95	Away	26-Nov-94	0-4		21,302	J.Worrall
1994-95	Home	4-Apr-95	0-1		16,508	R.Hart
1995-96	Away	19-Aug-95	0-1		25,932	A.Wilkie
1995-96	Home	13-Jan-96	0-1		13,957	G.Ashby

BOLTON WANDERERS

Season	Venue	Date	Res	Scorers	Attendance	Referee
1995-96	Away	30-Sep-95	1-0	Dichio (89)	17,362	J.Winter
1995-96	Home	16-Dec-95	2-1	Osborne (40); Impey (76)	11,456	S.Lodge

CHELSEA

Season	Venue	Date	Res	Scorers	Attendance	Referee
1992-93	Away	29-Aug-92	0-1		22,910	A.Buksh

1992-93	Home	27-Jan-93	1-1	Allen (88)	15,806	T.Ward
1993-94	Away	25-Aug-93	0-2		20,191	K.Burge
1993-94	Home	13-Apr-94	1-1	Ferdinand (66)	15,735	R.Milford
1994-95	Home	22-Mar-95	1-0	Gallen (62)	15,103	B.Hill
1994-95	Away	29-Apr-95	0-1		21,704	G.Ashby
1995-96	Home	2-Jan-96	1-2	Allen (71)	14,904	D.Elleray
1995-96	Away	23-Mar-96	1-1	Barker (20)	25,590	M.Reed

COVENTRY CITY

Season	Venue	Date	Res	Scorers	Attendance	Referee
1992-93	Away	26-Aug-92	1-0	Impey (45)	13,563	S.Lodge
1992-93	Home	20-Feb-93	2-0	OG (34, Pearce); Peacock (41)	12,453	P.Durkin
1993-94	Home	23-Oct-93	5-1	Ferdinand (15); Allen (30, 45); Impey (74);		G.Ashby
				Barker (88)	12,979	
1993-94	Away	22-Jan-94	1-0	White (25)	12,065	A.Wilkie
1994-95	Home	10-Sep-94	2-2	Penrice (35,37)	11,398	J.Worrall
1994-95	Away	1-Apr-95	1-0	Sinclair (85)	15,740	P.Danson
1995-96	Home	19-Dec-95	1-1	Barker (37)	11,189	M.Bodenham
1995-96	Away	13-Apr-96	0-1		22,916	K.Cooper

CRYSTAL PALACE

Season	Venue	Date	Res	Scorers	Attendance	Referee
1992-93	Home	12-Dec-92	1-3	Penrice (26)	14,571	R.Hart
1992-93	Away	3-Apr-93	1-1	Allen (23)	14,705	A.Wilkie
1994-95	Away	26-Dec-94	0-0		16,372	B.Hill
1994-95	Home	17-Apr-95	0-1		14,227	A.Wilkie

EVERTON

Season	Venue	Date	Res	Scorers	Attendance	Referee
1992-93	Home	28-Dec-92	4-2	Sinton (27, 51, 88); Penrice (46)	14,802	G.Ashby
1992-93	Away	12-Apr-93	5-3	Impey (6); Ferdinand (38, 47, 51); Bardsley (79)	19,057	S.Lodge
1993-94	Away	20-Nov-93	3-0	Allen (26, 51, 83)	17,326	R.Hart
1993-94	Home	16-Apr-94	2-1	White (66); Ferdinand (88)	13,330	M.Bodenham
1994-95	Away	17-Sep-94	2-2	Ferdinand (4,47)	27,285	R.Gifford
1994-95	Home	18-Mar-95	2-3	Ferdinand (36); Gallen (59)	14,488	K.Morton
1995-96	Away	22-Nov-95	0-2		30,009	P.Danson
1995-96	Home	8-Apr-96	3-1	Gallen (15); Hateley (42); Impey (61)	18,349	P.Durkin

IPSWICH TOWN

Season	Venue	Date	Res	Scorers	Attendance	Referee
1992-93	Home	5-Sep-92	0-0		12,806	D.Gallagher
1992-93	Away	9-Feb-93	1-1	White (80)	17,354	R.Milford
1993-94	Home	2-Oct-93	3-0	White (57, 62); Barker (65)	12,292	K.Cooper
1993-94	Away	26-Mar-94	3-1	Impey (64, 69); Ferdinand (71)	14,653	B.Hill
1994-95	Home	27-Aug-94	1-2	Ferdinand (90)	12,456	P.Danson
1994-95	Away	11-Apr-95	1-0	Ferdinand (68)	11,767	R.Gifford

LEEDS UNITED

Season	Venue	Date	Res	Scorers	Attendance	Referee
1992-93	Home	24-Oct-92	2-1	Bardsley (73); Ferdinand (85)	19,326	H.King
1992-93	Away	1-May-93	1-1	Ferdinand (16)	31,408	V.Callow

1993-94	Away	29-Dec-93	1-1	Meaker (62)	39,124	M.Reed
1993-94	Home	4-Apr-94	0-4		15,365	J.Worrall
1994-95	Home	19-Nov-94	3-2	Ferdinand (30,39); Gallen (68)	17,416	M.Bodenham
1994-95	Away	24-Jan-95	0-4		28,780	K.Morton
1995-96	Away	16-Sep-95	3-1	Dichio (15, 64); Sinclair (39)	31,504	S.Lodge
1995-96	Home	6-Mar-96	1-2	Gallen (30)	13,991	G.Powler

LEICESTER CITY

Season	Venue	Date	Res	Scorers	Attendance	Referee
1994-95	Away	31-Aug-94	1-1	OG (41, Willis)	18,695	S.Lodge
1994-95	Home	8-Mar-95	2-0	McDonald (71); Wilson (73)	10,189	M.Reed

LIVERPOOL

Season	Venue	Date	Res	Scorers	Attendance	Referee
1992-93	Home	23-Nov-92	0-1		21,056	R.Milford
1992-93	Away	10-Mar-93	0-1		30,370	K.Burge
1993-94	Home	18-Aug-93	1-3	Wilkins (24)	19,625	P.Durkin
1993-94	Away	8-Dec-93	2-3	Ferdinand (10); Barker (46)	24,561	V.Callow
1994-95	Home	31-Oct-94	2-1	Sinclair (28); Ferdinand (85)	18,295	T.Holbrook
1994-95	Away	11-Feb-95	1-1	Gallen (6)	35,996	D.Gallagher
1995-96	Away	30-Aug-95	0-1		37,548	S.Dunn
1995-96	Home	11-Feb-96	1-2	Dichio (66)	18,405	D.Gallagher

MANCHESTER CITY

Season	Venue	Date	Res	Scorers	Attendance	Referee
1992-93	Away	17-Aug-92	1-1	Sinton (47)	24,471	M.Bodenham
1992-93	Home	6-Feb-93	1-1	Wilson (66 pen)	13,003	M.Reed
1993-94	Away	11-Sep-93	0-3		24,445	A.Wilkie
1993-94	Home	5-Mar-94	1-1	Penrice (28)	13,474	S.Lodge
1994-95	Home	15-Oct-94	1-2	Wilson (62)	13,631	G.Willard
1994-95	Away	14-May-95	3-2	Ferdinand (13,89); Dichio (77)	27,850	M.Reed
1995-96	Home	26-Aug-95	1-0	Barker (31)	14,212	P.Danson
1995-96	Away	3-Feb-96	0-2		27,509	G.Poll

MANCHESTER UNITED

Season	Venue	Date	Res	Scorers	Attendance	Referee
1992-93	Away	26-Sep-92	0-0		33,287	D.Allison
1992-93	Home	18-Jan-93	1-3	Allen (42)	21,142	J.Martin
1993-94	Away	30-Oct-93	1-2	Allen (7)	44,663	S.Lodge
1993-94	Home	5-Feb-94	2-3	Wilson (44 pen); Ferdinand (65)	21,267	G.Poll
1994-95	Away	20-Aug-94	0-2		43,214	D.Gallagher
1994-95	Home	10-Dec-94	2-3	Ferdinand (24,64)	18,948	G.Poll
1995-96	Away	30-Dec-95	1-2	Dichio (68)	41,890	R.Hart
1995-96	Home	16-Mar-96	1-1	OG (63, Irwin)	18,817	R.Hart

MIDDLESBROUGH

Season	Venue	Date	Res	Scorers	Attendance	Referee
1992-93	Home	19-Sep-92	3-3	Ferdinand (57); Penrice (73); Sinton (90 pen)	12,272	J.Borrett
1992-93	Away	9-Jan-93	1-0	Ferdinand (72)	15,616	R.Dilkes
1995-96	Away	21-Oct-95	0-1		29,293	M.Reed
1995-96	Home	2-Dec-95	1-1	McDonald (15)	17,546	P.Durkin

NEWCASTLE UNITED

Season	Venue	Date	Res	Scorers	Attendance	Referee
1993-94	Away	16-Oct-93	2-1	Ferdinand (10); Allen (50)	33,801	K.Hackett
1993-94	Home	16-Jan-94	1-2	Penrice (20)	15,774	D.Gallagher
1994-95	Away	5-Nov-94	1-2	Dichio (60)	34,278	G.Ashby
1994-95	Home	4-Feb-95	3-0	Ferdinand (4,7); Barker (19)	16,576	K.Cooper
1995-96	Home	14-Oct-95	2-3	Dichio (43, 68)	18,254	P.Durkin
1995-96	Away	6-Apr-96	1-2	Holloway (53)	36,583	P.Sampson

NORWICH CITY

Season	Venue	Date	Res	Scorers	Attendance	Referee
1992-93	Away	17-Oct-92	1-2	Allen (77)	16,009	D.Gallagher
1992-93	Home	6-Mar-93	3-1	Ferdinand (18, 34); Wilson (78)	13,892	R.Gifford
1993-94	Home	18-Sep-93	2-2	Sinclair (29); Ferdinand (83)	13,359	R.Milford
1993-94	Away	12-Mar-94	4-3	Barker (49); Peacock (64); Penrice (70); White (84)	16,499	D.Allison
1994-95	Away	22-Oct-94	2-4	Barker (24); Gallen (61)	19,431	M.Reed
1994-95	Home	15-Mar-95	2-0	Ferdinand (66); Gallen (86)	10,519	G.Ashby

NOTTINGHAM FOREST

Season	Venue	Date	Res	Scorers	Attendance	Referee
1992-93	Away	24-Feb-93	0-1		22,436	R.Gifford
1992-93	Home	10-Apr-93	4-3	Ferdinand (38, 70, 73); Wilson (45pen)	15,815	P.Foakes
1994-95	Away	2-Oct-94	2-3	Ferdinand (54); Allen (84)	21,449	K.Morton
1994-95	Home	26-Feb-95	1-1	Barker (87)	13,363	P.Danson
1995-96	Home	28-Oct-95	1-1	Sinclair (76)	17,549	S.Dunn
1995-96	Away	5-May-96	0-3		22,910	G.Ashby

OLDHAM ATHLETIC

Season	Venue	Date	Res	Scorers	Attendance	Referee
1992-93	Home	5-Dec-92	3-2	Ferdinand (24,52); Penrice (33)	11,800	S.Lodge
1992-93	Away	20-Mar-93	2-2	Allen (68); Sinton (73)	10,946	M.Bodenham
1993-94	Home	27-Dec-93	2-0	White (56); Penrice (75)	13,218	K.Morton
1993-94	Away	2-Apr-94	1-4	Ferdinand (35)	10,440	K.Burge

SHEFFIELD UNITED

Season	Venue	Date	Res	Scorers	Attendance	Referee
1992-93	Home	22-Aug-92	3-2	Ferdinand (3); Barker (14); Bailey (84)	10,932	P.Foakes
1992-93	Away	30-Jan-93	2-1	Allen (19); Holloway (75)	16,366	V.Callow
1993-94	Home	1-Sep-93	2-1	Sinclair (15); Wilson (63 pen)	11,113	K.Barratt
1993-94	Away	16-Mar-94	1-1	Barker (12)	14,183	R.Gifford

SHEFFIELD WEDNESDAY

Season	Venue	Date	Res	Scorers	Attendance	Referee
1992-93	Away	19-Dec-92	0-1		23,164	J.Worrall
1992-93	Home	11-May-93	3-1	Allen (27, 31); Ferdinand (67)	12,177	D.Allison
1993-94	Home	1-Jan-94	1-2	Ferdinand (69)	16,858	P.Foakes
1993-94	Away	9-Apr-94	1-3	White (90)	22,437	K.Morton
1994-95	Home	24-Aug-94	3-2	Ferdinand (22); Sinclair (57); Gallen (78)	12,788	P.Jones
1994-95	Away	17-Dec-94	2-0	Maddix (60); Ferdinand (84)	22,766	P.Durkin
1995-96	Home	9-Sep-95	0-3		12,459	M.Reed
1995-96	Away	17-Feb-96	3-1	Barker (33, 67); Goodridge (87)	22,442	P.Durkin

SOUTHAMPTON

Season	Venue	Date	Res	Scorers	Attendance	Referee
1992-93	Home	19-Aug-92	3-1	Ferdinand (58, 86); Bardsley (70)	10,925	R.Bigger
1992-93	Away	12-Sep-92	2-1	Sinton (53); Channing (56)	14,125	A.Gunn
1993-94	Home	21-Aug-93	2-1	Penrice (13); Wilson (46 pen)	10,613	R.Dilkes
1993-94	Away	11-Dec-93	1-0	Ferdinand (2)	11,946	K.Barratt
1994-95	Home	28-Dec-94	2-2	Barker (7); Gallen (49)	16,078	K.Cooper
1994-95	Away	15-Apr-95	1-2	Ferdinand (63)	15,201	P.Jones
1995-96	Away	4-Nov-95	0-2		15,137	R.Dilkes
1995-96	Home	30-Mar-96	3-0	Brevett (25); Dichio (61); Gallen (76)	17,615	P.Jones

SWINDON TOWN

Season	Venue	Date	Res	Scorers	Attendance	Referee
1993-94	Away	24-Nov-93	0-1		14,674	G.Ashby
1993-94	Home	30-Apr-94	1-3	Ferdinand (71)	9,875	D.Elleray

TOTTENHAM HOTSPUR

Season	Venue	Date	Res	Scorers	Attendance	Referee
1992-93	Home	3-Oct-92	4-1	Holloway (52); Wilkins (59); Penrice (67, 79)	19,845	J.Worrall
1992-93	Away	27-Feb-93	2-3	Peacock (87); White (88)	32,341	D.Elleray
1993-94	Home	27-Nov-93	1-1	Ferdinand (1)	17,694	D.Elleray
1993-94	Away	7-May-94	2-1	Sinclair (36, 77)	26,105	A.Gunn
1994-95	Away	8-Oct-94	1-1	Impey (45)	25,799	P.Jones
1994-95	Home	6-May-95	2-1	Ferdinand (64,75)	18,367	G.Poll
1995-96	Home	25-Sep-95	2-3	Dichio (36); Impey (46)	15,659	D.Elleray
1995-96	Away	9-Dec-95	0-1		28,851	K.Cooper

WEST HAM UNITED

Season	Venue	Date	Res	Scorers	Attendance	Referee
1993-94	Away	28-Aug-93	4-0	Peacock (12); Ferdinand (47, 71); Penrice (53)	18,084	V.Callow
1993-94	Home	3-May-94	0-0		10,850	R.Dilkes
1994-95	Home	4-Dec-94	2-1	Ferdinand (2); Sinclair (37)	12,780	P.Don
1994-95	Away	3-May-95	0-0		22,932	G.Willard
1995-96	Away	25-Nov-95	0-1		21,504	P.Alcock
1995-96	Home	27-Apr-96	3-0	Ready (60); Gallen (70, 79)	18,828	G.Willard

WIMBLEDON

Season	Venue	Date	Res	Scorers	Attendance	Referee
1992-93	Away	7-Nov-92	2-0	Allen (25); Wilkins (42)	6,771	P.Don
1992-93	Home	13-Mar-93	1-2	Ferdinand (3)	12,270	P.Don
1993-94	Away	27-Sep-93	1-1	McDonald (18)	9,478	P.Don
1993-94	Home	19-Mar-94	1-0	Peacock (70)	11,368	M.Reed
1994-95	Home	24-Sep-94	0-1		11,061	K.Burge
1994-95	Away	4-Mar-95	3-1	Ferdinand (24,60); Holloway (49)	9,176	G.Willard
1995-96	Home	23-Aug-95	0-3		11,837	G.Poll
1995-96	Away	20-Jan-96	1-2	Hateley (56)	9,123	S.Dunn

INTRODUCTION

Founded 1889 as a professional club to fulfil the needs of those in charge at Bramhall Lane Cricket Club, including those associated with Sheffield United Cricket Club. The club failed in its application to join the Football Alliance in that competition's first season and played in the Midland League, moving to the Northern for 1891-92.

Failed too in its application for a place in Football League Division One in 1892, but joined the League instead as a founder member of Division Two. Played in all four divisions of the Football League and was a founder member of the Premier League in 1992.

Ground:	Bramall Lane Ground, Sheffield, S2 4SU
Nickname:	The Blades
Internet:	www.sheffutd.co.uk

HONOURS

Football League Div 1:	Champions 1897-98
	Runners-up 1896-97, 1899-1900
Football League Div 2:	Champions 1952-53
	Runners-up 1892-93, 1938-39, 1960-61, 1970-71, 1989-90
Football League Div 4:	Champions 1981-82.
FA Cup:	Winners 1899, 1902, 1915, 1925
	Runners-up 1901, 1936

EUROPEAN RECORD

Champions' League
Cup-Winners' Cup
UEFA Cup

FAPL RECORD SUMMARY

Most Total:	BRADSHAW, Carl	72
Most Starts:	BRADSHAW, Carl	63
Most Subs:	CORK, Alan	28
Most SNU:	KELLY, Alan	15
Most PS:	GANNON, John	11
Most Goals:	DEANE, Brian	15
Most Yel:	WHITEHOUSE, Dane	10
Most Red:	BRADSHAW, Carl	2

PLAYING RECORD – SEASON TOTALS

Season	Pn	P	W	D	L	F	A	Pts
1992-93	14	42	14	10	18	54	53	52
1993-94	20	42	8	18	16	42	60	42
Totals		84	22	28	34	96	113	94

PLAYING RECORD – HOME TOTALS

Season	Pn	P	W	D	L	F	A	Pts
1992-93	14	21	10	6	5	33	19	36
1993-94	20	21	6	10	5	24	23	28
Totals		42	16	16	10	57	42	64

PLAYING RECORD – AWAY TOTALS

Season	Pn	P	W	D	L	F	A	Pts
1992-93	14	21	4	4	13	21	34	16
1993-94	20	21	2	8	11	18	37	14
Totals		42	6	12	24	39	71	30

HIGHEST HOME ATTENDANCES

	Attendance	Opponents	Date	Season
1	30,044	Sheffield W.	23-Oct-93	1993-94
2	30,039	Sheffield W.	8-Nov-92	1992-93
3	29,013	Newcastle U.	30-Apr-94	1993-94
4	28,070	Manchester U.	15-Aug-92	1992-93
5	26,744	Manchester U.	7-Dec-93	1993-94

LOWEST HOME ATTENDANCES

	Attendance	Opponents	Date	Season
1	13,646	West Ham U.	28-Mar-94	1993-94
2	14,183	QPR	16-Mar-94	1993-94
3	14,628	Oldham A.	22-Feb-93	1992-93
4	15,135	Everton	11-Dec-93	1993-94
5	15,184	Middlesbrough	9-Feb-93	1992-93

TOP SCORER – SEASON BY SEASON

Season	Player	Goals
1992-93	Deane	15

PLAYERS WITH MOST PREMIERSHIP APPEARANCES

Tot	Player	St	Sb	Gls
72	BRADSHAW, Carl	63	9	2
64	BEESLEY, Paul	61	3	2
63	KELLY, Alan	61	2	0
62	HODGES, Glyn	47	15	6
52	ROGERS, Paul	50	2	6
52	WHITEHOUSE, Dane	49	3	10
48	GAGE, Kevin	43	5	0
48	WARD, Mitch	42	6	1
46	LITTLEJOHN, Adrian	30	16	11
46	CORK, Alan	18	28	5

CLUB-BY-CLUB RESULTS

ARSENAL

Season	Venue	Date	Res	Scorers	Attendance	Referee
1992-93	Home	19-Sep-92	1-1	Whitehouse (48)	19,105	R.Dilkes
1992-93	Away	9-Jan-93	1-1	Littlejohn (87)	23,818	G.Ashby
1993-94	Away	29-Dec-93	0-3		27,035	R.Milford
1993-94	Home	4-Apr-94	1-1	Rogers (54)	20,019	D.Frampton

ASTON VILLA

Season	Venue	Date	Res	Scorers	Attendance	Referee
1992-93	Home	29-Aug-92	0-2		18,773	R.Milford
1992-93	Away	27-Jan-93	1-3	Deane (74)	20,266	K.Burge
1993-94	Away	20-Nov-93	0-1		24,686	D.Frampton
1993-94	Home	16-Apr-94	1-2	Littlejohn (17)	18,402	G.Poll

BLACKBURN ROVERS

Season	Venue	Date	Res	Scorers	Attendance	Referee
1992-93	Away	19-Dec-92	0-1		16,057	D.Gallagher
1992-93	Home	17-Apr-93	1-3	Hodges (8)	18,186	D.Allison
1993-94	Away	18-Oct-93	0-0		14,276	T.Holbrook
1993-94	Home	15-Jan-94	1-2	OG (18, Hendry)	19,124	P.Foakes

CHELSEA

Season	Venue	Date	Res	Scorers	Attendance	Referee
1992-93	Away	31-Oct-92	2-1	Littlejohn (40); Deane (57)	13,763	D.Allison
1992-93	Home	8-May-93	4-2	Scott (7); Rogers (16); Whitehouse (43, 48)	24,850	A.Gunn
1993-94	Home	27-Nov-93	1-0	OG (32, Clarke)	16,119	R.Milford
1993-94	Away	7-May-94	2-3	Flo (29); Hodges (60)	21,782	K.Cooper

COVENTRY CITY

Season	Venue	Date	Res	Scorers	Attendance	Referee
1992-93	Home	28-Nov-92	1-1	OG (37, Pearce)	15,625	P.Don
1992-93	Away	24-Mar-93	3-1	Whitehouse (69); Deane (75); Littlejohn (87)	12,993	P.Wright
1993-94	Away	31-Oct-93	0-0		10,439	A.Gunn
1993-94	Home	12-Feb-94	0-0		15,394	J.Worrall

CRYSTAL PALACE

Season	Venue	Date	Res	Scorers	Attendance	Referee
1992-93	Away	5-Dec-92	0-2		12,361	H.King
1992-93	Home	20-Mar-93	0-1		18,857	J.Martin

EVERTON

Season	Venue	Date	Res	Scorers	Attendance	Referee
1992-93	Home	12-Dec-92	1-0	Littlejohn (34)	16,266	K.Morton
1992-93	Away	4-May-93	2-0	Bradshaw (15); Hodges (26)	15,197	V.Callow
1993-94	Away	21-Aug-93	2-4	Whitehouse (1); Cork (89)	24,177	D.Gallagher
1993-94	Home	11-Dec-93	0-0		15,135	V.Callow

IPSWICH TOWN

Season	Venue	Date	Res	Scorers	Attendance	Referee
1992-93	Away	26-Sep-92	0-0		16,353	R.Groves
1992-93	Home	16-Jan-93	3-0	Deane (31, 72, 75)	16,758	D.Allison
1993-94	Home	28-Aug-93	1-1	Flo (25)	17,932	P.Foakes
1993-94	Away	22-Feb-94	2-3	Cork (23); Carr (49)	11,468	K.Burge

LEEDS UNITED

Season	Venue	Date	Res	Scorers	Attendance	Referee
1992-93	Away	17-Oct-92	1-3	Beesley (53)	29,706	R.Lewis
1992-93	Home	6-Apr-93	2-1	Rogers (24); Deane (86)	20,562	K.Barratt
1993-94	Away	18-Sep-93	1-2	OG (45, Kelly)	33,879	P.Don
1993-94	Home	13-Mar-94	2-2	Flo (74); Gayle (90)	19,425	R.Dilkes

LIVERPOOL

Season	Venue	Date	Res	Scorers	Attendance	Referee
1992-93	Away	19-Aug-92	1-2	Deane (35)	33,107	D.Elleray
1992-93	Home	12-Sep-92	1-0	Littlejohn (4)	20,632	J.Martin
1993-94	Home	26-Dec-93	0-0		22,932	A.Wilkie
1993-94	Away	2-Apr-94	2-1	Flo (46, 72)	36,642	T.Holbrook

MANCHESTER CITY

Season	Venue	Date	Res	Scorers	Attendance	Referee
1992-93	Away	26-Dec-92	0-2		27,455	K.Barratt
1992-93	Home	9-Apr-93	1-1	Deane (69)	18,231	K.Cooper
1993-94	Home	25-Sep-93	0-1		20,067	D.Elleray
1993-94	Away	19-Mar-94	0-0		25,448	A.Gunn

MANCHESTER UNITED

Season	Venue	Date	Res	Scorers	Attendance	Referee
1992-93	Home	15-Aug-92	2-1	Deane (5, 50 pen)	28,070	B.Hill
1992-93	Away	6-Feb-93	1-2	Carr (7)	36,156	M.Bodenham
1993-94	Away	18-Aug-93	0-3		41,949	G.Ashby
1993-94	Home	7-Dec-93	0-3		26,744	A.Gunn

MIDDLESBROUGH

Season	Venue	Date	Res	Scorers	Attendance	Referee
1992-93	Away	5-Sep-92	0-2		15,179	A.Buksh
1992-93	Home	9-Feb-93	2-0	Carr (38); Deane (60)	15,184	T.Ward

NEWCASTLE UNITED

Season	Venue	Date	Res	Scorers	Attendance	Referee
1993-94	Away	24-Nov-93	0-4		35,029	J.Worrall
1993-94	Home	30-Apr-94	2-0	Blake (63, 90)	29,013	J.Worrall

NORWICH CITY

Season	Venue	Date	Res	Scorers	Attendance	Referee
1992-93	Away	21-Nov-92	1-2	Cork (71)	14,874	M.Peck
1992-93	Home	10-Mar-93	0-1		15,583	R.Lewis
1993-94	Home	6-Nov-93	1-2	Whitehouse (43 pen)	18,254	K.Burge
1993-94	Away	23-Apr-94	1-0	Blake (31)	18,474	R.Hart

NOTTINGHAM FOREST

Season	Venue	Date	Res	Scorers	Attendance	Referee
1992-93	Home	24-Oct-92	0-0		19,152	R.Hart
1992-93	Away	1-May-93	2-0	Hodges (30); Gayle (73)	26,752	P.Durkin

OLDHAM ATHLETIC

Season	Venue	Date	Res	Scorers	Attendance	Referee
1992-93	Home	22-Feb-93	2-0	Gannon (45); Littlejohn (77)	14,628	G.Ashby
1992-93	Away	13-Apr-93	1-1	Hoyland (44)	14,795	P.Foakes
1993-94	Home	1-Jan-94	2-1	Whitehouse (23 pen); Ward (32)	17,066	R.Hart
1993-94	Away	3-May-94	1-1	Cork (9)	14,779	A.Wilkie

QPR

Season	Venue	Date	Res	Scorers	Attendance	Referee
1992-93	Away	22-Aug-92	2-3	Cork (4); Deane (63)	10,932	P.Foakes
1992-93	Home	30-Jan-93	1-2	Hoyland (88)	16,366	V.Callow
1993-94	Away	1-Sep-93	1-2	Flo (10)	11,113	K.Barratt
1993-94	Home	16-Mar-94	1-1	Blake (48)	14,183	R.Gifford

SHEFFIELD WEDNESDAY

Season	Venue	Date	Res	Scorers	Attendance	Referee
1992-93	Home	8-Nov-92	1-1	Littlejohn (61)	30,039	M.Reed
1992-93	Away	21-Apr-93	1-1	Deane (44)	38,688	K.Redfern
1993-94	Home	23-Oct-93	1-1	Hodges (7)	30,044	K.Cooper
1993-94	Away	22-Jan-94	1-3	Whitehouse (87 pen)	34,959	K.Cooper

SOUTHAMPTON

Season	Venue	Date	Res	Scorers	Attendance	Referee
1992-93	Home	3-Oct-92	2-0	Whitehouse (4); Littlejohn (26)	15,842	K.Redfern
1992-93	Away	27-Feb-93	2-3	Gayle (37); Bryson (83)	13,814	J.Borrett
1993-94	Away	2-Oct-93	3-3	Falconer (72); Flo (80, 90)	11,619	G.Poll
1993-94	Home	26-Mar-94	0-0		19,522	D.Elleray

SWINDON TOWN

Season	Venue	Date	Res	Scorers	Attendance	Referee
1993-94	Home	14-Aug-93	3-1	Falconer (21); Bradshaw (76); Rogers (83)	20,904	J.Borrett
1993-94	Away	4-Dec-93	0-0		12,882	T.Holbrook

TOTTENHAM HOTSPUR

Season	Venue	Date	Res	Scorers	Attendance	Referee
1992-93	Away	2-Sep-92	0-2		21,322	I.Mitchell (G.Pearson, 72)
1992-93	Home	2-Mar-93	6-0	Carr (13); OG (21, Gray); Bryson (28, 29); Deane (73); Rogers (87)	16,654	J.Worrall
1993-94	Home	11-Sep-93	2-2	Littlejohn (47, 62)	21,325	K.Morton
1993-94	Away	5-Mar-94	2-2	Gayle (57); Blake (86)	25,741	D.Allison

WEST HAM UNITED

Season	Venue	Date	Res	Scorers	Attendance	Referee
1993-94	Away	3-Jan-94	0-0		20,365	M.Reed
1993-94	Home	28-Mar-94	3-2	Whitehouse (40); Gayle (48); Rogers (73)	13,646	P.Durkin

WIMBLEDON

Season	Venue	Date	Res	Scorers	Attendance	Referee
1992-93	Home	25-Aug-92	2-2	Beesley (48); Hodges (67)	15,463	K.Barratt
1992-93	Away	20-Feb-93	0-2		3,979	R.Hart
1993-94	Home	24-Aug-93	2-1	Flo (43); Falconer (58)	15,555	A.Wilkie
1993-94	Away	18-Dec-93	0-2		6,728	P.Durkin

INTRODUCTION

Founded in 1867 by members of the Wednesday Cricket Club and played at Highfield before moving to Myrtle Road. Were first holders of the Sheffield FA Cup. The club played at Sheaf House then Endcliff and became professionals in 1886. In 1887 moved to Olive Grove. Refused admission to the Football League, the club was founder member, and first champions, of the Football Alliance in 1889. In 1892 most Alliance clubs became founder members of Football League Division Two, but Wednesday were elected to an enlarged top division. The club moved to Hillsborough in 1899. Founder members of the Premier League 1992.

Ground: Hillsborough, Sheffield, S6 1SW
Nickname: The Owls
Internet: www.swfc.co.uk

HONOURS

Football League Div 1:	Champions 1902-03, 1903-04, 1928-29, 1929-30 Runners-up 1960-61
Football League Div 2:	Champions 1899-1900, 1925-26, 1951-52, 1955-56, 1958-59 Runners-up 1949-50, 1983-84
FA Cup:	Winners 1895-96, 1906-07, 1934-35. Runners-up 1889-90, 1965-66, 1992-93
Football League Cup:	Winners 1990-91 Runners-up 1992-93

EUROPEAN RECORD

Champions' League (0):	–
Cup-Winners' Cup (0):	–
UEFA Cup (3):	61-62 (QF), 63-64 (2), 92-93 (2)

FAPL RECORD SUMMARY

Most Total:	WALKER, Des	264
Most Starts:	WALKER, Des	264
Most Subs:	HYDE, Graham	40
Most SNU:	CLARKE, Matt	91
Most PS:	HIRST, David	32
Most Goals:	BRIGHT, Mark	48
Most Yel:	ATHERTON, Peter	34
Most Red:	HIRST, David	2

PLAYING RECORD – SEASON TOTALS

Season	Pn	P	W	D	L	F	A	Pts
1992-93	7	42	15	14	13	55	51	59
1993-94	7	42	16	16	10	76	54	64
1994-95	13	42	13	12	17	49	57	51
1995-96	15	38	10	10	18	48	61	40
1996-97	7	38	14	15	9	50	51	57
1997-98	16	38	12	8	18	52	67	44
1998-99	12	38	13	7	18	41	42	46
1999-00	19	38	8	7	23	38	70	31
Totals		316	101	89	126	409	453	392

PLAYING RECORD – HOME TOTALS

Season	Pn	P	W	D	L	F	A	Pts
1992-93	7	21	9	8	4	34	26	35
1993-94	7	21	10	7	4	48	24	37
1994-95	13	21	7	7	7	26	26	28
1995-96	15	19	7	5	7	30	31	26
1996-97	7	19	8	10	1	25	16	34
1997-98	16	19	9	5	5	30	26	32
1998-99	12	19	7	5	7	20	15	26
1999-00	19	19	6	3	10	21	23	21
Totals		158	63	50	45	234	187	239

PLAYING RECORD – AWAY TOTALS

Season	Pn	P	W	D	L	F	A	Pts
1992-93	7	21	6	6	9	21	25	24
1993-94	7	21	6	9	6	28	30	27
1994-95	13	21	6	5	10	23	31	23
1995-96	15	19	3	5	11	18	30	14
1996-97	7	19	6	5	8	25	35	23
1997-98	16	19	3	3	13	22	41	12
1998-99	12	19	6	2	11	21	27	20
1999-00	19	19	2	4	13	17	47	10
Totals		158	38	39	81	175	266	153

HIGHEST HOME ATTENDANCES

	Attendance	Opponents	Date	Season
1	39,640	Manchester U.	2-Feb-00	1999-00
2	39,475	Manchester U.	21-Nov-98	1998-99
3	39,427	Manchester U.	7-Mar-98	1997-98
4	38,943	Liverpool	11-May-97	1996-97
5	38,688	Sheffield U.	21-Apr-93	1992-93

LOWEST HOME ATTENDANCES

	Attendance	Opponents	Date	Season
1	16,229	Coventry C.	3-Dec-95	1995-96
2	16,390	Nottingham F.	18-Nov-96	1996-97
3	17,657	Leicester C.	2-Sep-96	1996-97
4	18,077	Wimbledon	2-Oct-99	1999-00
5	18,136	Aston Villa	5-Apr-00	1999-00

SHEFFIELD WEDNESDAY

TOP SCORER – SEASON BY SEASON

Season	Player	Goals
1992-93	Bright	11
1993-94	Bright	19
1994-95	Bright	11
1995-96	Hirst	13
1996-97	Booth	10
1997-98	Di Canio	12
1998-99	Carbone	8
1999-00	De Bilde	10

133	BRIGHT, Mark	112	21	48
115	BOOTH, Andy	107	8	25
113	WHITTINGHAM, Guy	90	23	22
109	WADDLE, Chris	94	15	10
109	BART-WILLIAMS, Chris	83	26	16
105	HIRST, David	93	12	34
100	SHERIDAN, John	91	9	6
96	CARBONE, Benito	86	10	25
93	PEMBRIDGE, Mark	88	5	12
77	BRISCOE, Lee	48	29	1
76	HINCHCLIFFE, Andy	76	0	5
76	RUDI, Petter	70	6	8
75	ALEXANDERSSON, Niclas	73	2	8

PLAYERS WITH 100 APPEARANCES OR MORE

Tot	Player	St	Sb	Gls
264	WALKER, Des	264	0	0
213	ATHERTON, Peter	213	0	9
207	PRESSMAN, Kevin	205	2	0
165	NOLAN, Ian	164	1	4
157	HYDE, Graham	117	40	11

CLUB-BY-CLUB RESULTS

ARSENAL

Season	Venue	Date	Res	Scorers	Attendance	Referee
1992-93	Away	29-Aug-92	1-2	Hirst (33)	23,389	P.Durkin
1992-93	Home	6-May-93	1-0	Bright (19)	23,645	R.Hart
1993-94	Home	21-Aug-93	0-1		26,023	R.Hart
1993-94	Away	12-Dec-93	0-1		22,026	D.Gallagher
1994-95	Away	6-Nov-94	0-0		33,705	R.Gifford
1994-95	Home	4-Feb-95	3-1	Petrescu (8); Ingesson (25); Bright (90)	23,468	K.Burge
1995-96	Away	21-Nov-95	2-4	Hirst (9); Waddle (20)	34,556	R.Dilkes
1995-96	Home	8-Apr-96	1-0	Degryse (61)	24,349	S.Dunn
1996-97	Away	16-Sep-96	1-4	Booth (25)	33,461	M.Reed
1996-97	Home	26-Dec-96	0-0		23,245	R.Dilkes
1997-98	Home	22-Nov-97	2-0	Booth (42); Whittingham (86)	34,373	K.Burge
1997-98	Away	28-Mar-98	0-1		38,087	S.Dunn
1998-99	Home	27-Sep-98	1-0	Briscoe (89)	27,949	P.Alcock
1998-99	Away	9-Mar-99	0-3		37,792	D.Elleray
1999-00	Home	3-Jan-00	1-1	Sibon (56)	26,155	M.Reed
1999-00	Away	9-May-00	3-3	Sibon (58); De Bilde (60); Quinn (70)	37,271	J.Winter

ASTON VILLA

Season	Venue	Date	Res	Scorers	Attendance	Referee
1992-93	Home	5-Dec-92	1-2	Bright (26)	29,964	R.Hart
1992-93	Away	20-Mar-93	0-2		38,024	R.Milford
1993-94	Home	18-Aug-93	0-0		28,450	P.Foakes
1993-94	Away	8-Dec-93	2-2	Bart-Williams (24); OG (69, Teale)	20,304	P.Foakes
1994-95	Away	27-Nov-94	1-1	Atherton (58)	25,082	G.Poll
1994-95	Home	18-Feb-95	1-2	Bright (71)	24,063	D.Gallagher
1995-96	Away	6-Mar-96	2-3	Blinker (8, 63)	27,893	D.Elleray
1995-96	Home	16-Mar-96	2-0	Whittingham (58); Hirst (87)	22,964	P.Jones

1996-97	Home	17-Aug-96	2-1	Humphreys (56); Whittingham (84)	26,861	R.Dilkes
1996-97	Away	29-Jan-97	1-0	Booth (69)	26,726	P.Alcock
1997-98	Away	27-Sep-97	2-2	Collins (25); Whittingham (42)	32,044	N.Barry
1997-98	Home	2-May-98	1-3	Sanetti (88)	34,177	M.Bodenham
1998-99	Home	29-Aug-98	0-1		25,989	K.Burge
1998-99	Away	28-Dec-98	1-2	Carbone (8)	39,217	G.Barber
1999-00	Away	18-Dec-99	1-2	De Bilde (20 pen)	23,885	S.Bennett
1999-00	Home	5-Apr-00	0-1		18,136	G.Poll

BARNSLEY

Season	Venue	Date	Res	Scorers	Attendance	Referee
1997-98	Home	8-Dec-97	2-1	Stefanovic (19); Di Canio (88)	29,086	G.Willard
1997-98	Away	11-Apr-98	1-2	Sefanovic (86)	18,692	P.Alcock

BLACKBURN ROVERS

Season	Venue	Date	Res	Scorers	Attendance	Referee
1992-93	Home	31-Oct-92	0-0		31,044	R.Lewis
1992-93	Away	8-May-93	0-1		14,956	P.Don
1993-94	Away	25-Sep-93	1-1	Hyde (55)	14,495	V.Callow
1993-94	Home	20-Mar-94	1-2	Watson (40)	24,655	R.Dilkes
1994-95	Home	2-Nov-94	0-1		24,207	R.Hart
1994-95	Away	12-Feb-95	1-3	Waddle (32)	22,223	P.Jones
1995-96	Home	23-Aug-95	2-1	Waddle (18); Pembridge (83)	25,544	P.Danson
1995-96	Away	20-Jan-96	0-3		24,732	G.Willard
1996-97	Home	19-Oct-96	1-1	Booth (3)	22,191	P.Danson
1996-97	Away	22-Apr-97	1-4	Carbone (84 pen)	20,845	G.Willard
1997-98	Away	25-Aug-97	2-7	Carbone (7, 46)	19,618	J.Winter
1997-98	Home	26-Dec-97	0-0		33,502	J.Winter
1998-99	Home	12-Sep-98	3-0	Atherton (18); Hinchcliffe (33); Di Canio (87)	20,846	A.Wilkie
1998-99	Away	20-Feb-99	4-1	Sonner (20); Rudi (40, 43); Booth (82)	24,643	A.Wilkie

BOLTON WANDERERS

Season	Venue	Date	Res	Scorers	Attendance	Referee
1995-96	Home	1-Jan-96	4-2	Kovacevic (22, 45); Hirst (54 pen, 60)	24,872	P.Durkin
1995-96	Away	23-Mar-96	1-2	Whittingham (37)	18,368	J.Winter
1997-98	Home	8-Nov-97	5-0	Booth (28, 33, 48); Di Canio (20); Whittingham (26)	25,067	M.Reed
1997-98	Away	14-Mar-98	2-3	Booth(28); Atherton (58)	24,847	G.Poll

BRADFORD CITY

Season	Venue	Date	Res	Scorers	Attendance	Referee
1999-00	Away	14-Aug-99	1-1	OG (39, Dreyer)	18,276	D.Gallagher
1999-00	Home	15-Jan-00	2-0	Alexandersson (52); OG (67, O'Brien)	24,682	J.Winter

CHARLTON ATHLETIC

Season	Venue	Date	Res	Scorers	Attendance	Referee
1998-99	Home	12-Dec-98	3-0	Booth (13); Carbone (64); Rudi (77)	26,010	D.Gallagher
1998-99	Away	16-May-99	1-0	Sonner (79)	20,043	M.Reed

CHELSEA

Season	Venue	Date	Res	Scorers	Attendance	Referee
1992-93	Home	22-Aug-92	3-3	Hirst (27, 37 pen); Wilson (81)	26,338	R.Dilkes
1992-93	Away	30-Jan-93	2-0	Warhurst (3); Harkes (89)	16,261	P.Foakes
1993-94	Away	28-Aug-93	1-1	Bright (12)	16,652	K.Morton
1993-94	Home	30-Mar-94	3-1	Bart-Williams (6); Palmer (21); Sheridan (85 pen)	20,433	D.Allison
1994-95	Home	29-Oct-94	1-1	Bright (67)	25,450	M.Reed
1994-95	Away	14-Jan-95	1-1	Nolan (90)	17,285	G.Willard
1995-96	Away	4-Nov-95	0-0		23,216	P.Danson
1995-96	Home	17-Apr-96	0-0		25,094	G.Willard
1996-97	Home	7-Sep-96	0-2		30,983	P.Jones
1996-97	Away	28-Dec-96	2-2	Pembridge (23); Stefanovic (90)	27,467	P.Durkin
1997-98	Home	20-Dec-97	1-4	Pembridge (81)	28,334	G.Barber
1997-98	Away	19-Apr-98	0-1		29,075	G.Willard
1998-99	Away	28-Nov-98	1-1	Booth (67)	34,451	N.Barry
1998-99	Home	25-Apr-99	0-0		21,652	S.Dunn
1999-00	Away	29-Dec-99	0-3		32,938	A.D'Urso
1999-00	Home	15-Apr-00	1-0	Jonk (51 pen)	21,743	P.Durkin

COVENTRY CITY

Season	Venue	Date	Res	Scorers	Attendance	Referee
1992-93	Home	2-Sep-92	1-2	Bart-Williams (62)	22,874	R.Gifford
1992-93	Away	3-Mar-93	0-1		13,206	K.Cooper
1993-94	Home	20-Nov-93	0-0		23,379	G.Poll
1993-94	Away	16-Apr-94	1-1	Jones (50)	13,052	R.Hart
1994-95	Home	28-Dec-94	5-1	Bright (14,45); Waddle (38); Whittingham (57,64)	26,056	K.Morton
1994-95	Away	15-Apr-95	0-2		17,015	G.Willard
1995-96	Away	21-Oct-95	1-0	Whittingham (16)	14,002	J.Winter
1995-96	Home	3-Dec-95	4-3	Whittingham (25); Hirst (39); Degryse (60); Bright (73)	16,229	M.Reed
1996-97	Away	26-Oct-96	0-0		17,267	K.Burge
1996-97	Home	1-Feb-97	0-0		21,793	M.Bodenham
1997-98	Home	20-Sep-97	0-0		21,087	G.Willard
1997-98	Away	7-Feb-98	0-1		18,375	G.Ashby
1998-99	Away	18-Oct-98	0-1		16,006	D.Elleray
1998-99	Home	3-Apr-99	1-2	Rudi (51)	28,136	K.Burge
1999-00	Home	23-Oct-99	0-0		23,296	M.Riley
1999-00	Away	6-May-00	1-4	De Bilde (81)	19,921	S.Bennett

CRYSTAL PALACE

Season	Venue	Date	Res	Scorers	Attendance	Referee
1992-93	Away	25-Aug-92	1-1	Williams,P. (66)	14,005	J.Martin
1992-93	Home	20-Feb-93	2-1	Warhurst (27); Wilson (71)	26,459	M.Reed
1994-95	Home	3-Dec-94	1-0	Bart-Williams (19)	21,930	K.Cooper
1994-95	Away	14-Mar-95	1-2	Whittingham (31)	10,422	P.Don
1997-98	Home	25-Oct-97	1-3	Collins (57)	22,072	D.Gallagher
1997-98	Away	10-May-98	0-1		16,876	M.Reed

DERBY COUNTY

Season	Venue	Date	Res	Scorers	Attendance	Referee
1996-97	Home	21-Sep-96	0-0		23,934	G.Barber
1996-97	Away	19-Feb-97	2-2	Collins (9); Hirst (76)	18,060	P.Alcock
1997-98	Home	24-Sep-97	2-5	Di Cannio (5); Carbone (13 pen)	22,391	M.Reed
1997-98	Away	28-Feb-98	0-3		30,203	A.Wilkie
1998-99	Away	9-Sep-98	0-1		26,209	P.Jones
1998-99	Home	30-Jan-99	0-1		24,440	D.Elleray
1999-00	Home	25-Aug-99	0-2		20,943	M.Reed
1999-00	Away	5-Feb-00	3-3	De Bilde (22); Sibon (68); Donnelly (89)	30,100	D.Elleray

EVERTON

Season	Venue	Date	Res	Scorers	Attendance	Referee
1992-93	Away	15-Aug-92	1-1	Pearson (15)	27,687	K.Morton
1992-93	Home	6-Feb-93	3-1	Warhurst (16); Harkes (17); Waddle (62)	24,979	K.Morton
1993-94	Away	27-Dec-93	2-0	Bright (34); Palmer (44)	16,471	R.Dilkes
1993-94	Home	2-Apr-94	5-1	Jones (11); Bart-Williams (43); Worthington (76); Bright (81, 87)	24,080	G.Ashby
1994-95	Away	26-Dec-94	4-1	Bright (39); Whittingham (42,79); Ingesson (47)	37,080	T.Holbrook
1994-95	Home	17-Apr-95	0-0		27,880	M.Reed
1995-96	Away	25-Nov-95	2-2	Bright (2, 35)	35,898	M.Bodenham
1995-96	Home	27-Apr-96	2-5	Hirst (9); Degryse (64)	32,724	M.Reed
1996-97	Away	28-Sep-96	0-2		34,160	P.Alcock
1996-97	Home	11-Jan-97	2-1	Pembridge (22); Hirst (50)	24,175	A.Wilkie
1997-98	Home	4-Oct-97	3-1	Carbone (78, 82 pen); Di Cannio (89)	24,486	P.Durkin
1997-98	Away	25-Apr-98	3-1	Pembridge (5, 38); Di Canio (90)	35,497	G.Barber
1998-99	Home	24-Oct-98	0-0		26,952	J.Winter
1998-99	Away	5-Apr-99	2-1	Carbone (52, 68)	35,270	M.Reed
1999-00	Home	11-Sep-99	0-2		23,539	M.Halsey
1999-00	Away	4-Mar-00	1-1	Quinn (49)	32,020	G.Barber

IPSWICH TOWN

Season	Venue	Date	Res	Scorers	Attendance	Referee
1992-93	Home	21-Nov-92	1-1	OG (16, Thompson)	24,270	K.Barratt
1992-93	Away	10-Mar-93	1-0	Hirst (35)	16,538	T.Ward
1993-94	Away	6-Nov-93	4-1	Jemson (19, 50); Bright (54); Palmer (76)	14,767	V.Callow
1993-94	Home	23-Apr-94	5-0	OG (6, Linighan); Watson (16); Pearce (56); Bart-Wiliams (69); Bright (90)	23,854	J.Worrall
1994-95	Away	16-Oct-94	2-1	Bright (8); Hirst (89)	13,073	M.Reed
1994-95	Home	14-May-95	4-1	Whittingham (7,58); Williams (55); Bright (89)	30,213	G.Poll

LEEDS UNITED

Season	Venue	Date	Res	Scorers	Attendance	Referee
1992-93	Away	12-Dec-92	1-3	Nilsson (37)	29,770	J.Borrett
1992-93	Home	4-May-93	1-1	Hirst (90)	26,855	R.Milford
1993-94	Home	30-Oct-93	3-3	Waddle (2); Jones (43); Bright (68)	31,892	P.Durkin
1993-94	Away	3-May-94	2-2	Bart-Williams (20); Watson (50)	33,575	A.Gunn
1994-95	Home	26-Sep-94	1-1	Bright (15)	23,227	A.Wilkie
1994-95	Away	4-Mar-95	1-0	Waddle (11)	33,750	K.Cooper
1995-96	Away	30-Sep-95	0-2		34,076	D.Allison

Season	Venue	Date	Res	Scorers	Attendance	Referee
1995-96	Home	16-Dec-95	6-2	Degryse (5, 25); Whittingham (18); Bright (67); Hirst (72, 86)	24,573	R.Hart
1996-97	Away	20-Aug-96	2-0	Humphreys (14); Booth (90)	31,011	J.Winter
1996-97	Home	22-Mar-97	2-2	Hirst (20); Booth (51)	30,373	P.Danson
1997-98	Home	13-Aug-97	1-3	Hyde (70)	31,520	P.Durkin
1997-98	Away	17-Jan-98	2-1	Newsome (51); Booth (83)	33,166	M.Bodenham
1998-99	Away	8-Nov-98	1-2	Booth (3)	30,012	K.Burge
1998-99	Home	13-Mar-99	0-2		28,142	G.Poll
1999-00	Away	16-Oct-99	0-2		39,437	G.Barber
1999-00	Home	30-Apr-00	0-3		23,416	R.Harris

LEICESTER CITY

Season	Venue	Date	Res	Scorers	Attendance	Referee
1994-95	Away	31-Dec-94	1-0	Hyde (40)	20,624	M.Reed
1994-95	Home	8-Apr-95	1-0	Whittingham (38)	22,551	G.Ashby
1996-97	Home	2-Sep-96	2-1	Humphreys (25); Booth (51)	17,657	G.Willard
1996-97	Away	7-May-97	0-1		20,793	G.Ashby
1997-98	Home	30-Aug-97	1-0	Carbone (55)	24,851	P.Alcock
1997-98	Away	28-Dec-97	1-1	Booth (85)	20,800	G.Poll
1998-99	Home	26-Dec-98	0-1		33,513	M.Reed
1998-99	Away	6-Feb-99	2-0	Jonk (48); Carbone (78)	20,113	G.Willard
1999-00	Away	30-Oct-99	0-3		19,046	P.Alcock
1999-00	Home	14-May-00	4-0	Quinn (14); Booth (40); Alexandersson (49); De Bilde (61)	21,656	D.Elleray

LIVERPOOL

Season	Venue	Date	Res	Scorers	Attendance	Referee
1992-93	Away	3-Oct-92	0-1		35,785	M.Bodenham
1992-93	Home	27-Feb-93	1-1	Anderson (82)	33,964	V.Callow
1993-94	Away	14-Aug-93	0-2		43,792	H.King
1993-94	Home	4-Dec-93	3-1	OG (30, Ruddock); OG (58, Wright); Bright (80)	32,177	J.Borrett
1994-95	Away	1-Oct-94	1-4	Nolan (33)	31,493	G.Willard
1994-95	Home	25-Feb-95	1-2	Bart-Williams (14)	31,932	D.Elleray
1995-96	Away	19-Aug-95	0-1		40,535	P.Durkin
1995-96	Home	13-Jan-96	1-1	Kovacevic (7)	32,747	D.Elleray
1996-97	Away	7-Dec-96	1-0	Whittingham (21)	39,507	M.Reed
1996-97	Home	11-May-97	1-1	Donaldson (25)	38,943	D.Elleray
1997-98	Away	13-Sep-97	1-2	Collins (81)	34,705	G.Poll
1997-98	Home	14-Feb-98	3-3	Carbone (7); Di Canio (63); Hinchcliffe (69)	35,405	M.Reed
1998-99	Away	19-Dec-98	0-2		40,003	A.Wilkie
1998-99	Home	8-May-99	1-0	Cresswell (87)	27,383	P.Jones
1999-00	Home	7-Aug-99	1-2	Carbone (88)	34,853	G.Poll
1999-00	Away	5-Dec-99	1-4	Alexandersson (18)	42,517	P.Durkin

MANCHESTER CITY

Season	Venue	Date	Res	Scorers	Attendance	Referee
1992-93	Home	5-Sep-92	0-3		27,169	R.Bigger
1992-93	Away	23-Feb-93	2-1	Anderson (72); Warhurst (82)	23,619	M.Bodenham
1993-94	Away	27-Nov-93	3-1	Jones (65, 75); Jemson (84)	23,416	H.King
1993-94	Home	7-May-94	1-1	Watson (25)	33,589	T.Holbrook
1994-95	Home	17-Sep-94	1-1	Watson (76)	26,776	D.Gallagher

SHEFFIELD WEDNESDAY

1994-95	Away	18-Mar-95	2-3	Whittingham (13); Hyde (21)	23,355	K.Burge
1995-96	Home	18-Nov-95	1-1	Hirst (14 pen)	24,422	G.Poll
1995-96	Away	13-Apr-96	0-1		30,898	R.Hart

MANCHESTER UNITED

Season	Venue	Date	Res	Scorers	Attendance	Referee
1992-93	Home	26-Dec-92	3-3	Hirst (2); Bright (6); Sheridan (62)	37,708	A.Buksh
1992-93	Away	10-Apr-93	1-2	Sheridan (65 pen)	40,102	M.Peck
						(J.Hilditch, 61)
1993-94	Home	2-Oct-93	2-3	Bart-Williams (47); Bright (86)	34,548	D.Allison
1993-94	Away	16-Mar-94	0-5		43,669	M.Bodenham
1994-95	Home	8-Oct-94	1-0	Hirst (44)	33,441	P.Danson
1994-95	Away	7-May-95	0-1		43,868	B.Hill
1995-96	Home	23-Sep-95	0-0		34,101	K.Burge
1995-96	Away	9-Dec-95	2-2	Bright (59); Whittingham (78)	41,849	P.Jones
1996-97	Home	18-Dec-96	1-1	Carbone (57)	37,671	P.Danson
1996-97	Away	15-Mar-97	0-2		55,267	P.Durkin
1997-98	Away	1-Nov-97	1-6	Whittingham (66)	55,529	G.Ashby
1997-98	Home	7-Mar-98	2-0	Atherton (26); Di Canio (88)	39,427	P.Jones
1998-99	Home	21-Nov-98	3-1	Alexandersson (14, 73); Jonk (55)	39,475	D.Elleray
1998-99	Away	17-Apr-99	0-3		55,270	N.Barry
1999-00	Away	11-Aug-99	0-4		54,941	M.Reed
1999-00	Home	2-Feb-00	0-1		39,640	S.Dunn

MIDDLESBROUGH

Season	Venue	Date	Res	Scorers	Attendance	Referee
1992-93	Away	24-Oct-92	1-1	Bright (29)	18,414	P.Wright
1992-93	Home	1-May-93	2-3	Bart-Williams (45); OG (78, Morris)	25,949	B.Hill
1995-96	Home	15-Oct-95	0-1		21,177	G.Ashby
1995-96	Away	5-Apr-96	1-3	Pembridge (54)	29,751	K.Cooper
1996-97	Away	18-Jan-97	2-4	Pembridge (29, 80)	29,485	P.Durkin
1996-97	Home	1-Mar-97	3-1	Booth (21); Hyde (42); Pembridge (90 pen)	28,206	G.Willard
1998-99	Away	3-Oct-98	0-4		34,163	R.Harris
1998-99	Home	27-Feb-99	3-1	Booth (11, 80); Sonner (77)	24,534	M.Riley
1999-00	Home	26-Dec-99	1-0	Atherton (28)	28,531	B.Knight
1999-00	Away	25-Mar-00	0-1		32,748	A.D'Urso

NEWCASTLE UNITED

Season	Venue	Date	Res	Scorers	Attendance	Referee
1993-94	Away	13-Sep-93	2-4	Sinton (26, 47)	33,519	R.Dilkes
1993-94	Home	5-Mar-94	0-1		33,153	P.Durkin
1994-95	Away	22-Oct-94	1-2	Taylor (55)	34,408	G.Poll
1994-95	Home	21-Jan-95	0-0		31,215	R.Gifford
1995-96	Home	27-Aug-95	0-2		24,815	P.Alcock
1995-96	Away	3-Feb-96	0-2		36,567	P.Danson
1996-97	Away	24-Aug-96	2-1	Atherton (14); Whittingham (79)	36,452	P.Jones
1996-97	Home	13-Apr-97	1-1	Pembridge (57)	33,798	G.Barber
1997-98	Away	9-Aug-97	1-2	Carbone (7)	36,771	P.Jones
1997-98	Home	10-Jan-98	2-1	Di Canio (1); Newsome (51)	29,446	D.Elleray
1998-99	Away	14-Nov-98	1-1	Rudi (80)	36,698	P.Jones
1998-99	Home	21-Apr-99	1-1	Scott (52)	21,545	P.Alcock

| 1999-00 | Away | 19-Sep-99 | 0-8 | | 36,619 | N.Barry |
| 1999-00 | Home | 26-Feb-00 | 0-2 | | 29,212 | M.Riley |

NORWICH CITY

Season	Venue	Date	Res	Scorers	Attendance	Referee
1992-93	Away	19-Sep-92	0-1		14,367	R.Nixon
1992-93	Home	10-Jan-93	1-0	Worthington (42)	23,360	D.Allison
1993-94	Home	1-Sep-93	3-3	Bart-Williams (51); Bright (59); Sinton (62)	25,175	A.Wilkie
1993-94	Away	25-Feb-94	1-1	Watson (75)	18,311	V.Callow
1994-95	Home	31-Aug-94	0-0		25,072	K.Cooper
1994-95	Away	8-Mar-95	0-0		13,530	P.Danson

NOTTINGHAM FOREST

Season	Venue	Date	Res	Scorers	Attendance	Referee
1992-93	Home	19-Aug-92	2-0	Hirst (16, 78)	29,623	P.Don
1992-93	Away	12-Sep-92	2-1	Warhurst (39); Hyde (57)	19,420	G.Ashby
1994-95	Away	10-Sep-94	1-4	Hyde (56)	22,022	P.Don
1994-95	Home	1-Apr-95	1-7	Bright (52 pen)	30,060	A.Wilkie
1995-96	Away	26-Dec-95	0-1		27,810	G.Ashby
1995-96	Home	3-Mar-96	1-3	Kovacevic (50)	21,930	G.Poll
1996-97	Home	18-Nov-96	2-0	Trustfull (63); Carbone (85)	16,390	S.Dunn
1996-97	Away	5-Mar-97	3-0	Carbone (52, 86); Blinker (57)	21,485	P.Jones
1998-99	Home	7-Dec-98	3-2	Alexandersson (22); Carbone (53,58)	19,321	R.Harris
1998-99	Away	1-May-99	0-2		20,480	J.Winter

OLDHAM ATHLETIC

Season	Venue	Date	Res	Scorers	Attendance	Referee
1992-93	Home	17-Oct-92	2-1	Palmer (9); Bright (17)	24,485	R.Groves
1992-93	Away	7-Apr-93	1-1	Watson (65)	12,312	A.Wilkie
1993-94	Home	24-Nov-93	3-0	Watson (7, 32); Jemson (64)	18,509	K.Barratt
1993-94	Away	30-Apr-94	0-0		12,973	P.Foakes

QPR

Season	Venue	Date	Res	Scorers	Attendance	Referee
1992-93	Home	19-Dec-92	1-0	Bright (39)	23,164	J.Worrall
1992-93	Away	11-May-93	1-3	Bright (78)	12,177	D.Allison
1993-94	Away	1-Jan-94	2-1	Bright (78); Watson (79)	16,858	P.Foakes
1993-94	Home	9-Apr-94	3-1	Bright (7, 31); Sheridan (21pen)	22,437	K.Morton
1994-95	Away	24-Aug-94	2-3	Sheridan (38); Hyde (74)	12,788	P.Jones
1994-95	Home	17-Dec-94	0-2		22,766	P.Durkin
1995-96	Away	9-Sep-95	3-0	Bright (56, 60); Donaldson (78)	12,459	M.Reed
1995-96	Home	17-Feb-96	1-3	Hyde (22)	22,442	P.Durkin

SHEFFIELD UNITED

Season	Venue	Date	Res	Scorers	Attendance	Referee
1992-93	Away	8-Nov-92	1-1	Hirst (84)	30,039	M.Reed
1992-93	Home	21-Apr-93	1-1	Warhurst (71)	38,688	K.Redfern
1993-94	Away	23-Oct-93	1-1	Palmer (12)	30,044	K.Cooper
1993-94	Home	22-Jan-94	3-1	Bright (58); Pearce (61); Watson (70)	34,959	K.Cooper

SOUTHAMPTON

Season	Venue	Date	Res	Scorers	Attendance	Referee
1992-93	Away	28-Dec-92	2-1	Sheridan (12 pen); Hirst (63)	17,426	R.Milford
1992-93	Home	12-Apr-93	5-2	Bright (37); Bart-Williams (43, 71, 81); King (50)	26,183	K.Morton
1993-94	Home	18-Sep-93	2-0	Sheridan (58 pen); Hirst (80)	22,503	R.Gifford
1993-94	Away	12-Mar-94	1-1	Bart-Williams (67)	16,391	D.Crick
1994-95	Home	2-Jan-95	1-1	Hyde (19)	28,424	R.Dilkes
1994-95	Away	29-Apr-95	0-0		15,189	J.Worrall
1995-96	Home	23-Dec-95	2-2	Hirst (14 pen, 50 pen)	25,115	J.Winter
1995-96	Away	20-Mar-96	1-0	Degryse (1)	13,216	M.Bodenham
1996-97	Home	2-Nov-96	1-1	Newsome (14)	20,106	A.Wilkie
1996-97	Away	22-Feb-97	3-2	Hirst (49, 55); Booth (78)	15,062	M.Reed
1997-98	Away	29-Nov-97	3-2	Atherton (27); Collins (68); Di Canio (84)	15,442	S.Dunn
1997-98	Home	4-Apr-98	1-0	Carbone (79)	29,677	P.Jones
1998-99	Home	31-Oct-98	0-0		30,078	M.Riley
1998-99	Away	21-Mar-99	0-1		15,201	R.Harris
1999-00	Away	28-Aug-99	0-2		14,815	P.Alcock
1999-00	Home	12-Feb-00	0-1		23,470	A.Wiley

SUNDERLAND

Season	Venue	Date	Res	Scorers	Attendance	Referee
1996-97	Away	23-Nov-96	1-1	Oakes (64)	20,644	G.Barber
1996-97	Home	12-Mar-97	2-1	Hirst (42); Stefanovic (63)	20,294	D.Gallagher
1999-00	Away	25-Sep-99	0-1		41,132	A.Wiley
1999-00	Home	22-Apr-00	0-2		28,072	M.Reed

SWINDON TOWN

Season	Venue	Date	Res	Scorers	Attendance	Referee
1993-94	Home	29-Dec-93	3-3	Bright (8); Watson (67, 70)	30,570	P.Don
1993-94	Away	4-Apr-94	1-0	Watson (69)	13,927	A.Gunn

TOTTENHAM HOTSPUR

Season	Venue	Date	Res	Scorers	Attendance	Referee
1992-93	Home	27-Sep-92	2-0	Bright (6); Anderson (32)	24,895	M.Peck
1992-93	Away	16-Jan-93	2-0	Bright (54); Hirst (88)	25,702	K.Morton
1993-94	Home	3-Jan-94	1-0	Bright (5)	32,514	K.Burge
1993-94	Away	5-Feb-94	3-1	Coleman (17); Bright (54, 62)	23,078	D.Frampton
1994-95	Home	20-Aug-94	3-4	Petrescu (54); OG (66, Calderwood); Hirst (83)	34,051	B.Hill
1994-95	Away	10-Dec-94	1-3	Nolan (37)	25,912	M.Bodenham
1995-96	Home	16-Sep-95	1-3	Hirst (8)	26,565	D.Gallagher
1995-96	Away	24-Feb-96	0-1		32,047	M.Reed
1996-97	Away	21-Dec-96	1-1	Nolan (16)	30,996	M.Riley
1996-97	Home	9-Mar-97	2-1	Atherton (18); Booth (70)	22,667	A.Wilkie
1997-98	Away	19-Oct-97	2-3	Collins (71); Di Cannio (84)	25,097	J.Winter
1997-98	Home	21-Feb-98	1-0	Di Canio (33)	29,871	M.Bodenham
1998-99	Away	22-Aug-98	3-0	Atherton (26); Di Canio (35); Hinchcliffe (78)	32,129	M.Reed
1998-99	Home	9-Jan-99	0-0		28,204	G.Willard
1999-00	Home	21-Aug-99	1-2	Carbone (23 pen)	24,027	A.D'Urso
1999-00	Away	22-Jan-00	1-0	Alexandersson (38)	35,897	M.Riley

WATFORD

Season	Venue	Date	Res	Scorers	Attendance	Referee
1999-00	Home	6-Nov-99	2-2	di Bilde (56 pen, 78)	21,658	J.Winter
1999-00	Away	18-Mar-00	0-1		15,840	N.Barry

WEST HAM UNITED

Season	Venue	Date	Res	Scorers	Attendance	Referee
1993-94	Away	25-Aug-93	0-2		19,441	J.Worrall
1993-94	Home	18-Dec-93	5-0	OG (35, Marsh); Bright (47); Waddle (51); Jemson (72); Palmer (87)	26,350	D.Frampton
1994-95	Home	19-Nov-94	1-0	Petrescu (28)	25,350	G.Ashby
1994-95	Away	23-Jan-95	2-0	Waddle (32); Bright (82)	14,554	P.Danson
1995-96	Home	28-Oct-95	0-1		23,917	K.Cooper
1995-96	Away	5-May-96	1-1	Newsome (89)	23,790	R.Dilkes
1996-97	Home	30-Nov-96	0-0		22,231	P.Durkin
1996-97	Away	3-May-97	1-5	Carbone (82)	24,490	M.Riley
1997-98	Away	13-Dec-97	0-1		24,344	M.Riley
1997-98	Home	13-Apr-98	1-1	Magilton (59)	28,036	N.Barry
1998-99	Home	15-Aug-98	0-1		30,236	P.Durkin
1998-99	Away	16-Jan-99	4-0	Hinchcliffe (26); Rudi (31); Humphreys (68); Carbone (73 pen)	25,642	K.Burge
1999-00	Home	11-Mar-00	3-1	Cresswell (55); Hinchcliffe (63); Alexandersson (66)	21,147	P.Jones

WIMBLEDON

Season	Venue	Date	Res	Scorers	Attendance	Referee
1992-93	Away	28-Nov-92	1-1	Bart-Williams (14)	5,740	R.Milford
1992-93	Home	24-Mar-93	1-1	Bright (76)	20,918	J.Lloyd
1993-94	Home	16-Oct-93	2-2	Waddle (9); Jones (84)	21,752	R.Gifford
1993-94	Away	15-Jan-94	1-2	Pearce (67)	5,536	M.Bodenham
1994-95	Away	27-Aug-94	1-0	Watson (79)	7,453	R.Hart
1994-95	Home	11-Mar-95	0-1		20,395	J.Worrall
1995-96	Away	30-Aug-95	2-2	Degryse (10); Hirst (46)	6,352	A.Wilkie
1995-96	Home	10-Feb-96	2-1	Degryse (55); Watts (85)	19,085	M.Bodenham
1996-97	Away	12-Oct-96	2-4	Booth (4); Hyde (72)	10,512	M.Riley
1996-97	Home	19-Apr-97	3-1	Donaldson (42); Trustfull (78, 83)	26,957	J.Winter
1997-98	Away	23-Aug-97	1-1	Di Cannio (74)	11,503	A.Wilkie
1997-98	Home	31-Jan-98	1-1	Pembridge (14)	22,655	A.Wilkie
1998-99	Away	19-Sep-98	1-2	Di Canio (84)	13,163	N.Barry
1998-99	Home	3-Mar-99	1-2	Thome (60)	24,116	P.Jones
1999-00	Home	2-Oct-99	5-1	Jonk (9); de Bilde (23, 82); Rudi (70); Sibon (90)	18,077	P.Durkin
1999-00	Away	12-Apr-00	2-0	De Bilde (39); Sibon (88)	8,248	A.Wiley

INTRODUCTION

Formed 1885 by members of the St Mary's Young Men's Association, St Mary's FC. The church link was dropped, though the name retained, in 1893. In 1895 applied for a Southern League place, but were refused, only to be invited to fill a subsequent vacancy. 'St Mary's' was dropped after two seasons. Moved from the County Cricket Ground to the Dell in 1898.

Six times Southern League champions, Southampton were founder members of Football League Division Three in 1920 (this becoming Division Three (South) the following season), of Division Three at the end of regionalisation in 1958, and of the Premier League, 1992.

Ground:	The Dell, Milton Road, Southampton, SO9 4XX
Nickname:	The Saints
Internet:	www.saintsfc.co.uk

HONOURS

Football League Div 1:	Runners-up 1983-84
Football League Div 2:	Runners-up 1965-66, 1977-78
Football League Div 3S:	Champions 1921-22
	Runners-up 1920-21
Football League Div 3:	Champions 1959-60
FA Cup:	Winners 1975-76
	Runners-up 1900, 1902
Football League Cup:	Runners-up 1978-79
Zenith Data Systems Cup:	Runners-up 1991-92

EUROPEAN RECORD

Champions' League (0):	–
Cup-Winners' Cup (1):	76-77 (QF)
UEFA Cup (5):	69-70 (3), 71-72 (1), 81-82 (2), 82-83 (1), 84-85 (1)

FAPL RECORD SUMMARY

Most Total:	LE TISSIER, Matthew	258
Most Starts:	LE TISSIER, Matthew	232
Most Subs:	HUGHES, David	32
Most SNU:	MOSS, Neil	86
Most PS:	LE TISSIER, Matthew	49
Most Goals:	LE TISSIER, Matthew	101
Most Yel:	LE TISSIER, Matthew	50
Most Red:	BENALI, Francis	5

PLAYING RECORD – SEASON TOTALS

Season	Pn	P	W	D	L	F	A	Pts
1992-93	18	42	13	11	18	54	61	50
1993-94	18	42	12	7	23	49	66	43
1994-95	10	42	12	18	12	61	63	54
1995-96	17	38	9	11	18	34	52	38
1996-97	16	38	10	11	17	50	56	41
1997-98	12	38	14	6	18	50	55	48
1998-99	17	38	11	8	19	37	64	41
1999-00	15	38	12	8	18	45	62	44
Totals		316	93	80	143	380	479	359

PLAYING RECORD – HOME TOTALS

Season	Pn	P	W	D	L	F	A	Pts
1992-93	18	21	10	6	5	30	21	36
1993-94	18	21	9	2	10	30	31	29
1994-95	10	21	8	9	4	33	27	33
1995-96	17	19	7	7	5	21	18	28
1996-97	16	19	6	7	6	32	24	25
1997-98	12	19	10	1	8	28	23	31
1998-99	17	19	9	4	6	29	26	31
1999-00	15	19	8	4	7	26	22	28
Totals		158	67	40	51	229	192	241

PLAYING RECORD – AWAY TOTALS

Season	Pn	P	W	D	L	F	A	Pts
1992-93	18	21	3	5	13	24	40	14
1993-94	18	21	3	5	13	19	35	14
1994-95	10	21	4	9	8	28	36	21
1995-96	17	19	2	4	13	13	34	10
1996-97	16	19	4	4	11	18	32	16
1997-98	12	19	4	5	10	22	32	17
1998-99	17	19	2	4	13	8	38	10
1999-00	15	19	4	4	11	19	40	16
Totals		158	26	40	92	151	287	118

HIGHEST HOME ATTENDANCES

	Attendance	Opponents	Date	Season
1	19,654	Tottenham H.	15-Aug-92	1992-93
2	19,105	Blackburn R.	16-Apr-94	1993-94
3	19,087	Aston Villa	30-Jan-93	1992-93
4	18,803	Aston Villa	30-Apr-94	1993-94
5	18,306	Liverpool	14-Feb-94	1993-94

LOWEST HOME ATTENDANCES

	Attendance	Opponents	Date	Season
1	9,028	Ipswich T.	8-Dec-93	1993-94
2	10,827	Oldham A.	31-Oct-92	1992-93
3	11,221	Wimbledon	17-Oct-92	1992-93
4	11,619	Sheffield U.	2-Oct-93	1993-94
5	11,946	QPR	11-Dec-93	1993-94

TOP SCORER – SEASON BY SEASON

Season	Player	Goals
1992-93	Le Tissier	15
1993-94	Le Tissier	25
1994-95	Le Tissier	20
1995-96	Shipperley	8
1996-97	Le Tissier	13
1997-98	Le Tissier, Ostenstad	11
1998-99	Le Tissier, Ostenstad	7
1999-00	Pahars	13

PLAYERS WITH MOST PREMIERSHIP APPEARANCES

Tot	Player	St	Sb	Gls
258	LE TISSIER, Matthew	232	26	101
235	BENALI, Francis	216	19	1
220	DODD, Jason	208	12	8

198	MONKOU, Ken	190	8	10
151	MADDISON, Neil	141	10	17
130	MAGILTON, Jim	124	6	13
125	OAKLEY, Matthew	107	18	9
120	LUNDEKVAM, Claus	114	6	0
113	CHARLTON, Simon	104	9	2
100	JONES, Paul	100	0	0
99	HALL, Richard	98	1	9
98	KENNA, Jeff	95	3	4
96	OSTENSTAD, Egil	80	16	29
92	DOWIE, Iain	90	2	21
88	BEASANT, Dave	86	2	0
72	WIDDRINGTON, Tommy	65	7	3

CLUB-BY-CLUB RESULTS

ARSENAL

Season	Venue	Date	Res	Scorers	Attendance	Referee
1992-93	Home	5-Dec-92	2-0	Maddison (16); Dowie (53)	17,286	J.Key
1992-93	Away	20-Mar-93	3-4	Dowie (4); Adams (30); Le Tissier (50)	24,149	K.Barratt
1993-94	Away	25-Sep-93	0-1		26,902	K.Morton
1993-94	Home	19-Mar-94	0-4		16,790	D.Frampton
1994-95	Home	19-Nov-94	1-0	Magilton (60)	15,201	R.Dilkes
1994-95	Away	24-Jan-95	1-1	Magilton (74)	27,213	D.Gallagher
1995-96	Away	23-Sep-95	2-4	Watson (24); Monkou (45)	38,136	R.Hart
1995-96	Home	9-Dec-95	0-0		15,238	P.Danson
1996-97	Away	4-Dec-96	1-3	Berkovic (81)	38,033	P.Jones
1996-97	Home	15-Mar-97	0-2		15,144	J.Winter
1997-98	Home	23-Aug-97	1-3	Maddison (25)	15,246	D.Elleray
1997-98	Away	31-Jan-98	0-3		38,056	P.Jones
1998-99	Away	17-Oct-98	1-1	Howells (67)	38,027	J.Winter
1998-99	Home	3-Apr-99	0-0		15,255	P.Jones
1999-00	Home	18-Sep-99	0-1		15,242	G.Barber
1999-00	Away	26-Feb-00	1-3	Richards (51)	38,044	J.Winter

ASTON VILLA

Season	Venue	Date	Res	Scorers	Attendance	Referee
1992-93	Away	22-Aug-92	1-1	Adams (79)	17,894	K.Morton
1992-93	Home	30-Jan-93	2-0	Banger (39); Dowie (63)	19,087	P.Wright
1993-94	Away	24-Nov-93	2-0	Le Tissier (50, 62)	16,180	K.Morton
1993-94	Home	30-Apr-94	4-1	Le Tissier (19, 77); Monkou (39); Maddison (89)	18,803	S.Lodge
1994-95	Away	24-Aug-94	1-1	Le Tissier (89)	24,179	P.Don
1994-95	Home	19-Dec-94	2-1	Hall (8); Le Tissier (90)	13,874	S.Lodge
1995-96	Home	20-Nov-95	0-1		13,582	D.Elleray
1995-96	Away	8-Apr-96	0-3		34,059	P.Danson
1996-97	Home	7-Dec-96	0-1		15,232	S.Lodge
1996-97	Away	11-May-97	0-1		39,339	G.Willard
1997-98	Away	20-Dec-97	1-1	Ostenstad (22)	29,343	D.Elleray

1997-98	Home	18-Apr-98	1-2	Le Tissier (19)	15,238	A.Wilkie
1998-99	Home	14-Nov-98	1-4	Le Tissier (53)	15,242	N.Barry
1998-99	Away	10-Apr-99	0-3		32,203	N.Barry
1999-00	Away	6-Nov-99	1-0	Richards (84)	26,474	A.D'Urso
1999-00	Home	18-Mar-00	2-0	Davies (39, 63)	15,218	M.Riley

BARNSLEY

Season	Venue	Date	Res	Scorers	Attendance	Referee
1997-98	Home	8-Nov-97	4-1	Le Tissier (2); Palmer (5); Davies (35); Hirst (53)	15,018	G.Ashby
1997-98	Away	14-Mar-98	3-4	Ostenstad (25); Le Tissier (41, 71)	18,368	G.Ashby

BLACKBURN ROVERS

Season	Venue	Date	Res	Scorers	Attendance	Referee
1992-93	Home	22-Nov-92	1-1	Le Tissier (22)	16,626	M.Bodenham
1992-93	Away	9-Mar-93	0-0		13,566	S.Lodge
1993-94	Away	20-Nov-93	0-2		17,343	K.Cooper
1993-94	Home	16-Apr-94	3-1	Dowie (28); Allen (39); Le Tissier (69 pen)	19,105	J.Worrall
1994-95	Home	20-Aug-94	1-1	Banger (15)	14,209	K.Cooper
1994-95	Away	10-Dec-94	2-3	Le Tissier (65,78)	23,372	A.Wilkie
1995-96	Away	14-Oct-95	1-2	Maddison (90)	26,780	M.Reed
1995-96	Home	6-Apr-96	1-0	Le Tissier (80)	14,793	D.Elleray
1996-97	Away	30-Nov-96	1-2	Ostenstad (62)	23,018	R.Dilkes
1996-97	Home	3-May-97	2-0	Slater (22); Le Tissier (73)	15,247	G.Ashby
1997-98	Away	18-Oct-97	0-1		24,130	G.Willard
1997-98	Home	21-Feb-98	3-0	Ostenstad (19, 88); Hirst (75)	15,162	U.Rennie
1998-99	Away	21-Nov-98	2-0	Oakley (4); Basham (89)	22,812	S.Dunn
1998-99	Home	17-Apr-99	3-3	Marsden (22); Hughes,M. (61); Pahars (85)	15,209	G.Barber

BOLTON WANDERERS

Season	Venue	Date	Res	Scorers	Attendance	Referee
1995-96	Home	25-Nov-95	1-0	Hughes (74)	14,404	P.Jones
1995-96	Away	27-Apr-96	1-0	Le Tissier (26)	18,795	G.Ashby
1997-98	Home	9-Aug-97	0-1		15,206	M.Bodenham
1997-98	Away	10-Jan-98	0-0		23,333	G.Willard

BRADFORD CITY

Season	Venue	Date	Res	Scorers	Attendance	Referee
1999-00	Home	3-Jan-00	1-0	Davies (55)	15,027	D.Elleray
1999-00	Away	8-Apr-00	2-1	OG (56, Windass); Pahars (76)	17,439	D.Elleray

CHARLTON ATHLETIC

Season	Venue	Date	Res	Scorers	Attendance	Referee
1998-99	Away	22-Aug-98	0-5		16,488	R.Harris
1998-99	Home	9-Jan-99	3-1	Kachloul (8); Colleter (52); Beattie (89)	15,222	G.Poll

CHELSEA

Season	Venue	Date	Res	Scorers	Attendance	Referee
1992-93	Away	26-Dec-92	1-1	Dowie (2)	18,344	A.Gunn
1992-93	Home	10-Apr-93	1-0	Banger (49)	15,135	K.Burge
1993-94	Home	27-Dec-93	3-1	Widdrington (28); Dowie (65); Bennett (89)	14,221	P.Durkin

SOUTHAMPTON

Season	Venue	Date	Res	Scorers	Attendance	Referee
1993-94	Away	2-Apr-94	0-2		19,801	M.Reed
1994-95	Home	3-Dec-94	0-1		14,404	R.Gifford
1994-95	Away	12-Apr-95	2-0	Shipperley (10); Le Tissier (32)	16,738	A.Wilkie
1995-96	Away	16-Sep-95	0-3		26,237	P.Alcock
1995-96	Home	24-Feb-96	2-3	Widdrington (60); Shipperley (38)	15,226	G.Ashby
1996-97	Home	18-Aug-96	0-0		15,186	M.Bodenham
1996-97	Away	19-Mar-97	0-1		28,079	S.Lodge
1997-98	Away	30-Aug-97	2-4	Davies (25); Monkou (59)	30,008	A.Wilkie
1997-98	Home	29-Dec-97	1-0	Davies (16)	15,231	M.Bodenham
1998-99	Home	26-Dec-98	0-2		15,253	D.Elleray
1998-99	Away	6-Feb-99	0-1		34,920	R.Harris
1999-00	Home	26-Dec-99	1-2	Davies (80)	15,232	P.Alcock
1999-00	Away	25-Mar-00	1-1	Tessem (69)	34,956	D.Gallagher

COVENTRY CITY

Season	Venue	Date	Res	Scorers	Attendance	Referee
1992-93	Home	12-Dec-92	2-2	Maddison (9); Dowie (61)	12,306	R.Nixon
1992-93	Away	3-Apr-93	0-2		10,463	K.Cooper
1993-94	Away	16-Oct-93	1-1	Charlton (56)	9,837	J.Worrall
1993-94	Home	15-Jan-94	1-0	Le Tissier (44 pen)	12,397	P.Don
1994-95	Away	24-Sep-94	3-1	Dowie (34,55); Ekelund (81)	11,784	K.Morton
1994-95	Home	4-Mar-95	0-0		14,505	K.Morton
1995-96	Away	1-Jan-96	1-1		16,822	K.Cooper
1995-96	Home	25-Mar-96	1-0	Dodd (2)	14,461	S.Lodge
1996-97	Away	13-Oct-96	1-1	Le Tissier (17)	15,485	P.Durkin
1996-97	Home	19-Apr-97	2-2	Evans (27); Ostenstad (47)	15,251	P.Jones
1997-98	Away	13-Sep-97	0-1		18,659	U.Rennie
1997-98	Home	18-Feb-98	1-2	Le Tissier (79 pen)	15,091	P.Alcock
1998-99	Home	24-Oct-98	2-1	Le Tissier (23); Ostenstad (44)	15,152	R.Harris
1998-99	Away	5-Apr-99	0-1		21,402	U.Rennie
1999-00	Away	7-Aug-99	1-0	Ostenstad (85)	19,915	P.Jones
1999-00	Home	4-Dec-99	0-0		15,168	J.Winter

CRYSTAL PALACE

Season	Venue	Date	Res	Scorers	Attendance	Referee
1992-93	Away	26-Sep-92	2-1	Dowie (44, 88)	13,829	J.Borrett
1992-93	Home	16-Jan-93	1-0	Maddison (50)	13,397	P.Don
1994-95	Away	26-Nov-94	0-0		14,186	P.Danson
1994-95	Home	3-May-95	3-1	Le Tissier (1,85); Watson (9)	15,151	G.Poll
1997-98	Home	27-Aug-97	1-0	Davies (57)	15,032	J.Winter
1997-98	Away	26-Dec-97	1-1	Oakley (39)	22,853	P.Alcock

DERBY COUNTY

Season	Venue	Date	Res	Scorers	Attendance	Referee
1996-97	Home	21-Dec-96	3-1	Watson (9); Oakley (12); Magilton (89 pen)	14,901	P.Danson
1996-97	Away	9-Apr-97	1-1	OG (90, Powell D.)	17,839	G.Willard
1997-98	Away	27-Sep-97	0-4		25,625	K.Burge
1997-98	Home	2-May-98	0-2		15,202	M.Riley
1998-99	Home	28-Nov-98	0-1		14,762	S.Lodge
1998-99	Away	24-Apr-99	0-0		26,557	A.Wilkie

| 1999-00 | Home | 4-Oct-99 | 3-3 | Pahars (22); Oakley (35); Ripley (66) | 14,208 | G.Poll |
| 1999-00 | Away | 24-Apr-00 | 0-2 | | 29,403 | P.Jones |

EVERTON

Season	Venue	Date	Res	Scorers	Attendance	Referee
1992-93	Away	19-Dec-92	1-2	Le Tissier (5)	14,051	M.Peck
1992-93	Home	17-Apr-93	0-0		16,911	M.Bodenham
1993-94	Home	14-Aug-93	0-2		14,051	K.Cooper
1993-94	Away	4-Dec-93	0-1		13,265	K.Burge
1994-95	Home	8-Oct-94	2-0	Ekelund (19); Le Tissier (72)	15,163	B.Hill
1994-95	Away	6-May-95	0-0		36,840	T.Holbrook
1995-96	Away	26-Aug-95	0-2		33,668	J.Winter
1995-96	Home	3-Feb-96	2-2	Watson (46); Magilton (77)	15,136	D.Elleray
1996-97	Away	16-Nov-96	1-7	Ostenstad (39)	35,669	M.Riley
1996-97	Home	5-Mar-97	2-2	Slater (59); OG (62, Short)	15,134	P.Durkin
1997-98	Away	2-Nov-97	2-0	Le Tissier (24); Davies (54)	29,958	A.Wilkie
1997-98	Home	7-Mar-98	2-1	Le Tessier (69); Ostenstad (86)	15,102	D.Elleray
1998-99	Away	12-Dec-98	0-1		32,073	A.Wilkie
1998-99	Home	16-May-99	2-0	Pahars (24, 68)	15,254	G.Barber
1999-00	Away	21-Aug-99	1-4	Pahars (70)	31,755	B.Knight
1999-00	Home	22-Jan-00	2-0	Tessem (47); Oakley (56)	15,232	A.D'Urso

IPSWICH TOWN

Season	Venue	Date	Res	Scorers	Attendance	Referee
1992-93	Away	7-Nov-92	0-0		15,722	R.Dilkes
1992-93	Home	13-Mar-93	4-3	Hall (17); Le Tissier (65 pen, 90); Kenna (84)	15,428	D.Elleray
1993-94	Away	17-Aug-93	0-1		14,958	A.Wilkie
1993-94	Home	8-Dec-93	0-1		9,028	G.Ashby
1994-95	Home	1-Oct-94	3-1	Maddison (53); Ekelund (65); Dowie (90)	13,246	G.Ashby
1994-95	Away	25-Feb-95	1-2	Maddison (38)	16,067	P.Jones

LEEDS UNITED

Season	Venue	Date	Res	Scorers	Attendance	Referee
1992-93	Home	19-Sep-92	1-1	Groves (43)	16,229	A.Buksh
1992-93	Away	9-Jan-93	1-2	Dixon (19)	26,071	R.Groves
1993-94	Home	11-Sep-93	0-2		13,511	K.Burge
1993-94	Away	5-Mar-94	0-0		30,829	R.Hart
1994-95	Home	29-Oct-94	1-3	Maddison (44)	15,202	R.Gifford
1994-95	Away	14-Jan-95	0-0		28,953	S.Dunn
1995-96	Home	30-Aug-95	1-1	Widdrington (81)	15,212	K.Cooper
1995-96	Away	3-Apr-96	0-1		26,077	M.Bodenham
1996-97	Home	23-Nov-96	0-2		15,241	K.Burge
1996-97	Away	12-Mar-97	0-0		25,913	G.Ashby
1997-98	Home	24-Sep-97	0-2		15,102	S.Lodge
1997-98	Away	28-Feb-98	1-0	Hirst (54)	28,791	K.Burge
1998-99	Away	8-Sep-98	0-3		30,637	A.Wilkie
1998-99	Home	30-Jan-99	3-0	Kachloul (31); Oakley (62); Ostenstad (86)	15,236	S.Dunn
1999-00	Home	11-Aug-99	0-3		15,206	A.Wiley
1999-00	Away	28-Nov-99	0-1		39,288	R.Harris

SOUTHAMPTON

LEICESTER CITY

Season	Venue	Date	Res	Scorers	Attendance	Referee
1994-95	Away	15-Oct-94	3-4	Dowie (78,90); Le Tissier (90)	20,020	R.Hart
1994-95	Home	14-May-95	2-2	Monkou (21); Le Tissier (55)	15,101	K.Burge
1996-97	Away	21-Aug-96	1-2	Le Tissier (68)	17,562	M.Riley
1996-97	Home	22-Mar-97	2-2	Ostenstad (31); van Gobbel (50)	15,044	K.Burge
1997-98	Home	13-Dec-97	2-1	Le Tissier (11); Benali (53)	15,121	S.Lodge
1997-98	Away	14-Apr-98	3-3	Ostenstad (17, 27); Hirst (49)	20,708	G.Poll
1998-99	Away	5-Dec-98	0-2		18,423	D.Gallagher
1998-99	Home	1-May-99	2-1	Marsden (36); Beattie (74)	15,228	P.Alcock
1999-00	Away	16-Oct-99	1-2	Pahars (84)	19,556	B.Knight
1999-00	Home	29-Apr-00	1-2	Kachloul (4)	15,178	M.Reed

LIVERPOOL

Season	Venue	Date	Res	Scorers	Attendance	Referee
1992-93	Away	1-Sep-92	1-1	Dixon (51)	30,024	R.Hart
1992-93	Home	13-Feb-93	2-1	Maddison (23); Banger (73)	17,216	A.Buksh
1993-94	Away	30-Oct-93	2-4	Le Tissier (40, 79)	32,818	D.Gallagher
1993-94	Home	14-Feb-94	4-2	Maskell (6); Le Tissier (1, 42 pen, 50 pen)	18,306	P.Foakes
1994-95	Home	31-Aug-94	0-2		15,190	M.Bodenham
1994-95	Away	5-Apr-95	1-3	Hall (13)	29,881	S.Lodge
1995-96	Home	22-Oct-95	1-3	Watson (3)	15,245	D.Gallagher
1995-96	Away	2-Dec-95	1-1	Shipperley (60)	38,007	R.Hart
1996-97	Away	7-Sep-96	1-2	Magilton (57)	39,189	A.Wilkie
1996-97	Home	29-Dec-96	0-1		15,222	S.Dunn
1997-98	Home	20-Sep-97	1-1	Davies (48)	15,252	P.Jones
1997-98	Away	7-Feb-98	3-2	Hirst (8 pen, 90); Ostenstad (85)	43,550	J.Winter
1998-99	Home	16-Aug-98	1-2	Ostenstad (37)	15,202	P.Alcock
1998-99	Away	16-Jan-99	1-7	Ostenstad (59)	44,011	U.Rennie
1999-00	Home	23-Oct-99	1-1	Soltvedt (39)	15,241	N.Barry
1999-00	Away	7-May-00	0-0		44,015	P.Alcock

MANCHESTER CITY

Season	Venue	Date	Res	Scorers	Attendance	Referee
1992-93	Away	24-Oct-92	0-1		20,089	P.Don
1992-93	Home	1-May-93	0-1		16,730	J.Lloyd
1993-94	Away	28-Dec-93	1-1	Dowie (26)	24,712	A.Wilkie
1993-94	Home	4-Apr-94	0-1		16,377	B.Hill
1994-95	Away	5-Nov-94	3-3	Hall (26); Ekelund (62,66)	21,589	M.Reed
1994-95	Home	4-Feb-95	2-2	OG (24, Coton); Le Tissier (60)	14,902	P.Durkin
1995-96	Home	31-Jan-96	1-1	Shipperley (66)	15,172	S.Dunn
1995-96	Away	16-Mar-96	1-2	Tisdale (64)	29,550	J.Winter

MANCHESTER UNITED

Season	Venue	Date	Res	Scorers	Attendance	Referee
1992-93	Home	24-Aug-92	0-1		15,623	R.Lewis
1992-93	Away	20-Feb-93	1-2	Banger (77)	36,257	R.Lewis
1993-94	Home	28-Aug-93	1-3	Maddison (12)	16,189	A.Gunn
1993-94	Away	4-May-94	0-2		44,705	T.Holbrook
1994-95	Home	31-Dec-94	2-2	Magilton (45); Hughes (73)	15,204	M.Bodenham
1994-95	Away	10-May-95	1-2	Charlton (5)	43,479	P.Danson

SOUTHAMPTON

1995-96	Away	18-Nov-95	1-4	Shipperley (85)	39,301	P.Danson
1995-96	Home	13-Apr-96	3-1	Monkou (11); Shipperley (23); Le Tissier (43)	15,262	G.Poll
1996-97	Home	26-Oct-96	6-3	Berkovic (6, 83); Le Tissier (34); Ostenstad (44, 85); OG (89, Neville,G.)	15,253	J.Winter
1996-97	Away	1-Feb-97	1-2	Ostenstad (10)	55,269	M.Riley
1997-98	Away	13-Aug-97	0-1		55,008	G.Barber
1997-98	Home	19-Jan-98	1-0	Davies (3)	15,241	M.Riley
1998-99	Home	3-Oct-98	0-3		15,251	D.Elleray
1998-99	Away	27-Feb-99	1-2	Le Tissier (90)	55,316	P.Jones
1999-00	Away	25-Sep-99	3-3	Pahars (17); Le Tissier (51, 73)	55,249	S.Dunn
1999-00	Home	22-Apr-00	1-3	Pahars (83)	15,245	N.Barry

MIDDLESBROUGH

Season	Venue	Date	Res	Scorers	Attendance	Referee
1992-93	Home	29-Aug-92	2-1	Le Tissier (80); Banger (83)	13,003	R.Gifford
1992-93	Away	26-Jan-93	1-2	Le Tissier (58)	13,921	P.Foakes
1995-96	Away	12-Sep-95	0-0		29,188	P.Jones
1995-96	Home	20-Jan-96	2-1	Shipperley (64); Hall (71)	15,151	K.Burge
1996-97	Home	28-Sep-96	4-0	Oakley (10); Le Tissier (28, 47); Watson (82)	15,230	R.Dilkes
1996-97	Away	11-Jan-97	1-0	Magilton (58)	29,509	G.Ashby
1998-99	Home	7-Nov-98	3-3	Monkou (61); Beattie (82); Ostenstad (85)	15,202	P.Alcock
1998-99	Away	14-Mar-99	0-3		33,387	M.Reed
1999-00	Away	11-Sep-99	2-3	Kachloul (15); Pahars (55)	32,165	S.Lodge
1999-00	Home	4-Mar-00	1-1	Pahars (44)	15,223	S.Dunn

NEWCASTLE UNITED

Season	Venue	Date	Res	Scorers	Attendance	Referee
1993-94	Home	24-Oct-93	2-1	Le Tissier (62, 87)	13,804	P.Don
1993-94	Away	22-Jan-94	2-1	Maddison (5); Le Tissier (83)	32,067	A.Gunn
1994-95	Away	27-Aug-94	1-5	Banger (53)	34,181	D.Elleray
1994-95	Home	22-Mar-95	3-1	Heaney (86); Watson (90); Shipperley (90)	14,676	J.Worrall
1995-96	Home	9-Sep-95	1-0	Magilton (65)	15,237	G.Ashby
1995-96	Away	17-Apr-96	0-1		36,554	D.Gallagher
1996-97	Home	18-Jan-97	2-2	Maddison (88); Le Tissier (90)	15,251	M.Reed
1996-97	Away	1-Mar-97	1-0	Le Tissier (55)	36,446	M.Bodenham
1997-98	Away	22-Nov-97	1-2	Davies (6)	37,759	D.Gallagher
1997-98	Home	28-Mar-98	2-1	OG (68, Pearce); Le Tissier (85 pen)	15,251	G.Barber
1998-99	Away	12-Sep-98	0-4		36,454	M.Riley
1998-99	Home	20-Feb-99	2-1	Beattie (16); Dodd (43 pen)	15,244	G.Poll
1999-00	Home	15-Aug-99	4-2	Kachloul (58, 68); Pahars (66); M.Hughes (78)	15,030	D.Elleray
1999-00	Away	16-Jan-00	0-5		35,623	N.Barry

NORWICH CITY

Season	Venue	Date	Res	Scorers	Attendance	Referee
1992-93	Away	5-Sep-92	0-1		12,452	K.Hackett
1992-93	Home	10-Feb-93	3-0	Hall (9); Adams (25); Banger (79)	12,969	J.Worrall
1993-94	Home	1-Jan-94	0-1		16,556	G.Poll
1993-94	Away	9-Apr-94	5-4	OG (44, Ulathorne); Le Tissier (58, 63 pen, 72); Monkou (90)	17,150	K.Cooper
1994-95	Home	2-Nov-94	1-1	Le Tissier (89 pen)	12,976	P.Durkin
1994-95	Away	11-Feb-95	2-2	Hall (33); Magilton (36)	18,361	R.Hart

NOTTINGHAM FOREST

Season	Venue	Date	Res	Scorers	Attendance	Referee
1992-93	Away	28-Nov-92	2-1	Le Tissier (21); Adams (63)	19,942	D.Elleray
1992-93	Home	24-Mar-93	1-2	Le Tissier (72)	18,005	M.Reed
1994-95	Home	17-Sep-94	1-1	Le Tissier (54 pen)	14,185	M.Reed
1994-95	Away	18-Mar-95	0-3		24,146	K.Cooper
1995-96	Home	19-Aug-95	3-4	Le Tissier (10 pen, 68 pen, 81)	15,165	G.Willard
1995-96	Away	13-Jan-96	0-1		23,321	S.Lodge
1996-97	Home	4-Sep-96	2-2	Dryden (53); Le Tissier (89)	14,450	P.Danson
1996-97	Away	5-Apr-97	3-1	Magilton (7); Evans (85, 89)	25,134	A.Wilkie
1998-99	Home	29-Aug-98	1-2	Le Tissier (89pen)	14,942	D.Gallagher
1998-99	Away	28-Dec-98	1-1	Kachloul (48)	23,456	M.Reed

OLDHAM ATHLETIC

Season	Venue	Date	Res	Scorers	Attendance	Referee
1992-93	Home	31-Oct-92	1-0	Hall (58)	10,827	P.Durkin
1992-93	Away	8-May-93	3-4	Le Tissier (34, 67, 85)	14,597	H.King
1993-94	Away	5-Feb-94	1-2	Le Tissier (26)	9,982	K.Morton
1993-94	Home	30-Mar-94	1-3	Le Tissier (59)	14,101	V.Callow

QPR

Season	Venue	Date	Res	Scorers	Attendance	Referee
1992-93	Away	19-Aug-92	1-3	Le Tissier (31)	10,925	R.Bigger
1992-93	Home	12-Sep-92	1-2	Le Tissier (11)	14,125	A.Gunn
1993-94	Away	21-Aug-93	1-2	Dowie (88)	10,613	R.Dilkes
1993-94	Home	11-Dec-93	0-1		11,946	K.Barratt
1994-95	Away	28-Dec-94	2-2	Dodd (14); Hughes (71)	16,078	K.Cooper
1994-95	Home	15-Apr-95	2-1	Shipperley (50); Watson (67)	15,201	P.Jones
1995-96	Home	4-Nov-95	2-0	Dodd (2); Le Tissier (76)	15,137	R.Dilkes
1995-96	Away	30-Mar-96	0-3		17,615	P.Jones

SHEFFIELD UNITED

Season	Venue	Date	Res	Scorers	Attendance	Referee
1992-93	Away	3-Oct-92	0-2		15,842	K.Redfern
1992-93	Home	27-Feb-93	3-2	Moore (2); Kenna (5); Dowie (39)	13,814	J.Borrett
1993-94	Home	2-Oct-93	3-3	Monkou (29); Maddison (53); Kenna (77)	11,619	G.Poll
1993-94	Away	26-Mar-94	0-0		19,522	D.Elleray

SHEFFIELD WEDNESDAY

Season	Venue	Date	Res	Scorers	Attendance	Referee
1992-93	Home	28-Dec-92	1-2	Monkou (80)	17,426	R.Milford
1992-93	Away	12-Apr-93	2-5	Dodd (68); Dowie (86)	26,183	K.Morton
1993-94	Away	18-Sep-93	0-2		22,503	R.Gifford
1993-94	Home	12-Mar-94	1-1	Monkou (78)	16,391	D.Crick
1994-95	Away	2-Jan-95	1-1	Le Tissier (70 pen)	28,424	R.Dilkes
1994-95	Home	29-Apr-95	0-0		15,189	J.Worrall
1995-96	Away	23-Dec-95	2-2	Heaney (7); Magilton (80 pen)	25,115	J.Winter
1995-96	Home	20-Mar-96	0-1		13,216	M.Bodenham
1996-97	Away	2-Nov-96	1-1	Le Tissier (55 pen)	20,106	A.Wilkie

1996-97	Home	22-Feb-97	2-3	Ostenstad (28); Le Tissier (32 pen)	15,062	M.Reed
1997-98	Home	29-Nov-97	2-3	Hirst (47); Palmer (55)	15,442	S.Dunn
1997-98	Away	4-Apr-98	0-1		29,677	P.Jones
1998-99	Away	31-Oct-98	0-0		30,078	M.Riley
1998-99	Home	21-Mar-99	1-0	Le Tissier (41)	15,201	R.Harris
1999-00	Home	28-Aug-99	2-0	Kachloul (53); Oakley (84)	14,815	P.Alcock
1999-00	Away	12-Feb-00	1-0	Tessem (26)	23,470	A.Wiley

SUNDERLAND

Season	Venue	Date	Res	Scorers	Attendance	Referee
1996-97	Home	19-Oct-96	3-0	Dodd (38); Le Tissier (53pen); Shipperley (89)	15,225	G.Willard
1996-97	Away	22-Apr-97	1-0	Ostenstad (22)	21,521	M.Riley
1999-00	Away	18-Dec-99	0-2		40,860	M.Reed
1999-00	Home	1-Apr-00	1-2	Le Tissier (89 pen)	15,245	P.Durkin

SWINDON TOWN

Season	Venue	Date	Res	Scorers	Attendance	Referee
1993-94	Home	25-Aug-93	5-1	Le Tissier (12, 52); Kenna (57); Dowie (62); Maddison (79)12,505		P.Durkin
1993-94	Away	18-Dec-93	1-2	Le Tissier (38)	13,565	D.Elleray

TOTTENHAM HOTSPUR

Season	Venue	Date	Res	Scorers	Attendance	Referee
1992-93	Home	15-Aug-92	0-0		19,654	V.Callow
1992-93	Away	7-Feb-93	2-4	Dowie (21); Hall (66)	20,098	K.Redfern
1993-94	Home	6-Nov-93	1-0	Maddison (60)	16,017	D.Allison
1993-94	Away	23-Apr-94	0-3		25,959	P.Durkin
1994-95	Away	12-Sep-94	2-1	Le Tissier (75,89)	22,387	A.Wilkie
1994-95	Home	2-Apr-95	4-3	Heaney (13); Le Tissier (44,58); Magilton (62)	15,105	G.Willard
1995-96	Home	26-Dec-95	0-0		15,238	P.Durkin
1995-96	Away	2-Mar-96	0-1		26,320	K.Burge
1996-97	Home	14-Sep-96	0-1		15,251	P.Alcock
1996-97	Away	26-Dec-96	1-3	Le Tissier (39)	30,549	G.Barber
1997-98	Home	25-Oct-97	3-2	OG (54, Vega); Hirst (67, 79)	15,225	N.Barry
1997-98	Away	10-May-98	1-1	Le Tissier	35,995	P.Jones
1998-99	Home	19-Sep-98	1-1	Le Tissier (64)	15,204	K.Burge
1998-99	Away	2-Mar-99	0-3		28,580	A.Wilkie
(S.Tomlin 23)						
1999-00	Home	20-Nov-99	0-1		15,248	S.Bennett
1999-00	Away	11-Mar-00	2-7	Tessem (26); El Khalej (33)	36,024	M.Halsey

WATFORD

Season	Venue	Date	Res	Scorers	Attendance	Referee
1999-00	Away	28-Dec-99	2-3	Boa Morte (61); Davies (63)	18,459	M.Riley
1999-00	Home	15-Apr-00	2-0	Davies (4); Pahars (75)	15,242	A.Wilkie

WEST HAM UNITED

Season	Venue	Date	Res	Scorers	Attendance	Referee
1993-94	Home	29-Nov-93	0-2		13,258	M.Bodenham
1993-94	Away	7-May-94	3-3	Le Tissier (45, 65pen); Maddison (52)	26,952	G.Ashby
1994-95	Away	22-Oct-94	0-2		18,853	J.Worrall
1994-95	Home	15-Mar-95	1-1	Shipperley (48)	15,178	K.Burge
1995-96	Home	2-Oct-95	0-0		13,568	G.Poll
1995-96	Away	16-Dec-95	1-2	OG (22, Bishop)	18,501	A.Wilkie
1996-97	Away	24-Aug-96	1-2	Heaney (17)	21,227	D.Elleray
1996-97	Home	12-Apr-97	2-0	Evans (12); Berkovic (36)	15,244	S.Dunn
1997-98	Home	4-Oct-97	3-0	Ostenstad (64); Davies (65); Dodd (69)	15,212	M.Riley
1997-98	Away	25-Apr-98	4-2	Le Tissier (39); Ostenstad (63, 85); Palmer (79)	25,878	D.Gallagher
1998-99	Away	28-Sep-98	0-1		23,153	U.Rennie
1998-99	Home	6-Mar-99	1-0	Kachloul (10)	15,240	D.Gallagher
1999-00	Home	5-Feb-00	2-1	Pahars (54); OG (86, Charles)	15,257	B.Knight
1999-00	Away	8-Mar-00	0-2		23,484	S.Lodge

WIMBLEDON

Season	Venue	Date	Res	Scorers	Attendance	Referee
1992-93	Home	17-Oct-92	2-2	Dowie (57); Groves (83)	11,221	K.Barratt
1992-93	Away	6-Mar-93	2-1	Le Tissier (33); Moore (73)	4,534	A.Gunn
1993-94	Away	31-Aug-93	0-1		6,036	K.Hackett
1993-94	Home	26-Feb-94	1-0	Le Tissier (74)	14,790	D.Gallagher
1994-95	Home	26-Dec-94	2-3	Dodd (10); Le Tissier (43)	14,603	G.Poll
1994-95	Away	17-Apr-95	2-0	Le Tissier (9); Magilton (30)	10,521	G.Ashby
1995-96	Away	28-Oct-95	2-1	Shipperley (9, 75)	7,982	J.Winter
1995-96	Home	5-May-96	0-0		15,172	M.Reed
1996-97	Away	23-Sep-96	1-3	Oakley (76)	8,572	P.Durkin
1996-97	Home	26-Feb-97	0-0		14,418	A.Wilkie
1997-98	Away	7-Dec-97	0-1		12,009	M.Reed
1997-98	Home	11-Apr-98	0-1		14,815	M.Reed
1998-99	Home	19-Dec-98	3-1	Ostenstad (11, 68); Kachloul (64)	14,354	M.Reed
1998-99	Away	8-May-99	2-0	Beattie (72); Le Tissier (84)	24,068	S.Dunn
1999-00	Away	30-Oct-99	1-1	Pahars (67)	15,754	S.Lodge
1999-00	Home	14-May-00	2-0	Bridge (57); Pahars (79)	15,249	S.Lodge

INTRODUCTION

Formed in 1879 as The Sunderland and District Teachers' Association FC by James Allan, a Scottish school teacher. Originally membership was restricted to teachers only, but this requirement was soon removed. Became Sunderland AFC in 1880 and had their first ground at the Blue House pub. Played at a number of grounds until they moved to their current Roker Park site in 1898. Elected to Division 2 of the Football League in 1890 and best remembered for their famous FA Cup win over Leeds United in 1973. Had one previous season in FAPL (1996-97) but were immediately relegated, but were promoted again at the end of the 1998-99 campaign and had a very successful 1999-00 season.

Ground:	Stadium of Light, Sunderland, SR5 1SU
Nickname:	The Rokermen
Internet::	www.sunderland-afc.com

HONOURS

Football League Div 1:	Champions: 1891-92, 1892-93, 1894-95, 1901-02, 1912-13, 1935-36, 1995-96, 1998-99
	Runners-up: 1893-94, 1897-88; 1900-01, 1922-23, 1934-35
Football League Div 2:	Champions: 1975-76
	Runners-up: 1963-64, 1979-80
Football League Div 2:	Champions: 1987-88
FA Cup :	Winners: 1936-37, 1972-73
	Runners-up: 1912-13, 1991-92
Football League Cup	Runners-up: 1984-85

EUROPEAN RECORD

Champions' League (0):	–
Cup-Winners' Cup (1):	1973-74 (2)
UEFA (0):	–

FAPL RECORD SUMMARY

Most Total:	GRAY, Michael	68
Most Starts:	GRAY, Michael	64
Most Subs:	RUSSELL, Craig	19
Most SNU:	MARRIOTT, Andy	37
Most PS:	GRAY, Michael	16
Most Goals:	PHILLIPS, Kevin	30
Most Yel:	RAE, Alex	13
Most Red:	ORD, Richard	2

PLAYING RECORD – SEASON TOTALS

Season	Pn	P	W	D	L	F	A	Pts
1996-97	18	38	10	10	18	35	53	40
1999-00	7	38	16	10	12	57	56	58
Totals		76	26	20	30	92	109	98

PLAYING RECORD – HOME TOTALS

Season	Pn	P	W	D	L	F	A	Pts
1996-97	18	19	7	6	6	20	18	27
1999-00	7	19	10	6	3	28	17	36
Totals		38	17	12	9	48	35	63

PLAYING RECORD – AWAY TOTALS

Season	Pn	P	W	D	L	F	A	Pts
1996-97	18	19	3	4	12	15	35	13
1999-00	7	19	6	4	9	29	39	22
Totals		38	9	8	21	44	74	35

HIGHEST HOME ATTENDANCES

	Attendance	Opponents	Date	Season
1	42,192	Newcastle U.	5-Feb-00	1999-00
2	42,026	Manchester U.	28-Dec-99	1999-00
3	42,015	Liverpool	20-Nov-99	1999-00
4	42,013	Middlesbrough	18-Mar-00	1999-00
5	41,947	Leeds U.	23-Jan-00	1999-00

LOWEST HOME ATTENDANCES

	Attendance	Opponents	Date	Season
1	18,642	West Ham U.	8-Sep-96	1996-97
2	19,262	Leicester C.	17-Aug-96	1996-97
3	19,459	Coventry C.	21-Sep-96	1996-97
4	19,672	Wimbledon	7-Dec-96	1996-97
5	19,683	Chelsea	14-Dec-96	1996-97

TOP SCORER – SEASON BY SEASON

Season	Player	Goals
1996-97	Russell	4
1999-00	Phillips	30

PLAYERS WITH MOST PREMIERSHIP APPEARANCES

Tot	Player	St	Sb	Gls
68	GRAY, Michael	64	4	3
49	QUINN, Niall	43	6	17
48	RAE, Alex	34	14	6
43	BALL, Kevin	38	5	3
38	BRACEWELL, Paul	38	0	0
37	SORENSEN, Thomas	37	0	0
36	PHILLIPS, Kevin	36	0	30
36	WILLIAMS, Darren	23	13	2
34	MAKIN, Chris	34	0	1
33	ORD, Richard	33	0	2

CLUB-BY-CLUB RESULTS

ARSENAL

Season	Venue	Date	Res	Scorers	Attendance	Referee
1996-97	Away	28-Sep-96	0-2		38,016	P.Danson
1996-97	Home	11-Jan-97	1-0	OG (66, Adams)	21,154	M.Riley
1999-00	Home	14-Aug-99	0-0		41,680	U.Rennie
1999-00	Away	15-Jan-00	1-4	Quinn (46)	38,039	P.Alcock

ASTON VILLA

Season	Venue	Date	Res	Scorers	Attendance	Referee
1996-97	Home	26-Oct-96	1-0	Stewart (25)	21,059	P.Alcock
1996-97	Away	1-Feb-97	0-1		32,491	S.Lodge
1999-00	Home	18-Oct-99	2-1	Phillips (60 pen, 82)	41,045	D.Elleray
1999-00	Away	29-Apr-00	1-1	Quinn (85)	33,949	A.D'Urso

BLACKBURN ROVERS

Season	Venue	Date	Res	Scorers	Attendance	Referee
1996-97	Home	18-Jan-97	0-0		20,850	P.Alcock
1996-97	Away	1-Mar-97	0-1		24,208	R.Dilkes

BRADFORD CITY

Season	Venue	Date	Res	Scorers	Attendance	Referee
1999-00	Away	2-Oct-99	4-0	Rae (17); Quinn (68); Phillips (88, 90pen)	18,204	S.Bennett
1999-00	Home	24-Apr-00	0-1		40,628	S.Lodge

CHELSEA

Season	Venue	Date	Res	Scorers	Attendance	Referee
1996-97	Home	14-Dec-96	3-0	OG (30, Duberry); Ball (48); Russell (67)	19,683	M.Bodenham
1996-97	Away	16-Mar-97	2-6	Stewart (57); Rae (59)	24,072	G.Willard
1999-00	Away	7-Aug-99	0-4		34,831	M.Riley
1999-00	Home	4-Dec-99	4-1	Quinn (1, 38); Phillips (23, 36)	41,377	S.Dunn

COVENTRY CITY

Season	Venue	Date	Res	Scorers	Attendance	Referee
1996-97	Home	21-Sep-96	1-0	Agnew (51)	19,459	M.Riley
1996-97	Away	1-Jan-97	2-2	Bridges (6); Agnew (18 pen)	17,700	G.Poll
1999-00	Home	29-Aug-99	1-1	Phillips (72)	39,427	S.Lodge
1999-00	Away	12-Feb-00	2-3	Phillips (57); Rae (88)	22,101	P.Alcock

DERBY COUNTY

Season	Venue	Date	Res	Scorers	Attendance	Referee
1996-97	Away	14-Sep-96	0-1		17,692	D.Elleray
1996-97	Home	26-Dec-96	2-0	Ord (73); Russell (87)	22,512	J.Winter
1999-00	Away	18-Sep-99	5-0	McCann (24); Phillips (42, 52, 85); Quinn (55)	28,264	P.Jones
1999-00	Home	26-Feb-00	1-1	Rae (62)	41,940	A.Wiley

EVERTON

Season	Venue	Date	Res	Scorers	Attendance	Referee
1996-97	Away	30-Nov-96	3-1	Russell (54); Bridges (74, 87)	40,087	P.Jones
1996-97	Home	3-May-97	2-0	Stewart (35); Waddle (57); Johnston (68)	22,108	K.Burge
1999-00	Away	26-Dec-99	0-5		40,017	S.Lodge
1999-00	Home	25-Mar-00	2-1	Summerbee (7); Phillips (77)	41,934	S.Bennett

LEEDS UNITED

Season	Venue	Date	Res	Scorers	Attendance	Referee
1996-97	Away	2-Nov-96	0-3		31,667	S.Dunn
1996-97	Home	22-Feb-97	0-1		21,890	G.Poll
1999-00	Away	21-Aug-99	1-2	Phillips (37 pen)	39,064	P.Alcock
1999-00	Home	23-Jan-00	1-2	Phillips (52)	41,947	P.Jones

LEICESTER CITY

Season	Venue	Date	Res	Scorers	Attendance	Referee
1996-97	Home	17-Aug-96	0-0		19,262	S.Lodge
1996-97	Away	29-Jan-97	1-1	Williams (18)	17,883	G.Ashby
1999-00	Home	11-Sep-99	2-0	Butler,P. (28); McCann (82)	40,105	A.D'Urso
1999-00	Away	5-Mar-00	2-5	Phillips (53); Quinn (75)	20,432	N.Barry

LIVERPOOL

Season	Venue	Date	Res	Scorers	Attendance	Referee
1996-97	Away	24-Aug-96	0-0		40,503	M.Bodenham
1996-97	Home	13-Apr-97	1-2	Stewart (52)	21,938	D.Gallagher
1999-00	Home	20-Nov-99	0-2		42,015	D.Gallagher
1999-00	Away	11-Mar-00	1-1	Phillips (77 pen)	44,693	G.Poll

MANCHESTER UNITED

Season	Venue	Date	Res	Scorers	Attendance	Referee
1996-97	Away	21-Dec-96	0-5		55,081	P.Durkin
1996-97	Home	8-Mar-97	2-1	Gray (52); Mullin (76)	22,225	P.Jones
1999-00	Home	28-Dec-99	2-2	McCann (2); Quinn (13)	42,026	J.Winter
1999-00	Away	15-Apr-00	0-4		61,612	P.Jones

MIDDLESBROUGH

Season	Venue	Date	Res	Scorers	Attendance	Referee
1996-97	Home	14-Oct-96	2-2	Rae (21 pen); Russell (61)	20,936	G.Poll
1996-97	Away	19-Apr-97	1-0	Williams (45)	30,106	G.Ashby
1999-00	Away	6-Nov-99	1-1	Reddy (78)	44,793	G.Barber
1999-00	Home	18-Mar-00	1-1	Quinn (66)	42,013	D.Elleray

NEWCASTLE UNITED

Season	Venue	Date	Res	Scorers	Attendance	Referee
1996-97	Home	3-Sep-96	1-2	Scott (20 pen)	22,037	J.Winter
1996-97	Away	5-Apr-97	1-1	Gray (31)	36,582	P.Durkin
1999-00	Away	25-Aug-99	2-1	Quinn (64); Phillips (75)	36,500	G.Poll
1999-00	Home	5-Feb-00	2-2	Phillips (22, 82)	42,192	D.Gallagher

NOTTINGHAM FOREST

Season	Venue	Date	Res	Scorers	Attendance	Referee
1996-97	Away	21-Aug-96	4-1	Gray (7); Quinn (16, 31); Ord (42)	22,874	G.Barber
1996-97	Home	22-Mar-97	1-1	Ball (61)	22,120	P.Alcock

SHEFFIELD WEDNESDAY

Season	Venue	Date	Res	Scorers	Attendance	Referee
1996-97	Home	23-Nov-96	1-1	Melville (68)	20,644	G.Barber
1996-97	Away	12-Mar-97	1-2	Ball (28)	20,294	D.Gallagher
1999-00	Home	25-Sep-99	1-0	Schwarz (51)	41,132	A.Wiley
1999-00	Away	22-Apr-00	2-0	Phillips (86, 90)	28,072	M.Reed

SOUTHAMPTON

Season	Venue	Date	Res	Scorers	Attendance	Referee
1996-97	Away	19-Oct-96	0-3		15,225	G.Willard
1996-97	Home	22-Apr-97	0-1		21,521	M.Riley
1999-00	Home	18-Dec-99	2-0	Phillips (30, 90)	40,860	M.Reed
1999-00	Away	1-Apr-00	2-1	Quinn (14); Phillips (86 pen)	15,245	P.Durkin

TOTTENHAM HOTSPUR

Season	Venue	Date	Res	Scorers	Attendance	Referee
1996-97	Away	16-Nov-96	0-2		31,867	M.Reed
1996-97	Home	4-Mar-97	0-4		20,785	M.Riley
1999-00	Home	31-Oct-99	2-1	Quinn (10, 21)	41,904	M.Riley
1999-00	Away	14-May-00	1-3	Makin (20)	36,070	M.Riley

WATFORD

Season	Venue	Date	Res	Scorers	Attendance	Referee
1999-00	Home	10-Aug-99	2-0	Phillips (62 pen, 86)	40,630	J.Winter
1999-00	Away	27-Nov-99	3-2	Phillips (24, 33); McCann (70)	21,590	U.Rennie

WEST HAM UNITED

Season	Venue	Date	Res	Scorers	Attendance	Referee
1996-97	Home	8-Sep-96	0-0		18,642	G.Poll
1996-97	Away	28-Dec-96	0-2		24,077	R.Dilkes
1999-00	Away	24-Oct-99	1-1	Phillips (24)	26,081	M.Halsey
1999-00	Home	6-May-00	1-0	Phillips (14)	41,684	N.Barry

WIMBLEDON

Season	Venue	Date	Res	Scorers	Attendance	Referee
1996-97	Home	7-Dec-96	1-3	Rae (53)	19,672	K.Burge
1996-97	Away	11-May-97	0-1		21,338	D.Gallagher
1999-00	Away	3-Jan-00	0-1		17,621	G.Poll
1999-00	Home	8-Apr-00	2-1	Quinn (54); Kilbane (82)	41,592	G.Barber

INTRODUCTION

Founded as Spartans around 1881 by cricketers from Swindon Spartans. Amalgamated with St Mark's Young Men's Friendly Society to become Swindon Town around 1883. First holders of the Wiltshire Senior Cup 1887. Founder member of the Southern League First Division 1894. Turned professional in 1895 and, having played on several sites, moved to the County Ground. FA Cup semi-finalists in 1912 and Southern League champions 1914. Founder members of Football League Division Three in 1920 (this becoming Division Three (South) the following season) and of Division Three at the end of regionalisation in 1958. Denied promotion to the top division for disciplinary reasons 1991.

Ground: County Ground, Swindon,
               Wiltshire, SN1 2ED
Nickname: The Robins
Internet: www.swindonfc.co.uk

HONOURS

Football League Div 3:	Runners-up 1962-63, 1968-69
Football League Div 4:	Champions 1985-86 (with record 102 points)
Football League Cup:	Winners 1968-69
Anglo-Italian Cup:	Winners 1970

EUROPEAN RECORD

Never qualified

FAPL RECORD SUMMARY

Most Total:	TAYLOR, Shaun	42
Most Starts:	TAYLOR, Shaun	42
Most Subs:	FJORTOFT, Jan-Aage	10
Most SNU:	HAMMOND, Nicky	29
Most PS:	LING, Martin	9
Most Goals:	FJORTOFT, Jan-Aage	12
Most Yel:	MONCUR, John	5
Most Red:	MUTCH, Andy	1

PLAYING RECORD – SEASON TOTALS

Season	Pn	P	W	D	L	F	A	Pts
1993-94	22	42	5	15	22	47	100	30
Totals		42	5	15	22	47	100	30

PLAYING RECORD – HOME TOTALS

Season	Pn	P	W	D	L	F	A	Pts
1993-94	22	21	4	7	10	25	45	19
Totals		21	4	7	10	25	45	19

PLAYING RECORD – AWAY TOTALS

Season	Pn	P	W	D	L	F	A	Pts
1993-94	22	21	1	8	12	22	55	11
Totals		21	1	8	12	22	55	11

HIGHEST HOME ATTENDANCES

	Attendance	Opponents	Date	Season
1	18,102	Manchester U.	19-Mar-94	1993-94
2	17,364	Liverpool	22-Aug-93	1993-94
3	17,228	Leeds U.	7-May-94	1993-94
4	17,214	Arsenal	27-Dec-93	1993-94
5	16,464	Tottenham H.	22-Jan-94	1993-94

LOWEST HOME ATTENDANCES

	Attendance	Opponents	Date	Season
1	11,940	Oldham A.	18-Aug-93	1993-94
2	12,882	Sheffield U.	4-Dec-93	1993-94
3	13,309	Wimbledon	23-Apr-94	1993-94
4	13,565	Southampton	18-Dec-93	1993-94
5	13,860	Ipswich T.	20-Nov-93	1993-94

TOP SCORER – SEASON BY SEASON

Season	Player	Goals
1993-94	Fjortoft	12

PLAYERS WITH MOST PREMIERSHIP APPEARANCES

Tot	Player	St	Sb	Gls
42	TAYLOR, Shaun	42	0	4
41	MONCUR, John	41	0	4
38	SUMMERBEE, Nicky	36	2	3
38	HORLOCK, Kevin	32	6	0
36	FJORTOFT, Jan-Aage	26	10	12
35	WHITBREAD, Adrian	34	1	1
33	LING, Martin	29	4	1
32	NIJHOLT, Luc	31	1	1
32	BODIN, Paul	28	4	7
30	MUTCH, Andy	27	3	6
28	DIGBY, Fraser	28	0	0
27	SCOTT, Keith	22	5	4
26	FENWICK, Terry	23	3	0

CLUB-BY-CLUB RESULTS

ARSENAL

Season	Venue	Date	Res	Scorers	Attendance	Referee
1993-94	Home	27-Dec-93	0-4		17,214	S.Lodge
1993-94	Away	2-Apr-94	1-1	Bodin (29 pen)	31,635	B.Hill

ASTON VILLA

Season	Venue	Date	Res	Scorers	Attendance	Referee
1993-94	Home	30-Oct-93	1-2	Bodin (33 pen)	16,322	K.Burge
1993-94	Away	12-Feb-94	0-5		27,637	R.Hart

BLACKBURN ROVERS

Season	Venue	Date	Res	Scorers	Attendance	Referee
1993-94	Home	2-Oct-93	1-3	Taylor (32)	15,847	D.Frampton
1993-94	Away	26-Mar-94	1-3	Fjortoft (4)	20,046	K.Morton

CHELSEA

Season	Venue	Date	Res	Scorers	Attendance	Referee
1993-94	Home	1-Jan-94	1-3	Mutch (90)	16,261	K.Hackett
1993-94	Away	27-Apr-94	0-2		11,180	B.Hill

COVENTRY CITY

Season	Venue	Date	Res	Scorers	Attendance	Referee
1993-94	Away	3-Jan-94	1-1	Mutch (89)	15,869	B.Hill
1993-94	Home	5-Feb-94	3-1	Fjortoft (9, 35 pen, 79 pen)	14,635	K.Burge

EVERTON

Season	Venue	Date	Res	Scorers	Attendance	Referee
1993-94	Home	16-Oct-93	1-1	Taylor (89)	14,437	K.Morton
1993-94	Away	15-Jan-94	2-6	Moncur (55); Bodin (61)	20,760	G.Ashby

IPSWICH TOWN

Season	Venue	Date	Res	Scorers	Attendance	Referee
1993-94	Home	20-Nov-93	2-2	Scott (45); Bodin (83 pen)	13,860	R.Dilkes
1993-94	Away	16-Apr-94	1-1	Fjortoft (15)	14,760	V.Callow

LEEDS UNITED

Season	Venue	Date	Res	Scorers	Attendance	Referee
1993-94	Away	27-Nov-93	0-3		32,630	V.Callow
1993-94	Home	7-May-94	0-5		17,228	M.Bodenham

LIVERPOOL

Season	Venue	Date	Res	Scorers	Attendance	Referee
1993-94	Home	22-Aug-93	0-5		17,364	P.Don
1993-94	Away	11-Dec-93	2-2	Moncur (60); Scott (74)	32,739	K.Morton

MANCHESTER CITY

Season	Venue	Date	Res	Scorers	Attendance	Referee
1993-94	Home	1-Sep-93	1-3	Summerbee (60)	16,067	K.Cooper
1993-94	Away	25-Feb-94	1-2	Fjortoft (7)	26,360	P.Foakes

MANCHESTER UNITED

Season	Venue	Date	Res	Scorers	Attendance	Referee
1993-94	Away	25-Sep-93	2-4	Mutch (77); Bodin (87 pen)	44,583	J.Worrall
1993-94	Home	19-Mar-94	2-2	Nijholt (36); Fjortoft (83)	18,102	B.Hill

NEWCASTLE UNITED

Season	Venue	Date	Res	Scorers	Attendance	Referee
1993-94	Home	18-Sep-93	2-2	Ling (60); Mutch (61)	15,393	H.King
1993-94	Away	12-Mar-94	1-7	Moncur (77)	32,219	M.Reed

NORWICH CITY

Season	Venue	Date	Res	Scorers	Attendance	Referee
1993-94	Away	28-Aug-93	0-0		17,614	D.Elleray
1993-94	Home	19-Feb-94	3-3	Taylor (18); Fjortoft (45, 50)	15,341	R.Gifford

OLDHAM ATHLETIC

Season	Venue	Date	Res	Scorers	Attendance	Referee
1993-94	Home	18-Aug-93	0-1		11,940	D.Gallagher
1993-94	Away	7-Dec-93	1-2	Mutch (71)	9,771	D.Allison

QPR

Season	Venue	Date	Res	Scorers	Attendance	Referee
1993-94	Home	24-Nov-93	1-0	Scott (37)	14,674	G.Ashby
1993-94	Away	30-Apr-94	3-1	Taylor (63); Fjortoft (76); Summerbee (90)	9,875	D.Elleray

SHEFFIELD UNITED

Season	Venue	Date	Res	Scorers	Attendance	Referee
1993-94	Away	14-Aug-93	1-3	Moncur (46)	20,904	J.Borrett
1993-94	Home	4-Dec-93	0-0		12,882	T.Holbrook

SHEFFIELD WEDNESDAY

Season	Venue	Date	Res	Scorers	Attendance	Referee
1993-94	Away	29-Dec-93	3-3	Mutch (6); Maskell (19,90)	30,570	P.Don
1993-94	Home	4-Apr-94	0-1		13,927	A.Gunn

SOUTHAMPTON

Season	Venue	Date	Res	Scorers	Attendance	Referee
1993-94	Away	25-Aug-93	1-5	Maskell (82 pen)	12,505	P.Durkin
1993-94	Home	18-Dec-93	2-1	Bodin (11); Scott (65)	13,565	D.Elleray

TOTTENHAM HOTSPUR

Season	Venue	Date	Res	Scorers	Attendance	Referee
1993-94	Away	23-Oct-93	1-1	Bodin (63 pen)	31,394	K.Barratt
1993-94	Home	22-Jan-94	2-1	Fjortoft (38); Whitbread (80)	16,464	P.Durkin

SWINDON TOWN

WEST HAM UNITED

Season	Venue	Date	Res	Scorers	Attendance	Referee
1993-94	Away	11-Sep-93	0-0		15,777	A.Gunn
1993-94	Home	5-Mar-94	1-1	Fjortoft (88)	15,929	R.Milford

WIMBLEDON

Season	Venue	Date	Res	Scorers	Attendance	Referee
1993-94	Away	6-Nov-93	0-3		7,758	S.Lodge
1993-94	Home	23-Apr-94	2-4	Summerbee (67); OG (80, Barton)	13,309	G.Poll

INTRODUCTION

Formed in 1882 by members of the schoolboys' Hotspur CC as Hotspur FC and had early church connections. Added 'Tottenham' in 1884 to distinguish club from London Hotspur FC. Turned professional in 1895 and elected to the Southern League in 1896 having been rebuffed by the Football League.

Played at two grounds (Tottenham Marshes and Northumberland Park) before moving to the site which became known as White Hart Lane in 1899. Joined the Football League Second Division in 1908. Having failed to gain a place in the re-election voting, they secured a vacancy caused by a late resignation. Premier League founder members 1992.

Ground:	748 High Road, Tottenham, London, N17 0AP
Nickname:	Spurs
Internet::	www.spurs.co.uk

HONOURS

Football League Div 1:	Champions 1950-51, 1960-61 Runners-up 1921-22, 1951-52, 1956-57, 1962-63
Football League Div 2:	Champions 1919-20, 1949-50 Runners-up 1908-09, 1932-33
FA Cup:	Winners 1900-01, 1920-21, 1960-61, 1961-62, 1966-67, 1163 980-81, 1981-82, 1990-91 Runners-up 1986-87
Football League Cup:	Winners 1970-71, 1972-73, 1998-99 Runners-up 1981-82
Cup-Winners' Cup:	Winners 1962-63 Runners-up: 1981-82
UEFA Cup:	Winners 1971-72, 1983-84 Runners-up: 1973-74

EUROPEAN RECORD

Champions' League (1):	61-62 (SF)
Cup-Winners' Cup (6):	62-63 (W), 63-64 (2), 67-68 (2), 81-82 (SF), 82-83 (2), 91-92 (QF)
UEFA Cup (6):	71-72 (W), 72-73 (SF), 73-74 (F), 83-84 (W), 84-85 (QF); 99-00

FAPL RECORD SUMMARY

Most Total:	WALKER, Ian	236
Most Starts:	WALKER, Ian	235
Most Subs:	ROSENTHAL, Ronny	33
Most SNU:	BAARDSEN, Espen	124
Most PS:	GINOLA, David	37
Most Goals:	SHERINGHAM, Teddy	74
Most Yel:	EDINBURGH, Justin	39
Most Red:	CALDERWOOD, Colin	3

PLAYING RECORD – SEASON TOTALS

Season	Pn	P	W	D	L	F	A	Pts
1992-93	8	42	16	11	15	60	66	59
1993-94	15	42	11	12	19	54	59	45
1994-95	7	42	16	14	12	66	58	62
1995-96	8	38	16	13	9	50	38	61
1996-97	10	38	13	7	18	44	51	46
1997-98	14	38	11	11	16	44	56	44
1998-99	11	38	11	14	13	47	50	47
1999-00	10	38	15	8	15	57	49	53
Totals		316	109	90	117	422	427	417

PLAYING RECORD – HOME TOTALS

Season	Pn	P	W	D	L	F	A	Pts
1992-93	8	21	11	5	5	40	25	38
1993-94	15	21	4	8	9	29	33	20
1994-95	7	21	10	5	6	32	25	35
1995-96	8	19	9	5	5	26	19	32
1996-97	10	19	8	4	7	19	17	28
1997-98	14	19	7	8	4	23	22	29
1998-99	11	19	7	7	5	28	26	28
1999-00	10	19	10	3	6	40	26	33
Totals		158	66	45	47	237	193	243

PLAYING RECORD – AWAY TOTALS

Season	Pn	P	W	D	L	F	A	Pts
1992-93	8	21	5	6	10	20	41	21
1993-94	15	21	7	4	10	25	26	25
1994-95	7	21	6	9	6	34	33	27
1995-96	8	19	7	8	4	24	19	29
1996-97	10	19	5	3	11	25	34	18
1997-98	14	19	4	3	12	21	34	15
1998-99	11	19	4	7	8	19	24	19
1999-00	10	19	5	5	9	17	23	20
Totals		158	43	45	70	185	234	174

TOTTENHAM HOTSPUR

HIGHEST HOME ATTENDANCES

	Attendance	Opponents	Date	Season
1	36,878	Chelsea	10-May-99	1998-99
2	36,521	Liverpool	5-Dec-98	1998-99
3	36,233	West Ham U.	6-Dec-99	1999-00
4	36,089	West Ham U.	24-Apr-99	1998-99
5	36,089	Watford	26-Dec-99	1999-00

LOWEST HOME ATTENDANCES

	Attendance	Opponents	Date	Season
1	17,452	Aston Villa	2-Mar-94	1993-94
2	17,744	Wimbledon	24-Nov-93	1993-94
3	20,098	Southampton	7-Feb-93	1992-93
4	21,322	Sheffield U.	2-Sep-92	1992-93
5	22,387	Southampton	12-Sep-94	1994-95

TOP SCORER – SEASON BY SEASON

Season	Player	Goals
992-93	Sheringham	21
1993-94	Sheringham	14
1994-95	Klinsmann	22
1995-96	Sheringham	16

1996-97	Sheringham	7
1997-98	Klinsmann	9
1998-99	Iversen	9
1999-00	Armstrong, Iversen	14

PLAYERS WITH MOST PREMIERSHIP APPEARANCES

Tot	Player	St	Sb	Gls
236	WALKER, Ian	235	1	0
234	CAMPBELL, Sol	225	9	8
201	ANDERTON, Darren	184	17	28
174	EDINBURGH, Justin	154	20	0
166	SHERINGHAM, Teddy	163	3	74
163	CALDERWOOD, Colin	152	11	6
143	HOWELLS, David	132	11	8
138	MABBUTT, Gary	132	6	2
136	CARR, Stephen	133	3	3
132	ARMSTRONG, Chris	114	18	46
124	AUSTIN, Dean	117	7	0
106	FOX, Ruel	95	11	13
100	GINOLA, David	100	0	13

CLUB-BY-CLUB RESULTS

ARSENAL

Season	Venue	Date	Res	Scorers	Attendance	Referee
1992-93	Home	12-Dec-92	1-0	Allen,P. (20)	33,709	A.Buksh
1992-93	Away	11-May-93	3-1	Sheringham (39); Hendry (46, 78)	26,393	K.Cooper
1993-94	Home	16-Aug-93	0-1		28,355	D.Elleray
1993-94	Away	6-Dec-93	1-1	Anderton (25)	35,669	P.Don
1994-95	Home	2-Jan-95	1-0	Popescu (22)	28,747	M.Reed
1994-95	Away	29-Apr-95	1-1	Klinsmann (74)	38,377	R.Hart
1995-96	Home	18-Nov-95	2-1	Sheringham (29); Armstrong (54)	32,894	A.Wilkie
1995-96	Away	15-Apr-96	0-0		38,273	M.Reed
1996-97	Away	24-Nov-96	1-3	Sinton (67)	38,264	D.Elleray
1996-97	Home	15-Feb-97	0-0		33,039	G.Poll
1997-98	Away	30-Aug-97	0-0		38,102	G.Willard
1997-98	Home	28-Dec-97	1-1	Nielson (28)	29,610	M.Riley
1998-99	Away	14-Nov-98	0-0		38,278	A.Wilkie
1998-99	Home	5-May-99	1-3	Anderton (43)	36,019	S.Dunn
1999-00	Home	7-Nov-99	2-1	Iversen (7); Sherwood (20)	36,085	D.Elleray
1999-00	Away	19-Mar-00	1-2	Armstrong (31)	38,131	P.Durkin

ASTON VILLA

Season	Venue	Date	Res	Scorers	Attendance	Referee
1992-93	Home	21-Nov-92	0-0		32,852	J.Borrett
1992-93	Away	10-Mar-93	0-0		37,727	K.Hackett
1993-94	Away	28-Aug-93	0-1		32,498	K.Cooper
1993-94	Home	2-Mar-94	1-1	Rosenthal (74)	17,452	K.Morton
1994-95	Home	19-Nov-94	3-4	Sheringham (39); Klinsmann (52 pen,72)	26,899	P.Durkin

Season	Venue	Date	Res	Scorers		Attendance	Referee
1994-95	Away	25-Jan-95	0-1			40,017	R.Hart
1995-96	Home	23-Aug-95	0-1			26,726	S.Dunn
1995-96	Away	21-Jan-96	1-2	Fox (26)		35,666	G.Poll
1996-97	Home	12-Oct-96	1-0	Nielsen (60)		32,847	P.Jones
1996-97	Away	19-Apr-97	1-1	Vega (54)		39,339	M.Bodenham
1997-98	Home	27-Aug-97	3-2	Ferdinand (15, 66); Fox (77)		26,317	M.Riley
1997-98	Away	26-Dec-97	1-4	Calderwood (59)		38,644	A.Wilkie
1998-99	Away	7-Nov-98	2-3	Anderton (65 pen); Vega (76)		39,241	R.Harris
1998-99	Home	13-Mar-99	1-0	Sherwood (88)		35,963	P.Jones
1999-00	Away	29-Dec-99	1-1	Sherwood (44)		39,217	G.Barber
1999-00	Home	15-Apr-00	2-4	Iversen (16); Armstrong (47)		35,304	R.Harris

BARNSLEY

Season	Venue	Date	Res	Scorers	Attendance	Referee
1997-98	Home	20-Dec-97	3-0	Nielson (5); Ginola (11, 17)	28,232	M.Reed
1997-98	Away	18-Apr-98	1-1	Calderwood (47)	18,692	M.Bodenham

BLACKBURN ROVERS

Season	Venue	Date	Res	Scorers	Attendance	Referee
1992-93	Away	7-Nov-92	2-0	Howells (67); Sheringham (81pen)	17,305	K.Barratt
1992-93	Home	5-May-93	1-2	Anderton (86)	23,097	K.Morton
1993-94	Away	30-Oct-93	0-1		17,462	A.Wilkie
1993-94	Home	12-Feb-94	0-2		30,236	J.Borrett
1994-95	Away	5-Nov-94	0-2		26,933	T.Holbrook
1994-95	Home	5-Feb-95	3-1	Klinsmann (18); Anderton (29); Barmby (79)	28,124	M.Bodenham
1995-96	Away	30-Dec-95	1-2	Sheringham (53)	30,004	P.Jones
1995-96	Home	16-Mar-96	2-3	Sheringham (61); Armstrong (80)	31,803	P.Durkin
1996-97	Away	17-Aug-96	2-0	Armstrong (33, 68)	26,960	P.Jones
1996-97	Home	29-Jan-97	2-1	Iversen (41); Sinton (83)	22,943	P.Danson
1997-98	Home	20-Sep-97	0-0		26,573	G.Barber
1997-98	Away	7-Feb-98	3-0	Berti (37); Armstrong (89); Fox (90)	30,388	G.Barber
1998-99	Home	9-Sep-98	2-1	Ferdinand (26); Nielsen (50)	28,338	P.Alcock
1998-99	Away	30-Jan-99	1-1	Iversen (61)	29,643	N.Barry

BOLTON WANDERERS

Season	Venue	Date	Res	Scorers	Attendance	Referee
1995-96	Home	23-Dec-95	2-2	Sheringham (53); Armstrong (71)	30,702	P.Danson
1995-96	Away	20-Mar-96	3-2	Howells (17); Fox (54); Armstrong (60)	17,829	S.Dunn
1997-98	Away	23-Sep-97	1-1	Armstrong (71)	23,433	U.Rennie
1997-98	Home	1-Mar-98	1-0	Nielsen (45)	29,032	P.Jones

BRADFORD CITY

Season	Venue	Date	Res	Scorers	Attendance	Referee
1999-00	Away	12-Sep-99	1-1	Perry (76)	18,141	A.Wilkie
1999-00	Home	4-Mar-00	1-1	Iversen (14)	35,472	P.Jones

CHARLTON ATHLETIC

Season	Venue	Date	Res	Scorers	Attendance	Referee
1998-99	Home	2-Nov-98	2-2	Nielsen (50); Armstrong (57)	32,202	M.Reed
1998-99	Away	20-Apr-99	4-1	Iversen (58); Campbell (78); Dominguez (89); Ginola (90)	20,043	D.Gallagher

CHELSEA

Season	Venue	Date	Res	Scorers	Attendance	Referee
1992-93	Home	5-Dec-92	1-2	Campbell (88)	31,540	R.Dilkes
1992-93	Away	20-Mar-93	1-1	Sheringham (31 pen)	25,157	R.Dilkes
1993-94	Home	1-Sep-93	1-1	Sheringham (85 pen)	27,567	V.Callow
1993-94	Away	27-Feb-94	3-4	Sedgley (18); Dozzell (19); Gray (72 pen)	19,398	J.Lloyd
1994-95	Home	23-Nov-94	0-0		27,037	G.Willard
1994-95	Away	11-Feb-95	1-1	Sheringham (8)	30,812	P.Durkin
1995-96	Away	25-Nov-95	0-0		31,059	S.Lodge
1995-96	Home	27-Apr-96	1-1	Armstrong (73)	32,918	A.Wilkie
1996-97	Away	26-Oct-96	1-3	Armstrong (41)	28,373	R.Dilkes
1996-97	Home	1-Feb-97	1-2	Howells (82)	33,027	P.Alcock
1997-98	Home	6-Dec-97	1-6	Vega (43)	28,476	D.Gallagher
1997-98	Away	11-Apr-98	0-2		34,149	P.Durkin
1998-99	Away	19-Dec-98	0-2		34,881	G.Poll
1998-99	Home	10-May-99	2-2	Iversen (38); Ginola (64)	36,878	D.Elleray
1999-00	Away	12-Jan-00	0-1		34,969	N.Barry
1999-00	Home	5-Feb-00	0-1		36,041	G.Poll

COVENTRY CITY

Season	Venue	Date	Res	Scorers	Attendance	Referee
1992-93	Home	19-Aug-92	0-2		24,388	D.Gallagher
1992-93	Away	14-Sep-92	0-1		15,348	M.Bodenham
1993-94	Home	1-Jan-94	1-2	Caskey (43)	26,015	T.Holbrook
1993-94	Away	9-Apr-94	0-1		14,487	M.Reed
1994-95	Away	31-Dec-94	4-0	OG (7, Darby); Barmby (67); Anderton (77); Sheringham (81)	19,951	G.Ashby
1994-95	Home	9-May-95	1-3	Anderton (83)	24,134	A.Wilkie
1995-96	Away	4-Nov-95	3-2	Fox (20); Sheringham (25); Howells (46)	17,545	J.Winter
1995-96	Home	30-Mar-96	3-1	Sheringham (50); Fox (51, 64)	26,808	R.Hart
1996-97	Away	7-Dec-96	2-1	Sheringham (26); Sinton (75)	19,675	G.Willard
1996-97	Home	11-May-97	1-2	McVeigh (44)	33,029	M.Bodenham
1997-98	Away	13-Dec-97	0-4		19,499	S.Dunn
1997-98	Home	13-Apr-98	1-1	Berti (68)	33,463	M.Riley
1998-99	Away	26-Dec-98	1-1	Campbell (17)	23,098	K.Burge
1998-99	Home	6-Feb-99	0-0		34,376	S.Lodge
1999-00	Home	19-Sep-99	3-2	Iversen (7); Armstrong (50); Leonhardsen (51);	35,224	A.D'Urso
1999-00	Away	26-Feb-00	1-0	Armstrong (82)	23,077	P.Durkin

CRYSTAL PALACE

Season	Venue	Date	Res	Scorers	Attendance	Referee
1992-93	Home	22-Aug-92	2-2	Durie (16); Sedgley (88)	25,237	P.Don
1992-93	Away	30-Jan-93	3-1	Sheringham (15, 30); Gray (26)	20,937	D.Elleray
1994-95	Home	27-Dec-94	0-0		27,730	G.Willard
1994-95	Away	14-Apr-95	1-1	Klinsmann (87)	18,149	P.Don
1997-98	Home	24-Nov-97	0-1		25,634	P.Durkin
1997-98	Away	28-Mar-98	3-1	Berti (55); Armstrong (72); Klinsmann (77)	26,116	M.Reed

DERBY COUNTY

Season	Venue	Date	Res	Scorers	Attendance	Referee
1996-97	Home	21-Aug-96	1-1	Sheringham (33)	28,219	K.Burge
1996-97	Away	22-Mar-97	2-4	Rosenthal (29); Dozzell (50)	18,083	S.Dunn
1997-98	Home	23-Aug-97	1-0	Calderwood (45)	25,886	M.Bodenham
1997-98	Away	31-Jan-98	1-2	Fox (46)	30,187	G.Willard
1998-99	Away	3-Oct-98	1-0	Campbell (60)	30,083	D.Gallagher
1998-99	Home	27-Feb-99	1-1	Sherwood (69)	35,392	J.Winter
1999-00	Away	16-Oct-99	1-0	Armstrong (37)	29,815	P.Durkin
1999-00	Home	29-Apr-00	1-1	Clemence (90)	33,044	N.Barry

EVERTON

Season	Venue	Date	Res	Scorers	Attendance	Referee
1992-93	Home	5-Sep-92	2-1	Allen,P. (79); Turner (90)	26,303	R.Hart
1992-93	Away	10-Feb-93	2-1	Mabbutt (26); Allen (69)	16,164	K.Barratt
1993-94	Home	3-Oct-93	3-2	Sheringham (58); Anderton (88); Caskey (90)	27,487	R.Milford
1993-94	Away	26-Mar-94	1-0	Sedgley (70)	23,460	K.Barratt
1994-95	Home	24-Aug-94	2-1	Klinsmann (21,35)	24,553	G.Willard
1994-95	Away	17-Dec-94	0-0		32,809	K.Cooper
1995-96	Away	22-Oct-95	1-1	Armstrong (37)	33,629	R.Dilkes
1995-96	Home	2-Dec-95	0-0		32,894	S.Dunn
1996-97	Home	24-Aug-96	0-0		29,696	L.Dilkes
1996-97	Away	12-Apr-97	0-1		36,380	G.Willard
1997-98	Away	29-Nov-97	2-0	Vega (71); Ginola (75)	36,670	P.Jones
1997-98	Home	4-Apr-98	1-1	Armstrong (73)	35,624	A.Wilkie
1998-99	Away	29-Aug-98	1-0	Ferdinand (5)	39,378	P.Jones
1998-99	Home	28-Dec-98	4-1	Ferdinand (24); Armstrong (63, 76, 81)	36,053	G.Poll
1999-00	Home	14-Aug-99	3-2	Sherwood (34); Leonhardsen (82); Iversen (86)	34,539	P.Alcock
1999-00	Away	15-Jan-00	2-2	Armstrong (24); Ginola (28)	36,144	A.Wiley

IPSWICH TOWN

Season	Venue	Date	Res	Scorers	Attendance	Referee
1992-93	Away	30-Aug-92	1-1	Cundy (29)	20,100	K.Hackett
1992-93	Home	27-Jan-93	0-2		23,738	S.Lodge
1993-94	Away	26-Sep-93	2-2	Sheringham (28); Dozzell (87)	19,437	G.Ashby
1993-94	Home	19-Mar-94	1-1	Barmby (56)	26,653	G.Ashby
1994-95	Away	30-Aug-94	3-1	Klinsmann (15,38); Dumitrescu (28)	22,559	R.Gifford
1994-95	Home	8-Mar-95	3-0	Klinsman (2); Barmby (15); OG (83, Youds)	24,930	B.Hill

LEEDS UNITED

Season	Venue	Date	Res	Scorers	Attendance	Referee
1992-93	Away	25-Aug-92	0-5		28,218	M.Reed
1992-93	Home	20-Feb-93	4-0	Sheringham (8, 37, 67pen); Ruddock (48)	32,040	G.Ashby
1993-94	Home	20-Nov-93	1-1	Anderton (80)	31,275	J.Worrall
1993-94	Away	17-Apr-94	0-2		33,658	R.Milford
1994-95	Away	15-Oct-94	1-1	Sheringham (27)	39,224	K.Cooper
1994-95	Home	14-May-95	1-1	Sherringham (30)	33,040	P.Durkin
1995-96	Home	9-Sep-95	2-1	Howells (27); Sheringham (66)	30,034	P.Durkin
1995-96	Away	2-May-96	3-1	Armstrong (18); Anderton (24, 66)	30,061	M.Bodenham
1996-97	Away	14-Dec-96	0-0		33,783	P.Durkin
1996-97	Home	15-Mar-97	1-0	Anderton (26)	33,040	D.Gallagher

1997-98	Home	1-Nov-97	0-1		26,441	K.Burge
1997-98	Away	4-Mar-98	0-1		31,394	P.Alcock
1998-99	Home	27-Sep-98	3-3	Vega (14); Iversen (71); Campbell (90)	35,535	P.Durkin
1998-99	Away	10-Mar-99	0-2		34,521	N.Barry
1999-00	Home	28-Aug-99	1-2	Sherwood (36)	36,012	M.Reed
1999-00	Away	12-Feb-00	0-1		40,127	D.Gallagher

LEICESTER CITY

Season	Venue	Date	Res	Scorers	Attendance	Referee
1994-95	Away	17-Sep-94	1-3	Klinsmann (88)	21,300	G.Ashby
1994-95	Home	18-Mar-95	1-0	Klinsmann (82)	30,851	S.Lodge
1996-97	Home	22-Sep-96	1-2	Wilson (64 pen)	24,159	A.Wilkie
1996-97	Away	19-Mar-97	1-1	Sheringham (90)	20,593	R.Dilkes
1997-98	Away	13-Sep-97	0-3		20,683	A.Wilkie
1997-98	Home	14-Feb-98	1-1	Calderwood (51)	28,355	S.Lodge
1998-99	Away	19-Oct-98	1-2	Ferdinand (12)	20,787	M.Riley
1998-99	Home	3-Apr-99	0-2		35,415	N.Barry
1999-00	Home	3-Oct-99	2-3	Iversen (26, 35)	35,591	G.Barber
1999-00	Away	19-Apr-00	1-0	Ginola (90)	19,764	J.Winter

LIVERPOOL

Season	Venue	Date	Res	Scorers	Attendance	Referee
1992-93	Home	31-Oct-92	2-0	Nayim (63); Ruddock (72)	32,917	G.Ashby
1992-93	Away	8-May-93	2-6	Sheringham (46); Sedgley (77)	43,385	S.Lodge
1993-94	Away	25-Aug-93	2-1	Sheringham (30 pen, 42)	42,456	K.Barratt
1993-94	Home	18-Dec-93	3-3	Samway (36); Hazard (68 pen); Caskey (76)	31,394	R.Hart
1994-95	Away	26-Nov-94	1-1	OG (77, Ruddock)	35,007	S.Lodge
1994-95	Home	22-Mar-95	0-0		31,988	P.Danson
1995-96	Home	26-Aug-95	1-3	Dumitrescu (87)	31,254	K.Cooper
1995-96	Away	3-Feb-96	0-0		40,628	S.Lodge
1996-97	Home	2-Dec-96	0-2		32,899	G.Poll
1996-97	Away	3-May-97	1-2	Anderton (5)	40,003	M.Reed
1997-98	Away	8-Nov-97	0-4		38,005	S.Lodge
1997-98	Home	14-Mar-98	3-3	Klinsmann (12); Ginola (48); Vega (80)	30,245	U.Rennie
1998-99	Home	5-Dec-98	2-1	Fox (26); OG (50, Carragher)	36,521	G.Barber
1998-99	Away	1-May-99	2-3	OG (13, Carragher); Iversen (35)	44,007	S.Lodge
1999-00	Home	3-Jan-00	1-0	Armstrong (23)	36,044	A.Wilkie
1999-00	Away	9-Apr-00	0-2		44,536	S.Lodge

MANCHESTER CITY

Season	Venue	Date	Res	Scorers	Attendance	Referee
1992-93	Away	28-Nov-92	1-0	Watson (77)	25,496	D.Allison
1992-93	Home	24-Mar-93	3-1	Anderton (23); Nayim (43); Bergsson (87)	27,247	J.Martin
1993-94	Home	21-Aug-93	1-0	Sedgley (70)	24,535	K.Hackett
1993-94	Away	11-Dec-93	2-0	Dozzell (64,88)	21,566	G.Poll
1994-95	Away	22-Oct-94	2-5	Dumitrescu (29 pen,46)	25,473	D.Elleray
1994-95	Home	11-Apr-95	2-1	Howells (53); Klinsmann (85)	27,410	A.Wilkie
1995-96	Away	19-Aug-95	1-1	Sheringham (33)	30,827	G.Poll
1995-96	Home	13-Jan-96	1-0	Armstrong (65)	31,438	D.Gallagher

MANCHESTER UNITED

Season	Venue	Date	Res	Scorers	Attendance	Referee
1992-93	Home	19-Sep-92	1-1	Durie (52)	33,296	R.Groves
1992-93	Away	9-Jan-93	1-4	Barmby (88)	35,648	M.Peck
1993-94	Away	16-Oct-93	1-2	Caskey (72)	44,655	K.Burge
1993-94	Home	15-Jan-94	0-1		31,343	R.Milford
1994-95	Home	27-Aug-94	0-1		24,502	K.Burge
1994-95	Away	15-Mar-95	0-0		43,802	K.Morton
1995-96	Home	1-Jan-96	4-1	Sheringham (35); Campbell (45); Armstrong (48, 66)	32,852	G.Ashby
1995-96	Away	24-Mar-96	0-1		50,157	G.Ashby
1996-97	Away	29-Sep-96	0-2		54,943	G.Willard
1996-97	Home	12-Jan-97	1-2	Allen (43)	33,028	M.Bodenham
1997-98	Home	10-Aug-97	0-2		26,359	G.Poll
1997-98	Away	10-Jan-98	0-2		55,281	P.Alcock
1998-99	Home	12-Dec-98	2-2	Campbell (70, 90)	36,070	U.Rennie
1998-99	Away	16-May-99	1-2	Ferdinand (24)	55,189	G.Poll
1999-00	Home	23-Oct-99	3-1	Iversen (37); OG (40, Scholes); Carr (71)	36,072	J.Winter
1999-00	Away	6-May-00	1-3	Armstrong (20)	61,629	A.Wilkie

MIDDLESBROUGH

Season	Venue	Date	Res	Scorers	Attendance	Referee
1992-93	Home	17-Oct-92	2-2	Sheringham (70 pen); Barmby (73)	24,735	P.Durkin
1992-93	Away	20-Apr-93	0-3		14,472	D.Allison
1995-96	Away	21-Nov-95	1-0	Armstrong (71)	29,487	M.Reed
1995-96	Home	8-Apr-96	1-1	Armstrong (84)	32,036	P.Jones
1996-97	Away	19-Oct-96	3-0	Sheringham (21, 89); Fox (23)	30,215	S.Lodge
1996-97	Home	24-Apr-97	1-0	Sinton (71)	29,947	P.Durkin
1998-99	Home	13-Sep-98	0-3		30,437	S.Dunn
1998-99	Away	20-Feb-99	0-0		34,687	R.Harris
1999-00	Away	18-Dec-99	1-2	Vega (7)	33,129	S.Dunn
1999-00	Home	3-Apr-00	2-3	Armstrong (31); Ginola (83)	31,796	A.Wiley

NEWCASTLE UNITED

Season	Venue	Date	Res	Scorers	Attendance	Referee
1993-94	Away	14-Aug-93	1-0	Sheringham (36)	34,565	D.Allison
1993-94	Home	4-Dec-93	1-2	Barmby (60 pen)	30,780	M.Reed
1994-95	Home	3-Dec-94	4-2	Sheringham (14,38,70); Popescu (79)	28,002	D.Gallagher
1994-95	Away	3-May-95	3-3	Barmby (22); Klinsmann (24); Anderton (26)	35,603	D.Gallagher
1995-96	Home	29-Oct-95	1-1	Armstrong (21)	32,279	M.Bodenham
1995-96	Away	5-May-96	1-1	Dozzell (57)	36,589	D.Gallagher
1996-97	Home	7-Sep-96	1-2	Allen (28)	32,535	P.Durkin
1996-97	Away	28-Dec-96	1-7	Nielsen (88)	36,308	G.Ashby
1997-98	Away	4-Oct-97	0-1		36,709	M.Bodenham
1997-98	Home	25-Apr-98	2-0	Klinsmann (31); Ferdinand (72)	35,847	J.Winter
1998-99	Home	24-Oct-98	2-0	Iversen (40, 76)	36,047	G.Barber
1998-99	Away	5-Apr-99	1-1	Anderton (50 pen)	36,655	M.Riley
1999-00	Home	9-Aug-99	3-1	Iversen (29); Ferdinand (45); Sherwood (61)	28,701	R.Harris
1999-00	Away	28-Nov-99	1-2	Armstrong (44)	36,460	P.Alcock

NORWICH CITY

Season	Venue	Date	Res	Scorers	Attendance	Referee
1992-93	Away	26-Dec-92	0-0		19,413	J.Martin
1992-93	Home	9-Apr-93	5-1	Ruddock (27); Sheringham (30, 77); Barmby (55); Nayim (83)	31,425	K.Barratt
1993-94	Home	27-Dec-93	1-3	Barmby (74)	31,130	A.Gunn
1993-94	Away	2-Apr-94	2-1	Sheringham (56); OG (76, Woodthorpe)	21,181	A.Wilkie
1994-95	Away	26-Dec-94	2-0	Barmby (11); Sheringham (90)	21,814	R.Dilkes
1994-95	Home	17-Apr-95	1-0	Sheringham (36)	32,304	R.Gifford

NOTTINGHAM FOREST

Season	Venue	Date	Res	Scorers	Attendance	Referee
1992-93	Home	28-Dec-92	2-1	Barmby (35); Mabbutt (85)	32,118	M.Reed
1992-93	Away	12-Apr-93	1-2	Sedgley (44)	25,682	A.Wilkie
1994-95	Home	24-Sep-94	1-4	Dumitrescu (32)	24,558	R.Hart
1994-95	Away	4-Mar-95	2-2	Sheringham (79); Calderwood (87)	28,711	G.Ashby
1995-96	Home	14-Oct-95	0-1		32,876	R.Hart
1995-96	Away	6-Apr-96	1-2	Armstrong (80)	27,053	P.Alcock
1996-97	Away	19-Jan-97	1-2	Sinton (1)	27,303	J.Winter
1996-97	Home	1-Mar-97	0-1		32,805	J.Winter
1998-99	Home	21-Nov-98	2-0	Armstrong (59); Nielsen (69)	35,832	S.Lodge
1998-99	Away	17-Apr-99	1-0	Iversen (62)	25,181	G.Willard

OLDHAM ATHLETIC

Season	Venue	Date	Res	Scorers	Attendance	Referee
1992-93	Away	19-Dec-92	1-2	Sheringham (61)	11,735	R.Milford
1992-93	Home	17-Apr-93	4-1	Sheringham (58pen, 82pen); Anderton (70); Turner (84)	26,663	K.Hackett
1993-94	Home	18-Sep-93	5-0	Sedgley (5,8); Sheringham (6); Durie (62); Dozzell (86)	24,614	A.Gunn
1993-94	Away	5-May-94	2-0	Samways (37); Howells (78)	14,283	R.Gifford

QPR

Season	Venue	Date	Res	Scorers	Attendance	Referee
1992-93	Away	3-Oct-92	1-4	Sheringham (28)	19,845	J.Worrall
1992-93	Home	27-Feb-93	3-2	Sheringham (8, 34); Anderton (61)	32,341	D.Elleray
1993-94	Away	27-Nov-93	1-1	Anderton (87)	17,694	D.Elleray
1993-94	Home	7-May-94	1-2	Sheringham (39)	26,105	A.Gunn
1994-95	Home	8-Oct-94	1-1	Barmby (79)	25,799	P.Jones
1994-95	Away	6-May-95	1-2	Sheringham (45)	18,367	G.Poll
1995-96	Away	25-Sep-95	3-2	Sheringham (48 pen, 75); Dozzell (73)	15,659	D.Elleray
1995-96	Home	9-Dec-95	1-0	Sheringham (3)	28,851	K.Cooper

SHEFFIELD UNITED

Season	Venue	Date	Res	Scorers	Attendance	Referee
1992-93	Home	2-Sep-92	2-0	Sheringham (43); Durie (46)	21,322	I.Mitchell (G.Pearson, 72)
1992-93	Away	2-Mar-93	0-6		16,654	J.Worrall
1993-94	Away	11-Sep-93	2-2	Sheringham (15,51)	21,325	K.Morton
1993-94	Home	5-Mar-94	2-2	Scott (64); Dozzell (90)	25,741	D.Allison

SHEFFIELD WEDNESDAY

Season	Venue	Date	Res	Scorers	Attendance	Referee
1992-93	Away	27-Sep-92	0-2		24,895	M.Peck
1992-93	Home	16-Jan-93	0-2		25,702	K.Morton
1993-94	Away	3-Jan-94	0-1		32,514	K.Burge
1993-94	Home	5-Feb-94	1-3	Rosenthal (66)	23,078	D.Frampton
1994-95	Away	20-Aug-94	4-3	Sheringham (19); Anderton (30); Barmby (71); Klinsmann (82)	34,051	B.Hill
1994-95	Home	10-Dec-94	3-1	Barmby (60); Klinsmann (70); Calderwood (79)	25,912	M.Bodenham
1995-96	Away	16-Sep-95	3-1	Sheringham (32, 65 pen); OG (6, Walker)	26,565	D.Gallagher
1995-96	Home	24-Feb-96	1-0	Armstrong (31)	32,047	M.Reed
1996-97	Home	21-Dec-96	1-1	Neilson (29)	30,996	M.Riley
1996-97	Away	9-Mar-97	1-2	Nielsen (43)	22,667	A.Wilkie
1997-98	Home	19-Oct-97	3-2	Ginola (45); Dominguez (6); Armstrong (39)	25,097	J.Winter
1997-98	Away	21-Feb-98	0-1		29,871	M.Bodenham
1998-99	Home	22-Aug-98	0-3		32,129	M.Reed
1998-99	Away	9-Jan-99	0-0		28,204	G.Willard
1999-00	Away	21-Aug-99	2-1	Ferdinand (19); Leonhardsen (41)	24,027	A.D'Urso
1999-00	Home	22-Jan-00	0-1		35,897	M.Riley

SOUTHAMPTON

Season	Venue	Date	Res	Scorers	Attendance	Referee
1992-93	Away	15-Aug-92	0-0		19,654	V.Callow
1992-93	Home	7-Feb-93	4-2	Sheringham (54, 59); Barmby (56); Anderton (57)	20,098	K.Redfern
1993-94	Away	6-Nov-93	0-1		16,017	D.Allison
1993-94	Home	23-Apr-94	3-0	Sedgley (5); Samways (67); Anderton (89)	25,959	P.Durkin
1994-95	Home	12-Sep-94	1-2	Klinsmann (6)	22,387	A.Wilkie
1994-95	Away	2-Apr-95	3-4	Sheringham (17); Klinsmann (35,59)	15,105	G.Willard
1995-96	Away	26-Dec-95	0-0		15,238	P.Durkin
1995-96	Home	2-Mar-96	1-0	Dozzell (63)	26,320	K.Burge
1996-97	Away	14-Sep-96	1-0	Armstrong (65 pen)	15,251	P.Alcock
1996-97	Home	26-Dec-96	3-1	Iversen (1, 30); Nielsen (63)	30,549	G.Barber
1997-98	Away	25-Oct-97	2-3	Dominguez (41); Ginola (54)	15,225	N.Barry
1997-98	Home	10-May-98	1-1	Klinsmann (27)	35,995	P.Jones
1998-99	Away	19-Sep-98	1-1	Fox (25)	15,204	K.Burge
1998-99	Home	2-Mar-99	3-0	Armstrong (19); Iversen (68); Dominguez (90)	28,580	A.Wilkie (S.Tomlin 23)
1999-00	Away	20-Nov-99	1-0	Leonhardsen (81)	15,248	S.Bennett
1999-00	Home	11-Mar-00	7-2	OG (28, Richards); Anderton (39); Armstrong (41, 64); Iversen (45, 78, 90)	36,024	M.Halsey

SUNDERLAND

Season	Venue	Date	Res	Scorers	Attendance	Referee
1996-97	Home	16-Nov-96	2-0	Sinton (13); Sheringham (82)	31,867	M.Reed
1996-97	Away	4-Mar-97	4-0	Iversen (2, 9, 64); Nielsen (26)	20,785	M.Riley
1999-00	Away	31-Oct-99	1-2	Iversen (63)	41,904	M.Riley
1999-00	Home	14-May-00	3-1	Anderton (11 pen); Sherwood (73); Carr (83)	36,070	M.Riley

SWINDON TOWN

Season	Venue	Date	Res	Scorers	Attendance	Referee
1993-94	Home	23-Oct-93	1-1	Dozzell (50)	31,394	K.Barratt
1993-94	Away	22-Jan-94	1-2	Barmby (30)	16,464	P.Durkin

WATFORD

Season	Venue	Date	Res	Scorers	Attendance	Referee
1999-00	Home	26-Dec-99	4-0	Ginola (28); Iversen (33); Sherwood (56, 83)	36,089	M.Reed
1999-00	Away	25-Mar-00	1-1	Armstrong (51)	20,050	U.Rennie

WEST HAM UNITED

Season	Venue	Date	Res	Scorers	Attendance	Referee
1993-94	Away	28-Dec-93	3-1	Dozzell (34); Hazard (42); Anderton (77)	20,787	G.Ashby
1993-94	Home	4-Apr-94	1-4	Sheringham (66pen)	31,502	P.Don
1994-95	Home	29-Oct-94	3-1	Klinsmann (18); Sheringham (48); Barmby (63)	26,271	K.Morton
1994-95	Away	14-Jan-95	2-1	Sheringham (59); Klinsmann (79)	24,573	B.Hill
1995-96	Away	30-Aug-95	1-1	Rosenthal (54)	23,516	M.Reed
1995-96	Home	12-Feb-96	0-1		29,781	J.Winter
1996-97	Home	2-Nov-96	1-0	Armstrong (67)	32,999	J.Winter
1996-97	Away	24-Feb-97	3-4	Sheringham (6); Anderton (28); Howells (53)	23,998	G.Willard
1997-98	Away	13-Aug-97	1-2	Ferdinand (81)	25,354	S.Lodge
1997-98	Home	17-Jan-98	1-0	Klinsmann (7)	30,284	D.Elleray
1998-99	Away	28-Nov-98	1-2	Armstrong (72)	26,044	D.Gallagher
1998-99	Home	24-Apr-99	1-2	Ginola (73)	36,089	U.Rennie
1999-00	Away	7-Aug-99	0-1		26,010	P.Durkin (D.Elleray 16)
1999-00	Home	6-Dec-99	0-0		36,233	P.Jones

WIMBLEDON

Season	Venue	Date	Res	Scorers	Attendance	Referee
1992-93	Away	25-Oct-92	1-1	Barmby (48)	8,628	A.Gunn
1992-93	Home	1-May-93	1-1	Anderton (39)	24,473	R.Lewis
1993-94	Home	24-Nov-93	1-1	Barmby (5)	17,744	K.Hackett
1993-94	Away	30-Apr-94	1-2	Sheringham (72 pen)	20,875	D.Allison
1994-95	Away	1-Oct-94	2-1	Sheringham (26); Popescu (61)	16,802	M.Reed
1994-95	Home	25-Feb-95	1-2	Klinsmann (49)	27,258	D.Gallagher
1995-96	Home	30-Sep-95	3-1	Sheringham (7, 32); OG (63, Elkins)	25,321	G.Ashby
1995-96	Away	16-Dec-95	1-0	Fox (85)	16,193	D.Elleray
1996-97	Away	3-Sep-96	0-1		17,506	S.Dunn
1996-97	Home	5-Apr-97	1-0	Dozzell (81)	32,654	K.Burge
1997-98	Home	27-Sep-97	0-0		26,261	P.Durkin
1997-98	Away	2-May-98	6-2	Ferdinand (17); Klinsmann (41,54,58,60); Saib (79)	25,820	G.Barber
1998-99	Away	15-Aug-98	1-3	Fox (75)	23,031	G.Poll
1998-99	Home	16-Jan-99	0-0		32,422	M.Riley
1999-00	Away	26-Sep-99	1-1	Carr (76)	17,368	G.Poll
1999-00	Home	22-Apr-00	2-0	Armstrong (8); Anderton (36)	33,086	D.Gallagher

INTRODUCTION

Founded in 1881 as Watford Rovers, they became West Herts in 1893 and then 'absorbed' Watford St Mary's FC in 1898 to become Watford FC. The club played its early football at the West Herts Sports Ground in Cassio Road. Playing in the Southern League they gained entry to the newly formed Football League Division 3 in 1920. In 1922 the team moved into a new ground at the Vicarage Road site, where they have played ever since. From 1982-88 they played in the old Division 1, finishing runners-up in their first season, when they were managed by current manager Graham Taylor. Taylor returned to the club and became team manager in May 1997 and immediately led them to successive promotions and a place in the Premier League via the play-offs.

Ground:	Vicarage Road Stadium, Watford, WD1 8ER
Nickname:	The Hornets
Internet:	www.watfordfc.co.uk

HONOURS

Football League Div 1:	Runners-up 1982-83
Football League Div 2:	Champions 1997-98
	Runners-up 1981-82
Football League Div 3:	Champions 1968-69
	Runners-up 1978-79
Football League Div 4:	Champions 1977-78
FA Cup:	Runners-up 1983-84

EUROPEAN RECORD

Champions' League (0) –
Cup-Winners' Cup (0) –
UEFA (1)   1983-84

FAPL RECORD SUMMARY

Most Total:	PALMER, Steve	38
Most Starts:	PALMER, Steve	38
Most Subs:	SMITH, Tommy	9
Most SNU:	DAY, Chris	27
Most PS:	NGONGE, Michel	11
Most Goals:	HELGUSON, Heidar	6
Most Yel:	PAGE, Robert	13
Most Red:	COX, Neil	1

PLAYING RECORD – SEASON TOTALS

Season	Pn	P	W	D	L	F	A	Pts
1999-00	20	38	6	6	26	35	77	24
Totals		38	6	6	26	35	77	24

PLAYING RECORD – HOME TOTALS

Season	Pn	P	W	D	L	F	A	Pts
1999-00	20	19	5	4	10	24	31	19
Totals		19	5	4	10	24	31	19

PLAYING RECORD – AWAY TOTALS

Season	Pn	P	W	D	L	F	A	Pts
1999-00	20	19	1	2	16	11	46	5
Totals		19	1	2	16	11	46	5

HIGHEST HOME ATTENDANCES

	Attendance	Opponents	Date	Season
1	21,590	Sunderland	27-Nov-99	1999-00
2	21,367	Liverpool	15-Jan-00	1999-00
3	21,244	Chelsea	18-Sep-99	1999-00
4	20,250	Manchester U.	29-Apr-00	1999-00
5	20,050	Tottenham H.	25-Mar-00	1999-00

LOWEST HOME ATTENDANCES

	Attendance	Opponents	Date	Season
1	15,511	Wimbledon	7-Aug-99	1999-00
2	15,564	Bradford C.	21-Aug-99	1999-00
3	15,840	Sheffield W.	18-Mar-00	1999-00
4	16,081	Middlesbrough	24-Oct-99	1999-00
5	16,184	Leicester C.	12-Feb-00	1999-00

TOP SCORER – SEASON BY SEASON

Season	Player	Goals
1999-00	Helguson, Ngonge, Smart	5

PLAYERS WITH MOST PREMIERSHIP APPEARANCES

Tot	Player	St	Sb	Gls
38	PALMER, Steve	38	0	0
36	PAGE, Robert	36	0	1
34	HYDE, Micah	33	1	3
32	ROBINSON, Paul	29	3	0
27	CHAMBERLAIN, Alec	27	0	0
23	JOHNSON, Richard	20	3	3
23	NGONGE, Michel	16	7	5
22	WILLIAMS, Mark	20	2	1
22	SMITH, Tommy	13	9	2
21	COX, Neil	20	1	0
20	WOOTER, Nordin	16	4	1
18	KENNEDY, Peter	17	1	1

CLUB-BY-CLUB RESULTS

ARSENAL

Season	Venue	Date	Res	Scorers	Attendance	Referee
1999-00	Away	25-Sep-99	0-1		38,127	P.Durkin
1999-00	Home	23-Apr-00	2-3	Helguson (58); Hyde (60)	19,670	R.Harris

ASTON VILLA

Season	Venue	Date	Res	Scorers	Attendance	Referee
1999-00	Home	24-Aug-99	0-1		19,161	S.Bennett
1999-00	Away	5-Feb-00	0-4		27,647	P.Jones

BRADFORD CITY

Season	Venue	Date	Res	Scorers	Attendance	Referee
1999-00	Home	21-Aug-99	1-0	Mooney (71)	15,564	R.Harris
1999-00	Away	22-Jan-00	2-3	Hyde (33); Helguson (88)	16,864	P.Alcock

CHELSEA

Season	Venue	Date	Res	Scorers	Attendance	Referee
1999-00	Home	18-Sep-99	1-0	Smart (57)	21,244	M.Reed
1999-00	Away	26-Feb-00	1-2	Smart (39)	34,920	S.Dunn

COVENTRY CITY

Season	Venue	Date	Res	Scorers	Attendance	Referee
1999-00	Away	31-Oct-99	0-4		21,700	P.Durkin
1999-00	Home	14-May-00	1-0	Helguson (43)	18,977	U.Rennie

DERBY COUNTY

Season	Venue	Date	Res	Scorers	Attendance	Referee
1999-00	Away	3-Jan-00	0-2		28,072	B.Knight
1999-00	Home	8-Apr-00	0-0		16,579	S.Bennett

EVERTON

Season	Venue	Date	Res	Scorers	Attendance	Referee
1999-00	Home	18-Dec-99	1-3	Ngonge (60)	17,346	A.Wilkie
1999-00	Away	1-Apr-00	2-4	Smart (35); Hyde (80)	31,960	S.Dunn

LEEDS UNITED

Season	Venue	Date	Res	Scorers	Attendance	Referee
1999-00	Home	3-Oct-99	1-2	Williams (42)	19,677	A.D'Urso
1999-00	Away	3-May-00	1-3	Foley (25)	36,324	P.Alcock

LEICESTER CITY

Season	Venue	Date	Res	Scorers	Attendance	Referee
1999-00	Away	30-Aug-99	0-1		17,920	N.Barry
1999-00	Home	12-Feb-00	1-1	Wooter (47)	16,184	A.D'Urso

LIVERPOOL

Season	Venue	Date	Res	Scorers	Attendance	Referee
1999-00	Away	14-Aug-99	1-0	Mooney (14)	44,174	A.Wilkie
1999-00	Home	15-Jan-00	2-3	Johnson,R. (44); Helguson (46)	21,367	S.Lodge

MANCHESTER UNITED

Season	Venue	Date	Res	Scorers	Attendance	Referee
1999-00	Away	16-Oct-99	1-4	Johnson,R. (68)	55,188	P.Jones
1999-00	Home	29-Apr-00	2-3	Helguson (33); Smith (78)	20,250	S.Lodge

MIDDLESBROUGH

Season	Venue	Date	Res	Scorers	Attendance	Referee
1999-00	Home	24-Oct-99	1-3	Smith (53)	16,081	A.Wiley
1999-00	Away	6-May-00	1-1	Ward (68)	32,930	P.Jones

NEWCASTLE UNITED

Season	Venue	Date	Res	Scorers	Attendance	Referee
1999-00	Home	20-Nov-99	1-1	Ngonge (53)	19,539	S.Dunn
1999-00	Away	11-Mar-00	0-1		36,433	A.Wiley

SHEFFIELD WEDNESDAY

Season	Venue	Date	Res	Scorers	Attendance	Referee
1999-00	Away	6-Nov-99	2-2	Ngonge (21); Page (59)	21,658	J.Winter
1999-00	Home	18-Mar-00	1-0	Smart (88)	15,840	N.Barry

SOUTHAMPTON

Season	Venue	Date	Res	Scorers	Attendance	Referee
1999-00	Home	28-Dec-99	3-2	Perpetuini (17); Gravelaine (31, 65)	18,459	M.Riley
1999-00	Away	15-Apr-00	0-2		15,242	A.Wilkie

SUNDERLAND

Season	Venue	Date	Res	Scorers	Attendance	Referee
1999-00	Away	10-Aug-99	0-2		40,630	J.Winter
1999-00	Home	27-Nov-99	2-3	Ngonge (4); Johnson,R. (49 pen)	21,590	U.Rennie

TOTTENHAM HOTSPUR

Season	Venue	Date	Res	Scorers	Attendance	Referee
1999-00	Away	26-Dec-99	0-4		36,089	M.Reed
1999-00	Home	25-Mar-00	1-1	Smart (78)	20,050	U.Rennie

WEST HAM UNITED

Season	Venue	Date	Res	Scorers	Attendance	Referee
1999-00	Away	11-Sep-99	0-1		25,310	D.Gallagher
1999-00	Home	4-Mar-00	1-2	Helguson (61)	18,619	M.Reed

WIMBLEDON

Season	Venue	Date	Res	Scorers	Attendance	Referee
1999-00	Home	7-Aug-99	2-3	Kennedy (17 pen); Ngonge (71)	15,511	S.Lodge
1999-00	Away	4-Dec-99	0-5		14,021	A.Wiley

INTRODUCTION

Thames Ironworks founded 1895, to give recreation for the shipyard workers. Several different grounds were used as the club entered the London League (1896) and won the championship (1898). In 1899, having become professional, won the Southern League Second Division (London) and moved into Division One.

On becoming a limited liability company the name was changed to West Ham United. Moved from the Memorial Ground to a pitch in the Upton Park area, known originally as 'The Castle', in 1904. Elected to an expanded Football League Division Two for the 1919-20 season and never subsequently out of the top two divisions.

Ground: Boleyn Ground, Green Street,
             Upton Park, London E13 9AZ
Nickname: The Hammers
Internet: www.westhamunited.co.uk

HONOURS

Football League Div 1:	Runners-up 1992-93
Football League Div 2:	Champions 1957-58, 1980-81
	Runners-up 1922-23, 1990-91
FA Cup:	Winners 1964, 1975, 1980
	Runners-up 1922-23
Football League Cup:	Runners-up 1966, 1981
Cup-Winners' Cup:	Winners 1964-65
	Runners-up 1975-76

EUROPEAN RECORD

Champions' League (0):	–
Cup Winners' Cup (4):	64-65 (W), 65-66 (SF), 75-76 (F), 80-81 (QF)
UEFA Cup (1):	99-00

FAPL RECORD SUMMARY

Most Total:	POTTS, Steve	196
Most Starts:	POTTS, Steve	175
Most Subs:	POTTS, Steve	21
Most SNU:	SEALEY, Les	92
Most PS:	MONCUR, John	25
Most Goals:	HARTSON, John	24
Most Yel:	MONCUR, John	42
Most Red:	LOMAS, Steve	3

PLAYING RECORD – SEASON TOTALS

Season	Pn	P	W	D	L	F	A	Pts
1993-94	13	42	13	13	16	47	58	52
1994-95	14	42	13	11	18	44	48	50
1995-96	10	38	14	9	15	43	52	51
1996-97	14	38	10	12	16	39	48	42
1997-98	8	38	16	8	14	56	57	56
1998-99	5	38	16	9	13	46	53	57
1999-00	9	38	15	10	13	52	53	55
Totals		274	97	72	105	327	369	363

PLAYING RECORD – HOME TOTALS

Season	Pn	P	W	D	L	F	A	Pts
1993-94	13	21	6	7	8	26	31	25
1994-95	14	21	9	6	6	28	19	33
1995-96	10	19	9	5	5	25	21	32
1996-97	14	19	7	6	6	27	25	27
1997-98	8	19	13	4	2	40	18	43
1998-99	5	19	11	3	5	32	26	36
1999-00	9	19	11	5	3	32	23	38
Totals		137	66	36	35	210	163	234

PLAYING RECORD – AWAY TOTALS

Season	Pn	P	W	D	L	F	A	Pts
1993-94	13	21	7	6	8	21	27	27
1994-95	14	21	4	5	12	16	29	17
1995-96	10	19	5	4	10	18	31	19
1996-97	14	19	3	6	10	12	23	15
1997-98	8	19	3	4	12	16	39	13
1998-99	5	19	5	6	8	14	27	21
1999-00	9	19	4	5	10	20	30	17
Totals		137	31	36	70	117	206	129

HIGHEST HOME ATTENDANCES

	Attendance	Opponents	Date	Season
1	28,382	Manchester U.	26-Feb-94	1993-94
2	26,952	Southampton	7-May-94	1993-94
3	26,106	Liverpool	23-Apr-94	1993-94
4	26,081	Sunderland	24-Oct-99	1999-00
5	26,044	Tottenham H.	28-Nov-98	1998-99
=	26,044	Leeds U.	14-May-00	1999-00

LOWEST HOME ATTENDANCES

	Attendance	Opponents	Date	Season
1	14,554	Sheffield W.	23-Jan-95	1994-95
2	15,777	Swindon T.	11-Sep-93	1993-94
3	16,605	Manchester C.	1-Nov-93	1993-94
4	16,959	Crystal P.	8-Oct-94	1994-95
5	17,211	Oldham A.	20-Nov-93	1993-94

TOP SCORER – SEASON BY SEASON

WEST HAM UNITED

Season	Player	Goals
1993-94	Morley	13
1994-95	Cottee	13
1995-96	Cottee	10
1996-97	Kitson	8
1997-98	Hartson	15
1998-99	Wright	9
1999-00	Di Canio	16

Tot	Player	St	Sb	Gls
196	POTTS, Steve	175	21	0
169	MIKLOSKO, Ludek	169	0	0
143	BREACKER, Tim	134	9	3
134	BISHOP, Ian	131	3	4
133	MONCUR, John	118	15	6
118	LAMPARD, Frank	102	16	16
115	FERDINAND, Rio	110	5	2
110	DICKS, Julian	110	0	21
95	LOMAS, Steve	95	0	4
90	RIEPER, Marc	83	7	5

PLAYERS WITH MOST PREMIERSHIP APPEARANCES

CLUB-BY-CLUB RESULTS

ARSENAL

Season	Venue	Date	Res	Scorers	Attendance	Referee
1993-94	Home	24-Nov-93	0-0		20,279	P.Durkin
1993-94	Away	30-Apr-94	2-0	Morley (77); Allen,M. (88)	33,700	R.Milford
1994-95	Home	25-Sep-94	0-2		18,498	K.Cooper
1994-95	Away	5-Mar-95	1-0	Hutchison (20)	36,295	B.Hill
1995-96	Away	16-Sep-95	0-1		38,065	A.Wilkie
1995-96	Home	24-Feb-96	0-1		24,217	D.Elleray
1996-97	Away	17-Aug-96	0-2		38,056	P.Durkin
1996-97	Home	29-Jan-97	1-2	OG (64, Rose)	24,382	M.Bodenham
1997-98	Away	24-Sep-97	0-4		38,012	P.Alcock
1997-98	Home	2-Mar-98	0-0		25,717	P.Durkin
1998-99	Away	26-Dec-98	0-1		38,098	P.Jones
1998-99	Home	6-Feb-99	0-4		26,042	J.Winter
1999-00	Home	3-Oct-99	2-1	Di Canio (29, 72)	26,009	M.Reed
1999-00	Away	2-May-00	1-2	Di Canio (40)	38,093	P.Durkin

ASTON VILLA

Season	Venue	Date	Res	Scorers	Attendance	Referee
1993-94	Home	16-Oct-93	0-0		20,416	S.Lodge
1993-94	Away	15-Jan-94	1-3	Allen,M. (30)	28,869	S.Lodge
1994-95	Home	17-Sep-94	1-0	Cottee (86)	18,326	S.Lodge
1994-95	Away	18-Mar-95	2-0	Moncur (11); Hutchison (49)	28,682	M.Bodenham
1995-96	Home	4-Nov-95	1-4	Dicks (85 pen)	23,637	P.Jones
1995-96	Away	17-Apr-96	1-1	Cottee (84)	26,768	S.Dunn
1996-97	Home	4-Dec-96	0-2		19,105	M.Riley
1996-97	Away	15-Mar-97	0-0		35,995	D.Elleray
1997-98	Home	29-Nov-97	2-1	Hartson (18, 47)	24,976	P.Alcock
1997-98	Away	4-Apr-98	0-2		39,372	S.Dunn
1998-99	Home	17-Oct-98	0-0		26,002	P.Alcock
1998-99	Away	2-Apr-99	0-0		36,813	G.Willard
1999-00	Away	16-Aug-99	2-2	OG (7, Southgate); Sinclair (90)	26,250	M.Riley
1999-00	Home	15-Jan-00	1-1	Di Canio (78)	24,237	G.Poll

BARNSLEY

Season	Venue	Date	Res	Scorers	Attendance	Referee
1997-98	Away	9-Aug-97	2-1	Hartson (56); Lampard (77)	18,667	A.Wilkie
1997-98	Home	10-Jan-98	6-0	Lampard (5); Abou (28, 52); Moncur (57);		
				Hartson (45); Lazaridis (89)	23,714	N.Barry

BLACKBURN ROVERS

Season	Venue	Date	Res	Scorers	Attendance	Referee
1993-94	Away	18-Sep-93	2-0	Chapman (33); Morley (71)	14,437	K.Hackett
1993-94	Home	27-Apr-94	1-2	Allen,M. (64)	22,186	T.Holbrook
1994-95	Away	2-Jan-95	2-4	Cottee (33); Dicks (58)	25,503	K.Morton
1994-95	Home	30-Apr-95	2-0	Rieper (50); Hutchison (83)	24,202	K.Morton
1995-96	Home	21-Oct-95	1-1	Dowie (25)	21,776	S.Lodge
1995-96	Away	2-Dec-95	2-4	Dicks (75 pen); Slater (86)	26,638	K.Burge
1996-97	Home	26-Oct-96	2-1	Porfirio (76); OG (83, Berg)	23,947	M.Reed
1996-97	Away	1-Feb-97	1-2	Ferdinand (64)	21,994	A.Wilkie
1997-98	Away	20-Dec-97	0-3		21,653	G.Ashby
1997-98	Home	18-Apr-98	2-1	Hartson (6, 26)	24,733	P.Durkin
1998-99	Away	3-Oct-98	0-3		25,213	K.Burge
1998-99	Home	27-Feb-99	2-0	Pearce (28); Di Canio (31)	25,529	S.Dunn

BOLTON WANDERERS

Season	Venue	Date	Res	Scorers	Attendance	Referee
1995-96	Away	18-Nov-95	3-0	Bishop (46); Cottee (68); Williamson (89)	19,047	P.Durkin
1995-96	Home	13-Apr-96	1-0	Cottee (28)	23,086	A.Wilkie
1997-98	Home	18-Oct-97	3-0	Berkovic (69); Hartson (78, 89)	24,867	G.Ashby
1997-98	Away	21-Feb-98	1-1	Sinclair (66)	25,000	P.Alcock

BRADFORD CITY

Season	Venue	Date	Res	Scorers	Attendance	Referee
1999-00	Away	28-Aug-99	3-0	Di Canio (34); Sinclair (44); Wanchope (49)	17,936	P.Jones
1999-00	Home	12-Feb-00	5-4	Sinclair (35); Moncur (43); Di Canio (65 pen);		
				Cole (70); Lampard (83)	25,417	N.Barry

CHARLTON ATHLETIC

Season	Venue	Date	Res	Scorers	Attendance	Referee
1998-99	Away	24-Oct-98	2-4	OG (17, Rufus); Berkovic (40)	20,043	N.Barry
1998-99	Home	5-Apr-99	0-1		26,041	S.Dunn

CHELSEA

Season	Venue	Date	Res	Scorers	Attendance	Referee
1993-94	Home	2-Oct-93	1-0	Morley (43)	18,917	R.Hart
1993-94	Away	26-Mar-94	0-2		19,545	M.Bodenham
1994-95	Away	2-Oct-94	2-1	Allen (53); Moncur (67)	18,696	P.Don
1994-95	Home	25-Feb-95	1-2	Hutchison (11)	21,500	G.Ashby
1995-96	Home	11-Sep-95	1-3	Hutchison (73)	19,228	R.Hart
1995-96	Away	17-Feb-96	2-1	Dicks (62); Williamson (72)	25,252	G.Willard
1996-97	Away	21-Dec-96	1-3	Porfirio (11)	28,315	A.Wilkie
1996-97	Home	12-Mar-97	3-2	Dicks (54 pen); Kitson (68, 90)	24,502	K.Burge
1997-98	Away	9-Nov-97	1-2	Hartson (84 pen)	34,382	G.Barber

1997-98	Home	14-Mar-98	2-1	Sinclair (67); Unsworth (73)	25,829	M.Bodenham
1998-99	Home	8-Nov-98	1-1	Ruddock (4)	26,023	G.Barber
1998-99	Away	13-Mar-99	1-0	Kitson (75)	34,765	S.Lodge
1999-00	Away	7-Nov-99	0-0		34,935	M.Riley
1999-00	Home	18-Mar-00	0-0		26,041	S.Dunn

COVENTRY CITY

Season	Venue	Date	Res	Scorers	Attendance	Referee
1993-94	Away	21-Aug-93	1-1	Gordon (44)	12,864	S.Lodge
1993-94	Home	11-Dec-93	3-2	Breacker (11); Butler (40); Morley (59 pen)	17,243	K.Cooper
1994-95	Home	26-Nov-94	0-1		17,251	M.Reed
1994-95	Away	18-Feb-95	0-2		17,556	R.Dilkes
1995-96	Home	31-Jan-96	3-2	Rieper (46); Cottee (59); Dowie (85)	18,884	G.Poll
1995-96	Away	2-Mar-96	2-2	Cottee (2); Rieper (22)	17,448	M.Bodenham
1996-97	Home	21-Aug-96	1-1	Rieper (78)	21,580	S.Dunn
1996-97	Away	22-Mar-97	3-1	Hartson (27); Ferdinand (33)	22,291	M.Reed
1997-98	Away	27-Aug-97	1-1	Kitson (64)	18,289	N.Barry
1997-98	Home	26-Dec-97	1-0	Kitson (17)	22,477	G.Poll
1998-99	Away	29-Aug-98	0-0		20,818	N.Barry
1998-99	Home	28-Dec-98	2-0	Wright (7); Hartson (68)	25,662	P.Durkin
1999-00	Away	25-Sep-99	0-1		19,993	D.Elleray
1999-00	Home	22-Apr-00	5-0	Carrick (7); Margas (14); di Canio (48, 67); Kanoute (83)	24,719	A.D'Urso

CRYSTAL PALACE

Season	Venue	Date	Res	Scorers	Attendance	Referee
1994-95	Home	8-Oct-94	1-0	Hutchinson (71)	16,959	G.Poll
1994-95	Away	6-May-95	0-1		18,224	S.Lodge
1997-98	Home	3-Dec-97	4-1	Hartson (30); Berkovic (45); Unsworth (47); Lomas (71)	23,335	D.Elleray
1997-98	Away	5-May-98	3-3	OG (4, Curcic); Omoyimni (68, 89)	19,129	G.Poll

DERBY COUNTY

Season	Venue	Date	Res	Scorers	Attendance	Referee
1996-97	Home	23-Nov-96	1-1	Bishop (16)	24,576	S.Lodge
1996-97	Away	15-Feb-97	0-1		18,057	G.Ashby
1997-98	Away	6-Dec-97	0-2		29,300	A.Wilkie
1997-98	Home	11-Apr-98	0-0		25,155	G.Barber
1998-99	Away	22-Nov-98	2-0	Hartson (7); Keller (72)	31,666	A.Wilkie
1998-99	Home	17-Apr-99	5-1	Di Canio (19); Berkovic (28); Wright (55); Ruddock (64); Sinclair (68)	25,485	K.Burge
1999-00	Home	28-Dec-99	1-1	Di Canio (21)	24,998	A.Wiley
1999-00	Away	15-Apr-00	2-1	Wanchope (15, 32)	31,202	M.Halsey

EVERTON

Season	Venue	Date	Res	Scorers	Attendance	Referee
1993-94	Away	1-Jan-94	1-0	Breacker (6)	19,602	J.Lloyd
1993-94	Home	9-Apr-94	0-1		20,243	P.Foakes
1994-95	Away	1-Nov-94	0-1		28,338	M.Bodenham
1994-95	Home	13-Feb-95	2-2	Cottee (22,60)	21,081	M.Reed
1995-96	Home	23-Sep-95	2-1	Dicks (7 pen, 41 pen)	21,085	P.Durkin
1995-96	Away	11-Dec-95	0-3		31,778	M.Reed

1996-97	Away	12-Oct-96	1-2	Dicks (85 pen)	36,571	G.Barber
1996-97	Home	19-Apr-97	2-2	Kitson (10, 32)	24,525	P.Alcock
1997-98	Away	23-Aug-97	1-2	OG (23, Watson)	34,356	P.Jones
1997-98	Home	31-Jan-98	2-2	Sinclair (9, 47)	25,905	M.Reed
1998-99	Home	19-Dec-98	2-1	Keller (19); Sinclair (75)	25,998	R.Harris
1998-99	Away	8-May-99	0-6		40,049	A.Wilkie
1999-00	Away	19-Sep-99	0-1		35,154	S.Bennett
1999-00	Home	26-Feb-00	0-4		26,025	P.Alcock

IPSWICH TOWN

Season	Venue	Date	Res	Scorers	Attendance	Referee
1993-94	Away	27-Dec-93	1-1	Chapman (77)	20,988	G.Poll
1993-94	Home	2-Apr-94	2-1	Rush (17); Morley (75)	18,307	D.Elleray
1994-95	Home	26-Dec-94	1-1	Cottee (16)	20,542	P.Durkin
1994-95	Away	17-Apr-95	1-1	Boere (90)	19,099	M.Bodenham

LEEDS UNITED

Season	Venue	Date	Res	Scorers	Attendance	Referee
1993-94	Away	17-Aug-93	0-1		34,588	R.Dilkes
1993-94	Home	8-Dec-93	0-1		20,468	J.Borrett
1994-95	Home	20-Aug-94	0-0		18,610	K.Burge
1994-95	Away	10-Dec-94	2-2	Boere (45,78)	28,987	R.Hart
1995-96	Home	19-Aug-95	1-2	Williamson (5)	22,901	K.Burge
1995-96	Away	13-Jan-96	0-2		30,658	P.Danson
1996-97	Home	20-Jan-97	0-2		19,441	G.Poll
1996-97	Away	1-Mar-97	0-1		30,575	P.Jones
1997-98	Away	23-Nov-97	1-3	Lampard (65)	30,031	G.Ashby
1997-98	Home	30-Mar-98	3-0	Hartson (7); Abou (22); Pearce (68)	24,107	A.Wilkie
1998-99	Away	5-Dec-98	0-4		36,320	J.Winter
1998-99	Home	1-May-99	1-5	Di Canio (48)	25,997	R.Harris
1999-00	Away	30-Oct-99	0-1		40,190	G.Poll
1999-00	Home	14-May-00	0-0		26,044	G.Barber

LEICESTER CITY

Season	Venue	Date	Res	Scorers	Attendance	Referee
1994-95	Home	5-Nov-94	1-0	Dicks (77 pen)	18,780	R.Dilkes
1994-95	Away	4-Feb-95	2-1	Cottee (28); Dicks (43 pen)	20,375	J.Worrall
1996-97	Home	19-Oct-96	1-0	Moncur (77)	22,285	M.Riley
1996-97	Away	23-Apr-97	1-0	Moncur (75)	20,327	G.Hegley
1997-98	Away	27-Oct-97	1-2	Berkovic (58)	20,021	M.Reed
1997-98	Home	10-May-98	4-3	Lampard (15); Abou (31, 74); Sinclair (65)	25,781	U.Rennie
1998-99	Home	14-Nov-98	3-2	Kitson (37); Lomas (56); Lampard (76)	25,642	S.Lodge
1998-99	Away	10-Apr-99	0-0		20,402	J.Winter
1999-00	Home	21-Aug-99	2-1	Wanchope (29); di Canio (53)	23,631	A.Wiley
1999-00	Away	22-Jan-00	3-1	Wanchope (13, 45); Di Canio (60)	19,019	D.Elleray

LIVERPOOL

Season	Venue	Date	Res	Scorers	Attendance	Referee
1993-94	Away	6-Nov-93	0-2		42,254	K.Barratt
1993-94	Home	23-Apr-94	1-2	Allen,M. (1)	26,106	S.Lodge

1994-95	Away	10-Sep-94	0-0		30,907	P.Danson
1994-95	Home	10-May-95	3-0	Holmes (28); Hutchison (60,62)	22,446	P.Durkin
1995-96	Home	22-Nov-95	0-0		24,324	J.Winter
1995-96	Away	8-Apr-96	0-2		40,326	P.Alcock
1996-97	Home	29-Sep-96	1-2	Bilic (15)	25,064	K.Burge
1996-97	Away	11-Jan-97	0-0		40,102	J.Winter
1997-98	Home	27-Sep-97	2-1	Hartson (14); Berkovic (64)	25,908	D.Gallagher
1997-98	Away	2-May-98	0-5		44,414	J.Winter
1998-99	Home	12-Sep-98	2-1	Hartson (4); Berkovic (51)	26,029	J.Winter
1998-99	Away	20-Feb-99	2-2	Lampard (24 pen); Keller (74)	44,511	N.Barry
1999-00	Away	27-Oct-99	0-1		44,012	S.Lodge
1999-00	Home	27-Nov-99	1-0	Sinclair (44)	26,043	G.Barber

MANCHESTER CITY

Season	Venue	Date	Res	Scorers	Attendance	Referee
1993-94	Home	1-Nov-93	3-1	Burrows (3); Chapman (29); Holmes (69)	16,605	K.Morton
1993-94	Away	12-Feb-94	0-0		29,118	V.Callow
1994-95	Away	24-Aug-94	0-3		19,150	R.Hart
1994-95	Home	17-Dec-94	3-0	Cottee (6,9,57)	17,286	T.Holbrook
1995-96	Away	1-Jan-96	1-2		24,024	M.Reed
1995-96	Home	23-Mar-96	4-2	Dowie (21, 53); Dicks (83); Dani (84)	24,017	K.Cooper

MANCHESTER UNITED

Season	Venue	Date	Res	Scorers	Attendance	Referee
1993-94	Away	1-Sep-93	0-3		44,613	R.Milford
1993-94	Home	26-Feb-94	2-2	Chapman (69); Morley (72)	28,382	A.Wilkie
1994-95	Away	15-Oct-94	0-1		43,795	R.Gifford
1994-95	Home	14-May-95	1-1	Hughes (30)	24,783	A.Wilkie
1995-96	Away	23-Aug-95	1-2	OG (56, Bruce)	31,966	D.Gallagher
1995-96	Home	22-Jan-96	0-1		24,197	S.Lodge
1996-97	Home	8-Dec-96	2-2	Raducioiu (77); Dicks (79 pen)	25,045	P.Jones
1996-97	Away	12-May-97	0-2		55,249	S.Lodge
1997-98	Away	13-Sep-97	1-2	Hartson (14)	55,068	D.Elleray
1997-98	Home	11-Mar-98	1-1	Sinclair (6)	25,892	G.Willard
1998-99	Home	22-Aug-98	0-0		26,039	P.Jones
1998-99	Away	10-Jan-99	1-4	Lampard (89)	55,180	M.Reed
1999-00	Home	18-Dec-99	2-4	Di Canio (23, 52)	26,037	U.Rennie
1999-00	Away	1-Apr-00	1-7	Wanchope (11)	61,611	M.Riley

MIDDLESBROUGH

Season	Venue	Date	Res	Scorers	Attendance	Referee
1995-96	Away	23-Dec-95	2-4	Cottee (80); Dicks (86)	28,640	S.Dunn
1995-96	Home	9-Mar-96	2-0	Dowie (1); Dicks (62 pen)	23,850	M.Reed
1996-97	Away	3-Sep-96	1-4	Hughes (57)	30,060	P.Jones
1996-97	Home	9-Apr-97	0-0		23,988	P.Jones
1998-99	Away	12-Dec-98	0-1		34,623	K.Burge
1998-99	Home	16-May-99	4-0	Lampard (4); Keller (26); Sinclair (75); Di Canio (78)	25,902	G.Willard
1999-00	Away	17-Oct-99	0-2		31,862	U.Rennie
1999-00	Home	29-Apr-00	0-1		25,472	B.Knight

NEWCASTLE UNITED

Season	Venue	Date	Res	Scorers	Attendance	Referee
1993-94	Away	25-Sep-93	0-2		34,179	M.Reed
1993-94	Home	19-Mar-94	2-4	Breacker (57); Martin (81)	23,132	K.Morton
1994-95	Home	31-Aug-94	1-3	Hutchison (87 pen)	18,580	B.Hill
1994-95	Away	8-Mar-95	0-2		34,595	T.Holbrook
1995-96	Home	21-Feb-96	2-0	Williamson (7); Cottee (82)	23,843	P.Alcock
1995-96	Away	18-Mar-96	0-3		36,331	S.Lodge
1996-97	Away	16-Nov-96	1-1	Rowland (22)	36,552	P.Danson
1996-97	Home	6-May-97	0-0		24,617	G.Poll
1997-98	Home	20-Sep-97	0-1		25,884	S.Dunn
1997-98	Away	7-Feb-98	1-0	Lazaridis (16)	36,736	U.Rennie
1998-99	Away	31-Oct-98	3-0	Wright (56, 90); Sinclair (76)	36,744	G.Poll
1998-99	Home	21-Mar-99	2-0	Di Canio (17); Kitson (82)	25,997	P.Durkin
1999-00	Away	3-Jan-00	2-2	Lampard (84); Stimac (88)	36,314	R.Harris
1999-00	Home	12-Apr-00	2-1	Wanchope (60,89)	25,817	P.Alcock

NORWICH CITY

Season	Venue	Date	Res	Scorers	Attendance	Referee
1993-94	Away	23-Oct-93	0-0		20,175	J.Worrall
1993-94	Home	24-Jan-94	3-3	OG (37, Sutton); Jones (46); Morley (84)	20,738	J.Worrall
1994-95	Away	27-Aug-94	0-1		19,110	P.Jones
1994-95	Home	11-Mar-95	2-2	Cottee (82,88)	21,464	A.Wilkie (M.Sims 35)

NOTTINGHAM FOREST

Season	Venue	Date	Res	Scorers	Attendance	Referee
1994-95	Home	31-Dec-94	3-1	Cottee (24); Bishop (26); Hughes (44)	20,544	D.Gallagher
1994-95	Away	8-Apr-95	1-1	Dicks (65)	28,361	G.Poll
1995-96	Away	26-Aug-95	1-1	Allen (14)	26,645	G.Ashby
1995-96	Home	3-Feb-96	1-0	Slater (19)	21,257	K.Burge
1996-97	Away	21-Sep-96	2-0	Bowen (44); Hughes (53)	23,352	G.Willard
1996-97	Home	1-Jan-97	0-1		22,358	P.Durkin
1998-99	Away	19-Sep-98	0-0		28,463	M.Reed
1998-99	Home	13-Feb-99	2-1	Pearce (35); Lampard (39)	25,458	R.Harris

OLDHAM ATHLETIC

Season	Venue	Date	Res	Scorers	Attendance	Referee
1993-94	Home	20-Nov-93	2-0	Martin (43); Morley (75)	17,211	D.Allison
1993-94	Away	16-Apr-94	2-1	Allen,M. (2); Morley (29)	11,669	K.Barratt

QPR

Season	Venue	Date	Res	Scorers	Attendance	Referee
1993-94	Home	28-Aug-93	0-4		18,084	V.Callow
1993-94	Away	3-May-94	0-0		10,850	R.Dilkes
1994-95	Away	4-Dec-94	1-2	Boere (90)	12,780	P.Don
1994-95	Home	3-May-95	0-0		22,932	G.Willard
1995-96	Home	25-Nov-95	1-0	Cottee (84)	21,504	P.Alcock
1995-96	Away	27-Apr-96	0-3		18,828	G.Willard

SHEFFIELD UNITED

Season	Venue	Date	Res	Scorers	Attendance	Referee
1993-94	Home	3-Jan-94	0-0		20,365	M.Reed
1993-94	Away	28-Mar-94	2-3	Bishop (8); Holmes (30)	13,646	P.Durkin

SHEFFIELD WEDNESDAY

Season	Venue	Date	Res	Scorers	Attendance	Referee
1993-94	Home	25-Aug-93	2-0	Allen,C. (79,84)	19,441	J.Worrall
1993-94	Away	18-Dec-93	0-5		26,350	D.Frampton
1994-95	Away	19-Nov-94	0-1		25,350	G.Ashby
1994-95	Home	23-Jan-95	0-2		14,554	P.Danson
1995-96	Away	28-Oct-95	1-0	Dowie (40)	23,917	K.Cooper
1995-96	Home	5-May-96	1-1	Dicks (72)	23,790	R.Dilkes
1996-97	Away	30-Nov-96	0-0		22,231	P.Durkin
1996-97	Home	3-May-97	5-1	Kitson (4, 12, 88); Hartson (29, 65)	24,490	M.Riley
1997-98	Home	13-Dec-97	1-0	Kitson (69)	24,344	M.Riley
1997-98	Away	13-Apr-98	1-1	Berkovic (7)	28,036	N.Barry
1998-99	Away	15-Aug-98	1-0	Wright (85)	30,236	P.Durkin
1998-99	Home	16-Jan-99	0-4		25,642	K.Burge
1999-00	Away	11-Mar-00	1-3	Lampard (10)	21,147	P.Jones

SOUTHAMPTON

Season	Venue	Date	Res	Scorers	Attendance	Referee
1993-94	Away	29-Nov-93	2-0	Morley (30); Chapman (38)	13,258	M.Bodenham
1993-94	Home	7-May-94	3-3	Williamson (11); Allen,M. (62); OG (89, Monkou)	26,952	G.Ashby
1994-95	Home	22-Oct-94	2-0	Allen (49); Rush (62)	18,853	J.Worrall
1994-95	Away	15-Mar-95	1-1	Hutchison (38)	15,178	K.Burge
1995-96	Away	2-Oct-95	0-0		13,568	G.Poll
1995-96	Home	16-Dec-95	2-1	Cottee (80; Dowie (82)	18,501	A.Wilkie
1996-97	Home	24-Aug-96	2-1	Hughes (72); Dicks (81 pen)	21,227	D.Elleray
1996-97	Away	12-Apr-97	0-2		15,244	S.Dunn
1997-98	Away	4-Oct-97	0-3		15,212	M.Riley
1997-98	Home	25-Apr-98	2-4	Sinclair (41); Lomas (82)	25,878	D.Gallagher
1998-99	Home	28-Sep-98	1-0	Wright (60)	23,153	U.Rennie
1998-99	Away	6-Mar-99	0-1		15,240	D.Gallagher
1999-00	Away	5-Feb-00	1-2	Lampard (65)	15,257	B.Knight
1999-00	Home	8-Mar-00	2-0	Wanchope (18); Sinclair (48)	23,484	S.Lodge

SUNDERLAND

Season	Venue	Date	Res	Scorers	Attendance	Referee
1996-97	Away	8-Sep-96	0-0		18,642	G.Poll
1996-97	Home	28-Dec-96	2-0	Bilic (35); Raducioiu (89)	24,077	R.Dilkes
1999-00	Home	24-Oct-99	1-1	Sinclair (89)	26,081	M.Halsey
1999-00	Away	6-May-00	0-1		41,684	N.Barry

SWINDON TOWN

Season	Venue	Date	Res	Scorers	Attendance	Referee
1993-94	Home	11-Sep-93	0-0		15,777	A.Gunn
1993-94	Away	5-Mar-94	1-1	Morley (48)	15,929	R.Milford

TOTTENHAM HOTSPUR

Season	Venue	Date	Res	Scorers	Attendance	Referee
1993-94	Home	28-Dec-93	1-3	Holmes (11)	20,787	G.Ashby
1993-94	Away	4-Apr-94	4-1	Jones (38); Morley (60 pen, 73); Marsh (80)	31,502	P.Don
1994-95	Away	29-Oct-94	1-3	Rush (41)	26,271	K.Morton
1994-95	Home	14-Jan-95	1-2	Boere (10)	24,573	B.Hill
1995-96	Home	30-Aug-95	1-1	Hutchison (24)	23,516	M.Reed
1995-96	Away	12-Feb-96	1-0	Dani (4)	29,781	J.Winter
1996-97	Away	2-Nov-96	0-1		32,999	J.Winter
1996-97	Home	24-Feb-97	4-3	Dicks (19, 71); Kitson (21); Hartson (36)	23,998	G.Willard
1997-98	Home	13-Aug-97	2-1	Hartson (3); Berkovic (70)	25,354	S.Lodge
1997-98	Away	17-Jan-98	0-1		30,284	D.Elleray
1998-99	Home	28-Nov-98	2-1	Sinclair (39, 46)	26,044	D.Gallagher
1998-99	Away	24-Apr-99	2-1	Wright (5); Keller (66)	36,089	U.Rennie
1999-00	Home	7-Aug-99	1-0	Lampard (45)	26,010	P.Durkin (D.Elleray 16)
1999-00	Away	6-Dec-99	0-0		36,233	P.Jones

WATFORD

Season	Venue	Date	Res	Scorers	Attendance	Referee
1999-00	Home	11-Sep-99	1-0	Di Canio (48)	25,310	D.Gallagher
1999-00	Away	4-Mar-00	2-1	Lomas (3); Wanchope (35)	18,619	M.Reed

WIMBLEDON

Season	Venue	Date	Res	Scorers	Attendance	Referee
1993-94	Home	14-Aug-93	0-2		20,369	K.Burge
1993-94	Away	4-Dec-93	2-1	Chapman (44,79)	10,903	D.Gallagher
1994-95	Away	28-Dec-94	0-1		11,212	P.Don
1994-95	Home	13-Apr-95	3-0	Dicks (41 pen); Boere (76); Cottee (78)	21,804	M.Reed
1995-96	Away	16-Oct-95	1-0	Cottee (18)	9,411	D.Gallagher
1995-96	Home	6-Apr-96	1-1	Dicks (6)	20,402	P.Durkin
1996-97	Home	14-Sep-96	0-2		21,924	R.Dilkes
1996-97	Away	17-Mar-97	1-1	Lazaridis (89)	15,771	J.Winter
1997-98	Home	30-Aug-97	3-1	Hartson (47); Rieper (54); Berkovic (55)	24,516	G.Poll
1997-98	Away	28-Dec-97	2-1	OG (30, Kimble); Kitson (54)	22,087	P.Durkin
1998-99	Home	9-Sep-98	3-4	Hartson (7); Wright (14, 27)	25,311	G.Barber
1998-99	Away	30-Jan-99	0-0		23,035	P.Durkin
1999-00	Away	26-Dec-99	2-2	Sinclair (45); Lampard (81)	20,394	S.Dunn
1999-00	Home	26-Mar-00	2-1	Di Canio (8); Kanoute (59)	22,438	R.Harris

INTRODUCTION

Founded 1889 as Wimbledon Old Centrals, an old boys' side of the Central School playing on Wimbledon Common. Member of the Southern Suburban League, the name was changed to Wimbledon in 1905. Moved to Plough Lane in 1912. Athenian League member for two seasons before joining the Isthmian League in 1921.

FA Amateur Cup winners 1963 and seven times Isthmian League champions. Turned professional in 1965, joining the Southern League, of which they were champions three times before being elected to Football League Division Four in 1977. Started ground sharing at Selhurst Park in 1991 and founder member of the Premier League 1992.

Ground:	Selhurst Park, South Norwood, London SE25 6PY
Nickname:	The Dons
Internet:	www.wimbledon-fc.co.uk

HONOURS

Football League Div 3:	Runners-up 1983-84
Football League Div 4:	Champions 1982-83
FA Cup:	Winners 1987-88
FA Amateur Cup:	Winners 1963.

EUROPEAN RECORD

Never qualified.

FAPL RECORD SUMMARY

Most Total:	EARLE, Robbie	244
Most Starts:	EARLE, Robbie	240
Most Subs:	CLARKE, Andy	70
Most SNU:	HEALD, Paul	109
Most PS:	GAYLE, Marcus	63
Most Goals:	HOLDSWORTH, Dean	58
Most Yel:	JONES, Vinny	39
Most Red:	JONES, Vinny	6

PLAYING RECORD – SEASON TOTALS

Season	Pn	P	W	D	L	F	A	Pts
1992-93	12	42	14	12	16	56	55	54
1993-94	6	42	18	11	13	56	53	65
1994-95	9	42	15	11	16	48	65	56
1995-96	14	38	10	11	17	55	70	41
1996-97	8	38	15	11	12	49	46	56
1997-98	15	38	10	14	14	34	46	44
1998-99	16	38	10	12	16	40	63	42
1999-00	18	38	7	12	19	46	74	33
Totals		316	99	94	123	384	472	391

PLAYING RECORD – HOME TOTALS

Season	Pn	P	W	D	L	F	A	Pts
1992-93	12	21	9	4	8	32	23	31
1993-94	6	21	12	5	4	35	21	41
1994-95	9	21	9	5	7	26	26	32
1995-96	14	19	5	6	8	27	33	21
1996-97	8	19	9	6	4	28	21	33
1997-98	15	19	5	6	8	18	25	21
1998-99	16	19	7	7	5	22	21	28
1999-00	18	19	6	7	6	30	28	25
Totals		158	62	46	50	218	198	232

PLAYING RECORD – AWAY TOTALS

Season	Pn	P	W	D	L	F	A	Pts
1992-93	12	21	5	8	8	24	32	23
1993-94	6	21	6	6	9	21	32	24
1994-95	9	21	6	6	9	22	39	24
1995-96	14	19	5	5	9	28	37	20
1996-97	8	19	6	5	8	21	25	23
1997-98	15	19	5	8	6	16	21	23
1998-99	16	19	3	5	11	18	42	14
1999-00	18	19	1	5	13	16	46	8
Totals		158	37	48	73	166	274	159

HIGHEST HOME ATTENDANCES

	Attendance	Opponents	Date	Season
1	30,115	Manchester U.	9-May-93	1992-93
2	28,553	Manchester U.	16-Apr-94	1993-94
3	26,309	Manchester U.	22-Nov-97	1997-98
4	26,129	Manchester U.	26-Feb-00	1999-00
5	26,121	Manchester U.	3-Apr-99	1998-99

LOWEST HOME ATTENDANCES

	Attendance	Opponents	Date	Season
1	3,039	Everton	26-Jan-93	1992-93
2	3,386	Oldham A.	12-Dec-92	1992-93
3	3,759	Coventry C.	22-Aug-92	1992-93
4	3,979	Sheffield U.	20-Feb-93	1992-93
5	4,534	Southampton	6-Mar-93	1992-93

TOP SCORER – SEASON BY SEASON

Season	Player	Goals
1992-93	Holdsworth	19
1993-94	Holdsworth	17
1994-95	Ekoku	9
1995-96	Earle	11
1996-97	Ekoku	11
1997-98	Cort, Ekoku, Euell, M. Hughes, Leaburn	4
1998-99	Euell	10
1999-00	Cort, Hartson	9

PLAYERS WITH MOST PREMIERSHIP APPEARANCES

Tot	Player	St	Sb	Gls
244	EARLE, Robbie	240	4	45
204	GAYLE, Marcus	174	30	34
201	CUNNINGHAM, Kenny	200	1	0
181	KIMBLE, Alan	168	13	0
179	SULLIVAN, Neil	178	1	0
177	JONES, Vinny	171	6	12
170	ARDLEY, Neal	141	29	12
169	HOLDSWORTH, Dean	148	21	58
165	PERRY, Chris	157	8	2
157	BLACKWELL, Dean	143	14	0
124	CLARKE, Andy	54	70	11
123	EKOKU, Efan	102	21	37
118	SEGERS, Hans	116	2	0
105	EUELL, Jason	85	20	22
101	BARTON, Warren	99	2	6
86	THATCHER, Ben	82	4	0
82	ELKINS, Gary	75	7	2
79	HUGHES, Michael	70	9	9
76	LEONHARDSEN, Oyvind	73	3	13
73	CORT, Carl	54	19	16
73	FEAR, Peter	51	22	4
72	SCALES, John	72	0	1
72	McALLISTER, Brian	64	8	0

CLUB-BY-CLUB RESULTS

ARSENAL

Season	Venue	Date	Res	Scorers	Attendance	Referee
1992-93	Home	5-Sep-92	3-2	Sanchez (39); Fashanu (80); Earle (86)	12,906	K.Burge
1992-93	Away	10-Feb-93	1-0	Holdsworth (19)	18,253	P.Don
1993-94	Home	1-Jan-94	0-3		16,584	G.Ashby
1993-94	Away	19-Apr-94	1-1	Earle (37)	21,292	R.Gifford
1994-95	Home	8-Oct-94	1-3	Jones (81)	10,842	G.Ashby
1994-95	Away	4-May-95	0-0		32,822	R.Gifford
1995-96	Away	30-Dec-95	3-1	Earle (38, 67); Holdsworth (50)	37,640	S.Lodge
1995-96	Home	16-Mar-96	0-3		18,335	D.Gallagher
1996-97	Home	2-Nov-96	2-2	Jones (44); Gayle (69)	25,521	P.Alcock
1996-97	Away	23-Feb-97	1-0	Jones (21)	37,854	P.Jones
1997-98	Home	11-Mar-98	0-1		22,291	D.Gallagher
1997-98	Away	18-Apr-98	0-5		38,024	P.Jones
1998-99	Home	21-Nov-98	1-0	Ekoku (77)	26,003	M.Riley
1998-99	Away	19-Apr-99	1-5	Cort (70)	37,982	S.Lodge
1999-00	Away	18-Dec-99	1-1	Cort (7)	38,052	G.Barber
1999-00	Home	1-Apr-00	1-3	Lund (12)	25,858	U.Rennie

ASTON VILLA

Season	Venue	Date	Res	Scorers	Attendance	Referee
1992-93	Home	3-Oct-92	2-3	Miller (34); Clarke (90)	6,849	S.Lodge
1992-93	Away	27-Feb-93	0-1		34,496	S.Lodge
1993-94	Home	21-Aug-93	2-2	Holdsworth (40); Fashanu (86)	7,564	J.Borrett
1993-94	Away	11-Dec-93	1-0	Holdsworth (77)	17,940	A.Gunn
1994-95	Home	9-Nov-94	4-3	Barton (8 pen); Ardley (60); Jones (83); Leonhardson (90)	6,221	D.Elleray
1994-95	Away	11-Feb-95	1-7	Barton (11)	23,982	B.Hill
1995-96	Away	16-Sep-95	0-2		26,928	D.Elleray
1995-96	Home	24-Feb-96	3-3	Goodman (10, 48); Harford (90)	12,193	J.Winter
1996-97	Away	22-Dec-96	0-5		28,875	S.Dunn
1996-97	Home	9-Apr-97	0-2		9,015	R.Dilkes
1997-98	Away	18-Oct-97	2-1	Earle (39); Cort (62)	32,087	K.Burge

1997-98	Home	21-Feb-98	2-1	Euell (10); Leaburn (38)	13,131	G.Ashby
1998-99	Away	12-Sep-98	0-2		32,959	D.Elleray
1998-99	Home	21-Feb-99	0-0		15,582	P.Alcock
1999-00	Away	23-Oct-99	1-1	Earle (26)	27,160	U.Rennie
1999-00	Home	6-May-00	2-2	OG (15, Ehiogu); Hartson (90)	19,188	M.Halsey

BARNSLEY

Season	Venue	Date	Res	Scorers	Attendance	Referee
1997-98	Home	23-Sep-97	4-1	Cort (49); Earle (64); C.Hughes (67); Ekoku (83)	7,976	J.Winter
1997-98	Away	28-Feb-98	1-2	Euell (72)	17,102	G.Barber

BLACKBURN ROVERS

Season	Venue	Date	Res	Scorers	Attendance	Referee
1992-93	Home	19-Sep-92	1-1	Ardley (24)	6,117	M.Bodenham
1992-93	Away	9-Jan-93	0-0		14,504	R.Hart
1993-94	Away	5-Feb-94	0-3		17,264	A.Wilkie
1993-94	Home	29-Mar-94	4-1	Fahanu (50); OG (75, Berg); Holdsworth (79); Earle (82)	10,537	J.Lloyd
1994-95	Home	3-Dec-94	0-3		12,341	P.Jones
1994-95	Away	22-Feb-95	1-2	Ekoku (39)	20,586	S.Lodge
1995-96	Home	23-Dec-95	1-1	Earle (82)	7,105	M.Bodenham
1995-96	Away	17-Apr-96	2-3	Earle (22); Gayle (48)	24,174	R.Hart
1996-97	Home	14-Dec-96	1-0	Holdsworth (85)	13,246	A.Wilkie
1996-97	Away	15-Mar-97	1-3	Ekoku (39)	23,333	G.Poll
1997-98	Home	4-Oct-97	0-1		15,600	D.Gallagher
1997-98	Away	25-Apr-98	0-0		24,848	G.Poll
1998-99	Home	31-Oct-98	1-1	Earle (76)	12,526	G.Willard
1998-99	Away	21-Mar-99	1-3	Euell (65)	21,754	G.Willard

BOLTON WANDERERS

Season	Venue	Date	Res	Scorers	Attendance	Referee
1995-96	Home	19-Aug-95	3-2	Ekoku (5); Earle (23); Holdsworth (55)	9,317	K.Cooper
1995-96	Away	13-Jan-96	0-1		16,216	M.Reed
1997-98	Away	29-Nov-97	0-1		22,703	J.Winter
1997-98	Home	4-Apr-98	0-0		11,356	M.Bodenham

BRADFORD CITY

Season	Venue	Date	Res	Scorers	Attendance	Referee
1999-00	Home	16-Oct-99	3-2	Hartson (22, 36); Cort (75)	10,029	P.Alcock
1999-00	Away	30-Apr-00	0-3		18,276	J.Winter

CHARLTON ATHLETIC

Season	Venue	Date	Res	Scorers	Attendance	Referee
1998-99	Home	26-Dec-98	2-1	Euell (33); Hughes,M. (51)	19,106	G.Barber
1998-99	Away	8-Feb-99	0-2		20,002	D.Elleray

CHELSEA

Season	Venue	Date	Res	Scorers	Attendance	Referee
1992-93	Home	28-Dec-92	0-0		14,687	D.Elleray
1992-93	Away	12-Apr-93	2-4	Holdsworth (55); Sanchez (88)	13,138	D.Elleray

1993-94	Home	17-Aug-93	1-1	Fashanu (80)	11,263	M.Reed
1993-94	Away	16-Mar-94	0-2		11,903	K.Morton
1994-95	Away	31-Dec-94	1-1	Ekoku (74)	16,105	K.Morton
1994-95	Home	10-Apr-95	1-1	Goodman (56)	7,022	K.Morton
1995-96	Away	26-Dec-95	2-1	Earle (35); Ekoku (39)	21,906	D.Gallagher
1995-96	Home	2-Mar-96	1-1	OG (38, Clarke)	17,048	P.Jones
1996-97	Away	19-Oct-96	4-2	Earle (4); Ardley (18); Gayle (64); Ekoku (78)	28,020	D.Elleray
1996-97	Home	22-Apr-97	0-1		14,601	P.Danson
1997-98	Home	26-Aug-97	0-2		22,237	M.Bodenham
1997-98	Away	26-Dec-97	1-1	Hughes,M. (28)	34,100	G.Willard
1998-99	Away	14-Nov-98	0-3		34,757	J.Winter
1998-99	Home	11-Apr-99	1-2	Gayle (88)	21,577	G.Willard
1999-00	Home	28-Aug-99	0-1		22,167	S.Dunn
1999-00	Away	12-Feb-00	1-3	Lund (73)	34,826	P.Jones

COVENTRY CITY

Season	Venue	Date	Res	Scorers	Attendance	Referee
1992-93	Home	22-Aug-92	1-2	Holdsworth (73)	3,759	J.Borrett
1992-93	Away	30-Jan-93	2-0	Holdsworth (4); Clarke (55)	11,774	R.Gifford
1993-94	Home	26-Dec-93	1-2	Holdsworth (38)	4,739	M.Bodenham
1993-94	Away	2-Apr-94	2-1	Castledine (32); Holdsworth (40)	11,312	M.Bodenham
1994-95	Away	20-Aug-94	1-1	Castledine (55)	10,962	R.Gifford
1994-95	Home	10-Dec-94	2-0	Leonhardson (4); Harford (17)	7,349	R.Dilkes
1995-96	Away	25-Nov-95	3-3	Jones (28 pen); Goodman (43); Leonhardsen (58)	12,496	R.Hart
1995-96	Home	27-Apr-96	0-2		15,540	S.Dunn
1996-97	Home	16-Nov-96	2-2	Earle (45); Gayle (54)	10,307	M.Bodenham
1996-97	Away	3-Mar-97	1-1	Ekoku (32)	15,273	D.Elleray
1997-98	Home	1-Nov-97	1-2	Cort (27)	11,210	U.Rennie
1997-98	Away	29-Apr-98	0-0		17,968	J.Winter
1998-99	Home	5-Dec-98	2-1	Euell (71, 83)	11,717	S.Dunn
1998-99	Away	1-May-99	1-2	Hartson (74)	21,200	G.Poll
1999-00	Home	14-Aug-99	1-1	Cort (67)	10,635	M.Halsey
1999-00	Away	15-Jan-00	0-2		19,012	S.Bennett

CRYSTAL PALACE

Season	Venue	Date	Res	Scorers	Attendance	Referee
1992-93	Away	26-Dec-92	0-2		16,825	R.Lewis
1992-93	Home	9-Apr-93	4-0	Earle (20, 53); Holdsworth (24, 46)	12,275	V.Callow
1994-95	Away	17-Sep-94	0-0		12,366	K.Cooper
1994-95	Home	18-Mar-95	2-0	Jones (37); Gayle (60)	8,835	D.Gallagher
1997-98	Home	20-Sep-97	0-1		16,747	P.Alcock
1997-98	Away	9-Feb-98	3-0	Leaburn (47,51); Euell (57)	14,410	K.Burge

DERBY COUNTY

Season	Venue	Date	Res	Scorers	Attendance	Referee
1996-97	Away	28-Sep-96	2-0	Earle (49); Gayle (70)	17,022	A.Wilkie
1996-97	Home	11-Jan-97	1-1	Gayle (60)	11,467	R.Dilkes
1997-98	Away	22-Oct-97	1-1	OG (70, Rowett)	28,595	U.Rennie
1997-98	Home	17-Jan-98	0-0		13,031	P.Jones
1998-99	Away	22-Aug-98	0-0		25,747	J.Winter
1998-99	Home	9-Jan-99	2-1	Euell (8); Roberts (83)	12,732	A.Wilkie

| 1999-00 | Home | 11-Sep-99 | 2-2 | Hartson (62); Euell (63) | 12,282 | A.Wiley |
| 1999-00 | Away | 4-Mar-00 | 0-4 | | 28,384 | A.D'Urso |

EVERTON

Season	Venue	Date	Res	Scorers	Attendance	Referee
1992-93	Away	29-Aug-92	0-0		18,118	H.King
1992-93	Home	26-Jan-93	1-3	Fashanu (75)	3,039	K.Hackett
1993-94	Home	27-Nov-93	1-1	Berry (49)	6,934	M.Reed
1993-94	Away	7-May-94	2-3	Holdsworth (4 pen); OG (20, Ablett)	31,233	R.Hart
1994-95	Home	2-Jan-95	2-1	Harford (3,8)	9,506	K.Burge
1994-95	Away	29-Apr-95	0-0		33,063	P.Danson
1995-96	Home	1-Jan-96	2-3		11,121	A.Wilkie
1995-96	Away	23-Mar-96	4-2	Gayle (12); Castledine (65); Clarke (85); Goodman (88)	31,382	R.Dilkes
1996-97	Home	7-Sep-96	4-0	Ardley (33); Gayle (46); Earle (58); Ekoku (73)	13,684	K.Burge
1996-97	Away	28-Dec-96	3-1	Ekoku (59); Leonhardsen (70); Gayle (76)	36,733	M.Bodenham
1997-98	Away	13-Dec-97	0-0		28,533	G.Ashby
1997-98	Home	13-Apr-98	0-0		15,131	K.Burge
1998-99	Home	3-Oct-98	1-2	Roberts (8)	16,054	P.Alcock
1998-99	Away	27-Feb-99	1-1	Ekoku (14)	32,574	N.Barry
1999-00	Away	25-Aug-99	0-4		32,818	J.Winter
1999-00	Home	6-Feb-00	0-3		13,172	G.Barber

IPSWICH TOWN

Season	Venue	Date	Res	Scorers	Attendance	Referee
1992-93	Home	18-Aug-92	0-1		4,954	R.Hart
1992-93	Away	12-Sep-92	1-2	Holdsworth (27)	13,333	S.Lodge
1993-94	Home	25-Oct-93	0-2		7,756	A.Gunn
1993-94	Away	22-Jan-94	0-0		11,849	B.Hill
1994-95	Home	23-Aug-94	1-1	Holdsworth (19)	6,341	J.Worrall
1994-95	Away	16-Dec-94	2-2	Holdsworth (2); Goodman (62)	11,367	D.Elleray

LEEDS UNITED

Season	Venue	Date	Res	Scorers	Attendance	Referee
1992-93	Away	15-Aug-92	1-2	Barton (76)	25,795	G.Ashby
1992-93	Home	6-Feb-93	1-0	Holdsworth (61)	6,704	V.Callow
1993-94	Away	2-Oct-93	0-4		30,255	J.Worrall
1993-94	Home	26-Mar-94	1-0	Fear (3)	9,035	K.Burge
1994-95	Away	5-Nov-94	1-3	Ekoku (25)	27,284	B.Hill
1994-95	Home	4-Feb-95	0-0		10,211	G.Ashby
1995-96	Home	23-Sep-95	2-4	Holdsworth (43); Reeves (59)	13,307	R.Dilkes
1995-96	Away	9-Dec-95	1-1	Leonhardsen (4)	27,984	G.Poll
1996-97	Away	26-Aug-96	0-1		25,860	M.Reed
1996-97	Home	16-Apr-97	2-0	Holdsworth (18); Castledine (74)	7,979	P.Alcock
1997-98	Home	25-Oct-97	1-0	Ardley (28)	15,718	G.Barber
1997-98	Away	10-May-98	1-1	Ekoku (88)	38,172	S.Dunn
1998-99	Home	29-Aug-98	1-1	M.Hughes (72)	16,437	S.Dunn
1998-99	Away	29-Dec-98	2-2	Earle (41); Cort (83)	39,816	P.Jones
1999-00	Home	7-Nov-99	2-0	Hartson (31); Gayle (65)	18,747	P.Jones
1999-00	Away	19-Mar-00	1-4	Euell (2)	39,256	A.Wiley

WIMBLEDON

LEICESTER CITY

Season	Venue	Date	Res	Scorers	Attendance	Referee
1994-95	Home	10-Sep-94	2-1	Harford (28); OG (44, Willis)	7,683	G.Poll
1994-95	Away	1-Apr-95	4-3	Goodman (63,90); Leonhardson (65,85)	15,489	D.Elleray
1996-97	Away	18-Jan-97	0-1		18,927	S.Lodge
1996-97	Home	1-Mar-97	1-3	Holdsworth (67)	11,487	G.Ashby
1997-98	Away	10-Nov-97	1-0	Gayle (50)	18,553	M.Riley
1997-98	Home	14-Mar-98	2-1	Roberts (14); Hughes,M. (61)	13,229	M.Riley
1998-99	Away	28-Sep-98	1-1	Earle (74)	17,725	A.Wilkie
1998-99	Home	6-Mar-99	0-1		11,801	R.Harris
1999-00	Away	20-Nov-99	1-2	Gayle (21)	18,255	A.Wiley
1999-00	Home	11-Mar-00	2-1	Ardley (33 pen); Cort (87)	14,316	P.Alcock

LIVERPOOL

Season	Venue	Date	Res	Scorers	Attendance	Referee
1992-93	Away	26-Sep-92	3-2	Fashanu (12); Earle (27, 76)	29,574	R.Milford
1992-93	Home	16-Jan-93	2-0	Fashanu (36 pen); Cotterill (64)	11,294	R.Dilkes
1993-94	Away	28-Dec-93	1-1	Fashanu (40)	32,232	K.Cooper
1993-94	Home	4-Apr-94	1-1	Elkins (90)	13,819	J.Borrett
1994-95	Away	22-Oct-94	0-3		31,139	P.Jones
1994-95	Home	2-May-95	0-0		12,041	T.Holbrook
1995-96	Home	9-Sep-95	1-0	Harford (28)	19,530	K.Burge
1995-96	Away	13-Mar-96	2-2	Ekoku (54); Holdsworth (60)	34,063	G.Willard
1996-97	Away	23-Nov-96	1-1	Leonhardsen (67)	39,027	P.Danson
1996-97	Home	6-May-97	2-1	Euell (41); Holdsworth (55)	20,016	P.Durkin
1997-98	Home	9-Aug-97	1-1	Gayle (56)	26,106	G.Willard
1997-98	Away	10-Jan-98	0-2		38,011	M.Bodenham
1998-99	Home	13-Dec-98	1-0	Earle (48)	26,080	G.Willard
1998-99	Away	16-May-99	0-3		41,902	N.Barry
1999-00	Away	28-Dec-99	1-3	Gayle (64)	44,107	N.Barry
1999-00	Home	16-Apr-00	1-2	Andresen (70)	26,102	M.Riley

MANCHESTER CITY

Season	Venue	Date	Res	Scorers	Attendance	Referee
1992-93	Home	1-Sep-92	0-1		4,714	M.Reed
1992-93	Away	21-Apr-93	1-1	Miller (50)	19,524	H.King
1993-94	Home	20-Sep-93	1-0	Earle (55)	8,533	K.Barratt
1993-94	Away	12-Mar-94	1-0	Earle (31)	23,981	D.Frampton
1994-95	Away	26-Nov-94	0-2		21,131	A.Wilkie
1994-95	Home	21-Mar-95	2-0	Thorn (59); Elkins (76)	5,268	R.Gifford
1995-96	Away	22-Nov-95	0-1		23,617	P.Durkin
1995-96	Home	8-Apr-96	3-0	Earle (40, 47); Ekoku (52)	11,844	G.Poll

MANCHESTER UNITED

Season	Venue	Date	Res	Scorers	Attendance	Referee
1992-93	Away	31-Oct-92	1-0	Sanchez (79)	32,622	K.Morton
1992-93	Home	9-May-93	1-2	Holdsworth (81)	30,115	J.Worrall
1993-94	Away	20-Nov-93	1-3	Fashanu (63)	44,748	J.Lloyd
1993-94	Home	16-Apr-94	1-0	Fashanu (22)	28,553	T.Holbrook
1994-95	Away	31-Aug-94	0-3		43,440	T.Holbrook
1994-95	Home	7-Mar-95	0-1		18,224	R.Hart

1995-96	Away	26-Aug-95	1-3	Earle (64)	32,226	P.Durkin
1995-96	Home	3-Feb-96	2-4	Gayle (68); Ewell (76)	24,432	P.Durkin
1996-97	Home	17-Aug-96	0-3		25,786	D.Elleray
1996-97	Away	29-Jan-97	1-2	Perry (61)	55,314	M.Reed
1997-98	Home	22-Nov-97	2-5	Ardlley (67); Hughes,M. (70)	26,309	P.Durkin
1997-98	Away	28-Mar-98	0-2		55,306	D.Gallagher
1998-99	Away	17-Oct-98	1-5	Euell (39)	55,265	G.Willard
1998-99	Home	3-Apr-99	1-1	Euell (5)	26,121	G.Barber
1999-00	Away	18-Sep-99	1-1	Badir (16)	55,189	R.Harris
1999-00	Home	26-Feb-00	2-2	Euell (1); Cort (62)	26,129	D.Elleray

MIDDLESBROUGH

Season	Venue	Date	Res	Scorers	Attendance	Referee
1992-93	Away	21-Nov-92	0-2		14,524	J.Worrall
1992-93	Home	9-Mar-93	2-0	Scales (32); Holdsworth (74)	5,821	M.Reed
1995-96	Home	18-Nov-95	0-0		13,780	K.Cooper
1995-96	Away	13-Apr-96	2-1	Earle (12); Ekoku (64)	29,192	G.Ashby
1996-97	Away	26-Oct-96	0-0		29,758	S.Dunn
1996-97	Home	1-Feb-97	1-1	OG (22, Cox)	15,046	G.Barber
1998-99	Home	24-Oct-98	2-2	Gayle (26, 76)	14,114	S.Lodge
1998-99	Away	5-Apr-99	1-3	Cort (75)	33,999	P.Durkin
1999-00	Home	10-Aug-99	2-3	Cort (17); Hartson (86)	11,036	B.Knight
1999-00	Away	27-Nov-99	0-0		31,400	P.Durkin

NEWCASTLE UNITED

Season	Venue	Date	Res	Scorers	Attendance	Referee
1993-94	Away	30-Oct-93	0-4		33,371	V.Callow
1993-94	Home	12-Feb-94	4-2	Earle (9); Blissett (25); Fashanu (56); Holdsworth (64)	13,358	J.Lloyd
1994-95	Home	19-Nov-94	3-2	Clarke (1); Ekoku (27); Harford (46)	14,203	P.Don
1994-95	Away	25-Jan-95	1-2	Ekoku (78)	34,374	M.Reed
1995-96	Away	21-Oct-95	1-6	Gayle (6)	36,434	G.Poll
1995-96	Home	3-Dec-95	3-3	Holdsworth (19, 65); Ekoku (21)	18,002	G.Ashby
1996-97	Away	21-Aug-96	0-2		36,385	S.Lodge
1996-97	Home	23-Mar-97	1-1	Leonhardsen (27)	23,175	S.Lodge
1997-98	Away	13-Sep-97	3-1	Cort (1); Perry (58); Ekoku (75)	36,256	M.Reed
1997-98	Home	31-Mar-98	0-0		15,478	N.Barry
1998-99	Away	28-Nov-98	1-3	Gayle (34)	36,623	U.Rennie
1998-99	Home	24-Apr-99	1-1	Hartson (24)	21,172	P.Jones
1999-00	Away	21-Aug-99	3-3	Hughes,M. (44); Ainsworth (68,90)	35,809	M.Reed
1999-00	Home	22-Jan-00	2-0	Earle (48); Gayle (69)	22,118	D.Gallagher

NORWICH CITY

Season	Venue	Date	Res	Scorers	Attendance	Referee
1992-93	Away	5-Dec-92	1-2	Sanchez (53)	14,161	R.Groves
1992-93	Home	20-Mar-93	3-0	Holdsworth (16, 82); Ardley (29)	10,875	K.Cooper
1993-94	Away	11-Sep-93	1-0	Sanchez (56)	14,851	G.Ashby
1993-94	Home	5-Mar-94	3-1	Earle (7, 65); Holdsworth (75)	7,206	A.Gunn
1994-95	Home	30-Oct-94	1-0	Ekoku (62)	8,242	D.Gallagher
1994-95	Away	14-Jan-95	2-1	Reeves (44); Ekoku (49)	18,261	M.Bodenham

NOTTINGHAM FOREST

Season	Venue	Date	Res	Scorers	Attendance	Referee
1992-93	Away	20-Dec-92	1-1	Clarke (13)	19,362	R.Hart
1992-93	Home	17-Apr-93	1-0	Clarke (32)	9,358	K.Barratt
1994-95	Away	17-Oct-94	1-3	Gayle (82)	20,187	R.Hart
1994-95	Home	13-May-95	2-2	Holdsworth (35,40 pen)	15,341	S.Lodge
1995-96	Away	6-Nov-95	1-4	Jones (11)	20,810	P.Alcock
1995-96	Home	30-Mar-96	1-0	Holdsworth (81)	9,807	K.Burge
1996-97	Home	30-Nov-96	1-0	Earle (37)	12,608	M.Reed
1996-97	Away	3-May-97	1-1	Leonhardsen (15)	19,865	G.Barber
1998-99	Away	7-Nov-98	1-0	Gayle (23)	21,362	G.Poll
1998-99	Home	13-Mar-99	1-3	Gayle (79)	12,149	K.Burge

OLDHAM ATHLETIC

Season	Venue	Date	Res	Scorers	Attendance	Referee
1992-93	Home	12-Dec-92	5-2	Ardley (18, 26); Holdsworth (22, 52); Clarke (51)	3,386	K.Hackett
1992-93	Away	3-Apr-93	2-6	Holdsworth (61, 68)	11,606	J.Martin
1993-94	Away	28-Aug-93	1-1	Jones (6)	9,633	P.Durkin
1993-94	Home	26-Apr-94	3-0	Holdsworth (32,47,55)	6,766	R.Milford

QPR

Season	Venue	Date	Res	Scorers	Attendance	Referee
1992-93	Home	7-Nov-92	0-2		6,771	P.Don
1992-93	Away	13-Mar-93	2-1	Fashanu (7); Earle (78)	12,270	P.Don
1993-94	Home	27-Sep-93	1-1	OG (42, Ferdinand)	9,478	P.Don
1993-94	Away	19-Mar-94	0-1		11,368	M.Reed
1994-95	Away	24-Sep-94	1-0	Reeves (48)	11,061	K.Burge
1994-95	Home	4-Mar-95	1-3	Holdsworth (12)	9,176	G.Willard
1995-96	Away	23-Aug-95	3-0	Leonhardson (30); Holdsworth (56); Goodman (83)	11,837	G.Poll
1995-96	Home	20-Jan-96	2-1	Leonhardsen (40); Clarke (74)	9,123	S.Dunn

SHEFFIELD UNITED

Season	Venue	Date	Res	Scorers	Attendance	Referee
1992-93	Away	25-Aug-92	2-2	Barton (34); Holdsworth (74)	15,463	K.Barratt
1992-93	Home	20-Feb-93	2-0	Fashanu (1); Dobbs (44)	3,979	R.Hart
1993-94	Away	24-Aug-93	1-2	Clarke (59)	15,555	A.Wilkie
1993-94	Home	18-Dec-93	2-0	Barton (50); Holdsworth (67)	6,728	P.Durkin

SHEFFIELD WEDNESDAY

Season	Venue	Date	Res	Scorers	Attendance	Referee
1992-93	Home	28-Nov-92	1-1	Jones (89 pen)	5,740	R.Milford
1992-93	Away	24-Mar-93	1-1	Holdsworth (90)	20,918	J.Lloyd
1993-94	Away	16-Oct-93	2-2	Blissett (46); Jones (89)	21,752	R.Gifford
1993-94	Home	15-Jan-94	2-1	Ardley (12); Fashanu (42)	5,536	M.Bodenham
1994-95	Home	27-Aug-94	0-1		7,453	R.Hart
1994-95	Away	11-Mar-95	1-0	Reeves (63)	20,395	J.Worrall
1995-96	Home	30-Aug-95	2-2	Goodman (17); Holdsworth (84 pen)	6,352	A.Wilkie
1995-96	Away	10-Feb-96	1-2	Gayle (60)	19,085	M.Bodenham
1996-97	Home	12-Oct-96	4-2	Ekoku (3); Earle (32); Leonhardsen (66); Jones (86)	10,512	M.Riley
1996-97	Away	19-Apr-97	1-3	Goodman (85)	26,957	J.Winter
1997-98	Home	23-Aug-97	1-1	Euell (17)	11,503	A.Wilkie

1997-98	Away	31-Jan-98	1-1	Hughes,M. (21)	22,655	A.Wilkie
1998-99	Home	19-Sep-98	2-1	Euell (1, 50)	13,163	N.Barry
1998-99	Away	3-Mar-99	2-1	Ekoku (8); Gayle (31)	24,116	P.Jones
1999-00	Away	2-Oct-99	1-5	Hartson (14)	18,077	P.Durkin
1999-00	Home	12-Apr-00	0-2		8,248	A.Wiley

SOUTHAMPTON

Season	Venue	Date	Res	Scorers	Attendance	Referee
1992-93	Away	17-Oct-92	2-2	Cotterill (50, 67)	11,221	K.Barratt
1992-93	Home	6-Mar-93	1-2	Holdsworth (22)	4,534	A.Gunn
1993-94	Home	31-Aug-93	1-0	Barton (34)	6,036	K.Hackett
1993-94	Away	26-Feb-94	0-1		14,790	D.Gallagher
1994-95	Away	26-Dec-94	3-2	Holdsworth (20,72 pen); Harford (37)	14,603	G.Poll
1994-95	Home	17-Apr-95	0-2		10,521	G.Ashby
1995-96	Winter	28-Oct-95	1-2	Ewell (64)	7,982	J.Winter
1995-96	Away	5-May-96	0-0		15,172	M.Reed
1996-97	Home	23-Sep-96	3-1	Gayle (13); Ekoku (38, 74)	8,572	P.Durkin
1996-97	Away	26-Feb-97	0-0		14,418	A.Wilkie
1997-98	Home	7-Dec-97	1-0	Earle (17)	12,009	M.Reed
1997-98	Away	11-Apr-98	1-0	Leaburn (38)	14,815	M.Reed
1998-99	Away	19-Dec-98	1-3	Gayle (76)	14,354	M.Reed
1998-99	Home	8-May-99	0-2		24,068	S.Dunn
1999-00	Home	30-Oct-99	1-1	Gayle (90)	15,754	S.Lodge
1999-00	Away	14-May-00	0-2		15,249	S.Lodge

SUNDERLAND

1996-97	Away	7-Dec-96	3-1	Ekoku (8, 29); Holdsworth (89)	19,672	K.Burge
1996-97	Home	11-May-97	1-0	Euell (85)	21,338	D.Gallagher
1999-00	Home	3-Jan-00	1-0	Cort (30)	17,621	G.Poll
1999-00	Away	8-Apr-00	1-2	OG (73, Craddock)	41,592	G.Barber

SWINDON TOWN

Season	Venue	Date	Res	Scorers	Attendance	Referee
1993-94	Home	6-Nov-93	3-0	Fashanu (29); Blissett (67); Holsworth (71)	7,758	S.Lodge
1993-94	Away	23-Apr-94	4-2	Fashanu (13); Earle (71, 75); Holdsworth (81)	13,309	G.Poll

TOTTENHAM HOTSPUR

Season	Venue	Date	Res	Scorers	Attendance	Referee
1992-93	Home	25-Oct-92	1-1	Gibson (38)	8,628	A.Gunn
1992-93	Away	1-May-93	1-1	Earle (64)	24,473	R.Lewis
1993-94	Away	24-Nov-93	1-1	Holdsworth (71)	17,744	K.Hackett
1993-94	Home	30-Apr-94	2-1	Holdsworth (58); Clarke (63)	20,875	D.Allison
1994-95	Home	1-Oct-94	1-2	Talboys (28)	16,802	M.Reed
1994-95	Away	25-Feb-95	2-1	Ekoku (38,64)	27,258	D.Gallagher
1995-96	Away	30-Sep-95	1-3	Earle (39)	25,321	G.Ashby
1995-96	Home	16-Dec-95	0-1		16,193	D.Elleray
1996-97	Home	3-Sep-96	1-0	Earle (3)	17,506	S.Dunn
1996-97	Away	5-Apr-97	0-1		32,654	K.Burge
1997-98	Away	27-Sep-97	0-0		26,261	P.Durkin
1997-98	Home	2-May-98	2-6	Fear (21, 29)	25,820	G.Barber
1998-99	Home	15-Aug-98	3-1	Earle (48); Ekoku (60, 88)	23,031	G.Poll

1998-99	Away	16-Jan-99	0-0		32,422	M.Riley
1999-00	Home	26-Sep-99	1-1	Hartson (57)	17,368	G.Poll
1999-00	Away	22-Apr-00	0-2		33,086	D.Gallagher

WATFORD

Season	Venue	Date	Res	Scorers	Attendance	Referee
1999-00	Away	7-Aug-99	3-2	Cort (10); Gayle (28); OG (78, Johnson,R.)	15,511	S.Lodge
1999-00	Home	4-Dec-99	5-0	Cort (15), Earle (32), Hartson (61); Euell (67); Gayle (78)	14,021	A.Wiley

WEST HAM UNITED

Season	Venue	Date	Res	Scorers	Attendance	Referee
1993-94	Away	14-Aug-93	2-0	Fashanu (64); Sanchez (72)	20,369	K.Burge
1993-94	Home	4-Dec-93	1-2	Holdsworth (83)	10,903	D.Gallagher
1994-95	Home	28-Dec-94	1-0	Fear (57)	11,212	P.Don
1994-95	Away	13-Apr-95	0-3		21,804	M.Reed
1995-96	Home	16-Oct-95	0-1		9,411	D.Gallagher
1995-96	Away	6-Apr-96	1-1	Jones (9)	20,402	P.Durkin
1996-97	Away	14-Sep-96	2-0	Clarke (54); Ekoku (84)	21,924	R.Dilkes
1996-97	Home	17-Mar-97	1-1	Harford (19)	15,771	J.Winter
1997-98	Away	30-Aug-97	1-3	Ekuko (80)	24,516	G.Poll
1997-98	Home	28-Dec-97	1-2	Solbakken (89)	22,087	P.Durkin
1998-99	Away	9-Sep-98	4-3	Gayle (30, 77); Euell (64); Ekoku (81)	25,311	G.Barber
1998-99	Home	30-Jan-99	0-0		23,035	P.Durkin
1999-00	Home	26-Dec-99	2-2	Hreidarsson (33); Ardley (85)	20,394	S.Dunn
1999-00	Away	26-Mar-00	1-2	Hughes,M. (75)	22,438	R.Harris

THE PLAYERS

AN A-Z OF EVERY PLAYER TO HAVE APPEARED IN THE FA PREMIER LEAGUE 1992-93 TO 1999-00

ABLETT, Gary

FULLNAME: Gary Ian Ablett
DOB: 19-Oct-65, Liverpool

Club History	Signed	Fee
Liverpool	11/83	Amateur
Derby Co.	1/85	Loan
Hull C.	9/86	Loan
Everton	1/92	£750,000

Season	Team	Tot	St	Sb	Snu	Ps	Gls
92-93	Everton	40	40	0	0	0	0
93-94	Everton	32	32	0	0	0	1
94-95	Everton	26	26	0	0	3	4
95-96	Everton	13	13	0	0	3	0
	Total	111	111	0	0	6	5

ABOU, Samassi

FULLNAME: Samassi Abou
DOB: 04-Apr-73, Gabona, Ivory Coast

Club History	Signed	Fee
Cannes		
West Ham U.	10/97	£400,000

Season	Team	Tot	St	Sb	Snu	Ps	Gls
97-98	West Ham U.	19	12	7	4	6	5
98-99	West Ham U.	3	2	1	7	1	0
99-00	West Ham U.	0	0	0	3	0	0
	Total	22	14	8	14	7	5

ADAMS, Micky

FULLNAME: Michael Richard Adams
DOB: 08-Nov-61, Sheffield

Club History	Signed	Fee
Gillingham	11/79	
Coventry C.	7/83	£75,000
Leeds U.	1/87	£110,000
Southampton	3/89	£25,000
Stoke C.	3/94	Loan

Season	Team	Tot	St	Sb	Snu	Ps	Gls
92-93	Southampton	38	38	0	0	0	4
93-94	Southampton	19	17	2	1	1	0
	Total	57	55	2	1	1	4

ADAMS, Neil

FULLNAME: Neil James Adams
DOB: 23-Nov-65, Stoke

Club History	Signed	Fee
Stoke C.	7/85	
Everton	7/86	£150,000
Oldham A.	1/89	Loan
Oldham A.	6/89	£100,000
Norwich C.	2/94	£250,000

Season	Team	Tot	St	Sb	Snu	Ps	Gls
92-93	Oldham A.	32	26	6	5	3	9
93-94	Oldham A.	13	7	6	1	1	0
93-94	Norwich C.	14	11	3	0	3	0
94-95	Norwich C.	33	23	10	1	8	3
	Total	92	67	25	7	15	12

ADAMS, Tony

FULLNAME: Anthony Alexander Adams
DOB: 10-Oct-66, Romford

Club History	Signed	Fee
Arsenal	1/84	Amateur

Season	Team	Tot	St	Sb	Snu	Ps	Gls
92-93	Arsenal	35	33	2	0	2	0
93-94	Arsenal	35	35	0	0	3	0
94-95	Arsenal	27	27	0	0	4	3
95-96	Arsenal	21	21	0	0	0	1
96-97	Arsenal	28	27	1	0	2	3
97-98	Arsenal	26	26	0	0	0	3
98-99	Arsenal	26	26	0	0	0	1
99-00	Arsenal	21	21	0	0	0	0
	Total	219	216	3	0	11	11

AGNEW, Steve

FULLNAME: Stephen Mark Agnew
DOB: 09-Nov-65, Shipley

Club History	Signed	Fee
Barnsley	11/83	Amateur
Blackburn R.	6/91	£700,000
Portsmouth	11/92	Loan
Leicester C.	2/93	£250,000
Sunderland	1/95	£250,000

Season	Team	Tot	St	Sb	Snu	Ps	Gls
94-95	Leicester C.	11	7	4	2	1	0
96-97	Sunderland	15	11	4	4	4	2
	Total	26	18	8	6	5	2

AGOGO, Junior

FULLNAME: Manuel Agogo
DOB: 01-Aug-79, Accra

Club History	Signed	Fee
Sheffield W.	10/96	Free from Non-League

Season	Team	Tot	St	Sb	Snu	Ps	Gls
97-98	Sheffield W.	1	0	1	0	0	0
98-99	Sheffield W.	1	0	1	4	0	0
	Total	2	0	2	4	0	0

AIJOFREE, Hasney

FULLNAME: Hansey Aijofree
DOB: 11-Jul-78, Manchester

Club History	Signed	Fee			
Bolton Wanderers		Trainee			

Season	Team	Tot	St	Sb	Snu	Ps	Gls
97-98	Bolton W.	2	2	0	5	0	0
	Total	2	2	0	5	0	0

AINSWORTH, Gareth

FULLNAME: Gareth Ainsworth
DOB: 10-May-73, Blackburn

Club History	Signed	Fee
Preston NE	1/92	Free NL
Cambridge U.	8/92	Free
Preston NE	12/92	Free
Lincoln C.	10/95	£25,000
Port Vale	9/97	£500,000
Wimbledon	10/98	£2m

Season	Team	Tot	St	Sb	Snu	Ps	Gls
98-99	Wimbledon	8	5	3	2	3	0
99-00	Wimbledon	2	0	2	1	0	2
	Total	10	5	5	3	3	2

AISTON, Sam

FULLNAME: Samuel James Aiston
DOB: 21-Nov-76, Newcastle-on-Tyne

Club History	Signed	Fee
Sunderland	7/95	Free from Newcastle Jnrs
Chester C.	2/97	Loan

Season	Team	Tot	St	Sb	Snu	Ps	Gls
96-97	Sunderland	2	0	2	9	0	0
	Total	2	0	2	9	0	0

AKINBIYI, Ade

FULLNAME: Adeola Peter Akinbiyi
DOB: 10-Oct-74, Hackney

Club History	Signed	Fee
Norwich C.	2/93	Trainee

Season	Team	Tot	St	Sb	Snu	Ps	Gls
93-94	Norwich C.	2	0	2	1	0	0
94-95	Norwich C.	13	6	7	0	5	0
	Total	15	6	9	1	5	0

ALBERT, Philippe

FULLNAME: Philippe Albert
DOB: 10-Aug-67, Bouillon, Belgium

Club History	Signed	Fee
Anderlecht		
Newcastle U.	8/94	£2.65m

Season	Team	Tot	St	Sb	Snu	Ps	Gls
94-95	Newcastle U.	17	17	0	0	1	2
95-96	Newcastle U.	23	19	4	5	1	4

Season	Team	Tot	St	Sb	Snu	Ps	Gls
96-97	Newcastle U.	27	27	0	5	1	2
97-98	Newcastle U.	23	21	2	7	3	0
98-99	Newcastle U.	6	3	3	4	0	0
	Total	96	87	9	21	6	8

ALEXANDERSSON, Niclas

FULLNAME: Niclas Alexandersson
DOB: 29-Dec-71, Halmstad, Sweden

Club History	Signed	Fee
IFK Gothenburg		
Sheffield W.	12/97	£750,000

Season	Team	Tot	St	Sb	Snu	Ps	Gls
97-98	Sheffield W.	6	5	1	1	2	0
98-99	Sheffield W.	32	31	1	0	9	3
99-00	Sheffield W.	37	37	0	0	8	5
	Total	75	73	2	1	19	8

ALLAN, Derek

FULLNAME: Derek Allan
DOB: 24-Dec-74, Irvine

Club History	Signed	Fee
Ayr U.		
Southampton	3/93	£70,000

Season	Team	Tot	St	Sb	Snu	Ps	Gls
92-93	Southampton	1	0	1	0	0	0
94-95	Southampton	0	0	0	1	0	0
	Total	1	0	1	1	0	0

ALLEN, Bradley

FULLNAME: Bradley James Allen
DOB: 13-Sep-71, Romford

Club History	Signed	Fee
QPR	9/88	Junior
Charlton A.	3/96	£400,000

Season	Team	Tot	St	Sb	Snu	Ps	Gls
92-93	QPR	25	21	4	3	1	10
93-94	QPR	21	14	7	3	2	7
94-95	QPR	5	2	3	4	0	2
95-96	QPR	8	5	3	1	3	1
98-99	Charlton A.	0	0	0	0	0	0
	Total	59	42	17	11	6	20

ALLEN, Chris

FULLNAME: Christopher Anthony Allen
DOB: 18-Nov-72, Oxford

Club History	Signed	Fee
Oxford U.	5/91	Trainee
Nottingham F.	2/96	Loan

Season	Team	Tot	St	Sb	Snu	Ps	Gls
95-96	Nottingham F.	3	1	2	1	0	1
96-97	Nottingham F.	24	16	8	10	4	0
	Total	27	17	10	11	4	1

ALLEN, Clive

FULLNAME: Clive D Allen
DOB: 20-May-61, Stepney

Club History	Signed	Fee
QPR	9/78	
Arsenal	6/80	£1.25m
Crystal P.	8/80	£1.25m
QPR	5/81	£425,000
Tottenham H.	8/84	£750,000
Bordeaux, France	5/88	£1m
Manchester C.	8/89	£1.1m
Chelsea	12/91	£250,000
West Ham U.	3/92	£275,000

Season	Team	Tot	St	Sb	Snu	Ps	Gls
93-94	West Ham U.	7	7	0	2	2	2
	Total	7	7	0	2	2	2

ALLEN, Graham

FULLNAME: Graham Allen
DOB: 08-Apr-77, Franworth

Club History	Signed	Fee
Everton	12/94	Free

Season	Team	Tot	St	Sb	Snu	Ps	Gls
95-96	Everton	0	0	0	2	0	0
96-97	Everton	1	0	1	8	1	0
97-98	Everton	5	2	3	6	1	0
	Total	6	2	4	16	2	0

ALLEN, Malcolm

FULLNAME: Malcolm Allen
DOB: 21-Mar-67, Caernarfon

Club History	Signed	Fee
Watford	3/85	Amateur
Aston Villa	9/87	Loan
Norwich C.	8/88	£175,000
Millwall	3/90	£400,000
Newcastle U.	8/93	£300,000

Season	Team	Tot	St	Sb	Snu	Ps	Gls
93-94	Newcastle U.	9	9	0	5	2	5
94-95	Newcastle U.	1	0	1	3	0	0
	Total	10	9	1	8	2	5

ALLEN, Martin

FULLNAME: Martin James Allen
DOB: 14-Aug-65, Reading

Club History	Signed	Fee
QPR	6/83	Amateur
West Ham U.	8/89	£675,000

Season	Team	Tot	St	Sb	Snu	Ps	Gls
93-94	West Ham U.	26	20	6	4	2	6
94-95	West Ham U.	29	26	3	1	5	2
95-96	West Ham U.	3	3	0	0	0	1
	Total	58	49	9	5	7	9

ALLEN, Paul

FULLNAME: Paul Kevin Allen
DOB: 28-Aug-62, Reading

Club History	Signed	Fee
West Ham U.	8/79	Amateur
Tottenham H.	6/85	£400,000
Southampton	9/93	£550,000

Season	Team	Tot	St	Sb	Snu	Ps	Gls
92-93	Tottenham H.	38	38	0	0	4	3
93-94	Tottenham H.	1	0	1	0	0	0
93-94	Southampton	32	29	3	3	2	1
94-95	Southampton	11	11	0	1	1	0
	Total	82	78	4	4	7	4

ALLEN, Rory

FULLNAME: Rory William Allen
DOB: 17-Oct-77, Beckenham

Club History	Signed	Fee
Tottenham H.	3/96	Trainee

Season	Team	Tot	St	Sb	Snu	Ps	Gls
96-97	Tottenham H.	12	9	3	12	3	2
97-98	Tottenham H.	4	1	3	2	1	0
98-99	Tottenham H.	5	0	5	4	0	0
	Total	21	10	11	18	4	2

ALLON, Joe

FULLNAME: Joe Allon
DOB: 12-Nov-66, Gateshead

Club History	Signed	Fee
Newcastle U.	11/84	Trainee
Swansea C.	8/87	Free
Hartlepool U.	11/88	Free
Chelsea	8/91	£250,000

Season	Team	Tot	St	Sb	Snu	Ps	Gls
92-93	Chelsea	3	1	2	4	1	0
	Total	3	1	2	4	1	0

ALLOU, Barnard

FULLNAME: Barnard Allou
DOB: 19-Jun-75, Ivory Coast

Club History	Signed			Fee		
Grampus 8						
Nottingham F.	3/99			Free		

Season	Team	Tot	St	Sb	Snu	Ps	Gls
98-99	Nottingham F.	2	0	2	3	0	0
	Total	2	0	2	3	0	0

ALMEIDA, Marco

FULLNAME: Marco Almeidea
DOB:

Club History	Signed			Fee		
Sporting Lisbon						
Southampton	7/99			Loan		

Season	Team	Tot	St	Sb	Snu	Ps	Gls
99-00	Southampton	1	0	1	4	0	0
	Total	1	0	1	4	0	0

ALOISI, John

FULLNAME: John Aloisi
DOB: 05-Feb-76, Australia

Club History	Signed			Fee		
Cremonese						
Portsmouth	8/97			£300,000		
Coventry C.	12/98			£650,000		

Season	Team	Tot	St	Sb	Snu	Ps	Gls
98-99	Coventry C.	16	7	9	2	3	5
99-00	Coventry C.	7	3	4	0	2	2
	Total	23	10	13	2	5	7

ALVES, Paolo

FULLNAME: Paolo Alves
DOB: 10-Dec-69, Mateus Villareal, Portugal

Club History	Signed			Fee		
Sporting Lisbon						
West Ham U.	11/97			Loan		

Season	Team	Tot	St	Sb	Snu	Ps	Gls
97-98	West Ham U.	4	0	4	4	0	0
	Total	4	0	4	4	0	0

AMBROSETTI, Gabriele

FULLNAME: Gabriele Ambrosetti
DOB: 07-Aug-73, Italy

Club History	Signed			Fee		
Vicenza						
Chelsea	8/99			£3.5m		

Season	Team	Tot	St	Sb	Snu	Ps	Gls
99-00	Chelsea	16	9	7	6	7	0
	Total	16	9	7	6	7	0

AMOKACHI, Daniel

FULLNAME: Daniel Amokachi
DOB: 30-Dec-72, Groko, Nigeria

Club History	Signed			Fee		
FC Bruge						
Everton	8/94			£3m		

Season	Team	Tot	St	Sb	Snu	Ps	Gls
94-95	Everton	18	17	1	2	4	4
95-96	Everton	25	17	8	6	4	6
	Total	43	34	9	8	8	10

ANDERSEN, Trond

FULLNAME: Trond Andersen
DOB: 06-Jan-75, Norway

Club History	Signed			Fee		
Molde						
Wimbledon	8/99			£2.5m		

Season	Team	Tot	St	Sb	Snu	Ps	Gls
99-00	Wimbledon	36	35	1	0	4	0
	Total	36	35	1	0	4	0

ANDERSON, Viv

FULLNAME: Vivian Anderson
DOB: 29-Aug-56, Nottingham

Club History	Signed			Fee		
Nottingham F.	8/74			Amateur		
Arsenal	8/84			£250,000		
Manchester U.	7/87			£250,000		
Sheffield W.	1/91			Free		

Season	Team	Tot	St	Sb	Snu	Ps	Gls
92-93	Sheffield W.	26	24	2	1	2	3
	Total	26	24	2	1	2	3

ANDERSSON, Andreas

FULLNAME: Andreas Claus Andersson
DOB: 10-Apr-76, Stockholm

Club History	Signed			Fee		
Milan						
Newcastle U.	1/98			£3.6m		

Season	Team	Tot	St	Sb	Snu	Ps	Gls
97-98	Newcastle U.	12	10	2	2	5	2
98-99	Newcastle U.	15	11	4	3	7	2
	Total	27	21	6	5	12	4

ANDERSSON, Patrik

FULLNAME: Patrik Andersson
DOB: 18-Aug-71, Borgeby

Club History	Signed	Fee
Malmo, Sweden		
Blackburn R.	12/92	£800,000
Borussia Monchengladbach		

Season	Team	Tot	St	Sb	Snu	Ps	Gls
92-93	Blackburn R.	11	6	5	4	3	0
93-94	Blackburn R.	1	1	0	2	1	0
97-98	Blackburn R.	4	1	3	8	1	0
98-99	Blackburn R.	0	0	0	2	0	0
	Total	16	8	8	16	5	0

ANDERTON, Darren

FULLNAME: Darren Robert Anderton
DOB: 03-Mar-72, Southampton

Club History	Signed	Fee
Portsmouth	2/90	Trainee
Tottenham H.	6/92	£1.75m

Season	Team	Tot	St	Sb	Snu	Ps	Gls
92-93	Tottenham H.	34	32	2	0	7	6
93-94	Tottenham H.	37	35	2	1	4	6
94-95	Tottenham H.	37	37	0	0	2	5
95-96	Tottenham H.	8	6	2	0	1	2
96-97	Tottenham H.	16	14	2	0	7	3
97-98	Tottenham H.	15	7	8	1	5	0
98-99	Tottenham H.	32	31	1	0	4	3
99-00	Tottenham H.	22	22	0	1	2	3
	Total	201	184	17	3	32	28

ANDRESEN, Martin

FULLNAME: Martin Andreson
DOB: 02-Feb-77, Norway

Club History	Signed	Fee
Stabaek		
Wimbledon	10/99	£1.8m

Season	Team	Tot	St	Sb	Snu	Ps	Gls
99-00	Wimbledon	14	4	10	6	3	1
	Total	14	4	10	7	4	1

ANDREWS, Ian

FULLNAME: Ian Edmund Andrews
DOB: 01-Dec-64, Nottingham

Club History	Signed	Fee
Leicester C.	12/82	Apprentice
Swindon Town	1/84	Loan
Celtic	7/88	£300,000
Leeds U.	12/88	Loan
Southampton	12/89	£200,000

Season	Team	Tot	St	Sb	Snu	Ps	Gls
92-93	Southampton	0	0	0	42	0	0
93-94	Southampton	5	5	0	37	0	0
	Total	5	5	0	79	0	0

ANELKA, Nicolas

FULLNAME: Nicolas Anelka
DOB: 24-Mar-79, Versailles

Club History	Signed	Fee
Paris St Germain		Trainee
Arsenal	1/97	£500,000

Season	Team	Tot	St	Sb	Snu	Ps	Gls
96-97	Arsenal	4	0	4	1	0	0
97-98	Arsenal	26	16	10	8	13	6
98-99	Arsenal	35	34	1	2	15	17
	Total	65	50	15	11	28	23

ANGELL, Brett

FULLNAME: Brett Ashley Angell
DOB: 20-Aug-68, Marlborough

Club History	Signed	Fee
Derby Co.	2/88	£40,000 from NL
Stockport Co.	10/88	£33,000
Southend U.	8/90	£100,000
Everton	9/93	Loan
Everton	1/94	£500,000

Season	Team	Tot	St	Sb	Snu	Ps	Gls
93-94	Everton	16	13	3	2	5	1
94-95	Everton	4	3	1	4	1	0
	Total	20	16	4	6	6	1

ANTHROBUS, Steve

FULLNAME: Stephen Anthony Anthrobus
DOB: 10-Nov-68, Lewisham

Club History	Signed	Fee
Millwall	8/86	Juniors
Wimbledon	2/90	£150,000

Season	Team	Tot	St	Sb	Snu	Ps	Gls
92-93	Wimbledon	5	4	1	0	0	0
	Total	5	4	1	0	0	0

APPLEBY, Matty

FULLNAME: Matthew Wilfred Appleby
DOB: 16-Apr-72, Middlesbrough

Club History	Signed	Fee
Newcastle U.	5/90	Trainee
Darlington	11/93	Loan
Darlington	9/94	Free
Barnsley	8/97	£250,000

Season	Team	Tot	St	Sb	Snu	Ps	Gls
93-94	Newcastle U.	1	1	0	3	0	0
97-98	Barnsley	15	13	2	7	5	0
	Total	16	14	2	10	5	0

320

ARDLEY, Neal

FULLNAME: Neal Christopher Ardley
DOB: 01-Sep-72, Epsom

Club History	Signed	Fee
Wimbledon	7/91	Trainee

Season	Team	Tot	St	Sb	Snu	Ps	Gls
92-93	Wimbledon	26	24	2	0	5	4
93-94	Wimbledon	16	14	2	1	3	1
94-95	Wimbledon	14	9	5	2	1	1
95-96	Wimbledon	6	4	2	2	1	0
96-97	Wimbledon	34	33	1	1	4	2
97-98	Wimbledon	34	31	3	0	6	2
98-99	Wimbledon	23	16	7	4	9	0
99-00	Wimbledon	17	10	7	2	4	2
	Total	170	141	29	12	33	12

ARMSTRONG, Alun

FULLNAME: Alun Armstrong
DOB: 22-Feb-75, Gateshead

Club History	Signed	Fee
Newcastle U.	10/93	Trainee
Stockport Co.	6/94	£50,000
Middlesbrough	2/98	£1.5m

Season	Team	Tot	St	Sb	Snu	Ps	Gls
98-99	Middlesbrough	6	0	6	2	0	1
99-00	Middlesbrough	12	3	9	11	3	1
	Total	18	3	15	13	3	2

ARMSTRONG, Chris

FULLNAME: Christopher Peter Armstrong
DOB: 19-Jun-71, Newcastle

Club History	Signed	Fee
Wrexham	3/89	Free NL
Millwall	8/91	£50,000
Crystal P.	9/92	£1m
Tottenham H.	7/94	£4.5m

Season	Team	Tot	St	Sb	Snu	Ps	Gls
92-93	Crystal P.	35	35	0	0	2	15
94-95	Crystal P.	40	40	0	0	1	8
95-96	Tottenham H.	36	36	0	0	1	15
96-97	Tottenham H.	12	12	0	0	2	5
97-98	Tottenham H.	19	13	6	2	5	5
98-99	Tottenham H.	34	24	10	1	5	7
99-00	Tottenham H.	31	29	2	0	8	14
	Total	207	189	18	3	24	69

ARMSTRONG, Craig

FULLNAME: Steven Craig Armstrong
DOB: 23-May-75, South Shields

Club History	Signed	Fee
Nottingham F.	6/92	Trainee

Season	Team	Tot	St	Sb	Snu	Ps	Gls
92-93	Nottingham F.	0	0	0	4	0	0
95-96	Nottingham F.	0	0	0	1	0	0
96-97	Nottingham F.	0	0	0	1	0	0
98-99	Nottingham F.	22	20	2	2	4	0
	Total	22	20	2	8	4	0

ARPHEXAD, Pegguy

FULLNAME: Pegguy Michel Arphexad
DOB: 18-May-73, Guadeloupe

Club History	Signed	Fee
Racing Club Paris		
Leicester C.	8/97	Free

Season	Team	Tot	St	Sb	Snu	Ps	Gls
97-98	Leicester C.	5	5	0	23	0	0
98-99	Leicester C.	4	2	2	34	0	0
99-00	Leicester C.	11	9	2	27	0	0
	Total	20	16	4	84	0	0

ASANOVIC, Aijosa

FULLNAME: Aijosa Asanovic
DOB: 14-Dec-65, Split, Croatia

Club History	Signed	Fee
Hajduk Split		
Derby Co.	7/96	£1m

Season	Team	Tot	St	Sb	Snu	Ps	Gls
96-97	Derby Co.	34	34	0	0	11	6
97-98	Derby Co.	4	3	1	1	3	1
	Total	38	37	1	1	14	7

ASPRILLA, Tino

FULLNAME: Faustino Hernon Asprilla
DOB: 10-Nov-69, Colombia

Club History	Signed	Fee
Parma		
Newcastle U.	2/96	£6.7m

Season	Team	Tot	St	Sb	Snu	Ps	Gls
95-96	Newcastle U.	14	11	3	0	3	3
96-97	Newcastle U.	24	17	7	4	12	4
97-98	Newcastle U.	10	8	2	0	3	2
	Total	48	36	12	4	18	9

ATHERTON, Peter

FULLNAME: Peter Atherton
DOB: 06-Apr-70, Orrell

Club History	Signed	Fee
Wigan A.	2/88	Trainee
Coventry C.	8/91	£300,000

Sheffield W.   6/94   £800,000

Season	Team	Tot	St	Sb	Snu	Ps	Gls
92-93	Coventry C.	39	39	0	0	0	0
93-94	Coventry C.	40	39	1	1	0	0
94-95	Sheffield W.	41	41	0	0	2	1
95-96	Sheffield W.	35	35	0	1	0	0
96-97	Sheffield W.	37	37	0	0	1	2
97-98	Sheffield W.	27	27	0	0	2	3
98-99	Sheffield W.	38	38	0	0	0	2
99-00	Sheffield W.	35	35	0	0	1	1
	Total	292	291	1	2	6	9

ATKINS, Mark

FULLNAME: Mark Nigel Atkins
DOB: 14-Aug-68, Doncaster

Club History	Signed	Fee
Scunthorpe U.	7/86	Juniors
Blackburn R.	6/88	£45,000

Season	Team	Tot	St	Sb	Snu	Ps	Gls
92-93	Blackburn R.	31	24	7	6	3	5
93-94	Blackburn R.	15	8	7	5	1	1
94-95	Blackburn R.	34	30	4	4	7	6
95-96	Blackburn R.	4	0	4	0	0	0
	Total	84	62	22	15	11	12

ATKINSON, Dalian

FULLNAME: Dalian Robert Atkinson
DOB: 21-Mar-68, Shrewsbury

Club History	Signed	Fee
Ipswich Town	6/85	Juniors
Sheffield W.	7/87	£450,000
Real Sociedad	8/90	£1.7m
Aston Villa	7/91	£1.6m

Season	Team	Tot	St	Sb	Snu	Ps	Gls
92-93	Aston Villa	28	28	0	0	4	11
93-94	Aston Villa	29	29	0	0	3	8
94-95	Aston Villa	16	11	5	2	5	3
	Total	73	68	5	2	12	22

AUSTIN, Dean

FULLNAME: Dean Barry Austin
DOB: 26-Apr-70, Hemel Hempstead

Club History	Signed	Fee
Southend U.	3/90	£12,000
Tottenham H.	6/92	£375,000

Season	Team	Tot	St	Sb	Snu	Ps	Gls
92-93	Tottenham H.	34	33	1	1	7	0
93-94	Tottenham H.	23	20	3	6	3	0
94-95	Tottenham H.	24	23	1	1	0	0
95-96	Tottenham H.	28	28	0	0	0	0
96-97	Tottenham H.	15	13	2	8	2	0

97-98	Tottenham H.	0	0	0	0	0	0
	Total	124	117	7	16	12	0

BAARDSEN, Espen

FULLNAME: Espen Baardsen
DOB: 07-Dec-77, San Rafael, Ca.

Club History	Signed	Fee
San Francisco All Blacks		
Tottenham H.	7/96	Free

Season	Team	Tot	St	Sb	Snu	Ps	Gls
96-97	Tottenham H.	2	1	1	36	0	0
97-98	Tottenham H.	9	9	0	26	0	0
98-99	Tottenham H.	12	12	0	25	0	0
99-00	Tottenham H.	0	0	0	37	0	0
	Total	23	22	1	124	0	0

BABAYARO, Celestine

FULLNAME: Celestine Babayaro
DOB: 29-Aug-78, Nigeria

Club History	Signed	Fee
Anderlecht		
Chelsea	4/97	£2.25m

Season	Team	Tot	St	Sb	Snu	Ps	Gls
97-98	Chelsea	8	8	0	1	1	0
98-99	Chelsea	28	26	2	0	3	3
99-00	Chelsea	25	23	2	0	1	0
	Total	61	57	4	1	5	3

BABB, Phil

FULLNAME: Phillip Andrew Babb
DOB: 30-Nov-70, London

Club History	Signed	Fee
Millwall	4/89	Trainee
Bradford C.	8/90	Free
Coventry C.	7/92	£500,000
Liverpool	9/94	£3.6m

Season	Team	Tot	St	Sb	Snu	Ps	Gls
92-93	Coventry C.	34	27	7	5	0	0
93-94	Coventry C.	40	40	0	0	1	3
94-95	Coventry C.	3	3	0	0	0	0
94-95	Liverpool	34	33	1	1	1	0
95-96	Liverpool	28	28	0	0	1	0
96-97	Liverpool	22	21	1	2	4	1
97-98	Liverpool	19	18	1	8	1	0
98-99	Liverpool	25	24	1	2	3	0
	Total	205	194	11	18	11	4

BADIR, Walid

FULLNAME: Walid Badir
DOB: 13-Mar-74, Israel

Club History	Signed	Fee
Hapoel Petah Tikva		
Wimbledon	7/99	£1.0m

Season	Team	Tot	St	Sb	Snu	Ps	Gls
99-00	Wimbledon	21	12	9	8	8	1
	Total	21	12	9	8	8	1

BAIANO, Francesco

FULLNAME: Francesco Baiano
DOB: 24-Feb-68, Napoli

Club History	Signed	Fee
Fiorentina	92	
Derby Co.	8/97	£650,000

Season	Team	Tot	St	Sb	Snu	Ps	Gls
97-98	Derby Co.	33	30	3	0	16	12
98-99	Derby Co.	22	17	5	3	14	4
99-00	Derby Co.	9	5	4	0	4	0
	Total	64	52	12	3	34	16

BAILEY, Dennis

FULLNAME: Dennis Lincoln Bailey
DOB: 13-Nov-65, Lambeth

Club History	Signed	Fee
Crystal P.	12/87	£10,000
Bristol R.	2/89	Loan
Birmingham C.	8/89	£80,000
Bristol R.	3/91	Loan
QPR	6/91	£175,000

Season	Team	Tot	St	Sb	Snu	Ps	Gls
92-93	QPR	15	13	2	2	6	1
93-94	QPR	0	0	0	2	0	0
	Total	15	13	2	4	6	1

BAKALLI, Adrian

FULLNAME: Adrian Bakalli
DOB: 22-Nov-76, Brussels

Club History	Signed	Fee
"Molenbeek"		
Watford		

Season	Team	Tot	St	Sb	Snu	Ps	Gls
99-00	Watford	2	0	2	2	0	0
	Total	2	0	2	2	0	0

BAKAYOKO, Ibrahima

FULLNAME: Ibrahima Bakayoko
DOB: 31-Dec-76, Seguela, Ivory Coast

Club History	Signed	Fee
Montpellier		
Everton	10/99	£4.5m

Season	Team	Tot	St	Sb	Snu	Ps	Gls
98-99	Everton	23	17	6	3	10	4
	Total	23	17	6	3	10	4

BAKER, Clive

FULLNAME: Clive Edward Baker
DOB: 14-Mar-59, N. Walsham

Club History	Signed	Fee
Norwich C.	7/77	Trainee
Barnsley	8/84	Free
Coventry C.	8/91	Free
Ipswich Town	8/92	Free

Season	Team	Tot	St	Sb	Snu	Ps	Gls
92-93	Ipswich T.	31	30	1	7	0	0
93-94	Ipswich T.	15	15	0	26	0	0
94-95	Ipswich T.	2	2	0	23	0	0
	Total	48	47	1	56	0	0

BAKER, Steve

FULLNAME: Steven Richard Baker
DOB: 08-Sep-78, Pontefract

Club History	Signed	Fee
Middlesbrough	7/97	Trainee

Season	Team	Tot	St	Sb	Snu	Ps	Gls
98-99	Middlesbrough	1	1	0	5	0	0
99-00	Middlesbrough	0	0	0	1	0	0
	Total	1	1	0	6	0	0

BAKKE, Eirik

FULLNAME: Eirik Bakke
DOB: 13-Sep-77, Norway

Club History	Signed	Fee
Sogndal	1/98	
Leeds U.	5/99	£1.75m

Season	Team	Tot	St	Sb	Snu	Ps	Gls
99-00	Leeds U.	29	24	5	3	5	2
	Total	29	24	5	3	5	2

BALL, Kevin

FULLNAME: Kevin Anthony Ball
DOB: 12-Nov-64, Hastings

Club History	Signed	Fee
Coventry C.		Juniors
Portsmouth	10/82	Free
Sunderland	7/90	£350,000

Season	Team	Tot	St	Sb	Snu	Ps	Gls
96-97	Sunderland	32	32	0	0	2	3
99-00	Sunderland	11	6	5	2	3	0
	Total	43	38	5	2	5	3

BALL, Michael

FULLNAME: Michael Ball
DOB: 02-Oct-77, Liverpool

Club History	Signed	Fee
Everton	10/96	Trainee

Season	Team	Tot	St	Sb	Snu	Ps	Gls
96-97	Everton	5	2	3	3	1	0
97-98	Everton	25	21	4	6	2	1
98-99	Everton	37	36	1	0	1	3
99-00	Everton	25	14	11	5	3	1
	Total	92	73	19	14	7	5

BANGER, Nicky

FULLNAME: Nicholas Lee Banger
DOB: 25-Apr-71, Southampton

Club History	Signed	Fee
Southampton	4/89	Trainee

Season	Team	Tot	St	Sb	Snu	Ps	Gls
92-93	Southampton	27	10	17	4	0	6
93-94	Southampton	14	4	10	2	2	0
94-95	Southampton	4	4	0	3	0	2
	Total	45	18	27	9	2	8

BANNISTER, Gary

FULLNAME: Gary Bannister
DOB: 22-Jul-60, Warrington

Club History	Signed	Fee
Coventry C.	5/78	Apprentice
Sheffield W.	8/81	
QPR	8/84	
Coventry C.	3/88	
WBA	3/90	
Oxford U.	3/92	Loan
Nottingham F.		

Season	Team	Tot	St	Sb	Snu	Ps	Gls
92-93	Nottingham F.	31	27	4	5	3	8
	Total	31	27	4	5	3	8

BARDSLEY, David

FULLNAME: David John Bardsley
DOB: 11-Sep-64, Manchester

Club History	Signed	Fee
Blackpool	11/82	Apprentice
Watford	11/83	£150,000
Oxford U.	9/87	£265,000
QPR	9/89	£500,000

Season	Team	Tot	St	Sb	Snu	Ps	Gls
92-93	QPR	40	40	0	0	0	3
93-94	QPR	32	32	0	0	0	0
94-95	QPR	30	30	0	0	0	0

Season	Team	Tot	St	Sb	Snu	Ps	Gls
95-96	QPR	29	28	1	1	3	0
	Total	131	130	1	1	3	3

BARKER, Simon

FULLNAME: Simon Barker
DOB: 04-Nov-64, Farnworth

Club History	Signed	Fee
Blackburn R.	11/82	Apprentice
QPR	7/88	£400,000

Season	Team	Tot	St	Sb	Snu	Ps	Gls
92-93	QPR	24	21	3	3	2	1
93-94	QPR	37	35	2	0	2	5
94-95	QPR	37	37	0	0	4	4
95-96	QPR	33	33	0	0	4	5
	Total	131	126	5	3	12	15

BARLOW, Andy

FULLNAME: Andrew John Barlow
DOB: 24-Nov-65, Oldham

Club History	Signed	Fee
Oldham A.	7/84	Juniors
Bradford C.	11/93	Loan

Season	Team	Tot	St	Sb	Snu	Ps	Gls
92-93	Oldham A.	7	7	0	0	1	0
93-94	Oldham A.	6	3	3	4	0	0
	Total	13	10	3	4	1	0

BARLOW, Stuart

FULLNAME: Stuart Barlow
DOB: 16-Jul-68, Liverpool

Club History	Signed	Fee
Everton	6/90	Free from Non League

Season	Team	Tot	St	Sb	Snu	Ps	Gls
92-93	Everton	26	8	18	3	3	5
93-94	Everton	22	6	16	3	3	3
94-95	Everton	11	7	4	11	1	2
95-96	Everton	3	0	3	3	0	0
	Total	62	21	41	20	7	10

BARMBY, Nicky

FULLNAME: Nicholas Jonathan Barmby
DOB: 11-Feb-74, Hull

Club History	Signed	Fee
Tottenham H.	4/91	Trainee
Middlesbrough	8/95	£5.25m
Everton	10/96	£5.75m

Season	Team	Tot	St	Sb	Snu	Ps	Gls
92-93	Tottenham H.	22	17	5	1	9	6
93-94	Tottenham H.	27	27	0	0	6	5
94-95	Tottenham H.	38	37	1	1	9	9

95-96	Middlesbrough	32	32	0	0	0	7
96-97	Middlesbrough	10	10	0	1	1	1
96-97	Everton	25	22	3	1	5	4
97-98	Everton	30	26	4	1	7	2
98-99	Everton	24	20	4	2	9	3
99-00	Everton	37	37	0	0	12	9
	Total	245	228	17	7	58	46

BARNARD, Darren

FULLNAME: Darren Sean Barnard
DOB: 30-Nov-71, Rinteln, Germany

Club History	Signed	Fee
Chelsea	5/90	£50,000 nl
Reading	11/94	Loan
Bristol C.	10/95	£175,000
Barnsley	8/97	£750,000

Season	Team	Tot	St	Sb	Snu	Ps	Gls
92-93	Chelsea	13	8	5	2	3	1
93-94	Chelsea	12	9	3	3	3	1
97-98	Barnsley	35	33	2	0	2	2
	Total	60	50	10	5	8	4

BARNES, David

FULLNAME: David Barnes
DOB: 16-Nov-61, Paddington

Club History	Signed	Fee
Coventry C.	5/79	
Ipswich Town	5/82	
Wolverhampton W	10/84	£35,000
Aldershot	8/87	£25,000
Sheffield U.	7/87	£50,000

Season	Team	Tot	St	Sb	Snu	Ps	Gls
92-93	Sheffield U.	13	13	0	0	2	0
93-94	Sheffield U.	2	2	0	0	0	0
	Total	15	15	0	0	2	0

BARNES, John

FULLNAME: John Charles Bryan Barnes
DOB: 07-Nov-63, Jamaica, West Indies

Club History	Signed	Fee
Watford	7/81	Free NL
Liverpool	6/87	£900,000
Newcastle	8/97	Free
Charlton A.	2/99	Free

Season	Team	Tot	St	Sb	Snu	Ps	Gls
92-93	Liverpool	27	26	1	0	0	5
93-94	Liverpool	26	24	2	0	6	3
94-95	Liverpool	38	38	0	0	3	0
95-96	Liverpool	36	36	0	0	2	3
96-97	Liverpool	35	34	1	2	2	4
97-98	Liverpool	0	0	0	1	0	0

97-98	Newcastle U.	26	22	4	8	8	6
98-99	Newcastle U.	1	0	1	3	1	0
98-99	Charlton A.	12	2	10	2	0	0
	Total	201	182	19	16	22	21

BARNESS, Tony

FULLNAME: Anthony Barness
DOB: 25-Mar-73, Lewisham, London

Club History	Signed	Fee
Charlton A.	3/91	Trainee
Chelsea	9/92	£350,000
Middlesbrough	8/93	Loan
Southend U.	2/96	Loan
Charlton A.	8/96	£165,000

Season	Team	Tot	St	Sb	Snu	Ps	Gls
92-93	Chelsea	2	2	0	0	0	0
94-95	Chelsea	12	10	2	1	3	0
95-96	Chelsea	0	0	0	1	0	0
98-99	Charlton A.	3	0	3	10	0	0
	Total	17	12	5	12	3	0

BARNWELL-EDINBORO, Jamie

FULLNAME: James Barnwell-Edinboro
DOB: 26-Dec-75, Hull

Club History	Signed	Fee
Coventry C.	7/94	Trainee

Season	Team	Tot	St	Sb	Snu	Ps	Gls
95-96	Coventry C.	1	0	1	0	0	0
	Total	1	0	1	0	0	0

BARRETT, Earl

FULLNAME: Earl Delisser Barrett
DOB: 28-Apr-67, Rochdale

Club History	Signed	Fee
Manchester C.	4/85	Trainee
Chester C.	3/86	Loan
Oldham Ath.	11/87	£35,000
Aston Villa	2/92	£1.7m
Everton	1/95	£1.7m
Sheffield Wed.	2/98	Free

Season	Team	Tot	St	Sb	Snu	Ps	Gls
92-93	Aston Villa	42	42	0	0	0	1
93-94	Aston Villa	39	39	0	0	0	0
94-95	Aston Villa	25	24	1	0	1	0
94-95	Everton	17	17	0	0	0	0
95-96	Everton	8	8	0	0	0	0
96-97	Everton	36	36	0	0	0	0
97-98	Everton	13	12	1	4	5	0
97-98	Sheffield W.	10	10	0	0	2	0
98-99	Sheffield W.	5	0	5	3	0	0
	Total	195	188	7	7	8	1

BARRETT, Graham

FULLNAME: Graham Barrett
DOB: 06-Oct-81, Dublin

Club History	Signed	Fee				
Arsenal	7/97	Trainee				
Season	Team	Tot	St	Sb	Snu	Ps	Gls
99-00	Arsenal	2	0	2	2	0	0
	Total	2	0	2	2	0	0

BARRON, Michael

FULLNAME: Michael James Barron
DOB: 22-Dec-74, Salford

Club History	Signed	Fee				
Middlesbrough	2/93	Trainee				
Season	Team	Tot	St	Sb	Snu	Ps	Gls
95-96	Middlesbrough	1	1	0	2	0	0
	Total	1	1	0	2	0	0

BARRY, Gareth

FULLNAME: Gareth Barry
DOB: 23-Feb-81, Hastings

Club History	Signed	Fee				
Brighton & HA		Trainee				
Aston Villa	2/98	Disputed				
Season	Team	Tot	St	Sb	Snu	Ps	Gls
97-98	Aston Villa	2	1	1	1	0	0
98-99	Aston Villa	32	27	5	4	4	2
99-00	Aston Villa	30	30	0	1	0	1
	Total	64	58	6	6	4	3

BART-WILLIAMS, Chris

FULLNAME: Christopher Gerald Bart-Williams
DOB: 16-Jun-74, Freetwon, Sierra Leone

Club History	Signed	Fee				
Leyton Orient	7/91	Trainee				
Sheffield W.	11/91	£275,000				
Nottingham F.	7/95	£2.5m				
Season	Team	Tot	St	Sb	Snu	Ps	Gls
92-93	Sheffield W.	34	21	13	4	5	6
93-94	Sheffield W.	37	30	7	1	14	8
94-95	Sheffield W.	38	32	6	0	7	2
95-96	Nottingham F.	33	33	0	2	1	0
96-97	Nottingham F.	16	16	0	1	3	1
98-99	Nottingham F.	23	19	4	1	5	3
	Total	181	151	30	9	35	20

BARTLETT, Neal

FULLNAME: Neal Bartlett
DOB: 07-Apr-75, Southampton

Club History	Signed	Fee				
Southampton	7/93					
Season	Team	Tot	St	Sb	Snu	Ps	Gls
92-93	Southampton	1	0	1	0	0	0
93-94	Southampton	7	4	3	1	3	0
	Total	8	4	4	1	3	0

BARTON, Warren

FULLNAME: Warren Dean Barton
DOB: 19-Mar-69, Stoke Newington

Club History	Signed	Fee				
Maidstone U.	7/87	£10,000				
Wimbledon	6/90	£300,000				
Newcastle U.	6/95	£4m+				
Season	Team	Tot	St	Sb	Snu	Ps	Gls
92-93	Wimbledon	23	23	0	0	0	2
93-94	Wimbledon	39	37	2	1	4	2
94-95	Wimbledon	39	39	0	0	2	2
95-96	Newcastle U.	31	30	1	4	4	0
96-97	Newcastle U.	18	14	4	10	0	1
97-98	Newcastle U.	23	17	6	1	3	3
98-99	Newcastle U.	24	17	7	11	4	0
99-00	Newcastle U.	34	33	1	0	2	0
	Total	231	210	21	27	19	10

BARTRAM, Vince

FULLNAME: Vincent Lee Bartram
DOB: 07-Aug-68, Birmingham

Club History	Signed	Fee				
Wolverhampton W	8/85	Juniors				
Blackpool	10/89	Loan				
Bournemouth	7/91	£65,000				
Arsenal	8/94	£400,000				
Season	Team	Tot	St	Sb	Snu	Ps	Gls
94-95	Arsenal	11	11	0	30	0	0
95-96	Arsenal	0	0	0	15	0	0
96-97	Arsenal	0	0	0	9	0	0
	Total	11	11	0	54	0	0

BASHAM, Steve

FULLNAME: Steve Basham
DOB: 02-Dec-77, Southampton

Club History	Signed	Fee				
Southampton	5/96	Trainee				
Wrexham	2/98	Loan				
Season	Team	Tot	St	Sb	Snu	Ps	Gls
96-97	Southampton	6	1	5	14	0	0
97-98	Southampton	9	0	9	1	0	0
98-99	Southampton	4	0	4	5	0	1
	Total	19	1	18	20	0	1

BATTY, David

FULLNAME: David Batty
DOB: 02-Dec-68, Leeds

Club History	Signed	Fee
Leeds U.	7/87	trainee
Blackburn R.	10/93	£2.75m
Newcastle U.	2/96	£3.75m
Leeds U.	12/98	£4.4m

Season	Team	Tot	St	Sb	Snu	Ps	Gls
92-93	Leeds U.	30	30	0	0	5	1
93-94	Leeds U.	9	8	1	1	0	0
93-94	Blackburn R.	26	26	0	0	3	0
94-95	Blackburn R.	5	4	1	1	0	0
95-96	Blackburn R.	23	23	0	0	1	1
95-96	Newcastle U.	11	11	0	0	0	1
96-97	Newcastle U.	32	32	0	0	1	1
97-98	Newcastle U.	32	32	0	0	1	1
98-99	Newcastle U.	8	6	2	0	0	0
98-99	Leeds U.	10	10	0	0	1	0
99-00	Leeds U.	16	16	0	0	1	0
	Total	202	198	4	2	13	5

BEAGRIE, Peter

FULLNAME: Peter Sydney Beagrie
DOB: 28-Nov-65, Middlesbrough

Club History	Signed	Fee
Middlesbrough	9/83	Juniors
Sheffield Wed	8/86	£35,000
Stoke C.	6/88	£210,000
Everton	11/89	£750,000
Sunderland	9/91	Loan
Manchester C.	3/94	£1.1m
Bradford C.	7/97	£50,000
Everton	3/98	Loan

Season	Team	Tot	St	Sb	Snu	Ps	Gls
92-93	Everton	22	11	11	0	2	3
93-94	Everton	29	29	0	0	6	3
93-94	Manchester C.	9	9	0	0	0	1
94-95	Manchester C.	37	33	4	0	3	2
95-96	Manchester C.	5	4	1	0	1	0
97-98	Everton	6	4	2	2	3	0
99-00	Bradford C.	35	30	5	0	7	7
	Total	143	120	23	2	22	16

BEARDSLEY, Peter

FULLNAME: Peter Andrew Beardsley
DOB: 18-Jan-61, Newcastle

Club History	Signed	Fee
Carlisle U.	8/79	Trail
Vancouver	4/81	£275,000
Manchester U.	9/82	£300,000
Vancouver (US)	9/83	
Newcastle U.	9/83	£150,000
Liverpool	7/87	£1.9m
Everton	8/91	£1m
Newcastle U.	7/93	£1.4m
Bolton Wanderers	8/97	£450,000

Season	Team	Tot	St	Sb	Snu	Ps	Gls
92-93	Everton	39	39	0	0	1	10
93-94	Newcastle U.	35	35	0	0	1	21
94-95	Newcastle U.	34	34	0	0	4	13
95-96	Newcastle U.	35	35	0	0	2	8
96-97	Newcastle U.	25	22	3	12	4	5
97-98	Newcastle U.	0	0	0	1	0	0
97-98	Bolton W.	17	14	3	6	7	2
	Total	185	179	6	19	19	59

BEASANT, Dave

FULLNAME: David John Beasant
DOB: 20-Mar-59, Willesden

Club History	Signed	Fee
Wimbledon	8/79	£1,000
Newcastle U.	6/88	£800,000
Chelsea	1/89	£725,000
Grimsby Town	10/92	Loan
Wolverhampton W.	1/93	Loan
Southampton	11/93	£300,000
Nottingham F.	11/97	Free

Season	Team	Tot	St	Sb	Snu	Ps	Gls
92-93	Chelsea	17	17	0	6	0	0
93-94	Southampton	25	25	0	4	0	0
94-95	Southampton	13	12	1	29	0	0
95-96	Southampton	36	36	0	1	0	0
96-97	Southampton	14	13	1	20	0	0
98-99	Nottingham F.	26	26	0	11	0	0
	Total	131	129	2	71	0	0

BEATTIE, James

FULLNAME: Southampton
DOB: 27-Feb-78, Lancaster

Club History	Signed	Fee
Blackburn R.	9/95	Trainee
Southampton	7/98	£1m

Season	Team	Tot	St	Sb	Snu	Ps	Gls
96-97	Blackburn R.	1	1	0	0	0	0
97-98	Blackburn R.	3	0	3	5	0	0
98-99	Southampton	35	22	13	3	8	5
99-00	Southampton	18	8	10	3	5	0
	Total	57	31	26	11	13	5

BECK, Mikkel

FULLNAME: Mikkel Beck
DOB: 12-May-73, Denmark

Club History	Signed	Fee
Fortuna Koln		
Middlesbrough	8/96	Free
Derby Co.	3/98	£500,000

Season	Team	Tot	St	Sb	Snu	Ps	Gls
96-97	Middlesbrough	25	22	3	3	2	5
98-99	Middlesbrough	27	13	14	2	5	5
98-99	Derby Co.	7	6	1	0	3	1
99-00	Derby Co.	11	5	6	2	2	1
	Total	70	46	24	7	12	12

BECKFORD, Darren

FULLNAME: Darren Richard Beckford
DOB: 12-May-67, Manchester

Club History	Signed	Fee
Manchester C.	8/84	Trainee
Bury	10/85	Loan
Port Vale	3/87	£15,000
Norwich C.	7/91	£925,000
Oldham A.	3/93	£300,000

Season	Team	Tot	St	Sb	Snu	Ps	Gls
92-93	Norwich C.	8	7	1	4	5	1
92-93	Oldham A.	7	6	1	0	1	3
93-94	Oldham A.	22	13	9	0	3	6
	Total	37	26	11	4	9	10

BECKHAM, David

FULLNAME: David Robert Beckham
DOB: 02-May-75, Leytonstone

Club History	Signed	Fee
Manchester U.	1/93	Trainee

Season	Team	Tot	St	Sb	Snu	Ps	Gls
94-95	Manchester U.	4	2	2	1	1	0
95-96	Manchester U.	33	26	7	4	5	7
96-97	Manchester U.	36	33	3	1	3	8
97-98	Manchester U.	37	34	3	0	2	9
98-99	Manchester U.	34	33	1	3	6	6
99-00	Manchester U.	31	30	1	1	7	6
	Total	175	158	17	10	24	36

BEENEY, Mark

FULLNAME: Mark Raymond Beeney
DOB: 30-Dec-67, Tunbridge Wells

Club History	Signed	Fee
Gillingham	8/85	Juniors
Maidstone U.	2/87	Free
Aldershot	3/90	Loan
Brighton & H A	3/91	£30,000
Leeds U.	4/93	£350,000

Season	Team	Tot	St	Sb	Snu	Ps	Gls
92-93	Leeds U.	1	1	0	0	0	0

93-94	Leeds U.	22	22	0	20	0	0
94-95	Leeds U.	0	0	0	42	0	0
95-96	Leeds U.	10	10	0	6	0	0
96-97	Leeds U.	1	1	0	37	0	0
97-98	Leeds U.	1	1	0	35	0	0
98-99	Leeds U.	0	0	0	4	0	0
	Total	35	35	0	144	0	0

BEESLEY, Paul

FULLNAME: Paul Beesley
DOB: 21-Jul-65, Liverpool

Club History	Signed	Fee
Wigan A.	22/9/84	Free - Marine
Leyton Orient	20/10/89	£175,000
Sheffield U.	10/7/90	£300,000
Leeds U.	8/95	£250,000

Season	Team	Tot	St	Sb	Snu	Ps	Gls
92-93	Sheffield U.	39	39	0	0	3	2
93-94	Sheffield U.	25	22	3	3	2	0
95-96	Leeds U.	10	8	2	9	1	0
96-97	Leeds U.	12	11	1	4	1	0
	Total	86	80	6	16	7	2

BEHARALL, David

FULLNAME: David Beharall
DOB: 13-Apr-79, Jarrow

Club History	Signed	Fee
Newcastle U.	7/97	Trainee

Season	Team	Tot	St	Sb	Snu	Ps	Gls
98-99	Newcastle U.	4	4	0	3	0	0
99-00	Newcastle U.	2	0	2	2	0	0
	Total	6	4	2	5	0	0

BEINLICH, Stefan

FULLNAME: Stefan Beinlich
DOB: 13-Jan-72, Berlin, Germany

Club History	Signed	Fee
Bergmann		
Aston Villa	10/91	£100,000

Season	Team	Tot	St	Sb	Snu	Ps	Gls
92-93	Aston Villa	7	1	6	2	0	0
93-94	Aston Villa	7	6	1	2	1	1
	Total	14	7	7	4	1	1

BENALI, Francis

FULLNAME: Francis Vincent Benali
DOB: 30-Dec-68, Southampton

Club History	Signed	Fee
Southampton	1/87	Apprentice

Season	Team	Tot	St	Sb	Snu	Ps	Gls
92-93	Southampton	33	31	2	2	6	0
93-94	Southampton	37	34	3	2	3	0
94-95	Southampton	35	32	3	1	3	0
95-96	Southampton	30	29	1	0	3	0
96-97	Southampton	18	14	4	4	2	0
97-98	Southampton	33	32	1	1	2	1
98-99	Southampton	23	19	4	1	1	0
99-00	Southampton	26	25	1	9	2	0
	Total	235	216	19	20	22	1

BENNETT, Frankie

FULLNAME: Frank Bennett
DOB: 03-Jan-69, Birmingham

Club History	Signed	Fee
Southampton	2/93	£7,500

Season	Team	Tot	St	Sb	Snu	Ps	Gls
93-94	Southampton	8	0	8	7	0	1
95-96	Southampton	11	5	6	4	5	0
	Total	19	5	14	11	5	1

BENT, Marcus

FULLNAME: Marcus Bent
DOB: 19-May-98, Hammersmith

Club History	Signed	Fee
Brentford	7/95	Trainee
C.Palace	1/98	£150,000>

Season	Team	Tot	St	Sb	Snu	Ps	Gls
97-98	Crystal P.	16	10	6	1	3	5
	Total	16	10	6	1	3	5

BERESFORD, David

FULLNAME: David Beresford
DOB: 11-Nov-76, Middlesbrough

Club History	Signed	Fee
Oldham A.	7/94	Trainee

Season	Team	Tot	St	Sb	Snu	Ps	Gls
93-94	Oldham A.	1	0	1	1	0	0
	Total	1	0	1	1	0	0

BERESFORD, John

FULLNAME: John Beresford
DOB: 04-Sep-66, Sheffield

Club History	Signed	Fee
Manchester C.	9/83	Apprentice
Barnsley	8/86	Free
Portsmouth	3/89	£300,000
Newcastle U.	7/92	£650,000
Southampton	2/98	£1.5m

Season	Team	Tot	St	Sb	Snu	Ps	Gls
93-94	Newcastle U.	34	34	0	0	2	0
94-95	Newcastle U.	33	33	0	0	0	0
95-96	Newcastle U.	33	32	1	1	2	0
96-97	Newcastle U.	19	18	1	5	0	0
97-98	Newcastle U.	18	17	1	0	3	2
97-98	Southampton	10	10	0	0	1	0
98-99	Southampton	4	1	3	1	1	0
99-00	Southampton	3	0	3	1	0	0
	Total	154	145	9	8	9	2

BERESFORD, Marlon

FULLNAME: Marlon Beresford
DOB: 02-Sep-69, Lincoln

Club History	Signed	Fee
Sheffield W.	9/87	Trainee
Bury	8/89	Loan
Northampton Town	9/90	Loan
Crewe Alex.	2/91	Loan
Northampton Town	8/91	Loan
Burnley	8/92	£95,000
Middlesbrough	3/98	£500,000

Season	Team	Tot	St	Sb	Snu	Ps	Gls
92-93	Sheffield W.	0	0	0	2	0	0
98-99	Middlesbrough	4	4	0	31	0	0
99-00	Middlesbrough	1	1	0	28	0	0
	Total	5	5	0	61	0	0

BERG, Henning

FULLNAME: Henning Berg
DOB: 01-Sep-69, Eidsvell

Club History	Signed	Fee
Lillestrom		
Blackburn R.	1/93	£400,000
Manchester U.	8/97	£5.0m

Season	Team	Tot	St	Sb	Snu	Ps	Gls
92-93	Blackburn R.	4	2	2	0	0	0
93-94	Blackburn R.	41	38	3	0	0	1
94-95	Blackburn R.	40	40	0	0	0	1
95-96	Blackburn R.	38	38	0	0	0	0
96-97	Blackburn R.	36	36	0	0	0	2
97-98	Manchester U.	27	23	4	8	2	2
98-99	Manchester U.	16	10	6	8	0	0
99-00	Manchester U.	22	16	6	8	0	1
	Total	224	203	21	24	2	7

BERGER, Patrik

FULLNAME: Patrik Berger
DOB: 10-Nov-73, Prague

Club History	Signed	Fee
Borussia Dortmund	1995	
Liverpool	8/96	£3.25m

Season	Team	Tot	St	Sb	Snu	Ps	Gls
96-97	Liverpool	23	13	10	9	5	6
97-98	Liverpool	22	6	16	9	2	3
98-99	Liverpool	32	30	2	0	9	7
99-00	Liverpool	34	34	0	0	5	9
	Total	111	83	28	18	21	25

BERGKAMP, Dennis

FULLNAME: Dennis Nicolaas Bergkamp
DOB: 18-May-69, Amsterdam, Netherlands

Club History	Signed	Fee
Internazionale	7/93	£12m
Arsenal	7/95	£7.5m

Season	Team	Tot	St	Sb	Snu	Ps	Gls
95-96	Arsenal	33	33	0	0	1	11
96-97	Arsenal	29	28	1	0	8	12
97-98	Arsenal	28	28	0	0	2	16
98-99	Arsenal	29	28	1	1	6	12
99-00	Arsenal	28	23	5	1	15	6
	Total	147	140	7	2	32	57

BERGSSON, Gundi

FULLNAME: Gudni Bergsson
DOB: 21-Jul-65, Iceland

Club History	Signed	Fee
Tottenham H.	12/88	£100,000
Bolton Wanderers	3/95	£65,000

Season	Team	Tot	St	Sb	Snu	Ps	Gls
92-93	Tottenham H.	5	0	5	4	0	0
95-96	Bolton W.	34	34	0	0	2	4
97-98	Bolton W.	35	34	1	0	1	2
	Total	74	68	6	4	3	6

BERKOVIC, Eyal

FULLNAME: Eyal Berkovic
DOB: 02-Apr-72, Haifa

Club History	Signed	Fee
Maccabi Haifa	1992	
Southampton	9/96	£1m
West Ham U.	6/97	£1.75m

Season	Team	Tot	St	Sb	Snu	Ps	Gls
96-97	Southampton	28	26	2	2	11	4
97-98	West Ham U.	35	34	1	1	12	7
98-99	West Ham U.	30	28	2	4	12	3
	Total	93	88	5	7	35	14

BERNARD, Paul

FULLNAME: Paul Robert James Bernard
DOB: 30-Dec-72, Edinburgh

Club History	Signed	Fee
Oldham A.	7/91	

Season	Team	Tot	St	Sb	Snu	Ps	Gls
92-93	Oldham A.	33	32	1	2	0	4
93-94	Oldham A.	32	32	0	0	4	5
	Total	65	64	1	2	4	9

BERRY, Greg

FULLNAME: Gregory John Berry
DOB: 05-Mar-71, Grays

Club History	Signed	Fee
Leyton Orient	7/89	£2,000
Wimbledon	8/92	£250,000

Season	Team	Tot	St	Sb	Snu	Ps	Gls
92-93	Wimbledon	3	2	1	2	1	0
93-94	Wimbledon	4	4	0	1	2	1
	Total	7	6	1	3	3	1

BERTI, Nicola

FULLNAME: Nicola Berti
DOB: 14-Apr-67, Salsomaggiore Terme

Club History	Signed	Fee
Internazionale		
Tottenham H.	1/98	Free

Season	Team	Tot	St	Sb	Snu	Ps	Gls
97-98	Tottenham H.	17	17	0	0	5	3
98-99	Tottenham H.	4	4	0	3	2	0
	Total	21	21	0	3	7	3

BETTS, Robert

FULLNAME: Robert Betts
DOB: 21-Dec-81, Doncaster

Club History	Signed	Fee
Doncaster		Schoolboy
Coventry C.	8/98	

Season	Team	Tot	St	Sb	Snu	Ps	Gls
99-00	Coventry C.	2	0	2	0	0	0
	Total	2	0	2	0	0	0

BEWERS, Jonathan

FULLNAME: Jonathan Bewers
DOB:

Club History	Signed	Fee
Aston Villa	8/99	Trainee

Season	Team	Tot	St	Sb	Snu	Ps	Gls
99-00	Aston Villa	1	0	1	2	0	0
	Total	1	0	1	2	0	0

BILIC, Slaven

FULLNAME: Slaven Bilic
DOB: 11-Sep-68, Croatia

Club History	Signed	Fee
Karlsruhe		
West Ham U.	12/95	£1.3m
Everton	5/97	£4.5m

Season	Team	Tot	St	Sb	Snu	Ps	Gls
95-96	West Ham U.	13	13	0	0	1	0
96-97	West Ham U.	35	35	0	0	3	2
97-98	Everton	24	22	2	3	1	0
98-99	Everton	4	4	0	2	0	0
	Total	76	74	2	5	5	2

BILLING, Peter

FULLNAME: Peter G. Billing
DOB: 24-Oct-64, Liverpool

Club History	Signed	Fee
Everton	1/86	From Non League
Crewe Alex	12/86	
Coventry C.	6/89	

Season	Team	Tot	St	Sb	Snu	Ps	Gls
92-93	Coventry C.	3	3	0	4	1	0
	Total	3	3	0	4	1	0

BILLIO, Patricio

FULLNAME: Patrico
DOB: 19-Apr-74, Treviso, Italy

Club History	Signed	Fee
Milan		
Crystal P.	2/98	Loan

Season	Team	Tot	St	Sb	Snu	Ps	Gls
97-98	Crystal P.	3	1	2	0	1	0
	Total	3	1	2	0	1	0

BISHOP, Ian

FULLNAME: Ian William Bishop
DOB: 29-May-65, Liverpool

Club History	Signed	Fee
Everton	5/83	Apprentice
Crewe Alexandra	3/84	Loan
Carlisle U.	10/84	£15,000
Bournemouth	7/88	£35,000
Manchester C.	8/89	£465,000
West Ham U.	12/89	Exchange
Manchester C.	3/98	Free

Season	Team	Tot	St	Sb	Snu	Ps	Gls
93-94	West Ham U.	36	36	0	0	4	1
94-95	West Ham U.	31	31	0	2	2	1

95-96	West Ham U.	35	35	0	0	3	1
96-97	West Ham U.	29	26	3	2	9	1
97-98	West Ham U.	3	3	0	12	0	0
	Total	134	131	3	16	18	4

BJORNEBYE, Stig Inge

FULLNAME: Stig Inge Bjornebye
DOB: 11-Dec-69, Norway

Club History	Signed	Fee
Rosenborg		
Liverpool	12/92	£600,000

Season	Team	Tot	St	Sb	Snu	Ps	Gls
92-93	Liverpool	11	11	0	2	0	0
93-94	Liverpool	9	6	3	2	3	0
94-95	Liverpool	31	31	0	0	7	0
95-96	Liverpool	2	2	0	0	0	0
96-97	Liverpool	38	38	0	0	3	2
97-98	Liverpool	25	24	1	3	4	0
98-99	Liverpool	23	20	3	6	4	0
	Total	139	132	7	13	23	2

BLACK, Kingsley

FULLNAME: Kingsley Black
DOB: 22-Jun-68, Luton

Club History	Signed	Fee
Luton Town	7/86	Juniors
Nottingham F.	9/91	£1.5m

Season	Team	Tot	St	Sb	Snu	Ps	Gls
92-93	Nottingham F.	24	19	5	7	3	5
94-95	Nottingham F.	10	5	5	4	1	2
95-96	Nottingham F.	2	1	1	0	1	0
	Total	36	25	11	11	5	7

BLACK, Tommy

FULLNAME: Thomas Robert Black
DOB: 26-Nov-79, Chigwell

Club History	Signed	Fee
Arsenal	7/96	Trainee

Season	Team	Tot	St	Sb	Snu	Ps	Gls
99-00	Arsenal	1	0	1	1	0	0
	Total	1	0	1	1	0	0

BLACKMORE, Clayton

FULLNAME: Clayton Graham Blackmore
DOB: 23-Sep-64, Neath

Club History	Signed	Fee
Manchester U.	9/82	Apprentice
Middlesbrough	7/94	Free

Season	Team	Tot	St	Sb	Snu	Ps	Gls
92-93	Manchester U.	14	12	2	2	1	0

Season	Team	Tot	St	Sb	Snu	Ps	Gls
95-96	Middlesbrough	5	4	1	3	0	0
96-97	Middlesbrough	16	14	2	3	1	2
98-99	Middlesbrough	0	0	0	9	0	0
	Total	35	30	5	17	2	2

BLACKWELL, Dean

FULLNAME: Dean Robert Blackwell
DOB: 05-Dec-69, Camden

Club History	Signed	Fee
Wimbledon	7/88	Trainee

Season	Team	Tot	St	Sb	Snu	Ps	Gls
92-93	Wimbledon	24	19	5	2	2	0
93-94	Wimbledon	18	16	2	5	2	0
95-96	Wimbledon	8	8	0	0	0	0
96-97	Wimbledon	27	22	5	2	0	0
97-98	Wimbledon	35	35	0	0	2	0
98-99	Wimbledon	28	27	1	1	3	0
99-00	Wimbledon	17	16	1	6	5	0
	Total	157	143	14	16	14	0

BLAKE, Mark

FULLNAME: Mark Anthony Blake
DOB: 16-Dec-70, Nottingham

Club History	Signed	Fee
Aston Villa	7/89	Trainee
Wolverhampton W.	1/91	Loan
Portsmouth	8/93	£400,000
Leicester C.	3/94	£360,000

Season	Team	Tot	St	Sb	Snu	Ps	Gls
92-93	Aston Villa	1	0	1	1	0	0
94-95	Leicester C.	30	26	4	2	5	3
	Total	31	26	5	3	5	3

BLAKE, Nathan

FULLNAME: Nathan Alexander Blake
DOB: 27-Jan-72, Cardiff

Club History	Signed	Fee
Cardiff C.	8/90	Free from Chelsea Jnrs
Sheffield U.	2/94	£300,000
Bolton Wanderers	12/95	£1.5m
Blackburn R.	11/98	£4.25m

Season	Team	Tot	St	Sb	Snu	Ps	Gls
93-94	Sheffield U.	12	7	5	1	1	5
95-96	Bolton W.	18	14	4	0	7	1
97-98	Bolton W.	35	35	0	0	2	12
98-99	Blackburn R.	11	9	2	2	0	3
	Total	76	65	11	3	10	21

BLAKE, Robbie

FULLNAME: Robert James Blake
DOB: 04-Mar-76, Middlesbrough

Club History	Signed	Fee
Darlington	7/94	Trainee
Bradford C.	3/97	£300,000

Season	Team	Tot	St	Sb	Snu	Ps	Gls
99-00	Bradford C.	28	15	13	7	4	2
	Total	28	15	13	7	4	2

BLATHERWICK, Steve

FULLNAME: Steven Blatherwick
DOB: 20-Sep-73, Nottingham

Club History	Signed	Fee
Nottingham F.	8/92	N.Co. Juniors
Wycombe W.	2/94	Loan

Season	Team	Tot	St	Sb	Snu	Ps	Gls
96-97	Nottingham F.	7	7	0	4	2	0
	Total	7	7	0	4	2	0

BLINKER, Regi

FULLNAME: Regi Blinker
DOB: 02-Jun-69, Surinam

Club History	Signed	Fee
Feyenoord		
Sheffield W.	3/96	£275,000

Season	Team	Tot	St	Sb	Snu	Ps	Gls
95-96	Sheffield W.	9	9	0	0	4	2
96-97	Sheffield W.	33	15	18	2	5	1
	Total	42	24	18	2	9	3

BLISSETT, Gary

FULLNAME: Gary Paul Blissett
DOB: 29-Jun-64, Manchester

Club History	Signed	Fee
Crewe Alex	8/83	
Brentford	3/87	£60,000
Wimbledon	7/93	£350,000

Season	Team	Tot	St	Sb	Snu	Ps	Gls
93-94	Wimbledon	18	6	12	7	1	3
94-95	Wimbledon	9	4	5	1	2	0
95-96	Wimbledon	4	0	4	0	0	0
	Total	31	10	21	8	3	3

BLOMQVIST, Jesper

FULLNAME: Jesper Blomqvist
DOB: 05-Feb-74, Sweden

Club History	Signed	Fee
Parma	97	
Manchester U.	8/98	£4.4m

Season	Team	Tot	St	Sb	Snu	Ps	Gls
98-99	Manchester U.	25	20	5	6	14	1
	Total	25	20	5	6	14	1

BLONDEAU, Patrick

FULLNAME: Patrick Blondeau
DOB: 27-Jan-68, Marseille

Club History	Signed	Fee
Monaco		
Sheffield W.	7/97	£1.8m

Season	Team	Tot	St	Sb	Snu	Ps	Gls
97-98	Sheffield W.	6	5	1	3	0	0
	Total	6	5	1	3	0	0

BLUNT, Jason

FULLNAME: Jason Blunt
DOB: 16-Aug-77, Penzance

Club History	Signed	Fee
Leeds U.	1/95	Trainee

Season	Team	Tot	St	Sb	Snu	Ps	Gls
95-96	Leeds U.	3	2	1	0	1	0
96-97	Leeds U.	1	0	1	2	0	0
	Total	4	2	2	2	1	0

BOA MORTE, Luis

FULLNAME: Luis Boa Morte Pereira
DOB: 04-Aug-78, Lisbon

Club History	Signed	Fee
Sporting Lisbon		
Arsenal	7/97	£1.75m
Southampton	8/99	£500,000

Season	Team	Tot	St	Sb	Snu	Ps	Gls
97-98	Arsenal	15	4	11	8	2	0
98-99	Arsenal	8	2	6	4	1	0
99-00	Arsenal	2	0	2	0	0	0
99-00	Southampton	14	6	8	7	3	1
	Total	39	12	27	19	6	1

BOATENG, George

FULLNAME: George Boateng
DOB: 05-Sep-75, Accra, Ghana

Club History	Signed	Fee
Feyenoord		
Coventry C.	12/97	£250,000
Aston Villa	7/99	£4.5m

Season	Team	Tot	St	Sb	Snu	Ps	Gls
97-98	Coventry C.	14	14	0	0	4	1
98-99	Coventry C.	33	29	4	1	4	4
99-00	Aston Villa	33	30	3	1	12	2
	Total	80	73	7	2	20	7

BODEN, Chris

FULLNAME: Christopher Desmond Boden
DOB: 13-Oct-73, Wolverhampton

Club History	Signed	Fee
Aston Villa	12/91	

Season	Team	Tot	St	Sb	Snu	Ps	Gls
94-95	Aston Villa	1	0	1	2	0	0
	Total	1	0	1	2	0	0

BODIN, Paul

FULLNAME: Paul J Bodin
DOB: 13-Sep-64, Cardiff

Club History	Signed	Fee
Newport Co.	1/82	Chelsea Jrs
Cardiff C.	8/82	Free
Newport Co.	1/88	£15,000
Swindon Town	3/88	£30,000
Crystal P.	3/91	£550,000
Newcastle U.	12/91	Loan
Swindon Town	1/92	£225,000

Season	Team	Tot	St	Sb	Snu	Ps	Gls
93-94	Swindon T.	32	28	4	0	4	7
	Total	32	28	4	0	4	7

BOERE, Jeroen

FULLNAME: Jeroen Boere
DOB: 18-Nov-67, Arnheim, Belgium

Club History	Signed	Fee
Go Ahead Eagles		
West Ham U.	9/93	

Season	Team	Tot	St	Sb	Snu	Ps	Gls
93-94	West Ham U.	4	0	4	5	0	0
94-95	West Ham U.	20	15	5	0	3	6
95-96	West Ham U.	1	0	1	0	0	0
	Total	25	15	10	5	3	6

BOERTIEN, Paul

FULLNAME: Paul Boertien
DOB: 20-Jan-79, Haltwhistle

Club History	Signed	Fee
Carlisle U.	5/97	Trainee
Derby Co.	3/99	£250,000

Season	Team	Tot	St	Sb	Snu	Ps	Gls
98-99	Derby Co.	1	0	1	0	0	0
99-00	Derby Co.	2	0	2	4	1	0
	Total	3	0	3	4	1	0

BOHINEN, Lars

FULLNAME: Lars Bohinen
DOB: 08-Sep-69, Vadso, Norway

Club History	Signed	Fee
Young Boys Berne		
Nottingham F.	11/93	£450,000
Blackburn R.	10/95	£700,000
Derby Co.	3/98	£1.45m

Season	Team	Tot	St	Sb	Snu	Ps	Gls
94-95	Nottingham F.	34	30	4	1	6	6
95-96	Nottingham F.	7	7	0	0	3	0
95-96	Blackburn R.	20	18	2	0	1	4
96-97	Blackburn R.	23	17	6	7	0	2
97-98	Blackburn R.	16	6	10	7	2	1
97-98	Derby Co.	9	9	0	0	3	1
98-99	Derby Co.	32	29	3	0	11	0
99-00	Derby Co.	13	8	5	0	6	0
	Total	154	124	30	15	32	14

BOLAND, Willie

FULLNAME: Willie Boland
DOB: 06-Aug-75, Republic of Ireland

Club History	Signed	Fee
Coventry C.	11/92	Juniors

Season	Team	Tot	St	Sb	Snu	Ps	Gls
92-93	Coventry C.	1	0	1	0	0	0
93-94	Coventry C.	27	24	3	3	2	0
94-95	Coventry C.	12	9	3	1	3	0
95-96	Coventry C.	3	2	1	5	0	0
96-97	Coventry C.	1	0	1	13	0	0
97-98	Coventry C.	19	8	11	10	2	0
98-99	Coventry C.	0	0	0	0	0	0
	Total	63	43	20	32	7	0

BONALAIR, Thierry

FULLNAME: Thierry Bonalair
DOB: 14-Jun-66, Paris

Club History	Signed	Fee
Neuchatel Xamax		
Nottingham F.	6/97	Free

Season	Team	Tot	St	Sb	Snu	Ps	Gls
98-99	Nottingham F.	28	24	4	2	3	1
	Total	28	24	4	2	3	1

BONETTI, Ivano

FULLNAME: Ivano Bonetti
DOB: 01-Aug-64, Brescia, Italy

Club History	Signed	Fee
Torino		
Grimsby Town	9/95	

Tranmere R.	8/93	Free
Crystal P.	10/97	Free

Season	Team	Tot	St	Sb	Snu	Ps	Gls
97-98	Crystal P.	2	0	2	0	0	0
	Total	2	0	2	0	0	0

BONNOT, Alexandre

FULLNAME: Alexandre Bonnot
DOB:

Club History	Signed	Fee
Angers	8/98	
Watford	1/98	Loan
Watford	8/99	Signed

Season	Team	Tot	St	Sb	Snu	Ps	Gls
99-00	Watford	12	7	5	14	3	0
	Total	12	7	5	14	3	0

BOOGERS, Marco

FULLNAME: Marco Boogers
DOB: 12-Jan-67, Dordrecht

Club History	Signed	Fee
Sparta Rotterdam		
West Ham U.	7/95	£1m

Season	Team	Tot	St	Sb	Snu	Ps	Gls
95-96	West Ham U.	4	0	4	3	0	0
	Total	4	0	4	3	0	0

BOOTH, Andy

FULLNAME: Andrew David Booth
DOB: 06-Dec-73, Huddersfield

Club History	Signed	Fee
Huddersfield Town	7/92	Trainee
Sheffield W.	7/96	£2.7m

Season	Team	Tot	St	Sb	Snu	Ps	Gls
96-97	Sheffield W.	35	32	3	0	7	10
97-98	Sheffield W.	23	21	2	1	4	7
98-99	Sheffield W.	34	34	0	0	7	6
99-00	Sheffield W.	23	20	3	0	6	2
	Total	115	107	8	1	24	25

BOOTY, Martyn

FULLNAME: Martyn James Booty
DOB: 30-May-71, Kirby Muxloe

Club History	Signed	Fee
Coventry C.	5/89	Trainee

Season	Team	Tot	St	Sb	Snu	Ps	Gls
93-94	Coventry C.	2	2	0	0	2	0
	Total	2	2	0	0	2	0

BORBOKIS, Vass

FULLNAME: Vassilios Borbokis
DOB: 10-Feb-69, Serresm Greece

Club History	Signed	Fee
AEK Athens		
Sheffield U.	7/97	£900,000
Derby Co.	3/99	£600,000

Season	Team	Tot	St	Sb	Snu	Ps	Gls
98-99	Derby Co.	4	3	1	0	1	0
99-00	Derby Co.	12	6	6	2	4	0
	Total	16	9	7	2	5	0

BORROWS, Brian

FULLNAME: Brian Borrows
DOB: 20-Dec-60, Liverpool

Club History	Signed	Fee
Everton	4/80	Juniors
Bolton Wanderers	3/83	£10,000
Coventry C.	6/85	£80,000

Season	Team	Tot	St	Sb	Snu	Ps	Gls
92-93	Coventry C.	38	36	2	0	2	2
93-94	Coventry C.	29	29	0	0	1	0
94-95	Coventry C.	35	33	2	2	1	0
95-96	Coventry C.	19	19	0	1	2	0
96-97	Coventry C.	23	16	7	8	4	0
97-98	Coventry C.	1	1	0	1	0	0
	Total	145	134	11	12	10	2

BOSANCIC, Jovo

FULLNAME: Jovo Bosancic
DOB: 07-Aug-70, Novi Sad

Club History	Signed	Fee
Iniao Madeira		
Barnsley	8/96	Free

Season	Team	Tot	St	Sb	Snu	Ps	Gls
97-98	Barnsley	17	13	4	7	3	2
	Total	17	13	4	7	3	2

BOSNICH, Mark

FULLNAME: Mark John Bosnich
DOB: 13-Jan-72, Sydney, Australia

Club History	Signed	Fee
Croatia Sydney		
Manchester U.	6/89	Free
Croatia Sydney	8/91	
Aston Villa	2/92	Free
Manchester U.	6/99	Free

Season	Team	Tot	St	Sb	Snu	Ps	Gls
92-93	Aston Villa	17	17	0	12	0	0
93-94	Aston Villa	28	28	0	8	1	0
94-95	Aston Villa	30	30	0	6	0	0
95-96	Aston Villa	38	38	0	1	0	0
96-97	Aston Villa	20	20	0	3	2	0
97-98	Aston Villa	30	30	0	0	0	0
98-99	Aston Villa	15	15	0	2	0	0
99-00	Manchester U.	23	23	0	3	3	0
	Total	201	201	0	34	7	0

BOULD, Steve

FULLNAME: Stephen Andrew Bould
DOB: 16-Nov-62, Stoke

Club History	Signed	Fee
Stoke C.	11/80	Apprentice
Torquay U.	10/82	Loan
Arsenal	6/89	£390,000
Sunderland	7/99	£500,000

Season	Team	Tot	St	Sb	Snu	Ps	Gls
92-93	Arsenal	24	24	0	1	0	1
93-94	Arsenal	25	23	2	2	0	1
94-95	Arsenal	31	30	1	0	1	0
95-96	Arsenal	19	19	0	0	2	0
96-97	Arsenal	33	33	0	1	2	0
97-98	Arsenal	24	21	3	4	0	0
98-99	Arsenal	19	14	5	9	1	0
99-00	Sunderland	20	19	1	1	3	0
	Total	195	183	12	18	9	2

BOUND, Matthew

FULLNAME: Matthew Terence Bound
DOB: 09-Nov-72, Melksham

Club History	Signed	Fee
Soputhampton	5/91	Trainee

Season	Team	Tot	St	Sb	Snu	Ps	Gls
92-93	Southampton	3	1	2	5	1	0
93-94	Southampton	1	1	0	3	0	0
	Total	4	2	2	8	1	0

BOWEN, Mark

FULLNAME: Mark Rosslyn Bowen
DOB: 07-Dec-63, Neath

Club History	Signed	Fee
Tottenham H.	12/81	Apprentice
Norwich C.	7/87	£97,000
West Ham U.	7/96	Free
Shimizu S-Pulse (J)	3/97	Free
Charlton Ath	9/97	Free

Season	Team	Tot	St	Sb	Snu	Ps	Gls
92-93	Norwich C.	42	42	0	0	0	1
93-94	Norwich C.	41	41	0	0	1	5
94-95	Norwich C.	36	34	2	0	2	1

Season	Team	Tot	St	Sb	Snu	Ps	Gls
96-97	West Ham U.	17	15	2	5	5	1
97-98	Southampton	3	1	2	0	2	0
98-99	Charlton A.	6	2	4	3	1	0
	Total	145	135	10	8	11	8

BOWMAN, Rob

FULLNAME: Robert Bowman
DOB: 06-Aug-75, Durham

Club History	Signed	Fee
Leeds U.	11/92	Trainee

Season	Team	Tot	St	Sb	Snu	Ps	Gls
92-93	Leeds U.	4	3	1	0	0	0
95-96	Leeds U.	3	1	2	3	0	0
	Total	7	4	3	3	0	0

BOWRY, Bobby

FULLNAME: Robert Bowry
DOB: 19-May-71, Hampstead

Club History	Signed	Fee
QPR	8/90	
Crystal P.	4/92	Free

Season	Team	Tot	St	Sb	Snu	Ps	Gls
92-93	Crystal P.	11	6	5	1	2	1
94-95	Crystal P.	18	13	5	4	5	0
	Total	29	19	10	5	7	1

BOWYER, Lee

FULLNAME: Lee David Bowyer
DOB: 03-Jan-77, London

Club History	Signed	Fee
Charlton Ath	4/94	Trainee
Leeds U.	7/96	£3m

Season	Team	Tot	St	Sb	Snu	Ps	Gls
96-97	Leeds U.	32	32	0	0	4	4
97-98	Leeds U.	25	21	4	11	6	3
98-99	Leeds U.	35	35	0	0	2	9
99-00	Leeds U.	33	31	2	0	4	5
	Total	125	119	6	11	16	21

BOXALL, Danny

FULLNAME: Daniel James Boxall
DOB: 24-Aug-77, Croydon

Club History	Signed	Fee
Crystal P.	4/94	Trainee

Season	Team	Tot	St	Sb	Snu	Ps	Gls
97-98	Crystal P.	1	0	1	3	0	0
	Total	1	0	1	3	0	0

BOYLE, Wesley

FULLNAME: Wesley Boyle
DOB: 30-Mar-79, Potadown

Club History	Signed	Fee
Leeds U.		Trainee

Season	Team	Tot	St	Sb	Snu	Ps	Gls
96-97	Leeds U.	1	0	1	1	0	0
	Total	1	0	1	1	0	0

BOYLIN, Lee

FULLNAME: Lee Boylin
DOB: 02-Sep-78, Chelmsford

Club History	Signed	Fee
West Ham U.		Trainee

Season	Team	Tot	St	Sb	Snu	Ps	Gls
96-97	West Ham U.	1	0	1	0	0	0
98-99	West Ham U.	0	0	0	1	0	0
	Total	1	0	1	1	0	0

BOZINOSKI, Vlado

FULLNAME: Vlado Bozinoski
DOB: 30-Mar-64, Macedonia

Club History	Signed	Fee
Sporting Lisbon		
Ipswich Town	12/92	£100,000

Season	Team	Tot	St	Sb	Snu	Ps	Gls
92-93	Ipswich T.	9	3	6	4	2	0
	Total	9	3	6	4	2	0

BRACEWELL, Paul

FULLNAME: Paul William Bracewell
DOB: 19-Jul-62, Heswall, Cheshire

Club History	Signed	Fee
Stoke C.	2/80	Apprentice
Sunderland	7/83	£250,000
Everton	5/84	£425,000
Sunderland	8/89	£250,000
Newcastle U.	6/92	£250,000
Sunderland	5/95	£100,000

Season	Team	Tot	St	Sb	Snu	Ps	Gls
93-94	Newcastle U.	32	32	0	0	4	1
94-95	Newcastle U.	16	13	3	5	1	0
96-97	Sunderland	38	38	0	0	6	0
	Total	86	83	3	5	11	1

BRADLEY, Shayne

FULLNAME: Sayne Bradley
DOB: 08-Dec-79, Gloucester

Club History	Signed	Fee				
Southampton		Trainee				

Season	Team	Tot	St	Sb	Snu	Ps	Gls
98-99	Southampton	3	0	3	2	0	0
99-00	Southampton	1	0	1	0	0	0
	Total	4	0	4	2	0	0

BRADSHAW, Carl

FULLNAME: Carl Bradshaw
DOB: 02-Oct-68, Sheffield

Club History	Signed	Fee
Sheffield W.	8/86	
Barnsley	8/86	Loan
Manchester C.	9/88	£50,000
Sheffield U.	9/89	£50,000
Norwich C.	8/94	£500,000

Season	Team	Tot	St	Sb	Snu	Ps	Gls
92-93	Sheffield U.	32	24	8	0	5	1
93-94	Sheffield U.	40	39	1	1	2	1
94-95	Norwich C.	26	25	1	0	4	1
	Total	98	88	10	1	11	3

BRADY, Garry

FULLNAME: Garry Brady
DOB: 07-Sep-76, Glasgow

Club History	Signed	Fee
Tottenham H.	9/93	Trainee
Newcastle U.	7/98	£600,000

Season	Team	Tot	St	Sb	Snu	Ps	Gls
96-97	Tottenham H.	0	0	0	3	0	0
97-98	Tottenham H.	9	0	9	0	0	0
98-99	Newcastle U.	9	3	6	3	2	0
	Total	18	3	15	6	2	0

BRANAGAN, Keith

FULLNAME: Keith Branagan
DOB: 10-Jul-66, Fulham

Club History	Signed	Fee
Cambridge U.	8/83	Junior
Millwall	3/88	£100,000
Brentford	11/89	Loan
Gillingham	10/91	Loan
Bolton Wanderers	7/92	Free

Season	Team	Tot	St	Sb	Snu	Ps	Gls
95-96	Bolton W.	31	31	0	0	0	0
97-98	Bolton W.	34	34	0	0	2	0
	Total	65	65	0	0	2	0

BRANCA, Marco

FULLNAME: Marco Branca
DOB: 06-Jan-65, Vimercate, Italy

Club History	Signed	Fee				
Internazionale	1995					
Middlesbrough						

Season	Team	Tot	St	Sb	Snu	Ps	Gls
98-99	Middlesbrough	1	0	1	0	0	0
	Total	1	0	1	0	0	0

BRANCH, Michael

FULLNAME: Michael Paul Branch
DOB: 18-Oct-72, Liverpool

Club History	Signed	Fee
Everton	10/95	Trainee

Season	Team	Tot	St	Sb	Snu	Ps	Gls
95-96	Everton	3	1	2	0	1	0
96-97	Everton	25	13	12	7	7	3
97-98	Everton	6	1	5	1	1	0
98-99	Everton	7	1	6	5	1	0
	Total	41	16	25	13	10	3

BRANCO

FULLNAME: Claudio Ibraim Vaz Leal
DOB: 04-Apr-64, Bage, Brazil

Club History	Signed	Fee
Internacional	1994	
Middlesbrough	2/96	Free

Season	Team	Tot	St	Sb	Snu	Ps	Gls
95-96	Middlesbrough	7	5	2	3	2	0
96-97	Middlesbrough	2	1	1	5	0	0
	Total	9	6	3	8	2	0

BRAYSON, Paul

FULLNAME: Paul Brayson
DOB: 16-Sep-77, Newcastle

Club History	Signed	Fee
Newcastle U.	8/95	Trainee
Swansea C.	1/97	Loan
Reading	3/98	£100,000

Season	Team	Tot	St	Sb	Snu	Ps	Gls
95-96	Newcastle U.	0	0	0	1	0	0
96-97	Newcastle U.	0	0	0	4	0	0
97-98	Newcastle U.	0	0	0	1	0	0
	Total	0	0	0	6	0	0

BRAZIER, Matt

FULLNAME: Matthew Barzier
DOB: 02-Jul-76, Whipps Cross

Club History	Signed	Fee
QPR		

Season	Team	Tot	St	Sb	Snu	Ps	Gls
95-96	QPR	11	6	5	5	1	0
	Total	11	6	5	5	1	0

BREACKER, Tim

FULLNAME: Timothy Sean Breacker
DOB: 02-Jul-65, Bicester

Club History	Signed	Fee
Luton Town	5/83	Apprentice
West Ham U.	10/90	£600,000

Season	Team	Tot	St	Sb	Snu	Ps	Gls
93-94	West Ham U.	40	40	0	0	0	3
94-95	West Ham U.	33	33	0	0	0	0
95-96	West Ham U.	22	19	3	2	0	0
96-97	West Ham U.	26	22	4	1	5	0
97-98	West Ham U.	19	18	1	1	5	0
98-99	West Ham U.	3	2	1	9	1	0
	Total	143	134	9	13	11	3

BREEN, Gary

FULLNAME: Gary Patrick Breen
DOB: 12-Dec-73, Hendon

Club History	Signed	Fee
Maidstone U.	3/91	Free Charlton Jnrs
Gillingham	7/92	Free
Peterborough U.	8/94	£70,000
Birmingham C.	2/96	£400,000
Coventry C.	1/97	£2.5m

Season	Team	Tot	St	Sb	Snu	Ps	Gls
96-97	Coventry C.	9	8	1	4	0	0
97-98	Coventry C.	30	30	0	2	2	1
98-99	Coventry C.	25	21	4	6	5	0
99-00	Coventry C.	21	20	1	11	1	0
	Total	85	79	6	23	8	1

BREITKREUTZ, Matthias

FULLNAME: Matthias Breitkreutz
DOB: 12-May-71, Berlin, Germany

Club History	Signed	Fee
Bergmann B		
Aston Villa	11/91	£100,000

Season	Team	Tot	St	Sb	Snu	Ps	Gls
92-93	Aston Villa	3	2	1	2	2	0
93-94	Aston Villa	2	1	1	0	1	0
	Total	5	3	2	2	3	0

BRENNAN, Mark

FULLNAME: Mark Robert Brennan
DOB: 04-Oct-65, Rossendale

Club History	Signed	Fee
Ipswich Town	4/83	
Middlesbrough	7/88	£375,000
Manchester C.	7/90	£500,000
Oldham A.	11/92	

Season	Team	Tot	St	Sb	Snu	Ps	Gls
92-93	Oldham A.	14	14	0	1	4	3
93-94	Oldham A.	11	11	0	6	3	0
	Total	25	25	0	7	7	3

BREVETT, Rufus

FULLNAME: Rufus Emanuel Brevett
DOB: 24-Sep-69, Derby

Club History	Signed	Fee
Doncaster R.	6/88	Trainee
QPR	2/91	£250,000

Season	Team	Tot	St	Sb	Snu	Ps	Gls
92-93	QPR	15	14	1	5	0	0
93-94	QPR	7	3	4	15	1	0
94-95	QPR	19	17	2	3	1	0
95-96	QPR	27	27	0	0	2	1
	Total	68	61	7	23	4	1

BRIDGE, Wayne

FULLNAME: Wayne Bridge
DOB: 05-Aug-80, Southampton

Club History	Signed	Fee
Southampton	1/98	Trainee

Season	Team	Tot	St	Sb	Snu	Ps	Gls
98-99	Southampton	23	15	8	9	6	0
99-00	Southampton	18	15	3	4	1	1
	Total	41	30	11	13	7	1

BRIDGE-WILKINSON, Marc

FULLNAME: Marc Bridge-Wilkinson
DOB: 16-Mar-79, Nuneaton

Club History	Signed	Fee
Derby Co.	3/97	Trainee
Carlsile U.	3/99	Loan

Season	Team	Tot	St	Sb	Snu	Ps	Gls
97-98	Derby Co.	0	0	0	3	0	0
98-99	Derby Co.	1	0	1	4	0	0
	Total	1	0	1	7	0	0

BRIDGES, Michael

FULLNAME: Michael Bridges
DOB: 05-Aug-78, North Shields

Club History	Signed	Fee
Sunderland	11/95	Trainee
Leeds U.	7/99	£5.0m

Season	Team	Tot	St	Sb	Snu	Ps	Gls
96-97	Sunderland	24	10	14	5	9	3
99-00	Leeds U.	34	32	2	0	19	19
	Total	58	42	16	5	28	22

BRIGHT, Mark

FULLNAME: Mark Abraham Bright
DOB: 06-Jun-62, Stoke

Club History	Signed	Fee
Port Vale	10/81	Free NL
Leicester C.	7/84	£33,000
Crystal P.	11/86	£75,000
Sheffield W.	9/92	£375,000
Millwall	12/96	Loan
Charlton A.	4/97	Free

Season	Team	Tot	St	Sb	Snu	Ps	Gls
92-93	Crystal P.	5	5	0	0	0	1
92-93	Sheffield W.	30	28	2	0	0	11
93-94	Sheffield W.	40	36	4	0	5	19
94-95	Sheffield W.	37	33	4	0	8	11
95-96	Sheffield W.	25	15	10	0	1	7
96-97	Sheffield W.	1	0	1	0	0	0
98-99	Charlton A.	5	1	4	6	1	1
	Total	143	118	25	6	15	50

BRIGHTWELL, David

FULLNAME: David John Brightwell
DOB: 07-Jan-71, Lutterworth

Club History	Signed	Fee
Manchester C.	4/88	Juniors
Chester C.	3/91	Loan

Season	Team	Tot	St	Sb	Snu	Ps	Gls
92-93	Manchester C.	8	4	4	4	0	0
93-94	Manchester C.	22	19	3	6	1	1
94-95	Manchester C.	9	9	0	6	2	0
	Total	39	32	7	16	3	1

BRIGHTWELL, Ian

FULLNAME: Ian Robert Brightwell
DOB: 09-Apr-68, Lutterworth

Club History	Signed	Fee
Manchester C.	5/85	From Juniors
Coventry C.	6/97	Free

Season	Team	Tot	St	Sb	Snu	Ps	Gls
92-93	Manchester C.	21	21	0	0	1	1
93-94	Manchester C.	7	6	1	0	0	0
94-95	Manchester C.	29	28	1	0	2	0
95-96	Manchester C.	28	25	3	0	2	0
98-99	Coventry C.	0	0	0	0	0	0
	Total	85	80	5	0	5	1

BRISCOE, Lee

FULLNAME: Lee Stephen Briscoe
DOB: 30-Sep-75, Pontefract

Club History	Signed	Fee
Sheffield W.	5/94	Trainee

Season	Team	Tot	St	Sb	Snu	Ps	Gls
93-94	Sheffield W.	1	0	1	0	0	0
94-95	Sheffield W.	6	6	0	0	3	0
95-96	Sheffield W.	25	22	3	2	4	0
96-97	Sheffield W.	6	5	1	5	1	0
97-98	Sheffield W.	7	3	4	3	2	0
98-99	Sheffield W.	16	5	11	12	2	1
99-00	Sheffield W.	16	7	9	8	4	0
	Total	77	48	29	30	16	1

BROLIN, Tomas

FULLNAME: Tomas Brolin
DOB: 29-Nov-69, Hudiksvall, Sweden

Club History	Signed	Fee
Parma	1990	
Leeds U.	11/95	£4.5m
FC Zurich	8/96	Loan
Parma	1/97	Loan +£300,000
C.Palace	1/98	Free

Season	Team	Tot	St	Sb	Snu	Ps	Gls
95-96	Leeds U.	19	17	2	0	9	4
97-98	Crystal P.	13	13	0	0	4	0
	Total	32	30	2	0	13	4

BROOKER, Stephen

FULLNAME: Stephen Brooker
DOB:

Club History	Signed	Fee
Watford		Trainee

Season	Team	Tot	St	Sb	Snu	Ps	Gls
99-00	Watford	1	0	1	1	0	0
	Total	1	0	1	1	0	0

BROOMES, Marlon

FULLNAME: Marlon Charles Broomes
DOB: 28-Nov-77, Birmingham

Club History	Signed	Fee
Blackburn R.	11/4	Trainee

Season	Team	Tot	St	Sb	Snu	Ps	Gls
96-97	Blackburn R.	0	0	0	3	0	0
97-98	Blackburn R.	4	2	2	14	0	0
98-99	Blackburn R.	13	8	5	8	0	0
	Total	17	10	7	25	0	0

BROWN, Kenny

FULLNAME: Kenneth James Brown
DOB: 11-Jul-67, Barking

Club History	Signed	Fee
Norwich C.	7/85	Juniors
Plymouth Argyle	8/88	Free
West Ham U.	8/91	£175,000

Season	Team	Tot	St	Sb	Snu	Ps	Gls
93-94	West Ham U.	9	6	3	6	1	0
94-95	West Ham U.	9	8	1	4	0	0
95-96	West Ham U.	3	3	0	0	0	0
	Total	21	17	4	10	1	0

BROWN, Michael

FULLNAME: Michael Brown
DOB: 25-Jan-77, Hartlepool

Club History	Signed	Fee
Manchester C.	9/94	Trainee

Season	Team	Tot	St	Sb	Snu	Ps	Gls
95-96	Manchester C.	21	16	5	1	3	0
	Total	21	16	5	1	3	0

BROWN, Richard

FULLNAME: Richard Anthony Brown
DOB: 13-Jan-67, Nottingham

Club History	Signed	Fee
Sheffield Wed	12/84	£10,000
Blackburn R.	9/90	£15,000

Season	Team	Tot	St	Sb	Snu	Ps	Gls
92-93	Blackburn R.	2	2	0	0	0	0
	Total	2	2	0	0	0	0

BROWN, Steve

FULLNAME: Steven Byron Brown
DOB: 13-May-72, Brighton

Club History	Signed	Fee
Charlton A.	7/90	Trainee

Season	Team	Tot	St	Sb	Snu	Ps	Gls
98-99	Charlton A.	18	13	5	15	1	0
	Total	18	13	5	15	1	0

BROWN, Wes

FULLNAME: Wesley Michael Brown
DOB: 16-Mar-79, Manchester

Club History	Signed	Fee
Manchester U.	11/96	Trainee

Season	Team	Tot	St	Sb	Snu	Ps	Gls
97-98	Manchester U.	2	1	1	0	0	0
98-99	Manchester U.	14	11	3	6	3	0
	Total	16	12	4	6	3	0

BROWNE, Paul

FULLNAME: Paul Browne
DOB: 17-Feb-75, Glasgow

Club History	Signed	Fee
Aston Villa	7/93	Trainee

Season	Team	Tot	St	Sb	Snu	Ps	Gls
95-96	Aston Villa	2	2	0	0	0	0
	Total	2	2	0	0	0	0

BRUCE, Steve

FULLNAME: Stephen Roger Bruce
DOB: 31-Dec-60, Corbridge

Club History	Signed	Fee
Gillingham	10/78	Apprentice
Norwich C.	8/84	£125,000
Manchester U.	12/87	£800,000

Season	Team	Tot	St	Sb	Snu	Ps	Gls
92-93	Manchester U.	42	42	0	0	1	5
93-94	Manchester U.	41	41	0	0	1	3
94-95	Manchester U.	35	35	0	0	1	2
95-96	Manchester U.	30	30	0	2	5	1
	Total	148	148	0	2	8	11

BRYSON, Ian

FULLNAME: James Ian Cook Bryson
DOB: 26-Nov-62, Kilmarnock

Club History	Signed	Fee
Sheffield U.	8/88	£40,000

Season	Team	Tot	St	Sb	Snu	Ps	Gls
92-93	Sheffield U.	16	9	7	0	4	3
	Total	16	9	7	0	4	3

BULL, Gary

FULLNAME: Gary W Bull
DOB: 12-Jun-66, Tipton

Club History	Signed	Fee
Cambridge U.	3/88	from S'ton Jnrs
Barnet	3/89	£2,000
Nottingham F.	7/93	Free

Season	Team	Tot	St	Sb	Snu	Ps	Gls
94-95	Nottingham F.	1	1	0	2	0	1
	Total	1	1	0	2	0	1

BULLOCK, Martin

FULLNAME: Martin John Bullock
DOB: 05-Mar-75, Derby

Club History	Signed	Fee			
Barnsley 9/93		£15,000 from Non League			

Season	Team	Tot	St	Sb	Snu	Ps	Gls
97-98	Barnsley	33	23	10	4	9	0
	Total	33	23	10	4	9	0

BURLEY, Craig

FULLNAME: Craig William Burley
DOB: 24-Sep-71, Irvine

Club History	Signed	Fee
Chelsea	9/89	Trainee
Celtic	7/97	£2.5m
Derby Co.	12/99	£3m

Season	Team	Tot	St	Sb	Snu	Ps	Gls
92-93	Chelsea	3	1	2	7	0	0
93-94	Chelsea	23	20	3	0	4	3
94-95	Chelsea	25	16	9	0	7	2
95-96	Chelsea	22	16	6	1	5	0
96-97	Chelsea	31	26	5	1	8	2
99-00	Derby Co.	18	18	0	0	2	5
	Total	122	97	25	9	26	12

BURNETT, Wayne

FULLNAME: Wayne Burnett
DOB: 04-Sep-71, Lambeth

Club History	Signed	Fee
Leyton Orient	11/89	Trainee
Blackburn R.	8/92	£90,000
Plymouth Argyll	8/93	
Bolton Wanderers	10/95	£100,000

Season	Team	Tot	St	Sb	Snu	Ps	Gls
95-96	Bolton W.	1	0	1	3	0	0
	Total	1	0	1	3	0	0

BURRIDGE, John

FULLNAME: John Burridge
DOB: 03-Dec-51, Workington

Club History	Signed	Fee
Newcastle U.		
Dumbarton	10/94	Non-Contract
Manchester C.		

Season	Team	Tot	St	Sb	Snu	Ps	Gls
93-94	Newcastle U.	0	0	0	2	0	0
94-95	Newcastle U.	0	0	0	1	0	0
94-95	Manchester C.	4	3	1	10	0	0
	Total	4	3	1	13	0	0

BURROWS, David

FULLNAME: David Burrows
DOB: 25-Oct-68, Dudley

Club History	Signed	Fee
West Brom	10/86	Apprentice
Liverpool	10/88	£550,000
West Ham U.	9/93	Swap
Everton	9/94	Swap +
Coventry C.	3/95	£1.1m

Season	Team	Tot	St	Sb	Snu	Ps	Gls
92-93	Liverpool	30	29	1	0	0	2
93-94	Liverpool	4	3	1	1	2	0
93-94	West Ham U.	25	25	0	0	2	1
94-95	Coventry C.	11	11	0	0	1	0
94-95	Everton	19	19	0	0	3	0
94-95	West Ham U.	4	4	0	0	0	0
95-96	Coventry C.	13	13	0	0	2	0
96-97	Coventry C.	18	17	1	6	3	0
97-98	Coventry C.	32	32	0	0	0	0
98-99	Coventry C.	23	23	0	0	6	0
99-00	Coventry C.	15	11	4	2	3	0
	Total	194	187	7	9	22	3

BURTON, Deon

FULLNAME: Deon John Burton
DOB: 25-Oct-76, Ashford

Club History	Signed	Fee
Portsmouth	2/94	Trainee
Cardiff C.	12/96	Loan
Derby Co.	8/97	£1.0m

Season	Team	Tot	St	Sb	Snu	Ps	Gls
97-98	Derby Co.	29	12	17	3	8	3
98-99	Derby Co.	21	14	7	4	3	9
99-00	Derby Co.	19	15	4	2	8	4
	Total	69	41	28	9	19	16

BURTON, Sagi

FULLNAME: Sagi Burton
DOB: 25-Nov-77, Birmingham

Club History	Signed	Fee
Crystal P.		Trainee

Season	Team	Tot	St	Sb	Snu	Ps	Gls
97-98	Crystal P.	2	1	1	1	0	0
	Total	2	1	1	1	0	0

BUSST, David

FULLNAME: David John Busst
DOB: 30-Jun-67, Birmingham

Club History	Signed	Fee
Coventry C.	1/92	Free

Season	Team	Tot	St	Sb	Snu	Ps	Gls
92-93	Coventry C.	10	10	0	9	0	0
93-94	Coventry C.	3	2	1	2	1	0
94-95	Coventry C.	20	20	0	0	2	2

95-96	Coventry C.	17	16	1	0	1	2
	Total	50	48	2	11	4	4

BUTLER, Paul

FULLNAME: Paul John Butler
DOB: 02-Nov-72, Manchester

Club History	Signed	Fee
Rochdale	7/91	Trainee
Bury	7/96	£100,000
Sunderland	7/98	£900,000

Season	Team	Tot	St	Sb	Snu	Ps	Gls
99-00	Sunderland	32	31	1	1	1	1
	Total	32	31	1	1	1	1

BUTLER, Peter

FULLNAME: Peter J F Butler
DOB: 27-Aug-66, Halifax

Club History	Signed	Fee
Huddersfield Town	8/84	Apprentice
Cambridge U.	1/86	Loan
Bury	7/86	Free
Cambridge U.	12/86	Free
Southend U.	2/88	£75,000
Huddersfield Town	3/92	Loan
West Ham U.	8/92	£170,000

Season	Team	Tot	St	Sb	Snu	Ps	Gls
93-94	West Ham U.	26	26	0	0	1	1
94-95	West Ham U.	5	5	0	0	2	0
	Total	31	31	0	0	3	1

BUTLER, Thomas

FULLNAME: Thomas Butler
DOB: 25-Apr-81, Ballymun

Club History	Signed	Fee
Sunderland	8/98	Trainee

Season	Team	Tot	St	Sb	Snu	Ps	Gls
99-00	Sunderland	1	0	1	2	0	0
	Total	1	0	1	2	0	0

BUTT, Nicky

FULLNAME: Nicholas Butt
DOB: 21-Jan-75, Manchester

Club History	Signed	Fee
Manchester U.	1/93	Trainee

Season	Team	Tot	St	Sb	Snu	Ps	Gls
92-93	Manchester U.	1	0	1	0	0	0
93-94	Manchester U.	1	0	1	0	0	0
94-95	Manchester U.	22	11	11	8	5	1
95-96	Manchester U.	32	31	1	0	4	2
96-97	Manchester U.	26	24	2	0	8	5
97-98	Manchester U.	33	31	2	1	6	2
98-99	Manchester U.	31	22	9	1	5	2
99-00	Manchester U.	32	21	11	1	4	3
	Total	178	140	38	11	32	15

BUTTERWORTH, Ian

FULLNAME: Ian Stuart Butterworth
DOB: 25-Jan-64, Crewe

Club History	Signed	Fee
Coventry C.	8/81	
Nottingham F.	6/85	£250,000
Norwich C.	9/86	Loan
Norwich C.	12/86	£160,000

Season	Team	Tot	St	Sb	Snu	Ps	Gls
92-93	Norwich C.	26	26	0	1	2	1
93-94	Norwich C.	25	23	2	3	3	0
	Total	51	49	2	4	5	1

BYFIELD, Darren

FULLNAME: Darren Byfield
DOB: 29-Sep-76, Birmingham

Club History	Signed	Fee
Aston Villa	2/94	Trainee

Season	Team	Tot	St	Sb	Snu	Ps	Gls
97-98	Aston Villa	7	1	6	6	1	0
98-99	Aston Villa	0	0	0	1	0	0
	Total	7	1	6	7	1	0

BYRNE, Shaun

FULLNAME: Shaun Byrne
DOB:

Club History	Signed	Fee
West Ham U.	8/99	Trainee
Bristol C.	1/00	Loan

Season	Team	Tot	St	Sb	Snu	Ps	Gls
99-00	West Ham U.	1	0	1	0	0	0
	Total	1	0	1	0	0	0

BYWATER, Stephen

FULLNAME: Stephen Bywater
DOB: 07-Jun-81, Manchester

Club History	Signed	Fee
Rochdale		Trainee
West Ham U.	8/98	Undisc.

Season	Team	Tot	St	Sb	Snu	Ps	Gls
99-00	West Ham U.	4	3	1	6	0	0
	Total	4	3	1	6	0	0

CABALLERO, Fabian

FULLNAME: Fabian Caballero
DOB: 31-Jan-78, Argentina

Club History	Signed	Fee
Serra Portino, Paraguay		
Arsenal	10/98	Loan

Season	Team	Tot	St	Sb	Snu	Ps	Gls
98-99	Arsenal	1	0	1	2	0	0
	Total	1	0	1	2	0	0

CADAMARTERI, Danny

FULLNAME: Daniel Cadamarteri
DOB: 12-Oct-79, Bradford

Club History	Signed	Fee
Everton	10/96	Trainee

Season	Team	Tot	St	Sb	Snu	Ps	Gls
96-97	Everton	1	0	1	0	0	0
97-98	Everton	26	15	11	3	9	4
98-99	Everton	30	11	19	4	4	4
99-00	Everton	17	3	14	10	1	1
	Total	74	29	45	17	14	9

CADETE, Jorge

FULLNAME: Jorge Cadete
DOB: 27-Aug-68, Mozambique

Club History	Signed	Fee
Benfica		
Bradford C.	2/00	Loan

Season	Team	Tot	St	Sb	Snu	Ps	Gls
99-00	Bradford C.	7	2	5	0	2	0
	Total	7	2	5	0	2	0

CALDERWOOD, Colin

FULLNAME: Colin Calderwood
DOB: 20-Jan-65, Stranraer

Club History	Signed	Fee
Mansfield Town	3/82	Trainee
Swindon Town	7/85	£30,000
Tottenham H.	7/93	£1.25m
Aston Villa	3/99	£225,000

Season	Team	Tot	St	Sb	Snu	Ps	Gls
93-94	Tottenham H.	26	26	0	0	1	0
94-95	Tottenham H.	36	35	1	2	3	2
95-96	Tottenham H.	29	26	3	2	2	0
96-97	Tottenham H.	34	33	1	1	0	0
97-98	Tottenham H.	26	21	5	10	5	4
98-99	Tottenham H.	12	11	1	8	3	0
98-99	Aston Villa	8	8	0	0	2	0
99-00	Aston Villa	18	15	3	5	2	0
	Total	189	175	14	28	18	6

CAMARA, Titi

FULLNAME: Titi Camara
DOB: 07-Nov-72, Conakry, Guinea

Club History	Signed	Fee
Marseille		
Liverpool	6/99	£2.6m

Season	Team	Tot	St	Sb	Snu	Ps	Gls
99-00	Liverpool	33	22	11	1	13	9
	Total	33	22	11	1	13	9

CAMPBELL, Andy

FULLNAME: Andrew Paul Campbell
DOB: 18-Apr-79, Stockton

Club History	Signed	Fee
Middlesbrough	7-96	Trainee

Season	Team	Tot	St	Sb	Snu	Ps	Gls
95-96	Middlesbrough	2	1	1	2	1	0
96-97	Middlesbrough	3	0	3	2	0	0
98-99	Middlesbrough	8	1	7	4	1	0
99-00	Middlesbrough	25	16	9	3	10	4
	Total	38	18	20	11	12	4

CAMPBELL, Kevin

FULLNAME: Kevin Joseph Campbell
DOB: 04-Feb-70, Lambeth

Club History	Signed	Fee
Arsenal	2/88	Trainee
Leyton Orient	1/89	Loan
Leicester C.	11/89	Loan
Nottingham F.	6/95	£2.5m
Trabzonspor	8/98	£2.5m
Everton	3/98	Loan
Everton	7/99	£3m

Season	Team	Tot	St	Sb	Snu	Ps	Gls
92-93	Arsenal	37	32	5	1	4	4
93-94	Arsenal	37	28	9	2	0	14
94-95	Arsenal	23	19	4	1	0	4
95-96	Nottingham F.	21	21	0	1	7	3
96-97	Nottingham F.	17	16	1	0	2	6
98-99	Everton	8	8	0	0	1	9
99-00	Everton	26	26	0	0	0	12
	Total	169	150	19	5	14	52

CAMPBELL, Sol

FULLNAME: Sulzeer Jeremiah Campbell
DOB: 18-Sep-74, Newham, London

Club History	Signed	Fee
Tottenham H.	9/92	Trainee

Season	Team	Tot	St	Sb	Snu	Ps	Gls
92-93	Tottenham H.	1	0	1	0	0	1

93-94	Tottenham H.	34	27	7	5	5	0
94-95	Tottenham H.	30	29	1	0	5	0
95-96	Tottenham H.	31	31	0	1	10	1
96-97	Tottenham H.	38	38	0	0	2	0
97-98	Tottenham H.	34	34	0	0	2	0
98-99	Tottenham H.	37	37	0	0	0	6
99-00	Tottenham H.	29	29	0	0	2	0
	Total	234	225	9	6	26	8

CAMPBELL, Stuart

FULLNAME: Stuart Pearson Campbell
DOB: 09-Dec-77, Corby

Club History	Signed	Fee
Leicester C.	7/96	Trainee

Season	Team	Tot	St	Sb	Snu	Ps	Gls
96-97	Leicester C.	10	4	6	10	2	0
97-98	Leicester C.	11	6	5	13	5	0
98-99	Leicester C.	12	1	11	6	2	0
99-00	Leicester C.	4	1	3	5	0	0
	Total	37	12	25	34	9	0

CANTONA, Eric

FULLNAME: Eric Cantona
DOB: 24-May-66, Paris, France

Club History	Signed	Fee
Nimes	1991	£1m
Leeds U.	2/92	£900,000
Manchester U.	11/92	£1.2m

Season	Team	Tot	St	Sb	Snu	Ps	Gls
92-93	Leeds U.	13	12	1	0	3	6
92-93	Manchester U.	22	21	1	0	1	9
93-94	Manchester U.	34	34	0	0	2	18
94-95	Manchester U.	21	21	0	0	0	12
95-96	Manchester U.	30	30	0	0	1	14
96-97	Manchester U.	36	36	0	0	1	11
	Total	156	154	2	0	8	70

CARBON, Matt

FULLNAME: Matthew Carbon
DOB: 08-Jun-75, Nottingham

Club History	Signed	Fee
Lincoln C.	4/93	Trainee
Derby Co.	3/96	£385,000

Season	Team	Tot	St	Sb	Snu	Ps	Gls
96-97	Derby Co.	10	6	4	8	4	0
97-98	Derby Co.	4	3	1	2	2	0
	Total	14	9	5	10	6	0

CARBONARI, Horacio

FULLNAME: Horacio Angel Carbonari
DOB: 02-May-73, Argentina

Club History	Signed	Fee
Rosario Central		
Derby Co.	5/98	£2.7m

Season	Team	Tot	St	Sb	Snu	Ps	Gls
98-99	Derby Co.	29	28	1	3	4	5
99-00	Derby Co.	29	29	0	2	3	2
	Total	58	57	1	5	7	7

CARBONE, Benito

FULLNAME: Benito Carbone
DOB: 14-Aug-71, Bagnara Calabra, Italy

Club History	Signed	Fee
Internazionale	1995	
Sheffield W.	10/96	£3m
Aston Villa	10/99	Nominal

Season	Team	Tot	St	Sb	Snu	Ps	Gls
96-97	Sheffield W.	25	24	1	0	11	6
97-98	Sheffield W.	33	28	5	0	7	9
98-99	Sheffield W.	31	31	0	0	6	8
99-00	Sheffield W.	7	3	4	0	0	2
99-00	Aston Villa	24	22	2	1	9	3
	Total	120	108	12	1	33	28

CAREY, Brian

FULLNAME: Brian Patrick Carey
DOB: 31-May-68, Cork

Club History	Signed	Fee
Manchester U.	9/89	£100,000
Wrexham	1/91	Loan
Wrexham	12/91	Loan
Leicester C.	7/93	£250,000

Season	Team	Tot	St	Sb	Snu	Ps	Gls
94-95	Leicester C.	12	11	1	0	2	0
	Total	12	11	1	0	2	0

CARR, Franz

FULLNAME: Franz Alexander Carr
DOB: 24-Sep-66, Preston

Club History	Signed	Fee
Blackburn R.	7/84	
Nottingham F.	8/84	£100,000
Sheffield W.	12/89	Loan
West Ham U.	3/91	Loan
Newcastle U.	5/91	£250,000
Sheffield U.	1/93	£120,000
Leicester C.	9/94	Loan
Leicester C.	10/94	£100,000
Aston Villa	12/95	£250,000
Reggina	10/96	Free
Bolton	10/96	Free

Season	Team	Tot	St	Sb	Snu	Ps	Gls
92-93	Sheffield U.	8	8	0	1	5	3
93-94	Sheffield U.	10	10	0	0	2	1
94-95	Leicester C.	13	12	1	0	5	1
94-95	Aston Villa	2	0	2	2	0	0
95-96	Aston Villa	2	1	1	4	0	0
97-98	Bolton W.	5	0	5	4	0	0
Total		40	31	9	11	12	5

CARR, Stephen

FULLNAME: Stephen Carr
DOB: 29-Aug-76, Dublin

Club History	Signed	Fee
Tottenham H.	8/93	Trainee

Season	Team	Tot	St	Sb	Snu	Ps	Gls
93-94	Tottenham H.	1	1	0	0	1	0
96-97	Tottenham H.	26	24	2	7	3	0
97-98	Tottenham H.	38	37	1	0	3	0
98-99	Tottenham H.	37	37	0	0	1	0
99-00	Tottenham H.	34	34	0	0	0	3
Total		136	133	3	7	8	3

CARRAGHER, Jamie

FULLNAME: James Carragher
DOB: 28-Jan-78, Bootle

Club History	Signed	Fee
Liverpool	10/96	Trainee

Season	Team	Tot	St	Sb	Snu	Ps	Gls
96-97	Liverpool	2	1	1	7	0	1
97-98	Liverpool	20	17	3	10	2	0
98-99	Liverpool	34	34	0	0	2	1
99-00	Liverpool	36	33	3	1	1	0
Total		92	85	7	18	5	2

CARRICK, Michael

FULLNAME: Michael Carrick
DOB: 28-Jul-81, Wallsend

Club History	Signed	Fee
West Ham U.	8/98	Trainee

Season	Team	Tot	St	Sb	Snu	Ps	Gls
99-00	West Ham U.	8	4	4	14	0	1
Total		8	4	4	14	0	1

CARRUTHERS, Martin

FULLNAME: Martin Carruthers
DOB: 07-Aug-72, Nottingham

Club History	Signed	Fee
Aston Villa	7/90	Trainee
Hull C.	10/92	Loan

Season	Team	Tot	St	Sb	Snu	Ps	Gls
92-93	Aston Villa	1	0	1	0	0	0
Total		1	0	1	0	0	0

CARSLEY, Lee

FULLNAME: Lee Kevin Carsley
DOB: 28-Apr-74, Birmingham

Club History	Signed	Fee
Derby Co.	7/92	Trainee
Blackburn R.	3/99	£3.375m

Season	Team	Tot	St	Sb	Snu	Ps	Gls
96-97	Derby Co.	24	15	9	4	3	0
97-98	Derby Co.	34	34	0	1	1	1
98-99	Derby Co.	22	20	2	1	0	1
98-99	Blackburn R.	8	7	1	0	1	0
Total		88	76	12	5	5	2

CARTER, Jimmy

FULLNAME: James William Charles Carter
DOB: 09-Nov-65, Hammersmith

Club History	Signed	Fee
QPR	9/85	Free QPR App
Millwall	3/87	£15,000
Liverpool	1/91	£800,000
Arsenal	10/91	£500,000

Season	Team	Tot	St	Sb	Snu	Ps	Gls
92-93	Arsenal	16	11	5	1	3	2
94-95	Arsenal	3	2	1	0	1	0
Total		19	13	6	1	4	2

CASCARINO, Tony

FULLNAME: Anthony Guy Cascarino
DOB: 01-Sep-62, Orpington

Club History	Signed	Fee
Gillingham	1/82	Free
Millwall	6/87	£200,000
Aston Villa	3/90	£1.5m
Celtic	7/91	£1.1m
Chelsea	2/92	£750,000

Season	Team	Tot	St	Sb	Snu	Ps	Gls
92-93	Chelsea	9	8	1	0	0	2
93-94	Chelsea	20	16	4	2	5	4
Total		29	24	5	2	5	6

CASIRAGHI, Pier Luigi

FULLNAME: Pier Luigi Casiraghi
DOB: 04-Mar-69, Monza, Italy

Club History	Signed	Fee
Lazio	1993	
Chelsea	6/98	£5.4m

Season	Team	Tot	St	Sb	Snu	Ps	Gls
98-99	Chelsea	10	10	0	0	7	1
	Total	10	10	0	0	7	1

CASKEY, Darren

FULLNAME: Darren Mark Caskey
DOB: 21-Aug-74, Basildon

Club History	Signed	Fee
Tottenham H.	3/92	Trainee

Season	Team	Tot	St	Sb	Snu	Ps	Gls
93-94	Tottenham H.	25	16	9	3	3	4
94-95	Tottenham H.	4	1	3	8	1	0
95-96	Tottenham H.	3	3	0	2	0	0
	Total	32	20	12	13	4	4

CASPER, Chris

FULLNAME: Christopher Martin Casper
DOB: 28-Apr-75, Burnley

Club History	Signed	Fee
Manchester U.	3/2/93	Trainee

Season	Team	Tot	St	Sb	Snu	Ps	Gls
94-95	Manchester U.	0	0	0	1	0	0
95-96	Manchester U.	0	0	0	1	0	0
96-97	Manchester U.	2	0	2	3	0	0
97-98	Manchester U.	0	0	0	3	0	0
	Total	2	0	2	8	0	0

CASTLEDINE, Stewart

FULLNAME: Stewart Mark Castledine
DOB: 22-Jan-73, Wandsworth

Club History	Signed	Fee
Wimbledon	7/91	Trainee

Season	Team	Tot	St	Sb	Snu	Ps	Gls
93-94	Wimbledon	3	3	0	0	1	1
94-95	Wimbledon	6	5	1	0	1	1
95-96	Wimbledon	4	2	2	0	1	1
96-97	Wimbledon	6	4	2	0	0	1
97-98	Wimbledon	6	3	3	4	1	0
98-99	Wimbledon	1	1	0	4	1	0
	Total	26	18	8	8	5	4

CHALLIS, Trevor

FULLNAME: Trevor Challis
DOB: 23-Oct-75, Paddington

Club History	Signed	Fee
QPR		Trainee

Season	Team	Tot	St	Sb	Snu	Ps	Gls
95-96	QPR	11	10	1	5	2	0
	Total	11	10	1	5	2	0

CHAMBERLAIN, Alec

FULLNAME: Alec Francis Roy Chamberlain
DOB: 20-Jun-64, March, Cambs.

Club History	Signed	Fee
Ipswich Town	7/81	Free
Colchester U.	8/82	Free
Everton	7/87	£80,000
Tranmere R.	11/87	Loan
Luton Town	7/88	£150,000
Sunderland	7/93	Free
Watford	7/96	£40,000

Season	Team	Tot	St	Sb	Snu	Ps	Gls
92-93	Chelsea	0	0	0	6	0	0
94-95	Liverpool	0	0	0	5	0	0
99-00	Watford	27	27	0	5	0	0
	Total	27	27	0	16	0	0

CHANNING, Justin

FULLNAME: Justin Channing
DOB: 19-Nov-68, Reading

Club History	Signed	Fee
QPR	8/86	Apprentice

Season	Team	Tot	St	Sb	Snu	Ps	Gls
92-93	QPR	2	2	0	1	1	1
	Total	2	2	0	1	1	1

CHAPMAN, Lee

FULLNAME: Lee Chapman
DOB: 05-Feb-59, Lincoln

Club History	Signed	Fee
Stoke C.	6/78	Junior
Plymouth Argyle	12/78	Loan
Arsenal	8/82	£500,000
Sunderland	12/83	£200,000
Sheffield W.	8/84	£100,000
Niort, France	6/88	£350,000
Nottingham F.	10/88	£350,000
Leeds U.	1/90	£400,000
Portsmouth	8/93	£250,000
West Ham U.	9/93	£250,000
Southend U.	1/95	Loan
Ipswich T.	1/95	£70,000
Leeds U.	1/96	Loan

Season	Team	Tot	St	Sb	Snu	Ps	Gls
92-93	Leeds U.	40	36	4	0	2	15
93-94	West Ham U.	30	26	4	2	1	7
94-95	West Ham U.	10	7	3	2	2	0
94-95	Ipswich T.	16	9	7	2	2	1
95-96	Leeds U.	2	2	0	0	1	0
	Total	98	80	18	6	8	23

CHARLES, Gary

FULLNAME: Gary Andrew Charles
DOB: 13-Apr-70, Newham

Club History	Signed	Fee
Nottingham F.	11/87	Trainee
Leicester C.	3/89	Loan
Derby Co.	7/93	£750,000
Aston Villa	1/95	£2.9m
West Ham U.		

Season	Team	Tot	St	Sb	Snu	Ps	Gls
92-93	Nottingham F.	14	14	0	1	0	0
94-95	Aston Villa	16	14	2	2	0	0
95-96	Aston Villa	34	34	0	1	1	1
97-98	Aston Villa	18	14	4	11	3	1
98-99	Aston Villa	11	10	1	5	3	1
99-00	West Ham U.	4	2	2	7	1	0
	Total	97	88	9	26	8	3

CHARLES, Lee

FULLNAME: Lee Charles
DOB: 20-Aug-71, Hillingdon

Club History	Signed	Fee
QPR	8/95	£67,500 from Non League

Season	Team	Tot	St	Sb	Snu	Ps	Gls
95-96	QPR	4	0	4	0	0	0
	Total	4	0	4	0	0	0

CHARLTON, Simon

FULLNAME: Simon Thomas Charlton
DOB: 25-Oct-71, Huddersfield

Club History	Signed	Fee
Huddersfield Town	7/89	Trainee
Southampton	6/93	£250,000

Season	Team	Tot	St	Sb	Snu	Ps	Gls
93-94	Southampton	33	29	4	1	4	1
94-95	Southampton	25	25	0	1	5	1
95-96	Southampton	26	24	2	1	6	0
96-97	Southampton	26	24	2	1	8	0
97-98	Southampton	3	2	1	1	2	0
	Total	113	104	9	5	25	2

CHARVET, Laurent

FULLNAME: Laurent Jean Charvert
DOB: 08-May-73, Beizers, France

Club History	Signed	Fee
Cannes		
Chelsea	1/98	Loan
Newcastle U.	7/98	£520,000

Season	Team	Tot	St	Sb	Snu	Ps	Gls
97-98	Chelsea	11	7	4	1	0	2
98-99	Newcastle U.	31	30	1	0	0	1
99-00	Newcastle U.	2	1	1	2	0	0
	Total	44	38	6	3	0	3

CHETTLE, Steve

FULLNAME: Stephen Chettle
DOB: 27-Sep-68, Nottingham

Club History	Signed	Fee
Nottingham F.	8/86	Apprentice

Season	Team	Tot	St	Sb	Snu	Ps	Gls
92-93	Nottingham F.	30	30	0	7	0	0
94-95	Nottingham F.	41	41	0	0	0	0
95-96	Nottingham F.	37	37	0	0	0	0
96-97	Nottingham F.	32	31	1	3	0	0
98-99	Nottingham F.	34	32	2	1	2	2
	Total	174	171	3	11	2	2

CHIPPO, Youssef

FULLNAME: Youssef Chippo
DOB: 10-May-73, Morocco

Club History	Signed	Fee
FC Porto	8/98	
Coventry C.	5/99	£1.2m

Season	Team	Tot	St	Sb	Snu	Ps	Gls
99-00	Coventry C.	33	33	0	0	8	2
	Total	33	33	0	0	8	2

CHRISTIE, Malcolm

FULLNAME: Malcolm Neil Christie
DOB: 11-Apr-79, Peterborough

Club History	Signed	Fee
Derby Co.	10/98	£50,000 from Non League

Season	Team	Tot	St	Sb	Snu	Ps	Gls
95-96	Coventry C.	1	0	1	5	0	0
98-99	Derby Co.	2	0	2	9	0	0
99-00	Derby Co.	21	10	11	4	2	6
	Total	24	10	14	18	2	6

CLAPHAM, Jamie

FULLNAME: James Clapham
DOB: 07-Dec-75, Lincoln

Club History	Signed	Fee
Tottenham H.	7/94	Trainee
Ipswich Town	3/98	£300,000

Season	Team	Tot	St	Sb	Snu	Ps	Gls
96-97	Tottenham H.	1	0	1	1	0	0
97-98	Tottenham H.	0	0	0	1	0	0
	Total	1	0	1	2	0	0

CLARIDGE, Steve

FULLNAME: Stephen Edward Claridge
DOB: 10-Apr-66, Portsmouth

Club History	Signed	Fee
Bournemouth	11/84	
Crystal P.	10/88	
Aldershot	10/88	£14,000
Cambridge Utd	2/90	£75,000
Luton Town	7/92	£160,000
Cambridge Utd	11/92	£195,000
Birmingham C.	1/94	£350,000
Leicester C.	3/96	£1m

Season	Team	Tot	St	Sb	Snu	Ps	Gls
96-97	Leicester C.	32	29	3	1	7	12
97-98	Leicester C.	17	10	7	3	8	0
	Total	49	39	10	4	15	12

CLARK, Lee

FULLNAME: Lee Robert Clark
DOB: 27-Oct-72, Wallsend

Club History	Signed	Fee
Newcastle U.	12/89	Trainee

Season	Team	Tot	St	Sb	Snu	Ps	Gls
93-94	Newcastle U.	29	29	0	0	5	2
94-95	Newcastle U.	19	9	10	9	0	1
95-96	Newcastle U.	28	22	6	4	2	2
96-97	Newcastle U.	25	9	16	12	2	2
	Total	101	69	32	25	9	7

CLARKE, Adrian

FULLNAME: Adrian James Clarke
DOB: 28-Sep-74, Cambridge

Club History	Signed	Fee
Arsenal	7/93	Trainee

Season	Team	Tot	St	Sb	Snu	Ps	Gls
94-95	Arsenal	1	0	1	0	0	0
95-96	Arsenal	6	4	2	2	2	0
	Total	7	4	3	2	2	0

CLARKE, Andy

FULLNAME: Andrew Weston Clarke
DOB: 22-Jul-67, Islington

Club History	Signed	Fee
Barnet		Free
Wimbledon	2/91	£250,000

Season	Team	Tot	St	Sb	Snu	Ps	Gls
92-93	Wimbledon	33	23	10	3	11	5
93-94	Wimbledon	23	9	14	8	6	2
94-95	Wimbledon	25	8	17	2	3	1
95-96	Wimbledon	18	9	9	0	4	2
96-97	Wimbledon	11	4	7	9	2	1
97-98	Wimbledon	14	1	13	13	0	0
	Total	124	54	70	35	26	11

CLARKE, Matt

FULLNAME: Mathew John Clarke
DOB: 03-Nov-73, Sheffield

Club History	Signed	Fee
Rotherham	7/92	Trainee
Sheffield W.	7/96	£325,000
Bradford C.	6/99	Free

Season	Team	Tot	St	Sb	Snu	Ps	Gls
96-97	Sheffield W.	1	0	1	37	0	0
97-98	Sheffield W.	3	2	1	32	0	0
98-99	Sheffield W.	0	0	0	22	0	0
99-00	Bradford C.	21	21	0	10	1	0
	Total	25	23	2	101	1	0

CLARKE, Steve

FULLNAME: Stephen Clarke
DOB: 29-Aug-63, Saltcoats

Club History	Signed	Fee
St Mirren		
Chelsea	1/87	£422,000

Season	Team	Tot	St	Sb	Snu	Ps	Gls
92-93	Chelsea	20	18	2	0	2	0
93-94	Chelsea	39	39	0	0	2	0
94-95	Chelsea	29	29	0	0	1	0
95-96	Chelsea	22	21	1	1	0	0
96-97	Chelsea	31	31	0	1	1	0
97-98	Chelsea	26	22	4	2	2	1
	Total	167	160	7	4	8	1

CLEGG, Michael

FULLNAME: Michael Clegg
DOB: 03-Jul-77, Tameside

Club History	Signed	Fee
Manchester U.	7/95	Trainee

Season	Team	Tot	St	Sb	Snu	Ps	Gls
96-97	Manchester U.	4	3	1	1	1	0
97-98	Manchester U.	3	1	2	6	1	0
98-99	Manchester U.	0	0	0	0	0	0
99-00	Manchester U.	2	0	2	1	0	0
	Total	9	4	5	8	2	0

CLELAND, Alex

FULLNAME: Alexander Cleland
DOB: 10-Dec-70, Glasgow

Club History	Signed	Fee
Dundee U.	6/87	Juniors

Rangers 1/95
Everton 7/98 Free

Season	Team	Tot	St	Sb	Snu	Ps	Gls
98-99	Everton	18	16	2	3	4	0
99-00	Everton	9	3	6	3	2	0
	Total	27	19	8	6	6	0

CLEMENCE, Stephen

FULLNAME: Stephen Clemence
DOB: 31-Mar-78, Liverpool

Club History	Signed	Fee
Tottenham H.	4/95	Trainee

Season	Team	Tot	St	Sb	Snu	Ps	Gls
97-98	Tottenham H.	17	12	5	5	3	0
98-99	Tottenham H.	18	9	9	6	7	0
99-00	Tottenham H.	20	16	4	6	3	1
	Total	55	37	18	17	13	1

CLEMENT, Neil

FULLNAME: Neil Clement
DOB: 03-Oct-78, Reading

Club History	Signed	Fee
Chelsea		Trainee

Season	Team	Tot	St	Sb	Snu	Ps	Gls
96-97	Chelsea	1	1	0	5	1	0
98-99	Chelsea	0	0	0	0	0	0
99-00	Chelsea	0	0	0	1	0	0
	Total	1	1	0	6	1	0

CLEMENT, Philippe

FULLNAME: Philippe Clement
DOB: 22-Mar-74, Antwerp

Club History	Signed	Fee
Racing Genk		
Coventry C.	3/98	£500,000

Season	Team	Tot	St	Sb	Snu	Ps	Gls
98-99	Coventry C.	12	6	6	6	3	0
	Total	12	6	6	6	3	0

CLOUGH, Nigel

FULLNAME: Nigel Howard Clough
DOB: 19-Mar-66, Sunderland

Club History	Signed	Fee
Nottingham F.	9/84	Free from NL
Liverpool	6/93	£2.275m
Manchester C.	1/96	£1.5m
Nottingham F.	12/96	Loan
Sheffield W.		

Season	Team	Tot	St	Sb	Snu	Ps	Gls
92-93	Nottingham F.	42	42	0	0	1	10
93-94	Liverpool	27	25	2	6	4	7
94-95	Liverpool	10	3	7	15	0	0
95-96	Liverpool	3	2	1	3	0	0
95-96	Manchester C.	15	15	0	0	1	2
96-97	Nottingham F.	13	10	3	1	3	1
97-98	Sheffield W.	1	1	0	3	1	0
98-99	Sheffield W.	9	7	2	4	5	0
	Total	120	105	15	32	15	20

COCKERILL, Glenn

FULLNAME: Glen Cockerill
DOB: 25-Aug-59, Grimsby

Club History	Signed	Fee
Lincoln C.	11/76	Free NL
Swindon Town	12/79	£11,000
Lincoln C.	8/81	£40,000
Sheffield W.	3/84	£125,000
Southampton	10/85	£225,000

Season	Team	Tot	St	Sb	Snu	Ps	Gls
92-93	Southampton	23	21	2	1	1	0
93-94	Southampton	14	12	2	0	2	0
	Total	37	33	4	1	3	0

COLE, Andy

FULLNAME: Andrew Alexander Cole
DOB: 15-Oct-71, Nottingham

Club History	Signed	Fee
Arsenal	10/89	Trainee
Fulham	9/91	Loan
Bristol C.	3/92	£500,000
Newcastle U.	3/93	£1.75m
Manchester U.	1/95	£7m +

Season	Team	Tot	St	Sb	Snu	Ps	Gls
93-94	Newcastle U.	40	40	0	0	1	34
94-95	Newcastle U.	18	18	0	0	0	9
94-95	Manchester U.	18	17	1	0	0	12
95-96	Manchester U.	34	32	2	1	10	11
96-97	Manchester U.	20	10	10	3	2	6
97-98	Manchester U.	33	31	2	0	6	16
98-99	Manchester U.	32	26	6	2	7	17
99-00	Manchester U.	28	23	5	2	9	19
	Total	223	197	26	8	35	124

COLE, Ashley

FULLNAME: Ashley Cole
DOB: 20-Dec-80, Stepney, London

Club History	Signed	Fee
Arsenal		Trainee

Season	Team	Tot	St	Sb	Snu	Ps	Gls
99-00	Arsenal	1	1	0	1	0	0
	Total	1	1	0	1	0	0

COLE, Joe

FULLNAME: Joseph John Cole
DOB: 08-Nov-81, London

Club History	Signed	Fee
West Ham U.	12/98	Trainee

Season	Team	Tot	St	Sb	Snu	Ps	Gls
98-99	West Ham U.	8	2	6	4	2	0
99-00	West Ham U.	22	17	5	6	3	1
	Total	30	19	11	10	5	1

COLEMAN, Chris

FULLNAME: Christopher Coleman
DOB: 10-Jun-70, Swansea

Club History	Signed	Fee
Swansea C.	9/87	From Man.C. Jnrs
Crystal P.	7/91	£275,000
Blackburn R.	12/95	£2.8m

Season	Team	Tot	St	Sb	Snu	Ps	Gls
92-93	Crystal P.	38	31	7	1	6	5
94-95	Crystal P.	35	35	0	0	2	1
95-96	Blackburn R.	20	19	1	0	1	0
96-97	Blackburn R.	8	8	0	0	2	0
97-98	Blackburn R.	0	0	0	0	0	0
	Total	101	93	8	1	11	6

COLEMAN, Simon

FULLNAME: Simon Coleman
DOB: 13-Mar-68, Worksop

Club History	Signed	Fee
Mansfield Town	7/85	Juniors
Middlesbrough	9/89	£400,000
Derby Co.	8/91	£300,000
Sheffield W.	1/94	£250,000
Bolton Wanderers	10/94	£350,000

Season	Team	Tot	St	Sb	Snu	Ps	Gls
93-94	Sheffield W.	15	10	5	0	0	1
94-95	Sheffield W.	1	1	0	1	0	0
95-96	Bolton W.	12	12	0	0	1	1
97-98	Bolton W.	0	0	0	1	0	0
	Total	28	23	5	2	1	2

COLGAN, Nick

FULLNAME: Nick Colgam
DOB: 19-Sep-73, Drogheda

Club History	Signed	Fee
Chelsea	10/92	Trainee
Oldham A.		Loan

Season	Team	Tot	St	Sb	Snu	Ps	Gls
92-93	Chelsea	0	0	0	12	0	0
93-94	Chelsea	0	0	0	2	0	0
93-94	Oldham A.	0	0	0	1	0	0
94-95	Chelsea	0	0	0	11	0	0
95-96	Chelsea	0	0	0	1	0	0
96-97	Chelsea	1	1	0	15	0	0
97-98	Chelsea	0	0	0	1	0	0
	Total	1	1	0	43	0	0

COLLETER, Patrick

FULLNAME: Patrick Colleter
DOB: 06-Nov-65, Brest, France

Club History	Signed	Fee
Marseille		
Southampton	3/12	£300,000

Season	Team	Tot	St	Sb	Snu	Ps	Gls
98-99	Southampton	16	16	0	1	3	1
99-00	Southampton	8	8	0	7	4	0
	Total	24	24	0	8	7	1

COLLETT, Andy

FULLNAME: Andrew Alfred Collett
DOB: 28-Oct-73, Stockton

Club History	Signed	Fee
Middlesbrough	6/92	Trainee

Season	Team	Tot	St	Sb	Snu	Ps	Gls
92-93	Middlesbrough	2	2	0	8	0	0
	Total	2	2	0	8	0	0

COLLINS, John

FULLNAME: John Angus Paul Collins
DOB: 31-Jan-68, Gallashiels

Club History	Signed	Fee
Hibernian	8/84	Free from Non League
Celtic	7/90	
Monaco	7/96	
Everton	8/98	£2.5m

Season	Team	Tot	St	Sb	Snu	Ps	Gls
98-99	Everton	20	19	1	0	2	1
99-00	Everton	35	33	2	2	1	2
	Total	55	52	3	2	3	3

COLLINS, Wayne

FULLNAME: Wayne Collins
DOB: 04-Mar-69, Manchester

Club History	Signed	Fee
Crewe Alex	7/93	£10,000 NL
Sheffield W.	8/96	£600,000

Season	Team	Tot	St	Sb	Snu	Ps	Gls
96-97	Sheffield W.	12	8	4	7	3	1
97-98	Sheffield W.	19	8	11	1	4	5
	Total	31	16	15	8	7	6

COLLYMORE, Stan

FULLNAME: Stanley Victor Collymore
DOB: 22-Jan-71, Stone

Club History	Signed	Fee
Crystal P.	1/91	£100,000
Southend U.	11/92	£100,000
Nottingham F.	7/93	£2.0m
Liverpool	7/95	£8.5m
Aston Villa	5/97	£7m
Leicester C.	2/00	£500,000

Season	Team	Tot	St	Sb	Snu	Ps	Gls
92-93	Crystal P.	2	0	2	4	0	0
94-95	Nottingham F.	37	37	0	0	1	23
95-96	Liverpool	30	29	1	2	6	14
96-97	Liverpool	30	25	5	5	9	12
97-98	Aston Villa	25	23	2	1	3	6
98-99	Aston Villa	20	11	9	1	3	1
99-00	Leicester C.	6	6	0	0	1	4
	Total	150	131	19	13	23	60

COOK, Paul

FULLNAME: Paul A Cook
DOB: 22-Feb-67, Liverpool

Club History	Signed	Fee
Wigan A.	7/84	Trainee
Norwich C.	5/88	£73,000
Wolverhampton W.	11/89	£250,000
Coventry C.	8/94	£600,000

Season	Team	Tot	St	Sb	Snu	Ps	Gls
94-95	Coventry C.	34	33	1	0	3	3
95-96	Coventry C.	3	2	1	0	2	0
	Total	37	35	2	0	5	3

COOKE, Terry

FULLNAME: Terence John Cooke
DOB: 05-Aug-76, Marston Green

Club History	Signed	Fee
Manchester U.	7/94	Trainee

Season	Team	Tot	St	Sb	Snu	Ps	Gls
95-96	Manchester U.	4	1	3	0	1	0
96-97	Manchester U.	0	0	0	0	0	0
	Total	4	1	3	0	1	0

COOPER, Colin

FULLNAME: Colin Terence Cooper
DOB: 28-Feb-67, Durham

Club History	Signed	Fee
Middlesbrough	7/84	Juniors
Millwall	7/91	£300,000
Nottingham F.	6/93	£1.7m

Middlesbrough   8/98   £2.5m

Season	Team	Tot	St	Sb	Snu	Ps	Gls
94-95	Nottingham F.	35	35	0	0	1	1
95-96	Nottingham F.	37	37	0	0	1	5
96-97	Nottingham F.	36	36	0	0	1	2
98-99	Middlesbrough	32	31	1	0	2	1
99-00	Middlesbrough	26	26	0	0	1	0
	Total	166	165	1	0	6	9

CORK, Alan

FULLNAME: Alan Graham Cork
DOB: 04-Mar-59, Derby

Club History	Signed	Fee
Derby Co.	7/77	
Lincoln C.	9/77	Loan
Wimbledon	2/78	Free
Sheffield U.		

Season	Team	Tot	St	Sb	Snu	Ps	Gls
92-93	Sheffield U.	27	11	16	7	4	2
93-94	Sheffield U.	19	7	12	2	2	3
	Total	46	18	28	9	6	5

CORT, Carl

FULLNAME: Carl Edward Richard Cort
DOB: 01-Nov-77, London

Club History	Signed	Fee
Wimbledon	6/96	Trainee

Season	Team	Tot	St	Sb	Snu	Ps	Gls
96-97	Wimbledon	1	0	1	0	0	0
97-98	Wimbledon	22	16	6	3	5	4
98-99	Wimbledon	16	6	10	6	3	3
99-00	Wimbledon	34	32	2	0	6	9
	Total	73	54	19	9	14	16

COTON, Tony

FULLNAME: Anthony Philip Coton
DOB: 19-May-61, Tamworth

Club History	Signed	Fee
Birmingham C.	10/78	
Watford	9/84	£300,000
Manchester C.	7/90	£1m
Manchester U.	1/96	£500,000
Sunderland	7/96	£350,000

Season	Team	Tot	St	Sb	Snu	Ps	Gls
92-93	Manchester C.	40	40	0	1	0	0
93-94	Manchester C.	31	31	0	2	0	0
94-95	Manchester C.	22	21	1	1	2	0
95-96	Manchester C.	0	0	0	9	0	0
95-96	Manchester U.	0	0	0	2	0	0
96-97	Sunderland	10	10	0	0	1	0
	Total	103	102	1	15	3	0

COTTEE, Tony

FULLNAME: Anthony Richard Cottee
DOB: 11-Jul-65, West Ham

Club History	Signed	Fee
West Ham U.	9/82	Apprerntice
Everton	8/88	£2.3m
West Ham U.	9/94	Swap+£300,000
Selangor	10/96	£750,000
Leicester C.	8/97	£500,000

Season	Team	Tot	St	Sb	Snu	Ps	Gls
92-93	Everton	26	25	1	0	2	12
93-94	Everton	39	36	3	1	5	16
94-95	Everton	3	3	0	0	1	0
94-95	West Ham U.	31	31	0	0	0	13
95-96	West Ham U.	33	30	3	1	11	10
96-97	West Ham U.	3	2	1	0	2	0
97-98	Leicester C.	19	7	12	6	4	4
98-99	Leicester C.	31	29	2	0	8	10
99-00	Leicester C.	33	30	3	2	18	13
	Total	218	193	25	10	51	78

COTTERELL, Leo

FULLNAME: Leo Spencer Cotterell
DOB: 02-Sep-74, Cambridge

Club History	Signed	Fee
Ipswich Town	7/93	Trainee

Season	Team	Tot	St	Sb	Snu	Ps	Gls
94-95	Ipswich T.	2	0	2	0	0	0
	Total	2	0	2	0	0	0

COTTERILL, Steve

FULLNAME: Stephen John Cotterill
DOB: 20-Jul-64, Cheltenham

Club History	Signed	Fee
Wimbledon	2/89	From Non League

Season	Team	Tot	St	Sb	Snu	Ps	Gls
92-93	Wimbledon	7	4	3	3	0	3
	Total	7	4	3	3	0	3

COUZENS, Andy

FULLNAME: Andrew Couzens
DOB: 04-Jun-75, Shipley

Club History	Signed	Fee
Leeds U.	3/93	Trainee

Season	Team	Tot	St	Sb	Snu	Ps	Gls
94-95	Leeds U.	4	2	2	1	0	0
95-96	Leeds U.	14	8	6	4	4	0
96-97	Leeds U.	10	7	3	4	7	1
	Total	28	17	11	9	11	1

COWAN, Tom

FULLNAME: Thomas Cowan
DOB: 28-Aug-69, Bellshill

Club History	Signed	Fee
Rangers		
Sheffield U.	7/91	£350,000

Season	Team	Tot	St	Sb	Snu	Ps	Gls
92-93	Sheffield U.	21	21	0	0	2	0
93-94	Sheffield U.	4	4	0	0	0	0
	Total	25	25	0	0	2	0

COWANS, Gordon

FULLNAME: Gordon Sidney Cowans
DOB: 27-Oct-58, Cornforth

Club History	Signed	Fee
Aston Villa	9/76	Apprentice
Bari (Italy)	7/85	£500,000
Aston Villa	7/88	£250,000
Blackburn R.	11/91	£200,000
Aston Villa	8/93	Free

Season	Team	Tot	St	Sb	Snu	Ps	Gls
92-93	Blackburn R.	24	23	1	4	5	1
93-94	Aston Villa	11	9	2	2	1	0
	Total	35	32	3	6	6	1

COX, Ian

FULLNAME: Ian Gary Cox
DOB: 25-Mar-71, Croydon

Club History	Signed	Fee
Crystal P.	3/94	£35,000 from Non League

Season	Team	Tot	St	Sb	Snu	Ps	Gls
94-95	Crystal P.	11	1	10	3	1	0
	Total	11	1	10	3	1	0

COX, Neil

FULLNAME: Neil James Cox
DOB: 08-Oct-71, Scunthorpe

Club History	Signed	Fee
Scunthorpe U.	3/90	Trainee
Aston Villa	2/91	£400,000
Middlesbrough	7/94	£1m
Bolton Wanderers	5/97	£1.5m
Watford	11/99	£500,000

Season	Team	Tot	St	Sb	Snu	Ps	Gls
92-93	Aston Villa	15	6	9	8	0	1
93-94	Aston Villa	20	16	4	10	1	2
95-96	Bolton W.	5	2	3	1	1	0
95-96	Middlesbrough	35	35	0	0	0	2
96-97	Middlesbrough	31	29	2	4	0	0
97-98	Bolton W.	21	20	1	2	1	1

99-00	Watford	21	20	1	0	4	0
	Total	148	128	20	25	7	6

COYNE, Chris

FULLNAME: Christopher Cole
DOB: 20-Dec-78, Brisbane

Club History	Signed	Fee
Perth SC		
West Ham U.	1/96	150,000

Season	Team	Tot	St	Sb	Snu	Ps	Gls
97-98	West Ham U.	0	0	0	7	0	0
98-99	West Ham U.	1	0	1	4	0	0
99-00	West Ham U.	0	0	0	2	0	0
	Total	1	0	1	13	0	0

CRADDOCK, Jody

FULLNAME: Jody Darryl Craddock
DOB: 25-Jul-75, Bromsgrove

Club History	Signed	Fee
Cambridge U.	8/93	From NL
Sunderland	8/97	£300,000

Season	Team	Tot	St	Sb	Snu	Ps	Gls
99-00	Sunderland	19	18	1	1	1	0
	Total	19	18	1	1	1	0

CRAMB, Colin

FULLNAME: Colin Cramb
DOB: 11-Jul-65, Southampton

Club History	Signed	Fee
Hamilton Academicals		
Southampton	8/93	£150,000

Season	Team	Tot	St	Sb	Snu	Ps	Gls
93-94	Southampton	1	0	1	0	0	0
	Total	1	0	1	0	0	0

CRAWFORD, Jimmy

FULLNAME: James Crawford
DOB: 01-May-73, Chicago, USA

Club History	Signed	Fee
Bohemians (Ire)		
Newcastle U.	3/95	£75,000

Season	Team	Tot	St	Sb	Snu	Ps	Gls
95-96	Newcastle U.	0	0	0	0	0	0
96-97	Newcastle U.	2	0	2	6	0	0
97-98	Newcastle U.	0	0	0	4	0	0
	Total	2	0	2	10	0	0

CREANEY, Gerry

FULLNAME: Gerald Thomas Creany
DOB: 13-Apr-70, Coatbridge

Club History	Signed	Fee
Celtic	5/87	From Juniors
Portsmouth	1/94	£500,000
Manchester C.	9/95	£1.5m

Season	Team	Tot	St	Sb	Snu	Ps	Gls
95-96	Manchester C.	15	6	9	7	1	3
	Total	15	6	9	7	1	3

CRESSWELL, Richard

FULLNAME: Richard Paul Wesley Cresswell
DOB: 20-Sep-77, Bridlington

Club History	Signed	Fee
York C.	11/95	Trainee
Mansfield T.	3/97	Loan
Sheffield W.	3/99	£950,000

Season	Team	Tot	St	Sb	Snu	Ps	Gls
98-99	Sheffield W.	7	1	6	1	0	1
99-00	Sheffield W.	20	2	18	12	0	1
	Total	27	3	24	13	0	2

CRITTENDEN, Nicky

FULLNAME: Nicolas Crittenden
DOB: 11-Nov-78, Bracknell

Club History	Signed	Fee
Chelsea	7/97	Trainee

Season	Team	Tot	St	Sb	Snu	Ps	Gls
97-98	Chelsea	2	0	2	1	0	0
	Total	2	0	2	1	0	0

CROFT, Gary

FULLNAME: Gary Croft
DOB: 17-Feb-74, Burton on Trent

Club History	Signed	Fee
Grimsby Town	7/92	Trainee
Blackburn R.	3/96	£1.7m

Season	Team	Tot	St	Sb	Snu	Ps	Gls
95-96	Blackburn R.	0	0	0	4	0	0
96-97	Blackburn R.	5	4	1	10	0	0
97-98	Blackburn R.	23	19	4	5	5	1
98-99	Blackburn R.	12	10	2	14	3	0
	Total	40	33	7	33	8	1

CROOK, Ian

FULLNAME: Ian Stuart Crook
DOB: 18-Jan-63, Romford

Club History	Signed	Fee
Tottenham H.	8/80	
Norwich C.	6/86	£80,000

Season	Team	Tot	St	Sb	Snu	Ps	Gls
92-93	Norwich C.	34	32	2	2	3	3
93-94	Norwich C.	38	38	0	0	0	0
94-95	Norwich C.	34	33	1	0	7	0
	Total	106	103	3	2	10	3

CROSBY, Gary

FULLNAME: Gary Crosby
DOB: 08-May-64, Sleaford

Club History	Signed	Fee
Lincoln C.	8/86	
Non League		
Nottingham F.	12/87	£20,000

Season	Team	Tot	St	Sb	Snu	Ps	Gls
92-93	Nottingham F.	23	20	3	6	3	1
	Total	23	20	3	6	3	1

CROSSLEY, Mark

FULLNAME: Mark Geoffrey Crossley
DOB: 16-Jun-69, Barnsley

Club History	Signed	Fee
Nottingham F.	7/87	Trainee

Season	Team	Tot	St	Sb	Snu	Ps	Gls
92-93	Nottingham F.	37	37	0	5	0	0
94-95	Nottingham F.	42	42	0	0	0	0
95-96	Nottingham F.	38	38	0	0	0	0
96-97	Nottingham F.	33	33	0	0	0	0
98-99	Nottingham F.	12	12	0	26	0	0
	Total	162	162	0	31	0	0

CRUYFF, Jordi

FULLNAME: Johan Jordi Cruyff
DOB: 09-Feb-74, Amsterdam

Club History	Signed	Fee
Barcelona	1994	
Manchester U.	8/96	£1.4m

Season	Team	Tot	St	Sb	Snu	Ps	Gls
96-97	Manchester U.	16	11	5	8	6	3
97-98	Manchester U.	5	3	2	1	1	0
98-99	Manchester U.	5	0	5	4	1	2
99-00	Manchester U.	8	1	7	6	1	3
	Total	34	15	19	19	9	8

CUDICINI, Carlo

FULLNAME: Carlo Cudicini
DOB: Italy

Club History	Signed	Fee
Castel Di Sangro	8/98	
Chelsea	7/99	Loan

Season	Team	Tot	St	Sb	Snu	Ps	Gls
99-00	Chelsea	1	1	0	34	0	0
	Total	1	1	0	34	0	0

CULKIN, Nicky

FULLNAME: Nicholas Culkin
DOB: 06-Jul-78, York

Club History	Signed	Fee
York C.	8/94	Trainee
Manchester U.	9/95	£250,000

Season	Team	Tot	St	Sb	Snu	Ps	Gls
97-98	Manchester U.	0	0	0	2	0	0
98-99	Manchester U.	0	0	0	3	0	0
99-00	Manchester U.	1	0	1	4	0	0
	Total	1	0	1	9	0	0

CULVERHOUSE, Ian

FULLNAME: Ian Brett Culverhouse
DOB: 22-Sep-64, Bishops Stortford

Club History	Signed	Fee
Tottenham H.	9/82	Apprentice
Norwich C.	10/85	£50,000

Season	Team	Tot	St	Sb	Snu	Ps	Gls
92-93	Norwich C.	41	41	0	0	0	0
93-94	Norwich C.	42	42	0	0	0	1
	Total	83	83	0	0	0	1

CUMMINS, Michael

FULLNAME: Michael Cummins
DOB: 01-Jun-78, Dublin

Club History	Signed	Fee
Middlesbrough	7/95	Trainee

Season	Team	Tot	St	Sb	Snu	Ps	Gls
98-99	Middlesbrough	1	1	0	0	0	0
99-00	Middlesbrough	1	0	1	0	0	0
	Total	2	1	1	0	0	0

CUNDY, Jason

FULLNAME: Jason Victor Cundy
DOB: 12-Nov-69, Wandsworth

Club History	Signed	Fee
Chelsea	8/88	Trainee
Tottenham H.	3/92	£750,000
Crystal P.	12/95	Loan

Season	Team	Tot	St	Sb	Snu	Ps	Gls
92-93	Tottenham H.	15	13	2	1	1	1
94-95	Tottenham H.	0	0	0	0	0	0
95-96	Tottenham H.	1	0	1	0	0	0
	Total	16	13	3	1	1	1

CUNNINGHAM, Kenny

FULLNAME: Kenneth Edward Cunningham
DOB: 28-Jun-71, Dublin

Club History	Signed	Fee
Millwall	9/89	Free NL
Wimbledon	11/94	£1.3m +

Season	Team	Tot	St	Sb	Snu	Ps	Gls
94-95	Wimbledon	28	28	0	0	0	0
95-96	Wimbledon	33	32	1	0	3	0
96-97	Wimbledon	36	36	0	0	2	0
97-98	Wimbledon	32	32	0	0	1	0
98-99	Wimbledon	35	35	0	0	0	0
99-00	Wimbledon	37	37	0	0	1	0
	Total	201	200	1	0	7	0

CURCIC, Sasa

FULLNAME: Sasa Curcic
DOB: 14-Feb-72, Belgrade

Club History	Signed	Fee
Partizan Belgrade	1993	
Bolton Wanderers	10/95	£1.5m
Aston Villa	8/95	£4m
C.Palace	2/98	£1.0m

Season	Team	Tot	St	Sb	Snu	Ps	Gls
95-96	Bolton W.	28	28	0	0	4	4
96-97	Aston Villa	22	17	5	6	10	0
97-98	Aston Villa	7	3	4	6	3	0
97-98	Crystal P.	8	6	2	0	3	1
	Total	65	54	11	12	20	5

CURETON, Jamie

FULLNAME: James Cureton
DOB: 28-Aug-75, Bristol

Club History	Signed	Fee
Norwich C.	2/93	Trainee

Season	Team	Tot	St	Sb	Snu	Ps	Gls
94-95	Norwich C.	17	9	8	1	5	4
	Total	17	9	8	1	5	4

CURLE, Keith

FULLNAME: Keith Curle
DOB: 14-Nov-63, Bristol

Club History	Signed	Fee
Bristol R.	11/81	Apprentice
Torquay U.	11/83	£5,000
Bristol C.	3/84	£10,000
Reading	10/87	£150,000
Wimbledon	10/88	£500,000
Manchester C.	8/91	£2.5m

Season	Team	Tot	St	Sb	Snu	Ps	Gls
92-93	Manchester C.	39	39	0	0	0	3
93-94	Manchester C.	29	29	0	0	2	1
94-95	Manchester C.	31	31	0	0	1	2
95-96	Manchester C.	32	32	0	0	0	0
	Total	131	131	0	0	3	6

CURTIS, John

FULLNAME: John Curtis
DOB: 03-Sep-78, Nuneaton

Club History	Signed	Fee
Manchester U.	10/95	Trainee

Season	Team	Tot	St	Sb	Snu	Ps	Gls
97-98	Manchester U.	8	3	5	5	1	0
98-99	Manchester U.	4	1	3	2	0	0
99-00	Manchester U.	1	0	1	4	0	0
	Total	13	4	9	11	1	0

CUTLER, Neil

FULLNAME: Neil Anthony Cutler
DOB: 03-Sep-76, Birmingham

Club History	Signed	Fee
WBA	3/96	Trainee
Chester C.	3/96	Loan
Crewe Alex.	7/96	Signed
Chester C.	8/96	Loan
Chester C.	7/98	Free
Aston Villa		

Season	Team	Tot	St	Sb	Snu	Ps	Gls
99-00	Aston Villa	1	0	1	13	0	0
	Total	1	0	1	13	0	0

DABIZAS, Nikos

FULLNAME: Nikolaos Dabizas
DOB: 03-Aug-73, Amyndaeo, Greece

Club History	Signed	Fee
Olympiakos		
Newcastle U.	3/98	£2.0m

Season	Team	Tot	St	Sb	Snu	Ps	Gls
97-98	Newcastle U.	11	10	1	0	0	1
98-99	Newcastle U.	30	25	5	1	1	3
99-00	Newcastle U.	29	29	0	0	1	3
	Total	70	64	6	1	2	7

DACOURT, Olivier

FULLNAME: Olivier Dacourt
DOB: 25-Sep-74, Montreuil, France

Club History	Signed	Fee
Strasbourg		
Everton	8/98	£4m

Season	Team	Tot	St	Sb	Snu	Ps	Gls
98-99	Everton	30	28	2	1	1	2
	Total	30	28	2	1	1	2

DAHLIN, Martin

FULLNAME: Martin Dahlin
DOB: 16-Apr-68, Lund (Sweden)

Club History	Signed	Fee
AS Roma		
B.Monchengladbach		Loan
Blackburn R.	7/97	£2.0m

Season	Team	Tot	St	Sb	Snu	Ps	Gls
97-98	Blackburn R.	21	11	10	5	7	4
98-99	Blackburn R.	5	2	3	0	0	0
	Total	26	13	13	5	7	4

DAILLY, Christian

FULLNAME: Christian Dailly
DOB: 23-Oct-73, Dundee

Club History	Signed	Fee
Dundee U.	1990	Juniors
Derby Co.	8/96	£1m
Blackburn R.	8/98	£5.3m

Season	Team	Tot	St	Sb	Snu	Ps	Gls
96-97	Derby Co.	36	31	5	0	6	3
97-98	Derby Co.	30	30	0	1	0	1
98-99	Derby Co.	1	1	0	0	0	0
98-99	Blackburn R.	17	14	3	4	1	0
	Total	84	76	8	5	7	4

DAISH, Liam

FULLNAME: Liam Sean Daish
DOB: 23-Sep-68, Portsmouth

Club History	Signed	Fee
Portsmouth	8/86	Apprentice
Cambridge U.	7/88	Free
Birmingham C.	1/94	£50,000
Coventry C.	2/96	£1.5m

Season	Team	Tot	St	Sb	Snu	Ps	Gls
95-96	Coventry C.	11	11	0	0	0	1
96-97	Coventry C.	20	20	0	0	2	1
98-99	Coventry C.	0	0	0	1	0	0
	Total	31	31	0	1	2	2

DALEY, Tony

FULLNAME: Anthony Mark Daley
DOB: 18-Oct-67, Birmingham

Club History	Signed	Fee
Aston Villa	5/85	Apprentice

Season	Team	Tot	St	Sb	Snu	Ps	Gls
92-93	Aston Villa	13	8	5	0	2	2
93-94	Aston Villa	27	19	8	0	2	1
	Total	40	27	13	0	4	3

DALGLISH, Paul

FULLNAME: Paul Dalglish
DOB: 18-Feb-77, Glasgow

Club History	Signed	Fee
Celtic	7/95	Juniors
Liverpool	8/96	Free
Newcastle U.	11/97	Free

Season	Team	Tot	St	Sb	Snu	Ps	Gls
98-99	Newcastle U.	11	6	5	2	4	1
	Total	11	6	5	2	4	1

DALLA BONA, Samuele

FULLNAME: Samuele Dalla Bona
DOB: 06-Feb-81, Italy

Club History	Signed	Fee
Atalanta	8/98	
Chelsea	10/98	

Season	Team	Tot	St	Sb	Snu	Ps	Gls
99-00	Chelsea	2	0	2	3	0	0
	Total	2	0	2	3	0	0

DANI

FULLNAME: Daniel Da Cruz Carvalho
DOB: 02-Nov-76, Lisbon

Club History	Signed	Fee
Sporting Lisbon		
West Ham U.	1/96	Loan

Season	Team	Tot	St	Sb	Snu	Ps	Gls
95-96	West Ham U.	10	3	7	1	2	2
	Total	10	3	7	1	2	2

DARBY, Julian

FULLNAME: Julian T Darby
DOB: 03-Oct-67, Bolton

Club History	Signed	Fee
Bolton Wanderers	7/86	Trainee
Coventry C.	10/93	£150,000

Season	Team	Tot	St	Sb	Snu	Ps	Gls
93-94	Coventry C.	26	25	1	2	0	5
94-95	Coventry C.	29	27	2	1	2	0
95-96	Coventry C.	0	0	0	4	0	0
	Total	55	52	3	7	2	5

DARCHEVILLE, Jean-Claude

FULLNAME: Jean-Claude Darcheville
DOB: 25-Jul-75, French Guyana

Club History	Signed	Fee
Stade Rennais		
Nottingham F.	6/98	Loan

Season	Team	Tot	St	Sb	Snu	Ps	Gls
98-99	Nottingham F.	16	14	2	6	12	2
	Total	16	14	2	6	12	2

DAVIDSON, Callum

FULLNAME: Callum Davidson
DOB: 25-Jun-76, Stirling

Club History	Signed	Fee
St. Johnstone	6/94	Juniors
Blackburn R.	2/98	£1.75m

Season	Team	Tot	St	Sb	Snu	Ps	Gls
97-98	Blackburn R.	1	1	0	3	1	0
98-99	Blackburn R.	34	34	0	0	1	1
	Total	35	35	0	3	2	1

DAVIES, Gareth

FULLNAME: Gareth Melville Davies
DOB: 11-Dec-73, Hereford

Club History	Signed	Fee
Hereford U.	4/92	Trainee
Crystal P.	7/95	£120,000

Season	Team	Tot	St	Sb	Snu	Ps	Gls
97-98	Crystal P.	1	0	1	2	0	0
	Total	1	0	1	2	0	0

DAVIES, Kevin

FULLNAME: Kevin Cyril Davies
DOB: 26-Mar-77, Sheffield

Club History	Signed	Fee
Chesterfield	4/94	Trainee
Southampton	5/97	£750,000
Blackburn R.	5/98	£7.5m
Southampton	8/99	£1.2m

Season	Team	Tot	St	Sb	Snu	Ps	Gls
97-98	Southampton	25	20	5	1	4	9
98-99	Blackburn R.	21	9	12	9	6	1
99-00	Southampton	23	19	4	2	2	6
	Total	69	48	21	12	12	16

DAVIES, Simon

FULLNAME: Simon Daviews
DOB: 23-Oct-79, Haverfordwest

Club History	Signed	Fee
Peterborough U.	7/97	Trainee
Tottenham H.	12/99	£700,000

Season	Team	Tot	St	Sb	Snu	Ps	Gls
99-00	Tottenham H.	3	1	2	1	0	0
	Total	3	1	2	1	0	0

DAVIES, Simon

FULLNAME: Simon Ithel Davies
DOB: 23-Apr-74, Winsford

Club History	Signed	Fee
Manchester U.	7/92	Trainee

Season	Team	Tot	St	Sb	Snu	Ps	Gls
94-95	Manchester U.	5	3	2	1	3	0
95-96	Manchester U.	6	1	5	2	1	0
96-97	Manchester U.	0	0	0	0	0	0
	Total	11	4	7	3	4	0

DAVIS, Neil

FULLNAME: Neil Davis
DOB: 15-Aug-73, Bloxwich

Club History	Signed	Fee
Aston Villa	5/91	From NL
Wycombe W.	10/96	Loan

Season	Team	Tot	St	Sb	Snu	Ps	Gls
95-96	Aston Villa	2	0	2	0	0	0
96-97	Aston Villa	0	0	0	1	0	0
	Total	2	0	2	1	0	0

DAVIS, Paul

FULLNAME: Paul Vincent Davis
DOB: 09-Dec-61, Dulwich

Club History	Signed	Fee
Arsenal	7/79	Apprentice

Season	Team	Tot	St	Sb	Snu	Ps	Gls
92-93	Arsenal	6	6	0	0	1	0
93-94	Arsenal	22	21	1	2	6	0
94-95	Arsenal	4	3	1	1	1	1
	Total	32	30	2	3	8	1

DAVISON, Aidan

FULLNAME: Aidan Davison
DOB: 11-May-68, Sedgefield

Club History	Signed	Fee
Notts Co.	3/88	
Bury	7/10/89	£6,000
Millwall	8/91	Free
Bolton Wanderers	7/93	£25,000
Hull	11/96	Loan
Bradford C.	3/97	Free

Grimsby Town	7/97		Free			
Sheffied U.			Free			
Bradford C.	3/00		Free			

Season	Team	Tot	St	Sb	Snu	Ps	Gls
95-96	Bolton W.	2	2	0	17	0	0
99-00	Bradford C.	6	5	1	16	0	0
	Total	8	7	1	33	0	0

DAVISON, Bobby

FULLNAME: Robert Davison
DOB: 17-Jul-59, South Shields

Club History	Signed	Fee
Huddersfield T.	7/80	From Non League
Halifax T.	8/81	
Derby Co.	12/82	
Leeds U.	11/87	
Derby Co.	9/91	Loan
Sheffield U.	3/92	

Season	Team	Tot	St	Sb	Snu	Ps	Gls
93-94	Sheffield U.	9	8	1	3	4	0
	Total	9	8	1	3	4	0

DAY, Chris

FULLNAME: Christopher Day
DOB: 28-Jul-75, Whipps Cross, London

Club History	Signed	Fee
Tottenham	1992	Trainee
Crystal P.	8/96	£225,000
Watford	7/97	£225,000

Season	Team	Tot	St	Sb	Snu	Ps	Gls
92-93	Tottenham H.	0	0	0	2	0	0
93-94	Tottenham H.	0	0	0	7	0	0
94-95	Tottenham H.	0	0	0	20	0	0
95-96	Tottenham H.	0	0	0	22	0	0
99-00	Watford	11	11	0	27	0	0
	Total	11	11	0	78	0	0

DAY, Mervyn

FULLNAME: Mervyn R. Day
DOB: 26-Jun-55, Chelmsford

Club History	Signed	Fee
West Ham U.	3/73	Apprentice
Leyton Orient	7/79	
Aston Villa	8/83	
Leeds U.	1/85	

Season	Team	Tot	St	Sb	Snu	Ps	Gls
92-93	Leeds U.	2	2	0	39	0	0
	Total	2	2	0	39	0	0

DE BILDE, Gilles

FULLNAME: Gilles De Bilde
DOB: 09-Jun-71, Belgium

Club History	Signed	Fee
PSV Eindhoven		
Sheffield W.	7/99	£3.0m

Season	Team	Tot	St	Sb	Snu	Ps	Gls
99-00	Sheffield W.	38	37	1	0	17	10
	Total	38	37	1	0	17	10

DE FREITAS, Fabian

FULLNAME: Fabian De Freitas
DOB: 28-Jul-72, Surinam

Club History	Signed	Fee
Volendam		
Bolton W.	8/94	£400,000

Season	Team	Tot	St	Sb	Snu	Ps	Gls
95-96	Bolton W.	27	17	10	3	2	5
	Total	27	17	10	3	2	5

DE GOEY, Ed

FULLNAME: Edward De Goey
DOB: 20-Dec-66, Gouda (Holland)

Club History	Signed	Fee
Feyenoord		
Chelsea	7/97	£2.5m

Season	Team	Tot	St	Sb	Snu	Ps	Gls
97-98	Chelsea	28	28	0	0	0	0
98-99	Chelsea	35	35	0	1	1	0
99-00	Chelsea	37	37	0	1	0	0
	Total	100	100	0	2	1	0

DE ZEEUW, Arjan

FULLNAME: Adrianus Johannes De Zeeuw
DOB: 16-Apr-70, Holland

Club History	Signed	Fee
Telstar		
Barnsley	11/95	£250,000

Season	Team	Tot	St	Sb	Snu	Ps	Gls
97-98	Barnsley	26	26	0	1	0	0
	Total	26	26	0	1	0	0

DEANE, Brian

FULLNAME: Brian Christopher Deane
DOB: 07-Feb-68, Leeds

Club History	Signed	Fee
Doncaster R.	12/85	Juniors
Sheffield U.	7/88	£30,000

Leeds U.   7/93   £2.9m
Sheffield U.   7/97   £1.5m
Benfica   1/98
Middlesbrough   10/98   £3m

Season	Team	Tot	St	Sb	Snu	Ps	Gls
92-93	Sheffield U.	41	41	0	0	2	15
93-94	Leeds U.	41	41	0	0	1	11
94-95	Leeds U.	35	33	2	0	2	9
95-96	Leeds U.	34	30	4	0	3	7
96-97	Leeds U.	28	27	1	0	4	5
98-99	Middlesbrough	26	24	2	0	6	6
99-00	Middlesbrough	29	29	0	0	1	9
	Total	234	225	9	0	19	62

DEARDEN, Kevin

FULLNAME: Kevin Charles Dearden
DOB: 08-Mar-70, Luton

Club History	Signed	Fee
Tottenham H.	7/88	Trainee

Season	Team	Tot	St	Sb	Snu	Ps	Gls
92-93	Tottenham H.	1	0	1	14	0	0
	Total	1	0	1	14	0	0

DEGN, Peter

FULLNAME: Peter Degn
DOB: 06-Apr-77, Denmark

Club History	Signed	Fee
Aarhus		
Everton	2/99	£200,000

Season	Team	Tot	St	Sb	Snu	Ps	Gls
98-99	Everton	4	0	4	3	0	0
	Total	4	0	4	3	0	0

DEGRYSE, Marc

FULLNAME: Marc Degryse
DOB: 04-Sep-95, Roeselare, Belgium

Club History	Signed	Fee
Anderlecht		
Sheffield W.	8/95	£1.5m

Season	Team	Tot	St	Sb	Snu	Ps	Gls
95-96	Sheffield W.	34	30	4	1	9	8
	Total	34	30	4	1	9	8

DELANEY, Mark

FULLNAME: Mark Anthony Delaney
DOB: 13-May-76, Haverfordwest

Club History	Signed	Fee
Cardiff C.	7/98	Free NL
Aston Villa	3/99	£250,000

Season	Team	Tot	St	Sb	Snu	Ps	Gls
98-99	Aston Villa	2	0	2	3	0	0
99-00	Aston Villa	28	25	3	2	3	1
	Total	30	25	5	5	3	1

DELAP, Rory

FULLNAME: Rory John Delap
DOB: 06-Jul-76, Sutton Coalfield

Club History	Signed	Fee
Carlisle U.	7/94	Trainee
Derby Co.	2/98	£500,000>

Season	Team	Tot	St	Sb	Snu	Ps	Gls
97-98	Derby Co.	13	10	3	1	3	0
98-99	Derby Co.	23	21	2	0	5	0
99-00	Derby Co.	34	34	0	0	2	8
	Total	70	65	5	1	10	8

DESAILLY, Marcel

FULLNAME: Marcel Desailly
DOB: 07-Sep-68, Accra, Ghana

Club History	Signed	Fee
Milan	1994	
Chelsea	6/97	£4.6m

Season	Team	Tot	St	Sb	Snu	Ps	Gls
98-99	Chelsea	31	30	1	0	2	0
99-00	Chelsea	23	23	0	0	3	1
	Total	54	53	1	0	5	1

DESCHAMPS, Didier

FULLNAME: Didier Deschamps
DOB: 15-Oct-68, Bayonne, Belgium

Club History	Signed	Fee
Juventus		
Chelsea	6/99	£3.0m

Season	Team	Tot	St	Sb	Snu	Ps	Gls
99-00	Chelsea	27	24	3	0	8	0
	Total	27	24	3	0	8	0

DI CANIO, Paolo

FULLNAME: Paolo Di Canio
DOB: 09-Jul-68, Rome

Club History	Signed	Fee
Milan		
Celtic	7/96	
Sheffield W.	8/97	£3m
West Ham U.	1/99	£1.7m

Season	Team	Tot	St	Sb	Snu	Ps	Gls
97-98	Sheffield W.	35	34	1	0	8	12
98-99	Sheffield W.	6	5	1	0	2	3
98-99	West Ham U.	13	12	1	0	2	4

99-00	West Ham U.	30	29	1	0	2	16
	Total	84	80	4	0	14	35

DI MATTEO, Roberto

FULLNAME: Roberto Di Matteo
DOB: 29-May-70, Sciaffusa, Switzerland

Club History	Signed	Fee
Lazio	1993	
Chelsea	7/96	£4.9m

Season	Team	Tot	St	Sb	Snu	Ps	Gls
96-97	Chelsea	34	33	1	3	5	6
97-98	Chelsea	30	28	2	1	6	4
98-99	Chelsea	30	26	4	1	7	2
99-00	Chelsea	18	14	4	3	3	2
	Total	112	101	11	8	21	14

DIA, Ali

FULLNAME: Ali Dia
DOB: 20-Aug-65, Senegal

Club History	Signed	Fee
Lubeck		
Southampton	11/96	Free

Season	Team	Tot	St	Sb	Snu	Ps	Gls
96-97	Southampton	1	0	1	0	1	0
	Total	1	0	1	0	1	0

DIAWARA, Kaba

FULLNAME: Kaba Diawara
DOB: 16-Dec-75, Toulon, France

Club History	Signed	Fee
Bordeaux		
Arsenal	1/99	£2.5m

Season	Team	Tot	St	Sb	Snu	Ps	Gls
98-99	Arsenal	12	2	10	4	2	0
	Total	12	2	10	4	2	0

DIBBLE, Andy

FULLNAME: Andrew Gerald Dibble
DOB: 08-May-65, Cwmbran

Club History	Signed	Fee
Cardiff C.	8/82	
Luton Town	7/84	£125,000
Sunderland	2/86	Loan
Huddersfield Town	2/87	Loan
Manchester C.	7/88	£240,000

Season	Team	Tot	St	Sb	Snu	Ps	Gls
92-93	Manchester C.	2	1	1	7	0	0
93-94	Manchester C.	11	11	0	29	0	0
94-95	Manchester C.	16	15	1	15	0	0
	Total	29	27	2	51	0	0

DICHIO, Daniele

FULLNAME: Daniele Salvatore Ernest Dichio
DOB: 19-Oct-74, Hammersmith

Club History	Signed	Fee
QPR	5/93	Trainee
Barnet	3/94	Loan
Sampdoria	8/97	Free
Lecce		
Sunderland	1/98	£750,000

Season	Team	Tot	St	Sb	Snu	Ps	Gls
94-95	QPR	9	4	5	1	0	3
95-96	QPR	29	21	8	1	2	10
99-00	Sunderland	12	0	12	9	0	0
	Total	50	25	25	11	2	13

DICKOV, Paul

FULLNAME: Paul Dickov
DOB: 01-Nov-72, Livingstone

Club History	Signed	Fee
Arsenal	12/90	Trainee

Season	Team	Tot	St	Sb	Snu	Ps	Gls
92-93	Arsenal	3	1	2	0	0	2
93-94	Arsenal	1	0	1	0	0	0
94-95	Arsenal	9	4	5	1	0	0
95-96	Arsenal	7	1	6	3	0	1
96-97	Arsenal	1	0	1	0	0	0
	Total	21	6	15	4	0	3

DICKS, Julian

FULLNAME: Julian Andrew Dicks
DOB: 08-Aug-68, Bristol

Club History	Signed	Fee
Birmingham C.	4/86	Apprentice
West Ham U.	3/88	£300,000
Liverpool	9/93	£1.5m
West Ham U.	10/94	£500,000+

Season	Team	Tot	St	Sb	Snu	Ps	Gls
93-94	Liverpool	24	24	0	0	1	3
93-94	West Ham U.	7	7	0	0	0	0
94-95	West Ham U.	29	29	0	0	1	5
95-96	West Ham U.	34	34	0	0	0	10
96-97	West Ham U.	31	31	0	0	0	6
98-99	West Ham U.	9	9	0	0	0	0
	Total	134	134	0	0	2	24

DIGBY, Fraser

FULLNAME: Fraser C Digby
DOB: 23-Jan-67, Sheffield

Club History	Signed	Fee
Manchester U.	4/85	Apprentice

Oldham A.	1/86	Loan
Swindon Town	12/86	£32,000
Manchester U.	11/92	Loan

Season	Team	Tot	St	Sb	Snu	Ps	Gls
92-93	Manchester U.	0	0	0	8	0	0
93-94	Swindon T.	28	28	0	2	1	0
	Total	28	28	0	10	1	0

DIXON, Kerry

FULLNAME: Kerry Michael Dixon
DOB: 24-Jul-61, Luton

Club History	Signed	Fee
Tottenham H.	7/78	
Reading	7/80	£20,000
Chelsea	8/83	£175,000
Southampton		

Season	Team	Tot	St	Sb	Snu	Ps	Gls
92-93	Southampton	9	8	1	2	0	2
	Total	9	8	1	2	0	2

DIXON, Lee

FULLNAME: Lee Michael Dixon
DOB: 17-Mar-64, Manchester

Club History	Signed	Fee
Burnley	7/82	Juniors
Chester C.	2/84	Free
Bury	7/85	Free
Stoke C.	7/86	£40,000
Arsenal	1/88	£400,000

Season	Team	Tot	St	Sb	Snu	Ps	Gls
92-93	Arsenal	29	29	0	0	2	0
93-94	Arsenal	33	32	1	0	3	0
94-95	Arsenal	39	39	0	0	0	1
95-96	Arsenal	38	38	0	0	1	2
96-97	Arsenal	32	31	1	0	3	2
97-98	Arsenal	28	26	2	0	3	0
98-99	Arsenal	36	36	0	0	3	0
99-00	Arsenal	28	28	0	6	2	3
	Total	263	259	4	6	17	8

DOBBS, Gerald

FULLNAME: Gerald Francis Dobbs
DOB: 24-Jan-71, Lambeth

Club History	Signed	Fee
Wimbledon	7/89	

Season	Team	Tot	St	Sb	Snu	Ps	Gls
92-93	Wimbledon	19	16	3	0	8	1
93-94	Wimbledon	10	3	7	1	1	0
	Total	29	19	10	1	9	1

DOBSON, Tony

FULLNAME: Anthony John Dobson
DOB: 05-Feb-69, Coventry

Club History	Signed	Fee
Coventry C.	7/86	Apprentice
Blackburn R.	1/91	£300,000

Season	Team	Tot	St	Sb	Snu	Ps	Gls
92-93	Blackburn R.	19	15	4	2	2	0
	Total	19	15	4	2	2	0

DODD, Jason

FULLNAME: Jason Robert Dodd
DOB: 02-Nov-70, Bath

Club History	Signed	Fee
Southampton	3/89	£50,000

Season	Team	Tot	St	Sb	Snu	Ps	Gls
92-93	Southampton	30	27	3	2	2	1
93-94	Southampton	10	5	5	4	1	0
94-95	Southampton	26	24	2	1	0	2
95-96	Southampton	36	36	0	0	0	2
96-97	Southampton	23	23	0	0	3	1
97-98	Southampton	36	36	0	0	2	1
98-99	Southampton	28	27	1	1	0	1
99-00	Southampton	31	30	1	0	0	0
	Total	220	208	12	8	8	8

DOHERTY, Gary

FULLNAME: Gary Michael Thomas Doherty
DOB: 31-Jan-80, Cardonagh

Club History	Signed	Fee
Luton T.	7/97	Trainee
Tottenham H.	8/00	

Season	Team	Tot	St	Sb	Snu	Ps	Gls
99-00	Tottenham H.	2	0	2	0	0	0
	Total	2	0	2	0	0	0

DOIG, Chris

FULLNAME: Christopher Doig
DOB: 13-Feb-81, Dumfries

Club History	Signed	Fee
Nottingham F.	3/98	Trainee

Season	Team	Tot	St	Sb	Snu	Ps	Gls
98-99	Nottingham F.	2	1	1	0	0	0
	Total	2	1	1	0	0	0

DOMI, Didi

FULLNAME: Didier Domi
DOB: 02-May-78, Sarcelles

Club History	Signed	Fee
PSG		
Newcastle U.	12/98	£3.25m

Season	Team	Tot	St	Sb	Snu	Ps	Gls
98-99	Newcastle U.	14	14	0	0	0	0
99-00	Newcastle U.	27	19	8	0	4	3
	Total	41	33	8	0	4	3

DOMINGUEZ, Jose

FULLNAME: Jose manuel Martins Dominguez
DOB: 16-Feb-74, Lisbon

Club History	Signed	Fee
Benfica		
Birmingham C.	3/94	£180,000
Sporting CP	8/95	£1.8m
Tottenham H.	8/97	£1.6m

Season	Team	Tot	St	Sb	Snu	Ps	Gls
97-98	Tottenham H.	18	8	10	3	2	2
98-99	Tottenham H.	13	2	11	6	2	2
99-00	Tottenham H.	12	2	10	7	4	0
	Total	43	12	31	16	8	4

DONAGHY, Mal

FULLNAME: Malachy Martin Donaghy
DOB: 13-Sep-57, Belfast

Club History	Signed	Fee
Luton Town	6/87	£20,000
Manchester U.	10/88	£650,000
Luton Town	12/89	Loan
Chelsea	8/92	£150,000

Season	Team	Tot	St	Sb	Snu	Ps	Gls
92-93	Chelsea	40	39	1	0	3	2
93-94	Chelsea	28	24	4	1	7	1
	Total	68	63	5	1	10	3

DONALDSON, O'Neill

FULLNAME: O'Neill McKay Donaldson
DOB: 24-Nov-69, Birmingham

Club History	Signed	Fee
Shrewsbury Town	11/91	Free NI
Doncaster R.	8/94	Free
Mansfield Town	12/94	Loan
Sheffield W.	1/95	£50,000

Season	Team	Tot	St	Sb	Snu	Ps	Gls
94-95	Sheffield W.	1	0	1	0	0	0
95-96	Sheffield W.	3	1	2	1	1	1
96-97	Sheffield W.	5	2	3	4	0	2
97-98	Sheffield W.	5	1	4	0	1	0
	Total	14	4	10	5	2	3

DONIS, George

FULLNAME: Gerogio Donis
DOB: 29-Oct-69, Frankfurt

Club History	Signed	Fee
Panathinaikos (Greece)		
Blackburn R.	7/96	Free

Season	Team	Tot	St	Sb	Snu	Ps	Gls
96-97	Blackburn R.	22	11	11	9	4	2
	Total	22	11	11	9	4	2

DONNELLY, Simon

FULLNAME: Simon Donnelly
DOB: 01-Dec-74, Glasgow

Club History	Signed	Fee
Canberra Cosmos	8/92	
Celtic	5/93	
Sheffield W.	6/99	Free

Season	Team	Tot	St	Sb	Snu	Ps	Gls
99-00	Sheffield W.	12	3	9	2	3	1
	Total	12	3	9	2	3	1

DORIGO, Tony

FULLNAME: Anthony Robert Dorigo
DOB: 31-Dec-65, Melbourne, Australia

Club History	Signed	Fee
Aston Villa	7/83	Apprentice
Chelsea	7/87	£475,000
Leeds U.	6/91	£1.3m
Torino	8/97	Free
Derby Co.	11/98	Free

Season	Team	Tot	St	Sb	Snu	Ps	Gls
92-93	Leeds U.	33	33	0	0	1	1
93-94	Leeds U.	37	37	0	0	2	0
94-95	Leeds U.	28	28	0	0	2	0
95-96	Leeds U.	17	17	0	0	5	1
96-97	Leeds U.	18	15	3	0	1	0
98-99	Derby Co.	18	17	1	1	3	1
99-00	Derby Co.	23	20	3	2	8	0
	Total	174	167	7	3	22	3

DOW, Andy

FULLNAME: Andrew Dow
DOB: 07-Feb-73, Dundee

Club History	Signed	Fee
Dundee	11/90	
Chelsea	7/93	£250,000

Season	Team	Tot	St	Sb	Snu	Ps	Gls
93-94	Chelsea	14	13	1	0	5	0
95-96	Chelsea	1	1	0	1	0	0
	Total	15	14	1	1	5	0

DOWIE, Iain

FULLNAME: Iain Dowie
DOB: 09-Jan-65, Hatfield

Club History	Signed	Fee	
Luton Town	12/88	£30,000 from NL	
Fulham	9/89	Loan	
West Ham U.	3/91	£480,000	
Southampton	9/91	£500,000	
Crystal P.	1/95	£400,000	
West Ham U.	9/95	£125,000	+ player

Season	Team	Tot	St	Sb	Snu	Ps	Gls
92-93	Southampton	36	34	2	1	2	11
93-94	Southampton	39	39	0	0	3	5
94-95	Southampton	17	17	0	0	0	5
94-95	Crystal P.	15	15	0	0	2	4
95-96	West Ham U.	33	33	0	0	1	8
96-97	West Ham U.	23	18	5	6	0	0
97-98	West Ham U.	12	7	5	6	1	0
	Total	175	163	12	13	9	33

DOYLE, Maurice

FULLNAME: Maurice Doyle
DOB: 17-Oct-69, Ellesmere Port

Club History	Signed	Fee
Crewe Alexandra	7/88	Trainee
QPR	4/89	£120,000

Season	Team	Tot	St	Sb	Snu	Ps	Gls
92-93	QPR	5	5	0	2	1	0
93-94	QPR	1	1	0	0	0	0
	Total	6	6	0	2	1	0

DOZZELL, Jason

FULLNAME: Jason Alvin Winans Dozzell
DOB: 09-Dec-67, Ipswich

Club History	Signed	Fee
Ipswich Town	12/84	Apprentice
Tottenham H.	8/93	£1.9m

Season	Team	Tot	St	Sb	Snu	Ps	Gls
92-93	Ipswich T.	41	41	0	0	2	7
93-94	Tottenham H.	32	28	4	0	3	8
94-95	Tottenham H.	7	6	1	0	3	0
95-96	Tottenham H.	28	24	4	1	2	3
96-97	Tottenham H.	17	10	7	7	2	2
	Total	125	109	16	8	12	20

DRAPER, Mark

FULLNAME: Mark Draper
DOB: 11-Nov-70, Long Eaton

Club History	Signed	Fee
Notts Co.	12/88	Trainee

Leicester C.	7/94	£1.25m		
Aston Villa	7/95	£3.25m		

Season	Team	Tot	St	Sb	Snu	Ps	Gls
94-95	Leicester C.	39	39	0	0	3	5
95-96	Aston Villa	36	36	0	0	3	2
96-97	Aston Villa	29	28	1	2	10	0
97-98	Aston Villa	31	31	0	3	2	3
98-99	Aston Villa	23	13	10	6	7	2
99-00	Aston Villa	1	0	1	3	0	0
	Total	159	147	12	14	25	12

DREYER, John

FULLNAME: John Brian Dreyer
DOB: 11-Jun-63, Alnwick

Club History	Signed	Fee
Oxford U.	1/85	FreeNL
Torquay U.	2/85	Loan
Fulham	3/86	Loan
Luton Town	6/88	£140,000
Stoke C.	7/94	Free
Bolton W.	3/95	Loan
Bradford C.	11/96	£25,000

Season	Team	Tot	St	Sb	Snu	Ps	Gls
99-00	Bradford C.	14	11	3	12	2	1
	Total	14	11	3	12	2	1

DRYDEN, Richard

FULLNAME: Richard Andrew Dryden
DOB: 14-Jun-69, Stroud

Club History	Signed	Fee
Bristol R.	7/87	Trainee
Exeter C.	9/88	Loan
Exeter C.	3/89	
Notts Co.	8/91	£250,000
Plymouth Argle	11/92	Loan
Birmingham C.	3/93	£165,000
Bristol C.	12/94	£140,000
Southampton	8/96	£150,000

Season	Team	Tot	St	Sb	Snu	Ps	Gls
96-97	Southampton	29	28	1	4	3	1
97-98	Southampton	13	11	2	6	1	0
98-99	Southampton	4	4	0	6	0	0
99-00	Southampton	1	1	0	0	1	0
	Total	47	44	3	16	5	1

DUBERRY, Michael

FULLNAME: Michael Wayne Duberry
DOB: 14-Oct-75, London

Club History	Signed	Fee
Chelsea	6/93	Trainee
Bournemouth	9/95	Loan

Leeds U.   7/99   £4.5m

Season	Team	Tot	St	Sb	Snu	Ps	Gls
93-94	Chelsea	1	1	0	2	0	0
95-96	Chelsea	22	22	0	0	2	0
96-97	Chelsea	15	13	2	4	0	1
97-98	Chelsea	23	23	0	0	0	0
98-99	Chelsea	25	18	7	6	2	0
99-00	Leeds U.	13	12	1	14	1	1
	Total	99	89	10	26	5	2

DUBLIN, Dion

FULLNAME: Dion Dublin
DOB: 22-Apr-69, Leicester

Club History	Signed	Fee
Norwich C.	3/88	Trainee
Cambridge U.	8/88	Free
Manchester U.	8/92	£1m
Coventry C.	9/94	£2m
Aston Villa	11/98	£5.75m

Season	Team	Tot	St	Sb	Snu	Ps	Gls
92-93	Manchester U.	7	3	4	3	1	1
93-94	Manchester U.	5	1	4	5	0	1
94-95	Manchester U.	0	0	0	2	0	0
94-95	Coventry C.	31	31	0	0	0	13
95-96	Coventry C.	34	34	0	0	1	14
96-97	Coventry C.	34	33	1	0	2	14
96-97	Coventry C.	5	1	4	4	0	0
97-98	Coventry C.	36	36	0	0	0	18
97-98	Coventry C.	3	1	2	1	2	0
98-99	Coventry C.	10	10	0	0	0	3
98-99	Aston Villa	24	24	0	0	7	11
99-00	Aston Villa	26	23	3	0	6	12
	Total	215	197	18	15	19	87

DUDFIELD, Lawrie

FULLNAME: Lawrie Dudfield
DOB: 07-May-80, London

Club History	Signed	Fee
Leicester C.		From Non League

Season	Team	Tot	St	Sb	Snu	Ps	Gls
99-00	Leicester C.	2	0	2	3	0	0
	Total	2	0	2	3	0	0

DUFF, Damien

FULLNAME: Damien Anthony Duff
DOB: 02-Mar-79, Ballboden

Club History	Signed	Fee
Blackburn R.	3/96	Free NL

Season	Team	Tot	St	Sb	Snu	Ps	Gls
96-97	Blackburn R.	1	1	0	4	0	0
97-98	Blackburn R.	26	17	9	4	5	4
98-99	Blackburn R.	28	18	10	5	9	1
	Total	55	36	19	13	14	5

DUMAS, Franck

FULLNAME: Franck Dumas
DOB:

Club History	Signed	Fee
Monaco		
Newcastle U.	7/99	£500,000

Season	Team	Tot	St	Sb	Snu	Ps	Gls
99-00	Newcastle U.	6	6	0	0	1	0
	Total	6	6	0	0	1	0

DUMITRESCU, Ilie

FULLNAME: Ilie Dumitrescu
DOB: 06-Jan-69, Romania

Club History	Signed	Fee
Steaua Bucharest	7/88	
Tottenham H.	8/94	£2.6m
FC Seville	12/94	Loan
West Ham U.	1/95	£1.65m

Season	Team	Tot	St	Sb	Snu	Ps	Gls
94-95	Tottenham H.	13	11	2	1	3	4
95-96	Tottenham H.	5	5	0	0	1	1
95-96	West Ham U.	3	2	1	0	2	0
96-97	West Ham U.	7	3	4	5	2	0
	Total	28	21	7	6	8	5

DUNDEE, Sean

FULLNAME: Sean William Dundee
DOB: 07-Dec-72, South Africa

Club History	Signed	Fee
Karlsruhe		
Liverpool	6/98	£2m

Season	Team	Tot	St	Sb	Snu	Ps	Gls
98-99	Liverpool	3	0	3	1	0	0
	Total	3	0	3	1	0	0

DUNN, David

FULLNAME: David Dunn
DOB: 27-Dec-79, Blackburn

Club History	Signed	Fee
Blackburn R.		Trainee

Season	Team	Tot	St	Sb	Snu	Ps	Gls
98-99	Blackburn R.	15	10	5	5	6	1
	Total	15	10	5	5	6	1

DUNNE, Richard

FULLNAME: Richard Patrick Dunne
DOB: 21-Sep-79, Dublin

Club History	Signed	Fee
Everton	10/96	Trainee

Season	Team	Tot	St	Sb	Snu	Ps	Gls
96-97	Everton	7	6	1	4	1	0
97-98	Everton	3	2	1	4	0	0
98-99	Everton	15	15	0	1	1	0
99-00	Everton	31	27	4	2	4	0
	Total	56	50	6	11	6	0

DURIE, Gordon

FULLNAME: Gordon Scott Durie
DOB: 06-Dec-65, Paisley

Club History	Signed	Fee
Chelsea	4/86	£380,000
Tottenham H.	8/91	£2.2m

Season	Team	Tot	St	Sb	Snu	Ps	Gls
92-93	Tottenham H.	17	17	0	0	4	3
93-94	Tottenham H.	10	10	0	0	2	1
	Total	27	27	0	0	6	4

DURRANT, Iain

FULLNAME: Iain Durrant
DOB: 29-Oct-66, Glasgow

Club History	Signed	Fee
Rangers		
Everton	10/94	Loan

Season	Team	Tot	St	Sb	Snu	Ps	Gls
94-95	Everton	5	4	1	0	1	0
	Total	5	4	1	0	1	0

DURRANT, Lee

FULLNAME: Lee Roger Durrant
DOB: 18-Dec-73, Great Yarmouth

Club History	Signed	Fee
Ipswich T.	7/92	

Season	Team	Tot	St	Sb	Snu	Ps	Gls
93-94	Ipswich T.	7	3	4	1	1	0
	Total	7	3	4	1	1	0

DYER, Bruce

FULLNAME: Bruce Antonio Dyer
DOB: 13-Apr-75, Ilford

Club History	Signed	Fee
Watford	4/93	Trainee
Crystal P.	3/94	£1.1m

Season	Team	Tot	St	Sb	Snu	Ps	Gls
94-95	Crystal P.	16	7	9	7	4	1
97-98	Crystal P.	24	21	3	3	11	4
	Total	40	28	12	10	15	5

DYER, Kieron

FULLNAME: Kieron Courtney Dyer
DOB: 29-Dec-78, Ipswich

Club History	Signed	Fee
Ipswich Town	1/97	Trainee
Newcastle U.	7/99	£6.5m

Season	Team	Tot	St	Sb	Snu	Ps	Gls
99-00	Newcastle U.	30	27	3	0	9	3
	Total	30	27	3	0	9	3

DYKSTRA, Sieb

FULLNAME: Sieb Dykstra
DOB: 20-Oct-66, Kerkrade

Club History	Signed	Fee
Motherwell		
QPR	7/94	£250,000

Season	Team	Tot	St	Sb	Snu	Ps	Gls
94-95	QPR	11	11	0	30	0	0
95-96	QPR	0	0	0	1	0	0
	Total	11	11	0	31	0	0

EADEN, Nicky

FULLNAME: Nicholas Jeremy Eaden
DOB: 12-Dec-72, Sheffield

Club History	Signed	Fee
Barnsley	6/91	Juniors

Season	Team	Tot	St	Sb	Snu	Ps	Gls
97-98	Barnsley	35	32	3	0	0	0
	Total	35	32	3	0	0	0

EADIE, Darren

FULLNAME: Darren Eadie
DOB: 10-Jun-75, Chippenham

Club History	Signed	Fee
Norwich C.	2/93	Trainee
Leicester C.	12/99	£3m

Season	Team	Tot	St	Sb	Snu	Ps	Gls
93-94	Norwich C.	15	9	6	2	2	3
94-95	Norwich C.	26	22	4	0	2	2
99-00	Leicester C.	16	15	1	0	5	0
	Total	57	46	11	2	9	5

EARLE, Robbie

FULLNAME: Robert Gerald Earle
DOB: 27-Jan-65, Newcastle-under-Lyme

Club History	Signed	Fee
Port Vale	7/82	Juniors
Wimbledon	7/91	£775,000

Season	Team	Tot	St	Sb	Snu	Ps	Gls
92-93	Wimbledon	42	42	0	0	1	7
93-94	Wimbledon	42	42	0	0	0	9
94-95	Wimbledon	9	9	0	0	1	0
95-96	Wimbledon	37	37	0	0	2	11
96-97	Wimbledon	32	32	0	0	4	7
97-98	Wimbledon	22	20	2	2	2	3
98-99	Wimbledon	35	35	0	0	4	5
99-00	Wimbledon	25	23	2	4	9	3
	Total	244	240	4	6	23	45

EASTON, Clint

FULLNAME: Clint Jude Easton
DOB: 01-Oct-77, Barking

Club History	Signed	Fee
Watford	7/96	Watford

Season	Team	Tot	St	Sb	Snu	Ps	Gls
99-00	Watford	17	13	4	3	5	0
	Total	17	13	4	3	5	0

EBBRELL, John

FULLNAME: John Keith Ebbrell
DOB: 01-Oct-69, Bromborough

Club History	Signed	Fee
Everton	11/86	
Sheffield U.	2/97	£1m

Season	Team	Tot	St	Sb	Snu	Ps	Gls
92-93	Everton	24	24	0	0	2	1
93-94	Everton	39	39	0	0	1	4
94-95	Everton	26	26	0	0	2	0
95-96	Everton	25	24	1	2	1	4
96-97	Everton	7	7	0	3	2	0
	Total	121	120	1	5	8	9

EDGHILL, Richard

FULLNAME: Richard Arlon Edgehill
DOB: 23-Sep-74, Oldham

Club History	Signed	Fee
Manchester C.	7/92	Trainee

Season	Team	Tot	St	Sb	Snu	Ps	Gls
93-94	Manchester C.	22	22	0	0	0	0
94-95	Manchester C.	14	14	0	1	0	0
95-96	Manchester C.	13	13	0	0	2	0
	Total	49	49	0	1	2	0

EDINBURGH, Justin

FULLNAME: Justin Charles Edinburgh
DOB: 18-Dec-69, Brentwood

Club History	Signed	Fee
Southend U.	7/88	Trainee
Tottenham H.	7/90	£150,000

Season	Team	Tot	St	Sb	Snu	Ps	Gls
92-93	Tottenham H.	32	31	1	1	2	0
93-94	Tottenham H.	25	24	1	0	3	0
94-95	Tottenham H.	31	29	2	3	1	0
95-96	Tottenham H.	22	15	7	8	1	0
96-97	Tottenham H.	24	21	3	6	2	0
97-98	Tottenham H.	16	13	3	0	5	0
98-99	Tottenham H.	16	14	2	4	3	0
99-00	Tottenham H.	8	7	1	6	2	0
	Total	174	154	20	28	19	0

EDWARDS, Chris

FULLNAME: Christian Nicholas Howells
Edwards
DOB: 23-Nov-75, Caerphilly

Club History	Signed	Fee
Swansea C.	7/94	Trainee
Nottingham F.	3/98	£175,000

Season	Team	Tot	St	Sb	Snu	Ps	Gls
98-99	Nottingham F.	12	7	5	8	1	0
	Total	12	7	5	8	1	0

EDWORTHY, Marc

FULLNAME: Marc Edworthy
DOB: 24-Dec-74, Barnstaple

Club History	Signed	Fee
Plymouth Arg	3/91	Trainee
Crystal P.	6/95	£350,000
Coventry C.	8/98	£800,000

Season	Team	Tot	St	Sb	Snu	Ps	Gls
97-98	Crystal P.	34	33	1	0	0	0
98-99	Coventry C.	22	16	6	7	3	0
99-00	Coventry C.	10	10	0	1	1	0
	Total	66	59	7	8	4	0

EHIOGU, Ugo

FULLNAME: Ugochuku Ehiogu
DOB: 03-Nov-72, Hackney

Club History	Signed	Fee
WBA	7/89	Trainee
Aston Villa	7/91	£40,000

Season	Team	Tot	St	Sb	Snu	Ps	Gls
92-93	Aston Villa	4	1	3	6	1	0
93-94	Aston Villa	17	14	3	6	0	0

94-95	Aston Villa	39	38	1	0	0	3
95-96	Aston Villa	36	36	0	0	0	1
96-97	Aston Villa	38	38	0	0	0	3
97-98	Aston Villa	37	37	0	1	2	2
98-99	Aston Villa	25	23	2	1	1	2
99-00	Aston Villa	31	31	0	0	1	1
	Total	227	218	9	14	5	12

EKELUND, Ronnie

FULLNAME: Ronald Michael Ekelund
DOB: 21-Aug-72, Denmark

Club History	Signed	Fee
Barcelona		
Southampton	9/94	£500,000
Manchester C.	12/95	Loan

Season	Team	Tot	St	Sb	Snu	Ps	Gls
94-95	Southampton	17	15	2	0	4	5
95-96	Manchester C.	4	2	2	0	2	0
	Total	21	17	4	0	6	5

EKOKU, Efan

FULLNAME: Efangwu Goziem Ekoku
DOB: 08-Jun-67, Manchester

Club History	Signed	Fee
Bournemouth	5/90	£100,000
Norwich C.	3/93	£500,000
Wimbledon	10/94	£900,000

Season	Team	Tot	St	Sb	Snu	Ps	Gls
92-93	Norwich C.	4	1	3	2	0	3
93-94	Norwich C.	27	20	7	2	3	12
94-95	Norwich C.	6	5	1	0	4	0
94-95	Wimbledon	24	24	0	0	6	9
95-96	Wimbledon	31	28	3	0	15	7
96-97	Wimbledon	30	28	2	0	17	11
97-98	Wimbledon	16	11	5	1	4	4
98-99	Wimbledon	22	11	11	2	7	6
	Total	160	128	32	7	56	52

EL KHALEJ, Tahar

FULLNAME: Tahar El Khalej
DOB: Morocco

Club History	Signed	Fee
Benfica		
Southampton	3/00	£350,000

Season	Team	Tot	St	Sb	Snu	Ps	Gls
99-00	Southampton	11	11	0	0	1	1
	Total	11	11	0	0	1	1

ELKINS, Gary

FULLNAME: Gary Elkins
DOB: 04-May-66, Wallingford

Club History	Signed	Fee
Fulham	12/83	
Exeter C.	12/89	Loan
Wimbledon	8/90	£20,000

Season	Team	Tot	St	Sb	Snu	Ps	Gls
92-93	Wimbledon	18	17	1	1	1	0
93-94	Wimbledon	18	18	0	0	2	1
94-95	Wimbledon	36	33	3	0	3	1
95-96	Wimbledon	10	7	3	0	1	0
	Total	82	75	7	1	7	2

ELLIOTT, Matt

FULLNAME: Matthew Stephen Elliot
DOB: 01-Nov-68, Wandsworth

Club History	Signed	Fee
Charlton A.	9/88	£5000 (NL)
Torquay U.	3/89	£10,000
Scunthorpe U.	3/92	£50,000
Oxford U.	11/93	£150,000
Leicester C.	1/97	£1.6m

Season	Team	Tot	St	Sb	Snu	Ps	Gls
96-97	Leicester C.	16	16	0	0	0	4
97-98	Leicester C.	37	37	0	0	0	7
98-99	Leicester C.	37	37	0	0	2	3
99-00	Leicester C.	37	37	0	0	0	6
	Total	127	127	0	0	2	20

ELLIOTT, Paul

FULLNAME: Paul Marcellus Elliott
DOB: 18-Mar-64, Lewisham

Club History	Signed	Fee
Charlton A.	3/81	Trainee
Luton Town	3/83	£95,000
Aston Villa	12/85	£400,000
Pisa (Italy)	7/87	£400,000
Celtic	6/89	£600,000
Chelsea	7/91	£1.4m

Season	Team	Tot	St	Sb	Snu	Ps	Gls
92-93	Chelsea	7	7	0	0	1	0
	Total	7	7	0	0	1	0

ELLIOTT, Robbie

FULLNAME: Robert James Elliott
DOB: 25-Dec-73, Newcastle

Club History	Signed	Fee
Newcastle U.	4/91	Trainee
Bolton W.	7/97	£2.5m

Season	Team	Tot	St	Sb	Snu	Ps	Gls
93-94	Newcastle U.	15	13	2	2	2	0
94-95	Newcastle U.	14	10	4	0	2	2
95-96	Newcastle U.	6	5	1	13	0	0

96-97	Newcastle U.	29	29	0	6	1	7
97-98	Newcastle U.	0	0	0	3	0	0
97-98	Bolton W.	4	4	0	0	2	0
	Total	68	61	7	24	7	9

ELLIOTT, Steve

FULLNAME: Steven Elliott
DOB: 29-Oct-78, Derby

Club History	Signed	Fee
Derby Co.	3/97	Trainee

Season	Team	Tot	St	Sb	Snu	Ps	Gls
97-98	Derby Co.	3	3	0	5	2	0
98-99	Derby Co.	11	7	4	8	2	0
99-00	Derby Co.	20	18	2	5	3	0
	Total	34	28	6	18	7	0

ELLIS, Kevin

FULLNAME: Kevin Edward Ellis
DOB: 11-May-77, Tiptree

Club History	Signed	Fee
Ipswich T.		Trainee

Season	Team	Tot	St	Sb	Snu	Ps	Gls
94-95	Ipswich T.	1	1	0	0	1	0
	Total	1	1	0	0	1	0

EMBLEN, Neil

FULLNAME: Neil Robert Emblen
DOB: 19-Jun-71, Bromley

Club History	Signed	Fee
Millwall	11/93	£175,000NL
Wolverhampton W.	7/94	£600,000
C.Palace	8/97	£2m

Season	Team	Tot	St	Sb	Snu	Ps	Gls
97-98	Crystal P.	13	8	5	5	5	0
	Total	13	8	5	5	5	0

EMERSON,

FULLNAME: Emerson Moises Costa
DOB: 12-Apr-72, Rio de Janeiro, Brazil

Club History	Signed	Fee
FC Porto	1994	
Middlesbrough	7/96	£4m

Season	Team	Tot	St	Sb	Snu	Ps	Gls
96-97	Middlesbrough	32	32	0	0	6	4
	Total	32	32	0	0	6	4

ENCKELMAN, Peter

FULLNAME: Peter Enckelman
DOB: 10-Mar-77, Turku

Club History	Signed	Fee
TPS Turku		
Aston Villa		

Season	Team	Tot	St	Sb	Snu	Ps	Gls
98-99	Aston Villa	0	0	0	6	0	0
99-00	Aston Villa	10	9	1	14	0	0
	Total	10	9	1	20	0	0

ERANIO, Stefano

FULLNAME: Stefano Eranio
DOB: 29-Dec-66, Genova

Club History	Signed	Fee
Milan	1990	
Derby Co.	5/97	Free

Season	Team	Tot	St	Sb	Snu	Ps	Gls
97-98	Derby Co.	23	23	0	0	6	5
98-99	Derby Co.	25	18	7	3	7	0
99-00	Derby Co.	19	17	2	0	8	0
	Total	67	58	9	3	21	5

ERIKSSON, Jan

FULLNAME: Jan Eriksson
DOB: 24-Aug-67, Sundsvall

Club History	Signed	Fee
Helsingborg		
Sunderland	1/97	£250,000

Season	Team	Tot	St	Sb	Snu	Ps	Gls
96-97	Sunderland	1	1	0	9	0	0
	Total	1	1	0	9	0	0

ETHERINGTON, Matt

FULLNAME: Matthew Etherington
DOB: 14-Aug-81, Truro

Club History	Signed	Fee
Peterborough U.	8/98	Trainee
Tottenham H.	12/99	£500,000

Season	Team	Tot	St	Sb	Snu	Ps	Gls
99-00	Tottenham H.	5	1	4	2	1	0
	Total	5	1	4	2	1	0

EUELL, Jason

FULLNAME: Jason Euell
DOB: 06-Feb-77, South London

Club History	Signed	Fee
Wimbledon	6/95	Trainee

Season	Team	Tot	St	Sb	Snu	Ps	Gls
95-96	Wimbledon	9	4	5	2	0	2
96-97	Wimbledon	7	4	3	2	0	2
97-98	Wimbledon	19	14	5	2	10	4

		Tot	St	Sb	Snu	Ps	Gls
98-99	Wimbledon	33	31	2	0	6	10
99-00	Wimbledon	37	32	5	0	1	4
	Total	105	85	20	6	17	22

EUSTACE, John

FULLNAME: John Eustace
DOB: 03-Nov-79, Solihull

Club History	Signed	Fee
Coventry C.		Trainee

Season	Team	Tot	St	Sb	Snu	Ps	Gls
96-97	Coventry C.	0	0	0	1	0	0
97-98	Coventry C.	0	0	0	1	0	0
99-00	Coventry C.	16	12	4	13	4	1
	Total	16	12	4	15	4	1

EVANS, Micky

FULLNAME: Michael James Evans
DOB: 01-Jan-73, Plymouth

Club History	Signed	Fee
Plymouth Argyle	3/91	Trainee
Southampton	3/97	£500,000

Season	Team	Tot	St	Sb	Snu	Ps	Gls
96-97	Southampton	12	8	4	0	0	4
97-98	Southampton	10	6	4	0	2	0
	Total	22	14	8	0	2	4

EVTUSHOK, Alex

FULLNAME: Alex Evtushok
DOB: 11-Jan-70, Ukraine

Club History	Signed	Fee
Dnepr		
Coventry C.	1/97	£800,000

Season	Team	Tot	St	Sb	Snu	Ps	Gls
96-97	Coventry C.	3	3	0	4	2	0
	Total	3	3	0	4	2	0

EYRE, John

FULLNAME: John Eyre
DOB: 09-Oct-74, Humberside

Club History	Signed	Fee
Oldham A.	7/93	Trainee

Season	Team	Tot	St	Sb	Snu	Ps	Gls
93-94	Oldham A.	2	1	1	0	1	0
	Total	2	1	1	0	1	0

FAIRCLOUGH, Chris

FULLNAME: Courtney Huw Fairclough
DOB: 12-Apr-64, Nottingham

Club History	Signed	Fee
Nottingham F.	10/81	Apprentice
Tottenham H.	6/87	£387,000
Leeds U.	3/89	£500,000
Bolton W.	7/95	£500,000

Season	Team	Tot	St	Sb	Snu	Ps	Gls
92-93	Leeds U.	30	29	1	0	3	3
93-94	Leeds U.	40	40	0	1	0	4
94-95	Leeds U.	5	1	4	2	0	0
95-96	Bolton W.	33	33	0	1	4	0
97-98	Bolton W.	11	10	1	3	3	0
	Total	119	113	6	7	10	7

FALCONER, Willie

FULLNAME: William Henry Falconer
DOB: 05-Apr-66, Aberdeen

Club History	Signed	Fee
Aberdeen		
Watford	6/88	£300,000
Middlesbrough	8/91	£45,000
Sheffield U.	8/93	

Season	Team	Tot	St	Sb	Snu	Ps	Gls
92-93	Middlesbrough	28	22	6	1	0	5
93-94	Sheffield U.	23	21	2	0	3	3
	Total	51	43	8	1	3	8

FARLEY, Adam

FULLNAME: Adam John Farley
DOB: 12-Jan-80, Liverpool

Club History	Signed	Fee
Everton	2/98	Trainee

Season	Team	Tot	St	Sb	Snu	Ps	Gls
98-99	Everton	1	0	1	0	0	0
	Total	1	0	1	0	0	0

FARRELL, Dave

FULLNAME: David William Farrell
DOB: 11-Nov-71, Birmingham

Club History	Signed	Fee
Aston Villa	1/92	£45,000

Season	Team	Tot	St	Sb	Snu	Ps	Gls
92-93	Aston Villa	2	1	1	0	1	0
93-94	Aston Villa	4	4	0	1	3	0
95-96	Aston Villa	4	1	3	6	0	0
96-97	Aston Villa	3	1	2	15	0	0
	Total	13	7	6	22	4	0

FARRELLY, Gareth

FULLNAME: Gareth Farrelly
DOB: 28-Aug-75, Dublin

Club History	Signed	Fee
Aston Villa	1/92	Trainee
Rotherham U.	3/95	Loan
Everton	7/97	£700,000

Season	Team	Tot	St	Sb	Snu	Ps	Gls
97-98	Everton	26	18	8	5	6	1
98-99	Everton	1	0	1	6	0	0
	Total	27	18	9	11	6	1

FASHANU, John

FULLNAME: John Fashanu
DOB: 18-Sep-62, Kensington

Club History	Signed	Fee
Norwich C.	10/79	
Crystal P.	8/83	Loan
Lincoln C.	9/83	
Millwall	11/84	£55,000
Wimbledon	3/86	£125,000
Aston Villa	8/94	£1.35m

Season	Team	Tot	St	Sb	Snu	Ps	Gls
92-93	Wimbledon	29	27	2	1	3	6
93-94	Wimbledon	36	35	1	0	7	11
94-95	Aston Villa	13	11	2	0	4	3
	Total	78	73	5	1	14	20

FEAR, Peter

FULLNAME: Peter Stanley Fear
DOB: 10-Sep-73, Sutton

Club History	Signed	Fee
Wimbledon	7/92	Trainee

Season	Team	Tot	St	Sb	Snu	Ps	Gls
92-93	Wimbledon	4	2	2	0	0	0
93-94	Wimbledon	23	23	0	1	5	1
94-95	Wimbledon	14	8	6	2	3	1
95-96	Wimbledon	4	4	0	0	3	0
96-97	Wimbledon	18	9	9	11	0	0
97-98	Wimbledon	8	5	3	2	0	2
98-99	Wimbledon	2	0	2	3	0	0
	Total	73	51	22	19	11	4

FENN, Neale

FULLNAME: Neale Fenn
DOB: 18-Jan-77, Tottenham

Club History	Signed	Fee
Tottenham H.	7/95	Trainee

Season	Team	Tot	St	Sb	Snu	Ps	Gls
96-97	Tottenham H.	4	0	4	3	0	0
97-98	Tottenham H.	4	0	4	2	1	0
	Total	8	0	8	5	1	0

FENTON, Graham

FULLNAME: Graham Anthony Fenton
DOB: 22-May-74, Wallsend

Club History	Signed	Fee
Aston Villa	2/92	Trainee
WBA	1/94	Loan
Blackburn R.	12/95	£1.5m
Leicester C.	8/97	£1.1m

Season	Team	Tot	St	Sb	Snu	Ps	Gls
93-94	Aston Villa	12	9	3	0	1	1
94-95	Aston Villa	17	7	10	7	4	2
95-96	Aston Villa	3	0	3	5	0	0
95-96	Blackburn R.	14	4	10	2	4	6
96-97	Blackburn R.	13	5	8	6	0	1
97-98	Leicester C.	23	9	14	14	7	3
98-99	Leicester C.	9	3	6	12	3	0
99-00	Leicester C.	2	1	1	6	0	0
	Total	93	38	55	52	19	13

FENWICK, Terry

FULLNAME: Terence William Fenwick
DOB: 17-Nov-59, Seaham

Club History	Signed	Fee
Crystal P.	12/76	
QPR	12/80	£110,000
Tottenham H.	12/87	£550,000
Leicester C.	10/90	Loan
Swindon Town	9/93	Free

Season	Team	Tot	St	Sb	Snu	Ps	Gls
92-93	Tottenham H.	5	3	2	1	1	0
93-94	Swindon T.	26	23	3	1	1	0
	Total	31	26	5	2	2	0

FERDINAND, Les

FULLNAME: Leslie Ferdinand
DOB: 18-Dec-66, Acton

Club History	Signed	Fee
QPR	4/87	£15,000 NL
Brentford	3/88	Loan
Besiktas (Turkey)	6/88	Loan
Newcastle U.	6/95	£6m
Tottenham H.	7/97	£6m

Season	Team	Tot	St	Sb	Snu	Ps	Gls
92-93	QPR	37	37	0	0	4	20
93-94	QPR	36	35	1	0	3	16
94-95	QPR	37	37	0	0	5	24
95-96	Newcastle U.	37	37	0	0	1	25
96-97	Newcastle U.	31	30	1	0	8	16
97-98	Tottenham H.	21	19	2	0	7	5
98-99	Tottenham H.	24	22	2	0	7	5
99-00	Tottenham H.	9	5	4	1	3	2
	Total	232	222	10	2	38	113

FERDINAND, Rio

FULLNAME: Rio Gavin Ferdinand
DOB: 07-Nov-78, London

Club History	Signed	Fee
West Ham U.	11/95	Trainee
Bournemouth	11/96	Loan

Season	Team	Tot	St	Sb	Snu	Ps	Gls
95-96	West Ham U.	1	0	1	0	0	0
96-97	West Ham U.	15	11	4	2	3	2
97-98	West Ham U.	35	35	0	0	1	0
98-99	West Ham U.	31	31	0	0	2	0
99-00	West Ham U.	33	33	0	0	1	0
	Total	115	110	5	2	7	2

FERGUSON, Darren

FULLNAME: Darren Ferguson
DOB: 09-Feb-72, Glasgow

Club History	Signed	Fee
Manchester U.	7/90	Trainee

Season	Team	Tot	St	Sb	Snu	Ps	Gls
92-93	Manchester U.	15	15	0	0	2	0
93-94	Manchester U.	3	1	2	4	0	0
	Total	18	16	2	4	2	0

FERGUSON, Duncan

FULLNAME: Duncan Ferguson
DOB: 27-Dec-71, Stirling

Club History	Signed	Fee
Dundee	2/90	Free from Non League
Rangers	7/93	£4m
Everton	10/94	£4.4m
Newcastle U.	11/98	£7m

Season	Team	Tot	St	Sb	Snu	Ps	Gls
94-95	Everton	23	22	1	0	1	7
95-96	Everton	18	16	2	0	2	5
96-97	Everton	33	31	2	1	0	10
97-98	Everton	29	28	1	0	1	11
98-99	Everton	13	13	0	0	1	4
98-99	Newcastle U.	7	7	0	0	3	2
99-00	Newcastle U.	23	17	6	0	8	6
	Total	146	134	12	1	16	45

FERRER, Albert

FULLNAME: Albert Ferrer
DOB: 06-Jun-70, Spain

Club History	Signed	Fee
Barcelona		
Chelsea	7/98	£2.2m

Season	Team	Tot	St	Sb	Snu	Ps	Gls
98-99	Chelsea	30	30	0	1	2	0
99-00	Chelsea	25	24	1	0	2	0
	Total	55	54	1	1	4	0

FERRI, Jean-Michel

FULLNAME: Jean-Michel Ferri
DOB: 09-Sep-69, France

Club History	Signed	Fee
Istanbulspor		
Liverpool	11/98	£1.5m

Season	Team	Tot	St	Sb	Snu	Ps	Gls
98-99	Liverpool	2	0	2	6	0	0
	Total	2	0	2	6	0	0

FESTA, Gianluca

FULLNAME: Gianluca Festa
DOB: 12-Mar-69, Cagliari

Club History	Signed	Fee
Internazionale	1993	
Middlesbrough	1/97	£2.2m

Season	Team	Tot	St	Sb	Snu	Ps	Gls
96-97	Middlesbrough	13	13	0	0	0	1
98-99	Middlesbrough	25	25	0	0	2	2
99-00	Middlesbrough	29	27	2	0	1	2
	Total	67	65	2	0	3	5

FETTIS, Alan

FULLNAME: Alan William Fettis
DOB: 01-Feb-71, Belfast

Club History	Signed	Fee
Ards		
Hull C.	8/91	£50,000
WBA	11/95	Loan
Nottingham F.	1/96	£250,000
Blackburn R.	9/97	£300,000

Season	Team	Tot	St	Sb	Snu	Ps	Gls
95-96	Nottingham F.	0	0	0	1	0	0
96-97	Nottingham F.	4	4	0	32	0	0
97-98	Blackburn R.	8	7	1	20	0	0
98-99	Blackburn R.	2	2	0	13	0	0
99-00	Leicester C.	0	0	0	1	0	0
	Total	14	13	1	67	0	0

FEUER, Tony

FULLNAME: Ian Anthony Feuer
DOB: 20-May-70, Las Vegas

Club History	Signed	Fee
LA Salsa	8/93	
West Ham U.	3/94	£70,000

Peterborough U.	2/95	Loan
Luton T.	9/95	Loan
Luton T.	12/95	£580,000
Rushden	12/98	
Colorado Rapids	2/99	
Cardiff C.	12/99	
West Ham U.	2/00	Free

Season	Team	Tot	St	Sb	Snu	Ps	Gls
94-95	West Ham U.	0	0	0	16	0	0
99-00	West Ham U.	3	3	0	9	0	0
	Total	3	3	0	25	0	0

FILAN, John

FULLNAME: John Richard Filan
DOB: 08-Feb-70, Sydney, Australia

Club History	Signed	Fee
Budapest St George (Sydney)		
Cambridge U.	3/93	£40,000
Nottingham F.	12/94	Loan
Coventry C.	3/95	£300,000
Blackburn R.	7/97	£700,000

Season	Team	Tot	St	Sb	Snu	Ps	Gls
94-95	Nottingham F.	0	0	0	9	0	0
94-95	Coventry C.	2	2	0	5	0	0
95-96	Coventry C.	13	13	0	24	0	0
96-97	Coventry C.	1	0	1	37	0	0
97-98	Blackburn R.	7	7	0	3	1	0
98-99	Blackburn R.	26	26	0	7	1	0
	Total	49	48	1	85	2	0

FINN, Neil

FULLNAME: Neil Edward Finn
DOB: 29-Dec-78, London

Club History	Signed	Fee
West Ham U.		Trainee

Season	Team	Tot	St	Sb	Snu	Ps	Gls
95-96	West Ham U.	1	1	0	0	0	0
97-98	West Ham U.	0	0	0	1	0	0
	Total	1	1	0	1	0	0

FISH, Mark

FULLNAME: Mark Anthony Fish
DOB: 14-Mar-74, Capetown, South
Africa

Club History	Signed	Fee
Orlando Pirates (SA)		
Bolton W.	9/97	£2.0m

Season	Team	Tot	St	Sb	Snu	Ps	Gls
97-98	Bolton W.	22	22	0	3	4	2
	Total	22	22	0	3	4	2

FITZGERALD, Scott

FULLNAME: Scott Brian Fitzgerald
DOB: 13-Aug-69, Westminster

Club History	Signed	Fee
Wimbledon	7/87	Trainee

Season	Team	Tot	St	Sb	Snu	Ps	Gls
92-93	Wimbledon	20	18	2	1	1	0
93-94	Wimbledon	28	27	1	1	0	0
94-95	Wimbledon	17	14	3	2	0	0
95-96	Wimbledon	4	2	2	1	0	0
	Total	69	61	8	5	1	0

FJORTOFT, Jan-Aage

FULLNAME: Jan-Aage Fjortoft
DOB: 10-Jan-67, Aalesund, Norway

Club History	Signed	Fee
Rapid Vienna		
Swindon Town	7/93	£500,000
Middlesbrough	3/95	£1.3m
Sheffield U.	1/97	£700,000
Barnsley	1/98	£800,000

Season	Team	Tot	St	Sb	Snu	Ps	Gls
93-94	Swindon T.	36	26	10	2	8	12
95-96	Middlesbrough	28	27	1	5	6	6
96-97	Middlesbrough	5	2	3	7	0	1
97-98	Barnsley	15	12	3	0	9	6
	Total	84	67	17	14	23	25

FLATTS, Mark

FULLNAME: Mark Michael Flatts
DOB: 14-Oct-72, Islington

Club History	Signed	Fee
Arsenal	12/90	Trainee

Season	Team	Tot	St	Sb	Snu	Ps	Gls
92-93	Arsenal	10	6	4	0	2	0
93-94	Arsenal	3	2	1	0	1	0
94-95	Arsenal	3	1	2	1	1	0
	Total	16	9	7	1	4	0

FLECK, Robert

FULLNAME: Robert Fleck
DOB: 11-Aug-65, Glasgow

Club History	Signed	Fee
Rangers		
Norwich C.	12/87	£580,000
Chelsea	8/92	£2.1m

Season	Team	Tot	St	Sb	Snu	Ps	Gls
92-93	Chelsea	31	28	3	3	9	2
93-94	Chelsea	9	7	2	0	3	1
94-95	Chelsea	0	0	0	1	0	0
	Total	40	35	5	4	12	3

FLEMING, Craig

FULLNAME: Craig Fleming
DOB: 06-Oct-71, Halifax

Club History	Signed	Fee
Halifax Town	3/90	
Oldham A.	8/91	£80,000

Season	Team	Tot	St	Sb	Snu	Ps	Gls
92-93	Oldham A.	24	23	1	11	0	0
93-94	Oldham A.	37	37	0	0	4	0
	Total	61	60	1	11	4	0

FLEMING, Curtis

FULLNAME: Curtis Fleming
DOB: 08-Oct-68, Manchester

Club History	Signed	Fee
Middlesbrough	8/91	£50,000

Season	Team	Tot	St	Sb	Snu	Ps	Gls
92-93	Middlesbrough	24	22	2	0	1	0
95-96	Middlesbrough	14	14	0	0	1	1
96-97	Middlesbrough	30	30	0	1	0	0
98-99	Middlesbrough	14	12	2	0	1	1
99-00	Middlesbrough	27	27	0	3	3	0
	Total	109	105	4	4	6	2

FLEMING, Terry

FULLNAME: Terry Fleming
DOB: 05-Jan-73, Marston Green

Club History	Signed	Fee
Coventry C.	7/91	Trainee

Season	Team	Tot	St	Sb	Snu	Ps	Gls
92-93	Coventry C.	11	8	3	5	2	0
	Total	11	8	3	5	2	0

FLITCROFT, Garry

FULLNAME: Gary William Flitcroft
DOB: 06-Nov-72, Bolton

Club History	Signed	Fee
Manchester C.	7/91	Trainee
Bury	3/92	Loan
Blackburn R.	3/96	£3.2m

Season	Team	Tot	St	Sb	Snu	Ps	Gls
92-93	Manchester C.	32	28	4	6	1	5
93-94	Manchester C.	21	19	2	1	1	3
94-95	Manchester C.	37	37	0	0	5	5
95-96	Manchester C.	25	25	0	0	4	0
95-96	Blackburn R.	3	3	0	1	0	0
96-97	Blackburn R.	28	27	1	2	8	3
97-98	Blackburn R.	33	28	5	3	3	0
98-99	Blackburn R.	8	8	0	1	0	2
	Total	187	175	12	14	22	18

FLO, Jostein

FULLNAME: Jostein Flo
DOB: 03-Oct-64, Eid, Norway

Club History	Signed	Fee
Songdal		
Sheffield U.	8/93	£400,000

Season	Team	Tot	St	Sb	Snu	Ps	Gls
93-94	Sheffield U.	33	32	1	0	1	9
	Total	33	32	1	0	1	9

FLO, Tore Andre

FULLNAME: Tore Andre Flo
DOB: 15-Jun-73, Norway

Club History	Signed	Fee
SK Brann	1996	
Chelsea	8/97	£300,000

Season	Team	Tot	St	Sb	Snu	Ps	Gls
97-98	Chelsea	34	16	18	4	6	11
98-99	Chelsea	30	18	12	2	4	10
99-00	Chelsea	34	20	14	1	9	10
	Total	98	54	44	7	19	31

FLOWERS, Tim

FULLNAME: Timothy David Flowers
DOB: 03-Feb-67, Kenilworth

Club History	Signed	Fee
Wolves	8/84	Apprentice
Southampton	6/86	£70,000
Swindon Town	3/87	Loan
Swindon Town	11/87	Loan
Blackburn R.	11/93	£2.4m
Leicester C.	7/00	£1.1m

Season	Team	Tot	St	Sb	Snu	Ps	Gls
92-93	Southampton	42	42	0	0	0	0
93-94	Southampton	12	12	0	0	0	0
93-94	Blackburn R.	29	29	0	0	0	0
94-95	Blackburn R.	39	39	0	0	0	0
95-96	Blackburn R.	37	37	0	0	0	0
96-97	Blackburn R.	36	36	0	2	0	0
97-98	Blackburn R.	25	24	1	3	1	0
98-99	Blackburn R.	11	10	1	13	0	0
99-00	Leicester C.	29	29	0	3	2	0
	Total	260	258	2	21	3	0

FLYNN, Sean

FULLNAME: Sean Michael Flynn
DOB: 13-Mar-68, Birmingham

Club History	Signed	Fee
Coventry C.	12/91	£20,000 from Non League
Derby Co.	8/95	£250,000

Season	Team	Tot	St	Sb	Snu	Ps	Gls
92-93	Coventry C.	7	4	3	3	2	0
93-94	Coventry C.	36	33	3	0	4	3
94-95	Coventry C.	32	32	0	3	6	4
96-97	Derby Co.	17	10	7	8	3	1
	Total	92	79	13	14	15	8

FOLAN, Tony

FULLNAME: Anthony Folan
DOB: 18-Sep-78, Lewisham

Club History	Signed	Fee
Crystal P.	9/95	Trainee

Season	Team	Tot	St	Sb	Snu	Ps	Gls
97-98	Crystal P.	1	0	1	1	0	0
	Total	1	0	1	1	0	0

FOLEY, Dominic

FULLNAME: Dominic Joseph Foley
DOB: 07-Jul-76, Cork

Club History	Signed	Fee
Wolverhampton W.	8/95	£35,000 NL
Watford	2/98	Loan
Notts Co.	12/98	Loan
Watford	7/99	Free

Season	Team	Tot	St	Sb	Snu	Ps	Gls
99-00	Watford	12	5	7	3	5	1
	Total	12	5	7	3	5	1

FORD, Mark

FULLNAME: Mark Ford
DOB: 10-Oct-75, Pontefract

Club History	Signed	Fee
Leeds U.	3/93	Trainee

Season	Team	Tot	St	Sb	Snu	Ps	Gls
93-94	Leeds U.	1	0	1	0	0	0
95-96	Leeds U.	11	11	0	3	5	0
96-97	Leeds U.	16	15	1	13	6	1
	Total	28	26	2	16	11	1

FORREST, Craig

FULLNAME: Craig Lorne Forrest
DOB: 20-Sep-67, Vancouver, Canada

Club History	Signed	Fee
Ipswich Town	8/85	Apprentice
Colchester U.	3/88	Loan
Chelsea	3/97	Loan
West Ham U.	7/97	£500,000

Season	Team	Tot	St	Sb	Snu	Ps	Gls
92-93	Ipswich T.	11	11	0	12	0	0
93-94	Ipswich T.	27	27	0	3	0	0
94-95	Ipswich T.	36	36	0	0	0	0
96-97	Chelsea	3	2	1	1	0	0
97-98	West Ham U.	13	13	0	21	0	0
98-99	West Ham U.	2	1	1	31	0	0
99-00	West Ham U.	11	9	2	18	0	0
	Total	103	99	4	86	0	0

FORRESTER, Jamie

FULLNAME: Jamie Mark Forrester
DOB: 01-Nov-74, Bradford

Club History	Signed	Fee
Auxerre (France)		
Leeds U.	10/92	£60,000

Season	Team	Tot	St	Sb	Snu	Ps	Gls
92-93	Leeds U.	6	5	1	0	3	0
93-94	Leeds U.	3	2	1	2	2	0
	Total	9	7	2	2	5	0

FORSSELL, Mikael

FULLNAME: Mikael Forssell
DOB: 15-Mar-81, Steinfurt, Germany

Club History	Signed	Fee
HJK Helsinki		
Chelsea	11/98	Free

Season	Team	Tot	St	Sb	Snu	Ps	Gls
98-99	Chelsea	10	4	6	4	3	1
99-00	Chelsea	0	0	0	1	0	0
	Total	10	4	6	5	3	1

FORTUNE, Quinton

FULLNAME: Quinton Fortue
DOB: 21-May-77, CapeTown, South Africa

Club History	Signed	Fee
Atletico Madrid		
Manchester U.	8/99	£1.5m

Season	Team	Tot	St	Sb	Snu	Ps	Gls
99-00	Manchester U.	6	4	2	6	1	2
	Total	6	4	2	6	1	2

FOSTER, Colin

FULLNAME: Colin J Foster
DOB: 16-Jul-64, Chislehurst

Club History	Signed	Fee
Leyton Orient	2/82	Apprentice
Nottingham F.	3/87	£70,000
West Ham U.	9/89	£750,000

Season	Team	Tot	St	Sb	Snu	Ps	Gls
93-94	West Ham U.	5	5	0	0	0	0
	Total	5	5	0	0	0	0

FOSTER, John

FULLNAME: John Colin Foster
DOB: 19-Sep-73, Manchester

Club History	Signed	Fee
Manchester C.	7/92	Apprentice

Season	Team	Tot	St	Sb	Snu	Ps	Gls
93-94	Manchester C.	1	1	0	0	0	0
94-95	Manchester C.	11	9	2	3	1	0
95-96	Manchester C.	4	4	0	0	1	0
	Total	16	14	2	3	2	0

FOWLER, Robbie

FULLNAME: Robert Bernard Fowler
DOB: 09-Apr-75, Liverpool

Club History	Signed	Fee
Liverpool	4/92	Trainee

Season	Team	Tot	St	Sb	Snu	Ps	Gls
92-93	Liverpool	0	0	0	1	0	0
93-94	Liverpool	28	27	1	0	3	12
94-95	Liverpool	42	42	0	0	3	25
95-96	Liverpool	38	36	2	0	2	28
96-97	Liverpool	32	32	0	0	4	18
97-98	Liverpool	20	19	1	0	4	9
98-99	Liverpool	25	23	2	1	5	14
99-00	Liverpool	14	8	6	0	2	3
	Total	199	187	12	2	23	109

FOX, Ruel

FULLNAME: Ruel Adrian Fox
DOB: 14-Jan-68, Ipswich

Club History	Signed	Fee
Norwich C.	1/86	Apprentice
Newcastle U.	2/94	£2.25m
Tottenham H.	10/95	£4.2m

Season	Team	Tot	St	Sb	Snu	Ps	Gls
92-93	Norwich C.	34	32	2	0	2	4
93-94	Norwich C.	25	25	0	0	3	7
93-94	Newcastle U.	14	14	0	0	2	2
94-95	Newcastle U.	40	40	0	0	6	10
95-96	Newcastle U.	4	2	2	2	1	0
95-96	Tottenham H.	26	26	0	0	3	6
96-97	Tottenham H.	25	19	6	3	6	1
97-98	Tottenham H.	32	32	0	3	9	3
98-99	Tottenham H.	20	17	3	9	7	3
99-00	Tottenham H.	3	1	2	10	1	0
	Total	223	208	15	27	40	36

FRANCIS, Damien

FULLNAME: Damien Francis
DOB: 27-Feb-79, London

Club History	Signed	Fee
Wimbledon	3/97	Trainee

Season	Team	Tot	St	Sb	Snu	Ps	Gls
97-98	Wimbledon	2	0	2	5	0	0
98-99	Wimbledon	0	0	0	6	0	0
99-00	Wimbledon	9	1	8	6	1	0
	Total	11	1	10	17	1	0

FRANCIS, Trevor

FULLNAME: Trevor John Francis
DOB: 19-Apr-54, Plymouth

Club History	Signed	Fee
Birmingham C.	5/71	Apprentice
Nottingham F.	2/79	£1m
Manchester C.	9/81	£1.2m
Sampdoria (Italy)	9/82	£800,000
Atlanta (Italy)	7/86	
Rangers	9/87	£75,000
QPR	3/88	
Sheffield W.	2/90	

Season	Team	Tot	St	Sb	Snu	Ps	Gls
92-93	Sheffield W.	5	1	4	2	1	0
93-94	Sheffield W.	1	0	1	0	0	0
	Total	6	1	5	2	1	0

FRANDSEN, Per

FULLNAME: Per Frandsen
DOB: 06-Feb-70, Copenhagen

Club History	Signed	Fee
FC Copenhagen		
Bolton Wanderers	8/96	£1.25m

Season	Team	Tot	St	Sb	Snu	Ps	Gls
97-98	Bolton W.	38	38	0	0	5	2
	Total	38	38	0	0	5	2

FREDGAARD, Carsten

FULLNAME: Carsten Fredgaard
DOB: 20-May-76, Denmark

Club History	Signed	Fee
Lyngby		
Sunderland	3/99	£1.5m

Season	Team	Tot	St	Sb	Snu	Ps	Gls
99-00	Sunderland	1	0	1	3	0	0
	Total	1	0	1	3	0	0

FREEDMAN, Dougie

FULLNAME: Douglas Alan Freedman
DOB: 21-Jan-74, Glasgow

Club History	Signed	Fee
QPR	5/92	Trainee

Barnet	7/94		Free			
Crystal P.	9/95		£800,000			
Wolverhampton W.	10/97		£800,000			
Nottingham F.	8/98		£950,000			

Season	Team	Tot	St	Sb	Snu	Ps	Gls
97-98	Crystal P.	8	2	6	0	2	0
98-99	Nottingham F.	31	20	11	2	9	9
	Total	39	22	17	2	11	9

FREESTONE, Chris

FULLNAME: Christopher Mark Freestone
DOB: 04-Sep-71, Nottingham

Club History	Signed	Fee
Middlesbrough	12/94	£10,000 from Non League
Carlisle U.	3/97	Loan

Season	Team	Tot	St	Sb	Snu	Ps	Gls
95-96	Middlesbrough	3	2	1	0	1	1
96-97	Middlesbrough	2	0	2	8	0	0
	Total	5	2	3	8	1	1

FREUND, Steffen

FULLNAME: Steffen Freund
DOB: 19-Jan-70, Germany

Club History	Signed	Fee
Borussia Dortmund		
Tottenham H.	12/98	£750,000

Season	Team	Tot	St	Sb	Snu	Ps	Gls
98-99	Tottenham H.	17	17	0	0	3	0
99-00	Tottenham H.	27	24	3	0	2	0
	Total	44	41	3	0	5	0

FRIEDEL, Brad

FULLNAME: Bradley Howard Friedel
DOB: 18-May-71, USA

Club History	Signed	Fee
Colombus Crew		
Liverpool	12/97	£1.0m

Season	Team	Tot	St	Sb	Snu	Ps	Gls
97-98	Liverpool	11	11	0	7	0	0
98-99	Liverpool	12	12	0	24	0	0
99-00	Liverpool	2	2	0	17	0	0
	Total	25	25	0	48	0	0

FROGGATT, Steve

FULLNAME: Stephen Junior Froggatt
DOB: 09-Mar-73, Lincoln

Club History	Signed	Fee
Aston Villa	1/91	Trainee
Wolverhampton W.	7/94	£1m
Coventry C.	9/98	£1.9m

Season	Team	Tot	St	Sb	Snu	Ps	Gls
92-93	Aston Villa	17	16	1	0	8	1
93-94	Aston Villa	9	8	1	0	0	1
98-99	Coventry C.	23	23	0	0	0	1
99-00	Coventry C.	26	21	5	0	4	1
	Total	75	68	7	0	12	4

FRONTZECK, Michael

FULLNAME: Michael Frontzeck
DOB: 26-Mar-64, Odenkirchen, Germany

Club History	Signed	Fee
B. Monchengladbach		
Manchester C.	1/96	£350,000

Season	Team	Tot	St	Sb	Snu	Ps	Gls
95-96	Manchester C.	12	11	1	2	6	0
	Total	12	11	1	2	6	0

FUERTES, Esterban

FULLNAME: Esteban Fuertes
DOB: 0,

Club History	Signed	Fee
Colon de Santa Fe		
Derby Co.	8/99	£2.3m

Season	Team	Tot	St	Sb	Snu	Ps	Gls
99-00	Derby Co.	8	8	0	0	5	1
	Total	8	8	0	0	5	1

FULLARTON, Jamie

FULLNAME: James Fullarton
DOB: 20-Jul-74, Scotland

Club History	Signed	Fee
SC Bastia		
C.Palace	7/97	Free

Season	Team	Tot	St	Sb	Snu	Ps	Gls
97-98	Crystal P.	25	19	6	2	2	1
	Total	25	19	6	2	2	1

FUMACA

FULLNAME: Jose Rodriguez Alves Antunes
DOB: 15-Jul-76, Bahia, Brazil

Club History	Signed	Fee
Catuense		
Colchester U.	3/99	Free
Barnsley	3/99	Free
Crystal P.	9/99	Free
Newcastle U.	9/99	Free

Season	Team	Tot	St	Sb	Snu	Ps	Gls
99-00	Newcastle U.	5	1	4	9	1	0
	Total	5	1	4	9	1	0

FURLONG, Paul

FULLNAME: Paul Anthony Furlong
DOB: 01-Oct-68, Wood Green

Club History	Signed	Fee
Coventry C.	7/91	£130,000 NL
Watford	7/92	£250,000
Chelsea	5/94	£2.3m
Birmingham C.	7/96	£1.5m

Season	Team	Tot	St	Sb	Snu	Ps	Gls
94-95	Chelsea	36	30	6	0	3	10
95-96	Chelsea	28	14	14	4	2	3
	Total	64	44	20	4	5	13

FUTRE, Paulo

FULLNAME: Dos Santos Futre Jorge Paulo
DOB: 28-Feb-66, Montijo (Portugal)

Club History	Signed	Fee
Milan		
West Ham U.	7/96	Free

Season	Team	Tot	St	Sb	Snu	Ps	Gls
96-97	West Ham U.	9	4	5	0	2	0
	Total	9	4	5	0	2	0

GABBIADINI, Marco

FULLNAME: Marco Gabbiadini
DOB: 20-Jan-68, Nottingham

Club History	Signed	Fee
York C.	9/85	Apprentice
Sunderland	9/87	£80,000
Crystal P.	10/91	£1.8m
Derby Co.	1/92	£1m

Season	Team	Tot	St	Sb	Snu	Ps	Gls
96-97	Derby Co.	14	5	9	1	4	0
	Total	14	5	9	1	4	0

GAGE, Kevin

FULLNAME: Kevin William Gage
DOB: 21-Apr-64, Chiswick

Club History	Signed	Fee
Wimbledon	1/82	Apprentice
Aston Villa	7/87	£100,000
Sheffield U.	11/91	£150,000

Season	Team	Tot	St	Sb	Snu	Ps	Gls
92-93	Sheffield U.	27	27	0	0	2	0
93-94	Sheffield U.	21	16	5	1	3	0
	Total	48	43	5	1	5	0

GALE, Tony

FULLNAME: Anthony P Gale
DOB: 19-Nov-59, Westminster

Club History	Signed	Fee
Fulham	8/77	Apprentice
West Ham U.	7/84	£150,000
Blackburn R.	8/94	Free

Season	Team	Tot	St	Sb	Snu	Ps	Gls
93-94	West Ham U.	32	31	1	4	2	0
94-95	Blackburn R.	15	15	0	3	2	0
	Total	47	46	1	7	4	0

GALLACHER, Kevin

FULLNAME: Kevin William Gallacher
DOB: 23-Nov-66, Clydebank

Club History	Signed	Fee
Coventry C.	1/90	£900,000
Blackburn R.	3/93	£1.5m
Newcastle U.	10/99	£500,000

Season	Team	Tot	St	Sb	Snu	Ps	Gls
92-93	Coventry C.	20	19	1	0	4	6
92-93	Blackburn R.	9	9	0	0	0	5
93-94	Blackburn R.	30	27	3	0	9	7
94-95	Blackburn R.	1	1	0	2	1	1
95-96	Blackburn R.	16	14	2	2	3	2
96-97	Blackburn R.	34	34	0	0	10	10
97-98	Blackburn R.	33	31	2	0	5	16
98-99	Blackburn R.	16	13	3	0	7	5
99-00	Newcastle U.	20	15	5	0	9	2
	Total	179	163	16	4	48	54

GALLEN, Kevin

FULLNAME: Kevin Gallen
DOB: 21-Sep-75, Chiswick

Club History	Signed	Fee
QPR	9/92	Trainee

Season	Team	Tot	St	Sb	Snu	Ps	Gls
94-95	QPR	37	31	6	3	10	10
95-96	QPR	29	26	3	5	9	8
	Total	66	57	9	8	19	18

GALLOWAY, Mike

FULLNAME: Michael Galloway
DOB: 30-May-65, Oswestry

Club History	Signed	Fee
Celtic		
Leicester C.	1/95	Loan

Season	Team	Tot	St	Sb	Snu	Ps	Gls
94-95	Leicester C.	5	4	1	0	0	0
	Total	5	4	1	0	0	0

GANNON, John

FULLNAME: John Spencer Gannon
DOB: 18-Dec-66, Wimbledon

Club History	Signed	Fee
Wimbledon	12/84	
Crewe Alexandra	12/86	Loan
Sheffield U.	2/89	Free

Season	Team	Tot	St	Sb	Snu	Ps	Gls
92-93	Sheffield U.	27	26	1	0	8	1
93-94	Sheffield U.	14	14	0	0	3	0
	Total	41	40	1	0	11	1

GARDE, Remi

FULLNAME: Remi Garde
DOB: 03-Apr-66, L'Arbesle

Club History	Signed	Fee
RC Strasbourg	1995	
Arsenal	8/96	Free

Season	Team	Tot	St	Sb	Snu	Ps	Gls
96-97	Arsenal	11	7	4	2	5	0
97-98	Arsenal	10	6	4	3	1	0
98-99	Arsenal	10	6	4	8	2	0
	Total	31	19	12	13	8	0

GASCOIGNE, Paul

FULLNAME: Paul John Gascoigne
DOB: 27-May-67, Gateshead

Club History	Signed	Fee
Newcastle U.	1984	Trainee
Tottenham H.	7/88	£2m
Lazio	5/92	£5.5m
Rangers	7/95	£4.3m
Middlesbrough	3/98	£3.45m

Season	Team	Tot	St	Sb	Snu	Ps	Gls
98-99	Middlesbrough	26	25	1	1	12	3
99-00	Middlesbrough	8	7	1	3	3	1
	Total	34	32	2	4	15	4

GAUDINO, Maurizio

FULLNAME: Maurizio Gaudino
DOB: 12-Dec-66, Brule, Germany

Club History	Signed	Fee
Eintracht Frankfurt		
Manchester C.	12/94	Loan

Season	Team	Tot	St	Sb	Snu	Ps	Gls
94-95	Manchester C.	20	17	3	1	6	3
	Total	20	17	3	1	6	3

GAVILAN, Diego

FULLNAME: Diego Gavilan
DOB:

Club History	Signed	Fee
Cerro Porteno		
Newcastle U.	1/00	£2m

Season	Team	Tot	St	Sb	Snu	Ps	Gls
99-00	Newcastle U.	6	2	4	5	2	1
	Total	6	2	4	5	2	1

GAVIN, Jason

FULLNAME: Jason Gavin
DOB: 14-Mar-80, Dublin

Club History	Signed	Fee
Middlesbrough		Trainee

Season	Team	Tot	St	Sb	Snu	Ps	Gls
98-99	Middlesbrough	2	2	0	0	1	0
99-00	Middlesbrough	6	3	4	13	0	0
	Total	8	5	4	13	1	0

GAYLE, Brian

FULLNAME: Brian Wilbert Gayle
DOB: 06-Mar-65, Kingston

Club History	Signed	Fee
Wimbledon	10/84	Apprentice
Manchester C.	7/88	£325,000
Ipswich Town	1/90	£330,000
Sheffield U.	9/91	£750,000

Season	Team	Tot	St	Sb	Snu	Ps	Gls
92-93	Sheffield U.	31	31	0	0	0	2
93-94	Sheffield U.	13	13	0	0	0	3
	Total	44	44	0	0	0	5

GAYLE, John

FULLNAME: John Gayle
DOB: 30-Jul-64, Bromsgrove

Club History	Signed	Fee
Wimbledon	3/89	£30,000
Birmingham C.	11/90	£175,000
Walsall	8/93	Loan
Coventry C.	9/93	£100,000

Season	Team	Tot	St	Sb	Snu	Ps	Gls
93-94	Coventry C.	3	3	0	2	1	0
	Total	3	3	0	2	1	0

GAYLE, Marcus

FULLNAME: Marcus Anthony Gayle
DOB: 27-Sep-70, Hammersmith

Club History	Signed	Fee
Brentford	7/89	Trainee
Wimbledon	3/94	£250,000

Season	Team	Tot	St	Sb	Snu	Ps	Gls
93-94	Wimbledon	10	10	0	0	0	0
94-95	Wimbledon	23	22	1	0	12	2
95-96	Wimbledon	34	21	13	0	11	5
96-97	Wimbledon	36	34	2	0	12	8
97-98	Wimbledon	30	21	9	6	13	2
98-99	Wimbledon	35	31	4	0	7	10
99-00	Wimbledon	36	35	1	0	8	7
	Total	204	174	30	6	63	34

GEE, Phil

FULLNAME: Philip John Gee
DOB: 19-Dec-64, Pelsall

Club History	Signed	Fee
Derby Co.	9/85	£5,000
Leicester C.	3/92	Swap

Season	Team	Tot	St	Sb	Snu	Ps	Gls
94-95	Leicester C.	7	3	4	2	3	2
	Total	7	3	4	2	3	2

GEMMILL, Scot

FULLNAME: Scot Gemmill
DOB: 02-Jan-71, Paisley

Club History	Signed	Fee
Nottingham F.	1/90	Trainee
Everton	3/99	£250,000

Season	Team	Tot	St	Sb	Snu	Ps	Gls
92-93	Nottingham F.	33	33	0	1	1	1
94-95	Nottingham F.	19	19	0	4	6	1
95-96	Nottingham F.	31	26	5	3	7	1
96-97	Nottingham F.	24	18	6	10	4	0
98-99	Nottingham F.	21	19	2	0	6	0
98-99	Everton	7	7	0	0	1	1
99-00	Everton	14	6	8	8	4	1
	Total	149	128	21	26	29	5

GENAUX, Regis

FULLNAME: Regis Genaux
DOB: 31-Aug-73, Belgium

Club History	Signed	Fee
Standard Leige	1991	
Coventry C.	8/96	£1m

Season	Team	Tot	St	Sb	Snu	Ps	Gls
96-97	Coventry C.	4	3	1	6	1	0
	Total	4	3	1	6	1	0

GEORGIADIS, George

FULLNAME: George Georgiadis
DOB: 08-Mar-72, Kavala, Greece

Club History	Signed	Fee
Panathinaikos		
Newcastle U.	7/98	£500,000

Season	Team	Tot	St	Sb	Snu	Ps	Gls
98-99	Newcastle U.	10	7	3	2	3	0
	Total	10	7	3	2	3	0

GERRARD, Paul

FULLNAME: Paul William Gerrard
DOB: 22-Jan-73, Heywood

Club History	Signed	Fee
Oldham A.	11/91	Trainee
Everton	8/96	£1m

Season	Team	Tot	St	Sb	Snu	Ps	Gls
92-93	Oldham A.	25	25	0	2	0	0
93-94	Oldham A.	16	15	1	18	0	0
96-97	Everton	5	4	1	30	0	0
97-98	Everton	4	4	0	28	0	0
98-99	Everton	0	0	0	15	0	0
99-00	Everton	34	34	0	0	1	0
	Total	84	82	2	93	1	0

GERRARD, Steven

FULLNAME: Steven George Gerrard
DOB: 30-May-80, Whiston

Club History	Signed	Fee
Liverpool	2/98	Trainee

Season	Team	Tot	St	Sb	Snu	Ps	Gls
98-99	Liverpool	12	4	8	1	3	0
99-00	Liverpool	29	26	3	1	10	1
	Total	41	30	11	2	13	1

GHRAYIB, Naguan

FULLNAME: Naguan Ghrayib
DOB:

Club History	Signed	Fee
Hapoel Haifa		
Aston Villa	7/99	£1m

Season	Team	Tot	St	Sb	Snu	Ps	Gls
99-00	Aston Villa	5	1	4	10	1	0
	Total	5	1	4	10	1	0

GIALLANZA, Gaetano

FULLNAME: Gaetano Giallanza
DOB: 06-Jun-74, Dornach, Switzerland

Club History	Signed	Fee					
Nantes							
Bolton Wanderers	3/98	Loan					

Season	Team	Tot	St	Sb	Snu	Ps	Gls
97-98	Bolton W.	3	0	3	3	0	0
	Total	3	0	3	3	0	0

GIBBENS, Kevin

FULLNAME: Kevin Gibbens
DOB: 04-Nov-79, Southampton

Club History	Signed	Fee
Southampton	1/98	Trainee

Season	Team	Tot	St	Sb	Snu	Ps	Gls
97-98	Southampton	2	2	0	4	1	0
98-99	Southampton	4	2	2	4	1	0
	Total	6	4	2	8	2	0

GIBBS, Nigel

FULLNAME: Nigel James Gibbs
DOB: 20-Nov-65, St Albans

Club History	Signed	Fee
Watford	11/83	Watford

Season	Team	Tot	St	Sb	Snu	Ps	Gls
99-00	Watford	17	11	6	12	2	0
	Total	17	11	6	12	2	0

GIBSON, Terry

FULLNAME: Terence Bradley Gibson
DOB: 23-Dec-62, Walthamstow

Club History	Signed	Fee
Tottenham H.	1/80	
Coventry C.	8/83	£100,000
Manchester U.	1/86	£650,000
Wimbledon	8/87	£200,000

Season	Team	Tot	St	Sb	Snu	Ps	Gls
92-93	Wimbledon	8	6	2	0	3	1
	Total	8	6	2	0	3	1

GIGGS, Ryan

FULLNAME: Ryan Joseph Giggs

DOB:29-Nov-73, Cardiff

Club History	Signed	Fee
Manchester U.	12/90	Trainee

Season	Team	Tot	St	Sb	Snu	Ps	Gls
92-93	Manchester U.	41	40	1	0	8	9
93-94	Manchester U.	38	32	6	2	5	13
94-95	Manchester U.	29	29	0	0	6	1
95-96	Manchester U.	33	30	3	0	2	11
96-97	Manchester U.	26	25	1	1	6	3
97-98	Manchester U.	29	28	1	1	4	8
98-99	Manchester U.	24	20	4	1	8	3
99-00	Manchester U.	30	30	0	2	9	6
	Total	250	234	16	7	48	54

GILCHRIST, Phil

FULLNAME: Phil Alexander Gilchrist
DOB: 25-Aug-73, Stockton on Tees

Club History	Signed	Fee
Nottingham F.	12/90	Trainee
Middlesbrough	1/92	Free
Hartlepool U.	11/92	Free
Oxford U.	2/95	£100,000
Leicester C.		

Season	Team	Tot	St	Sb	Snu	Ps	Gls
99-00	Leicester C.	27	17	10	8	4	1
	Total	27	17	10	8	4	1

GILLESPIE, Gary

FULLNAME: Gary Thomson Gillespie
DOB: 05-Jul-60, Stirling

Club History	Signed	Fee
Falkirk	1977	Juniors
Coventry C.	3/78	£75,000
Liverpool	7/83	£325,000
Celtic	8/91	£925,000
Coventry	8/94	Free

Season	Team	Tot	St	Sb	Snu	Ps	Gls
94-95	Coventry C.	3	2	1	1	0	0
95-96	Coventry C.	0	0	0	1	0	0
	Total	3	2	1	2	0	0

GILLESPIE, Keith

FULLNAME: Keith Robert Gillespie
DOB: 18-Feb-75, Bangor

Club History	Signed	Fee
Manchester U.	2/93	Trainee
Wigan A.	9/93	Loan
Newcastle U.	1/95	£1m +
Blackburn R.	12/98	£2.25m

Season	Team	Tot	St	Sb	Snu	Ps	Gls
94-95	Manchester U.	9	3	6	1	2	1
94-95	Newcastle U.	17	15	2	0	1	2
95-96	Newcastle U.	28	26	2	5	11	4
96-97	Newcastle U.	32	23	9	5	8	1
97-98	Newcastle U.	29	25	4	2	8	4
98-99	Newcastle U.	7	5	2	1	1	0
98-99	Blackburn R.	16	13	3	0	2	1
	Total	138	110	28	14	33	13

GINOLA, David

FULLNAME: David Ginola
DOB: 25-Jan-67, Gassin, nr St. Tropez

Club History	Signed	Fee
PSG		
Newcastle U.	7/95	£2.5m
Tottenham H.	7/97	£2m

Season	Team	Tot	St	Sb	Snu	Ps	Gls
95-96	Newcastle U.	34	34	0	0	5	5
96-97	Newcastle U.	24	20	4	7	6	1
97-98	Tottenham H.	34	34	0	0	7	6
98-99	Tottenham H.	30	30	0	3	13	3
99-00	Tottenham H.	36	36	0	0	17	4
	Total	158	154	4	10	48	19

GINTY, Rory

FULLNAME: Rory Vincent Ginty
DOB: 23-Jan-77, Galway

Club History	Signed	Fee
Crystal P.	11/94	Trainee

Season	Team	Tot	St	Sb	Snu	Ps	Gls
97-98	Crystal P.	5	2	3	4	0	0
	Total	5	2	3	4	0	0

GIOACCHINI, Stefano

FULLNAME: Stefano Gioacchini
DOB: 25-Nov-76, Rome

Club History	Signed	Fee
Venezia		
Coventry C.	1/99	Loan

Season	Team	Tot	St	Sb	Snu	Ps	Gls
98-99	Coventry C.	3	0	3	3	0	0
	Total	3	0	3	3	0	0

GITTENS, Jon

FULLNAME: Jon Gittens
DOB: 22-Jan-64, Birmingham

Club History	Signed	Fee
Southampton	10/85	£10,000 from Non League
Swindon Town	7/87	£40,000
Southampton	3/91	£400,000
Middlesbrough	2/92	Loan
Middlesbrough	7/92	£200,000

Season	Team	Tot	St	Sb	Snu	Ps	Gls
92-93	Middlesbrough	13	13	0	8	0	0
	Total	13	13	0	8	0	0

GIVEN, Shay

FULLNAME: Seamus John Given
DOB: 20-Apr-76, Lifford

Club History	Signed	Fee
Blackburn R.	8/94	From Celtic
Swindon	8/95	Loan
Sunderland	1/96	Loan
Newcastle U.	7/97	£1.5m

Season	Team	Tot	St	Sb	Snu	Ps	Gls
94-95	Blackburn R.	0	0	0	3	0	0
95-96	Blackburn R.	0	0	0	1	0	0
96-97	Blackburn R.	2	2	0	36	0	0
97-98	Newcastle U.	24	24	0	11	0	0
98-99	Newcastle U.	31	31	0	4	1	0
99-00	Newcastle U.	14	14	0	11	0	0
	Total	71	71	0	66	1	0

GLASS, Stephen

FULLNAME: Stephen Glass
DOB: 25-May-76, Dundee

Club History	Signed	Fee
Aberdeen		
Newcastle U.	9/98	£650,000

Season	Team	Tot	St	Sb	Snu	Ps	Gls
98-99	Newcastle U.	22	18	4	0	8	3
99-00	Newcastle U.	7	1	6	5	0	1
	Total	29	19	10	5	8	4

GLOVER, Lee

FULLNAME: Edward Lee Glover
DOB: 24-Apr-70, Kettering

Club History	Signed	Fee
Nottingham F.	7/86	Apprentice

Season	Team	Tot	St	Sb	Snu	Ps	Gls
92-93	Nottingham F.	14	9	5	6	2	0
	Total	14	9	5	6	2	0

GODDARD, Paul

FULLNAME: Paul Goddard
DOB: 12-Oct-59, Harlington

Club History	Signed	Fee
QPR	7/77	
West Ham U.	8/80	£800,000
Newcastle U.	11/86	£415,000
Derby co.	8/88	£425,000
Millwall	12/89	£800,000
Ipswich Town	1/91	

Season	Team	Tot	St	Sb	Snu	Ps	Gls
92-93	Ipswich T.	25	19	6	6	9	3

93-94	Ipswich T.	4	3	1	1	2	0
	Total	29	22	7	7	11	3

GOLDBAEK, Bjarne

FULLNAME: Bjarne Goldbaek
DOB: 16-Aug-68, Denmark

Club History	Signed	Fee
FC Copenhagen		
Chelsea	11/98	£350,000

Season	Team	Tot	St	Sb	Snu	Ps	Gls
98-99	Chelsea	23	13	10	3	4	5
99-00	Chelsea	6	2	4	0	2	0
	Total	29	15	14	3	6	5

GOMA, Alain

FULLNAME: Alain Goma
DOB: 05-Oct-72, France

Club History	Signed	Fee
PSG		
Newcastle U.	6/99	£4.7m

Season	Team	Tot	St	Sb	Snu	Ps	Gls
99-00	Newcastle U.	14	14	0	2	2	0
	Total	14	14	0	2	2	0

GOODEN, Ty

FULLNAME: Ty Michael Gooden
DOB: 23-Oct-72, Canvey Island

Club History	Signed	Fee
Wycombe W.		
Swindon Town	9/93	Free

Season	Team	Tot	St	Sb	Snu	Ps	Gls
93-94	Swindon T.	4	2	2	0	1	0
	Total	4	2	2	0	1	0

GOODMAN, Jon

FULLNAME: Jonathan Goodman
DOB: 02-Jun-71, Walthamstow

Club History	Signed	Fee
Bromley		
Millwall	8/90	£50,000 NL
Wimbledon	11/94	£1.3m +

Season	Team	Tot	St	Sb	Snu	Ps	Gls
94-95	Wimbledon	19	13	6	0	5	4
95-96	Wimbledon	27	9	18	3	5	6
96-97	Wimbledon	13	6	7	6	6	1
98-99	Wimbledon	1	0	1	0	0	0
	Total	60	28	32	9	16	11

GOODRIDGE, Greg

FULLNAME: Gregory Ronald St Clair
Goodridge
DOB: 10-Feb-75, Barbados

Club History	Signed	Fee
Lambada (Barbados)		
Torquay U.	3/94	Free
QPR	8/95	£100,000

Season	Team	Tot	St	Sb	Snu	Ps	Gls
95-96	QPR	7	0	7	3	0	1
	Total	7	0	7	3	0	1

GOODWIN, Tommy

FULLNAME: Thomas Goodwin
DOB: 08-Nov-79, Leicester

Club History	Signed	Fee
Leicester C.	8/98	Trainee

Season	Team	Tot	St	Sb	Snu	Ps	Gls
99-00	Leicester C.	1	1	0	1	0	0
	Total	1	1	0	1	0	0

GORDON, Dale

FULLNAME: Dale Andrew Gordon
DOB: 09-Jan-67, Great Yarmouth

Club History	Signed	Fee
Norwich C.	1/84	Apprentice
Rangers	11/91	£1.2m
West Ham U.	8/93	£750,000

Season	Team	Tot	St	Sb	Snu	Ps	Gls
93-94	West Ham U.	8	8	0	1	3	1
	Total	8	8	0	1	3	1

GORDON, Dean

FULLNAME: Dean Dwight Gordon
DOB: 10-Feb-73, Croydon

Club History	Signed	Fee
Crystal P.	7/91	Trainee
Middlesbrough	7/98	£600,000

Season	Team	Tot	St	Sb	Snu	Ps	Gls
92-93	Crystal P.	10	6	4	2	1	0
94-95	Crystal P.	41	38	3	0	0	2
95-96	West Ham U.	1	0	1	0	0	0
97-98	Crystal P.	37	36	1	0	0	2
98-99	Middlesbrough	38	38	0	0	0	3
99-00	Middlesbrough	4	3	1	2	1	0
	Total	131	121	10	4	2	7

GOSS, Jeremy

FULLNAME: Jeremy Goss
DOB: 11-May-65, Cyprus

Club History	Signed	Fee
Norwich C.	3/83	

Season	Team	Tot	St	Sb	Snu	Ps	Gls
92-93	Norwich C.	25	25	0	3	4	1
93-94	Norwich C.	34	34	0	0	2	6
94-95	Norwich C.	25	19	6	0	1	2
	Total	84	78	6	3	7	9

GOUGH, Richard

FULLNAME: Richard Charles Gough
DOB: 05-Apr-62, Stockholm, Sweden

Club History	Signed	Fee
Dundee U.	3/80	From NL
Tottenham H.	8/86	£750,000
Rangers	10/87	£1.5m
N.Forest	3/99	Free
Everton		

Season	Team	Tot	St	Sb	Snu	Ps	Gls
98-99	Nottingham F.	7	7	0	1	1	0
99-00	Everton	29	29	0	0	1	1
	Total	36	36	0	1	2	1

GOULD, Jonathan

FULLNAME: Jonathon Alan Gould
DOB: 18-Jul-68, London

Club History	Signed	Fee
Halifax Town	7/90	Free
Coventry C.	7/92	Free

Season	Team	Tot	St	Sb	Snu	Ps	Gls
92-93	Coventry C.	9	9	0	32	0	0
93-94	Coventry C.	9	9	0	32	0	0
94-95	Coventry C.	7	7	0	34	0	0
95-96	Coventry C.	0	0	0	12	0	0
	Total	25	25	0	110	0	0

GRAHAM, Richard

FULLNAME: Richard Graham
DOB: 28-Nov-74, Dewsbury

Club History	Signed	Fee
Oldham A.	7/93	Trainee

Season	Team	Tot	St	Sb	Snu	Ps	Gls
93-94	Oldham A.	5	4	1	3	3	0
	Total	5	4	1	3	3	0

GRANT, Gareth

FULLNAME: Gareth Michael Grant
DOB: 06-Sep-80, Leeds

Club History	Signed	Fee
Bradford C.	4/98	Trainee

Season	Team	Tot	St	Sb	Snu	Ps	Gls
99-00	Bradford C.	1	0	1	1	0	0
	Total	1	0	1	1	0	0

GRANT, Tony

FULLNAME: Anthony James Grant
DOB: 14-Nov-74, Liverpool

Club History	Signed	Fee
Everton	7/93	Trainee

Season	Team	Tot	St	Sb	Snu	Ps	Gls
93-94	Everton	0	0	0	1	0	0
94-95	Everton	5	1	4	0	1	7
95-96	Everton	13	11	2	5	4	1
96-97	Everton	18	11	7	4	3	0
97-98	Everton	7	7	0	1	4	1
98-99	Everton	16	13	3	7	9	0
99-00	Everton	2	0	2	2	0	0
	Total	61	43	18	20	21	9

GRANVILLE, Danny

FULLNAME: Daniel Patrick Granville
DOB: 19-Jan-75, Islington

Club History	Signed	Fee
Cambridge U.	5/93	Trainee
Chelsea	3/97	£300,000
Leeds U.	6/98	£1.6m

Season	Team	Tot	St	Sb	Snu	Ps	Gls
96-97	Chelsea	5	3	2	2	0	0
97-98	Chelsea	13	9	4	6	2	0
98-99	Leeds U.	9	7	2	8	3	0
	Total	27	19	8	16	5	0

GRAVELAINE, Xavier

FULLNAME: Xavier Gravelaine
DOB:

Club History	Signed	Fee
PSG		
Watford	11/99	Free

Season	Team	Tot	St	Sb	Snu	Ps	Gls
99-00	Watford	7	7	0	0	1	2
	Total	7	7	0	0	1	2

GRAY, Andy

FULLNAME: Andrew Arthur Gray
DOB: 22-Feb-64, Lambeth

Club History	Signed	Fee
Crystal P.	11/84	£2,000
Aston Villa	11/87	£150,000
QPR	2/89	£425,000
Crystal P.	8/89	£500,000
Tottenham H.	2/92	£900,000

Season	Team	Tot	St	Sb	Snu	Ps	Gls
92-93	Tottenham H.	17	9	8	0	5	1
93-94	Tottenham H.	2	0	2	3	0	1
	Total	19	9	10	3	5	2

GRAY, Andy

FULLNAME: Andrew David Gray
DOB: 15-Nov-77, Harrogate

Club History	Signed	Fee
Leeds U.	7/95	Trainee
Nottingham F.	8/98	£175,000

Season	Team	Tot	St	Sb	Snu	Ps	Gls
95-96	Leeds U.	15	12	3	1	2	0
96-97	Leeds U.	7	1	6	4	1	0
97-98	Leeds U.	0	0	0	1	0	0
98-99	Nottingham F.	8	3	5	5	2	0
	Total	30	16	14	11	5	0

GRAY, Julian

FULLNAME: Julian Gray
DOB: 21-Sep-79, Lewisham

Club History	Signed	Fee
Arsenal	7/96	Trainee

Season	Team	Tot	St	Sb	Snu	Ps	Gls
99-00	Arsenal	1	0	1	2	0	0
	Total	1	0	1	2	0	0

GRAY, Michael

FULLNAME: Michael Gray
DOB: 03-Aug-74, Sunderland

Club History	Signed	Fee
Sunderland	7/92	Trainee

Season	Team	Tot	St	Sb	Snu	Ps	Gls
96-97	Sunderland	35	32	3	3	9	3
99-00	Sunderland	33	32	1	1	7	0
	Total	68	64	4	4	16	3

GRAY, Wayne

FULLNAME: Wayne Gray
DOB: 07-Nov-80, London

Club History	Signed	Fee
Wimbledon	8/99	Trainee
Swindon T.	3/00	Loan

Season	Team	Tot	St	Sb	Snu	Ps	Gls
99-00	Wimbledon	1	0	1	2	0	0
	Total	1	0	1	2	0	0

GRAYSON, Simon

FULLNAME: Simon Nicholas Grayson
DOB: 16-Dec-69, Ripon

Club History	Signed	Fee
Leeds U.	6/88	Trainee
Leicester C.	3/92	£50,000
Aston Villa	7/97	£1.35m

Season	Team	Tot	St	Sb	Snu	Ps	Gls
94-95	Leicester C.	34	34	0	0	6	0
96-97	Leicester C.	36	36	0	0	1	0
97-98	Aston Villa	33	28	5	4	5	0
98-99	Aston Villa	15	4	11	13	1	0
	Total	118	102	16	17	13	0

GREEN, Scott

FULLNAME: Scott Paul Green
DOB: 15-Jan-70, Walsall

Club History	Signed	Fee
Derby Co.	7/88	Trainee
Bolton W.	3/90	£50,000

Season	Team	Tot	St	Sb	Snu	Ps	Gls
95-96	Bolton W.	31	26	5	6	4	3
	Total	31	26	5	6	4	3

GREENING, Jonathan

FULLNAME: Jonathan Greening
DOB: 02-Jan-79, Scarborough

Club History	Signed	Fee
York C.	12/96	Trainee
Manchester U.	3/98	£1m

Season	Team	Tot	St	Sb	Snu	Ps	Gls
97-98	Manchester U.	0	0	0	1	0	0
98-99	Manchester U.	3	0	3	1	0	0
99-00	Manchester U.	4	1	3	2	1	0
	Total	7	1	6	4	1	0

GREENMAN, Chris

FULLNAME: Christopher Greenman
DOB: 22-Dec-68, Bristol

Club History	Signed	Fee
Coventry C.		Trainee

Season	Team	Tot	St	Sb	Snu	Ps	Gls
92-93	Coventry C.	2	1	1	0	1	0
	Total	2	1	1	0	1	0

GREGORY, David

FULLNAME: David Spencer Gregory
DOB: 23-Jan-70, Colchester

Club History	Signed	Fee
Ipswich Town	3/87	Trainee

Season	Team	Tot	St	Sb	Snu	Ps	Gls
92-93	Ipswich T.	3	1	2	1	0	1
93-94	Ipswich T.	0	0	0	2	0	0

94-95	Ipswich T.	1	0	1	2	0	0
	Total	4	1	3	5	0	1

GREGORY, Neil

FULLNAME: Neil Gregory
DOB: 07-Oct-70, Zambia

Club History	Signed	Fee
Ipswich Town		Trainee

Season	Team	Tot	St	Sb	Snu	Ps	Gls
92-93	Ipswich T.	0	0	0	1	0	0
94-95	Ipswich T.	3	1	2	1	1	0
	Total	3	1	2	2	1	0

GRIFFIN, Andy

FULLNAME: Andrew Griffin
DOB: 07-Mar-79, Billinge

Club History	Signed	Fee
Stoke C.	9/96	Trainee
Newcastle U.	1/98	£1.5m >

Season	Team	Tot	St	Sb	Snu	Ps	Gls
97-98	Newcastle U.	4	4	0	2	2	0
98-99	Newcastle U.	14	14	0	2	2	0
99-00	Newcastle U.	3	1	2	1	0	1
	Total	21	19	2	5	4	1

GRIFFITHS, Carl

FULLNAME: Carl Brian Griffiths
DOB: 16-Jul-71, Welshpool

Club History	Signed	Fee
Shrewsbury Town	9/88	Trainee
Manchester C.	10/93	£500,000

Season	Team	Tot	St	Sb	Snu	Ps	Gls
93-94	Manchester C.	16	11	5	2	4	4
94-95	Manchester C.	2	0	2	1	0	0
	Total	18	11	7	3	4	4

GRIMANDI, Gilles

FULLNAME: Gilles Grimandi
DOB: 11-Nov-70, Gap (France)

Club History	Signed	Fee
AS Monaco		
Arsenal	6/97	£1.5m

Season	Team	Tot	St	Sb	Snu	Ps	Gls
97-98	Arsenal	22	16	6	8	3	1
98-99	Arsenal	8	3	5	14	0	0
99-00	Arsenal	28	27	1	4	3	2
	Total	58	46	12	26	6	3

GROBBELAAR, Bruce

FULLNAME: Bruce David Grobbelaar
DOB: 06-Oct-57, Durban, South Africa

Club History	Signed	Fee
Crewe Alexandra	12/79	
Vancouver (Canada)	5/80	
Liverpool	3/81	£250,000
Stoke C.	3/93	Loan
Southampton	8/94	£250,000

Season	Team	Tot	St	Sb	Snu	Ps	Gls
92-93	Liverpool	5	5	0	12	0	0
93-94	Liverpool	29	29	0	10	1	0
94-95	Southampton	30	30	0	9	1	0
95-96	Southampton	2	2	0	25	0	0
97-98	Sheffield W.	0	0	0	5	0	0
	Total	66	66	0	61	2	0

GRODAS, Frode

FULLNAME: Frode Grodas
DOB: 24-Oct-69, Norway

Club History	Signed	Fee
Lillestrom	1990	
Chelsea	11/96	Free
Tottenham H.	1/98	£250,000

Season	Team	Tot	St	Sb	Snu	Ps	Gls
96-97	Chelsea	21	20	1	9	1	0
97-98	Tottenham H.	0	0	0	10	0	0
	Total	21	20	1	19	1	0

GROENENDIJK, Alphonse

FULLNAME: Alphonse Groenendijk
DOB: 17-May-64, Leiden, Holland

Club History	Signed	Fee
Ajax		
Manchester C.	8/93	£500,000

Season	Team	Tot	St	Sb	Snu	Ps	Gls
93-94	Manchester C.	9	9	0	0	5	0
	Total	9	9	0	0	5	0

GROUDIN, David

FULLNAME: David Groudin
DOB: 08-May-80, Paris, France

Club History	Signed	Fee
St Etienne		
Arsenal	7/98	£500,000

Season	Team	Tot	St	Sb	Snu	Ps	Gls
98-99	Arsenal	1	1	0	0	0	0
	Total	1	1	0	0	0	0

GROVES, Perry

FULLNAME: Perry Groves
DOB: 19-Apr-65, Bow

Club History	Signed	Fee
Colchester U.	6/82	
Arsenal	9/86	£50,000
Southampton	8/92	£750,000

Season	Team	Tot	St	Sb	Snu	Ps	Gls
92-93	Arsenal	1	0	1	0	0	0
92-93	Southampton	15	13	2	2	5	2
	Total	16	13	3	2	5	2

GUDMUNDSSON, Johann

FULLNAME: Johann Birnir Gudmundsson
DOB: 05-Dec-77, Reykjavik, Iceland

Club History	Signed	Fee
Keflavik		
Watford	3/98	

Season	Team	Tot	St	Sb	Snu	Ps	Gls
99-00	Watford	9	1	8	8	1	0
	Total	9	1	8	8	1	0

GUDMUNDSSON, Niklas

FULLNAME: Niklas Gudmundsson
DOB: 29-Feb-72, Halmstad

Club History	Signed	Fee
Halmstads		
Blackburn R.	12/95	£750,000

Season	Team	Tot	St	Sb	Snu	Ps	Gls
95-96	Blackburn R.	4	1	3	4	1	0
96-97	Blackburn R.	2	0	2	5	0	0
	Total	6	1	5	9	1	0

GUENTCHEV, Bontcho

FULLNAME: Bontcho Guentchev
DOB: 07-Jul-64, Bulgaria

Club History	Signed	Fee
Sporting Lisbon		
Ipswich Town	12/92	£250,000

Season	Team	Tot	St	Sb	Snu	Ps	Gls
92-93	Ipswich T.	21	19	2	2	3	3
93-94	Ipswich T.	24	9	15	6	3	2
94-95	Ipswich T.	16	11	5	1	2	1
	Total	61	39	22	9	8	6

GUINAN, Steve

FULLNAME: Stephen Guinan
DOB: 24-Dec-75, Birmingham

Club History	Signed	Fee
Nottingham F.	1/93	Trainee

Season	Team	Tot	St	Sb	Snu	Ps	Gls
95-96	Nottingham F.	2	1	1	0	1	0
96-97	Nottingham F.	2	0	2	3	0	0
	Total	4	1	3	3	1	0

GUIVARC'H, Stephane

FULLNAME: Stephane Guivarc'h
DOB: 06-Sep-70, Concarneau, France

Club History	Signed	Fee
Auxerre		
Newcastle	6/98	£3.5m

Season	Team	Tot	St	Sb	Snu	Ps	Gls
98-99	Newcastle U.	4	2	2	1	1	1
	Total	4	2	2	1	1	1

GULLIT, Ruud

FULLNAME: Dil Ruud Gullit
DOB: 01-Sep-62, Amsterdam, Netherlands

Club History	Signed	Fee
Sampdoria	7/93	
Chelsea	7/95	Free

Season	Team	Tot	St	Sb	Snu	Ps	Gls
95-96	Chelsea	31	31	0	0	2	3
96-97	Chelsea	12	6	6	2	2	1
97-98	Chelsea	6	0	6	1	0	0
	Total	49	37	12	3	4	4

GUNN, Bryan

FULLNAME: Bryan James Gunn
DOB: 22-Dec-63, Thurso

Club History	Signed	Fee
Norwich C.	10/86	£150,000

Season	Team	Tot	St	Sb	Snu	Ps	Gls
92-93	Norwich C.	42	42	0	0	0	0
93-94	Norwich C.	41	41	0	0	1	0
94-95	Norwich C.	21	21	0	0	1	0
	Total	104	104	0	0	2	0

GUNNLAUGSSON, Arnar

FULLNAME: Arnar Bergmann Gunnlaugsson
DOB: 06-Mar-73, Iceland

Club History	Signed	Fee
IA Akranes		
Bolton W.	7/97	£100,000
Leicester C.	2/99	£2m

Season	Team	Tot	St	Sb	Snu	Ps	Gls
97-98	Bolton W.	15	2	13	9	1	0
98-99	Leicester C.	9	5	4	3	5	0
99-00	Leicester C.	2	2	0	6	2	0
	Total	26	9	17	18	8	0

GUPPY, Steve

FULLNAME: Stephen Guppy
DOB: 29-Mar-69, Winchester

Club History	Signed	Fee
Wycombe W.	1989	
Newcastle U.	8/94	£150,000
Port Vale	11/94	£225,000
Leicester C.	2/97	£850,000

Season	Team	Tot	St	Sb	Snu	Ps	Gls
96-97	Leicester C.	13	12	1	0	1	0
97-98	Leicester C.	37	37	0	0	2	2
98-99	Leicester C.	38	38	0	0	0	4
99-00	Leicester C.	30	29	1	0	1	2
	Total	118	116	2	0	4	8

GUSTAFSSON, Thomas

FULLNAME: Thomas Gustafsson
DOB: 7-May-73

Club History	Signed	Fee
AIK Solna		
Coventry C.	12/99	

Season	Team	Tot	St	Sb	Snu	Ps	Gls
99-00	Coventry C.	10	7	3	3	2	0
	Total	10	7	3	3	2	0

GYNN, Micky

FULLNAME: Michael Gynn
DOB: 19-Aug-61, Peterborough

Club History	Signed	Fee
Peterborough U.		
Coventry C.		

Season	Team	Tot	St	Sb	Snu	Ps	Gls
92-93	Coventry C.	20	18	2	1	5	2
	Total	20	18	2	1	5	2

HAALAND, Alf Inge

FULLNAME: Alf Inge Rasdal Haaland
DOB: 23-Nov-72, Stavanger, Norway

Club History	Signed	Fee
Young Boys		
Nottinham F.	1/94	
Leeds U.	6/97	£1.6m

Season	Team	Tot	St	Sb	Snu	Ps	Gls
94-95	Nottingham F.	20	18	2	4	1	1

Season	Team	Tot	St	Sb	Snu	Ps	Gls
95-96	Nottingham F.	17	12	5	12	1	0
96-97	Nottingham F.	34	33	1	2	3	6
97-98	Leeds U.	32	26	6	1	2	7
98-99	Leeds U.	29	24	5	4	1	1
99-00	Leeds U.	13	7	6	13	0	0
	Total	145	120	25	36	8	15

HADJI, Musta

FULLNAME: Mustapha Hadji
DOB: Morocco

Club History	Signed	Fee
Deportivo La Coruna		
Coventry C.	7/99	£4.0m

Season	Team	Tot	St	Sb	Snu	Ps	Gls
99-00	Coventry C.	33	33	0	0	7	6
	Total	33	33	0	0	7	6

HALL, Gareth

FULLNAME: Gareth David Hall
DOB: 12-Mar-69, Croydon

Club History	Signed	Fee
Chelsea	4/86	Apprentice
Sunderland	12/95	£300,000

Season	Team	Tot	St	Sb	Snu	Ps	Gls
92-93	Chelsea	37	36	1	2	2	2
93-94	Chelsea	7	4	3	2	0	0
94-95	Chelsea	6	4	2	3	0	0
95-96	Chelsea	5	5	0	2	0	1
96-97	Sunderland	32	32	0	6	5	0
	Total	87	81	6	15	7	3

HALL, Marcus

FULLNAME: Marcus Hall
DOB: 24-Mar-76, Coventry

Club History	Signed	Fee
Coventry C.	7/94	Trainee

Season	Team	Tot	St	Sb	Snu	Ps	Gls
94-95	Coventry C.	5	2	3	1	0	0
95-96	Coventry C.	25	24	1	3	1	0
96-97	Coventry C.	13	10	3	6	2	0
97-98	Coventry C.	25	20	5	6	3	1
98-99	Coventry C.	5	2	3	3	0	0
99-00	Coventry C.	9	7	2	1	0	0
	Total	82	65	17	20	6	1

HALL, Paul

FULLNAME: Paul Anthony Hall
DOB: 03-Jul-72, Manchester

Club History	Signed	Fee
Torquay U.	7/90	Trainee

Portsmouth	3/93	£70,000
Coventry C.	8/98	£300,000

Season	Team	Tot	St	Sb	Snu	Ps	Gls
98-99	Coventry C.	9	2	7	4	2	0
99-00	Coventry C.	1	0	1	0	0	0
	Total	10	2	8	4	2	0

HALL, Richard

FULLNAME: Richard Anthony Hall
DOB: 14-Mar-72, Ipswich

Club History	Signed	Fee
Scunthorpe U.	3/90	Trainee
Southampton	2/91	£200,000
West Ham U.	7/96	£1.9m

Season	Team	Tot	St	Sb	Snu	Ps	Gls
92-93	Southampton	28	28	0	1	1	4
93-94	Southampton	4	4	0	0	1	0
94-95	Southampton	37	36	1	0	3	4
95-96	Southampton	30	30	0	0	1	1
96-97	West Ham U.	7	7	0	0	0	0
98-99	West Ham U.	0	0	0	0	0	0
	Total	106	105	1	1	6	9

HALLE, Gunnar

FULLNAME: Gunnar Halle
DOB: 11-Aug-65, Oslo, Norway

Club History	Signed	Fee
Lillestrom		
Oldham Ath	2/91	£280,000
Leeds U.	12/96	£400,000
Bradford C.	7/99	£200,000

Season	Team	Tot	St	Sb	Snu	Ps	Gls
92-93	Oldham A.	41	41	0	0	3	5
93-94	Oldham A.	23	22	1	0	0	1
96-97	Leeds U.	20	20	0	0	0	0
97-98	Leeds U.	33	31	2	3	3	2
98-99	Leeds U.	17	14	3	15	1	2
99-00	Bradford C.	38	37	1	0	7	0
	Total	172	165	7	18	14	10

HALLWORTH, Jon

FULLNAME: Jonathan Geoffrey Hallworth
DOB: 26-Oct-65, Stockport

Club History	Signed	Fee
Ipswich Town	5/83	Apprentice
Bristol R.	1/85	Loan
Oldham A.	2/89	£75,000

Season	Team	Tot	St	Sb	Snu	Ps	Gls
92-93	Oldham A.	16	16	0	0	0	0
93-94	Oldham A.	19	19	0	20	1	0
	Total	35	35	0	20	1	0

HAMANN, Dietmar

FULLNAME: Dietmar Hamann
DOB: 27-Aug-73, Waldsasson, Germany

Club History	Signed	Fee
Bayern Munich		
Newcastle U.	8/98	£5.25m
Liverpool	7/99	£8.0m

Season	Team	Tot	St	Sb	Snu	Ps	Gls
98-99	Newcastle U.	23	22	1	3	3	4
99-00	Liverpool	28	27	1	0	6	1
	Total	51	49	2	3	9	5

HAMILTON, Des

FULLNAME: Derrick Vivian Hamilton
DOB: 15-Aug-76, Bradford

Club History	Signed	Fee
Bradford C.	6/94	Trainee
Newcastle U.	3/97	£1.6m +

Season	Team	Tot	St	Sb	Snu	Ps	Gls
96-97	Newcastle U.	0	0	0	3	0	0
97-98	Newcastle U.	12	7	5	9	4	0
	Total	12	7	5	12	4	0

HAMMOND, Nicky

FULLNAME: Nicholas D Hammond
DOB: 07-Sep-67, Hornchurch

Club History	Signed	Fee
Arsenal	7/85	Apprentice
Bristol R.	1/86	Loan
Peterborough U.	9/86	Loan
Aberdeen	2/87	Loan
Swindon Town	7/87	

Season	Team	Tot	St	Sb	Snu	Ps	Gls
93-94	Swindon T.	13	11	2	29	1	0
	Total	13	11	2	29	1	0

HAMON, Chris

FULLNAME: Christopher Hamon
DOB: 27-Apr-70, Jersey

Club History	Signed	Fee
St Peter		
Swindon Town		

Season	Team	Tot	St	Sb	Snu	Ps	Gls
93-94	Swindon T.	1	0	1	0	0	0
	Total	1	0	1	0	0	0

HAREWOOD, Marlon

FULLNAME: Marlon Anderson Harewood
DOB: 25-Aug-79, Hampstead

Club History	Signed	Fee
Nottingham F.	9/96	Trainee

Season	Team	Tot	St	Sb	Snu	Ps	Gls
98-99	Nottingham F.	23	11	12	3	6	1
	Total	23	11	12	3	6	1

HARFORD, Mick

FULLNAME: Michael Gordon Harford
DOB: 12-Feb-59, Sunderland

Club History	Signed	Fee
Lincoln C.	7/77	
Newcastle U.	12/80	£180,000
Bristol C.	8/81	£160,000
Birmingham C.	3/82	£100,000
Luton Town	12/84	£250,000
Derby Co.	1/90	£450,000
Luton Town	9/91	£325,000
Chelsea	8/92	£300,000
Sundlerland	3/93	£250,000
Coventry C	7/93	£200,000
Wimbledon		

Season	Team	Tot	St	Sb	Snu	Ps	Gls
92-93	Chelsea	28	27	1	1	4	9
93-94	Coventry C.	1	0	1	1	0	1
94-95	Wimbledon	27	17	10	4	5	6
95-96	Wimbledon	21	17	4	2	10	2
96-97	Wimbledon	13	3	10	15	1	1
	Total	90	64	26	23	20	19

HARKES, John

FULLNAME: John Andrew Harkes
DOB: 08-Mar-67, New Jersey, USA

Club History	Signed	Fee
Sheffield W.	10/90	£70,000
Derby Co.	8/93	
West Ham U.	10/95	Loan
DC United		
Nottingham F.	1/99	Loan

Season	Team	Tot	St	Sb	Snu	Ps	Gls
92-93	Sheffield W.	29	23	6	3	4	2
95-96	West Ham U.	10	6	4	3	3	0
98-99	Nottingham F.	3	3	0	0	1	0
	Total	42	32	10	6	8	2

HARKNESS, Steve

FULLNAME: Steven Harkness
DOB: 27-Aug-71, Carlisle

Club History	Signed	Fee
Carlisle U.	3/89	Trainee
Liverpool	7/89	£75,000

Season	Team	Tot	St	Sb	Snu	Ps	Gls
92-93	Liverpool	10	9	1	1	0	1
93-94	Liverpool	11	10	1	3	1	0
94-95	Liverpool	8	8	0	3	0	1
95-96	Liverpool	24	23	1	1	3	1
96-97	Liverpool	7	5	2	5	0	0
97-98	Liverpool	25	24	1	8	3	0
98-99	Liverpool	6	4	2	11	3	0
	Total	91	83	8	32	10	3

HARLEY, Jon

FULLNAME: Jon Harley
DOB: 26-Sep-79, Maidstone

Club History	Signed	Fee
Chelsea	3/97	Trainee

Season	Team	Tot	St	Sb	Snu	Ps	Gls
97-98	Chelsea	3	3	0	0	3	0
98-99	Chelsea	0	0	0	0	0	0
99-00	Chelsea	17	13	4	1	3	2
	Total	20	16	4	1	6	2

HARPER, Alan

FULLNAME: Alan Harper
DOB: 01-Nov-60, Liverpool

Club History	Signed	Fee
Liverpool	4/78	Apprentice
Everton	6/83	£100,000
Sheffield W.	7/88	£275,000
Manchester C.	12/89	£150,000
Everton	8/91	£200,000

Season	Team	Tot	St	Sb	Snu	Ps	Gls
92-93	Everton	18	16	2	3	3	0
	Total	18	16	2	3	3	0

HARPER, Kevin

FULLNAME: Kevin Patrick Harper
DOB: 15-Jan-76, Oldham

Club History	Signed	Fee
Hibernian	8/92	
Derby Co.	9/98	£300,000

Season	Team	Tot	St	Sb	Snu	Ps	Gls
98-99	Derby Co.	27	6	21	4	5	1
99-00	Derby Co.	5	0	5	2	0	0
	Total	32	6	26	6	5	1

HARPER, Lee

FULLNAME: Lee Harper
DOB: 30-Oct-71, Sittingbourne

Club History	Signed	Fee
Arsenal	6/94	£150,000 from Non League

Season	Team	Tot	St	Sb	Snu	Ps	Gls
94-95	Arsenal	0	0	0	12	0	0
96-97	Arsenal	1	1	0	9	0	0
	Total	1	1	0	21	0	0

HARPER, Steve

FULLNAME: Stephen Alan Harper
DOB: 14-Mar-75, Easington

Club History	Signed	Fee
Newcastle U.	7/93	Free NL

Season	Team	Tot	St	Sb	Snu	Ps	Gls
94-95	Newcastle U.	0	0	0	3	0	0
98-99	Newcastle U.	8	7	1	20	0	0
99-00	Newcastle U.	18	18	0	16	0	0
	Total	26	25	1	39	0	0

HARRISON, Craig

FULLNAME: Craig Harrison
DOB: 10-Nov-97, Gateshead

Club History	Signed	Fee
Middlesbrough	7/96	Trainee

Season	Team	Tot	St	Sb	Snu	Ps	Gls
98-99	Middlesbrough	4	3	1	2	0	0
	Total	4	3	1	2	0	0

HARTE, Ian

FULLNAME: Ian Harte
DOB: 31-Aug-77, Drogheda

Club History	Signed	Fee
Leeds Utd	12/95	Trainee

Season	Team	Tot	St	Sb	Snu	Ps	Gls
95-96	Leeds U.	4	2	2	0	0	0
96-97	Leeds U.	14	10	4	21	0	2
97-98	Leeds U.	12	12	0	9	2	0
98-99	Leeds U.	35	34	1	0	1	4
99-00	Leeds U.	33	33	0	0	3	6
	Total	98	91	7	30	6	12

HARTFIELD, Charlie

FULLNAME: Charles Joseph Hartfield
DOB: 04-Sep-71, Lambeth

Club History	Signed	Fee
Arsenal	9/89	Trainee
Sheffield U.	8/91	Free

Season	Team	Tot	St	Sb	Snu	Ps	Gls
92-93	Sheffield U.	17	12	5	3	5	0
93-94	Sheffield U.	5	3	2	2	0	0
	Total	22	15	7	5	5	0

HARTSON, John

FULLNAME: John Hartson
DOB: 05-Apr-75, Swansea

Club History	Signed	Fee
Luton Town	12/92	Trainee
Arsenal	1/95	£2.5m
West Ham U.	2/97	£3.2m>£5m
Wimbledon	1/99	£6m

Season	Team	Tot	St	Sb	Snu	Ps	Gls
94-95	Arsenal	15	14	1	0	5	7
95-96	Arsenal	19	15	4	10	4	4
96-97	Arsenal	19	14	5	2	8	3
96-97	West Ham U.	11	11	0	0	0	5
97-98	West Ham U.	32	32	0	0	1	15
98-99	West Ham U.	17	16	1	1	1	4
98-99	Wimbledon	14	12	2	0	6	2
99-00	Wimbledon	16	15	1	0	3	9
	Total	143	129	14	13	28	49

HASLAM, Steven

FULLNAME: Steven Haslam
DOB: 06-Sep-79, Sheffield

Club History	Signed	Fee
Sheffield W.	9/96	Trainee

Season	Team	Tot	St	Sb	Snu	Ps	Gls
98-99	Sheffield W.	2	2	0	2	2	0
99-00	Sheffield W.	23	16	7	7	5	0
	Total	25	18	7	9	7	0

HASSELBAINK, Jimmy

FULLNAME: Jerrel Floyd Hasselbaink
DOB: 27-Mar-72, Surinam

Club History	Signed	Fee
Boavista		
Leeds U.	6/97	£2m

Season	Team	Tot	St	Sb	Snu	Ps	Gls
97-98	Leeds U.	33	30	3	3	7	16
98-99	Leeds U.	36	36	0	0	7	18
	Total	69	66	3	3	14	34

HATELEY, Mark

FULLNAME: Mark Wayne Hateley
DOB: 07-Nov-61, Liverpool

Club History	Signed	Fee
Coventry C.	12/78	Apprentice
Portsmouth	6/83	£220,000
Milan	6/84	£1m
Monaco	7/87	
Rangers	7/90	
QPR	11/95	£1.5m
Leeds U.	8/96	Loan

Season	Team	Tot	St	Sb	Snu	Ps	Gls
95-96	QPR	14	10	4	1	4	2
96-97	Leeds U.	6	5	1	1	1	0
	Total	20	15	5	2	5	2

HAWORTH, Simon

FULLNAME: Simon Haworth
DOB: 30-Mar-77, Cardiff

Club History	Signed	Fee
Cardiff C.	8/95	Trainee
Coventry C.	5/97	£500,000

Season	Team	Tot	St	Sb	Snu	Ps	Gls
97-98	Coventry C.	10	4	6	8	2	0
98-99	Coventry C.	1	1	0	2	0	0
	Total	11	5	6	10	2	0

HAZARD, Micky

FULLNAME: Michael Hazard
DOB: 05-Feb-60, Sunderland

Club History	Signed	Fee
Tottenham H.	2/78	
Chelsea	9/85	£310,000
Portsmouth	1/90	£100,000
Swindon Town	9/90	£130,000
Tottenham H.	11/93	£50,000

Season	Team	Tot	St	Sb	Snu	Ps	Gls
93-94	Swindon T.	9	7	2	0	2	0
93-94	Tottenham H.	17	13	4	0	1	2
94-95	Tottenham H.	11	2	9	2	2	0
	Total	37	22	15	2	5	2

HEALD, Paul

FULLNAME: Paul Andrew Heald
DOB: 20-Sep-68, Wath-on-Dearne

Club History	Signed	Fee
Sheffield U.	6/87	Trainee
Leyton Orient	12/88	Unknown
Coventry C.	3/92	Loan
Swindon Town	3/94	Loan
Wimbledon	8/95	£125,000

Season	Team	Tot	St	Sb	Snu	Ps	Gls
92-93	Crystal P.	0	0	0	15	0	0
93-94	Swindon T.	2	1	1	3	0	0
95-96	Wimbledon	18	18	0	0	1	0
96-97	Wimbledon	2	2	0	23	0	0
97-98	Wimbledon	0	0	0	38	0	0
98-99	Wimbledon	0	0	0	33	0	0
99-00	Wimbledon	1	1	0	15	0	0
	Total	23	22	1	127	1	0

HEANEY, Neil

FULLNAME: Neil Andrew Heaney
DOB: 03-Nov-71, Middlesbrough

Club History	Signed	Fee
Arsenal	11/89	Trainee
Hartlepool U.	1/91	Loan
Cambridge U.	1/92	Loan
Southampton	3/94	£300,000

Season	Team	Tot	St	Sb	Snu	Ps	Gls
92-93	Arsenal	5	3	2	0	0	0
93-94	Arsenal	1	1	0	0	1	0
93-94	Southampton	2	2	0	0	1	0
94-95	Southampton	34	21	13	1	6	2
95-96	Southampton	17	15	2	0	7	2
96-97	Southampton	8	4	4	0	5	1
	Total	67	46	21	1	20	5

HEDMAN, Magnus

FULLNAME: Magnus Hedman
DOB: 19-Mar-77, Sweden

Club History	Signed	Fee
AIK Stockholm		
Coventry C.	7/97	£500,000

Season	Team	Tot	St	Sb	Snu	Ps	Gls
97-98	Coventry C.	14	14	0	23	0	0
98-99	Coventry C.	36	36	0	1	0	0
99-00	Coventry C.	35	35	0	1	0	0
	Total	85	85	0	25	0	0

HEGGEM, Vegard

FULLNAME: Vegard Heggem
DOB: 13-Jul-75, Norway

Club History	Signed	Fee
Rosenborg		
Liverpool	7/98	£3.5m

Season	Team	Tot	St	Sb	Snu	Ps	Gls
98-99	Liverpool	29	27	2	1	8	2
99-00	Liverpool	22	10	12	3	2	1
	Total	51	37	14	4	10	3

HELDER, Glenn

FULLNAME: Glenn Helder
DOB: 28-Oct-68, Leiden, Holland

Club History	Signed	Fee
Vitesse Arnhem	1993	
Arsenal	2/95	£2.3m

Season	Team	Tot	St	Sb	Snu	Ps	Gls
94-95	Arsenal	13	12	1	0	5	0
95-96	Arsenal	24	15	9	5	5	1
96-97	Arsenal	2	0	2	3	0	0
	Total	39	27	12	8	10	1

HELDER, Rodrigues

FULLNAME: Rodrigues Helder
DOB:

Club History	Signed	Fee
Deportivo La Coruna		
Newcastle U.	11/99	Loan

Season	Team	Tot	St	Sb	Snu	Ps	Gls
99-00	Newcastle U.	8	8	0	1	2	1
	Total	8	8	0	1	2	1

HELGUSON, Heidar

FULLNAME: Heidar Helguson
DOB: 28-Aug-77, Iceland

Club History	Signed	Fee
Lillestrom	1/00	£1.5m

Season	Team	Tot	St	Sb	Snu	Ps	Gls
99-00	Watford	16	14	2	0	6	6
	Total	16	14	2	0	6	6

HELMER, Thomas

FULLNAME: Thomas Helmer
DOB: 21-Apr-65, Herford Germany

Club History	Signed	Fee
Bayern Munich		
Sunderland	7/99	Free

Season	Team	Tot	St	Sb	Snu	Ps	Gls
99-00	Sunderland	2	1	1	4	0	0
	Total	2	1	1	4	0	0

HENCHOZ, Stephane

FULLNAME: Stephane Henchoz
DOB: 07-Sep-74, Billens (Switzerland)

Club History	Signed	Fee
Hamburg SV	7/95	
Blackburn R.	7/97	£3m
Liverpool	7/97	£3.5m

Season	Team	Tot	St	Sb	Snu	Ps	Gls
97-98	Blackburn R.	36	36	0	0	4	0
98-99	Blackburn R.	34	34	0	0	4	0
99-00	Liverpool	29	29	0	1	1	0
	Total	99	99	0	1	9	0

HENDRIE, John

FULLNAME: John Hendrie
DOB: 24-Oct-63, Lennoxtown

Club History	Signed	Fee
Coventry C.	5/81	Apprentice
Hereford U.	1/84	Loan
Bradford C.	7/84	Free

Club History	Signed	Fee
Newcastle U.	6/88	£500,000
Leeds U.	6/89	£600,000
Middlesbrough	7/90	£550,000

Season	Team	Tot	St	Sb	Snu	Ps	Gls
92-93	Middlesbrough	32	31	1	0	1	9
95-96	Middlesbrough	13	7	6	4	1	1
96-97	Middlesbrough	0	0	0	8	0	0
97-98	Barnsley	20	7	13	3	3	1
	Total	65	45	20	15	5	11

HENDRIE, Lee

FULLNAME: Lee Andrew Hendrie
DOB: 18-May-77, Birmingham

Club History	Signed	Fee
Aston Villa	5/94	Trainee

Season	Team	Tot	St	Sb	Snu	Ps	Gls
95-96	Aston Villa	3	2	1	5	0	0
96-97	Aston Villa	4	0	4	12	0	0
97-98	Aston Villa	17	13	4	9	2	3
98-99	Aston Villa	32	31	1	0	5	3
99-00	Aston Villa	29	18	11	1	6	1
	Total	85	64	21	27	13	7

HENDRY, Colin

FULLNAME: Edward Colin James Hendry
DOB: 07-Dec-65, Keith

Club History	Signed	Fee
Blackburn R.	3/87	£30,000
Manchester C.	11/89	£700,000
Blackburn R.	11/91	£700,000
Rangers	8/98	£4m
Coventry C.	2/00	£750,000

Season	Team	Tot	St	Sb	Snu	Ps	Gls
92-93	Blackburn R.	41	41	0	0	0	1
93-94	Blackburn R.	23	22	1	0	0	0
94-95	Blackburn R.	38	38	0	0	1	4
95-96	Blackburn R.	33	33	0	0	1	1
96-97	Blackburn R.	35	35	0	0	3	1
97-98	Blackburn R.	34	34	0	0	4	1
99-00	Coventry C.	9	9	0	0	1	0
	Total	213	212	1	0	10	8

HENDRY, John

FULLNAME: John Hendry
DOB: 06-Jan-70, Glasgow

Club History	Signed	Fee
Tottenham H.	7/90	£50,000

Season	Team	Tot	St	Sb	Snu	Ps	Gls
92-93	Tottenham H.	5	2	3	2	2	2
93-94	Tottenham H.	3	0	3	4	0	0
	Total	8	2	6	6	2	2

HENRY, Nick

FULLNAME: Nicholas Ian Henry
DOB: 21-Feb-69, Liverpool

Club History	Signed	Fee
Oldham A.	7/87	Trainee

Season	Team	Tot	St	Sb	Snu	Ps	Gls
92-93	Oldham A.	32	32	0	0	6	6
93-94	Oldham A.	22	22	0	0	2	0
	Total	54	54	0	0	8	6

HENRY, Thierry

FULLNAME: Thierry Henry
DOB: 17-Aug-77, Paris, France

Club History	Signed	Fee
Juventus		
Arsenal	8/99	£10.5m

Season	Team	Tot	St	Sb	Snu	Ps	Gls
99-00	Arsenal	31	26	5	2	13	17
	Total	31	26	5	2	13	17

HESKEY, Emile

FULLNAME: Emile Heskey
DOB: 11-Jan-78, Leicester

Club History	Signed	Fee
Leicester C.	10/95	Trainee
Liverpool	3/00	£11.0m

Season	Team	Tot	St	Sb	Snu	Ps	Gls
94-95	Leicester C.	1	1	0	1	1	0
96-97	Leicester C.	35	35	0	0	4	10
97-98	Leicester C.	35	35	0	0	2	10
98-99	Leicester C.	30	29	1	0	3	6
99-00	Leicester C.	23	23	0	0	1	7
99-00	Liverpool	12	12	0	0	3	3
	Total	136	135	1	1	14	36

HIDEN, Martin

FULLNAME: Martin Hiden
DOB: 11-Mar-73, Stainz, Austria

Club History	Signed	Fee
Rapid Vienna		
Leeds U.	2/98	£1.3m

Season	Team	Tot	St	Sb	Snu	Ps	Gls
97-98	Leeds U.	11	11	0	0	1	0
98-99	Leeds U.	14	14	0	0	1	0
99-00	Leeds U.	1	0	1	4	0	0
	Total	26	25	1	4	2	0

HIGGINBOTHAM, Danny

FULLNAME: Daniel Higginbotham
DOB: 21-Dec-78, Manchester

Club History	Signed	Fee
Manchester U.		

Season	Team	Tot	St	Sb	Snu	Ps	Gls
97-98	Manchester U.	1	0	1	0	0	0
99-00	Manchester U.	3	2	1	1	2	0
	Total	4	2	2	1	2	0

HIGNETT, Craig

FULLNAME: Craig Hignett
DOB: 12-Jan-70, Prescot

Club History	Signed	Fee
Liverpool		Juniors
Crewe Alexandra	5/88	Free
Middlesbrough	11/92	£500,000

Season	Team	Tot	St	Sb	Snu	Ps	Gls
92-93	Middlesbrough	21	18	3	2	7	4
95-96	Middlesbrough	22	17	5	4	4	5
96-97	Middlesbrough	22	19	3	6	6	4
	Total	65	54	11	12	17	13

HILEY, Scott

FULLNAME: Scott Patrick Hiley
DOB: 27-Sep-68, Plymouth

Club History	Signed	Fee
Exeter C.	8/86	Trainee
Birmingham C.	3/93	£100,000
Manchester C.	2/96	£250,000
Southampton	8/98	Free

Season	Team	Tot	St	Sb	Snu	Ps	Gls
95-96	Manchester C.	5	2	3	2	1	0
98-99	Southampton	29	27	2	8	4	0
99-00	Southampton	3	3	0	1	0	0
	Total	37	32	5	11	5	0

HILL, Andy

FULLNAME: Andrew Rowland Hill
DOB: 20-Jan-65, Maltby

Club History	Signed	Fee
Manchester U.	1/83	
Bury	7/84	
Manchester C.	12/90	£200,000

Season	Team	Tot	St	Sb	Snu	Ps	Gls
92-93	Manchester C.	24	23	1	1	1	1
93-94	Manchester C.	17	15	2	0	2	0
94-95	Manchester C.	13	10	3	4	3	0
	Total	54	48	6	5	6	1

HILL, Colin

FULLNAME: Colin Frederick Hill
DOB: 12-Nov-63, Uxbridge

Club History	Signed	Fee
Arsenal	8/81	Apprentice
Maritime		Free
Colchester U.	10/87	Free
Sheffield U.	8/89	£85,000
Leicester C.	3/92	Loan
Leicester C.	7/92	£200,000

Season	Team	Tot	St	Sb	Snu	Ps	Gls
94-95	Leicester C.	24	24	0	0	3	0
96-97	Leicester C.	7	6	1	9	4	0
	Total	31	30	1	9	7	0

HILL, Danny

FULLNAME: Daniel Hill
DOB: 01-Oct-74, Enfield

Club History	Signed	Fee
Tottenham H.	9/92	Trainee

Season	Team	Tot	St	Sb	Snu	Ps	Gls
92-93	Tottenham H.	4	2	2	0	0	0
93-94	Tottenham H.	3	1	2	0	2	0
94-95	Tottenham H.	3	1	2	0	0	0
96-97	Tottenham H.	0	0	0	3	0	0
	Total	10	4	6	3	2	0

HILL, Keith

FULLNAME: Keith John Hill
DOB: 17-May-59, Bolton

Club History	Signed	Fee
Blackburn R.	5/87	Apprentice

Season	Team	Tot	St	Sb	Snu	Ps	Gls
92-93	Blackburn R.	1	0	1	0	0	0
	Total	1	0	1	0	0	0

HILLIER, David

FULLNAME: David Hillier
DOB: 19-Dec-69, Blackheath

Club History	Signed	Fee
Arsenal	2/88	Trainee

Season	Team	Tot	St	Sb	Snu	Ps	Gls
92-93	Arsenal	30	27	3	0	6	1
93-94	Arsenal	15	11	4	1	5	0
94-95	Arsenal	9	5	4	0	1	0
95-96	Arsenal	5	3	2	7	1	0
96-97	Arsenal	2	0	2	0	0	0
	Total	61	46	15	8	13	1

HILLS, John

FULLNAME: John David Hills
DOB: 21-Apr-78, Blackpool

Club History	Signed	Fee
Blackpool	10/95	Trainee
Everton	11/95	£90,000

Season	Team	Tot	St	Sb	Snu	Ps	Gls
96-97	Everton	3	1	2	4	0	0
	Total	3	1	2	4	0	0

HINCHCLIFFE, Andy

FULLNAME: Andrew George Hinchcliffe
DOB: 05-Feb-69, Manchester

Club History	Signed	Fee
Manchester C.	2/86	Apprentice
Everton	7/90	£800,000
Sheffield W.	1/98	£3.0m

Season	Team	Tot	St	Sb	Snu	Ps	Gls
92-93	Everton	25	25	0	1	1	1
93-94	Everton	26	25	1	0	0	0
94-95	Everton	29	28	1	2	2	2
95-96	Everton	28	23	5	2	4	2
96-97	Everton	18	18	0	0	2	1
97-98	Everton	17	15	2	0	1	0
97-98	Sheffield W.	15	15	0	0	0	1
98-99	Sheffield W.	32	32	0	0	2	3
99-00	Sheffield W.	29	29	0	0	2	1
	Total	219	210	9	5	14	11

HIRST, David

FULLNAME: David Eric Hirst
DOB: 07-Dec-67, Cudworth

Club History	Signed	Fee
Barnsley	11/85	Apprentice
Sheffield W.	8/86	£200,000
Southampton	10/97	£2.0m

Season	Team	Tot	St	Sb	Snu	Ps	Gls
92-93	Sheffield W.	22	22	0	0	6	11
93-94	Sheffield W.	7	6	1	0	2	1
94-95	Sheffield W.	15	13	2	0	4	3
95-96	Sheffield W.	30	29	1	0	9	13
96-97	Sheffield W.	25	20	5	0	11	6
97-98	Sheffield W.	6	3	3	0	0	0
97-98	Southampton	28	28	0	0	12	9
98-99	Southampton	2	0	2	0	0	0
	Total	135	121	14	0	44	43

HISLOP, Shaka

FULLNAME: Neil Shaka Hislop
DOB: 22-Feb-69, London

Club History	Signed	Fee
Reading	9/92	
Newcastle U.	8/95	£1.575m
West Ham U.	7/97	Free

Season	Team	Tot	St	Sb	Snu	Ps	Gls
95-96	Newcastle U.	24	24	0	2	1	0
96-97	Newcastle U.	16	16	0	22	0	0
97-98	Newcastle U.	13	13	0	18	0	0
98-99	West Ham U.	37	37	0	0	0	0
99-00	West Ham U.	22	22	0	0	2	0
	Total	112	112	0	42	3	0

HITCHCOCK, Kevin

FULLNAME: Kevin Joseph Hitchcock
DOB: 05-Oct-62, Canning Town

Club History	Signed	Fee
Nottingham F.	8/83	£15,000
Mansfield Town	2/84	Loan
Mansfield Town	6/84	£140,000
Chelsea	3/88	£250,000

Season	Team	Tot	St	Sb	Snu	Ps	Gls
92-93	Chelsea	20	20	0	7	0	0
93-94	Chelsea	2	2	0	40	0	0
94-95	Chelsea	12	11	1	25	0	0
95-96	Chelsea	12	12	0	23	0	0
96-97	Chelsea	12	10	2	9	1	0
97-98	Chelsea	0	0	0	36	0	0
98-99	Chelsea	3	2	1	35	0	0
99-00	Chelsea	0	0	0	3	0	0
	Total	61	57	4	178	1	0

HJELDE, Jon

FULLNAME: Jon Olav Hjelde
DOB: 20-Jul-72, Levanger, Norway

Club History	Signed	Fee
Rosenborg		
Nottingham F.	8/97	£600,000

Season	Team	Tot	St	Sb	Snu	Ps	Gls
98-99	Nottingham F.	17	16	1	4	2	1
	Total	17	16	1	4	2	1

HODDLE, Glenn

FULLNAME: Glenn Hoddle
DOB: 27-Oct-57, Hayes

Club History	Signed	Fee
Tottenham H.	4/75	
Monaco	7/87	£800,000
Swindon Town	8/91	
Chelsea	6/93	£75,000

Season	Team	Tot	St	Sb	Snu	Ps	Gls
93-94	Chelsea	19	16	3	2	1	1

		12	3	9	3	3	0
94-95	Chelsea	12	3	9	3	3	0
	Total	31	19	12	5	4	1

HODGE, Steve

FULLNAME: Stephen Brian Hodge
DOB: 25-Oct-62, Nottingham

Club History	Signed	Fee
Nottingham F.	10/80	
Aston Villa	8/85	£450,000
Tottenham H.	12/86	£650,000
Nottingham F.	8/88	£550,000
Leeds U.	7/91	£900,000
Derby Co.	8/94	Loan
QPR	10/94	£300,000

Season	Team	Tot	St	Sb	Snu	Ps	Gls
92-93	Leeds U.	23	9	14	2	2	2
93-94	Leeds U.	8	7	1	6	1	1
94-95	QPR	15	15	0	0	3	0
95-96	QPR	0	0	0	1	0	0
	Total	46	31	15	9	6	3

HODGES, Glyn

FULLNAME: Glyn Peter Hodges
DOB: 30-Apr-63, Streatham

Club History	Signed	Fee
Wimbledon	2/81	Apprentice
Newcastle U.	7/87	£200,000
Watford	10/87	£300,000
Crystal P.	7/90	£410,000
Sheffield U.	1/91	£450,000
Derby Co.	2/96	Free
Sin Tao (Hong Kong)		
Hull C.	8/97	Free
Nottingham F.	2/98	Free

Season	Team	Tot	St	Sb	Snu	Ps	Gls
92-93	Sheffield U.	31	28	3	1	5	4
93-94	Sheffield U.	31	19	12	1	5	2
98-99	Nottingham F.	5	3	2	0	1	0
	Total	67	50	17	2	11	6

HODGES, Lee

FULLNAME: Lee Leslie Hodges
DOB: 04-Sep-73, Epping

Club History	Signed	Fee
Tottenham H.	2/92	Trainee

Season	Team	Tot	St	Sb	Snu	Ps	Gls
92-93	Tottenham H.	4	0	4	0	0	0
	Total	4	0	4	0	0	0

HODGES, Lee

FULLNAME: Lee Leslie Hodges
DOB: 02-Mar-78, Plaistow

Club History	Signed	Fee
West Ham U.	3/95	Trainee

Season	Team	Tot	St	Sb	Snu	Ps	Gls
96-97	West Ham U.	0	0	0	1	0	0
97-98	West Ham U.	2	0	2	11	0	0
98-99	West Ham U.	1	0	1	3	0	0
	Total	3	0	3	15	0	0

HOGH, Jes

FULLNAME: Jes Hogh
DOB: 07-May-66, Aalborg, Denmark

Club History	Signed	Fee
Fenerbahce		
Chelsea	7/99	£300,000

Season	Team	Tot	St	Sb	Snu	Ps	Gls
99-00	Chelsea	9	6	3	11	2	0
	Total	9	6	3	11	2	0

HOLDEN, Rick

FULLNAME: Richard William
DOB: 09-Sep-64, Skipton

Club History	Signed	Fee
Burnley	3/86	
Halifax Town	9/86	
Watford	3/88	£125,000
Oldham A.	8/89	£165,000
Manchester C.	7/92	£900,000
Oldham A.	10/93	£450,000

Season	Team	Tot	St	Sb	Snu	Ps	Gls
92-93	Manchester C.	41	40	1	0	3	3
93-94	Manchester C.	9	9	0	0	1	0
93-94	Oldham A.	29	28	1	0	1	6
	Total	79	77	2	0	5	9

HOLDSWORTH, Dean

FULLNAME: Dean Christopher Holdsworth
DOB: 08-Nov-68, London

Club History	Signed	Fee
Watford	11/86	Apprentice
Carlisle U.	2/88	Loan
Port Vale	3/88	Loan
Swansea C.	8/88	Loan
Brentford	10/88	Loan
Brentford	9/89	£125,000
Wimbledon	7/92	£720,000
Bolton W.	10/97	£3.5m

Season	Team	Tot	St	Sb	Snu	Ps	Gls
92-93	Wimbledon	36	34	2	0	5	19
93-94	Wimbledon	42	42	0	0	3	17
94-95	Wimbledon	28	27	1	1	10	7
95-96	Wimbledon	33	31	2	0	11	10
96-97	Wimbledon	25	10	15	1	3	5
97-98	Wimbledon	5	4	1	2	4	0
97-98	Bolton W.	20	17	3	0	4	3
	Total	189	165	24	4	40	61

HOLLAND, Chris

FULLNAME: Christopher James Holland
DOB: 11-Sep-75, Whalley

Club History	Signed	Fee
Preston NE		Trainee
Newcastle U.	1/94	£100,000

Season	Team	Tot	St	Sb	Snu	Ps	Gls
93-94	Newcastle U.	3	2	1	0	1	0
95-96	Newcastle U.	0	0	0	2	0	0
	Total	3	2	1	2	1	0

HOLLIGAN, Gavin

FULLNAME: Gavin Victor Holligan
DOB: 13-Jun-80, Lambeth

Club History	Signed	Fee
West Ham U.	11/98	£100,000 from Non League

Season	Team	Tot	St	Sb	Snu	Ps	Gls
98-99	West Ham U.	1	0	1	0	0	0
	Total	1	0	1	0	0	0

HOLLOWAY, Darren

FULLNAME: Darren Holloway
DOB: 03-Oct-77, Bishop Auckland

Club History	Signed	Fee
Sunderland	10/95	Trainee

Season	Team	Tot	St	Sb	Snu	Ps	Gls
96-97	Sunderland	0	0	0	1	0	0
99-00	Sunderland	15	8	7	4	2	0
	Total	15	8	7	5	2	0

HOLLOWAY, Darren

FULLNAME: Darren Holloway
DOB: 03-Oct-77, Bishop Auckland

Club History	Signed	Fee
Sunderland	10/95	Trainee
Carlisle U.	8/97	Loan

Season	Team	Tot	St	Sb	Snu	Ps	Gls
96-97	Sunderland	0	0	0	1	0	0
99-00	Sunderland	15	8	7	4	2	0
	Total	15	8	7	5	2	0

HOLLOWAY, Ian

FULLNAME: Ian Scott Holloway
DOB: 12-Mar-63, Kingswood

Club History	Signed	Fee
Bristol R.	3/81	Apprentice
Wimbledon	7/85	£35,000
Brentford	3/86	£25,000
Torquay U.	1/87	Loan
Bristol R.	8/87	£10,000
QPR	8/91	£230,000

Season	Team	Tot	St	Sb	Snu	Ps	Gls
92-93	QPR	24	23	1	2	1	2
93-94	QPR	25	19	6	1	4	0
94-95	QPR	31	28	3	2	1	1
95-96	QPR	27	26	1	1	1	1
	Total	107	96	11	6	7	4

HOLMES, Matty

FULLNAME: Matthew Jason Holmes
DOB: 01-Aug-69, Luton

Club History	Signed	Fee
Bournemouth	8/88	Trainee
Cardiff C.	3/89	Loan
West Ham U.	8/92	£40,000
Blackburn R.	8/95	£1.2m (inc swap)

Season	Team	Tot	St	Sb	Snu	Ps	Gls
93-94	West Ham U.	34	33	1	1	9	3
94-95	West Ham U.	24	24	0	1	8	0
95-96	Blackburn R.	8	7	1	1	3	1
	Total	66	64	2	3	20	4

HOLMES, Paul

FULLNAME: Paul Holmes
DOB: 18-Feb-68, Wortley

Club History	Signed	Fee
Doncaster R.	2/86	Apprentice
Torquay U.	8/88	£6,000
Birmingham C.	6/92	£40,000
Everton	3/93	£100,000

Season	Team	Tot	St	Sb	Snu	Ps	Gls
92-93	Everton	4	4	0	1	0	0
93-94	Everton	15	15	0	1	2	0
94-95	Everton	1	1	0	1	0	0
95-96	Everton	1	1	0	0	0	0
	Total	21	21	0	3	2	0

HOOPER, Mike

FULLNAME: Michael Dudley Hooper
DOB: 10-Feb-64, Bristol

Club History	Signed	Fee
Bristol C.	1/84	
Wrexham	2/85	
Liverpool	10/85	£40,000
Leicester C.	9/90	Loan
Newcastle U.	9/93	£550,000

Season	Team	Tot	St	Sb	Snu	Ps	Gls
92-93	Liverpool	9	8	1	22	0	0
93-94	Liverpool	0	0	0	8	0	0
93-94	Newcastle U.	19	19	0	15	0	0
94-95	Newcastle U.	6	4	2	36	0	0
	Total	34	31	3	81	0	0

HOPKIN, David

FULLNAME: David Hopkin
DOB: 21-Aug-70, Greenock

Club History	Signed	Fee
Morton	1989	From Port Glasgow
Chelsea	9/92	£300,000
Crystal P.	7/95	£850,000
Leeds U.	7/97	£3.25m

Season	Team	Tot	St	Sb	Snu	Ps	Gls
92-93	Chelsea	4	2	2	0	2	0
93-94	Chelsea	21	12	9	0	7	0
94-95	Chelsea	15	7	8	1	1	1
97-98	Leeds U.	25	22	3	6	8	1
98-99	Leeds U.	34	32	2	0	2	4
99-00	Leeds U.	14	10	4	9	5	1
	Total	113	85	28	16	25	7

HORLOCK, Kevin

FULLNAME: Kevin Horlock
DOB: 01-Nov-72, Plumstead

Club History	Signed	Fee
West Ham U.	7/91	
Swindon Town	8/92	Free

Season	Team	Tot	St	Sb	Snu	Ps	Gls
93-94	Swindon T.	38	32	6	0	4	0
	Total	38	32	6	0	4	0

HORNE, Barry

FULLNAME: Barry Horne
DOB: 18-May-62, St Asaph

Club History	Signed	Fee
Wrexham	6/84	Free NL
Portsmouth	7/87	£60,000
Southampton	3/89	£700,000
Everton	8/92	£695,000

Season	Team	Tot	St	Sb	Snu	Ps	Gls
92-93	Everton	34	34	0	0	5	1
93-94	Everton	32	28	4	3	3	1

		Tot	St	Sb	Snu	Ps	Gls
94-95	Everton	31	31	0	0	0	0
95-96	Everton	26	25	1	5	1	1
99-00	Sheffield W.	7	7	0	2	6	0
	Total	130	125	5	10	15	3

HORNE, Brian

FULLNAME: Brian Horne
DOB: 05-Oct-67, Billericay

Club History	Signed	Fee
Millwall		Apprentice
Watford		Loan
Middlesbrough		Loan

Season	Team	Tot	St	Sb	Snu	Ps	Gls
92-93	Middlesbrough	4	3	1	2	0	0
	Total	4	3	1	2	0	0

HOTTIGER, Marc

FULLNAME: Marc Hottiger
DOB: 07-Nov-67, Lausanne

Club History	Signed	Fee
Sion		
Newcastle U.	8/94	£520,000
Everton	3/96	£700,000

Season	Team	Tot	St	Sb	Snu	Ps	Gls
94-95	Newcastle U.	38	38	0	2	2	1
95-96	Newcastle U.	1	0	1	2	0	0
95-96	Everton	9	9	0	0	1	0
96-97	Everton	8	4	4	22	1	0
	Total	56	51	5	26	3	2

HOUGHTON, Ray

FULLNAME: Raymond James Houghton
DOB: 09-Jan-62, Glasgow

Club History	Signed	Fee
West Ham U.	7/89	Juniors
Fulham	7/82	Free
Oxford U.	9/85	£147,000
Liverpool	10/87	£825,000
Aston Villa	7/92	£900,000
Crystal P.	3/95	£300,000

Season	Team	Tot	St	Sb	Snu	Ps	Gls
92-93	Aston Villa	39	39	0	0	1	3
93-94	Aston Villa	30	25	5	0	4	2
94-95	Aston Villa	26	19	7	1	7	1
94-95	Crystal P.	10	10	0	0	1	2
	Total	105	93	12	1	13	8

HOULT, Russell

FULLNAME: Russell Hoult
DOB: 22-Nov-72, Leicester

Club History	Signed	Fee
Leicester C.	3/91	Trainee
Lincoln C.	8/91	Loan
Bolton W.	11/93	Loan
Lincoln C.	8/94	Loan
Derby Co.	2/95	£300,000

Season	Team	Tot	St	Sb	Snu	Ps	Gls
94-95	Leicester C.	0	0	0	2	0	0
96-97	Derby Co.	32	31	1	5	0	0
97-98	Derby Co.	2	2	0	34	0	0
98-99	Derby Co.	23	23	0	11	1	0
99-00	Derby Co.	10	10	0	11	0	0
	Total	67	66	1	63	1	0

HOWE, Bobby

FULLNAME: Stephen Robert Howe
DOB: 06-Nov-73, Annitsford

Club History	Signed	Fee
Nottingham F.	12/90	Trainee

Season	Team	Tot	St	Sb	Snu	Ps	Gls
95-96	Nottingham F.	9	4	5	10	3	2
96-97	Nottingham F.	1	0	1	6	0	0
	Total	10	4	6	16	3	2

HOWELLS, David

FULLNAME: David Howells
DOB: 15-Dec-67, Guildford

Club History	Signed	Fee
Tottenham H.	1/85	Apprentice
Southampton	7/98	Free

Season	Team	Tot	St	Sb	Snu	Ps	Gls
92-93	Tottenham H.	18	16	2	1	4	1
93-94	Tottenham H.	18	15	3	1	8	1
94-95	Tottenham H.	26	26	0	0	5	1
95-96	Tottenham H.	29	29	0	0	5	3
96-97	Tottenham H.	32	32	0	0	6	2
97-98	Tottenham H.	20	14	6	0	2	0
98-99	Southampton	9	8	1	5	4	1
	Total	152	140	12	7	34	9

HOWEY, Lee

FULLNAME: Lee Matthew Howey
DOB: 01-Apr-69, Sunderland

Club History	Signed	Fee
Sunderland	3/93	Free from NL

Season	Team	Tot	St	Sb	Snu	Ps	Gls
96-97	Sunderland	12	9	3	8	1	0
	Total	12	9	3	8	1	0

HOWEY, Steve

FULLNAME: Stephen Norman Howey
DOB: 26-Oct-71, Sunderland

Club History	Signed	Fee
Newcastle U.	12/89	Trainee

Season	Team	Tot	St	Sb	Snu	Ps	Gls
93-94	Newcastle U.	14	13	1	0	1	0
94-95	Newcastle U.	30	29	1	2	1	1
95-96	Newcastle U.	28	28	0	0	2	1
96-97	Newcastle U.	8	8	0	1	0	1
97-98	Newcastle U.	14	11	3	5	4	0
98-99	Newcastle U.	14	14	0	1	1	0
99-00	Newcastle U.	9	7	2	0	0	0
	Total	117	110	7	9	9	3

HOWIE, Scott

FULLNAME: Scott Howie
DOB: 04-Jan-72, Glasgow

Club History	Signed	Fee
Norwich C.	8/93	£300,000

Season	Team	Tot	St	Sb	Snu	Ps	Gls
93-94	Norwich C.	2	1	1	39	0	0
94-95	Norwich C.	0	0	0	6	0	0
	Total	2	1	1	45	0	0

HOYLAND, Jamie

FULLNAME: Jamie William Hoyland
DOB: 23-Jan-66, Sheffield

Club History	Signed	Fee
Manchester C.	11/83	Apprentice
Bury	7/86	Free
Sheffield U.	7/90	£250,000

Season	Team	Tot	St	Sb	Snu	Ps	Gls
92-93	Sheffield U.	22	15	7	5	1	2
93-94	Sheffield U.	18	17	1	1	2	0
	Total	40	32	8	6	3	2

HREIDARSSON, Hermann

FULLNAME: Hermann Hreidarsson
DOB: 11-Jul-74, Iceland

Club History	Signed	Fee
IVB		
Crystal P.	8/97	£500,000
Brentford	9/98	£850,000
Wimbledon	10/99	£2.5m

Season	Team	Tot	St	Sb	Snu	Ps	Gls
97-98	Crystal P.	30	26	4	7	0	2
99-00	Wimbledon	24	24	0	0	0	1
	Total	54	50	4	7	0	3

HRISTOV, Georgi

FULLNAME: Georgi Hristov
DOB: 20-Jan-76, Bitola, Macedonia

Club History	Signed	Fee
Partizan Belgrade		
Barnsley	7/97	£1.5m

Season	Team	Tot	St	Sb	Snu	Ps	Gls
97-98	Barnsley	23	11	12	10	9	4
	Total	23	11	12	10	9	4

HUCKERBY, Darren

FULLNAME: Darren Carl Huckerby
DOB: 27-Apr-76, Nottingham

Club History	Signed	Fee
Lincoln C.	7/93	Trainee
Newcastle U.	11/95	£400,000
Millwall	9/96	Loan
Coventry C.	11/96	£1m
Leeds U.	8/99	£4.0m

Season	Team	Tot	St	Sb	Snu	Ps	Gls
95-96	Newcastle U.	1	0	1	1	0	0
96-97	Coventry C.	25	21	4	0	7	5
97-98	Coventry C.	34	32	2	0	9	14
98-99	Coventry C.	34	31	3	0	10	9
99-00	Coventry C.	1	1	0	0	1	0
99-00	Leeds U.	33	9	24	2	3	2
	Total	128	94	34	3	30	30

HUGHES, Aaron

FULLNAME: Aaron Hughes
DOB: 08-Nov-79, Magherafelt

Club History	Signed	Fee
Newcastle U.	3/97	Trainee

Season	Team	Tot	St	Sb	Snu	Ps	Gls
96-97	Newcastle U.	0	0	0	1	0	0
97-98	Newcastle U.	4	4	0	11	1	0
98-99	Newcastle U.	14	12	2	10	1	0
99-00	Newcastle U.	27	22	5	9	3	2
	Total	45	38	7	31	5	2

HUGHES, Ceri

FULLNAME: Ceri Morgan Hughes
DOB: 26-Feb-71, Pontypridd

Club History	Signed	Fee
Luton Town	7/89	Trainee
Wimbledon	7/97	£400,000

Season	Team	Tot	St	Sb	Snu	Ps	Gls
97-98	Wimbledon	17	13	4	8	5	1
98-99	Wimbledon	14	8	6	3	3	0

| 99-00 | Wimbledon | 0 | 0 | 0 | 1 | 0 | 0 |
| | Total | 31 | 21 | 10 | 12 | 8 | 1 |

HUGHES, David

FULLNAME: David Robert Hughes
DOB: 01-Feb-78, Wrexham

Club History	Signed	Fee
Aston Villa	5/96	Trainee

Season	Team	Tot	St	Sb	Snu	Ps	Gls
96-97	Aston Villa	7	4	3	5	1	0
97-98	Aston Villa	0	0	0	5	0	0
98-99	Aston Villa	0	0	0	2	0	0
	Total	7	4	3	12	1	0

HUGHES, David

FULLNAME: David Robert Hughes
DOB: 30-Dec-72, St Albans

Club History	Signed	Fee
Southampton	7/91	Juniors

Season	Team	Tot	St	Sb	Snu	Ps	Gls
93-94	Southampton	2	0	2	1	0	0
94-95	Southampton	12	2	10	3	1	2
95-96	Southampton	11	6	5	3	0	1
96-97	Southampton	6	1	5	1	0	0
97-98	Southampton	13	6	7	5	1	0
98-99	Southampton	9	6	3	2	3	0
	Total	53	21	32	15	5	3

HUGHES, Mark

FULLNAME: Leslie Mark Hughes
DOB: 01-Nov-63, Wrexham

Club History	Signed	Fee
Manchester U.	11/80	Apprentice
Barcelona	7/86	£2.5m
Bayern Munich	10/87	Loan
Manchester U.	7/88	£1.5m
Chelsea	7/95	£1.5m
Southampton	7/98	£650,000
Everton	3/00	Free

Season	Team	Tot	St	Sb	Snu	Ps	Gls
92-93	Manchester U.	41	41	0	0	4	15
93-94	Manchester U.	36	36	0	0	5	11
94-95	Manchester U.	34	33	1	0	6	8
95-96	Chelsea	31	31	0	0	3	8
96-97	Chelsea	35	32	3	0	5	8
97-98	Chelsea	29	25	4	4	4	9
98-99	Southampton	32	32	0	0	4	1
99-00	Southampton	20	18	2	6	4	1
99-00	Everton	9	9	0	0	4	1
	Total	267	257	10	10	39	62

HUGHES, Michael

FULLNAME: Michael Eamonn Hughes
DOB: 02-Aug-71, Larne

Club History	Signed	Fee
Manchester C.	8/88	Trainee
Strasbourg	7/92	£450,000
West Ham U.	11/94	Loan/Free
Wimbledon	9/97	£800,000

Season	Team	Tot	St	Sb	Snu	Ps	Gls
94-95	West Ham U.	17	15	2	0	4	2
95-96	West Ham U.	28	28	0	0	4	0
96-97	West Ham U.	33	31	2	0	1	3
97-98	West Ham U.	5	2	3	2	0	0
97-98	Wimbledon	29	29	0	1	2	4
98-99	Wimbledon	30	28	2	0	9	2
99-00	Wimbledon	20	13	7	1	5	3
	Total	162	146	16	4	25	14

HUGHES, Paul

FULLNAME: Paul Hughes
DOB: 19-Apr-76, Hammersmith

Club History	Signed	Fee
Chelsea	7/94	Trainee

Season	Team	Tot	St	Sb	Snu	Ps	Gls
96-97	Chelsea	12	8	4	3	6	2
	Total	12	8	4	3	6	2

HUGHES, Stephen

FULLNAME: Stephen John Hughes
DOB: 18-Sep-76, Reading

Club History	Signed	Fee
Arsenal	7/95	Trainee
Fulham		Loan
Everton	3/00	£3m

Season	Team	Tot	St	Sb	Snu	Ps	Gls
94-95	Arsenal	1	1	0	0	1	0
95-96	Arsenal	1	0	1	4	0	0
96-97	Arsenal	14	9	5	3	6	1
97-98	Arsenal	17	7	10	10	2	2
98-99	Arsenal	13	4	9	7	0	1
99-00	Arsenal	2	1	1	3	1	0
99-00	Everton	11	11	0	0	4	1
	Total	59	33	26	27	14	5

HUMPHREY, John

FULLNAME: John Humphrey
DOB: 31-Jan-61, Paddington

Club History	Signed	Fee
Wolverhampton W.	2/79	Trainee
Charlton A.	7/85	£60,000

Reading	12/93	Loan	
Crystal P.	6/90	£400,000	

Season	Team	Tot	St	Sb	Snu	Ps	Gls
92-93	Crystal P.	32	28	4	2	5	0
94-95	Crystal P.	21	19	2	2	1	0
	Total	53	47	6	4	6	0

HUMPHREYS, Richie

FULLNAME: Richard John Humphreys
DOB: 30-Nov-77, Sheffield

Club History	Signed	Fee
Sheffield W.	2/96	Trainee

Season	Team	Tot	St	Sb	Snu	Ps	Gls
95-96	Sheffield W.	5	1	4	0	1	0
96-97	Sheffield W.	29	14	15	8	11	3
97-98	Sheffield W.	7	2	5	10	2	0
98-99	Sheffield W.	19	10	9	7	4	1
99-00	Sheffield W.	0	0	0	1	0	0
	Total	60	27	33	26	18	4

HUNT, Andy

FULLNAME: Andrew Hunt
DOB: 09-Jun-70, Thurrock

Club History	Signed	Fee
Newcastle U.	1/91	£150,000 from Non League
WBA	3/93	£100,000
Charlton A.	7/98	Free

Season	Team	Tot	St	Sb	Snu	Ps	Gls
98-99	Charlton A.	34	32	2	0	14	6
	Total	34	32	2	0	14	6

HUNT, Jon

FULLNAME: Jonathan Richard Hunt
DOB: 02-Nov-71, Camden

Club History	Signed	Fee
Barnet	1989	Juniors
Southend U.	7/93	Free
Birmingham C.	9/94	£50,000
Derby Co.	7/97	£500,000

Season	Team	Tot	St	Sb	Snu	Ps	Gls
97-98	Derby Co.	19	7	12	7	3	1
98-99	Derby Co.	6	0	6	3	0	1
	Total	25	7	18	10	3	2

HURLOCK, Terry

FULLNAME: Terence Alan Hurlock
DOB: 27-Sep-58, Hackney

Club History	Signed	Fee
Brentford	8/80	£6,000
Reading	2/86	£82,000
Millwall	2/87	£95,000
Rangers	8/90	£325,000
Southampton	9/91	£400,000

Season	Team	Tot	St	Sb	Snu	Ps	Gls
92-93	Southampton	30	30	0	0	6	0
93-94	Southampton	2	2	0	1	2	0
	Total	32	32	0	1	8	0

HURST, Lee

FULLNAME: Lee Jason Hurst
DOB: 21-Sep-70, Nuneaton

Club History	Signed	Fee
Coventry C.	5/89	

Season	Team	Tot	St	Sb	Snu	Ps	Gls
92-93	Coventry C.	35	35	0	0	3	2
	Total	35	35	0	0	3	2

HUTCHISON, Don

FULLNAME: Donald Hutchison
DOB: 09-May-71, Gateshead

Club History	Signed	Fee
Hartlepool U.	3/90	Trainee
Liverpool	11/90	£175,000
West Ham U.	8/94	£1.5m
Sheffield U.	1/96	£1.2m
Everton	2/98	£1.0m

Season	Team	Tot	St	Sb	Snu	Ps	Gls
92-93	Liverpool	31	27	4	2	2	7
93-94	Liverpool	11	6	5	3	3	0
94-95	West Ham U.	23	22	1	1	6	9
95-96	West Ham U.	12	8	4	1	3	2
97-98	Everton	11	11	0	0	0	1
98-99	Everton	33	29	4	0	2	3
99-00	Everton	31	28	3	1	4	6
	Total	152	131	21	8	20	28

HYDE, Graham

FULLNAME: Graham Hyde
DOB: 10-Nov-70, Doncaster

Club History	Signed	Fee
Sheffield W.	5/88	Trainee

Season	Team	Tot	St	Sb	Snu	Ps	Gls
92-93	Sheffield W.	19	14	5	2	3	1
93-94	Sheffield W.	36	27	9	0	2	1
94-95	Sheffield W.	35	33	2	0	5	5
95-96	Sheffield W.	26	14	12	5	4	1
96-97	Sheffield W.	19	15	4	0	3	2
97-98	Sheffield W.	21	14	7	4	10	1
98-99	Sheffield W.	1	0	1	4	0	0
	Total	157	117	40	15	27	11

HYDE, Micah

FULLNAME: Micah Anthony Hyde
DOB: 10-Nov-74, Newham

Club History	Signed	Fee
Cambridge U.	5/93	Trainee
Watford	7/97	£225,000

Season	Team	Tot	St	Sb	Snu	Ps	Gls
99-00	Watford	34	33	1	0	3	3
	Total	34	33	1	0	3	3

HYYPIA, Sami

FULLNAME: Sami Hyypia
DOB: 7-Oct-73, Poorvo, Finland

Club History	Signed	Fee
Finland		
Liverpool	5/99	£3m

Season	Team	Tot	St	Sb	Snu	Ps	Gls
99-00	Liverpool	38	38	0	0	1	2
	Total	38	38	0	0	1	2

ILIC, Sasa

FULLNAME: Sasa Ilic
DOB: 18-Jul-72, Australia

Club History	Signed	Fee
Charlton A.	10/97	Free
West Ham U.	2/00	Loan

Season	Team	Tot	St	Sb	Snu	Ps	Gls
98-99	Charlton A.	23	23	0	6	2	0
99-00	West Ham U.	1	1	0	1	0	0
	Total	24	24	0	7	2	0

IMMEL, Eike

FULLNAME: Eike Immel
DOB: 27-Nov-60, Marburg, Germany

Club History	Signed	Fee
VfB Stuttgart		
Manchester C.	8/95	£400,000

Season	Team	Tot	St	Sb	Snu	Ps	Gls
95-96	Manchester C.	38	38	0	0	0	0
	Total	38	38	0	0	0	0

IMPEY, Andy

FULLNAME: Andrew Rodney Impey
DOB: 30-Sep-71, Hammersmith

Club History	Signed	Fee
QPR	6/90	£35,000 NL
West Ham U.	9/97	£1.3m
Leicester C.	11/98	£1.6m

Season	Team	Tot	St	Sb	Snu	Ps	Gls
92-93	QPR	40	39	1	1	3	2
93-94	QPR	33	31	2	2	3	3
94-95	QPR	40	40	0	0	3	3
95-96	QPR	29	28	1	1	5	3
97-98	West Ham U.	19	19	0	1	5	0
98-99	West Ham U.	8	6	2	3	1	0
98-99	Leicester C.	18	17	1	2	4	0
99-00	Leicester C.	29	28	1	3	6	1
	Total	216	208	8	13	30	12

INCE, Paul

FULLNAME: Paul Emerson Carlyle Ince
DOB: 21-Oct-67, Ilford

Club History	Signed	Fee
West Ham U.	7/85	Apprentice
Manchester U.	8/89	£125,000
Internazionale	6/95	£7.5m
Liverpool	7/97	£4.2m
Middlesbrough	7/00	£1.0m

Season	Team	Tot	St	Sb	Snu	Ps	Gls
92-93	Manchester U.	41	41	0	0	4	6
93-94	Manchester U.	39	39	0	0	2	8
94-95	Manchester U.	36	36	0	0	2	5
97-98	Liverpool	31	31	0	1	1	8
98-99	Liverpool	34	34	0	0	2	6
99-00	Middlesbrough	32	32	0	0	2	3
	Total	213	213	0	1	13	36

INGEBRIGTSEN, Kare

FULLNAME: Kare Ingebrigtsen
DOB: 11-Nov-65, Rosenborg, Norway

Club History	Signed	Fee
Rosenborg		
Manchester C.		

Season	Team	Tot	St	Sb	Snu	Ps	Gls
92-93	Manchester C.	7	2	5	4	1	0
93-94	Manchester C.	8	2	6	0	0	0
	Total	15	4	11	4	1	0

INGESSON, Klas

FULLNAME: Klas Ingesson
DOB: 20-Aug-68, Odeshog, Sweden

Club History	Signed	Fee
PSV Eindhoven		
Sheffield W.	9/94	£800,000

Season	Team	Tot	St	Sb	Snu	Ps	Gls
94-95	Sheffield W.	13	9	4	0	3	2
95-96	Sheffield W.	5	3	2	1	0	0
	Total	18	12	6	1	3	2

INGRAM, Rae

FULLNAME: Rae Ingram
DOB: 06-Dec-74, Manchester

Club History	Signed	Fee
Manchester C.	7/93	Trainee

Season	Team	Tot	St	Sb	Snu	Ps	Gls
93-94	Manchester C.	0	0	0	1	0	0
95-96	Manchester C.	5	5	0	0	1	0
	Total	5	5	0	1	1	0

IRELAND, Simon

FULLNAME: Simon P Ireland
DOB: 23-Nov-71, Barnstaple

Club History	Signed	Fee
Huddersfield Town	7/90	Apprentice
Wrexham	2/92	Loan
Blackburn R.	10/92	£200,000

Season	Team	Tot	St	Sb	Snu	Ps	Gls
92-93	Blackburn R.	1	0	1	0	0	0
	Total	1	0	1	0	0	0

IRONSIDE, Ian

FULLNAME: Ian Ironside
DOB: 08-Mar-64, Sheffield

Club History	Signed	Fee
Scarborough	3/88	Free from Non League
Middlesbrough	8/91	

Season	Team	Tot	St	Sb	Snu	Ps	Gls
92-93	Middlesbrough	12	11	1	24	1	0
	Total	12	11	1	24	1	0

IRVING, Richard

FULLNAME: Richard James Irving
DOB: 10-Sep-75, Halifax

Club History	Signed	Fee
Manchester U.	10/92	Trainee
Nottingham F.	7/95	£75,000

Season	Team	Tot	St	Sb	Snu	Ps	Gls
95-96	Nottingham F.	1	0	1	2	0	0
	Total	1	0	1	2	0	0

IRWIN, Denis

FULLNAME: Joseph Denis Irwin
DOB: 31-Oct-65, Cork

Club History	Signed	Fee
Leeds U.	11/83	Apprentice
Oldham A.	5/86	Free
Manchester U.	6/90	£625,000

Season	Team	Tot	St	Sb	Snu	Ps	Gls
92-93	Manchester U.	40	40	0	0	2	5
93-94	Manchester U.	42	42	0	0	1	2
94-95	Manchester U.	40	40	0	1	0	2
95-96	Manchester U.	31	31	0	0	2	1
96-97	Manchester U.	31	29	2	3	2	1
97-98	Manchester U.	25	23	2	1	4	2
98-99	Manchester U.	29	26	3	1	4	2
99-00	Manchester U.	25	25	0	2	7	3
	Total	263	256	7	8	22	18

ISAIAS, Marques

FULLNAME: Marques Soares Isaias
DOB: 17-Nov-63, Rio de Janeiro, Brazil

Club History	Signed	Fee
Benfica		
Coventry C.	7/95	£500,000

Season	Team	Tot	St	Sb	Snu	Ps	Gls
95-96	Coventry C.	11	9	2	2	1	2
96-97	Coventry C.	1	0	1	1	0	0
	Total	12	9	3	3	1	2

ISMAEL, Valerien

FULLNAME: Valerien Ismael
DOB: 28-Sep-74, France

Club History	Signed	Fee
Strasbourg		
C.Palace	1/98	£2.75m

Season	Team	Tot	St	Sb	Snu	Ps	Gls
97-98	Crystal P.	13	13	0	1	2	0
	Total	13	13	0	1	2	0

IVERSEN, Steffen

FULLNAME: Steffen Iversen
DOB: 10-Nov-76, Oslo (Norway)

Club History	Signed	Fee
Rosenborg	1995	
Tottenham H.	11/96	£2.7m

Season	Team	Tot	St	Sb	Snu	Ps	Gls
96-97	Tottenham H.	16	16	0	0	1	6
97-98	Tottenham H.	13	8	5	0	2	0
98-99	Tottenham H.	27	22	5	1	4	9
99-00	Tottenham H.	36	36	0	0	7	14
	Total	92	82	10	1	14	29

IZZET, Muzzy

FULLNAME: Mustafa Izzet
DOB: 31-Oct-74, Mile End, London

Club History	Signed	Fee
Chelsea	5/93	Trainee

Leicester C.   3/96   £800,000

Season	Team	Tot	St	Sb	Snu	Ps	Gls
95-96	Chelsea	0	0	0	1	0	0
96-97	Leicester C.	35	34	1	0	6	3
97-98	Leicester C.	36	36	0	0	3	4
98-99	Leicester C.	31	31	0	0	4	5
99-00	Leicester C.	32	32	0	0	3	8
	Total	134	133	1	1	16	20

JACKSON, Darren

FULLNAME: Darren Jackson
DOB: 25-Jul-66, Edinburgh

Club History	Signed	Fee
Meadowbank T.	5/85	From Non Laegue
Newcastle U.	10/86	£70,000
Dundee U.	12/88	
Hibernian	7/92	
Celtic	7/97	
Coventry C.	11/98	Loan

Season	Team	Tot	St	Sb	Snu	Ps	Gls
98-99	Coventry C.	3	0	3	3	0	0
	Total	3	0	3	3	0	0

JACKSON, Mark

FULLNAME: Mark Graham Jackson
DOB: 30-Sep-77, Leeds

Club History	Signed	Fee
Leeds U.	7/95	Trainee

Season	Team	Tot	St	Sb	Snu	Ps	Gls
95-96	Leeds U.	1	0	1	0	0	0
96-97	Leeds U.	17	11	6	11	1	0
97-98	Leeds U.	1	0	1	8	0	0
98-99	Leeds U.	0	0	0	1	0	0
	Total	19	11	8	20	1	0

JACKSON, Matt

FULLNAME: Matthew Alan Jackson
DOB: 19-Oct-71, Leeds

Club History	Signed	Fee
Luton Town	7/90	Juniors
Preston NE	3/91	Loan
Everton	10/91	£600,000

Season	Team	Tot	St	Sb	Snu	Ps	Gls
92-93	Everton	27	25	2	2	2	3
93-94	Everton	38	37	1	0	1	0
94-95	Everton	29	26	3	6	2	0
95-96	Everton	14	14	0	1	1	0
96-97	Everton	0	0	0	2	0	0
	Total	108	102	6	11	6	3

JACKSON, Richard

FULLNAME: Richard Jackson
DOB: 18-Apr-80, Whitby

Club History	Signed	Fee
Scarborough U.	3/98	Trainee
Derby Co.		

Season	Team	Tot	St	Sb	Snu	Ps	Gls
98-99	Derby Co.	0	0	0	5	0	0
99-00	Derby Co.	2	0	2	5	0	0
	Total	2	0	2	10	0	0

JACOBS, Wayne

FULLNAME: Wayne Graham Jacobs
DOB: 03-Feb-69, Sheffield

Club History	Signed	Fee
Sheffield W.	1/87	Apprentice
Hull C.	3/88	£27,000
Rotherham U.	8/93	Free
Bradford C.	8/94	Free

Season	Team	Tot	St	Sb	Snu	Ps	Gls
99-00	Bradford C.	24	22	2	2	5	0
	Total	24	22	2	2	5	0

JAMES, David

FULLNAME: David Benjamin James
DOB: 01-Aug-70, Welwyn Garden C.

Club History	Signed	Fee
Watford	7/88	Trainee
Liverpool	7/92	£1m
Aston Villa	6/99	£1.7m

Season	Team	Tot	St	Sb	Snu	Ps	Gls
92-93	Liverpool	29	29	0	7	0	0
93-94	Liverpool	14	13	1	20	0	0
94-95	Liverpool	42	42	0	0	0	0
95-96	Liverpool	38	38	0	0	0	0
96-97	Liverpool	38	38	0	0	0	0
97-98	Liverpool	27	27	0	11	0	0
98-99	Liverpool	26	26	0	12	0	0
99-00	Aston Villa	29	29	0	0	2	0
	Total	243	242	1	50	2	0

JANSEN, Matt

FULLNAME: Matthew Jansen
DOB: 20-Oct-77, Carlisle

Club History	Signed	Fee
Carlisle U.	1/96	Trainee
C.Palace	2/98	£1.0m
Blackburn R.	1/99	£4.1m

Season	Team	Tot	St	Sb	Snu	Ps	Gls
97-98	Crystal P.	8	5	3	0	1	3

		Tot	St	Sb	Snu	Ps	Gls
98-99	Blackburn R.	11	10	1	0	9	3
	Total	19	15	4	0	10	6

JEFFERS, Francis

FULLNAME: Francis Jeffers
DOB: 25-Jan-81, Merseyside

Club History	Signed	Fee
Everton	2/98	Trainee

Season	Team	Tot	St	Sb	Snu	Ps	Gls
97-98	Everton	1	0	1	3	0	0
98-99	Everton	15	11	4	2	5	6
99-00	Everton	21	16	5	2	9	6
	Total	37	27	10	7	14	12

JEFFREY, Mike

FULLNAME: Michael R Jeffrey
DOB: 11-Aug-71, Liverpool

Club History	Signed	Fee
Bolton W.	2/89	
Doncaster R.	3/92	£20,000
Newcastle U.	10/93	£60,000

Season	Team	Tot	St	Sb	Snu	Ps	Gls
93-94	Newcastle U.	2	2	0	1	1	0
94-95	Newcastle U.	0	0	0	1	0	0
	Total	2	2	0	2	1	0

JEMSON, Nigel

FULLNAME: Nigel Bradley Jemson
DOB: 10-Aug-69, Preston

Club History	Signed	Fee
Preston NE	6/87	Trainee
Nottingham F.	3/88	£150,000
Bolton W.	12/88	Loan
Preston NE	3/89	Loan
Sheffield W.	9/91	£800,000

Season	Team	Tot	St	Sb	Snu	Ps	Gls
92-93	Sheffield W.	13	5	8	2	4	0
93-94	Sheffield W.	18	10	8	7	6	5
	Total	31	15	16	9	10	5

JENKINS, Iain

FULLNAME: Iain Jenkins
DOB: 24-Nov-72, Prescot

Club History	Signed	Fee
Everton	6/91	Trainee

Season	Team	Tot	St	Sb	Snu	Ps	Gls
92-93	Everton	1	1	0	0	0	0
	Total	1	1	0	0	0	0

JENKINSON, Leigh

FULLNAME: Leigh Jenkinson
DOB: 09-Jul-69, Thorne

Club History	Signed	Fee
Hull C.	6/87	Trainee
Rotherham U.	9/90	Loan
Coventry C.	3/93	£300,000

Season	Team	Tot	St	Sb	Snu	Ps	Gls
92-93	Coventry C.	5	2	3	2	2	0
93-94	Coventry C.	16	10	6	2	2	0
94-95	Coventry C.	10	9	1	3	4	1
	Total	31	21	10	7	8	1

JENSEN, John

FULLNAME: John Jensen
DOB: 03-May-65, Copenhagen, Denmark

Club History	Signed	Fee
Brondby		
Arsenal	8/92	£1.1m

Season	Team	Tot	St	Sb	Snu	Ps	Gls
92-93	Arsenal	32	29	3	0	9	0
93-94	Arsenal	27	27	0	0	9	0
94-95	Arsenal	24	24	0	0	8	1
95-96	Arsenal	15	13	2	8	4	0
	Total	98	93	5	8	30	1

JERKAN, Nikola

FULLNAME: Nikola Jerkan
DOB: 08-Dec-64, Croatia

Club History	Signed	Fee
Real Oviedo		
Nottingham F.	7/96	£1m

Season	Team	Tot	St	Sb	Snu	Ps	Gls
96-97	Nottingham F.	14	14	0	8	4	0
	Total	14	14	0	8	4	0

JESS, Eoin

FULLNAME: Eoin Jess
DOB: 13-Dec-70, Aberdeen

Club History	Signed	Fee
Rangers		Juniors
Aberdeen	11/87	Free
Coventry C.	2/96	£1.75m

Season	Team	Tot	St	Sb	Snu	Ps	Gls
95-96	Coventry C.	12	9	3	0	1	1
96-97	Coventry C.	27	19	8	7	10	0
	Total	39	28	11	7	11	1

JEVONS, Phil

FULLNAME: Phillip Jevons
DOB: 01-Aug-79, Liverpool

Club History	Signed	Fee
Everton	11/97	Trainee

Season	Team	Tot	St	Sb	Snu	Ps	Gls
97-98	Everton	0	0	0	4	0	0
98-99	Everton	1	0	1	5	0	0
99-00	Everton	3	2	1	6	1	0
	Total	4	2	2	15	1	0

JOACHIM, Julian

FULLNAME: Julian Kevin Joachim
DOB: 12-Sep-74, Peterborough

Club History	Signed	Fee
Leicester C.	9/92	Trainee
Aston Villa	2/96	£1.5m

Season	Team	Tot	St	Sb	Snu	Ps	Gls
94-95	Leicester C.	15	11	4	0	2	3
95-96	Aston Villa	11	4	7	1	3	1
96-97	Aston Villa	15	3	12	21	2	3
97-98	Aston Villa	26	16	10	7	3	8
98-99	Aston Villa	36	29	7	2	7	14
99-00	Aston Villa	33	27	6	0	10	6
	Total	136	90	46	31	27	35

JOBSON, Richard

FULLNAME: Richard Ian Jobson
DOB: 09-May-63, Holderness

Club History	Signed	Fee
Watford	11/82	£22,000
Hull C.	2/85	£40,000
Oldham A.	8/90	£460,000
Leeds U.	10/95	£1m

Season	Team	Tot	St	Sb	Snu	Ps	Gls
92-93	Oldham A.	40	40	0	0	0	2
93-94	Oldham A.	37	37	0	0	1	5
95-96	Leeds U.	12	12	0	0	0	1
96-97	Leeds U.	10	10	0	0	0	0
	Total	99	99	0	0	1	8

JOHANSEN, Martin

FULLNAME: Martin Johansen
DOB: 22-Jul-72, Golstrup (Denmark)

Club History	Signed	Fee
FC Copenhagen		
Coventry C.	7/97	Free

Season	Team	Tot	St	Sb	Snu	Ps	Gls
97-98	Coventry C.	2	0	2	8	0	0
	Total	2	0	2	8	0	0

JOHANSEN, Michael

FULLNAME: Michael Johansen
DOB: 22-Jul-76, Glostrup, Denmark

Club History	Signed	Fee
FC Copenhagen		
Bolton Wanderers	8/96	£1m

Season	Team	Tot	St	Sb	Snu	Ps	Gls
97-98	Bolton W.	17	5	12	16	3	1
	Total	17	5	12	16	3	1

JOHANSEN, Stig

FULLNAME: Stig Johansen
DOB: 13-Jun-72, Norway

Club History	Signed	Fee
Bodo-Glimt		
Southampton	8/97	£600,000

Season	Team	Tot	St	Sb	Snu	Ps	Gls
97-98	Southampton	6	3	3	10	3	0
	Total	6	3	3	10	3	0

JOHNSEN, Erland

FULLNAME: Erland Johnsen
DOB: 05-Apr-67, Fredrikstad, Norway

Club History	Signed	Fee
Chelsea	12/89	£306,000

Season	Team	Tot	St	Sb	Snu	Ps	Gls
92-93	Chelsea	13	13	0	4	0	0
93-94	Chelsea	28	27	1	1	1	1
94-95	Chelsea	33	33	0	0	1	0
95-96	Chelsea	22	18	4	1	2	0
96-97	Chelsea	18	14	4	7	3	0
	Total	114	105	9	13	7	1

JOHNSEN, Ronny

FULLNAME: Jean Ronny Johnsen
DOB: 10-Jun-69, Norway

Club History	Signed	Fee
Besiktas	1996	
Manchester U.	7/96	£1.2m

Season	Team	Tot	St	Sb	Snu	Ps	Gls
96-97	Manchester U.	31	26	5	2	6	0
97-98	Manchester U.	22	18	4	1	7	2
98-99	Manchester U.	22	19	3	4	2	3
99-00	Manchester U.	3	2	1	0	1	0
	Total	78	65	13	7	16	5

JOHNSON, Andy

FULLNAME: Andrew James Johnson
DOB: 02-May-74, Bath

Club History	Signed	Fee
Norwich C.	3/92	Trainee
Nottingham F.	7/97	£2.2m

Season	Team	Tot	St	Sb	Snu	Ps	Gls
92-93	Norwich C.	2	1	1	2	0	1
93-94	Norwich C.	2	0	2	3	0	0
94-95	Norwich C.	7	6	1	0	1	0
98-99	Nottingham F.	28	25	3	0	4	0
	Total	39	32	7	5	5	1

JOHNSON, Damien

FULLNAME: Damien Johnson
DOB: 18-Nov-79, Blackburn

Club History	Signed	Fee
Blackburn R.		Trainee
Nottingham F.		Loan

Season	Team	Tot	St	Sb	Snu	Ps	Gls
97-98	Blackburn R.	0	0	0	0	0	0
98-99	Blackburn R.	21	14	7	5	5	1
	Total	21	14	7	5	5	1

JOHNSON, Gavin

FULLNAME: Gavin Johnson
DOB: 10-Oct-70, Eye

Club History	Signed	Fee
Ipswich Town	2/89	Trainee

Season	Team	Tot	St	Sb	Snu	Ps	Gls
92-93	Ipswich T.	40	39	1	0	3	5
93-94	Ipswich T.	16	16	0	0	3	1
94-95	Ipswich T.	17	14	3	4	1	0
	Total	73	69	4	4	7	6

JOHNSON, Richard

FULLNAME: Richard Mark Johnson
DOB: 27-Apr-74, Kurri Kurri, Australia

Club History	Signed	Fee
Watford	5/92	Trainee

Season	Team	Tot	St	Sb	Snu	Ps	Gls
99-00	Watford	23	20	3	0	3	3
	Total	23	20	3	0	3	3

JOHNSON, Seth

FULLNAME: Seth Johnson
DOB: 12-Mar-79, Birmingham

Club History	Signed	Fee
Crewe Alex.	8/94	Trainee
Derby Co.	5/99	£3m

Season	Team	Tot	St	Sb	Snu	Ps	Gls
99-00	Derby Co.	36	36	0	0	2	1
	Total	36	36	0	0	2	1

JOHNSON, Thomas

FULLNAME: Thomas Johnson
DOB:

Club History	Signed	Fee
Celtic		
Everton	9/99	Loan

Season	Team	Tot	St	Sb	Snu	Ps	Gls
99-00	Everton	3	0	3	3	0	0
	Total	3	0	3	3	0	0

JOHNSON, Tommy

FULLNAME: Thomas Johnson
DOB: 15-Jan-71, Newcastle

Club History	Signed	Fee
Notts Co.	1/89	Trainee
Derby Co.	3/92	£1.3m
Aston Villa	1/95	£2.9m

Season	Team	Tot	St	Sb	Snu	Ps	Gls
94-95	Aston Villa	14	11	3	3	6	4
95-96	Aston Villa	25	19	6	5	4	5
96-97	Aston Villa	20	10	10	6	2	4
	Total	59	40	19	14	12	13

JOHNSTON, Alan

FULLNAME: Alan Johnston
DOB: 14-Dec-73, Glasgow

Club History	Signed	Fee
Heart of Midlothian	1992	From Non League
Rennes	7/96	
Sunderland	3/97	£550,000

Season	Team	Tot	St	Sb	Snu	Ps	Gls
96-97	Sunderland	6	4	2	0	3	1
	Total	6	4	2	0	3	1

JOHNSTON, Mo

FULLNAME: Maurice T Johnston
DOB: 30-Apr-63, Glasgow

Club History	Signed	Fee
Watford	11/83	£200,000
Celtic	10/84	£400,000
Nantes	6/87	£1m
Rangers	7/89	£1.5m
Everton	11/91	£1.5m

Season	Team	Tot	St	Sb	Snu	Ps	Gls
92-93	Everton	13	7	6	1	3	3
	Total	13	7	6	1	3	3

JONES, Cobi

FULLNAME: Cobi N'Gai Jones
DOB: 16-Jun-70, Detroit

Club History	Signed	Fee
US Soccer Federation		
Coventry C.	9/94	£300,000

Season	Team	Tot	St	Sb	Snu	Ps	Gls
94-95	Coventry C.	21	16	5	5	2	2
	Total	21	16	5	5	2	2

JONES, Keith

FULLNAME: Keith Aubrey Jones
DOB: 14-Oct-65, Dulwich

Club History	Signed	Fee
Chelsea	8/83	Apprentice
Brentford	9/87	£40,000
Southend U.	10/91	£175,000
Charlton A.	9/94	£150,000

Season	Team	Tot	St	Sb	Snu	Ps	Gls
98-99	Charlton A.	22	13	9	9	3	1
	Total	22	13	9	9	3	1

JONES, Lee

FULLNAME: Philip Lee Jones
DOB: 29-May-73, Wrexham

Club History	Signed	Fee
Wrexham	7/91	Trainee
Liverpool	3/92	£300,000

Season	Team	Tot	St	Sb	Snu	Ps	Gls
94-95	Liverpool	1	0	1	2	0	0
96-97	Liverpool	2	0	2	15	0	0
	Total	3	0	3	17	0	0

JONES, Matt

FULLNAME: Matthew Graham Jones
DOB: 01-Sep-80, Llanelli

Club History	Signed	Fee
Leeds U.	9/97	Trainee

Season	Team	Tot	St	Sb	Snu	Ps	Gls
97-98	Leeds U.	0	0	0	3	0	0
98-99	Leeds U.	8	3	5	5	1	0
99-00	Leeds U.	11	5	6	9	1	0
	Total	19	8	11	17	2	0

JONES, Paul

FULLNAME: Paul Steven Jones
DOB: 18-Apr-67, Chick

Club History	Signed	Fee
Wolverhampton W.	7/91	£40,000 nl

Stockport Co.	7/96	£60,000					
Southampton	7/97	£900,000					

Season	Team	Tot	St	Sb	Snu	Ps	Gls
97-98	Southampton	38	38	0	0	0	0
98-99	Southampton	31	31	0	1	0	0
99-00	Southampton	31	31	0	0	2	0
	Total	100	100	0	1	2	0

JONES, Rob

FULLNAME: Robert Marc Jones
DOB: 05-Nov-71, Wrexham

Club History	Signed	Fee
Crewe Alexandra	12/88	Trainee
Liverpool	10/91	£300,000

Season	Team	Tot	St	Sb	Snu	Ps	Gls
92-93	Liverpool	30	30	0	1	2	0
93-94	Liverpool	38	38	0	0	1	0
94-95	Liverpool	31	31	0	0	2	0
95-96	Liverpool	33	33	0	0	8	0
96-97	Liverpool	2	2	0	4	1	0
97-98	Liverpool	21	20	1	3	6	0
	Total	155	154	1	8	20	0

JONES, Ryan

FULLNAME: Ryan Anthony Jones
DOB: 23-Jul-73, Sheffield

Club History	Signed	Fee
Sheffield W.	6/91	Trainee

Season	Team	Tot	St	Sb	Snu	Ps	Gls
92-93	Sheffield W.	9	9	0	0	3	0
93-94	Sheffield W.	27	24	3	1	1	6
94-95	Sheffield W.	5	3	2	0	1	0
	Total	41	36	5	1	5	6

JONES, Scott

FULLNAME: Scott Jones
DOB: 01-May-75, Sheffield

Club History	Signed	Fee
Barnsley	2/94	Trainee

Season	Team	Tot	St	Sb	Snu	Ps	Gls
97-98	Barnsley	12	12	0	0	5	1
	Total	12	12	0	0	5	1

JONES, Steve

FULLNAME: Stephen Gary Jones
DOB: 17-Mar-70, Cambridge

Club History	Signed	Fee
West Ham U.	11/92	£22,500
Bournemouth	10/94	150,000
West Ham U.	5/96	

Charlton A.   2/97   £400,000

Season	Team	Tot	St	Sb	Snu	Ps	Gls
93-94	West Ham U.	8	3	5	8	0	2
94-95	West Ham U.	2	1	1	0	0	0
96-97	West Ham U.	8	5	3	3	3	0
98-99	Charlton A.	26	7	19	0	1	1
	Total	44	16	28	11	4	3

JONES, Vinny

FULLNAME: Vincent Peter Jones
DOB: 05-Jan-65, Watford

Club History	Signed	Fee
Wimbledon	11/86	£10,000 from Non League
Leeds U.	6/89	£650,000
Sheffield U.	9/90	£700,000
Chelsea	8/91	£575,000
Wimbledon	9/92	£500,000
QPR	3/98	

Season	Team	Tot	St	Sb	Snu	Ps	Gls
92-93	Chelsea	7	7	0	0	0	1
92-93	Wimbledon	27	27	0	0	2	1
93-94	Wimbledon	33	33	0	0	1	2
94-95	Wimbledon	33	33	0	0	2	3
95-96	Wimbledon	31	27	4	0	1	3
96-97	Wimbledon	29	29	0	0	7	3
97-98	Wimbledon	24	22	2	0	5	0
	Total	184	178	6	0	18	13

JONK, Wim

FULLNAME: Wim Jonk
DOB: 12-Oct-66, Holland

Club History	Signed	Fee
PSV Eindhoven		
Sheffield W.	8/98	£2.5m

Season	Team	Tot	St	Sb	Snu	Ps	Gls
98-99	Sheffield W.	38	38	0	0	6	2
99-00	Sheffield W.	30	29	1	0	6	3
	Total	68	67	1	0	12	5

JOSEPH, Roger

FULLNAME: Roger Anthony Joseph
DOB: 24-Dec-65, Paddington

Club History	Signed	Fee
Brentford	10/84	Free NL
Wimbledon	8/88	£150,000

Season	Team	Tot	St	Sb	Snu	Ps	Gls
92-93	Wimbledon	32	31	1	3	4	0
93-94	Wimbledon	13	13	0	0	0	0
94-95	Wimbledon	3	3	0	0	0	0
	Total	48	47	1	3	4	0

JUDGE, Alan

FULLNAME: Alan G Judge
DOB: 14-May-60, Kingsbury

Club History	Signed	Fee
Luton Town	1/78	Juniors
Reading	9/82	Free
Oxford U.	12/84	£10,000
Lincoln C.	11/85	Loan
Cardiff C.	10/87	Loan
Hereford U.	7/91	Free
Chelsea	7/91	Free
Chelsea	8/94	Non-Contract

Season	Team	Tot	St	Sb	Snu	Ps	Gls
94-95	Chelsea	0	0	0	2	0	0
	Total	0	0	0	2	0	0

JUNINHO

FULLNAME: Junior Oswaldo Giroldo
DOB: 22-Feb-73, Sao Paulo, Brazil

Club History	Signed	Fee
Sao Paulo		From Ituano
Middlesbrough	11/95	£4.75m
Atletico Madrid		
Middlesbrough	9/99	Loan

Season	Team	Tot	St	Sb	Snu	Ps	Gls
95-96	Middlesbrough	21	20	1	1	5	2
96-97	Middlesbrough	35	34	1	0	4	12
99-00	Middlesbrough	28	24	4	2	9	4
	Total	84	78	6	3	18	18

JUPP, Duncan

FULLNAME: Duncan Alan Jupp
DOB: 25-Jan-75, Guildford

Club History	Signed	Fee
Fulham	7/93	Trainee
Wimbledon	6/96	£125,000

Season	Team	Tot	St	Sb	Snu	Ps	Gls
96-97	Wimbledon	6	6	0	9	2	0
97-98	Wimbledon	3	3	0	5	1	0
98-99	Wimbledon	6	3	3	4	0	0
99-00	Wimbledon	9	6	3	6	0	0
	Total	24	18	6	24	3	0

KAAMARK, Pontus

FULLNAME: Pontus Sven Kaamark
DOB: 05-Apr-69, Vasteras (Sweden)

Club History	Signed	Fee
IFK Gothenburg	1990	
Leicester C.	11/95	£840,000

Season	Team	Tot	St	Sb	Snu	Ps	Gls
96-97	Leicester C.	10	9	1	2	3	0
97-98	Leicester C.	35	35	0	1	4	0
98-99	Leicester C.	19	15	4	8	3	0
	Total	64	59	5	11	10	0

KACHLOUL, Hassan

FULLNAME: Hassan Kachloul
DOB: 19-Feb-73, Agadir, Morocco

Club History	Signed	Fee
St Etienne		
Southampton	10/98	£250,000

Season	Team	Tot	St	Sb	Snu	Ps	Gls
98-99	Southampton	22	18	4	3	5	5
99-00	Southampton	32	29	3	1	13	5
	Total	54	47	7	4	18	10

KAMARA, Chris

FULLNAME: Christopher Kamara
DOB: 25-Dec-57, Middlesbrough

Club History	Signed	Fee
Portsmouth	1/76	
Swindon Town	8/77	£20,000
Portsmouth	8/81	£50,000
Brentford	10/81	Part-Exchange
Swindon Town	8/85	£14,500
Stoke C.	7/88	£27,500
Leeds U.	1/90	£150,000
Luton Town	11/91	£150,000
Sheffield U.	12/92	Loan
Middlesbrough	2/93	Loan

Season	Team	Tot	St	Sb	Snu	Ps	Gls
92-93	Middlesbrough	5	3	2	0	1	0
92-93	Sheffield U.	8	6	2	0	1	0
93-94	Sheffield U.	16	15	1	0	4	0
	Total	29	24	5	0	6	0

KANCHELSKIS, Andrei

FULLNAME: Andrei Kanchelskis
DOB: 23-Jan-69, Kirovograd, USSR

Club History	Signed	Fee
Shakhtyor Donezts		
Manchester U.	3/91	£1.1m
Everton	7/95	£5m

Season	Team	Tot	St	Sb	Snu	Ps	Gls
92-93	Manchester U.	27	14	13	10	9	3
93-94	Manchester U.	31	28	3	4	7	6
94-95	Manchester U.	30	25	5	0	3	14
95-96	Everton	32	32	0	0	3	16
96-97	Everton	20	20	0	0	5	4
	Total	140	119	21	14	27	43

KANOUTE, Frederic

FULLNAME: Frederic Kanoute
DOB: 02-Sep-77

Club History	Signed	Fee
Lyon		
West Ham U.	3/00	Loan

Season	Team	Tot	St	Sb	Snu	Ps	Gls
99-00	West Ham U.	8	8	0	0	0	2
	Total	8	8	0	0	0	2

KANU, Nwankwo

FULLNAME: Nwankwo Kanu
DOB: 01-Aug-76, Owerri, Nireria

Club History	Signed	Fee
Internazionale	1996	
Arsenal	1/99	£4.5m

Season	Team	Tot	St	Sb	Snu	Ps	Gls
98-99	Arsenal	12	5	7	2	3	6
99-00	Arsenal	31	24	7	1	9	12
	Total	43	29	14	3	12	18

KARELSE, John

FULLNAME: John Karelse
DOB:

Club History	Signed	Fee
NAC Breda		
Newcastle U.	8/99	£800,000

Season	Team	Tot	St	Sb	Snu	Ps	Gls
99-00	Newcastle U.	3	3	0	5	0	0
	Total	3	3	0	5	0	0

KARL, Stefan

FULLNAME: Stefan Karl
DOB: 03-Feb-70, Hohemm-Oelsen

Club History	Signed	Fee
Manchester C.		

Season	Team	Tot	St	Sb	Snu	Ps	Gls
93-94	Manchester C.	6	4	2	3	3	1
	Total	6	4	2	3	3	1

KAVANAGH, Graham

FULLNAME: Graham Anthony Kavanagh
DOB: 03-Dec-73, Dublin

Club History	Signed	Fee
Middlesbrough	8/91	From Home Farm

Season	Team	Tot	St	Sb	Snu	Ps	Gls
92-93	Middlesbrough	10	6	4	3	3	0
95-96	Middlesbrough	7	6	1	3	3	1
	Total	17	12	5	6	6	1

KAVELASHVILI, Mikhail

FULLNAME: Mikhail Kavelashvili
DOB: 22-Jul-71, Tbilisi, Georgia

Club History	Signed	Fee
Sporting Vladikavkaz		
Manchester C.	3/96	£1.4m

Season	Team	Tot	St	Sb	Snu	Ps	Gls
95-96	Manchester C.	4	3	1	2	2	1
	Total	4	3	1	2	2	1

KEANE, Robbie

FULLNAME: Robert David Keane
DOB: 08-Jul-80, Dublin

Club History	Signed	Fee
Wolverhampton W.	7/97	Trainee
Coventry C.	8/99	£6.0m

Season	Team	Tot	St	Sb	Snu	Ps	Gls
99-00	Coventry C.	31	30	1	0	4	12
	Total	31	30	1	0	4	12

KEANE, Roy

FULLNAME: Roy Maurice Keane
DOB: 10-Aug-71, Cork

Club History	Signed	Fee
Cobh Ramblers		
Nottingham F.	6/90	£10,000
Manchester U.	7/93	£3.75m

Season	Team	Tot	St	Sb	Snu	Ps	Gls
92-93	Nottingham F.	40	40	0	0	2	6
93-94	Manchester U.	37	34	3	0	1	5
94-95	Manchester U.	25	23	2	0	4	2
95-96	Manchester U.	29	29	0	0	2	6
96-97	Manchester U.	21	21	0	0	1	2
97-98	Manchester U.	9	9	0	0	0	2
98-99	Manchester U.	35	33	2	0	6	2
99-00	Manchester U.	29	28	1	0	5	5
	Total	225	217	8	0	21	30

KEARTON, Jason

FULLNAME: Jason Brett Kearton
DOB: 09-Jul-69, Ipswich, Australia

Club History	Signed	Fee
Brisbane Lions		
Everton	10/88	Free

Season	Team	Tot	St	Sb	Snu	Ps	Gls
92-93	Everton	5	2	3	37	0	0
93-94	Everton	0	0	0	41	0	0
94-95	Everton	1	1	0	32	0	0
95-96	Everton	0	0	0	25	0	
	Total	6	3	3	135	0	0

KEELEY, John

FULLNAME: John Keeley
DOB: 27-Jul-61, Plaistow

Club History	Signed	Fee
Southend U.	7/79	Apprentice
Brighton & HA	8/86	From Non League
Oldham A.	8/90	

Season	Team	Tot	St	Sb	Snu	Ps	Gls
92-93	Oldham A.	1	1	0	28	0	0
	Total	1	1	0	28	0	0

KEIZERWEERD, Orpheo

FULLNAME: Orpheo Keizerweerd
DOB: 21-Nov-68,

Club History	Signed	Fee
Rodez (France)		
Oldham A.	3/93	Trial

Season	Team	Tot	St	Sb	Snu	Ps	Gls
92-93	Oldham A.	1	0	1	1	0	0
	Total	1	0	1	1	0	0

KELLER, Kasey

FULLNAME: Kasey Keller
DOB: 27-Nov-69, Washington USA

Club History	Signed	Fee
Millwall	02/92	Free
Leicester C.	08/96	£900,000

Season	Team	Tot	St	Sb	Snu	Ps	Gls
96-97	Leicester C.	31	31	0	0	0	0
97-98	Leicester C.	33	33	0	1	0	0
98-99	Leicester C.	36	36	0	2	2	0
	Total	100	100	0	3	2	0

KELLER, Marc

FULLNAME: Marc Keller
DOB: 14-Jan-68, Colmar, France

Club History	Signed	Fee
Racing Strasbourg, Karlsruhe		
West Ham U.	4/98	Free

Season	Team	Tot	St	Sb	Snu	Ps	Gls
98-99	West Ham U.	21	17	4	11	5	5
99-00	West Ham U.	23	19	4	12	5	0
	Total	44	36	8	23	10	5

KELLY, Alan

FULLNAME: Alan Thomas Kelly
DOB: 11-Aug-68, Preston

Club History	Signed	Fee
Preston NE	9/85	Apprentice

Sheffield U.   7/92   £150,000

Season	Team	Tot	St	Sb	Snu	Ps	Gls
92-93	Sheffield U.	33	32	1	9	2	0
93-94	Sheffield U.	30	29	1	6	2	0
	Total	63	61	2	15	2	0

KELLY, David

FULLNAME: David Thomas Kelly
DOB: 25-Nov-65, Birmingham

Club History	Signed	Fee
Walsall	12/83	Free from NL
West Ham U.	8/88	£600,000
Leicester C.	3/90	£300,000
Newcastle U.	12/91	£250,000
Wolverhampton W.	6/93	£750,000
Sunderland	9/95	£1m

Season	Team	Tot	St	Sb	Snu	Ps	Gls
96-97	Sunderland	24	23	1	3	3	0
	Total	24	23	1	3	3	0

KELLY, Gary

FULLNAME: Garry Kelly
DOB: 09-Jul-74, Drogheda

Club History	Signed	Fee
Leeds U.	9/91	Free Home Farm

Season	Team	Tot	St	Sb	Snu	Ps	Gls
93-94	Leeds U.	42	42	0	0	0	0
94-95	Leeds U.	42	42	0	0	3	0
95-96	Leeds U.	34	34	0	0	1	0
96-97	Leeds U.	36	34	2	0	2	2
97-98	Leeds U.	34	34	0	0	0	0
99-00	Leeds U.	31	28	3	2	0	0
	Total	219	214	5	2	6	2

KENNA, Jeff

FULLNAME: Jeffrey Jude Kenna
DOB: 27-Aug-70, Dublin

Club History	Signed	Fee
Southampton	4/89	Trainee
Blackburn R.	3/95	£1.5m

Season	Team	Tot	St	Sb	Snu	Ps	Gls
92-93	Southampton	29	27	2	8	1	2
93-94	Southampton	41	40	1	0	1	2
94-95	Southampton	28	28	0	0	1	0
94-95	Blackburn R.	9	9	0	0	0	1
95-96	Blackburn R.	32	32	0	0	1	0
96-97	Blackburn R.	37	37	0	0	3	0
97-98	Blackburn R.	37	37	0	0	0	0
98-99	Blackburn R.	23	22	1	1	1	0
	Total	236	232	4	9	8	5

KENNEDY, Mark

FULLNAME: Mark Kennedy
DOB: 15-May-76, Dublin, Republic of
Ireland

Club History	Signed	Fee
Millwall	5/92	Trainee
Liverpool	3/95	£1.5m
Wimbledon	3/98	£1.75m

Season	Team	Tot	St	Sb	Snu	Ps	Gls
94-95	Liverpool	6	4	2	0	1	0
95-96	Liverpool	4	1	3	10	0	0
96-97	Liverpool	5	0	5	20	0	0
97-98	Liverpool	1	0	1	1	0	0
97-98	Wimbledon	4	4	0	0	2	0
98-99	Wimbledon	17	7	10	15	2	0
	Total	37	16	21	46	5	0

KENNEDY, Peter

FULLNAME: Peter Henry James Kennedy
DOB: 13-Sep-73, Lurhan, N.Ireland

Club History	Signed	Fee
Portadown		
Notts Co.	8/96	£100,000
Watford	7/97	£130,000

Season	Team	Tot	St	Sb	Snu	Ps	Gls
99-00	Watford	18	17	1	0	3	1
	Total	18	17	1	0	3	1

KENNY, Billy

FULLNAME: William Aiden Kenny
DOB: 19-Sep-73, Liverpool

Club History	Signed	Fee
Everton	6/92	Trainee

Season	Team	Tot	St	Sb	Snu	Ps	Gls
92-93	Everton	17	16	1	1	4	1
	Total	17	16	1	1	4	1

KEOWN, Martin

FULLNAME: Martin Raymond Keown
DOB: 24-Jul-66, Oxford

Club History	Signed	Fee
Arsenal	1/84	Apprentice
Brighton & HA	2/85	Loan
Aston Villa	6/86	£200,000
Everton	8/89	£750,000
Arsenal	2/93	£2m

Season	Team	Tot	St	Sb	Snu	Ps	Gls
92-93	Everton	13	13	0	0	0	0
92-93	Arsenal	16	15	1	0	0	0
93-94	Arsenal	33	23	10	3	3	0

		Tot	St	Sb	Snu	Ps	Gls
94-95	Arsenal	31	24	7	2	3	1
95-96	Arsenal	34	34	0	0	3	0
96-97	Arsenal	33	33	0	0	2	1
97-98	Arsenal	18	18	0	0	1	0
98-99	Arsenal	34	34	0	0	3	1
99-00	Arsenal	27	27	0	2	1	1
	Total	239	221	18	7	16	4

KERNAGHAN, Alan

FULLNAME: Alan Nigel Kernaghan
DOB: 25-Apr-67, Otley

Club History	Signed	Fee
Middlesbrough	3/85	Apprentice
Charlton A.	1/91	Loan
Manchester C.	9/93	£1.6m

Season	Team	Tot	St	Sb	Snu	Ps	Gls
92-93	Middlesbrough	22	22	0	1	1	2
94-95	Manchester C.	22	18	4	2	0	1
95-96	Manchester C.	6	4	2	10	1	0
	Total	50	44	6	13	2	3

KERR, David

FULLNAME: David William Kerr
DOB: 06-Sep-74, Dumfries

Club History	Signed	Fee
Manchester C.	9/91	Trainee

Season	Team	Tot	St	Sb	Snu	Ps	Gls
92-93	Manchester C.	1	0	1	1	0	0
93-94	Manchester C.	2	2	0	0	0	0
94-95	Manchester C.	2	2	0	0	2	0
95-96	Manchester C.	1	0	1	0	0	0
	Total	6	4	2	1	2	0

KERR, Dylan

FULLNAME: Dylan Kerr
DOB: 14-Jan-67, Valetta

Club History	Signed	Fee
Leeds U.		

Season	Team	Tot	St	Sb	Snu	Ps	Gls
92-93	Leeds U.	5	3	2	0	0	0
	Total	5	3	2	0	0	0

KERSLAKE, David

FULLNAME: David Kerslake
DOB: 19-Jun-66, Stepney

Club History	Signed	Fee
QPR	6/83	Apprentice
Swindon Town	11/89	£110,000
Leeds U.	3/93	£500,000
Tottenham H.	9/93	£450,000

Season	Team	Tot	St	Sb	Snu	Ps	Gls
92-93	Leeds U.	8	8	0	0	1	0
93-94	Tottenham H.	17	16	1	1	1	0
94-95	Tottenham H.	18	16	2	0	1	0
95-96	Tottenham H.	2	2	0	0	1	0
96-97	Tottenham H.	0	0	0	3	0	0
	Total	45	42	3	4	4	0

KETSBAIA, Temuri

FULLNAME: Temuri Ketsbaia
DOB: 18-Mar-68, Gale, Georgia

Club History	Signed	Fee
AEK Athens		
Newcastle U.	7/97	Free

Season	Team	Tot	St	Sb	Snu	Ps	Gls
97-98	Newcastle U.	31	16	15	4	4	3
98-99	Newcastle U.	26	14	12	2	8	5
99-00	Newcastle U.	21	11	10	6	8	0
	Total	78	41	37	12	20	8

KEWELL, Harry

FULLNAME: Harold Kewell
DOB: 22-Sep-78, Australia

Club History	Signed	Fee
Australia	Academy of Sport	
Leeds U.	12/95	

Season	Team	Tot	St	Sb	Snu	Ps	Gls
95-96	Leeds U.	2	2	0	0	2	0
96-97	Leeds U.	1	0	1	4	0	0
97-98	Leeds U.	29	26	3	3	3	5
98-99	Leeds U.	38	36	2	0	9	6
99-00	Leeds U.	36	36	0	0	4	10
	Total	106	100	6	7	18	21

KEY, Lance

FULLNAME: Lance William Key
DOB: 13-May-68, Kettering

Club History	Signed	Fee
Sheffield W.	4/90	£10,000 from Non League
Oldham A.	10/93	Loan

Season	Team	Tot	St	Sb	Snu	Ps	Gls
92-93	Sheffield W.	0	0	0	1	0	0
93-94	Sheffield W.	0	0	0	10	0	0
93-94	Oldham A.	2	2	0	2	0	0
94-95	Sheffield W.	0	0	0	27	0	0
	Total	2	2	0	40	0	0

KHARINE, Dmitri

FULLNAME: Dmitri Kharine
DOB: 16-Aug-68, Moscow

413

Club History	Signed	Fee
CSKA Moscow		
Chelsea	12/92	£200,000

Season	Team	Tot	St	Sb	Snu	Ps	Gls
92-93	Chelsea	5	5	0	8	1	0
93-94	Chelsea	40	40	0	0	0	0
94-95	Chelsea	31	31	0	3	1	0
95-96	Chelsea	26	26	0	7	0	0
96-97	Chelsea	5	5	0	0	1	0
97-98	Chelsea	10	10	0	1	0	0
98-99	Chelsea	1	1	0	1	0	0
	Total	118	118	0	20	3	0

KILBANE, Kevin

FULLNAME: Kevin Daniel Kilbane
DOB: 01-Feb-77, Preston

Club History	Signed	Fee
Preston NE	7/95	Trainee
WBA	6/97	£1m
Sunderland	12/99	£2.2m

Season	Team	Tot	St	Sb	Snu	Ps	Gls
99-00	Sunderland	20	17	3	1	3	1
	Total	20	17	3	1	3	1

KILCLINE, Brian

FULLNAME: Brian Kilcline
DOB: 07-May-62, Nottingham

Club History	Signed	Fee
Notts Co.	5/80	
Coventry C.	6/84	£60,000
Oldham A.	8/91	£400,000
Newcastle U.	2/92	£250,000
Swindon Town		

Season	Team	Tot	St	Sb	Snu	Ps	Gls
93-94	Newcastle U.	1	1	0	8	0	0
93-94	Swindon T.	10	10	0	0	0	0
	Total	11	11	0	8	0	0

KILGANNON, Sean

FULLNAME: Sean Kilgannon
DOB:

Club History	Signed	Fee
Middlesbrough	8/99	Trainee

Season	Team	Tot	St	Sb	Snu	Ps	Gls
99-00	Middlesbrough	1	0	1	4	0	0
	Total	1	0	1	4	0	0

KIMBLE, Alan

FULLNAME: Alan Frank Kimble
DOB: 06-Aug-66, Dagenham

Club History	Signed	Fee
Charlton A.	8/84	Juniors
Exeter C.	8/85	Loan
Cambridge U.	8/86	Free
Wimbledon	7/93	£175,000

Season	Team	Tot	St	Sb	Snu	Ps	Gls
93-94	Wimbledon	14	14	0	0	1	0
94-95	Wimbledon	26	26	0	0	2	0
95-96	Wimbledon	31	31	0	0	1	0
96-97	Wimbledon	31	28	3	4	0	0
97-98	Wimbledon	25	23	2	4	0	0
98-99	Wimbledon	26	22	4	11	4	0
99-00	Wimbledon	28	24	4	4	4	0
	Total	181	168	13	23	12	0

KINDER, Vladimir

FULLNAME: Vladimir Kinder
DOB: 04-Mar-69, Bratislava

Club History	Signed	Fee
Slovan Bratislava	1990	
Middlesbrough	1/97	£1m

Season	Team	Tot	St	Sb	Snu	Ps	Gls
96-97	Middlesbrough	6	4	2	5	1	1
98-99	Middlesbrough	5	0	5	8	1	2
	Total	11	4	7	13	2	3

KING, Ledley

FULLNAME: Ledley King
DOB: 12-Oct-80, London

Club History	Signed	Fee
Tottenham H.		Trainee

Season	Team	Tot	St	Sb	Snu	Ps	Gls
98-99	Tottenham H.	0	0	0	2	0	0
99-00	Tottenham H.	3	2	1	5	0	0
	Total	3	2	1	7	0	0

KING, Phil

FULLNAME: Philip Geoffrey King
DOB: 28-Jan-67, Bristol

Club History	Signed	Fee
Exeter C.	1/85	
Torquay U.	7/86	£3,000
Swindon Town	2/87	£15,000
Sheffield Wed	11/89	£400,000
Notts Co.	10/93	Loan
Aston Villa	8/94	£250,000

Season	Team	Tot	St	Sb	Snu	Ps	Gls
92-93	Sheffield W.	12	11	1	0	4	1
93-94	Sheffield W.	10	7	3	0	1	0
94-95	Aston Villa	16	13	3	2	4	0
	Total	38	31	7	2	9	1

KINKLADZE, Georgi

FULLNAME: Georgiou Kinkladze
DOB: 06-Nov-73, Tbilisi, Georgia

Club History	Signed	Fee
Dinamo Tbilisi		
Manchester C.	8/96	£2m
Ajax		£5m
Derby Co.	11/99	Loan
Derby Co.	4/00	£3m

Season	Team	Tot	St	Sb	Snu	Ps	Gls
95-96	Manchester C.	37	37	0	0	4	4
99-00	Derby Co.	17	12	5	1	7	1
	Total	54	49	5	1	11	5

KINSELLA, Mark

FULLNAME: Mark Anthony Kinsella
DOB: 12-Aug-72, Dublin

Club History	Signed	Fee
Colchester U.	8/89	Free
Charlton A.	9/96	£150,000

Season	Team	Tot	St	Sb	Snu	Ps	Gls
98-99	Charlton A.	38	38	0	0	8	3
	Total	38	38	0	0	8	3

KITSON, Paul

FULLNAME: Paul Kitson
DOB: 09-Jan-71, Peterlee

Club History	Signed	Fee
Leicester C.	12/88	Trainee
Derby Co.	3/92	£1.3m
Newcastle U.	9/94	£2.25m
West Ham U.	2/97	£2.3m

Season	Team	Tot	St	Sb	Snu	Ps	Gls
94-95	Newcastle U.	26	24	2	0	5	8
95-96	Newcastle U.	7	2	5	5	2	2
96-97	Newcastle U.	3	0	3	9	0	0
96-97	West Ham U.	14	14	0	0	2	8
97-98	West Ham U.	13	12	1	1	7	4
98-99	West Ham U.	17	13	4	1	4	3
99-00	West Ham U.	10	4	6	10	2	0
	Total	90	69	21	26	22	25

KIWOMYA, Chris

FULLNAME: Christopher Mark Kiwomya
DOB: 02-Dec-69, Huddersfield

Club History	Signed	Fee
Ipswich Town	3/87	Trainee
Arsenal	1/95	£1.55m

Season	Team	Tot	St	Sb	Snu	Ps	Gls
92-93	Ipswich T.	38	38	0	0	2	10
93-94	Ipswich T.	37	34	3	0	4	5
94-95	Ipswich T.	15	13	2	0	2	3
94-95	Arsenal	14	5	9	0	0	3
96-97	Arsenal	0	0	0	0	0	0
	Total	104	90	14	0	8	21

KJELDBJERG, Jakob

FULLNAME: Jakob Kjeldbjerg
DOB: 21-Oct-69, Denmark

Club History	Signed	Fee
Silkeborg		
Chelsea	8/93	£400,000

Season	Team	Tot	St	Sb	Snu	Ps	Gls
93-94	Chelsea	29	29	0	1	0	1
94-95	Chelsea	23	23	0	1	2	1
95-96	Chelsea	0	0	0	0	0	0
	Total	52	52	0	2	2	2

KLINSMANN, Jurgen

FULLNAME: Jurgen Klinsmann
DOB: 30-Jul-64, Goppingen

Club History	Signed	Fee
Monaco		
Tottenham H.	8/94	£2m
Bayern Munich	7/95	
Tottenham H.	12/97	£175,000

Season	Team	Tot	St	Sb	Snu	Ps	Gls
94-95	Tottenham H.	41	41	0	0	1	22
97-98	Tottenham H.	15	15	0	0	2	9
	Total	56	56	0	0	3	31

KONCHESKY, Paul

FULLNAME: Paul Martyn Konchesky
DOB: 15-May-81, Barking

Club History	Signed	Fee
Charlton A.		Trainee

Season	Team	Tot	St	Sb	Snu	Ps	Gls
98-99	Charlton A.	2	1	1	6	0	0
	Total	2	1	1	6	0	0

KONJIC, Muhamed

FULLNAME: Muhamed Konjic
DOB: 14-May-70, Bosnia-Herzegovina

Club History	Signed	Fee
AS Monaco		
Coventry C.	1/99	£2m

Season	Team	Tot	St	Sb	Snu	Ps	Gls
98-99	Coventry C.	4	3	1	7	1	0

| 99-00 | Coventry C. | 4 | 3 | 1 | 12 | 1 | 0 |
| | Total | 8 | 6 | 2 | 19 | 2 | 0 |

KORSTEN, Willem

FULLNAME: Willem Korsten
DOB: 21-Jan-75, Boxtel, Holland

Club History	Signed	Fee
Vitesse Arnhem		
Leeds U.	2/99	Loan
Tottenham H.	7/99	

Season	Team	Tot	St	Sb	Snu	Ps	Gls
98-99	Leeds U.	7	4	3	0	1	2
99-00	Tottenham H.	9	4	5	9	2	0
	Total	16	8	8	9	3	2

KOVACEVIC, Darko

FULLNAME: Darko Kovacevic
DOB: 18-Nov-73, Yugoslavia

Club History	Signed	Fee
Rec Star Belgrade		
Sheffield W.	10/95	£2m

Season	Team	Tot	St	Sb	Snu	Ps	Gls
95-96	Sheffield W.	16	8	8	0	5	4
	Total	16	8	8	0	5	4

KOZLUK, Rob

FULLNAME: Robert Kozluk
DOB: 05-Aug-77, Mansfield

Club History	Signed	Fee
Derby Co.	2/96	Trainee

Season	Team	Tot	St	Sb	Snu	Ps	Gls
97-98	Derby Co.	9	6	3	11	2	0
98-99	Derby Co.	7	3	4	1	2	0
	Total	16	9	7	12	4	0

KOZMA, Istvan

FULLNAME: Istvan Kozma
DOB: 03-Dec-64, Paszto, Hungary

Club History	Signed	Fee
Bordeaux		
Dunfirmline A.		
Liverpool		

Season	Team	Tot	St	Sb	Snu	Ps	Gls
92-93	Liverpool	1	0	1	1	0	0
	Total	1	0	1	1	0	0

KRIZAN, Ales

FULLNAME: Ales Krizan
DOB: 25-Jul-71, Slovenia

Club History	Signed	Fee
Marbor Branik		
Barnsley	7/97	£400,000

Season	Team	Tot	St	Sb	Snu	Ps	Gls
97-98	Barnsley	12	12	0	4	5	0
	Total	12	12	0	4	5	0

KRUSZYNSKI, Detsi

FULLNAME: Zbigniew Kruszynski
DOB: 14-Oct-61, Divschav

Club History	Signed	Fee
FC Homburg		
Wimbledon	12/88	
Brentford	3/92	Loan
Peterborough U.		
Coventry C.		

Season	Team	Tot	St	Sb	Snu	Ps	Gls
93-94	Coventry C.	2	1	1	0	0	0
	Total	2	1	1	0	0	0

KUBICKI, Dariusz

FULLNAME: Dariusz Kubicki
DOB: 06-Jun-63, Warsaw, Poland

Club History	Signed	Fee
Legia Warsaw		
Aston Villa	8/91	£200,000
Sunderland	3/94	£100,000

Season	Team	Tot	St	Sb	Snu	Ps	Gls
92-93	Aston Villa	0	0	0	2	0	0
93-94	Aston Villa	2	1	1	0	1	0
96-97	Sunderland	29	28	1	2	3	0
	Total	31	29	2	4	4	0

KVARME, Bjorn Tore

FULLNAME: Bjorn Tore Kvarme
DOB: 17-Jul-72, Trondheim

Club History	Signed	Fee
Rosenborg	1990	
Liverpool	1/97	Free

Season	Team	Tot	St	Sb	Snu	Ps	Gls
96-97	Liverpool	15	15	0	0	2	0
97-98	Liverpool	23	22	1	8	3	0
98-99	Liverpool	7	2	5	12	1	0
	Total	45	39	6	20	6	0

LAKE, Mike

FULLNAME: Michael Charles Lake
DOB: 16-Nov-66, Manchester

Club History	Signed	Fee
Sheffield U.	10/89	£60,000

Season	Team	Tot	St	Sb	Snu	Ps	Gls
92-93	Sheffield U.	6	6	0	0	1	0
	Total	Z6	6	0	0	1	0

LAKE, Paul

FULLNAME: Paul Andrew Lake
DOB: 28-Nov-69, Denton

Club History	Signed	Fee
Manchester C.	5/87	

Season	Team	Tot	St	Sb	Snu	Ps	Gls
92-93	Manchester C.	2	2	0	0	2	0
	Total	2	2	0	0	2	0

LAMA, Bernard

FULLNAME: Bernard Lama
DOB: 17-Apr-63, Sain Symphorien

Club History	Signed	Fee
PSG		
West Ham U.	12/97	Loan

Season	Team	Tot	St	Sb	Snu	Ps	Gls
97-98	West Ham U.	12	12	0	6	0	0
	Total	12	12	0	6	0	0

LAMBOURDE, Bernard

FULLNAME: Bernard Lambourde
DOB: 11-May-71, Guadeloupe

Club History	Signed	Fee
Bordeaux		
Chelsea	6/97	£1.5m

Season	Team	Tot	St	Sb	Snu	Ps	Gls
97-98	Chelsea	7	5	2	8	0	0
98-99	Chelsea	17	12	5	7	2	0
99-00	Chelsea	15	12	3	6	1	2
	Total	39	29	10	21	3	2

LAMPARD, Frank

FULLNAME: Frank Lampard Jnr
DOB: 21-Jun-78, Romford

Club History	Signed	Fee
West Ham U.		Trainee

Season	Team	Tot	St	Sb	Snu	Ps	Gls
95-96	West Ham U.	2	0	2	0	0	0
96-97	West Ham U.	13	3	10	15	2	0
97-98	West Ham U.	31	27	4	2	0	4
98-99	West Ham U.	38	38	0	0	0	5
99-00	West Ham U.	34	34	0	0	0	7
	Total	118	102	16	17	2	16

LAMPTEY, Nii

FULLNAME: Nii Odartey Lamptey
DOB: 10-Dec-74, Accra, Ghana

Club History	Signed	Fee
Anderlecht		
Aston Villa	8/94	£1m
Udinese		
Coventry C.	8/95	£150,000

Season	Team	Tot	St	Sb	Snu	Ps	Gls
94-95	Aston Villa	6	1	5	1	0	0
95-96	Coventry C.	6	3	3	3	2	0
	Total	12	4	8	4	2	0

LAUDRUP, Brian

FULLNAME: Brian Laudrup
DOB: 22-Feb-69, Vienna, Austria

Club History	Signed	Fee
Fiorentina	1992	
Rangers	1994	
Chelsea	6/98	Free

Season	Team	Tot	St	Sb	Snu	Ps	Gls
98-99	Chelsea	7	5	2	0	3	0
	Total	7	5	2	0	3	0

LAUNDERS, Brian

FULLNAME: Brian Terrance Launders
DOB: 08-Jan-76, Dublin

Club History	Signed	Fee
C.Palace	9/93	From NL
Crewe Alexandra	8/96	Free
BV Veendam	7/97	Free
Derby Co.	9/98	Loan

Season	Team	Tot	St	Sb	Snu	Ps	Gls
94-95	Crystal P.	2	1	1	1	1	0
98-99	Derby Co.	1	0	1	2	0	0
	Total	3	1	2	3	1	0

LAURENT, Pierre

FULLNAME: Pierre Laurent
DOB: 13-Dec-70, Tulle, France

Club History	Signed	Fee
SC Bastia	1994	
Leeds U.	3/97	£500,000

Season	Team	Tot	St	Sb	Snu	Ps	Gls
96-97	Leeds U.	4	2	2	2	1	0
97-98	Leeds U.	0	0	0	3	0	0
	Total	4	2	2	5	1	0

LAURSEN, Jacob

FULLNAME: Jacob Laursen
DOB: 06-Oct-71, Denmark

Club History	Signed	Fee
Silkeborg		
Derby Co.	7/96	£500,000

Season	Team	Tot	St	Sb	Snu	Ps	Gls
96-97	Derby Co.	36	35	1	0	7	1
97-98	Derby Co.	28	27	1	0	5	1
98-99	Derby Co.	37	37	0	0	5	0
99-00	Derby Co.	36	36	0	0	4	1
	Total	137	135	2	0	21	3

LAWRENCE, Jamie

FULLNAME: James Hubert Lawrence
DOB: 08-Mar-70, Balham

Club History	Signed	Fee
Sunderland	10/93	From NL
Doncaster R.	3/94	£20,000
Leicester C.	1/95	£125,000
Bradford C.	6/97	£50,000

Season	Team	Tot	St	Sb	Snu	Ps	Gls
94-95	Leicester C.	17	9	8	1	1	1
96-97	Leicester C.	15	2	13	16	0	0
99-00	Bradford C.	23	19	4	2	5	3
	Total	55	30	25	19	6	4

LAWS, Brian

FULLNAME: Brian Laws
DOB: 14-Oct-61, Wallsend

Club History	Signed	Fee
Burnley	10/79	Amateur
Huddersfield Town	8/83	£10,000
Middlesbrough	3/85	£30,000
Nottingham F.	7/88	£120,000

Season	Team	Tot	St	Sb	Snu	Ps	Gls
92-93	Nottingham F.	33	32	1	1	1	0
	Total	33	32	1	1	1	0

LAZARIDIS, Stan

FULLNAME: Stanley Lazaridis
DOB: 16-Aug-72, Perth, W.Australia

Club History	Signed	Fee
West Adelaide		
West Ham U.	8/95	£300,000

Season	Team	Tot	St	Sb	Snu	Ps	Gls
95-96	West Ham U.	4	2	2	0	1	0
96-97	West Ham U.	22	13	9	3	6	1
97-98	West Ham U.	28	27	1	0	3	2
98-99	West Ham U.	15	11	4	9	3	0
	Total	69	53	16	12	13	3

LE SAUX, Graeme

FULLNAME: Graeme Pierre Le Saux
DOB: 17-Oct-68, Jersey

Club History	Signed	Fee
St Pauls, Jersey		
Chelsea	12/87	Free
Blackburn R.	3/93	Swap
Chelsea	8/97	£5m

Season	Team	Tot	St	Sb	Snu	Ps	Gls
92-93	Chelsea	14	10	4	2	4	0
92-93	Blackburn R.	9	9	0	0	0	0
93-94	Blackburn R.	41	40	1	0	1	2
94-95	Blackburn R.	39	39	0	0	0	3
95-96	Blackburn R.	15	14	1	0	2	1
96-97	Blackburn R.	26	26	0	0	1	1
97-98	Chelsea	26	26	0	0	1	1
98-99	Chelsea	31	30	1	0	6	0
99-00	Chelsea	8	6	2	0	3	0
	Total	209	200	9	2	18	8

LE TISSIER, Matthew

FULLNAME: Matthew Paul Le Tissier
DOB: 14-Oct-68, Guernsey

Club History	Signed	Fee
Southampton	10/86	Apprentice

Season	Team	Tot	St	Sb	Snu	Ps	Gls
92-93	Southampton	40	40	0	0	7	15
93-94	Southampton	38	38	0	0	2	25
94-95	Southampton	41	41	0	0	3	20
95-96	Southampton	34	34	0	0	1	7
96-97	Southampton	31	25	6	0	8	13
97-98	Southampton	26	25	1	2	15	11
98-99	Southampton	30	20	10	0	7	7
99-00	Southampton	18	9	9	6	6	3
	Total	258	232	26	8	49	101

LEABURN, Carl

FULLNAME: Carl Winston Leaburn
DOB: 30-Mar-69, Lewisham

Club History	Signed	Fee
Charlton A.	4/87	Apprentice
Wimbledon	1/98	£300,000

Season	Team	Tot	St	Sb	Snu	Ps	Gls
97-98	Wimbledon	16	15	1	0	3	4
98-99	Wimbledon	22	14	8	3	8	0
99-00	Wimbledon	18	5	13	5	5	0
	Total	56	34	22	8	16	4

LEBOEUF, Franck

FULLNAME: Franck Leboeuf
DOB: 22-Jan-68, Marseille

Club History	Signed		Fee			
Strasbourg	1991					
Chelsea	7/96		£2.5m			

Season	Team	Tot	St	Sb	Snu	Ps	Gls
96-97	Chelsea	26	26	0	1	1	6
97-98	Chelsea	32	32	0	0	4	5
98-99	Chelsea	33	33	0	0	3	4
99-00	Chelsea	28	28	0	2	4	2
	Total	119	119	0	3	12	17

LEE, Dave

FULLNAME: David Mark Lee
DOB: 05-Nov-67, Blackburn

Club History	Signed	Fee
Bury	8/86	
Southampton	8/91	£350,000
Bolton W.	11/92	£300,000

Season	Team	Tot	St	Sb	Snu	Ps	Gls
92-93	Southampton	1	0	1	0	0	0
95-96	Bolton W.	18	9	9	2	2	1
	Total	19	9	10	2	2	1

LEE, David

FULLNAME: David John Lee
DOB: 26-Nov-69, Kingswood

Club History	Signed	Fee
Chelsea	7/88	

Season	Team	Tot	St	Sb	Snu	Ps	Gls
92-93	Chelsea	25	23	2	2	0	2
93-94	Chelsea	7	3	4	2	0	1
94-95	Chelsea	14	9	5	6	0	0
95-96	Chelsea	31	29	2	0	2	1
96-97	Chelsea	1	1	0	5	1	1
97-98	Chelsea	1	1	0	2	0	0
	Total	79	66	13	17	3	5

LEE, Jason

FULLNAME: Jason Benedict Lee
DOB: 09-May-71, Newham

Club History	Signed	Fee
Charlton A.	6/89	Trainee
Stockport Co.	2/91	Loan
Lincoln C.	3/91	£35,000
Southend U.	7/93	undisclosed
Nottingham F.	3/94	£200,000

Season	Team	Tot	St	Sb	Snu	Ps	Gls
94-95	Nottingham F.	22	5	17	11	0	3
95-96	Nottingham F.	28	21	7	2	3	8
96-97	Nottingham F.	13	5	8	4	0	1
	Total	63	31	32	17	3	12

LEE, Robert

FULLNAME: Robert Martin Lee
DOB: 01-Feb-66, West Ham

Club History	Signed	Fee
Charlton A.	7/83	
Newcastle U.	9/92	£700,000

Season	Team	Tot	St	Sb	Snu	Ps	Gls
93-94	Newcastle U.	41	41	0	0	3	6
94-95	Newcastle U.	35	35	0	0	6	9
95-96	Newcastle U.	36	36	0	0	3	8
96-97	Newcastle U.	33	32	1	0	7	5
97-98	Newcastle U.	28	26	2	0	3	4
98-99	Newcastle U.	26	20	6	0	2	0
99-00	Newcastle U.	30	30	0	0	9	0
	Total	229	220	9	0	33	32

LEESE, Lars

FULLNAME: Lars Leese
DOB: 18-Aug-69, Germany

Club History	Signed	Fee
Bayer Laverkusen		
Barnsley	7/97	£250,000

Season	Team	Tot	St	Sb	Snu	Ps	Gls
97-98	Barnsley	9	8	1	23	0	0
	Total	9	8	1	23	0	0

LENNON, Neil

FULLNAME: Neil Francis Lennon
DOB: 25-Jun-71, Lurgan

Club History	Signed	Fee
Manchester C.	8/89	Trainee
Crewe Alexandra	9/90	Free
Leicester C.	2/96	£750,000

Season	Team	Tot	St	Sb	Snu	Ps	Gls
96-97	Leicester C.	35	35	0	0	0	1
97-98	Leicester C.	37	37	0	0	1	2
98-99	Leicester C.	37	37	0	0	2	1
99-00	Leicester C.	31	31	0	0	1	1
	Total	140	140	0	0	4	5

LEONHARDSEN, Oyvind

FULLNAME: Oyvind Leonhardsen
DOB: 17-Aug-70, Norway

Club History	Signed	Fee
Rosenborg	1992	
Wimbledon	1/95	£660,000
Liverpool	6/97	£3.5m
Tottenham H.	8/99	£3.0m

Season	Team	Tot	St	Sb	Snu	Ps	Gls
94-95	Wimbledon	20	18	2	0	3	4
95-96	Wimbledon	29	28	1	0	6	4
96-97	Wimbledon	27	27	0	1	8	5
97-98	Liverpool	28	27	1	0	7	6
98-99	Liverpool	9	7	2	4	2	1
99-00	Tottenham H.	22	21	1	0	5	4
	Total	135	128	7	5	31	24

LEWIS, Neil

FULLNAME: Neil Anthony Lewis
DOB: 28-Jun-74, Wolverhampton

Club History	Signed	Fee
Leicester C.	7/92	Trainee

Season	Team	Tot	St	Sb	Snu	Ps	Gls
94-95	Leicester C.	16	13	3	0	2	0
96-97	Leicester C.	6	4	2	2	4	0
	Total	22	17	5	2	6	0

LIDDELL, Andy

FULLNAME: Andrew Mark Liddell
DOB: 28-Jun-73, Leeds

Club History	Signed	Fee
Barnsley	7/91	Trainee

Season	Team	Tot	St	Sb	Snu	Ps	Gls
97-98	Barnsley	26	13	13	5	11	1
	Total	26	13	13	5	11	1

LIDDLE, Craig

FULLNAME: Craig George Liddle
DOB: 21-Oct-71, Chester le Street

Club History	Signed	Fee	
Middlesbrough	7/94	Free from Non League	

Season	Team	Tot	St	Sb	Snu	Ps	Gls
95-96	Middlesbrough	13	13	0	3	0	0
96-97	Middlesbrough	5	5	0	5	0	0
	Total	18	18	0	8	0	0

LIGHTBOURNE, Kyle

FULLNAME: Kyle Lavince Lightbourne
DOB: 29-Sep-68, Bermuda

Club History	Signed	Fee
Scarborough	11/12	
Walsall	9/93	Free
Coventry C.	7/97	£500,000

Season	Team	Tot	St	Sb	Snu	Ps	Gls
97-98	Coventry C.	7	1	6	8	1	0
	Total	7	1	6	8	1	0

LILLEY, Derek

FULLNAME: Derek Lilley
DOB: 09-Feb-74, Paisley

Club History	Signed	Fee
Greenock Morton		
Leeds U.	3/97	£500,000

Season	Team	Tot	St	Sb	Snu	Ps	Gls
96-97	Leeds U.	6	4	2	0	0	0
97-98	Leeds U.	12	0	12	13	0	1
98-99	Leeds U.	2	0	2	1	0	0
	Total	20	4	16	14	0	1

LIMPAR, Anders

FULLNAME: Anders Limpar
DOB: 24-Sep-65, Sweden

Club History	Signed	Fee
Arsenal	8/90	£1m
Everton	3/94	£1.6m

Season	Team	Tot	St	Sb	Snu	Ps	Gls
92-93	Arsenal	23	12	11	0	8	2
93-94	Arsenal	10	9	1	2	3	0
93-94	Everton	9	9	0	0	1	0
94-95	Everton	27	19	8	5	5	2
95-96	Everton	28	22	6	5	9	3
96-97	Everton	2	1	1	10	1	0
	Total	99	72	27	22	27	7

LING, Martin

FULLNAME: Martin Ling
DOB: 15-Jul-66, West Ham

Club History	Signed	Fee
Exeter C.	1/84	
Swindon T.	7/86	£25,000
Southend U.	10/86	£15,000
Mansfield T.	1/91	Loan
Swindon T.	3/91	Loan
Swindon T.	7/91	£15,000

Season	Team	Tot	St	Sb	Snu	Ps	Gls
93-94	Swindon T.	33	29	4	2	9	1
	Total	33	29	4	2	9	1

LINIGHAN, Andy

FULLNAME: Andrew Linighan
DOB: 18-Jun-62, Hartlepool

Club History	Signed	Fee
Hartlepool U.	9/80	
Leeds U.	5/84	£200,000
Oldham A.	1/86	£65,000
Norwich C.	3/88	£350,000
Arsenal	6/90	£1.25m
Crystal P.	1/97	£110,000

Season	Team	Tot	St	Sb	Snu	Ps	Gls
92-93	Arsenal	21	19	2	1	0	2
93-94	Arsenal	21	20	1	3	0	0
94-95	Arsenal	20	13	7	7	2	2
95-96	Arsenal	18	17	1	4	1	0
96-97	Arsenal	11	10	1	11	1	1
97-98	Crystal P.	26	26	0	5	3	0
Total		117	105	12	31	7	5

LINIGHAN, Brian

FULLNAME: Brian Linighan
DOB: 11-Nov-73, Hartlepool

Club History	Signed	Fee
Sheffield W.		Trainee

Season	Team	Tot	St	Sb	Snu	Ps	Gls
93-94	Sheffield W.	1	1	0	1	1	0
96-97	Sheffield W.	0	0	0	1	0	0
Total		1	1	0	2	1	0

LINIGHAN, David

FULLNAME: David Linighan
DOB: 09-Jan-65, Hartlepool

Club History	Signed	Fee
Hartlepool U.	3/82	
Derby Co.	8/86	£25,000
Shrewsbury Town	12/86	£30,000
Ipswich Town	6/88	£300,000

Season	Team	Tot	St	Sb	Snu	Ps	Gls
92-93	Ipswich T.	42	42	0	0	2	1
93-94	Ipswich T.	38	38	0	2	3	3
94-95	Ipswich T.	32	31	1	0	5	0
Total		112	111	1	2	10	4

LISBIE, Kevin

FULLNAME: Kevin Anthony Lisbie
DOB: 17-Oct-78, Hackney

Club History	Signed	Fee
Charlton A.	5/96	Trainee

Season	Team	Tot	St	Sb	Snu	Ps	Gls
98-99	Charlton A.	1	0	1	0	0	0
Total		1	0	1	0	0	0

LITTLEJOHN, Adrian

FULLNAME: Adrian Sylvester Littlejohn
DOB: 26-Sep-70, Wolverhampton

Club History	Signed	Fee
Walsall	5/89	Free
Sheffield U.	8/91	Free

Season	Team	Tot	St	Sb	Snu	Ps	Gls
92-93	Sheffield U.	27	18	9	2	4	8

93-94	Sheffield U.	19	12	7	1	5	3
Total		46	30	16	3	9	11

LIVINGSTONE, Steve

FULLNAME: Stephen Livingstone
DOB: 08-Sep-68, Middlesbrough

Club History	Signed	Fee
Coventry C.	7/86	
Blackburn R.	1/91	£450,000
Chelsea	3/93	Swap

Season	Team	Tot	St	Sb	Snu	Ps	Gls
92-93	Blackburn R.	2	1	1	3	0	0
92-93	Chelsea	1	0	1	0	0	0
Total		3	1	2	3	0	0

LJUNGBERG, Freddy

FULLNAME: Fredrik Ljungberg
DOB: 16-Apr-77, Halmstad

Club History	Signed	Fee
BK Halmstad		
Arsenal	9/98	£3m

Season	Team	Tot	St	Sb	Snu	Ps	Gls
98-99	Arsenal	16	10	6	1	8	1
99-00	Arsenal	26	22	4	1	7	6
Total		42	32	10	2	15	7

LOMAS, Steve

FULLNAME: Stephen Martin Lomas
DOB: 18-Jan-74, Hanover

Club History	Signed	Fee
Manchester C.	1/91	Trainee
West Ham U.	3/97	£1.6m

Season	Team	Tot	St	Sb	Snu	Ps	Gls
93-94	Manchester C.	23	17	6	6	3	0
94-95	Manchester C.	20	18	2	1	0	2
95-96	Manchester C.	33	32	1	1	5	3
96-97	West Ham U.	7	7	0	0	1	0
97-98	West Ham U.	33	33	0	0	0	2
98-99	West Ham U.	30	30	0	0	2	1
99-00	West Ham U.	25	25	0	0	2	1
Total		171	162	9	8	13	9

LOMBARDO, Attilio

FULLNAME: Attilio Lombardo
DOB: 06-Jan-66, Maria la Fossa, Italy

Club History	Signed	Fee
Juventus		
Crystal P.	8/97	£1.6m

Season	Team	Tot	St	Sb	Snu	Ps	Gls
97-98	Crystal P.	24	21	3	0	9	5
Total		24	21	3	0	9	5

LOUIS-JEAN, Matthieu

FULLNAME: Matthieu Louis-Jean
DOB: 22-Feb-72, Mont St Aigan

Club History	Signed	Fee
Le Harve		
Nottingham F.	9/98	Loan

Season	Team	Tot	St	Sb	Snu	Ps	Gls
98-99	Nottingham F.	15	14	1	2	1	0
	Total	15	14	1	2	1	0

LOWE, David

FULLNAME: David Anthony Lowe
DOB: 30-Aug-65, Liverpool

Club History	Signed	Fee
Wigan A.	6/83	Apprentice
Ipswich Town	6/87	£80,000
Port Vale	3/93	Loan
Leicester C.	7/92	£250,000

Season	Team	Tot	St	Sb	Snu	Ps	Gls
94-95	Leicester C.	29	19	10	2	5	8
	Total	29	19	10	2	5	8

LUKIC, John

FULLNAME: Jovan Lukic
DOB: 11-Dec-60, Chesterfield

Club History	Signed	Fee
Leeds U.	12/78	
Arsenal	7/83	£50,000
Leeds U.	6/90	£1m
Arsenal	7/96	Free

Season	Team	Tot	St	Sb	Snu	Ps	Gls
92-93	Leeds U.	39	39	0	2	0	0
93-94	Leeds U.	20	20	0	22	0	0
94-95	Leeds U.	42	42	0	0	0	0
95-96	Leeds U.	28	28	0	0	1	0
96-97	Arsenal	15	15	0	20	0	0
97-98	Arsenal	0	0	0	14	0	0
98-99	Arsenal	0	0	0	13	0	0
99-00	Arsenal	0	0	0	15	0	0
	Total	144	144	0	86	1	0

LUMSDON, Chris

FULLNAME: Christopher Lumsdon
DOB: 15-Dec-79, Newcastle

Club History	Signed	Fee
Sunderland	7/97	Trainee

Season	Team	Tot	St	Sb	Snu	Ps	Gls
99-00	Sunderland	1	1	0	0	1	0
	Total	1	1	0	0	1	0

LUND, Andreas

FULLNAME: Andreas Lund
DOB: 07-May-75, Norway

Club History	Signed	Fee
Molde		
Wimbledon	2/00	£2.8m

Season	Team	Tot	St	Sb	Snu	Ps	Gls
99-00	Wimbledon	12	10	2	1	5	2
	Total	12	10	2	1	5	2

LUNDEKVAM, Claus

FULLNAME: Claus Lundekvam
DOB: 22-Feb-73, Norway

Club History	Signed	Fee
SK Brann	1993	
Southampton	9/96	£400,000

Season	Team	Tot	St	Sb	Snu	Ps	Gls
96-97	Southampton	29	28	1	1	3	0
97-98	Southampton	31	31	0	0	3	0
98-99	Southampton	33	30	3	2	2	0
99-00	Southampton	27	25	2	5	2	0
	Total	120	114	6	8	10	0

LUZHNY, Oleg

FULLNAME: Oleg Luzhny
DOB: 05-Aug-68, Ukraine

Club History	Signed	Fee
Dynamo Kiev		
Arsenal	5/99	£1.8m

Season	Team	Tot	St	Sb	Snu	Ps	Gls
99-00	Arsenal	21	16	5	5	1	0
	Total	21	16	5	5	1	0

LYDERSEN, Pal

FULLNAME: Pal Lydersen
DOB: 10-Sep-65, Norway

Club History	Signed	Fee
Arsenal	9/91	£500,000

Season	Team	Tot	St	Sb	Snu	Ps	Gls
92-93	Arsenal	8	7	1	4	3	0
93-94	Arsenal	0	0	0	1	0	0
	Total	8	7	1	5	3	0

LYTTLE, Des

FULLNAME: Desmond Lyttle
DOB: 24-Sep-71, Wolverhampton

Club History	Signed	Fee
Leicester C.	9/90	Trainee

Swansea C.	7/92	£12,500					
Nottingham F.	7/93	£350,000					

Season	Team	Tot	St	Sb	Snu	Ps	Gls
94-95	Nottingham F.	38	38	0	0	1	0
95-96	Nottingham F.	33	32	1	3	3	1
96-97	Nottingham F.	32	30	2	4	4	1
98-99	Nottingham F.	10	5	5	6	2	0
99-00	Watford	11	11	0	2	2	0
	Total	124	116	8	15	12	2

MABBUTT, Gary

FULLNAME: Gary Vincent Mabbutt
DOB: 23-Aug-61, Bristol

Club History	Signed	Fee
Bristol R.	1/79	Apprentice
Tottenham H.	8/82	£105,000

Season	Team	Tot	St	Sb	Snu	Ps	Gls
92-93	Tottenham H.	29	29	0	0	0	2
93-94	Tottenham H.	29	29	0	0	1	0
94-95	Tottenham H.	36	33	3	3	1	0
95-96	Tottenham H.	32	32	0	0	1	0
96-97	Tottenham H.	1	1	0	0	1	0
97-98	Tottenham H.	11	8	3	11	2	0
	Total	138	132	6	14	6	2

MacLAREN, Ross

FULLNAME: Ross MacLaren
DOB: 14-Apr-62, Edinburgh

Club History	Signed	Fee
Rangers		
Shrewsbury T.	8/80	Free
Derby Co.	7/85	£67,000
Swindon T.	8/88	£165,000

Season	Team	Tot	St	Sb	Snu	Ps	Gls
93-94	Swindon T.	12	10	2	3	1	0
	Total	12	10	2	3	1	0

MADAR, Michael

FULLNAME: Michael Madar
DOB: 08-May-68, Paris

Club History	Signed	Fee
Deportivo La Coruna		
Everton	12/97	Free

Season	Team	Tot	St	Sb	Snu	Ps	Gls
97-98	Everton	17	15	2	0	11	6
98-99	Everton	2	2	0	1	2	0
	Total	19	17	2	1	13	6

MADDISON, Neil

FULLNAME: Neil Stanley Maddison
DOB: 02-Oct-69, Darlington

Club History	Signed	Fee
Southampton	4/88	Trainee
Middlesbrough	10/97	£250,000

Season	Team	Tot	St	Sb	Snu	Ps	Gls
92-93	Southampton	37	33	4	1	2	4
93-94	Southampton	41	41	0	0	1	7
94-95	Southampton	35	35	0	0	7	3
95-96	Southampton	15	13	2	6	3	1
96-97	Southampton	17	14	3	16	5	1
97-98	Southampton	6	5	1	3	2	1
98-99	Middlesbrough	20	10	10	10	5	0
99-00	Middlesbrough	13	6	7	14	4	0
	Total	184	157	27	50	29	17

MADDIX, Danny

FULLNAME: Daniel Shawn Maddix
DOB: 11-Oct-67, Ashford, Kent

Club History	Signed	Fee
Tottenham H.	7/85	
Southend U.	10/86	Loan
QPR	7/87	Free

Season	Team	Tot	St	Sb	Snu	Ps	Gls
92-93	QPR	14	9	5	15	1	0
93-94	QPR	0	0	0	2	0	0
94-95	QPR	27	21	6	6	0	1
95-96	QPR	22	20	2	2	1	0
	Total	63	50	13	25	2	1

MAGILTON, Jim

FULLNAME: James Magilton
DOB: 06-May-69, Belfast, N.Ireland

Club History	Signed	Fee
Liverpool	5/86	Apprentice
Oxford U.	10/90	£100,000
Southampton	2/94	£600,000
Sheffield W.	9/97	£1.6m

Season	Team	Tot	St	Sb	Snu	Ps	Gls
93-94	Southampton	15	15	0	0	0	0
94-95	Southampton	42	42	0	0	2	6
95-96	Southampton	31	31	0	1	2	3
96-97	Southampton	37	31	6	1	7	4
97-98	Southampton	5	5	0	0	0	0
97-98	Sheffield W.	20	13	7	7	4	1
98-99	Sheffield W.	6	1	5	9	1	0
	Total	156	138	18	18	16	14

MAHORN, Paul

FULLNAME: Paul Gladstone Mahorn
DOB: 13-Aug-73, Whipps Cross, Essex

Club History	Signed	Fee
Tottenham H.	1/92	

Season	Team	Tot	St	Sb	Snu	Ps	Gls
93-94	Tottenham H.	1	1	0	0	0	0
97-98	Tottenham H.	2	2	0	1	2	0
	Total	3	3	0	1	2	0

MAKEL, Lee

FULLNAME: Lee Robert Makel
DOB: 11-Jan-73, Sunderland

Club History	Signed	Fee
Newcastle U.	2/91	Trainee
Blackburn R.	6/92	£160,000

Season	Team	Tot	St	Sb	Snu	Ps	Gls
92-93	Blackburn R.	1	1	0	2	0	0
93-94	Blackburn R.	2	0	2	0	0	0
95-96	Blackburn R.	3	0	3	1	0	0
	Total	6	1	5	3	0	0

MAKIN, Chris

FULLNAME: Christopher Gregory Makin
DOB: 08-May-73, Manchester

Club History	Signed	Fee
Oldham A.	11/91	Trainee

Season	Team	Tot	St	Sb	Snu	Ps	Gls
92-93	Oldham A.	0	0	0	1	0	0
93-94	Oldham A.	27	26	1	0	2	1
	Total	27	26	1	1	2	1

MALZ, Stefan

FULLNAME: Stefan Malz
DOB: 15-Jun-72, Ludwigshafen,
Germany

Club History	Signed	Fee
1860 Munich		
Arsenal	6/99	£650,000

Season	Team	Tot	St	Sb	Snu	Ps	Gls
99-00	Arsenal	5	2	3	6	1	1
	Total	5	2	3	6	1	1

MANNINGER, Alex

FULLNAME: Alex Manninger
DOB: 04-Jun-77, Salzburg

Club History	Signed	Fee
Grazer AK	1996	
Arsenal	3/97	£500,000

Season	Team	Tot	St	Sb	Snu	Ps	Gls
97-98	Arsenal	7	7	0	24	0	0
98-99	Arsenal	6	6	0	24	0	0
99-00	Arsenal	15	14	1	22	0	0
	Total	28	27	1	70	0	0

MARCELINO, Elena

FULLNAME: Elena Marcelino
DOB: 26-Sep-71,

Club History	Signed	Fee
Mallorca		
Newcastle U.	6/99	£5.0m

Season	Team	Tot	St	Sb	Snu	Ps	Gls
99-00	Newcastle U.	11	10	1	5	1	0
	Total	11	10	1	5	1	0

MARCELLE, Clint

FULLNAME: Clint Sherwin Marcelle
DOB: 09-Nov-68, Port of Spain

Club History	Signed	Fee
Felgueiras		
Barnsley	8/96	Free

Season	Team	Tot	St	Sb	Snu	Ps	Gls
97-98	Barnsley	20	9	11	11	7	0
	Total	20	9	11	11	7	0

MARCOLIN, Dario

FULLNAME: Dario Marcolin
DOB: 28-Oct-71, Brescia, Italy

Club History	Signed	Fee
Lazio		
Blackburn R.	10/98	Loan

Season	Team	Tot	St	Sb	Snu	Ps	Gls
98-99	Blackburn R.	10	5	5	7	2	1
	Total	10	5	5	7	2	1

MARGAS, Javier

FULLNAME: Javier Margas
DOB: 10-May-69, Chile

Club History	Signed	Fee
Univ. Catolica		
West Ham U.	8/98	£2m

Season	Team	Tot	St	Sb	Snu	Ps	Gls
98-99	West Ham U.	3	3	0	5	0	0
99-00	West Ham U.	18	15	3	7	2	1
	Total	21	18	3	12	2	1

MARGETSON, Martyn

FULLNAME: Martyn Walter Margetson
DOB: 08-Sep-71, Neath

Club History	Signed	Fee
Manchester C.	7/90	
Bristol R.	12/93	Loan

Season	Team	Tot	St	Sb	Snu	Ps	Gls
92-93	Manchester C.	1	1	0	33	1	0
93-94	Manchester C.	0	0	0	11	0	0
94-95	Manchester C.	0	0	0	11	0	0
95-96	Manchester C.	0	0	0	19	0	0
	Total	1	1	0	74	1	0

MARIC, Silvio

FULLNAME: Silvio Maric
DOB: 20-Mar-79, Croatia

Club History	Signed	Fee
Croatia Zagreb		
Newcastle U.	3/99	£3.3m

Season	Team	Tot	St	Sb	Snu	Ps	Gls
98-99	Newcastle U.	10	9	1	0	5	0
99-00	Newcastle U.	13	3	10	6	4	0
	Total	23	12	11	6	9	0

MARINELLI, Carlos

FULLNAME: Carlos Marinelli
DOB:

Club History	Signed	Fee
Boca Juniors		
Middlesbrough	9/99	£1.5m

Season	Team	Tot	St	Sb	Snu	Ps	Gls
99-00	Middlesbrough	2	0	2	3	0	0
	Total	2	0	2	3	0	0

MARKER, Nicky

FULLNAME: Nicholas R T Marker
DOB: 03-Jun-65, Budleigh Salterton

Club History	Signed	Fee
Exeter C.	5/83	
Plymouth Argyle	10/87	£95,000
Blackburn R.	9/92	£250,000

Season	Team	Tot	St	Sb	Snu	Ps	Gls
92-93	Blackburn R.	15	12	3	8	3	0
93-94	Blackburn R.	23	16	7	9	1	0
94-95	Blackburn R.	0	0	0	1	0	0
95-96	Blackburn R.	9	8	1	3	2	1
96-97	Blackburn R.	7	5	2	22	0	0
	Total	54	41	13	43	6	1

MARKSTEDT, Peter

FULLNAME: Peter Markstedt
DOB: 11-Jan-72, Vasteras, Sweden

Club History	Signed	Fee
Vasteras SK		
Barnsley	11/97	£250,000

Season	Team	Tot	St	Sb	Snu	Ps	Gls
97-98	Barnsley	7	6	1	2	2	0
	Total	7	6	1	2	2	0

MARQUIS, Paul

FULLNAME: Paul Raymond Marquis
DOB: 29-Aug-72, Enfield

Club History	Signed	Fee
West Ham U.	7/91	Trainee

Season	Team	Tot	St	Sb	Snu	Ps	Gls
93-94	West Ham U.	1	0	1	0	0	0
	Total	1	0	1	0	0	0

MARRIOTT, Andy

FULLNAME: Andrew Marriott
DOB: 11-Oct-70, Nottingham

Club History	Signed	Fee
Arsenal	10/88	Trainee
Nottingham F.	6/89	£50,000
WBA	9/89	Loan
Blackburn R.	12/89	Loan
Colchester U.	3/90	Loan
Burnley	8/91	Loan
Wrexham	10/93	£200,000
Sunderland	8/98	£200,000

Season	Team	Tot	St	Sb	Snu	Ps	Gls
92-93	Nottingham F.	5	5	0	37	0	0
99-00	Sunderland	1	1	0	37	0	0
	Total	6	6	0	74	0	0

MARSDEN, Chris

FULLNAME: Christopher Marsden
DOB: 03-Jan-69, Sheffield

Club History	Signed	Fee
Sheffield U.	1/87	Apprentice
Huddersfield Town	7/88	Free
Coventry C.	11/93	Loan
Wolverhampton W.	1/94	£250,000
Notts Co.	11/94	£250,000
Stockport Co.	1/96	£70,000
Birmingham C.	10/97	£500,000
Southampton	1/99	£800,000

Season	Team	Tot	St	Sb	Snu	Ps	Gls
93-94	Coventry C.	7	5	2	2	0	0
98-99	Southampton	14	14	0	0	1	2
99-00	Southampton	21	19	2	2	3	1
	Total	42	38	4	4	4	3

MARSH, Mike

FULLNAME: Michael Andrew Marsh
DOB: 21-Jul-69, Liverpool

Club History	Signed	Fee
Liverpool	8/87	
West Ham U.	9/93	Swap
Coventry C.	12/94	£450,000
Galatasaray	7/95	£500,000
Southend	9/95	£500,000

Season	Team	Tot	St	Sb	Snu	Ps	Gls
92-93	Liverpool	28	22	6	3	5	1
93-94	Liverpool	2	0	2	1	0	1
93-94	West Ham U.	33	33	0	0	4	1
94-95	West Ham U.	16	13	3	1	1	0
94-95	Coventry C.	15	15	0	2	2	2
	Total	94	83	11	7	12	5

MARSHALL, Andy

FULLNAME: Andrew Marshall
DOB: 14-Apr-75, Bury St Edmunds

Club History	Signed	Fee
Norwich C.	7/93	Trainee

Season	Team	Tot	St	Sb	Snu	Ps	Gls
92-93	Norwich C.	0	0	0	2	0	0
93-94	Norwich C.	0	0	0	2	0	0
94-95	Norwich C.	21	20	1	14	0	0
	Total	21	20	1	18	0	0

MARSHALL, Dwight

FULLNAME: Dwight Marshall
DOB: 03-Oct-65, Jamaica, West Indies

Club History	Signed	Fee
Plymouth Argyle		
Middlesbrough		Loan

Season	Team	Tot	St	Sb	Snu	Ps	Gls
92-93	Middlesbrough	3	0	3	1	0	0
	Total	3	0	3	1	0	0

MARSHALL, Ian

FULLNAME: Ian Paul Marshall
DOB: 20-Mar-66, Liverpool

Club History	Signed	Fee
Everton	3/84	Apprentice
Oldham A.	3/88	£100,000
Ipswich T.	8/93	£750,000
Leicester C.	8/96	£800,000

Season	Team	Tot	St	Sb	Snu	Ps	Gls
92-93	Oldham A.	27	26	1	0	2	2
93-94	Ipswich T.	29	28	1	0	2	10
94-95	Ipswich T.	18	14	4	2	4	3
96-97	Leicester C.	28	19	9	1	4	8
97-98	Leicester C.	24	22	2	0	10	7
98-99	Leicester C.	10	6	4	5	2	3
99-00	Leicester C.	21	2	19	7	2	0
	Total	157	117	40	15	26	33

MARSHALL, Scott

FULLNAME: Scott Roderick Marshall
DOB: 01-May-73, Edinburgh

Club History	Signed	Fee
Arsenal	3/91	Trainee
Rotherham U.	12/93	Loan
Sheffield U.	8/94	Loan
Southampton	7/98	Free

Season	Team	Tot	St	Sb	Snu	Ps	Gls
92-93	Arsenal	2	2	0	0	0	0
94-95	Arsenal	0	0	0	1	0	0
95-96	Arsenal	11	10	1	2	1	1
96-97	Arsenal	8	6	2	10	1	0
97-98	Arsenal	3	1	2	9	0	0
98-99	Southampton	2	2	0	2	0	0
	Total	26	21	5	24	2	1

MARTIN, Alvin

FULLNAME: Alvin Edward Martin
DOB: 29-Jul-58, Liverpool

Club History	Signed	Fee
West Ham U.	8/74	Apprentice
Leyton Orient	8/96	Free

Season	Team	Tot	St	Sb	Snu	Ps	Gls
93-94	West Ham U.	7	6	1	0	0	2
94-95	West Ham U.	24	24	0	0	1	0
95-96	West Ham U.	14	10	4	7	1	0
	Total	45	40	5	7	2	2

MARTIN, Lee

FULLNAME: Lee Martin
DOB: 05-Feb-68, Hyde

Club History	Signed	Fee
Manchester U.		Trainee

Season	Team	Tot	St	Sb	Snu	Ps	Gls
92-93	Manchester U.	0	0	0	5	0	0
93-94	Manchester U.	1	1	0	1	0	0
	Total	1	1	0	6	0	0

MARTYN, Nigel

FULLNAME: Nigel Anthony Martyn
DOB: 11-Aug-66, St Austell

Club History	Signed	Fee
Bristol R.	8/87	From Non League

Crystal P.   11/89   £1m
Leeds U.   7/96   £2.25m

Season	Team	Tot	St	Sb	Snu	Ps	Gls
92-93	Crystal P.	42	42	0	0	0	0
94-95	Crystal P.	37	37	0	0	1	0
96-97	Leeds U.	37	37	0	0	0	0
97-98	Leeds U.	37	37	0	0	0	0
98-99	Leeds U.	34	34	0	1	1	0
99-00	Leeds U.	38	38	0	0	0	0
	Total	225	225	0	1	2	0

MASINGA, Philomen

FULLNAME: Philomen Masinga
DOB: 28-Jun-69, Johannesburg

Club History	Signed	Fee
Mamolodi Sun		
Leeds U.	8/94	£250,000

Season	Team	Tot	St	Sb	Snu	Ps	Gls
94-95	Leeds U.	22	15	7	3	8	5
95-96	Leeds U.	9	5	4	2	3	0
	Total	31	20	11	5	11	5

MASKELL, Craig

FULLNAME: Craig Dell Maskell
DOB: 10-Apr-68, Aldershot

Club History	Signed	Fee
Southampton	4/86	Apprentice
Huddersfield Town	5/88	£20,000
Reading	8/90	£250,000
Swindon Town	7/92	£225,000
Southampton	2/94	£250,000

Season	Team	Tot	St	Sb	Snu	Ps	Gls
93-94	Swindon T.	14	8	6	6	3	3
93-94	Southampton	10	6	4	3	4	1
94-95	Southampton	6	2	4	4	1	0
95-96	Southampton	1	0	1	0	0	0
	Total	31	16	15	13	8	4

MASON, Paul

FULLNAME: Paul Mason
DOB: 03-Sep-63, Liverpool

Club History	Signed	Fee
Aberdeen		
Ipswich Town	8/93	£400,000

Season	Team	Tot	St	Sb	Snu	Ps	Gls
93-94	Ipswich T.	22	18	4	2	3	3
94-95	Ipswich T.	21	19	2	4	4	3
	Total	43	37	6	6	7	6

MASSEY, Stuart

FULLNAME: Stuart Massey
DOB: 17-Nov-64, Crawley

Club History	Signed	Fee
Crystal P.	7/92	£20,000

Season	Team	Tot	St	Sb	Snu	Ps	Gls
92-93	Crystal P.	1	0	1	0	0	0
	Total	1	0	1	0	0	0

MATERAZZI, Marco

FULLNAME: Marco Materazzi
DOB: 18-Aug-73, Lecce, Italy

Club History	Signed	Fee
Perugia		
Everton	7/98	£2.8m

Season	Team	Tot	St	Sb	Snu	Ps	Gls
98-99	Everton	27	26	1	1	4	1
	Total	27	26	1	1	4	1

MATHIE, Alex

FULLNAME: Alexander Mathie
DOB: 20-Dec-68, Bathgate

Club History	Signed	Fee
Morton	8/91	£100,000
Port Vale	3/93	Loan
Newcastle U.	7/93	£285,000
Ipswich Town	2/95	£500,000

Season	Team	Tot	St	Sb	Snu	Ps	Gls
93-94	Newcastle U.	16	0	16	13	0	3
94-95	Newcastle U.	9	3	6	6	0	1
94-95	Ipswich T.	13	13	0	0	3	2
	Total	38	16	22	19	3	6

MATTEO, Dominic

FULLNAME: Dominic Matteo
DOB: 28-Apr-74, Dumfries

Club History	Signed	Fee
Liverpool	5/92	Trainee
Sunderland	3/95	Loan

Season	Team	Tot	St	Sb	Snu	Ps	Gls
93-94	Liverpool	11	11	0	4	4	0
94-95	Liverpool	7	2	5	2	2	0
95-96	Liverpool	5	5	0	8	2	0
96-97	Liverpool	26	22	4	7	1	0
97-98	Liverpool	25	24	1	0	0	0
98-99	Liverpool	20	16	4	4	0	1
99-00	Liverpool	32	32	0	2	1	0
	Total	126	112	14	27	10	1

MATTHEW, Damian

FULLNAME: Damian Matthew
DOB: 23-Sep-70, Islington

Club History	Signed	Fee
Chelsea	6/89	
Luton Town	9/92	Loan
Crystal P.	2/94	£150,000

Season	Team	Tot	St	Sb	Snu	Ps	Gls
92-93	Chelsea	4	3	1	1	3	0
94-95	Crystal P.	4	2	2	2	1	0
	Total	8	5	3	3	4	0

MATTHEWS, Lee

FULLNAME: Lee Joseph Matthews
DOB: 16-Jan-79, Slough

Club History	Signed	Fee
Leeds U.	2/96	Trainee

Season	Team	Tot	St	Sb	Snu	Ps	Gls
97-98	Leeds U.	3	0	3	5	0	0
	Total	3	0	3	5	0	0

MATTSSON, Jesper

FULLNAME: Jesper Bo Mattsson
DOB: 18-Apr-68, Sweden

Club History	Signed	Fee
Halmstads		
Nottingham F.	12/98	£500,000

Season	Team	Tot	St	Sb	Snu	Ps	Gls
98-99	Nottingham F.	6	5	1	1	1	0
	Total	6	5	1	1	1	0

MAUTONE, Steve

FULLNAME: Steve Mautone
DOB: 10-Aug-78, Myrtleford

Club History	Signed	Fee
Canberra Cosmos		
West Ham U.	1995	

Season	Team	Tot	St	Sb	Snu	Ps	Gls
96-97	West Ham U.	1	1	0	7	0	0
	Total	1	1	0	7	0	0

MAY, David

FULLNAME: David May
DOB: 24-Jun-70, Oldham

Club History	Signed	Fee
Blackburn R.	6/88	Trainee
Manchester U.	7/94	£1.4m

Season	Team	Tot	St	Sb	Snu	Ps	Gls
92-93	Blackburn R.	34	34	0	0	1	1
93-94	Blackburn R.	40	40	0	0	2	1
94-95	Manchester U.	19	15	4	3	3	2
95-96	Manchester U.	16	11	5	1	2	1
96-97	Manchester U.	29	28	1	1	2	3
97-98	Manchester U.	9	7	2	3	1	0
98-99	Manchester U.	6	4	2	5	1	0
99-00	Manchester U.	1	0	1	0	0	0
	Total	154	139	15	13	12	8

MAYBURY, Alan

FULLNAME: Alan Maybury
DOB: 08-Aug-78, Dublin

Club History	Signed	Fee
Leeds U.	8/95	

Season	Team	Tot	St	Sb	Snu	Ps	Gls
95-96	Leeds U.	1	1	0	0	1	0
97-98	Leeds U.	12	9	3	5	4	0
99-00	Leeds U.	0	0	0	4	0	0
	Total	13	10	3	9	5	0

MAYRLEB, Christian

FULLNAME: Christian Mayrleb
DOB: 08-Jun-72, Austria

Club History	Signed	Fee
FC Tirol		
Sheffield W.	1/98	Free

Season	Team	Tot	St	Sb	Snu	Ps	Gls
97-98	Sheffield W.	3	0	3	3	0	0
	Total	3	0	3	3	0	0

MAZZARELLI, Giuseppe

FULLNAME: Giuseppe Mazzarelli
DOB: 14-Aug-72, Switzerland

Club History	Signed	Fee
FC Zurich		
Manchester C.	3/96	Loan

Season	Team	Tot	St	Sb	Snu	Ps	Gls
95-96	Manchester C.	2	0	2	0	0	0
	Total	2	0	2	0	0	0

McALLISTER, Brian

FULLNAME: Brian McAllister
DOB: 30-Nov-70, Glasgow

Club History	Signed	Fee
Wimbledon	2/89	Trainee

Season	Team	Tot	St	Sb	Snu	Ps	Gls
92-93	Wimbledon	27	26	1	0	1	0
93-94	Wimbledon	13	13	0	1	2	0

95-96	Wimbledon	2	2	0	0	1	0
96-97	Wimbledon	23	19	4	8	2	0
97-98	Wimbledon	7	4	3	7	1	0
98-99	Wimbledon	0	0	0	2	0	0
	Total	72	64	8	18	7	0

McALLISTER, Gary

FULLNAME: Gary McAllister
DOB: 25-Dec-64, Motherwell

Club History	Signed	Fee
Leicester C.	8/85	£125,000
Leeds U.	6/90	£1m
Coventry C.		

Season	Team	Tot	St	Sb	Snu	Ps	Gls
92-93	Leeds U.	32	32	0	0	4	5
93-94	Leeds U.	42	42	0	0	0	8
94-95	Leeds U.	41	41	0	0	1	6
95-96	Leeds U.	36	36	0	0	0	5
96-97	Coventry C.	38	38	0	0	0	6
97-98	Coventry C.	14	14	0	0	2	0
98-99	Coventry C.	29	29	0	0	8	3
99-00	Coventry C.	38	38	0	0	3	11
	Total	270	270	0	0	18	44

McANESPIE, Steve

FULLNAME: Steve McAnespie
DOB: 01-Feb-72, Kilmarnock

Club History	Signed	Fee
Aberdeen	5/88	Juniors
Vasterhaninge	6/93	
Raith R.	1/94	
Bolton Wanderers	9/95	£900,000

Season	Team	Tot	St	Sb	Snu	Ps	Gls
95-96	Bolton W.	9	7	2	8	1	0
97-98	Bolton W.	2	1	1	6	1	0
	Total	11	8	3	14	2	0

McATEER, Jason

FULLNAME: Jason McAteer
DOB: 18-Jun-71, Birkenhead

Club History	Signed	Fee
Bolton Wanderers	1/92	From Non League
Liverpool	9/95	£4.5m
Blackburn R.	1/99	£4m

Season	Team	Tot	St	Sb	Snu	Ps	Gls
95-96	Bolton W.	4	4	0	0	0	0
95-96	Liverpool	29	27	2	2	0	0
96-97	Liverpool	37	36	1	0	2	1
97-98	Liverpool	21	15	6	3	2	2
98-99	Liverpool	13	6	7	5	1	0
98-99	Blackburn R.	13	13	0	0	0	1
	Total	117	101	16	10	5	4

McAVENNIE, Frank

FULLNAME: Frank McAvennie
DOB: 22-Nov-59, Glasgow

Club History	Signed	Fee
St. Mirren		
West Ham U.	6/85	
Celtic		
West Ham U.	3/89	
Aston Villa		
Celtic	12/92	
Swindon Town		

Season	Team	Tot	St	Sb	Snu	Ps	Gls
92-93	Aston Villa	3	0	3	1	0	0
93-94	Swindon T.	7	3	4	1	2	0
	Total	10	3	7	2	2	0

McCALL, Stuart

FULLNAME: Andrew Stuart Murray McCall
DOB: 10-Jun-64, Leeds

Club History	Signed	Fee
Bradford C.	6/82	Apprentice
Everton	6/88	£850,000
Rangers	8/91	£1.2m
Bradford C.	6/98	Free

Season	Team	Tot	St	Sb	Snu	Ps	Gls
99-00	Bradford C.	34	33	1	0	1	1
	Total	34	33	1	0	1	1

McCANN, Gavin

FULLNAME: Gavin Peter McCann
DOB: 10-Jan-78, Blackpool

Club History	Signed	Fee
Everton	7/95	Trainee
Sunderland	11/98	£500,000

Season	Team	Tot	St	Sb	Snu	Ps	Gls
96-97	Everton	0	0	0	1	0	0
97-98	Everton	11	5	6	3	1	0
99-00	Sunderland	24	21	3	0	7	4
	Total	35	26	9	4	8	4

McCARTHY, Alan

FULLNAME: Alan James McCarthy
DOB: 11-Jan-72, Wandsworth

Club History	Signed	Fee
QPR	12/89	
Watford	11/93	Loan
Plymouth Argyle	2/94	Loan

Season	Team	Tot	St	Sb	Snu	Ps	Gls
92-93	QPR	0	0	0	1	0	0

		Tot	St	Sb	Snu	Ps	Gls
93-94	QPR	4	4	0	1	0	0
94-95	QPR	2	0	2	1	0	0
	Total	6	4	2	3	0	0

McCARTHY, Sean

FULLNAME: Sean Casey McCarthy
DOB: 12-Sep-67, Bridgend

Club History	Signed	Fee
Swansea C.	10/85	From Non League
Plymouth Arg	8/88	£50,000
Bradford C.	7/90	£250,000
Oldham A.	12/93	£500,000

Season	Team	Tot	St	Sb	Snu	Ps	Gls
93-94	Oldham A.	20	19	1	0	3	4
	Total	20	19	1	0	3	4

McCLAIR, Brian

FULLNAME: Brian John McClair
DOB: 08-Dec-63, Bellshill

Club History	Signed	Fee
Motherwell	8/81	
Celtic	7/83	£100,000
Manchester U.	7/87	£850,000

Season	Team	Tot	St	Sb	Snu	Ps	Gls
92-93	Manchester U.	42	41	1	0	2	9
93-94	Manchester U.	26	12	14	10	4	1
94-95	Manchester U.	40	35	5	2	6	5
95-96	Manchester U.	22	12	10	4	4	3
96-97	Manchester U.	19	4	15	16	0	0
97-98	Manchester U.	13	2	11	17	2	0
	Total	162	106	56	49	18	18

McCLEN, Jamie

FULLNAME: Jamie McClen
DOB: 13-May-79, Newcastle

Club History	Signed	Fee
Newcastle U.		Trainee

Season	Team	Tot	St	Sb	Snu	Ps	Gls
98-99	Newcastle U.	1	1	0	3	1	0
99-00	Newcastle U.	9	3	6	5	1	0
	Total	10	4	6	8	2	0

McDONALD, Alan

FULLNAME: Alan McDonald
DOB: 12-Oct-63, Belfast, Nth Ireland

Club History	Signed	Fee
QPR	8/81	

Season	Team	Tot	St	Sb	Snu	Ps	Gls
92-93	QPR	39	39	0	0	1	0
93-94	QPR	12	12	0	1	1	1
94-95	QPR	39	39	0	0	1	1
95-96	QPR	26	25	1	1	2	1
	Total	116	115	1	2	5	3

McDONALD, David

FULLNAME: David Hugh McDonald
DOB: 02-Jan-71, Dublin, Republic of Ireland

Club History	Signed	Fee
Tottenham H.	7/88	

Season	Team	Tot	St	Sb	Snu	Ps	Gls
92-93	Tottenham H.	2	2	0	0	0	0
	Total	2	2	0	0	0	0

McDONALD, Neil

FULLNAME: Neil McDonald
DOB: 02-Nov-65, Wallsend

Club History	Signed	Fee
Newcastle U.	2/83	Amateur
Everton	8/88	£535,000
Oldham A.	10/91	£500,000

Season	Team	Tot	St	Sb	Snu	Ps	Gls
92-93	Oldham A.	4	2	2	4	0	0
93-94	Oldham A.	3	3	0	1	3	0
	Total	7	5	2	5	3	0

McDONALD, Paul

FULLNAME: Paul McDonald
DOB: 20-Apr-68, Motherwell

Club History	Signed	Fee
Hamilton Aca.		
Southampton	6/93	£75,000

Season	Team	Tot	St	Sb	Snu	Ps	Gls
94-95	Southampton	2	0	2	0	0	0
95-96	Southampton	1	0	1	1	0	0
	Total	3	0	3	1	0	0

McEWAN, David

FULLNAME: David McEwan
DOB:

Club History	Signed	Fee
Tottenham H.	1/00	Free from Non League

Season	Team	Tot	St	Sb	Snu	Ps	Gls
99-00	Tottenham H.	1	0	1	1	0	0
	Total	1	0	1	1	0	0

McGEE, Paul

FULLNAME: Paul McGee
DOB: 17-May-68, Dublin, Republic of Ireland

Club History	Signed	Fee
Colchester U.	2/89	£35,000
Wimbledon	3/89	£120,000

Season	Team	Tot	St	Sb	Snu	Ps	Gls
92-93	Wimbledon	3	1	2	1	1	0
	Total	3	1	2	1	1	0

McGIBBON, Pat

FULLNAME: Patrick McGibbon
DOB: 06-Sep-73, Lurgan

Club History	Signed	Fee
Portadown		
Manchester U.	8/92	£100,000

Season	Team	Tot	St	Sb	Snu	Ps	Gls
94-95	Manchester U.	0	0	0	1	0	0
95-96	Manchester U.	0	0	0	3	0	0
	Total	0	0	0	4	0	0

McGINLAY, John

FULLNAME: John McGinlay
DOB: 08-Apr-64, Inverness

Club History	Signed	Fee
Shrewsbury Town	2/89	
Bury	7/90	£175,000
Millwall	1/91	£80,000
Bolton W.	9/92	£125,000

Season	Team	Tot	St	Sb	Snu	Ps	Gls
95-96	Bolton W.	32	29	3	2	9	6
97-98	Bolton W.	8	5	3	0	2	0
	Total	40	34	6	2	11	6

McGOLDRICK, Eddie

FULLNAME: Edward John Paul McGoldrick
DOB: 30-Apr-65, Islington

Club History	Signed	Fee
Northampton T.	8/86	£10,000
Crystal P.	1/89	£200,000
Arsenal	7/93	£1m

Season	Team	Tot	St	Sb	Snu	Ps	Gls
92-93	Crystal P.	42	42	0	0	1	8
93-94	Arsenal	26	23	3	2	5	0
94-95	Arsenal	11	9	2	1	2	0
95-96	Arsenal	1	0	1	0	0	0
	Total	80	74	6	3	8	8

McGOVERN, Brian

FULLNAME: Brian McGovern
DOB: 28-Apr-80, Dublin

Club History	Signed	Fee
Arsenal	7/97	Trainee

Season	Team	Tot	St	Sb	Snu	Ps	Gls
99-00	Arsenal	1	0	1	0	0	0
	Total	1	0	1	0	0	0

McGOWAN, Gavin

FULLNAME: Gavin Gregory McGowan
DOB: 16-Jan-76, Blackheath

Club History	Signed	Fee
Arsenal	7/94	Trainee

Season	Team	Tot	St	Sb	Snu	Ps	Gls
92-93	Arsenal	2	0	2	0	0	0
94-95	Arsenal	1	1	0	0	1	0
95-96	Arsenal	1	1	0	0	0	0
96-97	Arsenal	1	1	0	0	1	0
97-98	Arsenal	1	0	1	0	0	0
	Total	6	3	3	0	2	0

McGRATH, Lloyd

FULLNAME: Lloyd Anthony McGrath
DOB: 04-Dec-65, Birmingham

Club History	Signed	Fee
Coventry C.	12/82	

Season	Team	Tot	St	Sb	Snu	Ps	Gls
92-93	Coventry C.	25	20	5	3	2	0
93-94	Coventry C.	11	10	1	1	2	0
	Total	36	30	6	4	4	0

McGRATH, Paul

FULLNAME: Paul McGrath
DOB: 04-Dec-59, Ealing

Club History	Signed	Fee
Manchester U.	4/82	£30,000
Aston Villa	8/89	£400,000
Derby Co.	10/96	£100,000

Season	Team	Tot	St	Sb	Snu	Ps	Gls
92-93	Aston Villa	42	42	0	0	1	4
93-94	Aston Villa	30	30	0	0	2	0
94-95	Aston Villa	40	36	4	1	0	0
95-96	Aston Villa	30	29	1	0	5	2
96-97	Aston Villa	0	0	0	7	0	0
96-97	Derby Co.	24	23	1	1	4	0
	Total	166	160	6	9	12	6

McGREGOR, Paul

FULLNAME: Paul Anthony McGregor
DOB: 17-Dec-74, Liverpool

Club History	Signed	Fee
Nottingham F.	12/91	Trainee

Season	Team	Tot	St	Sb	Snu	Ps	Gls
94-95	Nottingham F.	10	0	10	9	0	1

		Tot	St	Sb	Snu	Ps	Gls
95-96	Nottingham F.	14	7	7	7	5	2
96-97	Nottingham F.	5	0	5	4	0	0
	Total	29	7	22	20	5	3

McKEE, Colin

FULLNAME: Colin McKee
DOB: 22-Aug-73, Glasgow

Club History	Signed	Fee
Manchester U.		Trainee

Season	Team	Tot	St	Sb	Snu	Ps	Gls
93-94	Manchester U.	1	1	0	0	1	0
	Total	1	1	0	0	1	0

McKEEVER, Mark

FULLNAME: Mark McKeever
DOB: 16-Nov-78, Derry

Club History	Signed	Fee
Peterborough		
Sheffield W.		

Season	Team	Tot	St	Sb	Snu	Ps	Gls
98-99	Sheffield W.	3	1	2	2	0	0
99-00	Sheffield W.	2	1	1	1	1	0
	Total	5	2	3	3	1	0

McKENZIE, Leon

FULLNAME: Leon Mark McKenzie
DOB: 17-May-78, Croydon

Club History	Signed	Fee
Crystal P.	10/95	Trainee

Season	Team	Tot	St	Sb	Snu	Ps	Gls
97-98	Crystal P.	3	0	3	1	0	0
	Total	3	0	3	1	0	0

McKINLAY, Billy

FULLNAME: William McKinlay
DOB: 22-Apr-69, Glasgow

Club History	Signed	Fee
Dundee U.		
Blackburn R.	10/95	£1.75m

Season	Team	Tot	St	Sb	Snu	Ps	Gls
95-96	Blackburn R.	19	13	6	3	2	2
96-97	Blackburn R.	25	23	2	4	3	1
97-98	Blackburn R.	30	26	4	3	6	0
98-99	Blackburn R.	16	14	2	3	2	0
	Total	90	76	14	13	13	3

McKINNON, Ray

FULLNAME: Raymond McKinnon
DOB: 05-Aug-70, Dundee

Club History	Signed	Fee
Dundee U.		Trainee
Nottingham F.		

Season	Team	Tot	St	Sb	Snu	Ps	Gls
92-93	Nottingham F.	6	5	1	0	1	1
	Total	6	5	1	0	1	1

McLEARY, Alan

FULLNAME: Alan Terence McLeary
DOB: 06-Oct-64, Lambeth

Club History	Signed	Fee
Millwall	10/81	Apprentice
Sheffield U.	7/92	Loan
Wimbledon	10/92	Loan

Season	Team	Tot	St	Sb	Snu	Ps	Gls
92-93	Sheffield U.	3	3	0	0	1	0
92-93	Wimbledon	4	4	0	0	0	0
	Total	7	7	0	0	1	0

McMAHON, Gerry

FULLNAME: Gerard McMahon
DOB: 29-Dec-73, Belfast, Nth Ireland

Club History	Signed	Fee
Glenavon		
Tottenham H.	7/92	£100,000

Season	Team	Tot	St	Sb	Snu	Ps	Gls
94-95	Tottenham H.	2	2	0	0	1	0
95-96	Tottenham H.	14	7	7	4	4	0
96-97	Tottenham H.	0	0	0	1	0	0
	Total	16	9	7	5	5	0

McMAHON, Sam

FULLNAME: Samuel Keiron McMahon
DOB: 09-Feb-76, Newark

Club History	Signed	Fee
Leicester C.	7/94	Trainee

Season	Team	Tot	St	Sb	Snu	Ps	Gls
94-95	Leicester C.	1	0	1	3	0	0
96-97	Leicester C.	0	0	0	1	0	0
97-98	Leicester C.	1	0	1	0	0	0
98-99	Leicester C.	0	0	0	1	0	0
	Total	2	0	2	5	0	0

McMAHON, Steve

FULLNAME: Stephen McMahon
DOB: 20-Aug-61, Liverpool

Club History	Signed	Fee
Everton	8/79	
Aston Villa	5/83	£175,000
Liverpool	9/85	£375,000
Manchester C.	12/91	£900,000

Season	Team	Tot	St	Sb	Snu	Ps	Gls
92-93	Manchester C.	27	24	3	0	4	1
93-94	Manchester C.	35	35	0	0	2	0
94-95	Manchester C.	7	6	1	1	1	0
	Total	69	65	4	1	7	1

McMANAMAN, Steve

FULLNAME: Steven McManaman
DOB: 11-Feb-72, Bootle

Club History	Signed	Fee
Liverpool	2/90	Trainee

Season	Team	Tot	St	Sb	Snu	Ps	Gls
92-93	Liverpool	31	27	4	0	4	4
93-94	Liverpool	30	29	1	2	4	2
94-95	Liverpool	40	40	0	0	1	7
95-96	Liverpool	38	38	0	0	1	6
96-97	Liverpool	37	37	0	0	1	7
97-98	Liverpool	36	36	0	1	2	11
98-99	Liverpool	28	25	3	0	5	4
	Total	240	232	8	3	18	41

McPHAIL, Stephen

FULLNAME: Stephen McPhail
DOB: 09-Dec-79, London

Club History	Signed	Fee
Leeds U.	12/96	Trainee

Season	Team	Tot	St	Sb	Snu	Ps	Gls
97-98	Leeds U.	4	0	4	6	0	0
98-99	Leeds U.	17	11	6	3	4	0
99-00	Leeds U.	24	23	1	1	3	2
	Total	45	34	11	10	7	2

McSHEFFREY, Gary

FULLNAME: Gary McSheffrey
DOB: 13-Aug-82, Coventry

Club History	Signed	Fee
Coventry C.		Trainee

Season	Team	Tot	St	Sb	Snu	Ps	Gls
98-99	Coventry C.	1	0	1	0	0	0
99-00	Coventry C.	3	0	3	1	0	0
	Total	4	0	4	1	0	0

McVEIGH, Paul

FULLNAME: Paul McVeigh
DOB: 06-Dec-77, Belfast

Club History	Signed	Fee
Tottenham H.		

Season	Team	Tot	St	Sb	Snu	Ps	Gls
96-97	Tottenham H.	3	2	1	2	2	1
97-98	Tottenham H.	0	0	0	0	0	0
	Total	3	2	1	2	2	1

MEAKER, Michael

FULLNAME: Michael John Meaker
DOB: 18-Aug-71, Greenford

Club History	Signed	Fee
QPR	12/89	

Season	Team	Tot	St	Sb	Snu	Ps	Gls
92-93	QPR	3	3	0	0	0	0
93-94	QPR	14	11	3	0	3	1
94-95	QPR	8	7	1	0	2	1
	Total	25	21	4	0	5	2

MEAN, Scott

FULLNAME: Scott Mean
DOB: 12-Dec-73, Crawley

Club History	Signed	Fee
Bournemouth	8/92	Trainee
West Ham U.	11/96	

Season	Team	Tot	St	Sb	Snu	Ps	Gls
96-97	West Ham U.	0	0	0	2	0	0
97-98	West Ham U.	3	0	3	11	0	0
98-99	West Ham U.	0	0	0	3	0	0
	Total	3	0	3	16	0	0

MEGSON, Gary

FULLNAME: Gary John Megson
DOB: 02-May-59, Manchester

Club History	Signed	Fee
Plymouth Argyle	5/77	
Everton	12/79	£250,000
Sheffield Wed	8/81	£130,000
Nottingham F.	8/84	£175,000
Newcastle U.	11/84	£130,000
Sheffield Wed	12/85	£60,000
Manchester C.	1/89	£250,000
Norwich C.	7/92	Free

Season	Team	Tot	St	Sb	Snu	Ps	Gls
92-93	Norwich C.	23	20	3	2	3	1
93-94	Norwich C.	22	21	1	8	8	0
94-95	Norwich C.	1	1	0	0	1	0
	Total	46	42	4	10	12	1

MEIJER, Erik

FULLNAME: Erik Meijer
DOB:

Club History	Signed	Fee
B. Leverkusen		
Liverpool	7/99	Free

Season	Team	Tot	St	Sb	Snu	Ps	Gls
99-00	Liverpool	21	7	14	5	3	0
	Total	21	7	14	5	3	0

MELCHIOT, Mario

FULLNAME: Mario Melchoit
DOB: 04-Nov-76, Amsterdam, Holland

Club History	Signed	Fee
Ajax		
Chelsea	6/99	Free

Season	Team	Tot	St	Sb	Snu	Ps	Gls
99-00	Chelsea	5	4	1	0	1	0
	Total	5	4	1	0	1	0

MELTON, Stephen

FULLNAME: Stephen Melton
DOB: 03-Oct-78, Lincoln

Club History	Signed	Fee
Nottingham F.		Trainee

Season	Team	Tot	St	Sb	Snu	Ps	Gls
98-99	Nottingham F.	1	1	0	0	0	0
	Total	1	1	0	0	0	0

MELVILLE, Andy

FULLNAME: Andrew Roger Melville
DOB: 29-Nov-68, Swansea

Club History	Signed	Fee
Swansea C.	7/86	Trainee
Oxford U.	7/90	£275,000
Sunderland	8/93	

Season	Team	Tot	St	Sb	Snu	Ps	Gls
96-97	Sunderland	30	30	0	0	0	1
	Total	30	30	0	0	0	1

MENDEZ, Alberto

FULLNAME: Alberto Mendez Rodriguez
DOB: 24-Oct-74, Nurnberg (Germany)

Club History	Signed	Fee
FC Feucht		
Arsenal	7/97	£250,000

Season	Team	Tot	St	Sb	Snu	Ps	Gls
97-98	Arsenal	3	1	2	1	1	0
98-99	Arsenal	1	0	1	3	0	0
	Total	4	1	3	4	1	0

MENDONCA, Clive

FULLNAME: Clive Paul Mendonca
DOB: 09-Sep-68, Tullington

Club History	Signed	Fee
Sheffield U.	9/86	Apprentice
Doncaster R.	2/88	Loan
Rotherham U.	3/88	£35,000
Sheffield U.	8/91	£110,000
Grimsby T.	1/92	Loan
Grimsby Town	8/92	£85,000
Charlton A.	5/97	£700,000

Season	Team	Tot	St	Sb	Snu	Ps	Gls
98-99	Charlton A.	25	19	6	1	8	8
	Total	25	19	6	1	8	8

MERSON, Paul

FULLNAME: Paul Charles Merson
DOB: 20-Mar-68, Harlesden

Club History	Signed	Fee
Arsenal	12/85	Apprentice
Brentford	1/87	Loan
Middlesbrough	7/97	£5m
Aston Villa	9/98	£6.75m

Season	Team	Tot	St	Sb	Snu	Ps	Gls
92-93	Arsenal	33	32	1	0	11	6
93-94	Arsenal	33	24	9	1	7	7
94-95	Arsenal	24	24	0	0	5	4
95-96	Arsenal	38	38	0	0	2	5
96-97	Arsenal	32	32	0	2	5	6
98-99	Middlesbrough	3	3	0	0	0	0
98-99	Aston Villa	26	21	5	1	6	5
99-00	Aston Villa	32	24	8	5	8	5
	Total	221	198	23	9	44	38

MIDDLETON, Craig

FULLNAME: Craig Middleton
DOB: 10-Sep-70, Nuneaton

Club History	Signed	Fee
Coventry C.		Trainee

Season	Team	Tot	St	Sb	Snu	Ps	Gls
92-93	Coventry C.	1	1	0	0	0	0
	Total	1	1	0	0	0	0

MIKE, Adie

FULLNAME: Adrian Roosevelt Mike
DOB: 16-Nov-73, Manchester

Club History	Signed	Fee
Manchester C.	15/7/92	Trainee
Bury	25/3/93	Loan
Stockport Co.	8/95	£60,000

Season	Team	Tot	St	Sb	Snu	Ps	Gls
92-93	Manchester C.	3	1	2	5	1	0
93-94	Manchester C.	9	1	8	2	0	1
94-95	Manchester C.	2	1	1	7	1	0
	Total	14	3	11	14	2	1

MIKLOSKO, Ludek

FULLNAME: Ludek Miklosko
DOB: 09-Dec-61, Protesov,
Czechoslovakia

Club History	Signed	Fee
Banik Ostrava		
West Ham U.	2/90	£300,000

Season	Team	Tot	St	Sb	Snu	Ps	Gls
93-94	West Ham U.	42	42	0	0	0	0
94-95	West Ham U.	42	42	0	0	0	0
95-96	West Ham U.	36	36	0	0	0	0
96-97	West Ham U.	36	36	0	0	1	0
97-98	West Ham U.	13	13	0	0	0	0
	Total	169	169	0	0	1	0

MILLER, Alan

FULLNAME: Alan John Miller
DOB: 29-Mar-70, Epping

Club History	Signed	Fee
Arsenal	5/88	
Plymouth Argyle	11/88	Loan
West Bromwich Albion	8/91	Loan
Birmingham C.	12/91	Loan
Middlesbrough	8/94	£500,000

Season	Team	Tot	St	Sb	Snu	Ps	Gls
92-93	Arsenal	4	3	1	35	0	0
93-94	Arsenal	4	3	1	36	0	0
95-96	Middlesbrough	6	6	0	2	0	0
96-97	Middlesbrough	10	10	0	2	0	0
	Total	24	22	2	75	0	0

MILLER, Charlie

FULLNAME: Charles Miller
DOB: 18-Mar-76, Glasgow

Club History	Signed	Fee
Rangers	7/92	Juniors
Leicester C.	3/99	Loan
Watford	9/99	£450,000

Season	Team	Tot	St	Sb	Snu	Ps	Gls
99-00	Watford	14	9	5	3	4	0
	Total	14	9	5	3	4	0

MILLER, James

FULLNAME: James Miller
DOB:

Club History	Signed	Fee
Leicester C.		Trainee

Season	Team	Tot	St	Sb	Snu	Ps	Gls
98-99	Leicester C.	4	1	3	5	1	0
	Total	4	1	3	5	1	0

MILLER, Kevin

FULLNAME: Kevin Miller
DOB: 15-Mar-69, Falmouth

Club History	Signed	Fee
Exeter C.	3/89	NL
Birmingham C.	5/93	£500,000
Watford	8/94	128
Crystal P.		

Season	Team	Tot	St	Sb	Snu	Ps	Gls
97-98	Crystal P.	38	38	0	0	0	0
	Total	38	38	0	0	0	0

MILLER, Paul

FULLNAME: Paul Anthony Miller
DOB: 31-Jan-68, Woking

Club History	Signed	Fee
Wimbledon	8/87	

Season	Team	Tot	St	Sb	Snu	Ps	Gls
92-93	Wimbledon	19	11	8	1	3	2
93-94	Wimbledon	0	0	0	1	0	0
	Total	19	11	8	2	3	2

MILLIGAN, Jamie

FULLNAME: Jamie Milligan
DOB: 03-Jan-80, Blackpool

Club History	Signed	Fee
Everton		Trainee

Season	Team	Tot	St	Sb	Snu	Ps	Gls
98-99	Everton	3	0	3	3	0	0
99-00	Everton	1	0	1	2	0	0
	Total	4	0	4	5	0	0

MILLIGAN, Mike

FULLNAME: Michael Joseph Milligan
DOB: 20-Feb-67, Manchester

Club History	Signed	Fee
Oldham A.	2/85	
Everton	8/90	£1m
Oldham A.	7/91	£600,000
Norwich C.	8/94	£850,000

Season	Team	Tot	St	Sb	Snu	Ps	Gls
92-93	Oldham A.	42	42	0	0	1	3
93-94	Oldham A.	39	39	0	0	4	0
94-95	Norwich C.	26	25	1	1	5	2
	Total	107	106	1	1	10	5

MILLS, Danny

FULLNAME: Daniel John Mills
DOB: 18-May-77, Norwich

Club History	Signed	Fee
Norwich C.	11/94	Trainee
Charlton A.	3/98	£350,000
Leeds U.	6/99	£4m

Season	Team	Tot	St	Sb	Snu	Ps	Gls
98-99	Charlton A.	36	36	0	0	4	2
99-00	Leeds U.	17	16	1	17	1	1
	Total	53	52	1	17	5	3

MILLS, Gary

FULLNAME: Gary R Mills
DOB: 11-Nov-61, Northampton

Club History	Signed	Fee
Nottingham F.	11/78	
Seattle (US)		
Derby Co.	10/82	
Seattle (US)		
Nottingham F.	12/83	
Notts Co.	8/87	
Leicester C.	3/89	£150,000

Season	Team	Tot	St	Sb	Snu	Ps	Gls
94-95	Leicester C.	1	1	0	0	0	0
	Total	1	1	0	0	0	0

MILLS, Lee

FULLNAME: Rowan Lee Mills
DOB: 10-Jul-70, Mexborough

Club History	Signed	Fee
Wolverhampton W.	12/92	Free from Non League
Derby Co.	2/95	£400,000
Port Vale	8/95	£200,000
Bradford C.	8/98	£1m

Season	Team	Tot	St	Sb	Snu	Ps	Gls
99-00	Bradford C.	21	19	2	0	3	5
	Total	21	19	2	0	3	5

MILOSEVIC, Savo

FULLNAME: Savo Milosevic
DOB: 02-Sep-73, Bijeljina, Yugoslavia

Club History	Signed	Fee
Partizan Belgrade		
Aston Villa	7/95	£3.5m

Season	Team	Tot	St	Sb	Snu	Ps	Gls
95-96	Aston Villa	37	36	1	0	5	12
96-97	Aston Villa	30	29	1	0	8	10
97-98	Aston Villa	23	19	4	8	7	7
	Total	90	84	6	8	20	29

MILTON, Simon

FULLNAME: Simon Charles Milton
DOB: 23-Aug-63, Fulham

Club History	Signed	Fee
Ipswich Town	7/87	£5,500

Season	Team	Tot	St	Sb	Snu	Ps	Gls
92-93	Ipswich T.	12	7	5	1	3	2
93-94	Ipswich T.	15	11	4	1	1	1
94-95	Ipswich T.	25	19	6	1	2	2
	Total	52	37	15	3	6	5

MIMMS, Bobby

FULLNAME: Robert Andrew Mimms
DOB: 12-Oct-63, York

Club History	Signed	Fee
Halifax Town	8/81	
Rotherham U.	11/81	£15,000
Everton	5/85	£150,000
Notts Co.	3/86	Loan
Sunderland	12/86	Loan
Blackburn R.	1/87	Loan
Manchester C.	9/87	Loan
Tottenham H.	2/88	£325,000
Aberdeen	2/90	Loan
Blackburn R.	12/90	£250,000

Season	Team	Tot	St	Sb	Snu	Ps	Gls
92-93	Blackburn R.	42	42	0	0	0	0
93-94	Blackburn R.	13	13	0	29	0	0
94-95	Blackburn R.	4	3	1	38	0	0
95-96	Blackburn R.	2	1	1	25	0	0
	Total	61	59	2	92	0	0

MINETT, Jason

FULLNAME: Jason Minett
DOB: 12-Aug-71, Peterborough

Club History	Signed	Fee
Norwich C.		Trainee

Season	Team	Tot	St	Sb	Snu	Ps	Gls
92-93	Norwich C.	1	0	1	0	0	0
	Total	1	0	1	0	0	0

MINTO, Scott

FULLNAME: Scott Christopher Minto
DOB: 06-Aug-71, Heswall

Club History	Signed	Fee
Charlton A.	2/89	Trainee
Chelsea	5/94	£775,000
Benfica		
West Ham U.	1/99	£1m

Season	Team	Tot	St	Sb	Snu	Ps	Gls
94-95	Chelsea	19	19	0	0	0	0
95-96	Chelsea	10	10	0	0	2	0
96-97	Chelsea	25	24	1	4	6	4
98-99	West Ham U.	15	14	1	2	1	0

99-00	West Ham U.	18	15	3	3	3	0
	Total	87	82	5	9	12	4

MITCHELL, Paul

FULLNAME: Paul R Mitchell
DOB: 20-Oct-71, Bournemouth

Club History	Signed	Fee
Bournemouth	8/89	
West Ham U.	8/93	£40,000

Season	Team	Tot	St	Sb	Snu	Ps	Gls
93-94	West Ham U.	1	0	1	1	0	0
	Total	1	0	1	1	0	0

MOHAN, Nicky

FULLNAME: Nicholas Mohan
DOB: 06-Oct-70, Middlesbrough

Club History	Signed	Fee
Middlesbrough	11/87	
Hull C.	9/92	Loan
Leicester C.	8/94	£330,000

Season	Team	Tot	St	Sb	Snu	Ps	Gls
92-93	Middlesbrough	18	18	0	2	0	2
94-95	Leicester C.	23	23	0	1	1	0
	Total	41	41	0	3	1	2

MOLBY, Jan

FULLNAME: Jan Molby
DOB: 04-Jul-63, Jutland, Denmark

Club History	Signed	Fee
Liverpool	8/84	£575,000

Season	Team	Tot	St	Sb	Snu	Ps	Gls
92-93	Liverpool	10	8	2	0	1	3
93-94	Liverpool	11	11	0	1	2	2
94-95	Liverpool	14	12	2	2	3	2
	Total	35	31	4	3	6	7

MOLDOVAN, Viorel

FULLNAME: Viorel Dinu Moldovan
DOB: 08-Jul-72, Bistrita, Romania

Club History	Signed	Fee
Grasshopper		
Coventry C.	12/97	£3.25m

Season	Team	Tot	St	Sb	Snu	Ps	Gls
97-98	Coventry C.	10	5	5	6	3	1
	Total	10	5	5	6	3	1

MOLENAAR, Robert

FULLNAME: Robert Molenaar
DOB: 27-Feb-69, Zaandam, Holland

Club History	Signed	Fee
FC Volendam	1992	
Leeds U.	1/97	£1m

Season	Team	Tot	St	Sb	Snu	Ps	Gls
96-97	Leeds U.	12	12	0	4	0	1
97-98	Leeds U.	22	18	4	12	5	2
98-99	Leeds U.	17	17	0	0	2	2
	Total	51	47	4	16	7	5

MONCUR, John

FULLNAME: John Frederick Moncur
DOB: 22-Sep-66, Stepney

Club History	Signed	Fee
Tottenham H.	8/84	Apprentice
Doncaster R.	9/86	Loan
Cambridge U.	3/87	Loan
Portsmouth	3/89	Loan
Brentford	10/89	Loan
Ipswich Town	10/91	Loan
Nottingham F.	2/92	Loan
Swindon Town	3/92	£80,000
West Ham U.	6/94	£900,000

Season	Team	Tot	St	Sb	Snu	Ps	Gls
93-94	Swindon T.	41	41	0	0	3	4
94-95	West Ham U.	30	30	0	0	2	2
95-96	West Ham U.	20	19	1	0	5	0
96-97	West Ham U.	27	26	1	1	7	2
97-98	West Ham U.	20	17	3	1	5	1
98-99	West Ham U.	14	6	8	12	0	0
99-00	West Ham U.	22	20	2	6	7	1
	Total	174	159	15	20	29	10

MONK, Gary

FULLNAME: Gary Monk
DOB: 06-Mar-79, Bedford

Club History	Signed	Fee
Torquay		
Southampton		

Season	Team	Tot	St	Sb	Snu	Ps	Gls
98-99	Southampton	4	4	0	6	0	0
99-00	Southampton	2	1	1	3	0	0
	Total	6	5	1	9	0	0

MONKOU, Ken

FULLNAME: Kenneth John Monkou
DOB: 29-Nov-64, Necare, Surinam

Club History	Signed	Fee
Chelsea	3/89	£100,000
Southampton	8/92	£750,000

Season	Team	Tot	St	Sb	Snu	Ps	Gls
92-93	Southampton	33	33	0	0	2	1

Season	Team	Tot	St	Sb	Snu	Ps	Gls
93-94	Southampton	35	35	0	0	1	4
94-95	Southampton	31	31	0	0	3	1
95-96	Southampton	32	31	1	0	2	2
96-97	Southampton	13	8	5	1	0	0
97-98	Southampton	32	30	2	1	1	1
98-99	Southampton	22	22	0	1	1	1
	Total	198	190	8	3	10	10

MOODY, Paul

FULLNAME: Paul Moody
DOB: 13-Jun-67, Portsmouth

Club History	Signed	Fee
Southampton	7/91	£50,000

Season	Team	Tot	St	Sb	Snu	Ps	Gls
92-93	Southampton	3	2	1	0	2	0
93-94	Southampton	5	3	2	0	0	0
	Total	8	5	3	0	2	0

MOONEY, Tommy

FULLNAME: Thomas John Mooney
DOB: 11-Aug-71, Middlesbrough

Club History	Signed	Fee
Aston Villa	11/89	Trainee
Scarborough	7/90	Free
Southend U.	7//93	£100,000
Watford	3/94	

Season	Team	Tot	St	Sb	Snu	Ps	Gls
99-00	Watford	12	8	4	0	1	2
	Total	12	8	4	0	1	2

MOORE, Alan

FULLNAME: Alan Moore
DOB: 25-Nov-74, Dublin

Club History	Signed	Fee
Middlesbrough	12/91	Trainee

Season	Team	Tot	St	Sb	Snu	Ps	Gls
92-93	Middlesbrough	2	0	2	4	0	0
95-96	Middlesbrough	12	5	7	11	1	0
96-97	Middlesbrough	17	10	7	9	7	0
98-99	Middlesbrough	4	3	1	7	3	0
99-00	Middlesbrough	0	0	0	2	0	0
	Total	35	18	17	33	11	0

MOORE, Darren

FULLNAME: Darren Mark Moore
DOB: 22-Apr-74, Birmingham

Club History	Signed	Fee
Torquay U.	11/92	Trainee
Doncaster R.	7/95	£62,500
Bradford C.	6/97	£310,000

Season	Team	Tot	St	Sb	Snu	Ps	Gls
99-00	Bradford C.	0	0	0	3	0	0
	Total	0	0	0	3	0	0

MOORE, Ian

FULLNAME: Ian Ronald Moore
DOB: 26-Aug-76, Birkenhead

Club History	Signed	Fee
Tranmere R.	7/94	Trainee
Nottingham F.	3/97	£1m

Season	Team	Tot	St	Sb	Snu	Ps	Gls
96-97	Nottingham F.	5	1	4	2	0	0
	Total	5	1	4	2	0	0

MOORE, Jason

FULLNAME: Jason Moore
DOB: 16-Feb-79, Dover

Club History	Signed	Fee
West Ham U.		Trainee

Season	Team	Tot	St	Sb	Snu	Ps	Gls
97-98	West Ham U.	1	0	1	2	0	0
	Total	1	0	1	2	0	0

MOORE, Joe-Max

FULLNAME: Joe-Max Moore
DOB: 23-Feb-71, USA

Club History	Signed	Fee
New England Revolution		
Everton	12/99	Free

Season	Team	Tot	St	Sb	Snu	Ps	Gls
99-00	Everton	15	11	4	1	5	6
	Total	15	11	4	1	5	6

MOORE, Kevin

FULLNAME: Thomas Kevin Moore
DOB: 29-Apr-58, Grimsby

Club History	Signed	Fee
Grimsby Town	7/76	
Oldham A.	2/87	£100,000
Southampton	8/87	£125,000

Season	Team	Tot	St	Sb	Snu	Ps	Gls
92-93	Southampton	18	18	0	3	1	2
93-94	Southampton	14	14	0	3	3	0
	Total	32	32	0	6	4	2

MOORE, Neil

FULLNAME: Neil Moore
DOB: 21-Sep-72, Liverpool

Club History	Signed	Fee
Everton	6/91	Trainee

Season	Team	Tot	St	Sb	Snu	Ps	Gls
92-93	Everton	1	0	1	0	0	0
93-94	Everton	4	4	0	1	1	0
	Total	5	4	1	1	1	0

MORAN, Kevin

FULLNAME: Kevin Bernard Moran
DOB: 29-Apr-56, Dublin, Republic of Ireland

Club History	Signed	Fee
Manchester U.	2/78	
Gijon (France)	8/88	
Blackburn R.	1/90	

Season	Team	Tot	St	Sb	Snu	Ps	Gls
92-93	Blackburn R.	36	36	0	0	6	4
93-94	Blackburn R.	19	19	0	0	9	1
	Total	55	55	0	0	15	5

MORAN, Paul

FULLNAME: Paul Moran
DOB: 22-May-68, Enfield

Club History	Signed	Fee
Tottenham H.	7/85	

Season	Team	Tot	St	Sb	Snu	Ps	Gls
92-93	Tottenham H.	3	0	3	0	0	0
93-94	Tottenham H.	5	0	5	3	1	0
	Total	8	0	8	3	1	0

MORENO, Jaime

FULLNAME: Jaime Moreno
DOB: 19-Jan-74, Bolivia

Club History	Signed	Fee
Blooming (Bolivia)		
Middlesbrough		£250,000
Washignton	8/96	£100,000

Season	Team	Tot	St	Sb	Snu	Ps	Gls
95-96	Middlesbrough	7	2	5	13	0	0
	Total	7	2	5	13	0	0

MORGAN, Chris

FULLNAME: Chris Morgan
DOB: 13-Feb-78, Barnsley

Club History	Signed	Fee
Barnsley		Trainee

Season	Team	Tot	St	Sb	Snu	Ps	Gls
97-98	Barnsley	11	10	1	1	1	0
	Total	11	10	1	1	1	0

MORGAN, Philip

FULLNAME: Philip Morgan
DOB: 18-Dec-74, Stoke-on-Trent

Club History	Signed	Fee
Ipswich T.		

Season	Team	Tot	St	Sb	Snu	Ps	Gls
93-94	Ipswich T.	0	0	0	13	0	0
94-95	Ipswich T.	1	1	0	18	0	0
	Total	1	1	0	31	0	0

MORGAN, Steve

FULLNAME: Stephen Alphonso Morgan
DOB: 19-Sep-68, Oldham

Club History	Signed	Fee
Blackpool	8/86	Apprentice
Plymouth Argyle	7/90	£115,000
Coventry C.	7/93	£110,000

Season	Team	Tot	St	Sb	Snu	Ps	Gls
93-94	Coventry C.	40	39	1	0	4	2
94-95	Coventry C.	28	26	2	2	1	0
	Total	68	65	3	2	5	2

MORLEY, Trevor

FULLNAME: Trevor W Morley
DOB: 20-Mar-61, Nottingham

Club History	Signed	Fee
Northampton Town	6/85	£20,000
Manchester C.	1/88	£175,000
West Ham U.	12/89	£500,000

Season	Team	Tot	St	Sb	Snu	Ps	Gls
93-94	West Ham U.	42	39	3	0	5	13
94-95	West Ham U.	14	10	4	3	1	0
	Total	56	49	7	3	6	13

MORRIS, Chris

FULLNAME: Christopher Barry Morris
DOB: 24-Dec-63, Newquay

Club History	Signed	Fee	
Sheffield W.	10/82		
Celtic	8/87	£125,000	
Middlesbrough	8/92	£450,000	+ player

Season	Team	Tot	St	Sb	Snu	Ps	Gls
92-93	Middlesbrough	25	22	3	0	2	1
95-96	Middlesbrough	23	22	1	0	2	2
96-97	Middlesbrough	4	3	1	4	2	0
	Total	52	47	5	4	6	3

MORRIS, Jody

FULLNAME: Jody Morris
DOB: 22-Dec-78, London

Club History	Signed	Fee
Chelsea	01/96	Trainee

Season	Team	Tot	St	Sb	Snu	Ps	Gls
95-96	Chelsea	1	0	1	0	0	0
96-97	Chelsea	12	6	6	8	3	0
97-98	Chelsea	12	9	3	2	5	1
98-99	Chelsea	18	14	4	8	8	1
99-00	Chelsea	30	19	11	5	4	3
	Total	73	48	25	23	20	5

MORRIS, Lee

FULLNAME: Lee Morris
DOB: 30-Apr-80, Blackpool

Club History	Signed	Fee
Sheffield U.	12/97	Trainee
Derby Co.	10/99	£3m

Season	Team	Tot	St	Sb	Snu	Ps	Gls
99-00	Derby Co.	3	2	1	0	2	0
	Total	3	2	1	0	2	0

MORRISON, Andy

FULLNAME: Andrew C Morrison
DOB: 30-Jul-70, Inverness

Club History	Signed	Fee
Plymouth Argyle	7/88	
Blackburn R.	8/93	£500,000

Season	Team	Tot	St	Sb	Snu	Ps	Gls
93-94	Blackburn R.	5	1	4	1	1	0
	Total	5	1	4	1	1	0

MORRISON, Clint

FULLNAME: Clinton Morrison
DOB: 14-May-79, Tooting

Club History	Signed	Fee
Crystal P.		Trainee

Season	Team	Tot	St	Sb	Snu	Ps	Gls
97-98	Crystal P.	1	0	1	0	0	1
	Total	1	0	1	0	0	1

MORRISON, Owen

FULLNAME: John Owen Morrison
DOB: 08-Dec-81, Londonderry

Club History	Signed	Fee
Sheffield W.	1/99	Trainee

Season	Team	Tot	St	Sb	Snu	Ps	Gls
98-99	Sheffield W.	1	0	1	0	0	0
	Total	1	0	1	0	0	0

MORROW, Steve

FULLNAME: Stephen Joseph Morrow
DOB: 02-Jul-70, Bangor, Northern Ireland

Club History	Signed	Fee
Arsenal	5/88	

Season	Team	Tot	St	Sb	Snu	Ps	Gls
92-93	Arsenal	16	13	3	1	0	0
93-94	Arsenal	11	7	4	2	0	0
94-95	Arsenal	15	11	4	4	2	1
95-96	Arsenal	4	3	1	5	2	0
96-97	Arsenal	14	5	9	12	3	0
	Total	60	39	21	24	7	1

MORTIMER, Paul

FULLNAME: Paul Henry Mortimer
DOB: 08-May-68, Kensington

Club History	Signed	Fee
Charlton A.	9/87	
Aston Villa	7/91	£350,000
Crystal P.	10/91	£500,000
Brentford	1/93	Loan
Charlton A.	8/94	Swap

Season	Team	Tot	St	Sb	Snu	Ps	Gls
92-93	Crystal P.	1	1	0	0	1	0
98-99	Charlton A.	17	10	7	1	8	1
	Total	18	11	7	1	9	1

MOSES, Adrian

FULLNAME: Adrian Paul Moses
DOB: 15-Nov-68, Doncaster

Club History	Signed	Fee
Barnsley	7/93	Juniors

Season	Team	Tot	St	Sb	Snu	Ps	Gls
97-98	Barnsley	35	32	3	0	1	0
	Total	35	32	3	0	1	0

MOSS, Neil

FULLNAME: Neil Graham Moss
DOB: 10-May-75, New Milton

Club History	Signed	Fee
Bournemouth	1/93	Trainee
Southampton	12/95	£250,000
Gillingham	8/97	Loan

Season	Team	Tot	St	Sb	Snu	Ps	Gls
96-97	Southampton	3	3	0	14	0	0

		Tot	St	Sb	Snu	Ps	Gls
97-98	Southampton	0	0	0	20	0	0
98-99	Southampton	7	7	0	23	0	0
99-00	Southampton	9	7	2	29	0	0
	Total	19	17	2	86	0	0

MOULDEN, Paul

FULLNAME: Paul Moulden
DOB: 06-Sep-67, Farnworth

Club History	Signed	Fee
Manchester C.	9/84	Apprentice
Bournemouth	7/89	
Oldham A.	3/90	

Season	Team	Tot	St	Sb	Snu	Ps	Gls
92-93	Oldham A.	4	1	3	0	1	0
	Total	4	1	3	0	1	0

MULLIN, John

FULLNAME: John Mullin
DOB: 11-Aug-75, Bury

Club History	Signed	Fee
Burnley	8/92	Trainee
Sunderland	8/95	£40,000

Season	Team	Tot	St	Sb	Snu	Ps	Gls
96-97	Sunderland	10	9	1	1	4	1
	Total	10	9	1	1	4	1

MULRYNE, Phil

FULLNAME: Philip Mulryne
DOB: 01-Jan-78, Belfast

Club History	Signed	Fee
Manchester U.		Trainee

Season	Team	Tot	St	Sb	Snu	Ps	Gls
97-98	Manchester U.	1	1	0	5	0	0
98-99	Manchester U.	0	0	0	0	0	0
	Total	1	1	0	5	0	0

MURPHY, Danny

FULLNAME: Daniel Benjamin Murphy
DOB: 25-Feb-73, Manchester

Club History	Signed	Fee
Crewe Alex.	3/94	Trainee
Liverpool	7/97	£1.5m

Season	Team	Tot	St	Sb	Snu	Ps	Gls
97-98	Liverpool	16	6	10	10	4	0
98-99	Liverpool	1	0	1	3	0	0
99-00	Liverpool	23	9	14	5	8	3
	Total	38	15	25	18	12	3

MURRAY, Adam

FULLNAME: Adam David Murray
DOB: 30-Sep-81, Birmingham

Club History	Signed	Fee
Derby Co.	10/98	Trainee

Season	Team	Tot	St	Sb	Snu	Ps	Gls
98-99	Derby Co.	4	0	4	2	0	0
99-00	Derby Co.	8	1	7	4	1	0
	Total	12	1	11	6	1	0

MURRAY, Paul

FULLNAME: Paul Murray
DOB: 31-Aug-76, Carlisle

Club History	Signed	Fee
Carlisle U.	6/94	Trainee
QPR	3/96	£300,000

Season	Team	Tot	St	Sb	Snu	Ps	Gls
95-96	QPR	1	1	0	0	0	0
	Total	1	1	0	0	0	0

MURRAY, Scott

FULLNAME: Scott George Murray
DOB: 26-May-74, Aberdeen

Club History	Signed	Fee
Aston Villa	03/94	£35,000

Season	Team	Tot	St	Sb	Snu	Ps	Gls
95-96	Aston Villa	3	3	0	0	1	0
96-97	Aston Villa	1	1	0	8	1	0
97-98	Aston Villa	0	0	0	2	0	0
	Total	4	4	0	10	2	0

MUSCAT, Kevin

FULLNAME: Kevin Muscat
DOB: 07-Aug-73, Australia

Club History	Signed	Fee
South Melbourne		
Crystal P.	6/96	

Season	Team	Tot	St	Sb	Snu	Ps	Gls
97-98	Crystal P.	9	9	0	1	4	0
	Total	9	9	0	1	4	0

MUSTOE, Robbie

FULLNAME: Robin Mustoe
DOB: 28-Aug-68, Witney

Club History	Signed	Fee
Oxford U.	7/86	Junior
Middlesbrough	7/90	£375,000

Season	Team	Tot	St	Sb	Snu	Ps	Gls
92-93	Middlesbrough	23	21	2	0	4	1
95-96	Middlesbrough	21	21	0	0	2	1
96-97	Middlesbrough	31	31	0	0	1	2
98-99	Middlesbrough	33	32	1	0	3	4
99-00	Middlesbrough	28	18	10	2	1	0
	Total	136	123	13	2	11	8

MUTCH, Andy

FULLNAME: Andrew Todd Mutch
DOB: 28-Dec-68, Liverpool

Club History	Signed	Fee
Wolverhampton W.	2/86	Free from Non League
Swindon Town	8/93	£250,000

Season	Team	Tot	St	Sb	Snu	Ps	Gls
93-94	Swindon T.	30	27	3	2	7	6
	Total	30	27	3	2	7	6

MYERS, Andy

FULLNAME: Andrew John Myers
DOB: 03-Nov-73, Hounslow

Club History	Signed	Fee
Chelsea	6/91	Trainee
Bradford C.	7/99	£800,000

Season	Team	Tot	St	Sb	Snu	Ps	Gls
92-93	Chelsea	3	3	0	1	1	0
93-94	Chelsea	6	6	0	0	1	0
94-95	Chelsea	10	9	1	1	1	0
95-96	Chelsea	20	20	0	1	0	0
96-97	Chelsea	18	15	3	6	6	1
97-98	Chelsea	12	11	1	5	1	0
98-99	Chelsea	1	1	0	1	1	0
99-00	Bradford C.	13	10	3	6	2	0
	Total	83	75	8	21	13	1

MYHRE, Thomas

FULLNAME: Thomas Myhre
DOB: 16-Oct-73, Norway

Club History	Signed	Fee
Viking Stavanger		
Everton	11/97	

Season	Team	Tot	St	Sb	Snu	Ps	Gls
97-98	Everton	22	22	0	1	0	0
98-99	Everton	38	38	0	0	0	0
99-00	Everton	4	4	0	3	0	0
	Total	64	64	0	4	0	0

NAYIM

FULLNAME: Mohamed Ali Amar
DOB: 05-Nov-66, Morocco

Club History	Signed	Fee
Barcelona		
Tottenham H.		

Season	Team	Tot	St	Sb	Snu	Ps	Gls
92-93	Tottenham H.	18	15	3	0	4	3
	Total	18	15	3	0	4	3

NDAH, George

FULLNAME: George Ndah
DOB: 23-Dec-74, Dulwich

Club History	Signed	Fee
Crystal P.	8/92	Trainee
Swindon Town	11/97	£500,000

Season	Team	Tot	St	Sb	Snu	Ps	Gls
92-93	Crystal P.	13	4	9	4	2	0
94-95	Crystal P.	12	5	7	2	2	1
97-98	Crystal P.	3	2	1	1	1	0
	Total	28	11	17	7	5	1

NDLOVU, Peter

FULLNAME: Peter Ndlovu
DOB: 25-Feb-73, Bulawayo, Zimbabwe

Club History	Signed	Fee
Coventry C.	8/91	£10,000

Season	Team	Tot	St	Sb	Snu	Ps	Gls
92-93	Coventry C.	32	27	5	0	1	7
93-94	Coventry C.	40	40	0	0	0	11
94-95	Coventry C.	30	28	2	0	2	11
95-96	Coventry C.	32	27	5	0	5	5
96-97	Coventry C.	20	10	10	1	4	1
	Total	154	132	22	1	12	35

NEILSON, Alan

FULLNAME: Alan Bruce Neilson
DOB: 26-Sep-72, Wegburg, Germany

Club History	Signed	Fee
Newcastle U.	2/91	Trainee
Southampton	6/95	£500,000

Season	Team	Tot	St	Sb	Snu	Ps	Gls
93-94	Newcastle U.	14	10	4	5	0	0
94-95	Newcastle U.	6	5	1	6	0	0
95-96	Southampton	18	15	3	1	3	0
96-97	Southampton	29	24	5	3	2	0
97-98	Southampton	8	3	5	1	0	0
	Total	75	57	18	16	5	0

NELSON, Fernando

FULLNAME: Fernando Nelson
DOB: 05-Nov-71, Lisbon

Club History	Signed	Fee					
Sporting Lisbon	(1991)						
Aston Villa	7/96	£1.75m					

Season	Team	Tot	St	Sb	Snu	Ps	Gls
96-97	Aston Villa	34	33	1	1	4	0
97-98	Aston Villa	25	21	4	11	6	0
	Total	59	54	5	12	10	0

NETHERCOTT, Stuart

FULLNAME: Stuart David Nethercott
DOB: 21-Mar-73, Ilford

Club History	Signed	Fee
Tottenham H.	8/91	Trainee

Season	Team	Tot	St	Sb	Snu	Ps	Gls
92-93	Tottenham H.	5	3	2	3	2	0
93-94	Tottenham H.	10	9	1	1	0	0
94-95	Tottenham H.	17	8	9	15	3	0
95-96	Tottenham H.	13	9	4	5	0	0
96-97	Tottenham H.	9	2	7	19	2	0
	Total	54	31	23	43	7	0

NEVILLE, Gary

FULLNAME: Gary Alexander Neville
DOB: 18-Feb-75, Bury

Club History	Signed	Fee
Manchester U.	1/93	Trainee

Season	Team	Tot	St	Sb	Snu	Ps	Gls
93-94	Manchester U.	1	1	0	0	0	0
94-95	Manchester U.	18	16	2	2	2	0
95-96	Manchester U.	31	30	1	3	1	0
96-97	Manchester U.	31	30	1	3	2	1
97-98	Manchester U.	34	34	0	2	5	0
98-99	Manchester U.	34	34	0	0	3	1
99-00	Manchester U.	22	22	0	0	3	0
	Total	171	167	4	10	16	2

NEVILLE, Phil

FULLNAME: Philip John Neville
DOB: 21-Jan-77, Bury

Club History	Signed	Fee
Manchester U.	06/94	Trainee

Season	Team	Tot	St	Sb	Snu	Ps	Gls
94-95	Manchester U.	2	1	1	0	1	0
95-96	Manchester U.	24	21	3	3	6	0
96-97	Manchester U.	18	15	3	5	1	0
97-98	Manchester U.	30	24	6	3	6	1
98-99	Manchester U.	28	19	9	7	5	0
99-00	Manchester U.	29	25	4	8	4	0
	Total	131	105	26	26	23	1

NEVLAND, Erik

FULLNAME: Erik Nevland
DOB: 10-Nov-77, Stravanger, Norway

Club History	Signed	Fee
Viking Stavanger		
Manchester U.	7/97	

Season	Team	Tot	St	Sb	Snu	Ps	Gls
97-98	Manchester U.	1	0	1	1	0	0
98-99	Manchester U.	0	0	0	0	0	0
	Total	1	0	1	1	0	0

NEWBY, John

FULLNAME: John Newby
DOB: 19-Aug-80, Liverpool

Club History	Signed	Fee
Liverpool		Trainee

Season	Team	Tot	St	Sb	Snu	Ps	Gls
99-00	Liverpool	1	0	1	1	0	0
	Total	1	0	1	1	0	0

NEWELL, Mike

FULLNAME: Michael Colin Newell
DOB: 27-Jan-65, Liverpool

Club History	Signed	Fee
Crewe Alexandra	9/83	Free
Wigan A.	10/83	Free
Luton Town	1/86	£100,000
Leicester C.	9/87	£350,000
Everton	6/89	£1.1m
Blackburn R.	11/91	£1.1m
Birmingham C.		
West Ham U.	12/96	Loan

Season	Team	Tot	St	Sb	Snu	Ps	Gls
92-93	Blackburn R.	40	40	0	0	1	13
93-94	Blackburn R.	28	27	1	0	4	6
94-95	Blackburn R.	12	2	10	16	0	0
95-96	Blackburn R.	30	26	4	2	9	3
96-97	West Ham U.	7	6	1	0	2	0
	Total	117	101	16	18	16	22

NEWHOUSE, Aidan

FULLNAME: Aidan Robert Newhouse
DOB: 23-May-72, Wallasey

Club History	Signed	Fee
Chester C.	7/89	
Wimbledon	2/90	£100,000

Season	Team	Tot	St	Sb	Snu	Ps	Gls
92-93	Wimbledon	1	0	1	0	0	0
	Total	1	0	1	0	0	0

NEWMAN, Ricky

FULLNAME: Richard Adrian Newman
DOB: 05-Aug-70, Guildford

Club History	Signed	Fee
Crystal P.	1/88	

Season	Team	Tot	St	Sb	Snu	Ps	Gls
92-93	Crystal P.	2	1	1	0	0	0
94-95	Crystal P.	35	32	3	0	4	3
	Total	37	33	4	0	4	3

NEWMAN, Rob

FULLNAME: Robert Nigel Newman
DOB: 13-Dec-63, Bradford on Avon

Club History	Signed	Fee
Bristol C.	10/81	
Norwich C.	7/91	£600,000

Season	Team	Tot	St	Sb	Snu	Ps	Gls
92-93	Norwich C.	18	16	2	2	2	2
93-94	Norwich C.	32	32	0	0	2	2
94-95	Norwich C.	32	23	9	2	5	1
	Total	82	71	11	4	9	5

NEWSOME, Jon

FULLNAME: Jonathan Newsome
DOB: 06-Sep-70, Sheffield

Club History	Signed	Fee
Sheffield Wed	7/89	Trainee
Leeds U.	6/91	£150,000
Norwich C.	6/94	£1m
Sheffield W.	3/96	£1.6m

Season	Team	Tot	St	Sb	Snu	Ps	Gls
92-93	Leeds U.	37	30	7	2	5	0
93-94	Leeds U.	29	25	4	4	1	1
94-95	Norwich C.	35	35	0	0	0	3
95-96	Sheffield W.	8	8	0	0	0	1
96-97	Sheffield W.	10	10	0	1	0	1
97-98	Sheffield W.	25	25	0	0	2	2
98-99	Sheffield W.	4	2	2	14	0	0
99-00	Sheffield W.	6	5	1	3	0	0
	Total	154	140	14	24	8	8

NEWTON, Adam

FULLNAME: Adam Newton
DOB:

Club History	Signed	Fee
West Ham U.		Trainee

Season	Team	Tot	St	Sb	Snu	Ps	Gls
99-00	West Ham U.	2	0	2	11	0	0
	Total	2	0	2	11	0	0

NEWTON, Eddie

FULLNAME: Edward John Ikem Newton
DOB: 13-Dec-71, Hammersmith

Club History	Signed	Fee
Chelsea	5/90	Trainee

Season	Team	Tot	St	Sb	Snu	Ps	Gls
92-93	Chelsea	34	32	2	2	2	5
93-94	Chelsea	36	33	3	0	1	0
94-95	Chelsea	30	22	8	0	2	1
95-96	Chelsea	24	21	3	0	1	1
96-97	Chelsea	15	13	2	2	2	0
97-98	Chelsea	18	17	1	2	5	0
98-99	Chelsea	7	1	6	7	0	0
	Total	164	139	25	13	13	7

NEWTON, Shaun

FULLNAME: Shaun O'Neill Newton
DOB: 20-Aug-75, Camberwell

Club History	Signed	Fee
Charlton A.	7/93	Trainee

Season	Team	Tot	St	Sb	Snu	Ps	Gls
98-99	Charlton A.	16	13	3	2	8	0
	Total	16	13	3	2	8	0

NGONGE, Michel

FULLNAME: Felix Michel Ngonge
DOB: 10-Jan-67, Zaire

Club History	Signed	Fee
Samsunspor		
Watford	8/98	Free

Season	Team	Tot	St	Sb	Snu	Ps	Gls
99-00	Watford	23	16	7	2	11	5
	Total	23	16	7	2	11	5

NICHOLLS, Mark

FULLNAME: Mark Nicholls
DOB: 30-May-77, Hillingdon

Club History	Signed	Fee
Chelsea		Trainee

Season	Team	Tot	St	Sb	Snu	Ps	Gls
96-97	Chelsea	8	3	5	8	2	0
97-98	Chelsea	19	8	11	10	3	3
98-99	Chelsea	9	0	9	11	0	0
99-00	Chelsea	0	0	0	2	0	0
	Total	36	11	25	31	5	3

NICOL, Steve

FULLNAME: Stephen Nicol
DOB: 01-Dec-61, Irvine

Club History	Signed	Fee				
Liverpool	10/81	£300,000				
Notts Co.	1/95	Free				
Sheffield W.	11/95	Free				

Season	Team	Tot	St	Sb	Snu	Ps	Gls
92-93	Liverpool	32	32	0	0	0	0
93-94	Liverpool	31	27	4	4	3	1
94-95	Liverpool	4	4	0	1	0	0
95-96	Sheffield W.	19	18	1	3	2	0
96-97	Sheffield W.	23	19	4	9	8	0
97-98	Sheffield W.	7	4	3	6	2	0
	Total	116	104	12	23	15	1

NIELSEN, Allan

FULLNAME: Allan Nielsen
DOB: 13-Mar-71, Esbjerg

Club History	Signed	Fee				
Brondby	1996	£100,000				
Tottenham H.	9/96	£1.6m				

Season	Team	Tot	St	Sb	Snu	Ps	Gls
96-97	Tottenham H.	29	28	1	1	8	6
97-98	Tottenham H.	25	21	4	6	4	3
98-99	Tottenham H.	28	24	4	3	2	3
99-00	Tottenham H.	14	5	9	2	2	0
	Total	96	78	18	12	16	12

NIJHOLT, Luc

FULLNAME: Luc Nijholt
DOB: 29-Jul-61, Zaandam

Club History	Signed	Fee				
Motherwell						
Swindon Town	8/93	£175,000				

Season	Team	Tot	St	Sb	Snu	Ps	Gls
93-94	Swindon T.	32	31	1	0	1	1
	Total	32	31	1	0	1	1

NILSEN, Roger

FULLNAME: Roger Nilsen
DOB: 08-Aug-69, Tromso, Norway

Club History	Signed	Fee				
Viking Stavanger						
Sheffield U.	11/93	£550,000				
Tottenham H.	3/99	Free				

Season	Team	Tot	St	Sb	Snu	Ps	Gls
93-94	Sheffield U.	22	21	1	0	3	0
98-99	Tottenham H.	3	3	0	4	0	0
	Total	25	24	1	4	3	0

NILSSON, Roland

FULLNAME: Nils Lennart Roland Nilsson
DOB: 27-Nov-63, Helsingborg, Sweden

Club History	Signed	Fee				
IFK Gothenburg						
Sheffield W.	11/89	£375,000				
Helsingborg	5/94					
Coventry C.	7/97	£200,000				

Season	Team	Tot	St	Sb	Snu	Ps	Gls
92-93	Sheffield W.	32	32	0	0	4	1
93-94	Sheffield W.	38	38	0	0	2	0
97-98	Coventry C.	32	32	0	1	0	0
98-99	Coventry C.	28	28	0	1	6	0
	Total	130	130	0	2	12	1

NIMNI, Avi

FULLNAME: Avi Nimni
DOB:

Club History	Signed	Fee				
Maccabi Tel Aviv						
Derby Co.	11/99	Loan				

Season	Team	Tot	St	Sb	Snu	Ps	Gls
99-00	Derby Co.	4	2	2	4	2	1
	Total	4	2	2	4	2	1

NOEL-WILLIAMS, Gifton

FULLNAME: Gifton Ruben Elisha Noel-Williams
DOB: 21-Jan-80, Islington

Club History	Signed	Fee				
Watford	2/97	Trainee				

Season	Team	Tot	St	Sb	Snu	Ps	Gls
99-00	Watford	3	1	2	1	0	0
	Total	3	1	2	1	0	0

NOLAN, Ian

FULLNAME: Ian Robert Nolan
DOB: 09-Jul-70, Liverpool

Club History	Signed	Fee				
Preston NE		Trainee				
Tranmere R.	8/91	£10,000				
Sheffield W.	8/94	£1.5m				

Season	Team	Tot	St	Sb	Snu	Ps	Gls
94-95	Sheffield W.	42	42	0	0	1	3
95-96	Sheffield W.	29	29	0	0	3	0
96-97	Sheffield W.	38	38	0	0	1	1
97-98	Sheffield W.	27	27	0	0	2	0
99-00	Sheffield W.	29	28	1	4	2	0
	Total	165	164	1	4	9	4

NORFOLK, Lee

FULLNAME: Lee Norfolk
DOB: 17-Oct-75, New Zealand

Club History	Signed	Fee
Ipswich Town		

Season	Team	Tot	St	Sb	Snu	Ps	Gls
94-95	Ipswich T.	3	1	2	0	0	0
	Total	3	1	2	0	0	0

NORMANN, Runar

FULLNAME: Runar Normann
DOB:

Club History	Signed	Fee
Lillestrom		
Coventry C.	7/99	

Season	Team	Tot	St	Sb	Snu	Ps	Gls
99-00	Coventry C.	8	1	7	7	2	0
	Total	8	1	7	7	2	0

NUNEZ, Milton

FULLNAME: Milton Nunez
DOB: 20-Oct-72, Honduras

Club History	Signed	Fee
PAOK Salonika		
Sunderland	3/00	£1.6m

Season	Team	Tot	St	Sb	Snu	Ps	Gls
99-00	Sunderland	1	0	1	3	0	0
	Total	1	0	1	3	0	0

O'BRIEN, Andy

FULLNAME: Andrew James O'Brien
DOB: 29-Jun-79, Harrogate

Club History	Signed	Fee
Bradford C.	10/96	Trainee

Season	Team	Tot	St	Sb	Snu	Ps	Gls
99-00	Bradford C.	36	36	0	2	1	1
	Total	36	36	0	2	1	1

O'BRIEN, Liam

FULLNAME: Liam O'Brien
DOB: 05-Sep-64, Dublin

Club History	Signed	Fee
Shamrock R.		
Manchester U.	10/86	£60,000
Newcastle U.	11/88	£250,000

Season	Team	Tot	St	Sb	Snu	Ps	Gls
93-94	Newcastle U.	6	4	2	3	0	1
	Total	6	4	2	3	0	1

O'CONNOR, Jon

FULLNAME: Jonathon O'Connor
DOB: 29-Oct-76, Darlington

Club History	Signed	Fee
Everton	10/93	Trainee

Season	Team	Tot	St	Sb	Snu	Ps	Gls
95-96	Everton	4	3	1	2	0	0
96-97	Everton	0	0	0	3	0	0
97-98	Everton	1	0	1	4	0	0
	Total	5	3	2	9	0	0

O'DONNELL, Phil

FULLNAME: Phil O'Donnell
DOB:

Club History	Signed	Fee
Sheffield W.		

Season	Team	Tot	St	Sb	Snu	Ps	Gls
99-00	Sheffield W.	1	0	1	1	0	0
	Total	1	0	1	1	0	0

O'HALLORAN, Keith

FULLNAME: Keith James O'Halloran
DOB: 10-Nov-75, Dublin

Club History	Signed	Fee
Cherry Orchard		
Middlesbrough	9/94	

Season	Team	Tot	St	Sb	Snu	Ps	Gls
95-96	Middlesbrough	3	2	1	0	1	0
	Total	3	2	1	0	1	0

O'KANE, John

FULLNAME: John Andrew O'Kane
DOB: 15-Nov-74, Nottingham

Club History	Signed	Fee
Manchester U.	1/93	Trainee
Bury	10/96	Loan (x2)
Everton	1/98	£250,000>

Season	Team	Tot	St	Sb	Snu	Ps	Gls
95-96	Manchester U.	1	0	1	0	0	0
96-97	Manchester U.	1	1	0	0	1	0
97-98	Everton	12	12	0	0	4	0
98-99	Everton	2	2	0	2	2	0
	Total	16	15	1	2	7	0

O'LEARY, David

FULLNAME: David Anthony O'Leary
DOB: 02-May-58, Stoke Newington

Club History	Signed	Fee
Arsenal	7/75	
Leeds U.	6/93	Free

Season	Team	Tot	St	Sb	Snu	Ps	Gls
92-93	Arsenal	11	6	5	3	3	0
93-94	Leeds U.	10	10	0	0	3	0
	Total	21	16	5	3	6	0

O'NEIL, Brian

FULLNAME: Brian O'Neil
DOB: 06-Sep-72, Paisley

Club History	Signed	Fee
Celtic	1991	
Nottingham F.		Loan

Season	Team	Tot	St	Sb	Snu	Ps	Gls
96-97	Nottingham F.	5	4	1	2	1	0
	Total	5	4	1	2	1	0

O'NEILL, Keith

FULLNAME: Keith Padre Gerard O'Neill
DOB: 16-Feb-76, Dublin, Republic of Ireland

Club History	Signed	Fee
Norwich C.	7/94	Trainee
Middlesbrough	3/99	£700,000

Season	Team	Tot	St	Sb	Snu	Ps	Gls
94-95	Norwich C.	1	0	1	0	0	0
98-99	Middlesbrough	6	4	2	1	2	0
99-00	Middlesbrough	16	14	2	0	3	0
	Total	23	18	5	1	5	0

O'NEILL, Michael

FULLNAME: Michael Andrew Martin O'Neill
DOB: 05-Jul-69, Portadown

Club History	Signed	Fee
Coleraine		
Newcastle U.	10/87	
Dundee U.	8/89	
Hibernian	8/93	
Coventry C.	7/96	£500,000

Season	Team	Tot	St	Sb	Snu	Ps	Gls
96-97	Coventry C.	1	1	0	3	1	0
97-98	Coventry C.	4	2	2	4	2	0
	Total	5	3	2	7	3	0

OAKES, Andy

FULLNAME: Andrew Mark Oakes
DOB: 11-Jan-77, Northwich

Club History	Signed	Fee
Hull C.	12/98	Free from Non League
Derby Co.	6/99	£460,000

Season	Team	Tot	St	Sb	Snu	Ps	Gls
99-00	Derby Co.	0	0	0	19	0	0
	Total	0	0	0	19	0	0

OAKES, Michael

FULLNAME: Michael Oakes
DOB: 30-Oct-73, Northwich

Club History	Signed	Fee
Aston Villa	07/91	Trainee

Season	Team	Tot	St	Sb	Snu	Ps	Gls
92-93	Aston Villa	0	0	0	5	0	0
93-94	Aston Villa	0	0	0	8	0	0
94-95	Aston Villa	0	0	0	8	0	0
95-96	Aston Villa	0	0	0	16	0	0
96-97	Aston Villa	20	18	2	17	0	0
97-98	Aston Villa	8	8	0	29	0	0
98-99	Aston Villa	23	23	0	15	0	0
99-00	Aston Villa	0	0	0	9	0	0
	Total	51	49	2	107	0	0

OAKES, Scott

FULLNAME: Scott John Oakes
DOB: 05-Aug-72, Leicester

Club History	Signed	Fee
Leicester C.	5/90	Trainee
Luton Town	10/91	
Sheffield W.	8/96	£450,000

Season	Team	Tot	St	Sb	Snu	Ps	Gls
96-97	Sheffield W.	19	7	12	9	5	1
97-98	Sheffield W.	4	0	4	10	0	0
98-99	Sheffield W.	1	0	1	3	0	0
	Total	24	7	17	22	5	1

OAKES, Stefan

FULLNAME: Stefan Oakes
DOB: 06-Sep-78, Leicester

Club History	Signed	Fee
Leicester C.		Trainee

Season	Team	Tot	St	Sb	Snu	Ps	Gls
97-98	Leicester C.	0	0	0	1	0	0
98-99	Leicester C.	3	2	1	3	1	0
99-00	Leicester C.	22	15	7	11	5	1
	Total	25	17	8	15	6	1

OAKLEY, Matthew

FULLNAME: Matthew Oakley
DOB: 17-Aug-77, Peterborough

Club History	Signed	Fee
Southampton	7/95	Trainee

Season	Team	Tot	St	Sb	Snu	Ps	Gls
94-95	Southampton	1	0	1	0	0	0
95-96	Southampton	10	5	5	0	3	0
96-97	Southampton	28	23	5	0	11	3
97-98	Southampton	33	32	1	0	10	1
98-99	Southampton	22	21	1	0	8	2
99-00	Southampton	31	26	5	2	4	3
	Total	125	107	18	2	36	9

OGRIZOVIC, Steve

FULLNAME: Steven Ogrizovic
DOB: 12-Sep-57, Mansfield

Club History	Signed	Fee
Chesterfield	7/77	
Liverpool	11/77	£70,000
Shrewsbury Tn	8/82	£70,000
Coventry C.	6/84	£72,000

Season	Team	Tot	St	Sb	Snu	Ps	Gls
92-93	Coventry C.	33	33	0	8	0	0
93-94	Coventry C.	33	33	0	8	0	0
94-95	Coventry C.	33	33	0	2	0	0
95-96	Coventry C.	25	25	0	0	0	0
96-97	Coventry C.	38	38	0	0	1	0
97-98	Coventry C.	24	24	0	13	0	0
98-99	Coventry C.	2	2	0	27	0	0
99-00	Coventry C.	3	3	0	17	0	0
	Total	191	191	0	75	1	0

OLDFIELD, David

FULLNAME: David C Oldfield
DOB: 30-May-68, Perth, Australia

Club History	Signed	Fee
Luton Town	5/86	
Manchester C.	3/89	£600,000
Leicester C.	1/90	£150,000

Season	Team	Tot	St	Sb	Snu	Ps	Gls
94-95	Leicester C.	14	8	6	1	2	1
	Total	14	8	6	1	2	1

OLNEY, Ian

FULLNAME: Ian Douglas Olney
DOB: 17-Dec-69, Luton

Club History	Signed	Fee
Aston Villa	7/88	
Oldham A.	5/92	£700,000

Season	Team	Tot	St	Sb	Snu	Ps	Gls
92-93	Oldham A.	34	32	2	0	4	12
93-94	Oldham A.	10	10	0	0	3	1
	Total	44	42	2	0	7	13

OMOYIMNI, Emmanuel

FULLNAME: Emmanuel Omoyimni
DOB: 28-Dec-77, Nigeria

Club History	Signed	Fee
West Ham U.	5/95	Trainee

Season	Team	Tot	St	Sb	Snu	Ps	Gls
96-97	West Ham U.	1	0	1	0	0	0
97-98	West Ham U.	5	1	4	2	0	2
98-99	West Ham U.	3	0	3	4	0	0
99-00	West Ham U.	0	0	0	1	0	0
	Total	9	1	8	7	0	2

ORD, Richard

FULLNAME: Richard John Ord
DOB: 03-Mar-69, Murton

Club History	Signed	Fee
Sunderland	7/87	Trainee

Season	Team	Tot	St	Sb	Snu	Ps	Gls
96-97	Sunderland	33	33	0	0	0	2
	Total	33	33	0	0	0	2

ORLYGSSON, Toddy

FULLNAME: Thorvaldur Orlygsson
DOB: 02-Aug-66, Odense

Club History	Signed	Fee
FC Akureyri		
Nottingham F.	11/89	

Season	Team	Tot	St	Sb	Snu	Ps	Gls
92-93	Nottingham F.	20	15	5	9	2	1
	Total	20	15	5	9	2	1

ORMONDROYD, Ian

FULLNAME: Ian Ormondroyd
DOB: 22-Sep-64, Bradford

Club History	Signed	Fee
Bradford C.	9/85	
Oldham A.	3/87	Loan
Aston Villa	2/89	£600,000
Derby Co.	9/91	£350,000
Leicester C.	3/92	Swap

Season	Team	Tot	St	Sb	Snu	Ps	Gls
94-95	Leicester C.	6	6	0	1	3	1
	Total	6	6	0	1	3	1

OSBORN, Simon

FULLNAME: Simon Edward Osborn
DOB: 19-Jan-72, Croydon

Club History	Signed	Fee
Crystal P.	1/90	
Reading	8/94	£90,000
QPR		

Season	Team	Tot	St	Sb	Snu	Ps	Gls
92-93	Crystal P.	31	27	4	5	4	2
95-96	QPR	9	6	3	6	3	1
	Total	40	33	7	11	7	3

OSTENSTAD, Egil

FULLNAME: Egil Ostenstadt
DOB: 02-Jan-72, Haugesund

Club History	Signed	Fee
Viking FK	(1990)	
Southampton	10/96	£800,000

Season	Team	Tot	St	Sb	Snu	Ps	Gls
96-97	Southampton	30	29	1	0	5	10
97-98	Southampton	29	21	8	0	4	11
98-99	Southampton	34	27	7	1	8	7
99-00	Southampton	3	3	0	0	0	1
	Total	96	80	16	1	17	29

OSTER, John

FULLNAME: John Morgan Oster
DOB: 08-Dec-78, Boston

Club History	Signed	Fee
Grimsby Town	7/96	Trainee
Everton	7/97	£1.5m
Sunderland		

Season	Team	Tot	St	Sb	Snu	Ps	Gls
97-98	Everton	31	16	15	5	5	1
98-99	Everton	9	6	3	1	4	0
99-00	Sunderland	10	4	6	10	4	0
	Total	50	26	24	16	13	1

OVERMARS, Marc

FULLNAME: Marc Overmars
DOB: 29-Mar-73, Emst (Holland)

Club History	Signed	Fee
Ajax	7/92	
Arsenal	7/97	£7.0m

Season	Team	Tot	St	Sb	Snu	Ps	Gls
97-98	Arsenal	32	32	0	0	13	12
98-99	Arsenal	37	37	0	0	19	6
99-00	Arsenal	31	22	9	0	13	7
	Total	100	91	9	0	45	25

OWEN, Michael

FULLNAME: Michael James Owen
DOB: 14-Dec-79, Chester

Club History	Signed	Fee
Liverpool	12/96	Juniors

Season	Team	Tot	St	Sb	Snu	Ps	Gls
96-97	Liverpool	2	1	1	2	0	1
97-98	Liverpool	36	34	2	1	4	18
98-99	Liverpool	30	30	0	0	9	18
99-00	Liverpool	27	22	5	0	15	11
	Total	95	87	8	3	28	48

PAATELAINEN, Mixu

FULLNAME: Mixu Paatelainen
DOB: 03-Feb-67, Helsinki

Club History	Signed	Fee
Valkeakosken		
Dundee U.	10/87	
Aberdeen	3/92	
Bolton W.	8/94	£300,000

Season	Team	Tot	St	Sb	Snu	Ps	Gls
95-96	Bolton W.	15	12	3	6	5	1
	Total	15	12	3	6	5	1

PADAVANO, Michele

FULLNAME: Michele Padavano
DOB: 28-Aug-66, Turin, Italy

Club History	Signed	Fee
Juventus		
C.Palace	11/97	£1.7m

Season	Team	Tot	St	Sb	Snu	Ps	Gls
97-98	Crystal P.	10	8	2	1	8	1
	Total	10	8	2	1	8	1

PAGE, Robert

FULLNAME: Robert John Page
DOB: 03-Jul-74, Rhondda

Club History	Signed	Fee
Watford	4/93	Trainee

Season	Team	Tot	St	Sb	Snu	Ps	Gls
99-00	Watford	36	36	0	0	2	1
	Total	36	36	0	0	2	1

PAHARS, Marian

FULLNAME: Marians Pahars
DOB: 05-Aug-76, Latvia

Club History	Signed	Fee
Skonto Riga		
Southampton	3/99	£800,000

Season	Team	Tot	St	Sb	Snu	Ps	Gls
98-99	Southampton	6	4	2	0	3	3
99-00	Southampton	33	31	2	1	8	13
	Total	39	35	4	1	11	16

PALLISTER, Gary

FULLNAME: Gary Andrew Pallister
DOB: 30-Jun-65, Ramsgate

Club History	Signed	Fee
Middlesbrough	11/84	Free from Non League
Darlington	10/85	Loan
Manchester U.	8/89	£2.3m
Middlesbrough	7/98	£2.5m

Season	Team	Tot	St	Sb	Snu	Ps	Gls
92-93	Manchester U.	42	42	0	0	0	1
93-94	Manchester U.	41	41	0	0	0	1
94-95	Manchester U.	42	42	0	0	0	2
95-96	Manchester U.	21	21	0	0	1	1
96-97	Manchester U.	27	27	0	1	4	3
97-98	Manchester U.	33	33	0	0	5	0
98-99	Middlesbrough	26	26	0	0	2	0
99-00	Middlesbrough	21	21	0	0	2	1
	Total	253	253	0	1	14	9

PALMER, Carlton

FULLNAME: Carlton Lloyd Palmer
DOB: 05-Dec-65, Rowley Regis

Club History	Signed	Fee
WBA	12/84	Apprentice
Sheffield W.	2/89	£750,000
Leeds U.	6/94	£2.6m
Southampton	9/97	£1.0m
Nottingham F.	1/99	£1.1m
Coventry C.		

Season	Team	Tot	St	Sb	Snu	Ps	Gls
92-93	Sheffield W.	34	33	1	0	1	1
93-94	Sheffield W.	37	37	0	0	0	5
94-95	Leeds U.	39	39	0	0	0	3
95-96	Leeds U.	35	35	0	0	1	2
96-97	Leeds U.	28	26	2	1	1	0
97-98	Southampton	26	26	0	0	0	3
98-99	Southampton	19	18	1	0	0	0
98-99	Nottingham F.	13	13	0	0	0	0
99-00	Coventry C.	15	15	0	0	0	1
	Total	246	242	4	1	3	15

PALMER, Roger

FULLNAME: Roger Neil Palmer
DOB: 30-Jan-59, Manchester

Club History	Signed	Fee
Manchester C.	1/77	
Oldham A.	11/80	£70,000

Season	Team	Tot	St	Sb	Snu	Ps	Gls
92-93	Oldham A.	16	5	11	8	1	0
93-94	Oldham A.	8	1	7	2	0	0
	Total	24	6	18	10	1	0

PALMER, Steve

FULLNAME: Stephen Leonard Palmer
DOB: 31-Mar-68, Brighton

Club History	Signed	Fee
Ipswich Town	8/89	Trainee
Watford	9/97	£130,000

Season	Team	Tot	St	Sb	Snu	Ps	Gls
92-93	Ipswich T.	7	4	3	0	2	0
93-94	Ipswich T.	36	31	5	1	7	1
94-95	Ipswich T.	12	10	2	6	1	0
99-00	Watford	38	38	0	0	1	0
	Total	93	83	10	7	11	1

PANAYI, James

FULLNAME: James Panayi
DOB: 24-Jan-80, Hammersmith

Club History	Signed	Fee
Watford		Trainee

Season	Team	Tot	St	Sb	Snu	Ps	Gls
99-00	Watford	2	2	0	0	2	0
	Total	2	2	0	0	2	0

PARKER, Garry

FULLNAME: Garry Stuart Parker
DOB: 07-Sep-65, Oxford

Club History	Signed	Fee
Luton Town	5/83	Apprentice
Hull C.	2/86	£72,000
Nottingham F.	3/88	£260,000
Aston Villa	11/91	£650,000
Leicester C.	2/95	£300,000

Season	Team	Tot	St	Sb	Snu	Ps	Gls
92-93	Aston Villa	37	37	0	0	10	9
93-94	Aston Villa	19	17	2	2	2	2
94-95	Aston Villa	14	12	2	3	1	1
94-95	Leicester C.	14	14	0	0	0	2
96-97	Leicester C.	31	22	9	1	5	2
97-98	Leicester C.	22	15	7	6	8	3
98-99	Leicester C.	7	2	5	11	2	0
	Total	144	119	25	23	28	19

PARKER, Paul

FULLNAME: Paul Andrew Parker
DOB: 04-Apr-64, West Ham

Club History	Signed	Fee
Fulham	4/82	
QPR	6/87	£300,000
Manchester U.	8/91	£2m
Derby		
Sheffield U.	11/96	Monthly

Fulham
Chelsea   3/97   Free
Derby Co.   10/97   Free

Season	Team	Tot	St	Sb	Snu	Ps	Gls
92-93	Manchester U.	31	31	0	0	1	1
93-94	Manchester U.	40	39	1	0	5	0
94-95	Manchester U.	2	1	1	1	1	0
95-96	Manchester U.	6	5	1	10	1	0
96-97	Chelsea	4	1	3	2	1	0
96-97	Derby Co.	4	4	0	2	1	0
	Total	87	81	6	15	10	1

PARKER, Scott

FULLNAME: Scott Matthew Parker
DOB: 13-Oct-80, Lambeth

Club History	Signed	Fee
Charlton A.	10/97	Trainee

Season	Team	Tot	St	Sb	Snu	Ps	Gls
98-99	Charlton A.	4	0	4	4	0	0
	Total	4	0	4	4	0	0

PARKINSON, Gary

FULLNAME: Gary Parkinson
DOB: 10-Jan-68, Middlesbrough

Club History	Signed	Fee
Everton		Amateur
Middlesbrough		

Season	Team	Tot	St	Sb	Snu	Ps	Gls
92-93	Middlesbrough	4	4	0	2	1	0
	Total	4	4	0	2	1	0

PARKINSON, Joe

FULLNAME: Joseph Simon Parkinson
DOB: 11-Jun-71, Eccles

Club History	Signed	Fee
Wigan A.	4/89	Trainee
Bournemouth	7/93	£35,000
Everton	3/94	£250,000

Season	Team	Tot	St	Sb	Snu	Ps	Gls
93-94	Everton	0	0	0	1	0	0
94-95	Everton	34	32	2	2	6	0
95-96	Everton	28	28	0	0	3	3
96-97	Everton	28	28	0	0	4	0
	Total	90	88	2	3	13	3

PARLOUR, Ray

FULLNAME: Raymond Parlour
DOB: 07-Mar-73, Romford

Club History	Signed	Fee
Arsenal	3/91	Trainee

Season	Team	Tot	St	Sb	Snu	Ps	Gls
92-93	Arsenal	21	16	5	0	4	1
93-94	Arsenal	27	24	3	1	3	2
94-95	Arsenal	30	22	8	0	5	0
95-96	Arsenal	22	20	2	0	6	0
96-97	Arsenal	30	17	13	4	2	2
97-98	Arsenal	34	34	0	0	15	5
98-99	Arsenal	35	35	0	0	6	6
99-00	Arsenal	30	29	1	0	7	1
	Total	229	197	32	5	48	17

PATES, Colin

FULLNAME: Colin Pates
DOB: 10-Aug-61, Mitcham

Club History	Signed	Fee
Chelsea	7/79	Apprentice
Charlton A.	10/88	
Arsenal	1/90	

Season	Team	Tot	St	Sb	Snu	Ps	Gls
92-93	Arsenal	7	2	5	4	0	0
	Total	7	2	5	4	0	0

PATTERSON, Darren

FULLNAME: Darren Patterson
DOB: 15-Oct-69, Belfast

Club History	Signed	Fee
WBA	7/88	Trainee
Wigan A.	4/89	
Crystal P.		

Season	Team	Tot	St	Sb	Snu	Ps	Gls
92-93	Crystal P.	0	0	0	2	0	0
94-95	Crystal P.	22	22	0	2	4	1
	Total	22	22	0	4	4	1

PATTERSON, Mark

FULLNAME: Mark Andrew Patterson
DOB: 24-May-65, Darwen

Club History	Signed	Fee
Blackburn R.	5/83	Apprentice
Preston North End	6/88	£20,000
Bury	2/90	
Bolton W.	1/91	£65,000

Season	Team	Tot	St	Sb	Snu	Ps	Gls
95-96	Bolton W.	16	12	4	1	1	1
	Total	16	12	4	1	1	1

PAZ, Adrian

FULLNAME: Adrian Paz
DOB: 09-Sep-68, Montevideo

Club History	Signed	Fee
Penarol		
Ipswich Town	9/94	£900,000

Season	Team	Tot	St	Sb	Snu	Ps	Gls
94-95	Ipswich T.	17	13	4	1	5	1
	Total	17	13	4	1	5	1

PEACOCK, Darren

FULLNAME: Darren Peacock
DOB: 03-Feb-68, Bristol

Club History	Signed	Fee
Newport Co.	2/86	Apprentice
Hereford U.	3/89	
QPR	12/90	£200,000
Newcastle U.	3/94	£2.7m
Blackburn R.	6/98	Free

Season	Team	Tot	St	Sb	Snu	Ps	Gls
92-93	QPR	38	35	3	3	1	2
93-94	QPR	30	30	0	0	0	3
93-94	Newcastle U.	9	9	0	0	0	0
94-95	Newcastle U.	35	35	0	1	1	1
95-96	Newcastle U.	34	33	1	2	0	0
96-97	Newcastle U.	35	35	0	3	0	1
97-98	Newcastle U.	20	19	1	3	1	0
98-99	Blackburn R.	30	27	3	3	2	1
	Total	231	223	8	15	5	8

PEACOCK, Gavin

FULLNAME: Gavin Keith Peacock
DOB: 18-Nov-67, Welling, Kent

Club History	Signed	Fee
QPR	11/84	
Gillingham	10/87	£40,000
Bournemouth	8/89	£250,000
Newcastle U.	11/90	£150,000
Chelsea	8/93	£1.25m

Season	Team	Tot	St	Sb	Snu	Ps	Gls
93-94	Chelsea	37	37	0	0	4	8
94-95	Chelsea	38	38	0	0	2	4
95-96	Chelsea	28	17	11	1	8	5
96-97	Chelsea	0	0	0	2	0	0
	Total	103	92	11	3	14	17

PEAKE, Andy

FULLNAME: Andrew Peake
DOB: 01-Nov-61, Market Harborough

Club History	Signed	Fee
Leicester C.	1/79	Apprentice
Grimsby T.	8/85	
Charlton A.	9/86	
Middlesbrough	11/91	

Season	Team	Tot	St	Sb	Snu	Ps	Gls
92-93	Middlesbrough	33	33	0	0	2	0
	Total	33	33	0	0	2	0

PEARCE, Andy

FULLNAME: Andrew John Pearce
DOB: 20-Apr-66, Bradford on Avon

Club History	Signed	Fee
Coventry C.	5/90	£15,000
Sheffield W.	6/93	£500,000
Wimbledon	11/96	£600,000

Season	Team	Tot	St	Sb	Snu	Ps	Gls
92-93	Coventry C.	24	21	3	4	1	1
93-94	Sheffield W.	32	29	3	3	2	3
94-95	Sheffield W.	34	34	0	1	0	0
95-96	Sheffield W.	3	3	0	1	0	0
95-96	Wimbledon	7	6	1	7	2	0
	Total	100	93	7	16	5	4

PEARCE, Ian

FULLNAME: Ian Anthony Pearce
DOB: 07-May-74, Bury St Edmunds

Club History	Signed	Fee
Chelsea	8/91	Juniors
Blackburn R.	10/93	£300,000
West Ham U.	9/97	£1.6m>

Season	Team	Tot	St	Sb	Snu	Ps	Gls
92-93	Chelsea	1	0	1	0	0	0
93-94	Blackburn R.	5	1	4	5	1	1
94-95	Blackburn R.	28	22	6	7	0	0
95-96	Blackburn R.	12	12	0	1	1	1
96-97	Blackburn R.	12	7	5	3	1	0
97-98	Blackburn R.	5	1	4	1	0	0
97-98	West Ham U.	30	30	0	1	1	1
98-99	West Ham U.	33	33	0	0	1	2
99-00	West Ham U.	1	1	0	0	1	0
	Total	127	107	20	17	6	5

PEARCE, Stuart

FULLNAME: Stuart Pearce
DOB: 24-Apr-62, Shepherds Bush

Club History	Signed	Fee
Coventry C.	10/83	£25,000
Nottingham F.	6/85	£200,000
Newcastle U.	7/97	Free
West Ham U.	8/99	Free

Season	Team	Tot	St	Sb	Snu	Ps	Gls
92-93	Nottingham F.	23	23	0	0	0	2
94-95	Nottingham F.	36	36	0	0	0	8
95-96	Nottingham F.	31	31	0	0	0	3
96-97	Nottingham F.	33	33	0	0	2	5
97-98	Newcastle U.	25	25	0	2	1	0

98-99	Newcastle U.	12	12	0	3	0	0
99-00	West Ham U.	8	8	0	0	2	0
	Total	168	168	0	5	5	18

PEARS, Stephen

FULLNAME: Stephen Pears
DOB: 22-Jan-62, Brandon

Club History	Signed	Fee
Manchester U.	1/79	Apprentice
Middlesbrough	11/83	Loan
Middlesbrough	7/85	£80,000

Season	Team	Tot	St	Sb	Snu	Ps	Gls
92-93	Middlesbrough	26	26	0	1	1	0
	Total	26	26	0	1	1	0

PEARSON, Nigel

FULLNAME: Nigel Graham Pearson
DOB: 21-Aug-63, Nottingham

Club History	Signed	Fee
Shrewsbury T.	11/81	£5,000
Sheffield W.	10/87	£250,000
Middlesbrough	7/94	£500,000

Season	Team	Tot	St	Sb	Snu	Ps	Gls
92-93	Sheffield W.	16	13	3	0	0	1
93-94	Sheffield W.	5	4	1	0	1	0
95-96	Middlesbrough	36	36	0	0	3	0
96-97	Middlesbrough	18	17	1	1	2	0
	Total	75	70	5	1	6	1

PEDERSEN, Per

FULLNAME: Per Werner Pederson
DOB: 30-Mar-69, Aalberg, Norway

Club History	Signed	Fee
OB (Denmark)	1996	
Blackburn R.	2/97	£2.5m
Strasbourg	8/98	£900,000

Season	Team	Tot	St	Sb	Snu	Ps	Gls
96-97	Blackburn R.	11	6	5	1	8	1
97-98	Blackburn R.	0	0	0	1	0	0
	Total	11	6	5	2	8	1

PEDERSEN, Tore

FULLNAME: Tore Pedersen
DOB: 29-Sep-69, Fredrikstad (Norway)

Club History	Signed	Fee
SK Brann		
Oldham A.		
St Pauli		
Blackburn R.	9/97	£500,000
Wimbledon	7/99	Free

Season	Team	Tot	St	Sb	Snu	Ps	Gls
93-94	Oldham A.	10	7	3	1	1	0
97-98	Blackburn R.	5	3	2	12	0	0
98-99	Blackburn R.	0	0	0	1	0	0
99-00	Wimbledon	6	6	0	0	1	0
	Total	21	16	5	14	2	0

PEMBERTON, John

FULLNAME: John Matthew Pemberton
DOB: 18-Nov-64, Oldham

Club History	Signed	Fee
Rochdale	9/84	Free
Crewe Alex	3/85	£1,000
Crystal P.	3/88	£80,000
Sheffield U.	7/90	£300,000
Leeds U.	11/93	£250,000

Season	Team	Tot	St	Sb	Snu	Ps	Gls
92-93	Sheffield U.	19	19	0	0	0	0
93-94	Sheffield U.	8	8	0	0	0	0
93-94	Leeds U.	9	6	3	4	1	0
94-95	Leeds U.	27	22	5	4	0	0
95-96	Leeds U.	17	16	1	3	3	0
	Total	80	71	9	11	4	0

PEMBRIDGE, Mark

FULLNAME: Mark Anthony Pembridge
DOB: 29-Nov-70, Merthyr Tydfil

Club History	Signed	Fee
Luton Town	7/89	Trainee
Derby Co.	6/92	£1.25m
Sheffield W.	7/95	£900,000
Benfica		
Everton	8/99	£800,000

Season	Team	Tot	St	Sb	Snu	Ps	Gls
95-96	Sheffield W.	25	24	1	0	7	2
96-97	Sheffield W.	34	33	1	0	2	6
97-98	Sheffield W.	34	31	3	0	15	4
99-00	Everton	31	29	2	2	8	2
	Total	124	117	7	2	32	14

PENNYFATHER, Glenn

FULLNAME: Glenn Pennyfather
DOB: 11-Feb-63, Billericay

Club History	Signed	Fee
Southend U.	2/81	Apprentice
Crystal P.	11/87	
Ipswich T.	10/89	

Season	Team	Tot	St	Sb	Snu	Ps	Gls
92-93	Ipswich T.	4	2	2	3	0	0
	Total	4	2	2	3	0	0

PENRICE, Gary

FULLNAME: Gary Kenneth Penrice
DOB: 23-Mar-64, Bristol

Club History	Signed	Fee
Bristol R.	11/84	
Watford	11/89	£500,000
Aston Villa	3/91	£1m
QPR	10/91	£625,000

Season	Team	Tot	St	Sb	Snu	Ps	Gls
92-93	QPR	15	10	5	0	2	6
93-94	QPR	26	23	3	1	5	8
94-95	QPR	19	9	10	6	3	3
95-96	QPR	3	0	3	0	0	0
	Total	63	42	21	7	10	17

PEREZ, Lionel

FULLNAME: Lionel Perez
DOB: 24-Apr-67, Bagnols Coze, France

Club History	Signed	Fee
Stade Lavallois		
Bordeaux		
Sunderland	8/96	£200,000
Newcastle U.	6/98	Free

Season	Team	Tot	St	Sb	Snu	Ps	Gls
96-97	Sunderland	29	28	1	8	0	0
98-99	Newcastle U.	0	0	0	12	0	0
99-00	Newcastle U.	0	0	0	4	0	0
	Total	29	28	1	24	0	0

PERPETUINI, Dave

FULLNAME: David Peter Perpetuini
DOB: 29-Sep-79, Hitchin

Club History	Signed	Fee
Watford	7/97	Trainee

Season	Team	Tot	St	Sb	Snu	Ps	Gls
99-00	Watford	13	12	1	5	5	1
	Total	13	12	1	5	5	1

PERRY, Chris

FULLNAME: Christopher John Perry
DOB: 26-Apr-73, Surrey

Club History	Signed	Fee
Wimbledon	7/91	Trainee
Tottenham H.	7/99	£4.0m

Season	Team	Tot	St	Sb	Snu	Ps	Gls
93-94	Wimbledon	2	0	2	9	0	0
94-95	Wimbledon	21	16	5	3	1	0
95-96	Wimbledon	36	35	1	0	1	0
96-97	Wimbledon	37	37	0	0	2	1
97-98	Wimbledon	35	35	0	0	1	
98-99	Wimbledon	34	34	0	0	1	0
99-00	Tottenham H.	37	36	1	0	1	1
	Total	202	193	9	12	6	3

PETIT, Manu

FULLNAME: Emmanuel Petit
DOB: 22-Sep-70, Dieppe

Club History	Signed	Fee
AS Monaco		
Arsenal	6/97	£3.5m

Season	Team	Tot	St	Sb	Snu	Ps	Gls
97-98	Arsenal	32	32	0	0	5	2
98-99	Arsenal	27	26	1	0	2	4
99-00	Arsenal	26	24	2	0	9	3
	Total	85	82	3	0	16	9

PETRESCU, Dan

FULLNAME: Dan Vasile Petrescu
DOB: 22-Dec-67, Bucharest

Club History	Signed	Fee
Genoa	7/93	
Sheffield W.	8/94	£1.25m
Chelsea	11/95	£2.3m

Season	Team	Tot	St	Sb	Snu	Ps	Gls
94-95	Sheffield W.	29	20	9	0	8	3
95-96	Sheffield W.	8	8	0	0	1	0
95-96	Chelsea	24	22	2	0	1	2
96-97	Chelsea	34	34	0	0	4	3
97-98	Chelsea	31	31	0	1	13	5
98-99	Chelsea	32	23	9	1	7	4
99-00	Chelsea	29	24	5	1	14	4
	Total	187	162	25	3	48	21

PETTERSON, Andy

FULLNAME: Andrew Keith Petterson
DOB: 26-Sep-69, Freemantle, Australia

Club History	Signed	Fee
Luton Town	12/88	
Swindon Town	10/89	Loan
Ipswich Town	3/92	Loan
Charlton A.	7/94	£85,000

Season	Team	Tot	St	Sb	Snu	Ps	Gls
92-93	Ipswich T.	1	1	0	7	0	0
98-99	Charlton A.	10	7	3	12	0	0
	Total	11	8	3	19	0	0

PEYTON, Gerry

FULLNAME: Gerald Joseph Peyton
DOB: 20-May-56, Birmingham

Club History	Signed	Fee
Burnley	5/75	
Fulham	12/76	£40,000
Southend U.	9/83	Loan
Bournemouth	7/86	
Everton	7/91	£80,000
Bolton W.	2/92	Loan
Brentford	9/92	Loan
Chelsea	1/93	Loan
West Ham U.	6/93	Free

Season	Team	Tot	St	Sb	Snu	Ps	Gls
92-93	Chelsea	1	0	1	2	0	0
93-94	West Ham U.	0	0	0	26	0	0
	Total	1	0	1	28	0	0

PHELAN, Mike

FULLNAME: Michael Christopher Phelan
DOB: 24-Sep-62, Nelson

Club History	Signed	Fee
Burnley	7/80	
Norwich C.	7/85	£60,000
Manchester U.	6/89	£750,000

Season	Team	Tot	St	Sb	Snu	Ps	Gls
92-93	Manchester U.	11	5	6	16	3	0
93-94	Manchester U.	2	1	1	2	0	0
	Total	13	6	7	18	3	0

PHELAN, Terry

FULLNAME: Terence Michael Phelan
DOB: 16-Mar-67, Manchester

Club History	Signed	Fee
Leeds U.	8/84	
Swansea C.	7/86	Free
Wimbledon	7/87	£100,000
Manchester C.	8/92	£2.5m
Chelsea	11/95	£900,000
Everton	12/96	£850,00

Season	Team	Tot	St	Sb	Snu	Ps	Gls
92-93	Manchester C.	37	37	0	0	1	1
93-94	Manchester C.	30	30	0	1	1	1
94-95	Manchester C.	27	26	1	0	3	0
95-96	Manchester C.	9	9	0	0	1	0
95-96	Chelsea	12	12	0	0	1	0
96-97	Chelsea	3	1	2	2	0	0
96-97	Everton	15	15	0	0	3	0
97-98	Everton	9	8	1	2	2	0
98-99	Everton	0	0	0	1	0	0
99-00	Everton	1	0	1	1	0	0
	Total	143	138	5	9	12	2

PHILLIPS, David

FULLNAME: David Owen Phillips
DOB: 29-Jul-63, Wegberg, Germany

Club History	Signed	Fee
Plymouth Argyle	8/81	Apprentice
Manchester C.	8/84	£65,000
Coventry C.	6/86	£150,000
Norwich C.	6/89	£525,000
Nottingham F.	8/93	£600,000

Season	Team	Tot	St	Sb	Snu	Ps	Gls
92-93	Norwich C.	42	42	0	0	2	9
94-95	Nottingham F.	38	38	0	0	1	1
95-96	Nottingham F.	18	14	4	9	1	0
96-97	Nottingham F.	27	24	3	5	3	0
	Total	125	118	7	14	7	10

PHILLIPS, Jimmy

FULLNAME: James Neil Phillips
DOB: 08-Feb-66, Bolton

Club History	Signed	Fee
Bolton Wanderers	8/83	Apprentice
Glasgow Rangers		£95,000
Oxford U.	8/88	£110,000
Middlesbrough	3/90	£250,000
Bolton W.	7/93	£250,000

Season	Team	Tot	St	Sb	Snu	Ps	Gls
92-93	Middlesbrough	40	40	0	0	2	2
95-96	Bolton W.	37	37	0	0	2	0
97-98	Bolton W.	22	21	1	11	3	1
	Total	99	98	1	11	7	3

PHILLIPS, Kevin

FULLNAME: Kevin Phillips
DOB: 25-Jul-73, Hitchin

Club History	Signed	Fee
Watford	19/94	£10,000 from Non League
Sunderland	7/97	£325,000

Season	Team	Tot	St	Sb	Snu	Ps	Gls
99-00	Sunderland	36	36	0	0	3	30
	Total	36	36	0	0	3	30

PHILLIPS, Martin

FULLNAME: Martin John Phillips
DOB: 13-Mar-76, Exeter

Club History	Signed	Fee
Exeter C.	7/94	Trainee
Manchester C.	11/95	£500,000

Season	Team	Tot	St	Sb	Snu	Ps	Gls
95-96	Manchester C.	11	2	9	5	1	0
	Total	11	2	9	5	1	0

PHILPOTT, Lee

FULLNAME: Lee Philpott
DOB: 21-Feb-70, Barnet

Club History	Signed	Fee
Peterborough U.	7/86	
Cambridge U.	5/89	Free
Leicester C.	11/92	£350,000

Season	Team	Tot	St	Sb	Snu	Ps	Gls
94-95	Leicester C.	23	19	4	1	5	0
	Total	23	19	4	1	5	0

PICKERING, Ally

FULLNAME: Albert Gary Pickering
DOB: 22-Jun-67, Manchester

Club History	Signed	Fee
Rotherham U.	2/90	£18,500
Coventry C.	10/93	£80,000
Stoke C.	8/96	£280,000

Season	Team	Tot	St	Sb	Snu	Ps	Gls
93-94	Coventry C.	4	1	3	5	0	0
94-95	Coventry C.	31	27	4	7	1	0
95-96	Coventry C.	29	26	3	4	3	0
	Total	64	54	10	16	4	0

PIECHNIK, Torben

FULLNAME: Torben Piechnik
DOB: 21-May-63, Copenhagen, Denmark

Club History	Signed	Fee
FC Copenhagen		
Liverpool	9/92	£500,000

Season	Team	Tot	St	Sb	Snu	Ps	Gls
92-93	Liverpool	16	15	1	6	1	0
	Total	16	15	1	6	1	0

PIERCY, John

FULLNAME: John Piercy
DOB: 18-Sep-79, Forest Gate

Club History	Signed	Fee
Tottenham H.		Trainee

Season	Team	Tot	St	Sb	Snu	Ps	Gls
99-00	Tottenham H.	3	1	2	0	1	0
	Total	3	1	2	0	1	0

PILKINGTON, Kevin

FULLNAME: Kevin William Pilkington
DOB: 08-Mar-74, Hitchin

Club History	Signed	Fee
Manchester U.	7/92	Trainee

Season	Team	Tot	St	Sb	Snu	Ps	Gls
94-95	Manchester U.	1	0	1	17	0	0
95-96	Manchester U.	3	2	1	3	0	0
96-97	Manchester U.	0	0	0	1	0	0
97-98	Manchester U.	2	2	0	6	0	0
	Total	6	4	2	27	0	0

PISTONE, Alessandro

FULLNAME: Alessandro Pistone
DOB: 27-Jul-75, Milan

Club History	Signed	Fee
Internazionale		
Newcastle U.	7/97	£4.3m

Season	Team	Tot	St	Sb	Snu	Ps	Gls
97-98	Newcastle U.	28	28	0	0	0	0
98-99	Newcastle U.	3	2	1	2	1	0
99-00	Newcastle U.	15	15	0	1	2	1
	Total	46	45	1	3	3	1

PITCHER, Darren

FULLNAME: Darren Edward Pitcher
DOB: 12-Oct-69, Stepney

Club History	Signed	Fee
Charlton A.	1/88	Trainee
Crystal P.	8/94	Swap+£40,000

Season	Team	Tot	St	Sb	Snu	Ps	Gls
94-95	Crystal P.	25	21	4	9	2	0
97-98	Crystal P.	0	0	0	1	0	0
	Total	25	21	4	10	2	0

PLATT, David

FULLNAME: David Andrew Platt
DOB: 10-Jun-66, Oldham

Club History	Signed	Fee
Crewe Alexandra	1/85	
Aston Villa	2/88	£200,000
Bari	7/91	£5.5m
Juventus		
Sampdoria		
Arsenal	7/95	£4.75m

Season	Team	Tot	St	Sb	Snu	Ps	Gls
95-96	Arsenal	29	27	2	0	0	6
96-97	Arsenal	28	27	1	0	5	4
97-98	Arsenal	31	11	20	1	3	3
	Total	88	65	23	1	8	13

PLATTS, Mark

FULLNAME: Mark Anthony Platts
DOB: 23-May-70, Sheffield

Club History	Signed	Fee
Sheffield W.	10/96	Trainee

Season	Team	Tot	St	Sb	Snu	Ps	Gls
95-96	Sheffield W.	2	0	2	2	0	0
	Total	2	0	2	2	0	0

PLUMMER, Chris

FULLNAME: Christopher Plummer
DOB: 12-Oct-76, Isleworth

Club History	Signed	Fee
QPR		Trainee

Season	Team	Tot	St	Sb	Snu	Ps	Gls
95-96	QPR	1	0	1	3	0	0
	Total	1	0	1	3	0	0

POBORSKY, Karel

FULLNAME: Karel Poborsky
DOB: 30-Mar-72, Trebon, Czech

Club History	Signed	Fee
Slavia Prague	1995	
Manchester U.	8/96	£3.5m

Season	Team	Tot	St	Sb	Snu	Ps	Gls
96-97	Manchester U.	22	15	7	15	10	3
97-98	Manchester U.	10	3	7	6	3	2
	Total	32	18	14	21	13	5

POINTON, Neil

FULLNAME: Neil Geoffrey Pointon
DOB: 28-Nov-64, Warsop, Vale

Club History	Signed	Fee
Scunthorpe U.	8/82	
Everton	11/85	£250,000
Manchester C.	7/90	£600,000
Oldham A.	7/92	£600,000

Season	Team	Tot	St	Sb	Snu	Ps	Gls
92-93	Oldham A.	33	33	0	0	4	3
93-94	Oldham A.	24	23	1	3	5	0
	Total	57	56	1	3	9	3

POLLOCK, Jamie

FULLNAME: Jamie Pollock
DOB: 16-Feb-74, Stockton

Club History	Signed	Fee
Middlesbrough	12/91	Trainee
Osasuna	9/96	Free
Middlesbrough	11/96	Free
Bolton W.	11/96	£1.5m

Season	Team	Tot	St	Sb	Snu	Ps	Gls
92-93	Middlesbrough	22	17	5	2	7	1
95-96	Middlesbrough	31	31	0	0	4	1
97-98	Bolton W.	26	25	1	1	5	1
	Total	79	73	6	3	16	3

POLSTON, John

FULLNAME: John David Polston
DOB: 10-Jun-68, Walthamstow

Club History	Signed	Fee
Tottenham H.	7/85	
Norwich C.	7/90	£250,000

Season	Team	Tot	St	Sb	Snu	Ps	Gls
92-93	Norwich C.	34	34	0	1	3	1
93-94	Norwich C.	24	24	0	1	1	0
94-95	Norwich C.	38	38	0	0	1	0
	Total	96	96	0	2	5	1

POOLE, Kevin

FULLNAME: Kevin Poole
DOB: 21-Jul-63, Bromsgrove

Club History	Signed	Fee
Aston Villa	6/81	Apprentice
Northampton T.	11/84	Loan
Middlesbrough	8/87	
Hartlepool U.	3/91	Loan
Leicester C.	7/91	£40,000

Season	Team	Tot	St	Sb	Snu	Ps	Gls
94-95	Leicester C.	36	36	0	6	0	0
96-97	Leicester C.	7	7	0	31	0	0
	Total	43	43	0	37	0	0

POOM, Mart

FULLNAME: Mart Poom
DOB: 03-Feb-72, Tallinn

Club History	Signed	Fee
FC Will		
Portsmouth	8/94	£200,000
FC Flora Tallinn		
Derby Co.	3/97	£500,000

Season	Team	Tot	St	Sb	Snu	Ps	Gls
96-97	Derby Co.	4	4	0	0	1	0
97-98	Derby Co.	36	36	0	1	0	0
98-99	Derby Co.	17	15	2	16	0	0
99-00	Derby Co.	28	28	0	3	0	0
	Total	85	83	2	20	1	0

POPESCU, Gica

FULLNAME: Gheorghe Posescu
DOB: 09-Oct-67, Calafat

Club History	Signed	Fee
PSV Eindhoven		
Tottenham H.	9/94	£2.9m

Season	Team	Tot	St	Sb	Snu	Ps	Gls
94-95	Tottenham H.	23	23	0	1	2	3
	Total	23	23	0	1	2	3

PORFIRIO, Hugo

FULLNAME: Hugo Cardoso Porfirio
DOB: 29-Sep-73, Lisbon, Portugal

Club History	Signed	Fee
Sporting Lisbon	8/96	
West Ham U.	9/96	Loan
Benfica		
Nottingham F.	1/99	Loan

Season	Team	Tot	St	Sb	Snu	Ps	Gls
96-97	West Ham U.	23	15	8	2	5	2
98-99	Nottingham F.	9	3	6	0	3	1
	Total	32	18	14	2	8	3

PORIC, Adem

FULLNAME: Adem Poric
DOB: 22-Apr-73, Australia

Club History	Signed	Fee
St George, Australia		
Sheffield W.	10/93	£60,000

Season	Team	Tot	St	Sb	Snu	Ps	Gls
93-94	Sheffield W.	6	2	4	6	0	0
94-95	Sheffield W.	4	1	3	1	1	0
95-96	Sheffield W.	1	1	0	0	0	0
97-98	Sheffield W.	3	0	3	2	0	0
	Total	14	4	10	9	1	0

POTTER, Graham

FULLNAME: Graham Stephen Potter
DOB: 20-May-75, Solihull

Club History	Signed	Fee
Birmingham C.	7/92	Trainee
Wycombe W.	9/93	Loan
Stoke C.	12/93	£75,000
Southampton	8/96	£250,000

Season	Team	Tot	St	Sb	Snu	Ps	Gls
96-97	Southampton	8	2	6	6	1	0
	Total	8	2	6	6	1	0

POTTS, Steve

FULLNAME: Steven John Potts
DOB: 07-May-67, Hartford, USA

Club History	Signed	Fee
West Ham U.	7/83	Trainee

Season	Team	Tot	St	Sb	Snu	Ps	Gls
93-94	West Ham U.	41	41	0	0	1	0
94-95	West Ham U.	42	42	0	0	2	0
95-96	West Ham U.	34	34	0	2	2	0
96-97	West Ham U.	20	17	3	5	3	0
97-98	West Ham U.	23	14	9	12	2	0
98-99	West Ham U.	19	11	8	11	2	0
99-00	West Ham U.	17	16	1	6	0	0
	Total	196	175	21	36	12	0

POWELL, Chris

FULLNAME: Christopher George Robin Powell
DOB: 08-Sep-69, Lambeth

Club History	Signed	Fee
Crystal P.	12/87	Trainee
Aldershot	1/90	Loan
Southend U.	8/90	Free
Derby Co.	1/96	£750,000
Charlton A.	6/98	£825,000

Season	Team	Tot	St	Sb	Snu	Ps	Gls
96-97	Derby Co.	35	35	0	0	4	0
97-98	Derby Co.	36	34	2	1	2	1
98-99	Charlton A.	38	38	0	0	2	0
	Total	109	107	2	1	8	1

POWELL, Darryl

FULLNAME: Darryl Anthony Powell
DOB: 15-Nov-71, Lambeth

Club History	Signed	Fee
Portsmouth	12/88	Trainee
Derby Co.	7/95	£750,000

Season	Team	Tot	St	Sb	Snu	Ps	Gls
96-97	Derby Co.	33	27	6	0	5	1
97-98	Derby Co.	24	13	11	1	4	0
98-99	Derby Co.	33	30	3	0	3	0
99-00	Derby Co.	31	31	0	0	1	2
	Total	121	101	20	1	13	3

POWELL, Lee

FULLNAME: Lee Powell
DOB: 02-Jun-73, Caerleon

Club History	Signed	Fee
Southampton	5/91	
Sunderland	8/93	Loan

Season	Team	Tot	St	Sb	Snu	Ps	Gls
92-93	Southampton	2	0	2	3	0	0
93-94	Southampton	1	1	0	0	0	0
	Total	3	1	2	3	0	0

POWER, Lee

FULLNAME: Lee Michael Power
DOB: 30-Jun-72, Lewisham

Club History	Signed	Fee
Norwich C.	7/90	

Season	Team	Tot	St	Sb	Snu	Ps	Gls
92-93	Norwich C.	18	11	7	1	3	6
93-94	Norwich C.	5	2	3	0	0	0
	Total	23	13	10	1	3	6

POYET, Gus

FULLNAME: Gustavo Augusto Poyet
DOB: 15-Nov-67, Montevideo

Club History	Signed	Fee
Real Zaragoza		
Chelsea	7/97	Free

Season	Team	Tot	St	Sb	Snu	Ps	Gls
97-98	Chelsea	14	11	3	0	1	4
98-99	Chelsea	28	21	7	0	7	11
99-00	Chelsea	33	25	8	0	7	10
	Total	75	57	18	0	15	25

PREECE, Andy

FULLNAME: Andrew Paul Preece
DOB: 27-Mar-67, Evesham

Club History	Signed	Fee
Northampton T.	8/99	Free from Non League
Worcester C.	7/89	Free
Wrexham	3/90	Free
Stockport Co.	12/91	£10,000
Crystal P.	6/94	£350,000

Season	Team	Tot	St	Sb	Snu	Ps	Gls
94-95	Crystal P.	20	17	3	1	5	4
	Total	20	17	3	1	5	4

PREKI

FULLNAME: Pedray Radosavijevic
DOB: 24-Jun-63, Belgrade, Yugoslavia

Club History	Signed	Fee
St Louis, USA		
Everton	9/92	£100,000
Portsmouth	7/94	£100,000

Season	Team	Tot	St	Sb	Snu	Ps	Gls
92-93	Everton	23	13	10	3	8	3
93-94	Everton	23	9	14	5	9	1
	Total	46	22	24	8	17	4

PRESSLEY, Steve

FULLNAME: Steven Pressley
DOB: 11-Oct-73, Elgin

Club History	Signed	Fee
Rangers		
Coventry C.	10/94	£600,000

Season	Team	Tot	St	Sb	Snu	Ps	Gls
94-95	Coventry C.	19	18	1	3	1	1
	Total	19	18	1	3	1	1

PRESSMAN, Kevin

FULLNAME: Kevin Paul Pressman
DOB: 06-Nov-67, Fareham

Club History	Signed	Fee
Sheffield W.	11/85	

Season	Team	Tot	St	Sb	Snu	Ps	Gls
92-93	Sheffield W.	3	3	0	37	0	0
93-94	Sheffield W.	32	32	0	10	0	0
94-95	Sheffield W.	34	34	0	5	0	0
95-96	Sheffield W.	30	30	0	0	1	0
96-97	Sheffield W.	38	38	0	0	1	0
97-98	Sheffield W.	36	36	0	0	1	0
98-99	Sheffield W.	15	14	1	15	0	0
99-00	Sheffield W.	19	18	1	19	0	0
	Total	207	205	2	86	3	0

PRICE, Chris

FULLNAME: Christopher Price
DOB: 30-Mar-60, Hereford

Club History	Signed	Fee
Hereford U.	1/78	Apprentice
Blackburn R.	7/86	
Aston Villa	5/88	
Blackburn R.	2/92	

Season	Team	Tot	St	Sb	Snu	Ps	Gls
92-93	Blackburn R.	6	2	4	1	0	0
	Total	6	2	4	1	0	0

PRINGLE, Martin

FULLNAME: Martin Ulf Pringle
DOB: 18-Nov-70, Sweden

Club History	Signed	Fee
Benfica		
Charlton A.	1/99	£800,000

Season	Team	Tot	St	Sb	Snu	Ps	Gls
98-99	Charlton A.	18	15	3	0	5	3
	Total	18	15	3	0	5	3

PRIOR, Spencer

FULLNAME: Spencer Justin Prior
DOB: 22-Apr-71, Hockley

Club History	Signed	Fee
Southend U.	5/89	
Norwich C.	6/93	£200,000
Leicester C.	8/96	£600,000
Derby Co.	8/98	£700,000

Season	Team	Tot	St	Sb	Snu	Ps	Gls
93-94	Norwich C.	13	13	0	2	3	0
94-95	Norwich C.	17	12	5	1	1	0
96-97	Leicester C.	34	33	1	1	4	0

		Tot	St	Sb	Snu	Ps	Gls
97-98	Leicester C.	30	28	2	2	5	0
98-99	Derby Co.	34	33	1	0	1	1
99-00	Derby Co.	20	15	5	5	2	0
	Total	148	134	14	11	16	1

PROCTOR, Mark

FULLNAME: Mark Proctor
DOB: 30-Jan-61, Middlesbrough

Club History	Signed	Fee
Middlesbrough	9/78	Apprentice
Nottingham F.	8/81	
Sunderland	3/83	
Sheffield W.	9/87	
Middlesbrough	3/89	

Season	Team	Tot	St	Sb	Snu	Ps	Gls
92-93	Middlesbrough	11	6	5	5	2	0
	Total	11	6	5	5	2	0

PRUNIER, William

FULLNAME: William Prunier
DOB: 14-Aug-67, Montreuil

Club History	Signed	Fee
Bordeaux		
Manchester U.	12/95	Loan

Season	Team	Tot	St	Sb	Snu	Ps	Gls
95-96	Manchester U.	2	2	0	0	0	0
	Total	2	2	0	0	0	0

QUASHIE, Nigel

FULLNAME: Nigel Francis Quashie
DOB: 20-Jul-78, Peckham

Club History	Signed	Fee
QPR	8/95	Trainee
Nottingham F.	8/98	£2.5m

Season	Team	Tot	St	Sb	Snu	Ps	Gls
95-96	QPR	11	11	0	0	4	0
98-99	Nottingham F.	16	12	4	1	6	0
	Total	27	23	4	1	10	0

QUIGLEY, Mike

FULLNAME: Michael Anthony Quigley
DOB: 02-Oct-70, Manchester

Club History	Signed	Fee
Manchester C.	7/89	

Season	Team	Tot	St	Sb	Snu	Ps	Gls
92-93	Manchester C.	5	1	4	4	0	0
93-94	Manchester C.	2	2	0	4	2	0
	Total	7	3	4	8	2	0

QUINN, Alan

FULLNAME: Alan Quinn
DOB: 13-Jun-79, Dublin

Club History	Signed	Fee
Sheffield W.	12/97	Free NL

Season	Team	Tot	St	Sb	Snu	Ps	Gls
97-98	Sheffield W.	1	0	1	0	0	1
98-99	Sheffield W.	1	1	0	0	1	0
99-00	Sheffield W.	19	18	1	0	4	3
	Total	21	19	2	0	5	4

QUINN, Barry

FULLNAME: Barry Scott Quinn
DOB: 09-May-79, Dublin

Club History	Signed	Fee
Coventry C.	11/96	Trainee

Season	Team	Tot	St	Sb	Snu	Ps	Gls
98-99	Coventry C.	7	6	1	3	1	0
99-00	Coventry C.	11	5	6	6	3	0
	Total	18	11	7	9	4	0

QUINN, Mick

FULLNAME: Michael Quinn
DOB: 02-May-62, Liverpool

Club History	Signed	Fee
Derby Co.		
Wigan A.	9/79	Free
Stockport Co.	6/82	Free
Oldham A.	1/84	£50,000
Portsmouth	3/86	£150,000
Newcastle U.	8/89	£680,000
Coventry C.	11/92	£250,000

Season	Team	Tot	St	Sb	Snu	Ps	Gls
92-93	Coventry C.	26	26	0	0	2	17
93-94	Coventry C.	32	28	4	7	5	8
94-95	Coventry C.	6	3	3	3	0	0
	Total	64	57	7	10	7	25

QUINN, Niall

FULLNAME: Niall John Quinn
DOB: 06-Oct-66, Dublin, Republic of Ireland

Club History	Signed	Fee
Arsenal	11/83	Juniors
Manchester C.	3/90	£800,000
Sunderland	8/96	£1.3m

Season	Team	Tot	St	Sb	Snu	Ps	Gls
92-93	Manchester C.	39	39	0	0	3	9
93-94	Manchester C.	15	14	1	0	1	5
94-95	Manchester C.	35	24	11	3	2	8

		Tot	St	Sb	Snu	Ps	Gls
95-96	Manchester C.	31	23	8	1	5	8
96-97	Sunderland	12	8	4	1	4	3
99-00	Sunderland	37	35	2	0	9	14
	Total	169	143	26	5	24	47

QUINN, Robert

FULLNAME: Robert John Quinn
DOB: 08-Nov-76, Sidcup

Club History	Signed	Fee
Crystal P.	3/95	Trainee

Season	Team	Tot	St	Sb	Snu	Ps	Gls
97-98	Crystal P.	1	0	1	12	0	0
	Total	1	0	1	12	0	0

RACHEL, Adam

FULLNAME: Adam Rachel
DOB: 10-Dec-76, Birmingham

Club History	Signed	Fee
Aston Villa	5/95	Trainee

Season	Team	Tot	St	Sb	Snu	Ps	Gls
96-97	Aston Villa	0	0	0	14	0	0
97-98	Aston Villa	0	0	0	3	0	0
98-99	Aston Villa	1	0	1	12	0	0
	Total	1	0	1	29	0	0

RADEBE, Lucas

FULLNAME: Lucas Radebe
DOB: 12-Apr-69, Johannesburg

Club History	Signed	Fee
Kaiser Chiefs		
Leeds U.	9/94	£250,000

Season	Team	Tot	St	Sb	Snu	Ps	Gls
94-95	Leeds U.	12	9	3	8	5	0
95-96	Leeds U.	13	10	3	3	2	0
96-97	Leeds U.	32	28	4	2	3	0
97-98	Leeds U.	27	26	1	0	2	0
98-99	Leeds U.	29	29	0	0	3	0
99-00	Leeds U.	31	31	0	0	2	0
	Total	144	133	11	13	17	0

RADUCIOIU, Florin

FULLNAME: Florin Raducioiu
DOB: 17-Mar-70, Bucharest

Club History	Signed	Fee
Espanyol	1994	
West Ham U.	7/96	£2.4m
Espanyol	1/97	£1.6m

Season	Team	Tot	St	Sb	Snu	Ps	Gls
96-97	West Ham U.	11	6	5	2	4	2
	Total	11	6	5	2	4	2

RAE, Alex

FULLNAME: Alexander Scott Rae
DOB: 30-Sep-69, Glasgow

Club History	Signed	Fee
Falkirk	1987	Free from NL
Millwall	8/90	£100,000
Sunderland	7/96	£750,000

Season	Team	Tot	St	Sb	Snu	Ps	Gls
96-97	Sunderland	22	12	10	6	5	3
99-00	Sunderland	26	22	4	7	5	3
	Total	48	34	14	13	10	6

RAHMBERG, Marino

FULLNAME: Marino Rahmberg
DOB: 07-Aug-74, Orebro

Club History	Signed	Fee
Degerfors		
Derby Co.	1/97	Loan

Season	Team	Tot	St	Sb	Snu	Ps	Gls
96-97	Derby Co.	1	0	1	3	0	0
	Total	1	0	1	3	0	0

RANKIN, Isiah

FULLNAME: Isiah Rankin
DOB: 22-May-78, London

Club History	Signed	Fee
Arsenal	9/95	Trainee
Colchester U.	9/97	Loan
Bradford C.	8/98	£1.3m

Season	Team	Tot	St	Sb	Snu	Ps	Gls
96-97	Arsenal	0	0	0	3	0	0
97-98	Arsenal	1	0	1	2	0	0
99-00	Bradford C.	9	0	9	3	0	0
	Total	10	0	10	8	0	0

RANSON, Ray

FULLNAME: Raymond Ranson
DOB: 12-Jun-60, St Helens

Club History	Signed	Fee
Manchester C.	6/77	Amateur
Birmingham C.	11/84	£15,000
Newcastle U.	12/88	£175,000
Manchester C.	1/93	Loan

Season	Team	Tot	St	Sb	Snu	Ps	Gls
92-93	Manchester C.	17	17	0	1	1	0
	Total	17	17	0	1	1	0

RAVANELLI, Fabio

FULLNAME: Fabrizio Ravanelli
DOB: 11-Dec-68, Perugia, Italy

Club History	Signed	Fee
Juventus	1992	
Middlesbrough	7/96	£7m

Season	Team	Tot	St	Sb	Snu	Ps	Gls
96-97	Middlesbrough	33	33	0	0	4	16
	Total	33	33	0	0	4	16

READY, Karl

FULLNAME: Karl Ready
DOB: 14-Aug-72, Neath

Club History	Signed	Fee
QPR	8/90	

Season	Team	Tot	St	Sb	Snu	Ps	Gls
92-93	QPR	3	2	1	4	0	0
93-94	QPR	22	19	3	5	0	1
94-95	QPR	13	11	2	6	1	1
95-96	QPR	21	16	5	9	3	1
	Total	59	48	11	24	4	3

REDDY, Michael

FULLNAME: Michael Reddy
DOB: 24-Mar-80, Graignamangh

Club History	Signed	Fee
Sunderland	8/99	Trainee

Season	Team	Tot	St	Sb	Snu	Ps	Gls
99-00	Sunderland	8	0	8	7	0	1
	Total	8	0	8	7	0	1

REDFEARN, Neil

FULLNAME: Neil David Redfearn
DOB: 20-Jun-65, Dewsbury

Club History	Signed	Fee
Bolton W.	6/82	N.Forest Jnrs
Lincoln C.	3/84	£8,250
Doncaster R.	8/86	
Crystal P.	7/87	£100,000
Watford	11/88	£150,000
Oldhan A.	1/90	£150,000
Barnsley	9/91	£150,000
Charlton A.	6/98	£1m
Bradford C.	7/99	£250,000

Season	Team	Tot	St	Sb	Snu	Ps	Gls
97-98	Barnsley	37	37	0	0	0	10
98-99	Charlton A.	30	29	1	0	9	3
99-00	Bradford C.	17	14	3	2	4	1
	Total	84	80	4	2	13	14

REDKNAPP, Jamie

FULLNAME: Jamie Frank Redknapp
DOB: 25-Jun-73, Barton on Sea

Club History	Signed	Fee
Bournemouth	6/90	Trainee
Liverpool	1/91	£350,000

Season	Team	Tot	St	Sb	Snu	Ps	Gls
92-93	Liverpool	29	27	2	0	6	2
93-94	Liverpool	35	29	6	0	0	4
94-95	Liverpool	40	36	4	2	1	3
95-96	Liverpool	23	19	4	2	3	3
96-97	Liverpool	23	18	5	6	0	3
97-98	Liverpool	20	20	0	0	2	3
98-99	Liverpool	34	33	1	0	4	8
99-00	Liverpool	22	18	4	0	2	3
	Total	226	200	26	10	18	29

REDMOND, Steve

FULLNAME: Stephen Redmond
DOB: 02-Nov-67, Liverpool

Club History	Signed	Fee
Manchester C.	12/84	
Oldham A.	7/92	£300,000

Season	Team	Tot	St	Sb	Snu	Ps	Gls
92-93	Oldham A.	31	28	3	5	1	0
93-94	Oldham A.	33	31	2	4	0	1
	Total	64	59	5	9	1	1

REEVES, Alan

FULLNAME: Alan Reeves
DOB: 19-Nov-67, Birkenhead

Club History	Signed	Fee
Norwich C.	9/88	
Chester C.	8/89	£10,000
Rochdale	7/91	Free
Wimbledon	9/94	£300,000

Season	Team	Tot	St	Sb	Snu	Ps	Gls
94-95	Wimbledon	32	32	0	0	1	3
95-96	Wimbledon	25	21	4	2	0	1
96-97	Wimbledon	2	0	2	11	0	0
97-98	Wimbledon	0	0	0	9	0	0
	Total	59	53	6	22	1	4

REGIS, Cyrille

FULLNAME: Cyrille Regis
DOB: 09-Feb-58, French Guyana

Club History	Signed	Fee
WBA	5/77	From Non League
Coventry C.	10/84	
Aston Villa	7/91	

Season	Team	Tot	St	Sb	Snu	Ps	Gls
92-93	Aston Villa	13	7	6	3	3	1
	Total	13	7	6	3	3	1

REID, Peter

FULLNAME: Peter Reid
DOB: 20-Jun-56, Huyton

Club History	Signed	Fee
Bolton W.	5/74	
Everton	12/82	£60,000
QPR	2/89	Free
Manchester C.	12/89	Free
Southampton		

Season	Team	Tot	St	Sb	Snu	Ps	Gls
92-93	Manchester C.	20	14	6	14	5	0
93-94	Manchester C.	4	1	3	0	0	0
93-94	Southampton	7	7	0	0	3	0
	Total	31	22	9	14	8	0

RENNIE, David

FULLNAME: David Rennie
DOB: 29-Aug-64, Edinburgh

Club History	Signed	Fee
Leicester C.	5/82	
Leeds U.	1/86	£50,000
Bristol C.	7/89	£175,000
Birmingham C.	2/92	£120,000
Coventry C.	3/93	£100,000

Season	Team	Tot	St	Sb	Snu	Ps	Gls
92-93	Coventry C.	9	9	0	0	1	0
93-94	Coventry C.	34	34	0	2	2	1
94-95	Coventry C.	28	28	0	1	2	0
95-96	Coventry C.	11	9	2	1	2	2
	Total	82	80	2	4	7	3

RIBEIRO, Bruino

FULLNAME: Bruino Ribeiro
DOB: 22-Oct-75, Setubal, Portugal

Club History	Signed	Fee
Vitoria Setubal		
Leeds U.	6/97	£500,00

Season	Team	Tot	St	Sb	Snu	Ps	Gls
97-98	Leeds U.	29	28	1	0	6	3
98-99	Leeds U.	13	7	6	11	6	1
	Total	42	35	7	11	12	4

RICARD, Hamilton

FULLNAME: Hamilton Cuesta Ricard
DOB: 12-Jan-74, Colombia

Club History	Signed	Fee
Deportivo Cali		
Middlesbrough	2/98	£2m

Season	Team	Tot	St	Sb	Snu	Ps	Gls
98-99	Middlesbrough	36	32	4	1	14	15
99-00	Middlesbrough	34	28	6	0	13	12
	Total	70	60	10	1	27	27

RICHARDS, Dean

FULLNAME: Dean Ivor Richards
DOB: 09-Jun-74, Bradford

Club History	Signed	Fee
Bradford C.	7/92	Trainee
Wolverhampton W.	3/95	£1.85m
Southampton	7/99	Free

Season	Team	Tot	St	Sb	Snu	Ps	Gls
99-00	Southampton	35	35	0	0	0	2
	Total	35	35	0	0	0	2

RICHARDSON, Kevin

FULLNAME: Kevin Richardson
DOB: 04-Dec-62, Newcastle

Club History	Signed	Fee
Everton	12/80	Apprentice
Watford	9/86	£225,000
Arsenal	8/87	£200,000
Real Sociedad	6/90	£750,000
Aston Villa	8/91	£450,000
Coventry C.	2/95	£300,000
Southampton	9/97	£150,000

Season	Team	Tot	St	Sb	Snu	Ps	Gls
92-93	Aston Villa	42	42	0	0	1	2
93-94	Aston Villa	40	40	0	0	2	5
94-95	Aston Villa	19	18	1	1	1	0
94-95	Coventry C.	14	14	0	0	0	0
95-96	Coventry C.	33	33	0	0	1	0
96-97	Coventry C.	28	25	3	7	2	0
97-98	Coventry C.	3	3	0	2	0	0
97-98	Southampton	28	25	3	5	9	0
	Total	207	200	7	15	16	7

RIDEOUT, Paul

FULLNAME: Paul David Rideout
DOB: 14-Aug-64, Bournemouth

Club History	Signed	Fee
Swindon Town	8/81	
Aston Villa	6/83	£200,000
Bari (Italy)	7/85	£400,000
Southampton	7/88	£430,000
Swindon Town	3/91	Loan
Notts Co.	9/91	£250,000

Rangers	1/92	£500,000
Everton	8/92	£500,000

Season	Team	Tot	St	Sb	Snu	Ps	Gls
92-93	Everton	24	17	7	0	7	3
93-94	Everton	24	21	3	0	7	6
94-95	Everton	29	25	4	1	2	14
95-96	Everton	25	19	6	1	3	6
96-97	Everton	9	4	5	15	2	0
	Total	111	86	25	17	21	29

RIEDLE, Karlheinz

FULLNAME: Karlheinz Riedle
DOB: 16-Sep-65, Weiler, Germany

Club History	Signed	Fee
Borussia Dortmund		
Liverpool	7/98	£1.75m

Season	Team	Tot	St	Sb	Snu	Ps	Gls
97-98	Liverpool	25	18	7	5	9	6
98-99	Liverpool	34	16	18	1	3	5
99-00	Liverpool	1	0	1	0	0	0
	Total	60	34	26	6	12	11

RIEPER, Marc

FULLNAME: Marc Rieper
DOB: 05-Jun-63, Rodoure, Denmark

Club History	Signed	Fee
Brondby		
West Ham U.	12/94	£500,000

Season	Team	Tot	St	Sb	Snu	Ps	Gls
94-95	West Ham U.	21	17	4	3	1	1
95-96	West Ham U.	36	35	1	1	0	2
96-97	West Ham U.	28	26	2	3	3	1
97-98	West Ham U.	5	5	0	0	0	1
	Total	90	83	7	7	4	5

RIGGOTT, Chris

FULLNAME: Christopher Riggott
DOB: 01-Sep-80,

Club History	Signed	Fee
Derby Co.		Trainee

Season	Team	Tot	St	Sb	Snu	Ps	Gls
99-00	Derby Co.	1	0	1	4	0	0
	Total	1	0	1	4	0	0

RIPLEY, Stuart

FULLNAME: Stuart Edward Ripley
DOB: 20-Nov-67, Middlesbrough

Club History	Signed	Fee
Middlesbrough	11/85	Apprentice
Bolton W.	2/86	Loan

Blackburn R.	7/92	£1.3m
Southampton	7/98	£1.5m

Season	Team	Tot	St	Sb	Snu	Ps	Gls
92-93	Blackburn R.	40	38	2	0	7	7
93-94	Blackburn R.	40	40	0	0	9	4
94-95	Blackburn R.	37	36	1	0	8	0
95-96	Blackburn R.	27	27	0	1	10	0
96-97	Blackburn R.	13	5	8	4	3	0
97-98	Blackburn R.	29	25	4	2	14	2
98-99	Southampton	22	16	6	2	9	0
99-00	Southampton	23	18	5	0	7	1
	Total	231	205	26	9	67	14

RITCHIE, Andy

FULLNAME: Andrew Timothy Ritchie
DOB: 28-Nov-60, Manchester

Club History	Signed	Fee
Manchester U.	12/77	
Brighton & HA	10/80	£500,000
Leeds U.	3/83	£150,000
Oldham A.	8/87	£50,000

Season	Team	Tot	St	Sb	Snu	Ps	Gls
92-93	Oldham A.	12	10	2	2	5	3
93-94	Oldham A.	22	13	9	6	5	1
	Total	34	23	11	8	10	4

RIX, Graham

FULLNAME: Graham Rix
DOB: 23-Oct-57,

Club History	Signed	Fee
Arsenal	8/77	Apprentice
Brentford	12/87	Loan
Caen		
Chelsea	8/92	Free

Season	Team	Tot	St	Sb	Snu	Ps	Gls
94-95	Chelsea	1	0	1	0	0	0
	Total	1	0	1	0	0	0

ROBERTS, Andy

FULLNAME: Andrew James Roberts
DOB: 20-Mar-74, Dartford

Club History	Signed	Fee
Millwall	10/91	Trainee
Crystal P.	7/95	£2.52m
Wimbledon	3/98	£1.2m>

Season	Team	Tot	St	Sb	Snu	Ps	Gls
97-98	Crystal P.	25	25	0	0	1	0
97-98	Wimbledon	12	12	0	0	0	1
98-99	Wimbledon	28	23	5	4	3	2
99-00	Wimbledon	16	14	2	5	5	0
	Total	81	74	7	9	9	3

ROBERTS, Ben

FULLNAME: Benjamin James Roberts
DOB: 22-Jun-95, Bishop Auckland

Club History	Signed	Fee
Middlesbrough	3/93	Trainee

Season	Team	Tot	St	Sb	Snu	Ps	Gls
92-93	Middlesbrough	0	0	0	5	0	0
96-97	Middlesbrough	10	9	1	25	0	0
99-00	Middlesbrough	0	0	0	10	0	0
	Total	10	9	1	40	0	0

ROBERTS, Iwan

FULLNAME: Iwan Wyn Roberts
DOB: 26-Aug-68, Bangor, Wales

Club History	Signed	Fee
Watford	7/86	Trainee
Huddersfield T.	8/90	£275,000
Leicester C.	11/93	£100,000

Season	Team	Tot	St	Sb	Snu	Ps	Gls
94-95	Leicester C.	37	32	5	2	2	9
	Total	37	32	5	2	2	9

ROBERTS, Tony

FULLNAME: Anthony Mark Roberts
DOB: 04-Aug-69, Holyhead

Club History	Signed	Fee
QPR	7/87	

Season	Team	Tot	St	Sb	Snu	Ps	Gls
92-93	QPR	28	28	0	14	1	0
93-94	QPR	16	16	0	26	0	0
94-95	QPR	31	31	0	10	0	0
95-96	QPR	5	5	0	3	0	0
	Total	80	80	0	53	1	0

ROBERTSON, David

FULLNAME: David Roberston
DOB: 17-Oct-68, Aberdeen

Club History	Signed	Fee
Aberdeen	1986	
Rangers	1991	
Leeds U.	5/97	£500,000

Season	Team	Tot	St	Sb	Snu	Ps	Gls
97-98	Leeds U.	26	24	2	0	0	0
	Total	26	24	2	0	0	0

ROBERTSON, Sandy

FULLNAME: Alexander Robertson
DOB: 26-Apr-71, Edinburgh

Club History	Signed	Fee
Rangers		
Coventry C.	1/94	£250,000

Season	Team	Tot	St	Sb	Snu	Ps	Gls
93-94	Coventry C.	3	0	3	4	0	0
94-95	Coventry C.	1	0	1	0	0	0
	Total	4	0	4	4	0	0

ROBINS, Mark

FULLNAME: Mark Gordon Robins
DOB: 22-Dec-69, Ashton-under-Lyne

Club History	Signed	Fee
Manchester U.	12/86	Apprentice
Norwich C.	8/92	£800,000
Leicester C.	1/95	£1m

Season	Team	Tot	St	Sb	Snu	Ps	Gls
92-93	Norwich C.	37	34	3	3	8	15
93-94	Norwich C.	13	9	4	4	4	1
94-95	Norwich C.	17	14	3	0	7	4
94-95	Leicester C.	17	16	1	0	1	5
96-97	Leicester C.	8	5	3	18	4	1
	Total	92	78	14	25	24	26

ROBINSON, John

FULLNAME: John Robert Campbell Robinson
DOB: 29-Aug-71, Bilawayo, Zimbabwe

Club History	Signed	Fee
Brighton & HA	4/89	Trainee
Charlton A.	9/92	£75,000

Season	Team	Tot	St	Sb	Snu	Ps	Gls
98-99	Charlton A.	30	27	3	0	9	3
	Total	30	27	3	0	9	3

ROBINSON, Mark

FULLNAME: Mark James Robinson
DOB: 21-Nov-68, Manchester

Club History	Signed	Fee
WBA	1/87	
Barnsley	6/87	Free
Newcastle U.	3/93	£450,000

Season	Team	Tot	St	Sb	Snu	Ps	Gls
93-94	Newcastle U.	16	12	4	2	1	0
	Total	16	12	4	2	1	0

ROBINSON, Marvin

FULLNAME: Marvin Leon St Robinson
DOB: 11-Apr-80, Crewe

Club History	Signed	Fee
Derby Co.	7/98	Trainee

Season	Team	Tot	St	Sb	Snu	Ps	Gls
98-99	Derby Co.	1	0	1	2	0	0
99-00	Derby Co.	8	3	5	2	2	0
	Total	9	3	6	4	2	0

ROBINSON, Matt

FULLNAME: Matthew Richard Robinson
DOB: 23-Dec-74, Exeter

Club History	Signed	Fee
Southampton	7/93	Trainee

Season	Team	Tot	St	Sb	Snu	Ps	Gls
94-95	Southampton	1	0	1	0	0	0
95-96	Southampton	6	0	6	5	0	0
96-97	Southampton	7	3	4	1	1	0
97-98	Southampton	1	0	1	3	0	0
	Total	15	3	12	9	1	0

ROBINSON, Paul

FULLNAME: Paul Robinson
DOB: 15-Oct-79, Beverley

Club History	Signed	Fee
Leeds U.		Trainee

Season	Team	Tot	St	Sb	Snu	Ps	Gls
97-98	Leeds U.	0	0	0	4	0	0
98-99	Leeds U.	5	4	1	29	0	0
99-00	Leeds U.	0	0	0	38	0	0
	Total	5	4	1	71	0	0

ROBINSON, Paul

FULLNAME: Paul Robinson
DOB: 20-Nov-78, Sunderland

Club History	Signed	Fee
Darlington		Trainee
Newcastle U.		

Season	Team	Tot	St	Sb	Snu	Ps	Gls
99-00	Newcastle U.	11	2	9	0	1	0
	Total	11	2	9	0	1	0

ROBINSON, Paul

FULLNAME: Paul Peter Robinson
DOB: 14-Dec-78, Watford

Club History	Signed	Fee
Watford	2/97	Trainee

Season	Team	Tot	St	Sb	Snu	Ps	Gls
99-00	Watford	32	29	3	1	0	0
	Total	32	29	3	1	0	0

ROBINSON, Stephen

FULLNAME: Stephen Robinson
DOB: 10-Dec-74, Lisburn

Club History	Signed	Fee
Tottenham H.	1/93	

Season	Team	Tot	St	Sb	Snu	Ps	Gls
93-94	Tottenham H.	2	1	1	0	2	0
	Total	2	1	1	0	2	0

ROBSON, Bryan

FULLNAME: Bryan Robson
DOB: 11-Jan-57, Witton Gilbert

Club History	Signed	Fee
WBA	8/74	
Manchester U.	10/81	£1.5m
Middlesbrough	5/94	Free

Season	Team	Tot	St	Sb	Snu	Ps	Gls
92-93	Manchester U.	14	5	9	2	0	1
93-94	Manchester U.	15	10	5	9	6	1
95-96	Middlesbrough	2	1	1	1	0	0
96-97	Middlesbrough	2	1	1	1	0	0
	Total	33	17	16	13	6	2

ROBSON, Mark

FULLNAME: Mark A Robson
DOB: 22-May-69, Stratford, London

Club History	Signed	Fee
Exeter C.	10/86	
Tottenham H.	7/87	£50,000
Reading	3/88	Loan
Watford	10/89	Loan
Plymouth Argyle	12/89	Loan
Exeter C.	1/92	Loan
West Ham U.	8/92	Free

Season	Team	Tot	St	Sb	Snu	Ps	Gls
93-94	West Ham U.	3	1	2	1	0	0
	Total	3	1	2	1	0	0

ROBSON, Stewart

FULLNAME: Stewart Ian Robson
DOB: 06-Nov-64, Billericay

Club History	Signed	Fee
Arsenal	11/81	
West Ham U.	1/87	£700,000
Coventry C.	3/91	Free

Season	Team	Tot	St	Sb	Snu	Ps	Gls
92-93	Coventry C.	15	14	1	0	1	0
93-94	Coventry C.	1	1	0	0	1	0
	Total	16	15	1	0	2	0

ROCASTLE, David

FULLNAME: David Carlyle Rocastle
DOB: 02-May-67, Lewisham

Club History	Signed	Fee
Arsenal	12/84	Apprentice
Leeds U.	8/92	£2m
Manchester C.	12/93	£2m
Chelsea	8/94	£1.25m

Season	Team	Tot	St	Sb	Snu	Ps	Gls
92-93	Leeds U.	18	11	7	3	4	1
93-94	Leeds U.	7	6	1	2	5	1
93-94	Manchester C.	21	21	0	0	3	2
94-95	Chelsea	28	26	2	1	17	0
95-96	Chelsea	1	1	0	0	0	0
	Total	75	65	10	6	29	4

RODGER, Simon

FULLNAME: Simon Lee Rodger
DOB: 03-Oct-71, Shoreham

Club History	Signed	Fee
Crystal P.	7/90	£1,000

Season	Team	Tot	St	Sb	Snu	Ps	Gls
92-93	Crystal P.	23	22	1	0	1	2
94-95	Crystal P.	4	4	0	0	2	0
97-98	Crystal P.	29	27	2	1	4	2
	Total	56	53	3	1	7	4

RODRIGUES, Dani

FULLNAME: Daniel Ferreira Rodrigues
DOB: 03-Mar-80, Madeira

Club History	Signed	Fee
CS Farense		
Bournemouth	10/98	Loan
Southampton	3/99	£170,000

Season	Team	Tot	St	Sb	Snu	Ps	Gls
99-00	Southampton	2	0	2	3	0	0
	Total	2	0	2	3	0	0

RODRIGUEZ, Bruno

FULLNAME: Bruno Rodriguez
DOB:

Club History	Signed	Fee
Lens		
Bradford C.	9/99	Loan

Season	Team	Tot	St	Sb	Snu	Ps	Gls
99-00	Bradford C.	2	0	2	1	0	0
	Total	2	0	2	1	0	0

ROGERS, Alan

FULLNAME: Alan Rogers
DOB: 03-Jan-77, Liverpool

Club History	Signed	Fee
Tranmere R.	7/95	Trainee
Nottingham F.	7/97	£2m

Season	Team	Tot	St	Sb	Snu	Ps	Gls
98-99	Nottingham F.	34	34	0	1	4	4
	Total	34	34	0	1	4	4

ROGERS, Paul

FULLNAME: Paul Anthony Rogers
DOB: 21-Mar-65, Portsmouth

Club History	Signed	Fee
Sheffield U.	1/92	£35,000

Season	Team	Tot	St	Sb	Snu	Ps	Gls
92-93	Sheffield U.	27	26	1	0	1	3
93-94	Sheffield U.	25	24	1	1	3	3
	Total	52	50	2	1	4	6

ROLLING, Franck

FULLNAME: Franck Jacques Rolling
DOB: 23-Aug-68, Colmar, France

Club History	*Signed	Fee
FC Pau		
Ayr U.	8/94	
Leicester C.	9/95	£100,000

Season	Team	Tot	St	Sb	Snu	Ps	Gls
96-97	Leicester C.	1	1	0	6	1	0
	Total	1	1	0	6	1	0

ROSARIO, Robert

FULLNAME: Robert Michael Rosario
DOB: 04-Mar-66, Hammersmith

Club History	Signed	Fee
Norwich C.	12/83	
Wolverhampton W	12/85	Loan
Coventry C.	3/91	£600,000
Nottingham F.	3/93	£400,000

Season	Team	Tot	St	Sb	Snu	Ps	Gls
92-93	Coventry C.	28	28	0	0	2	4
92-93	Nottingham F.	10	10	0	0	2	1
94-95	Nottingham F.	1	0	1	1	0	0
	Total	39	38	1	1	4	5

ROSE, Matthew

FULLNAME: Matthew Rose
DOB: 24-Sep-75, Dartford

Club History	Signed	Fee
Arsenal	7/94	Trainee

Season	Team	Tot	St	Sb	Snu	Ps	Gls
95-96	Arsenal	4	1	3	7	0	0
96-97	Arsenal	1	1	0	12	1	0
97-98	Arsenal	0	0	0	0	0	0
	Total	5	2	3	19	1	0

ROSENTHAL, Ronny

FULLNAME: Ronny Rosenthal
DOB: 11-Oct-63, Haifa, Israel

Club History	Signed	Fee
Liverpool	3/90	£1m
Tottenham H.	1/94	£250,000

Season	Team	Tot	St	Sb	Snu	Ps	Gls
92-93	Liverpool	27	16	11	3	9	6
93-94	Liverpool	3	0	3	0	0	0
93-94	Tottenham H.	15	11	4	0	3	2
94-95	Tottenham H.	20	14	6	1	1	0
95-96	Tottenham H.	33	26	7	2	5	1
96-97	Tottenham H.	20	4	16	6	0	1
	Total	118	71	47	12	18	10

ROSLER, Uwe

FULLNAME: Uwe Rosler
DOB: 15-Nov-68, Attenburg

Club History	Signed	Fee
D Dresden		
Manchester C.	3/94	£750,000

Season	Team	Tot	St	Sb	Snu	Ps	Gls
93-94	Manchester C.	12	12	0	0	3	5
94-95	Manchester C.	31	29	2	0	5	15
95-96	Manchester C.	36	34	2	0	5	9
	Total	79	75	4	0	13	29

ROUSSEL, Cedric

FULLNAME: Cendric Roussel
DOB: Belgium

Club History	Signed	Fee
Gent		
Coventry C.	10/99	Loan
Coventry C.	1/00	£1.2m

Season	Team	Tot	St	Sb	Snu	Ps	Gls
99-00	Coventry C.	22	18	4	1	8	6
	Total	22	18	4	1	8	6

ROWETT, Gary

FULLNAME: Gary Rowett
DOB: 06-Mar-74, Bromsgrove

Club History	Signed	Fee
Cambridge U.	9/91	
Everton	5/94	£200,000
Blackpool	1/95	Loan
Derby Co.	7/95	£300,000

Season	Team	Tot	St	Sb	Snu	Ps	Gls
93-94	Everton	2	0	2	2	0	0
94-95	Everton	2	2	0	1	0	0
96-97	Derby Co.	35	35	0	0	2	2

Season	Team	Tot	St	Sb	Snu	Ps	Gls
97-98	Derby Co.	35	32	3	3	2	1
	Total	74	69	5	6	4	3

ROWLAND, Keith

FULLNAME: Keith Rowland
DOB: 01-Sep-71, Portadown, Northern Ireland

Club History	Signed	Fee
Bournemouth	10/89	Trainee
Coventry C.	1/93	Loan
West Ham U.	8/93	£110,000

Season	Team	Tot	St	Sb	Snu	Ps	Gls
92-93	Coventry C.	2	0	2	1	0	0
93-94	West Ham U.	23	16	7	6	1	0
94-95	West Ham U.	12	11	1	8	2	0
95-96	West Ham U.	23	19	4	4	5	0
96-97	West Ham U.	15	11	4	11	8	1
97-98	West Ham U.	7	6	1	11	0	0
	Total	82	63	19	41	16	1

ROY, Bryan

FULLNAME: Bryan Edward Roy
DOB: 12-Feb-70, Amsterdam, Netherlands

Club History	Signed	Fee
Foggia	11/92	
Nottingham F.	8/94	£2.5m

Season	Team	Tot	St	Sb	Snu	Ps	Gls
94-95	Nottingham F.	37	37	0	0	16	13
95-96	Nottingham F.	28	25	3	0	9	8
96-97	Nottingham F.	20	8	12	12	7	3
	Total	85	70	15	12	32	24

ROY, Eric

FULLNAME: Eric Roy
DOB: 26-Sep-67, Nice, France

Club History	Signed	Fee
Marseille		
Sunderland	8/99	£200,000

Season	Team	Tot	St	Sb	Snu	Ps	Gls
99-00	Sunderland	24	19	5	6	10	0
	Total	24	19	5	6	10	0

ROYCE, Simon

FULLNAME: Simon Ernest Royce
DOB: 09-Sep-71, Forest Gate

Club History	Signed	Fee
Southend U.	10/91	£35,000 from Non League
Charlton A.	7/98	Free

Season	Team	Tot	St	Sb	Snu	Ps	Gls
98-99	Charlton A.	8	8	0	11	1	0
	Total	8	8	0	11	1	0

RUDDOCK, Neil

FULLNAME: Neil Ruddock
DOB: 09-May-68, Wandsworth

Club History	Signed	Fee
Millwall	3/86	Apprentice
Tottenham H.	4/86	£50,000
Millwall	6/88	£300,000
Southampton	2/89	£250,000
Tottenham H.	7/92	£750,000
Liverpool	7/93	£2.5m
QPR	3/98	Loan
West Ham U.		

Season	Team	Tot	St	Sb	Snu	Ps	Gls
92-93	Tottenham H.	38	38	0	0	1	3
93-94	Liverpool	39	39	0	0	1	3
94-95	Liverpool	37	37	0	0	1	2
95-96	Liverpool	20	18	2	1	1	5
96-97	Liverpool	17	15	2	17	3	1
97-98	Liverpool	3	2	1	2	1	0
98-99	West Ham U.	27	27	0	0	2	2
99-00	West Ham U.	15	12	3	5	1	0
	Total	196	188	8	25	11	16

RUDI, Petter

FULLNAME: Petter Rudi
DOB: 17-Sep-73, Norway

Club History	Signed	Fee
Molde		
Sheffield W.	10/97	£800,000

Season	Team	Tot	St	Sb	Snu	Ps	Gls
97-98	Sheffield W.	22	19	3	0	5	0
98-99	Sheffield W.	34	33	1	0	7	6
99-00	Sheffield W.	20	18	2	2	8	2
	Total	76	70	6	2	20	8

RUFUS, Richard

FULLNAME: Richard Raymond Rufus
DOB: 12-Jan-75, Lewisham

Club History	Signed	Fee
Charlton A.	7/93	Trainee

Season	Team	Tot	St	Sb	Snu	Ps	Gls
98-99	Charlton A.	27	27	0	0	2	1
	Total	27	27	0	0	2	1

RUSH, Ian

FULLNAME: Ian James Rush
DOB: 20-Oct-61, St Asaph

Club History	Signed	Fee
Chester C.	9/79	Apprentice
Liverpool	5/80	£300,000
Juventus (Italy)	6/87	£3.8m
Liverpool	8/88	£2.2m
Leeds U.	6/96	Free
Newcastle U.	8/97	Free

Season	Team	Tot	St	Sb	Snu	Ps	Gls
92-93	Liverpool	32	31	1	0	2	14
93-94	Liverpool	42	41	1	0	2	14
94-95	Liverpool	36	36	0	0	5	12
95-96	Liverpool	20	10	10	8	2	5
96-97	Leeds U.	36	34	2	0	4	3
97-98	Newcastle U.	10	6	4	8	2	0
	Total	176	158	18	16	17	48

RUSH, Matthew

FULLNAME: Matthew James Rush
DOB: 06-Aug-71, Hackney

Club History	Signed	Fee
West Ham U.	24/3/90	Trainee

Season	Team	Tot	St	Sb	Snu	Ps	Gls
93-94	West Ham U.	10	9	1	1	3	1
94-95	West Ham U.	23	15	8	1	3	2
	Total	33	24	9	2	6	3

RUSSELL, Craig

FULLNAME: Craig Stewart Russell
DOB: 04-Feb-74, Jarrow

Club History	Signed	Fee
Sunderland	7/92	Trainee

Season	Team	Tot	St	Sb	Snu	Ps	Gls
96-97	Sunderland	29	10	19	3	3	4
	Total	29	10	19	3	3	4

SAHA, Louis

FULLNAME: Louis Saha
DOB: 08-Aug-78, Paris, France

Club History	Signed	Fee
Metz		
Newcastle U.	1/99	Loan

Season	Team	Tot	St	Sb	Snu	Ps	Gls
98-99	Newcastle U.	11	5	6	0	3	1
	Total	11	5	6	0	3	1

SAIB, Moussa

FULLNAME: Moussa Saib
DOB: 15-Mar-69, Theniet-al-Had, Algeria

Club History	Signed	Fee					
Valencia							
Tottenham H.	2/98	£2.3m					

Season	Team	Tot	St	Sb	Snu	Ps	Gls
97-98	Tottenham H.	9	3	6	0	1	1
98-99	Tottenham H.	4	0	4	0	0	0
	Total	13	3	10	0	1	1

SALAKO, John

FULLNAME: John Akin Salako
DOB: 11-Feb-69, Nigeria

Club History	Signed	Fee
Crystal P.	11/86	Apprentice
Swansea C.	8/89	Loan
Coventry C.	8/95	£1.5m >£3m
Bolton W.	3/98	Free

Season	Team	Tot	St	Sb	Snu	Ps	Gls
92-93	Crystal P.	13	12	1	0	3	0
94-95	Crystal P.	39	39	0	0	6	4
95-96	Coventry C.	37	34	3	1	2	3
96-97	Coventry C.	24	23	1	0	2	1
97-98	Coventry C.	11	11	0	2	2	0
97-98	Bolton W.	7	0	7	2	1	0
	Total	131	119	12	5	16	8

SAMUEL, J Lloyd

FULLNAME: J Lloyd Samuel
DOB: 29-Mar-81, Trinidad

Club History	Signed	Fee
Charlton A.		
Aston Villa		

Season	Team	Tot	St	Sb	Snu	Ps	Gls
98-99	Aston Villa	0	0	0	8	0	0
99-00	Aston Villa	9	5	4	5	0	0
	Total	9	5	4	13	0	0

SAMWAYS, Vinny

FULLNAME: Vincent Samways
DOB: 27-Oct-68, Bethnal Green

Club History	Signed	Fee
Tottenham H.	10/85	
Everton	7/94	£2m

Season	Team	Tot	St	Sb	Snu	Ps	Gls
92-93	Tottenham H.	34	34	0	0	3	0
93-94	Tottenham H.	39	39	0	0	2	3
94-95	Everton	19	14	5	1	2	1
95-96	Everton	4	3	1	0	0	1
	Total	96	90	6	1	7	5

SANCHEZ, Lawrie

FULLNAME: Lawrence Philip Sanchez
DOB: 22-Oct-79, Lambeth

Club History	Signed	Fee
Reading	9/76	
Wimbledon	12/84	£29,000
Swindon Town		

Season	Team	Tot	St	Sb	Snu	Ps	Gls
92-93	Wimbledon	27	23	4	6	3	4
93-94	Wimbledon	15	15	0	0	1	2
93-94	Swindon T.	8	6	2	0	2	0
	Total	50	44	6	6	6	6

SANETTI, Francesco

FULLNAME: Francesco Sanetti
DOB: 11-Jan-79, Rome

Club History	Signed	Fee
Genoa		
Sheffield W.	4/98	Free

Season	Team	Tot	St	Sb	Snu	Ps	Gls
97-98	Sheffield W.	2	1	1	0	0	0
98-99	Sheffield W.	3	0	3	5	0	0
	Total	5	1	4	5	0	0

SANSOM, Kenny

FULLNAME: Kenneth Philip Sansom
DOB: 26-Sep-58, Camberwell

Club History	Signed	Fee
Crystal P.	12/75	
Arsenal	8/80	£955,000
Newcastle U.	12/88	£300,000
QPR	6/86	£300,000
Coventry C.	1/91	£100,000
Everton		Free

Season	Team	Tot	St	Sb	Snu	Ps	Gls
92-93	Coventry C.	21	21	0	0	2	0
92-93	Everton	7	6	1	1	0	1
	Total	28	27	1	1	2	1

SAUNDERS, Dean

FULLNAME: Dean Nicholas Saunders
DOB: 21-Jun-64, Swansea

Club History	Signed	Fee
Swansea C.	6/82	
Cardiff C.	3/85	Loan
Brighton & HA	8/85	
Oxford U.	3/87	£60,000
Derby Co.	10/88	£1m
Liverpool	7/91	£2.9m
Aston Villa	9/92	£2.3m

Galatasaray 7/95 £1.5m
Nottingham F. 7/96 £1.5m
Bradford C. 8/99 Free fm Benfica

Season	Team	Tot	St	Sb	Snu	Ps	Gls
92-93	Liverpool	6	6	0	0	3	1
92-93	Aston Villa	35	35	0	0	0	13
93-94	Aston Villa	38	37	1	1	4	9
94-95	Aston Villa	39	39	0	0	5	15
96-97	Nottingham F.	34	33	1	0	11	3
99-00	Bradford C.	34	28	6	1	10	3
	Total	186	178	8	2	33	44

SAVAGE, Robbie

FULLNAME: Robert William Savage
DOB: 18-Oct-74, Wrexham

Club History	Signed	Fee
Manchester U.	7/93	Trainee
Crewe Alex.	7/94	Free
Leicester C.	7/97	£400,000

Season	Team	Tot	St	Sb	Snu	Ps	Gls
97-98	Leicester C.	35	28	7	2	6	2
98-99	Leicester C.	34	29	5	0	6	1
99-00	Leicester C.	35	35	0	0	9	1
	Total	104	92	12	2	21	4

SCALES, John

FULLNAME: John Robert Scales
DOB: 04-Jul-66, Harrogate

Club History	Signed	Fee
Bristol R.	7/85	
Wimbledon	7/87	£70,000
Liverpool	9/94	£3.5m
Tottenham H.	12/96	£2.6m

Season	Team	Tot	St	Sb	Snu	Ps	Gls
92-93	Wimbledon	32	32	0	0	1	1
93-94	Wimbledon	37	37	0	0	0	0
94-95	Wimbledon	3	3	0	0	0	0
94-95	Liverpool	35	35	0	0	3	2
95-96	Liverpool	27	27	0	0	1	0
96-97	Liverpool	3	3	0	1	2	0
96-97	Tottenham H.	12	10	2	0	1	0
97-98	Tottenham H.	10	9	1	9	1	0
98-99	Tottenham H.	7	7	0	2	1	0
99-00	Tottenham H.	4	3	1	6	0	0
	Total	170	166	4	18	10	3

SCHMEICHEL, Peter

FULLNAME: Peter Boleslaw Schmeichel
DOB: 18-Nov-68, Glodsone, Denmark

Club History	Signed	Fee
Brondby		
Manchester U.	8/91	£550,000

Season	Team	Tot	St	Sb	Snu	Ps	Gls
92-93	Manchester U.	42	42	0	0	0	0
93-94	Manchester U.	40	40	0	0	1	0
94-95	Manchester U.	32	32	0	0	1	0
95-96	Manchester U.	36	36	0	0	1	0
96-97	Manchester U.	36	36	0	0	0	0
97-98	Manchester U.	32	32	0	0	1	0
98-99	Manchester U.	34	34	0	0	1	0
	Total	252	252	0	0	5	0

SCHNOOR, Stefan

FULLNAME: Stefan Schnoor
DOB: 18-Apr-71, Germany

Club History	Signed	Fee
Hamburg		
Germany	6/97	Free

Season	Team	Tot	St	Sb	Snu	Ps	Gls
98-99	Derby Co.	23	20	3	5	7	2
99-00	Derby Co.	29	22	7	4	6	0
	Total	52	42	10	9	13	2

SCHOLES, Paul

FULLNAME: Paul Scholes
DOB: 16-Nov-74, Salford

Club History	Signed	Fee
Manchester U.	1/93	Trainee

Season	Team	Tot	St	Sb	Snu	Ps	Gls
94-95	Manchester U.	17	6	11	4	3	5
95-96	Manchester U.	26	16	10	9	11	10
96-97	Manchester U.	24	16	8	7	7	3
97-98	Manchester U.	31	28	3	0	10	8
98-99	Manchester U.	31	24	7	3	9	6
99-00	Manchester U.	31	27	4	2	7	9
	Total	160	117	43	25	47	41

SCHWARZ, Stefan

FULLNAME: Stefan Schwarz
DOB: 18-May-69, Sweden

Club History	Signed	Fee
Benfica		
Arsenal	5/94	£1.75m
Fiorentina		
Valencia		
Sunderland	7/99	£4m

Season	Team	Tot	St	Sb	Snu	Ps	Gls
94-95	Arsenal	34	34	0	0	1	2
99-00	Sunderland	27	27	0	0	4	1
	Total	61	61	0	0	5	3

SCHWARZER, Mark

FULLNAME: Mark Schwarzer
DOB: 06-Oct-72, Australia

Club History	Signed	Fee
1.FC Kaiserslautern	1995	
Bradford C.	11/96	£350,000
Middlesbrough	2/97	£1.5m

Season	Team	Tot	St	Sb	Snu	Ps	Gls
96-97	Middlesbrough	7	7	0	1	1	0
98-99	Middlesbrough	34	34	0	3	0	0
99-00	Middlesbrough	37	37	0	0	0	0
	Total	78	78	0	4	1	0

SCIMECA, Ricky

FULLNAME: Riccardo Scimeca
DOB: 13-Aug-75, Leamington

Club History	Signed	Fee
Aston Villa	7/93	

Season	Team	Tot	St	Sb	Snu	Ps	Gls
95-96	Aston Villa	17	7	10	7	2	0
96-97	Aston Villa	17	11	6	9	0	0
97-98	Aston Villa	21	16	5	7	3	0
98-99	Aston Villa	18	16	2	4	5	2
	Total	73	50	23	27	10	2

SCOTT, Andy

FULLNAME: Andrew Scott
DOB: 02-Aug-72, Epsom

Club History	Signed	Fee
Sheffield U.	11/92	£50,000 from Non League

Season	Team	Tot	St	Sb	Snu	Ps	Gls
92-93	Sheffield U.	2	1	1	0	0	1
93-94	Sheffield U.	15	12	3	1	5	0
	Total	17	13	4	1	5	1

SCOTT, Keith

FULLNAME: Keith Scott
DOB: 10-Jun-67, London

Club History	Signed	Fee
Lincoln C.		
Wycombe W.		
Swindon Town		

Season	Team	Tot	St	Sb	Snu	Ps	Gls
93-94	Swindon T.	27	22	5	0	5	4
	Total	27	22	5	0	5	4

SCOTT, Kevin

FULLNAME: Kevin Watson Scott
DOB: 17-Dec-66, Easington

Club History	Signed	Fee
Newcastle U.	12/84	
Tottenham H.	2/94	£850,000

Season	Team	Tot	St	Sb	Snu	Ps	Gls
93-94	Newcastle U.	18	18	0	2	0	0
93-94	Tottenham H.	12	12	0	0	1	1
94-95	Tottenham H.	4	4	0	1	0	0
95-96	Tottenham H.	2	0	2	2	0	0
	Total	36	34	2	5	1	1

SCOTT, Martin

FULLNAME: Martin Scott
DOB: 07-Jan-68, Sheffield

Club History	Signed	Fee
Rotherham U.	1/86	Apprentice
Bristol C.	12/90	£200,000
Sunderland	12/94	£750,000

Season	Team	Tot	St	Sb	Snu	Ps	Gls
96-97	Sunderland	15	15	0	0	0	1
	Total	15	15	0	0	0	1

SCOTT, Philip

FULLNAME: Philip Scott
DOB: 14-Nov-74, Perth

Club History	Signed	Fee
St Johnstone		
Sheffield W.	3/99	

Season	Team	Tot	St	Sb	Snu	Ps	Gls
98-99	Sheffield W.	4	0	4	0	0	1
99-00	Sheffield W.	5	2	3	0	1	0
	Total	9	2	7	0	1	1

SEALEY, Les

FULLNAME: Leslie Jesse Sealey
DOB: 29-Sep-57, Bethnal Green

Club History	Signed	Fee
Coventry C.	3/76	
Luton Town	8/83	£100.000
Plymouth Argyle	10/84	Loan
Manchester U.	12/89	Loan
Manchester U.	3/90	Loan
Manchester U.	6/90	Free
Aston Villa	7/91	Free
Coventry C.	3/92	Loan
Birmingham C.	10/92	Loan
Manchester U.		Free
West Ham U.		Free

Season	Team	Tot	St	Sb	Snu	Ps	Gls
92-93	Aston Villa	0	0	0	10	0	0
92-93	Manchester U.	0	0	0	20	0	0
93-94	Manchester U.	0	0	0	39	0	0

94-95	West Ham U.	0	0	0	26	0	0
95-96	West Ham U.	2	1	1	27	0	0
96-97	West Ham U.	2	1	1	22	0	0
97-98	West Ham U.	0	0	0	10	0	0
98-99	West Ham U.	0	0	0	6	0	0
99-00	West Ham U.	0	0	0	1	0	0
	Total	4	2	2	161	0	0

SEAMAN, David

FULLNAME: David Andrew Seaman
DOB: 19-Sep-63, Rotherham

Club History	Signed	Fee
Leeds U.	9/81	Apprentice
Peterborough Utd	8/82	£4,000
Birmingham C.	10/84	£100,000
QPR	8/86	£225,000
Arsenal	5/90	£1.3m

Season	Team	Tot	St	Sb	Snu	Ps	Gls
92-93	Arsenal	39	39	0	0	1	0
93-94	Arsenal	39	39	0	0	0	0
94-95	Arsenal	31	31	0	0	0	0
95-96	Arsenal	38	38	0	0	0	0
96-97	Arsenal	22	22	0	0	0	0
97-98	Arsenal	31	31	0	0	0	0
98-99	Arsenal	32	32	0	0	0	0
99-00	Arsenal	24	24	0	0	1	0
	Total	256	256	0	0	2	0

SEDGLEY, Steve

FULLNAME: Stephen Philip Sedgley
DOB: 26-May-68, Enfield

Club History	Signed	Fee
Coventry C.	5/86	
Tottenham H.	7/89	£750,000
Ipswich Town	6/94	£1m

Season	Team	Tot	St	Sb	Snu	Ps	Gls
92-93	Tottenham H.	22	20	2	0	1	3
93-94	Tottenham H.	42	42	0	0	2	6
94-95	Ipswich T.	26	26	0	0	1	4
	Total	90	88	2	0	4	13

SEDLOSKI, Goce

FULLNAME: Goce Sedloski
DOB: 10-Apr-75, Macedonia

Club History	Signed	Fee
Hajduk Split		
Sheffield W.	2/98	£750,000>

Season	Team	Tot	St	Sb	Snu	Ps	Gls
97-98	Sheffield W.	4	3	1	0	1	0
	Total	4	3	1	0	1	0

SEGERS, Hans

FULLNAME: Johannes Segers
DOB: 30-Oct-71, Eindhoven

Club History	Signed	Fee
Nottingham F.	8/84	£50,000
Stoke C.	2/87	Loan
Sheffield U.	11/87	Loan
Dunfermline Ath	3/88	Loan
Wimbledon	9/88	£180,000
Wolverhampton W.	8/96	Non Contract
Tottenham H.		

Season	Team	Tot	St	Sb	Snu	Ps	Gls
92-93	Wimbledon	41	41	0	1	0	0
93-94	Wimbledon	41	41	0	1	1	0
94-95	Wimbledon	32	31	1	10	0	0
95-96	Wimbledon	4	3	1	2	0	0
98-99	Tottenham H.	1	1	0	2	0	0
99-00	Tottenham H.	0	0	0	1	0	0
	Total	119	117	2	17	1	0

SELLARS, Scott

FULLNAME: Scott Sellars
DOB: 27-Nov-65, Sheffield

Club History	Signed	Fee
Leeds U.	7/83	
Blackburn R.	7/86	£20,000
Leeds U.	7/92	£800,000
Newcastle U.	3/93	£700,000
Bolton W.	12/95	£750,000

Season	Team	Tot	St	Sb	Snu	Ps	Gls
92-93	Leeds U.	7	6	1	1	4	0
93-94	Newcastle U.	30	29	1	2	1	3
94-95	Newcastle U.	12	12	0	0	4	0
95-96	Newcastle U.	6	2	4	2	0	0
95-96	Bolton W.	22	22	0	0	1	3
97-98	Bolton W.	22	22	0	0	3	2
	Total	99	93	6	5	13	8

SELLEY, Ian

FULLNAME: Ian Selley
DOB: 14-Jun-74, Chertsey

Club History	Signed	Fee
Arsenal	5/92	

Season	Team	Tot	St	Sb	Snu	Ps	Gls
92-93	Arsenal	9	9	0	0	0	0
93-94	Arsenal	18	16	2	4	0	0
94-95	Arsenal	13	10	3	0	4	0
96-97	Arsenal	1	0	1	3	0	0
	Total	41	35	6	7	4	0

SERRANT, Carl

FULLNAME: Carl Serrant
DOB: 12-Sep-75, Bradford

Club History	Signed	Fee
Oldham A.	7/94	Trainee
Newcastle U.	7/98	£500,000

Season	Team	Tot	St	Sb	Snu	Ps	Gls
98-99	Newcastle U.	4	3	1	0	2	0
99-00	Newcastle U.	2	2	0	1	2	0
	Total	6	5	1	1	4	0

SHARP, Graeme

FULLNAME: Graeme Marshall Sharpe
DOB: 16-Oct-60, Glasgow

Club History	Signed	Fee
Everton	4/80	£125,000
Oldham A.	7/91	£500,000

Season	Team	Tot	St	Sb	Snu	Ps	Gls
92-93	Oldham A.	21	20	1	0	1	7
93-94	Oldham A.	34	31	3	1	1	9
	Total	55	51	4	1	2	16

SHARP, Kevin

FULLNAME: Kevin Phillip Sharp
DOB: 19-Sep-74, Ontario, Canada

Club History	Signed	Fee
Auxerre		
Leeds U.	10/92	£60,000

Season	Team	Tot	St	Sb	Snu	Ps	Gls
92-93	Leeds U.	4	4	0	0	1	0
93-94	Leeds U.	10	7	3	1	3	0
94-95	Leeds U.	2	0	2	1	0	0
95-96	Leeds U.	1	0	1	0	0	0
	Total	17	11	6	2	4	0

SHARPE, Lee

FULLNAME: Lee Stuart Sharpe
DOB: 27-May-71, Halesowen

Club History	Signed	Fee
Torquay U.	5/88	Trainee
Manchester U.	5/88	£185,000
Leeds U.	7/96	£4.5m
Bradford C.	3/98	Loan
Bradford C.	6/99	£200,000

Season	Team	Tot	St	Sb	Snu	Ps	Gls
92-93	Manchester U.	27	27	0	0	2	1
93-94	Manchester U.	30	26	4	2	5	9
94-95	Manchester U.	28	26	2	0	6	3
95-96	Manchester U.	31	21	10	2	4	4
96-97	Leeds U.	26	26	0	3	4	5

98-99	Leeds U.	4	2	2	5	1	0
99-00	Bradford C.	18	13	5	9	4	0
	Total	164	141	23	21	26	22

SHAW, Paul

FULLNAME: Paul Shaw
DOB: 04-Sep-73, Burnham

Club History	Signed	Fee
Arsenal	9/91	Trainee

Season	Team	Tot	St	Sb	Snu	Ps	Gls
94-95	Arsenal	1	0	1	0	0	0
95-96	Arsenal	3	0	3	2	0	0
96-97	Arsenal	8	1	7	17	1	2
	Total	12	1	11	19	1	2

SHAW, Richard

FULLNAME: Richard Edward Shaw
DOB: 11-Sep-68, Brentford

Club History	Signed	Fee
Crystal P.	9/86	Apprentice
Hull C.	12/89	Loan
Coventry C.	11/95	£1m

Season	Team	Tot	St	Sb	Snu	Ps	Gls
92-93	Crystal P.	33	32	1	0	4	0
94-95	Crystal P.	41	41	0	0	1	0
95-96	Coventry C.	21	21	0	1	0	0
96-97	Coventry C.	35	35	0	2	2	0
97-98	Coventry C.	33	33	0	2	1	0
98-99	Coventry C.	37	36	1	1	0	0
99-00	Coventry C.	29	27	2	1	0	0
	Total	229	225	4	7	8	0

SHEARER, Alan

FULLNAME: Alan Shearer
DOB: 13-Aug-70, Newcastle

Club History	Signed	Fee
Southampton	4/88	
Blackburn R.	7/92	£3.6m
Newcastle U.	7/96	£15m

Season	Team	Tot	St	Sb	Snu	Ps	Gls
92-93	Blackburn R.	21	21	0	0	3	16
93-94	Blackburn R.	40	34	6	1	2	31
94-95	Blackburn R.	42	42	0	0	2	34
95-96	Blackburn R.	35	35	0	0	0	31
96-97	Newcastle U.	31	31	0	0	1	25
97-98	Newcastle U.	17	15	2	0	0	2
98-99	Newcastle U.	30	29	1	0	2	14
99-00	Newcastle U.	37	36	1	0	0	23
	Total	253	243	10	1	10	176

SHEERIN, Joe

FULLNAME: Joseph Earman Sheerin
DOB: 28-Aug-74, Edinburgh

Club History	Signed	Fee
Chelsea		Trainee

Season	Team	Tot	St	Sb	Snu	Ps	Gls
96-97	Chelsea	1	0	1	0	0	0
97-98	Chelsea	0	0	0	1	0	0
	Total	1	0	1	1	0	0

SHEFFIELD, Jon

FULLNAME: Jonathan Sheffield
DOB: 01-Feb-69, Bedworth

Club History	Signed	Fee
Norwich C.	2/98	Trainee
Aldershot	8/89	Loan (x2)
Cambridge U.	3/91	Free
Colchester U.	12/94	Loan
Swindon T.	1/94	Loan

Season	Team	Tot	St	Sb	Snu	Ps	Gls
93-94	Swindon T.	2	2	0	1	1	0
	Total	2	2	0	1	1	0

SHEPHERD, Paul

FULLNAME: Paul Shepherd
DOB: 17-Nov-77, Leeds

Club History	Signed	Fee
Leeds U.	9/95	Trainee

Season	Team	Tot	St	Sb	Snu	Ps	Gls
96-97	Leeds U.	1	1	0	0	0	0
	Total	1	1	0	0	0	0

SHERIDAN, Darren

FULLNAME: Darren Stephen Sheridan
DOB: 01-Oct-64, Stretford

Club History	Signed	Fee
Barnsley	8/93	£10,000 from Non League

Season	Team	Tot	St	Sb	Snu	Ps	Gls
97-98	Barnsley	26	20	6	5	5	0
	Total	26	20	6	5	5	0

SHERIDAN, John

FULLNAME: John Joseph Sheridan
DOB: 01-Oct-64, Manchester

Club History	Signed	Fee
Leeds U.	3/82	
Nottingham F.	7/89	£650,000
Sheffield W.	11/89	£500,000
Birmingham C.	2/96	Loan
Bolton W.	12/96	£180,000

Season	Team	Tot	St	Sb	Snu	Ps	Gls
92-93	Sheffield W.	25	25	0	0	3	3
93-94	Sheffield W.	20	19	1	0	6	3
94-95	Sheffield W.	36	34	2	0	6	0
95-96	Sheffield W.	17	13	4	2	6	0
96-97	Sheffield W.	2	0	2	2	0	0
97-98	Bolton W.	12	12	0	3	3	0
	Total	112	103	9	7	24	6

SHERIDAN, Tony

FULLNAME: Anthony Joseph Sheridan
DOB: 21-Oct-74, Dublin, Republic of Ireland

Club History	Signed	Fee
Coventry C.	10/91	

Season	Team	Tot	St	Sb	Snu	Ps	Gls
92-93	Coventry C.	1	1	0	1	1	0
93-94	Coventry C.	8	4	4	1	3	0
94-95	Coventry C.	0	0	0	1	0	0
	Total	9	5	4	3	4	0

SHERINGHAM, Teddy

FULLNAME: Edward Paul Sheringham
DOB: 02-Apr-66, Walthamstow

Club History	Signed	Fee
Millwall	1/84	Apprentice
Aldershot	2/85	Loan
Nottingham F.	7/91	£2m
Tottenham H.	8/92	£2.1m
Manchester U.	6/97	£3.5m

Season	Team	Tot	St	Sb	Snu	Ps	Gls
92-93	Nottingham F.	3	3	0	0	1	1
92-93	Tottenham H.	38	38	0	0	0	21
93-94	Tottenham H.	19	17	2	0	1	13
94-95	Tottenham H.	42	41	1	0	0	17
95-96	Tottenham H.	38	38	0	0	1	16
96-97	Tottenham H.	29	29	0	0	0	5
97-98	Manchester U.	31	28	3	3	5	9
98-99	Manchester U.	17	7	10	2	2	2
99-00	Manchester U.	27	15	12	7	5	5
	Total	244	216	28	12	15	91

SHERON, Mike

FULLNAME: Michael Nigel Sheron
DOB: 11-Jan-72, Liverpool

Club History	Signed	Fee
Manchester C.	7/90	
Norwich C.	8/94	£1m

Season	Team	Tot	St	Sb	Snu	Ps	Gls
92-93	Manchester C.	38	33	5	2	6	11
93-94	Manchester C.	33	29	4	3	5	6
94-95	Norwich C.	21	17	4	0	5	1
	Total	92	79	13	5	16	18

SHERWOOD, Tim

FULLNAME: Timothey Alan Sherwood
DOB: 06-Feb-69, St Albans

Club History	Signed	Fee
Watford	2/87	Trainee
Norwich C.	7/89	£175,000
Blackburn R.	2/92	£500,000
Tottenham H.	3/99	£3.8m

Season	Team	Tot	St	Sb	Snu	Ps	Gls
92-93	Blackburn R.	39	38	1	1	2	3
93-94	Blackburn R.	38	38	0	0	1	2
94-95	Blackburn R.	38	38	0	0	1	6
95-96	Blackburn R.	33	33	0	1	2	4
96-97	Blackburn R.	37	37	0	0	3	3
97-98	Blackburn R.	31	29	2	0	3	5
98-99	Blackburn R.	19	19	0	0	0	3
98-99	Tottenham H.	14	12	2	0	0	2
99-00	Tottenham H.	27	23	4	0	2	8
	Total	276	267	9	2	14	36

SHILTON, Sam

FULLNAME: Sam Shilton
DOB: 21-Jul-78, Nottingham

Club History	Signed	Fee
Plymouth Argyle		Trainee
Coventry C.	10/95	£12,500

Season	Team	Tot	St	Sb	Snu	Ps	Gls
95-96	Coventry C.	0	0	0	3	0	0
96-97	Coventry C.	0	0	0	2	0	0
97-98	Coventry C.	2	2	0	5	1	0
98-99	Coventry C.	5	1	4	11	1	0
	Total	7	3	4	21	2	0

SHIPPERLEY, Neil

FULLNAME: Neil Shipperley
DOB: 30-Oct-74, Chatham

Club History	Signed	Fee
Chelsea	9/92	Trainee
Watford	12/94	Loan
Southampton	1/95	£1.25m
Crystal P.	10/96	£1m
Nottingham F.	9/98	£1.5m

Season	Team	Tot	St	Sb	Snu	Ps	Gls
92-93	Chelsea	3	2	1	0	1	1
93-94	Chelsea	24	18	6	1	7	4
94-95	Chelsea	10	6	4	1	3	2

Season	Team	Tot	St	Sb	Snu	Ps	Gls
94-95	Southampton	19	19	0	0	2	4
95-96	Southampton	37	37	0	0	4	8
96-97	Southampton	10	9	1	0	3	1
97-98	Crystal P.	25	17	8	2	3	7
98-99	Nottingham F.	20	12	8	4	3	1
	Total	148	120	28	8	26	28

SHIRTLIFF, Peter

FULLNAME: Peter Andrew Shirtliff
DOB: 06-Feb-61, Hoyland

Club History	Signed	Fee
Sheffield W.	10/78	
Charlton A.	7/86	£125,000
Sheffield W.	7/89	£500,000
Wolverhampton W.	8/93	£250,000
Barnsley	8/95	£125,000

Season	Team	Tot	St	Sb	Snu	Ps	Gls
92-93	Sheffield W.	20	20	0	1	1	0
97-98	Barnsley	4	4	0	0	2	0
	Total	24	24	0	1	3	0

SHORT, Craig

FULLNAME: Craig Short
DOB: 25-Jun-68, Bridlington

Club History	Signed	Fee
Scarborough	10/87	Free from Non League
Notts Co	7/89	£100,000
Derby Co.	9/92	£2.5m
Everton	7/95	£2.7m

Season	Team	Tot	St	Sb	Snu	Ps	Gls
95-96	Everton	23	22	1	5	2	2
96-97	Everton	23	19	4	6	4	2
97-98	Everton	31	27	4	1	6	0
98-99	Everton	22	22	0	4	3	0
	Total	99	90	9	16	15	4

SHUTT, Carl

FULLNAME: Carl Steven Shutt
DOB: 10-Oct-61, Sheffield

Club History	Signed	Fee
Sheffield W.	5/85	
Bristol C.	10/87	£55,000
Leeds U.	3/89	£50,000
Manchester C.		

Season	Team	Tot	St	Sb	Snu	Ps	Gls
92-93	Leeds U.	14	6	8	3	4	0
93-94	Manchester C.	6	5	1	1	1	0
	Total	20	11	9	4	5	0

SIBON, Gerald

FULLNAME: Gerald Sibon
DOB: 19-Apr-74, Holland

Club History	Signed	Fee
Ajax		
Sheffield W.	7/99	£2.0m

Season	Team	Tot	St	Sb	Snu	Ps	Gls
99-00	Sheffield W.	28	12	16	5	5	5
	Total	28	12	16	5	5	5

SILENZI, Andrea

FULLNAME: Andrea Silenzi
DOB: 10-Feb-66, Rome

Club History	Signed	Fee
Nottingham F.	8/95	£1.8m
Vicenza	10/96	Loan

Season	Team	Tot	St	Sb	Snu	Ps	Gls
95-96	Nottingham F.	10	3	7	6	1	0
96-97	Nottingham F.	2	1	1	0	1	0
	Total	12	4	8	6	2	0

SILVESTRE, Mikael

FULLNAME: Mikael Silvestre
DOB: 09-Aug-77, Chambray-Les-Tour, France

Club History	Signed	Fee
Internazionale		
Manchester U.	9/99	£4.0m

Season	Team	Tot	St	Sb	Snu	Ps	Gls
99-00	Manchester U.	31	30	1	0	2	0
	Total	31	30	1	0	2	0

SILVINHO

FULLNAME: Sylvio Mendes Campos Junor
DOB: 12-Apr-74, Sao Paulo, Brazil

Club History	Signed	Fee
Corinthians		
Arsenal	6/99	£4m

Season	Team	Tot	St	Sb	Snu	Ps	Gls
99-00	Arsenal	31	23	8	2	3	1
	Total	31	23	8	2	3	1

SIMONSEN, Steve

FULLNAME: Steven Preben Simonsen
DOB: 03-Apr-79, South Shield

Club History	Signed	Fee
Tranmere R.	10/96	Trainee
Everton	9/98	£3.3m

Season	Team	Tot	St	Sb	Snu	Ps	Gls
92-93	Manchester C.	29	27	2	4	4	1
98-99	Everton	0	0	0	22	0	0
99-00	Everton	1	0	1	34	0	0
	Total	30	27	3	60	4	1

SIMPSON, Fitzroy

FULLNAME: Fitzroy Simpson
DOB: 26-Feb-70, Bradford on Avon

Club History	Signed	Fee
Swindon Town	6/7/88	Trainee
Manchester C.	6/3/92	£500,000

Season	Team	Tot	St	Sb	Snu	Ps	Gls
93-94	Manchester C.	15	12	3	2	4	0
94-95	Manchester C.	16	10	6	2	2	2
	Total	31	22	9	4	6	2

SIMPSON, Paul

FULLNAME: Paul David Simpson
DOB: 26-Jul-66, Carlisle

Club History	Signed	Fee
Manchester C.	8/83	Apprentice
Oxford U.	10/88	£200,000
Derby Co.	2/92	£500,000

Season	Team	Tot	St	Sb	Snu	Ps	Gls
96-97	Derby Co.	19	0	19	12	0	2
97-98	Derby Co.	1	1	0	4	1	0
	Total	20	1	19	16	1	2

SINCLAIR, Frank

FULLNAME: Frank Mohammed Sinclair
DOB: 03-Dec-71, Lambeth

Club History	Signed	Fee
Chelsea	5/90	Trainee
WBA	12/91	Loan
Leicester C.	8/98	£2m

Season	Team	Tot	St	Sb	Snu	Ps	Gls
92-93	Chelsea	32	32	0	0	1	0
93-94	Chelsea	35	35	0	0	0	0
94-95	Chelsea	35	35	0	0	1	3
95-96	Chelsea	13	12	1	1	3	1
96-97	Chelsea	20	17	3	6	0	1
97-98	Chelsea	22	20	2	0	4	1
98-99	Leicester C.	31	30	1	1	2	1
99-00	Leicester C.	34	34	0	0	3	0
	Total	222	215	7	8	14	7

SINCLAIR, Trevor

FULLNAME: Trevor Sinclair
DOB: 02-Mar-73, Dulwich

Club History	Signed	Fee
Blackpool	8/90	Trainee
QPR	8/93	£750,000
West Ham U.	1/98	£2.3m

Season	Team	Tot	St	Sb	Snu	Ps	Gls
93-94	QPR	32	30	1	0	8	4
94-95	QPR	33	32	1	2	3	4
95-96	QPR	37	37	0	0	2	2
97-98	West Ham U.	14	14	0	0	1	7
98-99	West Ham U.	36	36	0	0	3	7
99-00	West Ham U.	36	36	0	0	0	7
	Total	188	185	3	2	17	31

SINNOTT, Lee

FULLNAME: Lee Sinnott
DOB: 12-Jul-65, Pelsall

Club History	Signed	Fee
Walsall	11/82	Apprentice
Watford	9/83
Bradford C.	7/87
Crystal P.	8/91

Season	Team	Tot	St	Sb	Snu	Ps	Gls
92-93	Crystal P.	19	18	1	1	2	0
	Total	19	18	1	1	2	0

SINTON, Andy

FULLNAME: Andrew Sinton
DOB: 19-Mar-66, Newcastle

Club History	Signed	Fee
Cambridge U.	4/83	Apprentice
Brentford	12/85	£25,000
QPR	3/89	£350,000
Sheffield W.	8/93	£2.75m
Tottenham H.	1/96	£1.5m

Season	Team	Tot	St	Sb	Snu	Ps	Gls
92-93	QPR	36	36	0	0	6	7
93-94	Sheffield W.	25	25	0	0	6	3
94-95	Sheffield W.	25	22	3	1	7	0
95-96	Sheffield W.	10	7	3	3	0	0
95-96	Tottenham H.	9	8	1	0	3	0
96-97	Tottenham H.	33	32	1	0	9	6
97-98	Tottenham H.	19	14	5	2	6	0
98-99	Tottenham H.	22	12	10	4	4	0
	Total	179	156	23	10	41	16

SKINNER, Justin

FULLNAME: Justin James Skinner
DOB: 17-Sep-72, Dorking

Club History	Signed	Fee
Wimbledon	7/91	Trainee

Season	Team	Tot	St	Sb	Snu	Ps	Gls
92-93	Wimbledon	1	1	0	0	0	0
95-96	Wimbledon	1	1	0	0	1	0
	Total	2	2	0	0	1	0

SLADE, Steve

FULLNAME: Steve Slade
DOB: 06-Oct-75, Romford

Club History	Signed	Fee
Tottenham H.	

Season	Team	Tot	St	Sb	Snu	Ps	Gls
95-96	Tottenham H.	5	1	4	5	1	0
	Total	5	1	4	5	1	0

SLATER, Robbie

FULLNAME: Robert David Slater
DOB: 22-Nov-64, Skelmersdale

Club History	Signed	Fee
Lens	
Blackburn R.	8/94	£300,000
West Ham U.	8/95	£600,000
Southampton	8/96	£250,000

Season	Team	Tot	St	Sb	Snu	Ps	Gls
94-95	Blackburn R.	18	12	6	5	3	0
95-96	West Ham U.	22	16	6	2	7	2
96-97	West Ham U.	3	2	1	0	1	0
96-97	Southampton	30	22	8	1	3	2
97-98	Southampton	11	3	8	3	3	0
	Total	84	55	29	11	17	4

SLATER, Stuart

FULLNAME: Stuart Ian Slater
DOB: 27-Mar-69, Sudbury

Club History	Signed	Fee
West Ham U.	4/87	Apprentice
Celtic	8/92	£1.5m
Ipswich Town	9/93	£750,000

Season	Team	Tot	St	Sb	Snu	Ps	Gls
93-94	Ipswich T.	28	28	0	0	3	1
94-95	Ipswich T.	27	22	5	0	4	1
	Total	55	50	5	0	7	2

SLAVEN, Bernie

FULLNAME: Bernard Slaven
DOB: 13-Nov-60, Paisley

Club History	Signed	Fee
Morton	
Airdrieonians	
Queens of the South	
Albion R.	
Middlesbrough	9/85

Season	Team	Tot	St	Sb	Snu	Ps	Gls
92-93	Middlesbrough	18	13	5	4	2	4
	Total	18	13	5	4	2	4

SMALL, Bryan

FULLNAME: Bryan Small
DOB: 15-Nov-71, Birmingham

Club History	Signed	Fee
Aston Villa	7/90	
Birmingham C.	9/94	Loan
Bolton W.	3/96	Free

Season	Team	Tot	St	Sb	Snu	Ps	Gls
92-93	Aston Villa	14	10	4	6	2	0
93-94	Aston Villa	9	8	1	1	3	0
94-95	Aston Villa	5	5	0	0	0	0
95-96	Bolton W.	1	1	0	1	0	0
	Total	29	24	5	8	5	0

SMART, Allan

FULLNAME: Allan Andrew Colin Smart
DOB: 08-Jul-74, Perth

Club History	Signed	Fee
Preston NE	11/94	£15,000
Carlisle U.	11/95	Loan
Northampton T.	9/96	Loan
Carlisle U.	10/96	
Watford	7/98	£75,000

Season	Team	Tot	St	Sb	Snu	Ps	Gls
99-00	Watford	14	13	1	1	6	5
	Total	14	13	1	1	6	5

SMICER, Vladimir

FULLNAME: Vladimir Smicer
DOB: 24-May-73, Decin, Czech Republic

Club History	Signed	Fee
Lens		
Liverpool	7/99	£4.2m

Season	Team	Tot	St	Sb	Snu	Ps	Gls
99-00	Liverpool	21	13	8	1	9	1
	Total	21	13	8	1	9	1

SMITH, Alan

FULLNAME: Alan Smith
DOB: 28-Oct-80, Wakefield

Club History	Signed	Fee
Leeds U.		Trainee

Season	Team	Tot	St	Sb	Snu	Ps	Gls
98-99	Leeds U.	22	15	7	2	3	7
99-00	Leeds U.	26	20	6	3	11	4
	Total	48	35	13	5	14	11

SMITH, Alan

FULLNAME: Alan Martin Smith
DOB: 21-Nov-62, Bromsgrove

Club History	Signed	Fee
Leicester C.	6/82	£22,000
Arsenal	5/87	£800,000

Season	Team	Tot	St	Sb	Snu	Ps	Gls
92-93	Arsenal	31	27	4	0	2	3
93-94	Arsenal	25	21	4	2	3	3
94-95	Arsenal	19	17	2	0	4	2
	Total	75	65	10	2	9	8

SMITH, David

FULLNAME: David Smith
DOB: 29-Mar-68, Gloucester

Club History	Signed	Fee
Coventry C.		

Season	Team	Tot	St	Sb	Snu	Ps	Gls
92-93	Coventry C.	6	6	0	0	2	1
92-93	Norwich C.	6	5	1	1	0	0
93-94	Norwich C.	7	5	2	9	2	0
	Total	19	16	3	10	4	1

SMITH, David

FULLNAME: David Christopher Smith
DOB: 26-Dec-70, Liverpool

Club History	Signed	Fee
Norwich C.	7/89	

Season	Team	Tot	St	Sb	Snu	Ps	Gls
92-93	Coventry C.	6	6	0	0	2	1
92-93	Norwich C.	6	5	1	1	0	0
93-94	Norwich C.	7	5	2	9	2	0
	Total	19	16	3	10	4	1

SMITH, Jamie

FULLNAME: James Jade Anthony Smith
DOB: 17-Sep-74, Birmingham

Club History	Signed	Fee
Wolverhampton		Trainee
Crystal P.	10/97	swap

Season	Team	Tot	St	Sb	Snu	Ps	Gls
97-98	Crystal P.	18	16	2	1	2	0
	Total	18	16	2	1	2	0

SMITH, Martin

FULLNAME: Martin Geoffrey Smith
DOB: 13-Nov-74, Sunderland

Club History	Signed	Fee			
Sunderland	9/92	Trainee			

Season	Team	Tot	St	Sb	Snu	Ps	Gls
96-97	Sunderland	10	6	4	8	3	0
	Total	10	6	4	8	3	0

SMITH, Richard

FULLNAME: Richard G Smith
DOB: 03-Oct-70, Lutterworth

Club History	Signed	Fee
Leicester C.	12/88	

Season	Team	Tot	St	Sb	Snu	Ps	Gls
94-95	Leicester C.	12	10	2	2	3	0
	Total	12	10	2	2	3	0

SMITH, Tommy

FULLNAME: Thomas William Smith
DOB: 22-May-80, Hemel Hempstead

Club History	Signed	Fee
Watford	10/97	Trainee

Season	Team	Tot	St	Sb	Snu	Ps	Gls
99-00	Watford	22	13	9	7	3	2
	Total	22	13	9	7	3	2

SNEEKES, Richard

FULLNAME: Richard Sneekes
DOB: 30-Oct-68, Amsterdam

Club History	Signed	Fee
Fortuna Sitard		
Bolton W.	8/94	£200,000

Season	Team	Tot	St	Sb	Snu	Ps	Gls
95-96	Bolton W.	17	14	3	3	1	1
	Total	17	14	3	3	1	1

SNODIN, Ian

FULLNAME: Ian Snodin
DOB: 15-Aug-63, Rotherham

Club History	Signed	Fee
Doncaster R.	8/80	
Leeds U.	5/85	£200,000
Everton	1/87	£840,000

Season	Team	Tot	St	Sb	Snu	Ps	Gls
92-93	Everton	20	19	1	0	8	1
93-94	Everton	29	28	1	1	2	0
94-95	Everton	3	2	1	0	0	0
	Total	52	49	3	1	10	1

SOLANO, Norberto

FULLNAME: Norberto Salano
DOB: 12-Dec-74, Lima, Peru

Club History	Signed	Fee
Boca Juniors		
Newcastle U.	8/98	£2.5m

Season	Team	Tot	St	Sb	Snu	Ps	Gls
98-99	Newcastle U.	29	24	5	6	14	6
99-00	Newcastle U.	30	29	1	1	15	3
	Total	59	53	6	7	29	9

SOLBAKKEN, Stalle

FULLNAME: Stalle Solbakken
DOB: 27-Feb-68, Norway

Club History	Signed	Fee
Lillestrom		
Wimbledon	10/97	£250,000

Season	Team	Tot	St	Sb	Snu	Ps	Gls
97-98	Wimbledon	6	4	2	5	0	1
	Total	6	4	2	5	0	1

SOLIS, Mauricio

FULLNAME: Mauricio Mora Solis
DOB: 13-Dec-72, Costa Rica

Club History	Signed	Fee
CS Heridiano		
Derby Co.	3/97	£600,000

Season	Team	Tot	St	Sb	Snu	Ps	Gls
96-97	Derby Co.	2	0	2	2	0	0
97-98	Derby Co.	9	3	6	6	3	0
	Total	11	3	8	8	3	0

SOLSKJAER, Ole Gunnar

FULLNAME: Ole Gunnar Solskjaer
DOB: 26-Feb-73, Kristiansund

Club History	Signed	Fee
Molde	1995	
Manchester U.	7/96	£1.5m

Season	Team	Tot	St	Sb	Snu	Ps	Gls
96-97	Manchester U.	33	25	8	2	11	18
97-98	Manchester U.	22	15	7	4	4	6
98-99	Manchester U.	19	9	10	9	5	12
99-00	Manchester U.	28	15	13	7	8	12
	Total	102	64	38	22	28	48

SOLTVEDT, Trond

FULLNAME: Trond Egil Soltvedt
DOB: 15-Feb-67, Norway

Club History	Signed	Fee
Rosenborg		
Coventry C.	7/97	£500,000
Southampton	8/99	£300,000

Season	Team	Tot	St	Sb	Snu	Ps	Gls
97-98	Coventry C.	30	26	4	8	10	1
98-99	Coventry C.	27	21	6	11	6	2
99-00	Coventry C.	0	0	0	1	0	0
99-00	Southampton	24	17	7	11	4	1
	Total	81	64	17	31	20	4

SOMMER, Jurgen

FULLNAME: Jurgen Petersen Sommer
DOB: 27-Feb-69, New York, USA

Club History	Signed	Fee
Luton Town	9/91	
Brighton & HA	11/91	Loan
Torquay U.	10/92	Loan
QPR	8/95	£600,000

Season	Team	Tot	St	Sb	Snu	Ps	Gls
95-96	QPR	33	33	0	0	0	0
	Total	33	33	0	0	0	0

SONG, Rigobert

FULLNAME: Rigobert Song
DOB: 01-Jul-76, Cameroon

Club History	Signed	Fee
Salernitana		
Liverpool	1/99	£2.72m

Season	Team	Tot	St	Sb	Snu	Ps	Gls
98-99	Liverpool	13	10	3	1	5	0
99-00	Liverpool	18	14	4	10	4	0
	Total	31	24	7	11	9	0

SONNER, Danny

FULLNAME: Daniel Sonner
DOB: 09-Jan-72, Wigan

Club History	Signed	Fee
Wigan A.		Youth
Burnley	8/90	Free
Preussen Koln		Loan
Bury	11/92	Loan
Ipswich Town	6/96	Free
Sheffield W.	10/98	£75,000

Season	Team	Tot	St	Sb	Snu	Ps	Gls
98-99	Sheffield W.	26	24	2	3	6	3
99-00	Sheffield W.	27	18	9	5	6	0
	Total	53	42	11	8	12	3

SORENSEN, Thomas

FULLNAME: Thomas Sorensen
DOB: 12-Jun-76, Denmark

Club History	Signed	Fee
OB Odense		
Sunderland	£1m	8/98

Season	Team	Tot	St	Sb	Snu	Ps	Gls
99-00	Sunderland	37	37	0	0	0	0
	Total	37	37	0	0	0	0

SOUTHALL, Neville

FULLNAME: Neville Southall
DOB: 16-Sep-58, Llandudno

Club History	Signed	Fee
Bury	6/80	£6,000
Everton	7/81	£150,000
Port Vale	1/83	Loan
Southend	12/97	Loan
Stoke C.	3/98	Free
Torquay	12/98	Free
Bradford C.	2/00	Free

Season	Team	Tot	St	Sb	Snu	Ps	Gls
92-93	Everton	40	40	0	0	1	0
93-94	Everton	42	42	0	0	0	0
94-95	Everton	41	41	0	0	0	0
95-96	Everton	38	38	0	0	0	0
96-97	Everton	34	34	0	4	1	0
97-98	Everton	12	12	0	5	0	0
99-00	Bradford C.	1	1	0	4	0	0
	Total	208	208	0	13	2	0

SOUTHGATE, Gareth

FULLNAME: Gareth Southgate
DOB: 03-Sep-70, Watford

Club History	Signed	Fee
Crystal P.	1/89	Trainee
Aston Villa	7/95	£2.5m

Season	Team	Tot	St	Sb	Snu	Ps	Gls
92-93	Crystal P.	33	33	0	2	2	3
94-95	Crystal P.	42	42	0	0	0	3
95-96	Aston Villa	31	31	0	0	1	1
96-97	Aston Villa	28	28	0	0	1	1
97-98	Aston Villa	32	32	0	0	1	0
98-99	Aston Villa	38	38	0	0	0	1
99-00	Aston Villa	31	31	0	0	1	2
	Total	235	235	0	2	6	11

SPACKMAN, Nigel

FULLNAME: Nigel James Spackman
DOB: 02-Dec-60, Romsey

Club History	Signed	Fee
Bournemouth	5/80	
Chelsea	6/83	£40,000
Liverpool	2/87	£400,000
QPR	2/89	£500,000
Rangers	11/89	£500,000
Chelsea	8/92	£485,000

Season	Team	Tot	St	Sb	Snu	Ps	Gls
92-93	Chelsea	6	6	0	0	0	0
93-94	Chelsea	9	5	4	7	0	0
94-95	Chelsea	36	36	0	1	6	0
95-96	Chelsea	16	13	3	7	3	0
	Total	67	60	7	15	9	0

SPEDDING, Duncan

FULLNAME: Duncan Spedding
DOB: 07-Sep-77, Camberley

Club History	Signed	Fee
Southampton	5/96	Trainee

Season	Team	Tot	St	Sb	Snu	Ps	Gls
97-98	Southampton	7	4	3	2	3	0
	Total	7	4	3	2	3	0

SPEED, Gary

FULLNAME: Gary Andrew Speed
DOB: 08-Sep-69, Hawarden

Club History	Signed	Fee
Leeds U.	6/88	Trainee
Everton	7/96	£3.5m
Newcastle U.	2/98	£5.5m

Season	Team	Tot	St	Sb	Snu	Ps	Gls
92-93	Leeds U.	39	39	0	0	0	7
93-94	Leeds U.	36	35	1	0	2	10
94-95	Leeds U.	39	39	0	0	1	3
95-96	Leeds U.	29	29	0	0	1	2
96-97	Everton	37	37	0	0	0	9
97-98	Everton	21	21	0	0	0	7
97-98	Newcastle U.	13	13	0	0	0	1
98-99	Newcastle U.	38	34	4	0	3	4
99-00	Newcastle U.	36	36	0	0	0	9
	Total	288	283	5	0	7	52

SPEEDIE, David

FULLNAME: David Robert Speedie
DOB: 20-Feb-60, Glenrothes

Club History	Signed	Fee
Barnsley	10/78	
Darlington	6/80	Free
Chelsea	6/82	£70,000
Coventry C.	7/87	£750,000
Liverpool	2/91	£675,000
Blackburn R.	8/91	£450,000
Southampton	7/92	£400,000

Season	Team	Tot	St	Sb	Snu	Ps	Gls
92-93	Southampton	11	11	0	0	1	0
	Total	11	11	0	0	1	0

SPENCER, John

FULLNAME: John Spencer
DOB: 11-Sep-70, Glasgow

Club History	Signed	Fee
Rangers	1989	Juniors
Morton	3/89	Loan
Chelsea	8/92	£450,000
QPR	11/96	£2.5m
Everton	3/98	Loan

Season	Team	Tot	St	Sb	Snu	Ps	Gls
92-93	Chelsea	23	13	10	3	3	7
93-94	Chelsea	19	13	6	4	2	5
94-95	Chelsea	29	26	3	0	6	11
95-96	Chelsea	28	23	5	2	9	13
96-97	Chelsea	4	0	4	5	0	0
97-98	Everton	6	3	3	0	0	0
98-99	Everton	3	2	1	2	2	0
	Total	112	80	32	16	22	36

SPINK, Nigel

FULLNAME: Nigel Philip Spink
DOB: 08-Aug-58, Chelmsford

Club History	Signed	Fee
Aston Villa	1/77	£4,000

Season	Team	Tot	St	Sb	Snu	Ps	Gls
92-93	Aston Villa	25	25	0	15	0	0
93-94	Aston Villa	15	14	1	25	0	0
94-95	Aston Villa	13	12	1	27	0	0
95-96	Aston Villa	2	0	2	19	0	0
	Total	55	51	4	86	0	0

SRNICEK, Pavel

FULLNAME: Pavel Srnicek
DOB: 10-Mar-68, Ostrava,
Czechoslovakia

Club History	Signed	Fee
Banik Ostrava		
Newcastle U.	2/91	£350,000
Banik Ostrava	7/98	Free
Sheffield W.	8/98	Free

Season	Team	Tot	St	Sb	Snu	Ps	Gls
93-94	Newcastle U.	21	21	0	20	0	0
94-95	Newcastle U.	38	38	0	0	0	0
95-96	Newcastle U.	15	14	1	12	0	0
96-97	Newcastle U.	22	22	0	16	0	0
97-98	Newcastle U.	1	1	0	9	0	0
98-99	Sheffield W.	24	24	0	0	0	0
99-00	Sheffield W.	20	20	0	15	1	0
	Total	141	140	1	72	1	0

STAM, Jaap

FULLNAME: Jakob Stam
DOB: 17-Jul-72, Kampen, Holland

Club History	Signed	Fee
PSV Eindhoven		
Manchester U.	6/98	£10.5m

Season	Team	Tot	St	Sb	Snu	Ps	Gls
98-99	Manchester U.	30	30	0	0	5	1
99-00	Manchester U.	33	33	0	0	4	0
	Total	63	63	0	0	9	1

STAMP, Phil

FULLNAME: Phillip Lawrence Stamp
DOB: 12-Dec-75, Middlesbrough

Club History	Signed	Fee
Middlesbrough	2/93	Trainee

Season	Team	Tot	St	Sb	Snu	Ps	Gls
95-96	Middlesbrough	12	11	1	0	2	2
96-97	Middlesbrough	23	15	8	3	2	1
98-99	Middlesbrough	16	5	11	3	3	2
99-00	Middlesbrough	16	13	3	1	4	0
	Total	67	44	23	7	11	5

STAUNTON, Steve

FULLNAME: Stephen Staunton
DOB: 19-Jan-69, Drogheda

Club History	Signed	Fee
Liverpool	9/86	£20,000
Bradford C.	11/87	Loan
Aston Villa	8/91	£1.1m
Liverpool	7/98	Free

Season	Team	Tot	St	Sb	Snu	Ps	Gls
92-93	Aston Villa	42	42	0	0	1	2
93-94	Aston Villa	24	24	0	0	4	3
94-95	Aston Villa	35	34	1	0	5	5
95-96	Aston Villa	13	11	2	3	4	0
96-97	Aston Villa	30	30	0	0	5	2
97-98	Aston Villa	27	27	0	1	5	1
98-99	Liverpool	31	31	0	4	8	0
99-00	Liverpool	12	7	5	14	1	0
	Total	214	206	8	22	33	13

STEFANOVIC, Dejan

FULLNAME: Dejan Stefanovic
DOB: 28-Oct-74, Yugoslavia

Club History	Signed	Fee
Red Star Belgrade		
Sheffield W.	12/95	£2m

Season	Team	Tot	St	Sb	Snu	Ps	Gls
95-96	Sheffield W.	6	5	1	2	3	0
96-97	Sheffield W.	29	27	2	5	3	2
97-98	Sheffield W.	20	19	1	3	2	2
98-99	Sheffield W.	11	8	3	11	0	0
	Total	66	59	7	21	8	4

STEIN, Mark

FULLNAME: Mark Earl Sean Stein
DOB: 28-Jan-66, South Africa

Club History	Signed	Fee
Luton Town	1/84	Juniors
Aldershot	1/86	Loan
QPR	8/88	£300,000
Oxford U.	9/89	Swap
Stoke C.	9/91	£100,000
Chelsea	10/93	£1.5m

Season	Team	Tot	St	Sb	Snu	Ps	Gls
93-94	Chelsea	18	18	0	0	1	13
94-95	Chelsea	24	21	3	0	4	8
95-96	Chelsea	8	7	1	4	5	0
	Total	50	46	4	4	10	21

STEJSKAL, Jan

FULLNAME: Jan Stejskal
DOB: 15-Jan-62, Czechoslovakia

Club History	Signed	Fee
QPR	10/90	£600,000

Season	Team	Tot	St	Sb	Snu	Ps	Gls
92-93	QPR	15	14	1	25	0	0
93-94	QPR	26	26	0	16	0	0
	Total	41	40	1	41	0	0

STENSAAS, Stale

FULLNAME: Stale Stensaas
DOB: 07-Jul-71, Trondheim, Norway

Club History	Signed	Fee
Rosenborg		
Rangers	5/97	£1.75m
Nottingham F.	1/99	Loan

Season	Team	Tot	St	Sb	Snu	Ps	Gls
98-99	Nottingham F.	7	6	1	1	5	0
	Total	7	6	1	1	5	0

STERLAND, Mel

FULLNAME: Melvyn Sterland
DOB: 01-Oct-61, Sheffield

Club History	Signed	Fee
Sheffield W.	10/79	
Rangers	3/89	£800,000
Leeds U.	7/89	£600,000

Season	Team	Tot	St	Sb	Snu	Ps	Gls
92-93	Leeds U.	3	3	0	0	2	0
	Total	3	3	0	0	2	0

STEWART, Jordan

FULLNAME: Jordan Stewart
DOB:

Club History	Signed	Fee
Leicester C.	8/99	Trainee

Season	Team	Tot	St	Sb	Snu	Ps	Gls
99-00	Leicester C.	1	0	1	1	0	0
	Total	1	0	1	1	0	0

STEWART, Paul

FULLNAME: Paul Andrew Stewart
DOB: 07-Oct-64, Manchester

Club History	Signed	Fee
Blackpool	10/81	Apprentice
Manchester C.	3/87	£200,000
Tottenham H.	6/88	£1.7m
Liverpool	7/92	£2.3m
Crystal P.	1/94	Loan
Wolverhampton W.	9/94	Loan
Burnley	2/95	Loan
Sunderland	8/95	Free

Season	Team	Tot	St	Sb	Snu	Ps	Gls
92-93	Liverpool	23	20	3	2	6	1
93-94	Liverpool	8	7	1	0	1	0
94-95	Liverpool	0	0	0	1	0	0
96-97	Sunderland	24	20	4	2	6	3
	Total	55	47	8	5	13	4

STEWART, Simon

FULLNAME: Simon A Stewart
DOB: 01-Nov-73, Leeds

Club History	Signed	Fee
Sheffield W.	6/92	

Season	Team	Tot	St	Sb	Snu	Ps	Gls
92-93	Sheffield W.	7	6	1	0	2	0
	Total	7	6	1	0	2	0

STIMAC, Igor

FULLNAME: Igor Stimac
DOB: 06-Sep-67, Croatia

Club History	Signed	Fee
Hadjuk Split		
Derby Co.	10/95	£1.5m
West Ham U.	8/99	£600,000

Season	Team	Tot	St	Sb	Snu	Ps	Gls
96-97	Derby Co.	21	21	0	0	1	1

Season	Team	Tot	St	Sb	Snu	Ps	Gls
97-98	Derby Co.	22	22	0	0	2	1
98-99	Derby Co.	14	14	0	0	2	0
99-00	West Ham U.	24	24	0	1	3	1
	Total	81	81	0	1	8	3

STOCKDALE, Robbie

FULLNAME: Robert Keith Stockdale
DOB: 30-Nov-79, Middlesbrough

Club History	Signed	Fee
Middlesbrough		Trainee

Season	Team	Tot	St	Sb	Snu	Ps	Gls
98-99	Middlesbrough	19	17	2	9	5	0
99-00	Middlesbrough	11	6	5	6	2	1
	Total	30	23	7	15	7	1

STOCKWELL, Mike

FULLNAME: Michael Thomas Stockwell
DOB: 14-Feb-65, Chelmsford

Club History	Signed	Fee
Ipswich Town	12/82	

Season	Team	Tot	St	Sb	Snu	Ps	Gls
92-93	Ipswich T.	39	38	1	0	2	4
93-94	Ipswich T.	42	42	0	0	0	1
94-95	Ipswich T.	15	14	1	0	0	0
	Total	96	94	2	0	2	5

STONE, Steve

FULLNAME: Steven Brian Stone
DOB: 20-Aug-71, Gateshead

Club History	Signed	Fee
Nottingham F.	5/89	Trainee
Aston Villa	3/99	£5.5m

Season	Team	Tot	St	Sb	Snu	Ps	Gls
92-93	Nottingham F.	12	11	1	5	1	1
94-95	Nottingham F.	41	41	0	0	1	5
95-96	Nottingham F.	34	34	0	0	1	7
96-97	Nottingham F.	5	5	0	0	2	0
98-99	Nottingham F.	26	26	0	0	1	3
98-99	Aston Villa	10	9	1	0	1	0
99-00	Aston Villa	24	10	14	3	3	1
	Total	152	136	16	8	10	17

STRACHAN, Gavin

FULLNAME: Gavin Strachan
DOB: 23-Dec-78, Aberdeen

Club History	Signed	Fee
Coventry C.		Trainee

Season	Team	Tot	St	Sb	Snu	Ps	Gls
97-98	Coventry C.	9	2	7	11	2	0
99-00	Coventry C.	3	1	2	15	1	0
	Total	12	3	9	26	3	0

STRACHAN, Gordon

FULLNAME: Gordon David Strachan
DOB: 09-Feb-57, Edinburgh

Club History	Signed	Fee
Manchester U.	8/84	£500,000
Leeds U.	3/89	£300,000
Coventry C.	3/95	Free

Season	Team	Tot	St	Sb	Snu	Ps	Gls
92-93	Leeds U.	31	25	6	2	3	4
93-94	Leeds U.	33	32	1	1	4	3
94-95	Leeds U.	6	5	1	1	2	0
94-95	Coventry C.	5	5	0	0	1	0
95-96	Coventry C.	12	5	7	3	2	0
96-97	Coventry C.	9	3	6	9	3	0
	Total	96	75	21	16	15	7

STRANDLI, Frank

FULLNAME: Frank Strandli
DOB: 16-May-72, Norway

Club History	Signed	Fee
IK Start		
Leeds U.	1/93	£350,000

Season	Team	Tot	St	Sb	Snu	Ps	Gls
92-93	Leeds U.	10	5	5	0	3	2
93-94	Leeds U.	4	0	4	2	0	0
	Total	14	5	9	2	3	2

STRONG, Greg

FULLNAME: Gregory Strong
DOB: 05-Sep-75, Bolton

Club History	Signed	Fee
Wigan A.	10/92	Trainee
Bolton W.	9/95	

Season	Team	Tot	St	Sb	Snu	Ps	Gls
95-96	Bolton W.	1	0	1	0	0	0
97-98	Bolton W.	0	0	0	2	0	0
	Total	1	0	1	2	0	0

STRUPAR, Branko

FULLNAME: Branko Strupar
DOB: 0, Zagreb, Croatia

Club History	Signed	Fee
Genk		
Derby Co.	12/99	£3m

Season	Team	Tot	St	Sb	Snu	Ps	Gls
99-00	Derby Co.	15	12	2	0	3	5
	Total	15	12	2	0	3	5

STUART, Graham

FULLNAME: Graham Charles Stuart
DOB: 24-Oct-70, Tooting

Club History	Signed	Fee
Chelsea	6/89	Trainee
Everton	8/93	£850,000
Sheffield U.	11/97	£850,000
Charlton A.	3/99	£1.1m

Season	Team	Tot	St	Sb	Snu	Ps	Gls
92-93	Chelsea	39	31	8	0	6	9
93-94	Everton	30	26	4	1	3	3
94-95	Everton	28	20	8	3	3	3
95-96	Everton	29	27	2	0	2	9
96-97	Everton	35	29	6	2	3	5
97-98	Everton	14	14	0	0	1	2
98-99	Charlton A.	9	9	0	0	0	3
	Total	184	156	28	6	18	34

STUBBS, Alan

FULLNAME: Alan Stubbs
DOB: 06-Oct-71, Liverpool

Club History	Signed	Fee
Bolton W.	7/90	Trainee

Season	Team	Tot	St	Sb	Snu	Ps	Gls
95-96	Bolton W.	25	24	1	1	0	4
	Total	25	24	1	1	0	4

STURRIDGE, Dean

FULLNAME: Dean Constantine Sturridge
DOB: 27-Jul-73, Birmingham

Club History	Signed	Fee
Derby Co.	7/91	Trainee

Season	Team	Tot	St	Sb	Snu	Ps	Gls
96-97	Derby Co.	30	29	1	0	5	11
97-98	Derby Co.	30	24	6	0	7	9
98-99	Derby Co.	29	23	6	2	9	5
99-00	Derby Co.	25	14	11	0	7	6
	Total	114	90	24	2	28	31

SUKER, Davor

FULLNAME: Davor Suker
DOB: 01-Jan-68, Osijek, Croatia

Club History	Signed	Fee
Real Madrid		
Arsenal	8/99	£500,000

Season	Team	Tot	St	Sb	Snu	Ps	Gls
99-00	Arsenal	22	8	14	5	1	8
	Total	22	8	14	5	1	8

SULLIVAN, Neil

FULLNAME: Neil Sullivan
DOB: 24-Feb-70, Sutton

Club History	Signed	Fee					
Wimbledon	7/88	Trainee					

Season	Team	Tot	St	Sb	Snu	Ps	Gls
92-93	Wimbledon	1	1	0	32	0	0
93-94	Wimbledon	2	1	1	25	0	0
94-95	Wimbledon	11	11	0	30	1	0
95-96	Wimbledon	16	16	0	0	0	0
96-97	Wimbledon	36	36	0	1	0	0
97-98	Wimbledon	38	38	0	0	0	0
98-99	Wimbledon	38	38	0	0	0	0
99-00	Wimbledon	37	37	0	0	0	0
	Total	179	178	1	88	1	0

SUMMERBEE, Nicky

FULLNAME: Nicholas John Summerbee
DOB: 26-Aug-71, Altrincham

Club History	Signed	Fee					
Swindon T.	7/89	Trainee					
Manchester C.	6/94	£1.5m					
Sunderland	11/97	£1m					

Season	Team	Tot	St	Sb	Snu	Ps	Gls
93-94	Swindon T.	38	36	2	0	4	3
94-95	Manchester C.	41	39	2	1	2	1
95-96	Manchester C.	37	33	4	0	4	1
99-00	Sunderland	32	29	3	3	8	1
	Total	148	137	11	4	18	6

SUMMERBELL, Mark

FULLNAME: Mark Sumerbell
DOB: 30-Oct-76, Durham

Club History	Signed	Fee					
Middlesbrough	7/95	Trainee					
Cork	10/96	Loan					

Season	Team	Tot	St	Sb	Snu	Ps	Gls
95-96	Middlesbrough	1	0	1	0	0	0
96-97	Middlesbrough	2	0	2	4	0	0
98-99	Middlesbrough	11	7	4	9	1	0
99-00	Middlesbrough	19	16	3	4	2	0
	Total	33	23	10	17	3	0

SUTCH, Daryl

FULLNAME: Daryl Sutch
DOB: 11-Sep-71, Beccles

Club History	Signed	Fee					
Norwich C.	7/90						

Season	Team	Tot	St	Sb	Snu	Ps	Gls
92-93	Norwich C.	22	14	8	4	2	2
93-94	Norwich C.	3	1	2	0	1	0
94-95	Norwich C.	30	20	10	1	3	1
	Total	55	35	20	5	6	3

SUTTON, Chris

FULLNAME: Christopher Roy Sutton
DOB: 10-Mar-73, Nottingham

Club History	Signed	Fee					
Norwich C.	7/91	Trainee					
Blackburn R.	7/94	£5m					
Chelsea	7/99	£10.0m					

Season	Team	Tot	St	Sb	Snu	Ps	Gls
92-93	Norwich C.	38	32	6	1	2	8
93-94	Norwich C.	41	41	0	0	1	25
94-95	Blackburn R.	40	40	0	0	7	15
95-96	Blackburn R.	13	9	4	4	4	0
96-97	Blackburn R.	25	24	1	0	3	11
97-98	Blackburn R.	35	35	0	0	1	18
98-99	Blackburn R.	17	17	0	0	2	3
99-00	Chelsea	28	21	7	1	9	1
	Total	237	219	18	6	29	81

SWAILES, Chris

FULLNAME: Christopher Swailes
DOB: 19-Oct-70, Gateshead

Club History	Signed	Fee					
Doncaster R.							
Ipswich T.	3/95	£150,00 +					

Season	Team	Tot	St	Sb	Snu	Ps	Gls
94-95	Ipswich T.	4	4	0	0	0	0
	Total	4	4	0	0	0	0

SYMONS, Kit

FULLNAME: Christopher Jeremiah Symons
DOB: 08-Mar-71, Basingstoke

Club History	Signed	Fee					
Portsmouth	30/12/88	Trainee					
Manchester C.	8/95	£1.2m					

Season	Team	Tot	St	Sb	Snu	Ps	Gls
95-96	Manchester C.	38	38	0	0	0	2
	Total	38	38	0	0	0	2

TAGGART, Gerry

FULLNAME: Gerald Paul Taggart
DOB: 18-Oct-70, Belfast

Club History	Signed	Fee
Manchester C.	7/89	Trainee
Barnsley	1/90	£75,000
Bolton W.	8/95	£1.5m
Leicester C.		

Season	Team	Tot	St	Sb	Snu	Ps	Gls
95-96	Bolton W.	11	11	0	0	1	1
97-98	Bolton W.	15	14	1	2	1	0
98-99	Leicester C.	15	9	6	9	2	0
99-00	Leicester C.	31	30	1	0	6	6
	Total	72	64	8	11	10	7

TAIBI, Massimo

FULLNAME: Massimo Taibi
DOB: 18-Feb-70, Palermo, Italy

Club History	Signed	Fee
Venezia		
Manchester U.	8/00	£4.5m

Season	Team	Tot	St	Sb	Snu	Ps	Gls
99-00	Manchester U.	4	4	0	3	0	0
	Total	4	4	0	3	0	0

TALBOYS, Steve

FULLNAME: Steven John Talboys
DOB: 18-Sep-66, Bristol

Club History	Signed	Fee
Wimbledon	9/92	£10,000

Season	Team	Tot	St	Sb	Snu	Ps	Gls
92-93	Wimbledon	7	3	4	3	1	0
93-94	Wimbledon	7	6	1	3	2	0
94-95	Wimbledon	7	7	0	1	2	1
95-96	Wimbledon	5	3	2	1	1	0
	Total	26	19	7	8	6	1

TANNER, Adam

FULLNAME: Adam Tanner
DOB: 25-Oct-73, Malden

Club History	Signed	Fee
Ipswich Town		

Season	Team	Tot	St	Sb	Snu	Ps	Gls
92-93	Ipswich T.	0	0	0	1	0	0
94-95	Ipswich T.	10	9	1	0	2	2
	Total	10	9	1	1	2	2

TANNER, Nicky

FULLNAME: Nicholas Tanner
DOB: 24-May-65, Kingswood, Bristol

Club History	Signed	Fee
Bristol R.	6/85	
Liverpool	7/88	£20,000
Norwich C.	3/90	Loan
Swindon Town	9/90	Loan

Season	Team	Tot	St	Sb	Snu	Ps	Gls
92-93	Liverpool	4	2	2	5	0	0
	Total	4	2	2	5	0	0

TARICCO, Mauricio

FULLNAME: Mauricia Taricco
DOB: 10-Mar-73, Buenos Aires

Club History	Signed	Fee
Argentina Juniors		
Ipswich T.	9/94	£175,000
Tottenham H.	12/98	£1.8m

Season	Team	Tot	St	Sb	Snu	Ps	Gls
94-95	Ipswich T.	0	0	0	1	0	0
98-99	Tottenham H.	13	12	1	1	3	0
99-00	Tottenham H.	29	29	0	1	4	0
	Total	42	41	1	3	7	0

TAYLOR, Bob

FULLNAME: Robert Taylor
DOB: 03-Feb-67, Horden

Club History	Signed	Fee
Leeds U.	3/86	Free NI
Bristol C.	3/89	£175,000
WBA	1/92	£300,000
Bolton W.		Loan

Season	Team	Tot	St	Sb	Snu	Ps	Gls
97-98	Bolton W.	12	10	2	4	5	3
	Total	12	10	2	4	5	3

TAYLOR, Ian

FULLNAME: Ian Kenneth Taylor
DOB: 04-Jun-68, Birmingham

Club History	Signed	Fee
Port Vale	7/92	£15,000 NL
Sheffield W.	7/94	£1m
Aston Villa	12/94	£1m

Season	Team	Tot	St	Sb	Snu	Ps	Gls
94-95	Sheffield W.	14	9	5	1	2	1
94-95	Aston Villa	22	22	0	0	1	1
95-96	Aston Villa	25	24	1	2	2	3
96-97	Aston Villa	34	29	5	0	2	2
97-98	Aston Villa	32	30	2	0	3	6
98-99	Aston Villa	33	31	2	0	5	4
99-00	Aston Villa	29	25	4	0	1	5
	Total	189	170	19	3	16	22

TAYLOR, Maik

FULLNAME: Maik Stefan Taylor
DOB: 04-Sep-71, Germany

Club History	Signed	Fee
Barnet	6/95	From NLge
Southampton	12/96	£500,000

Season	Team	Tot	St	Sb	Snu	Ps	Gls
96-97	Southampton	18	18	0	0	0	0
97-98	Southampton	0	0	0	14	0	0
	Total	18	18	0	14	0	0

TAYLOR, Martin

FULLNAME: Martin Taylor
DOB: 09-Nov-79, Northumberland

Club History	Signed	Fee
Blackburn R.	8/97	Trainee

Season	Team	Tot	St	Sb	Snu	Ps	Gls
98-99	Blackburn R.	3	1	2	5	0	0
	Total	3	1	2	5	0	0

TAYLOR, Martin James

FULLNAME: Martin James Taylor
DOB: 09-Dec-66, Tamworth

Club History	Signed	Fee
Derby Co.	7/86	Free from Non League

Season	Team	Tot	St	Sb	Snu	Ps	Gls
96-97	Derby Co.	3	3	0	28	0	0
	Total	3	3	0	28	0	0

TAYLOR, Scott

FULLNAME: Scott Dean Taylor
DOB: 28-Nov-70, Portsmouth

Club History	Signed	Fee
Reading	6/89	Trainee
Leicester C.	7/95	£500,000

Season	Team	Tot	St	Sb	Snu	Ps	Gls
96-97	Leicester C.	25	20	5	4	9	0
	Total	25	20	5	4	9	0

TAYLOR, Scott

FULLNAME: Scott James Taylor
DOB: 05-May-76, Chertsey

Club History	Signed	Fee
Millwall	2/95	£15,000 from Non League
Bolton W.	3/96	£150,000

Season	Team	Tot	St	Sb	Snu	Ps	Gls
95-96	Bolton W.	1	0	1	0	0	0
	Total	1	0	1	0	0	0

TAYLOR, Shaun

FULLNAME: Shaun Taylor
DOB: 20-Feb-63, Bideford

Club History	Signed	Fee
Exeter C.	12/86	
Swindon T.	7/91	£200,000

Season	Team	Tot	St	Sb	Snu	Ps	Gls
93-94	Swindon T.	42	42	0	0	0	4
	Total	42	42	0	0	0	4

TEALE, Shaun

FULLNAME: Shaun Teale
DOB: 10-Mar-64, Southport

Club History	Signed	Fee
Bournemouth	22/1/89	£50,000 from Non League
Aston Villa	25/7/91	£300,000

Season	Team	Tot	St	Sb	Snu	Ps	Gls
92-93	Aston Villa	39	39	0	0	1	1
93-94	Aston Villa	38	37	1	0	1	1
94-95	Aston Villa	28	28	0	0	2	0
	Total	105	104	1	0	4	2

TELFER, Paul

FULLNAME: Paul Norman Telfer
DOB: 21-Oct-71, Edinburgh

Club History	Signed	Fee
Luton T.	11/88	Trainee
Coventry C.	7/95	£1.5m

Season	Team	Tot	St	Sb	Snu	Ps	Gls
95-96	Coventry C.	31	31	0	3	6	1
96-97	Coventry C.	34	31	3	1	2	0
97-98	Coventry C.	33	33	0	0	4	3
98-99	Coventry C.	32	30	2	2	4	2
99-00	Coventry C.	30	26	4	0	2	0
	Total	160	151	9	6	18	6

TEN HEUVEL, Laurens

FULLNAME: Laurens Ten Heuvel
DOB: Duivendretch, Holland

Club History	Signed	Fee
Den Bosch		
Barnsley	3/96	£75,000

Season	Team	Tot	St	Sb	Snu	Ps	Gls
97-98	Barnsley	2	0	2	1	0	0
	Total	2	0	2	1	0	0

TERRIER, Dave

FULLNAME: David Terrier
DOB: 04-Aug-73, Verdun, France

Club History	Signed	Fee
Metz		
West Ham U.	7/97	Free
Newcastle U.	1/98	Free

Season	Team	Tot	St	Sb	Snu	Ps	Gls
97-98	Newcastle U.	0	0	0	1	0	0
97-98	West Ham U.	1	0	1	2	0	0
	Total	1	0	1	3	0	0

TERRY, John

FULLNAME: John Terry
DOB: 07-Dec-80, London

Club History	Signed	Fee
Chelsea		Trainee

Season	Team	Tot	St	Sb	Snu	Ps	Gls
98-99	Chelsea	2	0	2	8	0	0
99-00	Chelsea	4	2	2	5	0	0
	Total	6	2	4	13	0	0

TESSEM, Joe

FULLNAME: Joe Tessem
DOB: 28-Feb-72, Norway

Club History	Signed	Fee
Molde		
Southampton	11/99	£600,000

Season	Team	Tot	St	Sb	Snu	Ps	Gls
99-00	Southampton	25	23	2	0	4	4
	Total	25	23	2	0	4	4

THATCHER, Ben

FULLNAME: Benjamin David Thatcher
DOB: 30-Nov-75, Swindon

Club History	Signed	Fee
Millwall	6/96	Trainee
Wimbledon	7/96	£1.8m

Season	Team	Tot	St	Sb	Snu	Ps	Gls
96-97	Wimbledon	9	9	0	0	1	0
97-98	Wimbledon	26	23	3	4	2	0
98-99	Wimbledon	31	31	0	0	2	0
99-00	Wimbledon	20	19	1	0	2	0
	Total	86	82	4	4	7	0

THELWELL, Alton

FULLNAME: Alton Thelwell
DOB: 05-Sep-80, London

Club History	Signed	Fee
Tottenham H.		Trainee

Season	Team	Tot	St	Sb	Snu	Ps	Gls
98-99	Tottenham H.	1	1	0	1	0	0
	Total	1	1	0	1	0	0

THIRLWELL, Paul

FULLNAME: Paul Thirlwell
DOB: 13-Feb-79, Washington

Club History	Signed	Fee
Sunderland	4/97	Trainee

Season	Team	Tot	St	Sb	Snu	Ps	Gls
99-00	Sunderland	8	7	1	5	2	0
	Total	8	7	1	5	2	0

THOMAS, Danny

FULLNAME: Daniel Thomas
DOB: 01-May-81, Leamington Spa

Club History	Signed	Fee
Nottingham F.	8/99	Trainee
Leicester C.		

Season	Team	Tot	St	Sb	Snu	Ps	Gls
99-00	Leicester C.	3	0	3	2	0	0
	Total	3	0	3	2	0	0

THOMAS, Geoff

FULLNAME: Geoffrey Robert Thomas
DOB: 05-Aug-64, Manchester

Club History	Signed	Fee
Rochdale	8/82	Free NL
Crewe Alex.	3/84	Free
Crystal P.	6/87	£50,000
Wolverhampton W.	6/93	£800,000
Nottingham F.	7/97	Free

Season	Team	Tot	St	Sb	Snu	Ps	Gls
92-93	Crystal P.	29	28	1	3	2	2
98-99	Nottingham F.	5	5	0	0	2	1
	Total	34	33	1	3	4	3

THOMAS, Michael

FULLNAME: Michael Lauriston Thomas
DOB: 24-Aug-67, Lambeth

Club History	Signed	Fee
Arsenal	12/84	Apprentice
Portsmouth	12/86	Loan
Liverpool	12/91	£1.5m

Season	Team	Tot	St	Sb	Snu	Ps	Gls
92-93	Liverpool	9	7	2	1	1	1
93-94	Liverpool	7	1	6	2	1	0
94-95	Liverpool	23	16	7	6	1	0
95-96	Liverpool	27	18	9	3	1	1
96-97	Liverpool	30	28	2	3	2	3
97-98	Liverpool	11	10	1	2	2	1
	Total	107	80	27	17	8	6

THOMAS, Scott

FULLNAME: Scott L Thomas
DOB: 30-Oct-74, Bury

Club History	Signed	Fee
Manchester C.	3/92	Trainee

Season	Team	Tot	St	Sb	Snu	Ps	Gls
94-95	Manchester C.	2	0	2	0	0	0
	Total	2	0	2	0	0	0

THOMAS, Tony

FULLNAME: Anthony Thomas
DOB: 12-Jul-71, Liverpool

Club History	Signed	Fee
Tranmere R.	2/89	Trainee
Everton	8/97	£400,000

Season	Team	Tot	St	Sb	Snu	Ps	Gls
97-98	Everton	7	6	1	6	3	0
98-99	Everton	1	0	1	1	0	0
	Total	8	6	2	7	3	0

THOME, Emerson

FULLNAME: Emerson August Thome
DOB: 30-Mar-72, Porto Alegra, Brazil

Club History	Signed	Fee
Benfica		
Sheffield W.	3/98	Free
Chelsea	12/99	£2.7m

Season	Team	Tot	St	Sb	Snu	Ps	Gls
97-98	Sheffield W.	6	6	0	2	1	0
98-99	Sheffield W.	38	38	0	0	1	1
99-00	Sheffield W.	17	16	1	0	0	0
99-00	Chelsea	20	18	2	1	0	0
	Total	81	78	3	3	2	1

THOMPSON, Alan

FULLNAME: Alan Thompson
DOB: 22-Dec-73, Newcastle

Club History	Signed	Fee
Newcastle U.	3/91	Trainee
Bolton W.	7/93	£250,000
Aston Villa	6/98	£4.5m

Season	Team	Tot	St	Sb	Snu	Ps	Gls
95-96	Bolton W.	26	23	3	2	4	1
97-98	Bolton W.	33	33	0	0	2	9
98-99	Aston Villa	25	20	5	4	7	2
99-00	Aston Villa	21	16	5	3	11	2
	Total	105	92	13	9	24	14

THOMPSON, Andy

FULLNAME: Andrew Thompson
DOB: 28-Mar-74, Swindon

Club History	Signed	Fee
Swindon Town		Trainee

Season	Team	Tot	St	Sb	Snu	Ps	Gls
93-94	Swindon T.	1	1	0	1	0	0
	Total	1	1	0	1	0	0

THOMPSON, David

FULLNAME: David Thompson
DOB: 12-Sep-77, Birkenhead

Club History	Signed	Fee
Liverpool		Trainee

Season	Team	Tot	St	Sb	Snu	Ps	Gls
96-97	Liverpool	3	1	2	2	0	0
97-98	Liverpool	5	1	4	5	0	1
98-99	Liverpool	14	4	10	10	2	1
99-00	Liverpool	27	19	8	1	13	3
	Total	49	25	24	18	15	5

THOMPSON, Garry

FULLNAME: Garry Lindsay Thompson
DOB: 07-Oct-59, Birmingham

Club History	Signed	Fee
Coventry C.	6/77	
WBA	2/83	£225,000
Sheffield W.	3/85	£450,000
Aston Villa	6/86	£450,000
Watford	12/88	£325,000
Crystal P.	3/90	£200,000
QPR	8/91	£125,000

Season	Team	Tot	St	Sb	Snu	Ps	Gls
92-93	QPR	4	0	4	1	0	0
	Total	4	0	4	1	0	0

THOMPSON, Neil

FULLNAME: Neil Thompson
DOB: 02-Oct-63, Beverley

Club History	Signed	Fee
Hull C.	11/91	Free
Scarborough	8/83	Free
Ipswich T.	6/89	£100,000
Barnsley	6/96	Free

Season	Team	Tot	St	Sb	Snu	Ps	Gls
92-93	Ipswich T.	31	31	0	0	1	3
93-94	Ipswich T.	32	32	0	1	2	0
94-95	Ipswich T.	10	9	1	0	0	0
97-98	Barnsley	2	2	0	1	1	0
	Total	75	74	1	2	4	3

THOMPSON, Steve

FULLNAME: Stephen J Thompson
DOB: 02-Nov-64, Oldham

Club History	Signed	Fee
Bolton W.	11/82	
Luton Town	8/91	£180,000
Leicester C.	10/91	Swap
Burnley	2/95	£200,000

Season	Team	Tot	St	Sb	Snu	Ps	Gls
94-95	Leicester C.	19	16	3	0	3	0
	Total	19	16	3	0	3	0

THOMSEN, Claus

FULLNAME: Claus Thomsen
DOB: 31-May-70, Aarhus, Denmark

Club History	Signed	Fee
AGF Aarhus	1990	
Ipswich Town	6/94	£250,000
Everton	1/97	£900,000

Season	Team	Tot	St	Sb	Snu	Ps	Gls
94-95	Ipswich T.	33	31	2	0	3	5
96-97	Everton	16	15	1	0	5	0
97-98	Everton	8	2	6	1	1	1
	Total	57	48	9	1	9	6

THORN, Andy

FULLNAME: Andrew Charles Thorn
DOB: 12-Nov-66, Carshalton

Club History	Signed	Fee
Wimbledon	11/84	Apprentice
Newcastle U.	8/88	£850,000
Crystal P.	12/89	£650,000
Wimbledon	10/94	Free

Season	Team	Tot	St	Sb	Snu	Ps	Gls
92-93	Crystal P.	34	34	0	0	4	1
94-95	Wimbledon	23	22	1	0	1	1
95-96	Wimbledon	14	11	3	6	3	0
	Total	71	67	4	6	8	2

THORNLEY, Ben

FULLNAME: Benjamin Lindsay Thornley
DOB: 21-Apr-75, Bury

Club History	Signed	Fee
Manchester U.	1/93	Trainee

Season	Team	Tot	St	Sb	Snu	Ps	Gls
93-94	Manchester U.	1	0	1	0	0	0
95-96	Manchester U.	1	0	1	0	0	0
96-97	Manchester U.	2	1	1	5	1	0
97-98	Manchester U.	5	0	5	5	0	0
	Total	9	1	8	10	1	0

THORSTVEDT, Erik

FULLNAME: Erik Thorstvedt
DOB: 28-Oct-62, Stavanger, Norway

Club History	Signed	Fee
IFK		
Tottenham H.	12/88	£400,000

Season	Team	Tot	St	Sb	Snu	Ps	Gls
92-93	Tottenham H.	27	25	2	8	1	0
93-94	Tottenham H.	32	32	0	3	1	0
94-95	Tottenham H.	1	1	0	21	0	0
95-96	Tottenham H.	0	0	0	16	0	0
	Total	60	58	2	48	2	0

TILER, Carl

FULLNAME: Carl Tiler
DOB: 11-Jan-70, Sheffield

Club History	Signed	Fee
Barnsley	8/88	Trainee
Nottingham F.	5/91	£1.4m
Swindon Town	11/94	Loan
Aston Villa	10/95	£750,000
Sheffield U.	3/97	£650,000
Everton	11/97	£500,000
Charlton A.	9/98	£700,000

Season	Team	Tot	St	Sb	Snu	Ps	Gls
92-93	Nottingham F.	37	37	0	1	0	0
94-95	Nottingham F.	3	3	0	0	0	0
95-96	Aston Villa	1	1	0	0	1	0
96-97	Aston Villa	11	9	2	7	1	1
97-98	Everton	19	19	0	0	1	1
98-99	Everton	2	2	0	3	0	0
98-99	Charlton A.	27	27	0	2	2	1
	Total	100	98	2	13	5	3

TINKLER, Eric

FULLNAME: Eric Tinkler
DOB: 30-Jul-70, Capetown, South Africa

Club History	Signed	Fee
Cagliari		
Barneley	7/97	650,000

Season	Team	Tot	St	Sb	Snu	Ps	Gls
97-98	Barnsley	25	21	4	2	7	2
	Total	25	21	4	2	7	2

TINKLER, Mark

FULLNAME: Mark Roland Tinkler
DOB: 24-Oct-74, Bishop Auckland

Club History	Signed	Fee
Leeds U.	11/91	Trainee

Season	Team	Tot	St	Sb	Snu	Ps	Gls
92-93	Leeds U.	7	5	2	2	1	0
93-94	Leeds U.	3	0	3	5	0	0
94-95	Leeds U.	3	3	0	5	1	0
95-96	Leeds U.	9	5	4	5	0	0
96-97	Leeds U.	3	1	2	1	1	0
	Total	25	14	11	18	3	0

TISDALE, Paul

FULLNAME: Paul Tisdale
DOB: 14-Jan-73, Malta

Club History	Signed	Fee
Southampton	6/91	Junior

Season	Team	Tot	St	Sb	Snu	Ps	Gls
94-95	Southampton	6	0	6	5	0	0
95-96	Southampton	9	5	4	3	0	1
	Total	15	5	10	8	0	1

TODD, Andy

FULLNAME: Andrew John James Todd
DOB: 21-Sep-74, Derby

Club History	Signed	Fee
Middlesbrough	6/3/92	Trainee
Swindon T.	27/2/95	Loan
Bolton W.	8/95	£250,000

Season	Team	Tot	St	Sb	Snu	Ps	Gls
95-96	Bolton W.	12	9	3	1	4	2
97-98	Bolton W.	25	23	2	7	1	0
	Total	37	32	5	8	5	2

TODD, Lee

FULLNAME: Lee Todd
DOB: 07-Mar-72, Hartlepool

Club History	Signed	Fee
Stockport Co.	7/90	Free
Southampton	7/97	£500,000
Bradford C.	8/98	£250,000

Season	Team	Tot	St	Sb	Snu	Ps	Gls
97-98	Southampton	10	9	1	7	1	0
99-00	Bradford C.	0	0	0	4	0	0
	Total	10	9	1	11	1	0

TOLSON, Neil

FULLNAME: Neil Tolson
DOB: 25-Oct-73, Wordsley

Club History	Signed	Fee
Walsall	12/91	
Oldham A.	3/92	£150,000

Season	Team	Tot	St	Sb	Snu	Ps	Gls
92-93	Oldham A.	3	0	3	5	0	0
93-94	Oldham A.	0	0	0	1	0	0
	Total	3	0	3	6	0	0

TOMASSON, Jon Dahl

FULLNAME: John Dahl Tomasson
DOB: 29-Aug-76, Copenhagen

Club History	Signed	Fee
SV Herenveen		
Newcastle U.	7/97	£2.2m

Season	Team	Tot	St	Sb	Snu	Ps	Gls
97-98	Newcastle U.	23	17	6	11	6	3
	Total	23	17	6	11	6	3

TOWNSEND, Andy

FULLNAME: Andrew David Townsend
DOB: 23-Jul-63, Maidstone

Club History	Signed	Fee
Southampton	1/85	£35,000
Norwich C.	8/88	£300,000
Chelsea	7/90	£1.2m
Aston Villa	7/93	£2.1m
Middlesbrough	7/97	£500,000

Season	Team	Tot	St	Sb	Snu	Ps	Gls
92-93	Chelsea	41	41	0	0	2	4
93-94	Aston Villa	32	32	0	0	5	3
94-95	Aston Villa	32	32	0	0	4	1
95-96	Aston Villa	31	30	1	0	3	2
96-97	Aston Villa	34	34	0	0	2	2
97-98	Aston Villa	3	3	0	0	0	0
98-99	Middlesbrough	35	35	0	0	6	1
99-00	Middlesbrough	5	3	2	1	1	0
	Total	213	210	3	1	23	13

TRACEY, Simon

FULLNAME: Simon Peter Tracey
DOB: 09-Dec-67, Woolwich

Club History	Signed	Fee
Wimbledon	2/86	
Sheffield U.	10/88	£7,500
Manchester C.	10/94	Loan
Norwich C.	12/94	Loan
Nottingham F.	8/95	Loan
Wimbledon	11/95	Loan

Season	Team	Tot	St	Sb	Snu	Ps	Gls
92-93	Sheffield U.	10	10	0	1	0	0
93-94	Sheffield U.	15	13	2	13	0	0
94-95	Manchester C.	3	3	0	2	0	0
94-95	Norwich C.	1	1	0	5	0	0
95-96	Nottingham F.	0	0	0	3	0	0
95-96	Wimbledon	1	1	0	0	0	0
	Total	30	28	2	24	0	0

TRAMEZZANI, Paolo

FULLNAME: Paolo Tramezzani
DOB: 20-Jul-70, Castelnovo ne Monti, Italy

Club History	Signed	Fee\
Piacenza	1996	
Tottenham H.	7/98	

Season	Team	Tot	St	Sb	Snu	Ps	Gls
98-99	Tottenham H.	6	6	0	0	1	0
	Total	6	6	0	0	1	0

TROLLOPE, Paul

FULLNAME: Paul Jonathan Trollope
DOB: 03-Jun-72, Swindon

Club History	Signed	Fee
Swindon T.	12/89	Trainee
Torquay U.	3/92	Free
Derby Co.	12/94	Loan
Derby Co.	1/95	£100,000

Season	Team	Tot	St	Sb	Snu	Ps	Gls
96-97	Derby Co.	14	13	1	2	1	1
97-98	Derby Co.	10	4	6	1	0	0
	Total	24	17	7	3	1	1

TRUSTFULL, Orlando

FULLNAME: Orlando Trustfull
DOB: 04-Aug-70, Amsterdam

Club History	Signed	Fee
Feyenoord	1992	
Sheffield W.	8/96	£750,000

Season	Team	Tot	St	Sb	Snu	Ps	Gls
96-97	Sheffield W.	19	9	10	7	8	3
	Total	19	9	10	7	8	3

TURNER, Andy

FULLNAME: Andrew Peter Turner
DOB: 23-May-75, Woolwich

Club History	Signed	Fee
Tottenham H.	4/92	Trainee

Season	Team	Tot	St	Sb	Snu	Ps	Gls
92-93	Tottenham H.	18	7	11	1	4	3
93-94	Tottenham H.	1	0	1	0	0	0
94-95	Tottenham H.	1	1	0	1	0	0
	Total	20	8	12	2	4	3

TUTTLE, David

FULLNAME: David Philip Tuttle
DOB: 06-Feb-72, Reading

Club History	Signed	Fee
Tottenham H.	2/90	
Peterborough U.	1/93	Loan
Sheffield U.	8/93	£350,000
Crystal P.	3/96	

Season	Team	Tot	St	Sb	Snu	Ps	Gls
92-93	Tottenham H.	5	4	1	1	1	0
93-94	Sheffield U.	31	31	0	0	2	0
97-98	Crystal P.	9	8	1	0	3	0
	Total	45	43	2	1	6	0

ULLATHORNE, Robert

FULLNAME: Robert Ullathorne
DOB: 11-Oct-71, Wakefield

Club History	Signed	Fee
Norwich C.	7/90	Trainee
Osasuna		
Leicester C.	2/97	£600,000

Season	Team	Tot	St	Sb	Snu	Ps	Gls
92-93	Norwich C.	0	0	0	1	0	0
93-94	Norwich C.	16	11	5	6	0	2
94-95	Norwich C.	27	27	0	0	7	2
96-97	Leicester C.	0	0	0	0	0	0
97-98	Leicester C.	6	3	3	1	1	1
98-99	Leicester C.	25	25	0	0	2	0
	Total	74	66	8	8	10	5

UNSWORTH, David

FULLNAME: David Gerald Unsworth
DOB: 16-Oct-73, Chorley

Club History	Signed	Fee
Everton	6/92	Trainee
West Ham U.	8/97	£1m
Aston Villa	7/98	
Everton	8/98	£3m

Season	Team	Tot	St	Sb	Snu	Ps	Gls
92-93	Everton	3	3	0	1	2	0
93-94	Everton	8	7	1	2	1	0
94-95	Everton	38	37	1	0	3	3
95-96	Everton	31	28	3	3	1	2
96-97	Everton	34	32	2	0	3	5
97-98	West Ham U.	32	32	0	0	1	2
98-99	Everton	34	33	1	0	1	1
99-00	Everton	33	32	1	1	5	6
	Total	213	204	9	7	17	19

UPSON, Matthew

FULLNAME: Matthew James Upson
DOB: 18-Apr-79, Hartismere

Club History	Signed	Fee
Luton Town	4/96	Trainee
Arsenal	5/97	£1m

Season	Team	Tot	St	Sb	Snu	Ps	Gls
97-98	Arsenal	5	5	0	6	1	0
98-99	Arsenal	5	0	5	4	0	0
99-00	Arsenal	8	5	3	4	1	0
	Total	18	10	8	14	2	0

VAN DEN HAUWE, Pat

FULLNAME: Patrick William Roger
Van Den Hauwe
DOB: 16-Dec-60, Dendermonde,
Belgium

Club History	Signed	Fee
Birmingham C.	8/78	
Everton	9/84	£100,000
Tottenham H.	8/89	£575,000

Season	Team	Tot	St	Sb	Snu	Ps	Gls
92-93	Tottenham H.	18	13	5	1	1	0
	Total	18	13	5	1	1	0

VAN DER GOUW, Raimond

FULLNAME: Raimond Van der Gouw
DOB: 24-Mar-63, Oldenzaal, Holland

Club History	Signed	Fee
Vitesse Arnhem	1990	
Manchester U.	7/96	undisclosed

Season	Team	Tot	St	Sb	Snu	Ps	Gls
96-97	Manchester U.	2	2	0	34	0	0
97-98	Manchester U.	5	4	1	26	0	0
98-99	Manchester U.	5	4	1	27	0	0
99-00	Manchester U.	14	11	3	21	1	0
	Total	26	21	5	108	1	0

VAN DER LAAN, Robin

FULLNAME: Robertus Petrus Van Der Laan
DOB: 05-Sep-68, Schiedam, Holland

Club History	Signed	Fee
Wageningen		
Port Vale	2/91	£80,000
Derby Co.	8/95	£475,000

Season	Team	Tot	St	Sb	Snu	Ps	Gls
96-97	Derby Co.	16	15	1	7	7	2
97-98	Derby Co.	10	7	3	6	5	0
	Total	26	22	4	13	12	2

VAN GOBBEL, Ulrich

FULLNAME: Ulrich Van Gobbel
DOB: 16-Jan-71, Surinam

Club History	Signed	Fee
Galatasaray	12/95	
Southampton	10/96	£1.3m

Season	Team	Tot	St	Sb	Snu	Ps	Gls
96-97	Southampton	25	24	1	1	3	1
97-98	Southampton	2	1	1	0	1	0
	Total	27	25	2	1	4	1

VAN HOOIJDONK, Pierre

FULLNAME: Peirre van Hooijdonk
DOB: 29-Nov-69, Steenbergen (Hol)

Club History	Signed	Fee
NAC Breda	1993	
Celtic	1/95	£1.5m
Nottingham F.	3/97	£3.5m

Season	Team	Tot	St	Sb	Snu	Ps	Gls
96-97	Nottingham F.	8	8	0	0	0	1
98-99	Nottingham F.	21	19	2	1	1	6
	Total	29	27	2	1	1	7

VARADI, Imre

FULLNAME: Imre Varadi
DOB: 08-Jul-59, Paddington

Club History	Signed	Fee
Sheffield U.	7/78	From Non League
Everton	3/79	
Newcastle U.	8/81	
Sheffield W.	8/83	
WBA	7/85	
Manchester C.	10/86	
Sheffield W.	9/88	
Leeds U.	2/90	

Season	Team	Tot	St	Sb	Snu	Ps	Gls
92-93	Leeds U.	4	2	2	0	0	1
	Total	4	2	2	0	0	1

VASSELL, Darius

FULLNAME: Darius Vassell
DOB: 13-Jun-80, Birmingham

Club History	Signed	Fee
Aston Villa	4/98	Trainee

Season	Team	Tot	St	Sb	Snu	Ps	Gls
97-98	Aston Villa	0	0	0	2	0	0
98-99	Aston Villa	6	0	6	15	0	0
99-00	Aston Villa	11	1	10	1	2	0
	Total	17	1	16	18	2	0

VAUGHAN, Tony

FULLNAME: Anthony John Vaughan
DOB: 11-Oct-75, Manchester

Club History	Signed	Fee
Ipswich T.	7/94	Trainee

Season	Team	Tot	St	Sb	Snu	Ps	Gls
94-95	Ipswich T.	10	10	0	0	1	0
	Total	10	10	0	0	1	0

VEART, Carl

FULLNAME: Carl Thomas Veart
DOB: 21-May-70, Whyalla, Australia

Club History	Signed	Fee
Adelaide C.		
Sheffield U.	7/94	£250,000
Crystal P.	3/96	

Season	Team	Tot	St	Sb	Snu	Ps	Gls
97-98	Crystal P.	6	1	5	4	0	0
	Total	6	1	5	4	0	0

VEGA, Ramon

FULLNAME: Ramon Vega
DOB: 14-Jun-71, Zurich

Club History	Signed	Fee
Cagliari	8/96	
Tottenham H.	1/97	£3.75m

Season	Team	Tot	St	Sb	Snu	Ps	Gls
96-97	Tottenham H.	8	8	0	0	2	1
97-98	Tottenham H.	25	22	3	0	0	3
98-99	Tottenham H.	16	13	3	5	1	2
99-00	Tottenham H.	5	2	3	5	0	1
	Total	54	45	9	10	3	7

VENISON, Barry

FULLNAME: Barry Venison
DOB: 16-Aug-64, Consett

Club History	Signed	Fee
Sunderland	1/82	Apprentice
Liverpool	7/86	£200,000
Newcastle U.	7/92	£250,000
Galatasaray	6/95	£750,000
Southampton	10/95	£850,000

Season	Team	Tot	St	Sb	Snu	Ps	Gls
93-94	Newcastle U.	37	36	1	0	1	0
94-95	Newcastle U.	28	28	0	0	1	1
95-96	Southampton	22	21	1	0	1	0
96-97	Southampton	2	2	0	0	0	0
	Total	89	87	2	0	3	1

VIALLI, Gianluca

FULLNAME: Gianluca Vialli
DOB: 09-Jul-64, Cremona

Club History	Signed	Fee
Juventus	1992	
Chelsea	6/96	Free

Season	Team	Tot	St	Sb	Snu	Ps	Gls
96-97	Chelsea	28	23	5	5	3	9
97-98	Chelsea	21	14	7	10	6	11

Season	Team	Tot	St	Sb	Snu	Ps	Gls
98-99	Chelsea	9	9	0	0	1	1
	Total	58	46	12	15	10	21

VICKERS, Steve

FULLNAME: Stephen Vickers
DOB: 13-Oct-67, Bishop Auckland

Club History	Signed	Fee
Tranmere R.	9/85	
Middlesbrough	12/93	£700,000

Season	Team	Tot	St	Sb	Snu	Ps	Gls
95-96	Middlesbrough	32	32	0	0	0	1
96-97	Middlesbrough	29	26	3	4	3	0
98-99	Middlesbrough	31	30	1	4	1	1
99-00	Middlesbrough	32	30	2	2	4	0
	Total	124	118	6	10	8	2

VIEIRA, Patrick

FULLNAME: Patrick Vieira
DOB: 23-Jun-76, Dakar, Senegal

Club History	Signed	Fee
Milan	1995	
Arsenal	8/96	£3.5m

Season	Team	Tot	St	Sb	Snu	Ps	Gls
96-97	Arsenal	31	30	1	0	3	2
97-98	Arsenal	33	31	2	0	4	2
98-99	Arsenal	34	34	0	0	5	3
99-00	Arsenal	30	29	1	0	0	2
	Total	128	124	4	0	12	9

VIVAS, Nelson

FULLNAME: Nelson Vivas
DOB: 18-Oct-69, San Nicolas, BA

Club History	Signed	Fee
Quilmes, Boca Juniors		
Lugano		Loan
Arsenal	8/98	£1.6m

Season	Team	Tot	St	Sb	Snu	Ps	Gls
98-99	Arsenal	23	10	13	2	1	0
99-00	Arsenal	5	1	4	4	0	0
	Total	28	11	17	6	1	0

VONK, Michael

FULLNAME: Michael Christian Vonk
DOB: 28-Oct-68, Netherlands

Club History	Signed	Fee
Manchester C.	3/92	£500,000

Season	Team	Tot	St	Sb	Snu	Ps	Gls
93-94	Manchester C.	35	34	1	2	1	1
94-95	Manchester C.	21	19	2	2	4	0
	Total	56	53	3	4	5	1

WADDLE, Chris

FULLNAME: Christopher Roland Waddle
DOB: 14-Dec-60, Felling

Club History	Signed	Fee
Newcastle U.	7/80	£1,000
Tottenham H.	7/85	£590,000
Marseille	7/89	£4.25m
Sheffield W.	7/92	£1m
Falkirk	9/96	Free
Bradford C.		
Sunderland	3/97	£75,000

Season	Team	Tot	St	Sb	Snu	Ps	Gls
92-93	Sheffield W.	33	32	1	0	7	1
93-94	Sheffield W.	19	19	0	0	0	3
94-95	Sheffield W.	25	20	5	1	6	4
95-96	Sheffield W.	32	23	9	0	7	2
96-97	Sunderland	7	7	0	0	2	1
	Total	116	101	15	1	22	11

WALKER, Des

FULLNAME: Desmond Sinclair Walker
DOB: 26-Nov-65, Hackney

Club History	Signed	Fee
Nottingham F.	11/83	Apprentice
Sampdoria	8/92	£1.5m
Sheffield W.	7/93	£2.70m

Season	Team	Tot	St	Sb	Snu	Ps	Gls
93-94	Sheffield W.	42	42	0	0	2	0
94-95	Sheffield W.	38	38	0	0	3	0
95-96	Sheffield W.	36	36	0	0	0	0
96-97	Sheffield W.	36	36	0	0	1	0
97-98	Sheffield W.	38	38	0	0	1	0
98-99	Sheffield W.	37	37	0	0	1	0
99-00	Sheffield W.	37	37	0	0	3	0
	Total	264	264	0	0	11	0

WALKER, Ian

FULLNAME: Ian Michael Walker
DOB: 31-Oct-71, Watford

Club History	Signed	Fee
Tottenham H.	12/89	Trainee
Oxford U.	8/90	Loan

Season	Team	Tot	St	Sb	Snu	Ps	Gls
92-93	Tottenham H.	17	17	0	15	2	0
93-94	Tottenham H.	11	10	1	31	0	0
94-95	Tottenham H.	41	41	0	1	0	0
95-96	Tottenham H.	38	38	0	0	0	0
96-97	Tottenham H.	37	37	0	0	1	0
97-98	Tottenham H.	29	29	0	0	0	0
98-99	Tottenham H.	25	25	0	11	0	0
99-00	Tottenham H.	38	38	0	0	0	0
	Total	236	235	1	58	3	0

WALKER, Richard

FULLNAME: Richard Walker
DOB: 08-Nov-77, Birmingham

Club History	Signed	Fee
Aston Villa		Trainee

Season	Team	Tot	St	Sb	Snu	Ps	Gls
97-98	Aston Villa	1	0	1	2	0	0
99-00	Aston Villa	5	2	3	4	2	2
	Total	6	2	4	6	2	2

WALLACE, Danny

FULLNAME: David Lloyd Wallace
DOB: 21-Jan-64, Greenwich

Club History	Signed	Fee
Southampton	1/82	
Manchester U.	9/89	£1.2m

Season	Team	Tot	St	Sb	Snu	Ps	Gls
92-93	Manchester U.	2	0	2	3	0	0
	Total	2	0	2	3	0	0

WALLACE, Ray

FULLNAME: Raymond George Wallace
DOB: 02-Oct-69, Greenwich

Club History	Signed	Fee
Southampton	4/88	
Leeds U.	5/91	£100,000

Season	Team	Tot	St	Sb	Snu	Ps	Gls
92-93	Leeds U.	6	5	1	2	1	0
93-94	Leeds U.	1	0	1	0	0	0
	Total	7	5	2	2	1	0

WALLACE, Rod

FULLNAME: Rodney Seymour Wallace
DOB: 02-Oct-69, Greenwich

Club History	Signed	Fee
Southampton	4/88	Trainee
Leeds U.	6/91	£1.6m

Season	Team	Tot	St	Sb	Snu	Ps	Gls
92-93	Leeds U.	32	31	1	1	9	7
93-94	Leeds U.	37	34	3	1	8	17
94-95	Leeds U.	32	30	2	0	7	4
95-96	Leeds U.	24	12	12	3	6	1
96-97	Leeds U.	22	17	5	8	7	3
97-98	Leeds U.	31	29	2	2	6	10
	Total	178	153	25	15	43	42

WALLEMME, Jean-Guy

FULLNAME: Jean-Guy Wallemme
DOB: 10-Aug-67, Maubeuge, France

Club History	Signed	Fee
RC Lens		
Coventry C.	6/97	£700,000

Season	Team	Tot	St	Sb	Snu	Ps	Gls
98-99	Coventry C.	6	4	2	2	1	0
	Total	6	4	2	2	1	0

WALLWORK, Ronnie

FULLNAME: Ronald Wallwork
DOB: 10-Sep-77, Manchester

Club History	Signed	Fee
Manchester U.		Trainee

Season	Team	Tot	St	Sb	Snu	Ps	Gls
97-98	Manchester U.	1	0	1	0	0	0
98-99	Manchester U.	0	0	0	0	0	0
99-00	Manchester U.	5	0	5	3	0	0
	Total	6	0	6	3	0	0

WALSH, Gary

FULLNAME: Gary Walsh
DOB: 21-Mar-68, Wigan

Club History	Signed	Fee
Manchester U.	4/85	Junior
Airdrieonians	8/88	Loan
Oldham A.	11/93	Loan
Middlesbrough	8/95	£250,000
Bradford C.	9/97	£500,000

Season	Team	Tot	St	Sb	Snu	Ps	Gls
92-93	Manchester U.	0	0	0	14	0	0
93-94	Manchester U.	3	2	1	2	0	0
94-95	Manchester U.	10	10	0	24	0	0
93-94	Oldham A.	6	6	0	0	0	0
95-96	Middlesbrough	31	31	0	1	0	0
96-97	Middlesbrough	12	12	0	5	0	0
99-00	Bradford C.	11	11	0	2	0	0
	Total	73	72	1	48	0	0

WALSH, Paul

FULLNAME: Paul A M Walsh
DOB: 01-Oct-62, Plumstead

Club History	Signed	Fee
Charlton A.	10/79	
Luton Town	7/82	£400,000
Liverpool	5/84	£700,000
Tottenham H.	2/88	£500,000
QPR	9/91	Loan
Portsmouth	6/92	£400,000
Manchester C.	3/94	£750,000

Season	Team	Tot	St	Sb	Snu	Ps	Gls
93-94	Manchester C.	11	11	0	0	1	4
94-95	Manchester C.	40	40	0	0	8	12
95-96	Manchester C.	4	4	0	0	1	0
	Total	55	55	0	0	10	16

WALSH, Steve

FULLNAME: Steven Walsh
DOB: 03-Nov-64, Preston

Club History	Signed	Fee
Wigan A.	9/82	Juniors
Leicester C.	6/86	£100,000

Season	Team	Tot	St	Sb	Snu	Ps	Gls
94-95	Leicester C.	5	5	0	0	0	0
96-97	Leicester C.	22	22	0	0	0	2
97-98	Leicester C.	26	23	3	1	6	3
98-99	Leicester C.	22	17	5	1	4	3
99-00	Leicester C.	11	5	6	7	1	0
	Total	86	72	14	9	11	8

WALTERS, Mark

FULLNAME: Mark Everton Walters
DOB: 02-Jun-64, Birmingham

Club History	Signed	Fee
Aston Villa	5/82	Apprentice
Rangers	12/87	£500,000
Liverpool	8/91	£1.25m
Stoke C.	3/94	Loan
Wolverhampton W.	9/94	Loan
Southampton	1/96	Free

Season	Team	Tot	St	Sb	Snu	Ps	Gls
92-93	Liverpool	34	26	8	3	5	11
93-94	Liverpool	17	7	10	3	3	0
94-95	Liverpool	17	7	10	7	5	0
95-96	Southampton	4	4	0	1	3	0
	Total	72	44	28	14	16	11

WANCHOPE, Paulo

FULLNAME: Pablo Cesar Wanchope
DOB: 31-Jul-76, Costa Rica

Club History	Signed	Fee
CS Heridiano		
Derby Co.	3/97	£600,000
West Ham U.	7/99	£3.5m

Season	Team	Tot	St	Sb	Snu	Ps	Gls
96-97	Derby Co.	5	2	3	0	2	1
97-98	Derby Co.	32	30	2	0	6	13
98-99	Derby Co.	35	33	2	0	3	9
99-00	West Ham U.	35	33	2	1	4	12
	Total	107	98	9	1	15	35

WARD, Ashley

FULLNAME: Ashley Stuart Ward
DOB: 24-Nov-70, Manchester

Club History	Signed	Fee
Manchester C.	8/89	Trainee
Wrexham	1/91	Loan
Leicester C.	7/91	£80,000
Blackpool	11/92	Loan
Crewe Alexandra	12/92	£80,000
Norwich C.	12/94	£500,000
Derby Co.	3/96	£1m
Barnsley	9/97	£1.3m
Blackburn R.	12/98	£4.25m

Season	Team	Tot	St	Sb	Snu	Ps	Gls
94-95	Norwich C.	25	25	0	0	0	8
96-97	Derby Co.	30	25	5	1	7	10
97-98	Derby Co.	3	2	1	0	0	0
97-98	Barnsley	29	28	1	0	3	8
98-99	Blackburn R.	17	17	0	0	0	5
	Total	104	97	7	1	10	31

WARD, Darren

FULLNAME: Darren Philip Ward
DOB: 13-Sep-78, Brentford

Club History	Signed	Fee
Watford	2/97	Trainee

Season	Team	Tot	St	Sb	Snu	Ps	Gls
99-00	Watford	9	7	2	0	0	1
	Total	9	7	2	0	0	1

WARD, Gavin

FULLNAME: Gavin John Ward
DOB: 30-Jun-70, Sutton Coldfield

Club History	Signed	Fee
Cardiff C.	10/89	Free from WBA
Leicester C.	7/94	£175,000
Bradford C.	7/95	£175,000
Bolton W.	3/96	£300,000

Season	Team	Tot	St	Sb	Snu	Ps	Gls
94-95	Leicester C.	6	6	0	33	0	0
95-96	Bolton W.	5	5	0	0	0	0
97-98	Bolton W.	6	4	2	28	0	0
	Total	17	15	2	61	0	0

WARD, Mark

FULLNAME: Mark William Ward
DOB: 10-Oct-62, Huyton

Club History	Signed	Fee
Oldham A.	7/83	£10,000
West Ham U.	8/85	£250,000
Manchester C.	12/89	£1m
Everton	8/91	£1.1m

Season	Team	Tot	St	Sb	Snu	Ps	Gls
92-93	Everton	19	19	0	0	6	1
93-94	Everton	27	26	1	0	5	1
	Total	46	45	1	0	11	2

WARD, Mitch

FULLNAME: Mitchum David Ward
DOB: 19-Jun-71, Sheffield

Club History	Signed	Fee
Sheffield U.	7/89	Trainee
Crewe Alex.	11/90	Loan
Everton	11/97	£850,000

Season	Team	Tot	St	Sb	Snu	Ps	Gls
92-93	Sheffield U.	26	22	4	1	4	0
93-94	Sheffield U.	22	20	2	2	7	1
97-98	Everton	8	8	0	0	2	0
98-99	Everton	7	4	3	8	3	0
99-00	Everton	10	6	4	11	5	0
	Total	73	60	13	22	21	1

WARHURST, Paul

FULLNAME: Paul Warhurst
DOB: 26-Sep-69, Stockport

Club History	Signed	Fee
Manchester C.	6/88	Trainee
Oldham A.	10/88	£10,000
Sheffield W.	7/91	£750,000
Blackburn R.	8/93	£2.7m
Crystal P.		

Season	Team	Tot	St	Sb	Snu	Ps	Gls
92-93	Sheffield W.	29	25	4	0	6	6
93-94	Sheffield W.	4	4	0	0	2	0
93-94	Blackburn R.	9	4	5	2	1	0
94-95	Blackburn R.	27	20	7	3	1	2
95-96	Blackburn R.	10	1	9	7	2	0
96-97	Blackburn R.	11	5	6	10	3	2
97-98	Crystal P.	22	22	0	1	8	3
	Total	112	81	31	23	23	13

WARK, John

FULLNAME: John Wark
DOB: 04-Aug-57, Glasgow

Club History	Signed	Fee
Ipswich T.	8/74	
Liverpool	3/84	£450,000
Ipswich T.	1/88	£100,000
Middlesbrough	8/90	£50,000
Ipswich T.	8/91	

Season	Team	Tot	St	Sb	Snu	Ps	Gls
92-93	Ipswich T.	37	36	1	0	1	6
93-94	Ipswich T.	38	38	0	0	6	3
94-95	Ipswich T.	26	26	0	0	4	4
	Total	101	100	1	0	11	13

WARNER, Phil

FULLNAME: Philip Warner
DOB: 02-Feb-79, Southampton

Club History	Signed	Fee
Southampton	5/97	Trainee

Season	Team	Tot	St	Sb	Snu	Ps	Gls
97-98	Southampton	1	0	1	2	0	0
98-99	Southampton	5	5	0	2	2	0
	Total	6	5	1	4	2	0

WARNER, Vance

FULLNAME: Vance Warner
DOB: 03-Sep-74, Leeds

Club History	Signed	Fee
Nottingham F.	9/91	Trainee

Season	Team	Tot	St	Sb	Snu	Ps	Gls
94-95	Nottingham F.	1	1	0	1	0	0
96-97	Nottingham F.	3	2	1	0	0	0
	Total	4	3	1	1	0	0

WARREN, Christer

FULLNAME: Christer Warren
DOB: 10-Oct-74, Bournemouth

Club History	Signed	Fee
Southampton	3/95	£40,000 from Non League

Season	Team	Tot	St	Sb	Snu	Ps	Gls
95-96	Southampton	7	1	6	1	0	0
96-97	Southampton	1	0	1	1	0	0
	Total	8	1	7	2	0	0

WARZYCHA, Robert

FULLNAME: Robert Warzycha
DOB: 20-Aug-63, Wielun, Poland

Club History	Signed	Fee
Everton	3/91	£300,000

Season	Team	Tot	St	Sb	Snu	Ps	Gls
92-93	Everton	20	15	5	1	9	1
93-94	Everton	7	3	4	1	2	0
	Total	27	18	9	2	11	1

WATKINSON, Russ

FULLNAME: Russ Watkinson
DOB: 03-Dec-77, Epsom

Club History	Signed	Fee
Southampton		From Woking

Season	Team	Tot	St	Sb	Snu	Ps	Gls
96-97	Southampton	2	0	2	1	0	0
	Total	2	0	2	1	0	0

WATSON, Dave

FULLNAME: David Watson
DOB: 20-Nov-61, Liverpool

Club History	Signed	Fee
Liverpool	5/79	Juniors
Norwich C.	11/80	£100,000
Everton	8/86	£900,000

Season	Team	Tot	St	Sb	Snu	Ps	Gls
92-93	Everton	40	40	0	0	0	1
93-94	Everton	28	27	1	0	2	1
94-95	Everton	38	38	0	0	2	2
95-96	Everton	34	34	0	0	0	1
96-97	Everton	29	29	0	0	2	1
97-98	Everton	26	25	1	2	2	0
98-99	Everton	22	22	0	7	2	0
99-00	Everton	6	5	1	9	0	0
	Total	223	220	3	18	10	6

WATSON, David

FULLNAME: David Neil Watson
DOB: 10-Nov-73, Barnsley

Club History	Signed	Fee
Barnsley	7/92	Trainee

Season	Team	Tot	St	Sb	Snu	Ps	Gls
97-98	Barnsley	30	30	0	6	1	0
	Total	30	30	0	6	1	0

WATSON, Gordon

FULLNAME: Gordon William George Watson
DOB: 20-Mar-71, Sidcup

Club History	Signed	Fee
Charlton A.	4/89	Trainee
Sheffield W.	2/91	£250,000
Southampton	3/95	£1.2m

Season	Team	Tot	St	Sb	Snu	Ps	Gls
92-93	Sheffield W.	11	4	7	3	0	1
93-94	Sheffield W.	23	15	8	3	3	12
94-95	Sheffield W.	23	5	18	1	3	2
94-95	Southampton	12	12	0	0	2	3
95-96	Southampton	25	18	7	3	7	3
96-97	Southampton	15	7	8	3	6	2
	Total	109	61	48	13	21	23

WATSON, Kevin

FULLNAME: Kevin Edward Watson
DOB: 03-Jan-74, Hackney

Club History	Signed	Fee
Tottenham H.	5/92	

Season	Team	Tot	St	Sb	Snu	Ps	Gls
92-93	Tottenham H.	5	4	1	0	3	1
	Total	5	4	1	0	3	1

WATSON, Mark

FULLNAME: Mark Watson
DOB: 28-Dec-73, Birmingham

Club History	Signed	Fee
West Ham U.	5/95	from NL

Season	Team	Tot	St	Sb	Snu	Ps	Gls
95-96	West Ham U.	1	0	1	0	0	0
	Total	1	0	1	0	0	0

WATSON, Steve

FULLNAME: Stephen Craig Watson
DOB: 01-Apr-74, North Shields

Club History	Signed	Fee
Newcastle U.	4/91	Trainee
Aston Villa	10/98	£4m

Season	Team	Tot	St	Sb	Snu	Ps	Gls
93-94	Newcastle U.	32	29	3	2	4	2
94-95	Newcastle U.	27	22	5	11	1	4
95-96	Newcastle U.	23	15	8	10	1	3
96-97	Newcastle U.	36	33	3	2	3	1
97-98	Newcastle U.	29	27	2	2	0	1
98-99	Newcastle U.	7	7	0	0	2	0
98-99	Aston Villa	27	26	1	1	6	0
99-00	Aston Villa	14	13	1	13	3	0
	Total	195	172	23	41	20	11

WATTS, Grant

FULLNAME: Grant Watts
DOB: 15-Nov-73, Croydon

Club History	Signed	Fee
Crystal P.		Trainee

Season	Team	Tot	St	Sb	Snu	Ps	Gls
92-93	Crystal P.	4	2	2	5	1	0
	Total	4	2	2	5	1	0

WATTS, Julian

FULLNAME: Julian Watts
DOB: 17-Mar-71, Sheffield

Club History	Signed	Fee
Rotherham U.	7/90	Trainee
Sheffield W.	3/92	£80,000
Shrewsbury Town	12/92	Loan
Leicester C.	3/96	£210,000

Season	Team	Tot	St	Sb	Snu	Ps	Gls
92-93	Sheffield W.	3	2	1	0	0	0
93-94	Sheffield W.	1	1	0	0	0	0
94-95	Sheffield W.	0	0	0	3	0	2
95-96	Sheffield W.	11	9	2	6	1	1
96-97	Leicester C.	26	22	4	8	4	1
97-98	Leicester C.	2	0	2	5	0	0
	Total	43	34	9	22	5	4

WEAH, George

FULLNAME: George Weah
DOB: 01-Oct-66, Liberia

Club History	Signed	Fee
Milan		
Chelsea	1/00	Loan

Season	Team	Tot	St	Sb	Snu	Ps	Gls
99-00	Chelsea	11	9	2	0	1	3
	Total	11	9	2	0	1	3

WEBB, Neil

FULLNAME: Neil John Webb
DOB: 30-Jul-63, Reading

Club History	Signed	Fee
Reading	11/80	
Portsmouth	7/82	£83,000
Nottingham F.	6/85	£250,000
Manchester U.	7/89	£1.5m
Nottingham F.	11/92	£800,000

Season	Team	Tot	St	Sb	Snu	Ps	Gls
92-93	Manchester U.	1	0	1	1	0	0
92-93	Nottingham F.	9	9	0	0	0	0
94-95	Nottingham F.	0	0	0	4	0	0
	Total	10	9	1	5	0	0

WEBSTER, Simon

FULLNAME: Simon Paul Webster
DOB: 20-Jan-64, Earl Shilton

Club History	Signed	Fee
Tottenham H.	12/81	
Exeter C.	11/83	Loan
Huddersfield T.	2/85	£15,000
Sheffield U.	3/88	£35,000
Charlton A.	9/90	£50,000
West Ham U.	7/93	£525,000

Season	Team	Tot	St	Sb	Snu	Ps	Gls
94-95	West Ham U.	5	0	5	0	0	0
	Total	5	0	5	0	0	0

WEGERLE, Roy

FULLNAME: Roy Connon Wegerle
DOB: 19-Mar-64, Johannesburg, South Africa

Club History	Signed	Fee
Tampa Bay		
Chelsea	6/86	£100,000
Swindon Town	3/88	Loan
Luton Town	7/88	£75,000
QPR	12/89	£1m
Blackburn R.	3/92	£1.2m
Coventry C.	3/93	£1m

Season	Team	Tot	St	Sb	Snu	Ps	Gls
92-93	Blackburn R.	22	11	11	8	1	4
92-93	Coventry C.	6	5	1	0	2	0
93-94	Coventry C.	21	20	1	0	4	6
94-95	Coventry C.	27	22	5	2	8	3
	Total	76	58	18	10	15	13

WEIR, David

FULLNAME: David Wier
DOB: 10-May-70, Falkirk

Club History	Signed	Fee
Falkirk	8/91	From Celtic BC
Hearts	8/92	
Everton	2/99	£250,000

Season	Team	Tot	St	Sb	Snu	Ps	Gls
98-99	Everton	14	11	3	0	0	0
99-00	Everton	35	35	0	0	1	2
	Total	49	46	3	0	1	2

WESTERVELD, Sander

FULLNAME: Sander Westerveld
DOB: 23-Oct-74, Enschede, Holland

Club History	Signed	Fee
Vitesse Arnhem		
Liverpool	6/99	£4.0m

Season	Team	Tot	St	Sb	Snu	Ps	Gls
99-00	Liverpool	36	36	0	0	0	0
	Total	36	36	0	0	0	0

WESTON, Rhys

FULLNAME: Rhyrs Weston
DOB: 27-Oct-80, Kingston, Surrey

Club History	Signed	Fee
Arsenal	7/97	Trainee

Season	Team	Tot	St	Sb	Snu	Ps	Gls
99-00	Arsenal	1	1	0	0	1	0
	Total	1	1	0	0	1	0

WESTWOOD, Ashley

FULLNAME: Ashley Michael Westwood
DOB: 31-Aug-76, Bridgnorth

Club History	Signed	Fee
Manchester U.	7/94	Trainee
Crewe Alex.	7/95	£40,000
Bradford C.	7/98	£150,000

Season	Team	Tot	St	Sb	Snu	Ps	Gls
99-00	Bradford C.	5	1	4	15	1	0
	Total	5	1	4	15	1	0

WETHERALL, David

FULLNAME: David Wetherall
DOB: 14-Mar-71, Sheffield

Club History	Signed	Fee
Sheffield W.	7/89	Trainee
Leeds U.	7/91	£125,000
Bradford C.	6/99	£1.4m

Season	Team	Tot	St	Sb	Snu	Ps	Gls
92-93	Leeds U.	13	13	0	1	2	1
93-94	Leeds U.	32	31	1	3	3	1
94-95	Leeds U.	38	38	0	0	2	3
95-96	Leeds U.	34	34	0	1	0	4
96-97	Leeds U.	29	25	4	7	3	0
97-98	Leeds U.	34	33	1	2	0	3
98-99	Leeds U.	21	14	7	17	1	0
99-00	Bradford C.	38	38	0	0	0	2
	Total	239	226	13	31	11	14

WHALLEY, Gareth

FULLNAME: Gareth Whalley
DOB: 19-Dec-73, Manchester

Club History	Signed	Fee
Crewe Alex.	7/92	Trainee
Bradford C.	7/98	£600,000

Season	Team	Tot	St	Sb	Snu	Ps	Gls
99-00	Bradford C.	16	16	0	6	6	1
	Total	16	16	0	6	6	1

WHELAN, Noel

FULLNAME: Noel Whelan
DOB: 30-Dec-74, Leeds

Club History	Signed	Fee
Leeds U.	3/93	Trainee
Coventry C.	12/95	£2m

Season	Team	Tot	St	Sb	Snu	Ps	Gls
92-93	Leeds U.	1	1	0	0	0	0
93-94	Leeds U.	16	6	10	4	4	0
94-95	Leeds U.	23	18	5	5	3	7
95-96	Leeds U.	8	3	5	2	2	0
95-96	Coventry C.	21	21	0	0	1	8
96-97	Coventry C.	35	34	1	0	9	6
97-98	Coventry C.	21	21	0	0	2	6
98-99	Coventry C.	31	31	0	0	2	10
99-00	Coventry C.	26	20	6	0	6	1
	Total	182	155	27	11	29	38

WHELAN, Phil

FULLNAME: Philip James Whelan
DOB: 07-Mar-72, Stockport

Club History	Signed	Fee
Ipswich T.	7/90	Juniors
Middlesbrough	3/95	£300,000

Season	Team	Tot	St	Sb	Snu	Ps	Gls
92-93	Ipswich T.	32	28	4	10	6	0
93-94	Ipswich T.	29	28	1	0	4	0
94-95	Ipswich T.	13	12	1	0	2	0
95-96	Middlesbrough	13	9	4	10	1	1
96-97	Middlesbrough	9	9	0	11	1	0
	Total	96	86	10	31	14	1

WHELAN, Ronnie

FULLNAME: Ronald A Whelan
DOB: 25-Sep-61, Dublin, Republic of Ireland

Club History	Signed	Fee
Liverpool	10/79	

Season	Team	Tot	St	Sb	Snu	Ps	Gls
92-93	Liverpool	17	17	0	0	1	1
93-94	Liverpool	23	23	0	1	2	1
	Total	40	40	0	1	3	2

WHISTON, Peter

FULLNAME: Peter M Whiston
DOB: 04-Jan-68, Widnes

Club History	Signed	Fee
Plymouth Argyle	12/87	
Torquay U.	3/90	Free
Exeter C.	9/91	£25,000
Southampton	8/94	£30,000

Season	Team	Tot	St	Sb	Snu	Ps	Gls
94-95	Southampton	1	0	1	4	0	0
	Total	1	0	1	4	0	0

WHITBREAD, Adrian

FULLNAME: Adrian Richard Whitbread
DOB: 22-Oct-71, Epping

Club History	Signed	Fee
Leyton Orient	11/89	
Swindon Town	8/93	£500,000
West Ham U.	8/94	Swap +

Season	Team	Tot	St	Sb	Snu	Ps	Gls
93-94	Swindon T.	35	34	1	1	4	1
94-95	West Ham U.	8	3	5	8	0	0
95-96	West Ham U.	2	0	2	1	0	0
	Total	45	37	8	10	4	1

WHITE, David

FULLNAME: David White
DOB: 30-Oct-67, Manchester

Club History	Signed	Fee
Manchester C.	10/85	
Leeds U.	12/93	Swap

Season	Team	Tot	St	Sb	Snu	Ps	Gls
92-93	Manchester C.	42	42	0	0	3	16
93-94	Manchester C.	16	16	0	0	2	1
93-94	Leeds U.	15	9	6	2	5	5
94-95	Leeds U.	23	18	5	2	4	3
95-96	Leeds U.	4	1	3	0	1	1
	Total	100	86	14	4	15	26

WHITE, Devon

FULLNAME: Devon W White
DOB: 02-Mar-64, Nottingham

Club History	Signed	Fee
Lincoln C.	12/84	
Bristol R.	8/87	Free
Cambridge U.	3/92	£100,000
QPR	1/93	£100,000

Season	Team	Tot	St	Sb	Snu	Ps	Gls
92-93	QPR	7	3	4	6	1	2
93-94	QPR	18	12	6	4	2	7
94-95	QPR	1	1	0	0	0	0
	Total	26	16	10	10	3	9

WHITE, Steve

FULLNAME: Stephen J White
DOB: 02-Jan-59, Chipping Sodbury

Club History	Signed	Fee
Bristol R.	7/77	
Luton T.	12/79	£200,000
Charlton A.	7/82	£150,000
Lincoln C.	1/83	Loan
Luton T.	2/83	Loan
Bristol R.	8/83	£45,000
Swindon T.	7/87	Free

Season	Team	Tot	St	Sb	Snu	Ps	Gls
93-94	Swindon T.	6	2	4	0	1	0
	Total	6	2	4	0	1	0

WHITEHOUSE, Dane

FULLNAME: Dane Lee Whitehouse
DOB: 14-Oct-70, Sheffield

Club History	Signed	Fee
Sheffield U.	7/89	

Season	Team	Tot	St	Sb	Snu	Ps	Gls
92-93	Sheffield U.	14	14	0	0	5	5

| 93-94 | Sheffield U. | 38 | 35 | 3 | 0 | 4 | 5 |
| | Total | 52 | 49 | 3 | 0 | 9 | 10 |

WHITLOW, Mike

FULLNAME: Michael William Whitlow
DOB: 13-Jan-68, Liverpool

Club History	Signed	Fee
Leeds U.	11/88	£10,000 from Non League
Leicester C.	3/92	£250,000
Bolton W.	9/97	£700,000

Season	Team	Tot	St	Sb	Snu	Ps	Gls
94-95	Leicester C.	28	28	0	0	2	2
96-97	Leicester C.	17	14	3	5	1	0
97-98	Leicester C.	1	0	1	2	0	0
97-98	Bolton W.	11	11	0	1	0	0
	Total	57	53	4	8	3	2

WHITTINGHAM, Guy

FULLNAME: Guy Whittingham
DOB: 10-Nov-64, Evesham

Club History	Signed	Fee
Portsmouth	6/89	Free from Non League
Aston Villa	7/93	£1.2m
Wolverhampton Wan	2/94	Loan
Sheffield W.	12/94	£700,000

Season	Team	Tot	St	Sb	Snu	Ps	Gls
93-94	Aston Villa	18	13	5	7	7	3
94-95	Aston Villa	7	4	3	0	0	2
94-95	Sheffield W.	21	16	5	0	4	9
95-96	Sheffield W.	29	27	2	2	2	6
96-97	Sheffield W.	33	29	4	1	10	3
97-98	Sheffield W.	28	17	11	7	6	4
98-99	Sheffield W.	2	1	1	5	1	0
	Total	138	107	31	22	30	27

WHITTON, Steve

FULLNAME: Stephen Paul Whitton
DOB: 04-Dec-60, East Ham

Club History	Signed	Fee
Coventry C.	9/78	
West Ham U.	7/83	£175,000
Birmingham C.	1/86	Loan
Birmingham C.	8/86	£60,000
Sheffield W.	3/89	£275,000
Ipswich Town	1/91	£150,000

Season	Team	Tot	St	Sb	Snu	Ps	Gls
92-93	Ipswich T.	24	20	4	1	3	3
93-94	Ipswich T.	11	7	4	8	1	1
	Total	35	27	8	9	4	4

WHYTE, Chris

FULLNAME: Christopher Anderson Whyte
DOB: 02-Sep-61, Islington

Club History	Signed	Fee
Arsenal	9/79	
Crystal P.	8/84	Loan
Los Angeles	7/86	
WBA	8/88	Free
Leeds U.	6/90	£400,000
Birmingham C.	8/93	£250,000
Coventry C.	12/95	Loan

Season	Team	Tot	St	Sb	Snu	Ps	Gls
92-93	Leeds U.	34	34	0	1	1	1
95-96	Coventry C.	1	1	0	0	0	0
	Total	35	35	0	1	1	1

WHYTE, Derek

FULLNAME: Derek Whyte
DOB: 31-Aug-68, Glasgow

Club History	Signed	Fee
Celtic		Juniors
Middlesbrough	8/92	

Season	Team	Tot	St	Sb	Snu	Ps	Gls
92-93	Middlesbrough	35	34	1	2	2	0
95-96	Middlesbrough	25	24	1	0	2	0
96-97	Middlesbrough	21	20	1	11	3	0
	Total	81	78	3	13	7	0

WIDDRINGTON, Tommy

FULLNAME: Thomas Widdrington
DOB: 01-Oct-71, Newcastle

Club History	Signed	Fee
Southampton	5/90	

Season	Team	Tot	St	Sb	Snu	Ps	Gls
92-93	Southampton	12	11	1	5	4	0
93-94	Southampton	11	11	0	2	3	1
94-95	Southampton	28	23	5	8	6	0
95-96	Southampton	21	20	1	3	3	2
	Total	72	65	7	18	16	3

WIJNHARD, Clyde

FULLNAME: Clyde Wijnhard
DOB: 09-Nov-73, Surinam

Club History	Signed	Fee
Willem II		
Leeds U.	7/98	1.5m

Season	Team	Tot	St	Sb	Snu	Ps	Gls
98-99	Leeds U.	18	11	7	16	8	3
	Total	18	11	7	16	8	3

WILCOX, Jason

FULLNAME: Jason Malcolm Wilcox
DOB: 15-Mar-71, Farnworth

Club History	Signed	Fee
Blackburn R.	6/89	Trainee
Leeds U.	12/99	£3.0m

Season	Team	Tot	St	Sb	Snu	Ps	Gls
92-93	Blackburn R.	33	31	2	0	5	4
93-94	Blackburn R.	33	31	2	1	3	6
94-95	Blackburn R.	27	27	0	0	4	5
95-96	Blackburn R.	10	10	0	0	2	3
96-97	Blackburn R.	28	26	2	2	5	2
97-98	Blackburn R.	31	24	7	2	6	3
98-99	Blackburn R.	30	28	2	1	8	3
99-00	Leeds U.	20	15	5	1	3	3
	Total	212	192	20	7	36	29

WILKINS, Ray

FULLNAME: Raymond Colin Wilkins
DOB: 14-Sep-56, Hillingdon

Club History	Signed	Fee
Chelsea	10/73	
Manchester U.	8/79	£825,000
Milan	7/84	£1.5m
Rangers	11/87	£250,000
QPR	11/89	Free
Crystal P.	5/94	Free
QPR	11/94	Free

Season	Team	Tot	St	Sb	Snu	Ps	Gls
92-93	QPR	27	27	0	0	0	2
93-94	QPR	39	39	0	1	7	1
94-95	Crystal P.	1	1	0	0	1	0
94-95	QPR	2	1	1	2	1	0
95-96	QPR	15	11	4	6	6	0
	Total	84	79	5	9	15	3

WILKINSON, Paul

FULLNAME: Paul Wilkinson
DOB: 30-Oct-64, Louth

Club History	Signed	Fee
Grimsby T.	11/82	Amateur
Everton	3/85	£250,000
Nottingham F.	3/87	£200,000
Watford	8/88	£300,000
Middlesbrough	8/91	£550,000
Oldham	10/95	Loan
Watford	12/95	Loan
Luton T.	3/96	Loan
Barnsley	7/96	free

Season	Team	Tot	St	Sb	Snu	Ps	Gls
92-93	Middlesbrough	41	41	0	0	1	15
95-96	Middlesbrough	2	1	1	2	0	0
97-98	Barnsley	5	4	1	1	2	0
	Total	48	46	2	3	3	15

WILLEMS, Ron

FULLNAME: Ron Willems
DOB: 20-Sep-66, Epe (Holland)

Club History	Signed	Fee
Grasshopper		
Derby Co.	7/95	£300,000

Season	Team	Tot	St	Sb	Snu	Ps	Gls
96-97	Derby Co.	16	7	9	8	7	2
97-98	Derby Co.	10	3	7	4	1	0
	Total	26	10	16	12	8	2

WILLIAMS, Andy

FULLNAME: Andrew Williams
DOB: 06-Oct-77, Bristol

Club History	Signed	Fee
Southampton	Jul-94	Trainee

Season	Team	Tot	St	Sb	Snu	Ps	Gls
97-98	Southampton	20	3	17	7	2	0
98-99	Southampton	1	0	1	3	0	0
	Total	21	3	18	10	2	0

WILLIAMS, Brett

FULLNAME: Brett Williams
DOB: 19-Mar-68, Dudley

Club History	Signed	Fee
Nottingham F.		Apprentice
Stockport Co.		Loan
Northampton T.		Loan
Hereford U.		Loan
Oxford U.		Loan

Season	Team	Tot	St	Sb	Snu	Ps	Gls
92-93	Nottingham F.	9	9	0	2	0	0
98-99	Nottingham F.	1	1	0	2	0	0
	Total	10	10	0	4	0	0

WILLIAMS, Darren

FULLNAME: Darren Williams
DOB: 28-Apr-77, Middlesbrough

Club History	Signed	Fee
York C.	6/95	Trainee
Sunderland	10/96	£50,000

Season	Team	Tot	St	Sb	Snu	Ps	Gls
96-97	Sunderland	11	10	1	3	1	2
99-00	Sunderland	25	13	12	3	3	0
	Total	36	23	13	6	4	2

WILLIAMS, Geraint

FULLNAME: D Geraint Williams
DOB: 05-Jul-62, Treorchy

Club History	Signed	Fee
Bristol R.	1/80	
Derby Co.	3/85	£40,000
Ipswich T.	7/92	£650,000

Season	Team	Tot	St	Sb	Snu	Ps	Gls
92-93	Ipswich T.	37	37	0	0	0	0
93-94	Ipswich T.	34	34	0	0	3	0
94-95	Ipswich T.	38	38	0	0	4	1
	Total	109	109	0	0	7	1

WILLIAMS, John

FULLNAME: John N Williams
DOB: 11-May-68, Birmingham

Club History	Signed	Fee
Swansea C.	8/91	£5,000
Coventry C.	7/92	£250,000
Notts Co.	10/94	Loan
Swansea C.	2/95	Loan

Season	Team	Tot	St	Sb	Snu	Ps	Gls
92-93	Coventry C.	41	38	3	1	5	8
93-94	Coventry C.	32	27	5	1	12	3
94-95	Coventry C.	7	1	6	1	0	0
95-96	Coventry C.	0	0	0	1	0	0
	Total	80	66	14	4	17	11

WILLIAMS, Mark

FULLNAME: Mark Stuart Williams
DOB: 28-Sep-70, Stalybridge

Club History	Signed	Fee
Shrewsbury T.	3/92	Free NL
Chesterfield T.	8/95	£50,000
Watford	7/97	Free

Season	Team	Tot	St	Sb	Snu	Ps	Gls
99-00	Watford	22	20	2	1	3	1
	Total	22	20	2	1	3	1

WILLIAMS, Mike

FULLNAME: Michael Anthony Williams
DOB: 21-Nov-69, Bradford

Club History	Signed	Fee
Sheffield W.	2/91	Free from Non League
Halifax T.	12/92	Loan
Huddersfield T.	10/96	Loan

Season	Team	Tot	St	Sb	Snu	Ps	Gls
92-93	Sheffield W.	3	2	1	0	1	0
93-94	Sheffield W.	4	4	0	2	3	0
94-95	Sheffield W.	10	8	2	1	0	1
95-96	Sheffield W.	5	2	3	3	2	0
96-97	Sheffield W.	1	0	1	0	0	0
	Total	23	16	7	6	6	1

WILLIAMS, Paul

FULLNAME: Paul A. Williams
DOB: 08-Sep-63, Sheffield

Club History	Signed	Fee
Preston NE	12/86	From Non League
Newport Co.	8/87	
Sheffield U.	3/88	
Hartlepool U.	10/89	
Stockport Co.	8/90	
WBA	3/91	
Coventry C.		Loan

Season	Team	Tot	St	Sb	Snu	Ps	Gls
92-93	Coventry C.	2	1	1	1	0	0
	Total	2	1	1	1	0	0

WILLIAMS, Paul

FULLNAME: Paul Anthony Williams
DOB: 16-Aug-65, Stratford, London

Club History	Signed	Fee
Charlton A.	2/87	£10,000
Brentford	10/87	Loan
Sheffield W.	8/90	£700,000
Crystal P.	9/92	Swap

Season	Team	Tot	St	Sb	Snu	Ps	Gls
92-93	Crystal P.	18	15	3	4	3	0
94-95	Crystal P.	4	2	2	0	0	0
92-93	Sheffield W.	7	7	0	0	0	1
	Total	29	24	5	4	3	1

WILLIAMS, Paul

FULLNAME: Paul Darren Williams
DOB: 26-Mar-71, Burton

Club History	Signed	Fee
Derby Co.	7/89	Trainee
Lincoln C.	11/89	Loan
Coventry C.	8/95	£975,000

Season	Team	Tot	St	Sb	Snu	Ps	Gls
95-96	Coventry C.	32	30	2	1	1	2
96-97	Coventry C.	32	29	3	2	1	2
97-98	Coventry C.	20	17	3	8	1	0
98-99	Coventry C.	22	20	2	8	2	0
99-00	Coventry C.	28	26	2	1	2	1
	Total	134	122	12	20	7	5

WILLIAMS, Paul

FULLNAME: Paul Richard Curtis Williams
DOB: 11-Sep-69, Leicester

Club History	Signed	Fee
Leicester C.		
Sockport Co.	5/7/89	Free
Coventry C.	12/8/93	£150,000

Season	Team	Tot	St	Sb	Snu	Ps	Gls
93-94	Coventry C.	9	3	6	1	0	0
94-95	Coventry C.	5	5	0	3	0	0
	Total	14	8	6	4	0	0

WILLIAMSON, Danny

FULLNAME: Daniel Alan Williamson
DOB: 05-Dec-73, Newham

Club History	Signed	Fee
West Ham U.	7/92	Trainee
Doncaster R.	10/93	Loan
Everton	8/97	£1.0+

Season	Team	Tot	St	Sb	Snu	Ps	Gls
93-94	West Ham U.	3	2	1	0	0	1
94-95	West Ham U.	4	4	0	3	0	0
95-96	West Ham U.	29	28	1	0	3	4
96-97	West Ham U.	15	13	2	0	2	0
97-98	Everton	15	15	0	0	5	0
	Total	66	62	4	3	10	5

WILLIS, Jimmy

FULLNAME: James Anthony Willis
DOB: 12-Jul-68, Liverpool

Club History	Signed	Fee
Stockport Co.	8/86	Free from Halifax
Darlington	3/88	£12,000
Leicester C.	12/91	£100,000

Season	Team	Tot	St	Sb	Snu	Ps	Gls
94-95	Leicester C.	29	29	0	1	0	2
	Total	29	29	0	1	0	2

WILMOT, Rhys

FULLNAME: Rhys J Wilmot
DOB: 21-Feb-62, Newport

Club History	Signed	Fee
Arsenal	2/80	
Hereford U.	3/83	Loan
Leyton Orient	5/84	Loan
Swansea C.	8/88	Loan
Plymouth Argyle	2/89	Loan
Plymouth Argyle	7/89	£100,000
Grimsby Town	7/92	£87,500
Crystal P.	8/94	£80,000

Season	Team	Tot	St	Sb	Snu	Ps	Gls
94-95	Crystal P.	6	5	1	36	0	0
	Total	6	5	1	36	0	0

WILMOTT, Chris

FULLNAME: Christopher Wilmott
DOB: 30-Sep-77, Bedford

Club History	Signed	Fee
Luton	8/95	Trainee
Wimbledon	7/99	£3.5m

Season	Team	Tot	St	Sb	Snu	Ps	Gls
99-00	Wimbledon	7	7	0	9	1	0
	Total	7	7	0	9	1	0

WILSON, Clive

FULLNAME: Clive Euclid Aklana Wilson
DOB: 13-Nov-61, Manchester

Club History	Signed	Fee
Manchester C.	12/79	Juniors
Chester C.	9/82	Loan
Chelsea	3/87	£250,000
QPR	7/90	£450,000
Tottenham H.	6/95	Free

Season	Team	Tot	St	Sb	Snu	Ps	Gls
92-93	QPR	41	41	0	0	3	3
93-94	QPR	42	42	0	0	0	3
94-95	QPR	36	36	0	0	3	2
95-96	Tottenham H.	28	28	0	2	0	0
96-97	Tottenham H.	26	23	3	3	1	1
97-98	Tottenham H.	16	16	0	1	7	0
98-99	Tottenham H.	0	0	0	3	0	0
	Total	189	186	3	9	14	9

WILSON, Danny

FULLNAME: Daniel J. Wilson
DOB: 01-Jan-60, Wigan

Club History	Signed	Fee
Wigan A.		
Bury	9/77	
Chesterfield	7/80	
Nottingham F.	1/83	
Scunthorpe U.	10/83	Loan
Brighton & HA	11/83	
Luton T.	7/87	
Sheffield W.	8/90	

Season	Team	Tot	St	Sb	Snu	Ps	Gls
92-93	Sheffield W.	26	21	5	1	8	2
	Total	26	21	5	1	8	2

WILSON, Mark

FULLNAME: Mark Wilson
DOB: 09-Feb-79, Scunthorpe

Club History	Signed	Fee				
Manchester U.		Trainee				

Season	Team	Tot	St	Sb	Snu	Ps	Gls
99-00	Manchester U.	3	1	2	2	1	0
	Total	3	1	2	2	1	0

WILSON, Stuart

FULLNAME: Stuart Kevin Wilson
DOB: 16-Sep-77, Leicester

Club History	Signed	Fee				
Leicester C.	7/96	Trainee				

Season	Team	Tot	St	Sb	Snu	Ps	Gls
96-97	Leicester C.	2	0	2	2	0	1
97-98	Leicester C.	11	0	11	15	0	2
98-99	Leicester C.	9	1	8	2	1	0
99-00	Leicester C.	0	0	0	3	0	0
	Total	22	1	21	22	1	3

WILSON, Terry

FULLNAME: Terence Wilson
DOB: 08-Feb-69, Broxburn

Club History	Signed	Fee				
Nottingham F.		Apprentice				

Season	Team	Tot	St	Sb	Snu	Ps	Gls
92-93	Nottingham F.	5	5	0	1	1	0
	Total	5	5	0	1	1	0

WINDASS, Dean

FULLNAME: Dean Windass
DOB: 01-Apr-69, Hull

Club History	Signed	Fee				
Hull C.	10/91	Free NL				
Aberdeen	12/97	£700,000				
Oxford U.	8/98	£475,000				
Bradford C.	3/99	£950,000				

Season	Team	Tot	St	Sb	Snu	Ps	Gls
99-00	Bradford C.	38	36	2	0	7	10
	Total	38	36	2	0	7	10

WINTERBURN, Nigel

FULLNAME: Nigel Winterburn
DOB: 11-Dec-63, Nuneaton

Club History	Signed	Fee				
Wimbledon	9/83	Free				
Arsenal	5/87	£407,000				

Season	Team	Tot	St	Sb	Snu	Ps	Gls
92-93	Arsenal	29	29	0	0	1	1
93-94	Arsenal	34	34	0	0	2	0
94-95	Arsenal	39	39	0	0	3	0
95-96	Arsenal	36	36	0	0	1	2
96-97	Arsenal	38	38	0	0	3	0
97-98	Arsenal	36	35	1	0	2	1
98-99	Arsenal	30	30	0	1	3	0
99-00	Arsenal	28	19	9	6	2	0
	Total	270	260	10	7	17	4

WIRMOLA, Jonas

FULLNAME: Jonas Wirmola
DOB: 17-Jul-69, Sweden

Club History	Signed	Fee				
Sparvagens						
Sheffield U.	8/93	£50,000				

Season	Team	Tot	St	Sb	Snu	Ps	Gls
93-94	Sheffield U.	8	8	0	1	1	0
	Total	8	8	0	1	1	0

WISE, Dennis

FULLNAME: Dennis Frank Wise
DOB: 15-Dec-66, Kensington

Club History	Signed	Fee				
Wimbledon	3/85					
Chelsea	7/90	£1.6m				

Season	Team	Tot	St	Sb	Snu	Ps	Gls
92-93	Chelsea	27	27	0	0	0	3
93-94	Chelsea	35	35	0	0	2	4
94-95	Chelsea	19	18	1	0	1	6
95-96	Chelsea	35	34	1	0	4	7
96-97	Chelsea	31	27	4	0	4	4
97-98	Chelsea	26	26	0	0	2	3
98-99	Chelsea	22	21	1	1	1	0
99-00	Chelsea	30	29	1	0	3	4
	Total	225	217	8	1	17	31

WITSCHGE, Richard

FULLNAME: Richard Witschge
DOB: 20-Sep-69, Amsterdam

Club History	Signed	Fee				
Bordeaux						
Blackburn R.	3/95	Loan				

Season	Team	Tot	St	Sb	Snu	Ps	Gls
94-95	Blackburn R.	1	1	0	2	0	0
	Total	1	1	0	2	0	0

WITTER, Tony

FULLNAME: Anthony Junior Witter
DOB: 12-Aug-65, London

Club History	Signed	Fee	
Crystal P.	10/90	£10,000	
QPR	8/91	£125,000	

Season	Team	Tot	St	Sb	Snu	Ps	Gls
92-93	QPR	0	0	0	1	0	0
93-94	QPR	1	1	0	1	0	0
	Total	1	1	0	2	0	0

WOAN, Ian

FULLNAME: Ian Simon Woan
DOB: 14-Dec-67, Heswall

Club History	Signed	Fee
Nottingham F.	3/90	£80,000

Season	Team	Tot	St	Sb	Snu	Ps	Gls
92-93	Nottingham F.	28	27	1	1	2	3
94-95	Nottingham F.	37	35	2	2	6	5
95-96	Nottingham F.	33	33	0	0	1	8
96-97	Nottingham F.	32	29	3	1	7	1
98-99	Nottingham F.	2	0	2	6	0	0
	Total	132	124	8	10	16	17

WOLLEASTON, Robert

FULLNAME: Robert Wolleaston
DOB: 21-Dec-79, Perivale

Club History	Signed	Fee
Chelsea		Trainee

Season	Team	Tot	St	Sb	Snu	Ps	Gls
99-00	Chelsea	1	0	1	2	0	0
	Total	1	0	1	2	0	0

WOOD, Steve

FULLNAME: Stephen Alan Wood
DOB: 02-Feb-63, Bracknell

Club History	Signed	Fee
Reading	2/81	
Millwall	6/87	£80,000
Southampton	10/91	£400,000

Season	Team	Tot	St	Sb	Snu	Ps	Gls
92-93	Southampton	4	4	0	0	0	0
93-94	Southampton	27	27	0	0	7	0
	Total	31	31	0	0	7	0

WOODGATE, Jonathan

FULLNAME: Jonathan Woodgate
DOB: 22-Jan-80, Middlesbrough

Club History	Signed	Fee
Leeds U.		Trainee

Season	Team	Tot	St	Sb	Snu	Ps	Gls
98-99	Leeds U.	25	25	0	2	2	2
99-00	Leeds U.	34	32	2	1	3	1
	Total	59	57	2	3	5	3

WOODS, Chris

FULLNAME: Christopher Charles Eric Woods
DOB: 14-Nov-59, Boston

Club History	Signed	Fee
Nottingham F.	12/76	Apprentice
QPR	7/79	£250,000
Norwich C.	3/81	£225,000
Rangers	7/86	£600,000
Sheffield W.	8/91	£1.2m
Reading	10/95	Loan
Colorado Rapids		
Southampton	10/96	Loan
Sunderland		Free

Season	Team	Tot	St	Sb	Snu	Ps	Gls
92-93	Sheffield W.	39	39	0	2	0	0
93-94	Sheffield W.	10	10	0	22	0	0
94-95	Sheffield W.	9	8	1	8	0	0
95-96	Sheffield W.	8	8	0	3	1	0
96-97	Southampton	4	4	0	0	1	0
96-97	Sunderland	0	0	0	6	0	0
	Total	70	69	1	41	2	0

WOODTHORPE, Colin

FULLNAME: Colin John Woodthorpe
DOB: 13-Jan-69, Ellesmere Port

Club History	Signed	Fee
Chester C.	9/86	
Norwich C.	7/90	£175,000

Season	Team	Tot	St	Sb	Snu	Ps	Gls
92-93	Norwich C.	7	5	2	12	1	0
93-94	Norwich C.	20	18	2	2	2	0
	Total	27	23	4	14	3	0

WOOTER, Nordin

FULLNAME: Nordin Wooter
DOB: 07-Jul-76, Surinam

Club History	Signed	Fee
Real Zaragoza		
Watford	9/99	£950,000

Season	Team	Tot	St	Sb	Snu	Ps	Gls
99-00	Watford	20	16	4	1	7	1
	Total	20	16	4	1	7	1

WORTHINGTON, Nigel

FULLNAME: Nigel Worthington
DOB: 04-Nov-61, Ballymena, Northern Ireland

Club History	Signed	Fee
Notts Co.	7/81	£100,000
Sheffield W.	2/84	£125,000
Leeds U.		£2.225m

Season	Team	Tot	St	Sb	Snu	Ps	Gls
92-93	Sheffield W.	40	40	0	0	0	1
93-94	Sheffield W.	31	30	1	0	1	1
94-95	Leeds U.	27	21	6	5	2	1
95-96	Leeds U.	16	12	4	7	2	0
	Total	114	103	11	12	5	3

WREH, Chris

FULLNAME: Christopher Wreh
DOB: 14-May-75, Monrovia

Club History	Signed	Fee
Monaco		
Arsenal	8/97	Free

Season	Team	Tot	St	Sb	Snu	Ps	Gls
97-98	Arsenal	16	7	9	3	7	3
98-99	Arsenal	12	3	9	4	4	0
99-00	Arsenal	0	0	0	1	0	0
	Total	28	10	18	8	11	3

WRIGHT, Alan

FULLNAME: Alan Geoffrey Wright
DOB: 28-Sep-71, Ashton-under-Lyme

Club History	Signed	Fee
Blackpool	4/89	Juniors
Blackburn R.	10/91	£400,000
Aston Villa	3/95	£1m

Season	Team	Tot	St	Sb	Snu	Ps	Gls
92-93	Blackburn R.	24	24	0	0	3	0
93-94	Blackburn R.	12	7	5	7	2	0
94-95	Blackburn R.	5	4	1	4	0	0
94-95	Aston Villa	8	8	0	0	1	0
95-96	Aston Villa	38	38	0	0	0	2
96-97	Aston Villa	38	38	0	0	0	1
97-98	Aston Villa	37	35	2	1	3	0
98-99	Aston Villa	38	38	0	0	1	0
99-00	Aston Villa	32	31	1	2	6	1
	Total	232	223	9	14	16	4

WRIGHT, Ian

FULLNAME: Ian Edward Wright
DOB: 03-Nov-63, Woolwich

Club History	Signed	Fee
Crystal P.	8/85	Free
Arsenal	9/91	£2.5m
West Ham U.	7/98	undisclosed

Season	Team	Tot	St	Sb	Snu	Ps	Gls
92-93	Arsenal	31	30	1	0	7	15
93-94	Arsenal	39	39	0	0	3	23
94-95	Arsenal	31	30	1	0	5	18
95-96	Arsenal	31	31	0	0	4	15
96-97	Arsenal	35	30	5	0	4	23
97-98	Arsenal	24	22	2	0	7	10
98-99	West Ham U.	22	20	2	0	6	9
	Total	213	202	11	0	36	113

WRIGHT, Johnny

FULLNAME: John Wright
DOB: 24-Nov-75, Belfast, Nth Ireland

Club History	Signed	Fee
Norwich C.	7/94	Trainee

Season	Team	Tot	St	Sb	Snu	Ps	Gls
94-95	Norwich C.	2	1	1	0	1	0
	Total	2	1	1	0	1	0

WRIGHT, Mark

FULLNAME: Mark Wright
DOB: 01-Aug-63, Dorchester on Thames

Club History	Signed	Fee
Oxford U.	8/80	
Southampton	3/82	£80,000
Derby Co.	8/87	£760,000
Liverpool	7/91	£2.2m

Season	Team	Tot	St	Sb	Snu	Ps	Gls
92-93	Liverpool	33	32	1	2	2	2
93-94	Liverpool	31	31	0	0	1	1
94-95	Liverpool	6	5	1	2	0	0
95-96	Liverpool	28	28	0	1	2	2
96-97	Liverpool	33	33	0	0	3	0
97-98	Liverpool	6	6	0	2	0	0
	Total	137	135	2	7	8	5

WRIGHT, Nick

FULLNAME: Nicholas John Wright
DOB: 15-Oct-75, Derby

Club History	Signed	Fee
Derby Co.	7/94	Trainee
Carlisle U.	11/97	£35,000
Watford	7/98	£100,000

Season	Team	Tot	St	Sb	Snu	Ps	Gls
99-00	Watford	4	1	3	1	1	0
	Total	4	1	3	1	1	0

WRIGHT, Richard

FULLNAME: Richard Ian Wright
DOB: 05-Nov-77, Ipswich

Club History	Signed	Fee
Ipswich Town	1/95	Trainee

Season	Team	Tot	St	Sb	Snu	Ps	Gls
94-95	Ipswich T.	3	3	0	1	0	0
	Total	3	3	0	1	0	0

WRIGHT, Tommy

FULLNAME: Thomas E. Wright
DOB: 10-Jan-66, Dunfermline

Club History	Signed	Fee
Leeds U.	1/83	Amateur
Oldham A.	10/86	£80,000
Leicester C.	8/89	£350,000
Middlesbrough	7/92	£650,000

Season	Team	Tot	St	Sb	Snu	Ps	Gls
92-93	Middlesbrough	36	34	2	0	7	5
	Total	36	34	2	0	7	5

WRIGHT, Tommy

FULLNAME: Thomas J Wright
DOB: 29-Aug-63, Belfast

Club History	Signed	Fee
Linfield		
Newcastle U.	3/88	£30,000
Hull C.	2/91	Loan
Nottingham F.	9/93	£450,000
Reading	10/96	Loan
Manchester C.	1/97	Loan
Manchester C.	3/97	£450,000
Newcastle U.		

Season	Team	Tot	St	Sb	Snu	Ps	Gls
93-94	Newcastle U.	3	2	1	4	0	0
94-95	Nottingham F.	10	0	0	9	0	0
96-97	Nottingham F.	1	1	0	1	0	0
99-00	Newcastle U.	3	3	0	2	0	0
	Total	17	6	1	16	0	0

XAVIER, Abel

FULLNAME: Abel Xavier
DOB: 30-Nov-72, Mozambique

Club History	Signed	Fee
PSV Eindhoven		
Everton	9/99	£1.5m

Season	Team	Tot	St	Sb	Snu	Ps	Gls
99-00	Everton	20	18	2	2	1	0
	Total	20	18	2	2	1	0

YALLOP, Frank

FULLNAME: Frank Walter Yallop
DOB: 04-Apr-64, Watford

Club History	Signed	Fee
Ipswich Town	1/82	

Season	Team	Tot	St	Sb	Snu	Ps	Gls
92-93	Ipswich T.	6	5	1	2	1	2
93-94	Ipswich T.	7	2	5	6	1	0

YATES, Dean

FULLNAME: Dean Richard Yates
DOB: 26-Oct-67, Leicester

Club History	Signed	Fee
Notts Co.	6/85	Apprentice
Derby Co.	1/95	£350,000

Season	Team	Tot	St	Sb	Snu	Ps	Gls
96-97	Derby Co.	10	8	2	3	2	0
97-98	Derby Co.	9	8	1	2	2	0
	Total	19	16	3	5	4	0

YATES, Steve

FULLNAME: Stephen Yates
DOB: 29-Jan-70, Bristol

Club History	Signed	Fee
Bristol R.	8/93	
QPR	8/93	£650,000

Season	Team	Tot	St	Sb	Snu	Ps	Gls
93-94	QPR	29	27	2	4	0	0
94-95	QPR	23	22	1	5	2	1
95-96	QPR	30	30	0	0	1	0
	Total	82	79	3	9	3	1

YEBOAH, Anthony

FULLNAME: Anthony Yeboah
DOB: 06-Jun-66, Kumasi, Ghana

Club History	Signed	Fee
Eintracht Frankfurt		
Leeds U.	1/95	£3.4m

Season	Team	Tot	St	Sb	Snu	Ps	Gls
94-95	Leeds U.	18	16	2	1	3	12
95-96	Leeds U.	23	23	0	0	3	12
96-97	Leeds U.	7	6	1	4	3	0
	Total	48	45	3	5	9	24

YORKE, Dwight

FULLNAME: Dwight Yorke
DOB: 03-Nov-71, Tobago, West Indies

Club History	Signed	Fee
Aston Villa	12/89	£120,000
Manchester U.	8/98	£12.6m

Season	Team	Tot	St	Sb	Snu	Ps	Gls
92-93	Aston Villa	27	22	5	7	8	6
93-94	Aston Villa	12	2	10	3	1	2
94-95	Aston Villa	37	33	4	0	6	6
95-96	Aston Villa	35	35	0	0	5	17
96-97	Aston Villa	37	37	0	0	3	17

Season	Team	Tot	St	Sb	Snu	Ps	Gls
97-98	Aston Villa	30	30	0	0	2	12
98-99	Aston Villa	1	1	0	0	0	0
98-99	Manchester U.	32	32	0	1	5	18
99-00	Manchester U.	32	29	3	3	5	20
	Total	243	221	22	14	35	98

YOUDS, Eddie

FULLNAME: Edward Paul Youds
DOB: 03-May-70, Liverpool

Club History	Signed	Fee
Everton	6/88	
Cardiff C.	12/89	Loan
Wrexham	2/90	Loan
Ipswich Town	11/91	£250,000
Bradford C.	1/95	£175,000
Charlton A.	3/98	£550,000

Season	Team	Tot	St	Sb	Snu	Ps	Gls
92-93	Ipswich T.	16	10	6	8	3	0
93-94	Ipswich T.	23	18	5	1	3	1
94-95	Ipswich T.	10	9	1	3	0	0
98-99	Charlton A.	22	21	1	2	0	2
	Total	71	58	13	14	6	3

YOUNG, Eric

FULLNAME: Eric Young
DOB: 25-Mar-60, Singapore

Club History	Signed	Fee
Brighton & HA	11/82	£10,000
Wimbledon	7/87	£70,000
Crystal P.	8/90	£850,000

Season	Team	Tot	St	Sb	Snu	Ps	Gls
92-93	Crystal P.	38	38	0	0	1	6
94-95	Crystal P.	13	13	0	0	3	0
	Total	51	51	0	0	4	6

YOUNG, Luke

FULLNAME: Luke Young
DOB: 19-Jul-79, Harlow

Club History	Signed	Fee
Tottenham H.		Trainee

Season	Team	Tot	St	Sb	Snu	Ps	Gls
98-99	Tottenham H.	14	13	1	6	1	0
99-00	Tottenham H.	20	11	9	11	2	0
	Total	34	24	10	17	3	0

ZAGORAKIS, Theo

FULLNAME: Theodoros Zagorakis
DOB: 27-Oct-71, Kavala, Greece

Club History	Signed	Fee
PAOK Salonika		
Leicester C.	2/98	£750,000

Season	Team	Tot	St	Sb	Snu	Ps	Gls
97-98	Leicester C.	14	12	2	0	7	1
98-99	Leicester C.	19	16	3	13	11	1
99-00	Leicester C.	17	6	11	16	2	1
	Total	50	34	16	29	20	3

ZELIC, Ned

FULLNAME: Ned Zelic
DOB: 04-Jul-71, Australia

Club History	Signed	Fee
Borussia Dortmund		
QPR	8/95	£1.25m

Season	Team	Tot	St	Sb	Snu	Ps	Gls
95-96	QPR	4	3	1	0	0	0
	Total	4	3	1	0	0	0

ZIEGE, Christian

FULLNAME: Christian Ziege
DOB: 01-Feb-72, Germany

Club History	Signed	Fee
Milan		
Middlesbrough	7/99	£4m

Season	Team	Tot	St	Sb	Snu	Ps	Gls
99-00	Middlesbrough	29	29	0	0	5	6
	Total	29	29	0	0	5	6

ZOHAR, Itzy

FULLNAME: Itzhik Zohar
DOB: 21-Oct-70, Tel Aviv, Israel

Club History	Signed	Fee
Royal Antwerp		
C.Palace	8/97	£1.2m

Season	Team	Tot	St	Sb	Snu	Ps	Gls
97-98	Crystal P.	6	2	4	8	1	0
	Total	6	2	4	8	1	0

ZOLA, Gianfranco

FULLNAME: Gianfranco Zola
DOB: 05-Jul-66, Oliena (Sardinia)

Club History	Signed	Fee
Parma	1993	
Chelsea	11/96	£4.5m

Season	Team	Tot	St	Sb	Snu	Ps	Gls
96-97	Chelsea	23	22	1	1	4	8
97-98	Chelsea	27	23	4	4	11	8
98-99	Chelsea	37	35	2	1	17	13
99-00	Chelsea	33	25	8	2	10	4
	Total	120	105	15	8	42	33

ZUNIGA, Ysrael

FULLNAME: Ysrael Zuniga
DOB:

Club History	Signed	Fee
Coventry C.		

Season	Team	Tot	St	Sb	Snu	Ps	Gls
99-00	Coventry C.	7	3	4	2	2	2
	Total	7	3	4	2	2	2